# The Diary of Ebenezer Parkman

Lebanon

Vermont

New Hampshire

Maine

Massachusetts

Deerfield

Northampton

Westfield    Springfield

Hartford

Wethersfield

Connecticut

New Haven

Windham

Norwich

Stonington

Rhode Island

Providence

Newport

Amesbury

Townsend    Dunstable

Groton    Chelmsford
Littleton
Harvard    Bedford
Concord

Princeton    Lancaster Stow
Sudbury
Marlborough    Weston
Barre    Boylston    Natick
Rutland    Framingham
Worcester    Westborough
Ware    Grafton    Hopkinton
Brookfield    Leicester
Medfield

Sutton    Upton
Oxford
Sturbridge

Bellingham

Andover

Rowley
Ipswich

Danvers

Reading
Lexington    Woburn
Saugus

Cambridge
Newton
Boston
Dorchester
Needham    Quincy
Dedham    Milton
Braintree    Weymouth

Newburyport
Newbury

Gloucester

Beverly
Saleı.ı
Marblehead

Lynn
Charlestown

Hull

Hingham
Scituate

Norwell
Hanover
Abington    Marshfield
Pembroke

Easton    Duxbury
Bridgewater    Plymouth

Taunton    Middleborough
Rehoboth

Sandwich

# THE DIARY OF
# EBENEZER PARKMAN
# 1703-1782

FIRST PART

THREE VOLUMES IN ONE

*1719-1755*

### Edited by Francis G. Walett

WITH A FOREWORD BY

CLIFFORD K. SHIPTON

*American Antiquarian Society · Worcester · 1974*

Copyright © 1974 by American Antiquarian Society
Library of Congress Catalog Card Number 68-30686
International Standard Book Number 0-912296-04-6
Printed in the United States of America
by the Davis Press, Inc., Worcester, Massachusetts

# TABLE OF CONTENTS

# FOREWORD

In the course of forty years of searching the source materials for the history of the American colonies in the eighteenth century for *Sibley's Harvard Graduates*, I have read all of the available diaries, which number in the hundreds, and have come to the conclusion that by far the most interesting and important is the journal which Ebenezer Parkman kept for sixty-two years. Here was a unique picture of New England life in the eighteenth century, a document unmatched indeed in any age or country. Ordinary diaries, like mine, are records of routine with occasional exceptional events. In Parkman's day, many of them are primarily stock-taking of the writers' souls, of little interest to any one but the author. Parkman was a typical literate American of that generation, interested in all human knowledge, and situated in a country town not too large to be revealed in full detail in his microscopic view. Fortunately for us he was less interested in the state of his own soul than in the life which flowed around him, its superstitions, faults, prejudices, beliefs, and goodnesses, and in the ideas which were brought to him by the flood of print.

In time of tragic epidemic, he records that some of his people thought they saw coffins in the sky. Living on the relatively safe edge of the frontier, he dreamt of Mohawk war-cries. His diary is rooted deep in American life, as the greater diary of Samuel Sewall was not, for the Judge was an Englishman, living in an American city, and not experiencing the feelings of a born American in the full sweep of American life. Far more important as a record of political life, Sewall's diary is much nearer its great English contemporaries.

When I began the publication of the Parkman Diaries serially in the *Proceedings* of the American Antiquarian Society, Lyman Butterfield remarked that I was surrendering the secret weapon with which I had combatted the theories of my fellows. The Parkman diaries cover three generations and the good part of a century, although the later years kept by other members of the family are not as informing. It is greatly to be hoped that the whole series will eventually be published.

This meticulously kept record of daily life in a typical New England town is a record of the social history of Massachusetts provincial life nowhere equalled for length, for completeness, or for sustained interest. This remarkably full journal was begun when Parkman was a student at Harvard and it comes to an end only with his death well over sixty years later. The diary is important for a variety of reasons. In the first place it illuminates in unique detail the life of a country parson and the history of the general area in which he lived in the colonial period. Parkman recorded a mass of facts concerning the routine of work and play, the problems and vexations as well as the joys of everyday life. Occasionally, great figures are mentioned in the diary, to the delight of biographers and historians. Students of local history and genealogy will find this a most important source of information. For those who are concerned with the development of language and eighteenth-century English usage this record will be helpful. Subjects that are treated by Parkman in a significant way include the Great Awakening, manners and morals, health and medicine, and numerous theological disputes. There is material in this diary for everyone interested in any aspect of American life and thought in that generation, and much that is recorded only here.

It is recorded with such charm that whenever exigencies of space compelled us to omit an installment in the serial printing in the *Proceedings*, there were cries of indignation from readers in many disciplines who stopped me on the street and said they always gave this document priority in their reading. That demand is a chief reason for the present decision to reissue the installments of the diary as three volumes in one, with an Introduction and a new index. To Parkman's text the editor, Professor Walett, has added copious notes drawn from the church records and similar material. For an extended account of Parkman, the reader is referred to *Sibley's Harvard Graduates*, VI, 510-527, and to the sketch which follows.

Clifford K. Shipton

Shirley Center, Massachusetts
November 1973

# INTRODUCTION

EBENEZER PARKMAN, the writer of this wonderfully long diary and the first settled minister of Westborough, Massachusetts, was born in Boston on September 5, 1703. He was a young son in the large and rather poor family of William Parkman, a shipwright of the north end of town, who was respected enough to become a ruling member of the New North Church in later years. Ebenezer was raised in a steady, pious home, as numerous entries in the diary will attest.

Despite the lean times of the Parkman family, Ebenezer was sent at sacrifice to the North Latin School, where he was greatly influenced by John Barnard, a young schoolmaster and former pastor of the First Church in Andover, Massachusetts. Several notations in Parkman's papers indicate that the boy had great respect for Barnard, was fond of his pious teacher, and thankful that this man had helped him to set his course in life. Perhaps it was inevitable that a lad of Parkman's serious disposition, subjected to such influences, would enter the ministry.

Although his conservative religious training was of commanding influence throughout Ebenezer Parkman's long life, he was a man interested in everything he saw about him. All aspects of life concerned Parkman and he commented on many different matters. The diary will wipe out any illusions about the narrowness of outlook of early New Englanders. Readers will always be grateful for his long, full, candid, and dutifully kept journal.

Ebenezer studied the classics under Barnard and prepared for Harvard College, where he was enrolled in the class of 1721. Parkman's own notations about avoidance of youthful indiscretions and the college faculty records reveal that he was a serious student, careful enough in conduct to avoid disciplinary action by the authorities. Some of his copy books have survived and show that he studied not only theology but was also interested in some modern authors. This breadth of interest was to continue throughout his life, and the numerous notations in the diary concerning books that Parkman read are of great value in gaining some insight on influences that touched an eighteenth-century country parson in New England.

After graduation Parkman read theology and shortly took his second degree. He kept school for a time at Newton while waiting for a call to the ministry. Ebenezer's experiences in these years have to be pieced together from miscellaneous papers because he later destroyed those portions of the diary he kept while at Harvard and in his early years thereafter. The ministry was his goal and he was working toward it in this period. Opportunities to preach soon came: his earliest effort seems to have been in Boston (perhaps in the New North) in September 1722. Shortly he went into the countryside to fill pulpits a number of times at Wrentham, Worcester, Westborough, and Hopkinton. The diary does tell of some of his experiences in this preliminary work and the efforts made to examine and entertain candidates. Although the salary of 80£ and 150£ settlement offered seemed small, Ebenezer Parkman accepted in June 1724 the call to the small frontier town of Westborough.

In the spring and summer of 1724 Parkman courted and won Mary Champney of Cambridge, who was to come with him to be the mistress of Westborough's first parsonage. It was a loving match tenderly remembered by the minister for many years on the anniversaries of Mrs. Parkman's death. On October 28, 1724, the young preacher was installed as the first minister of the newly-constituted church. The new pastor began his church records, which were a model of precision and detail, with this entry.

The Church of Christ in Westborough was
embodied and Ebenezer Parkman was Ordained
the Pastor thereof, October 28th, in the
Year of our Lord, 1724

After suitable observances, twelve besides the minister signed the Covenant of the church and with the good wishes of the town people and the ministers from neighboring towns Parkman began his long pastorate.

In the aftermath of King Philip's War, settlers had soon ventured forth from outlying towns. By 1690, a few pioneers built homes and established farms near Lake Chauncy, and garrison houses on Powder Hill (now Lyman School Hill) in the western part of the town of Marlborough. These homes were within the present limits of Westborough and Northborough. The menace of Indians was not entirely past, and in the early 1700s several Rice boys were carried away. In Parkman's early days in Westborough he carried a pistol with him for protection against hostile Indians. Shortly before his arrival settlers of the Chauncy region had petitioned the General Court to be set off as a new town. The legislature concurred and Westborough, the one hundredth town in Massachusetts, was incorporated, November 18, 1717.

The new town, with widely scattered people, was a few miles west of Marlborough, and about thirty-five miles from Boston. Early in Parkman's pastorate especially, Westborough was in wilderness. Life was difficult and at times dangerous: wolves, bears, and Indians were numerous; travel was hazardous; the settlers were removed from ready medical care, and disease took a terrible toll. Parkman went about his work in this area with youthful vigor and enthusiasm. His complete dedication to the task at hand was obvious, for he constantly helped parishioners, neighbors, friends, and passers-by in every possible way. In the face of disputes with the church, the town, and disgruntled townspeople at times, his work was almost always respected for its sincerity of purpose. Over the years Parkman struggled to make both ends meet and fought over salary matters, but nevertheless he served unstintingly for nearly sixty years.

Westborough, to which the new minister brought his bride, had begun to build a meeting house on Powder Hill immediately after incorporation. It was a small, rude, dirt-floor structure, and early meetings were held there despite there being no seats. The small building was barely finished when Parkman came to town. The town grew fairly rapidly at first and the first meeting house was soon too small, and as early as 1729, when there were 89 members of the church, the building was enlarged. Near the meeting house on the hill, Parkman built his first home and established his farm, which he would have to work to make both ends meet. The minister often complained that his promised supply of firewood had not been delivered, and sometimes only desperate efforts in the dead of winter pulled the Parkmans through. The diary is filled with notes on the many trials of the minister, the daily struggle to meet the family's needs, and with the many kindnesses of neighbors and friends.

Being a minister then called for much more than preaching, holding the Thursday lecture, catechizing the boys and girls, and making pastoral calls. Farming was the inevitable responsibility of the country pastor and one that kept him close to his people.

Parkman's family learned that farm work was never done. Each season brought its many chores: spring saw them planting corn, rye, oats, hops, flax, and vegetables of all kinds; summer meant tending crops, fruits, and making hay; with the busy autumn came the harvest—gathering crops, drying fruits, husking corn, making

and 'boyling' cyder, brewing beer, slaughtering animals, and salting the meat; in winter, the quietest farm season, it was still necessary to tend the livestock. Parkman had cows, oxen, sheep, pigs, and horses. At any time of the year 'spare' time might be spent fixing tools, making house repairs, and fetching cut wood for the yawning hearths—the only means of heating in a colonial homestead. There was never enough time for clearing fields of trees and rocks, splitting rails for fences, gathering rocks and making stone walls, searching for runaway domestic animals and watching for predatory wild beasts, and carting away 'muck' from around the barn and sheds. In all, there is no better primary source of information about colonial New England farming life than the Parkman diary.

Mr. Parkman had help of course, and especially when the children were small. Neighbors were generous with gifts and were good about donating time on the parsonage farm, but the minister often lamented that much remained undone and work was far behind schedule. Parkman hired help when he could, but day labor was not plentiful, nor was it easy, with ready money so short.

On one occasion he took on a white indentured servant, but this turned out to be a serious mistake. John Kidney was no bargain: the minister found him to be lazy, a thief, a liar, and a person of 'Rude and Vile Conduct.' Worst of all, once when the parents were away, Kidney assaulted Molly, the minister's fourteen-year-old daughter. The terrified girl escaped being raped, and fortunately suffered only cut and scratched arms. The minister seems to have been remarkably patient, considering the circumstances; he did not press charges against Kidney, but soon sold his indenture. No other indentured servants were hired by the Parkmans.

In his early days at Westborough, Ebenezer Parkman owned a slave that he purchased from his father, but Maro soon died and could not be replaced. It is very interesting to note that Mr. Parkman mourned Maro's loss as 'The First Death in my Family.'

The women of the parsonage had their share of responsibility too. In such a self-sufficient homestead, all able hands had to work. Processing flax and wool, spinning thread, making cloth and clothes were steady household tasks. The minister made a present of a flax wheel to his daughter Molly when she was five years old. Making butter and cheese, preserving food stuffs, baking and preparing food occupied much of the women's time. Parkman had a large family and there were always relatives, friends, and visitors to be entertained. Although the minister frequently grumbled in his diary that his Lord's Day preparations were sadly interrupted, the parsonage door was always open to callers, great and humble. When the Parkman girls were young, outsiders were brought in to help the minister's wife. One such helper was a French Acadian girl, who came with her exiled family to live in Westborough. Comments on the treatment of these aliens and Mr. Parkman's efforts in middle-age to learn enough French to read and write letters for his new neighbors and to catechize them are recorded.

Added to other womanly problems was the constant burden of child-bearing. Mary Parkman gave birth to five children before she died. The minister was soon searching for another wife, and after courting several ladies Parkman won Hannah Breck, the daughter of the Reverend Robert Breck of Marlborough. The new mistress of the Westborough parsonage bore the ardent minister eleven more children. All but two of Parkman's big brood survived childhood. The diary is filled with the joys and vexations of raising this large family.

Ebenezer Parkman, for many years the only man in Westborough who had been to college, was the intellectual leader of his community. He tried to keep up with the affairs of the province, the country, and the world by subscribing to newspapers, and by reading whatever he could get his hands on. Moreover, he made frequent trips to Cambridge and Boston, visiting family and friends, attending commencement, and reading innumerable sermons. Naturally his more provincial neighbors looked to the minister for news, advice, and different kinds of help. He often drafted deeds, wills, and business documents, for there was no lawyer in Westborough for many years. He occasionally did some teaching and in any event judged the qualifications of prospective schoolmasters for the town.

Parkman was often called upon for medical advice while on pastoral calls, and he carried with him a book of remedies and treatments for all kinds of ailments. The minister regularly recorded information about such illnesses and accidents which were suffered in the course of farm work or during well-diggings or house-raisings. His own mishaps from falls from horses, his young daughter's escape from serious injury after a tumble down the open bulkhead into the parsonage cellar, and his son's severe burns incurred when he pitched forward into the kitchen fireplace are examples of the misfortunes that Parkman described. The minister's diary is a major source of information about the early medical history of the area. Of particular significance is the material on the dreaded 'throat distemper' which took the lives of hundreds of people in southern and central New England in the 1740s and 1750s.

Ebenezer Parkman was rather conservative in theology and largely untouched by the liberal currents of his time, which were now being felt in colonial Massachusetts. He owned numerous religious classics but he also had many of the works of Jonathan Edwards, the most powerful figure of the Great Awakening. Edwards visited and preached in Westborough and was entertained by Parkman. Nevertheless when the great English evangelist George Whitefield came through the area in 1740 on one of his preaching raids, Parkman asked him to speak and invited the great revivalist to his home. But during the 1740s when there were many controversies over religion in most towns of Worcester County, Parkman took a conservative stand and tried to soothe troubles and to heal breaches. He deplored the excesses in nearby towns and the many separations that took place.

The Parkman diary reveals that troubles in nearby Grafton were great. When the Great Awakening arrived, the minister, Solomon Prentice, supported it eagerly and joined in the evangelistic fervor. Parkman noted that Grafton was in a state of turmoil for several years and the town divided against the minister. When Prentice's wife joined the Separatist church in the town and was baptized by a lay preacher, the minister was so angry that he punched his wife, tore her clothes, and fought with her friends. Ebenezer Parkman and other neighboring persons tried to settle the disputes in Grafton and to save Prentice in several Councils, but the minister was dismissed in 1747.

Church meetings in Westborough were usually orderly but there were disturbances. During the Great Awakening some agitated souls cried out or moaned loudly during the worship service, and Parkman was annoyed with the rather emotional Separatist meetings that took place in town. In January 1743, the minister said, 'A number of Children were suppos'd to be much fill'd with the Spirit and carry'd out in Spiritual Joy last Night at Mr. Fays. An Indian Girl in great Distress for her Brother—and Betty Fay in Terrors. . . .' Once when Mr. Parkman was preaching a woman 'cry'd out very much at the Time of a loud clap of Thunder.' She later told the minister that 'the Spirit of God struck her at the same Time with the Clap, and (having been in great Darkness for some Time before) she was filled very much with Terror by reason of her sins.'

As Westborough grew, its widely scattered people decided to create a second precinct,

Northborough, and the center of town was re-
located. Before a new meeting house in the first
precinct could be completed, meetings were being held in it. The wind blew through the open
windows and at one time it rained on Parkman
as he was preaching. As might be expected,
meetings were sometimes disturbed by mischievous boys and girls; once the tithingman had to
chastise Billy Parkman for his 'rude' behavior.
In one unhappy occasion the minister recorded
that his daughter Molly was hit by 'tobacco
spittle' from the gallery as she sat in the ministerial pew.

The Lord's Day was the most important of
the week, for meetings were held morning and
afternoon, and Parkman delivered long, scholarly, and dull sermons in each session. Preparing
these sermons and the weekly Thursday lecture
was a major responsibility of the minister. As
years went by, and when he didn't have time to
prepare something new, Parkman would read a
sermon that he had delivered before. Disgruntled listeners complained about this at
times. The common practice of exchanging pulpits gave some relief from the steady require-
ment of preparing long sermons and provided a
welcome change for parishioners. One day when
Job Cushing of Shrewsbury was preaching in
Westborough, Parkman confessed, 'I was sleepy
at Meeting, the Lord forgive this Sin!' On
winter days the services in the unheated meeting
house must have seemed interminable, and only
rarely were meetings cut short because of bitter
cold weather.

The numerous sermons of Parkman that have
been preserved reveal that he was a scholarly
but rather dry preacher. He depended almost
completely on his prepared texts, and read these
long discourses while standing. If he left his text
or his spectacles at home he could not preach.
How he read his microscopic handwriting (particularly with the poor lighting of that time) is
mystifying to his editor. As was true with most
people of this time, Parkman saw the hand of
God or the Devil everywhere: manifestations of
God's wrath or pleasure were noted frequently.
There was inevitably a moralizing sermon after
a victory or defeat in the Indian wars, with unusual weather or illness, or with such extraordinary events as comets or earthquakes.

The removal of the center of Westborough
created problems for Parkman. For many
months he continued to live in the old parsonage
and made about a five-mile round-trip each
time he came down to the new meeting house.
On the Lord's Day, the minister complained
more than once that no one invited him to dine,
and he asked the town to pay for his noon meal

to no avail. Parkman had to bring his lunch
with him. One cold day in January 1751 he told
the congregation that there would be only a
fifteen-minute intermission before the afternoon
services; he wrote, I ate a 'bit of Bread and
Cheese which my Maid brought to me in the
Pulpit and I was much refresh'd.'

When Parkman built his second home in the
new center of town, his commuting problem was
relieved, but he still owned and leased the old
parsonage farm, and this proved a troublesome
care for years. The minister's new home seemed
to some parishioners to be unnecessarily large
and they were critical of the minister's extravagance. Construction of the new parsonage took
several years and was described so fully in the
diary (with reference to the source and types of
material procured and the progress of the work)
that I doubt very much that the construction of
any mid-eighteenth-century New England home
has been chronicled in more detail.

Ebenezer Parkman did his best to uphold the
strict Calvinist moral code that was still part of
the law of the colony. The diary, church, and
town records are often revealing in this respect.
'Profane cursing' was a matter of some concern
to the vigilant parson; Cornelius Cook, Westborough's blacksmith, was one of a number that
the minister reprimanded. Young people have
ever been a cause of worry to their elders, and
Parkman complained about youthful frolics at
huskings, raisings, or on training days. Once he
admonished girls to release suitors who visited
them at an early hour. The usual variety of
social sins were noted in the diary, church, or
Marlborough Association records: Parkman
complained at times about intemperance and
people who were 'overcome with strong drink';
at least two early schoolmasters were found to
be unusually fond of gaming and frequenting
places where strong drink was sold. Intemperate
persons were sometimes denied church ordinances, and our twentieth-century sensibilities
may be taxed by the denial of baptism of a
seven-month-old baby because of the alleged sin
of the parents.

While Parkman was always seriously concerned about his own and his neighbor's behavior, he found time for amusement and good
fun. He often enjoyed 'handsome entertainments' and remarked at times about the good
fellowship of raisings, huskings, and the amusements of training days. There was alcoholic
drink at all such affairs and the minister was no
enemy of the use of strong drink in moderation.
There were always beer, cider, and stronger stuff
at the parsonage and even in the meeting house:
once the minister noted that Stephen Maynard

brought him '11½ gallons of Rhum' from Boston and was grateful that the cargo got through despite the fact that the cart was overturned on the way. Another time on a hurried visit to Grafton in March 1740, Parkman wrote of 'having taken Brank and drank some Beer without staying to Dine, I went to Meeting and I preach'd.'

There were recreational diversions, too. The minister liked to fish both for the sport of it and the good food obtained. 'Pickerells' or 'salmon-trouts' made the diet more interesting. In 1740 Ebenezer had a long session of salt-water fishing in Boston harbor: 'we got aground by the Castle and did not get up home till 2 o'Clock next Morning. A very Pleasant Time. We caught 12 Tom Codd.' Parkman thought that skating was enjoyable and when he was fifty-six, he got out his skates and joined his son on the ice. In an unusual instance of amusement he wrote that one 'Edward Burley Son' came through town in 1739 with 'his Cabbin with his Puppetts.' The minister was so fascinated by this that he watched two performances, calling for one in his own home.

Ebenezer Parkman served God wherever and in whatever way he could. Only his own serious illness kept him from making pastoral calls on sick, disturbed, needful, or quarrelsome people. Many of his visits were made to friends or troubled folk in nearby towns. Once he tried to straighten out Dr. Benjamin Gott of Marlborough who was 'well liquored' too often. He called on those who were in need of help or solace in or outside of Westborough.

On one occasion, fairly early in his pastorate, Parkman was the confessor of the unfortunate Hugh Henderson, alias John Hamilton, convicted of burglary in Westborough and imprisoned in Worcester. Parkman visited the condemned man and noted that Henderson admitted to 'licentiousness and drinking, breaking the Sabbath, cursing and swearing . . . lying and gaming' and stealing. Although Henderson confessed his guilt, he also complained about the jury 'not going by the laws of God and the Country in Condemning him, having but Circumstantial Evidence.' Ebenezer Parkman's diary contains notes on the prisoner's futile effort to escape and on the public execution in Worcester, November 24, 1737. Shortly an admonitory broadside, suitably embellished with a crude picture of Henderson hanging at the scaffold, printing the victim's confession to Parkman, was published in Boston.

As the American Revolution approached, Parkman saw little merit in the arguments and activities of the Massachusetts Whigs. Although he lived in the country, the Westborough parson had often visited persons of high social standing and political importance in and around Boston. He shared the viewpoint of prerogative men and deplored such excesses as the Stamp Act riots as 'A melancholly Occurrence!' In 1773 when Westborough adopted resolutions calling attention to the 'present critical and alaruming Situation of our publick affairs,' Ebenezer Parkman thought that the radicals were overly concerned about the colonists' rights. During the difficulties of the next year he continued to deplore inflammatory statements by the radicals. Sick at heart over the turbulence in Massachusetts, he lamented in his diary, 'Mobs and Riots, Whigs and Torys—as if our Happiness were nigh to an end! O God save us!' The minister refused to sign the resolutions of the town, but attempted to mollify his neighbors with a statement that he was 'heartily Set against Despotism and Oppression.' With the outbreak of hostilities in April 1775 Ebenezer Parkman's position became more difficult, and for 'Peace Sake, and to Avoid a Rupture among us,' he signed an 'Exceptionable' patriot document. He prayed for the 'just . . . Defence of our invaluable Rights, Laws, Libertys and Privileges,' but continued to hope for a reconciliation with Great Britain even after the Declaration of Independence.

The war period brought more problems for the aging Westborough parson and his family. He noted sorrowfully, time after time, that his finances were ever more desperate. Inflation brought soaring prices and Parkman often complained about his growing indebtedness. Town records and the diary record his running quarrel with the town over his financial plight and the arrears of his salary. An indication of the respect of the townspeople for their old minister was the fact that they kept him in service and paid him his salary, however slowly, though he was no revolutionist.

Parkman's long pastorate came to an end with his death on December 9, 1782. In spite of various ills of age and failing sight he had continued with his duties until he evidently suffered a stroke in November 1782. The old minister died and was buried in Memorial Cemetery, Westborough.

Ebenezer Parkman began to keep a journal or diary while he was a student at Harvard; he continued this detailed record throughout his long pastorate in Westborough. Although Parkman destroyed an early part of the diary himself because of what he called youthful indiscretions, the great bulk of the manuscript is preserved in the libraries of the Massachusetts Historical Society and the American Antiquarian Society.

The parts of the diary that can be accounted for, with locations indicated are as follows: January 1723 through September 1728, A.A.S.; February through November 1737, printed by the Westborough Historical Society; January 1738 through December 1740, A.A.S.; December 21-31, 1742, M.H.S.; January 1743 through December 1748, A.A.S.; January 1749 through December 1749, M.H.S.; January 1750 through December 1754, A.A.S.; January 1755 through December 1755, M.H.S.; January 1756 through May 1761, A.A.S.; June 1764 through December 1767, A.A.S.; January 1768 through June 1769, A.A.S.; August 1771 through November 1772, M.H.S.; November 10 through November 21, 1772, A.A.S.; November 1772 through June, 1773, M.H.S.; June 1773 through October 1778, A.A.S.; November 1778 through December 1780, printed by W.H.S.; January 1781 through December 1782, M.H.S. There are also a few miscellaneous Parkman papers in the American Antiquarian Society. Manuscript sermons that have survived are in the Congregational Library in Boston, the Westborough Historical Society, and the New York Public Library. The Diary from 1719 through 1755 was first published serially as edited herein in the *Proceedings* of the American Antiquarian Society, Volume 71 (1961) to Volume 76 (1966).

The Diary of Ebenezer Parkman is of great importance to many people for a variety of reasons. In the first place it is a virtually unequalled record of the social history of a typical eighteenth-century New England town: nearly all aspects of life in the rural community of Westborough are illuminated over a long period of time. In addition to this, Parkman regularly visited and commented on conditions in many towns of eastern Massachusetts and Worcester County. Considering the paucity of source material for reconstructing social history in this period, the lengthy and very full Diary is a veritable treasure-trove of invaluable information.

The life of a country parson with his many responsibilities, joys, and vexations is revealed in unique detail by Mr. Parkman. He recorded a mass of facts about his numerous pastoral duties, the difficulties he experienced in preparing many sermons, discourses, and council 'results,' and the problems associated with farming and raising a large family. Ebenezer Parkman recorded that providing free medical advice, composing legal documents, and occasionally teaching school were also parts of a rural minister's chores. His opinions on events of his time and his reaction to conditions he faced form a significant part of the Diary, too.

While great figures, large events, and colony-wide concerns find their way occasionally into Parkman's journal, it is the routine of work and play, the quarrels and satisfactions of ordinary people, that fill the many pages of the Diary. Comments on the Great Awakening, political problems and economic disputes are quite useful, but the greatness of this source lies in the vast amount of information it gives about the manners and morals and the everyday struggles of ordinary people to survive and to lead meaningful lives in provincial Massachusetts. For students of local history and genealogy, Parkman's journal will provide much interesting information: notations about the raising of a barn or house, the location of homesteads, unusual events, crimes, illnesses, etc., will enrich the study of the entire region.

Some influences on the mind of a New England minister in the eighteenth century can be gauged by references to books and other publications that Parkman owned and borrowed. Occasional comments he made on books that he read may be useful to those interested in the workings of the colonial mind. Those concerned with the development of language and eighteenth-century English usage in America could hardly find a better original source than Ebenezer Parkman's long journal.

## METHOD

The first part of the editorial task has been the transcription of the diary. This in itself has been a sizable job because of the length of the document and the microscopic handwriting of the author. Parkman had a system of writing with innumerable abbreviations and frequent variations in spelling. The policy of the editor has been to write out abbreviated words using Parkman's spelling when this could be determined, and in general to preserve the original spelling. A major part of the work has been the identification of the many people who appear in the diary. Not all persons could be, or probably should be, identified, though the names and titles of authors and books that are mentioned are a very interesting phase of the work. The editor has succeeded in most of these instances, but a few references of Parkman have been too vague and elusive to be identified. It has been considered necessary at times to supply additional information to clarify the text of the diary, and occasionally obsolete or obscure expressions have been explained.

The editor's judgment that the Parkman Diary was an invaluable primary source of information about colonial New England and ought to be published was enthusiastically supported by Clifford K. Shipton, who had used the manuscript to great advantage for years in *Sibley's Harvard Graduates*. His encouragement and frequent advice in the early stages of the task were very important to me. As Directors of the American Antiquarian Society, Shipton and his successor Marcus A. McCorison have generously made available the rich resources of the Society, thereby greatly facilitating the editorial work. The Society's Editor, James E. Mooney, has given his expert assistance in many ways to bring this publication to you. Members of the busy staff of the American Antiquarian Society aided the editor in innumerable ways. Others who helped with the huge task of transcribing the Diary were a succession of student assistants, Kathleen Gianakis, Susan Emerson, and David Harper. Mrs. Eleanor Adams typed the printer's copy of the manuscript. While the editor gratefully acknowledges the assistance of these people, he assumes full responsibility for any editorial errors that may have crept in.

Francis G. Walett

# I

## YOUNG PASTOR IN A NEW TOWN
### 1719-1738

## CAMBRIDGE AUGUST 24, 1719

Blessed be the name of the Lord that I am Continued unto this very Day. Nevertheless all my Backslidings from his Testimonies are commissions of So many great and heinous Sins as I have been guilty of The Mercy of God is Still lengthened out unto me and I receive the favours of life and Health and as I hope enjoy the day of Grace and Opportunity of getting good for My Immortall Soul; which must be first and Chiefly by Faith and Repentance. In order to which I do profess the Faith and Belief contained in the Nicene In the Apostolick Creed. . . . And according to the direction of the Sacred Word of God, and particularly According to the Direction of Mr. Robert Russell[1] have long purposed to make a Collection of First The Great Mercys That the Mighty JEHOVAH has favoured me with. And First, In That He, at My Birth (In the Year of Christ, 1703, September the fifth on Sabbath day Morning, between Six and Seven of the Clock) Caused me to See light; and that it was not Among Pagans, nor Mahometans, nor Jews, but among Christians; and That In (Boston) a place where the Grace of God, bringing Salvation, hath Appeared; and of Religious Parents also, by whom I was well Educated; being first Sent to the reading, and in the Year 1711, to Writing, to Mr. John Cole and having continued there almost two Year (which was till the founding A Grammar free School at the North end and near My Fathers dwelling) I went to Mr. Recompence Wadsworth,[2] to learn Lattin. This was on the twentieth of April in the Year 1713, and Mr. Wadsworth dying, Mr. John Barnard[3] (Afterwards an ordained Minister of the Church of Christ at Andover) was Settled in his place. And October in the Year 1714 I was visited with a Low fit of Sickness beginning with a fever and attended with the Meazells, and after that with great weakness and Infirmities as also great pain, which Set me upon thinking upon what would be the Estate, the Condition of My

Soul after my Dissolution, which was apprehended by all to be Nigh, often in My Mind repeating the Psalmists words Blessed is he whose Transgression is forgiven whose Sin is Covered, Heartyly wishing and praying that My many and great Iniquities might be all so pardoned and washed away in the Blood of the Lamb of God that taketh away the Sin of the World, promising allso that if God would in his great Mercy Spare my Life I would Spend it more to the Glory and praise of his great Name thro his grace assisting me; and God was pleas'd to look upon my Affliction and my Pain and to remember me in my Low Estate, . . . and the Lord Raised me from my Bed of long Sickness and Languishing renewing allso my Strength So that in the Latter end of December I went to School again and continued So doing till by the Often persuasions of the Reverend Mr. John Webb[4] and My Brother William[5] My Father Sent Me to Harvard College Cambridge where I was admitted on August 22, 1717, and had Pain,[6] Davis,[7] Champney[8] for my Chamber fellows for the first year; removing the Second I had Jenison,[9] Pierpont[10] and Wyman[11] (for my chamber fellows) In both which Years I had Mr. Hezekiah Gold[12] for my Particular friend for whose instructions advice and inculcations both in Temporalls and in Spiritualls, I Shall have occasion of praising God Throughout Eternity. On April 19 I had Some Strivings and Motions of the holy Spirit to turn and live, and on December 27 allso but they Soon vanished as the Morning Cloud and as the early Dew. The Blessing of My Mother, the Advice of my Brother William, and the instructions of Mr. Webb, are I hope not quite (though I fear almost) fruitless.

[1] The English divine, of Wadhurst, Sussex.

[2] (Harvard 1708). Clifford K. Shipton, *Biographical Sketches of Those Who Attended Harvard College*, V (Boston, 1937), 461–463. Subsequent reference: *Sibley*, V, 461–463

[3] (Harvard 1709). The minister at Andover, 1718–1757. *Sibley*, V, 475–479.

[4] (Harvard 1708). The minister of the New North Church of Boston, 1714–1750. *Sibley*, V, 463–471.

[5] Ebenezer Parkman's eldest brother.

[6] Stephen Paine (Harvard 1721). *Sibley*, VI, 510–511.

[7] Simon Davis (Harvard 1721). *Sibley*, VI, 469.

[8] Joseph Champney (Harvard 1721) was Parkman's future brother-in-law. *Sibley*, VI, 437–438.

[9] Samuel Jennison (Harvard 1720). *Sibley*, VI, 389–390.

[10] Thomas Pierpont (Harvard 1721). *Sibley*, VI, 547–549.

[11] John Wyman (Harvard 1721). *Sibley*, VI, 591.

[12] (Harvard 1719). Later the minister at Stratford, Conn. *Sibley*, VI, 311–314.

That I had the Reverend Mr. John Leveret[13] for my President and Mr. Thomas Robie[14] for my Tutor is no Small blessing.

Thro the deceitfullness of my heart I Neglected this work (the Collection of Mercys) to my great Shame and Sorrow till February 19, 1719/20. When again I was awakened out of my Sleepy Security of Sin, I was roused out of my Sloth, and the awakenings of my Conscience, which had for a long time been Quiet, giving me but now and then a touch and a Small hint that I remained in my unconverted State, began afresh upon me, the Divil and my own wicked and abominably Sinfull and polluted heart persuading me that there was no hopes of Salvation lest That the Door of Mercy was Shut and the Day of Grace over—and that No man had Bakslidden or apostatized as I had done; till Barrett put me in Mind of one passage in Scripture Jer. 3, 6, 14, 22 together with the following Hosea 14, 4. I was little encouraged, utterly ashamed of my self and hating my self I resolved I would return, and that I would once more Seek to God by Prayer. This I did, but soon grew Lookewarm Neither cold nor hot wherefore I might justly have been Spew'd out And Yet, through the Abundant, the Infinite grace and unparallel'd Mercy of the Eternal JEHOVAH I have such privileges Yet, the Lord knows how long they may be continued for there Never was any in the world So unworthy as I am.

### ANNO 1723

DIURNA: or An Account of the Remarkable Transactions of Every Day: No. 7. Being a Continuation of a Design form'd in the Year 1719/20, February 19th.

### AUGUST [1723]

1. I got to Cambridge by noon, return'd my Horse, paid ½ a Crown to Mrs. Fessenden.[1] Mr. Bridgewater[2] was at College. I went to Boston about 5 P.M. Met at Barrett's.[3] Green[4] was absent. Barrett pray'd first. I read part of a Discourse from I Sam. 16, 7, and concluded. I lodg'd at my Fathers.

2. I bid farewel at home in the Morning, and walked up to Cambridge in my Boots and Spurs in order to go to Worcester. Mr. Sturgeon[5] of Waterton (a Scotch minister) his Case pleaded to Day at the Cambridge Sessions. I din'd at Mrs. Bordman's.[6] Just after Dinner in the College Yard I met with Young Mr. Thomas Rice[7] from Worcester to accompany me up there. I prepar'd and rode away to Mr. Champney's,[8] where with sitting, etc., we tarried till near 4 o'Clock before we Set out. We reach'd to Lieutenant Jones's[9] at Weston (where I lodg'd) just before Dark.

3. In the Morning about 8 (having been Kindly entertain'd) I again Set out for Mr. Jenison's[10] where I had appointed to Meet Mr. Rice, From thence I had more Company, viz. Mr. Golding[11] (brother to Mrs. Jenison[12]). We set out about 10. We stop'd at Sundry Taverns (which particularly I do not remember) before we got to Mr. Bricks[13] of Marlborough; here I was well received though I never was in the least acquainted with the Gentleman til now. N.B. we arriv'd in here by ¼ after one and Set out between 3 and 4, having stop'd Twice or Thrice more, jolted and tired, I

entered Lieutenant Lee's[14] house at Worcester where I was Kindly received by Deacon Haywood,[15] etc. With Pains in my Head and a Sore Throat I went to Bed.

4. In the Morning I was much Better, but my Sore Throat continued. I preach'd all Day on I Sam. 16. 7. I din'd at Deacon Haywoods. I was obliged to retire to finish my Sermon at Noon Time. Sundry Persons (as Mr. Flagg,[16] etc.) came in to see me in the Evening.

5. Towards Night to my Great Joy and Reviving came Colonel Winthrop[17] and Colonel Minot,[18] and with them Mr. Adam Winthrop[19] of College.

6. Prayers and Breakfast Ended we took pleasant walks to See the Farms those Gentlemen had in the Town. While the Colonels and Lieutenant Lee were further Engaged about their Particular Country Managery, Mr. Winthrop, Mr. Flagg and I walk'd to a fine Brook and Fish'd. We Caught Salmon–Trouts, etc. These were very well taken; and we din'd richly on them, Colonel Minot himself dressing them. According to my own Assignation, there came the same young Mr. Rice that accompanyed me up, with purpose this Afternoon to go over to Sutton to visit Mr. Mc-Kinstry.[20] Thus I was obliged to leave this good Company and take my Ride, and we made no other Stop than at Mr. Rice's Lodging, a little. We did not gain Mr. McKinstry's House till just Dark, though twas counted but 6 Miles. I found them in good Health, and I was well Entertained. Here I lodged very pleasantly, (considering, ———). [Word crossed out].

7. It rain'd all this Day which prevented our Return home. Mr. McKinstry walked with me to his Meeting house, and to Lieutenant Kings[21] (a Sensible Man in the Neighborhood) and thus droll'd off the Time, without much Discourse on any head at all.

8. There was a Raising of an House, a Suiting Diversion for Mr. Rice, while Mr. McKinstry, his wife and I took a Ride to Oxford to See Mr. Cambell.[22] This is Six Miles and ½. This was very diverting, and I found Mrs. Cambel[23] in pretty Good Humour. We had a good Contrivance in or going to a Water Melon house, for Mrs. Cambel must ride upon the Easyest-going horse which was Mr. McKinstry's, and So my old Friend must ride with me. This was a lucky Stroke to bring me an opportunity to discourse of Matters and things formerly in Requests. She was more Contented with her Irish Mate than I expected to find her. She said he was a good-natur'd Soul indeed, and She wanted Nothing on Earth but to be a little nearer her Friends. She Desir'd I would come and live at Worcester, etc. Mr. McKinstry, his Wife and I returned to Sutton just about Dark. N.B. We pray'd in the Family by Turns.

9. Returned to Worcester. We call'd to See Captain Jones[24] but he was not at home. Here I had the Information by a Dispensation of Providence in the Burning of the House of Captain Keys[25] of Shrewsbury with 3 of his Sons and Two workmen finishing the house in it. It broke out about Midnight. I visited Mr. Gershom Rice[26] (the Man that first Invited me up) and Thence Strait home. Old Mr. Gray[27] and Mr. Flagg were to see me.

[13] (Harvard 1680). John L. Sibley, *Biographical Sketches of Graduates of Harvard University*, III (Cambridge, 1885), 180–198. Subsequent reference: Sibley, III, 180–198.

[14] (Harvard 1708). Sibley, V, 450–455.

[1] Sarah Fessenden, who was licensed to sell intoxicating liquors at retail. Lucius R. Paige, *History of Cambridge* (Boston, 1877), p. 227.

[2] Probably Edward Bridgewater (Harvard 1718) who was in Cambridge in August, 1723. Sibley, VI, 231–232.

[3] Samuel Barrett (1700–1772), son of Deacon Samuel Barrett of Boston. A classmat, and lifelong friend of Ebeneazer Parkman. First minister of Hopkinton. Sibley, VI 428–432.

[4] Joseph Green (Harvard 1720) of Boston. Minister at Barnstable, 1725–1770. Sibley, VI, 385–387.

[5] Robert Sturgeon, minister of an independent Congregational Church, Watertown, Mass., 1721–1722.

[6] Probably Mary Bordman, who was licensed to sell liquors.

[7] Thomas Rice (1701/2–1785).

[8] Samuel Champney, Sr., Parkman's future father-in-law.

[9] Lieutenant Josiah Jones, one of the founders of the town of Weston.

[10] William Jennison (1676–1744) of Sudbury. Later he moved to Worcester and became Judge of the Court of Common Pleas.

[11] Either Windsor Golding (b. 1675) or Thomas Golding (b. 1678).

[12] Elizabeth (Golding) Jennison (1673–1756).

[13] Reverend Robert Breck (1682–1731), (Harvard 1700). Minister at Marlborough, 1704–1731. Sibley, IV, 515–518.

[14] Lieutenant Henry Lee.

[15] Daniel Heywood (1695–1773). An early settler of Worcester, selectman for 20 years, and an officer in an early military company. William Lincoln, *History of Worcester* (Worcester, 1837), p. 42.

[16] Either Benjamin Flagg (1662–1741) or his son Captain Benjamin Flagg (1690–1751).

[17] Colonel Adam Winthrop (1676–1743), (Harvard 1694), Councillor of the Province. Sibley, IV, 209–214.

[18] Colonel Stephen Minot (1662–1732). Justice and selectman of Boston.

[19] Adam Winthrop (1706–1744), (Harvard 1724). Son of Colonel Winthrop. Sibley, VII, 446–447.

[20] Reverend John McKinstry (1677–1754). First minister of Sutton, Mass. William A. Benedict and Hiram A. Tracy, *History of Sutton* (Worcester, 1878), pp. 691–693.

[21] Lieutenant Jonathan King who had come to Sutton in 1717.

[22] Reverend John Campbell (1691–1761), first minister of the First Congregational Church, Oxford, Mass., 1721–1761. George F. Daniels, *History of Oxford* (Oxford, 1892), pp. 49–52.

[23] Esther Whittle, Wheatly, or Whately of Boston, who married the Reverend Mr. Campbell, Feb. 6, 1722. Daniels, *Oxford*, p. 426.

[24] Captain Nathaniel Jones.

[25] Captain John Keyes (1675–1768). The three sons were Solomon, John and Stephen. The carpenter's apprentices were Abiel Bragg and William Oakes. See *The Boston News-letter*, Aug. 15, 1723.

[26] Gershom Rice (1666–1768), the second settler of Worcester, who arrived in 1715. Lincoln, *Worcester*, pp. 40–41.

[27] John Gray, an early proprietor.

Lieutenant Lee being gone to Boston, It was very lonely During his Absence, for he was Sociable.

10. In the Morning I revolved [?], in order to prepare for the approaching Sabbath. While we Din'd, Mr. Joseph Dana[28] came in.

11. I preached all Day. Din'd as before at Deacon Haywoods. As I returned home I had the Benefit of very Heavenly Conversation from old Mr. Gray. Mr. Flagg was with me all the Evening. We had News by a Post that rode through the Town to day that a Number of Indians were coming to Scout from Canada to those out Towns under the Command of one Captain Nathaniel.

12. Lieutenant Rice[29] call'd to See me to Day. I went over to Mr. Grays. At Night Sundry Men of the Town, viz. Lieutenant Rice and his Brother James, The Two Deacons, viz. Haywood and Mores,[30] Mr. Flagg and Mr. Joseph Dana together with my Landlord, Lieutenant Lee (just return'd from Boston) treated with me about Settling as their minister, etc. I fix'd Tomorrow to be the Day for my returning to Boston. It was very Late when they Left me.

13. I was very much disturbed through the Peoples not providing a Horse for me to ride down upon, according to agreement. To my Shame I am oblig'd to add that I loll'd off the Day in Indolence.

14. Mr. Lee was very much disturbed for the Same Reason; took his Horse and Rode away to Know the Cause. He did not return till after Dinner. But he told me he had Secured my Journey, and about 3 o'Clock P.M. came Mr. James Rice with a very good horse, and we rode away about 4. He related many Particulars of the Story of Mr. Gardiner,[31] who had been dismissed from them—his Innocence, etc. We reach'd Marlborough at the Close of the Day. We met with Mr. Breck in the Street. He asked me into his house and to Lodge with him, but that would obstruct our getting down Time enough for Lecture the next Day. We Thank'd him for his Expressions of Kindness, remounted and rode along for Sudbury. It was too late to gain the Town. We stop'd at David How's Tavern,[32] and having Eaten part of a Fryed Gosling for supper, prayed, etc., we repair'd to repose. N.B. This was the first Time that I ever Lodged in a Tavern on the Road.

15. Very Early we prepared (viz. by Prayers, Eating, etc.), and Set out. Stop'd at Jenisons.[33] We call'd again at Willsons,[34] and next at Warham William's,[35] who had been Sick very lately. We din'd at Each's. Thence to Boston, But at Charleston Mr. Rice parted with me. I invited him home with me, but he had Business for an avocation. At home I found My Sister Elius[36] (as we Sometimes call her) with a Child that was born the Fourth of this Instant. We Miss'd of being at Lecture, but I walked up to Mr. Edwards's Shop to hear the News, and see my Friends. At Night our Society Met at Barretts, at which I first pray'd and Mr. Eliot[37] Discoursed from James 1, 5, and I Concluded. Thence I went to my Father's where I Lodged.

16. Mr. Barrett and Mr. Rice (My Companion down) came to See me; and they acquainted me with the Sad Story of Mr. Willard[38] and Four Children of Mr. Stevens[39] of Rutland taken Yesterday by the Indians. In the Close of the Day I walked to Cambridge.

17. Being Saturday, Mrs. Elizabeth Nutting[40] and I rode to Concord. We baited at Muzzie's[41] at Lexington. Our visit was to Major Prescot;[42] where we were well received. I had a Note in the Evening to preach all Day tomorrow from Mr. Whiting.[43] But though press'd very hard by the Major and Madame also to Comply, I wholly and vigorously Deny'd.

18. Mr. Whiting preach'd all Day. Mrs. Prescott went to her Sons in the Evening. The Major went to Sudbury and remain'd there, having in the Morning emitted a Warrant for a press for men to go against the Indians. We were very pleasantly Entertained by Mrs. Rebecca Prescot,[44] etc.

19. This Day Everything was managed Suitably to the Relation they bore to each and their own Figure. In the Afternoon we concluded to go back, and the Horse balked. We (though with Some Difficulty through the Immoderate Kicking) mounted and rode about a Mile, when we met with Sir Sparhawk,[45] by whose Earnest Desire we went back to Major Prescots and remain'd another Night.

20. Mr. Sparhawk, according to Appointment, came to us in the Morning and we remounted; and coming to the house where Mrs. Nutting was, Mr. Whiting came up to us, and passing his Compliment, told us he was Glad to Meet such Company, etc. He rode with us. We came to Lexington, baited, and left Sir Sparhawk. But Mr. Whiting was our Pleasant Company to the Top of an eminent Hill in a Farm of his, whence we had one of the most Delightfull Prospects that ever I had in my Life. From this Hill we Sunk a little to a Country House—into which this Good Gentleman Conducted us and bid us Welcome. Here we din'd and thence rode with very good Speed till we were obliged to Stop at an House upon Cambridge Common, being overtaken with an heavy Shower of Rain. But we reach'd home before Night. I went back to College and Lodged there.

21. In the Morning came Mr. Shattuck[46] of Westborough to Invite me to preach in That Town. After a Pause of about an hour and Debating with him, I agreed; and took an Horse that he Said he had brought Down; and rode down to Boston to prepare for going with him. There were Three Score Mohawks arrived at Boston just before Noon. I returned to Cambridge and rode over to Champneys[47] where my Horse was taken care of. N.B. Mr. Shattuck was sent over to Mr. Champney to Inquire for me.

22. I Set away for Larnard's[48] at Waterton where I had appointed to meet with Mr. Shattuck at 12 o'Clock. He was not Come. I Sat down and waited for him till he came. We began our Journey from this Tavern about ½ after 12; to Mr. Willsons where by Two. Thence at ½ after Two to Mr. Swift's[49] by 4. Thence at 5 to My assign'd Landlords, Mr. Maynard's[50] by dark. Prayers Ended I went to my Bed and Lodged (with Mr. Chandler of Concord, a House Carpenter, at work in finishing the Meeting house) very comfortably.

23, 24. There was nothing Remarkable these Two Days that I remember more than my Miscellaneous Discourses with this Chandler (who seems to be an Understanding Man) and my preparations for Sabbath Day.

25. I preach'd first at Westboro all Day. My text was 1 Samuel 16, 7. N.B. I set the Psalm.

26. I expected Barrett and was very Impatient that he did not come. In the Evening Mr. Ward[51] (as I remember) and one or two more were to See me, and he Appointed to go with me tomorrow to Hopkinton. Accordingly on the

---

[28] Originally of Cambridge; later of Oxford and Worcester.

[29] Gershom Rice, Jr. (1696-1781).

[30] Nathaniel Moore, third settler of Worcester, from Sudbury.

[31] Andrew Gardner (Harvard 1712), first minister of Worcester, 1719-1722. *Sibley*, V, 638-641.

[32] The Wayside Inn of Longfellow fame, in Sudbury, built by David Howe in the early 18th century. Alfred S. Hudson, *History of Sudbury* (Sudbury, 1889), pp. 591-599.

[33] Also in Sudbury.

[34] Probably Nathaniel Willson in Sudbury.

[35] Reverend Warham Williams of Waltham (Harvard 1719). *Sibley*, VI, 361-364.

[36] Elizabeth (Weld) Parkman, wife of Ebeneazer's brother Elias. The child was Elizabeth.

[37] Jacob Eliot of Boston (Harvard 1720), minister of the Third Church, Lebanon, Conn., 1729-1766. *Sibley*, VI, 380-382.

[38] Reverend Joseph Willard, while out hunting game, was killed by the Indians, Aug. 14, 1723. *Sibley*, VII, 650-651.

[39] Deacon Joseph Stevens. On Aug. 14, 1723, two sons, Samuel and Joseph, were killed, and two others, Phinehas and Isaac, were taken captive. Francis E. Blake, *Rutland & the Indian Troubles of 1723-1730* (Worcester, 1886), p. 7.

[40] Mrs. Jonathan Nutting of Cambridge.

[41] Benjamin Muzzy (1680-1764).

[42] Jonathan Prescott of Concord.

[43] Reverend John Whiting of Concord (Harvard 1700). *Sibley*, IV, 532-535.

[44] Mrs. Jonathan Prescott.

[45] Deacon Nathaniel Sparhawk, a selectman of Lexington.

[46] Isaac Shattuck.

[47] Samuel Champney, Parkman's father-in-law.

[48] Thomas Learned, tavern keeper.

[49] Reverend John Swift of Framingham (Harvard 1697). *Sibley*, IV, 387-390.

[50] David Maynard, an original settler at Westborough. A manuscript volume of Westborough Church Records, kept by Ebenezer Parkman and later ministers, is preserved by the Westborough Historical Society. At the beginning of this Parkman made a list of the first settlers of the town. The list is printed in Heman P. DeForest and Edward C. Bates, *History of Westborough* (Westborough, 1891), p. 46.

[51] Increase Ward.

27. My Landlord having borrowed me an horse (of his Neighbour Mr. David How) Mr. Ward and I rode away. We first call'd at Mr. Woods[52] but he was not at home. We rode to Mr. Barretts Lodgings but he was not there. We rested a While Smoak'd, etc., and took our Horses and went out to Meet him. Mr. Wood was riding with his Wife. Mr. Barrett we Saw, and brought Them home. I Lodg'd with Mr. Barrett. I had his very Strong Pressures to take up with Westburgh, etc.

28. I went out a hunting with Mr. Barrett, a Young Faun having been Seen not long Since—and Flocks of Turkeys. We Search'd the woods but Saw Nothing but Pigeons. We brought home Seven or Eight of Those. Towards Night Mr. Wood came to See us, etc. Lodg'd with Mr. Barrett.

29. At Mr. Woods—din'd there—they entertaining us handsomely. Went home alone.

30. Read Dr. Prideaux[53] and Spectators. Visit divers Neighbors. See Ammi Printer at Captain Fay's.[54]

31. Prepar'd for the Sabbath (but my Sermon already made.) N.B. On the 23 of this Month Deceas'd that Venerable Man Doctor Increase Mather, in his 85th Year.

26. I was sent for in the Evening to visit a sick Young Woman at Mr. Tomlin's.[55] I went and pray'd with her.

*I walked to the Meeting House with a Pistol in my Hand by reason of Danger of the Indians. When I return'd was much affrighted with the Sight of an Indian as I suppos'd; but drawing nigher I perceiv'd it was my Landlord. In the afternoon about 4 o'Clock, there was an Alarm in the North and people hastened with their Arms, But it came to little.

### (1723) SEPTEMBER. AT WESTBORO.

1. Preach'd all Day on 1 Cor. 3. 11. In the Evening visited Mrs. Tomlin. In the Night I was very restless.

2. Came away from Westborough.

### DECEMBER. 1723

1. Mr. Thatcher[1] A. M. Mr. Webb[2] P.M.

6. Mr. Prince[3] preach'd a Lecture.

8. I preach'd all Day at Newton for Mr. Cotton,[4] on 1 Sam. 16. 7. N.B. Mr. Joseph Champney[5] and Mr. Cotton.

15. I rode from Cambridge over to Waterton and preach'd at the Old Meeting house, both A and P.M. on 2 Cor. 3, 11. Entertain'd at Lieutenant Coolidges.[6] Return'd at night to Cambridge.

18. The Reverend Mr. Gee[7] was ordain'd Colleague Pastor of the Old North Church with Doctor Cotton Mather.

### JANUARY. 1724

1. To Day it was very Stormy or I should have (according to appointment) visited Mr. Breck.

2. Fair Pleasant Weather invited me to Visit Mr. Breck. I rode my Landlords horse. The Conversation was very instructing and very Pleasant. We Sat up very late discoursing of many Things miscellaneously. I read Edifying Letters of the Jesuits, Missioners to the East Indies; after I was a bed.

3. Mr. Breck oblig'd me to offer the morning Sacrifice. After Sundry Colloquys we took a Walk to Merchant Woods'.[1] I borrow'd the Spectator of him (volume 9). I din'd at Mr. Breck's.

[52] Captain John Wood of Hopkinton.
[53] Humphrey Prideaux, D.D. (1648-1724), Scots scholar. The work may have been *The Old and New Testament Connected, in the History of the Jews and Neighboring Nations* (London, 1716-1718), 2 vols.
[54] Captain John Fay, town Clerk of Westborough. See George H. Johnson, *Fay Family Tree* (Columbus, 1913).
[55] Deacon Isaac Tomlin.
*No date given.
[1] Reverend Peter Thatcher (Harvard 1696), of the New North Church, Boston. *Sibley*, IV, 303-308.
[2] Reverend John Webb (Harvard 1708), of the New North Church. *Sibley*, V, 463-471.
[3] Reverend Thomas Prince, of the Old South Church, Boston (Harvard 1707). *Sibley*, V, 341-368.
[4] Reverend John Cotton (Harvard 1710). *Sibley*, V, 510-524.
[5] Parkman's classmate (Harvard 1721). *Sibley*, VI, 437-439.
[6] Lieutenant Richard Coolidge, a representative of Watertown.
[7] Reverend Joshua Gee (Harvard 1717). *Sibley*, VI, 175-183.
[1] Benjamin Woods of Marlborough.

After a Dinner, a Pipe, and Some Discourse, of Mr. Ickyl's[2] Seat at Stow, of Westboro, etc., I repair'd home.

4. I prepar'd (partly) for Sabbath. In the Afternoon came Mr. Elmer[3] and Mr. Goddard[4] of Shrewsbury as they were passing to Sherborn. Mr. Elmer invited me in Mr. Barrett's Name to meet Mr. Barrett and the Company with his Wife, down at Framingham next Wednesday.

5. I preach'd at Westborough all Day. My Text was Math. 28, 6. In the Evening I was visited by Mr. Thomas Forbush.[5]

6. Town Meeting. In the Evening Captain Fay and Mr. Oliver Ward[6] with Mr. Daniel How were with me. Mr. Eliot and I nominated. Messers. Baker[7] and Holoway[8] committee.

7. I rode home, P.M., with Mr. Elmer who came to See me this morning. Upon Seeing Mrs. Elmer in lonely and dejected Circumstances I made many Reflections concerning my own Manner of Living in Future Times, etc. I went to Mr. Cushings[9] to See his Library and Discourse about Dr. Manton's[10] Works, 5 Volumes, which he had talk'd of Selling to Me. I rode back to Mr. Elmers, and (though by this Time it was very Dark) I rode home alone.

8. In the Morning came the Committee to treat with a Minister, to acquaint me that the Town had nominated Mr. Eliot with me in order to Choose one of us Minister for This Place. was moved with the Thought and manifested to them the Sens I had of the Weightiness of the Affair, And in Truth I was at a Stand (though I did not express any extraordinary hesitation) considering My incapacitie on Every head. But my Eyes and my Heart were directed to the Father of Lights from whom descends every Grace Sufficient that I might be endow'd and prepar'd in Some measure for which his providence might call me. Mr. Cushing by this Time was come and waited for me below. The Committee retir'd and I prepar'd to Ride. Mr. Cushing and I rode to Mr. Whoods to gain Intelligence. We were directed to Mr. Swifts. We rode down and got there about Dark. The Company was not arrived till 8 o'Clock. Mr. Barrett and his Wife, Two Fathers, Brother Thornton Barrett[11] and Sister Greaves.[12] Mr. Tilestone[13] and Son James[14] were there. Mr. Tylestone informed me of the Death of Uncle Clough[15] and Mr. John Mountfort[16] at Boston. We Sup'd very plentifully and for Rarity had a Pea-Hen roasted. I lodg'd there with Mr. Tilestone and Mr. Thornton Barrett.

9. In the Morning Mr. Swift oblig'd me to pray, and to return Thanks after Breakfast. Mr. Morris and Deacon Barrat[17] went Back to Boston. By the Deacon I convey'd a Letter to John Hicks[18] for me. Between 12 and 1 o'Clock we Set out from Mr. Swift's for Hopkinton. We stop'd at the Tavern (Maynards)[19] where there was a great Number of Hopkinton People, and at Mr. Jones's[20] we stop'd also. Colonel How[21] was in the Company and with great Ceremony congratulated me. We rode together on the Journey to Hopkinton, and he Gave me to Understand that he had been at Westborough at his Son Agar's where he was informed how Affairs were carry'd on. And the Colonel told me

[2] A Mr. Jekyl, an Englishman residing at the lower village in Stow, gave the town a small bell to hang in the meeting house in 1722. *Stow, Mass., 1683-1933* (Stow, n.d.), p. 11.
[3] Reverend Daniel Elmer (Yale 1713), who preceded Parkman as minister at Westborough. Dissension arose and Elmer was dismissed. He moved to Springfield in 1724, and in 1728 was ordained at Fairfield, New Jersey. DeForest and Bates, *Westborough*, p. 51. Franklin B. Dexter, *Biographical Sketches of the Graduates of Yale College . . . 1701-1745* (N.Y., 1885), pp. 110-111.
[4] Edward Goddard.
[5] One of the first settlers and selectman of Westborough. See Frederick C. Pierce, *Forbes and Forbush Genealogy* (n.p., 1892).
[6] A selectman of Westborough.
[7] Edward Baker.
[8] William Holloway.
[9] Reverend Job Cushing of Shrewsbury (Harvard 1714). *Sibley*, VI, 45-46.
[10] Thomas Manton, D.D. (1620-1677), Presbyterian divine, whose numerous works appeared in various editions.
[11] Of Hopkinton.
[12] Perhaps Rachel Graves, wife of Joseph Graves of Framingham.
[13] Probably James Tileston (1678-c. 1740) of Boston.
[14] James, Jr. (b. 1704), son of above.
[15] Ebenezer Clough, father-in-law of Ebenezer Parkman's brother, Elias.
[16] A prominent merchant of Boston.
[17] Samuel Barrett, father of Reverend Samuel Barrett of Hopkinton.
[18] Of Cambridge.
[19] Jonathan Maynard's tavern in Framingham.
[20] Colonel John Jones, then in Hopkinton (now Ashland).
[21] Thomas Howe of Marlborough.

of the Opposition Mr. Thomas Ward[22] endeavour'd to raise, of which I believe more may be Said hereafter. At Hopkinton there were very plentiful Provisions made, And there were many People. In the Evening we Sang a Psalm, the 128 by Mr. Deming[23] and Sundry Psalm Tunes. I had a great Deal of Discourse with Mr. Barret, of the Country, etc. Mr. Deming, Mr. Cushing and I rode home with Mr. Whood. Mr. Deming pray'd. Mr. Cushing and I lodg'd together.

10. In the Morning I was appointed to go back to Mr. How's (upon Mr. Cushing's Horse) to Bring Madame Greaves in Company with Mr. Barrett and Madame, Old Mr. How[24] and his Wife. We din'd at Mr. Whoods Upon roast Goose, roast Pea hen, Bak'd Stuff'd Venison, Beef, Pork, etc. After Dinner we Smoak'd a Pipe, read Governor Shute's[25] Memorial to the King and Mr. Cushing and I rode home. This Eve I visited Old Mr. Rice.[26] Ensign Newton[27] was with him. I borrow'd an Horse of him for my Service to Marlboro and to Stow. I returned Mr. Pratt's[28] Horse, which I had Us'd through all these Frolicks, by his young Son. In the Morning I rode to Marlboro. After Dinner (upon Roast Beef) with Mr. Breck, and our Concerting Measures upon Changing, Mr. Breck rode away for Westborough.

11. I preach'd all Day at Marlboro from 1 Sam. 16, 7. In the Evening Mr. Breck returned.

12. In the Forenoon Mr. Breck and I rode to Stow to Mr. Gardners[29] and over to See Mr. Ickyls Seat. We arrived again at Marlboro about Seven, Evening.

13. [no entry]

### FEBRUARY [1724]

28. I receiv'd the Vote of the Town of Westborough in which I am call'd to the great and arduous Work of the Gospel Ministry among them.[1]

### JUNE [1724]

5. Answer'd the Town of Westborough in the Affirmative, relying upon their Christian Goodness and Generosity (Since they Shew such fervent Affection to me) to maintain and Support me among them, according to which this Office they call me to shall require.

### JULY [1724]

1. Commencement. Happen'd to be the Day I receiv'd my Master's Degree.[1]

### AUGUST [1724]

1. I prepar'd for the Sabbath. Mr. John Prat came to Me concerning my Hay. He had bargain'd with me to take it by the Halves. But his Business now was to tell me that he had found that was like to be but about 7 Loads and he thought I had better profit all for my own Spending. He said he had got Two loads of it in Cock for me. I Should be welcome to his Labour therein and he would help Me in Mowing another Day if I could procure him Company. I was very thankful to his kind Disposition and determin'd to accept. About nine this Evening we had an Alarm all over Town but heard no Cause.

2. I preach'd all Day. My Text: Acts 2, 37, 38.

3. Rainy Weather. I went out to get Men to Mow and Make my Hay. I was at Mr. Rice's. His son Beriah[1] agreed. At Mr. Prats his Son agreed, and the old Man himself engag'd to See to the Making. This was very kind. But I got Mr. Clark[2] to help him. I was at Mr. Aaron Forbushes[3] and Bakers. Returning home I was caught in the Rain and was very Wet. Went into Mr. Prats to Dry and get a Coat. Thence home. The Next Day I was at the

4. Fast at Hopkington in order to Ordination. Mr. Baker A.M., Mr. Dor[4] and Mr. Swift P.M. They Read a Paper of Meeting to Pray and Confer, etc. N.B. We met in Mr. Barrett's New House. Immediately after Exercises I rode away for Cambridge and got down about Eleven. N.B. Mr. Hobby[5] speaker at Hopkinton.

5. Brother Hinds[6] talked very hot about Living at Westboro.

6. I rode round to Boston but did not get there till Lecture was over. The News was Malden Emerson's[7] House was Burnt last Friday Night. Four Men taken at Rutland, 3 kill'd and one Captur'd.[8] There was one more wounded. I rode up to Cambridge to Night though it rain'd all the way.

7. I rode to Framingham. Lodg'd at Mr. Jones's.[9] I visited Increase Ward.[10]

8. In the Morning I rode to Hopkinton. Mrs. Spencer here still. I read severall fine Poems, etc.

9. I preach'd at Hopkinton; Mr. Barrett at Westboro. My Text was Rev. 3, 20, and John 15, 14. N.B. The first (through forgetfullness) I preach'd the Second time in this place.

10. Mr. Barrett's Wife and Mrs. Spencer rode with Me to White Hall.[11] In the After noon we gathered Hazelnutts. Towards Evening rode home.

11. In My Study of King on Church.

12. Visited Landlord Maynard. He not at Home.

13. I rode to Marlboro Lecture. Mr. Cushing preach'd. After Lecture Mr. Gardner of Stow came to Mr. Brecks. Captain Fay[12] and Mr. Prat rode home with me.

14. Read Martin Mar Prelate, and prepar'd for the Sabbath this and

15th Day.

16. Preach'd all Day. Acts 2, 37, 38.

17. I rode to Cambridge through Framingham on Mr. Samuel Hardys[13] Horse. Met Deacon Haven[14] on the Roade. We Call'd at Captain Goddards and at Mr. Swifts. Here was Mr. Brintnal.[15] I asked him to help me. I got down in the Evening.

18 and 19 it rain'd so I was detain'd at Cambridge.

20. I rode to Boston. Mr. Sewall[16] preach'd. He is Chosen president of Harvard College. In the after noon I was at Mr. Gee's where were Mr. Thomas Foxcroft,[17] Mr. Wigglesworth,[18] Mr. Prince (Nathan),[19] Mr. Turell[20] and Mr. [blank], a Gentleman from the Bank. I return'd to Cambridge in the Evening.

[22] One of the first inhabitants of Westborough.

[23] Probably Daniel Deming (Harvard 1700) who had been minister at Needham, Mass., and was later supply pastor at Lyme, Conn. Sibley, IV, 518-519.

[24] Captain Thomas Howe of Marlborough.

[25] Governor Samuel Shute of Mass.

[26] Thomas Rice of Westborough. See Andrew H. Ward, A Genealogical History of the Rice Family (Boston, 1858).

[27] Thomas Newton of Westborough.

[28] John Pratt of Westborough.

[29] Reverend John Gardner (Harvard 1715). Sibley, VI, 88-90.

[1] See DeForest and Bates, Westborough, pp. 62-63. On Jan. 6, 1724 the Westborough town meeting appointed "a Commetee to Go to Sum Reverend ordained Elders that are a quanted with Mr. Ebenezer Parkman and Mr. Jacob Eliot, Both of Boston, and Candideats for the ministry, for their advice and Recommendation in order for Election as the Law Directs." In February Parkman was chosen minister and the town voted a yearly salary of £80, and £150 for "a settlement," the latter to be paid in three equal annual installments.

[1] Parkman married Mary Champney, a daughter of Samuel and Hannah Champney of Cambridge on July 7, 1724 in Cambridge. See Paige, Cambridge, p. 507 and Cambridge Vital Records, II, 299. DeForest and Bates, Westborough, p. 71, incorrectly give the place and date of the marriage as Boston, Sept. 14, 1724.

[1] Beriah Rice (b. 1702), son of Thomas Rice.

[2] Westborough Vital Records (Worcester, 1903) do not give any record of a Clark in this period.

[3] An early inhabitant of Westborough.

[4] Reverend Joseph Dorr (Harvard 1711) of Mendon, Mass. Sibley, V, 574-578.

[5] William Hobby (Harvard 1725). Later minister of First Church at Reading, now Wakefield, Mass. Sibley, VII, 530-537.

[6] Perhaps Jacob Hinds (1685-1764?) who lived at various times in Brookfield, Marlborough, Shrewsbury and West Boylston.

[7] Reverend Joseph Emerson (Harvard 1717) of Malden. Boston News-Letter, Aug. 6, 1724. Sibley, VI, 170-175.

[8] Boston News-Letter, Aug. 6, 1724. The three men who perished were James Clark, Joseph Wood and Uriah Wood. Eleazer Ball was wounded. The name of a boy captured is unknown. Blake, Rutland and the Indian Troubles, pp. 10-11.

[9] Colonel John Jones.

[10] The only Increase Ward noted lived in Westborough.

[11] A large pond in Hopkinton.

[12] Captain John Fay.

[13] Of Westborough.

[14] Moses Haven of Framingham.

[15] William Brintnall (Yale 1721), schoolmaster of Sudbury, 1722-1726. Dexter, pp. 244-245.

[16] Joseph Sewall (Harvard 1707), D.D., minister of the Old South Church, Boston. Sibley, V, 376-393.

[17] (Harvard 1714). Minister of the First Church in Boston. Sibley, VI, 47-58.

[18] Edward Wigglesworth (Harvard 1710), D.D., Professor of Divinity, Harvard College. Sibley, V, 546-555.

[19] (Harvard 1718). Tutor and fellow of Harvard College. Brother of Thomas Prince, the historian. Sibley, VI, 268-279.

[20] Reverend Ebenezer Turell (Harvard 1721), minister of Medford. Sibley, VI, 574-582.

21. I rode away for Westboro. Met Mrs. Martha Clark[21] and Sister with Mrs. Lasten by riding to Newton. Farther on the Road I met Mr. Bartlett[22] of Brookfield by whom I learnt Something Considerable of the Town. I stopt at Merchant Woods[23] at Marlboro. He walked with me to Mr. Brecks.[24] Mr. Breck I found ill. I lodged here. Early to Westboro in the morning (22) to prepare for the Sabbath.

23. Preach'd all Day. Tit. 2, 12. News that Captain Harmon[25] had slain 5 or 6 Score Indians at Norridgewock with Sebastian Ralle[26] the Old Jesuit and brought in his and 26 or 27 Scalps besides and Delivered Three Captives from the Enemy. Among those that were Slain of the Indians Bummageem was one. His wife and Two Sons were taken Captive and brought to York and Piscataqua. And in all we lost not a Man but an Indian, a Cape Fellow. *Deo Opt. Max. Gloria Triumphi.* Captain Harmon (it is storied) found an Iron Chest with the Jesuit which had many Letters in it, Some from Gentlemen at Boston (O Horrids) Betraying our Country.

25. I rode Early in the Morn to Marlboro. Mr. Breck ill yet. Then rode (with Deacon Peters) over to Stow to the Association[27] at Mr. Gardners. A Thin Meeting, Mr. Swift and Cushing, Mr. Jenison,[28] Mr. Barrett[29] and Mr. Brintnall. Mr. Ickyl, etc. up at Stow.

26. Mr. Barrett Preach'd but Mr. Jenison prayed. Good entertainment, but no great Matter of Business done. I rode away with the Rest about 5 o'Clock P.M. Mr. Brintnall to preach for Me. I rode to Cambridge. Cousin Sarah Champney[30] at Uncle Champneys.[31] Between 10 and eleven o'Clock.

27. Not very Well. I could not go to Boston.

28. I rode to Framingham; preach'd. The Text was John 15, 14. Deacon Robie lodged with me.

29. Mr. Brintnall came. We rode to Captain Goddards and to Westboro.

30. Mr. Brintnall preach'd for Me but he would not pray at all Save after the forenoon Sermon. He said he was indisposed. Indians at Northhampton and Westfield.

31. Workmen about the Chamber.

### SEPTEMBER [1724]

1. Those that were Members of the Committee[1] met at Mr. Pratts.

2. In the Morning I rode with My Landlord[2] over to Hopkinton to Mr. Barrett's Ordination. We met in Mr. Barretts New House. Mr. Appleton[3] Pray'd First; Mr. Webb of Boston Preach'd; Mr. Dor then pray'd; Mr. Swift gave the Charge; Mr. Brown[4] of Reading the right Hand of Fellowship; and Elder Lyman[5] Set the Psalm. We din'd handsomely. Mr. Cushing, Mr. Thornton Barrett,[6] Cousin Charles Coffin and I all Lodg'd at Mr. Woods. N.B. Mr. Webb, discourse in the Evening, of the Doctors of the Church. Viz. Tillotson, Scott, etc.

3. Mr. T. Fowle and Mrs. Spencer came over to us at Woods. We had a good Dinner. Mr. Cushing and I carried the Ladies home to Mr. Barretts and return'd to My Lodging at Westboro. Mr. Cushing Lodg'd with Me.

[21] Mrs. Uriah Clark of Framingham.
[22] Thomas Bartlet.
[23] Benjamin Woods.
[24] Reverend Robert Breck of Marlborough.
[25] Colonel Johnson Harmon.
[26] Father Sebastian Ralé, head of the Jesuit mission at Norridgewock, Maine. See James P. Baxter, *The Pioneers of New France in New England* (Albany, 1891).
[27] The accepted date and place for the formation of the Marlborough Association of ministers is June 5, 1725, at the house of Mr. Breck in Marlborough. From this entry in the Parkman diary it is clear that an association was in existence before that time. Levi A. Field, *An Historical Sketch of the First Congregational Church in Marlborough, Mass.* (Worcester, 1859), pp. 16–18. Joseph Allen, *The Worcester Association and Its Antecedents* (Boston, 1868), p. 5.
[28] William Jennison (Harvard 1724), later minister of the Second Church of Salem, Mass., 1728–1736. *Sibley*, VII, 371–374.
[29] Reverend Samuel Barrett of Hopkinton.
[30] Daughter of Joseph and Sarah Champney of Cambridge. Sister of Parkman's classmate, Joseph Champney.
[31] Joseph Champney, Sr.
[1] This meeting reached the decision to organize a church in Westborough. DeForest and Bates, *Westborough*, p. 69.
[2] David Maynard.
[3] Reverend Nathaniel Appleton (Harvard 1712) of Cambridge. *Sibley*, V, 599–609.
[4] Reverend Richard Brown, Jr.
[5] Deacon Caleb Lyman of the New North Church, Boston.
[6] Of Hopkinton.

4. Mr. Cushing went home P.M. The Members of the Church, with those that had offered themselves to join, Came to See me and acquainted Me with their Meeting last Tuesday, with their most happy Union; and to See what I thought necessary further to be done. Our Consultation lasted til sundown. We concluded with a Prayer.

5. I prepar'd for the Sabbath. O My own Inconstancy and instability in these unsettled Times!—when Steadiness is so much demanded.

6. I preach'd from Luke 10, 42 and James 1, 22.[7]

### OCTOBER [1724]

1. Dr. Mather[1] preach'd the Lecture, which was upon the Death of Gurdon Saltonstall, Governour of Connecticut. Mr. Green[2] was in Town but I could not come to Speak to him. I waited upon Mr. Webb[3] at Mr. Bromfields[4] for the covenant of our Church at Boston. Just at Night my consort and I went over to Charleston. She was very much affrighted indeed, But Mr. and Mrs. Appleton[5] were in the Boat. My Horse was put up at Boylstons.[6] We visited Mrs. Larkin.[7] I came up to Cambridge, though a little late.

2. I came up to Westboro. I din'd at Mr. Williams' (Weston).[8] I asked him to preach my Ordination Sermon. He made Some Provisos. I left him now by ¾ past 3, But got up to Mr. Brecks by Daylight in. He was very ill. He invited me to tarry with him tonight, but I had appointed to meet our Church at my Lodging and therefore left him. In riding thence home I met with a Sad Mischance. My Cloak (and van Mastericht wrapt in it) broke from my Portmanteau as it was buckled behind me. And it was very dark, but Still I thought it best to alight and look back for it. (I was not so far as Captain Wards). I did so; and keeping my horse in my hand, with my Eyes near the Ground, and Swinging my Cane for ¾ of a Mile back, I at length found it. I therefore did not get home till the people were gone. I got a very bad Cold and Sore Throat, But

3. I prepar'd for the Sabbath And

4. preach'd all Day from Josh. 24, 15.

5. In the Afternoon the Church Members met together.

6. I had my Landlords Horse to Ride to Marlboro to See Mr. Breck. I acquainted him with our Management and with Mr. Rice[9] and his Concern, etc. Mr. Breck said he did not Expect that he should be with us, however he had no thought of any such thing as Excepting against Mr. Rice. I call'd in at Merchant Amsdens.[10] Here were Captain Willard[11] of Sutton. Mr. Bailey[12] of Lancaster and Mr. Wilder.[13] N.B. Captain Willard concerning Mr. Cushing and I. I rode to Mr. Samuel Hows[14] in my way to Mr. Swifts.[15] I lodg'd at Mr. Swifts.

7. Mr. Stone[16] came to See Mr. Swift in the Morn. I inquir'd of Mr. Swift concerning a form of Letter to Send to Churches to request their Help in Ordination but was not satisfy'd. I rode to Mr. Jones'[17] where I heard of Mrs. Barrett[18] and the Death of her Child. She had been in Travail a long time and very hardly escaped herself. I rode up to Hopkinton and was in good Season for the funerall. A Sorrowful Time! I rode to Mr. Woods[19] and lodg'd there.

[7] On Sept. 24, 1724, a fast was held in Westborough preparatory to the gathering of a church and the ordination of Mr. Parkman. On Sept. 28 it was voted in town meeting to hold the ordination, Oct. 28, 1724.
[1] Cotton Mather.
[2] Joseph Green of Boston.
[3] Reverend John Webb of Boston.
[4] Edward Bromfield, selectman of Boston.
[5] Probably Reverend and Mrs. Nathaniel Appleton of Cambridge.
[6] Richard Boylston of Charlestown.
[7] Probably Mrs. Edward Larkin of Charlestown.
[8] Reverend William Williams (Harvard 1705). *Sibley*, V, 295–300.
[9] Probably Thomas Rice of Westborough.
[10] Captain Isaac Amsden of Marlborough.
[11] Jonathan Willard.
[12] Benjamin Bayley or Bailey, constable.
[13] Probably Ebenezer Wilder, also of Lancaster.
[14] Of Framingham.
[15] Reverend John Swift of Framingham.
[16] Probably Thomas Stone, selectman of Framingham. Josiah H. Temple, *History of Framingham* (Framingham, 1887), p. 708.
[17] Probably Colonel John Jones of Hopkinton (now Ashland).
[18] No indication of a Barrett death at this time in *Hopkinton Vital Records* (Boston, 1911).
[19] Captain John Wood of Hopkinton.

8. I return'd to Westboro. I call'd to see Mr. Increase Ward to discourse with him about his Entering into the Church, baptism, etc.

9. My Business about this time was reading Ordination Sermons and wherever the Minister's Duty was Explain'd, Especially van Mastricht, *De Ministaris Ecclesiastico*.

10. According to Mr. Barretts Desire I rode over to Hopkinton. On the road met Captain Fay and his Wife going to Mr. Woods.

11. I preach'd at Hopkinton and Mr. Barrett at Westboro. My text, Heb. 12, 1; James 1, 22. Mr. Barrett went and return'd to Day. Mr. Fowles good Company Here.

12. I return'd to Westboro. Mrs. Wood[20] at her house discours'd about Some Methods for the people in their provision for Ordination. In the Evening came a Committee to treat with my Landlord about providing, etc. There was much Caring about bringing up my Goods.

Memorandum. I formed Letters (by the Towns Desire) to be Sent to Severall Churches, (viz. Boston to Mr. Webb, Framingham Mr. Swift, Marlboro Mr. Breck, Lancaster Mr. Prentice[21] and (a Letter from myself to ask him to preach), Sudbury Mr. Loring,[22] and Mendon Mr. Dorr. These were drawn up on the 9th Day.

13. I read Sermons, etc. Mr. Edmund Rice[23] with me in the Evening.

14. This Day I Solemnly Dedicated to Humiliation and Prayer to prepare myself (by the grace of God) for the Awful Time approaching.

28. This was truely the Greatest Day I ever Yet Saw—The Day of my Solemn Separation to the Work of the Gospel Ministry and my Ordination to the Pastorate in Westborough.

The Solemnity came on and proceeded in the manner following.

In Order to the gathering the Church, a Covenant was prepar'd before hand; read, and consider'd by the Candidates for Membership, and was Sign'd.

N.B. An Ecclesiastical Council was form'd, and they having got all Things ready (as they apprehended) proceeded to the Meeting House.

N.B. Reverend Mr. Swift was Sent to, but he was detain'd by Sickness in his Family. Nevertheless the Church sent two Delegates, viz. Colonel Buckminster[24] and Captain Goddard.[25]

Reverend Mr. Breck was also Sent to, but he was himself so ill (of the Strangury) that he could not attend. Those ministers being Absent, the Council, with Consent, Admitted and requested Reverend Mr. Williams of Weston to Assist.

Being come to the House of God, the Reverend Mr. Dorr of Mendon open'd the Solemnity with Prayer. The Reverend Mr. Prentice of Lancaster preach'd a Suitable Sermon from 2 Cor. 12, 15. Afterwards The Reverend Mr. Williams of Weston aforesaid pray'd and gather'd the Church. There were 12 besides the Pastor Elect, who sign'd the Covenant and answered to their Names in the Assembly.

The Reverend Mr. Prentice gave the Solemn Charge.

The Reverend Mr. Loring of Sudbury the Right Hand of Fellowship.

The Ordain'd appointed the Psalm (part of the 68th) and gave the Blessing.

I wish Every Day throughout my Life, may bear a Suitable proportion to this Day! That I may be Strong in the Grace which is in Christ Jesus, and that I may grow then into the Glory of God and the Edification of His Church! Amen![26]

### SEPTEMBER, 1725

My Mother rode up with me to Westboro.

14. This Morning was very Cloudy, Not only abroad as to the weather but in the house with respect to my wife who for

about Three hours was in great Extremity. I thought I had not been earnest enough with God yet, notwithstanding what passt last night, etc. Then again Engaged in a Short but fervent Devotion, and Ten Minutes past Eight my wife was delivered of a Daughter. I cryed unto God most high, unto God who is a very present Help in time of Trouble and performeth all things for us, and He brought Salvation. He put joy and Gladness into our Hearts; and O that we may never forget his Benefits!

17. My Father came up to us.

19. The Child was Solemnly given up to God in Baptism (My Father holding it up). I call'd it (by my wife's Name) Mary.

28. My Father and Mother rode to Boston. My mother stopt at Marlboro being ill.

### OCTOBER [1725]

4. Mother Champney came up, being brought up by Father Champney.

My wife a very Sore Breast.

Breast Broke under Mrs. Whitcombs Care.

Breast Broke a Second Time.

### NOVEMBER [1725]

8. I rode down with Mother Champney to Cambridge.

9. I went to Boston with Sister Lydia.[1] My horse was carried back to Cambridge by a Boy. I Supp'd at Brother Alexander's[2] (who was married Last month, just after my Father left home for Westborough).

11. Mr. Thatcher[3] preach'd the Publick Lecture. The Boy having brought Back my Horse, I toward night prepar'd, and understanding, by Sister Lydia, that Mrs. Dorcas Bows[4] (my wife's Kinswoman) would ride up to Westboro with me, and that Mrs. Dorcas waited for me at Charleston, we went over by Ferry and we overtook her at Neck o' Land. We proceeded on Horseback with good pace; and Sister alighting at a place whence she Could with much Ease walk to Sister Hicks'.[5] I returned and took up Mrs. Dorcas and by these means we got up Comfortably.

12. Brother Champney[6] and Sister Lydia accompanied Mrs. Dorcas and Me to Westboro; and we got home in good Season. I was forc'd to ply myself to finish my Preparation for Sabbath, which besides what I could do at Boston must needs be Thought to take up the whole Thirteenth Day of the Month.

14. I preach'd A.M. and P.M. from Eccl. 9, 10.

15. I was call'd out to see Mrs. Tomlin[7] who was in Travail and in terrible Fits. She continued in them in a very awfull and Ghastly manner. The Infant was Dead at the Birth. When I return'd home I found Mr. Cushing[8] at our House.

16. Mrs. Tomlin dy'd, a Sore Trial to the Young Man, Who in such a mann'r Lost his First wife and Child.

17. Brother and Sister return'd home to Cambridge. Mrs. Tomlin Buried. Mrs. Dorcas rode with me to the Funerall and after it we went up to Captain Fays.[9]

20. I rode down with Mrs. Dorcas to Cambridge.

### JANUARY [1726]

1. Besides my making my preparations for the approaching Sabbath, I have little to remark concerning this Day, as it looks as if very many kindred and most of my Dayes have rolled away without anything worth noting upon them. Some are left Blank because of the Confusion I am put into by *Diem perdidi;* or because with all my Desire to Improve my time, I prove but of little importance either to Myself, or anyone Else.

I had through the whole of this Day crowds of imperfect Reflections upon the Consumption of Time and the misimprov-

[20] Mrs. Benjamin Wood.

[21] Reverend John Prentice (Harvard 1700). *Sibley*, IV, 529-532.

[22] Reverend Israel Loring (Harvard 1701). *Sibley*, V, 75-83.

[23] Of Westborough.

[24] Joseph Buckminster of Framingham. Temple, *Framingham*, p. 490.

[25] Captain Edward Goddard of Framingham. Temple, *Framingham*, p. 566.

[26] See DeForest and Bates, *Westborough*, pp. 81-84, and Westborough Church Records.

[1] Lydia Champney, Parkman's sister-in-law.

[2] Alexander Parkman (1699-1747) married Esther, widow of John Pilkins and daughter of George and Rebecca Walker, Oct. 1, 1725.

[3] Reverend Peter Thatcher of Boston.

[4] Mrs. Nicholas (Champney) Bowes, Mrs. Parkman's cousin.

[5] Mrs. John (Champney) Hicks, daughter of Samuel and Hannah Champney of Cambridge.

[6] Samuel Champney, Parkman's brother-in-law.

[7] Mrs. Isaac Tomlin of Westborough.

[8] Reverend Job Cushing of Shrewsbury.

[9] Captain John Fay of Westborough.

ment of my Talents. Late in the Evening when I had finished my Sermons, as my manner has often been to look into Myself and view the State of my Heart, that I may be in some Measure prepar'd for the Holy time and solemn Employments coming on; at this Season, I say, my Thoughts run more free from those Confusions and interruptions just mentioned, than in the Day, but were chiefly engag'd upon my grievous Neglect of the Affairs and Concerns of my Soul and preparations for Eternity, and particularly upon my omission of this Method of keeping a journal (or Diary) so long as I have. And I regret that when I did make a Business of it, there was so much time and pain spent in Vanity. I fix'd a Resolution to prosecute other Aims and purposes, and to confine myself more severely and strictly to Studies of Grave and Serious Subjects, to Enquirys into my own Deportment, and to such observations on the Demeanour and Conduct of these as that thereby I may learn the most Suitable regular method of forming my own Thoughts and Actions.

2. My Early Thoughts were upon the Revolutions of Time which will, none knows how soon with me, be swallowed up in Eternity, And upon the wondrous Grace of God in Continuing the Day and means of Salvation. Our Entertainments for this Day were raised from 1 Cor. 16, 22. Mr. Nehemiah How[1] and Mr. Joseph Wheeler[2] din'd with us. The Evening Reflections were much the Same as Last Night.

3. I began, in a Serious Manner, with the above said purpose of numbering my Dayes; and I beseach God to aid me by his Holy Spirit, that I may do it aright, and that I may apply my Heart to true Divine wisdom. And there is so much and more need of Dependence upon God, because I am very suspicious that without Such preternaturall power and assistance lent me, what through my wretched Inconstancy, Inadvertence and want of Resolution against which would interrupt the Affair, would either altogether Drop or loose its principal Design.

4. I went to Mr. Bakers,[3] Captain Fay and to his Brothers. At the Captain's we were much engag'd about the circumstances of my delivering my Quit Claim to Mr. Elmer's[4] Land to Captain Goddard,[5] etc.

5. My Chief Concern lay with the 1 volume of the Occasional Papers and with Sir Matthew Hale's Contemplations.

6. Captain Fay (with his Team), Mr. Charles Rice,[6] Mr. Miller,[7] Mr. Grow,[8] Mr. Baker, Mr. Campbel, Mr. Samuel Fay's Son, and an hand from Rice, came to Cut and Sled wood for me.

7. 8. Prepar'd for the Sabbath (that is with the Preparation made in the former part of the Week). I bought a Bearskin Muffler. Mr. Rice was with me about keeping his Man.

9. A.M. Our Contemplations were on Job 28, 28, and P.M. on John 17, 3.

10. Neighbor Clark dress'd Flax for me, and his Son thrash'd Oats. Mr. Rice brought his Mare to my Stable. Mr. Whood sent me a Peacock and Peahen.

11. I rectified Sundry of my Accounts.

12. A Spaniard, Oko Smiths, of Valencia came and offered himself to my Service. In the Evening I rode abroad to Captain Byles[9] who Complain'd much of Pains and Lameness. I pay'd him for four Barrells and a powdering Tub made for me. Thence I rode to Neighbor Brighams[10] Whose Son and Daughter were ill. N.B. This Morning my Peacock dy'd.

13. Hannah Warren[11] had my Man to go to Boston.

14. 15. Prepar'd for the Sabbath.

16. I preach'd upon Col. 3, 2. I observ'd a general delinquency in our people in coming to meeting, through which I am oblig'd to wait near half an hour or altogether, as it has Sometimes prov'd before I could begin the Exercises of Evening.

17. Last night was Exceeding Cold. This Morning One of my Summer Piggs I perceived was frozen to Death. Mr. Barrett[12] came to see us, and with Heavy Tidings of my Fathers being so very ill that my Brother by him sent me this word, that there was Ground to fear My Father would never go abroad again; and therefore it was much desir'd I would immediately go down. Hereupon I went first to Mr. David Maynards and then to Mr. Pratts[13] for an Horse, mine being not yet returned, but I succeeded not till Eleazer Pratt[14] went to Mr. David Goodno's and Obtained His. My Walking so far in the Cold, together with my Troubles and fears, and the Worries of my Mind, were such that I felt very uncomfortable, and I had an Uneasy Night, a bad Cold and grievous Head ach. And a Tedious Journey at this Season in Prospect, Besides the Melancholly Expectations of what I was altogether unprepar'd for.

18. Three quarters after nine in the Morning, I mounted from home upon a very poor dull Horse, which was another Affliction to meet this time. At Mr. David Hows[15] I saw Mr. McKinstry[16] of Sutton with his friend Briton. Very Snowy. In Weston I met my own Beast and it much rejoic'd me to Change. I got to Father Champney's[17] in good Season to have gone to Boston, But the Storm was so violent, the wind very high and no less Cold, and very Slippery Riding, Besides that I was so tired and faint that I was necessitated to tarry all night here, though my Resolution had been very Strong to have seen my Father if alive before I left. Father Champney was very melancholy and Dejected, a great Alteration from a few Months ago.

19. I got into Boston before noon, and joyfull to tell, my Father I saw Sitting up and in some Hopefull Way. *Soli Deo Omnipotenti Gratias ago maximas qui hodienas preces matutinas audiebat et a tanta miseria et Calamitate quanta involutus fui Eiexit.* I visited Mr. Thatcher in the Evening. Mr. Webb[18] came in, and the Conversation turned upon the Kingdom of Christ, the calling of the Jews, etc. I observ'd Mrs. Thatcher[19] to discourse with a great deal of pertinence and Solidity as well as Zeal upon the Side of the millenists. By and by Madame rose up and to Mr. Webb we'll go if you please Sir from the Jews to Spanish and Polish at which game [?] they play'd till near nine when I left them and went to Captain Boyse's[20] to see Cousin Dorcas Bowes. He was presently very Earnest about the Late Transactions at the wedding of Miss Sarah Champney[21] to John Lowell,[22] who were married the 23 of Last Month. To Day Mr. Lowell ordained at Newbury.

20. Mr. Gee[23] preach'd the publick Lecture on Psalm 122. I went in the Afternoon to Mr. Lewis's to see Mrs. Edwards, but she herself was so ill with a broken Breast, and her son was apprehended to be dying, that therefore I could not see her. Captain Storey[24] convers'd with me about his Sons living with me. His words were these about the Conditions of our Discourse. 'Take the Lad, Sir, Till about May, when I expect to return from Sea, but if it please God to prevent me, if you like the Boy keep him till he is 15 or 16 years old, when I would have him put to apprentice. All I Desire is that you keep him warm, and feed him Suitably. Instruct him Christianity. My main Expectation and hope is that you'll give him Education proper to such an One. Let him Serve you as he is able, impose not on him those heavy burthens that will either Cripple him or Spoil his Growth. But in all regards I am willing he should Serve you to his Utmost. Upon my Consenting to this he said he has no Hatt. Let him have one of yours, and if it should so happen that he doth not remain with you I'll pay for it.' Upon all which I got him a Hatt at my Brothers and took him with Me at the Entrance of the

---

[1] Of Westborough.
[2] Of Westborough.
[3] Edward Baker of Westborough.
[4] Reverend Daniel Elmer, formerly of Westborough.
[5] Edward Goddard of Shrewsbury. Andrew H. Ward, *History of Shrewsbury* (Boston, 1847), pp. 283–284.
[6] An early inhabitant of Westborough.
[7] James Miller of Westborough.
[8] Samuel Grow of Westborough.
[9] Captain Joseph Byles, an early inhabitant of Westborough.
[10] David Brigham.
[11] Of Westborough.
[12] Reverend Samuel Barrett of Hopkinton.
[13] John Pratt.
[14] Of Westborough.
[15] At the Wayside Inn in Sudbury.
[16] Reverend John McKinstry.
[17] Samuel Champney, Sr.
[18] Reverend John Webb of Boston.
[19] Wife of the Reverend Peter Thatcher of Boston.
[20] Samuel Boyce of Boston.
[21] Daughter of Noah and Sarah (Tunnell) Champney.
[22] Reverend John Lowell (Harvard 1721). *Sibley*, VI, 496–502.
[23] Reverend Joshua Gee of Boston.
[24] Probably Rowland Storey of Boston.

Evening. It was very Cold and for the Sake of the Boy I was forc'd to call in twice by the way to Cambridge. We got up to Father Champney's in good Season, but very Cold.

21. It was near Eleven before I could Mount for home. I Stopp'd and Din'd at Captain Brintnalls,[25] and got home before Day Light in. Engag'd in My Preparations for the Sabbath, which were now to Begin.

22. I was bound very Strict to my Study, and very little time for Reflections or Meditations.

23. I finish'd my Sermons before meeting time which were a further prosecution of my Thoughts upon Col. 3, 2. It was a very Extreme Cold Day, Especially the forenoon. Captain Fay din'd with me.

24. I visited Mr. Thomas Newton[26] who had been ill some time. I am thankfull to Mr. Pratt who came to my Family to assist them in my Absence, and to see what might be done for their Comfort, and today came himself and went to Mill for me. Much foul weather, frequent Snows.

25. In the Evening I was full of Reflections upon my Negligence and in Trouble upon that account. The Circumstances of my Family are such that I can't avoid inumerable interruptions and impediments as it has prov'd all this winter, that I have been much obstructed in my Studies. I pay'd Mr. Goodeno 15 shillings for Labour in last Hay time.

26. I visited Mr. Jonathan Howard[27] who has been ill. His Mother likewise was Some little time agoe much afflicted with a Tumor in her Throat. Returning I call'd in at Mr. Eager's[28] and supp'd there.

27. 28. 29. My Time was these Dayes taken up with Enquiries into my Subject for Next Lords Daye's Sermons and preparing them.

30. Our Text was Heb. 10, 25. Forenoon particularly was very Stormy and a great deal of Snow fell.

31. In the Evening I went down to see Lieutenant Forbush[29] who yet remains in Sad Circumstances and much pained. I Entertained My Self with St. Augustine of the City of God with the Notes of Ludovicus Dives. This Book to my Conceiving is of Superiour Value and usefullness.

### FEBRUARY [1726]

1. A Clear Day, except the first part of it, but the wind very high and blew the Snow about very much, Especially towards and in the Evening Exceeding Vehement and Cold.

I read likewise the account given of Madame De Maintenon by the Guardian.

2. This morning was bitter Cold. We have hitherto had a very Severe Winter as we have Scarcely had for many Years. I began my preparations for the Sabbath. I read the notes of Rescomen on Horace in part.

3. 4. 5. I was Employ'd upon my Subject consulting Dr. Merlock, Mr. Charnock,[1] etc.

6. I preach'd on Heb. 10, 25. In the morning I was put into great confusion and astonishment while Engag'd in the first prayer, to Such a Degree that it was with much difficulty that I proceeded, for I Entered upon the Sacred Employment with trembling and fear from the meditations I had all the morning upon my unworthyness and Sinfullness, my Slothfullness, negligence and unprofitableness in the most Exalted Trust and with Some of the highest Advantages. And the lively apprehension hereof so fill'd and possess'd my mind in the Holy Exercises that I could Scarce regard anything besides. I consider it as a righteous Castigation of God for my unfaithfullness to him in the great work to which he has called me, and I would humble myself before him and Implore his pardon through the Blood of Christ, and his grace to quicken and assist me. Both at noon and at night I Sadly reflected hereupon and offered prayers to God for Reconciliation and mercy.

7. Neighbor Clark[2] related the management of the Church of Stow in the Case of Richard Temple, a Member thereof. We got out a parcell of grain that was so full of Tares it was Scarce fit for use.

8. I was abroad at Mr. Oliver Wards and reckoned household with him. In the Evening Mr. Thurston[3] and his wife were here till it was Late. We reckoned etc.

9. I was at Mr. John Maynards[4] about noon. In the first of the Evening came Mr. McKinstry of Sutton and Mr. Walker,[5] one of his parish and they lodged with us.

10. 11. 12. I was chiefly taken up with my Sermons. Very pleasant weather because thawing.

13. I again preach'd on Heb. 10, 25.

14. I rode to Marlboro to Mr. Brecks.[6] We walk'd to Mr. Woods.[7] I paid up my account with Mr. Woods. We went into Mr. Amsdens[8] and Mr. Thomas[9] came in. My Full purpose was to return home, but Mr. Breck was so very Urgent with me, Since I had not been there for the Space of 3 months, that I tarried there all night.

15. After Dinner Mr. Breck appointed to go to his Daughters with me. I went to Mr. Edward Rice's[10] Shop and there, taking leave of Mr. Breck, I rode to Williams's[11] To see Mrs. Williams,[12] it being the first of my being in Town Since she was married. Returning home I call'd at Captain Wards[13] to warm me it being Cold and to spend a Little time in Conversation with the Captain but he had taken a fortnight ride into Connecticut.

16. I read Dr. Mathers Directions to a Candidate of the Ministry which pleased me very much.

17. I read Ned. Wards Trips to New England and Jamaica, P.M. The Evening I Enter'd upon my Sermons on which the reading Mr. Watts'[14] Guide to prayer I Employ'd the 18th and 19th Dayes.

20. I preach'd upon Gen. 12, 8.

21. 22. 23. I was oblig'd to Strict attention and Study. I sent Mr. Ward to Mr. Barretts but he was from Home, and therefore no Dependence to be had upon him.

24. We had a Lecture upon 2 Cor. 5, 17.

25. 26. I us'd utmost Diligence to prepare myself for the Approaching Solemnity, yet I was somewhat put to it to finish before I went to Bed on Saturday Night.

27. It was very Stormy and Consequently few Communicants to be Expected and 'Twas not without much Difficulty that my Wife surmounted the Wind and Snow. But I hope we all had much Reason to rejoice in the presence of God that we Enjoy'd at the Holy Supper of the Lord, which I administered, having preach'd upon Psalm 84, 1. In the Afternoon I again Discours'd on Gen. 12, 8. Our Exercises were very short.

28. I rode as far as Mr. Warrins and Mr. Amsdens. Mr. Amsden, upon Occasion of his Horse and a great number in the Neighborhood besides, and in every Town about us, gave out various Reflections upon the Sad Mortality and Destruction of Horses; and the sore visitations in the Extream scarcity of Corn and Hay at this Juncture, through which Multitudes are sorely Distress'd.

### MARCH [1726]

1. 2. Mrs. Whood and her Son with a Sled came and fetch'd away their Hay out of my Barn.

3. Mr. Cushing came to see us, and Mr. Woods of Marlboro

---

[25] William Brintnall of Sudbury. Hudson, Sudbury, pp. 299-301.
[26] An early inhabitant of Westborough. DeForest and Bates, Westborough, pp. 46-47.
[27] Of Westborough.
[28] James Eager, an early inhabitant of Westborough.
[29] Thomas Forbush of Westborough.
[1] Stephen Charnock (1628-1680), an English Puritan theologian.
[2] This person appears often in subsequent entries. Neither the Westborough town records nor the town history records any Clark in this period. Also Clark and Clarke genealogies do not reveal further information about this man.
[3] Joseph Thurston.
[4] Of Westborough.
[5] Lieutenant Obadiah Walker.
[6] Reverend Robert Breck of Marlborough.
[7] Benjamin Woods of Marlborough.
[8] Captain Isaac Amsden of Marlborough.
[9] William Thomas of Marlborough.
[10] Of Marlborough.
[11] Colonel Abraham Williams, a prominent resident of Marlborough. Charles Hudson, History of Marlborough (Boston, 1862), p. 470.
[12] Elizabeth Breck, daughter of the Reverend Robert Breck, married Abraham Williams, Dec. 22, 1725.
[13] Nahum Ward of Shrewsbury. Ward, Shrewsbury, pp. 457-459.
[14] Isaac Watts, D.D. (1674-1748), the famous English hymn writer.

was here at the same time. A Swine (given us by Mr. Holloway[1]) kill'd for us by Neighbor Clark and David Maynard. Mr. Cushing Lodg'd here. He gave us an account of Mr. Elmer and his Enfield People, etc.

4. He Returned Home. I in part prepar'd a Sermon.

5. I went on with my preparation till Noon, when I rode to Shrewsbury, and Mr. Cushing rode back my Horse to Westboro.

6. I preach'd at Shrewsbury upon John 12, 26, A.M. and P.M. Captain Keyes[2] over to see Me.

7. Mr. Cushing came in the morning to Me. We went over to Mr. Keyes's, where we had a strange Report about Mr. Breck's going to Merchant Wood's. Old Mr. Joslin[3] of Marlboro, a very grave and good man buried there. I wrote to Boston by Lieutenant Leonard[4] of Worcester. I return'd home.

8. Mr. Williams of Marlboro here to ask me to preach Mr. Brecks Lecture next Thursday.

9. I went to Captain Byle's and to Mr. Brighams to see his dau'ter in Law who continues Sick. At her Desire I pray'd with her. Mr. Brigham came home with me to prune my Trees. I went over to Neighbor Pratts to the Raising of his Barn.

10. This morning, tho not very good weather, I went to Marlboro to Lecture, But Mr. Cushing both pray'd and preach'd notwithstanding I was sent to, for I was not very well and I was glad I could persuade him. His Text was Mat. 11, 12. We went down to Mr. Woods and it became very Stormy and rain'd hard. Mr. Thomas was with us with many of his diverting amusements and adventures in London. Mr. Woods presented me a Girdle. Mr. Cushing Lodg'd with me at Mr. Brecks.

11. Captain Brigham[5] came in and gave us all an Invitation to Dinner with his Troop the last Tuesday of this Month. When we had din'd we left Mr. Brecks. I return'd home by way of Deacon Rices.[6] It was most Tedious Riding by the breaking in of the Horse. We were run into some Difficulty about going to Mill thro it being So long Stormy. But William Clark on the 12th went for us. Neighbor Clark brought Three Cows and Mr Oliver Ward an Horse to my Barn.

13. My Text this Day was Math. 6, 6.

14. 15. There is Need of again and again Remarking the Extream Difficulty and Distresses of People For themselves and their Beasts for want of Both Corn and Hay.

16. I was abroad at Mr. Increase Wards, Captain Fays,[7] etc., about my Spring Business, to hire Labourers, and make Enquiry after a Man to Live with me.

17. 18. 19. I further pursu'd my Subject of Secret worship and accordingly

20. I preach'd on the same Text as Last Sabbath. Jason Badcock an illegitimate born Child presented by Mr. Joseph Wheeler was Baptiz'd. That I might warrant this practice by Suitable Defence thereof I consulted our gravest New England Divines, Increase Mather, etc., First, and then Foreign most Judicious as van Masterickt (as well as those of our own Nation) Ames, etc.

21. 22. 23. I made it my Business to Enquire into the State of the Land and to Study the Causes of the Divine Judgement and what God is Demanding of Us by his Severe hands upon us. It is a Distressing time. Multitudes under heavy Sufferings for want of Hay for their Creatures.

24. A Publick Fast. My Text was Jas. 12, 4, A.M. and P.M. I Labour'd hard. When Exercises were over my mind was possess'd with it that God would be favourable to us this Year Ensuing.

25. 26. Very Strictly Engag'd in my Preparations.

27. I preach'd upon Ps. 25, 11.

28. About This Time Neighbor Green[8] was urgent with me to sell him part of my Land.

29. Mr. Rice Sundry Times visited me upon account of his Mare. Mr. John Pratt with me about my Meadows, etc.

30. No whither can one turn but the Calamity of the times are felt, Everyone Complaining and Lamenting. My Neighbor Clark tho a foreigner I could not but Comiserate, and I actually did put forth Myself to my utmost to succour him Every Way, By Grain, Hay, keeping Creatures, Money, etc. *O Miserere Deus!* Corn was Sold at Oxford for 8 shillings per Bushel, and in other places.

31. I rode down to Captain Wards to Engage Robert Henry to Live with me and I did so and Silence Bartlet, one for 23 t'other for 8 pounds per Year.

### APRIL [1726]

1. William Wilson of Concord, a poor Shiftless man Lodg'd with us Last night, and about the same time Simon Tainter[1] (who had been with me some time agoe) was with Me in a very Heavenly and Devout Time, Conversing of his State and preparations for his admittance into the Communion. I was upon My Preparations as also the 2nd Day.

3. I preach'd upon the Same Text as last Sabbath, Ps. 25, 11. John Whood of Hopkinton at Dinner with us. He rode home his Horse which I had had to keep.

4. One of Mr. Ward's Cows went home. What man would not think it worth Noting that [he] has Seen the mighty Contests and Brawlings that are often made about the most inconsiderable things of this kind, and the Reflections cast upon the honesty and uprightness of those of Sacred Character (because they ought to be Examples to observe), if there is not a peculiar preciseness and Exactness in making up the minutest part of an account.

5. Silence Bartlet came to Live with us. Two of Neighbor Clarks Cows went away. My Hay growing very short, or my Tenderness towards this man would not have suffer'd me to Send them away.

7. Mr. Rice's Mare went away after Lecture. I preach'd this Day on 2 Cor. 1, 12. I very Eagerly expected Mr. Barrett,[2] having sent to him in good Season, but (as it has happened these Three Times with him) I was disappointed.

8. Another of Mr. Wards Cows was Sent home.

9. This Day the Last of Mr. Wards Cows and his Horse went away. N.B. The 5th and 6th Neighbor Clark and his Son ploughed (with my Mare and Mr. Wards Horse) my Stubble, and the 8th and 9th Neighbor Clark with my Boy went on (as aforesaid) in ploughing and sowing of Wheat and Rye and Barley.

10. This Day was our sacrament. I preach'd upon Lamt. and 2 Cor. 1, 12. I have great Reason to express all gratitude to God for his presence with me, inasmuch as I trust I had much of the presence and spirit of God with me.

11. Robert Henry came to live with me. Neighbor Clark Sow'd My Oats, and Some Peas. William Clark Harrow'd till Eleven o'Clock and then Robert took the Work.

12. I rode down to Association at Marlboro. Present, Mr. Swift,[3] Mr. Breck, Mr. Prentice,[4] Mr. Loring,[5] Mr. McKinstry,[6] Mr. Cushing,[7] Mr. Gardner,[8] Mr. Cook,[9] Mr. Barrett, Mr. Burr[10] and myself. Mr. Swift opened the Association with prayer, and Mr. Thomas McKinstry[11] propos'd a Matter between himself and one of his parish, in which he requested our Sentiments and advice concerning the best Manner of Managing it. He had preach'd a Sermon from these words in Eph. 5, 20: "Giving

---

[1] Adam Holloway of Westborough.
[2] John Keyes of Shrewsbury. Ward, *Shrewsbury*, pp. 340–341.
[3] Nathaniel Joslin died March 5, 1726.
[4] Moses Leonard.
[5] Nathan Brigham of Marlborough. Hudson, *Marlborough*, p. 334.
[6] Caleb Rice of Marlborough. Hudson, *Marlborough*, p. 435.
[7] John Fay of Westborough.
[8] John Green.

[1] Of Westborough. He was admitted to the church, April 3, 1726. Westborough Church Records. Simon Tainter, who later became a deacon, and who lived until 1763, was a good friend of Parkman. Harriette M. Forbes, *The Diary of Rev. Ebenezer Parkman* (Westborough, 1899), pp. 11–12.
[2] Reverend Samuel Barrett of Hopkinton.
[3] Reverend John Swift of Framingham.
[4] Reverend John Prentice of Lancaster.
[5] Reverend Israel Loring of Sudbury.
[6] Reverend John McKinstry of Sutton. Benedict and Tracey, *Sutton*, pp. 33–35. He was not a member of the Marlborough Association. Allen, *Worcester Association*, pp. 5–7.
[7] Reverend John Cushing of Shrewsbury.
[8] Reverend John Gardner of Stow.
[9] Reverend William Cooke (Harvard 1716) of Wayland. *Sibley*, VI, 134–138.
[10] Reverend Isaac Burr (Yale 1717) of Worcester. Dexter, pp. 163–165.
[11] This should be Reverend John McKinstry.

Thanks alwayes for all things unto God and the Father in the name of our Lord Jesus Christ." In which Sermon he maintained that we ought to give Thanks to God not only for Prosperous but Even Adverse Dispensations. One Putnam (and Sundry others Combining) had been Set Against, and Still manifested uneasiness at Such Doctrine and this man was Resolute to make a stir about it. He had alwayes been Discontented with Mr. McKinstry but now Charges him as inorthodox. We therefore wrote a brief Declaration according to Mr. McKinstrys Request in This Wise.

Application being made to us the Subscribers, conven'd at Marlboro April 12, 1726, by the Reverend Mr. John McKinstry, Setting forth that he had delivered certain Doctrine as follows, viz., that the Children of God ought to give thanks to God at all Times for all his Providence to us, Whether they be prosperous or Afflictive, and the Doctrine was Dissatisfactory to some of his Brethren. Our Opinion hereupon being Desired we freely Declare that we judge said Doctrine to be agreeable to the Sacred Scriptures and Sentiments of the most Judicious Expositions of Orthodox Divines. Sign'd by Ebeneazer Parkman, John Swift, Robert Breck, John Prentice, Israel Loring, Job Cushing, John Gardner, William Cook. Having din'd, Mr. Axtil[12] of Marlboro Desir'd advice of the Association in his Case, who for irregular Behaviour and Discourse with respect to one Tabitha Rice[13] (who had laid a Child to his son), and the Church, likewise in Managing the Affair, was suspended. But his Infirmity of understanding rendered him incapable of the plainest Counsell and Direction which from Everyone given him. Mr. Cook also Propos'd a Cause between Two of his Parish who were uneasy with one another in a Bargain they had made about some Land. But some other Business Engaging me I took little notice of it, Seeing it was not in my Power to advantage it any manner of way.

Association Breaking up, I rode with Mr. Barrett as far as Mr. Eagers[14] of the Town where my Horse broke, but Lighting upon Mr. McCollisters[15] Son upon a Horse I rode home. My Beast was Safe at my own Barn. Brothers Champney[16] and Hicks[17] were to see us.

13. Our Brethren went to Hopkinton and so home. Neighbor Green Bought part of the South Side of my Land. In the Evening we gave writings.

14. Mr. Barrett came to see us.

15. 16. Gloomy Weather for the Season. We had Cold Storms for most of the week.

17. I preach'd upon 2 Cor. 1, 12 and Ps. 25, 15. I was Extreamly Tired in my Body so that I could not only not keep off the Bed but Scarce lye on it.

18. Neighbor Clark had my Beast to plough for him.

19. Neighbor Clark's last Cows went home.

20. I heard of Severall more Creatures Dead.

21. Neighbor Green paid me forty pounds upon first bonds. Planted Apple Trees.

22. Bright, warm, after long Cold Rainy Weather.

23. We were in a sad Comotion by the Hills being fir'd. Robert was Exceeding unfortunate to burn the Brush after long uneasiness through my fears of his persuasions. I gave him leave to set fire to the most Distant Heap and the last in the wind, but the Leaves were drie and the wind fresh so that it put us to great Labour to carry it. It burnt about 20 Rod of my fence and would have Consum'd without a period if I had not receiv'd Neighbor David Maynards Help, and been very Diligent my Self. But before Neighbor Maynard came, it raged to such a Degree that we grew so hot and faint as Severall times to give

up and Robert[18] Lay'd himself down in an Expiring posture, till quickened by a New Resolution. It got Lead upon the Fence before Help came. Through Divine favour we put a stop to it to our great Joy att about noon. It continued to burn indeed, but not to run and Spread. We were oblig'd to have an Eye over it continually, and I was not, manytimes, without fear of its catching again because Towards night there were great Gusts of Wind, Thunder and Lightning and very little if any Rain. This was the more terrible as happening in the middst of my Preparation for the Sabbath. But God was very Gracious.

24. I preach'd upon James 1, 21, both A. and P.M. I baptiz'd Josiah Newton's[19] Daughter Mary.[20]

25. I Catechized the Children at the Meeting house. Number above Twenty.

26. Mr. Ward came with his Cart and We Carted out 20 Load of Muck. I made up accounts with Mr. Ward.

27. Again Carted 12 Load of Muck.

28. I rode down to Marlboro and preach'd the Lecture from Acts 16, 24. After Lecture I paid Colonel How[21] £3. 10 for Beef I had of him and Mr. Wood 20£, which (with 10£ at one time and 20£ at another before) made up the 50£ I borrowed of him last Year. I paid him the Interest also which was 1£ 25 Shillings. I made up with him also for Sundrys had in his Shop. Here was Mr. Thomas. Mr. Wood presented Me a Dozen of long Pipes, and Mr. Amsden presented Me a pair of Tobacco Tongs. It was between 10 and 11 when I got home. Bass and Shadd sent to us.

29. Rob was Employed about Setting up New Fence. But I was taken up with my Preparations for the Sabbath.

30. Went on with my Compositions. Robert plough'd for Planting.

### MAY [1726]

1. I preach'd on James 1, 21 A. and P.M. I receiv'd Asher Rice[1] into our Communion. N.B. Captain Fay offer'd to Say Something concerning the Congregations tarrying to Such admissions, but having given Sufficient Notice in my Conversations of my whole Purpose and practice in these Regards I put a stop to him imediately and said no More.

2. I read Miscellaneously. Robert Plough'd part of the Day. Put up some Fence in 1st part.

3. Mr. Breck came to see me. Robert plough'd again till towards night, when (after I had been with Mr. Breck to Mr. S. Maynards) I rode with Mr. Breck to Shrewsbury where we lodg'd.

4. We walk'd to Mr. Cushing's house and thence to Mr. Smith's[2] (who kept our Horses last night) where we decently Entertained. We returned to Mr. Wards[3] to Dinner after which Both Mr. Breck and Mr. Cushing rode with Me to My house at Westborough. They parted a little before night. Robert did somewhat more at ploughing this afternoon.

5. Finished his Ploughing.

6. 7. He planted Indian Corn, But I confined myself, and for want of Some inspection it was so furrow'd I could have been Glad to have had it to have done again.

8. I preach'd upon James 1, 21, A.M., and on Phil. 3, 13, P.M. I baptized Neighbor Prat[4] Junior his Daughter Betty.[5]

9. I rode (with my Wife) to See Mr. Thomas Newton[6] for whom (and for the widow Record Ward[7]) Prayers were Yesterday

---

[12] Thomas Axtell. Axtell was the subject of several discussions by the Marlborough Association. See Allen, *Worcester Association*, pp. 12, 19–20.

[13] The daughter of Edward Rice of Marlborough. There is no record of the birth of her child close to this date, but there is a record of a daughter, Sarah, born to Tabatha Rice, July 10, 1723. Tabatha Rice married one Nathaniel Oakes or Oke, Feb. 20, 1726/7. *Marlborough Vital Records* (Worcester, 1908), p. 160, p. 304.

[14] Either Zachariah Eager or his brother Zerubbabel, both of whom were residents of Marlborough at this time.

[15] Probably John McCollister of Westborough.

[16] Samuel Champney, Jr., of Cambridge, Parkman's wife's brother.

[17] John Hicks of Cambridge, Parkman's brother-in-law.

[18] Robert Henry, Parkman's hired hand.

[19] One of the first inhabitants of Westborough.

[20] Born April 20, 1726.

[21] Thomas Howe of Marlborough, an Indian fighter, Justice of the Peace, and representative of the town. Hudson, *Marlborough*, pp. 382–383.

[1] Asher Rice was the son of Thomas Rice. In 1704, when eight years of age, he was captured by the French and Indians. Four years later he was recovered by his father. Asher was an eccentric who retained some habits acquired when living with the Indians. He later moved to that part of Leicester which became the town of Spencer in 1775. DeForest and Bates, *Westborough*, pp. 37–40. See also *The Story of the Rice Boys* (Westborough, 1906).

[2] Peter Smith of Shrewsbury, a founder of the church there. Ward, *Shrewsbury*, p. 431.

[3] Captain Nahum Ward, a prominent resident of Shrewsbury.

[4] John Pratt.

[5] Born May 8, 1726.

[6] An early resident and militia officer of Westborough.

[7] Widow of Increase Ward. Mother of Oliver Ward, selectman of Westborough.

publickly Desir'd. We were in also at John Pratt Juniors and P.M. at Neighbor Josiah Newtons. This Last gave Me a pair of Shooes for my Self and a pair for My Lad.

10. 11. Robert got Rails. I began my Sermon.

12. Captain Fay came to our house. I fell upon a Discourse about his Speaking in the church as above mentioned, without Notice given Me concerning it, etc., etc. Mr. Cushing came to see Me.

13. 14. I was Strictly Engag'd upon My Subject.

15. We were Entertain'd upon Phil. 3, 13, 14, A.M. and P.M. The widow Ward died.

16. Robert Went to Work at Mr. Oliver Wards, whose Mother, Record Ward was this Day Buried. I was at the funerall all 4[?] P.M., and then My Wife and Child I carried with me to Mr. Brecks Who we found was not Well, and did not go to Meeting yesterday in the Afternoon. We lodged here.

17. We rode to Cambridge. Call'd at my wives Uncles about 3 P.M. Convers'd and refresh'd and went to her Father's.[8] Here we lodg'd. I was not well after Evening prayer in the Family.

18. I rode to Boston. My Mother not well. My Brother John Tyley[9] return'd from Honduras, having been taken by Ned Low the Pirate. Towards Evening I went back to Charlston for my Horse at Boylstons,[10] where I met Mr. Cotton[11] of Newton and a Company of his Neighbours, Mr. Ephraim Williams,[12] etc., who had all been out a fishing. I rode with them to Cambridge and then parted to go to Father Champneys where I lodged.

19. In the Morning I got on my Journey home. I lit of one [blank] of Lancaster who behaved himself very handsomely and bore my Expenses of Eating and Drinking and oats at the Tavern. I stop'd at Mr. Swifts whose Family (Severall of them being very ill and the rest not well) was much afflicted. I got home seasonably but much fatigued.

20. 21. Strictly Employ'd in My Preparations. My Lip broke out and was very troublesome. Captain Ward here about Robert. Robert came from Mr. Oliver Wards.

22. I preach'd all Day upon Prov. 3, 6. Mr. Willard[13] of Hassenimisco's Child Hannah[14] was baptized.

23. In the morning about 7 or 8 I set out for Cambridge. I call'd at Neighbor Thurstons,[15] he being agoing out waited for his Horse. I tarried an hour and half and then went away without him, as far as Mr. William Johnsons,[16] where he came up with me. We rode to Mr. Swifts but did not 'Light. Mr. Swift very ill, Hence we went to Natick but Mr. Peabody[17] not at home. Madame persuaded us to tarry for him Since he would not be at the Election, and Seeing Mr. Hale was with him. They came in the Beginning of the Evening, and we had a very pleasant time till Two o'Clock in the Morning, when we forc'd our Conversation to break up. (N.B. The Family had Liberty to repose about 10 in the Evening and Neighbor Thurston then retir'd from us). I had the afflicting account of poor Mr. Osgood[18] our Classmate, his Recess from Topsfield. In the Morning we Sung a Psalm and I was call'd upon (for I refus'd it last night and Mr. Hale was desir'd thereupon) to perform the address to Heaven. Then we Walk'd about Mr. Peabodys Farm. We convers'd, we smoak'd, and we (hardly) parted. Mr. Hale with us we proceeded as far as Mr. Ephraim Williams of Newton, but he was not at home. From this Place we Urg'd our way to Father Champneys (Mr. Hale dropping us at the verge of Waterton) and thence to Boston, My Wife being carried thither by her Brother this Morning. I sent back my Horse to Cambridge.

25. Mr. Thatcher[19] preach'd an Excellent Sermon from those words Psalm 77, 20 "Thou leddest thy People like a Flock by the Hand of Moses and Aaron." But I was much interrupted by a Lip full of anguish that put me to great Trouble. I was not at the publick Dinner for this Reason, that our Family were gathered together at my Fathers and I was Obliged to dine with them. And this, and my Lip detained me from the Convention.

26. I was at the Convention (at Mr. Sewalls[20]). Mr. William Williams[21] of Hatfield preach'd. After it we din'd at Holmes's. Much Discourse of a true Representation of the affair of the Synod Concerted last year. Dr. Mather[22] acquainted us he had Sent some letters hereabouts, but I had no perfect account being absent yesterday, as aforesaid. I sent for my Horse but it was late and then I was Easily prevailed with to tarry till the Morning.

27. Mr. Coffin and Mr. Lee came in just before we Left Home. The Last walked with me to the Ferry. My wife was very Timerous. I waited for one Boat after another before we ventur'd. It was near 10 o'clock ere we mounted. We rode to Cambridge to Hick's and Fathers. Bundled up, Din'd a little after 12 and (with our Brother Champney) Set out. Call'd at My Wive's uncle Champney's[23] and Every now and then Stopt in the Road to fix the Child. We parted at Livermores,[24] where Mr. Breck,[25] Mr. Woods[26] and Rasto call'd us, and we rode (after Severall Hesitations for Mr. Breck and on account of the Child) to David Hows[27] where we tarry'd Several Hours. Notwithstanding (coming by the Farms in Marlboro) we reach'd home before Day Light in.

28. We Rested. Brother returned home.

29. Early in the morning I rode to Hopkinton, met Mr. Barrett a little on this Side his house. I preach'd all Day from Acts 24, 16. Mrs. Barrett did not make a Dining. I waited for Mr. & Mrs. Barrett (for Drugs for my Child) till it was too late to return home. Mr. Barrett Baptized Jedidiah[28] the Son of Peres and Lydia Rice.

30. I returned home. Robert began to weed the Corn. He had Mr. Oliver Wards Rocket and Horse to assist him. I read Bradleys General Treatise on Husbandry and Gardening and Extracted Observations.

31. I read Dr. Cotton Mathers *Ratio Disciplinae Fratrum Nov. Anglorum,*[29] a Book which I have long wish'd for, or something of this Kind. I apprehend there was great need of the Publication here of [it] and I have a great value for it. Before it I knew not where there was anything fixt and stated for our Regulation in the Lesser Circumstances; or what to do about Severall Modalities in our Ministrations. For My own Part, I hitherto had governed My Self Chiefly by what the Assembly at Westminster had given me; but for more minute Articles I consulted what was customary with the best men among us and as far as they agreed with my Sense I followed them in My Management. I have Likewise Laid before me our own Platform and Confession of Faith, and various other Books I have Consulted for the Formation of my Directory. Where there was Honey to be Extracted I have not refused to Suck even the Common Prayer Book of the Church of England. But the Book above mentioned has proved the most illuminating and Instructing Especially in Circumstantialls.

Silence Bartlet[30] not well. She went to the Doctors.

### JUNE [1726]

1. Robert came between 1 and 2 P.M. to Hoe for me.

2. Robert still at Howing. Perhaps there may be many more Tedious and Chafing things in Hirelings than ever Mention has

[8] Samuel Champney of Cambridge.

[9] Parkman's brother-in-law, husband of Elizabeth Parkman.

[10] Richard Boylston of Charlestown.

[11] Reverend John Cotton.

[12] Colonel Ephraim Williams who moved to Stockbridge in 1739.

[13] Major Joseph Willard went to live at Hassenemisco, an Indian village, in 1717. He was a founder of the town of Grafton. Frederick C. Pierce, *History of Grafton* (Worcester, 1879), pp. 49–50, 604.

[14] Born May 22, 1726, according to Westborough town records.

[15] Joseph Thurston.

[16] Of Marlborough.

[17] Oliver Peabody (Harvard 1721). Later minister of the First Congregational Church (the Indian church) in Natick. *Sibley*, VI, 529–534.

[18] William Osgood (Harvard 1721) had begun preaching in Topsfield in the fall of 1725. In July, 1726, he was dismissed by his congregation. *Sibley*, VI, 508–509.

[19] Reverend Peter Thatcher of Boston.

[20] Reverend Joseph Sewall (Harvard 1707) of the Old South Church, Boston. *Sibley*, V, 376–393.

[21] Reverend William Williams (Harvard 1683). *Sibley*, III, 263–269.

[22] Cotton Mather.

[23] Joseph Champney, Sr.

[24] Joseph Livermore of Framingham. Temple, *Framingham*, p. 625.

[25] Reverend Robert Breck of Westborough.

[26] Benjamin Woods of Marlborough.

[27] The Wayside Inn in Sudbury.

[28] Of Westborough. Date of birth in town records is May 29, 1726.

[29] Published in Boston, 1716.

[30] Mrs. Parkman's young helper in the house.

been made of. Silence Bartlett being much indispos'd went to Marlboro to take advice of the Phician.

3. Robert at the Same Business still with William Clark to assist him. I was at my Preparations. In all my Wayes, outward or Secular Wayes as well as Spirituall I acknowledge God.

4. It was very hot all Day. We have had a very fierce Sun and but little Rain for Some time. In the Evening I went down into my Cellar thin clad as I had been in the Day and got a bad Cold.

5. I rose much indispos'd. I went to public Worship which my wife urged very much against. I was very faint when I Entered the house, but (with much difficulty) I went thro the Exercises of the forenoon. In the Intermission I was still worse. I tarry'd at home, and sent Mr. Symms's[1] Sermon to delaying Sinners to be Read. Neighbor Thurston and Mr. Tomlin,[2] I was told, pray'd. I grew very ill, having pains thro my Limbs, oppression and sharp pains at my Stomach that caused much faintness. Just the way of Divine Providence I would acknowledge God.

6. My illness increased. My Wife was not well nor any Child. I sent John Storey to Marlboro for Silence Bartlett. Robert wrought for Neighbor Clark.

7. I sent for Mr. Barrett.

8. Robert had not finish'd Howing till 11 o'clock. And then I order'd him to get up my Mare and carry Silence Bartlet to Brookfield. After they were gone Mr. Barrett came to see Me.

9. Mr. Ward[3] Sent his Daughter Dinah to us. Robert returned just within Night.

10. 11. This week was a weary time. What I could read chiefly was the Arch Bishop of Cambrays Telemathus, by Boyer. Dinah Ward went home.

12. I could not go to Meeting. I would humble myself before God for my former Negligence and unfaithfullness on this Blessed Day which justly Deserves the Divine Frowns. I Beseech God to assist me by his Grace to greater Diligence and Zeal and Constancy in his Service, especially in my Great work on this Day for the Future.

I Sent a sermon to the meeting house but there being but 3 or 4 Men there they returned to my house. Most of the people were gone to Meeting in neighbouring Towns. There were Worcester people here for Mr. Burr[4] was ill. It was doubtfull whether there would be any Meeting at Shrewsbury for Mr. Cushing[5] Broke his Arm some Time since and has not been able to preach for 2 Sabbaths. The Time look'd very Melancholly. It show'd in a Lively Light the great Privilege of Comfortable free Enjoyment of the Lords Day.

13. I read Drydens Virgil from the 7th Aneid.

14. Training Day. The Officers sent importunate Addresses to me to have me dine with them. I rode as far as Mr. Maynards[6] (the next house) and it made me more chearfull. It was Town meeting also, in the Afternoon upon account of our Sutton neighbours that would be Set off to us.[7] Robert was at Moulding up my Indian Corn. He did not make that Heavy Business of the First part that he did before. I prosecuted some preparation for Next Sabbath.

15. I read in Sir Matthew Hales[8] Contemplations. Rebecca Paddison came to Live with us.

16. N.B. We kill'd our Calf. The inability and negligence of Robert! An Exceeding Dry time.

17. Most of us were ill with Colds, and many round about us also.

18. I finished my Preparations. I had Sundry Reflections upon my past unserviceableness that might Righteously detain me from Gods house not only a Day or Two, but forever.

19. I preach'd A.M. on Prov. 3, 6; P.M. on Eph. 5, 16. Cap-

tain Willard[9] din'd with me and Mrs. Holloway.[10] Concluding Exercises in the Afternoon, I was very much Spent. I was very Faint and my knees trembled very Sensibly and so I continued till I had rested my Self some time at home. I had in the Evening a good Season of Serious Enquirys unto my Self. God grant me more such and bless them to me.

20. I rode as far as Mr. Tainters[11] to raising his Barn. It was a pleasant time, but not altogether without Trouble and Toil.

21. I grew Weary of Robert Henry; having set me up Some Lengths (perhaps a Score) after his Manner, I made up accounts with him and gave him his Liberty.

22. Robert Henry went away. I reckon'd with Neighbor Clark. N.B. After a long time of Drought God in Mercy remembered us, and Last night and this morning (with not a little Thunder and Lightening) Sent us plentifull Showers of Rain. I remain faint thro pains in my Stomach which often Oblige me to desist Studying. Yesterday Rebecca Paddison, apprehending Some Dangerous Tumour in her Breast, returned to her Mother. Brother Champney[12] came up to See us.

23. Brother returned home. I felt much pain in My Stomach, which made any work very Heavy.

24. I Employ'd the Chief of this Week in My preparations for the Sabbath, for my Indispositions allow'd me but very little Liberty without a Respit and avocation.

25. Mr. Tainter and Bowman of Sutton mow'd for me.

26. I preach'd all Day and Administer'd the Sacrament, But I Scarce went thro the Business.

27. This Day, for want of all other Help than my little Boy, I rak'd and turn'd my Hay till just before Night. Neighbor Clark sent his Son to assist in making it up.

28. This Morning we had many refreshing Showers, which I look upon as a great Mercy notwithstanding I had near two Load of Hay Expos'd in it. Hannah Paddison came to live with us.

29. 30. We pol'd in our Hay. Neighbor Green[13] and William Clark, My Self and Boy. My Self and Neighbor Green.

Notwithstanding such Exercise last mentioned was my Diversion and Choice, yet I found it sometime tir'd me very much. It set me into Reflections upon the unhappy times we are fallen into and the Ingratitude of most of the people of the Country to their Ministers, very few besides the Boston ministers being able to Support themselves with what they Receive from their People. Certainly they are straight handed and if they Reap Sparingly no wonder since they Sow very Sparingly. He that would be just will attribute hereto and not to the want of Either sufficient parts or Eager Inclination if there are not so great men among us as were famous in New England in the Dayes of Fathers. Most ministers do groan under their pressures and it is an addition to the weight that Sinks them that the Generality of People are of the Sort and Spirit that it Scarce ever can prove to the Advantage of men to complain, but it is best to Suffer patiently, to obtain relief. They Desire to be left to their own Generosity, the Extent of which is Enough Demonstrated. This Reflection is the more melancholly when it is Evident Such Evil conceits are daily propated to the Dishonour of God with the Disparagement of his Ministry. For, trifling as the following observation is, it is true: That their [blot] inward Respect is much proportion'd to our Externall appearance; when therefore it becomes mean thro their neglect it will be in Danger of becoming worse thro their Contempt. But (Christo gratias) I have had little Experience, as yet.

## JULY [1726]

1. 2. Whatsoever I have done in the former part of the Week in Reading Either Commentarys or sermons upon my Subject, or collecting observations thereon, yet these Days I would spend in strictest Engagement in writing and reviewing my preparations for the Public.

3. I preach'd A.M. on Eph. 5, 16., P.M., on Jer. 4, 14.

[1] Thomas, Symmes, A Monitor for Delaying Sinners (Boston, 1719).
[2] Deacon Isaac Tomlin.
[3] Oliver Ward of Marlborough. Dinah (b. 1709) was his eldest daughter.
[4] Reverend Isaac Burr of Worcester.
[5] Reverend Job Cushing of Shrewsbury.
[6] David Maynard of Westborough.
[7] See DeForest and Bates, Westborough, p. 101.
[8] Hale (1609-1676) was the famous English jurist. His Contemplations Moral and Divine (London, 1676) appeared in numerous subsequent editions.
[9] Benjamin Willard, father of Major Joseph Willard.
[10] Mrs. William Holloway of Westborough.
[11] Simon Tainter of Westborough.
[12] Samuel Champney, Jr., Parkman's brother-in-law.
[13] John Green of Westborough.

4. I rode away to Mr. Brecks,[1] who acquainted me with what was done last association. Especially referring to Mr. McKinstrys[2] Cause, and Mr. Barretts[3] with Mr. How. Thence I rode to Mr. Woods. Thence to Mr. Cooks where I din'd on fry'd Pigeons. Thence to Livermores, from whence to Father Champney's.[4] My Journey hither was very Tedious but I proceeded to Boston. Thro my illness I was very much tired. Brother John,[5] I was informed was ready to sail for Dublin in a vessel belonging to the Family. Brother Alexanders[6] wife Last week was Delivered of a Daughter.[7]

5. I was about various Concerns but I was very faint and incapable of Business. I was at Mather Byles's[8] and he show'd me (at my Request) his Poem to Mr. Dowding on his Verses of Eternity, Sent in a Letter to Sir Byles. This Poem was published in the Courant No.——.[9] He repeated his own and Mr. Adams's[10] Poems on Captain Winslow[11] deceas'd with all which I was very well pleas'd. I was at various places but I was not well in Either. I was very much afflicted with the Oppressions at my Stomach. I was with Dr. [Louis] Dalhonde.

6. Commencement. I was much of a stranger at College, but my indispositions much prevented my making my Observations. The Batchelours had their Degrees in the Meeting house in the Morning. But there was so much rain at noon that the masters Disputations were in College-Hall and their Degrees given them in the Afternoon. I was at Sir Bridghams[12] Chamber at Dinner but I was not fit for any Conversation thro my Lifelessness. I was desir'd by Mr. Barrett to Meet here with our Association upon Mr. McKinstrys Cause, But no body came. Mr. Breck led me to Sir Saltonstalls[13] Chamber where there being little Company I had most Quiet. It was a very rainy Time which kept the Town full of People, full of Jollitys and no one knows what. At Night having borrowed a Large Sturdy Coat I ventured over to Father Champney's but it was very wet, uncomfortable. Here was Cousin Dorcas Bows[14] and Susan Champney.[15] We lodg'd Comfortably. But a little after midnight Mrs. Jerusha Fairweather and Mrs. Mary Gain Came over. I was awoke but they concluded I was asleep, and therefore I was never Troubled.

7. In the Morn I found that Two Young Gentlemen had waited upon the forementioned Ladies but Despairing of Room in the House, never Enquir'd and roll'd into the Barn. Yet one was Sir Clark[16] one of the Orators; the other Mr. Woodbridge,[17] son of Governor Woodbridge[18] of the Asiento Company in the West Indies. It was Dark weather but pleasant Company particularly Mrs. Gains, with whom I chiefly confin'd my Conversation. About Ten I return'd over to the Town. I met Mrs. Porter who had just before had a turn of Illness and was coming out of Colledge to take the Air. She Desir'd me to walk with her. I embraced the opportunity, and (with her Sister, Two Miss Charnocks[19] and their Gentlemen Mr. Baxter[20] and Mr. Baker[21])

we walk'd round the Common, a long walk for an ill Man and a woman but half reviv'd. We lodged Safe at Sir Balch's[22] and I bid them Adieu for I was Oblig'd to hasten to Boston, to finish the Rest of my Business. I did so and Returned back to Cambridge. I waited on Sir Clark, and gave up the Cause. I retir'd to Father Champneys again and was much Diverted by the Facetious Company of Mrs. Gain.

8. About Ten (as I remember) I took horse for home, Mother Champney[23] being with me. I was become much better and my Journey was Much Easier than I (fearfully) Expected it would be. We came home very Safely. (Deo Optimo Salvatori Gratas quam plurimas). Asher Rice had been here at work (Mowing). When I had been at home sometime and had Contented my Self with my appointment with Mr. Cushing to Change. I was Surpriz'd to hear that his Arm was very bad and he gone or going to Narragansett, upon which I was driven to Compose Discourses for Sabbath Day. But I was in a flutter and could write but four lines. I Examined myself concerning my Negligence. I considered my Journey as Necessary to seek advice touching my Health; that I had no Opportunity or Strength; and the Divine Providence intervening and removing the means of my assistance I had the more Solid grounds to proceed to Entreat the Divine Help.

9. Anyone will suppose me most strictly Engaged in My Study to Day. My first Sermon I finished and Some part of my Second before I Slept. I made addition both in the morning and at noon.

10. I preach'd all Day upon Jer. 4, 14. My Wife was Taken with a shivering and Trembling while in the afternoon Exercise, but Showed nothing to me till I was come out of meeting, when She walked very Slow and look'd more pale and sunk than I had ever seen her on any occasion that I remember. But she made a shift to get home and then grew somewhat better. I concluded it to be issue proceeding from the Procidantia Uteri which she had been Troubled with. This accident put us upon Weaning the Child which this Night began.

11. I went out to see my Hay; Mr. Rice[24] came to see me and he with my own people (Two of them) got it into Cock. The Boy, first with me and then the men, poled it in, there being appearance of foul Weather nigh, and the cocks standing round the Barn, very Easy at hand. Now and in the next Morning together we carry'd in above Thirty.

12. My Wife Rode with me to Mr. Cushings whose arm Continues very Stiff and Troublesome. Yet Patient Job was good Company. What a favour of heaven to have the mind Stock'd with wise, with Divine Principles whereby it is fortify'd and kept Even. My Wife Seem'd to have a comfortable Time, and I made my Observations upon the Pleasure she seem'd to take in this Ride. Yet I understood afterwards that while at Mr. Cushings She was not very well.

13. I read Sundry Poeticall Pieces as the Temple of Death essay on the Spleen[?]. I pursued my Preparations.

14. I was much taken up with Looking out for Labour about my Barley Harvest. Isaac and Hezekiah Pratt[25] mow'd it in the first of the afternoon. I was some time in Conversation at Neighbor Clarks with him and Mr. Rice. [Blot] Molly[26] not well.

15. My Wife Complaining of weakness. Neighbor Maynard came to make up my Barley and get it in. My Studys minded.

16. My Barley Secur'd by Neighbor Maynard and his son. Molly was much indispos'd and I sent Yesterday to Marlboro for Mrs. Williams but she was not there. To Day I sent Hannah Peterson to her house, but she sent me Reasons she thought Sufficient for her not coming. We were very low at the news my wife being oppress'd with Every illness: The Procidentia, etc., the turning of her Milk, Her Mouth Obstructed, pain in her Breast, and great pain and weakness in Every part.

17. My Wife rose out of Bed but exceeding ill, bound together with her Excessive pains; came down; I'm afraid took Some Air

[1] Reverend Robert Breck of Marlborough.
[2] Reverend John McKinstry of Sutton. Benedict and Tracey, *Sutton*, pp. 32–35.
[3] Reverend Samuel Barrett of Hopkinton.
[4] Samuel Champney, Sr., Parkman's father-in-law.
[5] Parkman's brother-in-law, John Tyley.
[6] Parkman's older brother, Alexander.
[7] Esther Parkman, born June 29, 1726.
[8] Mather Byles (Harvard 1725), poet, humorist, minister of the Hollis St. Church, Boston, 1732–1776. *Sibley*, VII, 464–493. For information on Byles' poetry see the Introduction by C. Lennart Carlson in the 1940 facsimile edition of Byles' *Poems on Several Occasions* (Boston, 1744).
[9] *The New England Courant*, No. 237, published in Boston. Dowding may have been Joseph, b. 1702.
[10] John Adams (Harvard 1721), poet, minister and classmate of Parkman. *Sibley*, VI, 424–427.
[11] Captain Josiah Winslow (Harvard 1721) was the commander of a fort on St. George's River in Maine, and was killed in an Indian engagement April 30, 1724. *Sibley*, VI, 587–589. Byles' poem was printed in his *Poems on Several Occasions* (Boston, 1744), and Adams' in his *Poems on Several Occasions* (Boston, 1745).
[12] James Bridgham (Harvard 1726). *Sibley*, VIII, 7–10.
[13] Nathaniel Saltonstall (Harvard 1727). *Sibley*, VIII, 263–265.
[14] Mrs. Parkman's cousin.
[15] Susanna Champney, daughter of Joseph Champney, and Mrs. Parkman's cousin.
[16] William Clark (Harvard 1726), later a Boston physician and political writer. *Sibley*, VIII, 533–535.
[17] Benjamin Woodbridge (Harvard 1728). *Sibley*, VIII, 533–535.
[18] Judge Dudley Woodbridge of Barbados.
[19] Elizabeth and Mary, daughters of John and Mary Charnock of Cambridge or Boston.
[20] Joseph Baxter (Harvard 1724). *Sibley*, VII, 304–305.
[21] Thomas Baker (Harvard 1724). *Sibley*, VII, 294–295.
[22] William Balch (Harvard 1724). *Sibley*, VII, 296–304.
[23] Mrs. Samuel Champney, Parkman's mother-in-law.
[24] Asher Rice of Westborough.
[25] Both of Westborough.
[26] Mrs. Parkman.

at the Door; grew much worse. I got her up Stairs in order to go to Bed again, but she almost swoon'd away. Recovering a little from her faintings, She demonstrated to us that she was in grievous agonies. She undress'd and with the Tenderest Help [of] her Mother and myself She was assisted to Bed. But Every maladie was Enraged, by Every weakness and discouragement left almost Lifeless. I walked a little in the Room, her mother holding in one hand her hand, her other laid upon her Head. I cast my Eyes now and then upon her and Concluded she was drowsing, but I went to her to look upon her, and Spoke to her. Receiving no kind of Return Her Mother put her hand to her mouth. I urg'd Some Testification or sign, but none being given; but she lay in a profound stillness when as tho had hitherto been vigorously strugling Her Teeth were set, her Limbs Cold, her Eyes Distorted, and very Little Life any where perceptible, when her Mother gave me the word that She was Dying. How I felt outgoes Description. I hastened the Maid to Mrs. Forbush. My Wife Lay for the space of 3 quarters of or altogether an hour I suppose in such a Condition. O Dismal Hour, wherein the Struggle with my heart for her Division was like the Rending the Soul from the Body! It was truly a most gloomy Time! Mrs. Forbush came just when She spoke, a Galbunum Plaister was taken off which was too strong for her. Something was given her and She Revid'd a little but Continued in the Last Extremitys. It was a Reprieve but it Seem'd a Short one. We Expected we must be Rent asunder this Day! It grew more and more Intollerable! I was full of prayers and anon I had Some Hope. I grew more Confirmed in Hope. It brought fresh to my Mind all the Bitter Sufferings of her Dark friday, Ever long, about nine Months before, wherein I had the Same prospects. The Salvations of God then, strengthened my Trust in him. She became more sensible. We Encouraged ourselves in the Lord and He show'd us his Mercy. While We have any being let us praise the Lord! It grew very Late, but Leaving her under the Divine Protection, and to the care of Mrs. Forbush and Madame Maynard I repair'd to the House of God. Our Devotions, if they were fervent, they were short. Mrs. Peterson came and by various Applications she grew more Easy. I was full of Thankfullness and went again to the public worship, Mrs. Bayles tarrying with her. Our Text A.M. and P.M. was Jer. 4, 14. She continued extream bad. I sent Daniel Hardy[27] to Mr. Barrett. Mrs. Peterson watch'd. I have almost utterly forgot what became of me that night. (Now I recollect). Mr. Barrett came. He said and did very little. He gave us an account of what Mrs. Whitcomb had sent. He gave us better Balsom of Fennel for her violent Fever, gave her some Tent wine.[28] He pray'd with us. We lodg'd together.

18. Molly was further revived, and tho she was very weak, yet she was all Day much more comfortable. Mr. Barrett went away about 8 o'Clock. Mrs. Maynard watch'd.

19. Molly grew worse by a vomiting and flux; the Morning very grievous. I sent Phinehas Hardy[29] to Mr. Barrett who sent us Some plaisters and more Tent. She was somewhat better in the Afternoon; by various Applications the Flux Stay'd till night. Mrs. Thurston[30] watch'd. These Dayes I could do little besides reading Mr. Shepherds Sincere Convert[31] and Dr. Edwards Exercitations Critic. Philosoph. Historic Theog. on Some S.S.[32] Martha Becom an Indian came.

20. And this morning Joshua Misco[33] and his Squa howed my Corn. I went in the Afternoon to seek Labourers. At Peres Rice's[34] was one Stearns[35] of Sutton, who was full of inconsistance about the Affairs of Mr. McKinstry and the Doctrines he had delivered. When I came home my wife had been (tho' without

any the least Reason) very much affrighted with the Indians, and full of fear of what they might do. And yet there was no greater peace and good Temper than they Demonstrated and went away soberly to their Lodging in the neighbourhood. She was not well pleas'd with her Mother; and left with me Notwithstanding Necessity call'd me forth; and I took a Season when Company was with her. But the Weakness of her Body brought strange apprehensions in the mind.

21. Asher Rice mow'd a part of the day. Fitting weather. The Indians finished my Corn and went off.

23. Father Champney came up.

24. I preach'd in the morn on Jer. 4, 14. Afternoon upon Prov. 29, 1. My wife recovering.

25. It was Father Champneys Design to have carryed Mother Home, yet She could not Safely leave her Dauter. My Father made up my Hay. I rak'd myself I suppose an hour. And before noon he went away for home. Whitcomb here all night.

26. Mr. Bowman[36] came again to Mow for me. Mr. Cushing here. Bowman pol'd what Remained of my Hay. Mr. Cushing returned home.

27. I read Occasionall papers, Vol. 2.

28. I preach'd a Lecture at Shrewsbury. My Text was 1 Cor. 16, 22. I was with Captain Keyes[37] at his Sons who treated us with Brandy and Brandy punch. I returned in the Evening. Neighbor Clark reaping my maslin.[38]

29. William Clark reap'd half the Day and this finish'd my maslin. Nothing obstructed my Diligent application to my Preparations.

30. The frequent showers so Engaged Everyone about his Corn and Hay that it was no Easy matter to Obtain Help. It was with great Difficulty I got Neighbor Clark and his son to Shock my grain, which having layn long in the Field in all weathers and a threatning storm nigh, I was Restless till the Grain my Chief Dependance was upon [was] Secur'd. Shall I note here the Answers given by Two persons that my wife remark'd when she sent to Neighbor Clarks for assistance. Neighbor Clarks grain was upon Spoil and he was reaping it. He had Many (I think Ten) load of Hay that had been very long in cock in the Meadows and must be Tho't to be rotting. Himself lame in his hand, besides his comon lameness in his Leggs. His Son, who was all his Help, had hurt his ancle, and therefore he directed the messinger to ask Neighbor Maynard who had his own, his sons David, Jesse, Josham, Jonathan and Ebenezer's Help, tho one or Two of the last were not like the others. His Business in Good forwardness. He [Maynard] Replys when my Grass and Corn will move into my Barn without hands I'll leave it to Help Mr. Parkman—not before. The Messenger returns to Neighbor Clark. He answers what shall I do? My own is really Suffering and Everything is backward for want of a Team, for I have none and can get none, But he is Labouring for our Souls and why Shall I refuse? and came away.

31. I preach'd A.M. and P.M. on Prov. 29, 1. I was very weary at noon, and I had the Toothach. Neighbor Grove din'd with me. At Night I was much more weary. Our Repetitions were omitted.

## AUGUST [1726]

1. I stir'd myself pritty much about my Hay, raking, etc. Just before Even I walk'd down to See Neighbor John Maynard who lay ill. I pray'd with him.

2. Our Mother Champney with my Child rode to Cambridge, stopping only at Livermores.[1] Got down about 5 P.M. tho we set out at almost 10 A.M. We had a comfortable Journey. But we found sister Ruth ill. Brother Samuel Parkman happened to come up here and return'd again. Sister Lydia[2] and I walk'd over to Brother Hicks'.[3] She went to the Docters and then we returned home.

---

[27] Of Westborough.

[28] A deep red wine of low alcoholic content obtained chiefly from Spain.

[29] Of Westborough.

[30] Mrs. Joseph Thurston of Westborough.

[31] Thomas Shepherd, *The Sincere Convert, Discovering the Small Number of True Believers, and the Great Difficulty of Saving Conversion* (Cambridge, 1664).

[32] One of the works of John Edwards, D.D. (1637-1716), the English divine. Parkman possessed several of the books of Edwards. See DeForest and Bates, *Westborough*, pp. 73-75.

[33] One of the Indian proprietors of Hassanamisco.

[34] Perez Rice of Westborough.

[35] Either Ebenezer Storns or Samuel Stearns.

[36] Probably James Bowman of Westborough.

[37] John Keyes of Shrewsbury.

[38] Mixed grain, especially rye mixed with wheat.

[1] Joseph Livermore of Framingham.

[2] Lydia Champney, Parkman's sister-in-law.

[3] John Hicks of Cambridge, Parkman's brother-in-law.

3. I rode to Boston. Brother Samuel Parkman rode my Beast to Cambridge. I was at Mr. Bakers,[4] Demings, Greens[5] and Boyce's.[6]

4. I bought Mr. Willard on the Catechism,[7] price 55 Shillings. My appointment was to go back to Cambridge this morning and to proceed as far on my Journey as the Time would permit. I sat tediously waiting for my Horse, but not coming I neither went to Lecture nor any whither else all Day. About Sun setting Brother came and then I came to Cambridge.

5. Leaving Sister Ruth[8] very ill I rode as far as Captain Brintnalls[9] where I waited for his Son some time, but not coming I hasted to Marlboro. I din'd at Mr. Woods.[10] Was at Mr. Brecks[11]—for there was no little need of Resting, it was so exceeding hot. Thence (Gladly) home. But here the Evening was very disconsolate! My Wife was on the Bed lonely but sadly weeping, oppress'd and discourag'd with her own Pains and ills, and with the Sicknesses of many in the Town. Sarjeant Rice,[12] and Son Eleazer,[13] Neighbor Maynard, Asher Rice, and Jeduthan Fay[14] all suddenly taken and very bad each with scorching fevers.

6. My Wife was better. I rested myself, till Mr. Cushing came in the Afternoon. I rode to Shrewsbury. Very hot indeed all the last 3 dayes.

7. I preach'd A.M. on Eccl. 11, 8; P.M. on Rom. 1, 20. The Heat to Day also was very Tedious. But after Exercises the Heavens grew Black and we had great Rains till Sunset when I rode Back home.

8. I went to see Mr. Maynard and then Mr. Rice and his Son with all which I pray'd.

9. I was Requested to Mr. Rice's to assist him in settling his worldly Estate and Setting his house in order. Here was his Brother Joshua Rice.[15] I pray'd with him and his son.

10. I was at Mr. Rices again to finish his Last will and testament. Here was Captain Brigham[16] and Deacon Rice.[17] I pray'd here again. I call'd in to see Neighbor Maynard as I went home, and I pray'd with him likewise. In the Afternoon I rode out to See the Sick in the other parts of Town—Peres Rice and Jeduthan Fay.

11. Another, one Nathanael Child, taken ill.

12. Finished my Preparations. Very Sickly in Mendon and severall other Towns. Phinehas Hardy mow'd in my Lot for himself.

13. Very Rainy. My wife not well.

14. I preach'd all Day upon John 2, 1. Edward Baker was propounded to the Church.

15. I was sent for to Mr. Rices. They apprehended him (according to his own phrase) near winding up. When I came to him the Springs of Life were very weak and Low. He could speak Yea or No but I had no Answer from him to many Questions I asked him. I pray'd Earnestly for him; I discoursed to his Wife and Children and Friends about the Bed and then Solemnly bid him Farewell. He gave me fervent tokens and I Left him. He dy'd about an hour after. Captain Fay[18] and Two Sons came to take care of Some Hay which Phinehas Hardy and Thomas Forbush, Junior[19] mow'd to Day for me.

16. In the Morning Prescot[20] a Young Scholar and my wife's remote Kinsman came to See us, but tarried but an hour or Two.

Mr. Edmund Rice's Funerall, after which I visited Nathaniel Child and Asher Rice (sick).

17. I prepar'd for my Lecture. Phinehas and his Brother Daniel[21] mow'd for me to Day. Captain Fay came and Two Sons (but one finding himself not well returned home) and with his Team and got in part of my Hay. He left his Team with me. My Wife rode away from us for Cambridge (the Lad John before her).

18. Captain Fay came again and Lieutenant Forbush to get up the Rest of my Hay. Mr. Thomas Forbush[22] lent them his hand after Meeting. I preach'd a Lecture from Rev. 22, 20.

19. 20. Having had Such avocations this week, no one can think me Idle these Two Dayes, seeing a Sacrament approaches.

21. Sacrament Day. I preach'd A.M. on Heb. 10, 22. Captain Willard,[23] Dr. Matthews,[24] Hezekiah Ward[25] and Mrs. Grove of Greenland Communicated with us. P.M. I preach'd upon 1 John 2, 1. Many Marlboro people, Mr. Breck I concluded to be absent.

22. So many of my Friends absent I was very lonely. I walk'd down to Neighbor Greens.[26] I read miscellaneously. I kill'd 8 Pidgeons (and how many more I know not) at a shot.

23. In my lowly State I wrote a letter to my wife which I never Design'd to Send. I had great opportunity to Discourse with my Maid servant of things of an Everlasting Importance. I improv'd it in some measure, but found she had received but very barely in her Education, being very unacquainted with the Principles of Religion, and not able to so much as to return any Answer to the Catechism taught our Smallest Children. Alas! The Irreligion and Ignorance of many (professedly Christian) Families among us of this Country, notwithstanding the Care universally taken for their Instruction!

24. Phinehas Hardy went to Boston. I wrote diverse letters. Several: to my Father, Deacon Henihman. I was at Lieutenant Forbushes.[27]

25. I read various things. Very Impatient Except when I was immers'd in Thought. I went down to Lieutenant's again expecting the Young Man, but he came not. Neighbor Clark with me in my Return home.

26. I receiv'd from Boston. Mr. Willard on the Catechism brought up to me.

27. I have been finely at Liberty this Week for my Preparations. Yet not finish'd till within Night sometime.

28. I preach'd again upon 1 John 2, 1, A. & P.M. I was much wearied at noon, and very unactive. Aged Mrs. Holloway[28] was Suddenly taken ill this morning. At Midnight Mr. Holloway came to me and desir'd me to rise and ride to his Mother. I did so. When I came to her she could Scarce Speak, but her understanding was Strong. I pray'd after which She Reviv'd and spake a great deal to me alone of her former Desires and the Comforts She had lately received from Deacon Keys[29] of Shrewsbury, etc.

29. About 4 o'Clock I went up and went to Bed. I return'd home about nine. I sent for Mr. Oliver Ward's Horse and about 11 Rode away for Cambridge. It was past one when I left Mr. Amsden[30] yet I got to my Father Champneys[31] whilst the Day light was visible.

30. Brother Champney[32] with us. We set out near Night, and without stopping at any Tavern we came to Westborough presently after sun-down.

31. My Corn Stalks were Cut (in part). My Child not well, she now breading her Eye Teeth.

---

[4] Thomas Baker (Harvard 1724).

[5] Probably the home of Parkman's friend Joseph Green (Harvard 1720).

[6] Samuel Boyce of Boston.

[7] Samuel Willard, *A Compleat Body of Divinity in Two Hundred and Fifty Expository Lectures on the Assembly's Shorter Catechism* (Boston, 1726). *Sibley*, II, 13–36.

[8] Ruth Champney, Parkman's sister-in-law.

[9] William Brintnall of Sudbury.

[10] Benjamin Woods of Marlborough.

[11] Reverend Robert Breck of Marlborough.

[12] Edmund Rice, an original settler of Westborough.

[13] Eleazer Rice lived in southwestern Marlborough but was admitted to the church in Westborough.

[14] Son of Samuel and Tabitha Fay.

[15] A proprietor of Worcester who later (unknown date) removed to Marlborough. Lincoln, *Worcester*, p. 45, 47.

[16] Nathan Brigham of Marlborough.

[17] Caleb Rice of Marlborough.

[18] Of Westborough.

[19] Son of the Westborough selectman.

[20] Peter Prescott (Harvard 1730). Son of Dr. Jonathan Prescott of Concord. *Sibley*, VIII, 772–774.

[21] Hardy brothers of Westborough.

[22] Selectman of Westborough.

[23] Benjamin Willard of Grafton.

[24] Dr. John Matthews, physician of Marlborough and Southborough.

[25] Of Marlborough.

[26] John Green of Westborough.

[27] Lieutenant Samuel Forbush of Westborough.

[28] Mother of William and/or Adam Holloway of Westborough.

[29] Deacon John Keyes should not be confused with Captain John Keyes, another resident of Shrewsbury. The ancestry of both is unclear. Ward, *Shrewsbury*, pp. 339–341.

[30] Captain Isaac Amsden of Marlborough.

[31] Samuel Champney, Sr., of Cambridge.

[32] Samuel Champney, Jr.

I have had very Sensible Perception of the Truth of the Apostles Saying 1 Cor. 7, 31. The Fashion of this World passeth away. Truly a very Slender observation makes it Obvious. Everything in Nature being in incessant Motion; and we living by Changes The Age Wears off and Time is at last to be small ow'd up in Eternity.

### SEPTEMBER [1726]

1. Brother Champney went from us. I went over to Neighbor Pratts[1] in the Eve, where was Neighbor Charles Rice, and Neighbor Baker[2] both under great Difficulty for grinding (the Mills about us being dry), and fearing they must be Oblig'd to go as far as Providence. William Clark cutt Stalks till noon.

2. Neighbor Pratt kill'd a Calf for me. In the Afternoon He Cutt the remaining part of My Stalks. Sundry Persons taken Sick among us of a burning ague: Neighbor Isaac Pratt and his wife, Noah Rice,[3] etc.; and Some of the Distemper (distinguishing from the former and) call'd the Fever and ague. My Contemplations were Governed by the Times and

4. I preach'd upon Hosea 4, 12. In the Eve as I had infinite Reason I reflected on my unusefullness and unprofitableness and my vile Ingratitude to God in Continuing in so [illegible] Commission of Sin and perfunctory Superficiall performance of Duty.

5. This Day being my Birth Day (when I enter'd into my 24th year) I had a great variety of Contemplations of the volubility of Time of the vast importance of making preparation for Eternity the great Business of Life. And I am urged to be the more Speedy and fervent by the Consideration of the Tenderness and infirmity of my naturall constitution through which I have long been much obstructed in my great work. But what have my Strongest Resolutions Many times come to? and what is my own sufficiency without assistance of Divine Grace? O that I may Live to Christ, and by the Faith only of the Son of God, that I may have the honour and Happiness of doing Some service to his interest, that I may be wise to win souls, and when I have preach'd to others may not be myself a Cast away

6. Our Child was very ill, and especially at nights very unquiet.

7. We were in great Concern about the Child.

8. We Sent to Dr. Matthews for Little Molly ill with a fever and violent flux. The cause was from her breading her Eye Teeth. We have Sometimes been up with her till after midnight. My wife has not had a Comfortable night's Rest this week. I reflected upon Davids case when his Child was Sick.

9. My Babe I hope is better and in some method of Recovery.

10. The Season of Strict Engagement. Mr. Baker, whose Desires I had before receiv'd and propounded openly, brought his Relation.

11. I preach'd all Day upon John 3, 19. Mr. Baker was admitted into our Church.

12. Dr. Matthews came in to see the Child, which was ill yet, but thro the Divine Goodness in a more hopefull Condition than heretofore.

13. I rose very Early, sometime before Day, and more than ¼ before sunrise was mounted on my horse and rode to Shrewsbury. With Mr. Cushing[4] I went to Lancaster where Ministers were Asociated. Severall persons were here besides the members: Mr. Andrew Gardner,[5] Mr. Cook,[6] Mr. Trowbridge,[7] Mr. Frink,[8] Brintnall,[9] Samuel Willard,[10] etc. What was of greatest moment that I remember was advice to Mr. McKinstry[11] concerning the Management of his Cause.

14. Mr. Loring[12] preach'd Excellently on the Text Ps. 119, 18. It was very stormy, so that We did not return home.

[1] John Pratt of Westborough.
[2] Edward Baker.
[3] Youngest son of Thomas Rice of Westborough.
[4] Reverend Job Cushing of Shrewsbury.
[5] Formerly the minister at Worcester.
[6] Reverend William Cooke of Wayland.
[7] Reverend Caleb Trowbridge (Harvard 1710) of Groton, Mass. *Sibley*, V, 545–546.
[8] Reverend Thomas Frink (Harvard 1722) of Rutland, Mass. *Sibley*, VII, 69–75.
[9] Reverend William Brintnall, minister and schoolmaster at Sudbury.
[10] (Harvard 1723). The preacher in the Stony Brook region of Marlborough and later the minister at Biddeford, Maine, 1730–1741. *Sibley*, VII, 281–287.
[11] Reverend John McKinstry of Sutton.
[12] Reverend Israel Loring of Sudbury.

15. Most of us mov'd off in the morning but Mr. Cushing and I tarried till after Dinner, and then came away together as far as Deacon Keyes, Some little way on this Side [at] whose house I turned away for home. The Weather was not Settled yet, but I got to my house Comfortably.

16. 17. I Employ'd myself only on my Preparations for the Sabbath approaching, When

18. I preach'd again A.M. and P.M. on the Same, John 3, 19, and baptiz'd Mr. Isaac Shattucks child Mary.[13]

19. Now I am Enter'd into a Busy Time and active wherein my Heart has often Trembled within Me, that is of assisting the sick in their preparations for Eternity. Mr. Isaac Pratt and his wife, and Mr. Tainter[14] and his wife ill. I visited and pray'd with them.

22. Mr. Pratt dy'd, and

24. was Buried.

25. I preach'd A.M. on 1 Pet. 4, 3 and P.M. likewise. In the Evening I formed Severall Designs (in my Secret Reflections) about my future more Extensive serviceableness and particularly in my Fathers Family when I go to Boston (from one time to another) to assist their Spiritual Welfare.

26. 27. 28. And this Week is full of Employments, my providing and preparing for my Lecture and Sacrament. And wonderfull is the Goodness and favour of God in carrying me so comfortably thro' hitherto; tho I have many times had more unavoidable Avocations than I hope others of my Brethren in the Ministry. On the 27, Mr. Maynard[15] of Shrewsbury brought in my Colt which had rang'd the Woods the Summer past.

29. I preach'd a Lecture on Acts 8, 21, preparatory to the Holy Communion. When the Sacred Exercises were over I Stop'd the Brethren to propose to them a Method of Supporting the Elements at Sacrament by a Contribution every Sacrament. For in time past they had proceeded in a Way that being more agreeable to what they were brought up in, they were urgent with me to allow, but it had frustrated the purpose.

30. I was Diligent in my Great Work, but God forgive my unprofitableness and Negligence! (I have reason to say so tho I have been never so Diligent). O that his Grace may Supply where I am insufficient.

### OCTOBER [1726]

1. The Sacrament drawing nigh it was much my Care to provide not only for the ordinary Sabbath Exercises, but for the Solemnity of that speciall Ordinance of Christ.

2. I preach'd A.M. on Heb. 10, 22 and Administered the Sacrament of the Lords Supper. P.M. my Text was 1 Pet. 4, 3. [Two illegible, blotted lines follow.]

3. Mr. Cushing was at our house before his Journey to Hingham. We began our Indian Corn Harvest, and I sent my Apples to the Cyder Mill at Mr. Forbush's.[1] I went down to Mr. Forbush's myself before the Team (which was Mr. Warrens[2]) came along. Neighbor Green assisted in a Lesser Third part of what I planted of Corn.

4. We Husked Corn. I myself did little besides.

5. I finish'd the 2nd Volume of the Occasional Papers and Sent it by Neighbor Green to the owner Mr. Woods of Marlboro.

6. 7. I made some preparation tho I expected Mr. Cushing. Captain Keyes of Shrewsbury lodg'd with us last night.

8. Mr. Cushing came to me according to our appointment on Monday Last, and I went to Shrewsbury.

9. I preach'd at Shrewsbury on Phil. 3, 13, 14, A.&P.M. Mr. Cushing came up on my Mare.

10. We walk'd over to Mr. Gershom Keyes'. It rain'd all Day but I went down to Mr. Eagers[3] and Sojourn'd. I read great part of Mr. Penhallows History of the Wars of New England with the Eastern Indians.[4]

[13] Of Westborough. The birth day is recorded as August 10, 1726.
[14] Simon Tainter of Westborough.
[15] Simon Maynard.

[1] Jonathan Forbush of Westborough.
[2] Daniel Warren of Westborough.
[3] James Eager of Westborough.
[4] Samuel Penhallow, *History of the Wars of New England, with the Eastern Indians* (Boston, 1726).

11. Mr. Breck[5] and Two of his Deacons (Rice[6] and Keyes) came to our House. Mr. Breck lodg'd with us.

12. I rode with Mr. Breck to Sutton where was form'd an Ecclesiasticall Council by the Desire of Mr. McKinstry, the Pastor of the Church of Sutton and the aggriev'd Part of the Town and Church upon occasion of their Differences. The Council consisted of 7 Churches, viz., Framingham, Marlboro, Lancaster, West and East Sudbury, Weston and Shrewsbury, The Pastors and Delegates. The Reverend Mr. Swift[7] of Framingham, Moderator; The Reverend Mr. Prentice[8] of Lancaster, Clerk. The Public Hearing Lasted for this Day till nine at night. Ministers were Entertain'd and lodg'd at Mr. McKinstrys; the Delegates in the Town.

13. We were again at the Meeting house and the former part of the Day was spent in further hearing. The Contending or opposing (I had rather than aggriev'd) party was very Resolute to use their Utmost to Carry their will, But very unhappily Expos'd themselves (especially Some few of them) very much. The Council had a great deal of Patience because they would guard against Every Exception that might render their Result invalid with any one. The Council Sat the Latter part of the Day and till 2 in the morning. I Spent Time with Mr. Campbell,[9] Mr. McKinstry, My Sister (who was here at her Brothers) and in the Evening with Mr. Dike[10] (a man of great understanding) and others of the Standing Party (as they Stil'd themselves), among whom I had many circumstances open'd much to my Content.

14. The Council Sat again this Forenoon. After noon the Result was publish'd, which advis'd them to methods of Pacification, when it had pass'd Censure upon the various allegations on both Sides. Mr. McKinstry manifested his acquiescence. Mr. Johnson,[11] Mr. Putnam,[12] etc. demonstrated dissatisfaction and Passion. The Council urg'd them to Consider and weigh what was done, but they were wholly intractable forward. And such was the Frame we left them in. I got home (safe) a little before night.

15. I Carry'd on my Preparations. Yesterday Mr. Brigham[13] (having gather'd my Corn the Day before) brought five Fat Creatures to my Pasture. Yesterday (or the Day before I know not which) Mr. Forbush Sent my Cyder home, 5½ Barrells. Neighbor Clark help'd me put it into the cellar.

16. I preach'd A.M. on 1 Pet. 4, 4; P.M., 1 Pet. 4, 17.

17. I finish'd Mr. Penhallow's History.

18. I was abroad in the Neibourhood at Mr. Peres Rices[14] where I discours'd with one Mr. Robins whose dauter my Wife would have to live with her. At old Mr. Rice's,[15] etc.

19. I was much indispos'd with a Cold, but went to Lieutenants.

20. My Cold increas'd and I had much Trouble from a Sore Throat, so I was Oblig'd to keep Close. I study'd the Blessings of [blotted] and the Mischiefs of Divisions among People and this I continued the 21 and 22.

23. I preach'd all Day upon Heb. 12, 14. But I had much difficulty to go thro the Exercises by Reason of my being Stuff'd with my Cold.

24. [no entry].

25. I rode to Marlboro, it being Ministers Meeting. We were generally together. Mr. McKinstry ask'd what advice we could give him to direct his future Behaviour and Managements. Upon his Request the Eleven Ministers assisted him With Their Counsel. Mr. Swift (Mr. Cushing having pray'd) discours'd upon a Sower went forth to sow. I rode with Mr. Cook and Mr. Frink and Sister Hicks to Sudbury. I lodg'd at Mr. Cook's.

26. I rose early, at day break, mounted my horse and rode away without disturbing anyone of the house (as I had premonish'd them). I came to Cambridge about Ten, and thence to Boston about 2 or 3 o'Clock P.M. I was with Mr. Samuel Mather[16] this Evening. He read to Me a Letter of his Father to Lord Chancellor.

27. Mr. Thatcher[17] of Milton preach'd the Lecture, on Ps. 63, 5. I was after Lecture with Mr. Byles,[18] and very well Satisfy'd with his Improvements especially in Poetry. Deacon Coffin[19] of Newbury was at My Father's. My very Good Friend Mr. Isaac Greenwood[20] returned from England about a Week or Ten Dayes Since and was now in Town; but all My Diligence and Eagerness could not bring me to a Light of him. It was Windy and Cold I declin'd returning back upon my Journey as I had propos'd. I bought Dr. Mather's Christian Philosopher,[21] Sermons on Prayer with a Pamphlet or Two, of Mr. Gerrish.[22]

28. It continued very Cold yet in the Afternoon I ventur'd out upon my Journey to Cambridge.

29. I returned home, Stopping only at Mr. Swifts and at Captain Goddards.[23]

30. I preach'd Two Sermons I had about a Twelve Month or more before upon Eccl. 12, 1, which I appriz'd My audience of in a Brief Sentence immediately after I read my Text. Old Mr. Rice din'd with me.

31. My Employment various.

## NOVEMBER [1726]

In my Seclusion from most of those Objects which Engage the Busy and active part of the world I find not daily such a number Observations to be made upon what is round about me where I am not plac'd in the midst of the Crowds, Employments and accidents that must be always before hand with the mind; we cannot have so many rare accounts as in those places of Concourse and action, that we are in Retirement chiefly taken up about our Domestick affairs, and personal concerns. And it is very rare that we can have any matter of very great importance or weight to interest the world in, when under Confinement to so narrow a Sphere of motion. Here Likewise it might be added that much of the time revolving is consumed in much the Same manner, the Same Business or Amusements; and other parts of it may be Equally divided by so great a number of Engagements that it may be hard to say which took us up most, and it would be too great a Labour to insert all. Indeed sometimes there is a close Relation and Dependence one upon another, and then the giving one may give us all, an hint being Sufficient to bring the whole circle of actions or accidents into our minds and view again. And it is not always an action that may be accounted of itself of the greatest importance, that is of the greatest moment and Necessity to be mention'd as an hint of the Rest that was done. For that which is but a Trifle above, may best Serve to direct us to the whole Series.

The First 4 or 5 Dayes of this Month I do not remember anything worthy my Observation in this place. Except that on the 4 I rode out in the afternoon, a thing I hitherto have never done before.

6. I preach upon Luke 5, 32, A. and P.M.

7. 8. Very Busy in preparing for the Solemnity approaching. I was at Mr. Wards at Supper after the Raising his Mill. N. B. We sang Ps. 128th after Supper.

9. Mr. Ward sent his Man with a Load of Wood, and he carted another Load for me.

---

[5] Reverend Robert Breck of Marlborough.
[6] Deacon Caleb Rice of Marlborough.
[7] John Swift.
[8] John Prentice.
[9] Reverend John Campbell of Oxford.
[10] Nathaniel Dike of Sutton.
[11] Elisha Johnson.
[12] Elisha Putnam.
[13] David Brigham, a neighbor of Parkman.
[14] Of Westborough.
[15] Probably Charles Rice of Westborough.

[16] Samuel Mather (Harvard 1723), the son of Dr. Cotton Mather, and later minister of the Second Church in Boston, 1732-1741 and the 10th Congregational Society, 1742-1785. *Sibley*, VII, 216-239.
[17] Reverend Peter Thacher (Harvard 1671), minister of Milton. Sibley, II, 370-379.
[18] Mather Byles of Boston.
[19] Deacon Nathaniel Coffin, also the town clerk of Newbury for nearly 40 years. John J. Currier, *Ould Newbury: Historical and Biographical Sketches* (Boston, 1896), pp. 170-171.
[20] (Harvard 1721). Classmate of Parkman and later the first Hollis Professor of Mathematics at Harvard College. *Sibley*, VI, 471-482.
[21] Cotton Mather, *The Christian Philosopher: a collection of the best discoveries in Nature, with religious improvements* (Boston, 1721).
[22] Samuel Gerrish, town clerk of Boston, and a well-known bookseller.
[23] Edward Goddard of Framingham.

10. Public Thanksgiving. I preach'd on Ps. 100, 4, 5. Many Private (as well as public) Mercies call forth all Expressions of Gratitude. Remember July 17, Last, with many other signall appearances of God for me.

12. Mr. Wheeler[1] brought Old Mrs. Holloway to Me. I hope God has had Compassion on this aged person, her Confessions, etc., appear very Cordial. The work of God appears manifestly in her. I would praise the Name of God if he has made me anyway instrumental for her Souls advantage.

13. I preach'd A.M. on Heb. 10, 22. Administer'd the Sacrament, but imediately before sacrament I admitted Mrs. Holloway into the Church. I preach'd P.M. on Luke 5, 32. I hope this has been a Good Day. The Grace of God be magnify'd.

14. I rode to Marlboro. I met Mr. Cushing a little before we Came to Mr. Brecks. We were Disappointed in our Visit to Mr. Breck, He being gone to Boston. We went to Mr. Woods',[2] and to Mr. Thomas's,[3] the last having been very ill, and continuing under Confinement. Mr. Cushing went away for Lancaster when I went into Colonel Hows[4] to clear off my Beef Score, and thence I returned immediately home.

15. 16. I gave my Self very much to my Subject, being persuaded I shall be Depriv'd of Opportunity to study in the Latter part of the Week.

17. In the Morning I rode to Shrewsbury to Mr. Cushing. There was Captain Baker of Brookfield. Mr. Cushing rode with me to Lancaster. Mr. Prentice was come out to go to Meeting. He had Some Expectation of my Coming. He gave me his Bible and I preach on (a Text I had not Design'd to, but I was straitned for Time and Could not Look over the whole of any Sermon and I therefore Chose one I had frequently and somewhat lately preach'd) Acts 16, 24. We tarried all night at Mr. Prentice's, and had good Entertainment.

18. After Dinner we returned home. Mr. Samuell Fay[5] and his Son[6] Cut and Carted me ½ Dozen Load of Wood.

19. I was very Strictly Engaged.

20. I preach'd all Day upon Mark 3, 33.

21. 22. I read and wrote some remarks upon a Book entitled Reliquiae Anti Baxteriance.

23. Captain Keyes of Shrewsbury was here to see Me.

24. 25. 26. I was very much afflicted with Toothach and an ague in My Face. Alas how Small a Matter will discompose and Obstruct those, who in the best plight have but just Sufficient powers to perform any Service at all! N. B. 24. I married Ebenezer Savage[7] and Mary Hamilton of Rutland, Mr. Parsons[8] Mr. Burr,[9] and Mr. Cushing being absent.

27. I was grievously exercis'd all last night with pains in my Face. In the morning I was easier and went to Meeting. The Text A. and P.M. was Eph. 2, 5. We were Inform'd that Mr. Breck Yesterday buried his Youngest Child.[10] It dy'd very Suddenly. Mrs. Willard,[11] Mrs. Maynard, Mr. Behman[12] and his wife Din'd with us.

28. I read the Occasional Paper vol. 3.

29. Mr. Cushing came to see Us and lodg'd with us.

30. Mr. Cushing return'd home. Mr. Thomas Forbes, Junior was with me upon the Business of his Admission into our Church. He made some Hesitation about Making a Relation, But I satisfy'd him of the usefullness of the Practice if well observ'd and therefore the Expedience thereof. He was So well persuaded that he presented me one to be Read to the Church.

[1] Joseph Wheeler of Westborough.
[2] Benjamin Woods of Marlborough.
[3] William Thomas of Marlborough.
[4] Thomas Howe of Marlborough.
[5] One of the earliest settlers of Westborough and the younger brother of Captain John Fay.
[6] Either Samuel, Jr. (b. 1705), Jeduthan (b. 1707), or Ebenezer (b. 1713).
[7] Given in *Westborough Vital Records* as Ebenezer Savige and Mary Hambleton, and in *Rutland Vital Records* as Ebenezer Savage and Mary Hambleton.
[8] Reverend David Parsons (Yale 1705), minister of the First Congregational Church of Leicester, Mass. Dexter, pp. 36–37.
[9] Reverend Isaac Burr of Worcester.
[10] Anna Breck (b. March 13, 1725).
[11] Probably Mrs. Martha Willard of Hassinimisco.
[12] Probably Eleazer and Hannah Beemon or Beamon of Westborough.

## DECEMBER [1726]

1. 2. 3. I Employ'd myself almost wholly upon the Subject I Design further to Entertain my people with.

4. I preach'd A. and P.M. on Eph. 2, 5. It was a very stormy Day and I had but few hearers. Mr. Jedediah How set the Tune and read the Line, P.M.

5. Mr. Thomas Forbush, Junior's youngest Child[1] dy'd very suddenly this morning, as I hear many Young Children in severall Towns round here. In the Eve my Little Dauter was ill, But

6. Thro the Divine Favour She was this Morning well recovered. In the Afternoon I was at the funerall of Mr. Forbush's Child.

7. I rode over to Mr. Eagers upon the Affair of my absent Heiffer, But he was gone to Marlboro. Hearing Mr. Thomas Ward[2] was at Mr. Allens[3] Mill I went Thither and met with him. Mr. Allen requested me to go in and see his Wife. I did and had an hour or Two's Discourse with her. I both found and left her in a poor Melancholly, dejected, distressed Condition. Frome hence I rode to Marlboro. I went down to Mr. John How's (who I heard had my Heiffer) first with Two Young Men, Nathaniel Oak[4] and Joshua Goardin, and then with Mr. Ward (who had kept the Creature all Sumer and winter Last) to prove it mine, if they were able to give Testimony. They said (upon Seeing her) that they were not only able but ready, if call'd thereto, to give oath it was mine. But these all not satisfying Mr. How we went over to Mr. Woods and Chose him and Mr. Jedediah Brigham[6] to Determine between us. Upon hearing us it fell with full Consent to me and I gave Mr. How 10 Shillings for keeping her. After this (it being Somewhat after nine o'Clock) I went to Mr. Brecks where I Lodg'd.

8. Mr. Breck walked with me to Mr. Woods's. Here was Old Mr. How[6] of Hopkington who told over the Manner and Methods of Mr. Barretts[7] coming into Hopkinton and Settling there. Mr. Woods went up with us to Mr. Brecks where we din'd upon a Turkey. When Near night I came away, but meeting Mr. Jacob Amsden[8] I went in with him into his Father Behmans,[9] and thence I came home with Mr. Amsden.

9. 10. My Sermons took up the whole of my Time. I sent John and Nathaniel Oak to Marlboro, and in the morn they brought the Heiffer home.

11. I preach'd again All Day upon Eph. 2, 5. Old Mrs. Forbush,[10] Mr. How[11] of Hassinemisco, and his wife, Mrs. Newton,[12] Mrs. Goodeno[13] din'd with us. An Exceeding Cold Day.

12. Very Cold. Our schoolmaster, Mr. Townsend[14] came into Town, and the School began.

13. I was at Captain Fay's,[15] Mr. Pratts,[16] etc., to get hands to Cut wood and kill my Swine.

14. Neighbor Pratt and Maynard[17] came and kill'd Two of my Swine. P.M. it was Stormy, Snow, etc. Mr. Ward Reckon'd with me.

[1] Thomas, Jr.
[2] Of Westborough.
[3] Ephraim Allen who lived in that part of Westborough which became Northborough in 1776.
[4] Nathaniel Oak (Oaks, Oakes), Jr. of Marlborough, later a resident of that part of Lancaster which became Bolton in 1738.
[5] Son of Samuel Brigham of Marlborough and the proprietor of a tannery in that town. Hudson, *Marlborough*, pp. 334–335.
[6] John How who was prominent in the establishment of the First Congregational Church in Hopkinton in 1724. *Manual of the First Congregational Church in Hopkinton* (Boston, 1881), p. 20.
[7] Reverend Samuel Barrett, first minister at Hopkinton.
[8] Of Marlborough.
[9] Jacob Amsden married Sarah Beaman, daughter of Thomas Beaman of Marlborough, October 28, 1719. Jacob Amsden, son of Isaac Amsden, Sr., of Marlborough lived in Westborough as early as 1722.
[10] Probably the wife of Deacon Thomas Forbush.
[11] Nehemiah How.
[12] Either Mrs. Thomas or Mrs. Josiah Newton of Westborough.
[13] Mrs. David Goodenow of Westborough.
[14] Joshua Townsend of Brookfield was engaged for £18 to teach six months in three parts of Westborough. For twelve or thirteen years he continued to be the schoolmaster. DeForest and Bates, *Westborough*, pp. 96–100.
[15] Captain John Fay of Westborough.
[16] Probably John Pratt, a neighbor of Parkman.
[17] David Maynard.

15. Very high Winds and Sharp Cold. Mr. John Pratt, Junior and his Brother Came and Cutt Several Load of wood for me. An High German Doctor was here.

16. I finish'd Mr. Addisons 3d volume containing His Dialogues upon Medals, The Present state of the War, 1707, and of the Christian Religion.

17. Upon My preparations.

18. I preach'd all Day upon Luk. 6, 46. Mr. Simeon Howard din'd with us.

19. Very Stormy. High winds and Rain.

20. William Clark Thrash'd Oates for me. Mr. Barrett[18] expected according to word sent us but Came not. Mr. Peres Rice here with Complaints against his uncle, Mr. Samuel Fay, etc. He told me Some in the Town were Examining whether my marrying the Rutland couple was according to Law. Mr. Breck sent home my Political State 12 volumes, and a Pamphlet, by his son Mr. Robert and young Rice[19] of College.

21. Very Cold and we but Short firewood.

22. In the morning I sent for Neighbor Clarks cart for my Lad to bring home wood upon. But there Came some young Men that both Cut and Carted a good supply (of 7 Load). Captain Fay's 2 sons and Team, Peres Rice's Servant and Nathaniel Child[20] were my men.

23. 24. My whole time is taken up about my subject, and I Desire no other Employment on these Dayes.

25. I preach'd upon Luk. 11, 26 A. and P.M. Mrs. Holloway[21] din'd with us.

26. A.M. I read Lowths[22] Directions for Reading the Scriptures. P.M. I read the Clergyman's Vade mecum.

27. I rode to Mr. Barretts. Here was Mrs. Ford[23] and Mrs. Leasingby.[24] O'bed I read Mr. Moodys[25] Memoirs of Joseph Quasson and Just Sentiments on the protestant Religion. I likewise dip'd into Mr. Cooper's[26] Account of Mr. John Coney.

28. Very Stormy and Cold, but notwithstanding the women, out of their humourousness and gaiety Rode along with me to Mrs. Woods.[27] I brought home my peacock, and got home well tho it was a difficult Time, for the Riding, the Cold Storm, and it being in the Evening.

29. The storm Continues very hard. I read in Mr. Coney's Life and it very much affected me as I very well knew the man. I could not but have the Saddest Reflections upon my Self when I see what men of far inferiour advantages attain to; and under no such bonds as I am by my Solemn Consecration to God, in my holy ordination.

30. Mr. Barrett, Mr. Burnay and Wood came over with Mrs. Wood, Mrs. Fowl[28] and Leasingby to our house, and they returned in the Evening.

31. Very backward in my preparations but as the Year Concluded, the week and the Day my Sermons were brought to a Sufficient Length (if Every Discourse could be as good as it is Long).

## 1727
### JANUARY

1. This Morning I preach'd upon [blank] And on the Same text in the Afternoon. It is very Necessary I should Strengthen my Resolutions and mend my pace in the Christian Course, if I

would finish Well. Alas! how many Seekers are those who trifle in vain Efforts; when it is our great Duty to Strive to Enter in at the Strait Gate. A Strait Gate truly is the Gate of Life (and so it ought to be) but do I not prove my Self the Author of many of the Difficulties that add to its Straitness? O that I might obtain the quickening Grace of God to inspirit me, and make me fervent and Constant to the End of my Life! but particularly this Year I am now Entering upon that I may have a more Comfortable reflection upon it, and account to give of it, than of the Year past. And as I beseech the Influence of the Divine spirit and Grace in My Soul, I would likewise the Divine Conduct in the Blessing upon my bodily and secular Affairs, that I may do and Enjoy Nothing but to the honour of God.

2. I rode to Mr. Swifts[1] according to appointment made with Mr. Barrett and Mrs. Leasingby to meet them there at one o'clock. And tho I was precisely at the hour, they did not wait for me. However, they were not So long gone before Me, but that I caught up with them a mile or Two further down. We were in at Livermore's[2] and din'd there. It was heavy riding and sometimes rainy; so that it was somewhat tedious! I lodg'd at Father Champneys.[3]

3. I rode to Boston and found my Fathers family comfortable (Thanks to God).

4. Towards night I went to Mrs. Edward's (the widow of my good Friend John Edwards[4]) and pay'd the Ballance of our Account. Thence I went to Deacon Greens[5] printing house and paid him for my years news, etc, etc. I had design'd to have been upon my Journey home, but it continued such dark and wet weather that I defer'd it.

5. I went to Lecture and heard Mr. Prince[6] Excellently preach on Prov. 27, 1. I met with my dear friend Mr. Greenwood after his long absence from me and was made acquainted with his Design of Setting up an experimental Course of Mechanical Philosophy. I hope it will be followed with the Divine Blessing and all his other good Designs succeeded. Mr. Gee[7] invited us to dine with him. I spent a part of my Afternoon with a great deal of Delight (there being other very good Friends there) but I was oblig'd to Engage my Self in my Necessary affairs. It was raining but I was much constrain'd to go as far as Cambridge and I reach'd there.

6. Brother Champney[8] and Sister Ruth[9] rode with me home. It was very Serene weather but as heavy travelling as I can remember thro the Late Excessive Rains. We got home very timely and I found my Family well. God has carry'd me thro many a Difficult Journey, and given me great occasion to magnifie his goodness, extended in this Last.

7. Mr. Barrett had appointed to Change on the Sabbath approaching, but I have heretofore met with so many disappointments there, I was very full of concern lest I should be put to some Difficulty. However I rode over to Hopkington, which when I came to I was wel Satisfy'd in finding him ready to ride to Westboro. Here was Elder Barrett[10] and Mr. Charles Coffin, which made me to be Chearfull again.

8. I preach'd at Hopkington (in their new Meeting house) on Phil. 3, 13, 14 A. and P.M. After the Exercises I found it necessary to return home, they having no Hay at all at Mr. Barretts and severall Horses to provide for.

9. It continues (as it has been ever since Friday) very foggy and rainy weather. Brother Champney much afflicted with the Tooth ach.

10. 11. 12. I was variously Employ'd in reading Mr. Joseph Addisons Works, vol. 1, 12, etc, etc. Captain Fay came desiring me to visit his son, but my circumstances would not allow me.

[18] Reverend Samuel Barrett of Hopkinton.

[19] Caleb Rice (Harvard 1730), youngest son of Caleb Rice of Marlborough. Later the first minister of Sturbridge, Mass., 1736–1759. *Sibley*, VIII, 774–775.

[20] Nathaniel Child of Westborough.

[21] Either Mrs. William or Mrs. Adam Holloway of Westborough.

[22] Probably the popular work *Directions for the profitable reading of the Holy Scriptures* by the English theologian, William Lowth, D.D. (1660–1732). The work first appeared in a London edition of 1708. Numerous other editions followed.

[23] Probably Mrs. Stephen Ford of Charlestown.

[24] This name appears several times but extensive search reveals no clue to the identity of the person.

[25] Samuel Moodey or Moody, *A Summary Account of the Life and Death of Joseph Quasson, an Indian* (Boston, 1726).

[26] William Cooper, *The Service of God . . . Preach'd on . . . the Death of Mr. John Coney* [*An Appendix, Containing a Further Account of Mr. John Coney, Collected from his Private Writings*] (Boston, 1726). Cooper (Harvard 1712) was minister of the Brattle Street Church in Boston, 1716–1743. *Sibley*, V, 624–634.

[27] The home of Captain John Wood of Hopkinton.

[28] Probably Mrs. John Fowle of Charlestown.

[1] Reverend John Swift of Framingham.

[2] Joseph Livermore of Framingham.

[3] Samuel Champney, Sr., Parkman's father-in-law.

[4] Of Charleston.

[5] Bartholomew Green (1666–1732) of Boston, printer of the *Boston News-Letter*.

[6] Reverend Thomas Prince of the Old South Church.

[7] Reverend Joshua Gee of Boston.

[8] Samuel Champney, Jr., Parkman's brother-in-law.

[9] Ruth Champney, Parkman's sister-in-law.

[10] Samuel Barrett, Sr., of Boston, the father of the Reverend Samuel Barrett of Hopkinton.

13. Brother Champney went home.

15. I preach'd on Luk. 13, 24, A. and P.M.

16. A fierce storm of Snow.

17. Mr. Holloway Sent his Lad for me to [see] his Child.[11] I rode over and found it but alive. I pray'd with them for it, and then the Child Chang'd and Expir'd while I continued to Instruct, Exhort and Support the Heavy and Sorrowfull Parents under the grievous Loss, it being a fine son of his own Name and in its 3d Year. Mr. Cushing[12] to see me and lodg'd with us.

18. I was at the Funeral of Mr. Holloways Child. I rode upon Mr. Holloways Horse both Yesterday and today. It was raw, bleak Weather and I find I caught a Cold. I could not go to the Grave but turn'd in at Mr. John Pratt Juniors.

19. I had a Sore troublesome night of the last, having the Teeth ach and ague in my face. Mr. John Fay, Junior sent a Man and horse fore me, but I was so ill and the weather so Wet that I was prevented.

20. Mr. Simeon Howard[13] and his Man with his Team came to get me a Supply of wood. I join'd William Clark with them.

21. I was pretty well recovered from my indisposition. Mr. Balley[14] came to our house Expecting to Meet Mr. Jenison,[15] whom they had engaged to preach at that part of Marlboro call'd Stony Brook,[16] but he came not.

22. I preach'd A.M. on Luk. 13, 24; P.M. on Heb. 4, 1. The Lord Graciously forgive my unprofitableness!

23. Mr. Pratt brought me his horse to ride to his Brother John Fays. I went up accordingly and found him in grievous pains. I pray'd with him and used my Endeavours to Comfort and Relieve him as far as Means so poor as those I am impower'd with, might be Effectual.

24. Mr. Cushing came to see me. I find next to inconceivable Benefit by having frequent Conversation with my friends, especially with my Brethren in the ministry. But I am griev'd they can have no greater advantage by me. The Father of Light communicate Wisdom to me but especially make me wise in the Things of God! Mr. Cushing lodg'd with me. Mr. Cushing return'd home. P.M. I was much affected with what I read in the Life of Mr. Mat. Henry, of his wonderfull Labours and Serviceableness. Example seems to have a far greater influence upon me than precept, since it so gratifies my under powers, my imagination, and curiosity; and thereby captivates my affections. Its sad that my understanding and Judgement are no more Employ'd upon the purity and perfection of the Divine Laws, and the infinite Justice, Supremacy and goodness of my God that injoins their observance! But I am glad I can any way be wrought upon, and brought to my Duty.

26. Attended to my Subject. Phinehas Hardy[17] came and first back'd my Colt.

27. Mr. Samuel Willard[18] of Boston Merchant was brought here by his Kinsman Mr. Simon Willard[19] of Hassinamisco. I noted well his excessive antipathy against Mr. Thomas Smith[20] (a Preacher) with whom he was formerly exceeding intimate. There is Sad work when Such sort of Companions fall out and rake into the Dirt and Dung hills of their Conversations to blaze the Mystery of iniquity about the world when it is Shamefull so much as to think of what is done of them in secret. But I hope God has given his grace to Mr. Smith and that he has truly repented of all his Youthfull Sins. God Grant Mr. Willard the Same, and I would not forget my Self. But I am Oblig'd to acknowledge the Goodness of God in the Restraints granted to Me, So that I never was carried to the prodigious Enormitys of Such.

Men. Yet God forbid I should Pharisaically Say I am not as other Men.

28. My Heart in the Evening too indifferent and Slightly [?] in my Examinations. O Lord Quicken thou me in thy Way! To the Dust my Soul cleavest fast.

29. This was a good Day in Several regards. I was much affected with the Sermons I Delivered from Ps. 95, 7. Today if ye will hear his voice. But it had been better if Mr. Willard of Boston and others at my house had not at noon been so full of unsuitable Discourse. God forgive wherein I in any ways countenanc'd it by my Criminal silence. The Evening I would not let go off without some very Serious Enquirys what if this be all the Day that Ever I shall hear the will of God in? What if I should die before another Morning? Let me now put My Self into some actual Readings for my Last hour.

30. What I did Chiefly was in the Clergymans Vade Mecum Volume 1.[21]

31. I rode to the South part of Marlboro (call'd Stony Brook) to Dr. Bellus's,[22] to see Mr. Willard, and here was his Kinsman that had been up with me. I tarried here till near night and then rode up to Mr. Brecks.

N.B. Captain Willard's Characters of Mr. Ebenezer Gee[23] and Mr. John Mountfort[24] at Boston.

FEBRUARY [1727]

1. Mr. Willard and his Kinsman, the Chearful Captain[1] came while we were at an Excellent Dinner on Roast Turkey, etc., at Mr. Brecks. Near Sundown I was very Eager and Earnest to come home. Mr. Breck urged Exceedingly to stay but I resisted his most pressing Importunity and took my leave. I mounted and my Business leading Me down to Mr. Woods's,[2] Messrs. Willards would walk thither. Mr. Wood treated us handsomely and we all Sang the more chearfully. Here I rose up not a few times to return home but Captain Willard hung upon Me and would by no means let me have my way. Mr. Jonathan How[3] (the Tavern keeper) came up from Boston while we were at Mr. Woods's and having several Haddock I bought one for my Wife; and we returned to Mr. Brecks, where We had Sad and Melancholly News of a Young Man Mr. Simon Bradstreet that last friday fell down very suddenly on Mr. Greenwoods wharf at Boston and next morning dyed. The News Letter had given an account of the very Surprizing and most Sudden Death of Mr. Samuell Hirst[4] A.M. of Harvard College, who not long Since fell down Dead on the long wharf at Boston, being in perfect Health (to appearance) the moment before. And one Lewis[5] Sometime publisher of the Boston Gazette, the same afternoon was taken with an Apoplectick fit and dy'd in Two Hours. O that I may also be ready, and that all Young Persons might fear and prepare, Since So many die in full strength, etc., to Demonstrate to us that in an hour that we think not our Lord cometh! I lodged at Mr. Brecks tonight also.

2. In the morning Jonathan How came and invited us to a fish dinner. Accordingly we all went up to his house and Din'd with him on Haddock. Here his Brother Hezekiah[6] of Westboro happen'd very Lukily, whom I implor'd to carry home my Fish and some necessarys. When we came from Mr. Hows, we parted with Mr. Breck and rode to Mr. William Jonson's[7] and thence up to my house, Messrs. Willards being with me. They lodg'd with us.

3. Messrs. Willards went to Stoney Brook, while I confin'd my Self in my Studys as also

4. This Day. It was exceeding Stormy and Snow'd hard.

[11] William, Jr., son of William Holloway of Westborough.

[12] Reverend Job Cushing of Shrewsbury.

[13] One of the original settlers of Westborough. In *Westborough Vital Records* the name is spelled Howard, Haywood and Hayward.

[14] Benjamin Bayley of Marlborough. Hudson, *Marlborough*, p. 321.

[15] William Jenison (Harvard 1724), later minister of the Second Church, Salem, Mass., 1728-1736. *Sibley*, VII, 371-374.

[16] In 1727 this part of Marlborough was incorporated in the new town of Southborough.

[17] Of Westborough.

[18] (Harvard 1723). Later minister at Biddeford, Maine (1730-1741). *Sibley*, VII, 281-287.

[19] Son of Benjamin Willard, one of the original proprietors of Grafton, Mass.

[20] (Harvard 1720). Son of a Boston merchant and later minister of Falmouth, now Portland, Maine, 1726-1795. *Sibley*, VI, 400-410.

[21] [John Johnson]. *The Clergy-Man's vade-mecum: or an account of the ancient and present Church of England . . .* Third edition (London, 1709).

[22] Isaac Bellows.

[23] (Harvard 1722). *Sibley*, VII, 76.

[24] (Harvard 1722). *Sibley*, VII, 101-102.

[1] Captain Benjamin Willard of Grafton.

[2] Benjamin Woods of Marlborough.

[3] Of Marlborough.

[4] (Harvard 1723). *Sibley*, VII, 190-192.

[5] Thomas Lewis.

[6] Hezekiah Howe was an original settler of Westborough.

[7] William Johnson of Marlborough.

5. I preach'd on Heb. 3, 14, both fore and afternoon. The hard weather allow'd me but a small Congregation.

6. My Brethren Elias and Samuel[8] came (with Lieutenant Samuell How of Framingham their Conductor) to See us.

7. Mr. How went home after Dinner. My Brethren acquainted me that my Sister Susanna[9] had been Twice publish'd to Captain Josiah Willard of Salem. A cold Season.

8. It being Somewhat warmer, my Brethren went away for Boston. Towards night came the Willards and lodg'd with us.

9. Mr. Willard preach'd my Lecture from Prov. 27, 1. I beseach God to grant this Young Gentlemans Endeavours may [be] [illegible] and accepted. He has undertaken for nine Sabbaths at Stoney Brook and I pray his Labours there and Everywhere besides may be Succeeded for the great good of many! After Lecture they went away. Mr. Jonathan How of Marlborough and Jedidiah How of This Town came to Sing. Mr. Bradish[10] came to Request my Prayers and Assistance in a Matter grievous and Burthensome to him respecting his Oath of Administrator to an Estate of a Kinswoman of his (when living) of Boston.

10. My Heart is so backward I fear my Preparation for the Sacrament Approaching will be none of the Best. I find all my Sufficiency must be of God.

11. It was Violently Stormy, Blustering Cold Snow, Extream Tedious and Difficult. The Snow Deep.

12. I was much afraid the Sacrament must have been put by, and Captain Fay[11] mention'd its being So; but provision being made and a Very Considerable number of Communicants present I proceeded tho truly it was a Very Severe Season. I preach'd on 2 John 8, A.M. and on Heb. 3, 12, P.M. I trust in the Meritts and advocation of Christ, but I'm sure my performances, some of them can recomend Me to God.

13. I began to Read the Synopsis Criticism[12] on the New Testament for a Morning Exercise. Captain Willard call'd here.

14. 15. I read miscellaneously. Chiefly Mr. Willard[13] on the 5th and 7th Commandments and the Art of Speaking.

16. I was Employ'd on my Subject as This is my Business and Employment, and such an one as calls for great Constancy and patience. So God grant I may So continue in it as in some measure to Deserve the Approbation and Comendation I Know thy services.

17. Mr. Cushing came to see Me. I would fain reap Some Benefit of Every Such Conversation.

18. I was taken up with my preparations.

19. I preach'd upon Heb. 3, 13 A. and P.M.

20. 21. I early (in the Week) began my Studies for my Sermons. I conceive many advantages would accrue by it, and I'm Sure not a few Disadvantages would be avoided by it.

22. 23. 24. Mr. Ball (Junior) cut wood for me. I could make but Slow progress in my Business because of my Affliction by the Toothach.

25. My Toothach continues; but I finish'd my sermons (to a very small matter) by almost an hour before Sunset, when Mr. Cushing came and requested me to go to Shrewsbury. But my indisposition Oblig'd me to tarry all night.

26. In the morning I rode to Shrewsbury and A.M. preach'd on Ps. 95, 7; P.M. on Phil. 1, 27. In the Even, Captain Keyes[14] visited me. I read Mr. Hancocks[15] Ordination Sermon by his Father,[16] and Mr. Ward Clarks[17] by his Father in Law.[18]

27. After I had gone with Mr. Cushing to his house, din'd, etc., I returned home. Many of the Town came in to see me, it having been Town meeting. Mr. Ball (Nathan)[19] brought me Tobacco.

## MARCH [1727]

1. 2. 3. 4. 5. 6. Notwithstanding the preparations I made for last week yet I proceeded to other. I preach'd on Phil. 12, A. and P.M. I rode to Stoney Brook, to Mr. Willard.[1] With him was Mr. Brintnall.[2] The last rode with me to Mr. Swifts. I was design [?] to Boston, but receiving a Letter from my mother by Mr. B. How at Framingham meeting house, I turned back. I rode to Mr. Hows[3] and lodg'd there.

7. In the morning I rode to Marlboro. Din'd at Mr. Woods (with Deacon Wilder[4]). I went with Mr. Breck[5] to his house and (it storming hard) I remained here all night.

8. The storm continued, but yet after dinner I removed. Mr. Breck went with me to his Son Williams[6] (his daughters[7] lately lying in). Thence I returned home.

9. Very high winds. I my Self Sleded home wood with my own Team (mare and sled).

10. 11. Considering my Appointment to go to Boston next week, I Employ'd my Self in preparing Sermons to serve one on the following Sabbath, for I had finished for the approaching Sabbath.

12. I preach'd all Day on Phil. 2, 12.

13. My Wife had Designed to go to Boston with me but it was so rainy that she was obliged to give up her intention. About Eleven it held up and I set out. I was at Mr. Coles[8] (the shoemaker) where I saw Distracted Mrs. Bowtel.[9] I got down to Cambridge between 7 and 8.

14. I rode to Charleston with Father Champney, (it being Court Time) and thence over to Boston with Brother Hicks.[10] I spent my Time at home.

15. We had very joyfull news from my Brother John.[11] In the Evening I was at Mr. Greenwoods[12] Lecture which was upon Projectile Motion. I can't but Conclude these Exercises by Experiments are the most beneficial as they Reduce all to Sensible Demonstration. When I return'd I went in with Mr. Greenwood to Dr. Clarks.[13] At home I saw Captain Willard[14] of Salem.

16. Mr. Sewal preach'd the Lecture on John 15, 5. I din'd at Brother Williams. In the Evening My Sister Susanna was marry'd to Captain Josiah Willard of Salem by Dr. Mather.[15] The Ceremony over we Sang Psalm [blank] and the Doctor had many uncommon Observations upon the Concluding words of the psalm and explained Several other Texts in that millenary Scheme. I must observe here that I had very much Concern upon my Mind lest Every Thing throughout this transaction should not be to the Glory of God, and devout in the Eyes of Men. But last of all did I Suspect my Self.

17. My Brother Elias gave me one of Mr. Webbs[16] books on the 4 Last things; and Deacon Henchman[17] gave me the Extraordinary binding. I visited my friend Mr. John Adams.[18] In the Evening we had much more Company than I thought of.

[8] Elias and Samuel Parkman of Boston.
[9] Susanna Parkman of Boston.
[10] James Bradish or Braddish, an original settler of Westborough.
[11] John Fay of Westborough.
[12] This may have been *Synopsis Criticorum aliorumque S. Scripturae Interpretum*, 1678.
[13] Reverend Samuel Willard (1640–1707), vice-president of Harvard College.
[14] Captain John Keyes of Shrewsbury.
[15] Reverend John Hancock (Harvard 1719), minister of First Church of Braintree (now Quincy), 1726–1744. He was the father of the patriot John Hancock, first signer of the Declaration of Independence. *Sibley*, VI, 316–319.
[16] Reverend John Hancock (Harvard 1689), minister of Lexington, 1698–1752. *Sibley*, III, 429–439.
[17] Reverend Ward Clark (Harvard 1723), minister of First Congregational Church of Kingston, N.H., 1725–1737. *Sibley*, VII, 156–158.
[18] Clark's ordination sermon was by John Odlin (Harvard 1702), minister of Exeter, N.H. Odlin was not Clark's father-in-law, for Clark married Mary Frost, the daughter of Charles Frost of Kittery, Maine. *Sibley*, V, 168–172 and VII, 156–158.

[19] An early settler of Westborough.

[1] Samuel Willard, the preacher at the Stoney Brook part of Marlborough.
[2] Reverend William Brintnall of Sudbury.
[3] Probably at the Wayside Inn in Sudbury, kept by David Howe.
[4] Deacon Joseph Wilder of Lancaster.
[5] Reverend Robert Breck of Marlborough.
[6] Reverend Breck's son-in-law, Abraham Williams, a prominent resident of Marlborough.
[7] Elizabeth Breck, daughter of Reverend Robert Breck, married Abraham Williams.
[8] Probably Samuel Cole of Framingham.
[9] This was perhaps a woman who had married one of the Boutwells of Reading, Mass. In 1728 Samuel Cole of Framingham married a Sarah Boutwell of Reading.
[10] John Hicks of Cambridge, Parkman's brother-in-law.
[11] Parkman's brother-in-law John Tyley.
[12] Isaac Greenwood, Parkman's classmate and later first Hollis Professor of Mathematics at Harvard College.
[13] John Clark (Harvard 1687), a physician of Boston. Professor Greenwood married Clark's daughter Sarah. *Sibley*, III, 375–379.
[14] Josiah Willard.
[15] Cotton Mather.
[16] Reverend John Webb of Boston. The work was *Practical Discourses on Death, Judgement, Heaven and Hell. In Twenty-four Sermons* (Boston, 1726).
[17] Daniel Henchman, publisher and bookseller in Boston.
[18] (Harvard 1721). Of Boston. A classmate of Parkman.

Mr. Secretary Willard,[19] our Cousens, Mrs. Sarah Porter and her Sister, Mrs. Dorcas Bows,[20] etc., etc. I have grievously and Sadly reflected upon my Levity this Evening. I am very much afraid that in the Eyes of Some of the Company my Demeanour was not altogether becoming. But there was nothing criminal in my Conduct with one that considers what a time of Joy it was with us. However I think I might have spent more time with the graver people, especially have improv'd the opportunity of acquainting my Self better with the Secretary and perhaps it had not been to my Disadvantage.

18. I had additional Trouble by some Discourse my brother Samuel had with me upon the articles of my tarrying no more in Boston when I went down; for it was very stormy weather and I was urgent to return home. It rain'd till between 10 and 11, when holding up a little I left home, truly with my heart full of Sadness. *Veruntamen in quoquo peccavi, vel mete vel oculo, vel olioquiu Sanguis pratiosus Jesu Mei per totum purgabit!* It was one o'clock (as I remember) when I set out from Cambridge. I lit upon Mr. Tainter[21] riding up with Hannah Warrin.[22] I rode to Dr. Bellows of Marlboro, Stoney Brook, where I stop'd, Mr. Willard being gone up to Westboro. I was not well, or I should have reach'd home, and there was almost Sunrise to have gone by. I went to Bed not very Well. I was exceedingly fatigued and very faint. But what Surprized one very much in the morning Mr. Willard came in—for my wife Expected that if I returned from Boston at all I should reach home though it were 12 at night first. He soon went back to Westboro and I preach'd at Stoney Brook (the South part of Marlboro) A. and P.M. on Prov. 3, 6. At Even I returned to my own house. I found all things Comfortable. *Deo Opt. Max. Grates.*

20. Mr. Willard left us to go to his Lodgings.

22. I had not very well got over my Journey yet. Mr. Cushing (I understood) brought home his wife. I a little wonder'd why I was not sent for but Time will open the Cause.

25. I received a Letter from Mr. Cushing which invited me to go to his house on the 21 to Meet his Wife, and the Letter was written some considerable Time ago, but miscarry'd till now.

26. I preach'd on Phil. 2, 12, A. and P.M.

27. 28. 29. I was closely and Strictly Engaged in My Sermons and in my Enquiries into [blot] of the Land and of my People, particularly that I might prepare my Self for the Solemnity drawing nigh. But it is to be remark'd that the 27th was a very Tempestuous, Cold, Snowy Time, at which my Brother John Parkman was Shipwreck'd at Cape Ann. The Thirtieth was Publick Fast. I preach'd upon Ps. 51, 10 all Day and Endeavour'd to improve the Day also as preparation for our Sacrament.

31. I apply'd my Self to my Study only.

### APRIL [1727]

1. I was Strictly Employ'd in my preparations for the Sabbath approaching.

2. Sacrament. I preach'd all Day upon 2 John 8. After Meetings my Wife gave me the Heavy Tidings of the Death of my Brother John Parkman, but I had no very certain account.

3. I went up to Mr. Fays[1] and Engaged him to go down with me, my Wife and Sister, But

4. On the Day appointed it rained hard and put all things off.

5. I sent to Mr. Fays but was disappointed, and in the afternoon I went away alone; To Mr. Swifts[2] first, the Association not being dispers'd. Thence I rode to Mr. Peabodys[3] with Mr. Baxter[4] and Wife,[5] and Mrs. Peabody and Mr. Bucknam.[6] At Mr. Peabodys was Major Quincy[7] of Braintree.

[19] Josiah Willard (Harvard 1698) of Boston, college tutor, preacher, shipmaster and Secretary of the Province. *Sibley*, IV, 425-432.
[20] Sarah (Champney) Porter was evidently either a cousin or a niece of Mrs. Dorcas Bowes, who was Mrs. Parkman's cousin.
[21] Simon Tainter of Westborough.
[22] Mrs. Hannah Warren of Westborough.
[1] Probably Samuel rather than Captain John Fay of Westborough.
[2] Reverend John Swift of Framingham.
[3] Oliver Peabody, minister of the Indian Church of Natick.
[4] Reverend Joseph Baxter (Harvard 1693), minister of Medfield, 1694-1745. *Sibley*, IV, 146-153.
[5] Baxter's third wife, Mercy Bridgham.
[6] Reverend Nathan Bucknam (Harvard 1721), minister of the First Church in East Medway (now Millis), 1724-1795. *Sibley*, VI, 434-437.
[7] Edmund Quincy (Harvard 1699), Councillor and justice of the Superior Court. *Sibley*, IV, 491-495.

6. I rode to Boston to gain Information concerning my Brother, and I was Certify'd that on the 27th of the Last Month My Brother John Parkman was coming in from Anguilla (having been at Barbadoes to which port he came from Cork) in a Vessel built by him at Dighton, And with the Building, fraughted rigged and mann'd at his Father's his Brethren's and his own charge. He was now laden with Cotton, Rhum and diverse valuable articles, no small quantity of Gold, but the Heavy and greatest part of his Lading was Salt. But that this (27th) Day proving very Stormy they were driven near Cape Ann and finding that all that remain'd for them to do was to shift for their Life because of the Dangers they were come into upon the Rocks, especially being nigh Normans Woe (a great Rock So call'd which they now drove upon). My Brother endeavoured by the help of the Fore tack, and taking the advantage of the heaving of the vessell, to swing off from the Vessel, if possible on upon the Rock. But the vessel unexpectedly and Suddenly hove back and brought him into the deep. The Tumultuating and raging Sea foaming upon him, and frustrating all Endeavours to recover him (tho they threw out Ropes to him that slip'd thro his hands and tho the Mate had him once by the hand as he came along by the fore Chains) Swallow'd him up, and he perish'd in the Deep. Alas! My Brother! that Sucked the Breast of my Mother, that was brought up with me, is Separated from me and his Eyes clos'd in the night of Death. But I would not utter my plaints as if I mourned without hope. I trust that Living and Especially that Dying he was the Lords. Neither would I do otherwise than humbly own and Submissively acknowledge the Sovereign Power and Dominion of God, and bow my Self down before the unsearchable wisdom, the reproachless holiness, and with all the infinite Goodness and Divine Tenderness of my heavenly Father, and would dutifully and reverently Say that it is the Lord—and since it is he, Let him do what Seemeth him good. His wayes tho full of wonder yet holy are they all, and righteous are they all, and Every of his Works for the honour of his glorious Name, and all his Dispensations towards us for our highest Benefit if we will duely Improve the Same. How broken was his Body and batter'd against the Rocks when the people of the Place found the lifeless Corps on the fatal shore in the morning! When I see the Blood afresh trickling down from his wounds my heart is again Set ableeding, and when I see his Ruddy Countenance and his athletick Constitution so soon triumph'd over and Subdued! But let me go back again and See what comes of the Rest of the Company and not let all my Care waste itself here. They were wondrously Sav'd on the large Rock (on which they had dropt from the Bowsprit of the vessel before She stove) and here they remain'd through the night tho in the greatest Danger all the while of being wash'd away with the Sea that broke over them. The vessel being broken to pieces Some of the Goods were wafted along by the Rock and the Men Sav'd Some Baggs of Wool. The rest of the Cargo Goods, etc. was Lost. On the 29th our People receiv'd the Message in the Evening. On the 30th (being Fast Day) My Remaining Brethren went to Cape Ann but could not get there timely enough to do anything to purpose. On the 31 They Solemnized the Funerall, and buried him in that Town. On Satur day (April 1) they returned home. This is a Brief and Melancholly account. I Beseach God to make it Spiritually advantagious, though outwardly it is So grievous to us.

7. 8. I Attended Mr. Thatchers[8] Lecture. Mr. Waldron[9] desired me to preach for him. I would fain have flattly Deny'd him, but my Father was by, and I knew his mind was Set. I did not dare to refuse. I was obliged to Study very hard to prepare my Self for the Publick Exercises. With much Labour I finished my Sermon before Bed time. But I could not but be greatly concern'd about So hasty Compositions.

9. I attended at Mr. Thatchers in the forenoon, therein embracing an Opportunity to Communicate with the Church I had relation to. It was a Sacred joyfull Season. I would hope my Soul was refresh'd therewith. I din'd at Mr. Waldrons and preach'd (tho in a poor, lame manner truly) to his Congregation

[8] Reverend Peter Thatcher of Boston.
[9] Reverend William Waldron (Harvard 1717), first minister of the New Brick Church of Boston. *Sibley*, VI, 214-219.

upon the Text 1 King 13, 30. It met with some kind acceptance in the Family and at their Request I repeated it in the Evening.

10. I Spent the Time chiefly in the Family.

11. I rode to Reading to Mr. Burts[10] to obtain his Daughter to Serve in our house. From thence I rode to Salem, to Brother Willards and lodged there.

12. It being Lecture at Mr. Stantons[11] I tarried beyond my Design in this Town. I din'd at Mr. Stantons where was Mr. Blowers,[12] Mr. Fisk,[13] Mr. Ward,[14] Mr. Chever[15] of Manchester, and Mr. Jeffords,[16] the last of which preach'd on Mat. 11, 30. Presently after Lecture Brother Willard and Mrs. Grafton rode with me to Boston.

13. Mr. Foxcroft[17] preach'd at the Publick Lecture. Sister Willard[18] went to make Salem her home, diverse of the Family with her, to accompany etc. I rode from Winnesimmet to Cambridge and there was taken very ill.

14. I continued so ill all Day that I scarce got up. I was confin'd to the Bed in the Day but in the Evening was worse. Mrs. Burt[19] by appointment brought her daughter.

15. The journey home look'd very discouraging I was so ill. But riding an Easy horse and Father Champney[20] with me, with the Girl, we reach'd home. I was very much unfitted for publick Service.

16. But resting well thro Divine Goodness I rose enlivened and repeated to my Congregation (with Some Additions and a few alterations) what I delivered last Sabbath upon the Death of my Brother. At night I was considerably better Still.

17. So that in the Morning My Wife and Child rode down with our Father Champney. I was concern'd that the Stubble was not plough'd for planting, according to agreement made with Mr. Hezikiah Ward,[21] nor was there any ploughing for Sowing.

18. I got Mr. Thurston[22] to plow and sow my Barley, and Mr. Hezikiah Ward ploughed part of the Stubble.

19. And again he ploughed in the Stubble.

20. And he ploughed a Morning Spell more.

21. Sometime after Sun down Lieutenant Forbush[23] came and requested me to go down to See his Wife who they thought was drawing near her End and wanted to See Me. I went down. When I Entered I Said Mrs. Forbush I am Sorry to See you So ill; I am come at your Desire; which way can I become the most Serviceable to you? She reply'd She was under apprehension of the approach of Death and she could not but be under fears on So great an Occasion. Upon which I proceeded to enquire into the grounds of her Fears telling withal that I should endeavour to remove them and (receiving Some very generall answers) to promote the matter the more readily I began to Say Something concerning true Repentance, universal Obedience and the unfeigned Love of God and to the People of God which finding in her might Shew to her the Truth of Grace to be wrought in her, which being demonstrated must necessarily make all things bright and clear and comfortable. But this process I managed in such an easy and familiar manner as this following.

1. I am hoping (Mrs. Forbush) you have freely repented of any sin that you have known your Self guilty of. She answer'd that She trusted she had, and was heartily willing to, of all that she

had been chargeable with that she had not particularly known of, etc.

2. You have told me heretofore that you have us'd your utmost to keep the Commands of God universally but especially now Since you have openly dedicated your Self to God, and join'd your Self to the Communion of the Lords people and waited upon Christ Table I conclude you have much ground for Satisfaction and Comfort. (You Should have if you have Sincerely and uprightly done your Duty). To which she [said] It has indeed been a Comfort to me and I am now glad that I have not that work to reproach my Self with the commission of, (or in these words) I am glad havn't that work to do now (having some reference I believe to the Trouble that many have been in at such an hour that they had never obey'd the Comand of Christ.) etc., etc., etc.

3. Well, Mrs. Forbush but to let you see things more plainly Still. Let Us a little further enquire. Don't you find in you Such a Love to God as has made you both repent of Sin and Obey his Comands from a Desire of his Glory? etc. etc.

But to find out some further proof of all this and to have some stronger evidence of your Love to God and Christ, have you a pure love to the Godly; do you love the Disciples of Christ, those that you think bear the Image of God unfeignedly?

She. I hope really that I do.

N. B. Mr. Thomas Forbush[24] and wife, Captain Byles[25] and wife, and Jedediah How[26] were in the Room, besides the family. But the person being look'd upon as near expiring I thought not to thrust those persons So well acquainted with the woman, as nearer She has not (except one), out of the room, and Seeing my discourse was generall and what anyone might hear. Yet when under any of those heads any particular private matters have occurr'd it has then been usuall with me to desire the Company to withdraw. But here I apprehended would be such things spoken as might be very profitable and suitable for all that heard, as I concluded these near Relatives were gratify'd not a little by them. However, upon some account or other it Seems Old Mr. Forbush[27] is displeased and tho at the most awful time when every thought was profoundly Serious and solemn Yet he thinks fit to [illegible] upon us in a sad passionate manner upon the last Sentence, spoken thus. Sir, We are grown folks. I turned about in great Surprize and calmly looking upon him and then as calmly Speaking asked what he had said. He repeated the Same words as before. I asked him what then? (Now raising my Self up in my Chair) why then (says he) we understand these things already have read in the Bible and Some other Books, and ourselves know these things being grown folks and come into years. Here up I Spoke the words following (his Wife, his Sisters, especially the apprehended Dying person besought him not to open his mouth any further, they being astonished as well as I and the woman declaring it much to her Comfort and benefit that I had proceeded as I had and that it was the End of her sending for me, etc.). Mr. Forbush, I am astonish'd at such an interruption at such a season, when I come upon my Commission and Charge to minister in the name of God to a Servant of his ready to leave the world, etc., etc. Says he, If I had been in your place I would not have asked Such Questions. I reply'd in defence of them. He Said Mr. Breck would not ask Such. I answer'd I was not now to enquire what Mr. Breck would ask, but I was able to affirm that the most Learned, the most pious and the most Judicious ministers would. I therewith pray'd him to Say which were improper and wherein. He appear'd not able to tell so much as what any one Question was that I had asked. Well, Said I, Seeing you won't or can't tell me which, etc., I'll endeavour to recollect all that I have said, though I did not Study before I came down what I should say, nor had I time; neither did I confine my Self strictly to any Method but Said what I thought of the greatest weight in the Case before me. I then recapitu-

[10] Thomas Burt, Jr. His daughter was Sarah (b. 1711) who later married Joseph Gilbert of Boston.

[11] Reverend Robert Stanton (Harvard 1712), minister of the Second Church of Salem. Sibley, V, 647–648.

[12] Reverend Thomas Blowers (Harvard 1695), minister of First Church at Beverly, 1701–1729. Sibley, IV, 225–228.

[13] Reverend Samuel Fiske (Harvard 1708), minister of the First Church at Salem, 1718–1735. Sibley, V, 413–424.

[14] Reverend Robert Ward (Harvard 1719), minister at Wenham, 1722–1732. Sibley, VI, 350–352.

[15] Reverend Ames Cheever (Harvard 1707), minister at Manchester, Mass., 1716–1743. Sibley, V, 326–329.

[16] Reverend Samuel Jefferds (Harvard 1722), minister at Wells, Maine, 1725–1752. Sibley, VII, 83–85.

[17] Reverend Thomas Foxcroft of Boston.

[18] Parkman's sister, Susanna.

[19] Of Reading.

[20] Samuel Champney, Sr., Parkman's father-in-law.

[21] Of Westborough.

[22] Joseph Thurston of Westborough.

[23] Samuel Forbush of Westborough.

[24] Slectman of Westborough, brother of Samuel.

[25] Joseph Byles, an original settler of Westborough.

[26] Of Westborough.

[27] The oldest Forbush in Westborough at this time was Thomas Forbush.

lated and demanded as I went along what exceptions he had to make and wherein they were so grossly injudicious as to be foundation enough for his So Strange interposition. 1. He Suppos'd She had repented before now and she had examin'd her Self before this time o'Day often and often no doubt. And then I had liv'd in the house and knew the woman long ago. So that I had no need to ask Questions now. Besides I had or Should have ask'd her when She was admitted into the Church. Truly, said he, if it was my wife you Should not have asked her whether she had repented of her sins. We hope She has done it long ago. To which I Said, This Person I knew So Well as that I Saw no danger from my asking generall Questions. She has had nothing Scandalous in all her Life that I know of, neither could any one think that I desir'd to rake into all the particulars of her past conversation in the world and managements in the Familie (not but that If I had made Such enquires She might I believe have produc'd what would have been very instructing). Were I examining a person that had been notoriously vicious and demanding a particular confession and before So many witnesses it had been another thing; but I have been endeavouring to assist this person in preparing actually to give up her account to the great Judge, and though she may have view'd it numberless times and we may have review'd and examin'd it together yet now at the awfull juncture before delivering it into his hands we act most wisely to look all over as carefully as possible to find out whatever escapes or flaws there may be, Since it can never be done after, throughout Eternity, and Eternity depends upon this account. Mr. Forbush those Questions appear injudicious to you; yet they are so far from being a reflection upon your Sister that the most advanc'd Christian that is on Earth won't Scruple to ask them and they are the very questions therefore that the gravest and profoundest Divines in the Christian Church do put in these Cases, etc. etc.

2. You ask (Say'd he) whether she had not comfort in her having been at the Sacrament. How needless that question. What do you think She went to it for, Sir? I admire at you Mr. Forbush. Your Sister's End was to testifie her Obedience to the Command of Christ, and to obtain of her Lord Divine Grace and Support under all Troubles and difficulties, to Engage Gods mercifull presence in a time of Extremity, especially when Death approaches. She has been I Say, for these great and important things and now when She needs them most of all I ask whether she has got her Errand and how she is Sure She has these things and This is impertinent, etc., etc.

3. And You asked whether She lov'd the Godly? What a Question that is! I know what you mean whether She loves all that Appear professedly to be Christians. I havn't a Charity for everybody because they make a profession. There is some that I know of that I won't have a Charity for tho they have join'd to the Church. To which I rejoin'd Mr. Forbush in trying whether true Grace be in the heart love to Christ's Disciples is always enquir'd into. I doubted not but your Sister doth So, yet it is ask'd to make all things as clear and fair as possible. By Christ's Disciples I mean the Same as Saint John doth by the Brethren by which are understood all that any way bear the Image and Resemblence of Christ, and Mr. Forbush notwithstanding what you have last Said as to your Charity I'll tell you mine is So extensive that there is not a person in all Westboro but I would charitably hope he may be a subject for the Divine Grace to work upon. Well, he would not, etc. It was time I should do what I could for the woman. I told him he had prevented me and unfitted me, etc., but I turn'd about and went on. Mr. Forbush ask'd I'd forgive him if he had said anything wrong but he thought he would not ask Such questions. So that I So far lost my labour with him. I told him if he was So much disturb'd about them, I would submit them to the Judgement to whatsoever ministers in the Country he should Choose. I pray'd him to consider his sister. He was willing with all Saying that he knew not how soon he should need me on the Same account and therefore again desire me to forgive his bluntness, but yet He could not desire me if ever I should to ask him such sort of Questions. Thus did he in a strange manner keep up the flame by throwing in oil when he pretended to cast in water to quench it. No, Mr. Forbush Said I with some earnestness, I'm afraid you would not care that I should deal feelingly with your soul. I now told him of my being oblig'd in Conscience to do my utmost for persons when as his Sister, etc. I shall take no further notice of the Strange reply he made me nor the long discourse he further occasion'd. I was griev'd heartily to See So much of his ignorance and passions. It grew very late. It was well the woman (it may be through her fright) was reviv'd. We came into So amicable a Composition as to go to prayer and we parted Friends. But both my Head and heart were full. It was Twelve when I got home. Sister Ruth discern'd my Trouble. I went to bed but could not Sleep for a long time. I beseach God to quicken me hereby in my work, and make me more diligent to accomplish my Self lest I meet with worse trialls than this. I remember and would take notice of it that the Suddenness and lateness of Lieutenant's coming for me prevented my usual address to heaven before such Ministrations. I would be humbled for my Sin and take the Punishment God inflicted for it.

22. Mr. Ward came with his Team and carted out Muck upon my Corn grounds. Mr. Ward in the afternoon plough'd a spot for flax and went home.

23. I preach'd on 1 Pet. 2, 11.

25. I went to Shrewsbury to see Mr. Cushing[28] after his Marriage though truly it has now been some time since. But the reason was his Letter which he Sent me just before his bringing his wife home miscarried.

26. Mr. Thomas Newton[29] came to see me and Mr. Townsend[30] the Schoolmaster.

27. Very stormy.

28. One of my Boars was cut, a somewhat dangerous adventure, but 'twas now cool after the storm.

30. I preach'd on 1 Pet. 2, 11.

### MAY [1727]

1. I went abroad to Mr. Josiah Newtons, etc. When I return'd I found my wife brought home by her brother.[1]

2. Brother carry'd Sister Ruth[2] down home.

4. Mr. William Nurse[3] came with his Team and plough'd for me for planting but he was late in the morning and many hindrances So that not much was accomplished.

6. Mr. Green[4] ploughed.

7. I preach'd on Ps. 119, 9.

8. Captain Fay[5] ploughed. All this before we could plant. And it was but 2½ Acres. I was at Mr. Bakers.

9. It rain'd So that Mr. Baker[6] could not come.

10. Mr. Baker and Mr. Charles Rices Son came and planted for me. I was afflicted with a Boar I lately Cutt, for there was Hazard So late. N. B. Lecture put by.

12. 13. My Child was very ill. In the morning I found the Boar dead.

14. I preach'd on Song 2, 3 and Administer'd the Sacrament; P.M. on 2 John 8.

15. I went to see Mr. Tainter[7] and Mr. Jonathan Forbush[8] who was sick. I Sent Some Hair to Boston by Mr. Baker.

16. I went down to Marlborough. I acquaint Mr. Breck[9] with my trouble with Mr. Forbush. He said tho he was known to be the plainest and bluntest Man, yet he wondered at his extream Ignorance, unguardedness, etc.

17. Mr. Stone,[10] Mrs. Goddard[11] and her son David were here.

[28] Reverend Job Cushing of Shrewsbury.
[29] Of Westborough.
[30] Joshua Townsend of Westborough.

[1] Samuel Champney, Jr., of Cambridge.
[2] Ruth Champney of Cambridge, Parkman's sister-in-law.
[3] Of Westborough. Not listed as one of the original settlers of the town.
[4] John Green, Parkman's neighbor.
[5] John Fay, the prominent early resident of Westborough.
[6] Edward Baker of Westborough.
[7] Simon Tainter of Westborough.
[8] The younger brother of Thomas and Samuel Forbush of Westborough. He changed the name to Forbes. He became a deacon of the church and died in 1768.
[9] Reverend Robert Breck of Marlborough.
[10] Lieutenant Isaac Stone of Shrewsbury, selectman of that town. Ward, *Shrewsbury*, pp. 423-424.
[11] Probably Mrs. Edward Goddard of Shrewsbury.

21. I preach'd on Ps. 119, 9.

22. I rode over with my Wife to Mr. Ephraim Allens[12] to see his poor afflicted wife. I had hair of her which I Sent to Boston by Mr. Hezikiah Ward for we returned by the way of Mr. Brighams.

23. In the Night I marry'd Mr. Daniel Warrin[13] to Mary Wetherby.

24. It was very Cold. Tis the Day appointed or the ordination of Mr. Amos Throop[14] at Woodstock. Gods presence be in his Church and with his Servant.

25. 26. 27. I had Sufficient Business with my Sermons, considering especially what my avocations may be next Week.

28. I preach'd again on Ps. 119, 9, A.M. but P.M. on Ps. 25, 7. I beseach God to bless these Courses of Sermons not only to the young people of this Town, but to me who stands in the greatest need of assistances of these kinds!

29. Early in the morning I rode to Mr. Brecks upon my Journey to Boston, but the weather being various he detain'd me till after dinner when I left him. I hit upon Judge Meinzies[15] and had his Company to Cambridge. He was very civil and generous to Me on the Road, though his Conversation I had no great Esteem of. I turn'd out of the Road to go to Father Champneys and thence proceeded to Boston, and was not much after nine at my Fathers House.

30. I was not abroad much, except among my Relatives.

31. Mr. Joseph Baxter of Medfield preach'd the Election sermon from 1 Tim. 2, 1, 2. Mr. Stimpson,[16] Mr. Greenwood,[17] Mr. Turell[18] and I din'd with the officers of the Town Militia and the company of Cadys which waited upon his Honor the Lieutenant Governour.[19] Mr. Turell Pray'd and it fell to me to return. The Afternoon was in greatest part Spent at Mr. Henchmans[20] Shop with Mr. Greenwood, Turell, Prince,[21] etc., etc. We went to Mr. Sewalls[22] to the Convention. In the Evening I was with Mr. Lowel[23] and his Wife[24] first at his and then at her Fathers. I was also at Captain Kings where Mr. Joseph Parsons[25] was with Mrs. Porter. I invited him to lodge with me. Accordingly he did. He told me sorrowfull News of Mr. Samuel Coffins[26] being far Spent in a Consumption and his Life dispair'd of.

### JUNE [1727]

1. In the morning (family exercises and breakfast ended) we walk'd up to Mr. Sewalls. Mr. President Wadsworth[1] preach'd in the Convention from Hagg. 1, 13. The Devotions over though there had been long contests and debates about the phrasing of the address drawn up by Mr. Colman[2] to be Sent to his Majestie from the ministers in New England. Yet there were very hot and very long oppositions today also. And upon no other than the calling themselves the Ministers of the Churches, and whether it should not be the Teaching Elders, etc. Mr. Williams[3] of Deerfield was chosen to preach the Next Year. We din'd at an house Some little way below Mr. Sewalls in the Same Street.

2. It was late in the morning before I could set out from Charlston upon my Journey. I din'd at Father Champneys. At Mr. Learneds[4] was Mr. Cheney of Brookfield and his wife; and thither came Breck[5] from College. We all rode up within the bounds of Marlboro together where I parted from my Company. I got home seasonably.

3. I was much Engag'd and Employ'd that I might make up my preparations for the Sabbath.

11. King George dy'd at his Brother Ernest's Palace at Osnaburg.

14. The sad News of the Kings Death arriv'd at Richmond and George II was proclaim'd at Leicester House.

### JULY [1727]

3. My Little Dauter Molly was extremely ill So that we thought between 9 and 10, She would have expir'd.

4. Mr. Jonathan Howard[1] dy'd. My Child was very bad about noon and continued So, Sometime. But it was Some Comfort that Captain Whoods Widow was with us.

17. I went to Cambridge.

18. To Boston and return'd to Cambridge.

20. I came home and our Mother Champney[2] with me.

### AUGUST [1727]

1. 2. It was exceeding hot So that I could scarce mind my Business; but was oblig'd to make Some preparation for my Lecture.

3. Mr. Cushing and his Wife happened to come to See us upon this Day. But he had no Notes with him and I had not finished my Sermon, so that I was debarred their Company very much. I Lectur'd on 1 Chron. 28, 19. Mr. Cushing pray'd. His Wife not at Meeting. After Meeting I had information that Mr. Tomlins[1] Dauter was dead. A Young Woman that had lain confin'd ever since I had been in Town; and dy'd unbaptis'd. (*O Jesu Misericors ne mihi imputatur*). I went over to the house and discours'd with Mr. Tomlin and with the family, etc.

4. She was buried. I was full of Concern. God Sanctifie her Death to others of her Age and Circumstance.

5. It continues very hot, and parching weather.

6. I had appointed on this Day to administer the Sacrament of the Lords Supper, but we were disappointed, the Elements not being brought up nor the Person (Thomas Ward) that went for them, return'd. God graciously forgive wherever he has Seen Guilt, and whatever Unpreparedness in his Servants that Should provoke him to debarr us therefrom! I preach'd on 1 Chron. 28, 9, A. and P.M. It was very hot and I was very faint and weary when the Exercises were over.

7. I went to Mr. Thomas Newton's, who had a great deal to Say about Mr. Peres Rice[2] and wanted much that he Should be brought under Church censure, Seeing the Court of Judicature had found him guilty of violating the Civil law, in the act against Selling drink without License. I was at said Rices also but not to Discourse with him, nor did I upon anything besides coming to Mow for me.

8. Father Champney came up to See us. It is a favour of heaven that we can hear of the welfare of our Friends, and ought to be thankfully acknowledged.

9. Mr. Bradish[3] came and by his Help we got in near a load of Hay which was mow'd by Nathaniel Child last Saturday.

10. Father Champney return'd from us. Near Night Captain Goddard[4] came. It has been a time of parching Drought, but God mercifully remembers us and sends us Rain.

[12] Of that part of Westborough that later became Northborough.

[13] Captain Daniel Warrin or Warren was an original settler of Westborough. His first wife was Rebecca Garfield.

[14] (Harvard 1721). Minister of the First Congregational Church, Woodstock, Conn., 1727-1735. *Sibley*, VI, 572-574.

[15] John Menzies, a Justice of the Peace of Middlesex County.

[16] Joseph Stimpson (Harvard 1720), of Charlestown. Later minister at Malden, 1735-1744. *Sibley*, VI, 410-411.

[17] Isaac Greenwood, Professor of Mathematics at Harvard College.

[18] Reverend Ebenezer Turell (Harvard 1721), minister of Medford, 1724-1778. *Sibley*, VI, 574-582.

[19] Lieutenant Governor William Dummer was acting governor at this time, pending the arrival of Governor William Burnet.

[20] Daniel Henchman, publisher and bookseller in Boston.

[21] Nathan Prince, tutor at Harvard and brother of the famous historian, Thomas Prince.

[22] Reverend Joseph Sewall of the Old South Church, Boston.

[23] John Lowell (Harvard 1721) of Boston was the first minister of Newburyport, 1725-1767. *Sibley*, VI, 496-502.

[24] Lowell married Sarah Champney, a cousin of Parkman's wife.

[25] (Harvard 1720). Minister of Bradford, 1726-1765. *Sibley*, VI, 393-396.

[26] Brocklebank Samuel Coffin (Harvard 1718) of Newbury. *Sibley*, VI, 234.

[1] Benjamin Wadsworth, President of Harvard College.

[2] Dr. Benjamin Colman (Harvard 1692), minister of the Brattle St. Church, Boston, 1699-1747. *Sibley*, IV, 120-137.

[3] Reverend John Williams (Harvard 1683), first minister of Deerfield, 1686-1729. *Sibley*, III, 249-262.

[4] Thomas Learned was a tavernkeeper in Watertown.

[5] Robert Breck, Jr. (Harvard 1730), son of the Reverend Robert Breck of Marlborough. Breck, Jr., was later minister of the First Church of Springfield, 1734-1784. *Sibley*, VIII, 661-680.

[1] Of Westborough, although the death is not recorded in the *Westborough Vital Records*.

[2] Mrs. Samuel Champney, Sr., Parkman's mother-in-law.

[1] Isaac Tomblin was an early settler of Westborough. The *Westborough Vital Records* do not give the death of this person.

[2] Son of Thomas Rice, one of the original settlers of Westborough.

[3] James Bradish, an original settler of Westborough.

[4] Captain Edward Goddard of Shrewsbury.

11. Rain by the Divine Mercy.

12. Mr. Thomas Weld[5] came up to us.

13. Mr. Weld preach'd A.M. on Ps. 63. 3. I administered the Sacrament of the Lords Supper. Mr. Weld preach'd P.M. on John 9, 4, former part. The whole of his performances were laudable. God make him an eminent Instrument of his Glory in his Church.

14. I accompanied Mr. Weld as far as into the Mendon Road (beyond Mr. Eams of Hopkinton) he being determined to go to Mr. Dorrs.[6] I was at Mr. Jonathan Forbes' where there were not a few Sick. Mrs. Forbes was not Recovered. Three of their Dauters had a strong fever and Rebecca Paterson lay very ill.

15. I went to see Mr. Amsden[7] who was Sick and had desired praying for him.

16. I read in Wollastons Religion of Nature.[8] I take it to be a very Excellent Piece.

17. I Study'd the Works of God beginning with Gods Efficiency in generall.

18. 19. I forwarded my preparations, considering my wife's Hour was before her, and in Expectation of it immediately. I had the News of the Kings Death.

19. In the Afternoon my wife was pained, but no great Complaint till the Evening when She grew very ill. I went to Bed Somewhat late but could lie but a very few minutes. I rose and (being, as I gathered about midnight) rode to Mrs. Forbush and brought her up But she was not very much Employ'd till morning.

20. I rode for Mrs. Byles and sent for other neighbouring women. My wife had many pains, But I Saw Liberty to go to Meeting at the proper hour. I delivered the morning Sermon upon 1 Chron. 28, 9. In the Afternoon I preach'd upon Rom. 11, 36 wherein I had occasion to Mention the Kings Death, and to give fair hints at the Circumstances of my Family. When I came home at Even my wife was Still full of pains but no imediate apprehension that she should be delivered. But, a little more than half an hour after sunset (having been no long time in Extremity) She was Delivered, and the will of God was to favour me in a very high Degree. God gave Me a Son, which I have set up for my Ebenezer, for hitherto the Lord hath Helped Me. We have indeed a great deal of Reason to praise and magnifie the name of our gracious God who So Signally and mercifully appears for us, and lays us under ten thousand the strongest obligations to him. O that I may never forget his Benefits! But O that I may both Live and Speak Gods praises! Were comfortably carry'd thro the night. Blessed be God!

21. I went down to Mr. Thomas Forbes'[9] and was intending to marry his Dauter[10] to Mr. Cornelius Cook,[11] but they could produce me No legal certificate But I discoursed to them of their unhappy Circumstances and their Sin and urg'd to serious unfeigned Repentance. Mr. Cook I advis'd to go and get another Certificate, while I tarried there. He went away but a storm coming up and night hastening on, and my people at home extreamly prone to be very much Scar'd, I left them and walked home, leaving word that Mr. Cook should bring home my Horse, which He did. It was a very Awfull and terrible night and we had very little Rest (the Thunder and Lightening were So sharp) till near Day break.

22. I again rode to Mr. Forbes' and married Cornelius Cook and Eunice Forbush (so they will Spell their Name). I hasted home, a storm arising as it did last night. I went to Mr. John Maynards and brought up his wife to watch with mine. It was a very terrible storm and far louder Thunder than the night before, but lasted not so long. By nine o'Clock it abated.

23. Major Prescott was here to See us and informed us that Mr. Thomas Forbush, Junior[12] his Barn was Shatter'd by the Thunder last night.

24. My Wife and Infant through the Divine Goodness in very hopefull and favourable Circumstances. Little or nothing that was difficult with us.

25. Colonel How[13] and Mr. Woods[14] of Marlborough visited me.

26. If on Saturdayes in Generall I am professedly more employ'd than on any other Dayes I am Surely to be thought to be more on this, and I Endeavoured to possess my Thoughts in all Seriousness, of the Weighty and Solemn Transaction of Dedicating my Son to God, and I would in the Fear of God Undertake this Sacred Business.

27. I Sincerely comitted the great Article of offering my Son unto God and implor'd the divine direction and assistance, with Confession of my Sins and Thankfull acknowledgements of all especially his Signal Mercies. I then proceeded to the Exercises of the Day, and preach'd in the Morning on Mat. 19, 13, 14, 15, as I did in the afternoon likewise on the Same. And then (I hope in the integrity of my Heart and with Souls Desire of the Glory of God and the invaluable Spirituall Blessings of the Covenant) I baptiz'd My Son Ebenezer and put him into the Arms of the Saviour that He might Bless Him according to the gracious Encouragement given to His People. And I hope I found Favours with the Lord. Mr. Joseph Wheeler presented His Son Aaron[15] at the Same time. The Lord has done great things for me for which I was filled with Joy and Gladness. O that Gods Grace may be given me that I may alwayes walk in a suitable manner Before Him. At this Season I improv'd the Opportunity [to] renew the Dedication of my Self and My Dauter Mary and all mine unto our glorious God in the Covenant of Grace.

28. I Catechiz'd the Children and I happen'd to appoint the Same hour and Place that the Town meeting was warn'd, but I was Earlier than they and they waited till our Exercise was finished. Diverse persons were at my house in the Evening. I heard Yesterday and again today that my sister Tyley[16] was very ill after Delivered in childbearing.

30. I took an opportunity by Mr. David Maynard[17] to send down to Boston.

31. A Letter was written by Mother certifying me of the Dangerous Circumstances of my Sister, desiring me (if by any means I could) to go down and See her in her last hours in Some measure triumphing over Death and rejoicing in hope of the Glory of God.

## [SEPTEMBER, 1727]

[No entry].

## [OCTOBER, 1727]

October 29. After 10 o'Clock at night the Sky clear, the air cold, there was a very terrible Earthquake which lasted Shaking Extreamly about a minute and half,—a trembling continued for a Considerable time Longer. And within 65 minutes 5 More Rumblings and quiverings might be perceiv'd, Especially the last of those 5. But yet this was not Like the First of all. In about 18 minutes more a Seventh, and near Two o'Clock an 8th, and between 5 and 6 in the morning (perhaps 35 minutes after 5) there was a Ninth. The First of all these, if not all the rest were heard (I am ready to think) all over New England.

October 31. In the night Sometime (the weather being Cloudy if not Rain) there was heard by Diverse persons, another Such noise.[1]

## [NOVEMBER, 1727]

November 1. In the night Likewise, it having been very Stormy Snow in the Day and the Storm not over, there was the same.

[5] (Harvard 1723). Later minister of Upton, 1738-1744, and Middleborough, 1744-1749. *Sibley*, VII, 273-277.

[6] Reverend Joseph Dorr of Mendon.

[7] Jacob Amsden of Westborough.

[8] William Wollaston, *The Religion of Nature delineated* (London, 1725). Numerous other editions followed.

[9] Thomas Forbush did not change his name to Forbes as did his brother Jonathan. Parkman was confused at this point.

[10] Eunice Forbush.

[11] Also of Westborough.

[12] Also of Westborough. Later a deacon and selectman for many years.

[13] Thomas Howe of Marlborough. Hudson, *Marlborough*, pp. 382-383.

[14] Benjamin Woods.

[15] Born July 7. 1727.

[16] Parkman's sister Elizabeth, who married John Tyley of Boston. She died August 30, 1727.

[17] One of Parkman's neighbors.

[1] The foregoing entries for Oct., 1727 were recorded in Parkman's Natalitia.

November 3. My Wife and the Young People of the house asserted that between 4 and 5 P.M. they heard the Like again. The Weather being Rainy or misty. And This was confirm'd by many other persons.

November 4. The Sun Shone thro a Dusky, Smoky Air and generally thro Thin Clouds, the wind Southerly and therefore the weather much chang'd, being pretty warm.

November 5. A Warm Southerly Wind, a very Thick, Smoaky air till night. In the Evening it So cleared away as to be bright Starlight. But it was while I was observing the weather that I Saw a Flash of Lightning. I was not able to discern any Clouds, Yet I am prone to think there was a thick Cloud low in the West. For it Could not be half an hour (I believe, if it was more than a Quarter) before it rain'd, and all of a Sudden beat down in Such mighty Showers that it Startled us very much. However it lasted not long. After a few Such violent Showers it almost Ceased.

The 6th was a Warm, bright, pleasant Day.

The 7th Likewise, the wind blowing, indeed Somewhat Fresh, from the S.W.[1]

## 1728

### JANUARY

1. A moderate pleasant day, My heart was filled with Joy before God for his wondrous Sparing Mercy in bringing Me to the Light of this Day beginning another Year which truly, considering the Deserts of Sin and the late threatenings of Providence, it was almost beyond my Expectations to See.

Oh that it might please God, through his abundant Mercy in Christ to remove away those Sins of mine and those of his people of this Land that brought down Tokens of Displeasure in Such distressing and fearfull Dispensations as those of the Last Year, lest if his anger be not turned away his hand Should be stretched out still this Year also, and our plagues be made wonderfull, if we be not brought to utter Desolation.

As to the Earthquake, being down at Mr. David Maynards in the Evening (requested to visit his 5 Sick children and pray with them) Mr. Daniel Maynard of Marlborough enquir'd whether any of us had heard it, intimating herewith to us that Some persons were afraid they had, and afraid that it had been heard Every Sabbath night Since the great shocks. When I came home I understood by Noah Rice[1] and Daniell Hardy that Mr. James Miller and Nathaniel Whitney[2] each of them were so apprehensive that they heard it in the night before last that they both got up. The Divine Compassion that Safeguards and Delivers us! O that God would still deliver us. I was not without Some hearty, tho I confess too weak and lame Endeavours after, as the pardon of the Miscarriages and offences of the Last year (particularly of March 17th which Oh that it may be blotted out of the book of Gods remembrance) to Such a Settled pious Disposition that this Year may be Spent wholly to the Glory of God, in a walk that may please him, and in Essayes to promote his Church's interest to the last of my Capacity.

2. I rode to Mr. Hezekiah How's. I went with him to Examine some of the Bounds of the ministerial Lot, that I might make some Improvement of it.

In the Evening Mrs. Mary Whiting[3] was with me requesting I would Examine her in order to her joining with our Church. I hope the work of grace is at least begun in her Heart.

3. Reading Mr. Foxcrofts Sermon on the Earthquake (preach'd by him before the Court).[4] I was mov'd I hope rather with justifiable emulation and ambition than Envy. But verily I was much Excited most of the Day to reflect on the progress and advancement he and Some few other persons of distinguish'd Characters had gain'd in both Piety and Learning. I could but draw up a Resolution that tho my powers are small yet according to my Measures I would by the Grace of Christ, lead a Religious,

Serviceable and contented Life, with Diligence and industry laying in what Store of Knowledge, and especially Striving after as many Divine Virtues to adorn and accomplish me, as I may be able.

Lieutenant Forbush[5] came to me in the Evening who among other things, Speaking of Samuell Hardy's Case[6] Express'd himself So as Convinced me I should meet with some Trouble in managing it.

4. Private Meeting at Mr. Pratts. I sent Dr. Increase Mathers Kingdom of Christ is approaching,[7] etc., by Mr. Thurston. Deacon Fay[8] and Mr. Abner Newton[9] and others came to see me in the Evening. Very cold. Mr. How brought me Store Geese.

5. Very Sharp Cold. Mr. Nathaniel Whiting came to be Examin'd in order to his admission to the Lords Supper.

6. The First of my Discourses on Ps. 60, 1, 2 took me up (tho began in no improper Season of the week) till 3 P.M. of this Day When I began the first of those Discourses on 1 Cor. 6, 9, 10, 11, and it was prepar'd before it was over late in the night. I Suppose it not much after Eleven when I was actually in my bed. It must be remembered that my Choice was determined upon the Subject tho I had not so much as laid my Scheme before the hour abovesaid.

7. I preach'd on the footnotes on 1 Cor. 6, 9, 10, 11, in the Afternoon on Ps. 60, 1, 2.

11. The Church (at my appointment) came together and I entertain'd them with a Discourse from Acts 6, 6 but I left the method we should proceed in to the Church's Consideration. Afterwards they came down to my house whereby Mr. Asher Rice[10] was no small [illegible] about Mr. Josiah Newton.[11]

13. A very Violent storm of Snow. Just before dark Mr. Campbel[12] of Oxford came in, being on his journey home. He lodg'd here.

16. David Farrar, Thomas Kendal, Phinehas and Aaron Hardy cut wood.

21. I preach'd both fore and after noon from 1 Cor. 6, 9, 10, 11. I rode to Mr. Pratts and to Mr. Increase Wards[13] and Ballanced with Constable Warrin.[14] Mr. Collister[15] came with his complaints and witnesses.

22. I rode to Mr. John Pratt junior where was Captain Fay. With him I had discourse concerning the Sad Broils in the Town. We went to Mr. Thomas Rice's[16] where it was continued till Evening. I rode over to see Mr. Shattuck[17] (which was my purpose in coming out) he being in a low state. We return'd to Mr. Rices and then I came home. There I found Father Champney[18] and Sister Lydia.[19] The Town is in great uneasiness and ready to fall together by the Ears for the management of their military officers but mostly for receiving money for writs and Summons

---

[1] Entries for Nov., 1727 are from the Natalitia.

[1] Son of Thomas Rice, one of the original settlers of Westborough.

[2] All of these were young men of Westborough.

[3] No record of a family of this name in Westborough at this time.

[4] Thomas Foxcroft, *The Voice of the Lord, from the Deep Places of the Earth. . . .* (Boston, 1727).

[5] Samuel Forbush of Westborough.

[6] The Westborough Church Records, Feb. 11, 1728 contain the following details. "Another Affair was also brought before the Church at this meeting. The Pastor took their Advice in what would be most warrantable and Regular to be done in the Case of Samuel Hardy and his wife who desir'd baptism for their Child born Three Dayes within Seven Months after the parents' Marriage. No opposition was made to proceeding to grant the Privilege, the Circumstances of the fright it was declar'd the mother was in, occasioning as was believed the hasty birth, together with their Serious Declaration that they were innocent, being all the Satisfaction the Church could have in a Case of this Nature." Parson Parkman may not have been convinced that this was the right decision. At any rate he brought this matter before the Marlborough Association where the advice given was that the child "be baptized." Allen, *Worcester Association*, p. 12. Finally on April 28, 1728, the Reverend Mr. Parkman baptized Elizabeth, the daughter of Daniel and Tabitha Hardy.

[7] Mather did not publish a work with this title. Possibly Parkman was referring to *The Glorious Throne: or A Sermon Concerning The Glory of the Throne of the Lord Jesus Christ, Which is now in Heaven, and shall quickly be seen on the Earth.* (Boston, 1702).

[8] Captain John Fay was one of the first deacons chosen by the Westborough church, Oct. 12, 1727. The other was Isaac Tomblin.

[9] The son of Thomas Newton.

[10] Son of Thomas Rice, one of the original settlers of Westborough.

[11] Josiah and Thomas Newton were cousins. Both were original settlers of Westborough. See DeForest and Bates, *Westborough*, pp. 46–47.

[12] Reverend John Campbell.

[13] Increase Ward operated a saw-mill in that part of Westborough that became Northborough.

[14] Daniel Warrin, an original settler in the eastern part of Westborough.

[15] John McCollister of Westborough.

[16] Believed to be the first settler of that part of Marlborough that became Westborough. DeForest and Bates, *Westborough*, p. 20.

[17] Isaac Shattuck.

[18] Samuel Champney, Sr., Parkman's father-in-law.

[19] Lydia Champney, Parkman's sister-in-law.

when he had none of the Justice. Hezekiah Pratt and Eleazer Ward cut wood.

23. Father Champney return'd. Mr. Ward sledded the wood, the young men Cut, Several Load.

24. Mr. Campbel preach'd in the forenoon from Jer. [blank]; in the Afternoon from Acts 16, 30. On the occasion of the Earthquake. Mr. Thurston came and Sledded 4 more.

25. Mr. Campbel left us. A great noise like a gun was heard in the air between 1 and 2 o'Clock P.M. in most Towns about us as in ours. The young men came to set up a society. We first pray'd and then I gave them Some Articles to Sign and they Sign'd them. I gave them what Counsel I was able and dis-miss'd them.

26. Mr. John Pratt junior and his brother Eliezer, with Mr. David Goodenow came, two to cut and one with a Team, to Sled wood and they Sledded 15 Small jaggs (their Team being Small But the Team did not tarry till night.)

28. Diverse young men were with me requesting advice and instruction touching their setting up a private society. I desir'd 'em to come again on this Sennight. This Eve Mr. Asher Rice and Mr. Josiah Newton were again with me endeavouring some-thing towards their reconciliation, but all means were in vain. Instead of healing new work was made for, Mr. Rice having charg'd Mr. Newton with having (not only deceived in the article they were upon) but a principle of falsehood in his heart, which was so high, and beyond his real intention to Speak, he acknowledg'd it was wrong to Speak So of his brother and was Sorry for what he had said. The Cause was rais'd to a difficult pitch, and little prospect of Concord or Composition. Extream cold. The Earthquake was heard as was reported and Some say, felt this Morning about or just after Break of Day. I preach'd again upon 1 Cor. 6, 9, 10, 11. In admitting [illegible] Tomlin[20] to the Church I was So much employ'd in my thoughts by in-corporating the Baptismal Covenant and Church Covenant to-gether that I forgot to go to prayer before I baptiz'd Him, which I remain'd thoughtless about till I went up into the Pulpit from the Basen. It put me into a Consternation. I went to Prayer in which I lamented the miscarriage and enlarg'd the Prayer with those petitions that might be proper on this occasion. But I desire to lay my Self low before God for so grievous an omission and would learn hence forward to be more carefull and watchfull but especially more strongly relying on the Divine aid.

29. Deacon Tomlin[21] was with me entreating me to do some-thing about Mr. McCollisters cause with Mr. Newton, before the next Sacrament.

30. I rode to Mr. Behmans,[22] and thence (with Mr. Wheeler)[23] to Marlboro. At Mr. Williams,[24] Mr. Breck[25] was, and imediately asked me whether I had heard the Earthquake about ¾ of an hour before (it being then after Two o'clock). I had not heard anything of it. It was heard and felt also by most persons. The Sound was great, and, with many, a shake was distinctly per-ceiv'd. Some were ready to say that it was heard every day for 4 or 5 dayes last past. Unto the Lord from whom cometh our help.

I had something of Difficulty in my trading with Mr. Williams.

I lodg'd at Mr. Brecks. We discours'd upon the Signs of the Times. We rode to Mr. Woods. A wedding was Solemnized at Mr. Brecks. Samuel Eday[26] was joined to Elizabeth Bellows.[27] I was compell'd to bear Some part.

31. The morning was very stormy, snow and Rain. But after dinner I rode Home. My Wife told me Mr. Ashur Rice had been here again with a great deal to say about peoples un-easiness at my refusing at least deferring to have a Church Meet-ing on the account of accomodating the Differences.

[At a later point in the diary Parkman inserted several entries for January, 1728, as follows].

28. it was heard by very many, and

30. almost all people heard it and many felt it shake the houses.

### FEBRUARY [1728]

1. I am in great Concern respecting first my own Spiritual State and fearing the Earthquake that great and terrible opera-tion of the Divine Hand has not been so Suitably regarded by me as to produce a due Effect, and The impressions that were made I fear May be Sadly wearing off; and my preparations to meet my God are very low and Scanty.

Secondly. I am concerned in my mind about the Troubles that threaten in this Town. I See my Self unable to manage a Quarrell and very much indispos'd towards it; but especially I would be afraid of the Interests of Religion Suffering; I would dread the Sins and mischiefs my people may be rushing into; and Contention has the blacker aspect in the Day wherein we see Such evident manifestations of the Divine Displeasure upon us.

Whereupon I, in the fear of God, would Set apart this Day, therein to seek the face of God, to avert the Evils threatening, to give me his Grace to quicken me, and savingly to Convert me unto him, to give me a sealed pardon of my sins, and assist me to walk before him according to his most Blessed will; graciously to interpose for his people of this Town and restore peace and unanimity to us (which Blessings, Gods name be praised, that we happily enjoyed so long; and O that God would forgive our mis-improvement of them). However, to prepare and accomplish me with wisdom from above, and vouchsafe his imediate assist-ance and Conduct thro all that may be before me; and grant the Issue may be his own Glory. And now the Lord be with me in the Dayes work and Show me his favour for his mercies Sake. Let also these my Endeavours contribute not a little to fit me for waiting upon God in the Solemnities of the Supper of the Lord. I religiously observed the Day according to the abovemen-tioned appointment of it, till I was interrupted by Mr. Tainter[1] who came from the Private Meeting (about 3 P.M.) desiring me to go to their Assistance in the Exercises. I went and Enter-tained my hearers with my Discourse (Sometime Since publickly deliver'd) upon Hoseah 4, 12. So that I had nevertheless, Op-portunity to carry along the Private Designs abovesaid. At least they (I took care) were not forgotten or neglected. I had design'd for the Sake of promoting peace among my Brethren, to have gone to them in the Evening and I therefore Desired them to take all Suitable Methods for pacification and Reconciliation. Mr. Newton[2] was gone home but Asher Rice imediately Step'd forward full of his bitter case, but was almost imediately oppos'd by Ensign Newton, and then almost everyone in the Room en-gag'd in an unsuitable Clamour, which it was hard to lay. The Subject was that a Church meeting would alone help our State and was the only method that could be taken. But at length by Mr. Bradishes[3] urging it that "inasmuch as it could not be Expected to have a Church Meeting before the Sacrament he thought our present Duty was to Endeavour if possible to obtain that Christian Disposition that might qualifie us to come ac-ceptably to God and comfortably to ourselves; or however to prosecute these Ends as far as we could in doing what was to be done, and after the Sacrament if need were he would advise to discourse about a Church Meeting or what else was Suitable." I thought it Sage and Sat in with it and entreated for a composure and sedateness of Spirit as considering how holy the order we were to put our Selves into preparation for. I ask'd whether they were so disquieted that they could not in a Christian Tem-per Sit down at the approaching ordinance. Tho I had no direct answer yet I found that many of the Church would be disquieted if Mr. Newton should be there; and Some, on the other Hand, would be disquieted if Mr. McCollister and Rice[4] should be present. I advised and Entreated therefore that a person or Two Should be with those three men together and improve the Time and their utmost Skill to compose them, And if no Methods

---

[20] From the Church Records it appears this was Hezekiah Tomlin.
[21] Isaac Tomblin.
[22] Eleazer Behman or Beeman of Westborough.
[23] Joseph Wheeler, an original settler of Westborough.
[24] Colonel Abraham Williams.
[25] Reverend Robert Breck of Marlborough.
[26] Samuel Eady or Eddy of Oxford.
[27] Daughter of John Bellows of Marlborough.

[1] Simon Tainter.
[2] Josiah Newton.
[3] James Bradish.
[4] Asher Rice.

could be Successfull, I desir'd those 3 persons to absent themselves from this administration rather than disturb the whole communion. And so requested nothing more might pass among us this Night but what might be of an healing and salving nature. And this met with universal acceptance and thereupon we broke up. So that I hope there was Some happy issue and Effect, notwithstanding that unlikely view I had in the foregoing part of the Evening. To God be the Glory of any Good enabled from him to do. And I hope it was not altogether without Benefit and Comfort in my own Soul that this Day has been set apart; though too much reason to reflect on my own unstableness and inexpertness, thro' which if it had not been, perhaps I had reap'd more the Mercy of God thro the Merits of Christ vouchsafe Remission.

2. 3. Prepar'd for the Sabbath but not without Troublesome casts doubting of a Reconciliation between those foresaid Dissenting persons, and Sorrowing that Things should be brought to that pitch among us already that any of us should be oblig'd to withdraw from the Sacrament through want of Peace and Christian agreement. Tabitha Hardy[5] with me.

4. I preach'd from [blank]. Mr. Newton withdrawing (the other Two I believe were not at meeting) was a melancholly Sight to me. I administer'd the Sacrament. I hope God was convers'd with. For any Communications I would praise his Name But I would humble my Self that I receiv'd no more Spiritual Benefit. In the Afternoon I preach'd upon the Same Text.

10. Mr. Jonathan Forbush came and requested I would go See his Son in law Isaac Shattuck before He dy'd, and gave me his sons Earnest Desire to see me. Accordingly I went. Found him low and decay'd in Body, almost beyond all Hopes, But with great Encouragement touching Eternall matters. Having discours'd and pray'd with him I took my leave.

11. I preach'd upon Isaiah 1, 4 A. and P.M. After the Exercises Sister Lydia rode with me to see Mr. Shattuck. Found him living and that appear'd to be all. Scarcely Speaking but manifesting great ground of hope thro the almighty grace of God thro' the merits of Christ. We thought he began to Change. We pray'd recomending him to God and his family to the Divine grace and protection in as brief an address as possible. I took my last leave. Returning Sister Lydia fell from the horse but more surpriz'd than dammag'd. At our house was Mr. Bows[6] who had preach'd at Southborough on the Day past.

12. I rode down with Mr. Bows to Cambridge, dining at Mr. Jonsons[7] of Southborough and calling in likewise at Mr. Briton's[8] of the Same Town and at Mr. Williams[9] at Weston.

13. Mr. Isaac Greenwood[10] was inaugurated in the College Hall, the overseers and a great number of Gentlemen being present and handsomely entertain'd at Dinner after. In the Exercise Mr. Flynt[11] first pray'd and then made a Latin oration. The statutes of his founder read. The oaths were administered and he made his Declaration according to Mr. Hollis's Statutes that he would religiously observe them, and Mr. Greenwood made an handsome Oration in Latin. Mr. Flynt renunciated or openly declar'd Mr. Greenwood Professor of Mathematicks and Naturall and Experimental Phylosophy according to Mr. Hollis's institution. Mr. Appleton[12] pray'd and we in Conclusion Sang Ps. 104, the 1st and 2 last Stanzas of Tate and Bradys Version. It was a Day of Solemnity and great Joy, and I hope Glory was given to God. I tarried at College chiefly with Mr. Greenwood till time to repair to Lodgings at Father Champney's. I was at College at Mr. Greenwoods over a Dish of Tea, Stay'd till Sundown and then I went to Boston. Kept my Horse at Mr. Gold-

thwaits. The Great Dr. Cotton Mather dy'd this morning 4 A.M. after Suffering of an asthma.

15. Mr. Colman[13] preach'd Dr. Mathers funeral Sermon from Gen. 5, 24. I went in the Evening to Mr. Gerrish's[14] Retail. Here was Mr. Sewal,[15] Mr. Prince,[16] Mr. Cooper[17] and Mr. Foxcroft. After Candle Light I rode out of Town, to Cambridge upon my journey home. Here I found my wife and Son who were brought down yesterday by William Clark of Westborough. It rain'd So I was detain'd. Now I had opportunity to see much of Father Champney's Methods which were much out of due Course through the violence of a Fever many years agoe. Great grief and Concern in the Family.

17. It Storm'd So that I was utterly prevented moving from the house, either to Westborough or to Boston.

18. Mr. Appleton A.M. on Eccl. 7, 2, for That is the End of all men. I preach'd P.M. from Acts 24, 16. Supp'd at Mr. Appletons. Mr. Marston Gibs and Fitch[18] of Piscataqua there, and afterwards Mr. Remington,[19] Mr. Wigglesworth[20] and Sir Rogers.[21] I return'd to Father Champney's at nine.

19. I rode to Boston to Dr. Mathers Funerall. It look'd very Sad—almost as if it were the funerall of the Country. A very Sad Breach. Oh for Sufficient portions of Gods Spirit upon surviving ministers! Vast Concourse Exceeding long Procession and numberless Spectators. Every heart Sad. This Evening at cousin Dorcas Bows[22] where was Mrs. Rebecca Adams and by and by Brother Samuell Parkman.

20. An Appointment to go to Salem. Brother Elias and his wife went over. I rode from Charleston to Mores at Lyn, where I met them. But sister Willard[23] being gone to Boston we returned back. Dr. Delhond, etc., in Company.

21. Stormy. But yet I rode to Cambridge with Father Champney who ferry'd his horse over though it was grown Dark.

22. I was much detain'd the forenoon by making writings, Deed, Bonds, etc. Father Champney bying woodland of Cousin Daniel Champneys Children. I stop'd at Mr. Williams's a little while, but it began to Snow and I hastened. The Storm increas'd greatly So that night coming on also I turn'd away to Mr. Winchesters,[24] and lodg'd there.

23. The Morning was much worse till near Eleven, and though the wind was very high and the snow blowing very much, yet the Clouds began to grow thinner. He rode with me into the Road, the Paths being very much blown up and indeed the Roads too. I met with great Difficulties. I hardly reach'd Mr. Moss's where I had refreshment for my Self and horse, and a Young Man offer'd to ride with me. We reach'd Mr. Nathan Brighams,[25] refresh'd again, and Mr. Brigham rode up into this Town. But it was a Sad time to be abroad in, the Snow being very deep and great Danger if happening out of the Path and yet the Path almost wholly blown up. But thro the Divine Goodness I arrived without Damage and found my people well. *Deo opt. nostro grates.*

24. I went on with my Preparations.

25. Ps. 60, 1, 2 both A. and P.M. Isaac Shattuck died last wednesday was Sennight. A good Character of his last minutes. Mr. Barrett[26] and presently Dr. Gott,[27] came to see me. Dr. Gott left us this Eve.

29. Mr. Barrett return'd home.

---

[5] Mrs. Samuel Hardy of Westborough.
[6] Nicholas Bowes (Harvard 1725), later the first minister of Bedford, 1730–1754. *Sibley,* VII, 455–457.
[7] William Johnson resided in that part of Marlborough that was incorporated as the new town of Southborough in July 1727.
[8] John Britton of Southborough.
[9] Reverend William Williams (Harvard 1705), minister at Weston, 1709–1750. *Sibley,* V, 295–300.
[10] First Hollis Professor of Mathematics at Harvard College.
[11] Henry Flynt (Harvard 1693), Tutor at Harvard College. *Sibley,* IV, 162–167.
[12] Reverend Nathaniel Appleton, D.D. (Harvard 1712), minister of the First Church of Cambridge, 1717–1784. *Sibley,* V, 599–609.

[13] Reverend Benjamin Colman of the Brattle Street Church.
[14] Samuel Gerrish, the bookseller.
[15] Reverend Joseph Sewall of the Old South Church, Boston.
[16] Reverend Thomas Prince also of the Old South Church.
[17] Reverend William Cooper (Harvard 1712), of the Brattle Street Church, 1716–1743. *Sibley,* V, 624–634.
[18] John Fitch (Harvard 1728) of Portsmouth, N. H. The son of the Reverend Jabez Fitch. *Sibley,* VIII, 426–427.
[19] Jonathan Remington (Harvard 1696), Tutor at Harvard College, a judge, and Councillor of the Province. *Sibley,* IV, 300–303.
[20] Edward Wigglesworth (Harvard 1710), Professor at Harvard College. *Sibley,* V, 546–555.
[21] John Rogers (Harvard 1728). *Sibley,* VIII, 480–481.
[22] Mrs. Dorcas Bowes, cousin of Mrs. Parkman.
[23] Parkman's sister Susanna, wife of Captain Josiah Willard of Salem.
[24] Probably Ebenezer Winchester, prominent citizen of Framingham. Temple, *Framingham,* p. 752.
[25] Captain Brigham of Marlborough.
[26] Reverend Samuel Barrett of Hopkinton.
[27] Benjamin Gott, a physician of Marlborough.

MARCH [1728]

3. I preach'd on Is. 1, 4, both A. and P.M. I was not a little affected in the afternoon. I request of God to make these sermons profitable to my Self as well as to others that I may deplore my own Iniquities with which as I have been laden with the guilt of them. So God grant that I may be after a godly Sort weary and heavy laden, so under a sense of them that I may be a true mourner for the Sins of others and lament over the Calamities of the Land!

4. My wife and Child brought home by brother Champney. It was a warm Day, the Snow therefore Soft and the wayes heavy and tiresome, but (Thanks to God alone) got home well. Dr. Gott here but not a long time.

5. I was at Mr. Newtons[1] where was The Ensign[2] and we had pritty much Discourse about our Troubles in Town and the Ensign Said Things had never laid Easy with a certain person ever Sins [sic] Our church Covenant was chosen and my refusing a Quitclaim to Mr. Elmer,[3] which that person had himself written and offer'd me to sign; and that Things Still lay brooding, etc.

6. Brother Champney went home. In the Afternoon Mr. Thomas Forbush[4] was here on the Business of his Children, parted quiet though there had been Some warm Discourse. Just after I was got to Bed (about ¾ after Eleven) we were afrighted by the awfull sound of the Earthquake. All that were awake heard it. I lay awake an hour and half, but hearing nothing I Compos'd to sleep. God be prais'd from my Soul for his wondrous Deliverances. Let me never forget his Benefits.

7. It being Family meeting at Mr. Forbush's and earnestly desir'd by him to be present thereat I went to Mr. Forbush's and repeated a Discourse from John [blank]. After the Exercises Mr. McCollister and Asher Rice requested a Church Meeting which I comply'd with, that is to See whether the Church would consider and Act upon it seeing it is a mix'd Case, etc. Visit'd Lieutenant's[5] wife who was very low. Riding home Mr. Wheeler set forth the uneasiness people were in on the account of Mr. Newton,[6] and that some, truly, could be scarcely kept from falling upon my Self Seeing I would not let it come forward, whereas I had alwayes declar'd that I waited for nothing more than to have it brought into a proper fitness for the Church to hear. Captain Fay[7] and his wife, Wheeler and James Ball stopt at my house.

8. 9. I was full of Concern and hearty Prayer on account of the threatening Evils.

10. Not very well in the morning and at noon but God strengthening I went thro the Exercises. Preach'd A. and P.M. from Isa. 1, 5. Church meeting appointed. Full of hearty Concern and I hope mainly for the Glory of God and the Interests of the Souls of Men, for I find no great value for whatever Temporal Interests I can find in this Town.[8]

11. The Church met. I had great fear of disorder but by the favour of God we went on smooth. Mr. Forbush, just before meeting began, told me I should have wisdom to take Care of my Self but people Said now Mr. Parkman's undone—but this person has frequently enough shown that his Passions forc'd him to Speak what makes much mischief, tho the most ungrounded. I having given a Serious Discourse to keep us all upon our guard in all church matters and Read the Platform Ch. 10. I laid open the case and advis'd first to an arbitration. It was accepted by all. The chief trouble was to find arbitrators. Mr. Bradish excepted against Peres Rice.[9] Said Mr. Newton had bragg'd he had got Mr. Parkman and Mr. Bradish of his Side and he car'd not for all the Church besides. This Information he said came from John Eames of Hopkinton. Mr. Newton declar'd he spake

no Such thing nor had he seen John Eames. I openly clear'd my Self from being of either side and by Gods Grace I will remain impartial. The Arbitrators went out and took up the Time. When they came in they declar'd it their Opinion that if Mr. Newton had taken the money by deceit he should return it, but they enquired whether they ought to bring it to Trial whether he had deceiv'd, etc. I reply'd their work was yet to do. I desir'd they would go on and finish it this Evening or Some day Speedily—for they ought to clear off all that was of a Secular Nature in the Cause. It grew Dark. There was opposition by Peres Rice that the witnesses ought to be sworn, etc. I dismiss'd this Business and propos'd another affair for the Church's Consideration, Advice and Concurrence in. That is the Case of Samuel Hardy and his Wife, etc. I desir'd the Brethren would give me their minds and make what opposition they would ever offer. When one or Two had spoke Peres Rice (who gave us more Trouble than any one this meeting) Said he thought we must either wait till the Civil part of the Case was dispatch'd, till either the Court had done with it or rather till it had been put to an arbitration (reflecting upon the manner of managing the other Business of his Brother Asher and Newton), but (though there's difficulty in keeping our Selves under Suitable Command under such girds) I calmly assur'd him it was a far different Case, etc.

The Church gave their Consent to my Proceeding with the said persons and granting them Priviledges if they should Seriously declare their innocence, etc., upon which we clos'd the Meeting. After prayer Asher desir'd it might still go on that He might be heard in what he had of a Distinct Case to be Heard. I told him the meeting was over. What if the Brethren Should hear it? I am indispos'd but they may mediate between you when I am retir'd home. It Satisfy'd him and the Church might, etc. His Speaking the word church confirmed me in it that he thought it would be as much the Church that would act in the Evening upon anything he should bring before them (as much I say) as before the prayer and Blessing and dismission of the meeting, and as much in my absence as when I was there. So that my Reply was thus, viz. But observe, it hasn't been known that a Church can act (as a Church) without the Pastor, or make acts without the Pastor, which dash'd the whole and I returned home desiring the Arbitrators to finish their work as [soon as] possible and give me notice of it and when they Should desire it there might be (if needfull) another Church Meeting. Diverse came into my house with me. Mr. Tainter Supp'd with me. He agreed to keep my mare, I being short of Hay. Thus finish'd this troublesome Day. My Soul praise the Lord for his gracious assistances and Restraints; and the Lord forgive Every offence by me, and all the offences of my Brethren this Day! For Scarcely do any come off innocent when involv'd in Dissensions.

13. I sent my Mare to Mr. Tainters to be kept at his Stable. In the Evening at Mr. Forbush with demands upon Samuel Hardy and his Wife touching their Child, and upon the midwife, etc., etc. Call'd to see Lieutenant's wife.

Read Dr. Sherlock on Divine Providence.[10]

14. Mr. Eager[11] with me in the Evening till late. Discourse the Quarrell with Mr. Newton. It was to have been our Lecture but, the above Said Troubles happening, and Mr. Barrett who was to have assisted me Sending word that He could not attend it, but Especially my Seeing reason for deferring the Sacrament, I put it by.

17. I preach'd on Mat. 10, 29, 30.

18. It appears to me of the Last Importance for the people of this Province to take heed to them Selves when they are proposing Holy Dayes to be kept unto God, for without they are duly observed they are Such grand pieces of Solemn Mockery that I cannot but Think God is greatly provok'd by them. They are Loathsome to him and he is weary to bear them. I cannot but conclude that one of the great Reasons of the Lords Controversie with this Land is taken from Hence. O therefore that

---

[1] Josiah Newton of Westborough.
[2] Thomas Newton, cousin of Josiah.
[3] Reverend Daniel Elmer, formerly a preacher at Westborough.
[4] Prominent early settler of Westborough.
[5] Samuel Forbush.
[6] Reference to the quarrel between Josiah Newton and Asher Rice.
[7] John Fay of Westborough.
[8] In the Church Records of this date it is indicated that a number of people were "Complaining of Josiah Newton's deceiving them in his administration in the office of Military Clerk."
[9] Son of Thomas Rice, an original settler, and brother of Asher Rice.
[10] William Sherlock, *A Discourse Concerning the Divine Providence* (London 1694). Numerous other editions were printed.
[11] James Eager of Westborough.

Care may be taken about the Approaching Fast that it may not be in vain but a Fast that God hath Chosen!

21. Publick Fast. I preach'd all Day upon Hosea 13, 9. I would Lament that there are So many others that profane these Dayes of our Solemn Assemblies, but I have chiefly Reason to Reflect upon and Condemn my Self who have not been suitably prepar'd for, nor have been So full and Sincere in my Humiliation to Day as I ought to have been.

22. Mr. Coolidge[12] (having preach'd at Southborough yesterday) came up to see me, being Conducted up by Mr. William Johnson, Junior,[13] who last night as he was, with Mr. Bigolo, at their Saw-Mill, was Surprised with a very Conspicuous Aurora Borealis. Mr. Coolidge desir'd to Change with me the Sabbath Approaching and truly it was not unacceptable to me Seeing the Labors of this week have been already very great. And a person Sick at Mr. Thorntons whom I was requested to visit yesterday. When Mr. Coolidge left me I rode from home to see Mr. Thorntons Daughter who was very Sick. At Mr. Eagers was Mr. Benjamin Flagg of Worcester who inform'd me of Mr. Elmer's Death.

23. Josiah Newton and John McCollister came to our house to hear the Arbitration of their Case, which the Arbitrators had sent by Edward Baker this morning. They (after I had discours'd a while with them) were heartily and lovingly reconcil'd (as things appear'd). I had some difficulty with Mrs. Byles[14] about her sons Child, as I told her of the various objections I met with to oppose my Baptizing it as Deacon Tomlins,[15] Mr. Wheelers[16] and Bakers,[17] etc. Mr. Coolidge being come hither I rode to Southborough and Lodg'd at Mr. William Johnsons.

24. I preach'd at Southborough in the forenoon from John 15, 14. Din'd at Mr. [blank] Johnsons. I preach'd in the afternoon from Ps. 95, 7. Mr. Coolidge came to Southboro in the Evening.

25. Mr. Coolidge and I rode to Marlboro. Upon the Road he gave me some account of the Sin and Misfortunes of Mr. Samuel Jeffords[18] at Wells. I lodg'd at Mr. Brecks.[19] I took advice of Mr. Breck touching our Affairs at Westborough.

26. Return'd to Westboro.

27. Great Disquietments among us. I had trouble enough Every Day and Yet all that came to Me had the Reconciliation of our Two Brethren read to them (as those Brethren desir'd it might be) and Every person went away with the greatest Satisfaction. It was Suspected that I favour'd Mr. Newton which (if I can judge) I acted against, and was full in it that he ought to give Satisfaction to those he had offended for the wrong done them by Him.

28. I Rode (with my wife) to Shrewsbury upon my Young Horse, and being disappointed by both Mr. and Mrs. Cushings[20] absence from Home we presently returned to Westborough, but not home, we having determined to Visit Mr. Paterson. We went not only there [Entry ends incomplete at this point].

### APRIL [1728]

### MAY [1728]

[Blank pages with headings for these months were left, but no entries were recorded].

### JUNE [1728]

13. Thomas Kendal began to work for me.
15. Thomas Kendal had my Mare to go down to Lexington.
16. [no entry].
17. [no entry].
18. I preach'd at the Young mens meeting at Mr. Wards.

---

[12] Samuel Coolidge (Harvard 1724), schoolmaster at Watertown. *Sibley*, VII, 326–331.
[13] Of Southborough.
[14] Wife of Captain Joseph Byles of Westborough.
[15] Isaac Tomlin.
[16] Joseph Wheeler.
[17] Edward Baker.
[18] Reverend Samuel Jefferds of Wells, Maine.
[19] Reverend Robert Breck of Marlborough.
[20] Reverend Job Cushing of Shrewsbury.

### JULY [1728]

1. [no entry].
2. [no entry].
3. My wife and Children were brought up in a Calash with brother Champney[1] and Sister Lydia.[2]
4. I lectur'd on Isa. 26, 9.
5. Brother and Sister rode down in the Calash.
6. My interruptions have been very great; but God graciously assists me.
7. I preach'd all Day upon Phil. 3, 8, 9, 10, 11, and in the forenoon I administered the Sacrament of the Lords Supper.
9. Mrs. Burt[3] came for her Dauter.[4]
10. Mrs. Burt carry'd away her Dauter. A great Affliction to us.
11. 12. 13. It was a time of much Trouble and Concern with us respecting our weakhandedness.
14. I preach'd all Day on Phil. 3, 8, 9, 10, 11.
15. I rode to Cambridge with Neighbor Green.[5] Found nobody at Father Champneys but sister Hannah[6] just when I was going away and there came two men that would go in for Cyder. I went in again and tarried till they went away. I rode with them to Boston. Trouble Brother Samuell[7] and Mr. Dorcas.[8]
16. 17. I visited my Relatives and acquaintances. At Mr. Thatchers.[9]
18. Mr. Sewall preach'd Excellently from Ps. 119, 115. Occasion, Phillips and Woodbridge Duel.[10] At Mr. Wilsteeds in the Eve. Here was Mr. Joseph Green[11] of Barnstable. The Governours[12] coming in Everyones motions. His Excellency's Family came to Dr. Cooks this Eve.
19. A very great Day. His Excellency's Entrance into Boston was truly very Stately and Splendid. I was at Mr. Eliots.[13] I din'd at Holmes's.[14] Sister Lydia rode with me to Cambridge. Earthquake at Newbury, etc.
20. I rode up home. Got home a little after noon. Prepar'd what I could for the Sabbath. I praise God for his goodness this Journey.
21. I preach'd in the forenoon on Phil. 3, 8, 9, 10, 11. Afternoon repeated the Sermon (Numb. 28) on Prov. 10, 28.
22. I rode up to see Mrs. Nurse[15] who Suffer'd by a fall into the Cellar. Earthquake at Boston, at Newbury, as far as York, and many think it was then heard among us.

[In another part of the diary the following note appears].

July 22 [1728]. At Boston a small shock but at Newbury the houses shook. Some thought they heard it among us at the Same time, viz. about break of Day. I am apt to think I heard it myself.

23. I rode to Mr. Barretts[16] but found him not, He being over at Holliston.
24. 25. 26. 27. As much time as I had Spent upon my preparations but I was greatly taken off by the affairs of my house and of this Busy Season abroad.
28. I preach'd all Day on Gen. 18, 25. Mr. Nurse ill and distracted was at our house when meeting was closing, and till our Evening Exercise was over. I was in no little concern of mind about the Earthquakes Continuing.
29. I assisted with my own hands in the Carting, etc.
30. Having got in my Hay, Rice, Barley, and Wheat, I dismiss'd Thomas Kendal for a while. Now we are intirely alone

---

[1] Samuel Champney, Jr. of Cambridge, Parkman's brother-in-law.
[2] Lydia Champney, Parkman's sister-in-law.
[3] Mrs. Thomas Burt of Reading.
[4] Sarah Burt had been Mrs. Parkman's helper.
[5] John Green.
[6] Hannah Champney, Mrs. Parkman's oldest sister.
[7] Samuel Parkman of Boston.
[8] The reference (clearly legible) to a "Mr. Dorcas" is a bit puzzling. Parkman was probably referring to Dorcas Bowes, who married Samuel Parkman Jan. 29, 1729.
[9] Reverend Peter Thatcher of Boston.
[10] Henry Phillips (Harvard 1724) killed Benjamin Woodbridge in a duel on Boston Common, July 3, 1728 and escaped to France. The affair caused much excitement and produced several sermons in Boston and elsewhere. *Sibley*, VII, 424–429. See Samuel G. Drake. *The History and Antiquities of Boston* (Boston, 1854), pp. 579–580.
[11] Reverend Joseph Green, minister of Barnstable, 1725–1770.
[12] Governor William Burnett.
[13] Jacob Eliot of Boston, later first minister of Lebanon, Connecticut.
[14] Ebenezer Holmes (Harvard 1724), a merchant of Boston. *Sibley*, VII, 368–371.
[15] Mrs. William Nurse of Westborough.
[16] Reverend Samuel Barrett of Hopkinton.

having no Servant nor any one in the House. Our Loneliness gives Scope for Thought. God Sanctifie our solitude, and help us to improve in acquaintance with Himself. There was much Lighting in the North almost the whole Evening.

31. A very hot Day. About 11 at Night came up a storm of Rain with Thunder and Lightning.

### AUGUST [1728]

1. Mr. Flynt[1] and Mr. Greenwood[2] (who had taken a Circular Ride) came to See us. Our sisters Lydia and Ruth[3] and Kinswomen Mrs. Abigail and Susan Champney[4] came likewise.

2. Mr. Flynt and Greenwood rode to Marlboro. The rest tarry'd. Sister Ruth and the rest (except Sister Lydia) left us. These Dayes were very hot.

4. I preach'd from Gen. 18, 25, and from Ps. 119, 68.

6. Early in the morning Sister Lydia and I rode (single) to Cambridge, from whence I proceeded to Boston.

7. I went to See Mr. Miles's[5] Library. His widow show'd me her house and Garden.

8. I entered into Obligation to my Father for the Negro Barrow. My Father gave me 5£. I pay'd him 3£ and gave a promissory Bill to pay 66£, the whole making 74£ which was the price of him.

Mr. Cooper[6] Lectur'd on Job 37, 16. I din'd at Mr. Coopers, Mr. Thatcher and Mr. Byles[7] also.

9. I rode to Cambridge, Barrow, alias Maro, running on foot. Tho somewhat rainy, it clear'd away after noon. After 4 o'Clock I set out, my Self on one horse and the Negro on the other. At Larnards[8] met Mr. Swift.[9] Rode to Mr. Swifts and lodged there.

10. We rode home by a little after noon. Prepar'd somewhat upon John 1, 46 and carry'd on the Exercises with the Applicatory Considerations in the Sermons on John 12, 26.

12. I was at Lieutenant Forbes's,[10] his wife being very ill.

13. There arose a storm of Thunder and Lightning in the Night.

14. About 2 in the morning the Thunder and Lightning were very Sharp and terrifying. Neither was it a Crack or Flash or Two, but it continued for (I Suppose) an hour and half exceeding dreadfull. Once it was So hard Thunder that the house Jarr'd in some sort as in an Earthquake.

Mr. Rice was here, and Goddard[11] from College. The latter Said the people of Framingham entertain'd disaffections to Mr. Swift. My heart is mov'd greatly; and I think merely for the Cause of God in these melancholly and divided Times.

15. 16. 17. The Remaining Dayes of the Week I abode more strictly by my Preparations for the Sabbath. Late on Saturday Night I was Sent for by Lieutenant Forbes to his wife who departed this Life (a little before 12 o'clock) before I could get to the house. A very meek, patient, Godly person, under the sufferings She bore through most of her Life, by Sickness and weakness.

18. I preach'd from Ps. 119, 68 both forenoon and afternoon.

19. Mrs. Forbes was buried. A Large funerall; many people from Marlboro being up here. Mr. Foxcroft[12] of Boston, Esquire Pool[13] of Reading and Lieutenant How of Framingham came to our house and lodged with us.

20. Those Gentlemen rode away to Leicester to be (with others) a Council upon the Difficulties of that people. Mr. Swift of Framingham, Elder Lymen and Mr. Loring of Boston came but rode quickly away upon the lastnam'd Concern. Esquire Pools advice and offers respecting Mrs. Burt.

22. Our Father and mother Champney, with aunt Champney[14] and her son John[15] came to See us.

23. Mr. Winchester[16] came to wait upon his mother in law back to Framingham.

24. Mr. Baxter[17] and his messinger came hither from the Council, with word that they had stood out the hearing but had drawn up no Result—but had appointed to meet at Sudbury to finish the Affair.

25. I preach'd A.M. on Ps. 119, 68, and administered the Sacrament. I preach'd P.M. on 1 Cor. 10, 16. I have no slender Reason to lament my insensibility, indolence and utter unfruitfullness under all Gods Goodness to me; and it is nothing else but the infinite Mercy of God to poor sinners, his infinite Patience and Compassion towards us under our manifest infirmities that has brought me to the Sacrament for my Conduct is Such that my unprofitableness and indifference might utterly debar me and leave me discouraged.

26. Father and Mother Champney returned home.

27. Under the Engagements of my Family by reason of our want of Help, our Negro being New, I am much taken off from my Work, but I trust in God it may be better with me and more leasure ere long.

28. 29. 30. 31. Much Concern in the minds of all people throughout the Province on the account of the Difficulties at Court about settling the Governours Sallery. And no prospect of its being any better between the Governour and the Lower House. Indeed the Governour has always been fair and pleasant and is not willing to make Complaint against the Province. But his Instructions from his Majesty oblige him to move in this Manner and the House think they loose all Priviledges if they comply. Its a difficult Time respecting our Credit in England, but the Heavens do Rule. God gives us Wisdom and turneth the Heart of the King which way Soever He will.

### SEPTEMBER [1728]

1. I preach'd upon Isa. 31, 2. I have great experience of the Divine Compassion showed me under my insufficiency and great unworthiness, in that he so graciously assists me in the performances of my Sacred function. God alone have the Praise. God keep me from Vain Glory.

2. Mr. Thomas Weld[1] (having preach'd yesterday at Southborough) came to see me, and lodg'd with us.

3. Mr. Weld rode with me to Framingham, expecting an Association. It was very rainy and very troublesome getting there; and yet we were disappointed thro Mr. Swifts mistake. He had told his Family that the Association would be there next week; and so he went to Sudbury to the Council upon the Difficulties at Leicester. Mr. Cushing was thus Disappointed with us, and we rode away to Colonel Buckminsters[2] and lodged there.

4. This morning after breakfast we rode from Colonel Buckminsters to Marlboro and din'd at Mr. Woods.[3] Thence Mr. Weld and I went first to Mr. Brecks door but he being gone to the foresaid Council we went with Mr. Park[4] to his Lodgings. With Mr. Park there was Sir Kent,[5] Schoolmaster at Framingham. Near Sunset we parted and I Came home. On the Road home I had many Reflections upon My Life Past, the unusefullness and unprofitableness of it. I was griev'd at my taking no better notice of the divine Dealings with me. I was jealous of my Self and Suspected whether there was not some undue End in taking

[8] Thomas Learned, tavern-keeper of Watertown.

[9] Reverend John Swift of Framingham.

[10] Samuel Forbush did not change his name to Forbes, but Parkman's reference is doubtless indicative of some confusion in the minds of townspeople.

[11] David Goddard (Harvard 1731) of Watertown and later the second minister of Leicester. Sibley, IX, 40–43.

[12] Reverend Thomas Foxcroft.

[13] Benjamin Poole, selectman of Reading. Tilley Eaton, Genealogical History of the Town of Reading (Boston, 1874), pp. 108, 282, 283.

[1] Henry Flynt, Tutor at Harvard College.

[2] Professor Isaac Greenwood of Harvard College.

[3] Ruth Champney of Cambridge.

[4] Abigail and Susan Champney, cousins of Mrs. Parkman.

[5] Reverend Samuel Myles (Harvard 1684), Rector of King's Chapel, Boston, 1689–1728. The library in question was sent over by the Bishop of London. Sibley suggests that it was "perhaps the best theological library in the country." The remnants of this library were deposited in the Boston Athenaeum in 1823. Sibley, III, 287–293.

[6] Reverend William Cooper (Harvard 1712) of the Brattle Street Church. Sibley, V, 624–634.

[7] Reverend Mather Byles of Hollis Street Church, Boston.

[14] Mrs. Joseph Champney.

[15] Mrs. Parkman's cousin.

[16] Ebenezer Winchester of Framingham.

[17] Reverend Joseph Baxter of Medfield.

[1] (Harvard 1723). Later minister in Upton, 1738–1744, and Middleborough, 1744–1749. Sibley, VII, 273–277.

[2] Joseph Buckminster, Sr. of Framingham. Temple, Framingham, p. 490.

[3] Benjamin Woods.

[4] Probably John Park of Framingham.

[5] Benjamin Kent (Harvard 1727). Sibley, VIII, 220–230.

the accounts in this Book, Seeing this Design had no better Success. I would humbly hope that the Glory of God and my Spiritual Emolument has and shall determine me in the writing this Journal. I was full of Enquiry how I should best Spend the Morrow to the Glory of the God of my Life and my highest Advantage. I resolv'd in the Fear and by the Grace of God to Separate the Day to Seeking the Face of God, and Enquiring out as under the divine Influence, the best Methods for the Conduct of the Future part of my Life, Respecting my whole Behaviour, and proceedings, in my Secret Walk, in my Studies, in my ministrations, and my Several Relations. And the Spirit of God purifie, Sanctifie, Assist and direct me, and grant his Blessing upon me in the Prosecution of this my Purpose!

N.B. See for the 5th Day, the Beginning of the Book entitled Some Remarkable Passages, etc.[6]

[Entries for September, 1728, end at this point. There is then a blank page in the diary, and then the following undated entry].

Several gracious Promises of God. Ps. 32, 8. I will instruct thee, and teach thee in the way which thou shalt go: I will guide thee with mine Eyes.

Zech. 10, 12. And I will Strengthen them in the Lord, and they Shall walk up and down in the name of the Lord.

September 5th At Westborough.[7]

This being my Birth Day it may be a most proper Season to look back upon my Life Past, that I may See what account I may give unto the Great Judge of all the Earth. What penitence and Contrition I ought to express for the many Sins of my Conversation in the world the Twenty-five years that I have liv'd in it, and What Praises I owe to the God of my Life for the innumerable and unspeakable Benefits he has most bountifully (though most undeservedly) bestowed upon me. I deem it suitable also and prudent to take this Time especially to renew my Covenant with my God, which I solemnly entered into before Him on Saturday September 5 in the year 1719. Furthermore it is most proper now to be anew proposing methods of future Conduct, that the future part of my Life may be more profitable, and fruitfull than the former has ever been.

Accordingly I committed my Self to God in a solemn address, and besought his direction and assistance in the Several parts of this important work above mention'd. And then I proceeded to look into my Life past where I discern'd innumerable articles that require deep Repentance—among the rest my Sad misimprovement of my Time in my Youth, as appears by the papers that give an account of the past of my Conversation. It must be Judg'd from the Said Papers that my Course of Life has been full of Impertinencies, except I was to Live Some Centuries. Then indeed it might prove more Excusable to take my methods to know men and Things (as my pretence was); or it had perhaps been laudable to Spend a Month or some Small part of ones whole Life in this manner. I consum'd a great part of my Time. I Endeavour'd to affect my Self with Grief herefore and proceeded with Exercises of fervent Devotion, Reading the Divine Oracles and Serious Meditations, I carried on the Day till 3 P.M., when Mr. Wheeler came, and I went with him to Captain Fays to the Private Meeting. I went in while the Captain was at Prayer. Our Exercise was upon Col. 3, 4. Christ who in our Life. I chose this because I would have Christ to be my Life, and I would be quickened and instructed at this season to live to him. God give me Grace to do so! I spent the day throughout as a Day of Devotion, and I beseech God to accept me herein. But I was not able to go thro all my Proposal about Searching out the Suitable methods of future Conduct. These I deferr'd to the first opportunity I may have therefor. Nor did I draw out in writing what I could remember of the mercies of God to me and my Family, But I propos'd to do [so] as Speedily as my Circumstances will favour me. My Covenant with God was not solemnly renewed in that express manner I had propos'd but read over and anew consented to. But a reason of its not being So expressly renewed might be my apprehending it convenient to tran *sc* rib a Covenant Somewhat more Correct, which I would Solemnly Sign before God (having some regard to the Directions of Mr.

Alliene,[8] in his sure Guide to Heaven, Dis: x. p. 127, Edition at London anno 1705, in that affair).

O Glorious God in Trinity, I pray Thee be my covenant God! I do now Solemnly Take Thee, O ETERNAL FATHER, to be my God, my Father, my Friend, and my only Portion. I take Thee O ETERNAL SON, to be my God, my only Mediator and Redeemer.

I take Thee O ETERNAL SPIRIT to be my God, my Guide, my Sanctifyer and Comforter.

And I Sacredly Devote and Dedicate my Self wholly, Soul and Body, all the Powers and Faculties, all the Members and organs of Each, to Thee, the one onely living and true God, to be Thy Servant, Renouncing all my Sins and Lusts my Self, the world, the Flesh and the Devil, and humbly beseeching the Pardon of all the Violations of all my Former Covenants and Obligations, with all my other Iniquities, through Jesus Christ, I Consecrate my Self to THEE alone. And Promise, by thy Grace, to perform the Duties of my holy Christian Profession, and to Discharge my ministerial work. To ratifie which, I subscribe, with my Heart and Hand, humbly, and I trust, Sincerely, Ebenezer Parkman. Westborough November 24, 1729. Renew'd January 1, 1730 and This Transcript made January 3.

Some Rules for my Conduct in my Religious, Ministerial, Civil, Domestic, and Relative Life.

1. I would that my Eyes and Heart be carry'd to God at first Waking; That every Morning when I awaken I may be Still with God, as God is Still with me.

2. That nothing be undertaken which may defer my early sett, Solemn Morning Devotions to God, that I may be sure to begin the Day with God, set out in his Fear, and Spend it to his Glory.

3. When I rise from Dinner Let the first Opportunity be laid hold of for a solemn Address to God.

4. Let there be some Serious Reflections in the Evening and a solemn Address to God—closing my Eyes with recommending my Self to the Lord my Keeper, who is the Great Keeper of Israel, who never slumbers nor sleeps.

## APRIL 1729[1]

15. About five months agoe I set down some account of the more remarkable Mercies of God to Me in the Course of His Providence in and Since that my memorable dangerous Sickness when I was a Young School Boy; Having made Some (though I confess very imperfect) Record of what went before, in a little Book bearing Date August 24, 1719, and Several other Dates from thence, but in a great deal of Confusion, and with too many other marks of my puerility, when I Scribbl'd them however honest and upright my intention was to have Some Remembrances of those (to me) important Things by me; Having of late experienc'd So much of the divine Goodness as gives me new and the greatest Reason forever to esteem and admire the various Expressions thereof to me, and every way to manifest my greatfull Returns to my unspeakable Benefactor for what He has, in infinite Tenderness done for Me, I have here transcrib'd a Sort of Catalogue or Memorandum of those abovesaid Mercies to God to Me, have carry'd it along with what I have received Since.

### Divine Benignity and Providence

1. Recovery from a very Dangerous Fit of Sickness, and of near, if not altogether 4 Months Continuance, at the Time of the Meazles rageing in this Country. I was taken in October—had a Fever, then the Meazles—then languished as aforesaid. But the Lord was gracious and redeemed my Life from Destruction.

2. My being Sent, and my admission into, Harvard College, in the Year 1717. Examin'd July 8, admitted July 11, and went up to dwell at Cambridge August 13. Under Mr. Leveret,[2] president, and Mr. Robie,[3] my Tutor.

3. The good measure of Health, and the Prosperity enjoy'd while I liv'd at College.

4. The Honours of Bachelor of Arts, conferr'd in the Year 1721, July 5.

[6] Another name for his Natalitia.
[7] The entry for Sept. 5 is entirely in his Natalitia.
[8] Richard Alleine, *Heaven Opened, Or a Brief and Plain Discovery of the Riches of Gods Covenant of Grace* (Boston, 1699).
[1] All of the material for April 1729 is found in the Natalitia.
[2] John Leveret (Harvard 1680).
[3] Thomas Robie (Harvard 1708).

5. What acceptance I met with (the Same year) in my keeping School at Newton, and Preservation from the Infection of the Small Pox, by which many of my Friends were remov'd into the Eternal World.

6. My Brother Elias's[4] Kindness and Bounty when he took me to Board in His House and allow'd good and pleasant accomodattions there, in April 7th, 1722 and continuing the same for Near a Year and half, that is, till my more frequently going into the Country to preach, which was July 27, 1723 at Hopkington (or rather August 2 at Worcester) more occasionally, and afterwards (August 21) at Westborough more constantly, during the latter part of which Time, I did also reside at Times at Cambridge, where I kept a Chamber with Mr. Edward Hunting.[5] Indeed from the time of my first preaching at Wrentham (which was April 14, 1723) or before I was not constantly at Boston, but divided a part of my Time at Cambridge. Nevertheless I account that near a year and half I was at my Brothers, because thither I went as to my home when I was at Boston and kept my Library, etc. there, and had a Chamber Study and entertainment occasionally there, for the Space of Two years I suppose.

7. My admission into the New North Church and the assistance in my preparation therefor, March 31, 1723.

8. The Assistance God was pleased to grant me, and what Acceptance I (undeservedly) met with in my Preaching, which began first of all (as abovesaid) at Wrentham, April 14, 1723. My Text was 1 Cor. 3, 11. "Other Foundation can no man lay."

9. The Honour of a Second Degree at Harvard College, viz. of Master of Arts, conferr'd July 1, 1724.

10. The Blessing afforded me by my Marriage July 7, 1724 to Miss Mary Champney, Dauter of Mr. Samuel Champney at Cambridge, at which the Reverend Mr. Appleton,[6] with gracefull Solemnity officiated. And here I would Bless God for his wondrous Grace in restraining me from the Sin of Fornication, and carrying me through so many Temptations as Those pass'd in the Time of Courtship.

11. The Distinguishing Honours, and gracious Presence of God, at my Ordination, October 28th in the same year 1724. N.B. The Reverend Mr. Dorr[7] open'd the solemnity with prayer. The Reverend Mr. Prentice[8] preach'd on 2 Cor. 2, 16. Reverend Mr. William Williams of Weston pray'd and gather'd the Church. Mr. Prentice gave the charge. Reverend Mr. Loring[9] of Sudbury the Right Hand. Sung Ps. 69, 17 to 21.

12. Recovery from the illness that debarr'd Me the public Exercises, immediately after my ordination, Two Dayes of Service.

13. I look upon those Kindnesses receiv'd from my Westborough Neibours, as the Favours of Providence to me and my Family, and do return Thanks to God for them.

14. Gods appearing for my Wife in her hour of Peril and giving us a Dauter (which was Mary) September 14, 1725.

15. Three weeks after her lying in my wife had a very Sore Breast, which broke twice, and brought us into a great Affliction. I would thankfully remember the Deliverance out of that Grievous Trouble.

16. My Fathers recovery out of dangerous Sickness in January 1725/6, I would always number amongst Gods mercies to Me, and particularly because I then look'd upon my Self very unprepar'd to entertain his Death, as I ought.

17. My Wife's Restoration and Recovery from her great pains and illness (Laps-uteri) July 1726, under the Care of the Reverend Mr. Barrett[10] and Mrs. Whitcomb. This is to be remembered as a Special appearance of God for us.

18. The Lords Compassion in healing My Dauter when very ill. July 3, 1727, is to be observ'd by Me.

19. Deliverance to my Wife when in Travel [sic] the Second Time, and giving me a Son, August 20, 1727. This I call'd Ebenezer, Saying with Gratitude Hitherto hath the Lord helped.

20. I would record the Salvation vouchsaf'd us in the Time of the uncommon Thunder, Lightning and Wind in this Month, August (1727).

21. Still greater and more memorable Salvations in the Great Earthquake, and I would that more Special Notice be taken of it because I would lay those Threatenings in Divine Providence, with the awakenings of His word publickly delivered the Day before; which compleating the Third year Since the gathering our Church and my own ordination, I preach'd on Luke 13, 7.

22. The Goodness of God to me in the time of uneasiness touching Mr. Josiah Newton and preventing Divisions among us. April 4, 1728.

23. Recovery of my Son out of Sickness which he Labour'd of in the Months of September and October, of this Year 1728.

24. My Recovery from my Ague in November, Seizing Me the 7th at Night and continuing to the 15th a great part of the time in much Extremity.

25. Healing my Son in December in the Same Year.

26. I would put into this Account the Favour of my Library, So much larger than (considering my Circumstances) I might have expected it to be, Though I would humbly wait for the Divine Goodness in further Additions to it still, but especially beg for Grace to improve it to the Glory of God.

27. I would reckon also the Comforts pour'd on in from my Farms. But I pray God to preserve me from Worldly mindedness and Covetousness which may prove to the Detriment of my Spirituall State, and to my Studies and Ministrations. And thereby not a little to the Dishonor of God, and the Holy Ministry, and to the Disservice of the Interests of Religion. To that I would be not a little concerned on this Score.

28. I must ever remember with hearty gratitude My Recovery out of Dangerous Sickness, weakness and Pains that I was brought low with in March 1729. I was first of all Seiz'd February 11 and kept from public Service the 16th, But was So well on the 23rd as to go to Meeting again. I was again disorder'd on the 28th and March 1, was faint and feeble the 2d, yet ventur'd to meeting and preach'd all Day and had extremity of pain in my Limbs, and oppression in my Stomach. The nights after the 7th and 8th I had such fits my Physician call'd my Distemper and Rheumatic Fever as were not without Difficulty to be born; and I fear'd a 3d would be more than Nature Could resist. The 9th I had, thro the omnipotent Mercy of God, a instigation, and escaped the Danger. I was in the beginning of my illness under the Care of Reverend Mr. Barrett and afterwards of Dr. Roby.[11] However I was under Confinement and in Weakness, in Pain and [illegible] for weeks after. April 6. I went to meeting part of the Day, the 13th all Day. On the 20th I preach'd in the forenoon but could not undertake more than to baptize a child, in the afternoon.

29. I would Set it down among the Divine Mercies that after the Difficulties, weakness, pains in my Stomach, faintness, etc., on my Journey to Boston June 2d, 3, 4 which put me and my Relatives into great Fears and Concern. I was carry'd thro and brought home to my Family June 6, though continuing in much feebleness and in Fear and Care about the Event. I would record my Thanks also that I found my Son So recovered from the illness he had been for some time labouring under, and that he was much afflicted by, when I went from home.

30. July 3, 1729. The Salvation of God was Seen, and my Wife brought forth a Second Son, and upon Consideration of God repeating his Blessing in this kind, as well as my having an ancestor of that Name, I call'd him Thomas.

31. August 18. The Goodness of God was manifested to us and to my little Dauter Mary in preserving her when She had Sadly wander'd away, and was a long time lost in the Swamp; and directing a Young Man (David Maynard, Jr.) to her Deliverance.

---

[4] Elias Parkman of Boston.

[5] Edward Hunting (Harvard 1725). *Sibley*, VII, 542–543.

[6] Reverend Nathaniel Appleton.

[7] Joseph Dorr of Mendon.

[8] John Prentice of Lancaster.

[9] Israel Loring.

[10] Samuel Barrett of Hopkinton.

[11] Ebenezer Roby (Harvard 1719), a physician of Sudbury. *Sibley*, VI, 336–339.

32. February 17, 1729/30. In my great Weakness, the Reverend Mr. Campbell[12] of Oxford visited me, and persuaded me to ride. We rode to Marlboro and then proceeded to Cambridge. My Wife also went with me but it was, above all, a kind and merciful God who sustain'd me. The Glory to His Name! The 19th Day was Fast at Westborough on my account.

N.B. The affectionate Regard which the Reverend Mr. Breck[13] show'd me in the Exercises at the Fast which was kept at Westboro on the foresaid occasion: in particular in his Sermon which was from that Text Phil. 2, 27. "For indeed he was sick" etc. Reverend Cushing[14] also assisted in the Fast.

33. Deliverance to my Wife when Travailing with my Second Dauter, September 20, 1731. On account of the Singular Love and Affection, and memberless kind Regards of my Wife's sister, Miss Lydia Champney, we Thought fit to call this Child by her name, Lydia.

### JULY, 1729[1]

8. I have warnings from God by my Infirmities, that I must remove from my Temporal Possessions (and I had them from God but for Temporal). This Clay Tabernacle I now inhabit Cracks and threatens me that it must Dissolve, 'tis but Earthenware, and it doth not Sound whole. A Little matter will dash it to pieces.

Now what do I know about any Right I have to an Eternal Inheritance, to a Building of God, an house not made with Hands Eternal in the Heavens, wherein I may Spend an Happy Immortality, Since I am upon the Move.

### SEPTEMBER 1729[1]

4. How Shall I best employ my Self to Day? It being the last Day of my 26th Year.

Answer 1. In Solemnly Praising God for his mercies throughout my Life, particularly in the Course of this Year.

2. In humbling my Self for my Sins especially those of this Year.

3. In preparing my Self for Tomorrow's Business. Reading over what I have heretofore done, and what others have transacted, on Such Dayes, etc.

All which may be well assisted (perhaps) by waiting upon the Exercises of the private Meeting at Mr. David Brighams to Day (when I am very much importun'd to be present.)

But (alas) the weakness of my Body, and the Confusion of my mind at Seeing So much Business to do, and So Slender Ability to accomplish it!

But besides, Providence calls me to Work for others, as well as for my Self to Day. I must attend to what may fit me there for, and then Return to my private Concerns. The Grace of God enable me, under my Infirmities, and magnifie His Power through my Weakness!

5. 1. Bless God for the Light and Liberties of This Morning, and petition Direction and assistance in Such an Observation of the Day as may be most for the Divine Glory, and my Souls Comfort.

2. Let the Exercises of the Family (although not formally or noticeably by others) contribute as much as may be to the Holy Business of this Day.

3. Thankfully review the Divine Mercie to me and mine through my Life past, particularly Such as we have receiv'd in the Course of this Year, and Solemnly offer unto God the Praise. Read and Sung Ps. 145 in Tate's Version.

4. Bewail my Iniquities before God.
   1. Sin, in General: its 1. Turpitude, Vileness, and Offensiveness especially to God most Holy and glorious
      2. Fatal Consequences.

2. In Particular:
   1. The Sin of my Nature, and thereby
      1. The Weakness and Darkness of my Intellectual Powers;
      2. The Perverseness and Corruptness of my Elective Powers.
   2. The Foolishness and wickedness of my Childhood and youth
      1. Falseness. Ps. 58, 3. Brother William, Mr. Fl. [?], Mr. L. [?].
      2. Thievishness, apples, corn.
   3. The Vainness, Impurity and Impiety of my Youth and more Mature age.
      1. The Vainness in  1. Dress
                          2. Company
                          3. Studies: Romances and Tales; Poems and Playes.
                          4. Waste of Time. Impertinence. Walking about Town, etc. See my Journals No. 1, 2, 3, 4, 5, 6.
      2. The Impurity.
         1. Heart uncleanness and adulterie, thro The Eye—Pictures, etc; The Ear—Songs, etc.
         2. Wantonness in Carriage and Actions in various Instances and Respecting which I have Great Cause Exceedingly to bewail.
      3. Impiety.
         1. Restraining Prayer sometimes.
         2. Superficial performance of that and other Duties and formal attendance upon ordinances, The Word, Sacraments, etc.
         3. Unaffectedness at Providences, Mercys—publick, private
            1. Public Calamities.
            2. Personal Sufferings.
            3. Domestic and Relative Evils, Deaths, Sickness, etc. My Father, Mother, etc., etc.
   4. Unfaithfullness of my whole Life unto
      1. God, under
         1. My Baptismal Covenant.
         2. My Covenant of September 15, 1719.
         3. My Profession Engagements, March 31, 1723
         4. My Marriage Covenants. July 7, 1724 and September 1, 1737.
         5. My Ordination Vows, October 28, 1724, O.S.
         6. My frequent, especially September 5, Pretences and daily Devotions (which are so many Engagements) to Walk with God.
         7. Special Providences, as
            1. Mercies: Deliverances and Recoveries, to me, my wife, children and other Relatives—and to my Friends.
            2. Afflictions. Sickness and pains: my own, my Wife's, my childrens.
      2. Man, unto
         1. Parents, Brothers, Sisters.
         2. Acquaintance and Friends.
         3. Christians in Communion with me.
         4. Wife
         5. Children and Servants.
         6. People of Westborough and other Congregations where I have preach'd.
         7. Neighbours.
   5. My Self, as to (1) My Outward, (2) and (3) Spiritual and Eternal Interests. My Unfaithfullness, Impiety, etc. of my more mature Life may be further set down in this form following.
      1. My Hypocrisie and Insincerity.
      2. My Slender, partial Obedience.

[12] John Campbell.
[13] Robert Breck of Marlborough.
[14] Job Cushing of Shrewsbury.

[1] All of the material for July 1729 is to be found in the Natalitia.

[1] All entries for Sept. 1729 are from the Natalitia.

3. Neglect of Divine Dealings with me.
4. Covetousness, Love of the World and Disrelish of Divine Things.
5. Disquietness, Discontent and Envying.
6. Slothfullness and Idleness. Unseasonable Sermonizing.
7. Forbearing to reprove Sin, through Fear, Favour.
8. Unsabbatical Behaviour.
9. Equivocating.
10. Eating and Drinking more than answer'd the Ends to be propos'd therein and what I count Exceeding Christian Laws therein.
11. Breaking out to angry Resentments.
12. Vain Glory, Self Conceit and Self Dependence.
13. Detractions.
14. Unbelief.

5. The Fifth Thing on this Day was that which next followeth, and which was in this Form.

5.[2] Whereas it hath pleased the Almighty Author of my Being and the God of my Life out of his abundant mercy and Grace, to permit my Lot in a Land of Gospel Light, my Birth of Religious Parents, my Dedication to Him Early by Baptism, and my Education not only in the Nurture and instruction of the Lord, but with some peculiar happy Circumstances, both to fit me for and Engage me to His Service and Glory. Since also I have openly profess'd my Self a Disciple of Christ and in a Sacred manner bound my Self to the Strict observance of His Divine Commands, and have been Moreover, with utmost Solemnity Consecrated and Set apart to Him and his peculiar work. To all which the Dispensations of his Providence of Grace have been added and conspir'd together to affect me with my indispensable obligations to Fidelity to Him. But inasmuch as by too many Evidences it appears that without the Special Restraints and Assistances of Divine Grace, my natural Corruption proves many times prevalent over all my Professions and Resolutions and even my most Sacred Ties; that I may do whatever in me lies for the [illegible] thereof, and that I may be the better defended against future Assaults and Temptations (Yet without Relying on any other Endeavours of Mine, but only upon the Mediation and Merits of my Blessed Lord Jesus Christ and the Aid of His Spirit) I would, as the best revealed Expedient, in Sacred Form Renew my Covenant with God and Solemnly Sign this Instrument. [N.B. The then design'd Instrument is that in page 2, but it was not drawn out till some time after this, though I now renew'd my Covenant Dedication.]

### NOVEMBER, 1729[1]

Westborough November 24, 1729.
A Solemn Covenant was drawn out fair and in all Seriousness (as I was able) sign'd and ratify'd before God. The Form was that in page 2.

### DECEMBER, 1729[1]

December 5, 1729. It is a Day of great Darkness and Distress with both me and my Family. My own Weakness and Infirmitys increasing daily upon me and troubles of my heart greatly enlarged by my Disorders mocking the force of all Medical methods with me hitherto. My Wife also, under much Indisposition and trouble with her Breast. The Children likewise afflicted with Cold and very peevish under their uneasinesses. But Especially Maro at the Point of Death. The waves and Billows roll and roar out of the Deeps. I would Cry: Lord hear my Voice! Let not the Water floods overflow us, neither let the Deep Swallow us up!

December 6. The Hand of God is still heavier upon us. Exceeding weak, low and faint, my Self, almost ready to lie down under my prevailing Infirmities. But when both my Flesh and Heart fail, God is still the Strength of my Heart, and my Portion for Ever. But Dark as it has been with us it is become much

[1] From the Natalitia.
[1] All entries for Dec. 1729 are from the Natalitia.
[2] This additional entry for Sept. 5, 1729 is also from the Natalitia.

Darker at or about the Sun setting. The Sun of Maro's Life Sat. The First Death in my Family! God enable me to See His Sovereign Mind, and Comport with his holy Will!

As my Servant is Summon'd to go before, So God only knows whether his Master is not Shortly to follow after; and so the former to prove as an Harbinger to the latter. O that the whole Family may be getting ready, in another Sort than ever heretofore! But Especially O that God would enable Me to Live apace, Seeing I am Dying apace; to give Diligance, to work with my might, and to stand Waiting all the few Dayes of my appointed time, till God Shall call; that when I hear the Summons, I may, with Serenity, Say, Speak Lord, thy Servant heareth, may Depart in Peace, and See the Salvation of God!

While God is Stripping me of Outward Enjoyments I humbly trust God will let me have more of Himself and bestow more of Spiritual, invaluable Blessings.

Every Comfort is that to us, that God makes it, and is so long with us as He pleases to Continue it.

### Conclusion of the Year 1729

It is Said in Psalm 55, 19. "Because they have no Changes, therefore they Fear not God." (By which it obviously appears to be intimated, that Changes are very usefull and proper, nay very needfull means to excite the Fear of God.) I would then, from these words, Infer 1. That they are to be well observ'd and esteem'd as they are Such excellent means of Grace and God is to be praised for them. 2. Such persons fall under a no less Severe, than just Reprehension, who, although they have Changes, yet fear not God, and 3. It is matter of Melancholly Consideration whom those that meet with many Changes, have notwithstanding, but Slender Effects wrought upon them, by So powerfull means and but little more (if any) of the Fear of God excited in them thereby.

### Reflections

I have pass'd through many Changes, Especially this Last Year has been a Year of Changes. I would Humbly and Devoutly take notice of the Hand of God in them. I would humbly acknowledge and revere the Sovereignty and Majesty, and adore and magnifie the Righteousness and Holiness, the Wisdom and Goodness of God therein. I would humbly submit and resign my Self to his Sovereign and all wise Disposal with Satisfaction, remembering that I am in my Faithfull Creator's and Compassionate Redeemer's Hands, and I would, with Religions Fear and Care, Enquire after the holy Ends and Designs of God in his Several Visitations; and would give my Self to all Endeavours (ζυν θεω) to answer the Divine Demands. But before I proceed any further I would Look back with Shame and Sorrow on the Provocations offered to God, to punish and afflict me, as He has, in the various Sufferings I have been brought into, and would with Regret and Grief Observe the but faint Influence I have permitted My Changes to have upon me, and that there are so few Signs of the true Fear of God in me. And Finally would Earnestly beseech God to accompany all his Methods with me, with his Almighty Grace, that they may not fail, hence forward, to produce both his own Glory and my Spiritual and Eternal Good. And Oh that the more and the Greater Changes I pass through the more I may fear, and glorifie God whom alone I am to acknowledge in them.

### JANUARY, 1730[1]

January 1. I would heartily bless God for carrying me through the great Difficulties, Infirmties and Sufferings of the Year Past, and vouchsafing me the Beginning of another. I would humble my Self for the Sins of the Year Past with the rest of my Life before. I would Humbly give my Self up to God and Solemnly Renew my Covenant Transactions with Him. I would Humbly refer and Comitt to him all the Events and accidents of my Sickness and Health, beseeching the Divine Pity, Support and Direction Still, and Finally, would Fervently Begg His Favour and Blessing this Year and all my Dayes on Earth, and Assistance to Discharge all Duty. And when Years and Dayes Shall finish

[1] From the Natalitia.

and when the Stream of Time shall be Swallow'd up in the Ocean of Eternity I may be Ever with the Lord. Through Jesus Christ alone, To whom be Glory forever. Amen.

### FEBRUARY, 1730[1]

February 19. This Day was observed at Westborough in a Religious Manner with Fasting and Prayer on the account of my remaining Infirmities. The Reverend Mr. Breck and the Reverend Mr. Cushing managed the Exercises. The former preach'd from those words in the Epistle to the Philippians 2, 27, For indeed he was Sick, etc. I was my Self at Cambridge and Endeavour'd to hold Communion with them. How I employ'd my Self is hinted in the Minutes in Loose Papers. O that God would hear and forgive and Do, for his own name's Sake!

### SEPTEMBER, 1730[1]

September 5. At Cambridge. Read Ps. 90 the Eve before. In the Morn Ps. 103 and 145. I was much affected with some Conversation with my Brother William on Spiritual Subjects. I was Earnestly Desirous that with finishing my 27th Year I might finish intirely my Course of Sin, that I might certainly take leave of the latter, as I do of the former, never to see anything of it more. And it was my passionate Request that if I never was yet Regenerated (as to my Grief I have not Evidence enough that I have been) This, This Day I may without fail be Born again, and This be my Glorious Birth Day to God!

I would 1. Bless God, for the Mercies of my whole Life, common and Signal, particularly this Years for upholding me through my many and Great Difficulties, weakness, etc., and bringing me to the return of this Day, through so many fears when my Life was So much being in Doubt. 2. I would Affect and humble my Self for my Sins, especially my September 5th. My Covenant Violations, etc. 3. I would humbly renew my Covenant Transactions with God. 4. I would study New and better Methods of Glorifying God. [This I propos'd for, and endeavoured to attend upon in the Forenoon]. [In The Afternoon what follows]. 5. I would devoutly committ the remainder of my Life to the providences and grace of God, and the Conduct of his good Spirits. 6. I would meditate on the Frailty and uncertainty of human Life. At Noon I read Isaiah 55 and made a Recollection of Solemn Repetition of my Covenant, and P.M. I read Ps. 39.

[I would perform none of these formalities as if I would thereby Merit anything before the Lord, but only in hopes they maybe some way beneficial to fix and excite and quicken my wandering, Vain heart].

On the above mention'd Day I resolv'd that I would, by Divine Assistance, Endeavour from this time forward 1. To make a great Business, a solemn, Set, Separated, Sanctify'd undiverted Business of Prayer; in Praying to Pray; to watch unto Prayer, and as much as I can to Delight in Prayer; 2. To make every part of my Life as directly to the purpose of Life as possible; 3. As far as possible to do some Good every where and in Every Thing; 4. To watch against Formalities and ostentatiousness, and against relying upon Good Works. 5. To enquire diligently after the Great Designs of God in his Severe Dispensations towards me, in his Severe Inflictions on my Body, and of long Continuance, and carefully to attend to answer them, as far as God shall enable me.

### SEPTEMBER, 1731[1]

September 5. At Westborough. Since my Birth Day fell out this Year on the Sabbath (as the Time of my Birth itself was, and My first Solemn Dedication by Baptism the Same Day in the afternoon) I turn'd the Course of my wonted public Exercises in some Measure to suit the Season with me, seeing my mind would be unavoidably employ'd much this way.

In my own retir'd Devotions I offer'd Thanks to God for the return of this Day, and Specially for the Divine Goodness in the

Course of this Year past in Vouchsafing me Such Measures of Recovery and Strength for the Divine Service; humbled my Self as I could for my innumerable Transgressions, the Sin of my Nature and the Vanity and impurity of my Childhood and Youth; and humbly Devoted my Self wholly to God and Committed my Self to Him in Covenant. Read Ps. 103 and then proceeded to the Family and Public Offices. I preach'd on Ps. 51, 10. I may Lament before God my Coldness, unhumbledness, my undedicatedness to God Seeing I am under So peculiar and unspeakable Obligations!

### SEPTEMBER, 1732[1]

September 5. At Westborough. Besides enlarging my Devotions according to my Custom on this Day, (in Praises for the Divine Mercies through my Life and particularly through this Year past, in reviewing my Life and humbling my Self for my past iniquitys, Vanitys, impuritys and impietys, and reading Such suitable passages of the Sacred Scriptures as Ps. 145, Dan. 9, a.m., Ps. 103 and Job 14, p.m.), I made it considerably my Business to try and prove my Self whether I have indeed had a work of Grace Savingly wrought in my heart—in answer to the Following Question.

Question. What are the Signs of Conversion, and are they to be found in me? (And I esteem it a proper Enquiry, on my Natural Birth Day, What I may be able to find of my Spiritual Birth unto God.)

Answer. 1. Sign. Ps. 18, 23. I was upright before him, for I kept my Self from my own Iniquity. Do I?

2 Sign. 2 Cor. 5, 17. If any man be in Christ he is a new Creature. Am I? Have I experienc'd this?

3 Sign. Gal. 5, 24. He that is Christ's hath Crucifyed the Flesh, with the Affections and Lusts. Have I?

4 Sign. Rom. 8, 9. If any man have not the Spirit of Christ, he is none of His. Have I the Spirit of Christ?

N.B. Mr. Guthrys Trial of a Saving Interest in Christ[2] of great use.

N.B. Interruption by a woman under great Trouble of mind. Her name was Crouch,[3] wife of William Crouch of Shrewsbury.

N.B. An Earthquake just about (or a little after) Noon.

### SEPTEMBER, 1733[1]

September 5. Westborough. See my Almanack for this Day. The Ordination of Mr. William Hobby at Reading (at which Solemnity I chose to be present) was manag'd with great Devotion by the principal Persons of the Council, who were ordainers. Mr. Appleton's[2] Sermon (on 2 Tim. 2, 21) was especially very instructing and moving, And I hope was not without Some good quickening Influence upon Me.

But I was not able to keep my Self through the whole (nor through so considerable part) of the Day, as I propos'd and hop'd for, upon my own particular Case—The Vanity of Company, Strangers, Old Friends, etc.; my being much a stranger in the place, and riding off again the Same Day, extreamly and unavoidably diverted me.

### SEPTEMBER, 1734[1]

September 5. Westborough. 1. Thanksgiving, general particular for the year past. 2. Confession, general, particular for the year past. Coldness and withdraws from God. Hypocriticalness and formalness. 3. Petition. 4. Renewed Dedication. 5. Serious purposes. 6. Before Each, Contemplation.

---

[1] From the Natalitia.
[2] William Guthrie, Scottish Presbyterian divine, published *The Christian's Great Interest* (c. 1658), which appeared in numerous later editions.
[3] Mrs. Hannah Croutch.

[1] From the Natalitia.
[2] Reverend Nathaniel Appleton of Cambridge.

[1] From the Natalitia. Although headings of pages of Parkman's birthday for the years 1736 through 1742 appear in the Natalitia, he recorded no observations.

---

[1] From the Natalitia.

[1] From the Natalitia.

## FEBRUARY, 1737[1]

by the means thereof. That we may be awares and have our Eyes open our minds apprehensive now, and not have the first thorow sense of those Things in the midst of the unhappy Experience of them.

14. I put off my Journey by means that it was Town Meeting.

15. I rode to Concord. Mr. Flagg[2] of Grafton my Company, from Biglo's in Marlboro. Mr. Whiting[3] and his wife had rid out. Captain Joseph Buckley Spent the evening with us. I had conversation an hour or two with Mrs. Israel Whiting, lodged here.

16. Lieutenant Trowbridge[4] came to Mr. Whiting's and was my Company to Watertown. Lodged at Father Champney's[5] at Cambridge.

17. Rode to Boston. My mother still in a measure of Comfort through the Blessing of God. I could not be seasonable for lecture. N.B. Captain Foot[6] and Sister Elizabeth[7] and Mrs. Mary Tilestone took a ride with me in a double Slay at evening to Captain Sharp's[8] at Brookline, and Brother Elias[9] came to us upon my Horse, after supper there. At 10 o'clock they returned in the Slay but I tarried. N.B. The discovery of my Inclinations to Captain Sharp and to Madame. By their urgent Persuasions I tarried and lodged there. N.B. Mrs. Susanna Sharp.[10]

18. I rode to Father Champney's and thence to Westborough. N.B. Mr. Tilestone and Captain William Roby of Boston my Company from Watertown to Sudbury.

19. Engaged in my preparations. N.B. I cast a handful or two of Salt into my Pump.

20. On Luke 16, 13. P.M. repeated Sermon on Heb. 12, 1. At evening visited Mr. Stephen Fay[11] who was very low etc.

21. The small matter of Salt which I cast into my Pump on the 19th wonderfully loosened the Spire though it had been frozen for a long time (See Downs') and to our Joy and Pleasure had the use of the Pump again. Very pleasant weather.

22. A number of Hands came to get wood. Mr. Grout[12] with his Team, Mr. Tainter[13] with his and Mr. Harrington[14] with his, Mr. Grow,[15] Daniel Hardy, Daniel Forbush,[16] Elias Rice, Noah Rice,[17] James Fay,[18] James Bowman, Zebulon Rice, Solomon Rice, John Rogers, Timothy Warren, Jonathan Forbush, Junior, Thomas Winchester, David Baverick, Ebenezer Nurse, Simon Tainter, junior and Samuel Bumpso.

23. Very stormy. Rain and Wind, especially very Windy in the Night. N.B. Sister Hicks[19] another son, born a little before night.

24. Had sent to Mr. Prentice[20] of Grafton and very much depended upon him to preach my Lecture, but he failed. I repeated Sermon on Heb. 7, 25. A very cold day—very slippery—few at Lecture. Heard by Cousen Winchester that Sister Ruth Champney at Cambridge was sick.

25. A very cold day again. Ensign Ward of Marlborough here to obtain my Evidence of what the Association which met at Framingham October 16, 1733 judged concerning Mr. Kent.[21] At eve I gave my Testimony, confirmed by an Oath before Justice Keyes.[22] Ensign Ward being there present.

26. At eve came Dr. Thyery but he would go and lodge at Ensign Maynard's.

27. A.M. on 2 Cor. 13, 14. Sacrament. Dr. Thyery and Deacon Fay and his wife dind with me. P.M. on Mat. 7, 3, 4, 5. Dr. Thyery at eve, but was called away to visit Stephen Fay.

28. The weather was very Raw Cold. The Wind was north and very bleak. I visited Mr. Beeman's[23] Family and Mr. David Brigham. The Dauter of the former and the Wife of the Latter were ill.

Monsieur Thyery came to my house P.M. and I had some Expectations of Mr. Prentice of Grafton, and his wife to visit me, but they did not come. The Doctor spent the evening and good part of the night with me, but presently after he got to Bed came Simon Tainter, Junior upon a most urgent message from Stephen Fay, to have the Doctor visit him forthwith. Howbeit he would not rise till he had taken several naps. I did not get to bed till past three o'clock. N.B. Town Meeting to add to the Seats in Meeting House.

## MARCH, 1737

1. It had been very Icy and now by a snow upon the Ice and it was very Slippery and Troublesome riding. I rode to Mr. Cook's[1] to fix my Horse. Called at Captain Forbush's.[2]

2. Sister Lydia rode down to Cambridge with me. N.B. We set out somewhat before 10 A.M., rode double, yet got to Father Champney's at Cambridge promptly at 5 P.M. N.B. Mr. John Jarvis was returning from his journey to Marlborough, whither he had been to wait upon Mrs. Hannah Breck,[3] who made a visit yesterday to her sister Mrs. Gott[4] in her illness.

From Father Champney's I rode to Roxbury, called at Mr. Increase Sumner's. Thence I rode to Boston, waited upon my mother, and then went and Supped at Brother Elias's. N.B. Mr. Bowman the wharfinger and his wife at Supper with us. My Horse sent to his Stables. Lodged at Brother Elias's.

3. Mr. Mather[5] Lectured on [blank] against Covetousness. Dined at Brother Samuel's.[6] P.M. visited Mrs. Pierpont,[7] Mrs. Hannah being at Marlborough. Mr. Pierpont also had taken a Journey to New Haven. Towards night I rode over to Roxbury. N.B. Mrs. Sumner[8] ill. I proceeded to Captain Sharp's.[9] By Captain Sharp's strong Solicitation I tarried all night. N.B. Mrs. Susan not very willing to go so far in the Country as Westborough, etc., etc., etc.

4. I rode to Father Champney's. Thence I went over to the Town. N.B. Mr. Jonathan Monnef, Junior at Father Champney's. I returned P.M. from Town and went again to Captain Sharp's. N.B. Captain Sharp and Madame gone to the Funeral of a Relative at Roxbury. I tarried whilst the Captain and his Spouse came home. Arguments which be fruitless with Mrs. Susan. I returned to Father Champney's between 8 and 9 in the Evening.

[1] The original of the diary from Sept. 1728 to Jan. 1740 has evidently been lost. Fortunately a portion of this (February 1737 to November 1737) was published by the Westborough Historical Society in *The Diary of Ebenezer Parkman* . . . , ed. by Harriette M. Forbes (Westborough, 1899). The present editor has been completely dependent upon the transcription of Mrs. Forbes, and only minor changes of form in her text have been made. This has meant, essentially, writing out abbreviated words as has usually been done throughout the diary. Some material from Mrs. Forbes' notes has been incorporated in this work, and numerous other references added.

[2] Eleazer Flagg.

[3] Reverend John Whiting of Concord.

[4] William Trowbridge of Newton, selectman and deacon.

[5] Father of Parkman's first wife, Mary Champney, who died Jan. 29, 1735/6.

[6] Probably Captain John Foote of Amesbury, Mass.

[7] Mrs. Elias Parkman.

[8] A prominent and wealthy resident of Brookline.

[9] Elias Parkman of Boston.

[10] The daughter of Captain Robert Sharp whose hand in marriage Reverend Parkman was seeking.

[11] The son of Captain John Fay. He survived this illness and later became a prominent citizen of Hardwick, Mass. Johnson, *Fay Family Tree*, pp. 26–27.

[12] Joseph Grout.

[13] Deacon Simon Tainter.

[14] Samuel Harrington.

[15] Samuel Grow.

[16] Son of Deacon Jonathan Forbush.

[17] Son of Thomas Rice.

[18] Son of Captain John Fay.

[19] Rebecca (Champney) Hicks, Parkman's first wife's sister.

[20] Reverend Solomon Prentice (Harvard 1727), minister of Grafton, 1731–1747. *Sibley*, VIII, 248–257.

[21] Benjamin Kent (Harvard 1727), minister at Marlborough, 1733 to 1735 was dismissed and tried as a heretic.

[22] Captain John Keyes of Shrewsbury.

[23] Ebenezer Beeman of Westborough.

[1] Cornelius Cook, the blacksmith of Westborough.

[2] Samuel Forbush.

[3] The daughter of the late Reverend Robert Breck of Marlborough who married Reverend Parkman of Westborough, Sept. 1, 1737.

[4] Sarah Breck, also a daughter of the Reverend Breck, married Dr. Benjamin Gott of Marlborough in 1728.

[5] Reverend Samuel Mather of the Old North Church, Boston.

[6] Samuel Parkman of Boston.

[7] Mary, the widow of Reverend James Pierpont (Harvard 1681) of New Haven. She was the daughter of Reverend Samuel Hooker of Farmington, Conn., and the granddaughter of Reverend Thomas Hooker, the first minister of Hartford. Parkman was very fond of Mrs. Pierpont and she appears in the diary numerous times. After her death, Nov. 1, 1740, Parkman wrote a long eulogy which he intended to publish but did not. The manuscript is in the library of the American Antiquarian Society. See Sibley, III, 222–230.

[8] Mrs. Increase Sumner.

[9] In Brookline.

5. Sister Lydia was willing to go up again to Westborough with me if the weather would allow. Upon her mentioning her carrying up some other Coloured clothes than her black, and our putting off our Mourning it (by Degrees) moved me very much and my Passions flowed almost beyond Controll, till I was obliged to retire away. Every matter most exceeding Sorrowful to me. The weather was very discouraging to Sister Lydia's Design, nor could she in prudence venture though I tarryed for her till 11 when I set out. It rained and I had a very wet troublesome Journey. I rode over the new Bridge in Sudbury and went to Captain Clark's[10] of Framingham. The Waters flow abundantly, Ice rotts away, the Snow melts again, the Rain beats and the Storm strong. Captain Clark very urgent to have me stay, but I was resolute to get as far as I could. I called at Mr. Stone's[11] at Southborough, and about nine at night reached home. *D.O.M. Gratia.*

6. Repeated Sermon on Acts 2, 37, 38. Dr. Thyery at meeting.

7. Dr. Thyery visited me and dind with me. I prayed with the Town before their Elections. Mr. Prentice of Grafton visited me, and note well that the Day I went from home last week both he and his wife came to see me, just after we were gone. A very fine pleasant Day.

8. Cloudy. Some Snow. N.B. Many of the People gone to Sudbury about Housetonic Rights.[12]

9. The water everywhere exceeding high. Visit Mr. Sam Fay, and Stephen Fay.

10. The Winds more than ordinarily violent. A Barn was blown down in Framingham. A man narrowly escaped drowning at Framingham River. The water being so deep, the Current so strong and the Winds so impetuous.

11. Divers Neighbours (Mr. Maynard, Mr. Grout, and Mr. Charles Rice), here in the Evening. Catechizing, but only 4 boys, besides my own. No catechizing P.M. No children came.

12. [No entry].

13. A.M. on Matt. 7, 6 and P.M. repeated Sermon 46 being the 4th on Act 2, 37, 38.

14. I visited Stephen Fay, Captain Fay and old Mr. Rice.[13] David went away.

15. Early in the morning to Mr. Whipples,[14] etc. At noon I was extremely indisposed. Faint etc. Storm, snow. P.M. Dr. Thyery was here, I grew better. D.G.

16. *Dies. Humill. and Proc. Secret.* See my own Memoirs. At eve, Mr. Whipple. N.B. An ewe that was gored very ill—fine pleasant Day. Roads extremely hollow. Some of the oldest persons declare they scarce ever knew the Earth to have been so frozen as this winter.

17. A.M. Storm of snow. Rain. Trouble with my sick ewe. Mr. Whipple to Boston.

18. P.M. I rode to Marlborough to Colonel Wood's.[15] Eve at Dr. Gott's.[16] Mrs. Gott had been very ill, but is recovering. Mrs. Hannah Breck with her, but I spent my time with the men, scil. the Doctor, Colonel, and Mr. Daniel Steward.[17] Late in the Evening Deacon Woods[18] came to request me to visit a young woman at his House (Dauter of Mr. Samuel Stow)[19] apprehended to be at the Point of Death. I went, prayed with her etc. I lodged at Colonel Wood's.

19. A.M. To Dr. Gott's but a short space with Mrs. Hannah.[20] At my Request, she had (she assured me) burnt my Letters,

Poems etc. P.M. Funeral of Captain Eleazer How.[21] Captain Brigham[22] informed of the Death of President Wadsworth,[23] the Night before last, also lately Part of Northampton Meeting-House fell and wounded many, in time of Divine Service, and the Burning of Young Colonel Chandler's[24] House at Woodstock, and three persons consumed in it, scil., Mrs. Wright, her son and a man who was asleep with him. I returned home. At eve, Dr. Thiery at my house in great Urgency going to Boston for Drugs, to relieve Stephen Fay, no persuading him to the Contrary altho the Roads are extreme Bad, the night Dark etc. N.B. A piece of Cotton Linnen of 12 yards from Mr. Caruths.

20. On Matt. 7, 7, 8. P.M. on Matt. 7, 9, 10, 11.

21. I visited Stephen Fay—was at the Captain's, find Thyery is not a man of Truth or Probity. At Cousin Winchester's etc.

22. Rain and Cloudy. Visited old Mr. Ward's[25] Family, reckoned with Mr. Josiah Newton. Rainy—came home in the Night and in the Rain.

23. Cold notherly wind. P.M. visited old David Monanaow,[26] Indian, he tells me he was 104 last Indian Harvest. Says the name of Boston was not Shawmut but Shanwawmuck. Chauncy Pond was called Nawgawwoomcom and Marlborough, [blank]. N.B. Mr. Seth Rice[27] here about this time to discourse with me on the life of his sister Thankful. I visited Mr. David Brigham's[28] family, and old Captain Byles.[29]

24. Froze hard again last night. Cold windy day.

25. I rode to Marlborough, din'd with Mr. Hovey at Mm. Madame Fish's. Spent the afternoon at Dr. Gott's—was at the Colonel's, but returned to Doctor's. Mr. Hovey there with a Bass Viol. N.B. Mrs. Hannah Breck at the Doctor's still. Our conversation of a piece with what it used to be. I mark her admirable Conduct, her Prudence and wisdom, her good manners and her distinguishing Respectfulness to me which accompany her Denyals. After it grew late in the Evening, I rode home to Westborough, through the Dark and the Dirt, but cheerfully and comfortably (comparatively). N.B. My Family all abed.

26. I had appointed to ride to Grafton in order to changing with Mr. Prentice tomorrow, but it proved so very Rainy all day that it was unpracticable.

27. Fair and pleasant Day. Matt. 7, 12 A.M., but P.M. repeated Sermon II, Acts 2, 37, 38. N.B. Mr. Silas Brigham[30] and Mr. Eleazer Pratt[31] of Shrewsbury had desired me to baptize their Children. Accordingly, in my manner I desired the Children might be brought forth to Baptism. But only one appeared. I looked about till I conceived that something had befallen the other or those concerned with it. I proceeded and baptized Mr. Pratt's (which was the Child that was brought) when the prayers were over we proceeded to the last Singing; in the Time of the last Singing Mr. Brigham and his Child came in. After the Blessing and when I was down in the Alley going out, Mr. Brigham asked me whether his child could not be baptized. I answered, it could not now. My Reasons are these. Besides that, when I am spent with the foregoing Services, it is too much to expect me to repeat over them again. Besides that, such a custom indulged would involve us in great irregularity and Difficulty, but this administration for my known Friends would have forced me to make it a custom, and besides the impatience of many of the Congregation to get away home, being they live 4, 5 or 6

[10] Isaac Clark.

[11] Reverend Nathan Stone (Harvard 1726), first minister of Southborough, 1730–1781. *Sibley*, VIII, 99–105.

[12] The development of Houssatonnuc townships was a matter of interest to numerous people in central Massachusetts. Reverend Parkman later purchased a share in the area that became Sheffield.

[13] Thomas Rice, an original settler of Westborough.

[14] Francis Whipple of Westborough.

[15] Colonel Benjamin Woods.

[16] Benjamin Gott of Marlborough.

[17] Daniel Stewart of Marlborough.

[18] There was no Deacon Woods in Marlborough at this time. James Woods was elected in 1741 and served many years.

[19] Mary Stow died March 20, 1737.

[20] Hannah Breck of Marlborough whom the Rev. Parkman was courting.

[21] Of Marlborough. The commander of a company of militia.

[22] Nathan Brigham of Marlborough.

[23] President Benjamin Wadsworth of Harvard College.

[24] Lieutenant-Colonel Thomas Chandler, Woodstock's first representative to the General Assembly of Conn. Clarence W. Bowen, *Woodstock An Historical Sketch* (New York, 1886), p. 47.

[25] Probably Thomas Ward, an original settler of Westborough.

[26] Sometimes spelled Munnanaw and Munnanaow. He fought with King Philip but afterwards returned to his home in Marlborough.

[27] Seth Rice and his sister Thankful were 2 of the children of Edmund Rice, an original settler of Westborough.

[28] One of Parkman's neighbors.

[29] Captain Joseph Byles of Westborough.

[30] Of Westborough. The child was Jemima, born 4 days before. On April 3, 1737 the child was baptized by Reverend Prentice of Grafton.

[31] Eleazer and Ruhamah Pratt lived in a part of Shrewsbury later added to Westborough. Their child, Sarah, was six months old.

miles off. Besides those Reasons, I would urge that is was so very sudden upon me that I could not judge which way I could vindicate it if I should proceed. Again, by the suddenness I was too much confused to have my Power at command to perform the Devotions; nor was I furnished therefor (Eccl. 5, 1, 2). So that it would have been nothing short of horrible Presumption for me to have done it. Lydia Cutting not well.

28. Lydia[32] worse, having a bad Ague in her face and it threw her wholly by; but it was so ordered in Providence, that Deborah Ward came to see us and she served us.

Adjournment of Town Meeting. N.B. Brother Hicks[33] had been chosen Constable, but gets off by virtue of a Commission to be Deputy Sheriff. (David Baverick diets here.)

29. Very Rainy. Lydia worse, considerable Fever. Benjamin How with David at his work and din'd with us. Neither of them to be persuaded to go for Dr. Gott for Lydia. Jonathan Rogers came to go, but we did not send.

30. Lydia somewhat better, very fine weather.

31. Publick Fast. I preached on Isa. 1, 9. N.B. Mr. Abraham Amsden[34] of Marlborough here to desire me to attend the Funeral of his Brother Thomas' only Son,[35] a youth near 21, and very hopeful, who died after a short illness of but a few Days. O that I and that the people of Westborough, at least some of them might be of that small Remnant which God has left of truely Godly Ones! and O that we might have Grace to Demean and to acquit ourselves as such; and that it might please God to keep off His Judgments that this Land may not be made as Sodom or like unto Gomorrah, but that the Divine Mercy might be afforded to us as we need it and that Glory may yet Dwell in our Land!

### APRIL, 1737

1. I rode down to Marlborough to the Funeral of Joseph Amsden's. Many youth present and seem to be affected. O that there might be abiding impression on their souls! and upon all of us. This is the second death in that near Neighbourhood of youth in Flower and Glory within a very little while. N.B. This Joseph Amsden was one of the Bearers of the other, scil, the young woman that Dyed at Deacon James Wood's on the 19th of last month. After Burial I returned to Captain Amsden's to afford him what consolation I could under his melancholy circumstances. N.B. Colonel Woods with me. N.B. Captain Nathan Brigham gave further accounts of the Fury of the Mob at Boston—assaulting the Town House etc. At Eve, I was at Dr. Gotts, Mrs. Hannah was thought to be gone up to Mr. Week's[1] or Captain Williams,[2] with design to lodge there, but she returned to the Doctors. And she gave me her Company till it was very late. Her Conversation was very Friendly, and with divers expressions of Singular and Peculiar Regard. Memorandum. Oscul. But she cannot yield to being a step mother. I lodged there, and with great satisfaction and Composure.

Memorandum. Ebenezer[3] has begun to learn his 2. Accidence and now makes a Business of it.

### SEPTEMBER, 1737

[blank] which were upon their journey to Connecticut came to see us, dind with us and prevented us (although Sister Lydia and Mrs. Bekky were gone already as Earnest of our Going) till so late in the P.M., then the Rain coming also that we were utterly disappointed.

21. We rode to Cousen Winchester,[1] but they being gone and

their neighbours also to Worcester, we struck along up to Mr. Prentice's at Grafton. N.B. Their son Nathaniel's finger had been wounded, the Top of one of his Fingers being cut off. N.B. Mrs. Sartel[2] of Groton here. Called at Captain Fay's as we returned home in evening.

22. Visited Captain Eager's[3] wife who had been some time sick.

23. John Clung[4] so urgent for his money (because of his journey to Pennsylvania) that I was obliged to ride about to gather it, till I succeeded at Treasurer Newton's.

24. Message from John Hamilton[5] under condemnation for Burglary requesting that I would visit him. N.B. Lydia sick and my wife[6] burthened with the Business of the Family. N.B. Fire raging in the Bushes on the west side of Powder Hill, drie by the Drought and the Frost and the Wind very high. Brother Hicks alone there, till I assisted him, and we succeeded. D.G.

25. Mr. Pierpont came to us this morning, having come from Boston but a little before sunset last evening. N.B. News that the vessel in which his goods were had struck upon Martha's Vineyard, but had got off again. He (as he can) pursues his journey to see in what condition they are at New Haven. A.M. I repeated on 1 Chron. 26, 9. P.M. I preached on 1 Pet. 3, 7.

26. Mr. Pierpont and his wife left us. I with my wife accompanied them to Shrewsbury. I still continued with them as far as Worcester and dined with them at Captain Howard's. P.M. having taken leave of those Excellent Friends, I rode to Mr. Burr's,[7] not finding him at home, I hastened to the Prison to see the Criminal. Among other Questions, I asked him his true Name? He answered Hugh Henderson. He acquainted me with his Birth and Baptism etc. He was much concerned and distressed about his state, and ready to confess himself a great Sinner, etc. I prayed with him. He requested I would come and see him again. I hastened to Shrewsbury and with my wife, returned in the evening. N.B. John McClung took leave of us.

27. We took up our Flax. We supp'd at Brother Hicks's.

28. I was much indisposed with Headache.

29. Lectured on 1 Sam. 15, 22. At eve Mr. Jarvis came from Boston.

30. [No entry].

### OCTOBER, 1737

1. [No entry].

2. Sacrament. Ps. 63, 8. Repeated on Is. 53, 1. Patience Forbush[1] came again.

3. Catechized at the Meeting House. Judge Dudley[2] on his return from Springfield made us a visit, and dind with us. Lydia Cutting left us.

4. Mr. Jarvis, Sister Lydia[3] and I rode to Cambridge. Mrs. Susé Champney[4] there. Mr. Jarvis lodged with me at Father Champney's.[5] N.B. I rode down to Mr. Dana's[6] Tavern about my Wife's Trunk.

5. Early this morning we rode to Mr. Dana's again, and saw the Trunk in good order, in the Team to be transported up, and then we proceeded to Boston. Dined at Brother Elias's. My honored Mother in good health. D.G. I returned to Cambridge. Found Mrs. Susé Champney there still.

---

[32] Lydia Champney, the sister of Parkman's first wife.

[33] John Hicks, Parkman's brother-in-law by his first marriage.

[34] Abraham and Thomas, as well as Captain Isaac, were sons of Isaac Amsden, an early resident of Marlborough.

[35] Joseph, who had died the day before.

[1] Supply Weeks of Marlborough.

[2] Captain Abraham Williams of Marlborough married Elizabeth Breck, sister of Hannah Breck.

[3] Parkman's first son, born Aug. 20, 1727.

[1] Elizabeth Champney, cousin of Parkman's first wife, was the second wife of Benjamin Winchester of Framingham.

[2] Probably a relative of Sarah Sartele (Sartell or Sawtell) who married Reverend Solomon Prentice of Grafton in 1732.

[3] James Eager of Westborough.

[4] Should be McClung.

[5] Otherwise known as Hugh Henderson, at that time in jail in Worcester awaiting execution.

[6] On Sept. 1, 1737, Hannah Breck, daughter of the late Reverend Robert Breck of Marlborough became Ebenezer Parkman's second wife. Hannah was 21, some 13 years younger than Reverend Ebenezer. She bore him 11 children and survived him nineteen years. She died in 1801 at the age of 81.

[7] Reverend Isaac Burr of Worcester.

[1] Daughter of Deacon Jonathan Forbush of Westborough.

[2] Paul Dudley (Harvard 1690), later Chief Justice of Massachusetts. Sibley, IV, 42–54.

[3] Lydia Champney.

[4] Susanna Champney, cousin of the first Mrs. Parkman.

[5] Samuel Champney, Sr., father of Parkman's first wife.

[6] Jonathan Dana kept a tavern near the center of Brookline.

6. N.B. I set out from Cambridge before Day—got to Harrington's before sun rising from there set out at sunrise, but did not get up to Westborough till nigh one. Visited Hannah Bond, who lay sick at Captain Forbush[7] After that dind at Home. Young men came to gather my Corn. Set them to work.

Went to the private meeting at Mr. Townsend's[8] and preached on 2 Pet. 1, 10. Visited Hannah Bond again. About 18 or 20 hands husked out all my Corn. N.B. In my absence Winter Apples gathered in.

7. Mr. John Pratt brought home my cyder which he had made.

8. Mr. Pratt brought home the remainder of my cyder. Susa Cutting came.

9. I repeated my Sermon IV upon Is. 53, 1 from John 10, 26. P.M. Sermon 11 on 1 Sam. 15, 22 from Ps. 40, 6, 8.

10. Visited Mrs. Dantforth[9] who is in a languishing state. Was also at Mr. Hayward's[10] and at Mr. Lock's.[11]

11. Visited Mrs. Rogers[12] who is sick, Hannah Bond and old Mrs. Pratt.[13] N.B. overtook some Travellers on Foot with their Muskets: one of them very unmannerly and saucy. P.M. Mr. Tozier[14] and his wife here. Old Mr. Rice[15] visited us. John McClung here.

12. I went to Worcester to see Hugh Henderson, found him in much the same distressed state that I left him in, but I hope more knowing and acquainted with his Condition and with his Duty. N.B. Mr. Burr at the Goal with me. I prayed with him, a multitude attending. He earnestly desired me to see him again and wishes over and over that I would preach to him.

N.B. When I called at Mr. Cushing's[16] as I went up, Colonel Woods was there, on his return from Rutland. As I returned in the evening, there rose a storm of Lightening and Rain. Mr. Lock came and carried in Corn.

13. John McClung (who lodged here last night) carried in more of the Corn from the Barn. Paid John the whole and he bid farewell. At evening Brother Hicks helped in more Corn.

14. Jonathan Rogers got in Pumpkins, and the remainder of the Corn.

15. Noah How helped in with Turnips and some of the Potatoes. At eve old Mr. Rice, Mr. Jarvis came up.

16. Mat. 3, 1-4. John 16, 8. N.B. I was called away between 8 and 9 in the morning to see old Captain Byles, who was very bad with his Throat and at night I visited him again. N.B. The Congregation disturbed P.M. by the burning of Mr. David Brigham's House but when people gathered in again, and were composed, I went on with the rest of my sermon. A very sorrowful Providence! a great Loss! but I trust them and all of us to profit by it, that our Hearts may be taken off from temporal transitory Enjoyments.

17. Rainy. Various Company all day and at Evening. N.B. Mr. James Fay dind with us. N.B. Mr. Wheeler[17] distressed in Conscience for Hugh Henderson. Captain Williams from Marlboro.

18. Visited Captain Byles who is grown exceeding bad again. Visited the wife of William Rogers, Junior and proceeded to Mr. Brigham's to see their Desolations. A Sorrowful Sight! I desire heartily to sympathize. Returned to Captain Byles. He dyed this evening. N.B. Mr. Jarvis went to Boston in the morning. N.B. Mr. Jonathan Forbes[18] at my house in the Evening and after him Messers. Edward and Benjamin Goddard.[19]

19. Mr. Brigham's son David fetched away divers things which we lent them in their necessity. Nathan Maynard P.M. digging Potatoes.

20. Funeral of Captain Joseph Byles. My Spouse, Mrs. Richard Burrough and my Dauter Molly all there with me. The deceased was a bright example of Diligence and Industry in his calling, Constancy at the House of God, diligent attention to the Worship and Word preached, Truth and Faithfulness to his word and exact Honesty in his Trading. To which add a singularly manly Heroic Spirit. Visited old Mrs. Pratt at Eve. Captain Eager came home with us.

21. Closely engaged in my preparations. At eve Brother William Parkman came from the Council at Concord, which had voted Mr. Whiting[20] unfit to sustain the holy ministry and advised the church of Concord to dismiss him, which they complied with. N.B. Mr. Francis Pierce here—finished with him about his Boards. N.B. My Brother left us. Dr. Gott called in, P.M. I rode to Shrewsbury and met with Mr. Burr at Mr. Cushing's. I proceeded to Worcester and stopped at the Goal at the Grates to speak with the Prisoner and to put him in mind of the preparations needful for him to make in order to keeping his Last Sabbath. I lodged at Mr. Burr's.

23. Early in the morning began to write my address to the Prisoner. A.M. on Eccl. 11, 9, a crowded assembly, poor Hugh Henderson present. P.M. on Job 3, 36. A very great congregation, it being in their apprehension the last Sabbath Sermon the poor Criminal is to hear. At evening called at Mr. Eaton's[21] and at the Sherrif's, who went with me to the Prison. I interrogated the Prisoner what was the occasion of his coming to this country—whether he had discovered and acknowledged all that was fit and proper for him to reveal? Whether he had any confederates? A great number flocked in the Goal when at his Request I prayed with him. I left him between 8 and 9. By that I went to Mr. Cushing's where I intended to lodge. They were all in Bed wherefore, though cold, I proceeded home to my own House. N.B. Mr. Jarvis came up last night in a chair.

24. Mr. Burr left us early in the morning. P.M. Mr. Jarvis, my wife, Mrs. Bekky and I rode to the Great Pond to Captain Warren's[22] and Captain Forbush's. N.B. Supped at Captain Forbush's.

25. Mr. Jarvis and Mrs. Bekky Burough left us. I rode to Hopkinton Association. All that came besides were Mr. Nathan Stone and Mr. Solomon Prentice. Mr. Barrett[23] concio on 1 Pet. 4, 11. If any man speaketh.

26. Public Lecture by Mr. Solomon Prentice on Job 12, 35. First part. N.B. I had a very Sudden Turn of Sharp Pain in my Side after Dinner, but through Mercy, I recovered.

Mr. Prentice went home with me and lodged at our House.

27. Rode with Mr. Prentice to Grafton and preached his Lecture on Jude 10, 21. Returned to Westboro at night. N.B. The Governor has reprieved Hugh Henderson for a month at the request of Mr. Burr and Mr. Prentice.

28. Ah! what sad grounds of Severe Reflection upon myself for my wretched negligence and unfaithfulness! How great need of renewing and fixing my Resolutions of Reformation. But especially of crying unto God for pardon of what is past and Grace to assist and quicken me henceforward!

29. [No entry].

30. All day on Job, 3, 36. Rain A.M. High winds at even. N.B. Mr. Chamberlain[24] din'd with us.

### NOVEMBER, 1737

1. Visited Mr. Danforth.

2. [No entry].

3. Stormy.

4. Very cold.

5. I rode to Southborough. Met Mr. Stone by Captain Warren's. Very cold. Mr. Peabody[1] and Mr. Moquet[2] of Framingham here.

[7] Captain Samuel Forbush of Westborough.
[8] Joshua Townsend of Westborough.
[9] Mrs. John Danforth.
[10] Simeon Hayward.
[11] Joshua Lock.
[12] Mrs. John Rogers.
[13] Probably Mrs. John Pratt.
[14] Richard Tozer of Westborough.
[15] Edmund Rice, an original settler of Westborough.
[16] Reverend Job Cushing of Shrewsbury.
[17] Joseph Wheeler.
[18] Deacon Jonathan Forbush was one of the first to change the name to Forbes.
[19] The Goddards were from Shrewsbury.

[20] Reverend John Whiting, minister of the First Church in Concord, 1712-1737.
[21] Joshua Eaton (Harvard 1735), the first lawyer to settle in Worcester and later the first minister of Spencer. Sibley, IX, 533-538.
[22] Daniel Warren.
[23] Reverend Samuel Barrett of Hopkinton.
[24] Ebenezer Chamberlain of Westborough.
[1] Reverend Oliver Peabody of Natick.
[2] Francis Moquet, an innkeeper. Temple, Framingham, pp. 642-643.

6. Preached at Southborough, on Job 3, 36 A. and P.M. At eve, Colonel Ward[3] and his wife came in to Mr. Stone's. N.B. The Colonel's exceptions against that passage in my forenoon sermon, p. 2—too Small for the Divine Oracle to have been exprest about either.

7. At Mr. Tim Brigham's.[4] Mr. Stone brought Mrs. Parkman to his House, we dind there, after which I rode to visit old Mrs. Morse[5] at Marlborough, confined by her Broken Bone, and in great distress of mind, whilst Mr. Stone went with my wife up to Dr. Gott's. There we tarried all night.

8. Called at Captain Williams, and at Mr. Ebenezer Beeman's on our way home. P.M. Funeral of one of Mrs. Seth Rice's Dauters[6] who dyed by a Quinsy. Rain. N.B. The Floor of the Room at Mr. Rice's broke under us.

9. Stormy.

10. I rode to Mr. Wheeler's, called at Mr. Danforth[7] as I went, but din'd at Mr. Wheeler's. N.B. Mr. Thomas Ward at Mr. Nathan Balls's. I was at Mr. Lawrence's[8] and at Mr. Gershom Fay's[9] and at Mr. McCollister's.[10] N.B. Disappointment about Swine notwithstanding my long Dependence.

11. We first tyed up our Cattle in the Barn. My oxen were at work for Mr. David Brigham's to cart stones for their chimneys. I was at Mr. Grout's about Beef.

12. Fine warm day.

13. John 3, 36 and P.M. on John 16, 8. Captain Eager sick.

14. Brother Hicks went to Cambridge upon my Horse.

15. Trooping and Training—prayed with the foot before Dinner and dind with the officers of both Horse and Foot—prayed with the whole Body at Eve. N.B. Captain Eager detained by his sickness and Lieutenant Baker[11] also absent. N.B. I wrote to Worcester by Captain Moses Rice,[12] being I could not visit the Prisoner.

16. Brother Hicks came up with Sister Willard.[13]

17. Mr. Tainter came to me before Sunrise and informed me of a most Sudden and awful accident in their neighbourhood. That the wife of Mr. Joshua Harrington (who came up with his Family to Dwell among us, but this Day three weeks) was Shot in the head last evening, a little before Sundown, by a servant named Ebenezer Chubb in his 15th year, and she dyed upon the Spot. Mr. Tainter was going for the Coroner. Public Thanksgiving. Preached on Lev. 3, 1. After the publick exercises, the Coroner's Inquest sat on the body of Mrs. Harrington and their verdict was Accidental Death.

18. My wife and Sister were with me at the funeral of Mrs. Harrington.

19. [No entry].

20. Sacrament. John 16, 8, repeated. Mat. 10, 29, 30 P.M. N.B. Mrs. Trewsdale[14] of Newton, mother of Mrs. Harrington, above mentioned, dind with us.

21. I rode up to Worcester to see Hugh Henderson again. Was sorry to find he had tried to make his escape by filing the Goal door. We talked more of other matters, and kept longer off from the main point of his case than heretofore. I'm more put to it to judge of his Frame. Mr. Burr came to me, requested me to preach to him on Wednesday. Hugh desires it of me, and several of the people repeatedly and urgently insist and plead for it. I prayed with the prisoner and took leave at about seven o'clock. N.B. His Discourses of the Jury, not going by the laws of God and the Country in Condemning him, having but Circumstantial Evidence. As to Newton, he offered him all reasonable

Satysfaction, etc. But he added, that he was guilty, and his many sins had provoked God to anger, etc.

I called at Mr. Cushings and supped there. Thence I rode home.

22. Deacon Miles of Concord here to bring the Request of the Church that I would assist in the Fast they have appointed in order to the Calling another Minister.

23. The wife and younger son of Mr. Increase Ward very bad. I visited them and old Mrs. Pratt A.M. P.M. I rode up to Worcester at the Request of the Criminal and others to preach to him. There were so many at the Goal that we were obliged to go to the Meeting-House. I preached on 1 Tim. 1, 15. Supped (with Mr. Campbell)[15] at Deacon Haywards.[16] We visited the Prisoner. He spoke of having a solemn warning taken from his mouth, but chose to have it deferred to the morning, but prayed I would be early. We lodged at Mr. Burr's.

24. I went to the Prisoner as early as I could, and Mr. Burr was with me to assist in penning down what the Prisoner had to deliver by way of Confession and Warning to the World before his Execution. In it I was as punctual and strict as I could be in inserting his own words as near as I could, and when any others were used. It [Here this portion of the diary ends].

### 1738

### JANUARY

1. Nothing less than Patience and Forbearance which is Divine could permit me another Year Still! A.M. on Mat. 8, 5—P.M., on Eccl. 1, 2. I would Committ to God the Events of this Year, and I would enter a fixed Resolution, by the Grace of God to Serve Him in Fidelity in Some preferable Degree to what I have done heretofore.

2. Was at the Funeral of the Young Child of Mr. Thomas Bruce.

3. Was at the Funeral of a Child[1] of Mr. Josiah Russell, of about 5 years old, an hopefull, desirable Child—The Third that has dyd of late by the Quincy, and the 10th that has dyd in 10 weeks.

4. Captain Eager calld me in the morning to go over to Upton to the Ordination of Mr. Thomas Weld.[2] Mr. Tainter also went over with us. The Churches sent to were, the Church in Mendon, Brookline, Hopkinton, Attlebury, Uxbridge and Grafton; Mr. Barrett prayd before Sermon, Mr. Allen[3] preach'd on Isa. 6, 8. Mr. Dorr[4] gave the Charge; Mr. Weld of Attlebury the right Hand. Entertainment was plentifull at Ensign Woods. N.B. Deacon Millins[5] of Hopkinton Disputes for Ruling Elders, in opposition to the Doctrine deliver'd to Day. A very fine, bright, moderate Day. Return'd at Evening.

5. At Private Meeting at Brother Hicks's. Preached on Ps. 73, 25. Received the melancholly news of the Death of Madame Chandler, who deceasd on [blank].

6. James Bradish, Junior, carryd away my Flax to dress it.

7. Visited Mr. Increase Wards Family, 4 of them being sick. Rebecca very low.

8. On Matt. 8, 5–1 Cor. 15, 31. Moderate Day. Large Company.

9. Visited Mr. Wards Family again. Rebecca still living, though exceeding bad. Sent by Mr. Whipple to Boston—Letters from New Haven. Moderate, bright Day. N.B. Mr. Campbell of Oxford here.

10. Visited old Mr. Forbush.[6] Returnd by Mr. Cooks[7] and Mr. Wards.

[3] Colonel William Ward of Southborough.

[4] Timothy Brigham was a distinguished citizen of Southborough, being town treasurer and selectman for many years.

[5] Widow of Joseph Morse.

[6] Ruth Rice died Nov. 7, 1737, age about 18 months.

[7] John Danforth of Westborough.

[8] Benjamin Lawrence of Westborough.

[9] Gershom Fay, Jr., the nephew of Captain John Fay lived in that part of Westborough that later became Northborough.

[10] John McCollister.

[11] Edward Baker, an original settler of Westborough.

[12] Keeper of a public house in Worcester.

[13] Parkman's sister, Susanna, wife of Captain Josiah Willard of Salem.

[14] *Newton Vital Records* indicate that Elizabeth Trusdall married Joshua Harrington in 1731.

[15] Reverend John Campbell of Oxford.

[16] Deacon Daniel Heywood of the Old South Church in Worcester.

[1] The death of neither child is recorded in *Westborough Vital Records*.

[2] (Harvard 1723). *Sibley*, VII, 273–279.

[3] Probably James Allin (Harvard 1710), the first minister of Brookline. *Sibley*, V, 506–510.

[4] Reverend Joseph Dorr of Mendon.

[5] Henry Mellen.

[6] Thomas Forbush.

[7] Cornelius Cook, son-in-law of Thomas Forbush.

11. Ensign Maynard here from Boston. Provisions exceeding Dear there.

12. I rode to visit the Indians, Old David,[8] etc., at their Wigwam. At Captain Warrin's about Pork; and rode up to Mr. Reuben Maynards on the same account but he not at home, being gone to Mr. Joseph Miles' wedding. N.B. I visited Mr. Samuel Fay and Family, and Mr. Bezaleel Smiths.

13. Mr. Elias Havin,[9] on his journey to preach at Leicester here and lodged here. N.B. Captain Fay here at Evening also, and Mr. Reuben Maynard. It has been a Week of remarkably warm, pleasant Weather little freezing even o'nights. N.B. I had visited Rebecca Ward, P.M. being called by Mr. Samuel Fay, junior.

14. Mr. Haven left us. Very high winds, but not very Cold. Rebecca Ward[10] dy'd.

15. Matt. 8, 14, 15. John 16, 8. Raw Cold. Many Weathers.

16. Very Cold. P.M. at Captain Warrins, but he was not at home.

17. Rebecca Ward was buried.

18. [No entry].

19. Rode up to Captain Fays, to Mr. Reuben Maynards and to Cousin Winchesters.

20. The Weather has been for Some Days wondrous fine and moderate.

21. [Blank] Miller, a Glazier, mended our Glass.

22. Matt. 8, 16, 17. Luk. 1, 6. My Spouse was taken into the Church. Raind hard in the night.

23. At Eve Mr. Miles (son of Deacon Miles) from Concord with a present of Onions. The same Eve Mr. Horn, Mr. Daniel Fay, and Mr. Joseph Woods of Southborough were here. In the Hands of the Former were a pair of Gloves for my wife and me from Colonel Chandler[11] of Worcester.

24. Read Dr. Edwards[12] on the Use and Abuse of Apparell.

25. Mr. Cushing made us a visit and tarried into Evening.

26. Mr. Increase Ward and his son had requested that we would keep this Day in humiliation and Prayer on account of the Frowns of Heaven upon them in their grievous Sickness and Bereavment. Considering also that the Providence of God had been remarkable in the Late Mortality. The Exercise was publickly mentiond in the Congregation the Sabbath past, but because of Mr. Ward's and his Familys Circumstances we kept it at his House. Mr. Prentice[13] came at our request and assisted in the Prayers. I preachd on John 2, 2. Repeating with some alterations and Additions, part of my sermon on 1 John 4, 10. Many were gathered together and the Family provided a decent refreshment afterwards.

27. Rain, Cold and windy. But in general the weather has been unusually Moderate, or rather warm.

28. My Kinsman[14] came up from College upon my Horse, which I sent down for him, by Ensign Maynard.

29. On Eph. 3, 10, a. and p.m.

30. How different my State from what it was 2 years agoe! God has Set one Thing over against another. We should Sing of the Mercys of the Lord for Ever, but not forgetting his Judgments! Mr. Seth Rice's wife here. We went down to Ensign Maynards in the Evening. N.B. Mr. Haden here.

31. Very Cold windy day. Dr. Gott and his wife and Mr. Timothy Harrington made us a Visit and din'd and spent the Afternoon among us, except what time divers of us were down at Ensign Maynards, where were a Meeting of Houssatunnoc Petitioners for the drawing their Lotts. N.B. Colonel Woods there also. Very Cold Evening but they all returnd to Marlborough.

January leaves us like itself, but the most of the month has been the moderatest that most can remember.

---

[8] David Monanaow or Munnanaw.

[9] Elias Haven (Harvard 1733), schoolmaster at Hopkinton and later minister of Franklin, 1738-1754. *Sibley*, IX, 304-309.

[10] Daughter of Increase Ward.

[11] John Chandler, Jr.

[12] A work by the English Calvinist divine, John Edwards (1637-1716).

[13] Reverend Solomon Prentice of Grafton.

[14] Elias Parkman (Harvard 1737), Ebenezer Parkman's nephew. *Sibley*, X, 223-224.

## FEBRUARY, 1738

1. [No entry].

2. I cannot but remember the Wormwood and the Gall of the Funeral Day Two years agoe[1] and Desire my Soul may still be humbled within me. But God has turned the mourning of the Day (Day Two years agoe) into rejoicing and my sorrow into Gladness. But O that I may neither forget the Blessing enjoyed in my Dear Molly, nor the holy, Severity of the most high in So Sorely and grievously bereaving me of her! [illegible] Storm of Snow. Clear'd Somewhat when it was towards Evening.

3. [No entry].

4. [No entry].

5. Matth. 8, 18, 19, 20. Eph. 5, 25. Rain a.m.

6. Cold. Slippery. Mr. Francis Whipple and his Wife visited us at Eve.

7. Considerable Storm of Snow. Ensign Maynard at Evening. Reading Potters Greek Antiquitys.[2]

8. Bright fine Day. Ensign Maynard went to Boston. I rode down to the South East of the Town, visited Mr. Bradish,[3] Goslin, Jonathan Bellows, Chamberlain, and at Evening Old Mr. Forbush.

9. We rode to Marlborough, our Kinsman in Company, he being accommodated with an Horse by Mr. Aaron Forbush.[4] Mr. Bliss[5] preach'd to the Young Societys in that Town, from Ps. 119, 9. N.B. Confusion in the Singing by the young man's reading the Longer meeter in Standish Tune, throughout the Singing. After Service we went to Dr. Gotts, where we were refresh'd for we did not dine at Captain Williams's where we call'd before meeting. Divers of us Spent the Eve at the Colonel's. My Spouse and I lodg'd at Dr. Gotts, but my Kinsman with Mr. Bliss.

10. Settled all accompts with Colonel Woods,[6] unto this Day. Visited Mr. David Goodenow of Westborough under Lameness and Confinement at Marlborough. Din'd at the Doctors and then rode up home. Snow'd while we were upon the way. Town Meeting at Westborough. N.B. I gave Mr. James Miller a request to be admitted into No. 3 of the Houssatunnocs. Ensign Maynard brought up divers Things from Boston for me. N.B. Oysters, Salt Fish, etc.

11. Ensign Maynard din'd with us upon Salt Fish, etc.

12. Mr. Grow[7] dind with us. Variable Weather. Eph. 5, 25. Repeated Sermon 2 on Matt. 20, 6. From 1 Tim. 5, 13.

13. Mr. Tainter came and kill'd our Hog. Weigh'd about 12 score. N.B. Mr. Tainters Cousen Kendal[8] of Suffield here. They din'd with us. N.B. I wrote to Mr. Timothy Woodbridge,[9] junior of Simsbury by Mr. Kendall. Brother Hicks just at night pinch'd up the Barn Floor, and cutt up and Salted my Pork at Evening. Potter's Antiquities.

14. Mr. Weld of Upton came to See me and [illegible].

15. Mr. Weld left us. Pleasant Day. Jotham Maynard thrashing Rye. One of my little last year Twin Lambs found Dead at the old House. At Evening Neighbor Hezekiah Pratt, Mr. Whipple,[10] Mr. Livermore,[11] and Mr. James Fay[12] here.

16. I visited Edward Fay Sick at Mr. Increase Wards. Jotham Maynard thrash'd Rye, and p.m. he clean'd it up. 5½ Bushels. N.B. I reckon'd with Mr. Josiah Newton. N.B. I deliver'd up to Mr. Hezekiah Pratt a Bond of 900£ which he had given his Parents and which was repos'd in my Hands.

17. Very Cold, windy. Dr. Gott din'd here.

---

[1] The first Mrs. Parkman died Jan. 29, 1736.

[2] John Potter, *Archaeologica Graeca: or the Antiquities of Greece*, 2 volumes (Oxford, 1697-99). Numerous other editions followed.

[3] James Bradish.

[4] Son of Deacon Thomas Forbush.

[5] Daniel Bliss (Yale 1732), later the minister at Concord, Mass., 1738-1764. Dexter, pp. 439-440.

[6] Benjamin Woods of Marlborough.

[7] Samuel Grow of Westborough.

[8] Susanna, daughter of Deacon Simon Tainter, married Thomas Kendall of Suffield, Conn.

[9] (Yale 1732), tutor at Yale College at this time and later minister in Hatfield, Mass., 1740-1770. Dexter, p. 469.

[10] Francis Whipple.

[11] Jonathan Livermore.

[12] Son of Captain John Fay.

18. Mr. Weld came at Candle Light. I had a troublesome Cold ride—got no further than to Mr. Phinehas Hardy at Grafton. Lodg'd there.

19. Mr. Hardy was so kind as to ride over to Upton with me. A Cold windy Day. I preach'd on Heb. 13, 17. Was entertain'd at Ensign Jonathan Woods. Went into Mr. Sadlers[13] after the afternoon service. Conversation on his wide Difference with Mr. Weld.

20. I rode down to Mrs. Dorrs at Mendon, and din'd there. Mr. Dorr acquainted me with the Disquietments at Bellingham and the late Councils there. Mr. Weld and my Kinsman came to Mendon. When we return'd from thence we call'd at Mr. Sadlers and at Captain Hazletines.[14] Late home and Cold. My wife had a very ill turn, and had been very ill for Two Dayes. Keeps her Chamber. Abort,[15] etc., etc.

21. My wife keeps Chamber. Mr. Stone[16] of Southborough made us a Visit.

22. Read Eusebius Hist. Eccl. by Valesius.[17] Mr. Maynard and Sister Hicks were kind in visiting my wife.

23. It was generally very good pleasant Weather.

24. Mr. Jonathan Whipple was So kind as to present me with a Store Pigg about Six weeks old.

25. [No entry.]

26. Matth. 8, 21, 22. Eph. 5, 25.

27. Very Cold. Brother Breck[18] of Springfield came at Evening.

28. My Spouse first got down stairs after her illness After Dinner Brother Breck and my Kinsman rode to Marlborough. I rode as far with them as my visit to old Mr. Forbush led me. Mr. Forbush in a very low State and not likely to Continue. At Evening wrote by Neighbor David Maynard, junior, to Brother Samuel Parkman by who I sent the Ballance of Mr. Billings (Taylor at Boston) Accompt, being 9£.

### MARCH [1738]

1. Expected my Kinsman but in vain. N.B. Our Brethrens Interest in Marlborough sold by auction for 113£.

2. Lecture on Gal. 6, 15. Church Meeting. See the Records.

3. Brother Breck and my Kinsman return'd and din'd with us. P.M. Brother Breck went from us on his Journey to Springfield.

4. Fine Weather—invites to Guardening. The Chive and parsely Sprung.

5. Rain. Sacrament. Heb. 10, 35. P.M. Exod. 18, 21. Mr. Greaves, Deacon Fay and his wife din'd with us. Very much tir'd at night.

6. Town meeting. Chose only 4 select men all Day. Rain, Cold.

7. Adjournment of Town Meeting. Grows Cold again. N.B. Mr. Jonathan Forbush helped me in laying a front Hearth Stone in my Study.

8. Cold, windy Day. Visited old Mr. Thomas Forbush. My Kinsman (accommodated with Mr. Francis Whipples Horse) rode with me to Shrewsbury. N.B. Mr. Cushing gone to Lancaster. N.B. A Meeting of the Proprietors of the Houssatunnoc Township No. 3[1] at Captain Daniel Hows. And on Consideration of my paying 15£ I was admitted into their Society. N.B. The peculiar Friendliness of those who were Westborough Members, and especially of Mr. James Miller, who in a Singular manner espoused my Cause. The remaining Right (of the Seven that were to be dispos'd of) was sold to the highest Bidder for 26£ 10s. Late in the night when we got home, and very Cold, but through the Goodness of God we got home Safe and well.

9. Catechizing at the Meeting House forenoon and Afternoon.

10. I visited old Mr. Thomas Forbush being esteemed to be near his End. He acknowledged his Passionateness, and rash

Speaking, especially in the Times of our Contention, and ask'd forgiveness.

11. A very sharp Storm,—the Snow deep for it fell all Day.

12. I had prepar'd a Discourse to Wives, but I did not care to deliver it because there were So few at meeting. I repeated a. and p.m. Sermon on Gal. 6, 15.

13. It was a Day appointed to get Wood for me, but the Depths of the Snow prevented Captain Eager and his Neibours. But Captain Warrin and his Son Jonas came with a good Strong Team, and Neighbor Aaron Hardy and his Boy, Samuel Forbush (son of the Ensign) and Charles Bruce, and in the afternoon John Rogers and John Bradish came; and they got me a good Pile, 10 very large Loads, though it was heavy, troublesome Stirring and but one Team.

14. A.M. John Rogers with their Oxen and mine sledded stones from the Chimney of the Old House, but the Rain prevail'd upon us in so much that we were beat off before noon. N.B. Lieutenant Holloway[2] brought News from my mother, Brother, etc., with Flower, etc. N.B. Mr. Wheeler here. Talk of Jason again.

15. Very much troubled with the Tooth ach by means of the Cold I took yesterday.

16. The Tooth ach prevails upon me.

17. With great difficulty attend'd at all to my Studys, by means of Pain.

18. Blistering relieves me as it has been wont, but am much indispos'd.

19. On Eph. 5, 22, 33. N.B. So ill a Night last that when I awak'd in the morning I concluded I Should not be able to go to meeting. But Samuel Forbush came with an Earnest Request from his dying Grandfather that I would step down to him. I rose, and wrapping up well 1 ventur'd, pray'd with him, etc. As the Day rose I grew more lively, and by Divine Favour I got through the Exercises. N.B. Mr. Samuel Mason[3] of Stonington din'd and Supp'd and lodg'd here.

20. Under Indisposition still and great Fear of the Return of the Rheumatism. N.B. Old Mr. Forbush dy'd last night about 10 o'Clock. Mr. Mason rode to Mr. Peabodys.

21. A Dull Day but I ventur'd out being it was the Funeral of old Mr. Forbush. N.B. Mr. Reuben Maynard of Shrewsbury brought home the Pork I bought of him. The weight was 239£. Mr. Tainter was so kind as to come and Cutt it out and Salt it down.

22. Obadiah Walker[4] here.

23. Mr. Daniel Whitney of Waterton here with Mr. Tainter, having been up to view Mr. Thomas Wards Farm.

24. [No entry].

25. [No entry].

26. On Ps. 146, 3, 4.

27. Captain Abraham Williams[5] here and din'd with us. P.M. My wife and Kinsman, with Captain Williams and me, rode to Cousin Winchester, who had lately lain in, and leaving my wife, we rode to Grafton. But Mr. Prentice was gone to Cambridge. Captain Williams, in returning, continued his Journey to Marlborough, but we stay'd So long at Cousen Winchester as to sup.

28. My Wife and Kinsman and I were at Ensign Maynards at Eve.

29. Proprietors Meeting of the Houssatunnock Township No. 3. N.B. A mistake of Date of what was transacted at last Meeting at Shrewsbury by which what was then done is render'd somewhat uncertain. N.B. Some Considerable writing done of Conveyance of Titles, etc.

30. My Kinsman left us, upon my Horse, accompany'd by Mr. Francis Whipple. Did something at Gardening.

31. [No entry].

### APRIL, 1738

1. Mr. Whipple return'd with my Horse from my Kinsman.

2. On Eph. 6, 4. Mr. Ebenezer Chamberlains Wife din'd with us.

[13] Captain John Sadler, one of the first selectmen of Upton. *Upton, Mass.*, 1735-1935 (Upton, 1936), pp. 11, 14.

[14] John Hazeltine, an early resident and prominent citizen of Upton.

[15] Old usage for an untimely birth or miscarriage.

[16] Reverend Nathan Stone.

[17] An English translation of Valesius' edition of Eusebius, *History of the Christian Church*, 3 volumes (Cambridge, 1720).

[18] Samuel Breck (Harvard 1741), Parkman's brother-in-law, married Elizabeth Cooley of Springfield, Mass., in 1744. He became a surgeon.

[1] Later the town of Sheffield, Mass.

[2] William Holloway of Westborough.

[3] Descendant of Captain John Mason of Pequot War fame.

[4] Of Marlborough.

[5] Parkman's brother-in-law of Marlborough.

3. Raw Cold.

4. I rode abroad for Help in my Farm Business. Went to Mr. David Brigham's and found their Dauter Deberah very ill of a Fever. I took a ride round by Captain Forbush[1] and old Mr. Wards.[2] Silas Brigham here at Evening, his sister Deborah being at the point of Death. Easterly lowering Weather.

5. Deborah Brigham very low and dangerously ill. A very great storm of Rain, Cold and tedious, especially in the Morning. When it was more moderate I went down to see Deborah Brigham. Our maid boiling Soap.

6. Mr. Pratt, with his Cattle, Brother Hicks's and my own, to which we added Mr. Rogers's in the Afternoon broke up the Grass Ground on the West and South of the old House. P.M. I visited Mr. Josiah Russells Child which was Sick. Cloudy and Raw weather yet. Mr. Pratt, p.m., plough'd Stubble Ground.

7. Easterly Wind, Cloudy, Cold—Rain at Times throughout the Day.

8. The Same Weather still. Captain Brigham[3] of Marlborough here. P.M. I rode to Shrewsbury and met Mr. Cushing[4] coming to Westborough. Mr. Burr[5] at Mr. Cushings.

9. I preach'd at Shrewsbury on Rev. 3, 1. Return'd at Eve, home, and there found Mr. Andrew Boardman[6] School Master of Hopkinton who lodg'd with us.

10. I rode to Marlborough. Mr. Burr (who preach'd at Marlborough yesterday for Mr. Bliss) was there when I went down. Conversation with him about Bedforth Lands in Connecticut. Din'd at Dr. Gotts. Talk'd with Ensign Gotham Ward touching what had been reported of the neiboring ministers in the Affair of Marlborough against Mr. Benjamin Kent.[7] In returning Home, had Colonel William Wards Company. N.B. Took down a Jack at Father Breck's.[8]

11. David Baverick wrought for me.

12. David Wrought to Day also, and Mr. Aaron Forbush wrought with my Team in Splitting Hills.

13. Fast. On Ps. 65, 2.

14. David Batherick again. He Sow'd Rye.

15. David Still. He Carted stuff and mended Fence. Neighbor Aaron Hardy came with a Yoke of Oxen and plough'd up the rest of the stubble ground. I was necessitated a.m. to assist at the Team my Self to my great Trouble and affliction. Sacrament. Repeated Isa. 50, 10. P.M. Eph. 6, 4.

17. I rode into the Southwest part of the Town for necessary Supplys for the occasion approaching. N.B. Mr. Hall of Sutton here. N.B. Mr. William Caruth planted Potatoes for me.

18. Brother Hicks and his wife rode upon my Horse to Cambridge. The Association met at our House, Viz. Mr. Prentice[9] of Lancaster, Mr. Loring,[10] Mr. Cushing, Mr. Stone of Southborough, Mr. Prentice of Grafton (who also brought his Spouse with him). Mr. Jabez Richardson[11] and Mr. Andrew Boardman likewise came. No Body was prepared to give a Concio. At their Request I repeated my Discourse on Eph. 3, 10. Our Conversation turn'd upon the Affairs of Marlborough as they respected the Settlement of Mr. Bliss among them. Mr. Stone and Mr. Boardman left us.

19. Mr. Bliss and Mr. Haven came. Mr. Prentice of Grafton laid some Difficultys he was labouring under, before us. Mr. Prentice the Moderator gave Mr. Bliss reasons why he Suppos'd the Association would not look upon themselves call'd to meddle with the Affairs of Marlborough. The Moderator preach'd the public Lecture on Ps. 73, 25. I pray'd the Church to receive

their Votes for a Deacon or Deacons. The First (which was not ripen'd till the 3d Trial) was for Brother Thomas Forbush, For whom (at last there were 24 Votes out of 36 Members). Then the Church unanimously mov'd for a second to be Chosen—to which I consented. But seeing the Association were waiting for me I (with the Church's Consent) appointed Deacon Fay to receive the Church's Votes whilst I withdrew. When I returned I found they had chosen Brother Seth Rice to be the other Deacon.[12]

20. John Rogers wrought for me—ploughed in Rye and Barley.

21. Simon Tainter, junior, came and wrought for me. He plough'd the remainder of the Stubble, with Brother Hicks's oxen join'd to mine. P.M. Plough'd in Barley, with only my Cattle. I planted Cucumbers, Squashes. At Eve visited Mr. Hezekiah How, his Dauter being Sick.

22. Rain a.m. Held up p.m., yet Brother Hicks comes not with the Children.

23. Eph. 6, 4. Very pleasant weather.

24. A Fine, forward season. Brother and Sister Hicks came up from Cambridge and brought home my Dauter Lucy, who had been at Cambridge for 2 Years, and through the Favours of Heaven she had a fine, Comfortable journey. D.G.

25. Mr. Haden here, and help'd me mend the Boxes of my Pump.

26. John Rogers wrought for me, plough'd my ground second Time.

27. Catechiz'd at the Meeting House. N.B. 42 Boys A.M. [blank] Girls p.m. Mr. William Caruth came and P.M. planted more potatoes.

28. The Spring advanc'd mightily, but today was very Cold. Suse Cutting had today to visit her Friends in the South of the Town.

29. Trees put out very much—begin to Bloom.

30. Eph. 6, 4. God grant that all Parents might have a due sense of the weighty Duty incumbent on them respecting the Education of their Children! their Important Chance and tremendous Reckoning!

### MAY, 1738

1. Mr. Habijah Bruce sent his son Charles with a Yoke of Oxen to cross my Grass-Ground and they began the work, but old Mr. Greaves gave me so much of his Experience of planting upon the sods, that offering also to assist me in it, we proceeded to have it harrowed and then planted it. His Brother Francis Pierce also help'd in it. N.B. Goodman Gore of Marlborough here. Pleasant weather. P.M. Charles ploughed over the rest of the stubble ground.

2. Hired James Bradish and Noah How to cart out Muck, but before noon came Mr. John Watkin from Upton and offer'd to undertake my Work for longer or shorter Time. Accordingly a little before noon he went to work. P.M. Noah went home, and Mr. Watkin wrought at the Team in his Stead. Cool, raw weather, p.m. Great Expectation of Rain at the dry Time, but Clouds fail.

3. Watkins burning Brush all Day on the Hill and in the Low Ground as well as on the south side.

4. Watkins carted muck and Harrowed. P.M. came Abraham Moss, whom I at Eve hired for 4 Months for 20£.

5. Abraham Moss began to work. Watkins work'd till noon and then, with Consent, left us. Carting Muck and harrowing and furrowing out.

6. Furrowing and planting. Fine refreshing Showers of Rain upon the Thirsty Earth.

7. Repeated the greatest part of Sermon 4 and 5 on Mat. 20, 6 from Rom. 12, 11 and P.M. preach'd on Eph. 6, 1, 2, 3.

8. Rode to Captain Forbush, Captain Warrins, and to Mr. Joslins. N.B. Mr. John Swift, junior[1] here. Abraham Moss planting.

[1] Samuel Forbush.

[2] Increase Ward.

[3] Nathan Brigham.

[4] Reverend Job Cushing of Shrewsbury.

[5] Reverend Isaac Burr of Worcester.

[6] Andrew Bordman (Harvard 1737), later minister of the First Congregational Church in Chilmark, 1746–1776. Sibley, X, 121–122.

[7] Minister of Marlborough.

[8] Home of the late Reverend Robert Breck of Marlborough, father of Parkman's second wife.

[9] Reverend John Prentice.

[10] Reverend Israel Loring of Sudbury.

[11] (Harvard 1730), an itinerant preacher and schoolmaster at Woburn. Sibley, VIII, 778.

[12] See Church Records, April 19 and May 25, 1738. Both Thomas Forbush, Jr., and Seth Rice declined election.

[1] (Harvard 1733), son of the Reverend John Swift of Framingham and later the first minister in Acton. Sibley, IX, 333–336.

9. High Cold winds. Moss plough'd up the lower south side Stubble. P.M. plough'd it again and furrow'd it out.

10. A.M. finish'd planting Corn. Abraham planted more Potatoes. I sent 5 Young Cattle into the Woods in the Drove of Captain Warrins,[2] etc. Susanna Cutting rode upon my Horse designing to visit her Parents at Waterton. P.M. a great Storm of Rain. Yesterday Mr. Bliss deny'd Marlborough.

11. [No entry.]

12. [No entry.]

13. Deacon Miles[3] of Concord and his Wife were here. P.M. I rode down to Southborough intending to Change with Mr. Stone; and Mr. Stone was accordingly dressing himself when Mr. Man[4] from College came and so earnestly requested and importuned me to change with him that (at Mr. Stones Desire also) I rode over to Marlborough whilst Mr. Man rode up to Westborough.

14. I preach'd at Marlborough on Rev. 3, 1. At the Doctors[5] at Eve, and lodg'd there.

15. Town Meeting at Marlborough to choose a Representative, and church meeting to choose a Pastor. My Business lay with divers persons at both the Meeting House and School House (at the former the Town, at the latter the church met), So that I was unavoidably up there—but lest I Should fall under some Reproach I refus'd to pray with the Church notwithstanding their Sollicitous Messages one after another. N.B. Discourse with Mr. John Sherman about Mr. Brecks pew which some had disorderly and clandestinely pull'd down in Marlborough Meeting House. Having call'd at Captain Warrens I returned home.

16. Susanna Cutting returned home.

17. Mr. Whiting and his Wife, with her Dauter Mrs. Hall made us a Visit and lodg'd.

18. They took leave for Concord.

19. Abraham Moss went to Framingham.

20. Eph. 6, 1, 2, 3.

21. Town Meeting to choose a Representative. Captain James Eager chosen. N.B. Mr. Thomas Baker, a Taylor, at work here. N.B. Abraham return'd. N.B. I rode to Mr. Beemans[6] and took up 20£ of Bills of the Colony of Rhode Island, of him, and gave him Bond.

23. Brother Hicks[7] rode to Cambridge and carry'd Ebenezer[8] down with him.

24. I rode into the South part of the Town as far as to Mr. Millers where I din'd and to Mr. Samuel Harringtons. N.B. at my returning there was at Captain Fays Mr. Whitman,[9] minister of Farmington, and one of his Sons. N.B. I visited Mr. Samuel Fays wife, but he was himself at New Medfield.

25. Lecture. Repeated Sermon on John 20, 28. Church was Stopp'd to receive the answers of the Brethren who were chosen Deacons.[10] They each of them answer'd in the Negative. There was much debating whether we Should accept Such Reasons as they Supported their Denyal with except what Brother Forbush offer'd concerning his Bodily Infirmities which considering the End and Design of our Choosing Deacons was esteemed of avail by all that Spoke. There were so many differing Sentiments that I was oblig'd to offer to them to Dissolve all that had been done hitherto upon this Business and adjourn to this Day fortnight. N.B. Mr. Livermore put down the New Box, which I had of Mr. Reed of Boston, into the Pump, on the long Spire that it might work in the lower Part of the pump.

26. Variously moving about from house to house for Horse and Tackling[11] for my wife to journey with me next week. N.B. The Pump works well and delivers the Water plentifully. N.B. Colonel William Ward[12] here just at Eve.

27. Benjamin Forbush came to lead Horse to plough. Sent him to Ensign Forbush's for his Horse for my Wife, and succeeded.

28. Sacrament on Heb. 10, 38, and Eph. 6, 1, 2, 3. N.B. Very Seasonable Rain.

29. When the Rain in the Morning permitted, My Wife rode with me first to Mr. Joslins[13] which was a great hindrance to our Journey; then we proceeded to Marlborough, but the Rain prevaild to such a Degree that we were confin'd there all Night. N.B. The Wooden Horse which some of the Rabble had fastened at Colonel Woods's Door. N.B. Proprietors Meeting but I had not Plot with me. N.B. This Rain a great Mercy.

30. We waited till after dinner for weather, but then ventur'd to undertake our Journey. Mr. Cushing of Shrewsbury and Master Harrington in Company. N.B. just at Evening from Captain Wells to Father Champney's[14] we were in a heavy Shower of Rain. Lodg'd at Cambridge.

31. We rode to Boston. Mr. Webb[15] on Isa. 9, 6. We din'd at Brother Parkman's. P.M. an Ague utterly indispos'd me for going abroad till the next Day. So that I was not at the Convention at Dr. Sewall's.[16] Lodg'd at Brother Elias's. N.B. Mr. Weld[17] of Upton and Mr. John Hunt[18] (preacher) Supp'd at Brothers. N.B. Ebenezer Rode with us from Cambridge to Boston, which he had not Seen Since he was a Babe, but he in no wise likes it, because of the Evil Smells etc. He is under great Infirmitys—weak and Sick and a bad cough.

### JUNE, 1738

1. Was not at the Convention, but was at the public Concio by Mr. Barnard[1] of Marblehead on Coloss. 1, 18. The Collection for propagating the Gospel amounted to 207£. I din'd at Mr. Edmund Quincy's[2] where also din'd Colonel Chandler[3] of Worcester. P.M. I visited my wife's Aunt Mrs. Loring,[4] and her Kinswoman Mrs. Keggell.[5] I also waited upon Dr. Delhonde[6] for Ebenezer who remains feeble, Sick and Coughing. In the Evening I was at Brother Alexander's where also was my Wife, and we lodged there.

2. Visited in divers places but particularly was at Mr. Thomas Tylers.[7] N.B. Discourse of Mr. Pierponts[8] Circumstances and Affairs at New Haven. P.M. My honored and aged Mother undertook the journey to Westborough with me, my wife riding Single and my mother behind me. We proceeded as far as Father Champney's at Cambridge and lodged there, but were oblig'd to leave poor Ebenezer behind at Boston.

3. We chang'd Horses and my wife rode upon mine and my mother and I upon Ensign Forbushes, and by these means my mother had a very Comfortable Journey, and got up in good Season whilst the sun was a Considerable Height through the great Goodness of God. N.B. Mr. Prentice[9] of Grafton with us. N.B. Weeding finish'd in my Absence.

4. Repeated Sermon on Ps. 119, 136. N.B. Very Crowded assembly by means of Shrewsbury people and Some of Grafton.

5. Abraham Clearing up on the Hill. N.B. My Ague hangs about me yet.

6. Abraham Clearing, hoeing Beans, Covering Potatoes.

7. Mr. Joslin here.

8. Mr. Prentice of Grafton, his wife, and little son Nathaniel with Mrs. Elizabeth Rolfe of Boston, here and din'd with us.

---

2 Daniel Warrin, one of the original settlers of Westborough.

3 Samuel Miles.

4 Hezekiah Man (Harvard 1731). *Sibley*, IX, 65–67.

5 Dr. Benjamin Gott, Parkman's brother-in-law.

6 Eleazer Beamon of Westborough.

7 John Hicks, Parkman's brother-in-law.

8 Parkman's oldest son.

9 Reverend Samuel Whitman (Harvard 1696). *Sibley*, IV, 315–317.

10 Thomas Forbush, Jr., and Seth Rice had been elected April 19, 1738.

11 An old term meaning the harness of a draft animal.

12 Of that part of Marlborough that became Southborough.

13 Joseph Joslin of Westborough.

14 Samuel Champney of Cambridge, father of Parkman's first wife.

15 Reverend John Webb of the New North Church.

16 Reverend Joseph Sewall of the Old South Church.

17 Reverend Thomas Weld.

18 (Harvard 1734). Hunt did some preaching and then settled down in his home town, Watertown, to become a prosperous merchant and Representative to the General Court. *Sibley*, IX, 414–418.

1 Reverend John Barnard (Harvard 1700), minister of the First Church of Marblehead, 1715–1770. *Sibley*, IV, 501–514.

2 (Harvard 1722). A well known resident of Boston. *Sibley*, VII, 106–116.

3 John Chandler.

4 Mrs. Daniel Loring.

5 Mrs. Parkman's cousin, Hannah Breck, married Abel Keggell, a merchant of Boston.

6 Louis Dalhonde, a physician of Boston.

7 (Harvard 1730). A Boston merchant. *Sibley*, VIII, 791–793.

8 James Pierpont, Jr. Son of the late Reverend James Pierpont (Harvard 1681) of New Haven.

9 Reverend Solomon Prentice.

P.M. was Church meeting. I was oblig'd to leave the Company. About 28 members were together. Brother Nathan Ball would not vote at all. The First Business was to Choose more Deacons. Brother Jonathan Forbush was elected by 17 votes out of 26 or 27. And Brother Josiah Newton by 15. N.B. I did not my Self vote for either. Brother Newton answered by way of Acceptance. I then enquir'd whether the Brother who did not vote or any other of the Church had any material objection against either the Churchs proceeding in this Affair or against the persons elected to be Deacons. But none was made. As to the other part of our Business See Church Records.[10] When I return'd home Mr. Hall of Sutton had been there to request me to preach for him next week. But All the Company abovesaid were gone off. N.B. Mr. Joseph Wheeler here after meeting, and we had Some more Discourse about the old Disquietment respecting Jason. He still goes away disquieted. A very Cold wind at Eve. N.B. I hear that this Day Captain Ephraim Williams of Newton with his Family are on their Journey to Houssatunnoc. N.B. Abraham Moss gone today Upon his Business at Sutton.

9. Cold wind to Day. Moss begins half hilling.

10. [No entry].

11. On Consideration of its being the first of our Sending a Representative to the general Court, and that he had obtain'd Liberty to come up, and was now in Town, and on Consideration of our having So much to do in the Affair of Deacons which calls men to Serviceableness, generousness and public Spiritedness, I preach'd on Act. 13, 36. N.B. A great Congregation, many Strangers here, and besides them, many Southborough people, Mr. Stone being gone to Harwich. Dr. Matthew's[11] wife din'd with us.

12. Captain Ware[12] of Sherborn came over from his Brother Williams's to See me. Catechiz'd at Lieutenant Holloways. Was at Mr. Billings's to have a plough made. Fragrant Showers. Abraham Setting plants, Clearing, etc.

13. I help'd in the ploughing among the Corn. Let Mr. Winchester[13] have my oxen to go to Boston.

14. [No entry].

15. My wife rode with me to Grafton. It look'd showery. When at Grafton it rain'd too hard for her to proceed with me according to Design, but Mr. Prentice went with me to Sutton Lecture. I preach'd on 2 Thess. 2, 16, 17. N.B. The Church of Sutton dissatisfy'd with Mr. Peres Rice.[14] Mr. Prentice and I at Mr. Rice's in the Evening and Justice Dudley[15] there also. Mr. Prentice and I rode down to Grafton, where I left my Spouse and we lodged there.

16. We returned from Grafton. N.B. Captain Fay[16] with us. Din'd at Captain Fays. P.M. Cousin Winchester brought up Ebenezer from Cambridge.

17. Abraham mowing about the Barn.

18. I preach'd on Act 13, 36. P.M. repeated Sermon Jam. 1, 21 from 2 Pet. 1, 20, 21.

19. Captain Eager[17] and Captain Warrin here at Evening.

20. Trooping and Training. Mr. Cushing pray'd with the Foot. At Association at Southborough, where were Mr. Prentice of Lancaster, Mr. Loring, Mr. Cushing, Mr. Seccomb,[18] Mr. Jabez Fox[19] and Mr. Josiah Brown.[20] See Association Records. Mr. Seccomb and Mr. Brown deliver'd each an exercise.

21. Mr. Loring at the public Lecture on 1 Thess. 5, 19. N.B. Colonel Woods[21] and Dr. Stanton Prentice[22] with us. N.B. receiv'd a Letter from Mr. Timothy Woodbridge Junior[23] at Hartford.

23. Hot Day. The Children went a Cherrying P.M. to Captain Fays. Abraham mowing Some Spots about the House.

24. Abraham mowing Bushes. P.M. Mr. Stone came up to change, without any previous agreement or Intimation of it. Yet I gratify'd him immediately and rode to Southborough. Hot Day.

25. Very Hot. I preach'd at Southborough on Rev. 3, 1 a. and p.m. Mr. Stone came at Evening. Hot night again.

26. Weather continues hot.

27. Kill'd a Calf which at Eve (though an hot Season) I sent to Boston by John Rogers at Eve. P.M. near Evening came our Two Brethren of Springfield, who lodged here.

28. Brother Breck[24] rode to Marlborough. Hot weather still. P.M. came Dr. Gott. And after him Dr. Crouch with Two more, from Hadley call'd a while.

29. My wife and Brother Samuel Breck[25] rode with me to Marlborough, the weather being cool, cloudy and pleasant, and we din'd at Dr. Gotts. P.M. I preach'd to Three societys of young men who were met together at the Meeting House, on Eccl. 11, 9. N.B. Mr. Jabez Fox of Woburn present. After meeting the Societys Sent me four of their Number with their Gratitude. N.B. I went to Mr. Peter Butler and agreed with him to make me a Side Saddle for my wife, And an Housing for my Self of Homespun Cloth which I carry'd to him. In our returning home we were late, in the Dark and Wet and alone— but our Family not o'Bed.

30. Wet forenoon. Moss went to Mr. Thomas Billings's for my plough which he made for me. N.B. Mr. Jonathan Forbush here p.m. Moss mowing southside, upper End. N.B. Benjamin How brought home an Irish or Foot Wheel which he had made for Molly.[26]

## JULY, 1738

1. Brother Samuel Breck return'd from Marlborough. Raking and getting in Hay.

2. On Mat. 8, 23–27, and on Acts 13, 36.

3. Undertook to wait upon my Honored Aged Mother to Cambridge. At the widow Harringtons[1] in Marlborough we were oblig'd to Stop; my Mother could not ride upon that Pillion which we us'd any longer. She lay down and was refresh'd. We borrow'd Mrs. Harringtons Pillion and remounted. We had a prosperous Journey by the will of God and got down in season to Father Champney's where we lodged.

4. We rode to Charlston and din'd at Cousen Solely's. My Mother in great Comfort return'd to her own House. Blessed be God for his sustaining Mercy to her in this observable undertaking!

(N.B. When my Mother took her Leave of my Family, and bless'd them among other of her Expressions, these were remarkable when She kiss'd my two Sons in the Language of the patriarch Jacob when he lay'd his aged hands upon Ephraim and Manasseh "God almighty bless the Lads and make them a Blessing," etc.).

I return'd to Cambridge at Evening. N.B. Mr. John Osborn junior, of Rowley, with his mistress lodg'd at Father Champneys. Mother Champney and Sister Lydia were disquieted with me that I had remark'd to Brother Hicks their Sending So over strict a Charge by Cousen Winchester, about Ebenezer, when she brought him from Cambridge to Westborough on June 16 last. N.B. Mrs. Suse Champney there.

---

[10] The church was also concerned with "the Conduct of Mr. Samuel Fay in keeping from our Communion himself, and withholding his Wife therefrom also, although he had permitted her to bind herself thereto by Solemn Covenant."

[11] Wife or widow of John Matthews, physician of Marlborough and Southborough.

[12] Joseph Ware, prominent citizen and operator of a grist mill in Sherborn. Abner Morse, *Genealogical Register . . . and History of the Towns of Sherborn and Holliston* (Boston, 1856), pp. 253–254.

[13] Benjamin Winchester of Brookline, who married Elizabeth (Champney) Chamberlain, the first Mrs. Ebenezer Parkman's cousin, was living in Westborough at this time. He later moved to Grafton where he died in 1762.

[14] A former resident of Westborough. Son of Thomas Rice.

[15] Paul Dudley, a judge of the Massachusetts Superior Court.

[16] John Fay of Westborough.

[17] James Eager of Westborough.

[18] Reverend John Seccomb of Harvard, Mass.

[19] (Harvard 1727). Son of the Reverend John Fox of Woburn, Mass. Jabez did some preaching but was not ordained. He became the notary public and representative of the port of Falmouth, Maine. *Sibley*, VIII, 134–137.

[20] Josiah Brown (Harvard 1735) sometime preacher and schoolmaster of Lancaster and Sterling, Mass. *Sibley*, IX, 476–478.

[21] Benjamin Woods of Marlborough.

[22] Stanton Prentice, son of the Reverend John Prentice of Lancaster. Charles J. F. Binney, *The History and Genealogy of the Prentice or Prentiss Family, in New England* (Boston, 1852), p. 178.

[23] A tutor at Yale College.

[24] Reverend Robert Breck of Springfield, Parkman's brother-in-law.

[25] (Harvard 1742). Parkman's brother-in-law, who later became a physician at Worcester and Great Barrington. *Sibley*, XI, 131–132.

[26] Mary, Parkman's oldest child, who was born Sept. 14, 1725.

[1] Mrs. David Harrington.

5. It being Commencement I was chiefly at the following Chambers, Scil.: Sir Lorings,[2] Sir Davis's.[3] I visited Several others, as Sir Tyler's,[4] where I broke fast. I din'd but poorly in the Hall. P.M. The Presidents[5] Oration was very excelling. Lodg'd at Father Champney's and Sir Mower[6] with me.

6. I was again at College. Broke fast at Sir Mowers. Din'd at Sir Davis's at the Chamber they kept over the Common. N.B. I admonish'd Daniel Champney, junior,[7] at Sir Davis's, for his Drinking. N.B. Mr. Robert Sharp[8] and his Sister Mrs. Susan[9] at College. Mr. Robert led me to his Sister at Sir Whites[10] Chamber, but it was at Eve and they were soon removing home. I lodg'd at Father Champney's. My Kinsman Parkman walk'd over with me.

7. In Riding to Boston I first call'd at Captain Sharps[11]— then I stop'd at Judge Dudleys and din'd there. N.B. Mr. James Cushing[12] and his wife there. The Judge very entertaining and instructing in his Conversation. He led me into his Gardens, into his Library, etc. Stop'd again at Mr. Benjamin Eaton's Hatter in Roxbury. At Boston my Honored Mother and sister Willard[13] were both ill and kept therein Bed, which was the occasion of my Staying in Town all night. Lodg'd at Brother Elias's.[14]

8. Mother Somewhat better. I rode to Cambridge and thence to Westborough. One Mr. Caleb Johnson of Shrewsbury my Company the upper part of the Journey. Found the Family, through the Favour of God well.

9. Repeated Sermon on Gal. 3, 14.

10. Mr. John Caruth here, whom I paid. Mrs. Bulah Bent[15] of Marlborough here.

11. Very dry Season. Yet there was a little Shower at Night. N.B. I put up a Flap at the pulpit.

12. Old Mr. Lord[16] of the Cape was here upon a journey upward. Mr. Rand[17] of Sunderland and Mr. Billings[18] here and din'd with us.

13. Brethren Breck and Samuel here returning to Springfield. N.B. Samuel has been Examin'd and accepted at College when some Number were turn'd by. My Lecture was on John 6, 53. Mr. Jonathan Forbush accepted of the Deaconship. The Committee from Mr. Samuel Fay advis'd that I should make him a visit for that he had intimated that he should be glad to See me. N.B. Mrs. Rice of Hopkinton who was heretofore Whood was with me.

14. My Wife began to Spin Worstead.

15. [No entry].

16. Sacrament. On Song. 4, 16. Heb. 10, 38.

17. Pol'd Hay from the lower South Side. Dry Time.

18. I rode to Mr. Ephraim Allen's[19] and to Mr. Daniel Bartletts.[20] A plentifull and very Mercifull Rain while I was at Mr. Bartletts, which detain'd me there (I suppose) Several Hours. When I Slack'd I got as far as Mr. Eliazar Hows[21] at Marlborough

where I was kept till almost night. My Business from thence carry'd me to Mr. Peter Butlers.[22] At Colonel Woods in the Eve, Colonel Sent for Mr. John Rogers[23] and Sir Loring, who came accordingly. I lodg'd there.

19. At various places. Din'd at Dr. Gotts. Raining, yet I was oblig'd to get home. I was very wett, rode hard and it pritty much indispos'd me.

20. Catechiz'd at the meeting House. Rain'd—not many Children. Moss mow'd p.m.

21. [No entry].

22. Mr. Jotham Brigham of Marlborough came up with the Request of Mrs. How the wife of Jonathan How, that I would go down to her Husband, who was under terrible Distraction, and Mr. Rogers would come up to Westborough to change tomorrow. We had a great Deal of Hay to take care of, but towards Night I rode down. Mr. Rogers came up but I miss'd of him. Mr. How was in a piteous State intirely wild and confus'd, continually talking and worrying and Several to hold him. When I had pray'd with them I repair'd to my Lodgings at Madame Fisks.

23. I preach'd at Marlborough on Luke 19, 42. Was very much tir'd and Spent at Evening. Mr. Rogers came from Westborough. I lodg'd at Madame Fisks again. N.B. A Frost in low Ground.

24. After having been at various places as my Business call'd, I visited Dr. Gott and (with him) Mr. Jonathan How again. N.B. In Time of prayer he had a very violent Convulsion fit. After prayer and a great part of an Hour Spent whilst he was yet Striving in his Convulsion, I return'd to the Doctor's and having din'd with them, I came up home.

25. I visited Mr. Samuel Fay as the Committee had desir'd on the 13th. He deny'd that he had Said any Thing as if he desir'd any visit from me. His chief objections and offence against me were what arose from my bringing in new Singing and my wearing a Wigg. I reply'd that I was not aware that I had at any time given him just Reason of Offence but if he judg'd I had and we could not succeed in Reconciling the matter our Selves it was our Wisdom to get the Assistance of Some prudent, Serious, Christian Brethren about us; and I desir'd him to choose who he pleas'd that were such and I would be advis'd and guided by them. N.B. I inform'd him of not only what notice I took of his Conduct when my Brother Parkman was with me at his House to make him a Visit and he would not So much as come down from the Chamber to Speak with us, and of what I have divers times heard of him having for Several Years kept himself from seeing me in the pulpit, etc.—Which he own'd with a Laugh. He was urg'd to choose some Christian men to hear his Grievances—but he gave no reply to any of those Proposals. He did vouchsafe to thank my visit when I withdrew. At Eve A black thunder Storm arose. I got Shelter at Lieutenant Bakers. There was an heavy Shower and Sharp Lightening—but it clear'd up finely before it was too late to come home.

26. Mr. Thomas Brigham of Marlborough came up to acquaint me that Mr. Jonathan How dy'd last Night and that his widow earnestly desir'd me to go down to the Funeral tomorrow. Our Barley was mow'd and rak'd.

27. My Wife and I rode down with Neighbor Hezekiah How and his wife to Marlborough to the Funeral of Mr. Jonathan How. At the Doctor's after Funeral. N.B. Mr. Dyer of Boston there trading with the Doctor for his House down in the street.

28. Moss began p.m. to mow in ministerial Meadow.

29. Moss mowing in the Ministerial Meadow again.

30. On Heb. 10, 38. O that it might please God to Succeed so moving matters!

31. I rode to South West part of Town. Sent to Boston and my Kinswoman Winchester was at Mr. Tainters[24] in the Evening. Moss raking in the meadow till Eve and then he went away to go up to Sutton.

---

[2] Jonathan Loring (Harvard 1738), the son of Reverend Israel Loring of Sudbury, who later became a lawyer in Marlborough. *Sibley*, X, 298-299.

[3] Jonathan Davies (Harvard 1738), later a Roxbury physician. *Sibley*, X, 285.

[4] Andrew Tyler (Harvard 1738), minister of First Congregational Church of Westwood, 1743-1772. *Sibley*, X, 329-334.

[5] Edward Holyoke (Harvard 1705) became the ninth President of Harvard College, Sept. 28, 1737. *Sibley*, V, 265-278.

[6] Richard Mower (Harvard 1738) of Lynn. *Sibley*, X, 306-307.

[7] Of Cambridge. He was the nephew of the first Mrs. Parkman.

[8] Son of Captain Robert Sharpe of Brookline.

[9] Susanna Sharp, whom Reverend Parkman had courted after the death of his first wife. See Diary for February 17, 1737 and March 3 and 4, 1737.

[10] Benjamin White (Harvard 1738), sometime schoolmaster at Gloucester. *Sibley*, X, 338.

[11] Robert Sharpe, Sr., of Brookline.

[12] (Harvard 1725). Minister of Plaistow, New Hampshire, 1730-1764. *Sibley*, VIII, 499-501.

[13] Parkman's sister Susanna, who married Josiah Willard of Salem.

[14] Elias Parkman of Boston.

[15] Daughter of Peter Bent.

[16] Reverend Joseph Lord (Harvard 1691), minister of Chatham, Mass., 1718-1748. He was also a schoolmaster and physician. *Sibley*, V, 101-106.

[17] Reverend William Rand (Harvard 1721), minister of Sunderland, Mass., 1723-1745, and Kingston, Mass., 1746-1779. *Sibley*, VI, 549-553.

[18] Edward Billing (Harvard 1731) of Sunderland, who later became the first minister of Belchertown, Mass., 1739-1752. *Sibley*, IX, 22-28.

[19] Of Westborough.

[20] Ensign Bartlett lived in Marlborough.

[21] Captain Eleazer Howe.

[22] Of Marlborough.

[23] (Harvard 1732). Later the first minister of Leominster. *Sibley*, IX, 189-198.

[24] Deacon Simon Tainter of Westborough.

## AUGUST, 1738

1. At the Earnest and repeated Sollicitation of Mr. Ebenezer Chamberlain my wife and I rode down to the South East Corner of the Town, took the most of the Familys, but din'd with him, and at an handsome Entertainment his wife having lately lain in, and Every Thing very flourishing with them. N.B. Captain Warrin's wife[1] in a languishing State, and N.B. whilst we were at Mr. Jonathan Bellows's, Mrs. Belknap had one of her Fitts. We were in a Second Time at Ensign Forbushs.[2]

2. Moss return'd from Sutton very Early this morning—laid down to Sleep but went to work afternoon. N.B. Jonathan Forbush junior and Simon Tainter junior came very kindly and gave me a Days work each of them in mowing at my Meadow. The widow Rice[3] (heretofore Oake) here. P.M. I rode over to the North Side of the Town and visited Seven Familys, particularly Silas Fay who buried a Still born child yesterday. My son Ebenezer has a bad Swelling behind his Ear. Dr. Matthews[4] call'd in, accidentally.

3. Rain. Moss gone to mow what he can in the Meadow. Captain Forbush[5] and others at work upon the highway before my Barn; but p.m. the Rain was heavy and beat Every Body off. All that we have done at the Meadow lyes expos'd in this wet Storm.

4. Rains very hard all the morning. Latter part of the forenoon Moss bor'd a pole for a Ladder. Captain Forbush mending the highway before my House.

5. Fair Weather. Moss rak'd and cock'd Some of the Hay at the Meadow and mow'd Some more, But the Meadow very wet.

6. A.M. on Mat. 8, 28–33, p.m. on 10, 34.

7. Early in the morning I rode down to Mr. Bradishes to get James to help me in the Meadow and mett him going there. Both Moss and he rak'd all Day except a little turn of mowing in the Morning. I went to see them and to Mr. Eliezer Rice's and Mr. James Maynard's[6] where I din'd. N.B. I was bit by Mr. Eliezer Rice's[7] Dog. Mr. Pannell reap'd part of my Rie.

8. Moss at the Meadow. Fair good weather. Captain Warrin and his wife and Joanna Tainter[8] here in order to their joining to the Church. Mrs. Baker[9] and Deacon Newton's[10] wife visited Mrs. Parkman. N.B. Mr. Pannel came again to reaping and finish'd my Rie.

9. Eliezer Rice and John Rogers carted Hay from the Meadow. Two Load apiece. Moss Mowing in the Morning and raking and Cocking the rest of the Day. At Night the Carters got in my Rie into the Barn, almost wholly. Mrs. Williams[11] and Mrs. Rachel Rice[12] visited Mrs. Parkman. Fine weather.

10. A fine Day again. Moss at the Meadow. Ebenezer being troubl'd with a bad swelling in his Neck went to Marlborough to wait upon Dr. Gott[13] for Advice. David Baverick wrought for me at the Meadow with Moss, in poling, mowing, etc.

11. Very good weather. John Rogers Carting Hay from the Meadow. Captain Forbush Sent for me to the Funeral of his Infant (Still born) and both my Wife and I went to the House but not to the grave because of the Hurry and Urgency of my Business at Home.

12. Was in Some perplexity for Some Hand to help Moss in poling and Carting the remainder of the Hay from the Meadow. Went to old Mr. Maynards[14] and talk'd with him again about agreeing with Hicks,[15] and he told me that as to the methods which I propos'd, he would think upon them. Ebenezer went to Marlborough again about his Neck and got a Plaister for it.

13. On Mat. 9, 1–8, a. and p.m.

14. Brother Samuel Breck (who came from Springfield last week) brought up Sister Gott here. Mr. Abraham Rice of Marlborough and his Wife here in order to their owning the Covenant. But I was engag'd to go to the Funeral of Mr. Simeon Howards Second Son who was about in his 5th year and dyed somewhat suddenly by a stoppage in his Throat yesterday morn. After the Funeral Captain Eager[16] and Lieutenant Holloway[17] Stood with me at the burying place discoursing, and the latter Shew'd his displeasure at my not coming over more frequently to visit their side of the Town, partialy my not being at the Funeral of Neighbor Silas Fays Child of late, and my not being at the Funeral of his own Child—but I Strongly vindicated my Conduct and gave my Reasons for each. Captain Eager came home with me and supp'd with me. N.B. They went down, at my earnest sollicitation to Old Mr. Maynards to try if possible to make up the Difference Subsisting there, and Stop the Law suit Commencing. Bezaleel Frost[18] of Framingham who had difference with Abraham Moss came up late in the Evening to be reconcil'd and I us'd my friendliest Endeavours to put a period to their Contest. He lodg'd here.

15. Both Hicks's and Moss's Law suits put by by persuasions and methods of peace and reconciliation. Borrow'd Colonel Nahum Wards[19] 1 Volume of Pools English Annotations.[20] Moss gone to Worcester with Bezaleel Frost.

16. Ebenezer rode with me to Marlborough to Captain Peter Rice's,[21] to the widow How's[22] who carry'd Ebenezer to Uncle Gott's (with Captain Amsden[23]), to Mr. Phelp's[24] Mr. Peter Butlers, to Mr. Brown[25] the whitesmith, Colonel Woods's, and to Dr. Gotts. When the Doctor had advis'd respecting the Sore upon Ebenezer's Neck, we return'd home, altho it was nigh nine when we set out from Marlborough. N.B. Moss return'd before Day, this morning. He mow'd over the Bushes.

17. Moss mowing Bushes. P.M. I rode up to Mr. David Crosbys in Shrewsbury to get him to make me a pair of Boots. Call'd at Mr. Cushings—supp'd there. Between 10 and 11 o'clock at night when I return'd.

18. Rainy Day.

19. [no entry].

20. On Coloss. 4, 1, a. and p.m.

21. In the forenoon I went over to Mr. Jonathan Whipples to desire him to be with me at Mr. Samuel Fay's and sent Ebenezer to Ensign Forbush's to request the Same of him. I proceeded to Mr. Winchesters by whom I sent to Boston, and then Return'd to Captain Fays to meet with Mr. Whipple and Ensign Forbush, The former of which was there. I went down to Mr. Samuel Fays and Mr. Whipple came to me. I us'd all the most Serious and affectionate Methods with Mr. Fay and improv'd Mr. Whipples assistance to compose a Reconcilement, but in vain. Upon which I took a formal Leave of him. N.B. In going up to Mr. Winchesters I met Mr. Campbel,[26] Mr. Hall,[27] Captain Larnard[28] etc. going to a Council at Concord. When I had been at home some time Captain Warrin and his wife came, upon the Affair of their Relations preparitory to their admission into the Church.

22. Rode to Lancaster Association not without being Sadly bewilderd in the Woods, having lost my way once and again in

[6] An original settler of Westborough.

[7] Eleazer Rice lived in Marlborough close to the boundary of Westborough.

[8] The daughter of Simon Tainter of Westborough.

[9] Mrs. Edward Baker of Westborough.

[10] Mrs. Josiah Newton of Westborough.

[11] Probably Mrs. Abraham Williams of Marlborough, the sister of Mrs. Parkman. Hudson, *Marlborough*, p. 470.

[12] Probably Mrs. Luke Rice of Marlborough.

[13] Benjamin Gott, the physician, of Marlborough.

[14] David Maynard, an original settler of Westborough.

[15] John Hicks of Westborough, Parkman's brother-in-law by his marriage.

[1] Mrs. Daniel Warrin or Warren of Westborough.

[2] Thomas Forbush, Jr., also selectman of Westborough.

[3] The widow of Thomas Rice, formerly Mary Oakes.

[4] Dr. John Matthews, the physician of Marlborough.

[5] Samuel Forbush, an original settler of Westborough.

[16] James Eager.

[17] William Holloway.

[18] The son of Samuel Frost of Framingham. Temple, *Framingham*, p. 554.

[19] Of Shrewsbury.

[20] Matthew Poole's *Annotations upon the Holy Bible* was first published in 1688. Other editions soon appeared.

[21] Prominent citizen and captain of the "train-band."

[22] Lydia Howe, widow of Jonathan Howe who died June 22, 1738. Hudson, *Marlborough*, p. 384.

[23] Isaac Amsden of Marlborough.

[24] John Phelps of Marlborough was a cordwainer. He moved to Rutland, Mass., about 1742.

[25] James Brown.

[26] Reverend John Campbell of Oxford.

[27] Reverend David Hall (Harvard 1724), second minister of Sutton, Mass. *Sibley*, VII, 345–356.

[28] Isaac Larned, selectman of Oxford, Mass. Daniels, *Oxford*, pp. 580–581.

going over. Mr. Loring,[29] Mr. Williams[30] of Weston, Mr. Cushing,[31] Mr. Nathan Stone,[32] Mr. Solomon Prentice, and Mr. Stearns[33] present. Mr. Loring's Concio on Acts 10, part of 38th example who went about doing good. See Association Records. N.B. One Mr. Carter[34] dyed over there—a person of some Worth.

23. I preach'd publickly on Isa. 53, 1. Very hot, Dry Time. N.B. Mr. Stearns propos'd to have Mr. Prentice of Lancaster Dismiss'd that he might assist in founding another Association to the Northward, but the Motion was oppos'd.[35] I rode to Marlborough, in Company Mr. Stone, Mr. Rogers[36] (preacher at Marlborough) and Captain Amsden. Lodg'd at Dr. Gott's.

24. Mr. Rogers and Dr. Gott rode up to our Lecture. Mr. Rogers preach'd on [blank].

25. My wife weaving Fringe for new, Horse Furniture.

26. Moss picking up Apples for Cyder.

27. Sacrament. Captain Warrin and his wife admitted notwithstanding her Waste and Languishment in her Limbs. Sermon on Song 4 and Heb. 10, 29. Captain Williams of Marlborough here. N.B. remarkable Thunder and Lightning, yet he went to Marlborough in the Evening when the Rain was over.

28. My wife rode behind Ebenezer to Marlborough and return'd Safe at Evening.

29. [no entry].

30. Mr. Silas Witherby and his Lad came to make the Leaves of my Front Gate.

31. Mr. Witherby and his Lad here Still at work upon the Gate. Moss carry'd a parcel of Apples over to Mr. Hezekiah How,[37] who made up a Barrell, and part of a Second, of Cyder.

### SEPTEMBER, 1738

1. Mr. Witherby finish'd and put up my Gate, and altho he Set the price of his work to be 20 Shillings, yet considering he frequently came to Meeting here, he gave in Ten thereof. He made an End and went off Sometime before Night. Mr. Pannell and his son came to my Rye-Thrashing. They went home at Night. Moss fetch'd home the Cyder from Mr. Hows and Cut Stalks A.M.; work'd at Brother Hicks's p.m.

2. Mr. Pannel and his son came again to Thrashing and finish'd the Rye, Moss gathering up and pikeing the Stalks.

3. On Coloss. 4, 1. Heb. 10, 39. N.B. Mrs. Leeds of Groton in Connecticut (sister of old Mr. John Greaves) and Mr. Livermore din'd with us. N.B. I acquainted the Congregation that I know not but that I should be absent on the next Lords Day, and therefore desir'd that all such as could would wait upon the Christian Assembly where they could go the most Conveniently to, and hop'd that those who could not go to other meetings would, as Gods people meet together and worship him here, and if they should do so I wish'd them the Divine Presence among them and Blessing upon them.

4. N.B. A very great Drought. Great Trouble about getting Corn Ground. A burning Day. N.B. Moss in a great Fret after Dinner. He gathered the little piece of Corn of the South side.

5. I interrupted greatly in my purpose and Endeavours of this Day by the kindly intended visits of Mr. John Barrett and Mr. Benjamin Gerrish[1] of Boston on their journey to Middleton in Connecticut, and of Mr. Cushing and his Wife. Vid. Natal.[2]

6. At about 9 a.m. my Wife and I set out upon our Journey to Springfield and New Haven, on my Own and Cousen Winchester's Horses. Mr. Tainter bore us Company to Mr. Cushings at Shrewsbury. N.B. I bought a Foot Wheel at Mr. Cushings which Mr. Tainter was So kind as to bring home. Din'd season-

ably and agreeably at Colonel Chandlers[3] at Worcester. P.M. rode to Richardsons at Brookfield by about ¼ after 5. N.B. These Richardsons were heretofore Malden Milk Folks to our Family at Boston. They were very obliging and would receive no pay but for our Oats. We got to Mr. Cheneys[4] a little before Candle Light, but were so unhappy as to find neither Mr. Cheney nor Madame at Home. Mr. Cheney was gone to wait upon a number of Gentlemen who were upon the Road, Scil. Colonel Wendell,[5] Mr. President Holyoke,[6] Mr. Appleton,[7] etc. We tarried with and were entertain'd decently by Mrs. Dolly Hanley expecting Mr. Cheneys Return, but he came not. Dr. Pyncheon[8] of Springfield came in and tarried over night likewise.

7. In the Morning, just as we were mounting, Mr. Cheney (who had lodg'd with Mr. Bridgham[9] at Brimfield) came, and stay'd us whilst we made a visit to Colonel Dwight.[10] N.B. Colonel engag'd in building a new House. About ¾ after 8 we set out with Dr. Pyncheons Company. Light at Ashleys.[11] Left Ashleys between 10 and 11. At ½ after one arriv'd weary and tir'd at Scots in Kingston. Din'd there. Left Scotts ½ after 2. One Mr. Ball of Springfield and an Irishman bound to Glascow added to the Company. At Lambs in Springfield ½ after 3. N.B. Norwich Indians at Lambs. Left Lambs 20 minutes after 4. Mr. Breck came out to meet us a little before we got up to the Town. We arriv'd by Day Light—and not so tir'd as last night, nor as I was at Scotts in Kingstown.

8. Rainy Day. The Heavy Showers were a great Blessing, it having been a Time when there has been an unusual Drought. Mr. President Holyoke remains in Town—takes up his Lodging at Colonel William Pyncheon.[12] Colonel Pyncheon din'd with us. The President with us p.m.

9. Fair, bright Day. I waited upon Colonel William Pyncheon after I had view'd the River, the burying Place, etc. N.B. Some remarkable Inscriptions. N.B. Whilst we were at Colonel Pyncheon's with the President, Mr. Williams[13] of Longmeadow came and after him Mr. Hopkins[14] of the other Parish. They shap'd a Scheme for my assisting Mr. Williams by Mr. Hopkins preaching there and my preaching on the west Side, which I consented to after we had all din'd together at Mr. Brecks. N.B. Mr. Breck and I paid our Regards to old Colonel Pyncheon and his son Captain William, And p.m. Mr. President, Mr. Breck and I waited upon old Madame Brewer.[15]

10. In the morning I cross'd the River and went up to Mr. Hopkins. N.B. The first and Second Drum beating to give Notice to the People. Preach'd on Luk. 16, 23. N.B. The Women all sat upon the wrong side of the Meeting House. Deacon Parsons[16] very Courteous to me, and walk'd with me to the Ferry at Eve. At Mr. Brecks Mr. Hopkins in his return from Longmeadow. Cold Night.

11. Mr. Holyoke and Some Number besides were going up to Mt. Tom (call'd So as Tradition has it from one Rowland Thomas) and to Mt. Holyoke, (call'd so from one of the Presidents ancestors) and from thence they purpos'd to Mr. Rands[17] at Sunderland. But we rode to Long Meadow, when the Frost of this Morning which was very great was in great Degree gone, met Mr.

[29] Reverend Israel Loring of Sudbury.
[30] Reverend William Williams.
[31] Reverend Job Cushing of Shrewsbury.
[32] (Harvard 1726). First minister of Southborough, Mass. *Sibley*, VIII, 99–105.
[33] Reverend David Stearns (Harvard 1728), *Sibley*, VIII, 496–498.
[34] Samuel Carter died August 22, 1738. He was a former selectman of Lancaster, Mass.
[35] See Allen, *Worcester Association*, p. 19.
[36] Probably John Rogers (Harvard 1732), later the first minister of Leominster, Mass. *Sibley*, IX, 189–198.
[37] An original settler. Parkman's neighbor and friend.
[1] He later moved to Halifax, Nova Scotia, and became a prosperous merchant.
[2] Despite Parkman's reference to the Natalitia there is no entry in it for this date.

[3] John Chandler, a very prominent citizen, who at one time or another held virtually all the offices in the town. Lincoln, *Worcester*, pp. 296–298.
[4] Reverend Thomas Cheney (Harvard 1711), first minister of Brookfield, Mass. *Sibley*, V, 561–563.
[5] Jacob Wendell, merchant of Boston, member of the Council of the province after 1737 and commander of the Ancient and Honorable Artillery.
[6] Edward Holyoke (Harvard 1705), President of Harvard College. *Sibley*, V, 265–278.
[7] Reverend Nathaniel Appleton of Cambridge, Mass.
[8] Joseph Pynchon (Harvard 1726), physician of Springfield, Mass. *Sibley*, VIII, 90–92.
[9] Reverend James Bridgham (Harvard 1726), minister of Brimfield, Mass. *Sibley*, VIII, 7–10.
[10] Timothy Dwight of Northampton, Mass.
[11] The Ashley family kept a tavern in Westfield, Mass., for many years.
[12] Of Springfield.
[13] Reverend Stephen Williams (Harvard 1713), minister of the First Congregational Church of Longmeadow, Mass., 1714–1782. *Sibley*, VI, 25–35.
[14] Reverend Samuel Hopkins (Yale 1718), minister at West Springfield, Mass., 1720–1755. Dexter, 184–187.
[15] Widow of Reverend Daniel Brewer (Harvard 1687) of Springfield, Mass.
[16] Ebenezer Parsons of West Springfield.
[17] Reverend William Rand (Harvard 1721), second minister of Sunderland, Mass., and one of Parkman's classmates. *Sibley*, VI, 549–553.

Allis[18] hastening to join the foresaid Company. Mr. Williams set out with us, so far as to guide us to the way to Enfield. We cross'd the Ferry and rode (with one Kebby in Company) to Mr. Devotions[19] at Suffield. N.B. A fine prospect on the North of Suffield Meeting House. After kind Entertainment, dining, etc. we set out from thence in the middle of the Afternoon, rode to Windsor and Hartford and were kindly entertain'd at Mr. Austins.[20] N.B. His Honor Governor Law,[21] Captain Wadsworth,[22] etc. at Mr. Austins. N.B. 500 Hogsheads of Tobacco ship'd off last year from Connecticut River to the West Indies and chiefly from Windsor.

12. Mr. Austin persuaded me to go up on the State House to take a View of the Town, the River, etc. We visited Mr. Secretary Willis.[23] There was Mr. Woodbridge[24] of Symsbury and Mr. Case,[25] who were going to New Haven. This therefore was our Company. Stopp'd at Beckleys[26]—at Aspinwalls[27] in Kensington. N.B. In Wallingford or North Haven, a vessel building some Miles from the Water. N.B. Corn field 5 miles Long. N.B. A Late sorrowful occurrence by Thunder; the steeple shiver'd and a man thrown down from it and kill'd. N.B. 4 Persons buryed in the highway for suicide. N.B. Pleasant Fields appear'd at an agreeable Distance on the North East side of the Mountain. We stopp'd again at Hammerstones[28] in North Haven. There Mr. Wheelock[29] who had been Some time with us on the Road left us. N.B. College illuminated, seen Two Miles off. Call'd first at old Madame Pierponts[30] where was Mr. Russells wife[31], of Middleton, Mr. Pierponts sister. Found Dear Mrs. Pierpont Well and our meeting was with reciprocal Joy. Mr. Pierpont[32] was Still at Boston.

13. Being the Day of their Commencement I attended at College and at the Meeting House. Mr. Gay[33] of Hingham, Mr. Storer[34] of Waterton, Mr. Pemberton[35] of New York, Mr. Smith[36] of Weymouth, and Mr. John Hunt[37] preacher, were there. N.B. Mr. Dickerson[38] of Elizabeth Town—divers Clergymen of the Church of England, especially Mr. Johnson[39] and Wetmore.[40] N.B. Mr. Elmer[41] of Cohanzy. N.B. Mr. John Barrett and Mr. Benjamin Gerrish, Merchants of Boston, there. I din'd in the Hall. The Exercises and Entertainments handsome and agreeable, and especially the Valedictory Oration. The Company was

not very numerous. The Custom of giving Diploma at the time of giving the Degree is most fit and proper in my Eye and what I could wish our College would come into.

14. Went up to College a.m. In returning I carry'd down with me to Mrs. Pierponts, to Dinner Mr. Bliss, Mr. Case and Mr. Hunt. P.M. Mr. Elmer and Mr. Pemberton came to us. N.B. Sarah Cunnabel, Mrs. Pierponts Maid in a Fit.

15. We (Scil. Mrs. Pierpont, my wife and I) din'd at Mr. Noyes's.[42] N.B. Mr. Edwards[43] of North Hampton with us. P.M. Mr. Noyes, Mr. Edwards and I visited Mr. Isaac Dickerman,[44] a middle Batchelour, who was in a Languishment. Visited Mr. Daniel Edwards[45]—the Rector—and went into the Library—still with Mr. Jonathan Edwards. Mr. Woodbridge accompany'd us home to Mrs. Pierponts. I was much indispos'd altho I kept about, and was in Variety of Company, but especially I was very uncomfortable in the Evening and through the Night.

16. Mr. Edwards of North Hampton came to see me and walk with me to College, which I attempted altho I was not well. Mr. Woodbridge[46] conducted us into the Library and I Spent Several Hours diligently in viewing the Books. A most Curious and Costly Collection. Din'd at Old Madame Pierponts. P.M. I return'd to the Library again. At Mr. Noyes's. I was very feeble, and my stomach deprav'd. Return'd to my Lodging before Night. N.B. Sarah Cunnabel another Fit.

17. Too much indispos'd still for my public Service, yet was oblig'd to try. Mr. Hunt preach'd a.m. on Tit. 3, 2. I din'd at Mr. Noyes's. N.B. I left my Bible at Home when I went to meeting p.m. I hastily fetch'd it. Mr. Noyes pray'd. I preach'd on Job 19, 25. Supp'd at Mr. Noyes's. N.B. Old Mr. Warham Mather,[47] the Rector and Mr. Daniel Edwards there after Supper. Walk'd to Mr. Prouts[48] where we were very kindly receiv'd. From thence we retir'd home. Several very Cool Nights.

18. Mr. Prout, his Lady and Dauter, Mr. Hunt and Sister, and Mr. Pomroy, all came in to see us at going off. Mr. Hezekiah Pierpont[49] came and waited upon Mrs. Pierpont Some Miles with us. I rode up to College and to the Rectors for Mr. Woodbridge who had appointed to go with us, but he did not go. Mr. Daniel Edwards and Mr. Belden of Norwalk were our Company. Sorrowful Leave-taking of our Friends. Mr. Pierpont and Madame his Sister rode as far as Hamesdens and there parted. We set out from thence at almost noon. We din't at Halls[50] in Merrydan, a Corner of Farmington (as I remember) at 3/4 after one. Set out again just an Hour after. Stop'd at Beckleys. Mr. Thomas Goodwin,[51] late of Boston, now of Weathersfield, in Company. We halted at Mr. Goodwins at Weathersfield, and then tho weary'd and tir'd we stood it out to Mr. Secretary Wyllys's in Hartford, and there were friendly receiv'd and lodg'd that Night. N.B. The Antient Pedigree of Wyllys.

19. In great Doubt in the Morning about prosecuting our Journey being it was so lowery—but Mr. Edwards being waiting, we mounted from Mr. Austins in order to go to Windham; but the rain prevail'd so much that we bid farewell to Mr. Edwards, who being Clerk of the Court was oblig'd to go, and we return'd to Mr. Austins and spent the Day. P.M. Mr. Ellery's[52] Musick. At Eve Mr. Ellery and I visited Mr. Whitman and Mr. Wyllys. We Lodg'd at Mr. Austins.

20. In the Morning Mr. Ellerys little son was Scall'd with hot Chocolat, which as it put every one into great affliction it much retarded us and prevent'd our journeying Early. Mr. Wyllys and Mr. Ellery were so good as to ride with us. N.B. One of our

[18] William Allis of Sunderland.

[19] Reverend Ebenezer Devotion (Harvard 1707), third minister of Suffield, Mass. (now Connecticut). *Sibley*, V, 329-331.

[20] John Austin of Hartford, a merchant of that town.

[21] Jonathan Law (Harvard 1695), Governor of Connecticut. *Sibley*, IV, 237-242.

[22] Joseph Wadsworth of Windsor, Conn.

[23] George Wyllys (Yale 1729), Secretary of the Colony of Connecticut. *Dexter*, 399-400.

[24] Reverend Timothy Woodbridge (Yale 1706), minister of Simsbury, Conn., 1710-1742. Dexter, pp. 57-58.

[25] Benajah Case (Yale 1733), later minister of New Fairfield, Conn., 1742-1753. Dexter, pp. 475-476.

[26] Lieutenant Joseph Beckley of Wethersfield, Conn., was the proprietor of an important tavern on the road between Hartford and New Haven.

[27] Eleazer Aspinwall of Farmington (Kensington Parish).

[28] John Hamaston, Jr. (1685-1767).

[29] Reverend Eleazer Wheelock (Yale 1733), minister of the third church of Lebanon (Columbia), Conn., 1735-1770; later the founder and first president of Dartmouth College.

[30] Mary (Hooker) Pierpont, the widow of the Reverend James Pierpont (d. 1714), survived until Nov. 1, 1738. She was the granddaughter of the Reverend Thomas Hooker, the first minister of Hartford, Conn. Her daughter, Sarah, married Jonathan Edwards, D.D., the president of Princeton College.

[31] Mary Pierpont was the wife of the Reverend William Russell (Yale 1709), minister of Middletown, Conn., 1715-1761. Dexter, 90-91.

[32] James Pierpont, Jr. (Yale 1718), son of the Reverend James Pierpont of New Haven. Dexter, 189-190.

[33] Reverend Ebenezer Gay (Harvard 1714), minister of Hingham, Mass., 1717-1787. *Sibley*, VI, 59-66.

[34] Reverend Seth Storer (Harvard 1720), minister of Watertown, Mass., 1724-1774. *Sibley*, VI, 412-414.

[35] Reverend Ebenezer Pemberton (Harvard 1721), minister of the Presbyterian Church, New York City, 1727-1753. *Sibley*, VI, 535-546.

[36] Reverend William Smith (Harvard 1725), minister of the First Congregational Church of Weymouth, Mass., 1734-1783. Reverend Smith's daughter, Abigail, became the wife of President John Adams. *Sibley*, VII, 588-591.

[37] (Harvard 1734), of Watertown, Mass. He preached at Dedham and at Bellington, but in 1740 became a merchant at Watertown. *Sibley*, IX, 414-418.

[38] Reverend Jonathan Dickinson (Yale 1706), minister of Elizabethtown (Union), New Jersey, 1709-1747, and later President of Princeton College. Dexter, 45-52.

[39] Reverend Samuel Johnson (Yale 1714), minister of Christ Church, Episcopal, Stratford, Conn., 1723-1754 and 1764-1772. He was the first President of King's (now Columbia) College, 1754-1763. Dexter, pp. 133-138.

[40] Reverend James Wetmore (Yale 1714), minister of Christ Church, Rye, New York, 1726-1760. Dexter, pp. 133-138.

[41] Daniel Elmer (Yale 1713). Formerly of Westborough, Mass., and at this time minister of the church of Christ of Cohansey, Fairfield, New Jersey, 1727-1755. Dexter, pp. 110-111.

[42] Reverend Joseph Noyes (Yale 1709), minister at New Haven, 1715-1761. Dexter, pp. 85-89.

[43] Reverend Jonathan Edwards (Yale 1720), the great divine of Northampton, Mass., and later President of Princeton College.

[44] (Yale 1736). Dexter, p. 558.

[45] (Yale 1720). Dexter, pp. 216-217.

[46] Probably Timothy Woodbridge, Jr., tutor at Yale College.

[47] (Harvard 1685), sometime preacher and teacher, and Judge of the Probate Court at New Haven, 1716-1727. Sibley, III, 319-320.

[48] John Prout (Yale 1708), a merchant of New Haven and Treasurer of Yale College. Dexter, pp. 76-77.

[49] The youngest son of the Reverend James Pierpont of New Haven.

[50] Reverend Theophilus Hall (Yale 1727), first minister of Meriden, Conn., 1728-1767. Dexter, pp. 352-353.

[51] (Harvard 1725). *Sibley*, VII, 517-518.

[52] John Ellery (Harvard 1732), originally of Boston, was a prominent merchant of Hartford. *Sibley*, IX, 148-150.

Horses blunder'd overboard of the Ferry Boat, wet the Side-saddle etc., but we receiv'd not much more Damage than the Hindrance to our Journey thereby. N.B. Our Great Suspence whether we Should ride Springfield Road again or to Windham. One Mr. Stebbins was going to Springfield. Many Arguments were us'd against Bolton and Ashford Road, but most of all my Wife's Circumstances prevail'd to go Springfield way. Mr. Willys and Mr. Ellery accompany'd us as far as Grants[53] Tavern, where we din'd, oated etc. and all at their Expence. At almost 3 p.m. we took leave of those Gentlemen, mounted from Grants. Call'd at Mr. Reynolds's[54] in Enfield. Continued on to Long Meadow where we overtook Dr. Pyncheon. Arriv'd at Mr. Brecks a little before Day Light down, nor were we so overtir'd as at some other Times.

21. Mr. Breck rode with us Two or Three miles. Stopp'd a little at Lambs but din'd at Scotts. Lost our way before we got to Ashleys and wander'd some but found our Road so seasonably as to get to Mr. Cheneys in the first of the Evening. Were cheerfully received and handsomely lodg'd.

22. We set out early from Brookfield. Saw nothing of Mr. Bliss at Richardsons as was appointed tho we tarried some while there. Din'd at Mr. Goddards's[55] at Leicester (whose wife had lately been deliver'd of a son). He set out with us for Worcester. Met Mr. Abijah Bruce of Westborough on the Road. Call'd at Mr. Burrs[56] and at Mr. Cushings. Got home in Safety and found all Things well and in Prosperity. Moss[57] went off the Monday morning after we departed. Blessed be the Lord who hath smil'd on our going out and returning Home, who hath been our Shade upon our Right Hand and preserved us and ours from all Evil. To His Name be Glory from henceforth and forever!

23. I had agreed with Mr. Brown[58] of Lexington to preach last Sabbath but he came not by which means our people were without preaching Two Sabbaths.

24. Repeated Sermon on Matt. 26, 41. Rainy.

25. Rainy. Town Meeting upon my Support and to See what is best to be done about a Meeting House. I put in a Memorial to the Town and they made my sallery and support 200£. The other Affair was adjourn'd for a Fortnight.

26. Abraham Moss came here, acknowledg'd his unfit Conduct and Language in his Passionate Heat on the 4th Instant. P.M. I rode out to Several near neighbours. Mrs. Byles,[59] etc. Raw Cold. Perplex'd concerning a well, my Pump and Well being altogether dry.

27. Rainy again, and continued all Day very Wett. Arbitrators of the Affair between old Mr. Maynard[60] and Brother Hicks met today. Scil. Colonel Wards[61] of Southborough, Captain Williams[62] of Marlborough, and Captain Eager[63] of Westborough.

28. Rainy Still. Old Mr. Maynard came and requested me to go over to his son in laws, Nathaniel Oakes[64] to see their Young Child. P.M. It held up. I went over with him. The Child was thought to be in great Danger of Death. They requested that I would baptize it. They sent about to the Neibours to come in. There came upward of 20 persons, and I baptiz'd it by the name of Ebenezer. After that Exercise I rode up to Lieutenant Holloways,[65] visited Silas and Timothy Fay, and call'd at Captain Eagers at Evening.

29. Silas and Timothy Fay came and began a New Well for me.

30. Stormy Day again.

## OCTOBER, 1738

1. Very Stormy. On Heb. 10, 39. P.M. repeated on Mat. 26, 41. Mr. Townsend[1] din'd, and by reason of the Storm continuing lodg'd here.

2. Rainy morning, but when it slack'd Mr. Townsend return'd home. Eleazer Rice call'd me to visit Mr. James Maynard and his Children who were sick. I went and found Mr. Maynard very bad. P.M. I was at the Funeral of Mr. Nathaniel Oakes young Child (vid. supr.).

3. Expecting Moss for his Money, I rode to Mr. Joslins to provide it for him. When I return'd home Colonel Richard Saltonstall[2] was at my House upon his Journey from Springfield Court. N.B. Mrs. Eager, Mrs. Holloway, and Mrs. Wheeler to visit my wife. At Evening having rode with Judge Saltonstall to See him well out of Town, I visited Mr. James Maynard again and those Two of his Children which were Still very Bad. N.B. John Rogers carted me 500 Bricks from Pelatiah Rice's.

4. [No entry].

5. Old Mr. Maynard Winnow'd 12 Bushels and nigh 3 Pecks of Rice for me. N.B. Mr. Pannel had winnow'd 2 Bushels before. Susan Cutting rode to Shrewsbury. At Eve rode to Mr. Grouts[3] where I Supp'd. Mr. Tainter and his wife, etc. there. N.B. Mrs. Tainters high Disgust at our Dining the Sabbath before last in the Kitchen—She Surmizing that it was done with design to keep People from coming to warm themselves, which had not entered into our Thoughts, but was done because the House was Cold by the Storm and we had no fire in the Dining Room. At Winchesters[4] and at old Mr. Samuel Fays.[5]

6. Visited Mr. James Maynard in the Morning, who grows Somewhat better. Thomas Winchester gather'd in our Beans, pick'd winter Apples, etc. Susan return'd from Shrewsbury at Night.

7. Children picking Apples.

8. On Eph. 6, 5, 6, 7, 8.

9. All the officers met together at Ensign Maynards upon the Affair of a Regemental Muster. Mr. Prentice[6] of Grafton, Mr. Cook,[7] preacher at Marlborough, Dr. Gott, etc., were here. Town Meeting by adjournment to See what Should be done about a Meeting House. Dissolv'd. Divers Neighbours kindly help'd David Baverick (who wrought for me to Day) in Cutting up my Corn and carting it into the Barn. N.B. Noah How help'd David a.m. in carting in stalks, and Noah and his Brother Daniel[8] carted my Apples to our Mill. At Night 10 or a Dozen young men and Lads Husk'd part of my Corn.

10. Rain'd hard in the morning. P.M. it ceas'd and then I rode to the Southermost Houses towards Hopkinton. Supp'd at old Mr. Graves's.[9] N.B. Colonel Ward,[10] Captain Williams and Captain Eager, Arbitrators upon Mr. Maynards and Hicks's Difference. They brought in to Hicks's Dissatisfaction.

11. David Baverick wrought for me carrying up Corn, making a Partition Fence. Susanna Cutting[11] left us. She rode to Waterton upon my Horse.

12. Receiv'd Three Barrells of My own Cyder from Mr. How's Mill, and 4 More of Mr. Whitney[12] which I bought for 11 shillings per Barrell. Mr. Prentice of Grafton and Mr. Samuel Cook came and din'd with me. Mr. Cook preach'd on 1 Cor. 6, ult. Church meeting after Lecture on the Affairs of Mr. Samuel Fay, etc., and Concerning the Fragments after the Lords Supper, and concerning Vessels of the Table and a Baptizing Bason. Adjourn'd to this Day sennight. Ebenezer Maynard brought 2½ Barrells more of my Cyder from Mr. How's.

[53] Ebenezer Grant (Yale 1726), a leading merchant and inn-keeper in the East parish of Windsor (now East Windsor). Dexter, p. 328.

[54] Reverend Peter Reynolds (Harvard 1720), minister of Enfield, Conn., 1724–1768. *Sibley*, VI, 396–399.

[55] Reverend David Goddard (Harvard 1731), second minister of Leicester, Mass., 1736–1754. *Sibley*, IX, 40–43.

[56] Reverend Isaac Burr of Worcester.

[57] Abraham Moss, Parkman's hired man.

[58] Josiah Brown (Harvard 1735), sometime preacher and schoolmaster of Lancaster and Sterling, Mass. *Sibley*, IX, 476–478.

[59] Mrs. Joseph Byles.

[60] David Maynard.

[61] William Ward, justice of the peace and holder of several town offices.

[62] Abraham Williams, Parkman's brother-in-law.

[63] James Eager.

[64] Nathaniel Oak married Keziah Maynard, June 7, 1736.

[65] William Holloway of Westborough.

[1] Joshua Townsend, the first schoolmaster of Westborough.

[2] (Harvard 1722). *Sibley*, VII, 117–121.

[3] Joseph Grout, selectman of Westborough.

[4] Benjamin Winchester of Westborough.

[5] An original settler of Westborough.

[6] Reverend Solomon Prentice.

[7] Samuel Cooke (Harvard 1735), later minister of the First Congregational Church of Arlington, Mass. *Sibley*, IX, 500–508.

[8] Sons of Parkman's neighbor, Hezekiah How.

[9] John Graves of Westborough.

[10] Nahum Ward of Shrewsbury.

[11] Mrs. Parkman's helper.

[12] Nathaniel Whitney, a selectman of Westborough.

13. We boyl'd Cyder this Forenoon.

14. [No entry].

15. The Lords Supper was administered. Preach'd on Matt. 22, 12, Eph. 6, 8. At Eve I visited Mrs. James Maynard who lay in an extremely Dangerous state. When I return'd from Mr. Maynards I found Mr. James Pierpont at my House, who this Evening came up from Marlborough, and was upon his Journey to New Haven.

16. I Catechiz'd at the Meeting House a. and p.m. Rain a.m. Did not clear off p.m. Yet Mr. Pierpont was intent upon his Journey home. Mr. David Buys[13] of New Glasgow being here and going upwards, Mr. Pierpont was not to be persuaded to stay. He design'd for Worcester tonight.

17. Mr. Stone and I rode up to Shrewsbury to Ministers Meeting. See Association Records. Mr. Aaron Whitney[14] offer'd himself voluntarily to Examination. Mr. Tainter here at Eve with Lads who Husk'd more of my Corn but did not finish it.

18. Mr. Stone preach'd a very useful Sermon on Col. 1, 27. N.B. Mr. Loring absent, 'tis Thought on the Affair of Woburn, where there was a large Council last Week. Mr. Stone return'd home with me.

19. Deacon Forbush[15] somewhat after noon. Church Meeting was not duely attended either by any Number of Members or Seasonably by those who did come. See Church Records. Mr. Whipple[16] and Mr. Bradish[17] here at Eve.

20. Neighbor Hezekiah How brought 500 more of Bricks home for me.

21. Mr. Williams here. P.M. Ensign Maynard[18] brought a Kegg of Rhum from Boston.

22. On Matt. 9, 9. P.M. on Ex. 10, 11. Mr. Chamberlain[19] din'd with us.

23. At Deacon Tomlins,[20] Seth Rice's, Jedediah How's. P.M. getting up Corn from the Barn.

24. Captain Forbush came and invited me to Dinner to Day at Ensign Maynards. Trooping and Training. I pray'd with the Company, din'd with the Officers and pray'd with the whole Body at Night and we sung part of Ps. 144.

25. Very Rainy Day. At Eve I rode to Ensign Forbush, Master Townsend's, etc.

26. Mr. Hezekiah How and Mr. Francis Whipple accompany'd me to Grafton Lecture. I preach'd on Jude 10, 21, 1st Clause. We return'd at Eve.

27.28. I desire to take some serious Notice of the Longsuffering of God towards me and his Church in this place in continuing under the precious advantage of the Gospel these fourteen Years. I see great Reason to humble myself for my unfaithfullness Negligence and Unprofitableness and I would penitently repair to God in Christ for forgiveness.

29. We meditated upon What it is to be in Christ, what Benefits there are thereof, the Great Advantages of having been in Christ some years, and the great Privilege, advantage and Comfort of Knowing and being Sure of this; with Reflections adapted to the present Time and our present Circumstances. From 2 Cor. 12,2.

30. Very rainy and exceeding high Winds.

31. Meeting of proprietors of Houssatunnoc No. 3 at Ensign Maynards. My admission (on Condition of my paying 15£ and 6£ more towards Meeting House, etc.) Confirm'd. Mr. Palmer, Mr. William Maning and Mr. Thomas Hastings came up.

### NOVEMBER, 1738

1. Mr. Palmer had my Horse to go to Worcester his own being Lame. Mr. Manning, Hastings and Hicks din'd with us. Mr. Palmer return'd and he and Mr. Manning lodg'd here.

2. Mr. Palmer etc. return'd home. Church Meeting. See Records.[1] Had a pair of Turkeys of Mr. Jonathan Bellows brought home.

3. [No entry].

4. The Boys dug potatoes. Aaron Forbush, junior, and his Brother Benjamin dug p.m.

5. 2 Cor. 12, 2 and 1 Pet. 4, 4.

6. Rainy. Town meeting again about a Meeting House, but it fell through for want of selectmen.

7. Mr. Tainter Sow'd and plough'd in Rye for me. John Hicks junior dug Potatoes. Captain Goddard[2] here. I visited Captain Warrins[3] wife. Very fine Weather.

8. Fine Weather Still. I rode up to Mr. Garfields Lime Kiln now in Burning. Return'd by James Maynards whom I visited as he is Slowly creeping up from his low Condition, and his little son John worse again. N.B. Molly[4] went with Mr. Tainter up to Mr. Joseph Miles's and then home with Mr. Tainter.

9. My wife rode with me to visit upon the North side of the Town. Din'd at Captain Eagers and proceeded up to the Bowkers. Supp'd at Lieutenant Holloways. N.B. I bought a Swine of him for which I agreed to give him 3£. In returning we visited Mr. Josiah Rice, whose wife was sick of a Fever.

10. Mr. Peter Smith[5] of Shrewsbury and his Daughter[6] here. A Glazier also (one Child of Roxbury) to mend up my Glass. Salt brought up gratis by the Teams which went from here.

11. Abraham Moss here. He mention'd a mistake he thought was made in the Counting the money which was paid him, which expos'd him to loose 20 shillings.

12. Mat. 9, 12, 13. Eccl. 9, 3. Mrs. Byles and widow Pratt[7] and others din'd. It was a Cold Day, and the more tedious as it came upon us Suddenly. First time of Snowing at all, this Year.

13. The Cold increas'd and was very pinching. Ty'd up as many Cattle as we could.

14. More Moderate. Training Day. Andrew Cwees [?] brought the Swine which I bought of Lieutenant Holloway last week, price 3£.

15. Sister Hicks[8] brought to bed of her 10th Child—my wife over there till 5 o'Clock this morning. Mr. Aaron Forbush came to go up to Wachuset. Ensign Maynard rode with us to Captain Eagers and Lieutenant Holloways but the Rain prevail'd so that we return'd back after dining with Lieutenant Holloways. N.B. snow'd this morning.

16. Rainy.

17. [No entry].

19. Eccl. 9, 3; Ps. 51, 15.

20. Sold Mr. Tainter 3 Largest Weathers I had. Eve I visited Mr. Noah Rice's wife who was very sick and dejected. Very cold Night.

21. Snow.

22. [No entry].

23. Thanksgiving. Heb. 13, 15, 16. Neighbor Joseph Green Supp'd with us. A very Cold Day.

24. Ensign Maynard and I reckon'd and settled accounts. Deacon Newton here at Evening.

25. Cold season. Dr. Gott[9] here. My Wife has for some time had her Limbs exceedingly swelling insomuch that she can't well go about.

26. Sacrament. Matth. 22, 12. Ps. 74, 17. Very cold. 3 Deacons and Neighbor Thomas Bruce din'd with us. P.M. Snow.

27. Out of wood, except very great Loggs. Stephen Maynard at my desire brought a Load. Town Meeting the 4th Time about

[13] Probably one of the Boies family of New Glasgow (Blandford), Mass.

[14] (Harvard 1737), later the first minister of the First Congregational Society of Petersham, Mass., 1738-1777. *Sibley*, X, 260–263.

[15] Thomas Forbush, an original settler of Westborough.

[16] Francis Whipple.

[17] James Bradish, an original settler of Westborough.

[18] Stephen Maynard.

[19] Ebenezer Chamberlin.

[20] Isaac Tomlin or Tomblin.

[1] The church debarred Samuel Fay from the communion because he had prevented his wife from coming to church. On Dec. 17, 1738 Fay's acknowledgement of his offence was accepted.

[2] Edward Goddard of Framingham.

[3] Mrs. Daniel Warrin of Westborough.

[4] Parkman's oldest child, Mary.

[5] One of the founders of the church in Shrewsbury.

[6] Elizabeth Smith, born Dec. 22, 1724.

[7] Mrs. John Pratt, Sr., mother of John Pratt, Jr., an original settler of Westborough.

[8] Mrs. John Hicks of Westborough, Parkman's sister-in-law.

[9] Benjamin Gott, the physician of Marlborough, Parkman's brother-in-law.

a Meeting House or repairing the old one, or Dividing the Town. N.B. 23 votes out of 47 for the first. Mr. Tainter[10] alone my Butcher in killing the old Cow. Weight 327, Tallow 42, Hide 50. Sold the hide to Captain Eager for 25 Shillings. I was at Ensign Maynards in the Eve. N.B. Lucy Forbush came to work for us.

28. Snow'd. Mr. Taynter and his wife here cutting up and Salting down my Beef. At Mr. Cornelius Cooks.[11] Evening at Deacon Newtons.[12]

29. Mrs. Dorothy Rice[13] here. We rode over to see sister Hicks. We supp'd there. Brother Samuel Breck[14] came up to see us, and tarried.

30. Read Andrew Marvels[15] Rehearsal transpos'd.[16] Evening made up accounts with Mr. Hezekiah How. N.B. Mr. Ebenezer Johnson of Southborough and others here.

### DECEMBER, 1738

1. Snowy Day. Brother Samuel Breck went to Marlborough. Mr. Tainter came and got up Wood for me.

2. Snow'd hard. My wife grows more and more indispos'd.

3. Bright Day. Mat. 9, 14–17. Ps. 119, 5. Mr. Bradish and Mr. Samuel Harrington din'd with us. Lucy Forbush went home at Eve.

4. Very Cold morning. I rode over to Old Mr. Ward[1] and got his Dauter to come and Serve us. Thence to Deacon Newtons and after that I went to Cambridge. A troublesome cold Journey. Sister Lydia[2] had been very ill but was recovering.

5. Rain & cold. Din'd at Father Champneys. P.M. I rode to Boston. Small Pox in Town, in several places. Lodg'd at Brother Elias's.[3] N.B. Brother Samuel[4] had bargain'd for an Irish Lad of 15 years, with Captain Solomon Lombard—for £7, 15, and he was lodg'd at Brother Elias's till my Coming to Town. The Boys Name was John Ridney, born in the county of Waterford in Ireland.

6. Din'd at Brother Elias's. P.M. at Brother Alexander's.[5] At Eve at Mr. Webbs[6] with Brother Elias. My aged Mother still in a measure of Comfort. D.G.

7. Mr. Checkley[7] on Amos 3, 2 at public Lecture. N.B. great Trouble occasion'd by my having an hat left me in the Pew which was not mine by (as I found the next Day) Mr. Daniel Lagg of Cambridge. Din'd at Brother Samuels. At Eve John consented to be bound and go up with me forthwith. Whilst I was concern'd about the means and way of getting John up to Westborough Brother Hicks was at Brother Elias's. By various impediments we were hinder'd going over the Ferry till after nine o'Clock at night, but they ferry'd over, Brother and John and my Self for 2/6. Rode to Cambridge. Lodg'd John at the blue Anchor,[8] whilst Brother and I with our Horses were taken care of at Mr. Whittemore's.[9] N.B. Mr. Whittemore and wife and their sister Fisher from Boston not till after 12. A Cold Night.

8. Finish'd the Indentures and binding of John. Was at Colonel Goffs[10] for my Hatt. At Brecks Chamber at College. Sent John over to Father Champney's and upon Brother Hick's mare I undertook my Journey home. N.B. Colonel Fullam[11] at

Mr. Woolson's[12] Tavern. Not home till very late and Cold and Spent. N.B. In my absence a good Ewe (that which Mr. Ball[13] presented me at the Setting up my Flock) fell into the old House Cellar and dy'd there.

9. Brother Hicks and John Ridney came up on my Horse. A very Cold Day. Jerusha Ward[14] went home.

10. Ps. 119, 5, and p.m. Repeated sermon 2 on Ps. 90, 9 from Ps. 39, 5.

11. Patience Forbush[15] tarried last night that She might Serve us two or Three Days. Mrs. Knowlton and Mrs. Whipple to visit my wife. Mrs. Maynard and Cousen Winchester here also. In the Evening her Husband came. They tarried and Supp'd with us.

12. Snow. Ensign Maynard.

13. Mr. Cushing[16] made me a kind visit. Patience went home at night.

14. I rode to Marlborough, Ebenezer[17] with me, to Colonel Woods's[18] (who was gone to Charleston) to Mr. Butlers,[19] Mr. Tainters and Dr. Gotts. At the last place was Mr. Samuel Cook and others. We return'd home though late.

15. Abiel Allen came p.m. to serve us. Mr. Grout at Eve to consult upon the affair of getting wood. Snowy Night.

16. My wife has not only Swell'd greatly in her Limbs but (besides her pregnancy) in her Body, and is exceeding full of Pain. I sent Ebenezer to Marlborough to the Doctor's. A warmish, thawy Day. Wind at Sundown.

17. Rom. 8, 16 occasioned in part by the growing extravagance of Velvet and scarlet among people of low Rank. P.M. repeated sermon on Ps. 119, 9. My wife very ill. Public Prayers for her. At night extream full of Pain, and continued all Night. N.B. Mr. Eliezer Bellows[20] and Granny Forbush[21] din'd with us. Exceeding Cold Night.

18. The Morning Exeeding Cold. Dr. Gott here. Mrs. Knowlton and Mrs. Williams here to see my wife. She continues Swell'd and full of Pain.

19. Mr. Grout with a Team, and Mr. Samuel Harrington with his oxen to make up another Team with my oxen and Sled, Mr. Groe,[22] Mr. Tainter, Mr. Beriah Rice,[23] Mr. Jonathan Forbush, junior, Thomas Winchester, Edwards Whipple, Ephraim Whitney,[24] Samuel Rogers, Thomas Whitney, junior. Mr. Aaron Forbush[25] came p.m. to Cut and sled me wood from the further side of the Hill. N.B. One Mr. Daniel Damon of Leicester, who was born near Sydmouth in old England hear with Dears Leather. Bought a skin and a Brass-Albany-Tobacco Box of him. Brother Samuel Breck came up from Marlborough and lodg'd here. With him came sister Gott[26] and Mrs. Bulah Bent,[27] and after them came Captain Williams. These latter went down to Marlborough at Eve. N.B. Mrs. Byles and Mrs. Bruce to visit my wife and at Eve Mrs. Susanna Forbush.[28] A very Cold Night.

20. Very Cold and windy. Brother Samuel rode away upon his Journey to Springfield.

21. The Cold Somewhat abated. Sister Hicks here.

---

[10] Deacon Simon Tainter.

[11] The blacksmith of Westborough.

[12] Josiah Newton

[13] Wife of Seth Rice, son of Edmund Rice, an original settler of Westborough.

[14] Parkman's brother-in-law, the son of the late Reverend Robert Breck of Marlborough.

[15] Andrew Marvell (1621–1678), an English poet and satirist.

[16] *The Rehearsal Transpros'd, or Animadversions upon a late book intituled 'A Preface showing what Grounds there are of Fears and Jealousies of Popery'* (1672).

[1] Increase Ward, an original settler of Westborough.

[2] Lydia Champney, Parkman's sister-in-law.

[3] Elias Parkman.

[4] Samuel Parkman of Boston.

[5] Alexander Parkman of Boston.

[6] Reverend John Webb of Boston.

[7] Reverend Samuel Checkley (Harvard 1715), later minister of the Second Church of Boston, 1747–1768. *Sibley*, VI, 74–78.

[8] An old tavern in Cambridge operated at this time by Joseph Bean. Paige, *Cambridge*, pp. 225–226.

[9] Probably Deacon Samuel Whittemore of Cambridge.

[10] Edmund Goffe (Harvard 1690) of Cambridge, onetime selectman and representative, who was commissioned colonel in 1724. *Sibley*, IV, 57–60.

[11] Francis Fulham of Weston, Mass. Bond, *Watertown*, p. 227.

[12] The Woolson family had operated a tavern in Watertown since 1686. Bond, *Watertown*, pp. 668–669.

[13] Nathan Ball, an early settler.

[14] Daughter of Increase Ward of Westborough.

[15] Daughter of Deacon Jonathan Forbush of Westborough.

[16] Reverend Job Cushing of Shrewsbury.

[17] Parkman's oldest son, now eleven years old.

[18] Benjamin Woods.

[19] Peter Butler of Marlborough.

[20] Eleazer Bellows came to Westborough in the 1720's. The *Westborough Vital Records* record the births of three daughters and one son to Eleazer and Sarah Bellows, August 18, 1728.

[21] Widow of Deacon Thomas Forbush who died in May 1738.

[22] Samuel Grow.

[23] Son of Thomas Rice, an original settler of Westborough. Beriah lived in Westborough until about 1742 when he removed to Annapolis, Nova Scotia.

[24] Son of Nathaniel Whitney of Westborough.

[25] Eldest son of the late Deacon Thomas Forbush.

[26] Parkman's sister-in-law, the wife of Dr. Benjamin Gott.

[27] Beulah was the daughter of Peter Bent of Westborough.

[28] Mrs. Aaron Forbush.

22. Snow. The Boys Sledding up the remainder of the wood which was cut on the 19.

23. Cold. Sledding again. N.B. My wife in much Trouble by Headach last night.

24. Rom. 8, 6. P.M. Snow. Storm'd hard at Evening and very Cold. N.B. very few at meeting. My wife's Headach extreme.

25. Moderate, pleasant, bright morning. Neighbor Oak came with a Team, neighbor Jacob Rice,[29] Jonathan Maynard,[30] John Oake and Lieutenant Holloways men came to get wood. Fitted up our Team to go with them but after 4 Turns our sled was crush'd down. It rain'd when they came to Dinner and the rain preval'd So as to prevent their going for any more.

26. A little after 4 in the morning my Wife call'd Me up by her extreme pains prevailing upon her and changing into signs of Travail. I rode over to Deacon Forbush's[31] and brought her [sic] over as our midwife. Sister Hicks, old Mrs. Knowlton, Mrs. Whipple, Mrs. Hephzibath Maynard,[32] Mrs. Byles and Mrs. Rogers were call'd and brought and stay'd all Day and Night. The Weather Moderate and plesant.

27. In the morning the Women Scattered away to their several Homes except Mrs. Forbush who did not leave us. At Eve Deacon Forbush and Mr. John Pannell here. N.B. My Two Youngest Cattle and one of my Oxen not well. We cut off a part of the Tails. Mr. Tainter here to mend the sled. At night it grew exceeding Cold.

28. At about 4 in the morning Mrs. Forbush call'd me up with great earnestness to gather some women together. It was very Cold, and I ran on foot to sister Hicks and to old Mrs. Knowlton—sent to Mrs. Maynard and rode to Mrs. Byles, all which came together by Daybreak. We were in the Article of Distress. About

Seven o'Clock my Fourth Daughter was born. An exceeding Small Child and great doubt whether it would continue alive. But my wife in a good State, through the wondrous Goodness and Mercy of God. A Cold Day. Sent Ebenezer Maynard to Dr. Gotts, and to call Mrs. Mary Sherman[33] to Nurse. N.B. Sear'd the Ox which continued bleeding. N.B. Suse Cutting,[34] being married to John Rogers, as I concluded, is come up to dwell at Neighbor Rogers's. Nurse watch'd.

29. Mrs. Forbush carried home by Ebenezer. N.B. Mrs. Tainter here to discourse with me upon the Offence I had manifested at her Dauters being the Introducers of Velvet whoods among young persons of low Rank in the Congregation and she in a Christian manner Submitted and ask'd forgiveness inasmuch as She had been the Author of it. Martha Maynard[35] watch'd.

30. My wife in great Pain. Mrs. Maynard here. At Evening my wife exceedingly pained under her Breasts—thought to be the Coming of her milk. Molly Lee and the Nurse watch'd.

31. Cold, p.m. Snowy. Concluded the Year with Rev. 20, 12 and Discourse before the Baptism of my Daughter Elizabeth God hath Sworn on Mal. 3, 17. My Wife Easier to Day. Rebecca Hicks[36] watch'd.

As I have renewed my Engagement unto God and given up my Self and mine to Him, So, on the other Hand, God himself hath Sworn that they that Fear Him Shall be His in the Day that He will make up his Jewells. And O that We might be of that number! And that this Dear Infant in particular may be a rich Jewell in the Cabinet of God!

In finishing the Year God enable me to have a reallizing thought of the finishing of all Things, and that Great Day of the Eternal Doom for all both Small and Great, that I may be found ready for it whenever it Shall break forth!

---

[29] Son of Jacob Rice of Marlborough. Jacob and his wife were admitted to the Westborough church in Dec. 1731.

[30] Son of David Maynard.

[31] Jonathan Forbush.

[32] Wife of Captain John Maynard.

[33] Mrs. John Sherman of Marlborough.

[34] John Rogers of Westborough married Susanna Cuttin in Watertown Dec. 26, 1738.

[35] Daughter of David Maynard of Marlborough.

[36] Mrs. John Hicks, Parkman's sister-in-law.

# ❧ II ❧

## *THE GREAT AWAKENING*

### *1739-1747*

## JANUARY, 1739.

It may with great Reason affect us that the Waste of Years which hasten us into Eternity, makes no more impression upon us, or no more abiding!

2. I rode to Marlborough round by Mr. Josiah Rice's[1] and Captain Eagers.[2] My Little son Thomas rode with me. Rode to Captain Joseph Hows,[3] Mr. Joseph Tainters[4] where we Din'd, to Mr. Peter Butlers, Colonel Woods's and to Dr. Gotts. The Cold prevail'd at Evening So much that I yielded to their persuasions, for the sake of my son, to tarry over night. An Exceeding Cold night.

3. A very Cold Day—but Thommè and I rode up home through a sharp Cold Wind. Call'd to see Captain Warrins Wife who is exceeding low and weak. Extreme Cold night. Hannah Maynard[5] watch'd, as Lucy Forbush[6] did with Nurse last Night.

4. My Wife makes no great Haste in Recovery, but the Child is very weak and feeble yet, and the sore Mouth has been prevailing upon it for some time. Abiel Allen watch'd. Cold Season.

5. My Wife very faint and weak, fainting in going from the bed to the Table. Ruth Hicks watch'd. Cold continues. Boys sled wood.

6. My Wife feeble. Childs Sore mouth continues Bad. Rebecca watch'd.

7. Moderate fine Day. On Rev. 20, 12. N.B. Mr. Daniel Stones Wife din'd here. At Eve Rebecca Taynter[7] tarried and watch'd. My wife somewhat more Comfortable. The Child in doubtfull State by its Sore Mouth. N.B. Publick Prayers for the Child.

8. Old Mrs. Knowlton and Mrs. Maynard here. Boys cutting wood within the Fence. Child very bad. Mrs. Maynard watch'd.

9. The Child extreme bad, especially the latter part of the Day. Boys sledded home wood. P.M. and Evening we thought the Child was dying—took nothing for many Hours, a Ghastly pale overspread the Visage and appear'd choak'd up; sometimes was Seemingly gone for some while together. We pray'd for it p.m. All night distress'd about it and expecting its last Gasp. Nurse and my Dauter Molly sat up with it.

10. Through the Great Mercy of God the Child is alive this morning—and Continues—the sore mouth abates—peels and clears off. I rode over to visit Mr. Lawrence's wife,[8] Mr. Samuel Gamels[9] and Jesse Maynards[10] Family. N.B. Jotham Maynard thrash'd Barley with John Kidney.[11]

11. Frequent Snows. Trees ever so loaded yesterday when I rode over to the North side of the Town that it was very difficult passing, It being very deep in the Roads, yet it Snow'd again to Day. The Child somewhat better. Martha Maynard Watch'd. Storm continues.

12. A very great Storm, Windy, Cold and Snow'd very fast. Nurse Watch'd.

13. Sent for to visit Captain Warrin's Wife who was deliver'd of a very large Child this morning, but herself in a very low distressing Condition. Abiel watch'd.

14. A Morning of great Trouble! The Childs soreness of Mouth had return'd for Two or Three Days, but we did not judge it in immediate Danger. There was nothing of this discover'd in the first of the Morning. But about nine o'Clock I was call'd down from my Study with the Alarm that the Child was dying! About 10 She ceas'd to breath! The will of the Lord be done! I preach'd on Rev. 20, 12. O that we might have a due sense of the Divine Mind Concerning us!

15. Deacon Newton[12] kindly came and brought Two Bottles of wine and offer'd to go to Marlborough upon what Errands would

be Necessary to be done there. Ensign Maynard went to Mr. Cushings. Ebenezer Maynard dugg the Grave. The Snow exceeding Deep, by which means it was very difficult to break away to get wood, for 3 Fires and one so long all night as well as Day, had wasted wood at a very great Rate. Yet we got a Supply.

16. Mr. Cushing and his Wife came to the Funeral of my Infant Elizabeth. The Weather was moderate. The Neighbours in very considerable Numbers, attended. I desire to interr my Dead in the Faith of the new Covenant and of the glorious Privilege of the Ressurection to Eternal Life. N.B. Nurse was bearer. No Friends from Marlborough. N.B. Mr. Cushing and his Wife could not go to the Grave. Jotham cut wood a.m.

17. My wife was exceeding full of pain. Jotham Maynard cut Wood all Day and my Boys Sledded home 7 Load. At Evening I visited Mrs. Warrin[13] who was exceeding Slow and nigh unto Death. Could not Speak to me for some time, but at length reviv'd and discours'd a little. N.B. Took my Leave of her. The Cold Continues. N.B. Dr. Gott here.

18. My wife easier this morning, but very weak. Ebenezer and John rode to Marlborough. Brother Samuel Breck came from Springfield and went to Marlborough. N.B. I wrote to Mrs. Pierpont[14] at New Haven and sent it to Boston for Conveyance.

19. My Wife exceeding full of pain again, weak and distress'd, her lower Limbs grow useless and one of her feet swells again. I wrote to Mr. Secretary Wyllys[15] and Mr. Austin[16] at Hartford, to be sent by Colonel Pyncheon of Springfield. N.B. The Moderatest and pleasantest Day that we have had a very great While. Divèrs Women to visit my Wife. N.B. Mrs. Warrin dy'd last Night. Mr. James Maynards wife watched.

20. Mrs. Warrin Buryed. N.B. I baptiz'd the Infant at the House before the Corps were mov'd. N.B. Mr. Sherbourn and Mr. S. Grant upon their Journey with Mr. Prentice[17] to Grafton, and thence designing to proceed to Connecticut. My Wife exceeding full of pain, very faint and weak and low. Granny Forbush watch'd. N.B. Simon Tainter, junior went for the Doctor at almost Eve.

21. On Rev. 20, 12. My Wife in great Extremity. The Doctor was here in the morning. Cousin Winchester[18] tarried after meeting and watch'd.

22. Cousin Winchester tarried till her Husband came at Eve. Mr. Cushing and Captain Flagg,[19] Sister Gott and Mrs. Bulah Bent here. My Wife very full of Pain yet! N.B. We kill'd the Pig which I bought Some Time agoe of Lieutenant Holloway. Weight 126£.

23. Dr. Gott here. My Wife's pains do not Cease. Nurse sat up what she could.

24. Mr. Stone[20] made us a visit. Din'd with us and before he went away at Evening he pray'd with us.

25. My [wife] has not been easy ever since the 17th Day. Divers Women here.

26. Dr. Gott and Captain Williams here. Dr. din'd. Captain Williams went to Ensign Maynards and when he return'd was in so great an Hurry that he would only Eat a mouthful of Bread and cheese altho Food was preparing for him. It was what gave us some vexation because I had invited him to Dinner.

27. My Wife Easyer and Stronger, but I was not very well.

28. A very Stormy Day. Snow'd hard. I went to Meeting House a.m. and preach'd Still on Rev. 20, 12 altho I was not well. P.M. the storm increasing greatly I sent for the people to my own House, and perform'd Divers services at Home. Preach'd on 2 Pet. 2, 11, Continuing the same Subject which I was upon in the forenoon.

29. Bright Day. P.M. I rode to Mr. Charles Rice's.[21]

---

[1] Of Hopkinton. The son of David Rice of Marlborough.
[2] James Eager of Westborough.
[3] Of Marlborough.
[4] Deacon of the Marlborough church. Hudson, *Marlborough*, p. 456.
[5] Mrs. David Maynard of Westborough.
[6] Louise or Lucee (b. December 7, 1719) was the daughter of Aaron Forbush.
[7] Mrs. Simon Tainter.
[8] Mrs. Benjamin Lawrence.
[9] Of Westborough. The name was also spelled Gamwell.
[10] Formerly of Marlborough. The son of David Maynard.
[11] Parkman's indentured servant. At first Parkman spelled the name Ridney.
[12] Josiah Newton.

[13] Mary, the widow of Captain Daniel Warrin.
[14] Widow of the Reverend James Pierpont of New Haven.
[15] George Wyllys, Secretary of the colony of Connecticut.
[16] John Austin, a merchant of Hartford.
[17] Reverend Solomon Prentice of Grafton.
[18] Elizabeth, Mrs. Benjamin Winchester.
[19] Benjamin Flagg, Jr., of Worcester. Also a selectman. Lincoln, *Worcester*, pp. 52, 55, 57.
[20] Reverend Nathan Stone of Southborough.
[21] An early resident of Westborough.

30. Sent various Errands by Mr. John Rogers, particularly to Brother Champney and to Mrs. Kiggell.

31. Mr. Aaron Forbush had my oxen to sled down a large stick of Ship Timber to Marlborough. My Wife lys ill yet, but gathers Some Strength and can begin to take a step or Two with Help.

### FEBRUARY, 1739.

1. Pleasant a.m. Rain at Eve. I preach'd at the Private Meeting at Brother Hicks's on Phil. 1, 21. The Snow wastes off space.

2. A fine Clear Day. Nurse rode to Grafton upon my Horse. My Wife begins to be Somewhat pain'd upon T'other side, Scil. from her Hip downwards. But in the forepart of the Day we had discours'd of Nurse's going home.

3. Nurse return'd from Grafton. Wife's pains increase greatly.

4. On 2 Pet. 3, 11. Sent John Kidney to Marlborough to the Doctor.

5. I have Heard that to Day the Town of Marlborough were to open Mr. Samuel Cooks answer to their Call.[1] N.B. Mr. Samuel Fay juniors Infant Child bury'd which bled to Death at the Navel. N.B. Very Cold. In at Mr. Samuel Williams at Evening. My Wife grows worse, her pains being Sharper for the Time than with the former Legg. N.B. Upon the Sorrowful News we had receiv'd by Edwards Whipple[2] of the Extreme illness of our sister Lydia Champney at Cambridge, Brother Hicks[3] and his Wife went down, but the Circumstances of my Wife did utterly forbid me.

6. Somewhat Cold, but bright and Clear. My Wife had a very distressing Night exceeding full of pain from her Hip to her Toe. The Day was like the Night. No Physic work'd yesterday nor to Day. Her spirits much depress'd. N.B. Captain Fay[4] here to see us and din'd with us.

7. A great deal of Company here, which together my wife's exceeding low Circumstances made it a Day of perpetual Hurry and Engagement—for as to my wife, the night was very distressing—full of Pain and anguish and very faint and Weak. Nurse watch'd last night as well as Sat up the most of the Night before, and my wife was very restless and as if Death could not be very far off. As to the Company there were especially Mr. (or Captain) Jonathan Sawyer of Harvard with the bitter and grievous Case of Mr. Seccomb[5] their Pastor. My Advice was That it was not fit for them to expect a Judgment of the Case unless both sides are fully heard, or that I could hear Facts and Allegations that went into the Merits of the Cause unless they were what were well supported and Mr. Seccomb present to make Reply. Secondly, That none of the Crimes charg'd against Mr. Seccomb (however those false Rumors were that flew about the world) were such but that upon his deep Humiliation and Reformation and endeavouring to Conduct Himself with peculiar Care respecting the Youth of the Flock he might be, nay and ought to be continued their Pastor. Thirdly, that it was not adviseable, by any means to have a Council of Churches (Seeing that would be Such a mean of further publishing and Spreading the Evil, already too great) if by any good methods they could heal their grievance at Home, and if it were granted, as complain'd, that many new Facts, or horrible Circumstances had arisen which gave Such sad Disquietment to even those members who, knowing no more than they did then, voted his Restoration that they are full of Dissatisfaction, yet perhaps a new Church Meeting and Reconsideration or Review of matters, might Still be Sufficient and Successfull. And if it should upon Trial be found that it did not or if such Church Meeting could not be obtained I would rather advise that Two or Three Fathers in the Ministry be apply'd to, to go up to Harvard and assist and Direct them in the Affair. I also told Mr. Sawyer that if Opportunity presented I should acquaint Mr. Seccomb with his having been here, and

the Errand he came upon, which he very freely and readily consented to or desir'd. N.B. There came with Mr. Sawyer, one Mr. Taylor of North Worcester. Mr. Williams here with Hinges to hang my Front Gate. Captain Forbush[6] and others here. Sundry Women to see my Wife. Brother Hicks return'd from Cambridge.

8. My Wife very Weak and low last Night, but by the help of her Anodyne slept better than for several Nights. Nurse went to bed about one. Dr. Gott here and left various new prescriptions and Encouragements. Company Daily—an unspeakable Hindrance to my Studys.

9. A windy, Cold Day. Neighbor Beeman[7] and his wife made us a kind, bountifull visit. Mr. Wheeler[8] here. My Wife exceedingly pained at Eve.

10. [No entry].

11. Repeated Sermon on 1 John 3, 14 a. and p.m. unto page 16, but p.m. from Deut. 32, 5. Dr. Gott visited my wife in Meeting Time as he was going to see old Mrs. Tomlin.[9] Snow Storm.

12. Sent Ebenezer to Marlborough to the Doctors and to Mr. Butlers, with the side saddle but he was removed to Rutland. Captain Warrins young Child bury'd. I went down in the Snow o'Foot, and the snow blowing into the Path made it very heavy and tiresome. N.B. Sent to Mr. Williams a Letter touching the Harvard Affair and to Brother Samuel Breck at College and to Brother Samuel Parkman at Boston all by Samuel Baker.[10] My Wife remains in much the Same State, except the very great Extremeity of Pain which is mitigated by her Anodyne.

13. Dr. Convers,[11] by Dr. Gotts message to him as he was at Sudbury, came up to visit my wife. Afterwards came Dr. Gott. They find her very low, her Blood exceeding Weak, her swelling in her Legg increased and advanc'd into her Body, her Urine has been to a great Degree Supprest'd ever since this Second Legg was Seiz'd with the Pain. Her medicines are Chalbiats[12] mix'd with Castor, and Ocul. Cancror with Sal. Nitr. Her bathing with spirits of wine continued but her Pultis ceases, her Teas of Horse Radish, Fennel and Parseley Roots, and we now lay on a Blister. P.M. Mr. Beeman again bountifully visits and Cousin Winchester here.

14. Rain. My Wife somewhat better.

15. Mr. Tainter and his Son Simon came (upon hire) to cut Wood. Very Cold.

16. High Cold Winds continue. Very Cold. A Last Year Lamb that had been hurt by the wanton Swine dy'd yesterday. Mrs. Byles[13] here p.m. Hollister Baker call'd here.

17. Snow. My Wife grows Still better. Nurse went home having been with us full seven Weeks. I was pritty Seasonable in my preparations.

18. On Rom. 8, 6.

19. Mr. John Pannell here with Linnen Cloth. Town Meeting in part to See what to do about making more room in the Meeting House. N.B. Mr. Parris here, and lodg'd here.

20. Mr. Parris went off. Dr. Gott here. Pruning Trees.

21. It rained somewhat but I rode over to Mr. Joseph Greens. N.B. Aiery Gate. N.B. Mr. Jonathan Whipple and his Wife here at Eve.

22. Mr. Cushing and his Wife made us a Visit. Sorrowfull News at Eve by John Hicks junior of Sister Lydia Champneys extreme Ill State.

23. Moderate weather. Lieutenant Baker[14] help'd me Trim my Apple Trees. Abraham Moss call'd here.

24. Brother Hicks came and trimmed Apple Trees all Day. Ensign Maynard brought up a Present from Brother Elias containing a considerable Variety. Scil. Chocolat, Flower, Raisins,

[1] Cooke declined the call.

[2] Of Westborough.

[3] John Hicks, Parkman's brother-in-law by his first marriage.

[4] John Fay, an early settler of Westborough.

[5] Reverend John Seccomb (Harvard 1728), the first minister of Harvard, Mass. Seccomb was charged at this time with unfaithfulness to his marriage vows. *Sibley*, VIII, 481-490. Henry S. Nourse, *History of the Town of Harvard* (Harvard, 1894), pp. 185-187.

[6] Samuel Forbush of Westborough.

[7] Eleazer Beeman.

[8] Joseph Wheeler of Westborough.

[9] Wife of Deacon Isaac Tomlin.

[10] Son of Edward Baker of Westborough.

[11] Josiah Convers (Harvard 1723), a physician of Watertown. *Sibley*, VII, 159-160.

[12] A chalybeate medicine was impregnated with or flavored with iron.

[13] Mrs. Joseph Byles.

[14] Edward Baker of Westborough.

Currants, Spices, Limes and Several sorts of Bisketts. Lowery thawing Weather.

25. Misty Day. On Rom. 8, 6 and Repeated from page 13 of Sermon on Phil. 1, 21 from 1 Cor. 3, 22—Death all are yours. Sharp Thunder and Lightning at Eve. N.B. My Wife walk'd across the room, a thing she has not done these Three weeks, and she din'd with us to Day. G.D.

26. The Doctor came to see my wife. I rode down to Cambridge on occasion of sister Lydia Champneys illness. Very bad riding by the Hollowness of the Earth by the Frost. Met with Dr. Convers at Mr. Harringtons[15] Tavern at Waltham. Found sister Lydia better. Her Face, Chin and Throat had been very much tumifyed [?] and enflam'd and lanc'd, and she was in great Extremity for some Days last week, but is much more comfortable. N.B. Trouble by Brother Champney's[16] courting one Abigail Stearns.[17]

27. I rode to Charlestown. I found that the great Mr. Thatcher[18] of the New North dy'd yesterday morning about 3 or 4 o'Clock. Din'd at my mothers. Supp'd at Brother Elias's and lodg'd there. N.B. Brother Elias's taking Care about the paying what I ow'd for John Kidney and my Horse at Mr. Webb the Butchers. N.B. Visited Dr. Cutler,[19] Physician for sister Lydia.

28. Din'd at Brother Elias's. N.B. Hezekiah How[20] din'd with us. Visited Captain James Marshall. N.B. Major Lockman there. Went up to see the Camel. N.B. Serious Discourse with Brother Elias about his son. At Eve, 9 o'Clock, rode Round to Cambridge.

### MARCH, 1739.

1. Rode over to Cambridge and to College. Thence up to Waterton for Neighbor Hezekiah Hows Company. Overtook him at Woolsons.[1] Stop'd by Mr. William Williams[2] about Harvard affair, and by Brother Breck in Sudbury. Visited Mr. Cook[3] and his Kinsman[4] who has receiv'd a renewed call to Marlborough. Having been handsomely refresh'd there I pursued my Journey to Hows Tavern,[5] where came Neighbor Townsen but I had his Company but 2 or 3 miles till I came to Dr. Gotts, and made it into Evening, Cold, heavy, Dirty and Weary Home.

2. Mr. Stone of Southborough brought with him Captain Whitney of Harvard, with a Letter from Deacons and Brethren, and from Mr. Seccomb. Mr. Stone preach'd my Lecture on Ps. 146, 8, last Clause. After Lecture Mr. Stone and I had long Conference and Debates upon Harvard Affair. We wrote to Captain Sawyer. Mr. Stone return'd home late. Captain Whitney lodged here.

3. John Kidney Clearing Land, and did considerable of it in the Time of my Absence.

4. Sacrament. On Rom. 8, 6. P.M. Repeated the latter part of Sermon on Phil. 1, 21. Very weary and not well at night.

5. Before the yearly Meeting there was a Town Meeting by adjournment about the Meeting House. Mr. Daniel Stone brought me Two Heath Hens and a Cock.

6. Storm of Snow. Mr. Tainter came and kill'd Two Swine for me. I read Mr. Samuel Mathers Apology for the Churches in New England.[6]

7. Snow Storm continues. Cold and Windy. Mr. Tainter came and cut out and Salted up my Pork. No Catechizing (altho it had been appointed this Day) because of the storm.

8. Fair. Ebenezer Maynard came upon my sending for him to cut wood—and John Kidney sledded. N.B. Ebenezer Maynard gave the Day.

9. Snow. We had prepared to carry a Pine Logg out of the Lot to the Saw Mill and Ebenezer Maynard came to help load it, but the Storm prevail'd and we gave over.

10. With Brother Hicks's Cattle and Neighbor Aaron Hardys joined to my own Team, Ebenezer Maynard and John Kidney carry'd a Large Logg to the Saw Mill.

11. Snow'd again. On Prov. 4, 7. N.B. but few at Meeting p.m. N.B. My Wife has been somewhat disconsolate by her Limbs Swelling.

12. Brother Hicks to Shrewsbury upon my Horse. He went to Cambridge. Ebenezer went down to Mr. Daniel Matthews[7] for Malt.

13. [No entry].

14. Catechizing—it having been appointed on this Day because of the Disappointment last Week by the Storm.

15. Storm of Rain and Hail.

16. I rode to Marlborough. Exceeding bad Travelling. To Mr. Tainters,[8] Phelps,[9] Colonel Woods's, Dr. Gotts at Evening and at Captain Williams[10] late. Yet returned home.

17. [No entry].

18. On Prov. 4, 7.

19. Mr. Jeremiah Townsend came to us from New Haven.

20. Captain Williams of Marlborough here and made up Accounts as Executor of Mr. Brecks[11] Will, as Administratee Upon Mr. Brecks Substance, and as Guardian to my Wife. P.M. I rode to Deacon Tomlins[12] and to Mr. Icabud Druce's.

21. Rode South. Lieutenant Bakers, Captain Fays, Mr. Samuel Fays, etc., etc. N.B. Mr. James Taylor[13] of Worcester here.

22. A Meeting of the Proprietors of Hoossatunnoc No. 3. N.B. The Committee for that Business had agreed with Captain Hazletine[14] of Upton to build a Saw Mill. I assisted 'em in Drawing Two Bonds.

23. Town Meeting upon the Article of the Meeting House, but still did nothing. Mr. Samuel Harrington took my Horse to keep.

24. My wife went to the Kitchen about this Time.

25. On Mat. 9, 18.

26. Town Meeting by Adjournment. N.B. Marlborough propos'd Meeting. I sent down, a second time, a Plot of Two acres and 30 Rod upon Powder Hill, by old Mr. Maynard,[15] but oppos'd by Mr. Richard Barns. N.B. some warm answer to old Mr. Maynard and Neighbor Williams[16] when they gave me account of the Proprietors not accepting it. N.B. began to Garden. We plough'd in some early Peas.

27. Very fine Weather.

28. Receiv'd from my Mother by Mr. Simon Goddard[17] Tulip Roots, etc. Mr. David Bell of Boston in his Journey to New Haven came to us at Evening in the Rain and Lodg'd here.

29. Public Fast. I preach'd on Ezek. 36, 25 to 32 and part of 37.

30. Mr. Bell pursued his Journey to New Haven bearing Letters from us, Scil. to Mr. Pierpoint[18] and to Mr. Daniel Edwards,[19] The Wind exceeding high last night. Rugged, Cold, windy Day.

31. I walk'd into the Neighbourhood as far as to Mr. Williams and I borrowed his Horse to Southborough, Mr. Stone having writ to me in the beginning of the Week, to Change with him.

[15] Daniel Harrington. Charles A. Nelson, *Waltham, Past and Present* (Cambridge, 1879), p. 88.

[16] Samuel Champney, Jr., of Cambridge, the brother of Parkman's first wife.

[17] Of Concord. Intention of marriage to Champney, was recorded on October 24, 1739. The marriage itself is not recorded. Paige, *Cambridge*, p. 507.

[18] Reverend Peter Thatcher.

[19] Dr. John Cutler. Drake, *Boston*, p. 633.

[20] Parkman's neighbor in Westborough.

[1] Joseph Woolson of Framingham.

[2] Minister at Weston.

[3] Reverend William Cooke of Wayland, Mass.

[4] Samuel Cooke, later minister at Arlington, Mass.

[5] The Wayside Inn.

[6] *An Apology for the Liberties of the Churches in New-England* (Boston, 1738). Mather (Harvard 1723) was the youngest son of Cotton Mather and at this time minister of the Second Church in Boston. Sibley, VII, 216–238.

[7] Of Marlborough, and later of Southborough.

[8] Deacon Joseph Tainter.

[9] John Phelps, a cordwainer of Marlborough. About 1742 he moved with his family to Rutland, Mass. Hudson, *Marlborough*, p. 428.

[10] Abraham Williams of Marlborough.

[11] The late Reverend Robert Breck of Marlborough.

[12] Isaac Tomlin of Westborough.

[13] An early proprietor of Worcester. Lincoln, *Worcester*, pp. 46–47.

[14] John Hazeltine.

[15] David Maynard.

[16] Eleazer Williams.

[17] Of Shrewsbury. He had previously lived in Hopkinton. Ward, *Shrewsbury*, p. 285.

[18] James Pierpont, Jr., of New Haven.

[19] (Yale 1720). Clerk of the Superior Court of Connecticut. Dexter, pp. 216–217.

I expected Mr. Stone, but he came not. I rode down to Southborough upon Mr. Williams's Horse, but it was nigh dark when I
got to Mr. Stones, So that he tarried till morning.

### APRIL, 1739.

1. Mr. Stone rode up to Westborough in the Morning. I
preach'd at Southborough on Heb. 10, 38, a. and p.m. William
Pierce had excepted against Mr. Stones form of baptizing because
of his using the word [into] instead of [in] the name, etc. and therefor entreated me to baptize his youngest Child.[1] Mr. Stone had
intimated the matter to me and consented freely that the Man
Should request me, but I first opened the matter to him, read him
Dr. Collins's annotation upon Mat. 28, 19 in the Continuation of
Mr. Pools[2] and demanded of him whether he had any Disgust
with Mr. Stone on any other, etc. The name of the Child was
Seth. At Evening I return'd to Westborough. Met Mr. Stone by
the way. N.B. Mr. Stone had forgot his Notes by changing his
Coat, and had none with him at Westborough. It was so late in
the morning that he could not return home to fetch 'em, but my
wife, at his request, Show'd him a parcell of my Sermons and he
chose them that are on Hos. 13, 9, and preach'd from them a. and
p.m. N.B. My Young Red Cow brought a fine large Cow Calf.

2. Jotham Maynard came to work and Molly Bruce[3] came as a
Taylor to make a Coat for Ebenezer.[4] Jotham beat off at Noon
by the Rain. Read in Mr. Clarks last volume of Lives.[5] Lost
Two Ewes, one yesterday, the other to Day.

3. Dull heavy Weather. Jotham Maynard at Work all Day
on the Fences of the Southside. At Night a great Storm. Windy,
Cold, rain, Snow.

4. The Snow a Considerable Depth, but the Storm over. N.B.
Mrs. Josselyn[6] here both yesterday and to Day.

5. Sister Hicks at Dinner with me. I preach'd at the private
Meeting at Mr. Whipple's on Rev. 3, 1.

6. The Boys plough'd p.m., the Snow being so gone. Hannah,
wife of Daniel Warrin junior here.

7. The Boys plough'd all Day.

8. All Day on 2 Cor. 2, 15, 16.

9. Boys at Plough again. Samuel Rogers at work for me.

10. I rode to Sudbury, in Company from Captain Williams of
Marlborough with Mr. Cushing.[7] Mr. Nathan Stone and Mr.
Seccomb at Mr. Lorings.[8] My Concio was on 2 Cor. 2, 15, 16.
The Occasion of this Discourse on this Text was the ill Conduct of
divers Ministers, but particularly of Mr. Seccomb of Harvard.
N.B. Seven Towns in that Neighbourhood had had ministers
guilty of Scandalous offences.

11. Mr. Prentice of Grafton preach'd the public Lecture on
Isa. 1, 16. N.B. Conversation with Mr. Samuel Cook upon the
Affair of his refusing Marlborough. Mr. Cushing, Mr. Stone, and
Mr. Prentice of Grafton rode with me up to Marlborough. I
turn'd away to Mr. Edmund Rice's at the urgent request of his
wife, to discourse with their Daughter in Law who was under
Spiritual Troubles. Was at Colonel Woods's and settled all
accounts with him to this Day. At the Doctors[9] at Eve. Mr.
Prentice my Company to Westborough but he stood along for
home. N.B. some free Conversation with him about his Preaching. N.B. Sammè Breck[10] at my House. Came up yesterday.
Jotham Maynard work'd half a Day.

12. Jotham Maynard work'd another half Day. Powder hill
on Blaze, in a dry Time and an high Wind. The Fire broke out of
Brother Hicks's Ground and burnt me up all the Fence upon the
South and the north and north East, although the wind was very
strong at South and south West. I preach'd the Lecture on Rev.
3, 1 latter part. N.B. Mr. Tainter[11] brought up from Cambridge
a 3 year old Heifer which I bought of Brother Champney for 10£.

13. Very fine spring Weather. Barley Sow'd. At Evening
there arose a Storm of Thunder and Lightning. N.B. My old
Bell sheep kill'd as 'twas Thought by a Wolf on my Hill in the
upper Clear'd Ground. I have now lost no less than Four grown
sheep this last winter and this spring.

14. Abiel Allen went home. Nor could anyone be got in his
room. P.M. I rode over to the Funeral of a Young Child of Mr.
John Pannell. Very Warm Day.

15. Sacrament. Preach'd on Mat. 22, 12. O that I had the
Wedding Garment of a prepared soul to wait upon my Dear and
blessed saviour in! O that his own Righteousness might cover
me that the Shame of my Spiritual Nakedness might not appear!
P.M. by means of my many avocations and Labours I was prevented Composing another Discourse, and therefor I repeated to
page 7 of Sermon on Ps. 116, 12.

16. Abiel Allen having tarried over night, wash'd and did other
heavy Business for my Wife. N.B. Robert Bradish came and
acknowledg'd his ill Conduct and Expressions at Two particular
Seasons when he was with me as particularly in my House on
October [blank] past, and on March 30, last at Evening and I for-
gave him and was reconcil'd to him. This I bless God for, it
having been an Article which I had much requested. Fine
weather—ploughing. N.B. Hicks carry'd his Dauter Hannah to
Cambridge.

17. Catechiz'd at the Meeting House. The Trees and divers of
them, Apple Trees and Popplers, very Green and the Grass considerably grown.

18. I went to Captain Fays with John Kidney who drove a
Team and got 3 hundred pounds of Hay. Neighbor John Rogers
at work for me. Splicing Rails and posts and Setting up Fence
upon the back of the settle upon the Hill. Receiv'd a Young Sow
Pigg from Mr. Williams.

19. A white Frost last Night. Neighbor John Rogers setting
up Fence for me. I went with John Kidney who drove my Team
to Mr. David Brighams to get Sand. My Wife went as far as old
Mr. Maynards. The Turkey Hen Set.

20. Mr. William Nurse here to request me to [go] up to a Sick
Child a mile or Two above his House in Shrewsbury, but for many
Reasons I could not.

21. Mr. Damon of Leicester here. We sow'd a few Oates.
N.B. It was showery Some parts of the Day.

22. On 2 Cor. 15, 16. Widow Pratt din'd with us.

23. Visited Neighbor Isaac Tomlin junior, he being in a very
languishing Condition. I had Neighbor Seth Rice's Colt to ride
upon from his House. N.B. Captain Eager[12] from Court gave
advice to Neighbor Rice[13] to go down to Boston to Confer with
Two men who had been Capivated from Groton when they were
but Ladds and had dwelt with the Indians ever since, whose
English names were Tarbell[14]—Captain Kellogg[15] being likewise
at Boston who was ready to serve them as an interpreter.

24. My old Red Cow Calv'd a fine large Bull Calf. N.B.
Colonel Woods, Mr. Stone of Southborough, Mr. John Burt[16]
preacher at Marlborough and Mr. Jonathan Loring,[17] their School
Master made me a Visit.

25. I walk'd to Mr. Noah Rice's[18] to visit his wife, being
under long Confinement and weakness, very discourag'd and
Melancholly. Continued my walk over to Mr. Tainters who had

---

[1] Baptism recorded in Westborough Church Records.

[2] Matthew Poole, a learned Non-Conformist divine published *Annotations on the Holy
Bible, wherein the Sacred Text is inserted, and various readings annexed*, 2 vols. (London,
1688). Poole wrote the portion as far as chapter 58 of Isaiah. Other writers continued the
work.

[3] Mary, daughter of Abijah Bruce of Westborough.

[4] Parkman's eldest son.

[5] Samuel Clarke (1599-1683), an English theologian, published *The Marrow of Ecclesi-
astical Historie, Conteined in the Lives of the Fathers, and Other Learned Men, and Famous
Divines* (London, 1650). This work was enlarged and published in a variety of subsequent
English editions.

[6] Mrs. Joseph Joslin. Sometimes spelled Joslen or Josling.

[7] Reverend Job Cushing of Shrewsbury.

[8] Reverend Israel Loring of Sudbury.

[9] Benjamin Gott, the physician of Marlborough.

[10] Samuel Breck, Parkman's brother-in-law.

[11] Deacon Simon Tainter of Westborough.

[12] James Eager of Westborough.

[13] Asher Rice, who had also been a captive of the Indians.

[14] See Samuel A. Green, *Groton During the Indian Wars* (Groton, 1883), pp. 116-120.

[15] Joseph Kellogg.

[16] (Harvard 1736). Later minister at Bristol, Rhode Island, 1740-1775. *Sibley*, X,
29-31.

[17] Son of the Reverend Israel Loring of Sudbury.

[18] Son of Thomas Rice, an original settler of Westborough.

kept my Horse Sometime, and so rode back. Call'd at Mr. Jonah Warrins. N.B. Mr. John Pratt moving his Family to a new place by Mr. James Fays. N.B. Mr. Peter Butler was at our House. N.B. John Hicks junior help'd John Kidney in Carting out Muck. Planted Peas, New Haven Squashes, etc. in the garden and sow'd various seeds.

26. Neighbor John Rogers help'd in Carting out muck. N.B. Brother Hicks lost his Black Ox. Divers went to look for him up—found him dead in the mire of the Meadow on the North West End of the Great Pond. My Wife rode to Marlborough. N.B. Neighbor Seth Rice came up from Boston where he had Conference with the Tarbells of Groton and with Captain Kellogg upon the Affair of his Brethrens coming down from Canada. N.B. He brought my wife some Honey Suckle Roots (for Vines for the Front Door) from Madame Lucy Dudley of Roxbury.

27. My Lads fetch'd home some Hay from Neighbor Seth Rice's Mr. Mead here. It continues a very dry Season. P.M. Brother Hicks help'd John in Carting Muck. My Wife return'd from Marlborough and my Horse was kept this Night (as it was also the Night before last) at old Mr. Maynard's.

28. John Hicks junior went on foot to Cambridge. Ebenezer to Captain Eagers to carry Mr. Peter Butler 3£, 10 Shillings. John Carting Muck Still. Ebenezer Rode my Horse to Mr. Jacob Amsdens to have him kept there.

29. On 2 Cor. 2, 15, 16. Very weary and faint at night, my Spirits having been greatly impress'd and my Body worry'd. N.B. There had been a small Shower this Morn. The wind Raw, and promising a Storm.

30. A Rainy Time and the Earth much soak'd, after a very dry Week. The praise to God for his Kindness and faithfulness. Abiel Allen tarried over last night to help my Wife for Two or Three Dayes.

## MAY, 1739.

1. John Kidney, with the Oxen help'd Brother Hicks in Carting out Muck.

2. Mr. Andrew Boardman[1] and his Sister, with Adonijah Church[2] and Mrs. Betty Woods[3] made us a Visit. N.B. It has been very cold ever Since the Storm on the 30th last. Abiel went home.

3. Very Cold still. John ploughing the Grounds over in order to planting.

4. [No entry].

5. A very grievous Cold continues upon me.

6. On Mat. 9, 27 to 31, and on Ps. 99, 5 and 9. Some of our Cows lye out.

7. We furrow'd the further piece of the north field and planted the most of it till the Rain increas'd so much that we were oblig'd to desist. N.B. Sent for my Horse from Mr. Jacob Amsdens. N.B. Mr. William Nurse brought me a fine Pig of Two Months old and receiv'd only 2/6 (which was Scarcely a Quarter Price) for it. N.B. Receiv'd also a Pig of a Month old from Brother Hicks. At Night the Storm prevail'd greatly.

8. A.M. Rain and Stormy winds. P.M. Clear'd off. N.B. Neighbor How[4] brought us a Quarter of Veal. Neighbor Aaron Hardy bought Hopps of us. P.M. furrow'd.

9. I sent out my Oxen under the Care of Ensign Maynard and Four Young Creatures under the Care of Captain Warrin,[5] into the Woods. The Boys Planting; a fine warm Day. P.M. Ruth Bradish[6] here to Discourse with me in order to her joining to the Church.

10. Finished Planting. Cool Season again.

11. Mr. John Green, of Brookfield, heretofore my near Neighbour, here. Cool Weather. N.B. Ebenezer rode to Marlborough to carry wool to be spun at the widow Bents[7] and to bring my great Coat from Mr. Tainters but succeeded not in the last.

12. Cold and high winds So that we cannot sow our Flax. Youngest Calf being disorder'd and as we judg'd Tail soaken, we cut off the End of his Tail.

13. On Mat. 9, 32 to 34. Ps. 99, 5, 9. N.B. Several Hopkinton people at Meeting, by Reason of Mr. Barretts[8] illness. N.B. Two Young Gentlemen of Boston at Meeting, whom I could not find out. Mrs. Rice, heretofore Whood, at Dinner with me.

14. Warm and pleasant. Sow'd our Flax. I walk'd down to see Mrs. Townsend[9] and went as far as Mrs. Byles's and borrow'd her Horse for my Wife to ride to Hopkinton, whither we went and din'd there and return'd in Safety at Evening. Mr. Barrett was walking about with great Currency but in an ill Habit.

15. Read the Life of Mr. Fairclough.[10] Very Hot.

16. Very Hot. Mr. Edward Barns[11] marry'd to the widow Grace Rice.[12] I walk'd to Deacon Tomlins[13] with Captain Forbush.[14] N.B. Talk with Deacon[15] about his Children, who had been guilty of fornication.

17. John Finish'd Shearing. My wife rode to Mr. James Maynard.

18. Rainy, Thunderstorm. Several men came to the Meeting House freely to work in putting up seats—Shut up middle alley. Visited Mr. Noah Rice's sick Child. In the Night Molly Hicks[16] dy'd, about 11 of the Clock. My Wife there all night. Hicks at Cambridge.

19. Mr. Bridgham[17] here going to Brimfield. Hicks returned.

20. Mat. 9, 35—to the End. Ps. 99, 5, 9. Funeral of Brother Hicks's young Child, leave having been obtained of the Select Men therefor, viz. of Captain Warrin,[18] Deacon Newton,[19] and Ensign Forbush.

21. Word having been brought by Brother Hicks and also by Mr. James Maynard of my Honored aged Mothers Illness and desire that I would go down to her, I set out, and rode through Southborough. N.B. Abraham Moss[20] with me on the Road to Framingham, visited Mr. Swift,[21] proceeded to Cambridge, but was somewhat late.

22. Rode to Boston. My Mother very low, weak, and Sick and dispirited, but yet somewhat better than She was last Week.

23. Din'd at Brother Samuels.[22] N.B. Mother in great Trouble respecting both Temporal and Eternal Things.

24. Mr. Edwards[23] of North Hampton preach'd the public Lecture on Tim. 2, 5. With Mr. Edwards at Elder Lymans. P.M. at Dr. Sewalls[24] and Din'd at Brother Alexanders altho invited to Dine with the Governor.[25]

25. I din'd at Mr. Gees[26] with Mr. Edwards. At Brother Samuels and at Mr. Samuel Hunts.[27] At Evening Mr. Edwards preach'd at Elder Lymans but I could not attend by means of variety of Business and my Mothers low state.

26. Brother Samuel Parkman sent up a Boy from Charleston early in the morning, to bring down my Horse from Cambridge. N.B. Mrs. Newton (Ebenezer's Wife of Southborough). I had a very wet Journey. The Rain was heavy upon me from Weston.

[1] The schoolmaster of Hopkinton.
[2] Of Marlborough.
[3] Daughter of Benjamin Woods of Marlborough.
[4] Hezekiah How.
[5] Daniel Warren.
[6] Daughter of James and Dameris Bradish of Westborough.
[7] Mrs. Peter Bent.
[8] Reverend Samuel Barrett.
[9] Mercy, wife of Joshua Townsend, the schoolmaster of Westborough.
[10] Samuel Fairclough (1594–1677), an English nonconformist divine. The only biography of Fairclough that seems to have been published at this time was in Samuel Clarke's *Lives of Sundry Eminent Persons in this Latter Age* (London, 1683).
[11] Of Marlborough, where he and his wife continued to live.
[12] Of Westborough. The widow of Simon Rice. Hudson, *Marlborough*, p. 315.
[13] Isaac Tomlin.
[14] Samuel Forbush of Westborough.
[15] Timothy Fay and Lydia Tomlin (or Tomblin) were married April 30, 1738. The following entry by the Reverend Mr. Parkman appears in the Westborough Church Records, February 30, 1740. "Timothy Fay and Lydia his wife offered their public Humiliations for their committing the sin of Fornication and were restor'd to Charity."
[16] Mary was the infant daughter of John and Rebecca Hicks of Westborough.
[17] Reverend James Bridgham (Harvard 1726), the second minister of Brimfield, Mass., 1736–1776. *Sibley*, VIII, 7–10.
[18] Daniel Warrin.
[19] Josiah Newton.
[20] One of Parkman's hired hands.
[21] Reverend John Swift.
[22] Samuel Parkman of Boston.
[23] Reverend Jonathan Edwards.
[24] Reverend Joseph Sewall of Boston.
[25] Jonathan Belcher, Governor of Massachusetts.
[26] Reverend Joshua Gee of Boston.
[27] A shipwright of Boston.

N.B. at Weston I met with Mr. David Ball of Boston who was come with Mrs. Pierpont, Mr. Stephen White[28] and Mrs. Sarah Noyes[29] from New Haven Yesterday, and the 3 last were at my House. At Sudbury I borrow'd a great Coat of one Mr. Herd, my own being wet through. At Mr. Baldwins was Mr. Joseph Biglo[30] who was my Company as far as to his Fathers in Marlborough where we were shelter'd, and Horse and Man refreshed. At Home I found the Friends aforesaid to my great rejoicing.

27. Mr. White of New Haven preach'd for me on Mat. 25, 46 former part. P.M. I repeated on 2 Pet. 1, 10.

28. I Spent the forenoon in setting my Family affairs to rights. Din'd and after 3 o'Clock Set out for Cambridge. Rode by Mr. Beemans where I call'd. Through Marlborough and Stopp'd with sister Gott[31] etc., yet got down about 10 o'Clock. N.B. Mr. Edwards of North Hampton (as my wife inform'd me at my return) came to our House at Eve and lodged here.

29. I rode with Brother Samuel Parkman and his Wife to Cambridge to visit their little son, designing to ride also to Mistick, to visit Cousen Bradshaw,[32] but the Rain prevailed so that we only went to Cambridge. Neither could we return to Boston, but went over to Father Champneys[33] and lodged there. N.B. Mr. Samuel Liscomb of Southborough this afternoon inform'd me that Jacob Johnson and Daniel Taylor of Southborough each of about 22 or 23 years were lost at the Pond in Westborough which is the Head of the Sudbury River,[34] and it was concluded they were drowned. Their Horses, Shooes and Stockings were found by the Pond, their Canoo, Hatts and Cranberrys floating but their Bodys not found, this Morning at 8 o'Clock.

30. We went from Cambridge. Mr. Clark[35] of Salem Village preach'd an Excellent sermon on Hos. 11, 12. Din'd at Brother Elias's. N.B. Mr. Jeffords[36] of Wells confirm'd a Letter to the Convention concerning the Conduct of the Irish Bretheren and the Presbytery at the Eastward.

31. N.B. Mr. Samuel Cook, Mr. Pierce[37] of Dartmouth etc. lodg'd at Brother Elias's. I lodg'd at Brother Williams. I was at the Convention. N.B. Letters from Mr. Holden of London. The Sermon by Mr. Eels[38] on 1 Sam. 4, 13. The Collection £171 and odd money. Din'd at Mr. Checkleys.[39] Return'd to the Convention p.m. Visited Mrs. Keggell,[40] Mrs. Clark, etc. Lodg'd at Brother Williams.

## JUNE, 1739.

1. Cousin Needham[1] of Salem and his Son at Mothers. After various Business, etc. I rode to Cambridge. N.B. Mr. Edward Larkin's offers for my Horse.

2. Return'd to Westborough. My Company from Harringtons were Mr. James Morris who came lately from Lisbon, and from the Isle of Wight. (N.B. That he Saw in January or February last one of my name in west Cows in the Isle of Wight, Tavernkeeper, who said he was our Relation.) Other Company up was Mr. Joseph Gardner[2] who was going to preach at Hopkinton, and Mr. Andrew Boardman[3] Schoolmaster at Shrewsbury. Mr. Boardman and his Brother din'd with me at Baldwins. Shav'd at Sudbury. Rode through Marlborough. Mr. Aaron Forbush

at Colonel Woods's[4] who rode up with me and acquaint'd me with the Rude and Vile Conduct of John Kidney towards my Dauter Molly, when alone with her, except little Lucy, her Mother being at Marlborough with Mrs. Pierpont and her other Friends, whom she waited upon thither the Day before. It was to my great Surprize, but Blessed be God who is the Refuge of all Distressed ones, and who appear'd for the Dear Child in the middst of her Troubles calling aloud upon His Mercifull and allmighty name, and wondrously Sav'd her, tho he had button'd the Door and assaulted and Striven with her, thrown her on the Ground and was very indecent towards her, Yet was not suffer'd to hurt her—except what was by the Fright and bruising her arms in struggling with her. When disengag'd She ran out to go to her uncles, but he ran after her and forc'd her back and made her wash the Blood from her arms, which she did upon his Swearing to her that he would not go into the House again till night. As soon as She had got him out to his work, She ran to Ensign Maynards who rode to Marlborough and at Eve brought up her Mother. Stephen Maynard lodg'd in the House that night and Noah How the next, My wife being afraid to be alone with so bruitish a Creature. When I came home I examin'd Molly very Strictly. Brother Hicks and Ensign Maynard were here, whose advice I needed at so important a Juncture. John upon his Knees ask'd my Pardon, and again fell on his Knees and ask'd his mistresses Pardon. It was difficult with me to know what was fittest to be done, the Sabbath being approaching and the Holy Exercises thereof to be prepar'd for. As Compos'd as I could I deferr'd the Matter till the beginning of the Week.

3. A.M. on Ps. 116, 12 from page 7. On Consideration of the Great Goodness of God to Me and my Dear Dauter Molly in her late Remarkable Deliverance. P.M. on Eccl. 9, 19, repeating the last Part of one of my sermons on Eccl. 11, 9. On Occasion of the Sudden Death of Jacob Johnson and David Taylor of Southborough last week by Drowning. N.B. Weary and much Spent at Night.

4. Rainy and confin'd at Home, meddled not with the Affair of John till I could take advice.

5. Rainy, Yet I rode up in the Morning to Shrewsbury. At Mr. Cushings[5] were some of his Friends from Hingham. I asked Mr. Cushing advice aside concerning John Kidneys Conduct. I also visited Colonel Ward[6] and propos'd several General Cases, made Enquirys and consulted his Law Books. N.B. I din'd at Colonel Wards and ministered to an aged maiden of 60, named Abigail Green, who was in great Extremity, fitts of Difficult Breathing etc. Visited Mr. Isaac Tomlin[7] as I returned home.

6. About Dinner Time I made a Business of talking to John Kidney but he answer'd me nothing. Mr. Cushing came and preach'd my Lecture on 1 Tim. 4, 7. It had been rainy for Some Days. It rain'd this forenoon, but the Sun broke out in the Afternoon. Cousen Winchester, both he and she,[8] were here after Lecture.

7. I rode (with my Wife) to the Private Meeting at Mr. Noah Rice's. N.B. His Family had been in affliction for some Time. His Wife out of Health and disconsolate; his little son in a Feaver of Continuance, etc. Text 2 Thess. 2, 16, 17.

8. Sent down my Horse to Mr. Edward Larkin of Charlestown by Mr. Tainter.[9] The Horse being 15 years old I had but £16 for him. N.B. Brother Hicks framing and making a Gate for the West Yard.

9. Brother Hicks sett up Posts and hung the West Gate.

10. Sacrament. Text a. and p.m. Col. 1, 12. N.B. old Neighbor Thurston[10] from Uxbridge at Communion and at Dinner as was old Mr. Johnson[11] of Southborough and Deacon Fay. N.B. Many of Southborough here Mr. Stone[12] being gone to Harwick. N.B. at Evening I was exceeding Faint and Spent.

[28] (Yale 1736). Later minister at Windham, Conn., 1740-1794. Dexter, pp. 567-569.

[29] Daughter of James Noyes of Stonington, Conn.

[30] Son of John Bigelow. Joseph lived in Shrewsbury.

[31] Mrs. Benjamin Gott.

[32] Parkman's brother William had a daughter Sarah who married Samuel Bradshaw.

[33] Samuel Champney, Sr., of Cambridge.

[34] The Sudbury River begins in the eastern part of Westborough where several brooks come together to form Cedar Swamp.

[35] Reverend Peter Clark (Harvard 1712), minister at Danvers, Mass., 1716-1768. Sibley, V, 616-623.

[36] Reverend Samuel Jeffers of Wells, Maine.

[37] Reverend Richard Pierce (Harvard 1724), minister at New Bedford, Mass., 1733-1749. Sibley, VII, 429-431.

[38] Reverend Nathaniel Eels (Harvard 1699), minister at Norwell, Mass., 1704-1750. Sibley, IV, 468-471.

[39] Reverend Samuel Checkley of Boston.

[40] Mrs. Abel Keggell, a cousin of Mrs. Parkman.

[1] Parkman's eldest sister married Daniel Needham in 1702. Both Mr. and Mrs. Needham had died before 1739. This reference in the diary is to some relative of this connection.

[2] (Harvard 1732). Later a minister at Newport, Rhode Island, 1740-1743. Sibley, IX, 156-159.

[3] Boardman had previously been the schoolmaster at Hopkinton.

[4] Benjamin Woods of Marlborough.

[5] Reverend Job Cushing.

[6] Nahum Ward of Shrewsbury.

[7] The Westborough deacon.

[8] Mr. and Mrs. Benjamin Winchester of Westborough.

[9] Deacon Simon Tainter of Westborough.

[10] David Thurston, formerly of Westborough.

[11] William Johnson, who died in 1757 at the age of 89.

[12] Reverend Nathan Stone of Southborough.

11. Training. After Prayer with the Company I din'd with the Officers. N.B. Captain Flagg[13] din'd with them also. Captain Flagg improv'd by me to talk with John Kidney who manifested some Degree of Humiliation and made Promises of great Reformation. But I remain'd dissatisfy'd unless he Should undergoe some suitable Punishment in some Kind or other.

12. Rainy Day.

13. I made a new Cellar window, at the East end of the Cellar. Read great part of Mr. Frinks[14] Dissertation against Ruling Elders. P.M. Mr. Benjamin Hows wife came.

14. Mr. Beacon[15] of Woodstock here with his sister Allen, and with Abiel Allen, who was going up to Woodstock with her uncle. It rain'd but I rode over in the Rain to Lieutenant Holloways to Catechizing. I rode on Neighbor Benjamin Hows Young Horse. Had but 8 Children, 4 Boys and 4 Girls. N.B. Some Talk I had with James Jeffrey about ship Mate John Kidney.

15. At Night John Kidney was charg'd with having pilfer'd his mistresses Comb—but he at once deny'd that he had seen it or knew any Thing about it. I immediately took up his Cloths and put my Hand into his Pocketts and found it there.

16. In the morning I was at Ensign Maynards but he could not go with me to a Justice against John Kidney, I return'd home and a new Contest arose. John having got on his Best stockings to go to work in the Bushes with, I bid him pull 'em off and put on his old ones which were fitt enough for his Business, but he was disobedient and worded it and delayed for some Time, till I added Resolution and severe Chiding, and oblig'd him to both pull 'em off and bring 'em to me, against his Stubborn Stomach and Saucy Answers but I gave him no Blows altho it much disturb'd me, and put me into much Trouble, for I resolved to bear with him no longer at all. I sent for Lieutenant Baker who came, and having discover'd to Him my present need of him and my purpose to carry John up to the House of Correction he presently return'd home to prepare himself for it. When he was ready and we had din'd I bid John shirt him and putt on his best Stockings that he might go with me. He delay'd and deny'd and began to shew himself as in the Morn but with my insisting and demanding it he went and dress'd himself and I Set him along before me on Mr. Townsends[16] Mare, whilst I rode, myself, Ensign Maynards. N.B. Ensign Maynards unseasonable Replys to me near his House and his talk of his readiness to have bought John, but Now etc. Lieutenant Baker[17] and I rode, with John before us, up to Major Keys.[18] After a great Deal of Consultation and Captain Flagg's advice join'd to the rest I accepted Johns Humiliation on his Knees with flowing Tears so far as to putt a stop to his going to the House of Correction. And with my Consent the Major committed him to John Clarks Custody, who liv'd on his son Gershoms place, till further Order, upon which I return'd home. N.B. Mr. Stephen White and Mrs. Sarah Noyes of New Haven, were come up from Boston to our House, the Meazles being in Boston, and They afraid of Infection. But Mrs. Pierpont who had heretofore had that disease remained behind.

17. On Ps. 99, 5, 9. Eph. 3, 8. Mr. White pray'd before the afternoon sermon.

18. Mr. White rode with me into the South part of the Town. Din'd at Winchesters. Were at Mr. Samuel Harringtons. Sent down to Boston by them at Eve. N.B. Mr. John Clark here from Shrewsbury and made offers to buy John Kidney.

19. I rode Mr. Aaron Forbush's Horse to Grafton to Association leaving Jonathan Rogers to plough and hoe among my Corn. N.B. had Neighbor David Maynard Juniors Horse to plough. As to what was done at Association See Association Records.[19]

20. It has been a Dark rainy season for a long Time. Rained this Forenoon. N.B. Difficulty with Mr. Axtell. N.B. only Mr. Prentice[20] and Mr. Loring,[21] Mr. Cushing and I. Mr. Cushing preach'd on 2 Pet. 3, 11. Company in returning home was Mr. Loring, Deacon Keys[22] and Mr. Daniel Steward.[23]

21. Was at the Funeral of Mr. Hezekiah Pratts child.

22. John Clark of Shrewsbury and his Brother in law, William Gray of Worcester here to buy John Kidney. I rode first to Ensign Maynards where were our Assessors with whom I advis'd, and then up to Major Keyes, and Brother Hicks with me, and for £12 I threw up the Indenture and Mr. Gray and John Sign'd new Indentures mutually. Mr. Gray pay'd me £7. 10. 0 in Cash and John Clark gave me a note for £4. 10. 0 more. N.B. Mr. Gershom Keys of Boston I met on the Road.

23. Call'd away early in the Morning to visit Mr. Cornelius Biglo's Child[24] which dy'd p.m. Mr. Tainter and one Son and Mr. James Millers son[25] came and Hoed a Considerable part of my Field. Very Hot. I was at Abner Newtons[26] and hit [?] of some Veal which was very agreeable on account of my Friends of New Haven who were still at my House.

24. Mr. White (of New Haven) a.m. on Luke 10, 42. P.M. on Job. 14, 1.

25. Funeral of Mr. Biglo's Child. Very Hot. Mr. Bridgham here.

26. Mr. Nathaniel Child work'd for me. The First Day of Mowing. Mr. White, Mrs. Sarah Noyes, my wife and I rode to Marlborough hoping to See Mrs. Pierpont, but she came not. N.B. I turn'd from the Company in going down and rode to Mr. Beemans[27] and from thence I rode to Mr. Allens[28] to see his son Samuel who had been ill of a fever but was recovering. I left my Wife, Mr. White and Mrs. Noyes at Marlborough and return'd home my Self.

27. Fine Day for my Hay. P.M. Benjamin Forbush[29] hoed. At Night a Thunder storm. Heavy Rain in the Night.

28. My Wife ill.

29. I rode unto the South part of the Town. At my return in the Evening I found Mrs. Pierpont and Mr. Earl who were come up in a Chair. Mrs. Pierpont Lame by a Fall from her Horse which she left at Watertown.

30. Mr. Pomroy[30] of New Haven came. He had been at Boston and Lancaster. Mr. White Studying a Sermon. Mr. Earl return'd to Boston. He carry'd Molly in his Chair. P.M. I rak'd and pol'd Hay. Mrs. Pomroy assisted me. At Evening Mr. John Jarvis came. N.B. Mr. John Rogers mowed for me the Square piece next above the Barn.

### JULY, 1739.

1. Mr. White preach'd A.M. on 1 Tim. 2, 6. I preach'd P.M. on Ps. 99, 5, 9.

2. I visited Mr. Isaac Tomlin on Mr. Pomroys Horse. John Rogers mowing P.M. The Gentlemen, viz. Mr. White, Mr. Pomroy, and Mr. Jarvis went afishing at the River by Neighbor Hows.[1] I went to raking Hay. At Evening came Brother Robert Breck[2] and with him Mr. Mirrick,[3] a preacher at Cold Spring.[4] N.B. We lodg'd Seven more than our own Family.

3. Mr. Pomroy took leave and Sett off for New Haven. N.B. Mrs. Pierpoint was very ill in the Night and this morning. My

---

[13] Benjamin Flagg, Jr., of Worcester.

[14] Reverend Thomas Frink of Rutland, Mass. There appears to be no record of a publication by Frink of this title or of this approximate date.

[15] Probably one of the numerous Bacons of this town.

[16] Joshua Townsend.

[17] Edward Baker of Westborough.

[18] John Keyes of Shrewsbury.

[19] The principal business of this meeting seems to have concerned Thomas Axtell of Marlborough, whose conduct had previously been a business of the Association. Despite the opposition of Deacon Keyes, the meeting recommended that the Marlborough Church "extend their compassions towards him, and he having removed his habitation to Grafton, to dismiss him thereto." Allen, *Worcester Association*, pp. 12, 19.

[20] Reverend Solomon Prentice of Grafton.

[21] Reverend Israel Loring of Sudbury.

[22] Of Shrewsbury.

[23] Daniel Stewart of Marlborough. Hudson, *Marlborough*, p. 450.

[24] "Pall Biglo" died June 23, 1739. *Westborough Vital Records*, p. 229.

[25] Probably James, Jr.

[26] Son of Thomas Newton of Westborough.

[27] Thomas Beamon of Marlborough.

[28] Ephraim Allen of Westborough.

[29] Son of Aaron Forbush of Westborough.

[30] Reverend Benjamin Pomeroy (Yale 1733), minister of Hebron, Conn. Dexter, pp. 485–488.

[1] Hezekiah How lived close by the Assabet River, the present boundary between Northborough and Westborough.

[2] Robert Breck, Jr., minister of Springfield, Mass.

[3] Noah Merrick (Yale 1731), later minister at Wilbraham, Mass., 1741–1776. Dexter, pp. 431–433.

[4] The plantation which became the town of Belchertown, Mass. in 1761.

Wife was up most of the night. Mr. White went for the Doctor early after break of Day, and he came, upon which She grew better. Mr. Breck, Mr. Mirrick, Mr. John Jarvis and I rode to Marlborough. Din'd at Dr. Gotts, Mr. Cushing and his wife and Mr. Caleb Rice[5] dining with us. Thence we proceeded to Cambridge. I lodg'd at Father Champneys.

4. Mr. Joseph Grants Mare which I rode down got out of the Pasture this morning, but I got Deacon Sparhawks[6] lad to go up the Road after her which she [sic] did. I rode to Boston to see my Mother and fetch my Cloths which I did before meeting. My Kinsman Elias[7] came over from Captain Sharps[8] where he has lodg'd for some Time because of his Infirmitys. I din'd in the Hall. N.B. a very great storm of Thunder, Rain and Wind, at Dinner Time. N.B. A Most agreeable Century Oration by the President.[9] N.B. Mr. Worthington[10] of Seabury and Mr. Parsons[11] of Lyme in Connecticutt at our Commencement. I was chiefly entertain'd at Sir Buckminsters.[12] Sir Woods[13] did not keep Commencement. No Company at Father Champney's, He being much disordered.

5. I was at College the forepart of the Day and din'd at Sir Buckminsters, but went to Boston P.M. N.B. the Meazles at Boston. My Aged and Honored Mother Weak and Sick and low. I return'd to Cambridge at Night and lodg'd as usual.

6. Brother Champney carry'd my Dauter Molly to Waterton to Mr. Benjamins[14] and from thence she rode up Mrs. Peirpoints Horse. We din'd at Baldwins.[15] Mr. Keyes of Boston din'd with us. Mr. Frink and Mr. Willard[16] of Biddeford with us up to Marlborough. John Rogers work'd Tuesday and Thursday most of the Day, but went home before night because he was sick. Mrs. Pierpont recovered.

7. Mr. White and I at our Preparations and my Boys raking Hay but carry'd none in.

8. Mr. White a.m. on Phil. 2, 12, 13. I preach'd p.m. on 1 John 1, 7, which I deliver'd on occasion of Mrs. Pierpoints being about to take her Journey from us to New Haven.

9. Mrs. Pierpoint, Mr. White and Mrs. Sarah Noyes Sett out upon their Journey, And my Wife and I accompany'd them up to Worcester. We call'd at Mr. Cushings,[17] going and returning. We din'd at Deacon Howards, and proceeded as far as Mr. Burrs,[18] where we parted. We return'd at Evening.

10. No Body at Work at Corn or Hay from Day to Day (except a Few Rows of Corn plough'd by Deacon Forbush)[19] John Rogers being Sick. Showery. N.B. Jonathan Witt[20] and Dinah Johnson[21] here in the showers. I walk'd out towards Eve as far as to Mr. Whipples.[22]

11. Fine Day but no Body at Work except my little Boys. I walk'd down to Ensign Maynards, where was Mr. Tainter[23] of Marlborough. P.M. he was at our House, as was also Mr. Caleb Rice. N.B. Mr. Rice acquainted me with the Affair of Lieutenant Ward[24] of Sturbridge and one Smith in Leicester.

12. I walk'd to Mr. Rogers's in the Morning. Dr. Daniel Forbush[25] and Zebulon Rice[26] came to Hoing my Corn. At

about 3 p.m. came Mr. Winchester[27] and Mr. James Fay[28] and mowed in my upper South Side. I rode on Mr. Winchesters Horse as far as Mr. Charles Rice's[29] for Hands to come to work and thence I rode up to Mr. John Pratt to see what he had done about the Ministerial Meadow, and I understood that he had mow'd and made 4 Load and a Half—that he began to Mow the Day before Commencement, and that of what he had made he had carted home half a Load. N.B. Colonel William Ward[30] was here again upon the Affair of his son, of Sturbridge, and he stay'd and din'd with us. In the Eve Simon Tainter, junior, and James Bradish brought Jonas Warrin and Charles Bruce to be admitted into the private Society.

13. Elijah and Adonijah Rice[31] and Phinehas Forbush[32] to help me. Elijah mow'd, the others hoed. Ensign Maynard's old Mare to plough. P.M. Charles and Ephraim Bruce[33] came and the first mow'd, the other hoed. Yet they did not get the hoing done. N.B. Mr. Breck, Mr. Merick and Colonel Phycheon here, and having din'd pursu'd their Journey.

14. Very much hinder'd by my Hay—yet study'd great part of the Day.

15. On Matt. 10, 1–4. P.M. Repeated sermon on Eph. 3, 8, page 10 to 17, from Eph. 2, 7. At noon I took advice with the Deacons about laying Brother Isaac Tomlins Circumstances before the Church, he being very languishing and his help gone from his Business, so that his Interest and Affairs and necessary provision for his and his Familys subsistence Suffer without any Body to pitty him. They advis'd me to lay it before them. N.B. Brother Abijah Bruce made some hasty reply, judging it unfit to be mentioned on the Lords Day. I answered that works of mercy, and providing for the distress'd Members of Christ was one of the most proper Dutys of the Lords Day.

16. Rainy.

17. I borrow'd Ebenezer Maynards Horse and rode to Grafton to Mr. Harwoods[34] to See his Mare, to Mr. Jonathan Morse's to see an Horse of his and to Mr. Prentices who rode with me to Deacon Whipples[35] Son's to look of his Beast, but I bought neither of them. In the Evening I was in at Mr. Phinehas Hardys,[36] and return'd home.

18. I was at the Funeral of Mr. Simeon Haywards Child. N.B. Discourse of the Meazles being at Shrewsbury Close by us.

19. Lecture on Isa. 55, 7. The Brethren of the Church Stop'd after Lecture to conferr about Some Relief to be afforded to Brother Isaac Tomlin junior. N.B. John Rogers mow'd my Barley this morning.

20. Deacon Forbush came and mowed all Day.

21. Mr. James Bridgham[37] here in his return to Brimfield. P.M. Mr. Lull sent to me to go and see his sick Child. Ebenezer Maynard came and carry'd in my Barley, whilst I visited Mr. Lull's Child.

22. Sacrament. Preach'd on Ps. 16, 2. Cousen Winchester din'd with us. P.M. Benjamin How[38] and his Wife made their Humiliation.

23. In the morning William, John and Jonathan Rogers and James Bradish were mowing for me (Upon Wages) and the last of them continued all Day, but the 3 Rogers's went home after Dinner. Cornelius Biglo also mow'd from 10 a.m. till night and then lodg'd with us. P.M. I rode over to the Funeral of Mr. Lull's Child. At my Return Mr. Cushing made me a visit.

---

[5] The deacon of Marlborough.
[6] Samuel Sparhawk of Cambridge.
[7] Reverend Parkman's brother, Elias Parkman of Boston.
[8] Robert Sharp of Brookline.
[9] Edward Holyoke, President of Harvard College.
[10] Reverend William Worthington (Yale 1716), minister at Westbrook (Saybrook), Conn., 1724–1756. Dexter, pp. 156–158.
[11] Reverend·Jonathan Parsons (Yale 1729), minister at Old Lyme, 1729–1745. Dexter, pp. 389–393.
[12] Joseph Buckminster (Harvard 1739), later minister at Rutland, Mass., 1752–1792. Sibley, X, 348–354.
[13] Benjamin Woods (Harvard 1739), the eldest son of Colonel Benjamin Woods of Marlborough. Sibley, X, 416.
[14] Daniel Benjamin, Jr., Selectman of Watertown. Bond, Watertown, p. 28.
[15] Captain Samuel Baldwin of Weston.
[16] Reverend Samuel Willard (Harvard 1723), minister at Biddeford, Maine, 1730–1741.
[17] Reverend Job Cushing of Shrewsbury.
[18] Reverend Isaac Burr of Worcester.
[19] Jonathan Forbush.
[20] Of Southborough. Hudson, Marlborough, p. 474.
[21] The daughter of Timothy Johnson of Southborough.
[22] Francis Whipple of Westborough.
[23] Deacon Joseph Tainter.
[24] Hezekiah Ward.
[25] Son of Deacon Jonathan Forbush.
[26] Son of Charles Rice of Westborough. He had recently married Abigail, daughter of Deacon Jonathan Forbush.

[27] Benjamin Winchester.
[28] Son of Captain John Fay.
[29] Son of Edmund Rice, an original settler of Westborough.
[30] One of the founders of the town of Southborough. A surveyor, extensive landowner, selectman, and representative of Marlborough and Southborough. Charles Martyn, The William Ward Genealogy (New York, 1925), pp. 85–86.
[31] Sons of Charles Rice.
[32] Son of Deacon Jonathan Forbush.
[33] Sons of Abijah Bruce.
[34] Benjamin Harwood.
[35] James Whipple of Grafton.
[36] Of Westborough.
[37] (Harvard 1726). The minister of Brimfield, Mass., 1736–1776. Sibley, VIII, 7–10.
[38] In the Westborough Church Records for this date Parkman wrote "Benjamin How and Tabitha his Wife made their Humiliations for the sin of Fornication and being restored to Charity, She was baptized and then their son Jonathan was baptized also." The child was born May 29, 1738.

24. Mr. Biglo work'd for me, mowing and raking. We had so much to rake that I rak'd with them all the Afternoon. N.B. Mr. Joshua Wheelers Son, of Lancaster, a Turner, here with his Wooden Ware. N.B. Mr. Jonah Warrin here at Evening.

25. Mr. Biglo work'd for me, mowing and Carting Hay in. I assisted what I could. At Eve Raking, Poling, etc. At night Mr. Biglo went home, asking wages only for the Two last Dayes.

26. Drisly weather. In the morning we pol'd in Hay. At noon walk'd as far as Jedidiah Hows where I had an Horse to ride to Shrewsbury Lecture. I did not get up there till Mr. Cushing had begun the Publick service. I preach'd on Jude 10, 21 to page [blank]. N.B. Dr. Stannton Prentice[39] and three of his Sisters there. After Lecture I visited Mr. Isaac Tomlin who yet remains in a very low Condition. Mrs. Brigham[40] of Marlborough (Mrs. Hepsibah Maynards[41] Mother) dy'd.

27. Mr. Belknap here at Evening.

28. Mr. Biglo began to reap my Rie. The Boys did not wholly finish our Hoeing till to Day. N.B. Mr. Francis Pierce here. The widow Brigham's (of Marlborough) Funeral. Mr. Stone officiated.

29. On 1 Cor. 6, 18. Former P.M. Mr. Tainter[42] and Mrs. Joslin[43] din'd here.

30. Cloudy weather. Brother Hicks to Cambridge. Mrs. Dolly Rice to Boston.

31. Fine Weather. Mr. Biglo reaping. At Evening I walk'd to the ministerial Meadow. Found that there were 4 Stacks of Hay, 3 Load in Cock and about as much in Swarth and that all the South part of the Meadow was mowed. In returning home visited Mr. Whipple who had been ill and confin'd by Rheumatism for some Time. Mr. Bigolo's sisters came to see him. Mr. Biglo lodged here.

### AUGUST, 1739.

1. Mr. Biglo with Mr. Whipples Cart and Oxen and Mr. David Maynards oxen added to them carted. Three Loads of the Ministerial Meadow Hay. Dr. Gott[1] here. P.M. I with my wife rode up to Mr. Isaac Tomlins where the private meeting was kept and I preached on Job 19, 25 etc. Jonas Warrin[2] was So kind as to come and Mow a Day for me.

2. Mr. Biglo at work—mowing and getting in Rie. I rode up to Neighbor Isaac Tomlins and assisted him in making his Will.

3. Mr. Biglo came (about nine this Morning) to my Work. My Wife and I rode up to Grafton and I preach'd a Lecture on Jude 5, 21. N.B. Madam Sartel[3] of Groton there. At Eve we return'd home. Mr. Francis Whipple and his Wife in Company. N.B. We rode upon Mr. Daniel Forbush's Mare.

4. Mr. Biglo at work still. A very dire Time.

5. On Ps. 73, 24. Hot dry Day. Widow Rice[4] and Mr. Biglo and his wife din'd here.

6. Rain'd hard in the night and all the Morning. A great Blessing! I sow'd Turnips in the Field. Mr. Varney,[5] late of Wilmington, and Mr. Stone of Southborough, here and din'd with us. P.M. Clear weather. At Evening Mr. Frink[6] came and lodg'd.

7. Mr. Frink went off, and Mr. Bridgham came, din'd with us, etc.

8. Mr. Biglo came to Work again were oblig'd to open the Hay that was made up on Saturday—about Two Load—but there came up a storm of Rain to Day and we could not get it in, and altho it was cock'd up yet, being weedy and Leavy Stuff it would not Save it Self. Read about 150 pages of the Mute

Philosopher, vol. 1. Ruth Bradish[7] here about her admission. Finish'd Mr. Frinks Dissertation upon Ruling Elders.

9. Mr. Isaac Tomlin junior dy'd last night. Mr. Biglo at work here. Reap'd Oates; did not open the Hay.

10. I rode a.m. to see Mr. Noah Rice's Youngest son who was exceeding bad and P.M. my wife and I rode to Mr. Isaac Tomlins Funeral.

11. I rode to the Funeral of Mr. Noah Rice's Child.[8]

12. On Ps. 73, 24, and p.m. repeated the latter part of Sermon on Eph. 3 from Eph. 2, 7.

13. We opened the Hay that had lain through Several Storms last week and rak'd it up, and having no Team to get it in we Cock'd it up.

14. Neighbor Hezekiah How came with his Team and got in Two Turns and somewhat more. N.B. a Puppett show at Ensign Maynards at Eve.

15. Mr. Joslin and Mr. Bruce going for Hay with their Teams refuse to help me in with what had lain out for near a fortnight, till Rain came upon it and prevented all further attempts about it.

16. Mr. Cornelius Biglo brought Two Hoggs for which I agreed to give him 6£ and 2/6 for bringing them, of which I gave him 3£ in hand. Charles Bruce here mowing the Leavy Grass in the New, low Ground.

17. My Wife rode down to Marlborough. Mr. Stone preach'd a preparatory Lecture there. Mr. Edward Burley Son came to my House in his Cabbin with his Puppetts, etc. there in. N.B. I had my Self Seen them in some measure my self Yesterday just at Evening. P.M. Charles Bruce work'd for me and finished my common mowing.

18. Mr. Jonah Warrin brought me home Two Small Turns of Hay from the ministerial Meadow. And I got Mr. Aaron Forbush to putt into Stack a parcel of Cocks which Mr. Pratt had left for Some Time in the Meadow. Eleazer Williams with a Team came and got up a Load from the low Ground at home and Mr. Warrin and he got up what was mowed by Charles Bruce. Near Night, Mr. Cushing came. I was exceeding Hott and sweatty, with walking and looking after my Folks and Business, and when I came to shirt me cool'd my Self too much. Rode Captain Forbush's[9] Horse up to Shrewsbury in the Evening and doubtless took Cold.

19. Preach'd at Shrewsbury a.m. on Jude 10, 21, p.m. on Phil. 1, 21. The Head-Ach all Day. At Eve the Pain Settled upon my stomack and Bowells—increas'd my Trouble to a great Degree. Mr. Cushing return'd. My Pains and sickness lasted till it was late in the Night. All Nature in great Disorder with me. Work'd downward many Times and upwards several. I went to Bed very ill indeed. N.B. Rain, Thunder and Lightning.

20. I rose better in the Morning, through the great Goodness and Mercy of God. Return'd home by the way of the widow Tomlins. Mrs. Tomlins Horse was brought for me to ride to Boston upon.

21. Finding myself Still better I undertook my Journey. Stopp'd a while at Mr. Amsdens,[10] at Mr. David Hows,[11] at Mr. Cooks,[12] at Dr. Robys,[13] at Woolsons[14] from where I had Captain Samuel Chandler's[15] (of Woodstock) Company—and at Mr. Benjamins at Waterton. Arriv'd at Father Champneys after Dark.

22. Rainy forenoon. Din'd at Father Champneys. N.B. Father in a very disquieted and distracted State—from home by Night and by Day—has not been in Bed for scarcely a month together. P.M. Showery yet I rode to Boston. My Mother in a

[39] The physician of Lancaster.
[40] The widow of Samuel Brigham. Hudson, *Marlborough*, p. 334.
[41] Mrs. John Maynard of Westborough.
[42] Deacon Simon Tainter of Westborough.
[43] Mrs. Joseph Joslin of Westborough.

[1] Benjamin Gott, the physician of Marlborough.
[2] Son of Daniel Warrin.
[3] Mrs. Nathaniel Sartell of Groton, Mass. Samuel A. Green, *Epitaphs from the Old Burying Ground* (Boston, 1878), pp. 251-252.
[4] Mrs. Elizer Rice of Westborough.
[5] Reverend James Varney (Harvard 1725), the minister of Wilmington, Mass., 1733-1739. He had recently been dismissed by the church. *Sibley*, VII, 601-602.
[6] Reverend Thomas Frink of Rutland, Mass.

[7] Daughter of James Bradish of Westborough. She was admitted to the Westborough Church, Sept. 2, 1739.
[8] Noah Rice, Jr., died Aug. 10, 1739, at age of nine months.
[9] Samuel Forbush.
[10] Captain Isaac Amsden of Marlborough.
[11] Proprietor of the Wayside Inn in Sudbury.
[12] Reverend Samuel Cooke of Wayland.
[13] Ebenezer Roby, the physician of Sudbury.
[14] In Watertown.
[15] The son of the prominent Colonel John Chandler, the Chief Justice of the Court of Common Pleas and General Sessions. Woodstock was originally in Massachusetts but after 1749 in Connecticut. Clarence W. Bowen, *Woodstock An Historical Sketch* (New York, 1886), pp. 33-35. George Chandler, *The Chandler Family* (Worcester, 1883), pp. 130-131.

low, Sick, feeble, Dangerous State. My Kinsman Elias lodges Still at Captain Sharps—So that I Saw him not, this Journey, Lodg'd at Brother Elias's.

23. Last Night very rainy indeed —and terrible with Thunders and Lightnings. The morning also exceeding rainy, and Dark. Broke Fast with my Cousen Elizabeth Corsser[16] heretofore Elizabeth Tyley. Dr. Colman[17] preach'd an Excellent and very Seasonable Sermon on Job 38, 28. After Lecture Mr. Quincy[18] carried me to his House and on the way at the Printers presented me a volume of Mr. Flynts[19] Sermons, and I took my own likewise (for I was my Self a Subscriber) which I devoted to my Cousen Corsser aforesaid. After Dining at Mr. Quincys I attended a variety of Business—walk'd to Brother Alexanders. N.B. The Meazles not out of Town yet. N.B. Mr. Alexander Wolcott[20] of New Haven who had left that Town because of the Snares of a Young Widow there, notwithstanding the endearments and great Fortune of his own Wife, Supposed to be in Boston and the said Widow likewise, who boldly and resolutely and against the Fears and entreatys of her parents, Sisters and her own Child mounted her Horse before their Eyes and rode after Mr. Wolcott. My Mother very low but I was oblig'd to ride to Cambridge that I might pursue my Journey. N.B. Sister Lydia Champney[21] at Boston.

24. On my Journey I met with Captain Samuel Chandler according to Appointment at Captain Saltmarshes.[22] We call'd at Mr. Warham Williams's[23] at Waltham. We din'd at Mr. Woolsons. Call'd at Mr. Cook's—and at Marlborough. Made it late home. N.B. The vast Damage done to the Hay upon Sudbury Meadows, etc. by the late Excessive Rains.

25. Mr. Williams had made up, and today brought home Two Barrells of Cyder, One of which we boil'd.

26. In the morning between 8 and 9 came in Mr. James Varney and preach'd for me in the forenoon on Job 14, 1. P.M. I preach'd on Ps. 73, 24.

27. Mr. Varney went off. The Water in the Pump fails.

28. Mr. Loring[24] came about Noon; after him Mr. Stone, Mr. Prentice of Grafton, Mr. Cushing and Mr. Frink. These made up the Association.[25] Mr. Stone gave us a very usefull and Excellent Discourse on 2 Cor. 4, 5. Most of us read our Collections which we had made for the Association. N.B. Two Horses Neighbor How took home with him, Two I had pastur'd at Ensign Maynards great Pasture, and the Fifth at Neighbor Pratts.[26] The Ministers all lodg'd in the House.

29. Mr. Loring preach'd a very profitable sermon on Deut. 32, 47. N.B. After Sermon I read the brief Representation of the Case of Mr. Torry[27] in Narraganset. N.B. Madam Sartel[28] and her daughter Prentice[29] here.

30. Last Night was very Cold—a Considerable Frost.

31. Another Considerable Frost. John Rogers mowed Rowing. P.M. he Sett anew the Fence before the old House and putt up the stone wall under it. N.B. We had been troubled with Brother Hicks's Hoggs breaking in.

[16] Elizabeth Tyley, Parkman's niece, married John Coarsa, June 22, 1738.

[17] Reverend Benjamin Colman of Boston.

[18] Edmund Quincy of Boston.

[19] Henry Flynt (Harvard 1693), tutor for many years at Harvard College. The work mentioned here is *Twenty Sermons on Various Subjects* (Boston, 1739).

[20] (Yale 1731). He was the fourth son of Roger Wolcott of Windsor, Conn., later Governor of the province. Alexander's first wife (Sarah Drake) left him in 1739, and he married Mary, the widow of Fitz John Allen of New Haven. He later became a respected physician of Windsor. Dexter, pp. 435-436.

[21] Of Cambridge. Parkman's sister-in-law.

[22] Thomas Saltmarsh, a former sea-captain, was an innkeeper at Watertown for many years. Bond, *Watertown*, pp. 414, 913.

[23] The minister of Waltham.

[24] Reverend Israel Loring of Sudbury.

[25] See Allen, *Worcester Association*, p. 19.

[26] John Pratt.

[27] Reverend Joseph Torrey (Harvard 1728), minister of the Congregational Church at Kingston, R. I., 1732–1791. He was also a physician. Immediately after his ordination Torrey was involved in a law suit defending his right as a Congregational minister to 300 acres of glebe land. In this complicated and extraordinary case which went as far as the Privy Council, the real issue was the democratic nature of the New England church system. The case dragged on for a number of years, and in 1739 the Boston ministers Colman and Prince headed a successful campaign to raise money to pay the cost of Torrey's defense. *Sibley*, VIII, 498-507.

[28] Wife of Captain Nathaniel Sartell (Sartel, Sartele, Sawtell) of Groton.

[29] October 26, 1732, Sarah Sartell, daughter of Captain Nathaniel, married Reverend Solomon Prentice of Grafton. *Groton Vital Records*, II, 148.

## SEPTEMBER, 1739.

1. Nigh Two Barrells of Cyder made of my Apples by Mr. Williams for Mr. Rogers and Townsend.

2. Sacrament. Preach'd on John 13, 17, and on 1 Cor. 6, 18 former part. After meeting I Stopp'd the Deacons of the Church and the Select men of the Town to Confer with them respecting a suitable Time for the Contribution which authority had recommended to us for the Assistance of Mr. Torry of South Kingstown in Narragansett.

3. A very rainy forenoon. Trooping and Training. Captain Warrins Company met at Captain Fay's, and Captain Eagers[1] with the Troops at Ensign Maynards. N.B. I pray'd in the meeting House only with Captain Eagers Company. Din'd at Ensign Maynards. I pray'd with those at Evening with whom I had din'd. N.B. Storm Clear'd off towards Night. Patience Forbush[2] went with James Bradish to Ensign Maynards where Some number of Young People met at a Frolick and continued late—to my great Trouble and disquietment.

4. I rode on Captain Warrins Mare to Cambridge. Met Mr. Warham Williams and Mr. William Williams junior[3] on their Journey to New Haven. At Mr. Woolsons[4] at Weston I met with Mr. Berry, Shipwright of Boston going up to Hopkinton.

5. Rode a.m. to Captain Sharps where my Kinsman Elias still Lodges, then proceeded to Boston. I rode to Brother Alexanders who sent my wife 3 Gallons of wine by Mr. Cornelius Biglo. Din'd at Alexanders. My Mother Still in a weak and low Condition. Benjamin Parkman[5] rode my Horse to his Brother Bradshaws.[6] I was greatly interrupted by all these means in my usual practice on this Day—and very much subverted in my Design of improving this Season which was to have Spent it with my Mother and Brethren, especially the Afternoon or Evening in a Religious Manner, and I carry'd with me a Discourse on Ps. 73, 24, and another on Job 19, 25 for the purpose—but their various Engagements, etc. prevented. Yet I would not omitt wholly my regards to this Day, although I was not able so strictly to observe it to the Lord as I would have done.

6. Mr. Prince's[7] Lecture on Jer. 31, 18. Din'd at Brother Samuels.[8] N.B. His son Samuel very low in Consumption.

7. Din'd at Brother Elias's. Mr. Thomas Weld[9] there. N.B. Conversation the Day before yesterday and to Day with Captain White of New Haven concerning Mr. Alexander Wolcott. P.M. Mr. Webbs[10] Lecture on 2 Chron. 30, 18, 19. N.B. Haynes Woodbridge[11] went to Cambridge for my Horse, and not coming Seasonably in the Evening it put us to great trouble, for a Small number went over to Charleston to accompany my Niece Elizabeth (Brother Elias's Dauter) who was going up with me. We lodg'd at Father Champney's.

8. Return'd to Westborough with my Niece aforesaid. On the Road Company Mr. Francis Harrington of Grafton and Mr. Barnard[12] of Sutton. At Marlborough was my wife who kindly came down to meet me.

9. Repeated on Isa. 55, 7. P.M. on 1 John 2, 15. Appointed the Contribution for Mr. Torry to be the next Lords Day.

10. My Fatt Cattle which were brought down by Ensign Maynard last week, were taken into my own Pasture. Charles Bruce mow'd Bushes. Boys cutting Stalks. N.B. They began last week.

11. Catechiz'd at the Meeting House. 43 Boys—30 Girls. P.M. visited Mr. Gamel[13] who is sick.

[1] James Eager of Westborough.

[2] Daughter of Deacon Thomas Forbush.

[3] The minister of Weston.

[4] Isaac Woolson kept a tavern in Weston. Daniel S. Lamson, *History of Weston* (Boston, 1913), p. 188.

[5] Benjamin was the son of Parson Parkman's brother, William.

[6] Sarah, daughter of William Parkman married John Bradshaw, Sept. 26, 1736.

[7] Reverend Thomas Prince of the Old South Church.

[8] Samuel Parkman of Boston.

[9] Reverend Thomas Weld of Upton, Mass.

[10] Reverend John Webb of the New North Church.

[11] Son of the Reverend Timothy Woodbridge, Jr., the minister of Hatfield, Mass.

[12] Isaac Barnard. William Benedict and Hiram A. Tracy, *History of Sutton* (Worcester, 1878), pp. 584-585.

[13] Mrs. Samuel Gamel of Westborough.

12. Visited Mrs. Cody[14] of Hopkinton, who is in a distracted frame at her Mother Clarks at Shrewsbury.

13. A.M. I walk'd over to Mr. Hezekiah Hows.[15] At noon Mr. Biglo din'd with me and he work'd the afternoon. Mow'd Bushes and pik'd stalks. I rode his Horse down to Mr. Daniel Maynards[16] at Marlborough to see his Horses; but he was gone from home. N.B. One [blank] Darby, a Young Man of Concord, rode with me. I was at Mr. Beemans[17] and Mr. David Brighams[18] as I return'd. Jerusha Ward[19] and Mercy Nurse here.

14. [No entry].

15. Samuel Bumpso work'd for me.

16. John 13, 17. 2 Cor. 8, 7. Contribution to assist Mr. Torry of South Kingston in Narragansett. Gather'd £8.8.0. Which God be pleas'd to accept as a sweet Savour through Christ!

17. Mr. Alleson[20] of Hopkinton here with a Mare offer'd to Sale.

18. Mr. David Maynard, junior of Sudbury here with an Horse offer'd to Sale. I rode over to Winchesters, Mr. Grout,[21] Captain Fay, old Mrs. Fay, etc. At my return found my Wife ill—overdone with worrying Yesterday. Great Frosts.

19. Mr. Allison here with his Mare again for me to ride her and try her. I rode to Mr. Grouts and to old Mrs. Fays. N.B. Jeduthan's[22] young Horse offer'd. Sam Bumpso work'd for me. My Four Young Cattle were brought home by Neighbor Abner Newton. N.B. Neighbor Amsden[23] brought in Father Champney[24] who in his distraction had worry'd up o'Foot from Cambridge, having Set out the Day before, and layn out last night in the Cold and Frost.

20. Sam Bumpso at Work mowing. Ebenezer[25] went over with a Load of Apples and took Cold.

21. The Commission officers of the Regiment met to consult about a Regimental Muster. Two Lieutenants came for me to dine with them. N.B. Mr. James Bridgham here in his return home to Brimfield. Cloudy and lowery.

22. Rainy. Tobacco hung up. Ebenezer grows worse with his Cough.

23. 1 John 2, 14.

24. [No entry].

25. Aaron Forbush junior at work for me, picking Apples for Store and for Cyder. Father Champney went to Cambridge. A Long Ladder made by Brother Hicks, Sett up to Day on the Barn.

26. Aaron Forbush and William Johnson at Work for me, picking Apples and carting them over. Part of Afternoon Splitting Rails. N.B. Captain Eager here. Ebenezer Maynard kill'd a Calf of 5 weeks old which came out of the woods. Weigh'd 57½ pounds and he Carry'd it to Boston at night. 4 Barrells brought me by Mr. Belknap.

27. I rode over to Neighbor Jesse Maynards[26] to see his Sick Child. At Mr. Gamels and at Mr. Lawrence's[27] N.B. Mr. Eleazer Russell with a Mare offer'd to sale. I return'd by the Mill. Eleazer Williams carted over a Load of Apples.

28. My Son Ebenezer continues very badd with his Cough. My wife ill. My House in great Trouble. Some Number of men clearing up the Training Field.

29. A Barrell of Cyder for me and one for Brother Hicks by Mr. Williams of my Apples.

30. Eph. 6, 30 to 18.

[14] Mrs. John Cody.
[15] Parson Parkman's old friend and neighbor.
[16] Brother of James Maynard of Westborough.
[17] Eleazer Beemon of Westborough.
[18] An original settler of Westborough who lived near Parkman. DeForest and Bates, *Westborough*, pp. 46-47.
[19] Young daughter of Increase Ward of Westborough.
[20] Joseph Elison.
[21] Joseph Grout.
[22] Jeduthan Fay, son of Samuel Fay of Westborough.
[23] Jacob Amsden.
[24] Samuel Champney of Cambridge, the father of the Reverend Parkman's first wife.
[25] Parkman's eldest son.
[26] Son of David Maynard, an original settler of Westborough.
[27] Benjamin Lawrence of Westborough.

## OCTOBER, 1739.

1. Mr. David Maynard, junior was here with a large Bay Horse which I agreed with him for, in presence of Mr. Francis Whipple and Mr. Abner Newton at the price of 35 pounds but with the Reserve and Condition that if I find that he doth not suit Me, he shall take him again, if he be return'd within a fortnights Time. This was written and Declar'd by both of us before the Witnesses. The Road which goes out south from my House handsomely clear'd up, and the Training field clear'd more Spaciously.

2. I rode up to Shrewsbury to John Clarks and to Mr. Cushings. Sam Bumpso thrash'd Rye for me.

3. The Regiment Under the Command of Colonel William Ward consisting of 11 Companys, muster'd and perform'd the Exercises proper on That Occasion. N.B. Mr. Dor[1] and his Brothers Daughter, Mr. Weld, Mr. Webb, Mr. Cushing, Mr. Stone, Mr. Solomon Prentice, and Mr. John Ballentine.[2] We march'd with the Field Officers in Viewing the Regiment as the Battalion were in array, the Officers in their Places, and performing the Standing Salute. Mr. Dorr pray'd. We were entertain'd by the Field Officers. It was worthy of Notice that the Exercises were perform'd so well, considering their Newness, that there was so little hurt Done, and that there was So little intemperance, Rabblement and Riot. N.B. The Regiment under Colonel Chandler[3] muster'd the same Day. Mr. Dorr and niece, Mr. Weld and Mr. Webb lodg'd here.

4. Mr. Dorr, etc. rode away, and my Dauter Molly, Single on her Horse rode with them, Mr. Weld carrying my Niece Elizabeth behind him. At Evening, Mr. Weld, Eliza, and Molly return'd, having been to Grafton. Major Keys[4] din'd with us, and Mrs. Miles[5] of Concord. P.M. John Oake,[6] James Geoffrey, James Eager and Samuel Allen[7] gather'd that part of the Corn by the old House and with Jotham[8] and Stephen Maynard and Noah How husk'd it out in the Evening. N.B. Abial Allen help'd us these Two or Three Days but to Day went home, and Lydia Harrington came to serve us a Day or Two. John Oake lodg'd here in order to his Working tomorrow. Mr. Weld Lodg'd here.

5. Very Rainy. Mr. Weld detain'd here by the Storm of Rain. John Oake went off without working.

6. Mr. Weld left us. I was not very well.

7. On Eph. 6, 13 all Day but improv'd Some of the Discourse on Ps. 144, 1, for I was under So great Indisposition that my preparation was much obstruct'd. At Night I was very ill and went to Bed not being able so much as to perform the Dutys of the Family.

8. I Sent Brother Hicks with Mr. David Maynard's Horse down to Sudbury to him again for I found he would not Suit me. William Johnson making Cyder for me at Mr. Hezekiah Hows Mill.

9. William Johnson making Cyder for me still. Captain Forbush[9] with his Team, Timothy Warrin and John Rogers came p.m. to get up and husk'd Corn.

10. Rainy. General Muster of the Regiment of Horse at Lancaster.

11. [No entry].

12. Samuel Bumpso thrashing Rye. William Johnson work'd for me.

13. Mr. Cabot[10] of Killingly[11] here, very much out of Health. Lodg'd here. William work'd for me.

14. Mr. Cabot would not venture to undertake any part of the Public Service but went to Meeting and to Communion with us.

[1] Reverend Joseph Dorr of Mendon.
[2] (Harvard 1735). Later minister at Westfield, Mass., 1741-1776. *Sibley*, IX, 468-472.
[3] John Chandler of Worcester.
[4] John Keyes of Shrewsbury.
[5] Wife of Deacon Samuel Miles.
[6] Son of Nathaniel Oakes of Marlborough. Hudson, *Marlborough*, p. 426.
[7] Son of Ephraim Allen of Westborough.
[8] Son of David Maynard.
[9] Samuel Forbush.
[10] Reverend Marston Cabot (Harvard 1724), the first minister of Thompson, Conn., 1729-1756. *Sibley*, VII, 320-324.
[11] Killingly included the region that became the separate town of Thompson in 1785.

I repeated Sermon on Mat. 26, 21, 22. P.M. on Eph. 3, 10 last Clause.

15. Mr. Cabot pursued his Journey to the Eastward. Mr. Abraham Knowlton came to lay my East Garrett Floor. Sam Bumpso and William Johnson at work for Me. In great Trouble for want of Womens Help in the House.

16. Mr. Knowlton at Work here. Very Rainy forenoon. Mr. Cushing[12] din'd with us. P.M. it held up and we rode to Association at Southborough. At Eve Mr. Fisk[13] of Killingly came. N.B. Mr. Cabot there before detain'd by the Storm. See Association Records. I lodg'd with Mr. Cushing at Ensign Brighams.

17. Mr. Loring, Mr. Barrett[14] etc. came to Association. I preach'd on 1 John 1, 17 at the Public Lecture.

18. Several Neibours on the South side of Town Mr. Bowman,[15] Stone,[16] Martin Pratt, Beriah Rice,[17] Jonathan Forbes, and Phinehas Walker, Dan Hardy, came and gather'd my Corn. Molly Wright[18] came to wash for my Wife.

19. Mr. Williams has undertook to make up the Rest of my apples—Carting to Day.

20. Rain.

21. Rain. On Eph. 3, 10.

22. Town Meeting to grant my Support. Unanimous for 200. Rainy. I was greatly exercis'd by the Creatures lying So much upon my apples and I was oblig'd to be much abroad in the Town. Both the Constables made up Accounts with me. Rebecca Hicks[19] helps us.

23. Mr. Bridgham and Mr. Wyman[20] here. Mr. Williams brought home 6 Barrells more of Cyder. I had design'd to go to Boston but So much Business prohibited it. Mr. Samuel Harrington brought me his Horse for my Journey, and greatly assisted me in getting down Cyder, etc. Boil'd Two Barrells of Cyder into one. Neighbor Maynards, Whipples, Forbushs etc Lads Husking. N.B. I made up Accounts with Ensign Maynard.

24. I rode down to Lexington on Mr. Samuel Harringtons Horse. N.B. Difficulty in finding the Way from Weston. One Segar and one Mellage my Pilots it being Night. I went to Captain Joseph Bowmans[21] and lodged there. Very kindly entertain'd by them.

25. View'd a Mare of Mr. Francis Bowmans. Rode to Cambridge at Father Champneys. Ferry'd over from Charleston. Visited my honored aged Mother who was much better. Lodg'd at Brother Elias's.

26. Rode to Mr. Tainters[22] and Browns[23] at Waterton. Met Mr. Francis Bowman and Mr. Samuel Harrington. Din'd at Mr. Strattons of Waltham. Bargained with Mr. Bowman for his Mare. Rode home with Mr. Harrington and a Considerable Company of Neighbors, etc. Ensign Forbush, etc. We rode over the new Bridge. Not well at Wards, but held up home between 10 and 11 at Night.

27. Not well, but yet in my Study. In the Night very ill.

28. Grew worse. Not able to go to Meeting. A.M.—P.M. preach'd on Rev. 2, 21 but with much Difficulty, being very ill and feeble.

29. Abroad in the forenoon, but in pain, chiefly in my left Hip and Groin. Dr. Gott occasionally here. P.M. could not walk. At Eve my pains exceedingly increas'd. Neighbor How came and got my Bed down into the lower room, and lifted me on to it. All night in great pain. My Wife got up twice. Took Flower of Brimstone, which purged Me.

30. I grew More helpless. Ebenezer rode to Grafton for a market for the rest of my Cyder, but in Vain. N.B. Mrs. Maynard, Sister Hicks,[24] etc. No Watcher yet.

31. Ebenezer rode to Dr. Gott but he came not. He Sent me the Turbith Mineral[25] which I did not venture to take. Mrs. Maynard and Brother Hicks watch'd.

## NOVEMBER, 1739.

1. Dr. Gott came—judg'd I am taken with an high Inflammatory Rhumatism. Bled me in the right arm—insisted upon my taking my Turbith if diminished. N.B. It work'd 5 Times up, and 30 or 40 Times downward. Nathan Maynard[1] was Sent for the Doctor but he did not come, but Sent a Plaister, etc. Nathan Maynard and Bekky Hicks[2] watch'd. Ensign Maynard getting wood for me.

2. The Doctor came and bleeds me again. Gave Something to prevent my purging. P.M. Neibours on the South side came and got wood. John Rogers and Sister Hicks watch'd. A Bad Night.

3. Still remain in a weak, pained State. Worried through the Day. Jotham Maynard and Bekky Hicks watch'd. A bad Night again.

4. No Preaching, but few at Meeting. Doctor came. Bleeds again and gave Rubarb which work'd kindly. Deacon Newton[3] and My Niece Eliza watch'd. A dismal Night!

5. Storm of Snow. Lieutenant Holloway[4] went for me to Jabez Rice's to bespeak a fat Cow, and came and gave me Notice of it. Jotham Maynard fixing up the Barn to house Creatures. Jedidiah How watch'd. Somewhat easier Night.

6. Doctor came. Found me with a very bad Sore Throat, my Head on the back part great disorder'd—tottering and pained— Yet he judg'd I was better, and did not bleed me. Mr. Stone visited me and pray'd with us. Several of my Neibours here. My Head grew worse and those Disorders were very troublesome. But I had some good Rest nevertheless. Samuel Baker[5] and Molly Lee watch'd.

7. In the Morning My Fever was much Worse, and p.m. the Use of my Right Hand (which hitherto I have been favor'd with when every other Limb was disenabled) was taken away, but through Gods Mercy to me my Left grew better. About 9 at Night my Stomach grew very full of pain. I lay Striving for Breath all Night. Mr. Whipple watch'd.

8. About 4 o'Clock in the Morning my Wife got up by reason of my great Extremity, and desir'd Mr. Whipple to go away for the Doctor which he did. The Doctor came about 10 o'Clock and saw my Distress'd State, bled me again and gave me a portion of Rubarb which work'd kindly and my Breath was better Somewhat. Yet it remained bad. Captain Eager watch'd. A very labouring Breath Still. My Niece Eliza carry'd down by Ensign Maynard.

9. A Cloudy Day. Mr. Tainter[6] watch'd.

10. Somewhat better, through Gods great Goodness. The Doctor Came, but left nothing new. In the Evening My Brother Parkman came to see me, to my great Joy. N.B. Samuel Bumpso work'd for me p.m. digging potatoes. Levi Brigham watch'd.

11. I was very faint and weak. No preaching—but a Thin Meeting. Simon Tainter junior watch'd.

12. Mr. Cushing made me a Visit and pray'd with us. I was very weak and feeble. N.B. David Maynard, junior and his Brother Jotham came and had Two Store Piggs of me. The one weigh'd 46, the other 54. At Eve Mr. Frink came to see me. N.B. Captain Eager brought home the Fatt Cow, bought of Mr. Jabez Rice[7] for £13.5.0. Mr. David Maynard junior watch'd. I

[12] Reverend Job Cushing of Shrewsbury.

[13] Reverend John Fiske (Harvard 1702), the first minister of Killingly, Conn., 1715–1741. *Sibley*, V, 144–147.

[14] Reverend Samuel Barrett of Hopkinton.

[15] James Bowman.

[16] Daniel Stone.

[17] Son of Edmund Rice, an original settler.

[18] Mary, daughter of Edward Wright of Framingham. Temple, *Framingham*, p. 755.

[19] Mrs. John Hicks.

[20] Reverend Ebenezer Wyman (Harvard 1731), minister at Union, Conn., 1738–1746. *Sibley*, IX, 116–117.

[21] Prominent citizen of Watertown. Bond, *Watertown*, p. 690.

[22] Captain John Tainter of Watertown, brother of Deacon Simon Tainter of Westborough.

[23] Deacon William Brown, a prominent resident of Waltham.

[24] Mrs. John Hicks of Westborough, Parson Parkman's sister-in-law.

[25] Turpeth Mineral, a basic mercuric sulphate used as a purgative.

[1] Son of David Maynard, one of the neighbors.

[2] Rebecca, daughter of John and Rebecca Hicks.

[3] Josiah Newton.

[4] William Holloway.

[5] Son of Edward Baker, an original settler.

[6] Deacon Simon Tainter.

[7] Son of Deacon Caleb Rice of Marlborough.

had the best night of any Since I was Sick, and it had been most pleasant to enjoy by Dear Brothers Company. D.G.

13. My kind brother left us. Mr. Grout and Mr. Tainter came and kill'd my Fat Cow. N.B. The Quarter weigh'd 20 Score and 16 pound. Mrs. Tainter came to help us in cleaning Tripe, etc. And we had also hired Sarah Forbush[8] to work for us to Day. I was (through the Divine Goodness) Still better. The Doctor was here. Left the Ethiops Mineral,[9] etc. Bekky Hicks watch'd and I rested pritty well. D.G.

14. I could walk from my Bed to the Fire. P.M. Mrs. Dorothy Rice[10] here and She watch'd. I did not rest quite so well as before.

15. In the Morning very feeble. N.B. The Town Met to provide preaching. My Wife watch'd with me till Two o'Clock, and had no other watcher. Edward Whipple was to have watch'd but came not.

16. Extreme Cold—froze up the Earth. My House unbank'd, my Potatoes the greatest part in the Ground. A purging has attended me and continues, but by the Cold we were prevented sending to the Doctor. Stephen Fay had engaged to watch tonight, but fail'd. My Wife Sat up again till past midnight, after which I did without. Old Mrs. Tomlin, wife of Deacon Tomlin,[11] dy'd on the 16th in the Night, having wash'd the forenoon before She complain'd some Hours before She dy'd and the Deacon and his Son Sat up with her, but when a Neibour whom they sent for came and went to her (they Supposing her to be drowzing) She was found breathless.

17. The Cold Something abated. I Sent Ebenezer to Marlborough to the Doctor. Mr. William Jenison[12] came up from Waterton to preach here. Ruth Hicks watch'd. I crawl up very Slowly, yet Sit up Considerably. My Joints, my Knees and Ankles especially, weak and feeble.

18. Mr. Jenison preach'd A.M. on Exod. 33, 18. P.M. on 2 Corinth. 12, 9. Mr. Tainter din'd with us. I could take but very Little. Stephen Fay watch'd.

19. Mr. Jenison, when the Committee (Scil. Ensign Maynard and Mr. Tainter) had been with him for further Service, went away to return to Waterton. Old Mr. Maynard came and winnow'd up my Beans. Jotham Maynard had another Store Pigg. Weigh'd 52. Asa Brigham[13] watch'd.

20. Dr. Gott here. Deacon Tomlin's Wife's Funeral. At Eve Mr. Cushing here. I Seem'd to be still growing Somewhat better. D.G.

21. A Cold Season for some Days together. Thomas Green (Brother of our former Neighbor John) here. Brother Hicks kill'd a Pigg for me of about 48 pounds to Send to Boston, and Fowls kill'd at Eve, that Mr. Winchester[14] going down for me upon the Errand of a Maid there, might not go empty.

22. Before I got up I was in great Pains in my Bowels. The Day was a very ill Day with me. I had eat Milk the night before with good appetite, and I thought it sat So well upon my stomach that I might eat boil'd milk this Morning, but I was thereupon greatly disorder'd. Sick, faint, and Vomited Several Times in the Day Casting up whatever I took down. Mr. Winchester went down to Boston for me upon my Mare to bring up a Maid, one Mary Wakefield from thence. At Evening, though exceeding ill, I marry'd Timothy Warrin and Rebecca Tainter.[15] Bekky Hicks watch'd.

23. A.M. I was Still weak and faint, appetite gone. P.M. Somewhat better.

24. Mr. Winchester came up last night without the Young Woman. Mr. Jenison came. I was Somewhat Comfortable, tho week.

[8] Mrs. Samuel Forbush.
[9] A name formerly given to certain black or dark-colored compounds of metals.
[10] Mrs. Seth Rice.
[11] Isaac Tomlin.
[12] Former minister of Salem, Mass., who had been dismissed by his congregation, Dec. 27, 1736.
[13] Son of neighbor David Brigham.
[14] Benjamin Winchester.
[15] Daughter of Deacon Simon Tainter.

25. Mr. Jenison on Mat. 8, 17, and John 19, 34. My Spirits low and Stomach weak at Dinner. But I Still repose my Self on God.

26. Mr. Jenison and my wife rode away together, the one for Southborough, the other for Marlborough, but return'd after a little Time, my wife having fallen from her Mare and hurt herself so as to incapacitate her for proceeding. Colonel Woods[16] and Mr. Smith[17] (preacher) from Marlborough to see me. They din'd, and tarry'd till Evening. At Evening Mr. Jenison rode with them. I was considerable Comfortable and lively, and had some Considerable Appetite; Slept also Comfortably.

27. Very pleasant Weather. Mr. Jenison return'd. Dr. Gott here, left me Bitters and Crocus Martis,[18] advis'd to take the Air by Degrees. My wife feels her hurt of Yesterday much more. But I was better than I had been any Day, and had a good Night, through the great goodness of God.

28. Pleasant Day—and I was very Comfortable. But my Family greatly afflicted by my wife's pains and Confinement—being very weak-handed and yet much to do. (Mr. Jenison here, etc.) Lieutenant Baker (one of the Committee to take Care of the pulpit) here. He went to Ensign Maynards and provided Molly Lee who came to help us. Father Champney came up again.

29. Public Thanksgiving. Mr. Jenison preach'd on Eph. 5, 20. Among the great and Signal Benefits receiv'd from a most merciful and gracious God, his redeeming my Life from Destruction, easing my Limbs and granting me a great measure of Comfort, and the mercy Shewn my wife at the time of her Fall on the 26th, is to be Celebrated with gratefull Joy and Praise. But O that it might not be with me as with Hezekiah in 2 Chron. 32, 25!

30. My wife So full of pain and So confin'd that she could not sit up, not So much as to dine with us. Several visitors p.m. Mr. Jenison continues with us. Several Neibours in the Evening, etc.

### DECEMBER, 1739.

1. Molly Lee continues here yet. My wife Still very much Confin'd and in grievous Smart. Dr. Gott call'd here as he was visiting Several patients. A Bath which he directed to, gave her much Ease. Mr. Jenison and I read alternately the Minute Philosopher Vol. 2. N.B. I went to the South Door, but did not venture to Step out. N.B. The Committee paid Mr. Jenison for the whole Time of his service even including tomorrow also.

2. Mr. Jenison on Job 14, 14. Molly Lee having gone home last night, Bekky Hicks came for to Day. N.B. Sister Hicks's kindness in coming over to dress my Wife's wound. Mrs. Harrington of Framingham din'd with us.

3. Mr. Jenison left us early in the Morning though it was rainy. Molly Lee again. Dr. Gotts Young Man, Hemingway, here. Molly Lee making Soap. Dark, misty weather.

4. Misty and Dull weather a.m. Mr. Williams bought my Calves and agreed to give me 50 shillings for one and 30 shillings for the other. He Shod my Mare round and cork'd her for the Winter.

5. My Wife in very great Pain and Distress all the forenoon. P.M. Easier. At Eve Captain Eager here. Brother Samuel Breck,[1] and Gad Hitchcock came from Springfield, after having had the Meazles up there. N.B. Samuel Baker[2] rode my Mare to Boston to bring up a Maid from thence, who Brother Elias[3] had recommended.

6. Breck and Hitchcock rode off very Early. A pleasant Day. I went out abroad in the middle of the Day. N.B. Father Champney continues among us—lodges at Brother Hicks and comes over to us in the Morning. At Eve Mr. Tainter and his Wife and his Brother Harrington of Framingham in their Return from Suffield, were here. At Midnight Samuel Baker came up, and brought with him Judith Rocke to serve us.

7. The Honorable Thomas Hutchinsons Funeral at Boston. Father Champney went home.

[16] Benjamin Woods of Marlborough.
[17] Aaron Smith (Harvard 1735), later the minister at Marlborough, 1740-1778. *Sibley*, IX, 575-578.
[18] Crocus of iron, sesquioxide or peroxide of iron.
[1] Parkman's brother-in-law, the physician of Springfield, Mass.
[2] Son of Edward Baker.
[3] Elias Parkman of Boston.

8. Mr. Tainter p.m. with his Team to get down Some Loggs.

9. Moderate Weather till Evening when it blew up Cold. Mr. Jenison on Ps. 110, 3 and Prov. 16, 31.

10. Mr. Jenison went away early. Cold Morning but pleasant sunshine. Town Met to grant Money for preaching. At Evening Sundry Neighbours here. N.B. Mr. Tainters advice to offer the Town to bear Some part of the Charge of preaching, he not duly Considering the great and extraordinary Charges which I was brought into by my Sickness. Began Mr. Chubbs[4] true Gospel etc.

11. Cloudy. Continue upon Chubb. Old Mrs. Howard bury'd. Mr. Cushing here.

12. Rain. Finish'd Chubb. Meazles go from house to House. Jotham Maynard dress'd Flax for us. Reckon'd with Samuel Bumpso and William Johnson. Wrote to Mrs. Pierpoint.[5]

13. Cold—windy. Old Mr. Green here. P.M. Major Keys[6]— Mr. Jonathan Hemingway.[7] Jeduthan Fay brought up his wife. David Baverick had my Mare to Meet the Company at Marlborough. I began to sermonize again.

14. Cold.

15. Cold decreas'd Somewhat. Mr. Timothy Harrington came.

16. Mr. Harrington[8] preach'd in Mr. Jenisons Stead, who preach'd at Marlborough. Mr. Harringtons Text Isa. 52, 7, P.M. 1 Tim. 4, 8, latter part. Fine Moderate Day, but the Earth too Damp and the Meeting House to chilling for me to Venture out yet.

17. Rainy Morn—Cloudy, Damp. Lieutenant Tainter came and waited upon his Kinsman to his House. N.B. Mr. David Baverick and Samuel Bumpso bargained with me to Clear my Swamp for 40 shillings per Acre and their Dinners while they work'd. I was not altogether So well as heretofore. Pains, Dullness, etc.

18. Bright and Warm in the Middle of the Day. Dr. Gott here and din'd with us. P.M. I was invited out by the fineness of the Day and I rode to the Barn and round the Field.

19. P.M. Dr. Deming[9] of Lime, heretofore Minister of Medway, came with Mr. Stone from Southborough to See me, and Mr. Deming tarry'd all night. Memorandum. Old Mr. Increase Ward[10] dy'd last Night. N.B. He was the first person I ever baptiz'd. He dy'd (according to the Testimony of him) very resign'd to the will of God. Dr. Matthews[11] of Southborough, who had been a very usefull Man among the sick for some years, deceas'd, being upward of Eighty years old.

20. Mr. Deming, having din'd, return'd to Marlborough. Lieutenant Tainter here. N.B. free, friendly mutual admonitions. Funeral of Mr. Ward. Mr. Cushing[12] here at Evening.

21. Pleasant Weather. I rode up to the Upper Grounds, and to the Edge of the Wood. Mr. Goddard[13] of Liecester and his Brother Ebenezer here at Evening.

22. Mr. Jenison came at Evening, I being at my Study.

23. Being a Fine pleasant Day I ventur'd to Meeting. I pray'd a.m. and Mr. Jenison preach'd on Numb. 23, 10. Mr. Jenison pray'd p.m. and I preach'd on Ps. 68, 20, and baptiz'd Two Children, But was so tir'd I was oblig'd to lye down immediately after the Exercises. Mr. Jenison also not well.

24. Mr. Jenison went away. N.B. Mr. Tainter with his Team p.m. and got us wood.

25. My Wife had been not well in the Night—continued ill at Times with Travail pains most of the Day, yet kept up, and din'd with us. I sent for Mrs. Clark of Shrewsbury but she was not at Home. I sent for Mrs. Forbush[14] and she came. Sister Hicks also was sent for and her Husband with her again about 10 o'Clock at Night to get us more help. About 12 (although she had gone but

about 5 Months) She was deliver'd of a tender, lifeless, Male Child, The Measure of which was 13½ Inches long. Immature for Birth, Yet with all its parts perfect. See Ps. 139 (Tate and Bradys Version) 10, 13, 15, 16. But my wife through the great Goodness and Mercy of God in an hopefull State. N.B. Captain Goddard[15] here.

26. It has been a very open, warm Season for Some Time, Insomuch that within these few Dayes Some People have plough'd and Sow'd. But this Morning was Snowy—a Snowy Day. I improv'd Ebenezer Maynard to Digg a Grave for the Stillborn, little Babe and Brother Hicks made a Coffin, but did not Colour it. Mrs. Forbush tarried with us. Neighbor John Rogers kill'd a Shoat for me. Weigh'd 47 pounds. I Sent over to Mrs. Rice[16] (widow) to come and Nurse my Wife, but she sent back word that she could not come. Granny Forbush therefore tarrys. The Deacon came in the Evening, and we improv'd him to bury the Infant.

27. The Cold I complain'd of Yesterday, increases upon me— some pains in my Limbs, but chiefly an hoarseness of Voice. Justice Lee[17] of Worcester here all Evening. Somewhat Cold.

28. Justice Lee here again in the Morning. David Baverick here also. My Cold continues and renders me uncomfortable on various accounts. N.B. Mrs. Forbush called up out of her Bed and carry'd off by Neighbour Thurston,[18] But my Wife in a fine way—had got up to Day.

29. Sent Ebenezer to Cousin Winchesters for Nurse Sherman who came. Pleasant Weather though Somewhat Cold. My Hoarseness remains.

30. I was under great Indisposition both by Pain and by Hoarseness and went out with much Difficulty and doubting of the Event, carrying with me a Book that if I should be oblig'd to return home they might Still keep up the Exercises. But through Divine Assistance I preach'd all Day. Text Ps. 68, 20, and administer'd the Order of Baptism. At Evening I was heavy and worried, But heartily willing to Commit my Self and my whole Cause unto God. Mr. Stone of Southborough Sick of the Meazles.

31. My Arms and Knees have frequent Darts of Pain. A.M. pleasant and warm; p.m. Cloudy. Mr. Prentice[19] of Grafton and his Wife made us a Visit. Came while we were at Dinner and tarried till Evening. How wondrous Swift my Time flys and my Life Wasted with Alas how Slender Improvement! God be pleas'd to humble me for my Negligence and unprofitableness and quicken me to New Fidelity!

## JANUARY, 1740.

1. Through the tender Mercy and Long suffering of God I am again permitted to begin another New Year. Blessed be His glorious Name for it! But I am under Infirmity and Pain in my Limbs and under Confinement So that although I can follow my studys yet, cannot go from Home, nor Venture to my Barn when it is very Cold or Damp weather. This Morning was rainy, but clear'd up and was moderate and pleasant a.m. P.M. was very rugged.

2. Very high winds and extreme Cold. Mr. Caleb Rice[1] of Stourbridge here and din'd with us. We were very Short of Wood and were oblig'd to Cut up an Old Hoggs Stye to burn. Jotham Maynard getting out Flax for us.

3. Very Cold. Captain Warrin[2] and Jotham Maynard p.m. got wood. In the Evening Deacon Newton,[3] Lieutenant Baker and Lieutenant Tainter[4] here to Enquire how I was [illegible] for wood. Mr. Joseph Crosby here with Leather and I bought a Skin for Breeches of him.

4. Mr. Crosby again. I dispos'd of 4 Sheep Skins to him. I sent Ebenezer to Southborough for Salt it being most Scarce round

4 Thomas Chubb (1679-1747), the English deist wrote *The True Gospel of Jesus Christ Asserted* (London, 1738).
5 Widow of the Reverend James Pierpont of New Haven, Conn.
6 John Keyes of Shrewsbury.
7 The son of Deacon Joshua Hemenway of Framingham.
8 Timothy Harrington (Harvard 1737), later the first minister at Swanzey, N. H., 1741-1748. *Sibley*, X, 188-195.
9 Reverend Daniel Deming of Lyme, Conn.
10 An original settler of Westborough.
11 John Matthews, the physician of Southborough.
12 Reverend Job Cushing of Shrewsbury.
13 Reverend David Goddard (Harvard 1731), minister at Leicester, Mass., 1736-1754. *Sibley*, IX, 40-43.
14 Mrs. Thomas Forbush of Westborough.

15 Edward Goddard of Shrewsbury.
16 Mrs. Edmund Rice of Westborough.
17 Henry Lee, a justice of the peace.
18 Mrs. Joseph Thurston.
19 Reverend Solomon Prentice.

1 (Harvard 1730). The first minister at Sturbridge, 1736-1759. *Sibley*, VIII, 774-775.
2 Daniel Warrin of Westborough.
3 Josiah Newton.
4 Simon Tainter, junior.

about us. Mr. Jonathan Whipple here with Check'd Linnen Cloth which he had wove for us. David Baverick clearing in my swamp, and Lodg'd here.

5. David Baverick, Ezekiel Pratt, and Jonathan Rogers clearing in the Swamp and din'd here. P.M. Two more, viz. Sam Bumpso and John Rogers at the same work.

6. Clear and somewhat Cold. To Day I first put on my usual Cloths. Text Ps. 68, 20. Mr. Miller,[5] lately recover'd from the Meazles din'd with us.

7. Mr. Ebenezer Nurse's eldest son, Ebenezer, a Youth of about 19, died last Friday of the Iliack passion, and this Day I was at his Funeral. Mr. Jedidiah How help'd by Noah kill'd Two Hogs for me. Weight of my Two Hoggs was 19 Score. A.M. the 3 young men Clearing. Mr. Peter Butler of Rutland sadler was here, and lodg'd.

8. Mr. Butler having rectify'd my Cloth Housing, new stuff'd my wife's side saddle, etc., and settled accounts with me. Went off. Some Number of Hands came to get wood. Lieutenant Baker with a Yoke of oxen, and Neighbor Benjamin Fay[6] with 2 Yoke and Cart, Lieutenant Tainter For Mr. Beriah Rice, Neighbor Grow[7] For Deacon Newton,[8] Harrington,[9] Seth Rice[10] with his Team p.m., Eliezer Rice,[11] James Maynard, Sam Bumpso, David Baverick,[12] Ezekiel Pratt, Hezekiah Pratt, John Rogers for Mr. Abner Newton,[13] Joseph Green junior, Eliezer Williams, Samuel Rogers from Mr. William Nurse, Phinehas Forbush,[14] and Thomas Whitney. The first Cart went with onely one Yoke of Oxen and therefore could not load up. The other Cart had one Yoke and an Horse, and loaded decently, the other Two Yoke of Oxen drew a sled which for want of Snow could not be loaded up. The Wood was cut on the East Side of the Hill, and was a great deal of it very Small, but they clear'd the Small Tract as they went, of such Turns as aforesaid they made (as they gave account) 39 by Duskish. Lieutenant Tainter tarried in the Evening and Cut up and Salted my Two Hoggs which were kill'd Yesterday. They weighed both of them about 19 Score.

9. Snow'd last Night. The 3 Young Men, Scil. David Baverick, Ezekiel Pratt and Sam Bumpso, came to clearing but the Rain beat them off. Nurse Sherman was carried Home by Ebenezer, not to Marlborough the Meazles being thick there and about there but to Grafton. Mr. Bowman and Mr. Daniel Hardy here at Eve.

10. Snow'd last Night but turns to rain this morning. Snow returns and the Storm of Snow and Rain continues all Day. My Wife greatly afflicted with the Tooth ach. Meazles at Ensign Maynards.

11. Bright, Clear Day. Stephen Maynard[15] missing ever since Wednesday. His Father, uncle James and Cousen David gone after him again to Day and brought him from Providence.

12. Pleasant Day. My Wife (Except her Toothach) so far recover'd through Gods Mercy, that today She went into the Kitchen. Samuel Bumpso thrash'd Barley.

13. I preach'd a. and p.m. on Rev. 2, 21. Mr. Cornelius Biglo din'd here. After Meeting Mr. Biglo came in and my wife improv'd him to pull out her Tooth.

14. Samuel Bumpso finish'd Thrashing Barley a.m. Mr. Daniel Warrin (who bought my Oxen) drove them down to Boston. Mr. Moses Pierce junior of Boston, on his Journey to Connecticut, by whom I wrote to Mr. Pierpont, my Acknowledgments for his Bounty in presenting Me Dr. Fuller's[16] Church History of Britain and History of Cambridge which I receiv'd last Saturday Night. Mr. Beman[17] came to call me to visit Matthias

Rice[18] who was sick of the Meazles, and I ventur'd to go. Mr. Abraham How of Marlborough came home with me. Mr. Bowman here in the Evening.

15. Great Storm of Snow. High winds and very Cold. Very Difficult for my Boys to tend the Cattle and get Wood.

16. Bright, Windy and Cold.

17. Mr. Nathaniel Oake here to desire me to visit John Caruths[19] Sick Child.

18. I rode over to see John Caruths sick child, and in returning I visited Deacon Tomlin.[20]

19. [No entry].

20. On Ps. 119, 59. P.M. My wife went to Meeting, the first after her lying in.

21. Lieutenant Holloway brought a Letter from Mrs. Pierpoint and acquainted me that my Friends at Boston were well, and in particular My Brother Elias whom he had din'd with.

22. It is a good Sledding Time but I have nobody to improve it.

23. Ensign Maynard brought me the Sorrowfull Tidings that my Brother Elias was struck with the Dead palsie (as its commonly call'd) on Monday last; that he was himself with him Yesterday, and he lay in a very dull, insensible state, and it was greatly to be fear'd whether he would get over it. At Eve Brother and Sister Hicks[21] were here.

24. I had many heavy Thoughts; very much desir'd to get down to see my Brother, but I was under So much Weakness and often in Pains that It could not be judg'd Safe for me to venture out in So Cold Weather upon such a Journey. Ensign Maynard here Sometime in the forenoon. Said it was very Sharp Cold, etc. At Eve Mr. Samuel Harrington here.

25. [No entry].

26. [No entry].

27. Ps. 119, 59. Mr. Moses Pierce junior was come from New Haven. I took him Home and he din'd and lodg'd with us.

28. Rode to Cambridge in Company of Mr. Pierce. We went through Marlborough. At Waltham we had more Company, Mr. Jabez Ward of Marlborough. Mr. Pierce rode with me to Father Champneys but thence he went to Boston—it proving Evening I durst not Venture further.

29. This Memorable and Melancholly Morning I was full of Wormwood and the Gall. I drank so deep of this Day Four Years since.[22] It was very Cold but I was too uneasy to keep from my Dear Brother Elias to whom especially I was making my Visit. At Roxbury at Mr. Davis's Shop I got my Mare new Shod that I might help her as to her stumbling. At Boston it was very grievous to see my Brother in So strange a Condition. He did not know me in some Time—but in the afternoon he undertook to tell over to me the whole Manner of his being taken, etc., which he went through very intelligibly and exactly, but which he had not till now, nor had appear'd So rational or Compos'd till now. Blessed be God for Such a measure of Mercy. My Venerable mother there with her son Continually, and in a Measure of Comfort and Health. I made this my Chief Residence although I Sometimes lodg'd and Din'd otherwhere.

30. A.M. I went to Christ's Church and heard Dr. Cutler[23] on Dan. 6, 21. P.M. at Mr. Condy's[24] Lecture on 2 Pet. 3, 18 forepart. After service Mr. Chauncy,[25] Mr. Condy, Mr. Gray[26] and I went to Mr. Welsteeds.[27] But at Evening I was at an Entertainment at Brother Alexanders, our Kinsman John Parkman having brought his Mistress to them at this Time.

31. Mr. Chauncy preach'd at the public Lecture on 2 Pet. 3, 16. Those words, In which are some Things hard to be under-

5 James Miller of Westborough.
6 The son of Captain John Fay. Benjamin became a frequent officeholder of Westborough. Johnson, *Fay Family Tree*, pp. 27–30.
7 Samuel Grow.
8 Josiah Newton.
9 Samuel Harrington.
10 Son of Edmund Rice.
11 From Marlborough, near the Westborough line.
12 David Batherick of Westborough.
13 Son of Thomas Newton.
14 Son of Deacon Jonathan Forbush.
15 Son of Captain John Maynard.
16 Thomas Fuller (1608–1661) wrote *The Church-History of Britain; from the Birth of Jesus Christ, until the Year 1648* (London, 1655). There were later English editions. This work included "The History of the University of Cambridge since the Conquest."
17 Eleazer Beemon or Beamon.
18 Son of Benjamin Rice of Marlborough. Hudson, *Marlborough*, p. 433.
19 Of Westborough.
20 Isaac Tomlin.
21 Mr. and Mrs. John Hicks of Westborough.
22 This was the anniversary of the first Mrs. Parkman's death.
23 Reverend Timothy Cutler (Harvard 1701), minister of Christ Church Episcopal in Boston, 1723–1765. *Sibley*, V, 45–67.
24 Reverend Jeremiah Condy, Jr. (Harvard 1726), who had recently returned from England and was minister of the First Baptist Church of Boston, 1738–1764. *Sibley*, VIII, 20–30.
25 Reverend Charles Chauncy (Harvard 1721), minister of the First Church of Boston, 1727–1787. *Sibley*, VI, 439–467.
26 Reverend Ellis Gray (Harvard 1734), minister of the New Brick Church of Boston, 1738–1752. *Sibley*, IX, 400–404.
27 Reverend William Welsteed (Harvard 1716), minister of the New Brick Church of Boston, 1728–1753. *Sibley*, VI, 153–158.

stood, a Sermon as no doubt, very pleasing to Some So very Disgusting to others. Very cold. At Eve Mr. Harb Dorr and Mr. Davenport (the Baker) at Brother Elias's. N.B. Brother Hicks brought a Letter from my wife, but I saw not him. N.B. Sorrowful News of Mr. John Adams's[28] (My old Friend) Death and of Mr. Ebenezer Hancock[29] of Lexington.

### FEBRUARY, 1740.

1. Extreme Cold. It was Dr. Colman's[1] Lecture but I durst not venture out. But at Eve Visited Mr. Webb.[2]

2. Mr. Webb came and pray'd with Brother, and came again p.m. on the Business of my preaching for him, but I was of a long Time preengaged to Mr. Gee,[3] who on that Condition releas'd me at the Time of my Marriage. P.M. Mr. Gees son came with his Request, etc. N.B. Mr. Gee was married in the beginning of the Week to Mrs. Sarah Gardner.[4] At Eve I waited upon Mr. Gee at his Father Gardners and to Mr. Mathers.[5]

3. Mr. Mather a.m. on Ps. 97, 11. I din'd up at Mr. Gardners with the Bridegroom and Bride. P.M. I preach'd for the Bridegroom on Jude 10, 21. At Eve at my Brother Elias's, and at Mr. Mathers, where was Captain Samuel Greenwood[6] and his Spouse, etc. and we all supp'd there but I lodg'd at my Brother Samuel's.

4. My Niece Elizabeth Corser's[7] Child Eliza ill.

5. Ensign Maynard brought me a Second Letter from my Wife. Mr. Webb pray'd with my Brother again. I visited and pray'd with Elizabeth Corser. Din'd at my Niece Procter's.[8]

6. Din'd at Brother Williams. N.B. Deacon Larrabee[9] kindly visited me there. The Weather much moderater. P.M. I visited Mr. Robert Breck,[10] one of my Old School Mates and my wife's Kinsman.

7. Very Pleasant. John White went to Cambridge for my Horse. It was late before I mounted at Charleston, being after 11. Stop'd at College at sister Barretts[11] and rode over to Father Champney's.[12] After 1 p.m. I set out from thence. N.B. Sister Lydia[13] rode up with Brother Hicks on the 4th in a Whirry. Levi Brigham—my Company part of the Way. Got home at 7½ in the Eve.

8. Ensign Maynard the Meazles. I visited him. Sister Lydia keeps at Hicks's.

9. Storm—Snow, etc. Sister Lydia came here and lodg'd here.

10. Repeated John 9, 4.

11. Sister Lydia rode with Brother Hicks to Cambridge on his own Mare. Visited Ensign Maynard. Neighbor Charles Rice, etc.

12. Visited Old Mr. Fay[14]—he, his wife and Family being Sick of the Meazles. Visited Captain Fay's wife who is exceeding Low and wasted.

13. I rode to Marlborough, the Doctor[15] having Sent for me to visit them, Sister and all the Children being sick, but his little son John of about 9 months old much the worst and lying at the point of Death. Din'd at Colonel Woods[16] with Mr. Aaron Smith.[17] At their earnest request I went to the Funeral of Two of Mr. Joseph Tainters[18] Children—4 others of his Children being at the Same Time sick, and one or more of them in a Dangerous state and all of the Throat Disease. At their Instant Desire I

pray'd upon this sorrowful Occasion. Return'd to Brother Gotts. The Rain prevail'd so as to forbid my going Home, besides their Importunity on the Account of the Child which was nigh Expiring. It dy'd about 8 of the Clock in the Eve, the Doctor being exceedingly distressed and impatient. I lodged there with the Doctor.

14. Captain Amsden[19] burnt my Mares Mouth for (what is call'd) the Lampers. I went to Mr. Zechariah Maynards,[20] the widow Hows,[21] and Mr. Joseph Rice's[22] where I din'd. Thence I rode up to Mr. Thomas Wards in Westborough and to Lieutenant Holloways whose Youngest Child was very bad after the Meazles. Captain Eager came from thence with me, whose son was Sick also of the Same Distemper. Very troublesome, hollow riding, the Earth being much open'd. N.B. David Baverick and Samuel Bumpso getting Rails.

15. I rode again to Marlborough to the Funeral of John Gott,[23] and return'd at Eve. David and Samuel again.

16. Mr. Aaron Smith from Marlborough made me a Visit. David and Samuel and Ezekiel Pratt at work again. Mr. Smith din'd and Spent the afternoon with us and then went to Southborough. Rain at Evening.

17. Rain. Act. 3, 19. Mr. Thurston[24] and Mr. James Fay[25] din'd here.

18. Visited Ensign Maynard. David, Samuel and Ezekiel getting Posts. P.M. Cold. At Eve Stephen Fay[26] came to desire me to visit his Mother, but I was too much indispos'd to venture out in So Searching an Air.

19. Visited Mrs. Fay, who was yet alive but very low. N.B. Mr. Sherman of Marlborough and Mr. Phinehas Rice of Stow my Company in going to Captain Fays.

20. Read the Life of Signor Roselli, an Italian.

21. Mr. Metcalf[27] and Mr. [blank] of Medway here a.m. Captain Eager P.M. The Children went to School at Mr. Townsends,[28] This being the first of my knowing the School was kept there, although it had been kept there this fortnight, as the Master told me. Mr. Goodenow[29] here in the Eve to begin to pay me Rates for the Current Year.

22. Samuel Bumpso and Ezekiel Pratt came to clear in the Swamp. David having the Meazles. The Sow discovered to have Eight Piggs. Old Mr. Whipple and Captain Warrin here at Evening.

23. At the Funeral of the Infant Child of Mr. Eliezer Rice. Dr. Gott din'd with us. Samuel Bumpso and Ezekial Pratt Clearing and finish'd afternoon.

24. Act. 3, 19. Mrs. Byles[30] and Mehitable Coddington din'd with us.

25. Town Meeting. N.B. I gave the Town a General Receipt in full written in the Town Book.

26. My Wife rode to Marlborough on Brother Hicks's Mare. I rode with her as far as Captain Forbush's.[31] I went to Mr. Cooks.[32] Got an Iron Hoop fitted for dirty Shoes at my west Door. Visited old Mrs. Forbush,[33] Ensign, Captain. Neighbor Barns[34]—N.B. their Child very Sick.

27. Neighbor Barns came up and dock'd my Mare. P.M. his Father came and Challeng'd part of my Land. We went down to the Bounds. At Evening my wife return'd safe. Fine Weather.

28. Fine Weather. I preach'd the Lecture on Gal. 5, 25.

29. Rain A.M. Clear P.M. Somewhat forward in my preparations.

---

[28] Parkman's classmate at Harvard College.
[29] Reverend Ebenezer Hancock (Harvard 1728), minister at Lexington, 1734-1739. Sibley, VIII, 427-429.
[1] Reverend Benjamin Colman, minister of the Brattle Street Church.
[2] Reverend John Webb of the New North Church.
[3] Reverend Joshua Gee of Boston.
[4] Sarah, daughter of Samuel Gardner of Boston was the Reverend Mr. Gee's third wife.
[5] Reverend Mr. Samuel Mather.
[6] (Harvard 1709). A merchant of Boston who was made a captain in the militia. Sibley, V, 481-483.
[7] Mrs. John Coarsa.
[8] Hannah, daughter of Parson Parkman's brother William, married Samuel Proctor.
[9] Richard Larabee, deacon of the Brattle Street Church. Drake, Boston, p. 661.
[10] Of Boston. A Cousin of Mrs. Parkman. Samuel Breck, Genealogy of the Breck Family (Omaha, 1889), p. 19.
[11] Ruth Champney, the sister of Parkman's first wife, married John Barrett, May 5, 1737. Paige, Cambridge, p. 507.
[12] Samuel Champney, Sr., of Cambridge, Parkman's first father-in-law.
[13] Lydia Champney, Parkman's sister-in-law.
[14] Captain John Fay of Westborough.
[15] Dr. Benjamin Gott, Parkman's brother-in-law.
[16] Benjamin Woods, the merchant of Marlborough.
[17] (Harvard 1735). Ordained later, June 11, 1740, in Marlborough. Sibley, IX, 575-578.
[18] The deacon of Marlborough.

[19] Isaac Amsden of Marlborough.
[20] Son of John Maynard, an early resident of Marlborough. Hudson, Marlborough, p. 413.
[21] Widow of Thomas Howe, tavernkeeper of Marlborough, who had died in 1733. Hudson, Marlborough, pp. 382-383.
[22] Of Marlborough.
[23] Infant son of Dr. Benjamin Gott.
[24] Joseph Thurston of Westborough.
[25] Son of Captain John Fay.
[26] Another son of Captain Fay.
[27] Jonathan Metcalf.
[28] Joshua Townsend.
[29] David Goodenow of Westborough.
[30] Mrs. Joseph Byles of Westborough.
[31] Samuel Forbush.
[32] Cornelius Cook, the blacksmith of Westborough.
[33] Widow of Thomas Forbush.
[34] Richard Barnes.

## MARCH, [1740]

1. Snowy Forenoon. To my great Comfort I was early in Sermon. Finish'd before Sundown. I visited Mr. Richard Barns's Sick Child at Evening.

2. Sacrament. Act. 3, 19 a. and p.m. Three Deacons and Deacon Newtons wife, Cousin Winchester, and Mehitable Coddington din'd here.

3. The Town Sent Two Men to me to request me to pray with them at their annual Meeting which I comply'd with.

4. Mr. Breck[1] from Springfield din'd with us. P.M. Mr. Jonathan Barns[2] from Marlborough to bring the Request of that people that I would asist them in their Fast next week, which they had appointed on account of the Sicknesses among them, the Meazles and the Throat Distemper, as well as on account of their remaining under the Frowns of Divine Providence in so unsettled Circumstances. Mr. Barns also brought a Letter from Mr. Aaron Smith with his Desires to Change next Sabbath. Colonel Woods hath two Daughters exceeding low and in a Dangerous State by the Throat Disease. Mrs. Betty and Mrs. Sarah. Mr. Jonathan Loring,[3] their Schoolmaster Sick of the Same likewise. Mr. Breck and Mr. Barns went to Marlborough together.

5. I rode to Captain Fays to see his wife in her low Condition. From thence, with Mr. Batchellor[4] in Company great part of the way, to Mr. Zebediah Smiths at Grafton to committ a piece of Pladd and a piece of Callimanco to be dy'd and wove. Return'd at Eve by Mr. Bezaleel Smiths and Eleazer Pratts,[5] at which places I call'd. It was raw Cold, and Evening before I could get home, by which I was very much indispos'd.

6. Catechiz'd at the Meeting House a.m. and p.m. but not so full numbers of Children as usual, on account of the Meazles, which are in many Houses. After Catechizing I preach'd at Brother Hicks's on Ps. 63, 8 former part. Moses Pratt[6] clean'd out my Barly. At Eve Bezaleel Smith here.

7. Snow Storm. Brother Hicks making a small reading Desk for me.

8. Storm in the Morning and very Cold. P.M. Clear and pleasant. Mr. Aaron Smith came up from Marlborough in whose stead I rode down there. Lodg'd at the Colonel's.

9. On Matth. 24, 44. Lodg'd as well as din'd at Colonel's. His Family very Sick Still.

10. I visited divers afflicted people a.m. Din'd at Captain Williams's,[7] who with old Captain Brigham[8] perswaded me to go to the proprietors Meeting to Speak to the proprietors in Answer to Mr. Richard Barns's Objection against Two Acres and Thirty Rods of Land which I took up on the North End of Powder Hill. To compass an Argreement we Chose Two Men, Mr. Barns chose Mr. Joseph Stratton,[9] and I chose Captain Nathan Brigham, and the Proprietors put in a Third, Scil. Justice Samuel Brigham, the Moderator of the Meeting. Then I return'd home. Here I met Neighbor James Fay who acquainted me with his Mothers[10] Death, and desir'd me to attend upon her Funeral which they had appointed to be on Wednesday, although they knew (being inform'd by Mr. Whipple[11] on Saturday) was the Day of the Fast at Marlborough which I had promis'd to attend.

11. Storm, Rain, Hail, Snow.

12. My Wife and I rode down to Marlborough to the Fast on account of the Sickness in that Town. Dr. Gotts Dauter Betty thought to be Dangerously ill. Colonel Woods ill, and under great Affliction respecting his Children. His Youngest son Dead and others remaining very ill yet. A.M. Mr. Stone[12] pray'd and I preach'd on 1 Pet. 5, 6. We were entertain'd at the widow Gates's.[13]

The Storm continued, and although in the Morning it was Still and moderate yet the Day prov'd Cold and Raw. At Evening as we were at Mrs. Gates's Mr. Smith ask'd our advice touching his Answer to the Call of that people to Settle among them.[14] The Substance of our Advice was that considering the peoples great unanimity in Desiring him, it might appear his Duty to Accept especially being that they had been heretofore of so remarkably divided a Spirit. But then he must plainly distinguish between this Advice resulting from the proceedings and Circumstances of the people, and any Advice grounded on his Qualifications for the Ministry, inasmuch as we were in no wise ripe for this Latter, being that we were in a great Degree Strangers to him, and being that there would be a Time and Method no Doubt appointed on Purpose for his Examination and Approbation. My wife and I lodg'd at Dr. Gotts.

13. Snows Still, Yet we return'd Home. Mr. Simon Goddard here with a Letter from his Father. Mr. Zebadiah Smith here upon the Business of Weaving me some Plad and Callimanco.

14. Mr. Hezekiah Stow Sifted over my Barley. Hicks to Boston.

15. At the Furneral of Neighbor Benjamin Hows youngest Child.[15] Hicks return'd.

16. On Act. 3, 19. I was very much tir'd at Night and oblig'd to go to bed early.

17. Pleasant Day. Lieutenant Holloway here. Mrs. Wheeler. At Eve Neighbor Aaron Forbush here, and Mr. Francis Whipple. Reckon'd with Samuel Bumpso and David Baverick.

18. Rainy Day.

19. Samuel Bumpso and David Baverick at work for me. A.M. Cutting wood and P.M. Splicing Rails. I rode to smith Allens to get my Mare shod. Din'd with Colonel Ward.[16] At Mr. Cushings[17]—his son Jacob Very ill of the Throat Distemper. I rode to Worcester. Meazles at Mr. Burrs,[18] his wife Sick thereof. N.B. Mr. Morse,[19] their Schoolmaster and young preacher at Mr. Burrs this Eve.

20. The Next Morning after some Discourse of Land at Hartford and Simsbury, etc. I rode with great Haste over to Sutton yet the Roads very bad, and wholly New to me. Mr. Hall[20] half a Mile from his House and his wife from Home. I went to him upon the Affair of Some Land which he had lately bought of Mr. Smith, Sugar Baker of Boston, but it was chiefly bargained away. At ¼ after one I left Mr. Hall and rode down to Grafton, to Mr. Prentice's[21] in about an Hour. But they were gone to Lecture. N.B. that Mr. Cushing was to have preach'd, but the sickness of his son prevented him. He spake to me Yesterday of it, Mr. Prentice being gone to Groton, but expected back. I answered nothing because of my Engagement upon my Business, but as I was riding the Road to Worcester was reflecting upon the Matter and that I had no Notes with me. As I was Riding on I met Benjamin Fay. Him I sent to Mrs. Parkman to desire her to wrap me up some sermons, which I remember'd to lye in the Drawer of the Table I wrote at; and the Said Fay must do his utmost to Convey them up to Grafton where I would endeavour to be. Accordingly the Notes were come to Mr. Prentice's. Thus having taken Brank[22] and drank some Beer without staying to Dine, I went to Meeting and I preach'd Sermon on Ps. 73, 24 to page [blank]. Return'd to Westborough in the Evening.

21. Lowery Morning David and Samuel came to work but were discourag'd by the Weather—but after Nine of the Clock they went to work digging stones up on the Hill. Mr. Timothy Fays[23] wife here.

22. David and Sam digging stones.

23. Act. 9, 6, latter part.

24. David and Sam here, Digging stones on the Southside.

[1] Reverend Robert Breck, Jr., of Springfield.
[2] Son of Deacon John Barnes.
[3] Son of the Reverend Israel Loring of Sudbury.
[4] David Batchellor or Bachellor of Grafton.
[5] Smith and Pratt lived in the southern part of Westborough.
[6] The son of Isaac Pratt of Westborough.
[7] Abraham Williams, Parkman's brother-in-law.
[8] Nathan Brigham of Marlborough.
[9] Of Marlborough.
[10] Mrs. John Fay.
[11] Francis Whipple of Westborough.
[12] Reverend Nathan Stone of Southborough.
[13] Sarah, the widow of Simon Gates of Marlborough.
[14] After their trouble with the Reverend Benjamin Kent the people of Marlborough were careful about the choice of his successor. Hudson, Marlborough, pp. 127–128.
[15] Benjamin How, Jr., about one week old, died March 14, 1740.
[16] Nahum Ward of Shrewsbury.
[17] Reverend Job Cushing of Shrewsbury.
[18] Reverend Isaac Burr of Worcester.
[19] Ebenezer Morse (Harvard 1737), later the first minister of the First Congregational Parish of Boylston, Mass. Sibley, X, 211–217.
[20] Reverend David Hall of Sutton.
[21] Reverend Solomon Prentice of Grafton.
[22] Old usage for buckwheat.
[23] The son of Gershom Fay of Westborough. Orlin P. Fay, Fay Genealogy (Cleveland, 1898), pp. 331–332.

Did something at Gardening. Looking up a Team to mow up Grass Ground on my south side.

25. David and Samuel Digging stones, still on the Southside. Sent down my Subscription to the Manufacture Bank[24] by Mr. Samuel Robinson of Hardwicke.

26. My wife was taken sick of the Meazles. Extreme Pain in her Teeth.

27. Publick Fast. A.M. on 1 King, 8, 44, 45, on occasion of the season and the War with Spain. P.M. repeated from 2 and 3 on Hos. 6, 1 from Hosea 14, 1. Mrs. Whipple here to Nurse my wife. But Sister Hicks watch'd.

28. Sam at work digging stones, on the South side. N.B. Mr. Prentice of Grafton came up from Marlborough, and Mr. Belcher Hancock from Grafton and din'd with us, as did Mr. Samuel Robinson who had done my Business at the Manufacture Bank. P.M. I rode to Captain Warrins. Great Disappointment about a Team. My wife very full of pain in her Teeth. Mrs. Whipple watch'd.

29. Sam work'd rigging up stone Wall. My wife very ill yet, but the Meazles are turning as we judge. Suse Rogers very ill. Mrs. Tainter[25] came and watch'd with my wife.

30. Mrs. Tainter stayed till Evening. I Repeated sermon on 2 Cor. 5, 1, having been greatly hindered from my studys. Benjamin Fays wife watch'd.

31. I rode abroad to buy a Yoke of Oxen. I went as far as to Bezaleel Smiths and Mr. James Fay with me. I was at Captain Fays, Winchesters, etc.

## APRIL, 1740

1. In the forenoon I was variously taken up. Early I was at Mr. Hezekiah Hows[1] for Oxen and obtain'd them for the first part of the Day. Sam and David work'd. A.M. Sledded Stones till by the Infirmity of the Oxen and a Storm of Snow they were oblig'd to knock off. I visited Susé Rogers who lay in a very low Condition. N.B. her Testimony of the Hope she had in her Death, a very Remarkable Declaration of her Custom and Manner of Life, when She was but young, whilst she liv'd at Mr. Storers and whilst She liv'd at my House, withdrawing her Affections from the world, giving her Self to a Life with God and earnestly begging ever Night and every Day an Interest in Christ, especially improving Sabbath mornings and Evenings for Retiring to Spend some Time with God and to begg this of him. This She said was her continual practice especially whilst she dwelt at my House. As to dying She hop'd she was ready, and was willing because she hop'd she had not sought God in vain (for He is a Mercifull God) (or to such purpose); but if should be his will that She should live and recover, that She might serve and glorify him still in the world She was desiring of it (but left the Matter quietly with God). But O what would become of her if she should live, and Should nevertheless forget these purposes of Serving God. O wo unto her, wo unto her if she should! As to her dear Infant She had given it to God before it was born; She gave it up to him when it was born and I give it up to him now, Said She, and Should be glad to do it in (his holy) (the Ordinance of) Baptism. Thus she continued her speech, though but a whisper, through her great weakness, for some length of Time, telling me She thought she should not live over another Night. The appearance of the Grace of God in her occasioned our Thanksgiving to God for her. Dr. Gott was at my House in the mean Time to see my wife, who he judg'd had the Canker in her throat. In the Afternoon the storm of Snow prevail'd greatly; and in the middst of it Mrs. Edwards[2] of Northampton, sister to Mrs. Pierpoint[3] of New Haven came to see us, a young man from her Neibourhood accompanying her. They had neither of 'em had the Meazles, and were much afraid; but I kept 'em in a Separate Chamber as safely as I could that they might be wholly easy.

2. A rough, Cloudy morning, yet Mrs. Edwards Set out for Boston. When the Morning got up it was warmer and the Day prov'd pleasant. I rode down the road with Mrs. Edwards as far as Mr. Ebenezer Newton of Southborough's hithermost Corner—and returning I visited Sarah Bradish at Mr. Amsdens,[4] Thomas Bruce's wife,[5] Abijah Bruce, Abigail Bruce,[6] who were sick and Susé Rogers who is yet alive.

3. Susé Rogers[7] departed this Life about one o'Clock in the Morning. Much perplex'd in the morning about our spring work, the Care of it crowding upon me at a very uncomfortable Rate. After having been other where with no success, as I walk'd to Neighbor Hezekiah Pratts (who I sought to come with his Oxen and draw off the Stones from Ground which we wanted to break up for Planting) I had many musings touching the Conduct of God's Providence in the world, especially where even his own work was more immediately at stake—but I was enabled to refer and rest matters with God. Mr. Pratt came—after him Mr. Daniel Forbush[8] with Two Yoke of Cattle, and they drew off the stones. This they did a.m. David Baverick also came and rigg'd up the Fences; So that my Business was like to get along—for which I thank God that so I might attend to his service without so much distraction. Mr. Samuel Crosby[9] inform'd me that Mr. Cushing had just lost Two Children, Mary and John, who dy'd the Day before yesterday of the Throat Disease, and another was at the point of Death. I rode over to the North side of the Town, to Mr. Caruths, to Mr. Haywards[10] and Bakers[11]—to Mr. Livermores,[12] Balls and Wheelers.[13] N.B. John Badcocks Conduct towards me as he accompany'd me part of the way back from Mr. Wheelers. Mr. David Forbush plough'd stubble p.m. A Letter from Mr. Cushing came while I was abroad.

4. Stormy a.m. P.M. I rode up to the Funeral of Two of Mr. Cushings Children, Scil. the Eldest Daughter and the youngest Son. Mr. Prentice of Lancaster had pray'd before I could get there by reason of the Storm.

5. Neighbour Richard Barns, junior here to acquaint me that the Committee were to come up next Tuesday, but I was oblig'd to write to Marlborough to have it alter'd because it would be Association Day.

6. Act 2, 41, 42. P.M. Repeated Sermon on 1 Pet. 4, 3, from Ezek. 44, 6.

7. Stormy a.m. P.M. Gardening. Mr. Morse from Worster here.

8. A morning of great Hurry and Engagement. Mr. James Fay and Eliezer Rice each of them with Two Yoke of Oxen to break up Some Grass Ground on my south side. But our plough (which I had of the widow Tomlin) soon broke and we were oblig'd to get another, first at Ensign Maynards but Chiefly at Stephen Fays—and his held, but the Ground was so Stoney (notwithstanding all our pains and charge in Digging many of the stones out) that they made but a poor Hand of it. When we had din'd I rode over to Lancaster to the Association. N.B. Mr. Livermore rode Two or Three Miles with me. I got to the Meeting in the middst of the Exercises. Mr. Loring, Mr. Solomon Prentice, Mr. Stone, Mr. Josiah Swan[14] and Mr. Smith from Marlborough were all that came to Day.

9. Mr. Seccomb,[15] Mr. Stearns,[16] etc. came. Mr. Stone preach'd the public Lecture upon Rom. 8, 37. N.B. Mr. Lorings Exceptions against the Doctrine deliver'd. After Dinner I rode with Captain Joseph Willard[17] and Deacon Cooper[18] of Grafton to Shrewsbury to the Funeral of a Third of Mr. Chushing's Children who dy'd by the Throat Disease. A Melancholly Time! I return'd home at Eve.

[24] This term was sometimes used for the Land Bank of 1740, a plan for providing a currency backed by real estate and redeemable in the future in commodities. Andrew M. Davis, *Currency and Banking in the Province of Massachusetts-Bay* (New York, 1901), II, 140.

[25] Wife of Deacon Simon Tainter.

[1] Parkman's neighbor and friend.

[2] Wife of the Reverend Jonathan Edwards, D.D.

[3] Widow of the Reverend James Pierpont.

[4] James Amsden of Westborough.

[5] Sarah Bruce.

[6] The daughter of Abijah and Mary Bruce of Westborough.

[7] The wife of Parkman's neighbor, John Rogers.

[8] Son of Deacon Jonathan Forbush.

[9] Of Shrewsbury. One of the founders of the church there. Ward, *Shrewsbury*, p. 255.

[10] Simeon Hayward.

[11] Edward Baker.

[12] Jonathan Livermore.

[13] Joseph Wheeler.

[14] Reverend Josiah Swan (Harvard 1733), the minister of Dunstable, Mass., 1738-1746. *Sibley*, IX, 331-332.

[15] Reverend John Seccomb of Harvard, Mass.

[16] Reverend David Stearns of Lunenberg.

[17] One of the founders of Grafton.

[18] Samuel Cooper.

10. My Daughter Molly Sick of the Meazles. A sorrowful Message by Ezekiel How[19] that sister Gott was taken suddenly about an Hour before sundown yesterday with an Apoplexy, but partly Epileptical also, and was not thought to continue. I preach'd (Repeated) on Ps. 119, 5, and after Lecture I rode to Marlborough and found the Sorrowful Case of sister Gott to be as aforesaid! Lucy with the Measles.

11. About Seven in the morning Sister Gott expir'd. A very Solemn Morning! I rode home when I had dispatch'd various Affairs at Marlborough. P.M. Ebenezer Maynard rode before my Wife to Marlborough who also return'd safe at Evening, My son Thomas and Ebenezer much indispos'd. Mrs. Whipple helps us.

12. Jonathan and Benjamin Tainter[20] came with Three Cattle and plough'd Stubble and Split Hills. N.B. Lieutenant Holloway[21] here with an Affair relating to his Brother Hayward. Molly Lee here last night and to Day. Ebenezer[22] the Meazles.

13. Sacrament. Act. 2, 41, 42. My wife at Meeting but my Children all Sick. P.M. on Job 7, 8. Repeat'd pieces of Sermon on Job 14, 2 and Ps. 90, 9 on occasion of Sister Gotts sudden Death.

14. We rode down to the Funeral of Sister Gott. There were Mr. Loring, Mr. Barrett,[23] Mr. Brintnall,[24] Mr. Smith, etc. O that God would make us to know our End, etc., and O that we might hear Christ Saying to us Be ye Ready also, for In Such an Hour as ye Think not, the son of man cometh! Brother Hicks and his son plough'd for me.

15. N.B. The Committee about the Land I had taken up had appointed to come to Day but did not come. N.B. Hicks graffing.[25] John Rogers wrought for me. Jonathan and Benjamin Tainter with their Team Carted Wood, Fencing stuff, ploughed in wheat, etc.

16. Jonathan Tainter and Sam Hicks ploughed in Rye. Mr. Aaron Forbush wrought for me. Brother Samuel Breck visited us. My Children all getting about again. D. Glor.!

17. Mr. Aaron Forbush and David Baverick wrought. In the middle of the Day Several Showers of Rain and Hail. Catechiz'd on the North side.

18. David wrought, and Aaron Forbush junior. Mr. Verney of Boston here. At Eve my black Heifer missing. Rain in the Night.

19. Several of my Neibours assisted in looking for my young Cow, and found her mired in the Meadow north of the Great pond. Cold Raw wind after the Rain.

20. A very Cold Day. A.M. on Ps. 109, 4 latter part. P.M. repeated sermon on 1 Pet. 4, 3 from Ezek. 44, 6.

21. Rode over to Mr. Eliezer Rice's. David and Samuel Bumpso here in the Evening. Weather warm and plesant. Planted Cucumbers.

22. [No entry].

23. Very warm, but yet windy. I rode to Captain Warrins that I might send to Boston by Mr. Samuel Harrington who was to call there. I sent also to Mr. Francis Bowman[26] of Lexington by the Same.

24. Very Dry windy weather. Ebenezer Rode to Mr. Robert Allen's, at Shrewsbury and got my Mare New Shod. Nigh to Evening came Mr. John Henry Lydius[27] from Boston, upon his return to Albany, and lodg'd here.

25. Mr. Lydius pursued his Intention Home. Mr. [blank] Morse[28] here from Medfield.

26. David Baverick made a Meal Chest for me. Shower of Rain after Drought.

27. On Ps. 109, 4. Mrs. Knowlton and Mrs. Whipple din'd here. Southborough people here at Meeting, Mr. Stone being gone to Harwich.

28. Rain. Mr. John Mead here. N.B. His Contest with Mr. Eliezer Bellows. Mr. Mead Lodged here. Visited Mr. Bowman.

29. I went with Mr. Mead to his Boards and bought them of him. Din'd at Deacon Forbush.

30. Hicks Carting Muck (having taken the Business of my Indian Corn for half the Crop of it). P.M. Mr. Francis Whipple came and work'd gratis for me. At Evening I sold him a Barrell of Cyder and another to Neighbour Eliezer Rice.

## MAY, 1740.

1. Preach'd at the private Meeting at Mr. Whipples on Rev. 3, 1. N.B. Hicks ploughed a.m. Mr. Rider[1] of Hopkinton here. Mr. Caruth[2] brought home a piece of Strip'd Cotton and Linnen Containing 16 Yards.

2. Rainy. Ensign Maynard here who had been to Boston and brought 6¾ Yards Callico for Judith and [illegible] from Mr. Jenison for me.

3. Rain. Some Thunder. P.M. Hicks Cart [blank] Load of Muck.

4. On Ps. 109, 4. Mr. John Pool of Reading din'd here. Southborough people at meeting, Mr. Stone not having return'd yet from Harwich.

5. Very Rainy Day. Read Several Centurys in Dr. Fuller besides his History of Waltham Abbey. Thunder and Lightning at Night.

6. Rainy Still. Four Young Cattle turn'd up into the woods. Very Cold.

7. Mr. Jonah Warrin[3] and Benjamin Forbush[4] Carted 13 Load Muck with Mr. Williams's[5] Cart and Oxen. Hicks ploughing here.

8. Samuel Forbush and Jonas Warrin junior Carted 13 Load with Captain Warrins Oxen.

9.10. Cold yet, so that we refrain Planted [sic]. My Hay in the Barn finish'd but have part of a stack abroad.

11. On Ps. 109, 4. Warmer Weather.

12. Planted all before Dinner that was to be done in the Fields. My Wife ventur'd to ride my Mare to Marlborough. I rode with Mr. James Fay[6] at Evening to visit Mr. James Cutler[7] of Grafton. My Body much Chill'd with the Cold, for we did not get there till between 10 and 11. Mr. Cutler lay in a very despairing or rather in a delirious State. I lodg'd at Deacon Whipple's,[8] and the next morning return'd to visit Mr. Cutler who was Somewhat more Compos'd yet not steadily rational. His Condition very hazzardous. I took leave between 10 and 11 a.m. and came Home. Mr. Cutler dy'd about 1 o'Clock. My wife return'd at Eve from Marlborough.

14. Brother Hicks Sow'd my Flax. P.M. I rode to Mr. Thomas Goodenows. Jonathan's—Jesse Brighams, etc. N.B. I sent down by Neighbour Benjamin How[9] 32 papers out of Governor Bradstreets[10] Bundles, to Mr. Thomas Prince[11] at Boston.

15. [No entry].

16. Mr. William Nurse[12] here with Mr. Calef's Book of the Witchcraft at Salem in the Year 1692.[13]

17. [No entry].

18. On Ps. 73, 28. Mrs. Chamberlain din'd here.

19. A.M. finish'd Dr. Increase Mathers Cases about Witchcraft.[14]

20. On this Day came up Mr. Richard Barns and his Brother Edward with the Committee to See whether the Land I had taken up on the East of my Line and bounding on the North side of the highway which goes over Powder Hill be common Land, and to be granted to me by the Proprietors, that So my Plott of it might

[19] Son of Thomas How of Marlborough.
[20] Sons of Deacon Simon Tainter.
[21] William Holloway of Westborough.
[22] Parkman's eldest son.
[23] Reverend Samuel Barrett of Hopkinton.
[24] Reverend William Brintnal of Sudbury.
[25] Old form of grafting.
[26] Prominent officeholder, magistrate and representative of the town in the General Court. Charles Hudson, History of the Town of Lexington (Boston, 1868), p. 17.
[27] Son of a Dutch minister at Albany. He later had to face charges brought against him in 1747 by the Council of New York for becoming a Roman Catholic and alienating the friendship of the Indians from the English. Collections on the History of Albany (Albany, 1871), IV, 144.
[28] Either Joshua or Samuel Morse. William S. Tilden, History of the Town of Medfield (Boston, 1887), pp. 441-442.

[6] Son of Captain John Fay.
[7] Pierce, Grafton, p. 475.
[8] James Whipple, one of the first deacons of Grafton.
[9] Son of Hezekiah How.
[10] Simon Bradstreet was Governor of Massachusetts from 1679-1686 and from 1689-1692.
[11] Reverend Thomas Prince, the historian of Boston.
[12] Of Westborough.
[13] Robert Calef (1648-1719) was a Boston merchant and writer who disputed with Cotton Mather over witchcraft. No printer in Boston would print his tract but it appeared in England as More Wonders of the Invisible World: or The Wonders of the Invisible World, display'd in Five Parts (London, 1700).
[14] Cases of Conscience Concerning Evil Spirits Personating Men, Witchcrafts, Infallible Proofs of Guilt in Such as are Accused with that Crime (Boston, 1693).
[1] Gideon Rider.
[2] John Caruth of Westborough.
[3] Son of Captain Daniel Warrin.
[4] Son of Aaron Forbush.
[5] Eleazer Williams of Westborough.

be accepted. The Committee were Samuel Brigham Esquire (put in by the Proprietors) Captain Nathan Brigham (chosen by me) and Mr. Joseph Stratton (chosen by Mr. Richard Barns) all of them of Marlborough. Old Mr. Maynard[15] came up also to see the Bounds. Upon a full view of the Bounds The aforesaid Gentlemen perswaded Mr. Barns to Consent to the following Terms. First, That I should Measure off Two Acres and a Quarter of the Common Land and get it accepted and that Mr. Barns should have the Rest being the Same more or less. Secondly, that the Bounds of our Old Lines, or the East and North East Should be now renewed and settled forever to prevent all further Controversie among us or our Heirs After us; which was accordingly done in the presence and by the Assistance of the Mentioned Committee and Mr. Edward Barns. N.B. Mr. Seth Rice who was absent in the forenoon came at Dinner and was with us in the Afternoon and assisted in the aforesaid Difficult Affairs. But to our mutual rejoicing we ended this Controversie so far in Peace.

21. Rainy. I rose very Early but was exceeding indispos'd. Neighbour Silas Brigham who had not perfectly recover'd from the Meazles, is now raving Distracted, and Sent for me but I was not able to go.

22. Disappointed of all Help in my Lecture. I began a Discourse this morning upon Tit. 1, 5 and p.m. preach'd it. After Lecture I stop'd the Church to see whether they would do any Thing about the Ordination of Deacons, and it was left to further consideration. Town Meeting to Choose a Representative. Deacon Newton chose first and refus'd. Lieutenant Baker chose and refus'd. Received divers Letters from New Haven, Dated the 13 instant. Reckoned with David Batherick and Sam Bumpso. Visited poor Neighbour Silas Brigham, whom I both found and left in the ravings of his Distemper. A very afflected Family!

23. Very Warm. Mr. Bridgham[16] and his Wife din'd here.

24. Rainy. Mr. Daniel Warrin work'd for me somewhat more than half a Day getting Riders for the Stone Wall, Yokes for the piggs, etc. Mr. Jonathan Goodenow here.

25. Sacrament. A.M. on Ps. 73, 28; p.m. on Mal. 3, 14. Deacon Fay,[17] Mrs. Miles[18] and Cousin Winchester[19] din'd. Mrs. Mile's Supp'd and lodg'd here.

26. Prevented going my journey by the Delays of the Constables. P.M. Rain. Eliezer Rice and Stephen Fay here. Old Mrs. Knowlton and Mrs. Whipple here.

27. Molly rode with me to Cambridge. I went by Southborough. Colonel Woods Company from Sudbury. Din'd by him on Fish at Thomas Harringtons. Before night at Father Champney's.[20]

28. I rode to Boston. Put up my Beast at Bracketts. Visited Brother Elias whose Affections were very flowing. Mr. Cooper[21] on Ps. 2, 10, 11, 12. Din'd at Brother Samuels.[22] P.M. at Convention. Mr. White[23] of Cape Ann, Moderator. Dr. Colman[24] communicated his Letter to Mr. Rutherford,[25] the Irish minister at the Eastward and Several Things relating to the Spreading the Success of the Kingdom of Christ. N.B. Count Zinzendorf[26] in Germany, a preacher of the Reformed Religion. N.B. The Money Collected in the Massachusetts for Mr. Torry[27] last year amounted to upwards of £1200 and in Connecticut upwards of £300. I lodg'd with Mr. Weld[28] of Upton at Brother Elias's.[29] N.B. Mr. Aaron Smith[30] lodg'd there also.

29. A.M. at Madame Thatchers[31] and bought out of the Library of her venerable Husband, Willards Body,[32] Shepherds Sincere Convert and sound Believer,[33] Flavell's[34] A Saint indeed, Small New Testament in Lattin, and a quarto of Clean Paper. Then we repair'd to the Convention. Lecture preach'd by Mr. Prince on Isa. 9, 7. The Collection amounted to £235. Din'd at Mr. Checkley's.[35] P.M. at the Sale of the late Mr. John Adams's[36] Books. I bought Melchior Adams' Lives of the German Divines,[37] Owen's Theologoumena, and Aristotles works in Greek and Latin, 4 Tomes. At Mr. Fennells bought Crudens Concordance. N.B. Conversation with Mr. Jacques[38] and Mr. Smith of Marlborough on the Affair of his settling there. Rode to Cambridge after Ten at night.

30. Father Champney absent and the Family in Concern. I rode over to College for Mr. Smith whose Company I had to Marlborough. Some Shower of Rain in the Journey. We din'd at Mr. Williams's[39] at Weston, but Mr. Williams not at Home. Late up to Marlborough by means of the Showers. Rain'd at Eve. Lodg'd at Dr. Gotts.

31. Sent my Portmantle home by Neighbor Beriah Rice.[40] I accompany'd Dr. Gott to Mr. Benjamin Bailys[41] where lay Sick John Hambleton, son in law to Mr. Gamel. The Doctor judg'd he could not live long, and I acquainted John with it. His distress was very great respecting his Eternal Condition. I did not return home till middle of the Afternoon, by means of his Urgency and Earnestness to have me tarry with him in his low Condition, to direct and assist him in his Repentance and closing with Christ. He was very humble and broken for sin, full of passionate and repeated Crys to God and Christ, Sent for his Companions to ask their forgiveness, and to call 'em to repentance and to charge 'em to turn from sin to God. He fill'd up his Time with these Exercises—But I warn'd him of the Danger of trusting to them and how rarely a late Repentance was true, proceeding so much from the present Extremity, which forc'd it. Hicks weeding our Corn.

### JUNE, 1740.

1. A.M. I preach'd on Matt. 22, 5, Repeating Sermon 808, 809. Lieutenant Ward[1] and his Wife and Child, of Sturbridge, and Mr. Benjamin Lawrence[2] din'd with us. John Hamleton alive yet. After Dinner came Mr. Park[3] of Westerly and his Brother of Holliston, from Grafton where there was no meeting. Mr. Park preach'd on Matt. 18, 3. N.B. Lieutenant Ward requested Baptism for his Child, but on Consideration of Disquietments between Him and the Church of Sturbridge, for some time Subsisting I pray'd him to wave the matter till I had Opportunity to examine into the State of his Case. He produc'd that Church's vote of Acquittance and Charity with him but it being Dated so long ago as November and he manifesting great uncharitableness and laying heavy Charges upon that Church I still pray'd him to forbear insisting for Special privileges (though he be a member of that Church) till further Consideration, and because likewise it happen'd to be a Sabbath upon which we had many strangers from divers Towns round about who would have no right to be in what had pass'd at Sturbridge, etc.—upon which he withheld. Mr. Park tarried and lodg'd, but his Brother return'd to Holliston.

2. I wrote to Mr. Rice[4] of Sturbridge by Mr. Stearns[5] of

[15] David Maynard, one of the original settlers of Westborough.

[16] Reverend James Bridgham of Brimfield, Mass.

[17] John Fay of Westborough.

[18] Wife of Deacon Samuel Miles of Concord.

[19] Mrs. Benjamin Winchester of Westborough. She was the sister of the first Mrs. Parkman.

[20] Samuel Champney, Sr., of Cambridge.

[21] Reverend William Cooper of the Brattle Street Church in Boston.

[22] Samuel Parkman of Boston.

[23] Reverend John White (Harvard 1698), minister of Gloucester 1703-1760. Sibley, IV, 421-424.

[24] Reverend Benjamin Colman.

[25] Robert Rutherford, a preacher of Brunswick and Topsham, Maine.

[26] Count Nilcolaus Ludvig von Zinzendorf (1700-1760), German religious leader and founder of the Moravian Brethren. He was encouraged by John Wesley and George Whitefield and came to Pennsylvania in 1741.

[27] Reverend Joseph Torrey of South Kingston, R.I.

[28] Reverend Thomas Weld.

[29] Elias Parkman of Boston, Parson Parkman's brother.

[30] The preacher of Marlborough.

[31] Widow of the Reverend Peter Thatcher of Boston.

[32] Samuel Willard, A Compleat Body of Divinity in Two Hundred and Fifty Expository Lectures on the Assembly's Shorter Catechism (Boston, 1726).

[33] Thomas Shepard, The Sincere Convert, Discovering the Small Number of True Believers, and the Great Difficulty of Saving Conversion (Cambridge, 1664).

[34] John Flavell, A Saint Indeed; or the Great Work of Salvation Opened and Press'd (Boston, 1726).

[35] Reverend Samuel Checkley of Boston.

[36] Preacher, poet, and classmate of Parson Parkman.

[37] Melchior Adamus, Vitae Germanorum Theologorum, Qui Superiori Seculo, Ecclesiam Christi Voce Scriptisque Porpagarunt et Propugnarunt (Heidelberg, 1620). Another edition appeared in Frankfurt in 1653.

[38] Reverend Richard Jaques of Gloucester.

[39] Reverend William Williams.

[40] Son of Thomas Rice.

[41] In Marlborough.

[1] Benjamin Ward.

[2] Of Westborough.

[3] Reverend Joseph Parke (Harvard 1724), minister of the First Congregational Church of Westerly, R.I., 1733-1777. Sibley, VII, 415-421.

[4] Reverend Caleb Rice.

[5] Ebenezer Stearns, later minister of the Baptist Church in Easton, Mass., 1761-1766. William L. Chaffin, History of the Town of Easton, Mass. (Cambridge, 1886), pp. 178-179.

Stoughton. Hicks[6] weeding. N.B. I rode to see John Hamble-ton, at his Request by Eliazar Johnson. Now he had Hope.

3. Lieutenant Ward[7] and his wife here again in their journey Home, and he more fully acquaint'd me with his Case. Late p.m. I rode over to Stephen Fays and Lieutenant Bakers. Had a Message that John Hambleton dy'd yesterday, but a little while after I left him. Hicks weeding. Mr Aaron Smith here whilst I was from home.

4. Rode over, and Mr. Hezekiah How with me, to the Burying of John Hambleton. My Conversation with Mr. McAllister[8] respecting his Troubles on account of his Dauter Elizabeth who was Suppos'd to have run away last Sabbath Night with John Hudson[9] of Marlborough to Hampton to be marryed. Hicks finish'd weeding.

5. Catechiz'd at the Meeting House. About 38 males and about 21 females. Showers most of the Day. Ebenezer went to Mr. Thurstons[10] with Cotton and Linnen yarn to be wove by him, and p.m. I rode to Mr. Luke Rice with Yarn to be wove into Coverlids.

6. Mr. Daniel Warrin wrought for me p.m. Splicing Cedar Rails which Mr. Aaron Forbush got for me in Mr. Joseph Rice of Marlborough's Swamp. Mr. Abraham Knowlton here. Troubles in Shrewsbury again upon the Affair of the Goddards.

7. Mr. Cornelius Biglo promis'd to work for me in Hay time, if he goes not to Spain to the war. Lieutenant Baker[11] brought a part of my Boards from Mr. Meads. Captain Forbush[12] gave me a Swarm of Bees. Hot weather.

8. Mal. 3, 14. P.M. repeated on Mat. 22, 5. Mrs. Stone of Thompson[13] in Killingley and Deacon Forbush's[14] wife din'd with us. N.B. read the Letter from Marlborough. See Church Records.[15]

9. Visited Neighbour Silas Brigham who remains in Distraction. Thence I rode to Mr. Thomas Goodenows. Mr. Jonathan Hemingway came for my Wife but she could not go.

10. Thomas Hall came for my wife and she went with him to Marlborough. I rode to Neighbour Seth Rices and Deacon Tomlins.[16] Lucy[17] ill in the Night. Hezekiah Tomlin[18] came into the House while we were asleep in the Night and lay in the Garret on the wool till the morning unperceiv'd—And went off as Slyly likewise.

11. Deacon Fay and Deacon Forbush accompany'd me to Marlborough to the Ordination of Mr. Aaron Smith. The Council being form'd, the Church was call'd. Mr. Jabez Ward,[19] Strengthened by Colonel Woods[20] and Mr. William Witt,[21] Objected First, against the Council, alledging that it was not what the Church of Marlborough had chose but what their Committee for appointing the Time of the Ordination and who had no Authority to go any further, had chose. This was answer'd from the Votes of the Church. Secondly that the Church were not ripe for ordaining Mr. Smith, for he had never seen, or Consented to their Original Covenant. This was removed by his Consenting to a Covenant which the Church, upon its being read to them, acknowledged and accepted. He further debated, and alledged many Things, and frequently repeated and insisted upon the Same over again. Mr. William Witt objected against the Council,

[6] John Hicks, Parkman's brother-in-law.
[7] The son of Increase Ward of Westborough.
[8] John McAllister (McCollester, McCollister) lived in the northern part of Westborough that later became Northborough.
[9] John and Elizabeth were married; they resided first in Marlborough and then in Berlin, Mass. He fought in the French and Indian War, and he and eight sons saw service in the Revolution. Hudson, *Marlborough*, p. 400.
[10] Joseph Thurston of Westborough.
[11] Edward Baker, selectman of Westborough.
[12] Samuel Forbush.
[13] Thompson was a district of Killingley, Conn., until 1785 when it was incorporated as a separate town.
[14] Jonathan Forbush.
[15] Marlborough requested the Reverend Mr. Parkman and two delegates from Westborough attend the ordination of Aaron Smith. Deacon Fay and Forbush were chosen. Westborough Church Records, June 8, 1740.
[16] Isaac Tomlin.
[17] Parkman's daughter, aged six.
[18] Son of the deacon.
[19] Ward was one of a group of residents of eastern Marlborough, who in the period 1738 to 1744 were endeavoring to divide the town. Hudson, *Marlborough*, pp. 128-130.
[20] Benjamin Woods.
[21] Son of John Witt of Marlborough.

and so not owning them as such had prepar'd no reasons, but had divers to offer if there might be a regular Council call'd, and time to prepare himself. The Council voted that the Church had been regular in their Calling and choosing of this Council, nor any infringement of their Privileges, it having been their own proper act, and that the agrieved had had Sufficient Time to prepare themselves with their Reasons. Colonel Woods offer'd (as he Said) not by way of Objection or Opposition, but by way of Self Defence, what the hasty and precipitant proceeding of the Church had been, and his great Dissatisfactions therewith, which the Council by Examining the Records or Minutes thereof found to be very different (in their Apprehension) from what the Colonel had represented, and especially as to the Choice, the coming to the Choice, and the renewing and strengthening of it—it being by Continuation and adjournment November latter End to December 24 and the last meeting not till some time in February. The Colonel urg'd that not thinking the Church would come to a Choice neither he nor many Others of them acted—But it was made Evident that both Church and Town were fully apprized Sufficient time beforehand what the Business was, and might have come and acted if they had pleas'd—but that those persons were plainly desirous to clogg and impede the Church's Settlement. When the Colonel declar'd his unpreparedness to offer his Reasons against Mr. Smiths settlement there, the Council desir'd him to reveal what the Reasons were if he did not offer the Defence of them. Colonel said he judg'd him unqualify'd for the Gospel ministry. Upon this the Council read the Testimonials of Sundry Ministers in the County of Essex concerning him; and the Moderator had given an Account of his Examination by a number of ministers at the Church's express Desire, and the Result of it. And as to ordaining him without hearing him preach, there being but few in the Council, to be sure of the ministers, but what had, They who were of that number, that had not gave the Council to understand that they had taken equivalent Methods for Satisfaction in his ability for public Exercises, and were satisfy'd. Then the Council voted that they were ready (having chose a person to give the Charge—This was done at the Churchs express Desire—and another to give the Right Hand) to proceed to the Public Service. And the Church likewise voted that they were ready. Four o'Clock p.m., Mr. Williams of Weston pray'd. Mr. Wigglesworth preach'd on 1 Tim. 4, 16. Mr. Prentice[22] gave the Charge, and Mr. Loring[23] the Right Hand. Sung Ps. 68, 18, 19, 20. After supper Mr. Stone, Mr. Daniel Rogers,[24] of College, and several others of us went to see the Colonel. N.B. Dr. Gott no hand in any of the Business of the Church or Council to Day. Deacon Brown[25] of Weston rode with us as far as Captain Warrins. Late before we got home.

12. Lieutenant King of Suffield, and his New marry'd wife (who was Mrs. Hannah Devotion)[26] was here and din'd with us. P.M. Mr. Wigglesworth,[27] Mr. Prentice, Deacon Thorn[28] and Mr. Adams (the Two last of Ipswich) came. Mr. Prentice went home to Grafton and Deacon Thorn to Shrewsbury. The rest went with my wife and me to a raising Supper at Ensign Maynards. Mr. Wigglesworth lodg'd here.

13. Mr. Wigglesworth's Horse and my Mare got out of the pasture and had got down to Mr. Jacob Amsdens[29] before sun rise. His young Man brought 'em back to us. My wife and I waited on Mr. Wigglesworth to Mr. Whipples where we din'd, and thence we rode up to Mr. Joseph Knowltons,[30] and they would fain have perswaded us to ride up with them to Mr. Abraham Knowltons but I return'd. Mr. Caleb Rice and his Brother Payson[31] here. N.B. Our Conversation on the Affair of Lieutenant Ward.

[22] Reverend Solomon Prentice of Grafton.
[23] Reverend Israel Loring of Sudbury.
[24] (Harvard 1725). A tutor at Harvard College, and later minister at Exeter, N.H., 1748-1785. *Sibley*, VII, 554-560.
[25] Benjamin Brown. Lamson, *Weston*, p. 12.
[26] Daughter of the Reverend Ebenezer Devotion of Suffield.
[27] Edward Wigglesworth, D.D., Professor of Divinity at Harvard College.
[28] John Thorn.
[29] Of Westborough.
[30] Joseph Knowlton and his wife Abigail were admitted to the Shrewsbury church in March, 1733. Ward, *Shrewsbury*, p. 348.
[31] Parson Rice had married Priscilla, daughter of Captain Jonathan Payson of Woodstock, January 8, 1737.

14. [No entry].

15. I was not very well in the Morning, But Mr. Smith came from Marlborough to preach for me, yet with this proviso that I would go and preach for Mr. Prentice of Grafton who was ill. I undertook it, but could not perform with Life and Vigour. A.M. I preach'd on Ps. 73, 24. P.M. on 2 Pet. 1, 10. At Eve there was So great likelihood of Storm of Rain that I rode home being oblig'd to preach the next Day. Mr. Smith went to Marlborough before I got home.

16. I preach'd a Sermon to Young people from John 21, 15, Which I wholly composed this Day. The Exercise at 3 P.M. N.B. Hicks Shingling the west End of my Barn.

17. Trooping and Training. I din'd with the Officers after Prayer. Colonel William Ward[32] here, and he took the Names of Six persons who enlisted for the Expedition to Spain. Hicks a.m. on the Barn.

18. Mr. Baynes[33] of Marlborough paving my back Yard. Mrs. Thankfull Rice here. Hicks on the Barn. Wrote to Mr. Noyes[34] of New-haven, and my Wife to Mrs. Pierpoints.[35] My wife and I din'd at Ensign Maynards, and after Dinner Mrs. Maynard rode with us over to Mr. Howards to see their sick Children, suppos'd to have the Throat Disease. Rainy Return home.

19. Baynes paving—Hicks shingling. My wife and I rode over to Deacon Forbush and din'd there. The Deacon and his wife with us, we went to Mr. Daniel Forbush, Mr. Millers and Lieutenant Tainters. Lieutenant Tainter and his wife accompany'd us home. Jotham Maynard and Abigail Allen were marry'd.

20. Baynes paving.

21. Mr. Baynes having finished his work, went home this Morning. My wife rode to Marlborough. Very Hot. P.M. my wife return'd before the great Thunder Storm which arose about 4 or 5 o'Clock. The Lightening very sharp. Rain'd very hard. Hicks at Half hilling part of the Day.

22. Matt. 10, 5 to 13. P.M. repeated the last Sermon on Matt. 22, 5. Very weary at Eve.

23. Hot yet windy.

24. I rode over to Mr. Thomas Goodenow's, To Mr. Allens,[36] Mr. McCallisters whose child was Sick, Caruths,[37] Oakes,[38] Captain Eagers.[39] Din'd at Mr. Bezaleel Eagers.[40] Mr. Maverick[41] of Stratford on his Journey home, overtook me as I was riding up to Mr. Robert Allens.[42] I rode with him as far as to Mr. Cushings, return'd home about 5 p.m. Mr. Lyon of New Haven, Brazier, here. At Eve came Brother Breck[43] from Springfield, and with him Brother Samuel Breck,[44] who was upon his Journey from College to Springfield. The Scholars being dispers'd by reason of the prevalency of Throat distemper at Cambridge for which Reason the Commencement is also deferr'd for Six weeks.

25. Mr. Breck to Boston, Brother Samuel to Springfield. I rode up to Grafton to their Fast on account of the Throat Distemper. P.M. Mr. Prentice pray'd and Mr. Hall preach'd on Job 5, 8, 9. Mr. Cushing pray'd p.m. and I preach'd on Hos. 14, 1. Rode home in the Eve accompany'd by Captain Fay and Mr. Jonathan Whipple.

26. Mr. John Baker came from Mr. Simeon Haywards to desire me to visit their Sick Children. One of them was very bad of the Throat Distemper. Visited Mr. Caruth. Sent to Boston by Lieutenant Holloway. Visited the widow Fay. N.B. her Discourse of Sallery, etc.

27. I rode out to provide Help in my Haying—and to provide for my Journey next week. N.B. Mr. Whipple undertakes to get my Meadow Hay. Zachary Hicks came Home.

28. I rode over (unsent for) to the Funeral of Mr. Haywards son Simeon who dy'd (as 'twas thought) of the Throat Distemper. N.B. a great Mortality at Cambridge by it, especially in president Holyokes[45] and Steward Boardmans[46] Familys. At Southborough also. N.B. Mr. Moody[47] of York at Sudbury that Mr. Loring might be with Mr. Edmund Brown at York, for the Murther of [blank] Bryant in the Gaol. Edward Whipple mowed for me, at the East End and back of the Barn.

29. I was in no Small Conflict of Mind about my Sermons, having been hindred and call'd from Home most of the Days this Week. At length I determined to repeat my sermon on Mat. 24, 44, from Luke 12, 40, the latter on the account of the terrible Judgment of the Throat Distemper. Lieutenant Holloway, Mrs. Miller, Mrs. Thurston and Mrs. Walker at Dinner. P.M. Rain.

30. My Wife, furnished with Lieutenant Tainters Horse, Set out with me for Cambridge. N.B. Several Familys on the Road in Southborough very Sick of the Throat Distemper. At Lieutenant Brighams, 5; at Mr. Ephraim Wards (who bury'd Two Children on Saturday last and his wife but a little before) Several. We got to Watertown so as to dine (at 2 or 3 o'Clock) at Mr. Benjamin's. We were at Cambridge so Seasonably as to go to Boston and Lead up our Horses. We lodg'd at Brother Parkmans. Our Honored Mother Comfortable. Brother Elias remains much as he was—Very unable to help himself, His Reason Good, but his Passions Weak, and Soon in Excess, of Joy, Grief, etc.

### JULY, 1740.

1. We din'd at Brother Elias's. P.M. Mr. Halyer and my Kinsman Elias perswaded me to go off into the Harbour to fish. We got aground by the Castle and did not get up home till 2 o'Clock next morning. A very Pleasant Time. We caught 13 Tom Codd. Had Mr. Langdons Boat. Mr. Halyer lodg'd with us. My Wife lodg'd at Brother Alexander's with sister Lydia Champney.

2. This Day was observ'd as a Day of Fasting and Prayer at Cambridge on the Account of the Throat Distemper there, which otherwise had been the Commencement. Din'd at Brother Samuel's and Brother Breck with us. P.M. We went to the Baptist Meeting where Mr. Callender[1] of Newport preach'd on 1 Cor. 11, 28. After Lecture we went to Mr. Condeys[2] Lodgings at Mr. Jarvis's[3] where were Mr. Chauncy,[4] Harrison Gray,[5] etc. At Eve at Mrs. Keggells,[6] old Mr. Lorings, etc. Lodg'd at Brother Elias's.

3. Mr. Webb[7] Lecture on Rev. 3, 1, 2. I din'd at Brother Alexander's. My Wife at Brother Samuels, and with her din'd Dr. Smith[8] of Shrewsbury. P.M. I was at Mr. John Barretts where were Mr. Barrett[9] of Hopkinton and Mr. Cabbot[10] of Thompson after which I was at Mr. Salters,[11] with a young Association of Batchelors. At Eve at Brother Samuels and lodg'd there.

4. Din'd at Brother Parkman's, his Son John and his Wife likewise there. P.M. Visited Mr. Robert Brecks wife—and Mr. John Breck. At Eve the Private Meeting which Should otherwise have been at Brother Samuels was remov'd to Brother Elias's and I preach'd on Heb. 12, 5. Lodg'd at Brother Elias's.

5. I was at Mr. Thatchers[12] and bought the whole works of the Author of the Whole Duty of Man.[13] Several Persons (Cousin

[32] Of Southborough.

[33] William Bains.

[34] Reverend Joseph Noyes of New Haven.

[35] Widow of the Reverend James Pierpont of New Haven.

[36] Ephraim Allen lived in that part of Westborough that later became Northborough.

[37] John Caruth.

[38] Nathaniel Oak.

[39] James Eager, an early resident of Westborough.

[40] Son of Captain James Eager.

[41] Paul Maverick. Samuel Orcutt, A History of the Old Town of Stratford and the City of Bridgeport, Conn. (New Haven, 1886), II, 1244.

[42] Of Shrewsbury.

[43] Reverend Robert Breck, Jr.

[44] (Harvard 1741). Later a surgeon of Springfield.

[45] Edward Holyoke, President of Harvard College.

[46] Andrew Bordman (Harvard 1719), the steward at Harvard College. Sibley, VI, 295-296.

[47] Reverend Samuel Moody (Harvard 1697), minister at York, Maine, 1698-1747. Sibley, IV, 356-365.

[1] Reverend John Callender (Harvard 1723), the Baptist minister at Newport, R.I., 1731-1748. Sibley, VII, 150-155.

[2] Reverend Jeremiah Condy (Harvard 1726), the minister of the First Baptist Church of Boston, 1738-1764. Sibley, VIII, 20-30.

[3] Nathaniel Jarvis of Boston.

[4] Reverend Charles Chauncy.

[5] Later the Treasurer of the Province, and one of the loyalists who left Boston in 1776. M. D. Raymond, Gray Genealogy (Tarrytown, 1887), p. 192.

[6] Mrs. Abel Keggell, the cousin of Mrs. Parkman.

[7] Reverend John Webb.

[8] Dr. Joshua Smith. Ward, Shrewsbury, p. 436.

[9] Reverend Samuel Barrett of Hopkinton.

[10] Reverend Marston Cabot (Harvard 1724), the first minister of Thompson, Conn., 1729-1756. Sibley, VII, 320-324.

[11] Richard Salter (Harvard 1739), later the minister at Mansfield, Conn., 1744-1787. Sibley, X, 404-409.

[12] Reverend Peter Thatcher.

[13] Richard Allestree, D.D. (1619-1681), the royalist divine, is generally held to have been the author of The Whole Duty of Man, which was first published in 1658, and went through more than thirty editions. The work Parkman refers to may have been his Forty Sermons whereof Twenty-one are now First Published, 2 vols. (London, 1684).

Elias, and Two Elizas) accompany'd us to Charlestown. My Dauter Molly, who had been at Boston Several Weeks, being now to return home with us. Mounted between 11 and 12. Din'd at Brother Barretts[14] at Cambridge, his wife having lately been deliver'd of a son. It was after one when we left Cambridge. N.B. The Distemper not so raging as last week, when no less than 8 dy'd therefrom. At Mr. Harringtons Tavern we had Mr. Belcher Hancocks Company to Marlborough. Got home between 9 and 10 and found all in Safety. D.G.

6. A.M. Repeated Sermon on Mat. 24, 44, from Luke 12, 40. P.M. repeated sermon on 1 Tim. 1, 15. A dry Time.

7. A very Mercifull Rain. Mrs. Hardy returning from her Brother Haywards acquaint'd me that he had lost another Child by the Throat Distemper.

8. In the Forenoon I was at the Funeral of Mr. Haywards Child. From thence I rode to Josiah Bowkers, call'd at John Bowkers[15] and thence proceeded to Mr. Cushing[16] to Association. Mr. Prentice, Mr. Loring[17] and Mr. Frink[18] were there. Mr. Loring gave us some account of his late Journey to York to visit Mr. Edmund Brown, late of Sudbury, under Condemnation for the Murther of [blank] Briant; and gave us a Concio on Eph. 6, 18 and part of 19. Mr. Meacham[19] of Coventry and Mr. Woodbridge[20] of Hatfield came in. At night I returned home, because of Several Workmen mowing today for me. Scil. Mr. Cornelius Biglo, Mr. John Caruth and Jonathan Green. Mr. Biglo stay'd over night. At Eve came Mr. Solomon Prentice.

9. I rode to Shrewsbury round by Mr. Whipple's. Mr. Biglo mow'd for me, made Hay etc. N.B. at Shrewsbury Mr. Prentice[21] of Lancaster preach'd the Lecture on Ezek. 33, 31–32.

10. Busy about my Hay part of the forenoon. Disappointed of all in my Lecture. I repeated Sermon on Ps. 43, 3, 4. After Lecture Lieutenant Tainter and Neighbor Thurston were very helpfull about my Hay—pitching up what was in Disorder in the Barn and poling in a Quantity that was abroad. A pritty hot Season.

12. Weather chang'd, windy and Cool. Jonas Warrin junior (Son of Jonas) mow'd. Mr. Biglo brought up Wheat, Books etc. in his Cart from Boston.

13. Sacrament. A.M. on Ps. 65, 4. N.B. the Number LXIV. P.M. on Mat. 10, 14, 15, 16. Deacon Fay[22] old Mrs. Knowlton, Mrs. Dinah Goodenow,[23] Mrs. Deliverance Fay,[24] Mrs. Grow[25] and Mrs. Walker[26] din'd with us.

14. Catechiz'd a. and p.m. at the meeting House. My Sons busy (except Catechizing Time) about the Hay.

15. I rode to my ministerial Meadow, found Edward and Benjamin Whipple mowing. It was already somewhat Brown and ought to have been cutt before this Day. I rode to Mr. Whipples, Captain Fays, Mr. Grouts,[27] Cousin Winchesters, Mr. Nathaniel Whitneys, Walkers, Tainters (where I din'd—N.B. Discourse with Bekkey),[28] old Mrs. Rice's and thence home about 2 p.m.

16. Sam Bumpso gave me a Day at my Meadow. Edward and Benjamin Whipple mowing there also. N.B. Neighbor Warrin mowing for me at Home. Zebadiah Smith brought home Plad and Calamaneo for my Gown.

17. Neighbor Warrin came between 10 and 11, mow'd till near noon then pitch'd up a great parcel of Hay in the Bay and Barn Floor and put the mow to rights. He mow'd a little and was so ill that he broke off before night, but help'd us in carrying in Hay. Mr. Eliezer Bellows carted home Boards for me, the Remainder of what I bought of Mr. Mead.

18. Mr. Francis Whipple carted home 4 Load of Hay from the Ministerial Meadow, His Father and Brother assisting him at the Meadow in poling, Loading, etc.

19. Mr. Caruth mow'd on the South side. P.M. the Boys pol'd in some Hay from the South side which was mow'd by Neighbor Warrin—and I rode to Shrewsbury.

20. In the Morning I walk'd with Dr. Smith to See Solomon Hapgood, second son of Captain Hapgood[29] who was very bad of the Throat Distemper. I preach'd on Hos. 6, 1 a. and p.m. After Services Mr. Cushing came home, and went to Captain Hapgoods—But the sun being sett I returned home.

21. Thomas Winchester and Thomas Whitney went with Edward Whipple to mow in the Meadow. Thomas Whitney soon cutt himself and went home. My little Boys considerable of Hay to take Care of and nobody to help 'em. P.M. Messers. Whipples brought home (with one Team) Two Load of Hay from the Meadow and got up one Load from below my old House and southside. Sold them a Barrell of Cyder for 16 Shillings. N.B. Neighbor Cook[30] and John Rogers in Contest before Colonel Nahum Ward.[31]

22. I rose early and rode as far as Mr. Biglo's. Met Mr. Eliezer Bellows going to work for Ensign Maynard[32] notwithstanding that he had promis'd to come and help me, for which I was disquieted with him. Call'd at Neighbor Abner Newtons and receiv'd £5. Neighbor Biglo and his Boy, neighbor Daniel Hardy and Jonas Warrin, junior mow'd for me. The weather Clear yet and the Earth very dry. The Staple in my Pump Handle drew out and Sunk down to the Box, which oblig'd me to pull up the pump Spire; and it being very long, Neighbor Hardy (who endeavor'd to hold it up) let it fall and broke off the Top nigh a foot and half which put us into much trouble for Water. N.B. Neighbor Jesse Maynard[33] and his wife here in order to their owning the Covenant. N.B. Solomon Hapgood and Mr. Daniel Drury, Child, of Shrewsbury, bury'd, both having dy'd of the Throat Distemper.

23. Tom Black, Boy to Mr. Biglo, came late in the Morning to work; afternoon it rain'd so that it beat him wholly off. Before the Rain prevail'd much Mr. Francis Whipple brought Home a Load of Hay from the meadow.

24. Rain still. The Seasonableness of the Rain may prevent our meadow repining for our Hay, though Two Load or more at the Meadow and 3 or 4 Days Mowing at home lyes expos'd. P.M. clear'd away and nigh ½ after 4 o'Clock Mr. Biglo came and Tom with him and mow'd till night the new ground above the Orchard and both of them lodg'd here.

25. Mr. Biglo went to the Meadow to mow the North Side of the Brook. Tom mow'd a little in the morning, and afterwards we all made and raked till night. N.B. Disappointed by Neighbor Daniel Warrin, whom I would fain have had for the afternoon although I willingly releas'd him to his own work in the morning. At Eve reckon'd with Neighbor Aaron Forbush. N.B. Timothy Warrin and wife here in the Evening.

26. Mr. Biglo went again to mow the north side of the Meadow. Tom Rak'd at Home. N.B. Neighbor Daniel Warrin came to work, but I had engag'd help Sufficient, and my Business being near finish'd I let him have his Choice to go or Stay upon which he went home. Mr. Aaron Forbush came between 10 and 11 a.m. with his Team and got in Two Turns of Hay. Mr. Biglo afternoon came and help'd rake and Cock the Hay at Home.

27. On Isa. 26, 20, 21. P.M. it rain'd.

28. Rain. Read Diogenese Laertius, volume 1.

29. Rode to Mr. Whipple's and to the Meadow. Hazey all Forenoon. Clear, p.m. Mr. Zebulon Smith here and din'd with us. Flax pull'd.

30. Mr. Whipple brought home 3 Turns of Hay from the Meadow, which finish'd the Bargain with him, and he brought up 8 or 9 Cocks from the Low Ground at Home, the rest being too Wett.

31. A Clear good Hay Day. We open'd and Spread what the Storms had Soak'd and recock'd it by the help of Neighbor Daniel

---

[14] John Barrett, who had married Ruth, the daughter of Samuel Champney, Sr., of Cambridge. Paige, *Cambridge*, p. 506.
[15] Of Westborough until 1741, when he moved to Marlborough. Hudson, *Marlborough*, p. 225.
[16] Reverend Job Cushing of Shrewsbury.
[17] Reverend Israel Loring of Sudbury.
[18] Reverend Thomas Frink of Rutland.
[19] Reverend Joseph Meacham (Harvard 1710), the minister of South Coventry, Conn., 1714–1752. *Sibley*, V, 533–536.
[20] Reverend Timothy Woodbridge, Jr., of Hatfield, Mass.
[21] Reverend John Prentice.
[22] Captain John Fay.
[23] Mrs. David Goodenow.
[24] Mrs. Samuel Fay.
[25] Mrs. Samuel Grow.
[26] Mrs. Josiah Walker.
[27] Joseph Grout.
[28] Mrs. Simon Tainter.
[29] Thomas Hapgood of Shrewsbury. Ward, *Shrewsbury*, p. 306.
[30] Cornelius Cook.
[31] The magistrate, of Shrewsbury.
[32] Stephen Maynard of Westborough.
[33] Son of David Maynard, an original settler.

Warrin who help'd me from noon till 4 o'Clock p.m. We pol'd in Some leavy Hay from the New Ground on the East Side of the upper Garden. At Night a Thunder Storm. The Two little Boys rak'd yesterday and today at the Meadow what Mr. Biglo mow'd, and Aaron Forbush junior (who went about the middle of the afternoon) cock'd it, about 28 Cocks. N.B. Girls to Huckleberrying.

### AUGUST, 1740.

1. Lowery. Mr. Joseph Crosby[1] of Worcester here, and din'd with us. Rainy still. Timothy Warrin[2] here at Evening as were several others.

2. Mr. Crosby having been to Southborough inform'd himself in the particulars of the Sudden Death of Mr. Jonathan Johnson there, which he related to us. How frequently doth God give us Warning, and call upon us to be ready also! Lowery Morning.

3. Cloudy. On Ps. 91, 1. Mr. Holloway din'd with us. Rainy Eve.

4. Rainy Day. Very great Frown of Providence on the Hay and Barley Harvest.

5. Lowery and Drizley Still. P.M. Clearer. Mr. Samuel Taylor of Southborough here. He inform'd me that Sometime agoe they had a Fast at Southborough on Account of the Throat Distemper, which Fast I never had heard a bitt of till now.

6. A bright Morning, which we have not had this long Time. I think ever since Thursday last. Mr. Barrett, going to Shrewsbury, call'd here. Letter from Mr. Lydius of Albany, informing that the Rices[3] of Canada desire one of their Brethren of New England would go up to Albany and meet them on September 6 next, in order to their making a Visit hither. Neibour Seth Rice[4] here with the Letter, himself under Indispositions.

7. We poled in the last of our Hay at Home, which was Cutt Several Weeks agoe.

8. Neighbor Caruth reap'd my Wheat. About 14 shock from less than half an Acre.

9. Mr. Biglo and How with him reap'd half an acre of Rye, so that it was all secur'd at once.

10. On Mat. 10, 17 to 20. Luke 12, 21. Dr. Smith of Shrewsbury here p.m. and supp'd with me. He had been to See Mr. Bradishes Family, Three of which had the Throat Distemper. Beriah Rice had also a Child sick of the Same.

11. My Wife rode with me to Marlborough. I visited Colonel Woods[5] who was much indispos'd by Hydropic and Asthmatic Disorders. I din'd with Mr. Smith, where also din'd Mr. Cushing and Master Loring. We visited the Colonel after Dinner and were also at the Doctors and at Captain Williams.[6] While we were at the Captain's a great storm of Rain arose. We rode home in the Evening after the Rain.

12. Our Water in the Pump So fails that we fetch'd up a Barrell from the old well on a pair of Thills I made for that purpose. P.M. Mr. Thomas Bruce here. I rode down to Mr. Bradish's[7] to see his Wife and Dauter who were sick.

13. I rode over to see Neighbor Beriah Rice's Child which had the Throat Distemper but was better. P.M. Dr. Smith here. I was inform'd that Mr. Simon Goddard[8] of Shrewsbury has lost a Third Child of the awful Disease.

14. I went to Mr. Aaron Forbush[9] and perswaded him to bring home the Hay which Mr. Biglo mow'd on the north side of the meadow the 25 and 26th of last month and he carted it home accordingly.

15. The Widow Mary Rice,[10] Neighbor Grow[11] here. I wrote and sent a Letter to my Nephew Benjamin Parkman,[12] who is gone to settle at Philadelphia.

16. Ebenezer rode over to Mr. Francis Pierce's.

17. On Luke 12, 21. Mrs. Bathsheba Pratt,[13] Mrs. Rebecca

Warrin,[14] Mrs. Joanna Forbush[15] and Mrs. Sarah Bruce[16] din'd with us. At Noon I receiv'd a Letter from Mr. Ebenezer Morse[17] to request me to preach at Rutland this Day sennight—Mr. Frink having abdicated, but it must be (by Divine Permission) our Communion Day. At Eve I sent an answer by Dr. Smith who had been to See Two more of Mr. James Bradish's Children Sick of the Throat Distemper. Scil. Jonas and Joseph.

18. Town Meeting respecting a Grammar Schoolmaster. A very rainy Day.

19. Mr. Asher Rice[18] here to take my Advice respecting his Journey to Albany.

20. Mrs. Rachel Bowker[19] visited us, and Din'd here, as did Dr. Smith likewise. Ebenezer to Shrewsbury and got the mare Shod.

21. Great Expectation of Mr. Barrett to preach but he came not. I repeated on Ps. 43, 3, 4. After Lecture Brother Hicks and David Baverick put up a Trough on Back Side of my House. N.B. Ebenezer and Samuel Hicks rode to Cambridge, the latter to bring up the Mare.

22. Very Rainy Day. Brother Samuel Breck came, being on his Journey from Springfield to Cambridge.

23. Clear Weather. Brother Samuel went on his Journey to Cambridge. Brother Hicks put up the Troughs at the Back side of my House. Samuel Hicks return'd from Cambridge.

24. Ps. 65, 4. Heb. 13, 20, 21. Sacrament.

25. Early in the Morning I visited Mr. Bradish's Family. Sarah very low, but Somewhat reviv'd. I found her Smoaking. I proceeded therefore on my Journey. Stopp'd at Mr. Swift's. Din'd at Two o'Clock at Cambridge. Went to Boston. Ebenezer went to Charlestown to bring back the mare to Cambridge. Brother Elias weak yet—he had a fitt this Day.

26. The Several Companys of Volunteers for the Expedition against Cuba, quarter'd in Boston, muster'd to Day to receive their Bounty Money from the Province. Four Companys were compleat in Arms, and five were unprovided. Din'd at Brother Samuels. P.M. at Mr. John Brecks. At Eve at Mr. Keggels, and Supp'd at Brother Alexander's.

27. Commencement. Din'd in the Hall. My Kinsman Elias[20] Receiv'd his Degree, but did not dispute. Lodg'd at Father Champney's, and Cousen Elizabeth,[21] Her Brother and Mr. Halyer at Deacon Sparhawks.[22] Sorrowful News of the Death of Mr. Stoddard[23] of Chelmsford, who dy'd in his Well.

28. A.M. at Sir Gay's[24] Chamber where was Mr. Obadiah Ayres,[25] Mr. Samuel Coolidge,[26] etc. Din'd at Sir Princes[27] Chamber. P.M. Negro Boys in Masquerade. Eve at Mr. Rogers.[28]

29. Brother Hicks goes to Boston dissatisfy'd about the Managements of the Directors of the Land Bank. Ebenezer so ill he could not go to Boston as was propos'd, that he might go to School. I undertook my Journey home. Call'd at Mr. John Hunts[29] at Watertown (who has lately set up a Still House there). There I found Mr. Cheney[30] of Brookfield who was riding home also. We din'd at Mr. Williams's[31] at Weston where were Mr. Seccomb[32] and Halery[33] of Newton (a young preacher). At Marlborough We found Colonel Woods in a low State of Health.

[1] An early settler. See Lincoln, *Worcester*, pp. 46–47.
[2] Son of Captain Daniel Warrin of Westborough.
[3] The story of the captivity of the Rice boys was recorded by Parkman. See *The Story of the Rice Boys* (Westborough, 1906).
[4] Son of Edmund Rice of Westborough.
[5] Benjamin Woods.
[6] Abraham Williams, Parkman's brother-in-law.
[7] James Bradish of Westborough.
[8] Formerly of Hopkinton. Ward, *Shrewsbury*, p. 285.
[9] Son of Deacon Thomas Forbush.
[10] Mrs. Thomas Rice.
[11] Samuel Grow.
[12] The son of William Parkman, Parson Parkman's brother.
[13] Mrs. John Pratt.
[14] Mrs. Timothy Warrin.
[15] Mrs. Jonathan Forbush, Jr.
[16] Mrs. Thomas Bruce.
[17] Later the minister at Boylston, Mass.
[18] Son of Thomas Rice. He had been captured by the Indians in 1704 and later was redeemed. DeForest and Bates, *Westborough*, pp. 37–39.
[19] The daughter of John Bowker of Marlborough. Hudson, *Marlborough*, p. 330.
[20] Elias Parkman (Harvard 1737) was the son of Elias Parkman of Boston. Elias, Jr., became a physician of Boston. *Sibley*, X, 223–224.
[21] Elizabeth, the daughter of Joseph Champney of Cambridge.
[22] Nathaniel Sparhawk. Paige, *Cambridge*, p. 657.
[23] Reverend Samson Stoddard (Harvard 1701), the minister at Chelmsford, 1706–1740. *Sibley*, V, 119–122.
[24] Samuel Gay (Harvard 1740). *Sibley*, X, 496.
[25] (Harvard 1710). The chaplain of Castle William. *Sibley*, V, 510–512.
[26] (Harvard 1724). He was the schoolmaster of Watertown. *Sibley*, VII, 326–331.
[27] Thomas Prince (Harvard 1740).
[28] Daniel Rogers (Harvard 1725), a tutor at Harvard College. *Sibley*, VII, 554–560.
[29] A Representative. Bond, *Watertown*, p. 304.
[30] Reverend Thomas Cheney.
[31] Reverend William Williams.
[32] Reverend John Seccomb of Harvard, Mass.
[33] Parkman probably meant Jonathan Helyer (Harvard 1738), who later was the minister at Newport. *Sibley*, X, 294–295.

Call'd at Dr. Gotts. Mr. Cheney rode to our House and lodged here.

30. Mr. Cheney went on his Journey. The Throat Distemper increases in Westborough. Sarah Bradish[34] (a Member of our Church) was bury'd the Day before Yesterday, and Joseph Bradish, her brother of about 7 or 8, was bury'd yesterday, and Some Number are Sick.

31. On Micah 6, 9 and p.m. on Zech. 7, 5, preparatory to the Fast which with the Advice of the Deacons of the Church and the Selectmen of the Town I appointed to be on Thursday next. The persons for whom prayers were ask'd to Day, being Sick of the Throat Distemper were Richard Barns, Hannah (wife of Noah) Rice, Robert Bradish, Miriam Fisk, Abigail Dunton, a child of Thomas Bruce, Four Children at Mr. Gamels.[35]

SEPTEMBER, 1740.

1. I visited Captain Warrins, Thomas Bruce's and Samuel Hardys Familys. N.B. Captain Warrins Son Silas ill with the Throat Distemper, but walks about. Mrs. Hardy ill with the Same and Several of their Children.

2. My Wife rode to Mr. Winchesters[1] a.m. and with me p.m. to Mr. Wheelers,[2] Mr. Balls,[3] etc. and thence over the Hill to Mr. Gamels, Jesse Maynards,[4] etc. Simon Tainter junior our Company back. Captain Hapgood of Shrewsbury burys his Eldest Son of the Throat Distemper to Day. Very Cool Evening.

3. A great Frost last night.

4. A Fast was kept by this Church and Town on occasion of the Throat Distemper coming among us. I began the Exercises. Mr. Cushing[5] preach'd on Amos 4, 10 the first and last Clauses. Mr. Cushing prayed p.m. and Mr. Prentice[6] of Grafton preach'd on Jonah 3, 10. Lieutenant Brigham[7] of Southboro and his wife, Mr. Phinehas Hardy and Neighbor Zebulon Rice's wife at Supper with us. At Eve I rode down to visit Neighbor Thomas Bruce's Family, Two of whose Children are very bad.

5. I improv'd the forenoon as Separately as I could to my usual Exercises. P.M. undertook to make a Visit to Colonel Woods who (as I hear) grows worse, but a great Storm of Rain, Thunder, etc. prevented my going any further than Captain Warrins where I was confin'd (much against my Inclination at this Time) Several Hours.

6. Mr. Samuel Coolidge here. He was riding to Leicester. I rode with him as far as Shrewsbury. I din'd at Mr. Cushings, and thence I rode to Rutland at the repeated Sollicitation of Mr. Ebenezer Morse, and Captain Howard by him, Mr. Frink having ceased to preach. I lodg'd at Mr. Frinks.

7. An exceeding rainy Day. I preach'd at Rutland a.m. on Ps. 122, 6 to the End. P.M. on Jude 10, 21. At Evening came Captain Stevens,[8] Ensign Moses How[9] and a Third to see me. Mr. Frink and I sat up till past 1 o'Clock upon his Farewell Sermon on July 27 last, from Rev. 3, 3.

8. A.M. I visited Ensign How and Jonathan Goodenow, and Mr. Frink accompanying me as far on my Journey as to the Grist Mill, there he stopp'd. I call'd to see Mr. Calwell[10] and old Mr. Clark, and Lieutenant Davis[11] who had Several Children sick of the Throat Distemper with whom I pray'd. N.B. Dr. Fletcher[12] accompany'd me down below Biglo's.

9. At the Burial of Thomas Bruce's Child who dy'd by the Throat Distemper.

10. My wife rode with me to Marlborough being ask'd by Dr. Gott[13] to meet with a young widow whom he purposed to bring from Boston to his House this Evening. We visited Colonel Woods whose illness So increases that this Day he is got up into his Chamber from which tis fear'd he will never come down. We waited at Evening for the Doctor at his House till we were weary, and then return'd home without seeing him.

11. I rode up to the Fast at Shrewsbury accompany'd by Mr. Stone.[14] Mr. Cushing pray'd and Mr. Stone preach'd on Ps. 57, 1. Mr. Prentice of Grafton pray'd p.m. and I preach'd from Mic. 6, 9. I return'd at Evening.

12. Ensign Forbush[15] sent his Son and a Yoke of Cattle, Sergeant Bruce a Son and a Yoke of Cattle and Captain Warrin[16] his Oxen, and plough and Harrow to plough and harrow my rugged Ground on the South Side.

13. Benjamin Forbush[17] work'd for me, a.m. mowing Bushes. P.M. took care of Stalks. Daniel How[18] came part of the afternoon and help'd.

14. On Mic. 6, 9. Eccl. 8, 11. Mrs. Billings[19] din'd with us.

15. P.M. Mr. Baxter[20] and Madam accompany'd by Captain Winchesters[21] wife of Framingham, came, and they lodged here. N.B. This Day arriv'd Neighbor Eliezer Rice from Albany with his Brother Ozorongoughton[22] and Mr. Tarbell[23] for a Companion and Interpreter.

16. Mr. Baxter and Madam, Captain Winchester and his wife rode from hence to go to Brimfield. I rode with them as far as Neighbor Seth Rice's, where I saw the Captives. P.M. at the Burying of another of Thomas Bruces Children and visited one of Captain Warrins which was very low of the Same Distemper. Towards Evening the Captives came to view to old House where Mr. Rice us'd to dwell, and they were at my House, Some number of the Neighbours accompanying them.

17. Mr. Baines[24] of Marlborough came to digg my Well. A.M. it rain'd. P.M. he wrought. I rode to the South and South west of the Town, was at old Mr. Rice's. The Chief had been there and remember'd the Old Gentleman. They were down with him to view the place where he was carry'd away Captive. N.B. I wrote to the Governor concerning the Captives.

18. The Funeral of Captain Warrins little Daughter, which dy'd by the Throat Distemper. The Strangers went from us to Groton to visit Captain Tarbell. They were at my House as they went. Mr. Baines went off in the Morning to look him up an hand to work with him, he having taken my well by the Great [?]. In the Bargain we agreed that he Should Dig till he found Water to my Reasonable Content, and Should Stone the Well compleat and be four feet within the wall at the Bottom, for Ten pounds and his own and a man's keeping, and I should draw him Stones convenient about the Well. And in Case he Should not find a good Spring this Season the well shall be covered up till another, only he Should receive five pounds of money and the remainder when the Well should be finished whenever it Shall be.

19. Very Cold, Windy but bright Morning. Mr. Baines came late from Marlborough and Sett to his work without an Hand. Mr. Whitefield[25] came last Night to Boston.

20. Baines at Work part of the Day—but went home about an Hour after Dinner. Mr. Rice return'd from Groton.

21. Ps. 126, chiefly 10, 3 and 4. P.M. Eccl. 8, 11.

22. Rain. P.M. Captain Eager[26] and Lieutenant Holloway[27] here.

23. Rain a.m. As Soon as I had din'd (Somewhat after one o'Clock) I Set out from Cambridge. At Sudbury lit on Mr. Samuel Bagnal going to Boston. I rode with him and got to Town before nine o'Clock. Lodg'd at Brother Elias'. N.B. Ebenezer[28] lodges there and goes to the North Latin School. This

[34] Daughter of James Bradish.
[35] Samuel Gamel or Gamwell.

[1] Benjamin Winchester of Westborough.
[2] Joseph Wheeler.
[3] Nathan Ball.
[4] Son of David Maynard.
[5] Reverend Job Cushing of Shrewsbury.
[6] Reverend Solomon Prentice.
[7] Nathan Brigham.
[8] Deacon Joseph Stevens of Rutland.
[9] Also of Rutland.
[10] John Caldwell of Rutland.
[11] Simon Davis of Rutland.
[12] Hezekiah Fletcher, the physician of Rutland. Jonas Reed, A History of Rutland (Worcester, 1836), pp. 115-116.
[13] Benjamin Gott.

[14] Reverend Nathan Stone of Southborough.
[15] Thomas Forbush, Jr.
[16] Daniel Warrin.
[17] Son of Aaron Forbush.
[18] Son of Parkman's neighbor, Hezekiah How.
[19] Hannah, wife of Thomas Billings of Westborough.
[20] Reverend Joseph Baxter of Medfield.
[21] Ebenezer Winchester.
[22] The Indian name of Timothy Rice who had been captured in 1704. Parson Parkman later spelled this name Oughtzorongoughton. See, The Story of the Rice Boys.
[23] John Tarbell. See Green, Groton during the Indian Wars, pp. 116-120.
[24] William Bains.
[25] Reverend George Whitefield, the famous revivalist.
[26] James Eager of Westborough.
[27] William Holloway of Westborough.
[28] Parkman's eldest son.

he has done nigh a fortnight. N.B. An Awfull Providence yesterday at Mr. Checkleys[29] meeting House in Boston. Three or Four Persons kill'd in the crowd, and many wounded—among the wounded sister Esther[30] and her Dauter. Mr. Whitefield preaches Twice every Day to the astonishment of all.

24. Having receiv'd no return from the Governor[31] touching the Captives with us, I waited on his Excellency, who told me the Governor and Council had directed the Secretary to write me an Answer and he had done it, but knew not where it lodg'd, or where it miscarried. It rained a.m. and detain'd me at Irelands till past 11. From thence I rode up to Dana's, on the South part of Cambridge, and to Father Champney's[32] from whence I went to College where Mr. Whitefield had been preaching. His Text was 2 Cor. 2, 17. I din'd at Brother Barretts[33] and thence went to Mr. Appletons[34] where Mr. Whitefield was. N.B. The Account which he gave of the Time and Manner of the powerful working of the Spirit of God upon him. P.M. He preach'd in the College Yard again; his Text was Mat. 11, 28. It was to incredible multitudes, and with wondrous power. N.B. I wrote to Captain Tarbell. At Eve I rode over to Medford with Mr. Turell[35] and his wife. Lodg'd at my Kinsman Bradshaws.[36]

25. Mr. Turell rode with me to Charleston. Mr. Whitefield preach'd the publick Lecture at Boston. His Text John 2, 11. P.M. he preach'd at Charlestown on John 3, 3. At Evening only Sister rode up with me to Cambridge. Mr. Tainter of Westborough having taken my Portmantle.

26. We rode to Dr. Robys[37] and din'd there. From thence to Marlborough to see Colonel Woods who was by this Time reduced to a very low State by the Hydrops Pectoris. In the middst of many Fears respecting his Sincerity, he maintained an humble Hope in God. I pray'd with him and took leave. Call'd at the Doctors and return'd Home (with my Sister Willard[38] with me). N.B. Mr. Baines came on the 23d near night, and the next Day his Young Man, one Merritt, and they both work'd daily at the Well. Sam Bumpso came on the 24 and pinch'd up my Thrashing Floor. Mr. Thomas Billings came for Lieutenant Holloway and Sow'd nigh Three pecks of Rye upon my New Ground on the South Side. And the Cattle were brought from the woods. Sam Bumpso and Ezekiel Pratt wrought wheat.

27. Sam Bumpso Thrashing. Mr. Baines and Merritt digging. Eliezer Rice rode to Groton for Mr. Tarbell in order to his going down, at the Command of the Governor, to Boston.

28. Repeated on John 3, 36. Mr. Tarbell came after meeting from Groton.

29. The Captives went to Boston. In the middle of the Night Mr. Sables came from the Secretary with another Letter concerning the Captives, the first having miscarried. But I had already taken effectual Care.

30. Rain. Sister Hicks was last night deliver'd of the Sixth Son. Father Champney came up. He brings word that Colonel Woods dy'd last night. Sam Bumpso thrash'd in the Morning. Thomas Winchester and Sam Bumpso righted my Fence which divides the upper from the lower Field.

#### OCTOBER, 1740.

1. Sam Bumpso Thrashing Wheat Still. Finish'd it somewhat before night, and winnow'd it over a first Time. Mr. Baxter and Madam in their return from Brimfield call'd here a while. P.M. I visited Thomas Bruces Wife, Ensign Forbushs Child, and Neighbor Cooks[1] Children who were sick, and had my Mare shod. Mrs. Fisher and Mrs. Whittemore visited Sister Hicks.

2. Thomas and Joshua Winchester gathering apples and Corn in the upper Field. Carry'd in Stalks, etc. I rode to the Fast at Hopkinton which was on account of the Throat Distemper. I pray'd and preach'd a.m. on 1 Pet. 5, 6 and at noon I rode to Marl-

borough to the Funeral of my worthy Friend Colonel Benjamin Woods. There were Mr. Swift,[2] Loring,[3] Cushing, Stone, Rice[4] (of Sturbridge). Mr. Swift pray'd. Colonel William Ward,[5] Major Keyes,[6] Captain Amsden,[7] Samuel Brigham Esquire,[8] Captain Williams[9] and Captain Barnard[10] were the Bearers. I lodg'd at Madam Woods's with Mr. Swift. N.B. Baines and Marritt came to work about noon at the well.

3. I return'd home. Baines and Marritt at the well. Exceeding Cold at Night.

4. Baines and Marritt at the Well. They have got down about 21 feet. Very Cold. Mr. John Ballantine[11] came from Hopkinton this Evening to preach for me. At the Funeral of Ensign Forbush's Child which dy'd of the Throat Distemper.

5. Greatly afflicted with the Cattle breaking into the Corn. Rainy Day. Mr. John Ballantine preach'd a.m. on 1 Tim. 5, 22. P.M. on Eccl. 1, 2. The Chief, Rice not well. Was at my House at Eve as he went from his Brother Wards to his Brother Seths. In the middle of the Night was call'd out of my Bed because the Cattle had broke into the Corn.

6. I rode with Mr. Ballantine a mile or Two towards Hopkinton. Was at Ensign Newtons,[12] Charles Rice's, and other Neighbors. Din'd with the Captain who was grown better. P.M. Lieutenant Baker[13] Sent his son and Team and Neighbor Pratt[14] his Moses to gather my Half of the Lower Field of Corn, Beans, etc. Several Neighbors at Eve.

7. Baines and Marritt again at the well. Paul Fay Sent by Cornet Howard to help me. He carted Stones for the well with Deacon Tomlins[15] Oxen and Neighbor Hows Cart. Cold winds, but bright Sun.

8. Baines and Marritt at the Well. The Captives went off, desiring Prayers in our Congregation for them. N.B. Captain Tarbell of Groton return'd home. I rode 2 or 3 Miles with him to Shew him the Road. N.B. His levelling Rice and his Brother, etc. I visited Mr. Jacob Rice[16] and his Family, and Mrs. Thankful Rice.[17]

9. In great perplexity in the fore part of the Day by Reason of the Cattle and Hoggs breaking in upon my few Apples, tossing about the piles of Stalks, etc. Old Mr. Maynard at my urgent request Sent his son Ebenezer who with his Cousens Team carted the Stalks into the Barn and the Apples over to Mr. Hows Mill. Mr. Cushing preach'd my Lecture on Luke 16, 11, 2 last words. Baines and Warrin work'd at the well, Marritts arm being sprain'd. Husk'd at Eve, but my wife not well.

10. Last Night my Wife had a terrible Convulsion Fitt, But through Gods great mercy it did not continue long. She by Degrees came to her Senses again. Brother Hicks was call'd and sent for Dr. Gott. His young man came, he being himself at Boston, celebrating his own Nuptials.[18] The young man attempted to Bleed my Wife but miss'd the Veins Some Number of Times; but when daily Light came on he succeeded and she bled freely. She was in her pregnancy 4 or 5 Months gone. The bleeding She judg'd was very beneficial to her. Mr. Baines went home.

11. Very Cold and Raw. Old Mr. Maynard[19] and his Son Nathan cut and Carted Home Two Load of Wood. Dr. Gott and his young man here.

12. Sacrament. I preach'd on Ps. 126, 3, 4 a. and p.m. Deacon Fay,[20] Mrs. Knowlton and Mrs. Whipple din'd with us. After meeting Mr. Ezekiel Upham of Sturbridge here.

[29] Reverend Samuel Checkley.
[30] The wife of Parkman's brother, Alexander.
[31] Jonathan Belcher, Governor of Massachusetts.
[32] Samuel Champney, Sr., Parkman's father-in-law.
[33] Parkman's brother-in-law, John Barrett of Cambridge.
[34] Reverend Nathaniel Appleton of Cambridge.
[35] Reverend Ebenezer Turell of Medford.
[36] Parkman's niece, Sarah, married Samuel Bradshaw of Cambridge.
[37] Ebenezer Roby, the physician of Sudbury.
[38] Mrs. Josiah Willard of Salem, Parkman's sister Susanna.
[1] Cornelius Cook, the blacksmith.

[2] Reverend Jonathan Swift of Framingham.
[3] Reverend Israel Loring of Sudbury.
[4] Reverend Caleb Rice.
[5] Of Southborough.
[6] John Keyes of Marlborough. Hudson, *Marlborough*, p. 409.
[7] Isaac Amsden of Marlborough.
[8] Prominent resident of the south part of Marlborough.
[9] Abraham Williams of Marlborough.
[10] Captain Robert Barnard of Marlborough.
[11] (Harvard 1735). Later the minister at Westfield, Mass. *Sibley*, IX, 468–472.
[12] Thomas Newton.
[13] Edward Baker.
[14] John Pratt.
[15] Isaac Tomlin.
[16] Jacob Rice of Westborough.
[17] Mrs. Josiah Rice of Westborough.
[18] Benjamin Gott married his second wife, Lydia Ward of Boston, Oct. 5, 1740.
[19] David Maynard.
[20] John Fay.

13. Dr. Gott and his young man here. Catechiz'd at the meeting House a. and p.m.

14. Notwithstanding that it was Somewhat rainy My Wife and I rode down to Marlborough to attend upon the preaching of the Reverend Mr. George Whitefield. My Neighbor Barns carried my Sister Willard, Daniel How carried my Dauter Molly, and old Mr. Green[21] carried Thomme. Mr. Whitefield preach'd at Sudbury in the forenoon, and came about ½ after 3 this afternoon. He preach'd to a great Assembly from Luke 18, 14. N.B. Governor Belcher present. In Dr. Gotts Name I asked Mr. Whitefield and his Fellow Travellers to his House and they accordingly went, but could not be perswaded to make any Stay nor to lodge Short of Worcester, even altho the weather was rainy. I Supp'd at Mr. Smiths[22] in Company with Mr. Dorr,[23] Mr. Stone, and Mr. Hemingway[24] of Townshend, but I lodg'd at the Doctors. My Sister rode home with Captain Warrin, and Thomme with Mr. Green, but My Wife and Molly Stay'd because of the Rain. N.B. Mr. Dorrs Account of their Troubles in Mendon Strengthened by the Testimony of Mr. Bruce[25] of the Same Town.

15. My wife Stays at Marlborough. Molly rode home with me. When I came home I had the Sorrowful Sight of the Mischief done by my Cattle breaking in upon my Corn which lay husk'd in the Barn, for I could have no Convenience to carry it up. The Disaster respecting the Corn was so much the more trouble some as my Corn was exceeding Short having but half the Field and what there was was exceeding poor and mean and soft. P.M. James Bradish so kind as to give me the cutting of Three Load of Wood, and the Carrying up the good Corn which I had in the Barn, which the Cattle did not get over to (but to the Soft Corn only). N.B. The Good Corn carry'd up from the Barn was 14 or 15 Basketts—and this was the biggest part of my Corn this Year.

16. Neighbor Daniel Warrin kill'd a small shoate for me which weigh'd 44 pound. Lieutenant Tainter Carted 3 Load of wood for me. P.M. at the Burial of the Child of Mr. Noah Rice. N.B. This is the Third Funeral at which I have been when Bearers have had Gloves and their minister none. Nigh Evening I rode up to Daniel Warrin, junior at Shrewsbury and to neighbor Eliezer Rice's. N.B. Dr. Gott brought home his Wife, but I could not wait upon him.

17. Brother Samuel Breck[26] brought up my wife from Marlborough, who had been there ever since Mr. Whitefields preaching there. Thome had rid down today to wait upon his Mother also.

18. Breck return'd. P.M. Mr. Dodge of Marlborough and Mr. Pomeroy[27] of New Haven here. The latter tarried over the Sabbath. N.B. The great hindrance by Company to me in my Studys.

19. On 1 Cor. 3, 9 a. and p.m. Repeating partly from Sermon on Acts 26, 16, 17, 18; the last Sermons on that Text from page 36 to 40, and from page 60 ad finem.

20. Mr. Pomeroy set out on his Journey. Town Meeting for my Support—granted an hundred and Twenty pounds (without mention of the wood, but a very cold season; Ground mostly covered with Snow in the Morning) in Case I supply the pulpit this Year.

21. Mr. Baynes came; went to work after noon. He had been absent so long that he spent all the Afternoon in emptying the water out of the well. Mr. Cushing here. Three Barrels and a part of a 4th of Cyder made by Mr. How, of my apples. N.B. Silas Warrin[28] brought the whole home. I rode to Neighbor Thomas Goodenows and to Mr. Elieser Beemans first of Evening. N.B. Samuel Allen with me.

22. Eleaser Williams help'd Mr. Baynes at the well. Mr. Baynes early in the morn kill'd a Shoate for me which weighed 60 and which I got Mr. Jesse Brigham to carry to my Mother at Boston. Marritt thrash'd Rie.

23. Mr. Daniel Warrin work'd with Mr. Baynes at the Well. Eliza Newton Sick.

24. Storm of Rain, a.m. Cold. Very difficultly perswaded Mr. Baynes to go on with the Work when it clear'd up, but Mr. Warrin came and was forward and then he consented. Greatly Troubled about my Trading with Mr. Warrin, he apprehending that I had sold him a young Sow which I did not judge I had properly and really bargained away to him.

25. No Sign of a Good Spring yet. They dugg till more than the Middle of the Afternoon and then broke off for this year.

26. On Mat. 10, 21, 22. 1 Cor. 3, 9. Mr. Pool[29] of Reading din'd here. At Eve I rode to Deacon Newtons[30] again to see his Dauter Eliza who was very bad with the Throat Distemper. P.M. I rode accompany'd by Mr. Whipple[31] to see Mr. Seth Hudson[32] who was sick. Call'd at Mr. Allens[33] and at Mr. Pilatiah Rice's.[34] Heard that Mr. Whitefield was taken up and carry'd off.

28. Ministers Meeting at my House. Rain P.M. Mr. Loring, Mr. Cushing, and Mr. Stone. Mr. Dorr also of Mendon came. I deliver'd a Concio on 1 Cor. 2, 9.

29. Mr. Dorr preach'd the Lecture on Prov. 29, 18. P.M. my sister and I rode to Mr. Tainters[35] to See a Child there Sick of the Throat Distemper.

30. Mr. Tainter, Mr. Harrington,[36] Mr. Aaron Forbush and Warrin came to take down my wild steer. They perswaded me rather to fell him and buy my Beef notwithstanding the keeping I had bestow'd and I consented and Sold him to Mr. Harrington for £13. Mr. Hezekiah Ward of Sturbridge here. We Shut up a Third Swine for Pork. Exceeding Cold for the Time of Year.

31. Mr. Hezekiah How and Eliezer Rice got down poles to cover my well with. I bought a pair of Steers one coming 4 which I had for 11£ 5 Shillings, and another coming 5 which was valued at 12£ 10, for which I was to give him a Young Cow with Calf, valued at 8£ 10, and a Red Steer coming 4 valued at 7£ 15, and he to give me in money 3£ 15. A.M. I rode to Marlborough to wait upon Mr. Aaron Smith in bringing home his New Wife. Lodg'd at Dr. Gotts upon whose new wife I now wished [blank] also.

### NOVEMBER, 1740.

1. In the Morning I got my Horse Shod at Mr. William Witts.[1] I broke fast at Mr. Smiths, brought up Sally Gott[2] to tarry a while at our House, but we rode first to the Burial of Joseph Warrin Son of Neighbour Thomas Warrin who dy'd of the Throat Distemper at Lieutenant Tainters,[3] and was buryed from thence. I din'd at Lieutenant Tainters. A Cold Season.

2. Repeated Isa. 26, 9. P.M. 2 Cor. 6, 1. Mrs. Ball (wife of Nathan) din'd with us. News that Mother Parkman was ill, Brother Elias worse, etc.

3. Brother Hicks carry'd down Sister Willard to Boston upon my Mare. Cold. Marritt and Dunton finish'd thrashing my Rye, and p.m. Cut Wood. Matthias Rice[4] here.

4. Snow storm. Neighbour John Rogers kill'd a Shoat for me (weigh'd 50).

5. A Thaw. Wett weather.

6. Covering up my well it being very pleasant weather and the Earth open. Much Dirt had drop'd into the well by means of the Frosts. Mr. Mead here and Mr. Billings;[5] the latter inform'd me

[21] John Green of Westborough.
[22] Reverend Aaron Smith of Marlborough.
[23] Reverend Joseph Dorr of Mendon.
[24] Reverend Phinehas Hemenway (Harvard 1730), the first minister at Townsend, Mass., 1734–1760. *Sibley*, VIII, 724–726.
[25] Benjamin Bruce. See John G. Metcalf, *Annals of the Town of Mendon* (Providence, 1880), pp. 237–238.
[26] Mrs. Parkman's brother.
[27] Reverend Benjamin Pomeroy, minister at Hebron, Conn.
[28] The son of Captain Daniel Warrin.
[29] Benjamin Poole.
[30] Josiah Newton.
[31] Francis Whipple of Westborough.
[32] Of Marlborough. Hudson, *Marlborough*, p. 399.
[33] Ephraim Allen, who lived in that part of Westborough that later became Northborough.
[34] Palatiah (Pallatiah) Rice lived in Westborough.
[35] Simon Tainter.
[36] Samuel Harrington.
[1] The son of John Witt who came to Marlborough in the early 1700's. Hudson, *Marlborough*, pp. 473–474.
[2] Sarah Gott was Parkman's niece.
[3] Joseph Tainter of Marlborough.
[4] The son of Benjamin Rice of Marlborough. The Westborough Church Records indicate that Matthias and Anna Rice were admitted to the church Nov. 23, 1740.
[5] Thomas Billings.

that the Committee for the School had sent for Mr. Jenison[6] to keep our school for Two Months over on the North side, and That Corner had met, agreed and rais'd Money for his preaching to them, all on the North of the Road; and Mr. Wheeler one of the said Committee was now down for him. Not a word of all which had I ever heard of till this Day.

7. Jejun. Priv. At Eve Mr. Matthias Rice and his wife here.

8. A very great Storm of Rain. The Rain exceeding plentifull.

9. 2 Cor. 6, 1. All Coran, [?] absent. Mr. Bradish and Mrs. Walker din'd with me. I begg of God we may not continue to receive his Grace in vain.

10. Mr. Matthias Rice bought a Barrow shoat, weight 52. Mr. Warrin winnow'd my Rye. 11 Bushels and a Peck.

11. Mr. Daniel Forbush[7] came and mended my Chimney, on the north side under the Roof of the House, a part of which we took off and clos'd up again. He pointed round the Chimney, and the Kitchen Jamms etc. My Wife rode to Marlborough with Brother Hicks upon my mare, to be blooded, and return'd at Evening. Lieutenant Tainter and Mr. Charles Rice[8] got me down several turns of wood with my Oxen. In the Evening Charles Woods[9] was married to Phebe Rice. A Considerable Number of young persons and others present. Put up the mare tonight in the Barn.

12. Squawly, Snowy, etc. last night. Cold blustering Winds this morning. Neibbour Cook here at Evening desiring a church meeting, which I promis'd him with all Convenient Speed. N.B. on the 12th Mr. Eliezer Rice here and took away my young brindled Cow, with Calf, and a young Steer coming 4, according to bargain for his Cattle. I am indebted to him 7.10.0, overplus.

13. Storm of Snow, very Cold, and the Meeting House very Cold and uncomfortable. Several of the Casements down and others very loose and open. I Spake to the people with some Resentment because I had twice Spoken in Private without Effect. I preach'd, tho through much Difficulty, on Eph. 5, 20. It continues to Snow, and is a very Difficult, Cold Time. My Cattle out yet.

14. Snowy and Cold. Could not Succeed to get my Barn fitted for my Cattle.

15. Very Cold. Got up Six of my Cattle. Ensign Maynard[10] got me 2 Turns of Wood. Rainy a.m. Reckon'd with Mr. Jonah Warrin.[11] N.B. Several men at the meeting House endeavoring to Mend the Windows.

16. Very Cold. On Isa. 26, 9. P.M. repeated sermon 1 on Ps. 5, 7. Mrs. Bellows (wife of Ithamar) din'd here.

17. Phinehas Forbush[12] p.m. cut wood gratis. Cattle got into the Barn. Eve Stormy.

18. A great Storm of Snow. Very Cold and tedious. Thomas not Well. The Business lay on me.

19. Sent by Brother Hicks to Ebenezer. At Evening Mr. Jenison and Mr. Wheeler and the rest of the school Committee. N.B. They agreed with Mr. Jenison to keep School for £65 per annum.

20. Neighbor Aaron Forbush and Hezekiah Pratt kill'd Three Swine for me. Weight 141, 118, 99. Neighbor Warrin building me a Hovel. At Evening a great Multitude were here to see Simon Tainter and Mary Bruce marry'd. Thirteen Horses, 12 of which double, came with them and about half a Dozen more came before them and a great number of Young Persons, So that the House was greatly fill'd with them.

21. Very fine pleasant Day, Such as we have not had for a long time. Neighbour Warrin finishing the Hovel. Major Keys here.[13] Mr. Simeon Hayward[14] here. Lieutenant Tainter cut up and salted my Pork this Evening.

22. Moderate weather. Friend Dyer of Marlborough here with Mr. Smiths[15] Horse, going to change him at Neighbour Hezekiah Pratts.

23. Cloudy, Sometimes Misty. Sacrament Day. A great Number of North Side Members absent—notwithstanding that it was the Day according to Custom; and notwithstanding that Mr. Jenison, Mr. Wheeler, and Mr. Hayward were here in the Course of the Week and were well inform'd and could inform others. I preach'd on Heb. 13, 20, 21. P.M. repeated sermon 2 on Ps. 5, 7.

24. Rainy, otherwise I should have expected a Number of Neighbours to get Wood for me. At Eve Neighbor Whipple and Eliezer Rice here.

25. Treasurer Newton[16] settled with me for the south part of the Rates of last year. Visited Neighbour Barns in his Confinement and weakness. Rain.

26. Mr. Davenport (who married a Tolman) here and din'd with us. Captain Fay and Eager here. Rain.

27. Very Rainy Still. Ebenezer Maynard, and Samuel Allen[17] here. Reading Sir Peter King's History of the Apostles Creed.[18]

28. Rainy Day. Mr. Garfield[19] of Shrewsbury here.

29. Rain continues. A most unusual Season. Benjamin Forbush[20] cutt wood a.m.

30. The Rain is not over yet. Mat. 10, 23, 4, 5. P.M. Repeated Sermon 3 on Ps. 89, 7. Appointed a Church meeting to be tomorrow at 2 p.m.

### DECEMBER, 1740.

1. Exceeding Rainy; The Earth fill'd with water and the Floods rais'd. No Church meeting—no Burial of widow Tomlins Child[1] as was appointed.

2. A.M. I went over to the Funeral of the widow Tomlins Child, and P.M. to the Funeral of Deacon Newtons Child[2] both of which dy'd of the Throat Distemper. A Third Grave was open'd this Day, Scil. for a Still born Infant of Daniel Stone. After the Funerals I went with Mr. Grout to Neighbour Beriah Rice's to see the Cow Mr. Tainter had bought for me and afterwards to Mr. Tainters. N.B. Richard King son of King the Cutler, etc.

3. I rode over to the north side to visit Thomas Warrins Family who had been long sick of the Throat Distemper. Evening when I return'd.

4. Mr. Tainter brought home Two of my Calves which he had kept a long time for me—and brought a Fat Cow from Neighbour Beriah Rice's and with Mr. Harringtons help kill'd her. Weight 17½ Score. Tallow 35, and the Hide 56. P.M. I was at old Mr. Rice's, where the private meeting mett. I preach'd on Ps. 89, 47.

5. Cloudy. Eve Mr. Tainter came and cutt and salted up my Beef.

6. Rainy. P.M. Neighbour Benjamin Fay[3] and his Wife came to discourse with me, but it was too late and I was too much engag'd in my Preparations to do them service.

7. Very Stormy Day—Rain, at night Snow. High Winds. I preach'd a.m. on Mat. 10, 26, 27, 28. P.M. on Jer. 2, 19.

8. Very Stormy Day, and we were nigh without wood. P.M. Mr. Seth Rice[4] here about his sister Thankful.[5] Neighbour Aaron Forbush here and reckoned with me. They both of them fetch'd wood. At Eve Ensign Maynard and Mr. Francis Whipple here, and Mr. Hall[6] of Sutton came and lodg'd here.

9. A bright fine pleasant Day. Mr. Hall went upon his Journey to Boston. Mr. Maynard here.

10. A very blustering Storm of Snow and Rain, and we out of wood. Ensign Maynard with his oxen came of his own accord and with young John Hicks got me two turns of wood.

11. A pritty good Day—but heavy, Dirty and Snowy under Foot. I rode to Marlborough and on my Way settl'd with and

[6] William Jenison, formerly a minister at Salem.
[7] Son of Deacon Jonathan Forbush.
[8] One of the early residents of Westborough.
[9] Of Southborough.
[10] Stephen Maynard.
[11] Son of Captain Daniel Warrin of Westborough.
[12] Son of Deacon Jonathan Forbush. Pierce, *Forbes and Forbush Genealogy*, pp. 23–26.
[13] Of Shrewsbury.
[14] Of the northern part of Westborough.
[15] Reverend Aaron Smith of Marlborough.
[16] Abner Newton.
[17] The son of Ephraim Allen of Westborough.
[18] *The History of the Apostles Creed: with Critical Observations on its Several Articles* (London, 1703). It appeared in several subsequent editions.
[19] Daniel Garfield. Ward, *Shrewsbury*, p. 290.
[20] Son of Aaron Forbush.
[1] Mary, the daughter of the late Isaac Tomblin, Jr., and Gemima, died November 28, 1740.
[2] *Westborough Vital Records* do not reveal which of Josiah Newton's children had died.
[3] The son of Captain John Fay.
[4] Son of Edmund Rice.
[5] Mrs. Josiah Rice.
[6] Reverend David Hall.

paid Mr. Beeman.[7] Was at Mr. Feltons,[8] Mr. Williams (the sadler) din'd at Mr. Tainter's. Visited Mrs. Lydia Barnard who was Sick at Mrs. Gates's.[9] Visited Mr. Smith and Dr. Gott, and return'd home in the Evening.

12. I was not well in the Forenoon having taken Cold last night.

13. James Eager here to inform of the Death of Mr. Thomas Warrins eldest son.

14. Cold Day, windy—but very little Wood. On Jer. 2, 19. Mr. Bradish and Mr. Samuel Fay, junior din'd with us.

15. Mr. Bradish Sent his son Jonas to cutt Wood for me, & he got down one Turn with my Oxen, whilst I was gone to the Funeral of Mr. Thomas Warrins Son, the third of his Children that had dy'd by the Throat Distemper. At Ensign Maynards as I return'd home.

16. Bright but Cold Weather. Mr. Taylor[10] of Sudbury and Lieutenant Brigham[11] of Southborough here and din'd with me. Their Errand was to request me to visit Captain Nathan Brigham of Marlborough labouring under great Trouble of Mind. Matthias Rice, Mr. Townsend,[12] Dr. Gott here. I visited Mr. Townsends youngest Child that was Sick.

17. A very Violent and tempestuous Storm of Snow, and we very Short of Wood. But through Gods great Mercy we are all in Health. John Hicks[13] sent to help us in cutting up what wood we had, etc. and help tend the Cattle, and lodg'd here.

18. I was according to appointment to have visited Captain Brigham and to have preach'd the Lecture in Marlborough but the drifted Snow, and the high, cold winds blowing the Snow about renders it exceeding difficult travelling. I rode with much trouble as far as Mr. Aaron Forbush and from thence to Mr. Whipples went upon Racketts and obtained Three young Men to come and cutt and sledd some wood. Ebenezer Maynard, Aaron Forbush, junior and Edward Whipple who in the Cold and Snow got down Six Load.

19. Cold, and difficult stirring in the Deep Snow—at the Funeral of Mrs. Townsends youngest Child. O that God would make it matter of quickening to Me, who am alas how far behind!

20. Cold, cloudy, Snow'd a little. My mare very lame. Lieutenant Hezekiah Ward[14] here.

21. Cold Day. Difficult getting to meeting. Jer. 2, 19. O that it may Convince and humble me for my forsaking God!

22. At Mr. Hows[15] in the Morning by whom I wrote to Mr. Cooper[16] of Boston. Dr. Smith,[17] Master Townsend and Mr. Hezekiah Pratt here. Dr. Smith din'd with us. Set up a Bedstead in the dining room.

23. Very Cold Season.

24. Very Cold. Dr. Smith here having again been to Mr. Townsends whose Wife and eldest son Sick. I visited Mr. Townsends Family and Neighbour Barns.[18] N.B. Neighbour Barns renew'd the Leave to me to cut wood in his Swamp. His Father Bruce[19] and his Brother Charles there. My son Thomas not well. Receiv'd from Boston by Ensign Maynard.

25. Cold. I rode to Deacon Newtons to see his Sick Children. Lieutenant Bakers,[20] old Mr. Rice's, Neighbour Daniel Forbush. Din'd at Mr. Harringtons. Visit Neighbour Grows, Thurstons,[21] John Pratts, James Fayes, Grouts, Captain Fays.[22] Cold Evening. Mr. Francis Whipple came to ask me to Joseph Greens Wedding, which I solemniz'd at Mr. Whipples and Supp'd there. Edward Whipple accompany'd me back.

26. Exceeding Cold. Cloudy a.m. Snow p.m. I rode to Captain Eagers[23] and to Ensign Bartletts[24] in the Storm. At Eve the Storm prevail'd much. Difficult getting Home. After I got Home the Storm was exceeding Vehement.

27. My Wife had been Somewhat ill all night but in the morning was so full of Pain that I rode away to fetch Granny Forbush to her. The Snow which fell last night added to the former (both being deep) made it extraordinary difficult passing. I was overmatch'd with it at old Mr. Maynards.[25] Ebenezer Maynard and Neighbour Pratt took their Horses and rode before me, by which means I succeeded. Brother Hicks carry'd up his wife, and fetch'd Mrs. How and Ensign Forbushs[26] wife. Ensign Maynard brought his wife and fetch'd Mrs. Whipple. Mr. Williams also brought over his. But we were in great Want of Wood through the Disappointments which I had met with. This Ensign Maynard help'd by chopping and sledding down a Load from the Hill. A Time of Remarkable Difficulty yet God was pleas'd to help us through.

28. I repeated sermon on Job 14, 5. The women still here A.M. At noon Mrs. Maynard and Mrs. How went Home. At Eve Mrs. Forbush (Ensigns wife) went home. My wife continuing yet about the Room. The Midwife, Mrs. Whipple, and Mrs. Williams Remain'd all night. Visited Mr. Townsends Family. Joshua very bad.

29. Eleazer Williams, Thomas Winchester,[27] Nathan Maynard[28] and Ezekiel Pratt after 11 a.m. Afterwards Lieutenant Tainter in the afternoon got wood. Captain Eager here.

30. Mr. James Fay with a Number of Hands came to get wood and brought one yoke of Oxen. The Hands with him were his Two Brethren, Robert Bradish, Jonas Child, Samuel Bumpso, Samuel Baker,[29] Elijah Rice,[30] Ephraim Whitney,[31] Noah How, and Stephen Maynard with a Team (paid for by Mr. Fay). Joshua Townsend aged 8 Dy'd, and Mr. Beemans youngest Dauter of 5 years of age. I rode to Mr. Beemans. Eleazer exceeding bad and all the rest sick. John McClung of Pensylvania, on his Journey, came at Night.

31. John McClung left us, carrying Letters for us, to my Kinsman Benjamin Parkman[32] at Philadelphia, and Mrs. Pierpoint[33] at New Haven. I went to the Funeral of Mr. Beemans little Daughter. His son Eleazer thought to be irrecoverable. Dr. Gotts young man, Hall, was my Company to Marlborough to Captain Nathan Brigham who was Still in a Melancholly, disconsolate Condition. I din'd late at Captain Brighams. Colonel Ward[34] there at Evening. Had his Company as far as his House, where I call'd; as I did also at Mr. Jacob Amsdens,[35] it being exceeding Cold. After I got home I marry'd Two Couple. Mr. Thomas Joslin[36] to Lucy Forbush[37] and Nathaniel Johnson[38] to Sarah Forbush.[39]

## [MARCH, 1741]

March 13, 1740/1.[1] Jejun. Priv. in Preparing Sacrament. Special Resolutions.

1. To Return or pay for the Books I have some Time agoe borrowed and negligently and unjustly detained for Some years from the owners thereof, at those times purposing to buy them, but to this Day have omitted it; by which I have involved my Self in the Guilt of Unrighteousness.

2. To quicken up my Self in the Several parts of my Ministerial Duty; in particular

[7] Eleazer Beeman of Westborough.
[8] Jacob Felton. Hudson, *Marlborough*, p. 362.
[9] Sarah, the widow of Simon Gates.
[10] Thomas Taylor.
[11] Timothy Brigham.
[12] Joshua Townsend of Westborough.
[13] Parkman's brother-in-law.
[14] Of Westborough.
[15] Parkman's neighbor, Hezekiah How.
[16] Reverend William Cooper of the Brattle Street Church.
[17] Joshua Smith, the physician of Shrewsbury.
[18] Richard Barnes.
[19] Elizabeth, the daughter of Abijah and Mary Bruce of Westborough, married Richard Barnes, Jr., of Marlborough, May 10, 1739.
[20] Edward Baker.
[21] Joseph Thurston.
[22] John Fay, an original settler.
[23] James Eager of Westborough.
[24] Daniel Bartlett of Marlborough.
[25] David Maynard.
[26] Thomas Forbush, Jr.
[27] Son of Benjamin Winchester.
[28] Son of David Maynard.
[29] Son of Edward Baker.
[30] Son of Charles Rice.
[31] Son of Nathaniel Whitney.
[32] Parson Parkman's nephew.
[33] Mrs. James Pierpont. Parkman must not have realized she had died Nov. 1, 1740.
[34] William Ward of Southborough.
[35] Of Westborough.
[36] Son of Nathaniel Joslin of Marlborough.
[37] Daughter of Aaron Forbush of Westborough.
[38] Son of John Johnson of Marlborough.
[39] Daughter of Aaron Forbush. She and her husband lived in Marlborough. Pierce, *Forbes and Forbush Genealogy*, pp. 26-27.

[1] The entry for this date is from the Natalitia.

In Sermonizing more Seasonable—

In Visiting my People if it be possible to get Opportunity for this in Some certain Course—

In Admonishing—To be more impartial and faithful that So I may deliver my own Soul, and keep clear from the Blood of all men.

And O that God would graciously please to assist me to abide by these Engagements to his Glory! Amen.

### DECEMBER, 1742.

21. Very fine moderate Weather. Mrs. Eager and Mrs. Barns here, and Mr. Smith[1] of Marlborough. He din'd with us and kindly tarried all the afternoon. Through Gods great Goodness I felt the best of any Day Since my Sickness. May God go on and perfect my Recovery!

22. Extraordinary pleasant Moderate Weather like Spring. 'Twas Said it did not so much as freeze last night. I was not So well as yesterday, yet ventur'd down to the Kitchen so much as to look about. Young Mr. Caleb Prentice[2] of Cambridge here. Told me of the Religious Commotions last Sabbath and last night at Grafton. Divers Neighbours to see me. Mrs. Dolly Rice,[3] Mrs. Winchester,[4] Mrs. Hephzibah Mainard,[5] old Mr. Mainard.[6] N.B. Life of Rev. Mr. George Frosse.

23. Very fine Weather Still. Several persons here. I went down below again and took the air of the Door by stepping into the for Yard.

24. Rainy Weather yet I was wondrous Comfortable and brisk. Read and Writ almost all Day and till nine at Night—Studying a Sermon on Isa. 33, 14. Glory to God!

25. Was too well yesterday to hold it. To Day I was dull and feeble and could not study. Mr. J. Mead a.m. and Mr. Jenison and Mr. James Fay[7] p.m.

26. A pleasant Day, but I felt feeble and weak; and therefore looked upon the work of the Day with Fear and Concern. The people met at my House. I undertook what I might with God's Help to be able to do. I pray'd 20 Minutes and preach'd 30, on Ps. 90, 1. At Noon lay down and refresh'd me and din'd also with Some, tho deprav'd, Appetite. P.M. attempted another Exercise and held out 50 minutes in my sermon on the Same Text. Immediately after lay down and after a while was greatly reviv'd, and had a pleasant Eve, thro the wondrous Goodness of God. Mr. Jenison, from the North Side here in the Evening. O might we all have due Reflections on our frail and dying State! Lord make me know etc!

27. Sent by Mr. Tainter[8] to Boston. Mr. Stone[9] here, din'd and Spent the P.M. I was very lively a.m. Went into the Yard—tho a Cold yet a Clear Day. P.M. and Eve not without feverishness and faintness. But Blessed be God I am so far recruited! O may I Spend my Strength to His Glory!

28. Was pritty Comfortable in the Day But was feverish at Eve. N.B. a remarkable meeting at Mr. Harwoods (upon the Borders) last night. Great awakenings there and several Children of Mr. William Nurse and one of Mr. James Fay much wrought on. N.B. An Indian Youth one [blank] Cole, greatly carry'd out at those Meetings. Some of Westborough people that were present greatly question'd their regularity and Soundness, particularly Mr. Eliezer Rice.[10] May the Spirit of Truth lead us and guide us into all Truth for his Name's Sake! Grant us by all Means the Blessing and preserve us from the Evil! Old Mr. Mainard settling his Estate. At Eve Mr. Edward Goddard[11] here. Thomas Winchester thrashing my Rye.

29. Thomas Winchester thrashing Rye. I rode out a little way about my Place. Could Study with Some Comfort.

30. Thomas clear'd up the Rye. Brother Hicks having heard of my Sickness came to see me. Rain P.M. At Eve Mr. Whipple,

Mr. James and Neighbour David Mainard and Mr. Abner Newton (all of them having been at the Meeting at Harwoods last Monday night) came to See me and discourse of those so uncommon Things.

31. Brother Hicks return'd to Sutton. Bright and pleasant. Thro Divine Goodness and Mercy I felt very comfortably and was Chearfull. At Eve Captain Eager and Lieutenant Holloway[12] here, who had not been to see me in all my sickness, and Scarcely any other North Side men, tho many had rid by my Door. However I was glad to see 'em at last. Receiv'd a Letter from Brother Breck dated the 27th. He writes that all New Light is almost Extinct—and God grant that all New Light may be, intirely that the Old the true Gospel Light may Shine forth the more gloriously and victoriously!

Now I come to finish the Year, what Shame and Sorrow I had need to be fill'd with for my Ingratitude, unprofitableness and insensibility, when God has been so wondrous patient, So mercifull So faithfull, So abundant in Goodness towards Me! How graciously he has conducted me through all the Changes of the Year! and in Special, let me never forget his Mercifull and Compassionate Beliefs in my Sickness, So that Neither my Rheumatism, nor my Fever prevail'd upon me! O that I might know the mind and will of God concerning me! and what shall I render to him for all his Benefits towards Me! The Lord prepare my Heart to render as I ought. But O may my great Redeemer both wash me from my sins in his own Blood, and grant me the gracious and Sanctifying influences of his Blessed Spirit. Without these I can neither be acceptable in his sight, nor offer any Thing to His Glory.

### 1743
### JANUARY

1. I bent my mind (as far as my present engagement in my Preparations for the Sabbath would allow) to consider the Lord's gracious dealings with me in granting me the Beginnings of another year, and begging that all my old sins might be done away; and that I might Spend all the residue of my Time to the will of God and would Committ all the Events of this Year to Him. For I entreat I may both putt on the New.

2. I preach'd on Ps. 116, 9 at the Meeting House, Sermons of Gratitude for the Favours conferr'd in my Recovery from sickness, and granting us the New Year. I endeavour'd in some poor Manner to Engage after the Manner of David that I would walk, etc. See a loose Paper. Receiv'd from New Haven of November 29. N.B. Wilson Rawson[1] here at Evening with a Message from Mr. Door.[2]

3. Molly in an afflicted State by the Pains of her Stomach. I would have gone to Mrs. Stone that has been long sick, but there rose a very raw Wind which prevented Me.

4. The people of Grafton (where have been peculiar awakenings of late especially among the Children) have agreed to Spend most of the Days of this Week in Exercises of Religion and have Sent to some Number of Ministers, Mr. Hall, Goddard,[3] Webb of Uxbridge,[4] Bliss,[5] Haven[6] to preach to them. To Day Mr. Hall p.m. and Mr. Goddard in the Eve. May God grant them the Assistance and Measures of Wisdom which they need at this Time, and succeed them to his Glory! Neighbour Rogers and Chamberlain kill'd a Hogg for me (which when lean I bought of Brother Hicks) weigh'd 188. Wet Day.

5. Jejun. priv. The New Year. The Late Frown of Heaven in my sickness through which I am much Weaken'd and sett back in my Business. The present Times among us—call'd for no less. We Sent Ebenezer to Grafton but tho I design'd he should wait upon what Exerciser he could yet he return'd without going to Meeting at all. Mr. Hall a.m. and Mr. Bliss p.m. Mr. Goddard at Eve. My own Mind wrought very much on my inward State

[1] Reverend Aaron Smith.
[2] Son of Deacon Henry Prentice.
[3] Mrs. Seth Rice.
[4] Mrs. Benjamin Winchester.
[5] Wife of Captain John Maynard.
[6] David Maynard, an original settler.
[7] Son of Captain John Fay.
[8] Deacon Simon Tainter.
[9] Reverend Nathan Stone of Southborough.
[10] Eleazer Rice lived in Marlborough but was a member of the Westborough Church.
[11] Of Shrewsbury.

[12] William Holloway.
[1] Samuel Rawson of Milford, Mass. Adin Ballou, History of the Town of Milford (Boston 1882), p. 983.
[2] Reverend Joseph Dorr of Mendon.
[3] Reverend David Goddard of Leicester.
[4] Reverend Nathan Webb (Harvard 1725), the first minister at Uxbridge, 1731–1772. Sibley, VII, 617–619.
[5] Reverend Daniel Bliss of Concord.
[6] Reverend Elias Haven of Franklin.

and upon what God is doing among his people. Mr. Wilson here to acquaint me with the Death of Mr. John Snells child. Very fine pleasant Weather, especially a.m. Mr. Prentice[7] sent me a Letter of the third which I receiv'd this Evening to acquaint me with and desire my assistance in their Solemnitys.

6. Rainy a.m. Clear'd up p.m. Mr. Cushing[8] after the Funeral of Mr. Snells Child, here. He is not Satisfy'd about the Grafton Exercises. Mr. Bliss preach'd at Grafton a.m., Mr. Haven p.m.

7. Cold, yet my Wife and I ventur'd out to Mr. Daniel Stones to see his Wife in her low Condition. This was my first going out among my Neibours. N.B. Mrs. Stone very low, weak and under grievous Sores which endanger'd her Life. N.B. Mr. Tyler[9] from Mendon, there, with a Letter to me from the Society call'd Mill River in order for a Council. Mr. Haven preach'd a.m. at Grafton (which finish'd the public Exercises). Mr. Prentice himself preach'd at Eve at a private Meeting. Much has been said of these Exercises—some Number being very dissatisfy'd with them. Others much applauding and praising God for the great Grace appearing in them.

8. Mr. Jenison here.

9. On Matt. 11, 25, 26. Isa. 33, 14. Mrs. Thurston din'd with us. O that God would deeply impress us with the solemn Things of his Word! And that this might not go over without an abiding Effect.

10. Bright Day. Mr. Bradish here and din'd with me. At Eve Mr. Williams, Beriah Rice and James Fay—much pro and con respecting the Times.

11. My Wife and I rode up to Mr. Snells and to Shrewsbury to a Lecture by Mr. Hall. He preach'd on Rom. 2, 4. Many present. N.B. Mr. Harwood in his Fitts, panting, heaving, etc. We return'd at Evening but there was also an Evening Exercise By the Same Gentleman, Reverend Mr. Cushing being passive therein.

12. A Letter from Messers. Stone and Smith concerning a Monthly Lecture in their respective Towns. A great variety of Company. Deacon Forbush[10] in great Soul Distresses, yet disapproving of several Things in the private meetings of the enlightened. Young Fitch[11] of Norwich here by whom I wrote to my Cousin Daniel Needham[12] and to Mr. Wight.[13] Deacon Whipple[14] of Grafton came with his Brother of this Town and spent the Evening with me. N.B. his account of his Conversion last February. Yet neither can he allow of divers Things at the Private Meetings of these Times. N.B. a Private Meeting this very Eve at Mr. James Fays. I allow'd Ebenezer[15] and Rebecca Hicks[16] (under Special Charge) to go. N.B. settled and Ballanced with Daniel Forbush.

13. A number of Children were suppos'd to be much fill'd with the Spirit and carry'd out in Spiritual Joy last Night at Mr. Fays. An indian Girl in great Distress for her Brother—and Betty Fay[17] in Terrors. Of which and other Things occurring at the Meeting, there are various Sentiments. Mrs. Woods[18] of Marlborough here. Dr. Gott[19] and Lieutenant Woods with him here and din'd with us. A very open, moderate season for many Days past. Rain at Eve.

14. John Hicks here and lodg'd. At Eve Deacon Fay, greatly mov'd with the present Times, made me a visit.

15. Ebenezer rode to Mr. Allens to secure some Pork I had bespoke, and he went to Marlborough upon divers Messages. N.B. his return without an answer from Mr. [The diary ends abruptly at this point because the remaining part for 1743 has been lost].

---

[7] Reverend Solomon Prentice of Grafton.
[8] Reverend Job Cushing of Shrewsbury.
[9] Probably Captain Nathan Tyler.
[10] Jonathan Forbush.
[11] One of the sons of the late James Fitch. John G. Fitch, *Genealogy of the Fitch Family* (Olmsted, Ohio), pp. 21–22.
[12] Parkman's oldest sister, Mary had married Daniel Needham in 1702.
[13] Reverend Jabez Wight (Harvard 1721), the minister of Preston, Conn., 1726–1782. *Sibley*, VI, 582–584.
[14] James Whipple. Pierce, *Grafton*, pp. 596–598.
[15] Parkman's eldest son.
[16] Daughter of John Hicks.
[17] Elizabeth, the daughter of John Fay, Jr.
[18] Widow of Benjamin Woods.
[19] Benjamin Gott, the physician of Marlborough.

## 1743 [SEPTEMBER]

September 5[1]. I have great Reason to fear that I have had too Strong a Reliance and Dependence upon Form; and my Soul may have been led away by the snare. I begg of God to Deliver me, for his Mercy Sake! I have especially been afraid of my Birth Day Formalitys; and have often omitted to write down any Thing of the 2 last years; but indeed might well omitt it to write since there was So little done; and what was done, was done so lamely, brokenly and sinfully.

But now it has pleas'd the glorious and gracious God, through His adorable Patience and Long-suffering, to grant me this Day, having now been continued Forty Years. I cannot but take some Distinct Notice of it.

September 6. I observ'd yesterday as a Day of Fasting and prayer from morning to Night, as I was able. I endeavour'd in it the following Things—

1. To Recollect what God has done for me. And through this long Space I find that passage very much Verified in Deut. 2, 7. "He knoweth thy walking thro this Great Wilderness: These Forty Years the Lord thy God hath been with thee—thou hast lacked nothing."

2. To Reflect how I have conducted towards Him. And I find that it has been so Contrary, evil and ungratefull that He might very justly say of me that I have tempted him and proved him, tho I saw his work—and He may reasonably add that bitter Complaint, "Forty Years long was I grieved" by him. For O how I have erred from God and have disregarded his ways! O how I have provok'd Him So that He might even Swear in His wrath that I should never enter into His Rest. Ps. 95, 9, 10, 11.

3. I endeavour'd in some Measure to Consider my Frailty; and would fain Reallize that I must Die—that I know not how soon. I took some notice of Ps. 90, 9. Ps. 39, 4, 5, 7, 12.

4. I took some pains in Examining my state anew—was not a little assisted by the Hints in the Life of Mr. Henry Gearing.[2] And tho there are Some Marks which I can't Speak plainly [?] to yet (Blessed be the name of God for his Grace to So vile a Wretch!) I found so much as gives me (I think) Ground to hope I am not utterly destitute of the Life of God. O may God be pleas'd to pity me in my Darkness and afford me Light, in my Corruptness, and subdue my sins and Lusts, and sanctify me; and in my Inability for this service, and furnish quicken and Strengthen me! I hope it is the Grief and Burthen of my Soul that I am So exceedingly behind, and so destitute, and empty, when others are springing forward, and ready for every good work.

5. I carry'd to God the State of Religion in this Day, in these Parts; and sought Divine Direction respecting the approaching Fast at Grafton, at which my Assistance is desir'd; and the State of this Town who are much Divided about building a meeting House, Or Houses, and are this Day Met upon that Affair.

6. I considered in some Imperfect Manner what God now expects from Me during my remaining Short Continuance in the World: and O that I may be able to give up a good Account when I shall be call'd out of it.

## 1744
### JANUARY

If I have heretofore taken Some Notice of the wondrous Patience and Longsuffering of God towards me in Time past, what far more increas'd Reason to now! O that Since God is vouchsafing and protecting His rich Mercys to me, it might please Him to add This Great Mercy to all the other Grace to enable me to make a right Improvement thereof!

The Thoughts and Conversation of People Seem to be very much engross'd by the Appearing and Continuance of the Comet in the West. I think it the Largest that I have ever Seen, and that it comes Nearer and Nearer to the Earth. I desire it may put me in Mind of the Greatness, Glory and Power, and the wisdom and So great Dominion of the infinite God whose works these are; And that I may bring to remembrance and have an abiding sense of that Day that Shall burn as an Oven, when this

---

[1] Entries for Sept. 1743, are from the Natalitia.
[2] [John Shower], *Some Account of the Holy Life and Death of Mr. Henry Gearing* (Boston, 1704).

Earth also shall be sett on Fire and, all the wicked shall be Consumed. Mal. 4, 1. 2 Epistle of Pet. 3, 7.

I preach'd on Col. 1, 21. Mr. Coolidge tho in Town yet not well nor at meeting.

2. Mr. Garfield of Shrewsbury here. Conversation mainly of the State of Religion in these Times.

3. Was to have assisted Mr. Cushing in keeping a Fast at the House of one Samuel Brown in Shrewsbury, who is in a distress'd if not distracted Frame and has been so for Several Years without Relief. But it was Such a storm of Snow that I was prevented. Short of Wood but Nathan Maynard kindly helpfull in Splitting what was at the Door, etc.

4. Nathan Maynard, Daniel Bellows,[1] Benjamin Whipple[2] and [blank] came and got me a present Supply of wood. P.M. Colonel Nahum Ward[3] here. Seems to have a Concern about Religion. At Eve Abner Maynard[4] of Shrewsbury here and brought me a Token of respect from the Society I had lately preach'd to in that Town. 20 shillings old Tenor from these Lads.

5. Preach'd at the private Meeting at Deacon Forbush's[5] on Matt. 11, 26. N.B. Lieutenant Tainter sick. N.B. after Meeting relating the Story of Mercy Wheeler[6] of Plainfield her wonderful Recovery, Mrs. Whitney Scarcely Contains. [?] N.B. My wife went with me and we were at old Mr. Rice's in the Evening.

6. I have been acquainting myself somewhat with that Excellent Man's Life and writings Mr. Robert Bolton.[7] May God Bless them to my highest Good!

7. [Blank].

8. Col. 1, 21, a. and p.m. Mr. Coollidge[8] here.

9. Another fruitless Town Meeting, concerning My Support and Dividing the Town. This Meeting was oversatt by the plan that several Men were not Warned. Brother Hicks here and lodged. I had Some perplexity by Means of Neighbour John Rogers his having promis'd me money and continually Disappointed me.

10. Dr. Smith here and din'd with us. P.M. I visited the Wife of Mr. Samuel Fay junior who has been long confin'd.

11. Pleasant Day again.

12. A Lecture to young People on Prov. 7, 7, and by my Closeness upon them with respect to Unclean Practices, and the [illegible] of Behaviour among Youth which lead thereto.

13. We kill'd a second Hogg, Weight 265, by Neighbour Ebenezer Maynard and Thomas Winchester.

14. Thomas Winchester cutts Wood for me in Neighbour Chamberlains Name Gratis.

15. On Coloss. 1, 21, a.m. On Prov. 7, 7, p.m. Mr. Coollidge here.

16. Cold, Windy. Neighbour Wheeler here, he brought 2 Bushels of Rie at 16 shillings per Bushel. John Roberts[9] of Grafton was also here, to ask my Advice concerning his applying to Books and Learning in order to his Education for the Ministry.

17. Thomas Winchester Came and Elijah Rice to dress Flax, but it was So very Cold that they could not Stand it, they broke off and got Wood for me a spurt and went off.

18. [Blank].

19. Mr. Cushing here. Troubles in Shrewsbury increase. Zebediah Johnson,[10] Lieutenant Stone,[11] etc. very uneasy as if they had not Spiritual Diet. Mr. Cushing and I din'd at Ensign Maynards[12] with Colonel Nahum Ward, Colonel Williams and others at the giving out a Number more of Commissions—and particularly Ensign Maynard is now Constituted a Captain. N.B.

Lieutenant Lee of Worcester his unguarded Talk, both at Captain Maynards and at my House.

20. Nine Men came and got Wood. Neighbour Hezekiah Pratt, James Bradish, Eleazer Williams, Noah How, Paul Newton,[13] Elijah Rice, Thomas Winchester, Solomon Baker[14] and James Maynard. 12 Large Load. N.B. Trouble in the Young Mens Society on account of Richard Roberts a young Man of Grafton who is hir'd to keep School on the South west Corner of the Town, and who being a serious and Religious person many are desirous should meet with them but Nathan Maynard chiefly opposes it (he being a New Light) and they bring the Difficulty to me. I sent for Nathan and he Came and gave his Reasons. But I advis'd that Roberts defer his meeting till the Society can be a little more Compos'd.

21. Thomas and Elijah at the Flax—but I was not well myself one Day after another.

22. Coloss. 1, 21, a.m. 2 Pet. 3, 9. Mr. Coollidge constantly dines with me on Lords Days, but it is grievous to me either to ask him to say Grace, or cast the Shame upon him at refusing him. My Heart akes exceedingly for him.

23. Reverend Mr. Smith[15] of Marlborough made a Visit. We don't meet without some Contests about the Times. He Thinks that there are as many and as deeply heart searching sermons among those Term'd opposers as any others whosoever etc. He din'd with me but it was at a Time when a Number of my Neighbours were here getting Wood. Viz. Mr. Grout,[16] Thomas Whitney, Harrington, Bowman[17] Daniel Forbush, Jonathan, Phinehas and Eli Forbush, Daniel Stone, Eliezer and Jeb Rice, Benjamin and Daniel Fay, each of which with a Team. Dan Warrin, James and Ebenezer Miller, Eleazer and Oliver Whitney, Samuel Baker. N.B. What wood was at the Door before and what there is now brought amounts to at least 50 Load now in the Piles, D. Gr.

24. At Dinner at Captain Maynards, both my wife and I with Captain Tyler who with a Considerable Number and Mr. Frost[18] their minister is conducting his New spouse[19] Home to Mendon.

25. I went out with Design to go to see Lieutenant Tainter who continues sick, but the Rain prevented my going any further than Captain Bakers. N.B. There was Mr. Marshal Baker and his wife.

26. Went to Lieutenant Tainters who is weak and feeble yet. Was also at Stephen Fays. His Brother James there. He acquaints me with Mr. Halls[20] going to Framingham shortly to preach there. Desir'd me to let him preach at his House. I chose he should at the Meeting House and wrote a Letter to Mr. Hall for that End, which he took the Care to Convey.

27. Letter from Brother Samuel Parkman. N.B. his wife distracted about the Comet. Moderate weather.

28. Cold. Storm of Snow.

29. On 2 Cor. 5, 20. Mr. Coollidge, Mrs. Chamberlain. At Eve Deacon Miles[21] of Concord and his wife at my House. Concord, by their Telling in much Disquietment Yet. At this Time I remembered the wormwood and the Gall.[22]

30. Another Town Meeting about my support etc. They voted but £200—Old Tenor. The North Side very Resolute. They urg'd that the Town gave me last year more than I needed or desir'd, that provisions were cheaper, etc., whereas I never gave so much as for both my Beef and my Rie—and also for Labour. The Moderator Mr. Livermore[23] would not as much as Send me any Committee or Message of what they had done—said it was not in the Warrant. The Year has been of far greater Labours than Ever with me for them and of far greater Charge on the Account of the Company etc., by means of the multiply'd Exercises, Lectures, etc. But God grant me an Even mind and resignation

[1] Son of Eleazer Bellows.
[2] Son of Francis Whipple.
[3] Of Shrewsbury.
[4] Son of Sergeant Simon Maynard, one of the founders of the Shrewsbury church.
[5] Jonathan Forbush.
[6] See Benjamin Lord, *God Glorified in His Works, of Providence and Grace. A Remarkable Instance of it, in the Various and Signal Deliverances, that Evidently Appears to be Wrought for Mrs. Mercy Wheeler, in Plainfield* (Boston, 1743).
[7] *The Works of the Reverend . . . Robert Bolton . . . as They were Finished by Himselfe in his Life Time. The Life and Death of the Author*, by E. B[aghaw].
[8] Samuel Coolidge, sometime schoolmaster and preacher.
[9] Roberts didn't pursue his interest. Later in 1746 he married Elizabeth Fay of Westborough. Pierce, *Grafton*, p. 559.
[10] Ward, *Shrewsbury*, p. 334.
[11] Isaac Stone, one of the first selectmen of Shrewsbury.
[12] Stephen Maynard of Westborough.
[13] Son of Deacon Josiah Newton.
[14] Son of Edward Baker.
[15] Aaron Smith.
[16] Joseph Grout.
[17] James Bowman.
[18] The Reverend Amariah Frost (Harvard 1740), the minister of Milford, Mass., 1742–1792. *Sibley*, X, 494–496.
[19] Mary, daughter of John Cloyes of Framingham.
[20] The Reverend David Hall of Sutton.
[21] Samuel Miles.
[22] The anniversary of the first Mrs. Parkman's death.
[23] Jonathan Livermore.

to His will! O that I may also have Grace to Examine my Ends, aims and Views, Mr. Whitneys Dauter Mary here—also Brother Hicks. At Evening Captain Warrin and Lieutenant Forbush[24] here.

31. Not willing to perplex myself any longer about Mr. Rogers's Small Debt, at his Request, made known to me by Mr. Chamberlain,[25] I transferred the Business, to Mr. Chamberlain—not willing to use the Law if by any means, tho to my Hurt, I could issue this troublesome Affair.

## FEBRUARY [1744]

1. Mr. Hall came and preach'd my Lecture on Luke 21, 36, which Lecture I was the more willing to appoint both because of our Standing so much in need of Quickening and Awakening—and because it happen'd to be the first Wednesday of the Month, according to the manner of our beginning the Lectures last Year. Reverend Mr. Cushing here. Mr. Coollidge also din'd with us. N.B. After Lecture Captain Hazeltine[1] came with a message from Upton Church to Mr. Hall and me, acquainting us with their increasing Divisions and praying that Five Ministers would go over on the 14 Day of the Month and endeavour their Help. The other Ministers Mr. Peabody,[2] Mr. Bliss, and Mr. Prentice of Grafton. But he brought no Letters for the Church did not go into the form of voting as a Church nor would Mr. Weld lead them into any, nor make any Records thereof—but they had mutually agreed to choose by Partys each side Two, and then to pitch upon one in which both could agree—and to these Things Mr. Weld[3] Consented—and he the said Messanger was come in the Name of the Church accordingly. We Consented to go and I wrote to Mr. Peabody, committing it to Mr. Hall who was going to Framingham to forward it. N.B. Mr. Jonathan Burnap[4] in the Evening here. Disturbances in Hopkinton are risen to great Heights and Richard and Nathaniel Smith[5] are sent to Jayl for breaking up the Worship last Sabbath. Great Troubles also in Leicester. Reverend Mr. Goddard[6] in such Darkness about his own State that the last Sabbath, though Communion Day, he went not out to preach, but Captain Denny[7] going to him he sent a Letter to the People.

2. I gave Mr. Coollidge what Serious and affectionate Admonitions I could. The Lord add his Blessing! My wife and I rode over to Mrs. McAllisters to visit her in great Trouble and near her Time. N.B. Mrs. Thankful Rice[8] met me with a Confession written with her own Hand of her Drunkenness—but could not give her Encouragement that I would read it, except she would reform, at least give better Tokens of it than she had ever yet done. The Comet appears larger, the Stream from it much greater than a Month agoe.

3. David Crossby[9] who lately made me a pair of Boots price 3. 12.0 which I paid him for. N.B. I had some free Converse with him concerning the Excesses of some in these Times. He din'd with us. Sent by him to Reverend Mr. Townshend[10] of Needham.

4. Somewhat Rainy. Expected Mr. Brown,[11] preacher, here that we might Change, but did not come from one Saturday to another.

5. On Ps. 110, 3 former part. Mr. Coollidge here. O might it please God to make it the Day of his power with our Souls! At Eve Mr. Pierce[12] took a Letter from me for Mr. Burnap to carry to Mr. Hobby[13] of Reading.

6. Mr. Cunnable of Boston, and his son, in their Return from Deerfield, here and din'd with me. Sent by him Monsieur Missons[14] vol. 1 to my Kinsman Parkman.

7. At Mr. Rogers[15] to see his wife who is sick. A Town Meeting respecting the Dividing the Town—but nothing Done.

8. Moderate Weather. The Comet large yet.

9. Old Mrs. Wheeler, aged 95, dy'd. Snow. Engag'd to go to her Funeral if good Weather.

10. [No entry].

11. A Smart Snow Storm, but clear'd off P.M. The Time appointed for Mrs. Wheelers buryal is the forenoon, so that I could not attend it. But in the afternoon I borrow'd an Horse and went to meet them at the Grave; but meeting the young man (who return'd the buryal Cloth) a little beyond Captain Maynards, I return'd. Have the trouble of daily dressing my Mares Legg ever since my ride to Mr. McAllisters.[16]

12. On Ps. 110, 3, former part. Mr. Coollidge. Mrs. Grow.

13. The Comet almost disappears in the Evening but I expect it may be Visible in the Morning. Mr. Francis Whipple brought his Brother Lambson to see me at Evening—as was also Captain Warrin. Religious Affairs more steddily manag'd at Ipswich than in Time past.

14. In my riding to Upton I call'd at Mr. Thurstons[17] who acquaints me that a Number of North Side people met those of the South, last night at Captain Fays[18] to gather subscriptions to a petition to the General Court that the Town may be divided. At the Same Meeting Eliezer Rice broke his legg by wrestling with Silas Pratt. I proceeded to Upton and met Mr. Prentice of Grafton on the Road. We went to Mr. Sadlers[19]—waited for Mr. Hall, but in Vain. Heard that neither Mr. Peabody nor Mr. Bliss were like to come. But we at length proceeded to Lieutenant Tafts,[20] where we were directed to Meet—and at 10 o'clock but I had no word of either Time or place whereas Mr. Prentice had a formal Letter from a Number of the Brethren Signifying both (I think) distinctly. At Lieutenant Tafts were the Brethren gather'd, and there we found not only Mr. Weld, but Mr. Peabody, who had been waiting an Hour or Two for our Coming. We din'd and then conferr'd together. Mr. Weld was with us when we pray'd by our Selves, (which fell to me to perform), But he was absent for an hour or Two after it while we Settl'd ourselves. When the Church came in Mr. Peabody pray'd. After which we made some Overtures but Considering that Five of those which the major part of the Church (as that party was who were against Mr. Weld) had chose, had not come they were against Submitting their Cause to us. We saw it was in Vain to try to reconcile them. Neither could we do any thing that would be likely to End well, and therefor determin'd to advise them to Choose a Council. This we conducted to Effect and assisted them in forming all the votes, and watch'd over them thro the whole Affair (Except in the Nominations, and upon their nominating Mr. Peabody and me we each of us as modestly as we could declin'd) but they finish'd the whole that night tho it was late and almost worried me down. Mr. Prentice pray'd before we broke up. Mr. Peabody is requested by Mr. Weld to preach a sermon in the forenoon tomorrow before he leaves the place, and I am desir'd to preach p.m. Thus we disperse. Mr. Peabody and I lodged together.

15. By Day we wake with the Silent sight of a Young Fellow in the room getting up from his Girl in the t'other Bed in the Same Room with us. Astonishing Boldness and Impudence! nor could we let the Girl go off without a brief Lecture. But we kept the matter for the Parents for the Time. We all broke Fast at Mr. Nelsons. Mr. Peabody preach'd an Excellent sermon on Col. 1, 27, latter part, and after sermon left us. I din'd in quiet at Deacon Nelsons with Mr. Weld, Mr. Dorr and his Dauter, for I had obtain'd leave to do as I would about the Afternoon Exercise, and I saw so much of the extra fervency of many of the people to

---

24 Samuel Forbush of Westborough.
25 Ebenezer Chamberlain of Westborough.

1 John Hazeltine, a prominent resident of Upton.
2 The Reverend Oliver Peabody of Natick.
3 The Reverend Thomas Weld of Upton.
4 Of Hopkinton.
5 See *Sibley*, VI, 430, and *Manual of the First Congregational Church in Hopkinton, Mass.* (Boston, 1881), pp. 27–28.
6 David Goddard, the New-Light Minister at Leicester.
7 Daniel Denny of Leicester. Emory Washburn, *Historical Sketches of the Town of Leicester* (Boston, 1860), pp. 354–355.
8 Wife of Josiah Rice.
9 The shoemaker of Shrewsbury.
10 The Reverend Jonathan Townsend (Harvard, 1716), the minister at Needham, 1720–1762. *Sibley*, VI, 150–153.
11 Probably Josiah Brown, sometime preacher and schoolmaster at Sterling.
12 William Pierce of Westborough.
13 The Reverend William Hobby.

14 François M. Misson, *A New Voyage to Italy* (London, 1695), 2 vols.
15 John Rogers of Westborough.
16 John McAllister of the north part of Westborough.
17 Joseph Thurston of Westborough.
18 Deacon John Fay of Westborough.
19 Captain John Sadler of Upton.
20 Elisha Taft.

have Mr. Prentice preach that I gave way. He din'd at Mr. Sadlers—and he preach'd p.m. on Exod. 5, 10 latter part, and 11, 12. At Eve I rode up to Captain Hazzletines and thence (accompany'd by Mr. Fisk[21] of Upton to pilot me) got over safe to Westborough and found my Family well, after the troublesome Turn.

16. Dr. Smith here with Mr. Bucknams[22] sermons. Paul Fay here. Captain Fay[23] at Evening who brot a Letter for our Young schoolmaster Richard Roberts, unbosoming his Troubles and griefs.

17. A Considerable Snow Storm.

18. [No entry].

19. On Job 36, 24, 25. Jer. 8, 5. I Stopp'd the Church to read Upton Church Letter. Voted to Comply with their Request But insisted for Two Delegates—and Two Brethren insisted for the Choices to be by written Votes. Deacon Forbush had the most votes the first Time, and Mr. Nathaniel Whitney the second but neither of them the majority of the whole. Some Debate arose and I was very uneasy to have this Interruption on the Lords Day; I therefore adjourn'd to next Tuesday one o'Clock. I inadvertently Said those persons were chose—designing no other than to let the Church know how the Votes stood—and that the Majority of the Church was not for them and I actually Said I know this is not the Mind of the Church, And it being the Sabbath I conceiv'd they would either confirm them that had the most Votes or take some other short Method. But Captain Baker in Heat Said it was Collusion etc. Upon which I meekly pray'd him to be satisfy'd and overlook it, for it was verily my own Inadvertence that I did not expect such a choice, was willing the Church Should have their own Choice. Mr. Coollidge here at noon.

20. I rode to Neighbour Thurstons and visited Neighbour Eliezer Rice under his Lameness. Was at James Fays and Winchesters. Richard Roberts gone to my House.

21. Jedidiah Rice[24] went Early in the Morn with a Letter to Mr. Prentice of Grafton, and return'd me Mr. Prentices answer. Brother Hicks for Cambridge. Robert Evans Leather Dresser and seller, here and I bought Two of him. He din'd with us. Church Meeting by Adjournment. After Prayer we proceeded to Choose Delegates for the Council at Upton. Brother Francis Whipple and Deacon Newton were Chosen, and no Difficulty arose. All, or the Chief, Debate we had was from my recommending it to them previous to the Choice that no Brother ought to be Chose who had Interest in that Town. The Members of the Council Should be disinterested persons. It was upon this mov'd to me that no Inhabitant of Upton might vote; which was freely yielded to. After this Affair I pray'd the Church to take into (which took off Brother Zebulon Rice) consideration the Case of Neighbour Cornelius Cook;[25] and the Church Saw cause to send a Committee to him, viz. Deacon Forbush, Brother James Bradish and Brother James Bradish junior. With prayer and Blessing the Meeting Concluded. Before Captain Baker went home I had a little Conference with him upon his unreasonable Warmth respecting my undesign'd and (as to me) innocent Oversight on the Lords Day, and I told him it may be he did not know the Meaning of the Word Collusion, which imply'd that there was intent to Deceive. He did not make any Reply to that, but said it look'd to him at the Juncture of my declaring those men Chosen that I design'd to let it go if they (He and Brother Whipple) had not Spoke—which verily I hope I should not. He Spake about a fair and full meeting of the Church, and upon asking him what he intended by that? He answer'd he meant when the North side was duly Notify'd. I told him the Church was notify'd publickly in the Appointed place; and if any did absent themselves I could not either go after them or hire a man to goe round like a Constable to Warn them. As for their drawing off, it had never been in such good Order as they ought to have done it in. They had never acquaint'd the Church tho under Covenant to hold Com-

munion and tho I had advis'd them to consider their Duty. I told him that Certainly as to Such peculiar pains and Trouble to notifie them they did not Deserve it. This expression he did not desire to hear. But for the foresaid Reasons and their late Conduct toward me in Cutting off my support, I thought to be just and fitt, upon which he declar'd himself Satisfy'd.

22. Mrs. Bacon of Needham and her Daughter Rice of Worcester here, brought me a Letter from Reverend Mr. Townsend[26] concerning Some Books he had of Mine (Lord Kings Biography) and some I had of his (Echards Eccl. His.).[27]

23. [No entry].

24. [No entry].

25. Snow Storm.

26. On Job 36, 24, 25 on occasion of the Comet. Mr. Coollidge and Mr. Thurston din'd with me. Letter from Mr. Hobby of Reading, that he Cannot come up into our parts of the Country tho he has desir'd it.

27. Mrs. Hannah Forbush (the Deacons wife) and Mrs. Mary Steward made us a Visit.

28. Fine Weather.

29. Heard that Roxbury new, handsome Meeting House was burnt down last sabbath by means of a stove in Judge Dudleys[28] Pew.

### MARCH [1744]

1. Preach'd my Lecture my Self. Repeated on Jude 10, 21. Stop'd the Church to See what their minds were respecting Grafton Members communicating with us—having been ask'd Several Times by John Bradish to grant this Privilege, and they (Several of them, viz. Mr. Miller,[1] Mr. Whipple, Deacon Newton,[2] as I remember all that Spake) manifested that they could not consent to have any Members of that Church come to Communion here whilst they were in Such Divisions, and were (as at that very Time) agitating and ripening their affairs on for a Council. After meeting Lieutenant Forbush and I admonish'd Brother Jonathan Bellows for his late Conduct and call'd him to Repentence. Conference in the Evening with Brother Seth Rice about his Sister Thankful who had Some Time agoe deliver'd me a Confession which I esteem'd Lame and unsound. He took a Note from me to her.

2. I understand the Comet has not been Seen for Some Dayes.

3. There arose a great Storm of Snow.

4. The Storm so great that but few came to Meeting. Deacon Forbush[3] came not with the Elements. Yet I went on with my Sermon on 1 Cor. 11, 26, though the Sacrament was not Celebrated. P.M. on Job 36, 24, 25. Deacon Fay, and Mr. Joseph Crosby of Worcester din'd with me.

5. Town Meeting. I pray'd with them. Sent in a Letter to the Town concerning their making so Slender a provision for my Support this Year, and sent a writing to the Moderator praying him in my name to notifie the people of the Communion next Lords Day, and a Sermon to be tomorrow to young people on the north side of the Town. N.B. I Sent another Letter (which I prepar'd last week) to Reverend Mr. Prentice[4] of Grafton per Mr. Benjamin Winchester.[5] Mr. Jonathan Burnap here and din'd with us. N.B. Reckon'd with Captain Maynard—fell in his Debt £9 old Tenor. N.B. The Middle of the Town so much the Lead at this Meeting as that the Select Men were Captain Warrin,[6] Captain Baker,[7] Deacon Newton, Captain Maynard,[8] Lieu-

[21] Ebenezer Fisk.

[22] The Reverend Nathan Bucknam, the minister of Medway published *Ability to, and Fidelity in the Ministry . . . Preach'd at Shrewsbury . . . October 26, 1743* (Boston, 1743).

[23] Captain John Fay.

[24] Son of Perez Rice.

[25] Cook was guilty of "profane swearing." In Jan., 1743, when Cook's confession of this offence was read to the church, not one member voted to accept it.

[26] Jonathan Townsend of Needham.

[27] Laurence Echard (1670?–1730), the English historian published *A General Ecclesiastical History from the Nativity of our Blessed Saviour to the First Establishment of Christianity by Humane Laws under Emperour Constantine the Great* (London, 1702).

[28] Paul Dudley, Justice of the Superior Court of Judicature. "On the Lord's day, February 26, 1743/4, soon after Divine service in the afternoon, a fire broke out in this Meeting House by which this large and costly building was burnt to the ground. It occurred as 'twas thought by a stove accidentally upset with fire in it unperceived which was left in a Pew after the assembly was dismissed." Walter E. Thwing, *History of the First Church in Roxbury* (Boston, 1908), p. 142.

[1] James Miller.

[2] Josiah Newton.

[3] Jonathan Forbush.

[4] Solomon Prentice.

[5] Of Westborough. He had married the first Mrs. Parkman's cousin.

[6] Daniel Warrin, an original settler.

[7] Edward Baker, an original settler.

[8] John Maynard.

tenant Forbush.[9] N.B. Thomas Winchester here at Evening but no agreement yet.

6. My Wife rode with Me to Mr. Nathaniel Oakes where I preach'd to Young people from Rom. 8, 7. After Meeting at Captain Eagers. May God grant Success.

7. Surpriz'd with an unaccountable Letter from Mr. Prentice of Grafton, who tells me that he read my Letter complaining that they did not call Wheeler to account in presence of People of their Church and that they were all of the Mind to prosecute the Affair and he was so desir'd to write to me to Come up to their Church meeting tomorrow and produce my Witnesses, etc. To which I return'd an Answer manifesting my Astonishment that he had Expos'd my Private Letter and friendly Communication with him as my Brother and that I Should not attend Said meeting. The Bearer of Each Letter was Thomas Winchester. P.M. Deacon Newton here, reckon'd with him and paid all except for his line. Mr. Richard Salter[10] from Mansfield here and lodg'd with us.

8. Mr. Matthew Rice here acquainting me with the Good Effect of the Sermon at Nathaniel Oakes the Day before Yesterday; and that they earnestly desire the Copy of it for the press, and will Satisfie me for my pains in preparing it for them. P.M. I rode over to Neighbour Seth Rice's to discourse with him about his sister Thankfulls Confession and what success he had had in his Endeavours with her. Thence I rode up to Colonel Nahum Wards[11] and conferr'd with him upon what the Law had provided in the Case of Secret Letters disclos'd, and whether the Author or the receiver is Chargeable with the Mischief arising from such Divulging? Return'd again the Same Evening. Mr. Salter left us, for Boston uncertain yet whether he shall settle at Mansfield.

9. A.M. Aaron Hardy and Simon Tainter of Grafton both here, concerned lest I had brought myself into a snare by sending such a Letter to Mr. Prentice for that it was much fear'd that the witnesses which I depended upon to Support my Charge, would fail me. They Staid and din'd with me. P.M. Mrs. Thankfull Rice here—and had no difficulty with her about Altering her Confession. I was exceeding uneasy at Evening what might be the Event of my Letter to Mr. Prentice—because if I should escape Trouble in the Law, yet Should fall under much Blame and reproach for my Credulousness and Abounding Charity towards the New Lights, who in many Instances have (Its said commonly) been found too forgetfull where they ought to remember both words and Facts. N.B. The proposals of a Council at Grafton thrown up for the present and a Fast is now appointed instead thereof but the aggriev'd resolve to have a Council

10. I rose very Early and Committing my Case to God I went (as I was able) in his Fear and trusting in his goodness to Phinehas Hardys of Grafton and thence to Deacon Miriams,[12] He being one of the witnesses etc. as above. He and his wife treated me with great Civility and Courteousness and generousness, of their own accord providing an Handsome Breakfast of Chocolat etc. etc. for me—and Deacon freely Said that what he remember'd of the Conversation we had with Wheeler he would faithfully relate and would Stand by Steadfastly. He affirm'd that tho he could not remember the particular words yet he did that the Drift and Substance of it imply'd his acknowledging that he was Guilty of Fornication with Lydia Pratt etc. He said moreover that he had not refus'd to testify—but had refus'd to Complain of Wheeler, because he had privately forgiven him—But when lawfully call'd was able and was willing to say much more. I ask'd him whether I could take minutes of what he said and he freely consented and Signed it. He having repeatedly assur'd me that he would not fail me, I took leave, and return'd by Simon Tainters and Phinehas Hardy. At Mr. Hardys I din'd. He told me that His wife and He had heard Deacon Miriam say that Wheeler had heretofore deny'd, and then had confess'd his Guiltiness etc.—and they had both of them heard Mr. Harwood affirm the Same Concerning Himself, that Wheeler had deny'd it and then confess'd it to Him.

But James Harrington (they Said) was but just gone from their House who was positive that Wheeler had first ly'd and then owned etc. Mr. Harrington was right in my road, so I took therefor a pen and Ink and Hardy and I went to him, who freely related the whole, was willing I should take minutes of it, and freely sign'd it before us who sign'd it as witnesses. Hardy was so kind as to ride with me to Winchesters who took of me my Letter of the 7th to Mr. Prentice, in order to Convey it—and he affirm'd before Mr. Hardy that the Letter he took of me was well seal'd; and that he deliver'd it So to John Cooper of Grafton to Convey it as directed. Having thus clear'd my way, I return'd Home about 3 p.m. to finish what preparations I could for the Sabbath, having look'd upon Myself as call'd and bound in Duty to look after this affair with what thoroughness I could, even though I Should be oblig'd to omitt making a fresh sermon for the afternoon tomorrow. But having had such success in my Endeavours to secure my Innocence I was both thankful to God and Calm in my own Breast. I would have visited Mr. Prentice if it had been another season—but as to his Injury done me in disclosing my Letter I look'd upon it as rather owing to his Inadvertence than wickedness and was ready to forgive it.

11. Lieutenant Tainter came to me in the Morning before Exercises and Spake to me of Mr. Coollidges[13] Communicating, but I immediately put an Effectual stop to it and told him I would not hear one word about it. Mr. Coollidge himself came to me but I would in no wise give way, but utterly refus'd. I preach'd on 1 Cor. 11, 26 and Celebrated the Communion. O might it prove for the Divine Glory and our highest Comfort! Mr. Coollidge din'd with me, as did Deacon Fay, Deacon Newton and wife and Jonathan Tainter. P.M. preach'd on John 15, 9 latter part repeating Sermon 2 on Jude 4, 21. Propounded Paul Fay[14] in order to his being Baptiz'd and took the Churchs Consent to my Baptizing on the North side of the Town, and particularly Mr. McAllisters[15] Child.

12. I rode down to Colonel Wards[16] at Southborough that I might Consult Dalton[17] and other Lawyers, upon Letters Sent for one friend to another in a private and Secret Manner upon Witnesses etc. Return'd without much Success, the Colonel being from home. I call'd at his son Elisha's, Dalton being there.

13. Deacon Newton, Brother Whipple and I rode to Upton. Arriv'd at Mr. Welds[18] House but a little after 10. Found Mr. Bucknam[19] and Peabody there, but understood to our grief that the Council were to be entertain'd at Separate Houses each Party their own churchs; nor was it possible to alter it. We waited till 3 p.m. before the rest came that we might form into a Council. Mr. Peabody having been more peculiarly chose by both sides than either of us, who were the Senior Ministers, he was thought the fittest for Moderator from that Circumstance as well as his Superior Powers and Abilitys. It was So late that we could do little more than receive their Papers and number them and hear a few Debates. I think we made some Overtures to the Contending Partys touching mutual Condescensions and Comprimising matters—but they were in Vain. Rachel Wheeler of Grafton, heretofore Woods of Upton, had reveal'd some of the Conduct of Reverend Mr. Weld who heretofore Courted her to her Husband—and her Evidence was given in by the Adverse party to Support one of their Charges—but it was given in such strong Terms that Mr. Weld had obtain'd a Warrant for her, and Mr. Bruce[20] the Sheriff was dedie in Diem at Mr. Welds all the Time of the Council. By means of this Affair all accommodations of Differences were clogg'd. Adjourn'd to the Meeting House Tommorrow.

14. See the Minutes of the Council. N.B. Justice Taft[21] Swore Rachel Wheeler at her Fathers House—which was a great obstruction to all Hopes of accommodation. N.B. The Councils

9 Thomas Forbush, Jr.

10 Richard Salter (Harvard 1739), who was ordained minister at Mansfield, Conn., June 27, 1744. Sibley, X, 404–409.

11 The prominent citizen of Shrewsbury.

12 Joseph Merriam, a pioneer of Grafton, who served as deacon for fifty-five years. Pierce, Grafton, pp. 532–533.

13 Samuel Coolidge.

14 The son of Gershom Fay of the north part of Westborough. Orlin P. Fay, Fay Genealogy (Cleveland, 1898), pp. 331–333.

15 John McAllister or McCollister.

16 William Ward, a justice of the peace.

17 A work of Michael Dalton (1584–1648?), the English lawyer. Perhaps The Countrey Justice, Conteyning the Practice of the Justices of the Peace out of Their Sessions (London, 1618). It also appeared in later editions.

18 The Reverend Thomas Weld.

19 The Reverend Nathan Bucknam of East Medway.

20 No Sheriff Bruce is recorded by William H. Whitmore, The Massachusetts Civil List (Albany, 1870).

21 Daniel Taft, justice of the peace.

affairs greatly delay'd by the other part of the Councils not attending in season. But we could not obtain to dine or Supp together— not alternately nor any Way what ever. At the Meeting House A.M. At Mr. Welds p.m. and Evening.

15. Often weary and despairing to bring any Thing to issue— but We attended publickly both a. and p.m., to hear etc. See the minutes. Three Things dampt the opposing Brethren. One, the confusion they were thrown into in trying to pick up their Reasons for Separating from 3 different papers—and the Immethodicalness of their paper of Complaints. 2. They were disappointed much in what they expected from Mrs. Matchetts Testimony— as they were in some others. 3. The great Acceptance that Mr. Welds Sermons met with in the Council and assembly instead of being condemn'd and despis'd, as they who had separated from him pretended they had reason to. In the Evening offers again made respecting accommodations but to little purpose—tho the adverse Brethren were much more dispos'd to it than heretofore. They were now heartily sorrowful for the Wheeler witness. The Council were to draw up something against the Morning for the Brethren them to Consider on.

16. Mr. Peabody, Bucknam and I had partly drawn up Something which when Mr. Hall[22] came to us conceiv'd to Contain More than the Separating Brethren would conform to so that he sat down to draw anew But when the Council met, neither would his Draught be accepted. Mr. Weld declar'd his utter and positive determination to have Nothing done respecting Rachel Wheeler till he had taken Advice; notwithstanding that Ensign Woods and his Wife, Dauter, Friends etc. were all of them very Desirous to throw all that Matter up and acknowledge both their folly and their sin. P.M. at Eve, tho we adjourn'd yet since it rain'd and storm'd we tarried and rested ourselves as well as we Could.

17. Clear and Comfortable. We return'd home but on our way visited Deacon Newtons Dauter Warrin[23] and their Brother Jonas's Family, and din'd at Neighbour Thurstons. Found my Family Well, thro the Goodness of God. At Eve came Mr. Josiah Brown to Change with me tomorrow. N.B. a most sorrowful piece of News at my Return. One Daniel Campbell who in Years past used to keep Maylems Stables at Boston, was lately murther'd at Rutland by (as tis Suspected) Edward Fitzpatrick who is apprehended accordingly and Imprison'd at Worcester.

18. I preach'd on the North Side, at the House of Mr. Nathaniel Oake, on Col. 1, 21. Din'd at Captain Eagers. Baptiz'd Mr. McAllisters Child; and Mr. John Caruths, which was born today. Return'd home at Evening. Mr. Brown preach'd on Ps. 32, 11 and on Prov. 8, 36.

19. Mr. Brown left us. But Mr. Stone[24] of Southboro came— din'd and Spent the p.m. with us. Which was singularly acceptable to me, as I was very dull and had got over my last Weeks Worry.

20. My Wife and I rode to Grafton Fast. Mr. Prentice[25] pray'd and Mr. Haven[25] preach'd on Hosea 11, 4. I drew therewith the Bands of Love. We went and refresh'd at Mr. Prentice's—and there were also Mr. Halls and Mr. Havens wives. N.B. Mr. Goddard[26] a.m. but went to Leceister p.m. At Eve Mr. Prentice sollicited me to Stay and assist them in their Church Meeting which was to be upon their sad Differences and Divisions among them—but I utterly declin'd—however the Church sent a Committee to me, Deacon Whipple[27] Deacon Miriam and Lieutenant Drury[28] to desire me, with the other ministers to go into Meeting. I comply'd for a few minutes—but could not tarry, my wife being in the cold, and a Young Child at home, the ways dirty and like to be Dark. I took leave and we rode to Winchesters and thence home.

21. Sent my Horse by Captain Maynard to Boston for Thomme. Sent by him also to Mrs. Catherine Foster, Clothier. Captain Forbush here, and told me that Considering the Town had not granted sufficiency for my Support he would send me a Bushel of English Grain, Wheat and Rye.

22. Snow Storm. We were anxious about Thomme on his Journey.

23. Thomme under the kind Care of Captain Maynard by the Favour of God came home Safe, they having lodg'd last night at Baldwins at Sudbury.

24. [No entry].

25. On Mat. 12, 17 to 21. Mr. Coollidge, Mrs. Grow, and Thomas Winchester din'd.

26. Captain Fay her. Mr. Mede. P.M. Jonas Child.

27. The Catechetical Exercises to young Women. I made use of my sermon on Exod. 33, 18. It being rainy I had but about 16 Hearers. At Evening Came James Bradish and with him Paul Newton, Elijah Warrin, and Jonas Brigham.

28. My Wife and I rode to Marlborough. P.M. visited old Mrs. Beeman under her Cancer. Visited Colonel Williams[29] but the Colonel not a home. We were also at Mr. Smiths[30] but were obliged to lodge at Dr. Gotts.[31]

29. A.M. at Mr. Tainters to hasten his making up the Cloths he had in Hand for Me and for Ebenezer, viz. Leather Breeches for Each of us and a Coat of light grey Broad Cloth for him. We din'd at Mr. Smiths and p.m. rode to Southborough and made a visit to Mr. Stones. At night return'd thro God's Mercy in safety.

30. A great Storm of Rain in the Morning. Mr. John Mathis of Southborough dropt down dead in the highway. An Awful Warning.

31. Mr. Ebenezer Wheeler of Grafton here. Treated him with kindness. Discover'd to him what Testimony I was able to give Concerning him and how it was Strengthen'd by Three others— but I did not perceive that he was inclin'd to make acknowledgement to the Church except he was forc'd to it, yet left me in a friendly manner.

### APRIL 1744

1. On Mat. 12, 22, a.m. On Matt. 3, 10. Repeated with some Additions on occasion of the Death of Mr. John Mathis of Southborough in so sudden and awful a Manner.

2. Rode thro Southborough to Cambridge. Call'd at the house of the late Mr. Mathis to Sympathize with the Widow and Children, and to obtain a particular and distinct account of the Deceas'd and the manner of his leaving the World. Was also at Mr. Stones and din'd there, where was also the Coroner viz. Lieutenant Hezekiah Ward. From Horns had Colonel Nahum Wards Company down. We call'd to pay our Regards to the good and aged Mr. Swift. Rainy before I got to Father Champneys, where I lodg'd.

3. To Boston. My Kinsman confin'd for Months past. I think ever since the 22d of last October and not able to go out of his Chamber yet. My aged Mother there with him to be Company for him. Pito carry'd back my Horse to Cambridge. N.B. Cousen Proctor[1] and Bradshaw[2] from Stoughton happen'd to be now at Boston. At Lecture this Evening at the New North. Mr. Prince[3] preach'd on Cant. 5, 16. A very excellent usefull moving sermon. I beg of God I may not loose the Savour of it. After Sermon I was at Mr. Eliots,[4] where was my Brother Peabody[5] of Natick. Lodg'd as usual at my Kinsmans.

4. Rain. Din'd at Brother Samuels—sister not in Health. P.M. at Mr. John Brecks. In the Evening at Mr. Simeon Skilling's Carver. Endeavouring to obtain a good place to bind my son Thomme out a'Prentice.

5. Mr. Checkly[6] preach'd the Publick Lecture (instead of Dr. Chauncy) on Tit. 3, 8. Din'd at Brother Samuels again with Mr. Eliot. P.M. a Young Man[7] Sat on the Gallows for attempting to

---

[22] The Reverend David Hall of Sutton.
[23] Elizabeth, daughter of Josiah Newton, had married Sials [Silas?] Warrin, Dec. 6, 1742.
[24] The Reverend Nathan Stone.
[25] The Reverend Elias Haven of Franklin.
[26] The Reverend David Goddard of Leicester.
[27] James Whipple of Grafton.
[28] Thomas Drury of Grafton.

[29] Abraham Williams, Parkman's brother-in-law.
[30] The Reverend Aaron Smith.
[31] Benjamin Gott, the physician.
[1] The Reverend Parkman's niece, Hannah, who married Samuel Proctor.
[2] Sarah, sister of Hannah of the last note, married John Bradshaw.
[3] The Reverend Thomas Prince.
[4] The Reverend Andrew Eliot, minister of the New North Church of Boston.
[5] The Reverend Oliver Peabody.
[6] The Reverend Samuel Checkley.
[7] Parkman must have referred to the following incident reported in *The Boston Gazette, or Weekly Journal*, March 27, 1744. "Early on Wednesday Morning last, one John Martin, Journeyman to Mr. Perkins, Chairmaker, hanged himself in the Chamber over the Shop, with a Piece of rotten Line that neither had Knot or Noose at either End, and he was found with one Foot on the Ground, and the other Knee on a Block. The Jury of Inquest having declared him a *Felo de se*, his Corps was carried in a Cart and buried near the Gallows."

Murther his Master. The world has also rung with Tom Bell's[8] conduct in Charlestown Jayl. N.B. P.M. Discours'd with Mr. Joshua Emms about his taking my son Thomme. John White from Brother Parkmans went for my Horse to Cambridge. At Eve I return'd there. N.B. Brother and sister Hicks[9] there.

6. Had Some serious Discourse with Brother Champney concerning their Domestic Contests. Return'd to Westborough. D.G. No Thomas Winchester yet. Little Sarah from Lameness in her left Arm, which we can't well account for.

7. [No entry].

8. On Matt. 12, 27. P.M. on Ps. 65, 2 preparatory to the Fast in the Ensuing Weeks.

9. Mr. Dunlop was So kind as to come and give me a Days Work. Thomas Winchester came again for another six Months (by Gods Leave) but insist'd for £40 old Tenor for it. P.M. my wife and I rode to the Burial of Silas Fays dead born Infant. N.B. at the Grave some Such Question were ask'd me by Mr. Fay by which I came to understand that his Brother Timothy held the odd opinion that an unborn Child had not a rational immortal soul and that he had been thus minded several Year. At Eve Brother Hicks and his wife here from Cambridge.

10. Thomas (who mended Fence Stone wall etc. yesterday) ploughing Hills.

11. Thomas Sowing Rie in the lower Field.

12. Publick Fast. On Isa. 66, 2. P.M. much Spent by that Time I began my afternoon sermon which was a carrying on the Same subject, but I improv'd part of my sermon on Zech. 12, 10. viz. from page 43 and onn. After Exercises Thankful Rice's[10] Confession read and she was restor'd. Committee from the Young Mens society acquainted me that they had receiv'd satisfaction and made up their Difference concerning which they were with me some Evenings since. The Committee also touching Mr. Cornelius Cooks[11] affair were with me at my Desire, because Mr. Cook Seem'd not to conform (a I judg'd) to what the Committee had brought me from him, in his Confession. Alas! how dull and dry, how weak and worthless in the Service of God and how unable to lead the people of God or profit them on such Days as this!

13. A.M. Thomas broke up the Grass Ground in the lower Orchard South side. I was at Deacon Newtons and Captain Bakers. P.M. Rain—ploughing and all work abroad thrown up. At Eve Captain Maynard. Also Cornelius Cook and James Bradish were here upon Mr. Cooks Confession.

14. Fine pleasant Day. Thomas ploughing up Stubble of the South side. Mr. Hezekiah Hows Oxen yesterday and to Day. Ebenezer to Marlborough. P.M. I rode over to Upton and Mr. Weld came here. I lodg'd at Captain Hazzletines.[12]

15. Captain Hazzeltine was in doubt what would become of me at Noon, but Mr. Fisk who liv'd nigher the Meeting House was so good as to ask me to Dinner as did also Captain Sadler[13] who was Still more conveniently Situated. Preach'd on Luke 19, 10. Din'd at Captain Sadlers. Captain Tyler[14] and his Wife of Still River there also. Some Number Seem'd to be greatly affected, especially one Mr. Peas[15] could not wholly contain himself. After Meeting I refresh'd at Captain Sadlers. Ensign Woods[16] greatly insisted upon my going to his House to See his Lad who had fallen from a Damm and grievously hurt his Jaw Bone. I went. Captain Hazzelton, Captain Sadler, Lieutenant Taft there also. Then return'd Evening. I came Home tho it was very Late.

16. A.M. Mr. Weld preach'd to great good Acceptance of those of our people who went to hear him, and especially commended each his last Prayers, but Mr. James Fay and his Brother Stephen hearing he was to preach went to Grafton. I ask'd Mr. Weld whether he would drop his Action against Mr. Ebenezer Wheeler and his Wife if they made an humble Submission? Or, why he would go on to prosecute them if they would? He reply'd he did not know what he might do in that matter if they Should, but no one person had been to him in such a way as yet. Neither had he any Reason to expect they would, for they had rather done all within their power to Stand by what had been done. Ex. gr. her taking her oath before Justice Taft, etc. He set out for Worcester. P.M. at Mr. E. Nurse's. At Eve Captain Mainard and Mr. Abner Newton here. Rainy Evening.

17. Thomme who had left me last night to go down to Boston in Company with Jonathan Rogers, went not away till the morning. I wrote by him to Mr. Joshua Emms of Boston, Goldsmith, with whom he was going to live. I had Mr. Williams's Mare to ride over to the Association at Lancaster. Mr. Loring[17] absent by reason of the late Death of his oldest son, Dr. John Loring[18] Physician at Boston. Mr. Gardner[19] read his Concio on Matt. 13, 27 and part of 28. Heard to Day the sorrowful News of the Burning of Mr. Emmersons[20] House at Nessitissett[21] lately.

18. Mr. Barrett[22] not being present I preach'd the public Lecture. Text Luke 16, 23. N.B. The first Time I preach'd in the New Meeting House. P.M. I got an Horse of Mr. Prentice,[23] and (Mr. Bowers[24] of Middletown in Connecticutt and Mr. Whitcomb[25] of Lancaster part of the way in Company) I rode to Luningburgh and to Townshend, lodg'd at Lieutenant Taylors,[26] but alas! the house in Tears for my kind Landlady, Mrs. Taylor, who lately deceas'd. N.B. Several Houses in Townshend fortified against the Indians.

19. I made Enquirys into the Situation of my Land in the upper part of Townshend but could not go to see it. Went to Mr. Hemmingways[27] and Mr. Samuel Clarks.[28] Committed the Sale of it to Lieutenant Taylor and return'd to Luninburgh, din'd with Mr. Thomas Prentice's[29] Wife he being himself gone to Boston and with him Reverend Mr. Stearns.[30] Return'd to Lancaster with all Speed, but was greatly retarded by a Thunder storm, which turn'd me in to one Clarks an Irishman, and again to Mr. Whitcombs—but reach'd Mr. Prentice's a little before night. I lodg'd there. Mr. Stephen Frost my Bedfellow. Nothing Specially noticeable but a general Dullness and indisposedness to the Things of religion, being principally engag'd in Things of a Temporal nature, Except at Townshend, where there was a very lively Sense of Spiritual and Divine and Eternal Things. I met with this among all of them that I convers'd with.

20. I return'd to Westborough as early as I could. Call'd to See the North Inhabitants on the Hill, but made what haste I could because of the Lecture I was to preach to Day. Preach'd from Ps. 24, 3. N.B. After Lecture Brother James and Stephen Fay, being dissatisfy'd with my changing with Mr. Weld, were here to discourse with me about it. To whom I gave the Reasons of my Conduct in that Matter.

21. [No entry].

22. I administered the Sacrament of the Lords Supper. The Fays were present. Preach'd on 1 Cor. 11, 26, and Ps. 24, 4.

[8] The following appeared in *The Boston Evening-Post*, March 19, 1744. "The famous *Tom Bell*, upon an Indictment of the Grand Jury for the County of Middlesex, was last Thursday convicted of Theft, and on Saturday had the following Sentence passed upon him, viz. *That he next Wednesday, between the Hours of Two and Three in the Afternoon, be whip'd at the publick Market at Charlestown, Twenty Stripes upon his naked Back; that he pay 75 Pounds Lawfull Money, being Trebel Damage, and cost of Prosecution, and stand committed till Sentence be performed; and that in Case he complies not with the Sentence, that he be sold for Three Years.*" See *Sibley*, IX, 375–386.

[9] Mr. and Mrs. John Hicks of Westborough.

[10] Wife of Josiah Rice. The Westborough Church Records reveal that Mrs. Rice "offer'd an humble and voluntary Confession of her sin of Drinking to Excess."

[11] The Westborough blacksmith got into various troubles. At this time he was charged with "profane swearing."

[12] John Hazeltine was a prominent citizen of Upton.

[13] John Sadler of Upton.

[14] Edward Tyler of Harvard, Mass.

[15] Josiah Pease.

[16] Jonathan Wood.

[17] The Reverend Israel Loring of Sudbury.

[18] (Harvard 1729). *Sibley*, VIII, 598–599.

[19] The Reverend John Gardner of Stow.

[20] The Reverend Daniel Emerson (Harvard 1739), the first minister of Hollis, N.H., 1743–1793. *Sibley*, X, 359–364. See *The Boston Gazette, or, Weekly Journal*, April 24, 1744.

[21] Nissitisset was the West Parish of Dunstable, Mass., later incorporated in 1746 as Hollis, N.H.

[22] The Reverend Samuel Barrett of Hopkinton.

[23] The Reverend John Prentice of Lancaster.

[24] The Reverend Benjamin Bowers (Harvard 1733), the minister of Haddam, Conn., 1740–1761. *Sibley*, IX, 278–279.

[25] Deacon David Whitcomb.

[26] Daniel Taylor. See Ithamar B. Sawtelle, *History of the Town of Townsend* (Fitchburg, 1878), p. 154.

[27] The Reverend Phinehas Hemenway (Harvard 1730), the minister at Townsend, 1734–1760. *Sibley*, VIII, 724–726.

[28] A deacon of the Townsend church. Sawtelle, *Townsend*, p. 116.

[29] Prentice was a prominent resident and officeholder.

[30] David Stearns of Lunenberg.

23. I receiv'd a note from Mr. Prentice of Grafton acquainting me that they had appoint'd a Church meeting to be on next Friday, praying that if I knew of any Evidences in the Affair of Mr. Wheeler I would help them to them.

24. Held a Catechatical Exercise at the Meeting House, but it was somewhat Thin. Deliver'd my Ninth Exercise on the Catechism, viz. on God is a Spirit.

25. Catechiz'd at the Meeting House a. and p.m.

26. My wife and I rode over with Captain Fay to Lieutenant Holloways where the Captain was marry'd to the widow Mary Rice, and we had an handsome Entertainment. N.B. the Bride's Grandson Jonathan Oake, who was before Lame and one-eyed has lately met with another Maim, his Uncle George having accidentally Splitt his Hand from the Finger to the wrist. I carry'd my wife to Bezaleel Eagers and left her there, that I might go up into Shrewsbury and Discourse with Colonel Nahum Ward upon the Wheeler Affair. I went as far as Mr. Cushings[31] (tho it was when their Lecture was done) but made no Stay. Was very friendly receiv'd by the Colonel, who as he advis'd me to go to Grafton tomorrow So at my request was willing to go over also. N.B. Several Northampton men at Eagers in the Eve. When we return'd home we found Lieutenant Holloway and Mr. Wheeler with their wives, who had been waiting upon the Bridegroom and Bride to their Lodgings at Young Mr. David Maynards.

27. I rode to Grafton—Call'd at Mr. James Harringtons and at Ensign Jonathan Halls, but went up to Mr. Wheelers to See whether upon his Seeing what Testimonys I had to prove that he had acknowledg'd his Fornication with Lydia Pratt he would not humble himself, but he was for having me go on and prove what I could. I was mov'd with Pity towards him especially Considering he was under great Trouble already by Means of Mr. Weld of Uptons prosecuting him in the Law in an action of £1000 for his wife's Defamation, but my Discourse avail'd Nothing, tho I stay'd with him and din'd also and strove every Way to gain him. I rode to Mr. Prentice's and after some Time came Colonel Nahum Ward as I had requested. I told Mr. Prentice how much rather I chose to have Wheeler labour'd with in private and that he would prevent public Ecclesiastical process. The Pastor and Brethren repair'd to the Meeting House, open'd their meeting and then adjourn'd for 1/4 hour that such Brethren as were so inclin'd might come with Wheeler to me. Several came. Essays were made to bring him to acknowledgment but in Vain. They return'd to Meeting and being requested by the Church to go to them I accordingly went read and gave in a Written Testimony of what I heard Mr. Wheeler Say. Then gave them what I had receiv'd from Deacon Miriam. After those Two Evidences Jason Whitney and James Harrington being sworn before Colonel Ward, gave in theirs. After various Questions put as the Brethren Saw Cause, and Conference with Wheeler and us who were Witnesses the meeting was adjourn'd to Thursday next 4 p.m. At Mr. Prentice's request I pray'd at breaking up. Colonel Ward went home but it having been rainy, and now very damp, cold and Late I ventur'd not but lodg'd at Mr. Prentice's. Thomas Winchester broke yesterday and this morning by going to look of Land nigh his Fathers.

28. Return'd as Early as I could, having much yet to do in my preparations for the Lords Day.

29. On John 4, 24 and P.M. repeated on 1 Pet. 3, 7. Mr. Coollidge in Town again (keeping School at the South East part of the Town) and din'd here.

30. Brother Breck went to Marlborough. Brother Hicks here. Captain Maynard rais'd another Large Barn. My Wife and I were there. N.B. One Goodhew, a Young Man from Boston residing among us, had a fall from the Frame and was led into the House much hurt, but afterwards recover'd. At Supper there were So many to be entertain'd that we were kept till 10 o'Clock. I manifested so much uneasiness that we were so detain'd that I concluded everybody would retire home as Soon as they might, but it prov'd otherwise. Many tarried long after I was got home and the Time run off; among the rest 3 of my own Family. After 12 I walk'd away towards the House again. Ebenezer and Thomas

_____
[31] The Reverend Job Cushing of Shrewsbury.

Needham were returning home—upon which I went to my Bed—but understanding that there were many yet behind and among them Some Heads of Family. I rose very uneasy and went down to the House, and having acquainted Captain Maynard with what Time of Night it was, I ask'd him whether he did not Consent to my going in among the Company that were Still diverting themselves at this unseasonable Time, I went in and admonish'd them, and sent them home. N.B. George Smith (the Taylor) and Robert Bradish made the Chief Stand—but Smith I Sent off and Bradish took up his Lodging there.

This Exerting my Authority gave me great uneasiness, but I was resolute to Shew Impartiality and not be partaker of other Mens Sins, as likewise to discharge my own Duty as Watchman in this Place and as having the Care of their Souls. N.B. Thomas Winchester last 1/2 Day.

MAY 1744

1. Robert Bradish and George Smith here in the Morning. I renewed my admonition. Bradish Submitted—but Smith was refractory and went off so. Thomas Winchester planting Corn south side. Dr. Gott and Brother Samuel Breck[1] came up from Marlborough and din'd with Me. My Wife walk'd with her Brethren to visit Captain Maynard.[2] Rainy p.m. Thomas is broke off. Brother Samuel tarried over Night and Hay being Short Sent his Horse to old Mr. Maynards. Brother Breck upon his Journey to Springfield purposing to buy and Settle in Worcester, there being now no Settled Physician there. Very pleasant—Thomas[3] Planting.

2. [No entry].

3. Preach'd at the Private Meeting at Mr. Grouts,[4] on 1 Cor. 3, 7. But few men, the Same Number of women. N.B. Bekky Hicks[5] rode with me. We call'd at Captain Fays[6] when we return'd. Mr. Stephen Fays [crossed out] Wife was there. She desir'd to Speak alone with me, the Conversation the most accountable and intolerable that ever I met with Making Exceptions against the most inexceptionable parts of my Sermon today; and declaring her great Dissatisfaction to my preaching in general, and to my Ministration, and yet in plain Terms said she could not given any Reason why. Upon my reproving her for her unreasonableness, She freely Submitted to it, and when I ask'd her whether She thought these Things proceeded from the Spirit of God, She freely acknowledg'd that She did think they did not, but from the Contrary. But She desir'd I would not be angry, for She knew it was the Effect of prejudice reigning and prevailing in her against me, and She pray'd me to tell her what She Should do to get rid of it, or what I could do to help her? I ask'd her whether She did not think She was under the influence of a Party Spirit. She Said it was most likely. I told her the Apostle directed me to rebuke her Sharply that She might be Sound in the Faith and this therefore (I told her) I now did, for it was great Sin and wickedness which She was guilty of herein, and I pray'd her to consider how horrible and how dangerous it was to be So much under the Influence of Adversary and bid her beware—with divers other Such Expressions—which She thank'd me for and we concluded.

When I came home Captain Timothy Brigham of Southborough was here on a Message from Madam Stone to request me to go to Mr. Stone's tomorrow, their Infant Child being deceas'd and Mr. Stone being gone to Norwich.

4. I was at the Funeral of Mr. Stone (of Southborough) his youngest Child.

5. Great Storm of Rain.

6. Rainy. On John 4, 24, a. and p.m. The widow of Thomas Bruce heretofore of this Town and Mrs. Ruth Fay (wife of Mr. Stephen) din'd here.

7. Visited Several Sick, viz. Amos Whitney,[7] who was ill of a Rheumatism, Eli Forbush,[8] Sick of a pleurisy, Jonathan Tainter

_____
[1] Mrs. Parkman's brother.
[2] John Maynard.
[3] Thomas Winchester, the hired hand.
[4] Joseph Grout.
[5] Daughter of John Hicks.
[6] John Fay.
[7] Son of Nathaniel Whitney.
[8] Eli Forbes (Harvard 1751), later minister of Brookfield and Gloucester.

in the Wastes of a Consumption, and daily (as tis thot) growing Worse. He has been propounded in order to admission into full Communion but has been a Journey since for his Health and it has prov'd to Much for him. Thomas picking up and burning Bushes.

8. Pleasant Weather. Read the Conversion of Mr. Benjamin Dutton a dissenting Minister in England. At Evening old Mr. Maynard and Mr. Francis Whipple here. Thomas picking up etc.

9. Heard that Ezekiel Cole's Case was try'd yesterday at our County Court at Worcester, and that he was fin'd etc. And inform'd likewise that to Day Reverend Mr. Welds against Rachel Wheeler of Grafton, comes on. Mr. Weld recover'd of Wheeler £400 old Tenor for Defamation—but both he and Wheeler appeal'd from the Judgement.

10. At Deacon Tomlins[9] and visited Jonathan Tainter.

11. Brother Samuel Parkman came at Evening from Dunstable.

12. Brother visited Captain Maynard and Captain return'd with him here, which I was glad of. See April 30 at night.

13. On Mat. 12, 28 and Ps. 47, 7. Mr. Coollidge din'd.

14. I accompany'd my Brother to the Borders of Hopkinton, and in returning I visited old Mr. Rice who lyes very weak and low. Town Meeting to see whether the Town will choose a Committee to make Reply to the Petition lately put in to the General Court to divide the Town. The Town voted to do so and chose Captain Warrin, Captain Maynard and Mr. Francis Whipple their Committee for that purpose. Reverend Mr. Warham Williams of Waltham here, with Delegates going up to a Council at Grafton chose by agriev'd Brethren there—viz. Aaron Hardy, Simon Tainter etc. At Eve Simon Tainter here to desire me to go up tomorrow, or draw up what I had to say about Wheeler, and about Mr. Prentice's being dismiss'd from the Association. But I could not gratify them with either, for 1.) my wife designs to go to Boston tomorrow. 2) There is no Time to apprize Mr. Prentice of it. 3.) I have not time to look up my papers and prepare.

15. My Wife undertook her Journey to Boston.

16. [No entry].

17. Mr. Barrett came from Grafton and acquainted me with what the Council had done there. N.B. but 3 Churches met—and they adjourn'd to August next, advising the aggrieved Brethren there to make fresh application to the Church to join with them in calling a Council mutually, which if they would not do, to add six churchs more to themselves to form another Council. Mr. Barrett din'd with me and Spent several Hours afternoon—walk'd to the great Pond etc. He tells me the separations in Hopkinton increase, and now both the Ruling Elders there are in Separation.

18. Mr. Buckminster of Rutland[10] here in his Return home.

19. My Wife return'd from Boston, informs me that my Honored Mother is not so well as heretofore. Mother Champney also very weak and languishing. My son Thomme much out of Health and Mr. Emms discourag'd about him and would have me send for him home.

20. On Mat. 12, 29, and p.m. repeat'd Sermon on 1 Cor. 14, 15, from Ps. 47, 7. Mr. Coollidge here at Dinner.

21. N.B. A Meeting of those Inhabitants who were against the Northside's petition; and they met at Captain Forbush's. Captain Maynard here. N.B. a Visit from Captain Eager and Mr. Livermore.

22. I rode to Marlborough to Mr. Tainters[11] and Madam Woods,[12] and proceeded to Mr. Stones at Southboro where I din'd, and thence to Hopkinton. On the Road to Major Jones's met Mr. Barrett and the Committee from the General Court to look into the affair of Malden Farm lying in Shrewsbury and Worcester. Had some opportunity to Confer with them upon the affair of the Petition of our Northside, particularly with Mr. Foxcroft,[13] Captain Watts, Dr. Hale,[14] etc. When I came home Mr. Ebenezer Chamberlain was here with Mrs. Rebecca Cotton of Newton. N.B. Thomas gone to Worcester the Morning.

23. Rainy Day, but old Mr. Rice lys in so low a state and sending for me I ventur'd to go and See him. Visited also Jonathan Tainter in his Waste. When I return'd home Mr. Breck from Springfield was here, but much indispos'd by a Sore Throat. At Eve Dr. Breck came. N.B. The Doctor has bought at Worcester and begins to build there.

24. Elijah Rice and Sarah Shattuck were married in the Morning. Mr. Breck and his Brother went to Marlborough.

25. I rode to Worcester to See the Prisoner Richard Fitz Patrick Committed for the Murther of Daniel Campbell of Rutland. I din'd at Mr. Cushings at Shrewsbury, had Colonel Ward[15] for my Company. Call'd at the high Sheriffs, Captain Flaggs,[16] who went with me to Reverend Mr. Burrs[17] and to the Jayl. Found the prisoner very Ignorant but desirous of Instruction. Having done what in me lay in Instructing him and Praying with him, I went into Colonel Chandlers[18] and refresh'd myself and so hastened home. At my House found Mrs. Edwards[19] of Northampton and her Dauter Jerusha, accompany'd by Reverend Mr. Hopkinton[20] of Sheffield.

26. Mr. Hopkins etc went off for Boston. Captain Baker[21] invites me to dine with him on the 28.

27. Repeated on 1 Cor. 6, 18, a. and p.m. N.B. in the Close I gave Warning with respect to 'Lection Diversions. Mr. Coollidge, Mr. Kendal[22] of Suffield with his wife din'd here. Likewise Mr. Harrington[23] of Framingham and wife and Mrs. Tainter din'd with us.

28. Din'd with Captain Baker and the other Officers at Captain Fays. N.B. Mr. Coollidge there. N.B. Mr. James and Stephen Fay oppose my sermon Yesterday because of my allowing Recreations of any kind. I visited Amos Whitney and old Mr. Rice who lies exceeding low. At my returning home a little before night Mr. Coollidge and Lieutenant Forbush[24] and others met me who acquaint'd me that Benjamin Fays wife Seeing the follys and vanitys of men and the extreme Brevity of Life, cry'd out with loud crys and Lamentations and fervent Beseechings to all about her which She for some time indeed labour'd to restrain And went into the back part of her House, but could not Stifle—which gather'd a throng about her and it lasted Some Time. Stephen Fay also, going down to market met me, and soon getting upon a strain concerning my sermons which I thought very unjust, I look'd upon myself bound in Duty to reprove and admonish him, advise and direct him, which I did Somewhat thoroughly and left it upon him to Reflect upon in his Journey to Boston. N.B. Mr. Cornelius Biglo Shot in the Thigh by Mr. Ebenezer Chamberlain, in their foolish Play and Diversion at Clark (Abner) Newtons.

29. Brother Hicks here—but I set out for Boston: call'd at Mr. Matthias Rice's to borrow money. Din'd there and then he went with me to his Brother Ephraim Hows and got me 50 Shillings new Tenor. Proceeded to Mr. Joseph Tainters where I was very long detain'd for my Coat which was not done. Could get no farther than Saltmarshes[25] at Watertown—lodg'd there, and N.B. Mr. Ballantine[26] of Westfield lodg'd in the Same House.

30. Early to Father Champneys. Mother poor and low and Consumptive. Proceeded to Boston, my mother weak and faint, and dejected in soul, yet (thro Divine Goodness) not so sick nor distress'd as in Time past. My Niece Elizabeth[27] very low also, having a pleuretic Fever—but her Brother Elias gets abroad a little. Mr. Allen[28] of Brookline on Isa. 6, 1. Din'd at Brother Samuels without any other Company. P.M. at the Convention

[9] Isaac Tomlin.
[10] Reverend Joseph Buckminster (Harvard 1739) had settled in Rutland in Sept., 1742. Sibley, X, 348–354.
[11] Deacon Joseph Tainter.
[12] Widow of Benjamin Woods.
[13] The Reverend Thomas Foxcroft of Boston.
[14] Nathan Hale was a physician of Newbury.
[15] Nahum Ward of Shrewsbury.
[16] Benjamin Flagg, Jr.
[17] Isaac Burr, the minister of Worcester.
[18] John Chandler, Jr.
[19] Wife of the great Reverend Jonathan Edwards.
[20] Samuel Hopkins.
[21] Edward Baker of Westborough.
[22] Thomas Kendall.
[23] Ebenezer Harrington, a selectman of Framingham. Temple, Framingham, p. 576.
[24] Samuel Forbush.
[25] Thomas Saltmarsh kept an inn for many years. Bond, Watertown, p. 414.
[26] The Reverend John Ballantine (Harvard, 1735), the minister of Westfield, Mass., 1741–1776. Sibley, IX, 468–472.
[27] Daughter of Elias Parkman of Boston.
[28] The Reverend James Allin.

Dr. Sewal[29] Moderator but Mr. Eels[30] pray'd who were chiefly Settling old accounts. Nothing of Contest to Day respecting the Times. At Eve I retir'd to Brother Alexanders[31] who was Lodg'd with my Kinsman Elias.

31. At Convention Sermon but went in late, for it began at 9 a.m. Dr. Chauncey[32] on Tit. 2, 15, last Clause—Let no man dispise thee. Din'd at Mr. Eliots[33] with above 20 more. Mr. Benjamin Bass,[34] Dexter,[35] Champney,[36] Tyler[37] etc. etc. Afterwards at Mr. Mathers[38] where there was a large Company also. Mr. Parsons[39] of Bradford, Barnard[40] of Newbury, Balch[41] of Bradford, Breck, Walter[42] etc. etc. I visited also Mr. Webb[43] and Mr. Gee.[44] N.B. Conversation with Mr. Hobby[45]—at Eve at Mr. Condy's[46]—So differently was my time Spent. Supp'd and lodg'd at Brother Samuels—my Kinsman and his Mother being at a Wedding at Mrs. Tylestones.

### JUNE [1744]

The Morning and most of the Forenoon I Spent with Mr. Thomas Stoddard who was very full of Experiences of the Lords work upon his Soul—accompany'd me to my mothers who lyes weak and cast down, yet hoping in God. I was full of Concern about my Son Thomme, my hopes all blasted respecting his living with Mr. Emms, who is discourag'd and throws up. I sought to Mr. Skelling the Carver, but in vain—to Mr. Samuel Jarvis, but not direct Success. I was also otherwise variously taken up—partly to make Some Interest in Court lest the Petition of our Coram side of the Town should be granted, which would be (Should it happen) to my inexpressible Detriment. Din'd at Brother Alexanders[1]—waited on Dr. Delhonde[2] and paid him for what he had done last year for my Daughter Molly. Exceeding Hot Season—can but just keep alive. At Eve took Very Solemn Leave of my Honor'd aged and dear Parent, and took Thomme to Cambridge.

2. Thomme rode behind me and we got home about 2 p.m., while my Family were at Dinner. N.B. I had Mr. Hall[3] and his Wife's Company from Wards Tavern. Blessed be God I find my Family in Health and peace.

3. On Mat. 12, 30, and p.m. Repeated sermon on Ps. 99, 5, 9 from Exod. 15, 11, with Some alterations. N.B. A Packet came from England into Boston yesterday and War was to be proclaim'd in the afternoon and was so about 5 o'clock between England and France. N.B. This proclamation of war immediately follow'd by a terrible Shock of an Earthquake about 10 o'Clock this Morning. N.B. Mr. James Fays wife cry'd out very much as Soon as I was come from the meeting House at Noon—and there was great crying out in the woods where a Number were retir'd at noon.

I Stop'd the Church at Eve at the request of Lieutenant Thomas Forbush to See if the Church would put in another Member to supply the place of Brother Whipple[4] at Upton Council, who is one of the Committee for answering the North Side's Petition to the general Court, but he holding he should not go to Boston as he conceiv'd.

[29] The Reverend Joseph Sewall of Boston.
[30] The Reverend Nathaniel Eels of Norwell.
[31] Alexander Parkman of Boston.
[32] The Reverend Charles Chauncey of Boston.
[33] The Reverend Andrew Eliot (Harvard 1737), the minister of the New North Church. Sibley, X, 128–161.
[34] The Reverend Benjamin Bass (Harvard 1715), the minister of Hanover, Mass., 1728–1756. Sibley, VI, 72–74.
[35] The Reverend Samuel Dexter (Harvard 1720), the minister of Dedham, Mass., 1724–1755. Sibley, VI, 376–380.
[36] The Reverend Joseph Champney of Beverly.
[37] The Reverend Andrew Tyler (Harvard 1738), the minister of Westwood, Mass., 1743–1772. Sibley, X, 329–334.
[38] The Reverend Samuel Mather.
[39] The Reverend Joseph Parsons.
[40] The Reverend Thomas Barnard (Harvard 1732), the minister of West Newbury, Mass., 1739–1752. Sibley, IX, 120–129.
[41] The Reverend William Balch of Groveland (Second Church in Bradford).
[42] The Reverend Nathaniel Walter (Harvard 1729), the minister of West Roxbury, 1734–1776. Sibley, VIII, 630–634.
[43] The Reverend John Webb of Boston.
[44] The Reverend Joshua Gee of Boston.
[45] The Reverend William Hobby of Reading.
[46] The Reverend Jeremiah Condy, the Baptist minister of Boston.
[1] Alexander Parkman of Boston.
[2] Louis Delhonde, the physician of Boston.
[3] The Reverend David Hall of Sutton.
[4] Francis Whipple.

4. Variety of Company all Day. Mr. Whipple is again induced to go to Boston. Mr. Beaman[5] and Josiah Rice with 8 or 9 more resolve to petition that they may not be laid to the design'd New Precinct.

5. Old Mr. Rice yet living. Made him the last Visit and pray'd with him in my way to Upton. It is this Day 20 Years Since I gave my Answer to Settle in this Town. Mr. Rice lives to See it, but dyes this very Day. Did not overtake Deacon Newton till I got to Mr. Fisks[6] in Upton. Council met at Mr. Welds,[7] and immediately adjourn'd to Captain Sadlers where we were to be entertain'd, and from whence we never stirr'd. All Things relating to the people Separating from Mr. Weld to hear Mr. Pain,[8] were conducted smoothly enough and then respecting Mr. Weld's Maintenance. And we lodg'd comfortably at Captain Sadlers.

6. But when we came to propose the Hearing of the Case relating to Rachel Wheeler, we had great Struggle. It was plain that Mr. Wheeler would never submit it, nor yield to any Thing that could be done about it. The Vote was put and there appear'd 8 for it and 7 against it, without the Moderator—but there was great Stir and noise on the Yea Side and Mr. Hall and Prentice[9] threaten'd that they would forthwith go home if it was to be kept out, and in short the Moderator upon Considering all the State of Things condescended to give his Vote for hearing it, insisting at the Same Time upon the Liberty to Enter his Dissent in the Result. How much we might then wish for the help of Brother Whipple who was gone to Boston! But at length even he came, whilst in the hearing of the Wheeler Case. See the Minutes of the Council for the rest of the Proceedings. Lieutenant Tainter came to me at Upton to request me to go to Old Mr. Thomas Rice's Funeral who deceas'd Yesterday, this Month 90 years old, a principal Instrument in obtaining the Grant and Settling of This Town.

7. Spent the Day in Debating, and passing Votes of Judgment upon what we had heard. I would have nothing to do with the Wheeler Case—and was Sorry to See Such a reigning Disposition in that part of the Council we were chose by the Dissatisfy'd to carry every thing they could to its height against Mr. Weld. It being very Hot and my Business in the Council Such as requir'd close Attention and continual Application I was very much worried and faint, and a bad Cold also Seiz'd upon me and kept me down.

8. Exceeding poor and weak, Sweating and fainting Last Night and very little sleep. But in the Morning when I got up and Stirr'd about I revived and was Better. We who were the Committee for drawing up a Result, could not be wholly alone without great Inconvenience. Mr. Hall who had drawn up the most of the Votes which had pass'd in the Council, undertook to draw up the rough Draught for the Result—of that part which was most Critical and difficult. N.B. the Church were call'd in (inadvertently) to hear it read, before the Committee themselves could have time to weigh and recommend it, But it was read. Upon my mentioning it to the Moderator how unfit till we had Scann'd and finish'd the Preparation of it—we had the privilege to be alone—and the Draughting the Result took us til late in the Afternoon. Not without many Strivings if not deep mutual Dissatisfactions. But at length it was finish'd, and pass'd in Council tho to my great Dislike in many respects. Just before sundown the people were summon'd, Mr. Prentice, as the Moderators desire Read the Result (in Captain Sadlers Entry, for we never went to the meeting House at all) and the Moderator concluded with prayer. Captain Hazzletine and others earnestly requested me to tarry over Night but I was determin'd Home if possible—and Home we came tho it was nigh Midnight first. N.B. there had been a press for Soldiers to go up and keep guard in Frontier Towns. Silas Pratt,[10] Silas Newton, Jacob Garfield went out of our South Company and Josiah Cutting and Benjamin Wilson out of the North. We Hear the Earthquake was very great at the Eastward

[5] Eleazer Beamon.
[6] Ebenezer Fiske.
[7] The Reverend Thomas Weld.
[8] Probably Elisha Paine, an itinerant Baptist preacher.
[9] The Reverend Solomon Prentice of Grafton.
[10] Son of John Pratt.

particularly Newbury, last Sabbath. It was much noted how this present war breaks forth with the Earthquake. It is Still a great increase of our Calamitys to have such intestine Broils and so furious Contentions among ourselves. N.B. Reverend Mr. Stone preach'd the Lecture in Westborough to day preparatory to the Communion.

9. Greatly disquieted with both the Actual Miscarriages and the Defects of the Council at Upton, and made some Remarks thereon. Prepar'd what I could of my sermon for the Communion tomorrow—and O that my own Soul were suitably prepar'd there for! Bekky[11] and Lucy[12] rode to Sutton. N.B. Mr. James Bowman took the Care of a Letter from me to Mr. Weld of Upton.

10. Relations of those who stood Candidates for Admission into the Church not brought till just before I went out to Meeting. Preach'd on 1 Cor. 11, 26. P.M. (as last Sabbath p.m.) on the Holiness of God. Mr. Coollidge having mov'd his Lodgings nigher meeting, viz. to Mr. Samuel Williams's, din'd at home. Captain Fay, Mrs. Adams [blank] din'd with us. O might it please God to Sanctifie both his Word and Sacraments to our highest Benefit!

11. Mr. Coollidge[13] opens School at Lieutenant Aaron Forbush's, and sent Ebenezer[14] there. Mr. Samuel Biglo and his wife, of Shrewsbury here upon their Spiritual Concerns. Mr. Weld came, and manifested his great Disgust at what the Council had done. He lodg'd here. Thomas mow'd the fore Yard and Garden.

12. Mr. Frost[15] of Mill-river in Mendon here with a Young Lady, in their Journey to Brookfield; soon after Mr. Weld had taken leave, and went up the Road to Shrewsbury. Mr. Salter[16] from Mansfield here also. Captain Maynard's Training. Great Ruffle and Contests in the Breasts and partly breaking forth in the Conduct and Conversations of many of the North side soldiers. N.B. Mr. Wheeler as I was going into the Meeting House to prayer, told me he thought they were hardly in a Frame fit for Such Things—but I ask'd him whether we ought not to labour to be Compos'd, at least so far forth to beg of God to prepare us? A great Favour that Colonel Nahum Ward and Colonel Williams[17] came, and were present at Reading the Laws, Viewing arms etc. that the unruly might be rebuk'd and kept down. N.B. It had been said that a certain Man on the North side [promised?] a Gallon of Rum if they would rebell against Captain Maynard—and a man was ready (as it was conceived) to head them. Mr. Wheeler was thot to be the first of these and Corporal Nathan Ball the other. But in Public and whenever I was present I saw no indecency for which I was greatly rejoic'd and that Captain Eager[18] and Lieutenant Holloway[19] din'd with us at Captain Maynards, as did Mr. Salter (who went down with me) likewise. P.M., Dr. Breck from Worcester here, but he went to Marlborough at Evening. N.B. Neighbour Chamberlain mov'd his Family and his Goods to Leicester, and Thomas Winchester had my Mare to help up their Children. N.B. Rebecca Hicks and my little Lucy return'd from Sutton, tho a Very hot Day.

13. Very hot again. Thomas and the Boys with him half hilling.

14. I had appoint'd a Catechetical Exercise for young Women today but a great Storm arose just at the Hour appointed which prevented their Coming.

15. [No entry].

16. [No entry].

17. On Mat. 12, 31, 32. A very awful Subject! O that we might have a right understanding of it and Suitably improve it!

18. [No entry].

19. Rode to the Association at Shrewsbury. See the Association Records. N.B. was at Smith Allens Shop to get my Horse Shod before I went up to Mr. Cushings.[20] Was also at Dr. Smiths[21] being much Concern'd for Mr. Jonathan Livermores wife who I understand is in a wasting state.

20. Mr. Loring[22] preach'd an Excellent sermon on Heb. 6, 11. After Dinner I rode to Worcester (accompany'd by Reverend Mr. Davis [23] of Holden) Visited Dr. Breck but my Special Design was to make a Visit to the poor prisoner.[24] I found him willing to submitt to Instruction, but in no very deep Concern about his State. I very familiarly explain'd to him 10 principal Heads of Christian Religion which I had drawn up for that purpose and which I left at the Jayl that they who were there might often read to him. I pray'd with him. Waited on Madam Chandler (the Colonel being at Boston) and return'd home to Westborough the same Night. N.B. accompany'd some Miles by Mr. Curtis of Worcester being very full of his Uneasiness with Mr. Burr, and how far they had proceeded about Calling a Council.

21. Mr. Dorr[25] of Mendon and Mr. Weld made me a Visit and din'd here; But they would not Stay to the Lecture (at 4 o'Clock p.m.)—full of remarks upon the late Result. I preach'd to a thin Auditory, from Tit. 2, 6. N.B. receiv'd a Letter from Mr. Hall requesting a Copy of our Result.

22. Richard Roberts here a.m. David Marble (from old Mr. Prentice's of Lancaster). Sent by those Young Men a Return to Mr. Halls request of the Result. P.M. Sudden Storms arose—of Thunder, Wind and Rain. Thomas got in part of a Load of Hay only: and that considerably wet before he could house it. N.B. Mrs. Rebecca Hayward[26] here about a Quarrill between her and Mrs. Townsend.[27]

23. I rode up to Deacon Cyprian Keyes's [28] in order to Change with Mr. Morse, but miss'd of Mr. Morse,[29] he having gone to our House in a different Road. Rainy Night.

24. Morning—preach'd at North Shrewsbury on Rom. 8, 7, a. and p.m. Din'd at Lieutenant Taylors.[30] N.B. Mr. Sparhawk[31] Schoolmaster in the Town din'd with me. After the Exercises Ebenezer Ball piloted me over to his uncle Livermore's, that I might See his Wife who was in a Wasting Languishing State, was told she was not like to live, and I understood that the way was shorter than I found it to be—but my Circumstances were like to be such that I could not visit her for Several Weeks. I return'd to my Family at Evening. Both Mr. Morse and Mr. Coollidge lodg'd here.

25. Mr. Morse went home. Mr. Coollidge din'd here. Sarah Tainter[32] here in order to her joining the Church.

26. [No entry].

27. Mr. Chamberlin from Leicester here. We had some disquietment about his delaying to pay Rogers's Debt which Should have been paid last February or rather (as it was due) last December 25, but I prevented much Contest and dismiss'd it for the present.

28. Publick Fast on account of the War and the Earthquake. I preach'd a.m. on Ps. 46, 6, p.m. on Isa. 1, 4.

29. Major Jones[33] of Hopkinton here. Mr. Lawrence here about Chamberlins Debt.

30. Have heard that there are 4 Indians gone down to Boston with the Commissioners that lately went to Albany to treat with them. Six Nations. One of the Said Indians is look'd upon as a Chief of the Whole Six Nations: and that they design to proceed to the Eastward.

## JULY [1744]

On Isa. 66, 2. N.B. p.m. there arose a great Storm of Rain and Thunder, just as we broke off our public Exercises which detain'd the Assembly in the Meeting House. I led them to Sing

---

[11] Rebecca Hicks, Parkman's niece.
[12] Parkman's daughter who was 10 years old.
[13] Samuel Coolidge.
[14] Parkman's eldest son.
[15] The Reverend Amariah Frost (Harvard 1740), the minister of the Second Church of Mendon (later the First Church of Milford, Mass.), 1742–1792. *Sibley*, X, 494–496.
[16] The Reverend Richard Salter of Mansfield, Conn.
[17] Abraham Williams of Marlborough.
[18] James Eager of Westborough.
[19] William Holloway of Westborough.
[20] The Reverend Job Cushing.
[21] Joshua Smith, the physician of Shrewsbury.
[22] The Reverend Israel Loring of Sudbury.
[23] The Reverend Joseph Davis (Harvard 1740), the first minister at Holden, Mass., 1742–1773. *Sibley*, X, 478–481.
[24] Edward Fitzpatrick.
[25] The Reverend Joseph Dorr.
[26] Mrs. Simon Hayward.
[27] Mrs. Joshua Townsend.
[28] In Shrewsbury. Ward, *Shrewsbury*, p. 342.
[29] The Reverend Ebenezer Morse (Harvard 1737), the minister of the North Parish in Shrewsbury, which later became the separate town of Boylston.
[30] Eleazer Taylor.
[31] John Sparhawk (Harvard 1723), formerly a schoolmaster and lawyer at Plymouth, Mass. *Sibley*, VII, 258–259.
[32] Daughter of Deacon Simon Tainter.
[33] John Jones.

part of Ps. 147. N.B. Mr. Stephen Fays Wife cry'd out very much at the Time of a loud Clap of Thunder. I discours'd with her at my House afterwards before She went home, and She said the Spirit of God struck her at the Same Time with that Clap, and (having been in great Darkness for some Time before) she was fill'd with much Terror by reason of her sins.

2. Mr. Livermore here to pay me some Money—not a little Discourse concerning the State of the Town—Dividing—Military Affairs etc. Mr. Morse of Shrewsbury and Master Timothy Pain with him on their Journey to Medfield in order to attend upon Commencement, and Mr. Timothy to be Examin'd for Entrance into College. Brother Hicks here.

3. Brother Hicks and I to Cambridge. On the Road Mr. Cushing[1] of Shrewsbury and Two of his Neighbours in Company. Mr. Fortunatus Woods[2] also. I got down so seasonably as to make a Visit over to Town. There was Mr. Messinger[3] of Wrentham my old Friend at College. Sir Williams's[4] and at the Buttery.

4. At Meeting the Gratulatory oration was delay'd till the Governor and the Mohawk Chiefs came. I din'd in the Hall. The Mohawks din'd there also. N.B. Great Disorder (we hear) were lately at Ipswich by means of one Woodberry[5] who with Mr. Gilman[6] of Durham has Sent Letters to many Ministers of the Province as from the King of Kings and Lord of Lords. N.B. I transcribed a Letter at Mr. Newmans[7] Study from Madam Christian Wainwright[8] of Ipswich to Madam Dudly[9] of Roxbury respecting the Ipswich Disorders in the last Month, horrible to relate. My Brother Samuel Parkman was present at Ipswich whilst some of those Facts were done.

5. Early in the Morning I rode to Boston. At Breakfast at Mr. Josiah Quincys[10] with the 4 Mohawks. Their Names Anerek (or Henrich) Thoyennoga, James, Kayea wire gowa, these Two were elderly men and Chiefs; Yonathan, Kayea wire gowa, and Joseph, Onondager. (N.B. I copy'd their Names from the Writing of Yonathan (or Jonathan) Kayea wire gowa.) Mrs. Kellogg of Suffield being Interpretress. Their Design was to go to the Eastward to bear a message to the Eastward Indians also. Thoyennogea was very ready, pleasant and intelligent, and especially gave free answers to our Enquiries concerning their Sentiments in matters of Religion. We understand that all these 4 are Baptiz'd and Submitt to the Instruction of an English minister who is settled among them for 2 Towns which are call'd Skenecktada—about 12 Miles above Albany. They tell us the Cagnaway's were afore hand of them in saying that in the War between France and England they must not meddle. They inform that Timothy Rice has been out of Health, and that his son has return'd from his warring with the Flatt Heads.

Mr. Barnard[11] of Marblehead preach'd the public Lecture on Gal. 2, 20 latter part on Assurance. I din'd with the Venerable Dr. Colman,[12] where also din'd Mr. Turell,[13] Mr. Josiah Cotton,[14] and Mr. Byles.[15] Am inform'd that Mr. Dutton a Baptist Minister, whose Life I not long Since read is lately come from England to Boston and preach'd to Day at Dorcester. My aged Mother very Feeble and scarcely able to go across the Room. I return'd to Cambridge at Evening. N.B. in my way was very mercifully preserv'd from being Crush'd by a 4 Wheel Chaise in a narrow Passage nigh Roxbury meeting House, but receiv'd not much

Hurt. D. G. plurimas! N.B. Cousin Winchester of Westborough lodg'd at Father Champneys.

6. Brother Hicks to Boston but Cousin Winchester and I rode together to Westborough. I call'd at Mr. Cooks[16] in Waterton to see his Books—Clarks Martyral and Lives.[17] I din'd at Mr. Darlings[18] on the Road. We stop'd also at old Mr. Shermans[19] in Marlborough—had a great deal of talk with my Kinswoman about the New Lights as they are term'd and particularly her own sourness and Disaffectedness and reprov'd her for many Things. Got home in the middle of the Afternoon.

7. Close engag'd in my Preparations. Thomas Winchester has carry'd on the Business and conducted the Boys in the Hilling and Haying. Nor any Evil befallen my Family in my absence. Blessed be God. Brother Hicks came up from Boston last night and lodged here, and to Day he went home.

8. I preach'd on Isa. 66, 2 and p.m. repeated my Exposition on Mat. 7, 22, 23. The Lord grant us Grace savingly to profit by the Means thereof.

9. John Rogers work'd with Thomas. A.M. They mow'd Barley. P.M. they went to the Meadow. I rode to some Number of Houses—old Mr. Whipples, Stephen Fays. Din'd at Captain Fays. Talk'd with Mr. Benjamin Fays wife concerning her Emotions and crying out on the Training Day at their House. Was at Mr. Grouts and made a Business of Visiting and discoursing with Mr. James Fay and his wife, Mr. Fay having been absent now four Days running from the public Assemblys. He told that he had not been so disgusted as to leave us, be we were Crowded at our Meeting House, and he liv'd almost as near and handy to Grafton. Besides that he intimated to me that the Grand Jury man (Mr. Miller) threatno to present them for Disorderly Behaviour because his wife cry'd out on the Day of the Earthquake. I could not find that our Conversation together would be serviceable towards a Reconcilement let me do or say even ever so much either Spiritually or Condescendingly and endearingly. I also Sometimes reprov'd—nor did I soon come away but tarry'd till the sun was not very high—but after all came away with Grief. He, in the Course of the Talk told me my Conversation was but a little of Spiritual Things—that Mr. Prentices Sermons were lively, profitable and Excellent—that as for me I very much affected such ministers as were opposite—but especially I was Sett against those whom he could not bear to hear a word against: Such as Mr. Bliss and Mr. Prentice. After visiting Mr. Fay I went to Mr. Whitneys where I found far Different Dispositions—and to Lieutenant Tainters. N.B. Jonathan I think wears away.

10. Thomas and Neighbour Rogers to the Meadow a.m. Thomas at home p.m. Neighbour Rogers p m work'd for Neighbour Maynard. No Barley [?] to reap tho much was expected. N.B. I visited William Clarks two Children that were sick. Met Mr. Lawrence who rode with me to Mr. Caruths.[20]

11. Thomas and Rogers at the Meadow but Rogers not till 10 o'Clock. A.M. showery. Mrs. Sibyl Child[21] here to be examin'd in order to her joining with the Church.

12. The Meadow waited on by all Hands, viz. Thomas, Neighbour Rogers and the Two Boys. My Wife not well. Last night we began to Wean Sarah. My wife to Marlboro. Ensign Bruce here in the Morning. Some time before noon he Sent me his son Jonathan who reap'd down my Winter Rye, 6 Shock, and we got it into the Barn at Evening. Held the Catechetical Exercise and preach'd on Ps. 27, 7.

13. Mr. Chamberlain here in the Morning. He hinder'd Neighbour Rogers part of the Morning. Rogers and Thomas at the Meadow. They Carted home 3 Load and finish'd Mowing the Meadow, for they Left a part which was so thin and Dead that they Concluded was not worth Cutting. N.B. That being late in the morning they work'd late at Evening for it. My wife return'd from Marlborough. N.B. The Child weans without Trouble.

[1] The Reverend Job Cushing.
[2] Son of Benjamin Woods of Marlborough. Sibley, XI, 336.
[3] The Reverend Henry Messenger (Harvard 1717), the minister at Wrentham, 1719-1751. Sibley, VI, 197-199.
[4] (Harvard 1744). The son of the Reverend Parkman's brother-in-law, Colonel Abraham Williams of Marlborough. Abraham, Jr., later became the minister of Sandwich, Mass. Sibley, XI, 498-502.
[5] Richard Woodbury was associated with the Reverend Gilman of Durham, who ordained him in a ceremony that produced numerous protests. See The Boston Gazette, July 24, 1744 and The Boston Evening Post, July 30, Aug. 6, 1744.
[6] The Reverend Nicholas Gilman (Harvard 1724), the minister at Durham, N.H., 1742-1748. He was "the wildest of the New-Lights." Sibley, VII, 338-344.
[7] John Newman (Harvard 1740), later the minister at Edgartown, Mass., 1747-1758. Sibley, X, 528-531.
[8] Mrs. John Wainwright.
[9] The wife of Justice Paul Dudley.
[10] Colonel Quincy (Harvard 1728) was a well-known merchant of Boston. Sibley, VIII, 463-475.
[11] The Reverend John Barnard.
[12] The Reverend Benjamin Colman.
[13] The Reverend Ebenezer Turell of Medford.
[14] (Harvard 1722). The minister of Providence, R.I. Sibley, VII, 50-56.
[15] The Reverend Mather Byles of Boston.
[16] Stephen Cook, Jr., of Watertown. Bond, Watertown, p. 163.
[17] Samuel Clarke, A Generall Martyrologie, Containing a Collection of all the Greatest Persecutions which have Befallen the Church of Christ from the Creation to our Present Times (London, 1651).
[18] Thomas Darling of Framingham.
[19] Mrs. John Sherman.
[20] John Caruth lived in the north part of Westborough.
[21] Cibel was the wife of Jonas Child.

14. Thomas and Rogers and the Boys at Work at the Meadow. Rak'd up all and brot home 2 Load. Have suffer'd myself to be hinder'd very little by these hurrys.

15. A. and p.m. on Joel 3, 13, former part. N.B. A very fervent Address to old people. N.B. Mr. Coollidge comes in commonly after the public Exercises and this Evening seems somewhat affected and awaken'd. The Lord grant these awakening Things may be a quickening to us all to improve our Golden Opportunity and Advantages!

16. Thomas with the Boys got home one Load of Meadow Hay before the Rain.

17. [No entry].

18. I went to Mr. Francis Whipples to take him with me to Mendon but he could not go. I proceeded to Lieutenant Tainters to see poor Jonathan who is very low in his Wasting and Consumption and not like to continue, yet Say, but little only that he is pritty much in the Dark, yet would hope in the Mercy of God. After prayer and Some Instructions I rode to Mendon. Mr. Webb[22] of Uxbridge and his wife, and Mr. Prentice[23] of Holliston at Mr. Dor's. Mr. Prentice could not Stay to Lecture. I preach'd on Luke 16, 23. O that after as many Times preaching this Sermon and I hope not altogether without Success to others I might obtain Grace from God to become truely Serious and Considerate myself! Rode back with Captain Tyler as far as to his House, and it rain'd so that I was oblig'd to lodge there all Night.

19. Very heavy Rains early in the Morning but clear'd off so afterwards that I return'd home. Captain Tyler being so good as to accompany me part of the way as far as Mr. Matthew Tafts. N.B. I call'd also at Mr. Freelands[24] in Hopkinton. P M I preach'd on Preparatory Lecture from Ps. 24, 4, 5. N.B. Mr. Coollidge here after meeting and I perceiv'd him to be free and ready in Classical Learning, except in Tullys Orations etc but upon several Occasions Dropping very Dark sentences about himself. Scil. his own Spiritual and Eternal State and Condition which were very terrible to hear—nor could he receive any Reply, Direction nor Encouragement that I could give him.

20. Thomas Carted home the last Load of the Meadow Hay. P.M. a very Considerable Thunder Storm but we and ours mercifully preserv'd. D.G. May we have, and ever Maintain the true, holy filial Fear of God and be Cur'd of a slavish Dread which keeps us in Bondage and gives Torment! For Blessed is the man that (truely) feareth alwayes!

21. Brother Hicks and his son Samuel going to Cambridge. N.B. Sammè is going to mow there. Brother Champney being ill and Father Champney too aged, so that their English Grass Stands from Week to Week uncutt, in great Part.

22. Sacrament. I preach'd a.m. on 1 Cor. 11, 26, pm on Joel 3, 13. Captain Fay and Mr. Coollidge at Dinner. At Eve Mr. William Williams of Mansfield[25] here.

23. Thomas mow'd at Lieutenant Tainters for Mr. Dunlops reaping Rye this Same Day for me. My Wife rode with me to see Mr. Samuel Fay, junior, his Wife who has lain confin'd for nigh 11 months, and Jonathan Tainter who is in a deep Consumption. We were also at Mr. Charles Rice's.[26]

24. The last of our Home Cutt Hay got into the Barn. Thomas Reap'd Rye the rest of the Day. I Catechiz'd a and pm. Very Faint and weak. Brother Hicks return'd from Cambridge. Read Dr. Peter Kings Biographic Ecclesiastica.[27] Very Hot. Thomas to Worcester middle of p.m.

25. [No entry].

26. Chiefly on my Preparations from Day to Day, having been for Some time greatly troubled at the Scantiness of them.

27. [No entry].

28. [No entry].

29. On Matt. 13, 39, a and pm. Deacon Forbush,[28] who had requested me to preach at his home next Thursday, told me of his

Brother Tainters[29] request for the Sake of his son Jonathan to move the Place of the Lecture by the Consent of the Brethren of the Meeting to his House, Jonathan being not like to go abroad again or long to continue; and upon their Consulting Such Brethren of the Meeting as they could light of and obtaining Consent thereto, I appointed the Lecture accordingly to be at said Tainters on the next Thursday 4 p.m. and likewise propounded the Desires of his Dauter Sarah to join in full Communion with the Church.

30. In the Morning I rode down to Mr. Beemans and Matthias Rice's. Thomas help'd Levi Brigham p.m.

31. Thomas work'd at Mr. Beemans. P.M. Mr. Jonathan Forbush came suddenly to call me to see his poor Brother Jonathan Tainter. I found him very low, but had his reason and could Speak a few words at a Time softly yet somewhat Audibly. He had no such direct Evidence as to give him much Comfort, but yet he hop'd and desir'd; and Hopes and Desires were the Chief of what I could get from him. Many were gather'd there. I pray'd with him, after what moving and Instructing Exhortations I could give both to him and the by-Standers. About sun setting I left him. N.B. Mrs. Dunlop rode with me part of the way back and she was under much Spiritual Trouble. N.B. Hannah Forbush (the Deacons youngest Dauter) in distressing Concern. I call'd in at Mr. Williams to see Mr. Coollidge as I return'd. My wife inform'd me that Mr. Andrew Boardman[30] and Sister Williams[31] had bin to visit me.

## AUGUST 1744

1. Thomas did not come here from Mr. Beemans till 11 o'Clock. Neighbour How[1] came in the morning and told me that Jonathan Tainter dy'd last Evening and This Day he was to be bury'd; and accordingly was so. N.B. Thomas at Burial, so that he wrought but about 2 Hours today, or but little more.

2. Mr. Matthias Rice informs me that the Mohawks on their Journey home came to Marlborough last night, and that several Canada Indians are expected down. I preach'd at Lieutenant Tainters on Isa. 40, 6, 7, 8, and may the Lord give it his peculiar Blessing! N.B. Among others Mrs. Stevens of Grafton there.

3. Thomas at Mr. Beeman's. I was devoted to my Business, in some Measure as I was able, but I was much indispos'd in Body, and could not make Dispatch.

4. Thomas at Mr. Beemans. Mr. John Sparhawk Schoolmaster at Shrewsbury came at Evening and lodg'd here. N.B. The School in the Middle of the Town over.

5. Mr. Sparhawk kept Sabbath here. I preach'd on Mat. 12, 33, 34, 35. P.M. on James 5, 9. Mr. Coollidge and Mr. Sparhawk Supp'd and Lodg'd there.

6. Mr. Sparhawk return'd to Shrewsbury in the Morning. Mr. Coollidge Stay'd and din'd. He seems to be in great Horrors and Despairs. N.B. Eli Forbush with me in the Morning very much engag'd in the Business of his Soul and appears to have experienc'd some Remarkable Convictions. Mrs. Stevens (wife of Israel) of Grafton having experienc'd wonderful awakenings, was here with me. She assures me she is not able to admitt many things which she finds among her Neibours—regard to Dreams, and holding most sensible Communion with God in sleep, etc. She and her sister Rice din'd with me. P.M. Mrs. Thankful Maynard[2] here desirous to join with the Church. At Eve Thunder storm arose. Thomas at Mr. Beemans.

7. I visited Mr. John Caruth's wife who languishes in Body and is very much distress'd in Mind. As I was riding over upon this visit Captain Forbush met me and acquaint'd me that a man was kill'd last night by his Cart near Ensign Bruce's in this Town. At my Return home I was requested to attend the Funeral of the Said poor Man, at 4 p.m. I had appointed with myself that this Afternoon I would visit in that Corner and my Wife and I accordingly rode down to Mr. Ebenezer Chamberlains and by means thereof we were till somewhat past 5 when I got to Ensign Bruce's,

22 The Reverend Nathan Webb (Harvard 1725), the minister of Uxbridge, 1731-1772. *Sibley*, VII, 617-619.
23 The Reverend Joshua Prentiss (Harvard 1738). *Sibley*, X, 312-314.
24 Thomas Freeland.
25 In Connecticut.
26 One of the original settlers of Westborough.
27 Lord King (1669-1733) was a nephew of John Locke.
28 Jonathan Forbush.

29 Deacon Simon Tainter.
30 The schoolmaster of Hopkinton.
31 Mrs. Abraham Williams of Marlborough.

1 Hezekiah How.
2 Mrs. Stephen Maynard.

the people being very much gather'd and long waiting. It was a very sorrowfull Time! The providence very awfull indeed. The man was of Sutton, one Mr. Samuel March of about 29 or 30 Years, originally from Newbury. His poor mournfull widow, the Dauter of Captain Sibley[3] of Sutton was there, with her Father and Some Number of Sutton Friends along with them. The Lord Sanctifie His holy Dispensation in peculiar to them and to his Mate (Mr. Holbrook) who was upon the Road with another Team just before Mr. March; but O that God would also enable all of us to make a Suitable Improvement of So awakening a Providence, and Convince us that we know not the Hour! For as Saith Solomon man also knoweth not his Time: as the Fishes etc. and as the Birds, etc. So are the sons of men Snared in an Evil Time, when it cometh Suddenly upon them. Eccl. 9, 12. N.B. I understand that 5 Indians of the Cagawaya's went to Boston last Friday; and that Some Considerable part of our Soldiers who were sent out to guard and Scout in our New Towns, were call'd in, and had return'd. Thomas at Mr. Beemans.

8. Rainy Day. Thomas came home from Mr. Beemans.

9. My Kinsman Needham[4] with his Wife from Norwich and they carry away their Son Thomas with them. N.B. I gave him everything that he carry'd away with him, except his Coat which Mr. Needham agrees to pay me for. P.M. Mrs. Eager and her Sister Mrs. Patty Ward rode here in their Chair to make us a Visit. Many Interruptions by Company almost from Morning till night. Thomas Set up a New Rail Fence between my Fore yard and Garden.

10. [No entry].

11. Mr. Matthew Bridge[5] going up to preach at North Sutton and Mr. John Brown[6] with him. They din'd here.

12. On Eccl. 9, 12, on occasion of the Sudden Death of Mr. Samuel March on the 6th Instant. May the Lord Sanctifie both his Word and Providence to us that we may be Quicken'd and O that we may be found ready how suddenly so ever we Should be Summon'd! Mr. Coollidge din'd with me.

13. The Towns Committee went down to the General Court to reply to the Petition of the North side. I wrote to Mr. Danforth by Ensign Rice. P.M. I was at Captain Bakers[7] an Hour of Two, he not being well, nor could go to Court. Rainy at my return in the Evening, found Mr. Brown and Bridge from Sutton at my House. And they lodg'd here.

14. They rode with me to Sudbury to Ministers Meeting. We went first to Mr. Smiths[8] at Marlborough and he requested my Mare might be put into his Chaise and we rode together. See Association Records for Mr. Barretts Concio On 2 Cor. 5, 20 etc. N.B. Mr. Gardner[9] an Excellent prayer in the Evening with the Family. N.B. Mr. Cook[10] came among us. Mr. Smith rode my mare to Mr. Cooks.

15. There was more Business done by the Association than usual—more Collections, etc. Mr. Swift[11] of Acton preach'd a Smart, bold Sermon on Mat. 13, 5, 6. After Dinner Mr. Wood,[12] Deacon Miles[13] and others from Concord came in among us to request the Ministers so far to Countenance Them of their Party as to preach among them in their Separation from Mr. Bliss.[14] But they were rather advis'd to seek out some suitable Young Gentleman to preach to them and leave it to him to Change with neighbouring Ministers as they Should incline or see prudentest. Return'd home through Marlborough and for the Sake of Mr. Cushings[15] and Mr. Morse's[16] Company, by Ensign Bartletts. Found Mr. Weld[17] here.

[3] Joseph Sibley.
[4] Parkman's eldest sister, Mary, had married Daniel Needham.
[5] (Harvard 1741). Later the minister of the First Congregational Church of Framingham, 1746-1775. *Sibley*, XI, 8-11.
[6] (Harvard 1741). Later the minister of Cohasset, 1747-1791. *Sibley*, XI, 12-17.
[7] Edward Baker.
[8] The Reverend Aaron Smith.
[9] The Reverend John Gardner of Stow.
[10] The Reverend William Cooke of Wayland.
[11] The Reverend John Swift, Jr., of Acton.
[12] Ephraim Wood. Lemuel Shattuck, *History of the Town of Concord* (Boston, 1835), p. 388.
[13] Samuel Miles.
[14] The Reverend Daniel Bliss.
[15] The Reverend Job Cushing of Shrewsbury.
[16] The Reverend Ebenezer Morse of the North Parish of Shrewsbury.
[17] The Reverend Thomas Weld of Upton.

16. Mr. Weld left us—but not before Ensign Wood of Upton also, came, both of them on Account of Council papers. Mr. Weld to return Some and Ensign Wood to take off a Copy of his Dauters Oath. N.B. Two Exercises yesterday and the like to Day at Grafton but I could not go up, having so newly come Home, and much Business lyes behind. At Eve Mr. Cornelius Cook[18] here, and was partly Examin'd in order to his joining with the Church.

17. Captain Maynard and Mr. Francis Whipple return'd from Boston and inform'd that having laid their Reply to the North side's Petition, before a Committee of the Honorable Board, viz. Judge Wilder,[19] Colonel Berry,[20] Captain Watts,[21] a Committee was appointed by the Two Houses to come up and View the Town and report accordingly. Said Committee were Captain Watts, Major James[22] and Mr. Dodge, to come up Next Tuesday come fortnight.

18. [No entry].

19. On Mat. 12, 36. P.M. repeat'd on Mat. 7, 24 to 27. Mr. Coollidge[23] din'd with me.

20. Ebenezer Wheeler brought me a summons to answer in Court tomorrow at Worcester Court in the Case depending between Reverend Mr. Weld of Upton and Rachel Wheeler of Grafton. N.B. Samuel Baker here to be examin'd in order to his joining with the Church. P.M. Mr. Cook with me on the Same Errand. At Eve Captain Maynard and Mr. Whipple here.

21. I early rode to Colonel Wards[24] to enquire whether the Business of the sessions would be likely to bring the Wheeler Case on to Day? The Reason of My Enquiry was, I had appointed the Catechetical Exercise to Young Women to be this afternoon before I had known any Thing of Mr. Wheelers summons. Who told me it would be Contrary to Custom of the Court if it was call'd, and assur'd me I might safely return home for to Day. Upon which I return'd accordingly. P.M. attended upon my Catechizing of Young Women, and deliver'd them a sermon on Ps. 25, 7. Hannah Forbush[25] full of Spiritual Concern came to my House, as her Brother Eli had been not long Since.

22. I rode up to Worcester Court—from Mr. Cushings had Dr. Stanton Prentice's[26] Company. Visited Mr. Burr[27] and Dr. Breck.[28] Mr. Solomon Prentice[29] came there and we went together to the Court—where I attended the forenoon. I din'd at Mr. Burrs with Mr. Loring[30] of Marlborough and Dr. Breck. P.M. a very lazy Time, whilst I neither Care to be at the Court, it being Sultry Hot, nor Ventur'd to go to the prisoner (Edward Fitz Patrick) but convers'd with Some of my old Neibours who had gone from us whom I occassionally light of, and at Eve was at Mr. Waldo's.[31] But I lodg'd with my Brother Breck. N.B. at Captain Daniel Wards[32] where I lodg'd. Mr. Ebenezer Wheeler and many of that Company had taken up their Quarters.

23. In the Morning after the Rain I went to the Jayl and Spent Some Time with the prisoner who is as Yet unhumbled—has talk'd of late in a Strain of denyal of the Fact, and grumbles at his Windows being Shutt up (tho at That tis thought he receiv'd ill Counsel) and Complains of the Room he is confin'd in etc—as if he was treated hardly because he was a Stranger. Mr. Campbell[33] of Oxford there and pray'd with him, and whilst we were in the Jayl the Wheeler Case was call'd at Court, and was thrown out of that Court. I din'd with Mr. Solomon Prentice at Mr. Eatons.[34]

[18] Westborough's profane blacksmith.
[19] Joseph Wilder was a Special Justice of the Superior Court.
[20] Thomas Berry was a Special Justice of the Superior Court.
[21] Samuel Watts was later Judge of the Inferior Court of Common Pleas in Suffolk County.
[22] John James of Medford.
[23] Samuel Coolidge of Westborough.
[24] Nahum Ward of Shrewsbury.
[25] Daughter of Thomas Forbush.
[26] The physician of Lancaster.
[27] The Reverend Isaac Burr of Worcester.
[28] Samuel Breck, the physician of Worcester.
[29] The Reverend Solomon Prentice of Grafton.
[30] Jonathan Loring, a lawyer.
[31] Cornelius Waldo, Jr., son of the prominent merchant of the same name in Boston. See Waldo Lincoln, *Genealogy of the Waldo Family* (Worcester, 1902), I, 71-72.
[32] The son of Obadiah Ward, an early settler of Worcester. See Andrew H. Ward, *Ward Family, Descendants of William Ward* (Boston, 1851), p. 23.
[33] The Reverend John Campbell.
[34] Joshua Eaton (Harvard 1735) was the first lawyer to settle in Worcester. He fell under the spell of George Whitefield, became a New-Light preacher, and the minister of the first church of Spencer, Mass., 1744-1772. *Sibley*, IX, 533-538.

P.M. return'd home having Mr. Dana[35] the Lawyers Company great part of the way, but he proceeded down the Road to Marlborough.

24. Mrs. Hephzibath Maynard[36] here p.m. but my wife gone to visit Neighbour Davids[37] wife who is ill. Thomas getts Fencing Stuff, having mow'd our Bushes over.

25. Thomas Cutt Stalks. I was (according to my Custom) confin'd closely in my Study as I was yesterday also, yet having met with So many hindrances all the fore part of the Week I was too much behind hand in my preparations.

26. A.M. on Matt. 12, 36, 37. P.M. on 10, 38, 39. Mr. Coollidge din'd with me. He appears very gloomy, very Despairing of his Eternal State. At Eve James Bradish, junior deliver'd me a Letter from the Separate Church in New Haven, praying assistance in Council on the 13th of September next.

27. Mr. Ebenezer Rice came about noon to get my Team to go to Boston. I rode to Mr. Winchesters[38] and obtain'd his Oxen to go with my own to Boston. Thomas went with the Team to Mr. Abraham Temple's at Grafton for the Load and so Set out with it before Day. Brother Hicks[39] and Deacon Hall[40] of Sutton here. They went to Boston.

28. Visited Captain Forbush who is sick of a Fever. A Council of Five Churches sat at Grafton, The Churches of Lancaster, Oxford, East Sudbury, Waltham and Southboro, being call'd by the agrieved only. I Hear that the North and south side of this Town have employ'd Major Jones[41] of Hopkinton to measure the Roads of this Town—and that they begin to Day.

29. Major Jones with his Chain Men accompany'd by Mr. Miller,[42] Deacon Forbush[43] and Beriah Rice,[44] are come, in their measuring, to my gate, and thence proceed to the South Eastward to go down to Mr. Belknaps Corner. At Eve I visited Captain Forbush who grows worse, yet sleeps very much Day and Night.

30. A.M. Major Hicks[45] of Salem, Deacon Whittemore[46] and Mr. Joseph Bradford, with Brother Hicks who met them on his Journey down, and return'd to Sutton with them, but was now proceeding on his Journey again. They din'd here and took Leave. P.M. I preach'd on John 1, 11, and after Exercise read the Letter from New Haven receiv'd last Sabbath. At Eve I visited Captain Forbush who is not much better. Major Jones Measuring again to Day. Heard that the Council at Grafton had perswaded the Church and agrieved Brethren to unite in Calling a Council consisting of the following Churches, Mr. Prescotts[47] of Salem, Mr. Wigglesworths[48] of Ipswich, Mr. Emersons[49] of Malden, Mr. Turells[50] of Medford, and Mr. Hobbys[51] of Reading.

31. Thomas return'd in safety from Boston in the Night; and it was the greater Favour as it prov'd a very rainy morning, which follow'd.

### SEPTEMBER 1744

1. Have understood that the prisoner FitzPatrick had made his Escape out of Worcester Jayl—But is taken again. Brother Hicks here who brought me a Letter from Reverend Mr. Webb[1] of Boston intimating to me that it is unlikely that he shall go to New Haven to be upon the Council there.

2. Sacrament Day. Mr. Coollidge, Captain Fay[2] and his Dauter Goodenow[3] din'd with me. I preach'd a.m. on 1 Cor. 11,

26. P.M. repeated Sermon on 2 John 8. A.M. not without some hope that God was among us—but yet we have very great Reason to be humbled under a sense of our Leanness and Blindness, our Negligence and sinfullness. I again laid the New Haven Letter before the Church but they did not see Cause to Consent to the Request thereof. They urg'd that they as it was far off So they could not come to any tolerable understanding of their Case; nor could Learn how that Society had Separated from Mr. Noyes,[4] etc. For my own part, I could not inform them, having never been inform'd myself, and I thought myself too nearly ally'd to Mr. Pierpont,[5] to warrant my pressing the matter upon them.

3. I visited Ensign Josiah Rice's Child, ill of the Cankers; and Captain Forbush who Still lyes sick of a Fever. The Lord look upon him and be gracious to him. N.B. Mr. Batchellour and his partner, Goodhew, flourish in their Coopering at Captain Maynards[6] and to Day sent a Load of Barrells to Boston. This is the first Load out of the Town.

4. The Gentlemen whom the General Court has Sent as their Committee to View this Town and judge of the Circumstances hereof, and make Report accordingly—viz. The Honorable Samuel Watts Esq. of Chelsey, Major Jones of Hopkinton and Mr. Dodge[7] of Wenham, are suppos'd to be at Hopkinton. P.M. Mr. Joseph Wheeler and Samuel Allen here good part of the Afternoon, but went south I suppose to wait (with others) upon the Said Gentlemen; but it was so rainy that they came not into Town. I wrote to the Society in New Haven which had lately sent to us.

5. The Rain prevail'd greatly and continued all Day. So that neither did the Courts Committee come to us to Day. An Exceeding Rainy Time. *Jejun. priv. vide Natal.* The Lord enable me to take due Notice of his adorable patience and long suffering towards me! I now enter upon my 42nd Year. The Rain so heavy that if I would ever So fain I could not go to Southborough to Day, as requested by Mr. Stone[8] to preach his Lecture.

[In the Natalitia is recorded the following under date of September 5.]

September 5. I endeavour'd to humble my Soul with Fasting, and I Spent the Day chiefly in acts of Religion and Devotion.

I first Consider'd and then endeavour'd to praise God for, His astonishing Patience and rich Goodness towards Me.

I reflected with some seriousness upon my ungratefull Returns to God—recollecting my past Conduct, and especially my youthfull; my Soul was fill'd with much both Shame and Grief. My late Transgressions also testifie against me, and ought deeply to humble me: the Defects of my Ministry and my own unprofitableness and unfaithfulness under my Christian Obligations.

I sought the Lord in prayer and supplication for Pardoning Mercy and sanctifying Grace. I sought for myself—for my Family—for my Flock. I carry'd their present state to God as they are now engag'd in the great Affair of Dividing the Town, and the General Courts Committee now here among us. I carry'd to God also, as I was able, the state of the Churches of this Land, as circumstanc'd at this Day. I renewed my Solemn Engagements before the Lord and my Resolutions to walk before Him (by his Grace assisting me) in Integrity all the Days of my Life.

6. But gratify'd Mr. Cushing (as far as I was able) by preaching to Day for him. Text John 1, 11. Very few at Meeting there. Mr. Samuel Biglo's wife with Me, in her soul Distresses still. Return'd at Evening. N.B. The Courts Committee view'd the south part of the Town. I was with them at Eve at Captain Maynards. N.B. Mr. Ebenezer Baker of Marlboro a great Interruption of our Conversation there.

7. So grievously broke in upon by the Various Matters of the View of the Town etc., that I could not attend to My Studys. Din'd with the Committee at Captain Eagers.[9] N.B. Lieutenant Holloway intimated to Me that it was agreeable to my own Desire

---

[35] Richard Dana (Harvard 1718) served various towns before settling in Boston, where he later became a prominent Son of Liberty. *Sibley,* VI, 236–239.
[36] Mrs. John Maynard.
[37] David Brigham.
[38] Thomas Winchester.
[39] Parkman's brother-in-law had moved from Westborough to Sutton about 1740.
[40] Percival Hall. Benedict and Tracy, *Sutton,* p. 654.
[41] John Jones.
[42] James Miller of Westborough.
[43] Jonathan Forbush.
[44] Son of Edmund Rice, an original settler.
[45] Joshua Hicks.
[46] Samuel Whittemore was a deacon of the Cambridge church for over 40 years. Paige, *Cambridge,* p. 688.
[47] The Reverend Benjamin Prescott (Harvard 1709) was the first minister of Peabody, Mass., 1713–1756. *Sibley,* V, 485–491.
[48] The Reverend Samuel Wigglesworth (Harvard 1707) was the first minister of Hamilton, Mass., 1714–1768. *Sibley,* V, 406–412.
[49] The Reverend Joseph Emerson.
[50] The Reverend Ebenezer Turell.
[51] The Reverend William Hobby.

[1] John Webb.
[2] John Fay.
[3] Dinah Fay had married David Goodenow of Marlborough. He later moved to Shrewsbury. Hudson, *Marlborough,* p. 373.

[4] The Reverend Joseph Noyes.
[5] James Pierpont, Jr., son of the Reverend James Pierpont, the predecessor of Noyes at New Haven, was a leader in the movement to establish a second church. Dexter, *Biographical Sketches,* pp. 189–190.
[6] John Maynard.
[7] Numerous persons of this name, several of them prominent, were living in Wenham. See Myron O. Allen, *The History of Wenham* (Boston, 1860), pp. 141–142.
[8] The Reverend Nathan Stone.
[9] James Eager of Westborough.

that I was with the Committee whereas it was in Conformity to their Special Request Sent me by Captain Eager and Captain Eagers own personal Request that I put myself to the Trouble to go over and din'd there. N.B. Captain Watt's advice that I would not engage myself in the Disputes of my Neighbours about Dividing the Town, The Rather because they all, universally express'd so much Love and Esteem etc. and were each of them desirous to enjoy me among them. Conformable to his Advice I Said nothing but after a little Space retir'd.

8. I had many close Reflections upon myself, Chastizing myself for my Pusillanimity that I did not boldly bear my Testimony against the slender Provisions in the Most Towns throughout the Country for the Maintenance of ministers, which withholding more than is Meet tendeth to Poverty and is one of the Principal Causes of the many Dissentions in the Land—but know not what the Event would be if I had Zealously appear'd in it since it might soon have involv'd me in what the Committee had so much advis'd me against. However my mind was Somewhat Eas'd when Major Jones and Mr. Dodge came along by my House in the forenoon in their return home, (Captain Watts going down the Road from Captain Eagers,) for though I could not have Opportunity to declare my mind last night yet I did to the fore-named Gentlemen to Day. Lieutenant Holloway and Mr. Jacob Rice being in Company with them. In which I expressly declar'd especially that I could not by any means Countenance Such Divisions of Towns or Parishes as incapacitated them for bearing the necessary Public Charge etc, and that notwithstanding all the Love which the Town express'd to Me yet I intimated that they certainly did not provide for me as was necessary to enable me to answer their Expectations from me. Captain Maynard at my House afterwards, and at noon Lieutenant Holloway and Rice—but would not stay to Dine. P.M. Mr. Coollidge returns from the North side and keeps School no more, being far gone in Despairs, Sordidness and viciousness (viz. Idleness and sloth, Smoaking and Drinking)—But he seem'd so much to Desire to remain with me over the Sabbath that I even told him he should be welcome.

9. Great Frost last night. On Consideration of the State of Things in the Town I repeated sermon on Ps. 103, 19 latter part. Mr. Coollidge and Mr. James Balls wife din'd with us. Mr. Coollidge says he is utterly without Hope.

10. My forenoon taken up in various necessary Things—fixing a Well—Buckett to the Pole etc. Mr. Coolidge went to Captain Maynards and din'd there, but return'd here. P.M. Spent mostly with him. At Eve I visited Captain Forbush. Thomas Winchester at his Fathers. Mr. Coollidge lodg'd here.

11. Mr. Coollidge went away to Lieutenant Tainters. I walk'd, tho not with Mr. Coollidge to Lieutenants and din'd there. At Eve Mr. Coollidge with Lieutenant for Watertown. At Eve Eli Forbush here at my House having wrote the Dealings of God with his soul, he gave it me. Mr. Cook was here after him and gave account of his Experiences and what he thought to be his Conversion; but when we were upon the most serious Concerns, and without any Sign of Provocation that I know of, except that I made no Difference between persons of our Country or another, he bitterly told me that he had been more abus'd by me, and by my wife and Children than ever he had been abus'd in All his Life, which with other Things I remember he Said to me nigh about those Times which he says he Experienc'd made me fear whether he who brot forth so Contrary Fruits to the Spirit had that glorious Spirit. After I had administered some Reproof and Reason'd with him and told him I Should make a minute of this he left me, and O that God would please to shew him his Errors and forgive them! N.B. Bekky Hicks to Day to Cambridge on my mare. Thomas at his Fathers.

12. Visited Captain Forbush[10] but the Doctor being there, and it appearing later than I thought for I did not make any long stay. Brother Samuel Breck was there also with Dr. Gott.[11] Dr. Breck din'd with us. P.M. I rode over to Lieutenant Holloways (favour'd with Neighbour Ebenezer Maynards Horse) to Catechizing. Had 27 Boys and 17 Girls. Lieutenant Holloway[12]

[10] Samuel Forbush.
[11] Benjamin Gott, the physician of Marlborough.
[12] William Holloway of the north side of Westborough.

gone to Brookfield. Call'd at Mr. Tim Fays after the Exercises. Rainy return home at Thomas[13] at his Fathers Still.

13. Captain Forbush grows worse. Sent for me. I went immediately—found him very low. I dealt very plainly and as thorowly as I could with him. O that I had Sooner and Continually, both with him and all others!

14. Visited Captain Forbush. Find him with but little hopes respecting his Spiritual State—but begging the Mercy of God. We could make no New Cyder. Neighbour Pratt[14] kindly offer'd to Send me a Barrell and did so.

15. Unusual Great Frosts from Night to Night.

16. Matt. 16, 26. Repeat'd sermon on Rev. 20, 12 from 2 Cor. 5, 10. O that the Lord would make His Sabbaths Days of true Spiritual Rest and Joy to my Soul!

17. Thomas Clearing. Mrs. Patty Ward[15] (Colonel Nahums Dauter) here. She and Molly rode to Marlboro. P.M. I visited old Mrs. Goodenow who lay very Sick. She gave me an Excellent Testimony of the Grace of God in her and the Evidences of a regular and thorow work from her early Age; of which may God have the Glory! And may we all pattern after her! Her children also testify that this had been the Substance of her Conversation among them all along thro her Life. N.B. I hear that David Crosby and 5 others break Jayl.

18. Thomas thrash'd rye. Samuel Baker here to be examin'd a.m. I visited Mr. Gibson of Hopkinton who lyes very bad, and Mr. Barrett[16] gone to Boston to his Brother Mr. Thornton Barretts Funeral. In my way I was at Mr. Bowmans.[17] Dr. Crawford return'd with me. N.B. Mrs. Thankfull Maynard here to be Examin'd. Molly return'd from Marlborough.

19. Rode up to Worcester. Mr. Welds[18] Case against Rachel Wheeler was try'd at Superior Court; but only as to the Libel, and did not go into the proof of the Facts—and was committed to a Jury—but they could not agree. So that it was put off to another Year. I din'd at Colonel Chandlers.[19] P.M. I was at Mr. Eatons, where were Mr. Hall[20] and Mr. Prentice with their Wives. In the Eve I was at Mr. John Chandlers, where was Mr. Johonnot[21] of Boston. While I was there a Messenger with Candle and Lanthorn to have me lodge at Colonel Chandlers, where were Several of the Judges—which I embrac'd.

20. The Trial of Edward Fitz Patrick, for Murthering Daniel Campbel of Rutland in March last. Mr. Campbel of Oxford pray'd at the opening the Court. The Trial began at 11 a.m. and lasted till 4 or 5 p.m. The ministers din'd with the Court at Captain Haywards. At Eve the Jury brought in their Verdict, Guilty. After Spending some Time in the Eve at Colonel Chandler with the Judges etc., Mr. Campbell and I were Conducted by Mr. Sheriff Curtis to the high sheriffs, Captain Flaggs,[22] where we lodg'd. Thomas at Worcester to Day.

21. We understand that the Prisoner took on much last Night when he had his Irons put on again. Mr. Campbell and I visited him before his Sentence. I receiv'd the Judges Request to pray with the Court. Judge Dudley[23] pronounc'd the sentence of Death upon him.[24] He Confess'd that what the Justice (Chandler) and the Minister (Mr. Burr) had Said (namely of his Confession in the Jayl at his first Committment) was true, tho he Stood to it that the Rutland men testify'd was, Two words to one, wrong. Din'd at Colonel Chandlers, and return'd home. Returning home heard that old Mrs. Goodenow was Dead, and this Day to be bury'd. Mr. Cushing was gone to the Funeral. I also hastened, waited at Ensign Rice's, and went to the Grave as the Corps pass'd to it. May God Sanctifie this Breach upon us!

[13] Thomas Winchester.
[14] John Pratt.
[15] Of Shrewsbury.
[16] The Reverend Samuel Barrett of Hopkinton.
[17] James Bowman of Westborough.
[18] The Reverend Thomas Weld of Upton.
[19] John Chandler, Jr. of Worcester.
[20] The Reverend David Hall of Sutton.
[21] Daniel Johonnot, a Huguenot refugee, was a distiller and merchant in Boston. See *The New England Historical and Genealogical Register*, VI (1852), 357-360.
[22] Benjamin Flagg of Worcester.
[23] Paul Dudley of the Superior Court of Judicature.
[24] Edward Fitzpatrick was sentenced to be executed Oct. 18, 1744. He was the first to be executed for murder in Worcester County. Jonas Reed, *A History of Rutland* (Worcester, 1836), pp. 183-184.

22. Mr. Gibson of Hopkinton I hear is Dead. I rode to Shrewsbury and Mr. Cushing to Westborough. N.B. Major Keys acquaints me that the Flagg of Truce from Cape Breton is detain'd by the Governour and that we are short of Ammunition.

23. I preach'd at Shrewsbury on Rom. 8, 7. Mr. Cushing at Westborough on Rom. 6, 23 and on Ps. 76, 7. I return'd home at Eve, as did Mr. Cushing also.

24. Visited Mr. Thurston a.m. and found him very bad. Mr. Gamel P.M. who is very ill likewise.

25. Visited old Mr. Samuel Fay. Was at Mr. Grouts and Winchesters. P.M. Catechized young Women. Exercise on Ps. 25, 7.

26. Sent for to visit Mr. Thurston again who grows worse, and is very Delirious. Yet it was Evident his soul was much engag'd in deep self Abasements. Cry'd out Ashes and Muck—rottenness etc.

27. Thomas made Cyder yesterday and to Day.

28. Thomas fetch'd 3 Barrells of Cyder from Mr. Grout and one from Mr. Miller. P.M. gathering Corn. Mr. Patteshall here in his way to Sutton. He lodg'd here.

29. Old Mr. Thurston came and acquaint'd Me that his son Joseph dy'd last night.

30. On 2 Cor. 5, 10. Repeating several parts of Sermon on Rev. 20, 12. Old Mr. Thurston din'd with me. N.B. Mrs. Beeman sick and pray'd for.

### OCTOBER, 1744

The Funeral of Mr. Joseph Thurston, a man well spoken of for his Seriousness and Graciousness. He leaves a Widow and six Children among us. Help Lord! the Godly man ceaseth etc. Deacon Whipple of Ipswich Hamlet here. At Eve Mr. Patteshall again; Mr. Turell and Two Messengers going to the Council at Grafton, viz. Captain Brooks and Mr. Tufts[1]—and they all 4 lodged here. Neibours Young Men came and Husk'd.

2. A.M. Mr. Emmerson of Malden and his Messengers, viz. Mr. Brainerd and Mr. Shute.[2] They all left us before Dinner and Mr. Patteshall rode with me to Mr. Beemans—and thence he went for Marlborough. The Judges Saltonstall[3] and Sewall[4] din'd with me. Mr. Zebulon Rice lay'd the Floor of my new Study.

3. I rode to Grafton Council (as an Auditor). Thomas Winchester at Grafton. Mr. Patteshall came into Captain Fays while I was there and was my Company up. We were at the Forenoon public Hearing but not at the Reading over Articles of Complaint. They heard but 11 of 23 Articles to Day and in the Evening. I lodg'd at Captain Willards.[5]

4. I rode to Worcester and din'd with Mr. Burr, where also din'd Captain Flagg. Mr. Burr asked Me to Change with him next Sabbath, but I freely told him it would Stir up great uneasiness among my people. He ask'd me to Preach the Execution sermon but I was oblig'd to deny him because of my design'd Journey to Boston. I visited the Prisoner, found him in a bad frame—dwelling upon his deplorable Condition but taking no Care to help himself, nor suitably betaking himself to God for Help. Unforgiving, Sour, very Sparing of Speech—not Confessing his Sin—refusing to say anything about it, but that We might think as we would—reflecting on his Trial. But I most solemnly Call'd him to Repentence and Confession, reprov'd, Charg'd him, pray'd with him and left him. Justice Brigham my Company to Grafton and to Westborough. Thomas at his Fathers.

5. George Reed came with a Message from Grafton from Drury and Hardy to go up. I rode up and p.m. the Council took under Consideration the aggrieved Brethrens Complaint of Reverend Mr. Prentice's Disgust at my sermon on their Fast in September 1743, and I was Desir'd to produce my Notes. At their request I read the disquieting Prayer—and after a Short Debate withdrew.

At Eve Mr. Hall preach'd a Lecture (while the Council were in their Debates in private) on Job 22, 21, a very savoury and usefull sermon. The Lord graciously bless it to my Spiritual Profit! Return'd home Mr. James Fay and wife being in Company.

6. The good and Learned Moderator of the Council, Reverend Mr. Wigglesworth came to me with Mr. Francis Whipple who waited on him—to preach for me tomorrow.

7. Mr. Wigglesworth a.m. on Jer. 8, 20. The Very Text and the Very Day on which I purpos'd myself to preach, that I might follow my summer sermons with the most solemn and awakening Warnings. But the Lord in his Providence has order'd wisest and best, that these should be dispers'd by So Superiour a messenger. P.M. on Mat. 11, 12 O that God would follow both sermons with an efficacious Blessing!

8. Mr. Wigglesworth return'd to the Council. Training Day, but I was overlook'd, and it suited me very well, not to be disturb'd, being in my Preparations for my Journey. Ebenezer went to Grafton and brought Madam Sartels Chaise. Mr. Millen[6] from Chauxit here, with his Call to settle there. Mr. Matthias Rice kindly lent me £50 old Tenor, for which I gave him a Bond.

9. My Wife and I with our little son William rode to Sudbury in Madam Sartels Chaise. We got down about 12. It was the Time of the Ministers Meeting at Mr. Cooks.[7] While dinner was preparing I borrow'd Mr. Lorings Horse and rode to Mr. Farrars[8] at Concord and paid him £50 old Tenor and return'd to Ministers Meeting. I read (for my Concio) the former part of my sermon on Heb. 13, 17.

10. We rode to Mr. Foxcrofts[9] and my Deeds from Mr. Lull were enter'd to be recorded. Proceeded to Boston. My aged Mother much more Comfortable than for a long Time. Blessed be God. We din'd with her. N.B. The Sorrowful Shocking News by Brother Samuel of Cousen Elias's[10] Fall into uncleanness with Mrs. Sally Hill. The Lord Sanctifie this sore Trial for our deep humbling! P.M. I was at Dr. Sewals. We lodg'd at Brother Samuels.

11. Mr. Byles Lecture on Tit. 2, 13, middle Sentence. Din'd at Brother Alexanders. P.M. at Mrs. Bennetts, where was Mr. Mather.[11] At Eve at Mr. Webbs[12] and at Mr. Eliots[13]—in these last visits, upon poor Parkmans Case. Lodg'd again at Brother Samuels.

12. We purpos'd to have gone to Cambridge but the rainy Weather prevented. I attempted to go over the Ferry, but the Rain increasing I prevail'd with the Ferryman to sett me ashore, as also Colonel Minot[14] of Concord. He walk'd up with me and broke fast at Brother Samuels. At Secretary Willards.[15] P.M. at Mr. Gee's.[16] So rainy that I concluded to stay over the Sabbath and engag'd to preach for Mr. Gee. At Eve waited on Mr. Wilsteads[17] Lecture. On Mat. 16, 26. Lodg'd at Sister Bettys. N.B. Mr. John Jarvis dy'd nigh a month agoe.

13. The Morning was So bright (tho windy) that I hasten'd to Mr. Gees to dissolve the above Obligation of preaching for him and tripp'd to Cambridge to my Horse (our Chaise having been left at Charlestown) and endeavour'd to Come up to my own Flock; but by loosing one pair of Gold Buttons out of my Sleave, and other Impediments I made it sundown before I got to David Hows[18]—and was much Chill'd with the Cold of the Night. Stopp'd at Mr. Smiths[19] of Marlborough and lodged there.

14. Lords Day Morning, rose early and was more Comfortable. Rode up Home and preach'd all Day, repeating (with

[1] John Tufts (Harvard 1708), of Amesbury, formerly the minister at West Newbury. Sibley, V, 457-461.

[2] Daniel Shute (Harvard 1743), of Malden, later minister of the Second Congregational Church of Hingham, 1746-1802. Sibley, XI, 304-309.

[3] Richard Saltonstall, justice of the Superior Court of Judicature.

[4] Stephen Sewall (Harvard 1721), justice of the Superior Court of Judicature. Sibley, VI, 561-567.

[5] Benjamin Willard, an early settler of Grafton.

[6] The Reverend John Mellen of Sterling.

[7] The Reverend William Cooke of Wayland.

[8] Deacon Samuel Farrar. See Shattuck, Concord, p. 370.

[9] The Reverend Thomas Foxcroft.

[10] Sibley, X, 223-224.

[11] The Reverend Samuel Mather.

[12] The Reverend John Webb.

[13] The Reverend Andrew Eliot (Harvard 1737), minister of the New North Church in Boston, 1741-1772. Sibley, X, 128-161.

[14] James Minott was Concord's representative in the General Court. Shattuck, Concord, p. 380.

[15] Josiah Willard, Secretary of the Province.

[16] The Reverend Joshua Gee of Boston.

[17] The Reverend William Welsteed (Harvard 1716) was minister of the New Brick Church in Boston, 1728-1753. Sibley, VI, 153-158.

[18] Proprietor of the Wayside Inn.

[19] The Reverend Aaron Smith.

alterations and additions) Sermon on Mat. 26, 41. This I was prevail'd with to do tho I had preach'd 'em once or Twice before, because they were so seasonable after Grafton Council—and suitable for us likewise seeing Such a Trying Time is before us, next week, when the General Courts Report on our Northside People's Petition is propos'd to be made. A Thin Congregation many having thot I would not return from Boston so soon.

15. Rode to Cambridge, partly in Company with Mr. Smith of Marlborough. We din'd at Mr. Woolsons at Weston. No Buttons found. I set up Notifications. So Early at Cambridge that I walk'd from thence to Boston, in Company with one Mr. Shaw shingler, of Boston South End. Lodg'd at Brother Samuels.

16. Din'd at Brother Parkman's. Our Conversations turn very much upon the Melancholly and afflicted Circumstances of my poor, Miserable Kinsman. But as to the Affair of Westboro Petitioners, there is little room for me to Say any Thing because our People are grown so jealous that there is my Design in being at Boston so much at this Time, viz. that I may undermine them[20] etc.—whereas this journey was appointed on Occasion of the Ministers Meeting at Mr. Cooks. At Eve was at Mr. Eliots Lecture on Jam. 5, 16, latter part. N.B. Mr. Buel,[21] Mr. Pomeroy,[22] and Mr. Parsons,[23] of Connecticut at meeting. I was at Mr. Eliots after Lecture. N.B. Mr. Whitefield expected at Portsmouth, Piscataqua. We lodg'd at my aged Mothers.

17. Din'd at Alexanders. Refus'd to apply to any Gentlemen of the Court about our Westborough Affair. Saw divers of the Committees of both Sides. Lieutenant Holloway very hot. We rode to Cambridge. Our Mare in the Chaise got away from Sister Barretts and ran over to Father Champneys. Broke one of the Thills and clear'd herself of her Tackling. But I found her again, and Deacon Whittemore[24] Sent over my wife and son in his Chaise to prevent further trouble.

18. Rainy. John and Samuel Hicks helpfull to get over my broken Chaise to Mr. Edward Mannings to be mended. Din'd at Mr. Whittemore. P.M. Mr. Manning and Mr. Moss (the Smith) prepar'd and fitted every Thing for the mended Shaft to be put on again. And in the Eve I visited Mr. Goff, Mr. Appleton[25] and Dr. Wigglesworth,[26] and supp'd with the Doctor before I return'd to Father Champneys.

19. So rainy that we were confin'd at Father Champneys all Day.

20. Tho the weather was thick and Sometimes Misty, yet being Saturday we Set out upon our Journey. Were at Baldwins by Twelve, at Hows before 2 p.m. Din'd at Mr. Darlings, and got home by Day Light, in Safety. The praise to God, who has protected both us and our Family in our Absence.

21. I preach'd on Heb. 10, 22, being mainly from what I had deliver'd in Time past tho with much alteration and addition. Eli Forbush[27] and Mrs. Thankfull Maynard[28] here before meeting with their Relations. P.M. they were admitted before the Communion. Preach'd p.m. on Mat. 16, 26. I beg it mayn't be without Effect!

22. Had the Chaise to mend at Mr. Williams Shop before it was carry'd home. Ebenezer went up with it to Grafton. N.B. Captain Baker at Mr. Williams Shop. Hear that the Petition of the North side was last week granted by the General Court. N.B. Captain Baker and I a great Deal of Talk of the Manner of my first Settlement in Westboro. Thomas Winchester work'd for Mr. Samuel Fay, junior. I visited Captain Forbush who is very weak yet.

23. At Mr. Beemans in the Morning. Catechiz'd a. and p.m. N.B. Mrs. Kelley present at the Catechizing. N.B. Mr. Cor-

nelius Cook here and as violent as ever. Thomas Winchester carting out Dung from the Cow Yard.

24. Thomas Winchester carting Dung and clear'd up Rye. I preach'd at Southboro on John 1, 11. Few at Meeting. When I return'd home Thomas was gone, and now changes his Home.

25. Mr. Smith having desir'd me to preach for him, but not hearing any Thing from him Since he went to Cape Ann, I rode as far as Mr. Matthias Rice's with whom I had some Business, that I might be more certain—but could not find from them or from there Neibours that any Lecture was appointed—so that I return'd home.

26. I preach'd at Mr. James Fays on Eph. 1, 4, and hope that thro the Grace of God there was Some good Effect. Wish it may have Suitable Impression upon my own Heart. A number of hearers immediately requested me to print the Sermon. N.B. Captain John Tainter of Watertown there, with his Wife.

27. Many Reflections on God's wonderful Patience towards me and his people in this Place.

28. The Lord's name be prais'd and magnify'd for his adorable Patience and Longsuffering towards Me and towards the Dear Flock in this place, that now we see the 20th Year Completed since our Founding and Ordination. Alas! My Barrenness and unprofitableness! How little good have I done in all these years, and how many Things are amiss also among the people! O that God would Pardon us through the Greatness of his Mercy! And Grant us his almighty Grace, to enable us to Repeat, and bring forth Fruits meet for Repentence. I preach'd a.m. on Gen. 31, 38 and p.m. on 2 Cor. 13, 9, Repeating part of Sermon on Heb. 13, 20, 21.[29] Captain John Tainter and his wife, with Lieutenants Wife also din'd with us. O that God would make it the Day of his power with us!

29. Mr. Weld[30] of Upton here. He Still thinks himself under grievous Oppression. Wants another Copy of our late Result, which I transcrib'd for him and let him have Copys of Several Papers. He din'd here, and p.m. being somewhat rainy he lodg'd here also. In the Eve Captain Maynard here, and John Oake in order to owning the Covenant. A.M. visited Mr. Jonathan Forbush's Sick Child.

30. A.M. Mr. Weld left us. P.M. came Mr. Peabody,[31] accompany'd by Deacon Felch[32] and Chickery, on their Journey to Worcester Council. O what Cause of Grief and Mourning that God has permitted So many unhappy Divisions and Contentions to arise among us! May God Sanctifie these Evils and hasten them to an End! New Perplexitys also arise respecting the Affairs of Upton. The Moderator at the Request of Sundry of the Upton Brethren has issued out Letters for the Council to meet the first Tuesday of November, but it falls out to be the week of West-Leicester Ordination at which Mr. Hall, Prentice and Goddard[33] are to officiate. So that it was concluded by the people at Upton that there must be another appointment which the Moderator refuses to make, but abides by his old Appointment, and requests me to Certifie Mr. Weld that he does; nor can attend at any other Time, unless it be adjourn'd till Spring. My Catechetical Exercise with young women could not be attended till it was too late for the Sermon, but the other parts of it were accomplished.

31. I went to Mr. Whipples[34] and Deacon Newtons[35] upon the Upton Business. Wrote to Reverend Mr. Weld and to Ensign Jonathan Wood.[36] N.B. Serjeant Miller undertook to Convey the Letters to Mr. Jonas Warrins[37] of Upton. Raw Cold season. Snow'd some part of the Day. Daniel How[38] work'd for me, Ploughing up Stubble of the lower Field.

---

[20] The north precinct of Westborough was created by the legislature, Oct. 20, 1744. Distance from the meeting house was one of the important factors motivating the northside people. See Josiah C. Kent, *Northborough History* (Newton, 1921), p. 14.

[21] The Reverend Samuel Buell (Yale 1741), an itinerant preacher and later minister at East Hampton, Long Island, 1746-1798. Dexter, *Biographical Sketches*, pp. 664-669.

[22] The Reverend Benjamin Pomeroy of Hebron, Conn.

[23] The Reverend Jonathan Parsons (Yale 1729), minister at Old Lyme, Conn., 1729-1745, and later at Newburyport, 1746-1776. Dexter, *Biographical Sketches*, pp. 389-393.

[24] Samuel Whittemore.

[25] The Reverend Nathaniel Appleton of Cambridge.

[26] Edward Wigglesworth, Hollis Professor of Divinity at Harvard College.

[27] Eli Forbes, *Sibley*, XIII.

[28] Mrs. Stephen Maynard.

[29] This sermon has been preserved and is printed in large part in DeForest and Bates, *Westborough*, pp. 126-129. It is regrettable that Parkman did not take this opportunity to give an historical summary of the previous period.

[30] The Reverend Thomas Weld.

[31] The Reverend Oliver Peabody of Natick.

[32] Ebenezer Felch of Natick.

[33] The Reverend David Goddard of Leicester.

[34] Francis Whipple of Westborough.

[35] Josiah Newton.

[36] A selectman of Upton.

[37] Jonas Warren was a deacon of the Upton church.

[38] Son of Parkman's neighbor, Hezekiah How.

## NOVEMBER [1744]

1. Mr. John Sparhawk,[1] Schoolmaster at Shrewsbury, here to see me. Lieutenant Tainter at Evening.

2. Mrs. Martha Warrin here to be examin'd again in order to her joining with the Church. At Evening came Captain Trowbridge[2] and Mr. Isaac Williams[3] (Delegates from Newtown Church), came from Worcester Council, who have adjourn'd to last Tuesday of this Month. Captain Trowbridge lodged here, Mr. Williams at his Brothers.

3. Captain Trowbridge left us. Benjamin Forbush[4] plough'd Stubble. Mr. Jonathan Forbush's Dauter[5] of about 3 Years old, bury'd a.m. I return'd in Haste to my House to meet with Mr. Peabody who was coming from Worcester. He was entering my House with his Delegates at the juncture that I return'd. They din'd with me. Mr. Peabody tells me he has receiv'd another Letter from the Brethren at Upton that beseeches him to put by the Council, and he has accordingly gratify'd them. I sent by Mr. Peabody a Line to Mr. Stone to change tomorrow, which he comply'd with and came up at Evening. I also rode to his House the Same Evening.

4. Preach'd at Southboro on Rom. 8, 7, a. and p.m. N.B. No preacher at Framingham—many of them at Southborough. Captain Goddard and Wife etc. I return'd home at Eve, as did Mr. Stone.

5. Benjamin Forbush finish'd ploughing my Stubble. P.M. Mr. Cotton[6] of Newtown, who preach'd yesterday at North Sutton, came to see me and lodged here.

6. Transcrib'd the Worcester Result and rode with Mr. Cotton to Mr. Ebenezer Chamberlains where we din'd. I spent the Afternoon in visiting that Corner of the Town.

7. We ty'd up our Cattle in the Barn. Grows Cold.

8. Mr. Belknap who has been baptiz'd, here with me for 5 Hours.

9. N.B. My Young Cattle viz. Three young Heiffers, which Lieutenant Tainter drove up to Cold Spring for summering, in the forepart of the Year, were all missing when the Drovers came in. But Lieutenant undertook a Journey after them on the sixth instant, and this Evening brought in Two of them, the Third as tis judg'd dy'd in the Woods Some time agoe; the Carcase was found but was greatly corrupted etc. Lieutenant had been out 27 Shilling, and there remained 10 shilling for the Herdsman; in all the Charge amounted to 37 Shilling. N.B. Thomas Winchester and Ebenezer Maynard kill'd two Shotes for me—the Weight about 100 apiece—the Markit so low we salted them up.

10. Cold.

11. On Mat. 16, 26. O that these Sermons might not be in Vain! My own Soul (I thank God) was somewhat warm'd thereby. I was earnestly desirous that there might be Some success. Mrs. Chamberlain, that lately liv'd near us, was here and din'd with us. P.M. We had a Contribution for Mr. Jedidiah Biglo of Grafton whose House was burnt down October 9. I read the proclamation for the Thanksgiving, and appointed an Assembly next Thursday for Young People.

12. Mr. Lull was here and inform'd me that Mr. Farrar of Concord would be here to Day. I rode to Mr. Beemans and hir'd £30 of him (old Tenor). Mr. Farrar accordingly came and I paid him the whole of my Bond to him and took it up. Captain Maynard train'd his Company. I pray'd with them both at the Beginning and Concluding their Exercises. Din'd at his House (Mr. Farrar with me.) N.B. At Eve Mr. Wheeler very full of bitter Complants that the Captain kept his Boys So late (and it was by this Time sundown), as also that they were abus'd etc. N.B. The Committee for the School viz. Lieutenant Holloway,[7]

and Messers. James Bowman and Seth Rice confer with me about Mr. Sparhawk for a Schoolmaster. N.B. Lieutenant Holloway and Mr. Livermore[8] request me to preach to the North Side Next Thursday forenoon. My Mind was engag'd upon a Variety of Things, and suffer'd their Urgency to overcome Me, tho I presently after regretted it.

13. Rose before Day a great while and Sent Thomme by break of Day with a [blotted] to Lieutenant Holloway and Mr. Livermore to prevent their Notifying the People and to Certifie them that I cannot preach, as propos'd last Night. N.B. Mrs. Chamberlin and her Twin Boys lodg'd here last Night.

14. Mr. Richard Barns[9] and Mr. Jonathan Rogers kill'd my old Red Cow which I formerly bought of old Mr. Holloway. P.M. Captain Tyler[10] of Mendon and his wife here.

15. I had a Lecture to Young People at the Request of the Society in the Middle of the Town. I preach'd on Prov. 14, 14, Repeating chiefly my Sermon of Heb. 10, 38. At Evening Deacon Forbush[11] and his wife here, and some others, Miller, Beriah Rice, Harrington, who had been over to the first Precinct Meeting on the north side here.

16. Mrs. Thankfull Rice[12] here. P.M. Mrs. Townsend (Joshua's wife) here, much concern'd about her Spiritual State etc. Towards Eve came Deacon Burnap[13] and one of his Sons—of whom I enquir'd concerning their great Divisions and Contentions in Hopkinton.

18. On Matt. 12, 40. Isa. 26, 20, 21, Repeat'd. Mrs. Grow[14] and Thomas Winchester din'd here.

19. Visited Mr. Benjamin Fays wife who is very ill in her lying in. N.B. Mr. Joseph Woods here with a message from Gideon Rice who lyes in Boston Jayl.

20. [No entry].

21. [No entry].

22. Thanksgiving. The first Very Cold Day. Preach'd on 1 Sam. 7, 12. Old Mr. Green[15] with me.

23. Mrs. Abigail Maynard[16] here.

24. A.M. Cloudy. P.M. Rain and Something of Snow but not to lie. At Eve came Mr. Cotton of Newton and Mr. Isaac Williams. They acquaint'd me that Captain Trowbridge who was with them in their other Journey to Worcester and lodg'd here, was lately bury'd. O that God would Shew us our End and make us know the Measure of our Days—how frail!

25. Mr. Cotton preach'd Two very awakening Sermons. A.M. from Luke 19, 14. P.M. on Ps. 119, 155. Mrs. Whitney[17] in great agitations and Sometimes was heard crying out Oh! Oh! At Evening in my Family service Mr. Cotton on Rom. 8, 9. May God give a Special Blessing!

26. Mr. Cotton to Worcester. P.M. Mr. Peabody and Deacon Felch—but left me, to prosecute their Journey to Worcester.

27. Rain. I had appointed the Young Womens Catechizing but the Weather prevented their coming. Thomas Winchester here and lodg'd here.

28. Thomas consenting to carry a Calf for us to Boston, Neighbour Hezekiah How came and kill'd it, but by Reason of the bad weather Thomas deferr'd his going.

29. Preach'd my Lecture myself, on Rom. 16, 20 first part. Repeated from Heb. 13, 20. Little Sarah greatly Exercis'd with Vomiting and purging. My wife detain'd from Lecture. Thomas to Boston with the Calf.

30. Brother Samuel Parkman having been at Hopkinton and rais'd his House there, at Eve came here, and lodg'd with us. A Cold Season.

---

1 (Harvard 1723). Sparhawk, who had been barred from the practice of law at Plymouth because of intemperance, kept school at Shrewsbury for a time. *Sibley*, VII, 258–259.

2 William Trowbridge was a selectman, slave owner, and deacon. He died later this month, Nov. 19, 1744. Francis B. Trowbridge, *The Trowbridge Genealogy* (New Haven, 1908), pp. 507–508.

3 Sometime selectman of Newton. Francis Jackson, *History of the Early Settlement of Newton* (Boston, 1854), pp. 441–442.

4 Son of Aaron Forbush of Westborough.

5 Joanna Forbush died Nov. 1, 1744.

6 The Reverend John Cotton (Harvard 1710) was the minister of Newton, 1714–1757. *Sibley*, V, 517–524.

7 William Holloway.

8 Jonathan Livermore.

9 One of Parkman's neighbors.

10 Nathan Tyler, a prominent citizen.

11 Jonathan Forbush.

12 Mrs. Josiah Rice.

13 Benjamin Burnap, Sr., *Manual of the First Congregational Church in Hopkinton* (Boston, 1881), p. 42.

14 Mrs. Samuel Grow of Westborough.

15 John Green, a neighbor.

16 Daughter of James Maynard of Westborough.

17 Mrs. Nathaniel Whitney.

## DECEMBER 1744

1. Brother Samuel return'd to Boston. At Eve Thomas Winchester return'd from there. Mr. Whitefield[1] preaching at Boston. I was rather more afore hand with my preparations for the Sabbath than was Common with me and had somewhat more freeness and Ease of Mind. But yet alas too unprepar'd.

2. Sacrament. A pritty Cold Day. A. and P.M. on Mat. 12, 41. Deacons Fay[2] and Newton din'd here. The Lord follow us with his almighty Influences and make us Stedfast! N.B. My Wife not out to Day by reason of her ague and Sarahs illness.

3. Mr. Samuel Williams and Mr. Charles Rice kill'd 2 Hoggs between 10 and 11 Score apiece. P.M. pray'd with Captain Maynards Company at their Training, and din'd with the Officers. N.B. Mr. Boynes met me who was Still uneasy about the Affair of the Well. I told him to come to my House and I would Settle with him, tho he had been very abusive to me.

4. Deacon Newton Mr. Whipple and I rode over (in the Cold) to Upton. The Council Sat; but Mr. Goddard[3] of Leicester and Captain Clark[4] of Medway hinder'd by their illness and could not come. We first of all Enquir'd into the Letter which now brought us together and whether the Church and pastor had Comply'd with our former Result etc. See the Minutes of the Council.

5. Methods improving for Accommodations without going into further hearing. Mr. Hall of Sutton greatly Sensible of Wrong done by the former Result. He endeavours to compose a New Plan, the main of which was afterwards Accepted.

6. We accomplish'd the Arduous and Sorrowful Affair of Mr. Welds Separation and Dismission from his people. Mr. Hall went away Home before the Solemn reading of the Result. Mr. Peabody Bucknam[5] and I invited Mr. Weld to our Pulpits and we all offer'd to preach a Lecture to the people at proper seasons. Mr. Peabody and Bucknam to preach tomorrow. Deacon Newton return'd Home in the Night, but Mr. Whipple stay'd to accompany me.

7. Mr. Peabody (our late Moderator) preached on Isaiah. After Dinner we took Leave. Mr. Bucknam to preach p.m. In my Journey home Mr. Whipple was my Company. We came by Solomon and Elijah Rice's where we call'd and at Neighbour Eliezers also.

8. May the Frowns of Heaven on the Ministry be duely Improv'd by Me! Ebenezers Lessons a great Hindrance to me.

9. I preach'd on the Occasion of the Dismission of Mr. Weld, and of Mr. Burr[6] the Week before, from Matt. 28, 20. And pray it may be follow'd with a Blessing to both myself and the people.

10. Sixteen came to get me Wood. Solomon Woods with a Team, Mr. Grow, Miller,[7] Harrington,[8] Daniel, Jonathan, Phinehas and Eli Forbush,[9] Beriah Rice, Dunlop, Daniel Warrin, Elijah Warrin, Benjamin Tainter, Jonathan Grout, Jonas Child and Zebulon Rice. The Swamp clear'd. My Team improv'd all Day. N.B. The Committee from the Northside with me, to make me their Offers according to the General Court which erected them into a precinct.[10] Neighbour Jedidiah How here in the Evening.

11. Four Persons came to get the rest of the wood which was cut yesterday, to the Door. Mr. Dunlop (who was the Means of the rest) Mr. Jonah Warrin, Mr. Hezikiah Pratt with his Oxen and Sled and Moses Nurse with his Oxen and Sled likewise. They improv'd my Team and got down a good Pile. The Young Women Catechizing. They Said the 3 last Answers. I deliver'd another Discourse on Ps. 25, 7, chiefly against Company keeping and Unchastity. At Eve Mr. Peter Bent[11] here from Marlborough to talk with me in Mr. Boynes Behalf. Snow'd in the Night.

12. My Wife and I rode to Marlborough. Call'd at Neighbour Matthias Rice's, where was Mr. Thomas Ward. My wife was blooded by Dr. Gott,[12] and we din'd with him. P.M. at Mr. Smiths[13] where was Mr. Edward Barns. N.B. Talk of Boyness's Conduct. I call'd at divers Places to hire money to pay Mr. Lull and Thomas Winchester but in Vain. We return'd by Matthias's, and were kindly and handsomely entertained by them.

13. Rain. Mr. John Pratt[14] of Lambstown relates the great Revival of Religion among them in that Town. He desires a Dismission for himself and wife from our Church.

14. Mr. Beeman and Mr. Bowman, Captain Warrin and Captain Maynard here p.m. at Evening.

15. At the Funeral of Mr. James Maynards Daughter Olive, who dy'd the Night before last, having been ill but a Day or Two, but I hastened home without going to the Grave. She was nigh 11 Years old.

16. On Mat. 12, 42. Deacon Fay and Mr. Solomon Woods's wife din'd here. P.M. Repeated on Ps. 146, 4.

17. Dr. Gott here. Mr. John Mead at Evening.

18. Mr. Mead and Mr. Jeduthan Fay din'd here.

19. [No entry].

20. Visited Mr. Samuel Fay junior's Wife who lies in a very low Condition—has not been at public worship these 16 months. At Eve Mrs. Baker (wife of Captain) here to be examin'd in order to joining with the Church. Mr. Jenison came from Lunenburg with his Cloths etc., in order to his keeping School in this Town again, but was now immediately going to Watertown first; he lodg'd here. One of my Oxen ill. Captain Maynard very kind and Friendly according to his Wont in my Difficultys. He blooded the Ox.

21. My Ox very ill—a Fever—bound up. Captain Maynard here administering to him. Lieutenant Tainter here. He rak'd the Ox. At Eve he was somewhat better. Mr. Jonas Warrin here from Upton. Sent word by him that Next Wednesday come sennight (by Divine Leave) I would preach at Upton. N.B. I had told Captain Hazzleton[15] the like a few Days agoe.

22. Great Snow Storm last night and to Day. N.B. Mr. Samuel Mower[16] of Worcester here to desire me in the Name of the Committee, to preach tomorrow come sennight at Worcester, Mr. Cushing[17] being to preach tomorrow. My Ox better. Captain Maynard here (in his kindness) to See him.

23. On Mat. 12, 43, 44, 45. P.M. Repeat'd Sermon on Heb. 13, 21, from 2 Cor. 13, 9. Thin Congregation but 2 or 3 Men from the Northside—bad Travelling.

24. At Mr. Cornelius Cooks and at Lieutenant Thomas Forbush's[18] a.m. P.M. I rode to Mr. Lulls and he Sign'd me another Deed of the 70 acre Lot in Townsend. Ensign Josiah Rice rode down with me and was one of the Witnesses. Mr. Thomas Billings the other.

---

[1] The Reverend George Whitefield, the great English evangelist, arrived at Boston from Portsmouth, Nov. 26, 1744. *The Boston Weekly News-Letter*, Nov. 29, 1744.
[2] Captain John Fay.
[3] The Reverend David Goddard.
[4] Edward Clark. E. O. Jameson, *Biographical Sketches . . . of Prominent Persons . . . in Medway, Mass.* (Millis, 1886), p. 131.
[5] The Reverend Nathan Bucknam of East Medway (now Millis).
[6] The Reverend Isaac Burr of Worcester.
[7] James Miller.
[8] Samuel Harrington.
[9] Daniel, Jonathan, Phinehas, and Eli were sons of Deacon Jonathan Forbush.
[10] Dec. 9, 1744, the north precinct had appointed a committee "to Treate with the Reverend Ebenezer Parkman to see if he will tack up with the offer of the precinct as it is sett forth in the act of Courte which has divided the Town into Two Precincts and come to be our minister, or whether he will stay in the first Precinct and Tack the Twelve pounds, Ten Shillings ordered the petitioners to pay and to give security for said money agreeable to said act." Kent, *Northborough History*, p. 20.

[11] Prominent citizen who later represented Marlborough in the General Court. Hudson, *Marlborough*, p. 324.
[12] Benjamin Gott, the physician of Marlborough.
[13] The Reverend Aaron Smith of Marlborough.
[14] Formerly of Westborough. Sometime after 1737 he moved to Lambstown plantation, which became the town of Hardwick, Mass., in 1739. Lucius R. Paige, *History of Hardwick, Mass.* (Boston, 1883), p. 456.
[15] John Hazeltine.
[16] See Caleb A. Wall, *Reminiscences of Worcester* (Worcester, 1877), p. 351.
[17] The Reverend Job Cushing of Shrewsbury.
[18] Deacon, town clerk and selectman of Westborough. Pierce, *Forbes and Forbush Genealogy*, p. 27.

25. [No entry].

26. The Rain abated and the Shining Sun about 11 a.m. in-duc'd me to ride to Marlboro to preach Mr. Smiths Lecture. Bad travelling and Clouds and rain return'd—but I had reason to think that he depended upon me. But when I through all my Difficul-tys got there he told me he had not appointed it. It was Such bad weather that he had not appointed the Sacrament. Neither did he expect me to come—Whereas he ought to have Sent me Word that he had put the Exercises aforesaid by—and as to my Coming he could not know that it would not be good Weather by that Time. This is the Second Time of Disappointment about his Lectures of Late. I din'd with him, and then rode to Mr. John Stows[19] on the Business of Thomas Winchester. At Dr. Gotts at Eve but lodg'd at Mr. Smiths.

27. I return'd home by Neighbour Matthias Rice's. Mr. Benjamin Burnap here. Hopkinton Troubles continue nor prospect of Issue. P.M. Leçture to the Ladds, on Hos. 11, 7. Repeat'd chiefly my Sermon on Heb. 10, 38. Brother Hicks[20] here. He brought me a packet from Reverend Mr. Hall contain-ing the Christian History No. 74[21] with Marginal Defence which he wrote at my Motion made to him when we were at Upton Council. Brother lodg'd here.

28. Mr. Thomas Rice[22] of Worcester (one of the Committee to Supply their Pulpit) here in his return from Southborough, having been to Mr. Stone[23] to prevail with him to go to Worcester next Sabbath come Sennight. (N.B. Mr. Rice was my Company up to Worcester and over to Sutton when I first preach'd there Twenty Years agoe.) He din'd with Me. My son Thomas rode down to Mr. Bristons for our Cloth but in Vain. Neighbour Jedidiah How was so kind as to bring Me a Load of Pitch Pine.

29. I rode up to Worcester, calling at Mr. Cushings. One Brown from Reading, going to work at Mr. Eatons,[24] my Com-pany. Met Captain Maynard coming out of Worcester just at or presently after sunsitting. I was directed to go to Colonel Chandlers, and accordingly there I was handsomely receiv'd by his Spouse, but She was in No Small anxiety about her Husband, who came not till 10 o'Clock but then the face of Care was chang'd to Joy.

30. Mr. Brown[25] of Chauxit (as I afterward heard) preach'd at Westborough whilst I Preach'd at Worcester. A.M. on 2 Thes. 3, 1. P.M. on Ps. 122 latter End. Pray for the peace of Jerusalem etc. I din'd at the Colonel's who vouchsaf'd to go to meeting p.m. tho he loung'd at Home and his wife with him a.m. and am Sorry that I did not exert myself in Reproving them for their Sloth and Negligence. At Eve I was a while at the Colonels, and there came Justice Lee[26] and others—but I retir'd to Dr. Brecks[27] whom I had not visited since he brought his Wife to that Town and I lodg'd there.

31. In the Morning I Sent a Messenger to Mr. Burrs to see if he was at home Who return'd that he was not in Town. In my return home Mr. John Chandler was my Company as far as Eager's. We met Dr. Smith, his wife and others going to Worces-ter upon an action of the Doctor's against the wife of Mr. Caleb Johnson for Depriving him of a Note given to the Doctor by her Husband. N.B. My Off Ox ill again. But through the tender Mercy of God My Wife, Children etc. enjoy much Comfort and Health hitherto of the Winter. I desire to mark it with hearty Thanks for it. Thus has pass'd another Year of God's Long-suffering! N.B. Mr. William Jenison began to keep School at Captain Maynards and Eli Forbush came to board at my House.

[19] Of Marlborough. Hudson, *Marlborough*, p. 453.
[20] Parkman's brother-in-law by his first marriage.
[21] [Thomas Prince], *The Christian History, Containing Accounts of the Revival and Propa-gation of Religion in Great Britain, America, etc.*, No. 74 [Boston], July 28, 1744. This issue contained the Reverend David Hall's account of the revival in Sutton, Mass.
[22] Son of Ephraim Rice, an original proprietor of Worcester. Wall, *Reminiscences of Worcester*, p. 43.
[23] The Reverend Nathan Stone of Southborough.
[24] The Reverend Joshua Eaton of Spencer.
[25] Josiah Brown (Harvard 1735), sometime preacher, was the schoolmaster of the West Parish of Lancaster which became the town of Sterling. Parkman used a shortened version of the Indian name for Sterling, Woonksechocksett. *Sibley*, IX, 476–478.

## JANUARY 1745

We began the Year with a Little Association at our House. Rev-erend Ministers Cushing, Stone and Smith came up and din'd with me, and Smok'd a Pipe. P.M. There were Two Things I wanted the Thoughts of my Brethen in the Ministry upon. My Circumstances in Westborough at this present Day—as the Town are like to Violate and Destroy the Covenant and Contract which has hitherto been between us. And there are Two Meetings before us, to be within a few Days. A Precinct Meeting to be on the Thursday and a Town Meeting (which is to be partly at my Request) next Monday. I was not willing that there Should be Such Affairs as these transacting among us without acquainting my Friends about Me therewith and Consulting them thereon. This therefore I did.

Another Thing was I found there was like to be some Difficulty arising if I ask'd Mr. Jenison[1] to preach for me, or if I Should recommend him to our North side or Countenance his preaching there as in Years past. Mr. Smith in particular had told me that for himself he Should not ask him—and he conceiv'd that Mr. Cushing would refuse to likewise nor merely on account of his living from his Wife (which had but a bad aspect) but on account of other Conduct in divers respects. This was therefore talk'd over at my House and all present discover'd their sentiments and their Resolutions, which were that he ought to be refus'd, untill those Matters complain'd of were clear'd up—and they engag'd to second and strengthen me if I found it needful to begin with him in a faithful Discovery of My Mind to him.

But N.B. some unhappy Contrast between Mr. Smith and me at Table on the Score of Mr. Hall, and his Letter concerning the revival of Religion in Sutton inserted in the Christian History. At Evening before Mr. Cushing went away I sent my Desire to Mr. Jenison to come and sup with me, Which gave me Oppor-tunity, as it did also Mr. Cushing to deal freely with him; and we improv'd it as we were able. And as far as was discoverable he took it well and was thankfull.

2. Thus the Year began with Difficult Dutys and Trials, and more follow'd immediately upon them for on the second I rode over to Upton according to my appointment and Message to them. Lieutenant Tainter (whose wife I visited as I went) Mr. Stratton of Waltham, his son Harrington and Mr. Grow, were my Com-pany over. We din'd at Captain Sadlers.[2] It was Somewhat lowery A.M. but was clearer P.M. Mr. Weld and Mr. Dorr[3] at Meeting. I preach'd on James 5, 9, latter part. After Sermon Israel Taft junior who had before hand acquaint'd me with his Right to Church Privilege and his Desire of Baptism for his Child, having Stood up, with his Child ready, I laid his Desires before the Church who manifested their Consent to proceeding—But Reverend Weld objected and after long debatings Still insisted that this was one that had not made him Satisfaction etc. Rev-erend Mr. Dorr said he thot I ought to abide by our own Result, which granted Privilege. Several Brethren would fain have drawn off but I besought them to tarry. Mr. Matthew Taft in particular, but he said he thot it had as good be Wav'd for the present Seeing So much was Said. As to myself I conceiv'd that being the Young Man publickly acknowledg'd he was to blame in leaving Mr. Weld to hear Mr. Pain,[4] and was willing to join in what the Brethren did in the Agreement with Mr. Weld previous to his Dismission, he ought to be restor'd and enjoy Privilege but since there was so much uncomfortable Debate and the Sun just sitting I chose to Wave it. And so I proceeded to Prayer, and dismiss'd the People. Mr. Dorr and Mr. Weld went down to Captain Sadlers where Mr. Weld manifested great Disquiet-ment with our last Result as well as the former. But I would not tarry to contest with him. We return'd home. N.B. I supp'd at Neighbour Harringtons with Mr. Stratton and others.

3. The First Precinct had their First Meeting, and chose Precinct Officers, and a Committee to treat with Me. By this Days Transactions all Enquiry whether the Town Submitts to

[1] William Jenison. *Sibley*, VII, 371–374.
[2] John Sadler, a selectman of Upton.
[3] The Reverend Joseph Dorr of Mendon.
[4] Probably the Reverend Seth Paine (Yale 1726), who had been dismissed by Stafford, Conn., and became an Episcopalian. Dexter, *Biographical Sketches*, pp. 334–335.

the General Courts Act in dividing the Town is Superseded: for this is an actual Submission thereto and proceeding accordingly. This Day therefore I look upon the Contract between this Town and my Self to be Shock'd and Violated. God grant me wisdom proportionable to the Trial![5] My Ox bad. Eliezer Rice rak'd him. Sent for Mr. Daniel Garfield.[6] On the 3 Mr. Daniel Forbush laid an Hearth in my New Study.

4. Bad Weather, yet Mr. William Caruth coming to call me to Visit Mr. Simon Howards young Child, I went over—and having admonish'd them for their Neglect in not bringing it to Baptism, now the third Month—I sent to all those Neighbours round about who could be thot to attend, who accordingly came; Several of the Church, viz. Mr. Nathan Ball, Mr. Livermore, Mr. Townsend,[7] and others—who all judging and Concluding that the Child[8] would not live but was near its End, I baptiz'd it by the name of Solomon. After which we Commended it to God. Sang a Psalm and dismiss'd them with the Blessing. Not well when I got home went early to bed. Mr. Garfield came to look at my Ox which grows rather better. He rak'd him.

5. Rose better. Mr. Lull here. I paid him £20 old Tenor. Mr. Stone here on his Journey to Worcester to preach there.

6. A.M. on Consideration of the Very Weighty Affairs which in Divine Providence are before me with relation to this Town I preach'd on Mat. 6, 25, and p.m. on Phil. 4, 6. Mr. Jenison and Mr. Stratton din'd here. It was not difficult for the Congregation to perceive that my Subject pointed at the purpos'd Business before us on the Morrow. The Lord prepare my Heart!

7. I sat up till nigh two o'Clock this Morning in preparing for the Meeting (which was this Day) of the Town, and when the Town had been some Time together they sent a Committee viz. Captain Eager and Captain Warrin to desire me to go to the Meeting House, which I did and deliver'd my mind to them, which being from a written Paper, See. It was a Matter that my Mind wrought in: and I endeavour'd in some measure, to Committ it to God the Fountain of all Knowledge and Grace and the supreme orderer and Disposer of all Events. At Eve I visited Captain Maynard and Mr. Jenison. There were several Neighbours—Mr. Francis Whipple, Lieutenant Aaron Forbush, etc. N.B. The Town Meeting was adjourn'd to next Friday.

8. A Stormy Day, otherwise I should have been Expected to be at Southborough where some Ministers propos'd to meet in order to calling our Association together that a public Testimony may be drawn up against Mr. Whitefield.[9]

9. Still foul weather.

10. [No entry].

11. The Town met again about my Affairs. They granted Money at the Rate of £220 per Year for my preaching from June 5 to the 19th of October when the Town was divided into Two Precincts. Captain Fay and Captain Warrin were the Committee to inform Me, to which I return'd a Written Answer. And So now I am after these Things to be thrown upon a Precinct, or out of Doors—our old Covenants and Contracts being nullify'd and dissolved—and this without any Consent of mine, or Opportunity from either the Court or the Town to Shew whether I consented or not. At Eve came Captain Eager, Lieutenant Holloway, Mr. Wheeler, Mr. Livermore, Mr. James Ball, Mr. Jesse Brigham, Mr. Nathaniel Oake and Lieutenant Tainter and several of them had not heard the Paper which I read to the Town on the 7th. I did not read it for it was nigh Dark and they were Moving; but I gave them the Substance and enquir'd whether any one had a Mind to say anything about the Things which had been offer'd—upon which Mr. Wheeler and I had a long Conference In which I prov'd the Necessity of Order, but especially of Reasonableness in Societys, and that what the Town had done had been opposite to both; and that especially by the breaking up of our Covenant I was become a great Sufferer. Constable Livermore paid me all.

[5] See DeForest and Bates, *Westborough*, p. 131.
[6] Given as Gafeld in *Westborough Vital Records*.
[7] Joshua Townsend.
[8] Neither the birth nor the death is recorded in *Westborough Vital Records*.
[9] Parkman's name was among those of the ministers who expressed their approval of the Reverend Mr. Whitefield's work in a letter to *The Boston Gazette or Weekly Journal*, Jan. 8, 1745.

12. Mr. Othniel Taylor[10] of Worster here. Tells me of great outcrys at Mr. Webbs[11] meeting at Boston last Wednesday Eve, at Mr. Whitefields preaching.

13. Preach'd on Phil. 4, 7. Very Moderate and pleasant Weather for the Season, and we had a pritty good Assembly, I Thank God. O that his word might do us Good as it does the upright! O that We might have the Peace of God reigning in our Hearts! and that we may, might it please God to help us to Cast all our Care upon Him and in Every Thing make our Requests known to Him.

14. I rode to Mr. Grouts to pay him £16 Old Tenor for Thomas Winchester and I was in at Mr. Jeduthan Fays. P.M. Captain Maynard kill'd a sow for me assisted by Lieutenant Aaron Forbush and Nathan Maynard—in order to his Carrying it down in his Cart to Boston. P.M. The Committee of the first Precinct, viz. Old Mr. Whipple, Deacon Newton and Lieutenant Thomas Forbush came to me to see whether I inclin'd to Stay in this Parish or no? To which I return'd this Answer that the Parish ought first to manifest whether they desire me to; and this might be Two ways first by public Vote, and then by suitable Provision etc. At eve John Hicks junior here and lodg'd.

15. Captain Maynard to Boston, having my sow in his Team, for the Market. Mr. Aaron Hardy of Grafton here at Evening who acquaints me that they are yet in great and increasing Troubles by means of Mr. Prentice's[12] Conduct and preaching; having no regard to the Result of the Council that sat there, and Says he never did come in with it. He informs me that Mr. Dutton was the most of last Week among them and that Mr. Prentice gave him a very high Commendation on the Lords Day after.

16. Mrs. Stevens[13] of Grafton here being under Difficultys and wanting Advice on a Cause depending between her and Mr. Jacob Whipple[14] of their Church.

17. The world full of Mr. Whitefield (as I hear) who is now preaching at Boston.

18. [No entry.]

19. Captain Maynard made but slender Returns for my Pork, but 11 d. per pound at Boston. But we have more to Say on Town Affairs. N.B. North Side petition the Court again. See the copy.

20. On Phil. 4, 7—beg the word may be bless'd to my own soul as well as to the People. A raw Cold Day. Mr. James Balls wife din'd here. Mr. James Fay after several Sabbaths absence, came to meeting again.

21. A bad Snow storm.

22. At the Request of Mr. Loring,[15] Mr. Cook[16] and Mr. Smith, divers ministers were to Meet at Marlborough in order to draw up and publish a Testimony against Mr. Whitefield. But I sent a Letter by Thomme to Mr. Stone directed to Mr. Smith containing my Reasons why I did not go. See the Letter. Thomme brought home a piece of White Cloth from Mr. Britons fulling mill, 10 yards and ¾. The Committee of the North Precinct here again for my answer but was not ready. The first Precinct having done nothing to Effect yet. Deacon Newton and Captain Maynard here in the Evening.

23. At Deacon Newtons in the Evening, to Solemnize the Marriage of his Dauter Mary to Asa Brigham,[17] now an inhabitant of Shrewsbury. N.B. Mr. Goodale[18] of Marlborough awhile there. After supper I return'd.

24. Reading Mr. Hubbards Absence of the Comforter,[19] and diligently at my Preparations.

25. At Eve Mr. Whipple and Ebenezer Maynard here. A Cold Storm of Snow at Eve. Eli rode to Lieutenant Holloways.

[10] A young man who later was a conspicuous opponent of British rule.
[11] The Reverend John Webb of the New North Church.
[12] The Reverend Solomon Prentice had been rebuked by an ecclesiastical council at Grafton, Oct. 2, 1744, for his unreserved New-Light preaching. *Sibley*, VIII, 249–250. Pierce, *Grafton*, pp. 173–178. On Jan. 22, 1745, Prentice asked to be dismissed from the Marlborough Association and that body consented. Allen, *Worcester Association*, p. 24.
[13] Hannah, Mrs. Israel Stevens.
[14] Son of Deacon James Whipple.
[15] The Reverend Israel Loring of Sudbury.
[16] The Reverend William Cooke of Wayland.
[17] Son of David Brigham of Westborough. He became the Captain of the South Militia Company of Shrewsbury and later moved to Fitzwilliam. Ward, *Shrewsbury*, p. 236.
[18] Benjamin Goodale.
[19] Nehemiah Hobart, *The Absence of the Comforter Described and Lamented, in a Discourse on Lam. I, 16* (New London, 1717).

26. Mr. Millen[20] in his way to Mr. Morse's,[21] in here. He inform'd me that all the association[22] but Mr. Barrett[23] and I met last Tuesday.

27. Luke 12, 15. P.M. repeated the last sermons on John 14, 21. N.B. Mr. Josiah Walker of No. 4 of the Tannick Townships, din'd here.

28. Mr. Millen who had chang'd with Mr. Morse din'd with me.

29. I desire to remember the Wormwood and the Gall; and may my Soul be humbled within Me! Nine Years have roll'd off Since the Lord was pleas'd to bereave me of the Desire of my Eyes by his holy Stroke![24] Jejun. and Consider. At Eve Neighbour Jedidiah How and Neighbour Daniel Hardy here. This Day an Ecclesiastical Council (as I have heard) Sitts At Hopkinton. Eli Forbush went home.

30. I rode to Ensign Newtons[25]—din'd at Mr. Ebenezer Rice's—visited Mr. Nathaniel Whitneys Family—Mr. Jonas Childs—was at Lieutenant Tainters. (The School began by Mr. Jenison at the South School House.) Conferr'd with Mrs. Martha Warrin (wife of Daniel) touching her Admission into the Church. I call'd also to talk with Captain Bakers wife who was desirous of the Same Privilege. Dr. Gott and Dr. Breck here whilst I was gone and din'd with my wife.

31. Very Cold. Kept Close to my Studys. Mr. Jeduthan Fay made up with me. N.B. Mr. James Fay here and Stay'd out the Evening. Thus finishes another Month of God's Long Suffering.

## FEBRUARY [1745]

1. More Moderate Air. Clear and pleasant for the Season tho Somewhat Cold. Ebenezer Maynard came from Boston Yesterday. Brought up several Pamphletts against Mr. Whitefield—of whom (and Fresh Provisions) he says, the Town is full. Two Essex associations Letters to the Ministers of Boston,[1] and the Determination of the Association at Cambridge. Mr. Nathaniel Henchman[2] of Lyn, his Letter[3] to Mr. Chase[4] of Lyn End against Mr. Whitefield. But have not yet Seen Mr. Foxcrofts Apology.[5] The world much divided. *Laudatur ab his Culpatur ab illis.* God grant us Wisdom, Grace and Peace!

2. Pleasant Day tho Somewhat Cold. Mr. George Smith the Taylor brought home a Great Coat which he had made for Ebenezer. His work 11/.

3. On Luke 12, 15. Repeat'd p.m. on Ps. 73, 25. Mr. Jenison and Mr. Tainter and Mrs. Biglo. At Eve Lieutenant Tainters Sister Hastings here.

4. A Beggar whose Feet had been froze, and one Cutt wholly off, the other all the Toes, here, his Name John Green, his Home Hartford. I could not but Sympathize with him. The Lord make me thankfull for my Limbs and faithful in improving them to the Divine Glory. Brother Hicks and his wife here going to Cambridge. Mrs. Martha Warrin here further to Discourse concerning her Admission into the Church. At Evening Reverend Prentice of Grafton, and his Wife, with their son Solomon here. Supp'd with me and return'd to Mr. Winchesters in order to their going Home.

5. I visited Mr. Samuel Fays (Junior) Wife, who lyes Still in her Languishment. P.M. The First Precinct Met to See whether they would by a publick Vote manifest their Desire of my Continuing their Minister; which Vote pass'd by Every one present. Also money for Support till next June, and that the Precinct would

take upon them the Obligations which the Town were under. N.B. A Considerable Number of the precinct were dissatisfy'd with the Warnings of the meeting, posted upon the Meeting House Door, which stood there on the Sabbath, and therefore did not care to be present—but came to my House; or if they were at the Meeting House at any Time, retir'd from acting in the Affair. Messers. Miller, Whitney, Jonah Warrin, Beriah Rice, Stephen Fay, etc. were of those who esteem'd the notification of the Precinct Meeting to be a Breach of the Sabbath.

6. Zipporah Wheeler[6] marry'd to Asaph Wilder[7] of Lancaster. Mrs. Baker here again in order to her joining in full Communion with the Church. A Committee from the first precinct to acquaint me with how far they proceeded at the late meeting—and to Consult me about what Distance from a Meeting House I could be easy with meeting. Training, on the South side. Was Requested by Lieutenant Forbush (Captain Baker being at Court) to be with them at Captain Fays—Pray with them and Dine among them—which I did. Mr. Jenison was there also. N.B. A Young Man there who came from the Town of Preston in Connecticutt who was much in Defence of Mr. Pain etc. The Proclamation was read to the Company by Lieutenant Forbush encouraging Men to 'List Volunteers in the Expedition to Cape Breton. But no one 'listed. N.B. Cornelius Cook[8] talk'd with but in Vain. At Eve in at Mr. Williams's. Conversation turn'd upon the Business of the Precinct tomorrow.

8. I Solemnly Committed to God the Business and Affairs of the Precinct this Day—and besought the Divine Direction in the drawing up my Thoughts which the precinct had desir'd Me to Send them. I drew them up and Sent them by Mr. Abner Newton (one of the Committee). N.B. Captain Maynards Company together afternoon and I pray'd with them. No one 'listed. The Precinct Met also this afternoon, by adjournment. N.B. Those who excepted against the Notification (as above) would not attend. At Eve Deacon Newton and Mr. Francis Whipple, Deacon Forbush, Mr. Abner Newton and others came to my House, and Deacon Newton Said that the Precinct had not appointed a Committee to wait upon me, for it was growing nigh Dark, but they desir'd their Moderator and Clark to come and give me an Account of what they had done, and they were now come accordingly. And then he desir'd Clark Whipple to read the Votes which had been pass'd that Day; who comply'd and read that the Precinct had voted £55 of New Tenor money (not Soldier money) to be my Yearly sallery from June 5 next—and that in Case the Meeting House be mov'd above 3/4 of a Mile from Me, that then the Precinct pay me £500 old Tenor. Upon which they dissolv'd the Meeting. It appear'd to me to be of God that they were so ready to provide for me, as the last meeting they were so universal in their Desire of my Continuance.[9] At Eve Brother and sister Hicks from Cambridge who inform that Father Champney has been ill, but is better. That Mrs. Susè Champney[10] dy'd at Hingham, etc. etc.

9. Brother and sister went home to Sutton. Mr. Joseph Batchellor[11] of Grafton here, Who agreed to take my Son Thomme a Prentice next April.

10. Luke 12, 15. Ps. 73, 25. Granny Forbush[12] din'd here. At Eve Thomas Winchester and Sarah Henry a Taylor, Stopp'd and lodg'd here. N.B. I propounded Mrs. Baker and Mrs. Warrin and appointed a Meeting to be next Thursday at Mr. Solemen Rice's in Upton. Cold Day.

11. Ebenezer who came home on Saturday last return'd to the School again this Morning. Thomas thrash'd Barley and Sarah Henry making a Coat for Ebenezer.

12. Thomas thrashing Barley. Sarah at work. P.M. Mr. A. Hardy of Grafton here.

13. Thomas and Sarah at Work. Visited at Charles Bruce's and Mr. David Brighams. Mr. John Oakes Wife here again in Order to her being propounded and having her Child baptiz'd,

[20] The Reverend John Mellen (Harvard 1741), the first minister of Sterling, Mass., 1744-1774. *Sibley*, XI, 40-52.
[21] The Reverend Ebenezer Morse of Boylston.
[22] See Allen, *Worcester Association*, p. 47.
[23] The Reverend Samuel Barrett of Hopkinton.
[24] The anniversary of the first Mrs. Parkman's death.
[25] Thomas Newton.

[1] Caleb Cushing, and others, *A Letter From Two Neighbouring Associations of Ministers in the Country . . . Relating to the Admission of Mr. Whitefield into Their Pulpits* (Boston, 1745).
[2] (Harvard 1717). The minister of Lynn, 1720-1761. *Sibley*, VI, 192-195.
[3] *Reasons Offered by Mr. Nathaniel Henchman . . . for Declining to Admit Mr. Whitefield into his Pulpit* [with an introductory note by Stephen Chase] (Boston, 1745).
[4] The Reverend Stephen Chase (Harvard 1728), the minister of Lynnfield, 1731-1747, was also hostile to Whitefield. *Sibley*, VIII, 382-385.
[5] Thomas Foxcroft, *An Apology in Behalf of the Reverend Mr. Whitefield* (Boston, 1745).

[6] Daughter of Joseph Wheeler of Westborough.
[7] Son of the late Colonel James Wilder, who had been a deacon of the Lancaster church.
[8] Westborough's profane and cantankerous blacksmith.
[9] See DeForest and Bates, *Westborough*, p. 131.
[10] Susanna was the cousin of Parkman's first wife.
[11] A weaver.
[12] Widow of Thomas Forbush of Westborough.

but am oblig'd still to delay gratifying her, not finding her acquainted with what is necessary to be known and understood of the main Principles of Religion. At night Thomas and Sarah went home.

14. I rode to Mr. Solomon Rice's, at Upton and preach'd there on Rom. 8, 7. The Lord add his effectual Blessing! N.B. Molly went with me. We design'd to have gone by Mr. Eliezer Rice's, but miss'd my way and went to Mr. Timothy Warrins—and they being at Dinner, we din'd there. But I rode up to Mr. Eliezer Rice's because I had told him of my Coming to his House to Day. When we return'd at Eve I visited Mr. Daniel Forbush's wife who was confin'd and greatly distress'd, and Expecting (at her Time) much Danger and Difficulty as her Circumstances are. Was also at Lieutenant Tainters, and Molly not well, but we (thro Divine Favour) got home safe.

15. Town Meeting to see if the Town would make an Answer to the North side's second Petition to the General Court; and voted it, and Captain Warrin, Mr. Francis Whipple, and Deacon Newton to be the Committee. Mr. Daniel Warrin trimming my Orchard. N.B. My wife has been generally much indispos'd for a Month or Two past, and grows much more uncomfortable—and is particularly very much so today.

16. A Thaw. High South Winds; Misty—the Snow gone. Ebenezer came home.

17. On Luke 12, 15 and p.m. on 1 Tim. 6, 2 those words—Partakers of the Benefit and therefrom repeated part of sermon on Eph. 3, 8th viz. from page 17 to page 24. Mr. Jenison, Mrs. Tainter and Mrs. Child din'd with us.

18. This Day The Committee from the Northside were with me to receive my determinate answer[13] to their Message on December 10 to go over and be their Minister. Lieutenant Holloway and Mr. Collister[14] here, but Mr. Matthias Rice did not come. Those who were here gave me their Bond for Security of £12, 10 s. I dealt somewhat freely with them about their last Petition to the Court and warn'd them against Unrighteousness and against Divisions, but wish I had been more faithfull on the Affair of the Petition, notwithstanding that I had it over with them time after Time. Mr. Dan Warrin trimming my Orchards. A Number of hands cutting and Carting Wood for me, viz. Benjamin Whipple with a Yoke of Oxen made up my Team. Mr. Benjamin Fay with his Cart and 2 Yoke of Oxen, and Jonas Brigham with his Cart and 2 Yoke. The Cutters were Mr. Harrington, Dunlop, Edwards Whipple, Noah How, Sam Baker, Silas Pratt, Levi Brigham, [blank] White, Charles and Artemas Bruce, Moses Warren, and Samuel Bumpso. And they got to my Door 50 Load of Wood. N.B. At Eve Samuel Baker discours'd with me touching his admission into the Church, but not without some Disputing on Visible and Real Right to Special Ordinances. Ebenezer return'd to the School.

19. Fine Day. Sarah took Physick. P.M. both Mrs. Whipples here to visit my wife.

20. I rode to Mr. Matthias Rice's, and to Mr. Thomas Goodenows but neither of them at home, I convers'd a while with the women at each House, and then proceeded to Mr. Allen's,[15] Mrs. Allen continuing in a Very disquieted, disorder'd State. I also visited at Captain Eagers to discharge my Duty to both Parents and Children under their Sad Fall, their Daughter Oake having lain in already and got about again.

21. My wife very hardly able to be about. Read Dr. Prestons Life.[16]

22. Mr. Upham[17] of Sturbridge here—din'd with us. Trundle Bedstead from Mr. Hows. Was Strenuous to have my preparations for the Sabbath in good Season, yet by Various hindrances much taken off.

23. Mr. Matthias Rice here to take my Advice about a Preacher for the North Precinct. N.B. Our Conversation about Mr. Jenison,[18] whom I could not recommend to them because of diverse Complaints in Neibouring Towns. See January 1. Ensign Josiah Rice has been here to request my advice about his and others (Captives as they are Call'd) petitioning the General Court again that they may be Excepted out of the North Precinct. Ebenezer came home. Thomme brought 49 lb. of cheese from Mr. Jabez Rice's.

24. On Luke 12, 15. P.M. on Isa. 5, 4. Old Mr. Bellows and Granny Forbush din'd here.

25. Captain Daniel Ward of Worcester here. Further talk with Mr. Cornelius Cook who remains very disorderly and under bitter prejudices. Ebenezer at Home. Mr. Jenison gone to Watertown. The Committee appointed by the Town to make answer to the North precincts Second Petition to the General Court, went to Boston. I wrote by them to my Brother Parkman.

26. [No entry].

27. Very Cold.

28. Public Fast on Occasion of the Expedition to Cape Briton, as well as the Ensuing Spring. On Joshua 7, 4, 13. P.M. on Isa. 1, 19, 20. Mr. Jenison (Schoolmaster) was not at meeting, being not well.

### MARCH 1745

1. Orders having Come to the Captains of the Companys in this Town last Night, to Beat up to Day again for Volunteers to go to Cape Briton the Companys were together, P.M. Colonel Nahum Ward[1] and Lieutenant Willard[2] (from Lancaster) came. After prayer I went down to Captain Maynards, at his urgent Request. But no man 'listed in this Town. A.M. Mrs. Martha Warrin here—took her Relation from her Mouth.

2. At night came a storm of Snow; but not so bad as last Year just before Sacrament. The Lord give me strength and Assistance!

3. Sacrament. Preach'd on 1 Tim. 6, 2. Those Words, Partakers of the Benefit. Mr. Jenison did not Stay to Communion. Said he was not very well. I told him I expected him to have communicated. He din'd with me as did also Deacon Forbush and Deacon Newton. Deacon Fay did not. P.M. Repeated sermon on Isa. 1, 20. At Night Very much Tir'd in Body, and much disquieted in my Mind, having had but too lifeless a Time of it. The Lord in much Mercy Pardon, and quicken me! N.B. Captain Tainters[3] (of Watertown) Dauter Rebecca here. N.B. Only Mr. Matthias Rice (of Men I think) from the Northside at Communion, though a pritty good Day for Stirring.

4. Though I have had Such a fine wood pile got me, yet I am very much without Loggs. Sent to Neighbour Ebenezer Maynard who came up, with his Brother Nathan and their Oxen and Sled, who, having Cut the Chief of them (and adding my Oxen) got me down 3 Turns of Loggs. The Town met. Deacon Forbush and Captain Warrin came to me from the Town to desire me to pray with them. Mr. Whipple (after Prayer) came to me and deliver'd me a Letter from my Aged and venerable Mother (writ by my Kinsman Elias) complaining of too long neglect, and informing me of Sister Dorcas's[4] low State. N.B. Our Affair upon which the Committee went down from the Town to the General Court, labours much and goes from House to House, and is undetermin'd. Ebenezer went this morning again to South School, having been taught by me Last Week. N.B. Lieutenant Tainter talks with me about a Chaise that he has bought with some View to me.

5. I visited Mr. Thomas Billings and Family, and din'd with him. Visited also Mr. John Oake and Wife, talk'd with them again touching their owning the Covenant. Rode up to Mr. Asa Bowkers,[5] and thence I proceeded (Major Keys[6] my Company

---

13 Mr. Parkman declined the offer of the northside people in his "determinate answer" which is printed in Kent, *Northborough History*, pp. 22–23. The northside committee reported Feb. 21, 1745: "we have accordingly applied ourselves to the Reverend Mr. Parkman and he hath chose to Tack the Twelve pound Ten Shillings, and we have accordingly given bond to the said Mr. Parkman of £12. 10s. to be paid by the first Day of May Nexte in sewing."

14 John McCollister.

15 Ephraim Allen of the northside.

16 Thomas Ball, *The Life of Doctor Preston* (London, 1641). John Preston (1587–1628) was the master of Emmanuel College, Cambridge University.

17 Ezekiel Upham.

18 William Jenison (Harvard 1724) had been dismissed by the East Parish of Salem in 1736. Thereafter he had taught school in Lexington, Worcester, Lunenberg, and Westborough. Jenison was eccentric and intemperate, was not living with his wife, and was opposed "on account of other conduct in divers respects." See entry in this diary, Jan. 1, 1745. See also *Sibley*, VII, 371–374, and Allen, *Worcester Association*, p. 28.

1 Prominent citizen of Shrewsbury.

2 Moses Willard.

3 John Tainter.

4 Parkman's sister-in-law, Mrs. Samuel Parkman.

5 Of Marlborough.

6 John Keyes of Marlborough.

from thence) to Mr. Cushings His little Dauter Molly (a Second Molly) being bad with the Throat Distemper. As I return'd at Eve, I call'd at Captain Maynards, the Captain going to Boston Early tomorrow morning. N.B. Mr. Francis Whipple. N.B. Talk of Justice Baker[7] (our New Justice) his judgment of the first Warrant for Precinct Meeting on this side the Town (which was issued out by Esquire Nahum Ward and directed to Constable Abner Newton) that was defective and all that has been done by Vertue of it (of Consequence) invalid. N.B. Brother Hicks[8] and Mr. Barnard[9] of Sutton din'd with my wife. By my Absence I could not see them. N.B. John Hicks junior has 'listed to go to Cape Briton.

6. Mr. Morse[10] of Shrewsbury here in his way home from Mendon etc. Mr. Dodge[11] of Brookfield here at the Same Time. And by and by Mr. Patteshall in his Journey from Killingley to Cambridge—But he soon went off with Mr. Morse.

7. Catechiz'd A. and P.M. at the Meeting House. 40 Boys, but 10 Girls. I know not whether the Private Meeting this afternoon might not be some reason for so small a number. N.B. Molly had a Ride to Cramberrying with Mrs. Thankfull Rice.

8. Fine Weather. I was induc'd to have Something done at Gardening. Mr. Jonas Warrin of Upton here to be Examin'd in order to his joining with our Church.

9. Captain Maynard, who came up from Boston last Night, brings Me Brother Samuels Mournfull Letter of the Death of his Wife,[12] on Monday Eve last, about 6 o'Clock. The Lord Awaken all of us to a due Sense of his holy Will! May He be very gracious to those more immediately Suffering under So Sore a Bereavement. And may we all be quicken'd to and assisted in all due preparation for our own Decease! Sister Dorcas had been long languishing and wasting, and much Confin'd from Publick Ordinances but I have learnt Nothing of the State of her Mind. N.B. Small pox Said to have been at Boston.

10. Greatly Unprepar'd for public Service (as I am any Sabbaths)—go to my work but very dully; my mind crowded with the Composing of my sermon. Preach'd a.m. on John 27, 3, but could not do justice to so grand and important a Subject. P.M. Repeat'd the remainder on Isa. 5, 4. Mr. Jenison din'd with us, as did old Mrs. Byles[13] and old Mrs. Whipple,[14] and Mrs. Rebecca Tainter of Watertown. Exceeding high Winds.

11. A Letter at Eve by Captain Maynard from Mr. Smith[15] of Marlborough again requesting me to preach his Lecture. N.B. Benjamin Whipple[16] and Nathan Maynard[17] here to desire that Some Neighbouring Minister might preach to their Society, which I very freely consented to.

12. I rode a.m. to Mr. Grouts, by whom I sent a Letter to Brother Samuel Parkman, Mr. Winchesters, Mr. Thomas Whitneys and Mr. Eleazer Pratts. Din'd at Home. Mr. Jonas Warrin here again on his Examination. See the Eighth Day. My Wife ill and in Pain from Day to Day, yet keeps about for the most Part. We are waiting the Will of the Sovereign God.

13. A Storm of Snow. My Wife grows very bad. No possibility of gratifying Mr. Smith in his Lecture: nor does he indeed Deserve it, having Twice Disappointed me, by engaging me to preach, without appointing the Lecture or Sending me Word, So that I went, once part of the way, and the other time wholly to the House expecting to preach, but behold! there was no Lecture appointed. But I am ready to forgive the Injury; and was very much upon going to Day were it not for my wife's Circumstances—and the Storm. Yet I wrote a Letter to give him word and Committed it to Captain Maynard for Conveyance. My Wife gave us the Alarm. I hasted to old Mr. Maynards and got Nathan to go for Mrs. Forbush,[18] who was brought. Nathan

went also for Divers other Women. We got as many together as were needed, before or by 12 o'Clock. By Gods Power and Mercy my wife was deliver'd of her Third but my Sixth Daughter, being my Ninth Living Child about 1/2 past 2 o'Clock. The Glory be to God! May We who are the Instruments of its Natural be under God, of its Spiritual Birth! And may the Lord yet magnifie his Mercy to His Handmaid and recover her to Health and Strength again! Nor We be unmindfull of God's Goodness or of our Obligations to Him therefor! The Women assisting to Mrs. Forbush were the following—viz. old Mrs. Whipple, Mrs. Rogers, Mrs. Maynard, Mrs. How, Captain Samuel Forbushs and Lieutenant Aaron Forbush Wife's. Our Eating was over before Night—prayer also—and Thomme began to carry Home the Women, tho some of them tarry'd in the Evening whilst others were returning. But Granny Forbush tarry'd all Night.

14. My Wife and Infant Child very Comfortable. Pleasant, warmish Day after the Storm. Mrs. Forbush carry'd Home by Thomme. May others in the Town experience (where they need it) the like Mercy and Power of God that we have done!

15. Brother Hicks (who has been at Cambridge Some time and whom we concluded to have gone Home) return'd, and brings the Sorrowful News that my Honoured Father in Law Mr. Samuel Champney departed this Life on the eighth instant and was bury'd on the thirteenth. May we mark the perfect man and behold the upright, for the End of this Man in peace! O what an heavenly mind; what Hours together Spent with God, what a Contempt of the World, what Concern for the true Interests of Religion and of the Land, what value for the truely Godly and pious—was discernible in this worthy Person, above most! May I, and all nearly related have Grace to imitate his Excellent Example in those Respects!

16. One Mr. Daniel Hubbard of Suffield here with Flax. Noah How came p.m. to raise up the west part of my red Fence which had been blown down by the late high winds, but he did not finish it.

17. A.M. Preparatory to the Solemnity of Dedicating my young Child I preach'd on Ps. 51, 15 and p.m. on Gen. 17, 7. It was baptiz'd by the Name of Susanna. God grant his Covenant may be with me and mine. Messers. Winchester of Brookline sons of old Captain—din'd here. Mr. Jenison not at Meeting. Mr. Martin[19] preaches to the North Precinct.

18. Mr. Martin made me a kind visit, and din'd with me. Mr. Jonas Warrins wife from Upton here and examin'd. Divers neighbours to see my wife—who, and the Child, are very comfortable and Strengthen apace. D.G.

19. Mr. Cushing here and din'd with me. N.B. The Committees of Each Precinct running the precinct Line. Captain Robert Goddard of Sutton, the Surveyor. P.M. I went to Deacon Tomlins,[20] who is under much Affliction and under many Temptations by reason of his being included in the North Precinct Line. I had much, and Earnest Discourse with the Deacon against the Baptists, whilst he entertain'd favourable Thoughts of their Tenets. I gave him affectionate Caution in such a Day of Temptation, and Strong Exhortation to Steadfastness, etc. His son Mr. Elisha Newton there—who was my Company to Bezaliel Eagers. In returning Mr. Ithamar Bellows with me. At Eve Captain Maynard brought Captain Goddard to see me, who tarried all Night.

20. Captain Goddard return'd to his work, in running the Line. I rode over to Visit Mr. Barrett[21]—in my way I call'd at Mr. William Pierce's[22]—Understanding that Mr. Dunlop had gone away clandestinely to Ship for Cape Breton. I visited his wife who was in great Distress for her Husband and two Sons. I din'd at Mr. Barretts. I return'd him his Henry vol. 5.[23] N.B. Major Jones there. In returning I call'd at Mr. Tainters where I view'd a Chaise which he had bought with a View to me, but I conceiv'd it too much worn, yet determin'd nothing.

21. Preach'd at Shrewsbury Lecture, Preparatory to the Communion, on Cant 1, 4.

[7] Edward Baker, Justice of the Peace for Worcester County.
[8] John Hicks, formerly of Westborough. Parkman's brother-in-law. Benedict and Tracy, *Sutton*, pp. 660–661.
[9] Isaac Barnard.
[10] The Reverend Ebenezer Morse of Boylston.
[11] Francis Dodge.
[12] Dorcas (Bowes) Parkman died March 14, 1745.
[13] Widow of Captain Joseph Byles.
[14] Mrs. Francis Whipple.
[15] The Reverend Aaron Smith.
[16] Son of Francis Whipple of Westborough.
[17] Son of David Maynard, an early resident.
[18] Widow of Thomas Forbush. She often served as midwife.
[19] The Reverend John Martyn, later the first minister of Northborough, 1746–1767.
[20] Isaac Tomlin of Westborough.
[21] The Reverend Samuel Barrett of Hopkinton.
[22] Of Westborough.
[23] Matthew Henry, *Exposition of the Old and New Testaments* (London, 1710), 5 vols.

22. Could not get to writing my preparations for the Sabbath till this Morning, to any purpose; and then with too many Burdens, Cares and Avocations. Heavy Showers and extreme high Winds. I was not a little concern'd on the account of Such of the forces as have sail'd for Canso,[24] the place of Rendezvous.

23. The Winds very high still; white flying Clouds. My old Barn so weak, and continually Cracking, is in Danger.

24. A.M. on Gen. 17, 7. P.M. on Ps. 91, 1. Mr. Jenison and Granny Forbush din'd with me. Mr. Jenison Supp'd and lodg'd with me. N.B. Propounded Mr. Jonas Warrin and Lydia his wife, for full Communion. N.B. Mr. Dunlop with me after meeting with various Spiritual Distresses.

25. In the Morning walk'd with Mr. Jenison to Merchant Rices. Was at Captain Bakers[25]—and at Abner and Deacon Newton's. This Last Consider'd me on account of the Towns being so long prevented being assess'd, and so the Rates for my Sallery and Support suspended—he paid me 5£ old Tenor. N.B. One David Dunsmore of Wrentham here. Bought a very large Deer Skin of him. P.M. Mr. Thomas Goodenow and Mr. Elijah Rice's wife here. In the Eve Mrs. Hephzibah Maynard. Heard that Mr. Seth Rice is so oppress'd with being forc'd into the North Precinct that he has mov'd his Family and stock out of it, and Deacon Tomlin is also preparing to build in this Parish.

26. Heard that Ensign Josiah Rice has mov'd out of the North Precinct into this, by means of his Uneasiness. Mr. Willson came to work. Mending Hearths and Jamms. At his Instigation I sent Thome up to Mr. Hastings[26] of Shrewsbury for Lime to whitewash but succeeded not.

27. Rode to Mr. Samuel Fays to see his Wife again who is in her Confinement and expecting the Hours of Travail. Proceeded to Mr. Gershom Brighams and din'd at Mr. Joseph Knowltons: with whom I agreed to take his Son Nathan (who is about 11 Years of Age) for a Twelve Month, feeding, Clothing and instructing him. In returning home Colonel Williams[27] of Marlborough in pursuit of a maid, overtook me, but could not visit his sister. N.B. Precinct Meeting to choose Precinct Officers. Mr. Belknap here with Me most of the afternoon. At Eve rain'd very hard. Mr. John Stow here. His Horse left him and tarried all Night.

28. Mr. Stow finds not his Horse. I went to Mr. Barns and obtain'd of him to wait upon Mr. Stow with his Horse—to Marlborough, but he chose to go o'foot. Windy and Cold. P.M. I visited Mr. Daniel Forbush's wife, who had been long Confin'd—but Somewhat to my surprise found She was brought to Bed, and has a fine son. Visited Mr. Millers[28] son Solomon whose Leg was lately broke by a Log. Was at Mr. James Fays who went with me to see Mr. Timothy Warrin who had a few Days Since, a Fit of Nervous Convulsions: and had another ill Turn last Night.

29. P.M. Some Number of Women to Visit my Wife. Samuel Baker[29] here. Captain Maynard, with his Evening Post, came at Evening which was an unspeakable Hindrance to me.

30. One Young, a Taylor, Travelling to Norwich, here. Our Young Child very sore Mouth. Ebenezer brought Samuel Bakers Relation.

31. On Gen. 17, 7. I am full of Hopes God was pleas'd to make the Sermon a Means of Good to the souls of Some. P.M. on 2 Cor. 6, 2. Mr. Jenison, Mrs. Tainter and Mrs. Child din'd here. N.B. a most pious and Religious Proclamation for another Fast.

## APRIL 1745

The School moves over to Lieutenant Holloways. Trouble in my neibourhood respecting Sheep hurt by Doggs. An Ewe and Lamb of mine in all likelihood kill'd. Had we purpos'd to go to Cambridge but the Weather So Stormy in the Morning (Rain and Snow) that I was prevented. N.B. Mr. Jenisson seems to be in some Frett on account of his missing the Employment of preach-ing on the North Side. Towards Night Thomas Winchester came, went to Work about the Fences and thereby began another half year with me, for the same Wages as last. N.B. Mr. Thomas Billings here.

2. I rode into my Neibourhood to Captain Bakers, whom I improv'd to bring up Sundry Things for me from Boston: Whitewashing Lime, Sugar and Corks, Lime juice, etc. to Captain Fays, Mr. James Fays, Mr. Winchesters—and got him to go up to Brother Hicks for me. At Eve Silas Pratt here.

3. I earnestly desire and request a Suitable Preparation for the Extraordinary Fast approaching! May the Lord prepare us all, this whole people to sanctifie it! Brother Hicks came here and went to Cambridge in order to put forward a settlement of Father Champneys Estate.

4. Publick Fast on occasion of the Enterprize and Expedition against Cape Breton.[1] I preach'd on Joel 2, 12, 13. P.M. Repeat'd on 2 Cor. 6, 2. Behold now, etc. O that God would accept this Fast and give Success or prepare us for what He may please to order out to be the Event! Mr. James Fay left me his mare at Eve for my Journey. My Wife got down to supper with us.

5. At 4 in the morning just when the Day broke I Set out for Cambridge and arriv'd there at 1/2 after 10. Din'd with my poor, afflicted, Bereaved Mother in Law, whom God graciously Sustains! P.M. at Mr. Remingtons[2] with Brother Hicks. But tho we were both of us come down on purpose to attend the Business of Settling Father Champney's Estate yet no word would the Judge Speak upon any such Head. We were driven to the Shift of attending upon what might be done by Mr. Danforth[3] and were sent to Him. But it happen'd also that Mr. Danforth was not at Home nor in Town. I was forc'd again to go to Boston to him if I would Speak with him. Brother Hicks Stay'd at Cambridge and I rode to Boston, put up at Mr. Larkins[4] of Charlestown. Visited my aged Mother, who thro the tender mercy of God is yet in a measure of Comfort. N.B. Mr. Danforth I could not find this Evening. Mr. Whitefield preaching at Dr. Sewalls[5] but I could not wait upon the Exercise. Supp'd at Brother Alexanders but lodg'd at Sister Bettys with my Kinsman. Mrs. Sally Hill I conclude is a Bed but my Kinsman persists in opposition—will not marry her, being otherwise engag'd, viz. to Mrs. Nabby White. I am full of Grief for his ruin'd state but can't help him. His Troubles still more and more retard and impede his engaging in Business, and he is as backward and undetermin'd as ever. N.B. Captain Hope, of New York, lodges there.

6. After much Enquiry I found Mr. Danforth and receiv'd his Advice and Directions. A Variety of Things hinder'd my getting to Cambridge much before Noon. Brother Hicks and I din'd with Mother Champney and Sett out at least half after one, if it was not even Two o'Clock, and thro God's great Mercy we were safe at my House before the Day light was gone. N.B. No news yet from our Fleet. Mr. Whitefield expounds every Morning at Boston, as well as preaches very frequently as heretofore. The Divisions on that occasion, I think, hotter than ever. The Lord have Mercy on us for his great Name's Sake. William Pierce[6] work'd with Thomas yesterday, putting up the remainder of the Stone Wall at the Lower Orchard.

7. I Repeat'd on 2 Cor. 6, 2. I receiv'd a bitter and ungrateful Letter from Mr. William Jenison,[7] Am sorry especially that I should be disturb'd with it on the Lords Day. The Lord grant me a patient and forgiving Spirit! Brother Hicks who lodg'd here, din'd with me as did Mrs. Tainter[8] and Mrs. Patience Woods.[9] At Eve Brother Hicks rode home, and Mr. Belcher

[24] In northeastern Nova Scotia, opposite the shore of Cape Breton Island.
[25] Edward Baker of Westborough.
[26] Daniel Hastings.
[27] Abraham Williams.
[28] James Miller of Westborough.
[29] Son of Captain Edward Baker.

[1] Governor William Shirley issued a proclamation, March 25, 1745, setting April 4, 1745, as a day of general fasting and prayer throughout Massachusetts in connection with the forthcoming expedition against Louisbourg, Cape Breton. See *Boston Weekly News-Letter*, March 28, 1745.
[2] Jonathan Remington, a Judge of the Superior Court, who died later this year, Sept. 30, 1745. Paige, *Cambridge*, pp. 639-640.
[3] Samuel Danforth of Cambridge.
[4] Edward Larkins.
[5] The Reverend Joseph Sewall of the Old South Church.
[6] William Pierce, Jr., of Westborough.
[7] Jenison was bitter because the Marlborough Association would not recommend him to fill the pulpit of the north precinct in Westborough.
[8] Mrs. Simon Tainter.
[9] Mrs. Solomon Woods.

Hancock,[10] who had preach'd at North Sutton, came, and lodged here.

8. Mr. Willson whitewashing a.m. No ploughing done by us yet tho our Neibours have, this fortnight. Captain Warrin has made me a new plough but we could not get it plated yet. Mr. Hancock returns to Cambridge. A fine Warm Day.

9. Return'd some Answer to Mr. Jenisons late tart Letter, and sent it by Benjamin Lull, junior. Such Contention fills me with Trouble—but the Lord preserve and restrain me! By and By Mr. Jenison (not having receiv'd the Letter) came to my House about the Time that the Ministers began to assemble to the Association, which met here to Day. The Gentlemen that came were, Mr. Loring,[11] who was Moderator. Messers Cushing, Gardner,[12] Barrett, Stone, Smith, Goss,[13] and Davis.[14] Mr. Martyn was also here present. Mr. Stone deliver'd a Concio on 2 Cor. 12, 2. At Eve Mr. Martyn deliver'd a large Confession of Faith. Debates upon his being approbated. Mr. Gardner made objection. N.B. Mr. Barrett told us that a Westborough man, he could not tell who, but he thinks one that was griev'd by the Line of the Precincts or in the Name of Deacon Tomlin was over at Hopkinton to enquire of his Brother Morris[15] after Mr. Commissary Price,[16] in order to joining with the Church of England there. N.B. Mr. Jenison and I some Warm Contest in presence of Messers Cushing, Stone and Smith with reference to my Discourse with him January 1 and afterwards my Conversation with Mr. Matthias Rice on February 23. Mr. Jenison went away dissatisfy'd, but I requested him to come tomorrow (not only to Lecture but) to dine with us. N.B. Captain Maynard took 2 Horses, 3 at old Mr. Maynards[17]—and one at Mr. Hows,[18] and 3 Gentlemen, Mr. Goss, Mr. Davis and Mr. Martyn lodg'd at Captain Maynards.

10. Resum'd the Conference about Mr. Martyn. Mr. Gardner and he were advis'd to retire together. They did so and came in reconcil'd. *Deo soli gloria!* Mr. Davis preach'd the public Lecture on Ps. 51, 17. Mr. Jenison at meeting and I invited him again to Dinner, and he came. P.M. We have further Debate, and were more successful and pacify'd. The Gentlemen who were with us, were of the opinion he had better wave his preaching any where, while he was in his present Circumstances tho they also told him they Should not pretend to lay an Embargo (as he himself had phras'd it) or Barr him from it. I gave him my Distinction between the Common privileges of Christians and those more public and special acts of Preaching, etc., and I told him I would have him come to the Sacrament next Sabbath. He answered me that he could not Say whether he Should or not, but yet went away more compos'd. N.B. I had offer'd him that if he would withdraw his Letter to me he might burn my Reply to him. To return to the Association—Mr. Martyn was further interrogated with regard to his disuse of the Tongues, the Sciences etc. In a word, he was approbated by a Certificate sign'd by every member. Old Mr. Axtell[19] here but we could do nothing for him.

11. Nathan Knowlton came to live with me. I visited old Deacon Tomlin who has not only rais'd him a New House in this Parish but this Day begins to move into it. I am Sorry to find the Deacon Shaken in Mind—but is dispos'd to listen to any Defence of the Church of England, or Opinions of the Baptists. I gave him earnest Cautions, Exhortations and Instructions, and then proceeded to Ensign Rice's where I found a New Common Prayer Book and a New Book publish'd by the Society for Propagating the Gospel in Defence of the Church of England. Ensign was not at Home. I left my Counsel and Charge with his Wife and visited Neighbour Jeduthan How. Went next over to

Brother Seths, with whom I also Seriously discours'd—but I found him, through Grace, Stedfast. I understand that his Brother Josiah is preparing to raise a New House in our parish— and being greatly Concern'd for him would not go home without seeing him, tho he was far off, Carting Stones. To my great Sorrow found him leaning to the Church. He had been with Mr. Price at Boston, etc. I discharg'd my Duty to him with Some fervency and left him—Committing this Cause to God. I call'd at Mr. James Maynards and at Eve return'd home.

12. Last night our Small Flock of Sheep Sett on by Doggs. A principal Ewe lay Dead, and mostly Eat up: her Lamb left to be brought up by Hand. A Weather also much bitt, that we much doubted of its Life. Thomme not well, and the Weather wet and Cold so that we defer his going to Mr. Batchellors at Grafton.

13. Fowl Weather and Thomme not well.

14. The Communion, and a bright good Day, yet the Earth too Damp and Cold for my wife who has not as yet us'd herself to the air to go out to meeting. I preach'd A.M. on John 17, 3, and P.M. on Gal. 6, 8.

15. At 3 in the Morning Brother Hicks call'd me out of my Bed. We Set out a little before Sun Rise (N.B. I had Neighbour Benjamin Hows Horse) upon our Journey to Cambridge—arrived before noon, din'd with Mother Champney, and went over to Mr. Danforth, Mr. Remington being incapable of any Business. According to Mr. Danforths Directions in the Methods of our Proceeding to Settle the Estate of our Deceas'd Father (Champney) we made Choice of the following Gentlemen to be prizers of the personal Estate, viz. Deacon Samuel Sparhawk, Captain Benjamin Dana, and Mr. Thomas Dana and the Message hereof and of our Desire that they would attend upon that Business tomorrow, was carry'd to them. At Mr. Morris's. N.B. Indignation and Contempt cast upon Mr. William Hobby[20] for his Vindication of Mr. Whitefield.[21] My Son Thomas went to Live with Mr. Joseph Batchelour of Grafton, Weaver. Ebenezer went up with him, in my absence upon my Journey to Cambridge.

16. The Prizers of the Personal Estate came, and view'd the Land, the House and Barn. I din'd with them in Brother Champneys Room. N.B. very unhappy Disagreements of Temper between Brother Champney and sister Lydia[22] which had Subsisted for Some Time, and were now foolishly and sinfully discover'd to my great Grief and Sorrow. My Brother and I were together in the Chamber looking over Brother Champneys Long accounts.

17. The Prizers of the Personal Estate at Mothers again, and Viewed Husbandry Tools, Wearing Apparell, Household Goods etc. We din'd in Mothers Room to Day, and with more composedness among those of the House. At Eve we laid Some Scheme respecting the Prizing the Real and made Choice of the following Gentlemen for that Purpose, viz. Captain Sharp, Captain Benjamin Dana (one of the other Committee of Prizers) Deacon Henry Prentice, Mr. Richard Gardner and Mr. Thomas Sparhawk.

18. Word was carry'd to Each of the last Mention'd Gentlemen; I was at Mr. Gardners[23] and at Captain Sharps.[24] Broke fast at Mrs. Keggells at Boston. Visited my Aged and honor'd Mother. Had so many difficult Affairs upon Me that I could not go to Lecture. Sad News came to Boston to Day by an Express from Captain Knowls at St. Kitts directed to Commodore Warrin who is gone to Cape Briton of 7 or 8 French Men of War and 28 Transports arrived at Martinece, bound we know not whither. Din'd at Brother Williams.[25] N.B. Our Dear Kinsman Elias[26] was unemploy'd yet, but Seems now to be about resolving—the Lord rouse him—for human Help is Vain! I hastened to Cambridge at Eve in prosecution of our affairs there, Tho to my great perplexity I miss'd of Mr. Danforth at Boston.

[10] (Harvard 1727). The tutor of Harvard College. *Sibley,* VIII, 137–140.

[11] The Reverend Israel Loring of Sudbury.

[12] The Reverend John Gardner of Stow.

[13] Thomas Goss (Harvard 1737), the minister at Bolton, 1741–1771. *Sibley,* X, 175–185.

[14] The Reverend Joseph Davis (Harvard 1740), the minister at Holden, 1742–1773. *Sibley,* X, 478–481.

[15] Theophilus Morris, a graduate of Trinity College, Dublin, was an Episcopal missionary who had settled at West Haven, Conn., 1740–1742.

[16] Roger Price was the rector of King's Chapel in Boston until Nov. 21, 1746. He later founded the Episcopal Church in Hopkinton. See Henry W. Foote, *Annals of King's Chapel* (Boston, 1882–1896), 2 vols.

[17] David Maynard.

[18] Hezekiah How.

[19] Thomas Axtell of Marlborough had been a concern to the Association before. Allen, *Worcester Association,* p. 19.

[20] Minister of Reading.

[21] William Hobby, *An Inquiry into the Itinerancy and the Conduct of the Rev. Mr. George Whitefield* (Boston, 1745).

[22] Lydia Champney, Parkman's sister-in-law.

[23] Richard Gardner of Cambridge.

[24] Captain Robert Sharp of Brookline.

[25] William Parkman of Boston.

[26] Parkman's nephew, the son of Elias Parkman (d. 1741).

19. Mr. Danforth was come up to Cambridge last night, So that this morning we went on with our Business; and Three of the Prizers, viz. Captain Sharp, Messers Gardner and Sparhawk were Sworn. Brother Hicks and I endeavour'd to Expedite Matters by Measuring the Land as we were able, but having no Compass, we only carry'd the Chain upon the Lines, and deferr'd the exact Calculating to such Time as we could have a Surveyor. We din'd in Mother's Room. N.B. Captain Dana came at the Beginning of the work, which was Somewhat after 11 o'Clock a.m. Deacon Prentice came at 3 P.M. At Eve the Gentlemen endeavour'd to persuade Brother Champney to Apply himself to the work of the Season.

20. Brother Champney refusing to take the Administration, Brother Hicks appear'd willing—and I left my Consent, bid farewell and rode home. N.B. refresh'd me at Goodenows Tavern in Sudbury, kept now by one Mountgomery. N.B. Company'd some part of the way by Mr. Thomas Marsh[27] who is going to preach at Worcester. Found my Family well about 5 P.M. Gr. D.

21. My Wife at Meeting again; the Lords Name be prais'd! Preach'd on Heb. 13, 17, and P.M. on Gal. 6, 8. Stopp'd the Church at noon. N.B. P.M. Dr. Gott[28] came to sermon but went out as Soon as it was over. (See Church Records[29] for Stopping the Church at Noon.)

22. Ephraim Bruce[30] Examin'd A.M. Recon'd also with Deacon Newton.[31] N.B. Deacon Tomlin here requesting a few Lines to be drawn by way of Petition to the North precinct. N.B. Edward Whipple's Wife Examin'd.

23. Brother Hicks came up from Cambridge who tells me he has given Bonds for administering on Father Champneys Estate. I Catechiz'd at the South Part of the Town, at the School-House. This was the first Time of my doing this. N.B. 51 Children. After Catechizing I visited the Widow Woods. N.B. I went there on foot, but rode Lieutenant Tainters Horse back. I had also din'd at his House.

24. Mr. Charles Bruce and his Wife here to be Examin'd. P.M. Ephraims Wife[32] also. Found her humble and penitent for her Youthful Sins and Follys.

25. Mr. Bacon[33] of Ashuelot here. Mr. Stone preach'd a Lecture to our Young Men from 1 Sam. 2, 26. After Meeting came a Messenger from Framingham (one of the Hemingways) with the Sorrowfull Tidings of the Death of the Reverend and Worthy Mr. Swift[34] of Framingham, Who in March last finish'd his 66th Year. A man of good Abilitys, natural and acquir'd—of a Sprightly Genius and delighting in Learning; a Valuable Pastor and an entertaining preacher, of great Goodness, affability and Courtesy and therefore Easy of access and pleasant to Converse with, was very Hospitable to all and none more affectionate to his Friends. He nevertheless met with much ill treatment among some of his ungrateful people, rigid Sticklers for the Church Discipline of Lay Elders, and disorderly New Lights, the Latter of which had even set up a Meeting House on purpose for Itineracy. The Troubles he was Exercis'd with in both his Flock and Family (of very different kinds indeed) might justly be conceiv'd to have given great advantage to his bodily Disorders which had prevail'd ever since he had an Apoplectick Shock a few Years past. Yesterday Morning When his End approach'd he had unusual appetite and would fain have some Cheese for his Breakfast, but that was conceiv'd hurtfull, and therefore they perswaded him to accept of Chocolat and a Toast. Whilst they were feeding with These he dy'd away at once, and reviv'd no more. Help Lord the

Godly Man Ceaseth! The Righteous fall from among the Children of Men! When Such Usefull Men are taken away alas how weak are we! We have lost much of our Strength and our Glory when any of the Pillars Fall, the Fabrick shakes. Yet with God is the residue of the Spirit. May he grant us his almighty Influences that We may dispatch our Work and get ready for our own Summons, and raise up Successors and give Pastors after his own Heart!

26. In the Morning I rode up to Mr. Samuel Fay junior whose Young Child is to be bury'd to day. He was not at home. I pray'd with his wife and told them who were there of the reason of my withdraw. Mr. Cushing came to my House with whom and Mr. Stone I (on Mr. Pratts Horse) rode to Framingham to the Funeral of Reverend Mr. Swift. The Coffin not being ready we waited till 6 o'Clock before the Corps mov'd. Mr. Loring, Mr. Cushing, Mr. Gardner and Mr. Cook,[35] Mr. Stone and I were Pall Bearers. The Deacons etc. were under Bearers, the Brethren of Church walking before the Corps, Mr. Loring having pray'd before moving. It was a very mournfull Time! There was So much mist and rain as made it uncomfortable, but Care was taken that all the Circumstances of the Funeral were very decent. The Grave was brick'd So high as to cover the Coffin with large flat Stones—and there was provision for a Monument. We Supp'd at the Sorrowfull Widows. Mr. Loring, Gardner and Peabody[36] retir'd to draw up a Character, Mr. Cushing and I rode home with Mr. Stone and lodged there.

27. I came home, Mr. Cushing accompanying me. Could have little Time for my Preparations for the Sabbath having Ebenezer to hear. John Oake here. John Oake told me that his Aunt Holloway was to do a message to me, viz. that the people over there desir'd me to go over next Tuesday to the raising their Meeting House, and they would have me be with them at 8 in the Morning to pray with them—and his aunt not coming he did the message by her Order. I told him I was in Some difficulty for want of an Horse, my mare having lately foal'd. N.B. Thomas gone from my business from Thursday noon to Saturday night.

28. With Some omissions, alterations etc. I repeated Sermon 2 Kings 2, 14. P.M. preach'd on Numb. 27, 16, 17. Appointed the Catechetical Exercise to be next Wednesday.

29. At Deacon Newtons and other Houses in that Neighbourhood in preparing for Thomas's Journey tomorrow to get Lime. Letter from Mr. Stone that his Lecture is next Wednesday. I sent word round the Parish that the young women's Catechizing must be on Thursday. Mr. Breck[37] and his wife din'd with us.

30. The Morning Rainy. The Deacon Newton brought his Cart and Oxen and Hoggsheads for Lime yet Thomas declin'd going whilst it was So Wet. I kept the Deacons Oxen till the Weather was better. No body from the North Side to bring me an Horse or accompany me over to the raising the meeting House there. Nor any one person of the Multitude who pass'd by my House from the South, so much as call'd to See whether I were to go or could go or no. Mr. Patteshall[38] (who had preach'd at Worcester last Sabbath) din'd here. P.M. I rode over to the North side on my own Mare, notwithstanding the inconvenience of it, and the misting, uncomfortable Weather. For tho I mislik'd many Things in their Conduct there, yet I found not enough to warrant my proclaiming War against them as my refusing to go to Day would do. I found Mr. Cushing and Mr. Morse there. Afterwards came Mr. Martin and Mr. Goss. The raising began about 10 A.M. and was finish'd about 4 P.M. without Hurt, thro the Great Mercy and Goodness of God. To him be the Glory! At their Request I pray'd after the work was finish'd, and we Sung Ps. 127, first Stanza, Ps. 125, first half Stanza and Ps. 128 beginning. Their Entertainment was in the Frame. The people brought their provisions in great Plenty.[39] Mr. Cushing

[27] Marsh was a deacon of the First Church at Mansfield, Conn. He was uneducated but was ordained by the Separatist Church in Mansfield, July 1, 1746.

[28] Benjamin Gott, the physician of Marlborough.

[29] "At Noon the Church was Stop'd to acquaint them with the Desire of Brother Samuel Fay junior to have not only his newborn Infant baptiz'd but a Child of about a Year and half old, which had been neglected in this Time of their Great Trouble and Affliction, for which he was Sorry, and desir'd the Compassion of the Church which was freely extended to him and May God please to overlook the Sin of this Neglect. Accordingly P. M. Hannah and Ebenezer, of Samuel and Deliverance Fay baptized." Westborough Church Records, April 21, 1745.

[30] Son of Abijah Bruce.

[31] Josiah Newton.

[32] Mrs. Ephraim Bruce.

[33] The Reverend Jacob Bacon (Harvard 1731) was the minister of Keene, N.H. (Upper Ashuelot), 1737-1747. Sibley, IX, 18-21.

[34] John Swift.

[35] The Reverend William Cooke of Wayland.

[36] The Reverend Oliver Peabody of Natick.

[37] The Reverend Robert Breck, Jr., the minister of Springfield. Parkman's brother-in-law.

[38] Richard Pateshall (Harvard 1735), a Boston schoolmaster, preached at many places. He bitterly opposed the New-Lights and attacked William Hobby for his defense of George Whitefield. Richard Pateshall, Pride Humbled, or, Mr. Hobby Chastised (Boston, 1745). See Sibley, IX, 558-560.

[39] Precinct records add "Allowed Jothan Bartlett £2 10 shillings for 2 barrells of cider for the raising."

crav'd and Mr. Martyn return'd. A number of us were at Captain Eagers[40] after supper. In returning home Captain Baker in Company and we had some earnest arguings all the way, but kept and parted in peace.

### MAY 1745

1. I preach'd Mr. Stones Lecture on John 14, 21. Rode Mr. Charles Bruce's Horse. Ebenezer went afishing at the great Pond this Evening, this being almost the very beginning of their Fishing this Season.

2. I held my Catechetical Exercise again—and preach'd to the Young Women on Ps. 25, 7.

3. Mr. Whitefield preach'd at Mill-River in Mendon the first instant.

4. Mr. Belcher Hancock came and din'd with me, perswaded me to go in his Stead to North Sutton. Had Lieutenant Aaron Forbush's Horse. Got up to my Lodging, at Lieutenant Issac Barnards just as the sun was Setting. N.B. Met my son Thomas going home.

5. Preach'd at North Sutton at the House of Mr. Singletary[1] by the Great Pond on Eph. 3, 8, last Clause, a. and p.m. Din'd at the Same House, and my Kinswoman Mrs. Susanna Fuller with me. After Exercises and refreshment I rode to Mr. Halls[2] which was nigher than my Landlord Barnards and lodg'd there. N.B. One Mr. Sears of Millford on Rye in Connecticutt there in the Evening.

6. Rode back. Went to Mr. Batchellors at Grafton tho Thomme[3] was gone to Westborough on a Visit. Very hot Day. Din'd at Mr. Prentice's.[4] Mrs. Prentice (I find) was very much in Raptures last Night, and was Somewhat full, at times, to Day. At Westborough understood that from Mr. Hancock yesterday Mr. Whitney and wife with others went over to hear Mr. Martyn[5], not being able to bear Mr. Hancocks Doctrine.

7. Thomme return'd to his master Batchellours. Captain Forbush's wife here to be Examin'd. Ephraim Bruce towards Eve. Sent Mr. Eaton of Leicester his Bolton by Robert Horn junior.

8. Neighbour Edwards Whipple here to be Examin'd previous to his joining with the Church. Nigh Eve came Mr. Bacon of Ashuelot and lodged here. N.B. About supper receiv'd a Letter dated yesterday from Mr. Smith of Marlborough to preach his Lecture next Wednesday—it being difficult to determine what Wednesday he Means.

9. Mr. Bacon upon his journey home and I rode to Mr. Nathan Balls to see his son Ebenezer who was in a Languishing State. N.B. Mr. Wheeler and Mr. Ball told me that their Northernmost part, being disappointed by their Brethren of the Precinct, were proposing to unite with a Number of Familys in Bolton and build Still another Meeting House. N.B. Ephraim Bruce's wife here. P.M. her Brother Charles's wife. At Eve Edwards Whipple's wife—all in order to their enjoying public privileges. N.B. Mrs. Winchester here at Eve.

10. My Wife to Marlborough on Nathan Maynards Mare to visit Mrs. Breck of Springfield.

11. Captain Maynard (in his Team) brot me up 14£ Sugar and my Kegg of 3 Gallons of Rum from Boston. P.M. Mr. Millen[6] here. He discover'd to me that it was by him that I sent Mr. Loring his Hubbards Absence of the Comforter.[7] At Eve came Brother Samuel Parkman from Hopkinton, bound up to Bolton and thence to Hartford. N.B. Ebenezer went to Lieutenant Tainters for his Chaise and brought it.

12. I preach'd on John 17, 3, a. and p.m. Propounded Edward Whipple and wife for Church Communion. Charles Bruce and his wife for public Humilliation and owning the Covenant.

13. My Brother went on his Journey. I went divers places for an Horse to go down to Cambridge but in Vain, particularly was at Jesse Brighams, Thomas Goodeno, Matthias Rice's, and to Mr.

Beeman's. Sister Hicks at our House at Evening from Sutton.

14. Try'd Jonas Brighams Horse in the Chaise, but he was too furious—broke Whipple-Tree and threw me out, but without Hurt. D.G. But he was a good Horse in the saddle. I rode him to Cambridge. I stop'd at Colonel Wards to Condole under his great Afflictions. Stopp'd also at Mr. Pattersons in Sudbury with my wife's Kinsman Williams,[8] the school master there. Yet got to Cambridge Some time before Night. Mother Champney has had a very ill Turn and tho much better than She was, especially last Friday, yet is very Weak and low.

15. In the Morning I went over to College—was with Mr. Mayhew[9] particularly. But I return'd over to Mothers. Mr. Winthrop improv'd to Survey Father Champneys Lands, to prepare the Work for the Prizers, who all came. I din'd with them. N.B. Brother Champney now reports he did not take the Administration instead of Hicks. I rode to Boston Early—broke fast at my Honor'd Mother's (who is in much Comfort, except her Trouble about her Negro, Pito, who gives her much Trouble). My Kinsman Elias (to my great Grief) is Still at home, unactive, Slothfull, disheartened and as far from engaging in any Business as ever. Mr. Checkley[10] the Public Lecture on John 4, 14. After I din'd at Brother Alexander's. I visited Dr. Sewal, and there came in Dr. Chauncey,[11] and afterward Mr. Gee. Mr. Whitefield the Subject, almost everywhere. Dr. Wigglesworths[12] Letter to him came out to Day. When I return'd to Mother Champneys at Evening the Prizers having done their Work, were gone home. At home, Mr. Devotion[13] of Windham, his wife and wife's sister Visited my Family; came at Eve and Lodg'd.

16. Mr. Devotion etc. detain'd at our House because of the Rain. Thomas Winchester went to Grafton, where a Fast is kept to Day, as there was also public Exercises both parts of the Day yesterday. The Rain was Such as might have hinder'd him from work Some Part of the Forenoon but not the rest of the Day. N.B. A Number of Ministers Met as an Association there—Nor did Mr. Prentice wholly omitt to invite me, but I was under Engagement to be at Cambridge for that very Time. Thomme came home ill from Mr. Batchellors.

17. I went over to College in the Morning. At Mr. Hancocks Chamber where were Mr. Flynt,[14] Mr. Mayhew and Mr. Nathaniel Gardner.[15] Bought Dr. Wigglesworths Letter to Mr. Whitefield of Mr. Flynt, and borrow'd Tennents Examiner Examined,[16] of Mr. Mayhew. On my Journey home I call'd at Dr. Robys,[17] at Sudbury, and found he was not averse to taking up my Kinsman Elias to study Physic with him, upon which I wrote to my Kinsman and committed it to the Care of the Doctor. I din'd at Mr. Pattersons with my Kinsman Williams, the Schoolmaster there. Rode into Marlboro to See Sister Breck[18] of Springfield who is ill yet at Dr. Gotts. At Home, Brother Hicks (who drove up his Oxen from Cambridge) and his wife who came up (also) from Cambridge, lodg'd with us.

18. My Brother Samuel Parkman returning from Hartford to Boston touch'd here this morning (having lodg'd at Worcester) presently after his taking Leave it Sett in for Rain, and p.m. was very Wet. Brother and sister Hicks went home Early.

19. Repeated Sermon on Eph. 3, 10 from page 18 to page 32, under that Text in Phil. 2, 8, a.m. and Ex. 9, p.m. Appointed the Communion and Preparatory Lecture.

20. Sent Thomme down to Dr. Gott that he might be under his advice and Directions: he rode before his mother who visited

[40] James Eager.
[1] John Singletary had come from Haverhill. Benedict and Tracy, Sutton, pp. 726–727.
[2] The Reverend David Hall of Sutton.
[3] Parkman's son, Thomas, had been apprenticed to Joseph Batchellor, a weaver.
[4] The Reverend Solomon Prentice of Grafton.
[5] The Reverend John Martyn of the north precinct.
[6] The Reverend John Mellen of Sterling.
[7] Nehemiah Hobart, The Absence of the Comforter Described and Lamented (New London, 1717).
[8] Abraham Williams, Jr. (Harvard 1744), of Marlborough. He later became the fifth minister of the First Congregational Church, Sandwich, Mass., 1749–1784, despite the fact that while in college he was convicted three times of "drinking prohibited Liquors and . . . Scandalous lying." Sibley, XI, 498–502.
[9] Jonathan Mayhew (Harvard 1744), the great preacher at the West Church at Boston, 1747–1766. Sibley, XI, 440–472.
[10] The Reverend Samuel Checkley of the New South Church in Boston.
[11] The Reverend Charles Chauncy of the First Church in Boston.
[12] Edward Wigglesworth, A Letter to the Reverend Mr. George Whitefield, by Way of a Reply to his Answer to the College Testimony against him and his Conduct (Boston, 1745).
[13] The Reverend Ebenezer Devotion.
[14] Henry Flynt, the old Tutor.
[15] (Harvard 1739). A Boston schoolmaster. Sibley, X, 366–368.
[16] Gilbert Tennent, The Examiner, Examined, or Gilbert Tennent, Harmonious (Philadelphia, 1743).
[17] Ebenezer Roby was the physician of Sudbury.
[18] Mrs. Samuel Breck, Parkman's wife's sister.

her sister Breck to Day and carry'd her Child; and Thomme return'd home with Mrs. Sally Gott[19] instead of his Mother.

21. Town Meeting to choose a Representative, but the Town were of the Mind to rely upon the Courts Goodness and would Send none considering the Towns New and heavy Burdens. Receiv'd from Mr. Edwards[20] of Northampton Proposals for printing his Treatise of Religious Affections.[21] Mr. Breck of Springfield came at Evening in his Chair and brought his Daughter Lois and lodg'd here.

22. In the Morning about 8 o'Clock I rode to Mr. Williams's and marry'd his Daughter to Mr. Reuben Maynard of Shrewsbury. Immediately return'd back to Mr. Breck who was waiting for my Company to Marlborough. He and his little Daughter rode in his Chair and Mrs. Sally Gott and I in Mr. Tainters Chaise. We call'd to see Colonel William Ward. We din'd at Dr. Gotts p.m. From Mr. Smiths Fence my Mare broke loose and ran away with the Chaise. Soon oversett it. Scrap'd one Thill in Sunder, clear'd herself of her Tackling and posted away for home, but was presently Stop'd by the Smith on the Hill. We gather'd up the broken Tackling, dragg'd the Chaise to Mr. Smiths, and I rode to Deacon Stevens's and got him to it to look upon it and make a new Thill. Thus I left the Chaise, and my wife and child rode with me on Horseback home at Evening.

23. Mr. Breck and Mr. Smith came up from Marlborough. They din'd with me and after Dinner Mr. Breck preach'd my Lecture from 1 Pet. 3, 15, a useful Sermon. May God Succeed it, and bless the Preacher. Not many North Side People at Lecture. N.B. Ebenezer Ball, in a Consumption brought low, was pray'd for. N.B. One Mr. Town of Oxford labouring under a Diabetes, and much enfeebled, was carry'd along in an Horse litter, some Framingham people assisting. Mr. Breck and Mr. Smith return'd to Marlborough. The former carrying off the works of the Author of the Whole Duty of Man,[22] for which he is to bring me all he has of Dr. Owen.[23]

24. Sent Ebenezer to Marlborough for the Chaise we left to be mended by Deacon Stevens;[24] and after much worry and trouble with the unruly Mare, he got home with it.

25. Neighbor Jedidiah How cutt 5 young Piggs for me. Captain Maynard here after his Journey to Boston—a great hindrance to me in my preparations and I am rarely without great Perplexity upon such occasions. Edwards Whipple, and afterwards his Wife with their Relations.

26. On John 17, 3 a.m. After admitting Edwards Whipple and his wife into the Church, I administered the Lords Supper.[25] N.B. the greatest Part of our Northern Brethren absent, to my great Grief. P.M. I consider'd the proneness of our Young People to run into great Extravagancys at the Election Time, and for some abatement of their ungodly Mirth I made an Essay on Luke 6, 25.

27. [No entry].

28. [No entry].

29. The first Election that I remember to have kept in Westborough. I read partly in my Family old Mr. Higginsons Election Sermon on the Cause of God and his People.[26] Had a good Dinner with my Family, rejoicing in the great goodness of God to his people in all the Memorable Works which He had wrought—and for that He continues to us our precious and pleasant Things—and after Dinner we Sung part of the first 8 Verses of Ps. 78, Tate and Bradys Version. P.M. a number of Elderly men came to see me. Old Mr. Maynard, Mr. Whipple and his Brother Lambson of

Ipswich. Upon the whole, I endeavour'd to keep the Day in humble gratitude to God, hearty Loyalty to the Government over me, and Communion with the Ministers in their General Convention, and in Chearfull Satisfaction with my own House, charging and watching over all under my Care that good order and good Hours be observ'd which (for any Thing has come to my knowledge) were So.

30. Thomas had gone to his Fathers and not being well return'd late this Morning—yet had struck no stroke at Weeding till to Day. I rode again to Mr. Nathan Balls to see his son Ebenezer who grows worse. I visited Mr. Livermores[27] Family, one of whose Dauters of about 11 years of age has been much troubled with Fitts. N.B. I took some pains, as I had Opportunity to Enquire into the Reasons of the absence of Such a Number of the Northside Members from the last Communion. Mr. Livermore prevented by his Dauters Fitts. Mrs. Hannah Ball and divers others disquieted in their minds with their Differences. Mr. Jacob Rice Said he could not leave his House, it being the place where the North Assembly meets—but there appeared to me no strength nor Validity in his Excuse.

31. Mr. Cushing and Mr. Morse came up from Boston; and they gave me Some Account of what had been done at the Election and at the Convention. In particular at the latter Mr. Clark[28] of Salem Village preach'd a Seasonable, Close sermon with regard to Mr. Whitefields Errors of mis-conduct—and both he and his wife were present. The Collection was large, £290 Old Tenor. In the Convention Mr. Gee[29] and others made proposals of Subscribing the Platform and Confession of Faith; or Some other good Draught—but it was rejected. Mr. Prince[30] no longer Clerk, but Mr. Turell[31] chose in his Room.

### JUNE [1745]

1. My Son Thomme much out of Health So that I sent him to Marlborough to Dr. Gotts that he might get suitable Directions and Druggs of him. Mr. Simon Goddard came here to ask whether his coming to Meeting here on sabbath Days would be disagreeable to Me? And in reply, I expressed to him in what Case and for what Reasons it would. His Father here presently after, but we had nothing upon his sons Errand.

2. On Sabbath Morning Mr. Breck[1] came up and preach'd for me all Day, A.M. on Ps. 130, 3, 4, P.M. Mat. 25, 1-13. He return'd to his wife at Marlborough after he had Supp'd. N.B. he brought up the Agreeable News of our Forces having Succeeded in the Capture of a French Man of War of 64 Guns. To God be praise and Glory!

3. [No entry].

4. Training in each part of the Town and beating up for Volunteers—but none as yet enlist for this Recruit. P.M. I held my Catechetical Exercise to the Young Women.

5. A.M. Mr. Townsend[2] from the Northside here, and very full of Discourse. I visited Neighbour William Rogers junior's Wife who lies Sick. P.M. I rode (with my wife) over to the raisings on the west side of the River. Mr. Seth Rice an House and Ensign Josiah a Barn. N.B. Brother Hicks was here a.m. and brought up yesterdays Gazette[3] containing a large and particular account of the Successes of both Army and Fleet.

6. Preach'd at Mr. Bradish's[4] on Isa. 66, 2. Mr. Cook[5] there. N.B. another fruitless Attempt of Reconcilement with him.

7. Thomme for my Malt at Mr. Matthias's and brought it. Mr. Green here for a Pigg I sold him. Weigh'd [blank].

8. Thomme return'd to his Master Batchellor at Grafton.

9. On John 17, 3, and P.M. on Mat. 6, 10. Received from

---

[19] Sarah, the daughter of Dr. Gott.

[20] The great Jonathan Edwards.

[21] *A Treatise Concerning Religious Affections, in Three Parts* (Boston, 1746).

[22] The work generally ascribed the English divine Richard Allestree. See note for July 5, 1740.

[23] Over 80 works of John Owen (1616–1683), the English divine, were published. One had recently been published in America. *Eshcol: a Cluster of the Fruit of Canaan Brought to the Borders* (Boston, 1744).

[24] Samuel Stevens.

[25] Westborough Church Records for this date include the following: "Ephraim Bruce and Mary his wife offer'd their Confession and acknowledgment of the Sin of Fornication and were restor'd."

[26] John Higginson, *The Cause of God and His People in New-England* (Cambridge, 1663).

[27] Jonathan Livermore of Westborough.

[28] The Reverend Peter Clark of Danvers.

[29] The Reverend Joshua Gee of Boston.

[30] The Reverend Thomas Prince of Boston.

[31] The Reverend Ebenezer Turell of Medford.

[1] The Reverend Robert Breck, Jr., of Springfield.

[2] Joshua Townsend.

[3] *The Boston Gazette, or Weekly Journal*, June 4, 1745.

[4] James Bradish, an original settler of Westborough.

[5] Cornelius Cook.

Reverend Mr. Salter[6] of Mansfield (who stop'd at Captain Fays[7] in his journey home) Mr. Solomon Williams's[8] Sermon on his Ordination and the Windham Associations Letter to the Several Societys in that County concerning Mr. Pain[9] etc. Mr. James Fay who brot these deliver'd me also a Book from Deacon Merriam[10] of Grafton, being Dr. Francke[11] against the Fear of Man.

10. At Mr. Hows in the Morning. At Mr. Ebenezer Nurse's to get an Horse to go to Ministers Meeting. Could not Succeed with him—but did with Mr. Hezekiah Pratt.

11. I have discover'd that though Ebenezer performs his Tasks of Lessons, yet he has an inward heavyness and drops now and then a word how glad he Shall be to be at Work upon the place, how much better the place Should Soon be if he Should labour etc. I therefore took the Opportunity this Morning to talk with him, and I once More still gave him Liberty to Choose what Method of Life Should Suit his Genius best. I rode to Boston by the Way of Captain Barnards[12] of Marlboro, to Association. The following were present. Messers. John Prentice,[13] Loring, Cushing, Cook, Barrett, Stone, Seccomb,[14] Smith, Goss, Marsh,[15] Morse, Millen; and Mr. Buckminster[16] was voted in. Mr. Martyn also and Mr. Nathaniel Gardner,[17] Candidates were there. After Prayer arose a Sharp and Vehement insisting for my transcribing into the Association Book, the minutes of the Meeting[18] at Mr. Smiths in Marlboro, last January when a Testimony was drawn up against Mr. Whitefield, but which I Strenuously deny'd and gave my Reasons for my Refusal of it. It was desir'd that Mr. Stone would but he refus'd also; and tho his Reason was that he had no more authority than anybody Else, he being Clerk only for that Meeting, yet when it was about to be put to Vote that he might be authoriz'd by the Association to do it, he still refus'd. I repeatedly offer'd, and entreated that I might resign the office of Clerk. I had now had the Burthen of it for 20 years, and it was Time Somebody else Should take a Turn. But it was not granted—except by a Member or Two—of which Mr. Marsh was chief, who several Times desir'd that a New Clerk might be Chose. After long Contest about recording those Minutes (it being of an out-of-Season, out-of-place Meeting, and when besides the Business of that Meeting, Two Members were admitted and one old Member dismissed) Mr. Barrett offer'd himself that if the Association Should appoint him to transcribe Mr. Stones Minutes into the Book, he would do it, which accordingly they did. Then Mr. Martyn (the Concionator not being present) deliver'd an Exercise on Mat. 16, 27, which no one Member (I think) was Satisfy'd with, he therein advancing that there would be no rewards in the future world according to Mens Works, untill the General Judgment. But the Chief Subject of Conversation was Mr. Whitefield. Collections were unthought of (I Suppose) by the Moderator. They were never call'd for. After Supper at Mr. Goss's, Mr. Stone and I went home with Mr. Martyn and lodged there.

12. In the Morning before the public Meeting, there was a free Conversation with Mr. Martyn about his Sermon Yesterday, the Scheme being New and some passages offensive, to us all. Mr. Cook preach'd the Public Lecture upon Amos 8, 11. In my returning I rode to Marlborough. Messers Barrett, Stone and Smith in Company. I visited Sister Breck who is yet at Marlborough.

13. I got Mr. Benjamin How to work for me to Day in Chang-

---

[6] Richard Salter (Harvard, 1739), the minister at Mansfield, Conn., 1744-1787. *Sibley*, X, 404-409.

[7] Captain John Fay.

[8] (Harvard 1719). The minister of the First Church in Lebanon, Conn., 1722-1776. The ordination sermon was *Ministers of the Gospel* (New London, 1744). See *Sibley*, VI, 352-361.

[9] Elisha Paine had been imprisoned in 1743 in Connecticut for preaching without a license. He is said to have founded the First Baptist Church in Harwich. The pamphlet Parkman mentioned is *A Letter from the Associated Ministers of the County of Windham* (Boston, 1745).

[10] Joseph Merriam.

[11] August Hermann Francke, *Nicodemus; or a Treatise Against the Fear of Man*, 3rd. ed. (Boston, 1745).

[12] Robert Barnard was a miller and tavern keeper. Hudson, *Marlborough*, p. 313.

[13] The Reverend John Prentice of Lancaster.

[14] The Reverend John Seccomb of Harvard.

[15] Thomas Marsh of Mansfield, Conn.

[16] The Reverend Joseph Buckminster (Harvard 1739), the minister of Rutland. *Sibley*, X, 348-354.

[17] (Harvard 1739). A Boston schoolmaster. *Sibley*, X, 366-368.

[18] See Allen, *Worcester Association*, p. 24.

---

ing the Doors of my Barn, and placing my Great Doors on the North. N.B. Ebenezer discovers by all his Conduct that he preferrs Labour to Studying—and tho it grievously wounds me, yet I yield the point finally.[19]

14. Ebenezer at work on the Smaller, South, Barn Doors. P.M. Mr. Miller here. Mr. Jenison (who has begun to keep school at Mr. Hezikiah Pratts, lodging at Mr. Williams's) came here P.M. and had some further talk, but yet seems to be resenting and goes away unquiet. Molly exercis'd much with Toothach goes to Hopkinton, to Mr. Barrett[20] to pull them out which troubled her. He pull'd Two.

15. Mr. John Chamberlain having bought of the Maynards the West End of the House which he himself us'd to live in, this Day mov'd it, upon Wheels, beyond Captain Maynards nigh the River. P.M. Thomme return'd home again from Grafton being in such Pain and under So great Discouragement that his master[21] sends all his Things Home with him. God grant the Grace and Wisdom needed under every Trial!

16. On John 17, 3. P.M. on 2 Tim. 3, 16. N.B. Mr. Jenison came in the Morning and also din'd with us. N.B. at Noon Time Mrs. Whitney went down the road near my Barn and there made a great Out Cry. N.B. Captain Baker (with my Consent obtain'd at noon) after the Public Exercises of the Day desir'd the Congregation to stop, and warn'd his Company to come together tomorrow Morning at 9 o'Clock.

17. I visited Mr. Hezikiah Pratts Child sick of a fever. Both Companys met to Show Arms and beat up for Volunteers, but I was with neither of them. Captain Maynard indeed came to my House to ask me but I was not at Home. N.B. Mr. Benjamin Burnap of Hopkinton here and din'd with us. N.B. David Warrin of Marlborough here, with a Message from Mr. Smith, who had again still asked me to preach a Lecture for him, and which by our Agreement was to have been tomorrow, but it So falls out that their Military Companys are then to meet, and therefore the Lecture is wav'd [sic]. N.B. Thomas Winchester gone part of today, as he was half of Saturday, p.m. of Friday helping Mr. Chamberlain, and p.m. Thursday last, at his Fathers raising.

18. Last Night a Night of Thunder and Lightning and Rain. My Wife not well. Thomas began to Mow the Garden and Fore Yard. Mr. Salter and his wife on their Journey home, came and lodg'd here. Their Horses had broke from them at Sudbury and Mr. More (Son of Deacon) waited on them hither with Two, who also return'd with the Evening. Mr. Salter brings Sad News from the Fleet and Camp at Cape Briton. Captain Smithhurst[22] missing in the Country Galley, and 140 Land soldiers cut off in their Attempt on the Island Battery. Yet God has deliver'd 3 French Sail into our Hands, Two 36-Gun-Company-Ships from France and a Quebeck Sloop with Flour and Peas.

19. A Young Man, one Laffland from Landlord Wards in Marlborough, brought Mr. Salters Stray Horses, and they proceeded upon their Journey. I rode with them as far as Captain Bakers. N.B. Reckon'd with Samuel Baker. P.M. Hard Thunder and heavy Rain. Towards Eve came Mr. Benjamin Goddard to talk with me about what is the Duty of a Christian that in his Conscience did Seriously judge that the Constant Preaching he sits under is not edifying, if So much as Safe. My Wife rather Worse.

20. My Wife ill yet. Sent to Dr. Gott. P.M. the Doctor came. Left divers Medicines both with regard to her Fever and pains in her Limbs, and likewise for her Sore, pained Breast. God grant us to make a good Improvement of his holy Corrections! My Family divers of them continue not well, Several of the Children as well as their Mother. My Concern at present great for Thomme yet he is Stirring about a little, but growing no better (I think) in the Main. Mr. Joseph Batchellor here and we finish'd with regard to Thomme.

21. I rode over to see Deacon Tomlin who lies ill. He answer'd me with great readiness respecting his State, and said he had such Hope, and such scripture ground for his Hope that he was not

[19] The Reverend Mr. Parkman was much disappointed that Ebenezer never did prepare to go to Harvard.

[20] The Reverend Samuel Barrett was a useful citizen.

[21] Joseph Batcheller, the weaver, of Grafton.

[22] Smithurst captained the *Prince of Orange*, a vessel of 16 guns. *The Boston Gazette, or Weekly Journal*, June 11, 1745.

afraid. I gave him some Cautions,—Strait the Gate—few etc.—the many deceiv'd—the Heart deceitful—the wiles of Satan—our own Sin—particularly warn'd him respecting Covetousness and loving the world—wanting to Live longer, how long soever we live. Pray'd with him and recommended him to the Grace of God. Neighbour Abner Newton[23] din'd with me, told me he heard that a Young man at Mill River was kill'd by the Lightning the Day before yesterday—as was another at Woodstock or Pomfret last Monday Night in his Bed. Mr. Jenison here, and pleasant.

22. Mrs. Hannah Rice (wife of Noah) from Sutton, here with 3 Children and din'd with me.

23. On 2 Tim. 3, 16. P.M. on Hos. 6, 3.

24. A very Spreading report that Mr. Whitefield is to preach at Grafton tomorrow. I visited Deacon Tomlin who lyes utterly insensible, breaths as if he was in a Sleep but cannot be wak'd, nor has Spake ever since about Sundown last Evening. Tis conceiv'd is in a dying State. Mr. Benjamin Burnap came to me at the Deacons. He has gather'd a Number of Subscriptions (under mine) for Mr. Edwards of Religious Affections. Old Ensign Newton here.

25. Early in the Morning to the House of Death, the late Deacon Tomlins, who deceas'd last Night. *Jejun. Priv. Speciatim propter Reverendi Domini Whitefield Approquinquationem: ut de Voluntate Dei gravis sim; ut nosque De Displiceani nec Quomodocumque opus eius impediam sed Sapientiam et Directionem omnem quae necessaria Set praesertim hoc Tempore, a Deo Fonte et Patre Luminum et Largitionem, obtineam.*

26. Deacon Tomlin was bury'd. Thunder Showers. At the request of the Widow—principal Heir and Executor, I stop'd at the House after the Funeral to read the Last Will and Testament of the Deceased. N.B. The Will disquieted the Daughters. Deacon Fay rode home with me and I show'd him Something that I had drawn up with regard to Mr. Whitefield. Mr. Whipple and his wife at my House at Eve.

27. Mr. Thomas Billing here. Neighbour Rogers Suffers Damage by Doggs among his sheep. People report here for the Fruits of my Garden. Cherrys and Currants. Thomas and Ebenezer mow Bushes instead of Grass, by Reason of the Cloudiness of the Weather. Nor have we done anything at Haying for several Days.

28. Thomas work'd for Mr. Chamberlin till noon, when Ensign Bruce came along with him home, having press'd him in his Majesty's Name to go up to the Western Frontiers. Somewhat Surpriz'd at Such a sudden and unexpected Turn, I had my Horse, left my Studys and Business and rode with the Ensign over to the Captain, who after a great deal of arguing told me that it was done out of Favour and regard to me, for that unless the young man be Secur'd he would soon Escape, and neither the King nor I Should have any Benefit from him. But I could not but Conceive that if that had been the Case the Affair would not have been carry'd on with all manner of Tokens of carrying him off, and no private hints given me of the Design, but every way oppressive to me under the Weight, not merely of my private, but of publick Business. I mention'd over the Young men of the Neighbourhood that might better have been pitch'd upon than Thomas—and tho I was willing to bear my part—a public Calamity, yet could by no means conceive it to be my place to suffer as yet in this way. We broke off with his assuring me he should be releas'd upon his promising him to Stick to my Business and not run away if there Should be further Occasion for young men and Necessity obliging them At Length to take him. I din'd there. P.M. The Companys train'd and beat up for Volunteers—but without sucess. In the North Company Captain Maynard pressed his own son or young man Merodach, [illegible] Lieutenant Forbush's son Noah and Ensign Rice's son Joseph. The last hir'd Silas Pratt to go in his sons stead. N.B. An Exceeding, great Storm of Thunder and Lightning (which rose among us) prevail'd as it pass'd into the East and the brightest rainbow follow'd. N.B. I saw Deacon Mirriam of Grafton going to Concord with an Horse for Mr. Whitefield. N.B. At

Evening Joshua Winchester was press'd. He was of them I nam'd when I mention'd over the Neighbourhood but I added I thought it might not do to take one out of that but I did not remember that they had one Son already in the Kings service, viz. Samuel gone to Cape Breton: for then I should have endeavour'd to have him excus'd.

29. Thomas went to Captain Bakers and home. After a while came his Mother, disquieted that I (as she said) was the means of having Joshua press'd. Ebenezer carry'd home Mr. Tainters Chaise which has stood in my Barn now some Time. Very letting Weather as to our Hay—so frequent showers and Shines. P.M. another Thunder Storm, but chiefly went away South. After which there was Still a great and dismal one which went from the North East to the South East but did not come up over us.

30. On Hos. 6, 3, former part. P.M. 1 John 3, 23, former part for this last I us'd an Exercise on the Catechism which I had deliver'd to Young Women. Eli Forbush[24] din'd here. N.B. He and Jonathan Bruce being press'd to go to Westward to guard the Frontier desir'd prayers for them. I was very much tir'd and worried with my Services to Day which were somewhat long. Memorandum. Mr. Whitefield preaches at Grafton to Day and Some number of my Southern Neighbours are gone to hear him. Thomas Winchester at his Fathers and went to hear Mr. Whitefield.

## JULY 1745

1. Thomas Winchester got off from going out a soldier. His Brother Joshua also got off as did divers others. But the seven that appear'd and that went this Morning from Captain Bakers to Colonel Wards in order to their going up to Colonel Hoddard of Northampton, were there. Jonathan Bruce, James Bradish, Ephraim Whitney, James Miller, Jonas Warrin, Elijah Rice and Eli Forbush. These out of Captain Maynards Company were Two only, viz. his own son, his only child Stephen, and Silas Pratt who went in the Room of Ensign Rice's son Joseph. N.B. I wrote a Letter in Eli's behalf to Mr. Edwards of Northampton. P.M. I rode down to Mr. Matthias Rices to get an Horse to go to Cambridge, but did not succeed. Went also to Mr. Seth Rice's and got one. Mr. Whitefield, I hear, preaches at Grafton to Day, a.m. and at Upton p.m.

2. My Dauter Molly accommodated with Captain Fays Horse rode to Cambridge with me. My Wife rode with me as far as Mr. Amsdens, whom I obtain'd to carry her (and her child) to Marlborough to see Sister Breck who was extreme urgent to have her be with her in her affliction and Confinement. N.B. Mr. Whitefield preach'd at Dr. Gotts and my wife heard him. An Hot Day. Molly and I rested at Lieutenant Biglo's at Waltham. Got to Mother Champneys just before a great storm of Thunder and Rain. N.B. Mother Champney in a Comfortable State of Health to what she has been.

3. This Morning going over to Cambridge met Mr. Matthias Rice, who inform'd me that our Forces had taken CAPE BRITON and that there was all manner of Joy thereat. The Exercises came to the Governor this morning early, and presently the Bells were rung, Guns fired, etc. Commencement was render'd the most gladsome Day. Everybody was full of the welcome story and wishing one another Joy. Was chiefly at Mr. Hancocks and at Sir Peabodys Chamber. N.B. Mr. Swift[1] of Acton his indecent Vociferation concerning my not being present at Mr. Smiths January 22 to bear my Testimony against Mr. Whitefield. I din'd in the Hall. N.B. Poor Mr. Samuel Coollidge[2]—his Distractions and Deliriums—pluck'd out of the presidents Chair in the Meeting House and dragg'd out on the Ground by a negro, like a Dead Dogg in presence of all the Assembly. Most piteous Sight! Molly din'd at Mr. Danforths.[3] N.B. Mr. Rand[4] of Sunderland has left

23 Son of Thomas Newton.

24 Eli Forbes. *Sibley*, XIII.

1 The Reverend John Swift, Jr.

2 (Harvard 1724). The former schoolmaster at Westborough and other places, who had become a public charge. *Sibley*, VII, 326–331.

3 Samuel Danforth.

4 The Reverend William Rand left Sunderland because he disliked the preaching of George Whitefield while many of his congregation evidently sympathized with the evangelist. John M. Smith, *History of the Town of Sunderland* (Greenfield, 1899), p. 61. Rand is believed to have written an address of the Hampshire County clergy to Whitefield which appeared in *The Testimony of the North Association in the County of Hartford* (Boston, 1745).

his people. Mr. Breck gives me word from my wife that Mr. Smith (who had engag'd to last Lecture when he came with Mr. Breck to my House) could not preach my Lecture. Lodg'd at Mother Champneys.

4. Molly and I rode to Boston. Broke fast at Brother Alexanders. Visited my Mother who is weak and sick. Mr. Gay[5] of Hingham preach'd the Lecture on 1 Sam. 14, 6, 7, 13. Din'd at Mrs. Thomas Hubbards. Mr. Niles,[6] Mr. Webb, Captain Dupre and others din'd also. N.B. My Kinsman at Dr. Delhonds[7] but is not well contented there. At Mrs. Thomas Stoddards and paid her about 12 pounds old Tenor. Return'd to Cambridge at Eve. N.B. Roxbury illuminated. Colleges illumin'd. Bonfire. Bell ringing, Drum beating etc. most of the Night.

5. It was Somewhat misty, but Molly and Mr. John Sparhawk[8] in Company we rode as far as Mrs. Bekky Walkers in Waltham, when Molly being indispos'd we Lit and stay'd the making and Eating of Chocolat. We got up so seasonably to Westborough that I preach'd my Lecture at the usual Time in the afternoon, on John 4, 24. My wife return'd from Marlborough a.m.

6. [No entry].

7. Sacrament. On 1 John 4, 11. P.M. Ps. 89, 15. N.B. Somewhat more of the Northside at Communion than Some seasons of late, for I had wrote a Letter to Mr. Martyn before last Sabbath to notifie them. Yet some Number were absent.

8. Read Lowman[9] on the Revelations.

9. Catechetical Exercise to young Women on the Eternally unchangeableness and wisdom of God.

10. An Hott Day. Ensign Bruce (who went up to Fort Shirley to bring back his son Jonathan) return'd—and informs that last Friday about 10 a.m. Mr. William Phipps was kill'd by the Indians about 30 Rods from the Garrison at [Putney] (nigh which lives Mr. Nehemiah How who went from Grafton) and his Body was treated inhumanly, Scalp'd, his Heart taken out etc.

11. Another Hot Day. Conformable to a Request from Reverend Stone of Southborough in behalf of Mr. Moses Fay and his wife of Said Town I went down there to a private Fast. Mr. Loring,[10] Barrett,[11] Stone,[12] and Smith[13] also at Mr. Fay's. N.B. Mrs. Fay had been languishing more than Seven Years and not at Meeting in that Time tho she has had six Children, and now suppos'd to be in a Consumption; her Case therefore calling for Pity and Prayers. Mr. Stone offer'd up the first Prayer. I preach'd on Ps. 65, 2. Mr. Barrett pray'd and Mr. Loring preach'd p.m. on Isa. 45, 22. A good Savoury Sermon which may the Lord bless to all Souls! Supp'd at Mr. Stones. I return'd at Evening. N.B. Mr. Smith inform'd me that Brother Breck was gone home, but a Number of Books which were all by Dr. Owen, he had bargain'd away to him, for which he had receiv'd and carry'd home with him Dr. Hammond.[14] Compare this Conduct with Mr. Brecks Engagement to Me May 23.

12. Hot Weather Still. Heard that Deacon Fisher[15] was lately kill'd at Ashualot by the Indians, and a post in this Day gone along to the Governor with the sad news of it.

13. [No entry].

14. A.M. on 1 John 4, 11. P.M. on Eph. 6, 13 to 18.

15. Mr. Jenison was here with divers important pieces of public News, in the Public Papers, in special our Loosing the Battle in Flanders near Tournay. N.B. Mr. Aaron Hardy of Grafton here, and is full of uneasiness about Mr. Prentices[16] preaching.

16. [No entry].

17. Isaac Newton of Southborough here, from Fort Shirley. Becky[17] and Molly rode to Sutton. Brother Hicks from Cambridge to Sutton.

18. In the Singular good Providence of God Lieutenant Tainter this Morning Sent us a large Quarter of Lamb. Otherwise we Should have been unprovided for any Special Entertainment at our Table to Day, which was THANKSGIVING on Account of the late Success at Cape Briton, on which Occasion I preach'd on Isa. 25, 1, 2, 9. N.B. Mr. Prentice and his wife went a while agoe along with Mr. Whitefield and his wife in their Journey to Northampton and are not return'd. A Number of Grafton at Meeting with us. Mr. John Collar and Deacon Cooper[18] and his wife din'd with us. At the Request of our Young Men Some while Since I appointed a Lecture to them to be in about 2 Hours, which I attended and preach'd on Rom. 2, 4, latter part.

19. Thomas and Ebenezer began at the Meadow. At Night there was Exceeding loud Cracks of Thunder and Sharp Lightning.

20. Thomas and Ebenezer at the Meadow. Rain p.m. Becky and Molly return'd from sutton. Thomas sow'd Turnips.

21. Repeat'd on Eph. 6, 13, and 1 John 3, 23. Mrs. Wheeler din'd here. It is my Grief that the North side are in so broken and unflourishing state.

22. Ebenezer having been somewhat poison'd by his working in the Meadow last week, goes not today with Thomas, but Reap'd Rye. I rode to Marlborough to Mr. Woods and return'd their Occasional Paper 3 vols. At Deacon Stevens's and paid him 10 shillings for mending Lieutenant Tainters Chaise May 22 last. I went to Mr. Smiths but he and his wife, old Mr. Loring and Sister Breck were gone down to Mr. Jonathan Lorings,[19] to dine there but I din'd at Dr. Gotts. After Dinner the Doctor and I rode to Mr. Lorings. They had not din'd. I was oblig'd to Sit down with them Mr. Loring insisting, when as I had heard he was (tho unreasonably) disgusted with me. My Design in going to Marlborough was very much this, to wait on Sister Breck to our House, but she was not to be perswaded. I return'd with Mr. Smith etc. to his House and thence home.

23. Thomas at the Meadow. Ebenezer at the Rye. P.M. I preach'd at Mr. Sam Fay juniors on Heb. 12, 5. Mrs. Fay not having been at publick worship for more than 2 years. Very few attended—it being so busy a season.

24. Cornelius Biglo Sick of a Fever. I visited him, and dealt plainly with him. At divers Neighbours. Visited also Mr. Daniel Forbush's wife who is confin'd again by weakness and illness. Din'd at home. Thomas at the Meadow. Ebenezer at the Rye. Towards Night Mrs. Maynard had my mare to ride to Mrs. Miles[20] at Shrewsbury. At Eve I help'd Ebenezer in his unloading Hay and Carting in a Turn of Rye.

25. [No entry].

26. Mr. Breck on his Journey from Springfield to Marlborough. I resented his Conduct in trading away Dr. Owens Books to Mr. Smith.

27. Mr. Breck and his wife came up from Marlborough and lodg'd here.

28. Mr. Breck a.m. on Luke 12, 48, and p.m. on Gal. 6, 14.

29. Rain. Mr. Breck and his wife detain'd by the wet weather. N.B. Stephen Maynard return'd last night from Fort Shirley. Mr. Breck and I walked down to Captain Maynards.

30. Mr. Breck and his wife undertook their Journey. My wife (favour'd with Mr. Benjamin Hows Horse) and I rode to Worcester with them—and we din'd at Dr. Brecks. N.B. Mr. Fessenden[21] there after dinner. P.M. We return'd, but tarried Some little Time at Colonel Chandlers and drank a Dish of Tea with Madam Chandler.[22] She inform'd me that there were about 40 French persons old and Young dispos'd of in their Town. Mr. Cushing So busy Carting Hay I Saw him not, either going or

[5] The Reverend Ebenezer Gay.
[6] The Reverend Samuel Niles (Harvard 1699), the minister of the Second Church of Braintree, 1711–1762. Sibley, IV, 485–491.
[7] Louis Delhonde, the physician of Boston.
[8] The Reverend John Sparhawk of Salem.
[9] Moses Lowman (1680–1752) was a non-conformist English divine. A Paraphrase and Notes on the Revelation of St. John (London, 1737).
[10] The Reverend Israel Loring of Sudbury.
[11] The Reverend Samuel Barrett of Hopkinton.
[12] The Reverend Nathan Stone of Southborough.
[13] The Reverend Aaron Smith of Marlborough.
[14] A work of Samuel Hammond, the English nonconformist divine who died in 1665.
[15] Josiah Fisher, one of the original proprietors of Upper Ashuelot, was killed and scalped by the Indians, July 10, 1745. Philip A. Fisher, The Fisher Genealogy (Everett, 1898), pp. 74–75.
[16] The Reverend Solomon Prentice of Grafton, who had been rebuked by an ecclesiastical council in Oct., 1744, continued his New-Light preaching until his resignation in 1747.
[17] Rebecca Hicks, daughter of John Hicks of Sutton, was Parkman's niece.
[18] Samuel Cooper of Grafton.
[19] Son of Parson Loring. Jonathan lived in Marlborough. Hudson, Marlborough, p. 410.
[20] The wife of Deacon Samuel Miles. Ward, Shrewsbury, p. 368.
[21] Stephen Fessenden (Harvard 1737) was the second lawyer to practice in Worcester. Sibley, X, 169.
[22] Wife of Colonel John Chandler.

returning. N.B. Mrs. Sarah Whipple took Care of our Sucking Child.

31. I visited Mrs. Grow who was Sick, and I din'd there. Visited Mrs. Harrington and Mr. Jonas Child and his wife, who wanted very much an Opportunity to discourse with Me about the grand Interests of their Souls. N.B. Mr. Whitney came in. I would rejoice to have this glorious work promoted, and do lament it is So behind hand.

### AUGUST [1745]

1. I went to Shrewsbury. Preach'd the Lecture on Mat. 13, 39. Few at Meeting. Return'd at Eve.

2. Thomas brot home 3 Load from the Meadow and got in one Load of Home Hay.

3. Thomas brought home the last Load from the Meadow altho it has been very wett and troublesome stirring in the Meadow this Season. At Eve Loud Cracks of Thunder and Sharp Lightning. Through God's great Goodness we were preserv'd and Safe.

4. Rainy a. and p.m. on 1 John 3, 23. Heavy Rains which caus'd a great Flood. N.B. James Dunlop from Cape Briton here, as I also daily hear of their Returning.

5. Din'd at Deacon Newtons on Salt Fish. P.M. rode to Southboro to Mr. Thomas Hudson. Paid his wife 15 shillings old Tenor, Interest of £50 for one Quarter. Mr. Hudson not being at Home. Mr. Stone not at Home. Return'd at Eve.

6. Read Thoughts on Religion[1] and a Letter to a Baptist concerning Some Important Discoverys in Phylosophy and Theology—an Entertaining Piece. N.B. Great Loss of Hay among our Neighbours by the Flood.

7. My Little Dauter Sarah ill. At Mr. Matthias Rice's to talk with him about our North Precincts delaying to pay their £50 tho I have waited upon them 3 months and paid Interest because of their Neglect. He told me he would go to Lieutenant Holloway and Endeavour that he Should come and See me, or do what might serve me. Was at Mr. Beemans[2]—at Levi Brighams, who has newly got to keeping House at old Mr. Brighams. At Eve found Mr. Gay[3] of Suffield and his wife here, being on their Journey Home. Brother Hicks here and his Son John from Cape Briton.

8. The Company went off. Thomas went to mowing at Mr. Beemans, but return'd without being able to do any thing the Waters were so high. Neighbour Stephen Maynard here and gave me a Narrative of his Excursion in the public service at Fort Shirley and of the good Behaviour of their Captain (Ephraim Williams junior) towards them. At Eve Mrs. Winchester here.

9. Thomas works at his Fathers. Ebenezer and the Two Boys clearing. Mr. Abner Newton here and paid me £20 old Tenor.

10. Thomas at his Fathers. Mr. Thomas Goodenow here. Gave him a Letter from me to Mr. Martyn.

11. On Acts 20, 21, and on Luke 18, 21.

12. Ezekiel Dodge[4] a Freshman of Harvard College here.

13. I rode to Harvard Association, by Marlborough. Was at Mr. Smiths Early, but he refus'd to go, tho he was at the appointment of the Meeting and was himself the appointed Lecturer; his main Objection was rais'd from this, that Mr. Seccomb[5] had ask'd Mr. Whitefield to preach, and he had accordingly preach'd at Harvard. But tho Mr. Smith and Several others were not there yet there was a considerable Number and Mr. Trowbridge[6] and his wife from Groton. Concior absent Mr. Loring repeated a sermon on Eph. 5, 25, last Clause, and gave himself for it among the Collections[?]. Mr. Stone's seem'd to be so much in Favour of Crying out that I could not help making my Remarks on it, how differently it would have been taken from some others (Ex gr. from me) if Such Collection had been brought by them.

14. A Number of us went with Mr. Seccomb to his Island[7] with great pleasure. Mr. Stone deliver'd an Excellent Sermon at the Public Lecture on Tit. 2, 14. N.B. Our Conversation on a Certain Meeting propos'd by some ministers to be at Boston September next to subscribe the Confession of Faith; but we determin'd nothing, unless to let it very much alone—wait and see. Mr. Barrett my Company to Marlborough. Supp'd at his Kinsman Barretts. Home late.

15. Hearing that Mrs. Tomlin (widow) was not well I visited her at Evening.

16. Mr. Smith came up from Marlborough a.m. P.M. preach'd my Lecture on John 14, 19.

17. Brother Hicks here, on his journey to Cambridge. Rain P.M.

18. Rain in the Morning—but So held up afterwards that we had a Comfortable Day. I preach'd on Isa. 25, 9. Mr. Nathaniel Parker[8] of Newton with us at Communion—and here at noon time but did not dine with us. Deacon Fay and Deacon Forbush din'd here. P.M. Repeated sermon on Luke 12, 21. Have great reason to mourn over my Dullness and want of Spiritual Taste etc.

19. Mr. Parker of Newton here—his Discourse very much of one Bird,[9] a preacher among them.

20. Catechetical Exercise to young Women. Thomas to Mr. Beemans for a Load of Hay, of him. At Night Thomas went to his Fathers to work some Days for himself.

21. A.M. Captain Bass of Dorchester and Mr. Daniel Henshaw of Boston here. Mr. Martyn[10] also. The last din'd and Spent the afternoon with me. He told me that he drew the Last Petition which our North side put in to the Court, but he did not know how the Case was Circumstanced but as he took it from Lieutenant Holloways mouth. We had some discourse of Changing after a while.

22. I visited Captain Forbush's wife who had been in some Spiritual Concern and Distress. Ebenezer went p.m. to Sutton to look up my Young Cattle which had not been heard of for some time.

23. Mr. Simon Goddard here—he brought me 2 Pamphlets to read, one of which was Mr. Shurtleffs Letter concerning Mr. Whitefield.[11] P.M. Mr. Abraham Knowlton who din'd with us.

24. Mr. Simon Goddard here again. I rode to Hopkinton on Mr. Edwards Whipples Horse. N.B. Ebenezer return'd from Sutton without any News of my Cattle. Thomas Winchester return'd at Eve from his Fathers.

25. Mr. Barrett preach'd here on Tit. 2, 11, The Grace of God. I preach'd at Hopkinton a. and p.m. on Song. 1, 7, 8. N.B. Mr. David Snowden of Boston there.

26. I return'd from Hopkinton. Thomas at my work again. Mr. James Fays son James Sick. N.B. Mr. Fay came yesterday to Westborough meeting a.m. but because Mr. Barrett preach'd he went to Grafton p.m. and desir'd prayers for his son there. Noah How p.m. sealing my new Closet (or little study). Mr. Thomas Hudson at Eve.

27. Catechiz'd the Children a. and p.m. at the Meeting House. Mr. Peabody[12] going to a Fast at Worcester din'd with me. Noah How at work at my new Study still. Mr. Whitney here to ask my Mind about Mr. Hales[13] preaching next week at some House on the Road as would best accommodate—to which I consented. N.B. Mr. Ball and Mr. Wheeler here. Ebenezer was ill, bad cold etc.

28. Thomas at Grafton a.m. hunting for my young Cattle, but in Vain. Very hot Season.

29. Visited Mr. Daniel Forbushs wife who lyes Sick, but has

---

[1] Probably [Blaise] Pascal, *Thoughts on Religion, and Other Subjects* (London, 1704).

[2] Eleazer Beeman of Westborough.

[3] The Reverend Ebenezer Gay, Jr. *Sibley*, X, 171-175.

[4] (Harvard 1749). Later the minister of Abington, 1750 to 1770. See Benjamin Hobart, *History of the Town of Abington* (Boston, 1866), pp. 96-98.

[5] The Reverend John Seccomb of Harvard.

[6] The Reverend Caleb Trowbridge of Groton.

[7] The Reverend Mr. Seccomb "built a substantial summer cottage, as a place of pleasant resort," on Grape Island in Bare Hill Pond. Henry S. Nourse, *History of the Town of Harvard* (Harvard, 1894), p. 187.

[8] The proprietor of a saw mill.

[9] The Reverend Samuel Bird attended Harvard College but was expelled, May 11, 1744, because he was "notoriously guilty of the most intollerable impudence, Arrogance and Contempt of Superiours, and especially of Ministers of the Gospel." He already had New-Light tendencies. He became the minister of Dunstable, 1747-1751, and later of the White Haven Church, New Haven, Conn. *Sibley*, XI, 359-364.

[10] The Reverend John Martyn of the North Precinct.

[11] William Shurtleff, *A Letter to Those of his Brethren in the Ministry Who Refuse to Admit the Rev. Mr. Whitefield into Their Pulpits* (Boston, 1745).

[12] The Reverend Oliver Peabody of Natick.

[13] The Reverend Moses Hale (Harvard 1734), later minister of the First Congregational Church of West Newbury, 1752-1779. *Sibley*, IX, 407-408.

her Senses. I not only convers'd with her but read part of Mathers Dead Faith[14] etc.

30. [No entry].

31. Brother Hicks here and Mrs. Peggy Whittemore din'd with us. It has been Sorrowful to hear of So many of those who have return'd from Cape Breton who have sicken'd and dy'd.

### SEPTEMBER, 1745

1. On Isa. 25, 9. P.M. repeated Sermon on Ps. 106, 5 on Spiritual Joy. Acquainted our Congregation that there would (God willing) be a Sermon tomorrow at Stephen Fay's at 11 o'Clock.

2. My wife and I rode to Stephen Fays. Mr. Hall was there, and many people. Mr. Hall[1] preach'd on Mat. 6, 10. Thy Kingdom Come. Mr. Winchester[2] a Candidate for the Ministry and preacher at Sutton was there also. N.B. an Handsome Entertainment after the Exercise. Mr. Hall on his Journey to Concord. N.B. Thomas Winchester (by agreement) went off. This I consented to, because my Two sons and Nathan Knowlton Suffic'd for my present Business and it was upon Condition that Thomas Should help me the month of April instead of this month: and as to his lost Time, he is to make it up in Cyder making and Thrashing. Moses Pratt had my Oxen to cross his Ground in Shrewsbury.

3. Having heard that one of Reverend Mr. Smiths little Daughters[3] was dead, I went (though not sent for) to the Funeral. Mr. Loring was there and pray'd. A very grievous Loss to the poor bereav'd Parents. The Lord be almightily present with them and Sustain them! Rode with Mr. Loring to his sons. Mr. Peabody return'd from Worcester, and tells me that Mr. Nathaniel Gardner is Chose their Pastor. N.B. Mr. Lorings great Concern at hearing of the Choice of Mr. Gardner at Worcester: and he wrote a Letter to Mr. Prentice[4] of Lancaster while I was present, to induce him to Converse with others in the Neighbouring Ministry about it. Mr. Josiah Brown the bearer as he was also of another from me to beseach Mr. Prentice to preach to our northside at their approaching Fast. I return'd from Sutton to Cambridge.

I carry'd to God those Important Articles—and the Particular State of Some of the Flock, more Especially the Condition of Mrs. Abigail Forbush (wife of Daniel) who lyes most dangerously ill, if yet alive; and that of James Bradish junior (if he be among the Living) very Sick and low, at Deerfield; The Contests also raised by Mr. James Fay and his Brother Stephen, chiefly on account of my disapproving of their going to other Towns, to Meeting on Lords Days. N.B. The Last of them last night in a great Flame, on sudden, about this Matter, but Came to me to Day to acknowledge his unguarded Passion and indecency at that time.

Besides these, the Case of my Family, my wife, Children—the Ministry—the Land, the Nation and Protestant Interests abroad, call for Concern and [illegible] Prayers. Upon the Whole I solemnly Reviewed my Engagements and Resolutions to be the Lords, relying upon the Merits and Reassurances of the Lord. Christ alone for Pardon and acceptance with God and the Aids of the Divine Spirit to enable me to adhere to and fulfill them. And May the Lord most mercifully watch over the future part of my (Short) Life, and prepare me for His whole will! Amen.

4. Visited Mr. Daniel Forbushs wife, but she had not her Reason. Visited Mr. James Fays family—much uncomfortable Complaint of me and my improving the Neibouring Ministers, Mr. Barrett Especially. N.B. Stephen Fay came and return'd as far as his house with me; and just before parting flew into a dreadful passion with me that I did not Consent to his going away to other Towns on the Lords Day: and immoderately rak'd up by Strict Charge given him about Mr. Elisha Paine. It griev'd me heartily to see him in such an high Ferment, but the Lord have Mercy on us and pardon us for his Name's Sake!

5. *Jejun. Priv. Vide Natalitia.* Stephen Fay here acknowledging his indecent Temper and Manner last Night, but stands to the Things that he Spoke. The Lord Shew him his Error!

[The following entry for September 5, 1745, was inserted in the Natalitia.]

May a gracious and merciful God accept what I have this Day been enabled to do, in humbling my soul before him, and offering up fervent Supplications to him; together with my hearty Thanksgivings for his Sparing Goodness to So Vile and unprofitable a Creature.

I had the following Special Occasions of Prayer before me this Day:

1. My own inward State which is not without much Darkness and Confusion and sometimes Distress yet. Besides what I needed with regard to my Self, my inward State, I wanted Direction and Assistance in my studys and Ministry.

2. There are Discouraging Symptoms among my people, not only Deadness and Coldness as to the things of God, but many Signs of Worldliness, Carnality, Contentiousness.

3. The North Side are taking Steps Preparitory to Settling a Minister and are next week to have a Fast.

6. At Eve Mr. Bezaleel Eager came from Mr. Billings with his Earnest request to have [me] go over to see his sick Children. I went and found his little son, his only Son, very nigh to Death, and Two little Dauters sick. Return'd at about ten and one-half to my Family. Their sickness is Fever and Flux[5] which greatly prevails in Shrewsbury and many children are taken away.

7. Moses Pratt return'd my Oxen Safe after their journey and work.

8. On Acts 20, 21, and Ps. 89, 47 p.m. on Occasion of Mr. Daniel Forbushs wifes Death last night. The Lord make us sensible of the worth of our opportunitys since our Time is so short, and the advantage of Reason and understanding so invaluable.

9. I rose early and went to Mr. Joseph Rice's at Marlborough. Took up £50 old Tenor of him to pay Mr. Hudson of Southboro and then attended Funeral of Mrs. Forbush. At Mr. Williams's after the Funeral.

10. In the Morning rode to Southboro to Mr. Hudsons and took up my Bond. N.B. Mr. Edy and his wife at Mr. Hudsons. N.B. Mr. Stone gone to Harwich. After my Return, my wife and I went to the Funeral of Two of Mr. Billings's[6] Children[7]—his little Son and a little Dauter who sabbath was Sennight went hand in hand to the House of God now lay in one Grave in one Coffin. They were buried by the New Meeting House, the first that have been buryed in that place.

11. N.B. Mr. Wolcott[8] of Salem and his wife at Bezaleel Eagers. Ebenezer and Thomme went to Grafton and brought down our young Cattle from Mr. David Batchellors. At Eve Mr. Ebenezer Rice and his wife here but I could not converse with them only directed them when to come to me. Mr. James Ball, Laurence and James Rice were here, and brought me a Paper sign'd by eleven persons of the North precinct Shewing that they were against their Brethrens appointing the Fast approaching in order to call and settle a minister. A Fast, they acknowledge, there is reason for and they are ready to join in one, but not for the Calling a Minister. N.B. I had so much hindrance that I could not without Difficulty prepare a Sermon.

12. Fast on the North Side. Mr. Cushing[9] Sent a Letter that the Sick and Dead among them prevented his Coming. Mr. Morse[10] Sent a Letter also that not only was there most distressing Sickness among his Neighbours, but he himself was Sick; nay and desir'd a Fast might be kept among them, next Week. Mr. Prentice of Lancaster neither Came nor sent why. Mr. Goss[11]

---

[14] Samuel Mather, *Dead Faith Anatomized* (Boston, 1740).

[1] The Reverend David Hall of Sutton.
[2] Jonathan Winchester (Harvard 1737) was later the first minister of the First Congregational Church of Ashburnham, 1760–1767. *Sibley*, X, 264–265.
[3] Anna, daughter of the Reverend Aaron Smith of Marlborough died Sept. 1, aged 4.
[4] The Reverend John Prentice.

[5] Excessive fluid discharge from the bowels.
[6] Thomas Billing or Billings of Westborough.
[7] Nathaniel died Sept. 8 and Mary Sept. 9. Still another child, Jane Billing died a few days later, Sept. 15, 1745.
[8] John Wolcott (Harvard 1721), a gentleman and merchant, who served as a Representative, Justice of the Peace, and High Sheriff of Essex County. *Sibley*, VI, 590–591.
[9] The Reverend Job Cushing of Shrewsbury.
[10] The Reverend Ebenezer Morse of Boylston.
[11] The Reverend Thomas Goss of Bolton.

came. Show'd him the paper I receiv'd last night. A.M. I pray'd and Mr. Goss preach'd on Lev. 44. P.M. Mr. Goss pray'd and I preach'd on 2 Chron. 15, 2. O that God might make it a Day of Atonement an Reconciliation, and that He would please truely to humble, direct prepare and Bless the precinct! We were entertain'd at Captain Eagers. At Evening came a Committee (viz. Messers. Livermore, McAllister, Townsend and Matthias Rice) to take Advice of the Ministers—and the Dissatisfy'd also came and brought their reasons against joining in the Fast. We heard much, yet deferr'd the matter to another Time when the other Ministers might be present: viz. next Monday come sennight, and to meet then at Lieutenant Holloways, at 12 o'Clock. N.B. Captain Fay my Company coming and going. N.B. News of the Mohawks Threatening.

13. Mr. Smith of Marlborough sent David Warrin to me, informing me that his wife was ill and he desir'd Earnestly to Change next Sabbath. P.M. went to Mr. Ebenezer Johnsons of Southboro to see his wife who was very sick and low, and Mr. Stone at Harwich was at Mr. Jacob Amsdens as I return'd home. N.B. Thomas Winchester at work for me both yesterday and today, making Cyder.

14. Thomas making and Ebenezer boyling Cyder. In all, have made 16 Barrells and boyl'd about 10. Mr. Smith came here, and I went to Marlborough. Thomas return'd home.

15. Mr. Smith preach'd here on John 1, 11. I preach'd at Marlborough on Luke 12, 15. I baptized Mr. Samuel Shermans son Jason. I return'd at Evening.

16. Was at the Funeral of another of Mr. Billings Children and Mrs. Billings ill. N.B. A Story has got about of a Dream of Mrs. Billings, and which I took the Freedom to enquire into and which She confirm'd, viz. that She Saw a man bring the Coffin of her youngest Child into the House, upon which She took on; but presently there came in another Man with a large Coffin, and said to her that She had not need to take on for her Child for here was a Coffin for herself also, for she Should die next. N.B. Mr. Hale who lives near the new burying place (tis said) saw a large Coffin (as well as a small one) in the air just over the Burying place last Tuesday Evening immediately after the burying Mr. Billings Two Children, which story much fright people about Mrs. Billings Death—but I reply'd that we have a more Sure word of Prophecy etc. Mr. John Oake and Mr. Jesse Brigham have Each of them a Child very bad of the Distemper, both which I visited and pray'd with. N.B. Dark riding home through the woods at Night, from Mr. Brighams, nor was it without Danger—but God was pleas'd to Preserve and Conduct me. Captain Fay told me that a Negro man from Mendon was committed to gaol last night for murthering his Mistress.

17. I visited Eunice Bradish a.m. she lying Sick. Messengers one after another of the Deaths and sickness among us. Mr. Brighams[12] and Oakes[13] Children dy'd last Night. Mrs. Billings very bad. Mrs. Dinah Goddenow taken last night, but better today. Mr. Ebenezer Rice's wife here to be Examin'd. Mrs. Thomas Kendal (that formerly liv'd with me) here to See me. Mr. Joseph Batchellor of Grafton, with Mr. Francis Whipple, here.

18. I went to the Funeral of Mr. Jesse Brighams Child, a little Dauter of about 3 and ½. From thence I went to the Funeral of Mr. John Oakes eldest Child between 2 and 3. By the way I visited Mrs. Billing also, who was very ill yet—and pray'd with her. N.B. Mr. Whipple accompany'd me when I went and return'd with me. Mrs. Daniel Goodenow was in great Distress, the night before last in such agony, that by means of the Trouble of her Mind under a sense of Gods Judgments and her own Hardness of heart.

19. A Public Fast on Occasion of the Warr lately Declar'd against the Indians, both at the Eastward, and Westward, and great Apprehensions that the 6 Nations, The Iroquois, viz. Mohawks etc. who have been from Early Times in Alliance with us, would break forth against us. A.M. I preach'd on 2 Chron. 20, 12. P.M. on Heb. 6, 7, 8. May it please God to accept the

Solemnity and bless and prosper his holy Word for our awakening and saving Benefit!

20. Mr. Wheeler here to desire to be put into a way to appear before the Ministers next Monday at Lieutenant Holloways. I told him if he had anything of Weight he might write it.

21. My honoured Mother this Day 85 years old. The Lord yet sustain and preserve her! etc.

22. Preach'd on Two very moving Subjects viz. a.m. on 2 Cor. 3, 15. P.M. Heb. 6, 7, 8. O that the word may not be as Water Spilt on the Ground!

23. Wrote to my Mother and Brother Samuel. Din'd at Lieutenant Holloways, with Mr. Prentice of Lancaster and Mr. Cushing; afterwards came Mr. Morse; but Mr. Goss was gone to Brookfield to see his Father who is sick. After Mr. Prentice had pray'd, The Committee appointed to wait on the Ministers for their Advice came in, viz. Messers. Livermore, Townsend, McAllister, Jacob and Matthias Rice, and by word of mouth express'd the Desire of the Precincts. There came in also Mr. Wheeler, Ball etc. who were dissatisfy'd with proceeding at the present to settle a minister. After hearing both sides at large, they withdrew and the ministers conferr'd one with another. We look'd as impartially as we could into each part of the Case, and drew up and sign'd our Advice to them which was also read to them. But when Mr. Wheeler heard it, he was not a little Disturb'd. Several of us in the Ministry address'd them with earnest Exhortations, Cautions etc. We Supp'd there—my Mare broke out of the Pasture there and ran home to her Colt. I rode Lieutenants Mare home. It was after Midnight when I got home, and my Family o'Bed.

24. Greatly Troubled at the Slender success of our Advice last night. Captain Maynard going to Boston. I sent Letters by him to Reverend Messers Webb[14] and Eliot[15] respecting the meeting of ministers this week at Boston to subscribe Confessions of Faith. At Eve Mr. Ebenezer Rice here to be Examin'd. I began a Letter to the Committee of the North Precinct—in which I would fain qualifie their Tempers so far as to be Condescending to their Brethren and induce them to proceed with moderation in their Affairs. Catechiz'd young Women. Preach'd to them on Mat. 13, 39.

25. Besides finishing my Letter to the Committee I wrote affectionately to the dissatisfy'd party if possible to Calm them a little under their uneasiness and Caution them against the evils to which they are now in great Danger—especially against prostituting and sacrificing the Interests of the Soul to Temporal etc., being afraid, from Some discourse from them that they are in Danger of turning to the Church of England. At Eve Stephen Fay here with his uneasinesses Still, for my reproofs at the Time of Mr. Elisha Pain and for my Saying at his Brother Fays that his [Stephens] wife had acknowledged to me that her disaffection to Me and my ministrations was from a wrong Spirit which was true. See her talk with me, May 3, 1744.

26. Divers poor Sickly Soldiers from Cape Breton here, bound for Suffield—whom I endeavour'd to refresh and they went on their way. Mr. Martyn came, din'd with me and preach'd my Lecture on John 8, 23 those words Ye are of this World. A reasonable and Excellent Sermon. May God make it usefull and Effectual to all of us! After Lecture many people were here. Captain Eager, Lieutenant Holloway. I deliver'd my Letter to the Committee to Mr. Livermore, McAllister and Matthias Rice (three of them) and manifested my hearty Concern for them and my Fears lest these Trials which Some of their Brethren (viz. the Dissatisfy'd) were brought into, would be too hard for them, and this I had the more reason for when they themselves told me that they heard that Mr (Commissary) Price[16] is design'd to preach a Lecture in a short time in Mr. Wheelers Chamber.

As to Mr. Martyn, I found that Captain Eager etc. were desirous of his coming over and preaching for me on Communion Day. I plainly intimated to him my Concurrence therewith, and desire of it. His answer left it at uncertaintys for a while,

[12] Persis Brigham died Sept. 17.
[13] Hannah Oake died Sept. 16.

[14] John Webb of Boston.
[15] Andrew Eliot of Boston.
[16] Roger Price, the Commissary or superintendent of Episcopal churches of New England.

but at length he consented I might depend upon Seeing him, God willing, next Saturday P.M.

Messers. James and Stephen Fay and their wives here, and had a long Conference with me about their Uneasiness. They judg'd that Seeing Ruths Offence against me (May 3, 1744) was private, I ought not to have divulg'd it. I Reply'd that if She had not done it herself I Should not made [sic] the Reply that I did at James's that She confess'd to me that her Disaffection to me was from a wrong Spirit. They said she had not done it, for they never knew of what was done or said at the Time referr'd to; she had not told them. I return'd that by their telling me that she was dissatisfy'd with me, and expressing themselves as they did I could not but take it that She had, for that was the principal if not only Time wherein she had manifested dissatisfaction and disaffection to me. But I added that if she had not I misapprehended them, and I was Sorry that I said a word about it; and I desir'd James and his wife to take notice of it; but I hop'd they would not be so unwise as to Make any Noise about these Things, but prudently Conceal them. Lydia Said I had pray'd them at their House not to mention what at that time I said of Ruth, and they did not intend to, but She drop'd something of it before she was aware. Stephen very much insisted and entreated I would humour him so much as to let him see what I had writ about his wifes Discourse with me. After some time refusing I gratify'd him (with her Consent) and putting the others into another Room, I read my Journal of that Time to them but she Seem'd not to Remember much about it. I said many things to them of the unreasonableness of their Disgusts, before they went away; and of my Grief to have persons that profess'd to be such Friends of the Interest of Christ to do So many Things for the Clogging and hindering it.

27. Very heavy Rains last night and this Morning. Mr. Thomas Goodenow here. He informs me of his infant's illness and requests me to go over and baptize it; but I was unwilling Considering that we should not be likely to have any Number of person together it being so near night, but especially I was not able to be out in the Evening and expose my Health—but I deferr'd the matter till tomorrow. We would God willing, See how the Child would be then, and what would be best to be done.

28. I went over to Mr. Thomas Goodenow's and baptiz'd his Infant Child. By the Name of [blank]. Brother Ephraim Allen, Matthias Rice etc. were present. It appear'd to those who were there that the Child was in Danger of Death. After that Baptism I visited Josiah Cutting who is taken sick of Fever and Flux, and grows very bad.

29. I expected Mr. Martyn last night, but he came no further than Lieutenant Holloways. He was at Communion with us and the Generality of the Northside, there being no Meeting there to Day. I preach'd on 2 Cor. 3, 14, and administered the Sacrament. Mr. Martyn, Deacon Fay etc. din'd with me. Mr. Martyn p.m. on Song 5, 16, last Clause, This is my Friend, O Dauters of Jerusalem. The Lord bless what has been done this Day for our Saving Benefit! Mr. Martyn lodg'd here: and his Conversation not disagreeable.

30. Was at the Burial of Mr. Thomas Goodenows Infant Child,[17] and afterwards visited Josiah Cutting (at Mr. Jesse Brighams) who grows worse. Mrs. Brigham and their son Timothy under the same Distemper.

### OCTOBER, 1745

1. Fast at Hopkinton on account of the sorrowful Divisions and Separations among them. Mr. Loring and Mr. Hall there, but Mr. Messinger,[1] who was sent to also, did not come. I began with Prayer A.M. and Mr. Hall preach'd on Mat. 6, 12. Mr. Loring P.M. both pray'd and preach'd. His Sermon on Mat. 5, 4. May it please God to accept this Day! and have Compassion on his People! We all lodg'd at Mr. Barretts. N.B. Mr. Commissary Price held a Lecture among his people to Day also; and I had reason to suppose that Mr. Joseph Wheeler of Westborough was with Mr. Price and solliciting him to preach a Lecture at his House.

2. We were desirous to return home, but the Church being, by agreement together for a Conference, importun'd us urgently to tarry and be present with them at the Meeting House and Mr. Loring open'd their meeting with prayer. Their Conference rose to no purpose. We left them and they soon dispers'd. We din'd and parted. I return'd home (having Lieutenant Aaron Forbushs Horse upon this Journey) tho very much griev'd that such a season for reconcilement was lost. At my House found Elihu Lyman[2] of Northampton (a young graduate of Yale College) and with him Mrs. Esther Edwards, on a Journey to Boston. And by and by came also Mr. Sergeant of Stockbridge and his wife, on their return home from Boston.

3. Our Company went off. N.B. Mary Graves, now Garfield, here confessing her Fornication and desiring a Line to Mr. Cushing if I was willing she should Make her public Humilliation there, Seeing She had dwelt in Shrewsbury about 3 years: which I consented to. P.M. Mr. Francis Whipple here. He in Conversation inform'd me that this Precincts Committee were to meet tomorrow Evening.

4. I wrote to the Precincts Committee that when they call a Meeting again they may insert a Clause relating to the Precincts hearing my answer to their Messages of February last.

5. Last Night Mr. Daniel Warrin of our North precinct brought a sad message of Dr. Gotts Wife[3] being at the Point of Death and his Desire to see me. I therefore left my Study and Preparations and rode to Marlborough, where was a sorrowful sight. Mrs. Gott was alive and sometimes seem'd to have some Understanding but was hardly able to Speak a Sentence: and but Rarely so much as a Yes. I stay'd and din'd there, and at the Doctors Desire pray'd with Mrs. Gott, but the Doctor was hurry'd up to Westborough to Mr. George Smiths wife, and to Mr. Jacob Rice—the last being sick and very bad of the Distemper. N.B. Captain Ward of Worcester at the Doctors Mr. Chandlers wife being very bad of a Nervous Fever. P.M. I was at Reverend Mr. Smiths—and in my return Home was at Mr. Matthias Rice's where Benoni Baily was Sick of the Common Distemper.

6. I preach'd on the Subject of Taking away the Vail, but us'd the 16th and part of the 17th verse [of 2 Cor. 3] for my Text: and by Reason of my many hindrances was forc'd to use Some parts of my Sermons on Col. 1, 21, from page 14. Lydia Cutting din'd with us. N.B. Old Mrs. Cheney[4] of Cambridge here, after Exercises.

7. I Catechiz'd at the South End, at the School House—upward of 40 Children. Mrs. Tainter[5] kindly ask'd me to Dinner, which I readily accepted of. N.B. Mr. Tainter[6] of Grafton there and Mr. Nathaniel Whitney. Finishing the Subscriptions among us for Mr. Edwards[7] of Northampton on Religious Affections. When I came home I found Sir Williams[8] from Sudbury here, and afterwards came Brother Hicks. The latter lodg'd here.

8. My wife rode to Marlborough p.m. to see Mrs. Gott, who is yet alive. Ebenezer and Nathan Knowlton (with some help of Ebenezer Maynard) made a Load of Cyder. Lieutenant Hezekiah Ward of Southborough here. Finish'd Missons Voiages into Italy[9]—After reading out Lowman on the Revelations.[10] I have for some time been reading his paraphrase of such of the Notes as can be profitable, in my Family.

9. Mr. Charles Roberts of Sutton, came for a Load of Cyder, for which he promis'd to pay me in six weeks.

10. In the Morning I rode up to Shrewsbury Fast, which was on occasion of the Mortal Sickness among them (the Fever and Flux). Mr. Hall was to have been there but he came not. My part was to perform the forenoon service since I could not be there in the afternoon. I preach'd on 1 Pet. 5, 6. At noon I took leave, Mr. Morse being with Mr. Cushing. I hasted to Mr.

---

17 Aaron Goodenow or Goodanow died Sept. 29.

1 The Reverend Henry Messenger of Wrentham.

2 (Yale 1745). Dexter, *Biographical Sketches*, II, 49–50.

3 Mrs. Parkman's sister.

4 Mrs. Benjamin Cheney.

5 Wife of Deacon Simon Tainter.

6 Simon Tainter, Jr., who had lived in Westborough.

7 The Reverend Jonathan Edwards.

8 Abraham Williams (Harvard 1744).

9 François Mission, *A New Voyage to Italy* (London, 1695), 2 vols.

10 Moses Lowman, *A Paraphrase and Notes on the Revelation of St. John* (London, 1737).

Francis Whipples in Westborough and preach'd at the Private Meeting there on Isa. 66, 2.

11. Ebenezer with the help of Neighbour Ebenezer Maynard makes Cyder.

12. Ebenezer got home the Cyder. [blank] Barrells. N.B. Mrs. Gott dy'd last night.

13. On Cor. 3, 16, 17. John 13, 17. N.B. Under the former repeated sermon on Col. 1, 21, page 25 to 31.

14. Early to Mr. Grouts to look at some Beef—he came to look of one of my own Cows to pass his Judgment. I took his advice and determin'd on my own. My Wife and I rode to Mrs. Gotts Funeral. Mr. Smith tho at the Funeral, was not well and could not Pray. I was oblig'd (tho it was so sudden) to pray. We return'd at Eve. N.B. Captain Hapgood[11] of Shrewsbury bury'd to Day also. N.B. Colonel Ward[12] said, of Captain Hapgoods repenting that he had talk'd so much against New Light People etc.

15. I rode to Association at Stow. As I went I call'd at Mr. Matthias Rice's (Mr. Francis Whipple being with me) and borrowed £8 Old Tenor of Mrs. Rice otherwise my Journey to Boston must have been stop'd, for tho I had £10 in my Pocket, my ocasions call'd for as much more. From Marlborough I had Mr. Smiths Company to Stow. Besides us Mr. Prentice, Loring, Barrett,[13] Stone, Seccomb, Swift[14] and Goss there. Mr. Swifts Concio tho Short, yet pritty well done. Mr. Ephraim Allen came with a Letter from our North Precinct to Messers Prentice and Cushing and Me, desiring us to Consult the Association what they had best do about Candidates for them, Seeing the Committee which they had chose to wait upon those Gentlemen as the Precinct had nominated would not go: and whether they might proceed to Call Mr. Martyn?[15] The Association did not Care to do nor Say any thing till they had receiv'd Satisfaction from Mr. Martyn respecting his Sermon at Bolton, and he not being now present the affair was deferr'd till tomorrow morning.

16. Mr. Martyn came and after some Debate he receded from the sentiments deliver'd in his sermon at Bolton, and sign'd a Paper drawn up to that Purpose, and upon that the Association wrote a Letter to our North precinct they had nothing to say why they might not proceed with respect to Mr. Martyn if the Committee etc. refus'd to wait upon the other Candidates nominated. N.B. Mr. Smith who was to have preach'd the Public Lecture was not well, and requested Mr. Loring to preach for him; which was accepted, and he preach'd from those words [blank] Pet. [blank] The Precious Blood of Christ. It was so late before we broke up that it was night by that I got to Mr. Lorings; and Mr. Seccomb being my Company in My Journey to Weston he induc'd me to lodge at his Father Williams.[16] But Mr. Williams was gone to Hatfield. Thomas Winchester Made Cyder a Day and Half, and gott in Corn a Day and half.

17. Proceeded on my Journey to Cambridge. N.B. Contest between sister Lydia and Brother Hicks, the administrators. I refus'd to engage in it: and hasten'd to Boston, but 'twas too late for Lecture. My Brother Samuel gone to Plymouth. My Mother wondrously Sustain'd by God and Comfortable. Blessed be God for this great Favour! but my sister Esther very low and confin'd to her Bed. I din'd at Judge Sewals[17] where was also his Brother Mitchel Sewal, and after Dinner Dr. Chauncy[18] and Mr. Rand[19] came. At Sister Eliza's who (with her Dauter) was sick. Lodg'd there with Parkman. My Mare at Mrs. Keggells.[20] N.B. The Negro that murder'd his Mistress at Mendon, was hanged, and Mr. Campbell preach'd the Lecture at Worcester.

18. At Mr. Webbs. Din'd with Mr. Eliot. P.M. gratify'd my Curiosity at the Chiming of the Ring of Bells at Dr. Cutlers[21]

Church—view'd the Bells—the Organs, Vestry etc. At Eve at Brother Alexanders. Took Solemn leave of sister Esther commending her to the Infinite Mercy and Grace of God, and return'd to Cambridge in good season.

19. Return'd to Westborough. Din'd at Mr. Cooks[22] at Sudbury, where was also Mr. Marsh[23] of College. N.B. Thomas Winchester work'd for me last Tuesday and Wednesday in making Cyder and gathering Corn. N.B. About 40 Barrells of Cyder this Year, 10 of them boyl'd. 30 now in the Cellar. Found my Family in Peace and Safety. Blessed be God for all his Benefits!

20. Repeated Sermon on Ps. 112, 3, and O that God would make it the Day of his Power with us, and us his Willing People upon it! The Sickness creeps in upon us in this Parish. The Lord prepare us to meet with Him in the way of his Judgments!

21. Visited Mr. Samuel Fay junior who lyes sick of the Distemper: and Mr. Gershom Brighams Family who have all been so sick of the Same, and has bury'd one Child whilst I was absent: Mrs. Brigham and the remaining Child, now sick. Visited Abigail Knowlton who is sick also.

22. I visited Mrs. Martha Warrin who lyes weak and low and some measure under the Distemper.

23. My Wife and I were at the Funeral of Mr. Gershom Brighams other Child. We visited Mr. Daniel Warrin of Shrewsbury who had several Convulsion Fitts of late, and was much concern'd. We also visited Mr. Samuel Fay junior who (with Several of his Children Sick likewise but himself) lyes very bad. When I came home found Mr. Mighel[24] here (See the Catalogue of Harvard Scholars 1704). He had been at my house and lodg'd here while I was on my late Journey to Boston—and now lodg'd again. Captain Warrin I understand has agreed with him to keep our School.

24. Mr. Mighel din'd here: bought 3 Weathers of me for 5 shillings per Head and paid me for them. P.M. I visited Susanna Ball who lies very bad of the Distemper, and Mrs. Wheeler who is ill of a plaister. My Boys have been much employ'd in Husking—for I was dissatisfy'd with late night Huskings.

26. Ebenezer plough'd Stubble Hills and had Nathan Maynards Oxen with mine, Nathan having my Mare a.m. to grind Apples. P.M. Deacon Thomas Greenwood of Newton here.

27. A.M. on 2 Cor. 3, 17 latter part. P.M. on Ps. 2, 8 on Occasion of the Return of our Ambassadors from the Treaty at Albany with the 6 Nations of Iroquois Indians. I took Occasion also to Mention God's wonderfull Mercy to Us, who were heretofore but a few generations back Heathen—but us in Special in this Place it being nigh Seven Times 3 Years that God has waited upon us, Since our first incorporating into a church state. N.B. Mr. John Sparhawk[25] from Shrewsbury here: din'd and lodg'd here.

28. I would thankfully mention the Loving Kindness of the Lord towards us in Sparing us untill this Day, now 21 years since the founding of this Church and my Ordination over it. O may the Blood of Jesus Christ cleanse me from all sin! and quicken me to new Care and Faithfullness. The fore Part of the Day I spent Separately—P.M. I was oblig'd to wait upon Captain Maynard and his Company in Arms with whom I pray'd, and before night I eat [sic] at Captain Maynards House. The Lord pardon my many Defects in my holy Ministry! and quicken and assist me hence forward—that the Blood of Immortal Souls may not be laid to my Charge!

29. Ebenezer clearing the back Yard of the Chips muck and manure which has lain in some Thickness from Year to Year there. Wondrous pleasant and Moderate Weather for the Season. Mrs. Anna Rice here. We finish'd reading Mr. Lowman on the Revelation in the Family, and began the Bible again, at Evening.

30. Wrote to Brother Sam Parkman by Mr. R. Banks. Began the New Testament in the Morning Family Reading.

31. I was in Strong Expectation of Mr. Seccomb to preach a Lecture which I appointed for my Young Men, but he came not. Mr. Cushing came and I prevail'd upon him to preach to them

11 Thomas Hapgood died Oct. 5, 1745. Ward, *Shrewsbury*, p. 306.
12 Nahum Ward.
13 The Reverend Samuel Barrett of Hopkinton.
14 The Reverend John Swift, Jr., of Acton.
15 The Reverend John Martyn.
16 The Reverend William Williams of Weston was the father-in-law of the Reverend Mr. Seccomb.
17 Stephen Sewall (Harvard 1721) Justice of the Superior Court of Judicature, later Chief Justice of Massachusetts. *Sibley*, VI, 561-567.
18 The Reverend Charles Chauncy of Boston.
19 The Reverend William Rand of Sunderland.
20 Mrs. Abel Keggell, Mrs. Parkman's cousin.
21 The Reverend Timothy Cutler, D.D., Episcopal minister of Boston.
22 The Reverend William Cooke of Wayland.
23 Perez Marsh (Harvard 1748).
24 Samuel Mighill (Harvard 1704), an itinerant schoolmaster. *Sibley*, V, 255-256.
25 The schoolmaster.

which he did from Rom. 7, 9. At Eve Deacon Andrew Rice of Marlborough and his wife here. N.B. Mr. Aaron Hardy was here in the Morning for advice relating to his being dismiss'd from Grafton Church, they being ready to give him both Dismission and Recommendation notwithstanding his not being in good Terms with themselves. I advis'd in the Negative.

## NOVEMBER, 1745

1. Ebenezer work'd for Noah How—had the Oxen with him: Noah sowing Rye. At Eve Mr. Winchester here. My wife gone to Mr. Ebenezer Maynards, his wife in Travail and had another son.[1]

2. Noah How work'd here, hewing Timber for a shed over my East Door.

3. A.M. on 2 Cor. 3, 18. P.M. Repeated on Col. 1, 12. Giving Thanks, etc. Mr. Rand[2] preach'd on the North Side. Mr. Bradish[3] and Patience Wood[4] din'd with me. Somewhat Cold, yet Pleasant Day. But O that God would enable us by his holy Spirit to see Things truely, as exhibited in the Glass of his Word! The Things of God and Christ, the Things of our Souls and an Eternal World!

4. Wrote to Mr. Hall of Sutton to preach a Lecture for me next Friday. In the Morning (which was very Cold) I rode over to Mr. Balls (in my way went into Lieutenant Holloways,[5] where was Mr. Rand). Susè Ball very low and distress'd. Fever, Flux and Canker. The Flux abates but the Canker eats. Was at Mr. Livermores, Mr. James Ball's, at Mr. Wheeler Senior and thence to Mr. Josiah Bowkers, to the Funeral of one of his Children,[6] another being very bad. After Funeral, went to see Captain Eager[7] who is unwell. Supp'd there. Mr. Abner Newton there and rode home with me. Rainy Evening.

5. Young Women Catechiz'd. I deliver'd an Extemporaneous Exercise on one of the answers: viz. of original Sin. At Eve Brother Hicks, who brought us some Wheat and lodg'd here. Visited Abraham Batchellor who lies sick at Captain Maynards.

6. Ebenezer Splitting Hills [sic]. Mr. Benjamin Burnap here. Lieutenant Holloway also, who informs us that Mr. Bowker has lost another Child and Captain Eager is worse. Lieutenant desir'd me to attend the Funeral of Mr. Bowkers Child[8] at 2 p.m. which I did. N.B. Receiv'd by Brother Hicks a Letter from Mr. Hall that he could not preach my Lecture next Friday but he desir'd my assistance at a Fast in Sutton (on account of the Sickness) next Wednesday.

7. Ebenezer ploughing and Sowing Wheat. The Sowing by Neighbour Ebenezer Maynard.

8. Was oblig'd to preach my Lecture myself. Repeated from 2 Cor. 5, 1. N.B. did not know that I had repeated this Sermon before. N.B. Ebenezer plough'd in Rye.

9. [No entry].

10. Sacrament. Preach'd on 2 Cor. 3, 18. N.B. Mr. Joseph Batchellor from Grafton at Communion. Tho I was not without fears that he would be objected against. Deacon Fay,[9] Mrs. Billings,[10] and Mrs. Caruth at Dinner here. Too few of the North side at Meeting. N.B. I publickly warn'd people who were wont to go away home on sacrament noons without returning again, that they beware of so ill a practice. P.M. I repeated Exposition on Mat. 13, 14, from Luke 13, 24.

11. Catechiz'd at Lieutenant Holloways. In the Exercise time came Mr. Goss and Mr. Martyn. I visited Captain Eager who is still confin'd by sickness.

12. The First (and which was a very Considerable) Snow Storm.

13. Notwithstanding the weather was rugged yet I ventur'd up to Sutton to the Fast on account of the Sickness there. It was almost noon when I got there. Exercise was begun. I turn'd into

the nearest Pew to the Door, after Mr. Hall had pray'd, and preach'd from 1 Thess. 5, 19. At Eve Mr. James Fay[11] at Mr. Halls. Mr. Prentice[12] not very well, return'd with Mr. Fay: but I tarry'd at Mr. Halls.

14. Through Gods Mercy, was very Comfortable tho I had been not without Fears of Rheumatic Turns! I rode to Sister Hicks's[13] (Brother being at Cambridge) thence to Grafton, Deacon Whipples[14] and Mr. Prentices. Found Mr. Prentice very ill of his Disorders (the Piles) his wife also much indispos'd. N.B. Dissentions among the Brethren in Grafton that used to adhere to Mr. Prentice, a Number (Ebenezer Wadsworth at their Head) take in with the Canterbury Men lately among them. N.B. Ebenezer hous'd the Cattle last night in the Barn.

15. My great Sow strangely disordered. Sent for Captain Forbush who help'd her. Dr. Gott here. N.B. Abraham Batchellor lyes Sick Still at Captain Maynards.

16. [No entry].

17. All Day on John 6, 12, on gathering up the very Fragments of Time. May give those (tho weak) Endeavours his Effectual Blessing! Mr. Rand preach'd to the North side, and came here at Evening. Lodg'd here. A worthy man! Could earnestly wish he might be resettled and in these parts as it might please God.

18. Mr. Rand was so good as to Stay and dine with me, but then left us. Town Meeting to grant money for the School tho we have been for a long time without any. At Eve Nathans Father came and told me they were now somewhat put to it for Boys Help and desir'd me if I could Spare him to release his son, which I did, and he went home with his Father. And may God be gracious to him!

19. I visited Mr. Bowman who is sick: and went to see Ebenezer Miller[15] who has return'd from Fort Shirley Feeble and Weakly. Was at Lieutenant Tainters at Eve. N.B. Dr. Gott had din'd with me to Day—he bountifully added £30 (Old Tenor) to what he had before given to my Daughter Sarah.

20. Lieutenant Tainter and Mr. Harrington kill'd a Cow for me which weigh'd nigh 360. Brother Hicks and his Two sons John and Joshua here in their return from Cambridge. Brother lodg'd here. I was much indispos'd in the Evening and Night.

21. Mr. Bowker bury'd a Third Child[16] with the Same Distemper. I attended on the Funeral and visited Captain Eager at Eve. His pains are abated but his Fever weakens him much. Colonel Williams and Dr. Gott etc. there. I also visited Abraham Batchellor who still continues sick.

22. Sent for early in the Morning to go to Mr. Grouts Three of his Children being bad with the Throat Distemper, viz. Mehitable, Jonathan and Sarah. Sarah was in an exceeding Dangerous State. Receiv'd a Letter from Mr. Pierpoint[17] of New Haven and at Eve a sorrowfull one from Brother Samuel Parkman, dated Yesterday, to inform me of the Dying Circumstances (as they conceiv'd) of our Dear sister Esther; and that Brother Alexander desir'd him to write to me. I was therefore Expected to go down as soon as possible. But I determin'd to tarry over the Sabbath apprehending that I should then be seasonable for her funeral.

23. Sent Ebenezer to Mr. Grouts to See how they did; who return'd me word that Sarah dy'd last night about 9 o'Clock. Thomme to Mr. Cooks[18] to get the Mare Shod—and we prepar'd for my Journey to Boston.

24. A.M. on John 6, 12. P.M. on Mic. 6, 9. At Eve my wife and I rode to Mr. Grouts distract'd Family, Sarah Dead and Two more ill. Concerning Sarah there was Testimony of her dying very hopefully. The Glory to God who has shown his Great Grace to Children!

25. I rose at 4 o'Clock. Mr. Abraham Batchelors Brother, Amos, and his sister Porter were my Company an Hour before

[1] Malachi Maynard.
[2] The Reverend William Rand of Sunderland.
[3] James Bradish, an original settler of Westborough.
[4] Mrs. Solomon Maynard.
[5] William Holloway of the north precinct.
[6] Damaris Bouker or Bowker died Nov. 2, 1745.
[7] James Eager.
[8] Prudence Bouker died Nov. 2, 1745.
[9] Captain John Fay.
[10] Mrs. Thomas Billings of the north precinct.

[11] Son of Captain John Fay.
[12] The Reverend Solomon Prentice of Grafton.
[13] Mrs. John Hicks of Sutton.
[14] James Whipple of Grafton.
[15] Son of James Miller of Westborough.
[16] Dority Bouker died Nov. 19, 1745.
[17] James Pierpont, Jr.
[18] Cornelius Cook, the Westborough blacksmith.

sunrise upon my Journey. Cold and Rough riding. Did not stop at Cambridge but proceeded to Boston—to Brother Alexanders and found his wife Alive notwithstanding all my bad news and sorrowfull Expressions. Put out my Horse at Cousen Proctors, and Lodg'd at Brother Alexanders.

26. Wrote to my wife by Deacon Amos Rice of Brookfield, that I was well etc. except somewhat of a sore throat. Din'd with my aged mother. But at Night I grew so bad of it that I was in great Trouble. Something of a Fever accompany'd it—and I had an ill night. N.B. Lay at Brother Alexanders—but it was a sick House without me, for besides Sisters low Condition, Mr. Walker continues in his Confinement by the Gout there, and Alexander Kelland lyes very low there, in a Consumption.

27. My Throat bad, but the Weather so moderate that I accepted Brother Samuels Invitation to go to his House and reside there. Was out no further than to Mr. Stoddards and Mr. Thayers, lodg'd at Brother Samuels my sore Throat increasing—but no Canker that I perceive.

28. Having heard that Mr. Gee[19] has been troubled with a sore Throat, I sent for him, who accordingly came and gave me his advice to use a Tea of Mullen, Cullenbine and Sage which I did at Night, and hope that this and other means, accompany'd with divine Blessing, had a good Effect. Brother Sam p.m. to Cambridge on my Mare. At Eve Brother William, Brother Alexander and our Kinsman Hearsy and wife to see me. Lodg'd at Brother Samuels.

29. Stormy. Mr. Parker of Grafton was so good as to carry up my Horse to Westborough. Mr. Ebenezer Maynard at Brother Samuels—where I still lodg'd.

30. Bright Day. Got abroad. Din'd at Mr. John Salters—lodg'd at sister Bettys. N.B. She is not only under much feebleness of Body, but under great Distress of mind; complaining much of an Hard Heart etc.

### DECEMBER [1745]

1. Mr. Vinal[1] was engag'd to preach to Day for Mr. Gee, So that though I had been oblig'd to preach for him the first Time I should be in Town, yet now I was at Liberty and chose to go to Mr. Checklys,[2] where I had the Benefit of being at Communion (after his sermon on Isa. 50, 10). Din'd with him and preach'd p.m. on John 1, 11. At Eve deliver'd a sermon to my mother and Brethren and divers other Relations on Gal. 2, 20. O that God would accompany with his Blessing. Lodg'd at sister.

2. A.M. Visited Mr. Gee—din'd at Mr. Webbs.[3] N.B. he made a present of one of Mr. Dickinsons Familiar Letters.[4] P.M. at Mr. John Brecks. At Eve at Mr. Foxcrofts[5]—first saw one of the Philadelphian Fire-places. Was with my Honour'd Mother also. Lodg'd at sister Bettys with Parkman.

3. Neighbour David Maynard junior brought my Mare to me at Brother Samuels with an Affectionate Letter from my Wife. Din'd at Brother Alexanders. P.M. I rode to Cambridge, was at Mr. Rands[6]—lodg'd at Mother Champneys, and thank God I am so Comfortable after my late Illness!

4. Rode Home. Mr. McAllister and Mr. Priest my Company some part of the way. Would Bless God that I find my Tabernacle in Peace, Especially in such a Time of Calamity as this, especially among some of my Neighbours. N.B. More of Mr. Grouts Family taken ill of the Throat Distemper, and Two of Mr. Winchesters.

5. Public Thanksgiving. On Rom. 12, 1. O may we be truly sensible of the Divine Benefits and of our Obligations to Him therefore! that we might present ourselves a living Sacrifice etc. which is our Reasonable Service!

6. Visited at both Winchesters and Grouts. Having receiv'd a Petition from Mr. David Crosby in Worcester Gaol that there might be a Contribution here for him, I Yesterday desir'd the Deacons of the Church and the Selectmen of the Town to meet at my House this Day. And they accordingly came; but they all declin'd our complying with Said Petition. N.B. Mr. Wheeler and James Ball here, and were full of Grievance and perplexity about the proceedings of the North Precinct. N.B. Had the sorrowful News of the Sudden Death of Mr. Joseph Rice of Marlborough, who was going last Tuesday to [illegible] but dy'd before he got home.

7. Sarah Henry came last night, and works here this Day, making a pair of Leather Breeches for William.

8. Repeated the Remainder of Sermon on Rom. 12, 1. Mrs. Kelly and her sister Dunlop and Mr. Jonathan Bellows wife din'd here. At Eve visited Mr. Seth Rice's little Dauter lying at the Point of Death.

9. Great Concern upon my Heart respecting our Northern Brethren who this Day meet to Elect a Minister. The Lord grant them Grace and direction and overrule their spirits to do what may be for the Divine Glory and for their own truest peace and Welfare! Old Mr. Maynard here to have some alterations made in his will. N.B. Mr. Seth Rice's little Dauter Hannah (of 2 and ½) dy'd last night.

10. At the Funeral of Mr. Seth Rice's Daughter. At Eve visited Abraham Batchellor who is on the Recovery. At Eve also Mr. Wheeler and Mr. Jedidiah How were at my Home. Mr. Wheeler very full in informing me what their North Precinct had done Yesterday. That about 30 Voters were present—that 20 chose Mr. Martyn and 10 were against him; and he said a number more, tho not Voters yet of interested persons joined in the opposition. Mr. Wheeler would fain have me, write a Letter to Mr. Martyn to inform him how the Case is Circumstanc'd that he may not be abus'd with a false Representation. But I utterly declin'd it—especially could not from hearing only one Side. He ask'd me what I had against his doing it (or to that purpose). I told him no one could hinder his writing to him, if he Should do it in a suitable Manner. He pull'd out a paper in which he said a number of them had drawn up something of that kind, and would fain have me look of it to See whether I could approve of it; but I utterly declin'd it and refus'd so much as to look of it. But he seem'd much taken with my yielding that he himself and those who join'd with him against the Vote might write to Mr. Martyn to inform him of it.[7] Open, but dull, cloudy Raw Weather. Heard that Boston was rejoic'd with the Return of the Governour from Louisburgh, and thence the Joy Spreads over all the Province.

11. I Visited at Moses Winchesters where Betty Chamberlin was ill of Sore Throat—at James Fays, where Silas Pratt was ill of a Fever; and Mr. Grouts whose Children were much better: at Mr. Williams's also whose Wife continues ill. N.B. In my going today had some Earnest Talk with Justice Baker on the Affair (which our Committee are now gone to Boston upon) respecting the Petition of the North side to the General Court last year, to be freed from paying my Sallery from June 5 to October 20.

12. North side Committee for waiting on Mr. Martyn with their Call, not going over to Bolton yesterday when the appointment was (for they refus'd to go over because Mr. Wheeler, Mr. Ball and other opposers would go over with them) went over to him to Day. Very Moderate, pleasant Weather.

13. Molly rode to Grafton, to see whether her Gown was done at Mr. Batchellors.

14. Lieutenant Aaron Forbush kill'd a Pigg which weigh'd 114 for me. At Eve Jacob Rice.

15. I had chose to repeat Old Sermons last Sabbath that I might be both in Season with my Preparations and might Deliver the whole of what I Should have to say upon the Subject in one Day, but tho I had provided a Matter of 16 pages yet I could not finish the Subject without waiting upon the Sabbath, the Things which occurr'd to my Mind were so needfull and as I thought would be so usefull that I could not omitt them. My Text was Rom. 6, 13, middle Clause. In the Close I was very fervent, the

[19] The Reverend Joshua Gee of Boston.

[1] William Vinal (Harvard 1739), later minister of the First Congregational Church at Newport, R.I., 1746-1768. *Sibley*, X, 412-415.
[2] The Reverend Samuel Checkley.
[3] The Reverend John Webb.
[4] Jonathan Dickinson, *Familiar Letters to a Gentleman upon a Variety of Seasonable and Important Subjects in Religion* (Boston, 1745).
[5] The Reverend Thomas Foxcroft.
[6] John Rand (Harvard 1748), later the minister at Lyndeborough, N.H., 1757-1762. See D[ennis] Donovan and Jacob A. Woodward, *The History of the Town of Lyndeborough* (n.p., 1906), pp. 614-615.

[7] See Kent, *Northborough History*, pp. 23-24.

Lord grant it may not be in Vain! As to the Weather, Cold Day.

16. Mr. Wheeler here all the afternoon. Selectmen met and having receiv'd Order from the Council Board that the Town Should be assess'd, issued Orders accordingly to the Assessors for that Purpose. Cold Weather.

17. Mr. Cushing[8] din'd with Me and spent the afternoon with me. Ebenezer today (*Ah! Quantum mutatus ab Expectione nostra*) work'd with Daniel How in the Cedar Swamp in making Shingles.

18. As we have had a fine Moderate Season except the last Three Days, So of no Snow since that which fell November 12. But now comes a fierce storm, Cold, Windy, Snow.

19. P.M. I rode over to talk with Deacon Newton about his Success at the General Court in the Affair of my last Years Sallery. At Eve came my Kinsman Hearsey from Boston and lodged here.

20. Mr. Hearsey goes to Oxford to wait on his wifes Aunt Griffin. Old Mr. Maynard Signs and Declares another Last Will and Testament. Lieutenant Aaron Forbush and Edward Whipple the Witnesses. Snow. Ebenezer sledds Wood. N.B. Old Mr. Maynards Sledd.

21. Lieutenant Tainter here. He bemoans the Condition of his Brother Thomas Harrington at Waltham.

22. Cold, cloudy Day. I preach'd a.m. on Heb. 9, 27. P.M. I repeat'd from Col. 3, 4, the Introduction but fill'd up the Exercise with the first part of sermon on Phil. 1, 21, the first 12 pages. O that since it is settled by the Decree of Heaven that I must die I may So reallize that my Life may be a truely Christian Life— that for me to Live may be Christ and to die Gain!

23. Captain Maynard here and informs me that the soldiers are not likely to return from the Frontiers, according to their Expectations. That therefore he does not expect to see his son much before Spring. Would be glad (being there is now opportunity) if I would write him a Line—which Request I readily comply'd with.

24. Daniel How thrashing Rye with Ebenezer. Thomas Winchester came and Thrash'd a.m. and p.m. kill'd Two Piggs which weigh'd about 100 apiece. Deacon Forbush[9] to Worcester with his Dauter Hannah to keep Mr. Jenisons House.

25. Thomas Winchester went to Boston with the Two Piggs on my Mare. I borrow'd Mr. Williams's Mare and rode (tho not sent for, yet a bright Comfortable Day inviting and hearing that a number of Ministers were to be there) to Grafton Fast. I arriv'd just at 12 yet forenoon Prayer was not much more than half done. I sat in Mr. Prentice's Pew. Mr. Bliss[10] and Mr. Hall[11] were the Ministers that were come to Assist. Mr. Bliss preach'd on Heb. 4, 16. At Noon at Mr. Prentice's. Mr. Hall pray'd p.m. and Mr. Bliss preach'd again. His Text Mat. 5, 16. Stay'd to Supper. Mr. James Fay requested that Mr. Bliss might preach at his House tomorrow at 11 o'Clock. I did not sett myself against it, but permitted it, but did not give much Encouragement that I should be there myself, having divers Things before me that would be like to hinder me. At coming away had Some Talk with Mr. Prentice respecting his Disgust with me which arose (and as I conceive continues) from my Sermon at a Former Fast there, but he said that was all over with him. What he waited for was that I would come out—boldly for the Cause of God and let him come freely into my Pulpit and then He Should be free to ask me into his. I told him it was necessary to regard my people (by this Time Mr. Bliss came to us) and I know well that my people would be greatly disgusted and I did not think it wise or prudent to give way to it. I ask'd Mr. Bliss to my House. N.B. Mr. Hall agreed to preach a Lecture to my Young People this Day fortnight. I call'd at Cornet Shermans and at Abraham Temple's. From Temple's Mr. Abner Newton was my Company to Westborough. Found my Tabernacle in Peace, and myself comfortable tho it was a Cold Evening. To God be the Glory! and may here be an abiding Influence of what I have heard!

26. Tho it was last night a most Clear and bright Night yet this Morn was thick Cloudy, and anon it snow'd; and it prov'd a Stormy Day. Wrote Mr. Bliss a Letter and sent it to Captain

Fays by my son Thomme. N.B. Mr. Williams here while I wrote it. P.M. Justice Baker here, enquiring after a Colt, which he thought might probably strole away last night after me as I pass'd by his House, but I saw none.

27. When the Storm Clear'd away last night the Wind rose very high. It was a Night of Strong Gusts that rock'd and Shook the House very much, but God Mercifully preserv'd us and upheld our Dwelling. It prov'd a Windy and Cold Day. Ebenezer and Thomme thrash'd Rye. Brother Hicks from Cambridge lodg'd here last Night. P.M. Mr. Matthias Rice and Mr. Thomas Goodenow here. They told me that Mr. Wheeler had said among them [the Northside People] and particularly to Mr. Livermore that he was advis'd by an Angel to turn among them; and also in what he did in going over to Mr. Martyn (at the Time that their Committee went to Carry his Call) that it was the Angel of the Church in Westborough. I reply'd that Mr. Wheeler was here, but that I refus'd to meddle with their Affair: nor did then see Mr. Wheelers Paper not a word of it nor know I what was in it. And this I now repeated to them, that I did not desire to have Concern with their Affairs nor to meddle with them. At Eve Thomas Winchester return'd from Boston—got 12 *d* per pound for the Pork and brought up ½ Bushel Salt, but it being Rainy while he was in Town he went to none of my Friends as I had appointed him to.

28. Thomas broke out Flax A.M. P.M. he went home. Moderate, pleasant Day. Ebenezer winnow'd some Rye. Thomme I sent to Mr. James Maynards, he being Collector for the Parish.

29. A.M. on Heb. 9, 27, and P.M. Repeat'd on Mat. 13, 39. It being the Last Sabbath of the Year I was Desirous to Meditate on the Last Day Each Mans Life, and the Last Day of the World. May it please God to make the word Savingly Efficacious to our Souls! I endeavour'd to impress these Serious Things upon my Family—and may God be pleas'd to accompany what I have done with his Blessing!

30. A tedious Snow Storm. Adhere to a Custom I am in of Reading Lowth in the Morning. Have not yet finish'd Fullers Church History, but keep on in it. P.M. Old Mr. Maynard, Old Mr. Whipple and Captain Maynard here.

31. Storm continues. At my preparations for the Sabbath. At Night Very high Winds.

Might it please God of his abundant Mercy to grant a suitable Sense of the Transitoriness of Time! humble Me for and thro the Blood of his Dear son pardon, the sins of the Year past, and of my whole Life! And O might I be ready for the Close of my Life, as well as the Close of the Year!

### JANUARY, 1746.

What Shall we render to the Lord for all his Benefits towards us! As high as the Heavens are above the Earth So great is his Graciousness to Me and Mine: In Special through the Course of the Year past. The last night a Very Sharp Cold as most we have felt. The Power and Greatness of God are manifest by this Work of his. I retir'd from Incumbrance. I review'd my Old Journals— in particular those of my 16, 17, 18 Year. I find them of much Use to me as they display my egregious folly and Vanity, and fill me with Shame and Grief. The Lord, of his infinite Mercy Pardon Me thro the Blood of the Great Sacrifice! O what a Price had I in my Hand to get Wisdom—but how little Heart to improve it!

At Eve Captain Maynard and Mr. William Pierce here. Nothing Singular, but the Cold.

2. Continued my Review of my old Journals, for my deep Abasement and Sorrow before God. Lord, remember not against me the sins of my Youth and my Transgressions. After thy Mercy remember me, for they Graciousness sake, O Lord!

3. Thomas Winchester and Ebenezer gett out Flax. More moderate weather.

4. Thomas and Ebenezer thrash'd Rye. Ebenezer was hurt on his Eye and Cheek Bone by the breaking of Thomas's Swingill, or beating his own against him. Little Suse begins to go alone. Weather Pleasant.

[8] The Reverend Job Cushing of Shrewsbury.
[9] Jonathan Forbush.
[10] The Reverend Daniel Bliss of Concord.
[11] The Reverend David Hall of Sutton.

5. On Heb. 9, 27, former part. May God be pleas'd to add his Special Blessing, that this Serious Subject may suitably affect both me and the people!

6. Mr. Martyn came to see me; din'd with me and Spent the Afternoon. Tells me has not determin'd what he shall do with regard to our North Side, purposes to Visit the disaffected, and particularly Mr. Wheeler,[1] that he may know the better what to do. N.B. Lieutenant Thomas Forbush and Mr. Simon Goddard of Shrewsbury here.

7. Sent a Letter by Ebenezer Maynard to Messers Rogers and Fowle for December Magazine, and to let them know that I would have them Sent no longer. Another Letter by the Same Hand for my Portmantle at Cousin Proctors, in which I expect Cloth for a great Coat, provided for me, by Brother Alexander. Sent 5 Musk Squash Skins to Mr. Eaton, Hatter at Boston, by Noah How. Thomas Winchester breaking Flax and Ebenezer Shingles. Moderate and bright, but Exceeding high winds, p.m.

8. Mr. Hall of Sutton preach'd a Lecture to Young People on 1 K. 18, 12. Several from other Towns at Meeting. After Meeting Ward[2] (Colonel Nahums son) from College with his Two sisters viz. Mrs. Eager and Mrs. Patty Ward, here. Mr. Hall went home. Mr. Benjamin Burnap and Mr. James Fay spent the Eve here. N.B. Mr. Fay has not been at our Meeting for a number of sabbaths (I think 3) but that I might have no Jarr at this Time I Said Nothing to him about it. Thomas Winchester thrash'd a.m. Bright tho Somewhat Cold.

9. I read various Things—Dickinsons Letters—Magazine—Tillotson—Hopkins[3]—Richard Taylor[4] on Eph. 2, 8. Thomas Thrashing. Receiv'd a Blue Great Coat from Brother Alexander at Boston per Ebenezer Maynard. Stormy. Snow—Rain.

10. Thomas Thrashing Rye Still. Ebenezer daily with him. Thomas and I reckon'd up the Loss Time which he had agreed to make up, and there is due to me (on that Account) 26 this Evening. That is, 6 more of these Winter Days. Exceeding Cold Night.

11. Thomas and Ebenezer dressing Flax. Pleasant but Cold Day. Lieutenant Tainter here—he brought the Journal which contains Father Patrick Graham, Almoner and Confessor to the Young Pretender, his Letter to Father Benedict York, giving an account of their proceedings, successes and Designs.

12. Pleasant. A.M. on John 17, 15. Repeating from page 15 to 19 of Sermon on Jer. 2, 19. P.M. on Eph. 2, 8. My Wife not well—could Scarce tarry at Meeting during the forenoon Exercise, but was not able to go to Meeting at all p.m. At Eve Very much of a Fever.

13. My Wife somewhat better a.m. (having been sweated the Night before). I rode to Mr. Jesse Rice's at Marlborough to talk with him about the Bond which I gave his Father (now deceas'd) for £50 Old Tenor. Borrow'd of him Fenner on Conscience.[5] At my Return home found my Wife was grown Very ill again, the Fever strong upon her. Mrs. Maynard here and took Susè down to their House, her dauter in Law being able to suckle. N.B. Mr. Brown[6] of Cambridge (young Preacher) from Worcester here whilst I was gone to Marlborough, as was also Mr. Millen[7] of Chauxit. They inform that Mr. Morse[8] of North Shrewsbury carry'd home his wife last Tuesday. N.B. At Eve came Esquire Williams of Stockbridge and Mr. Lydius of Albany and lodg'd here. And Captain Ephraim Williams junior and his Brother Thomas at Captain Maynards. Sent for the Latter to Visit my wife, who accordingly came. He thinks She is going to have the long Fever. The forenam'd Gentlemen are going to Boston to promote an Expedition against Crown Point.

14. Our Company prosecuted their Journey to Boston. Sent Thome to Dr. Gotts and Mr. Britons.[9] Dr. Gott came, but my

Wife was better. Thanks to God! Neighbour Samuel Hardy came late a.m. to Swingle Flax. P.M. he join'd with a Number that were here to get me some Wood, for Lieutenant Tainter and Neighbour Samuel Harrington were here yesterday while I was absent, and rigg'd up my Sled, and they Two, with Neighbour Hezekiah Pratt (who brought a Team of Oxen), Beriah Rice, and Eleazer Rice, came and got me a Pile of Wood. N.B. Neighbour Sam Hardy join'd them. P.M. At Eve we sent for Susè home from Captain Maynards.

15. Rode to Neighbour Cooks on purpose to talk with him, but I found Neighbours Josselin[10] and Belknap there, for which Reason I proceeded further to visit the South East Corner. N.B. Mr. Belknap walk'd with me and we had Some Conversation about Mr. Cook. He told me Mr. Cook had desir'd him some Time ago to go up with him to my House. I pray'd him to meet me towards Eve at Mr. Cooks—he consented. He told me likewise that he himself had been admitted into the Southborough Church. I went to Mr. Bradish's and pray'd him to meet me at Mr. Cooks by and by (he being also a Man that I knew Mr. Cook would ken to). Visited Mr. Jonathan Bellows Family; he was not at Home. I din'd at Mr. Chamberlains. At Parting he told me that Mr. Cook had heretofore desir'd him to go up with him to discourse with me, and upon that I told him I Should be glad to see him at Neighbour Cooks this Very Evening. Visited Neighbours Ithamar Bellows and Family and Josselin's. Afterward I return'd to Mr. Cooks, found the Three Men aforesaid there. I acquaint'd them with my Conduct towards Neighbour Cook in my proceedings with him; and intimated what his had been towards Me. He also made his Replys; in his own boisterous and coarse Manner, and the Brethren mediated and endeavour'd to bring him to a right Understanding and Submission; but (whilst I was there) in Vain. I lamented my unsuccessfullness in my Attempts: and at Parting offer'd him my Hand in Token of my readiness to be reconcil'd if he would Comply; but ineffectually. When I was mounted on my Horse to return home, he came out and seem'd to express his desire of Forgiveness; and thereupon—giving him my Hand told him I was willing if he acknowledg'd, and was Sorry for his undutifull Conduct towards me in Time past, and would Carry it (by the Help of Grace) in a Suitable Manner becoming his Relation to me, for the future. This he seem'd once to Consent to, but afterwards drew back from it; and Seem'd to expect an acknowledgment from Me also with regard to my Carriage towards him—which I could see no ground for; and ask'd whether it could be expected when I admonish'd those under my Pastoral Care whom I found defective, if it came Close to them and they should frett at it if it was no more than was necessary for them, and my own indispensible Duty? I left him with the Brethren, hoping that if he was truely Sensible, and reform'd I Should soon know it; but any thing that was only Sudden and Strain, would (I conceiv'd) not last long. N.B. his unaccountable ways of Softening his Several harsh allegations against me, and heavy Complaints of me from Time to Time. Exceeding great his Explanation of his Saying "I had abus'd him more than any Man in the world—why," he said, "one word from me, from Mr. Parkman was worse than any body else could Speak." Again, when he told me that a main Thing he had against me was "That I was an Enemy of the Work of God." This he said he meant thus, that we all had naturally an Enmity against God and his work: and the ministers being at Variance one with another was a great Hindrance and discouragement, and that I had taken Such ways and methods as he could not judge were so prudent and fit to promote the Work of the late Times: and he likewise endeavour'd to enervate and interpret away his Strange Message by Noah How to me, "that he felt So towards me and Sometimes that he could Bite Me." Nothing being effected, nor much prospect of it, and my wife being ill at Home, I came home.

16. My Wife took Physic, though unsuitable Wett Weather. At Eve Jonas Brigham was marry'd to Persis Baker. Have read out Fullers Church History of Britain.[11]

17. My Wife continues ill, her Physic does not cease Working.

[1] Joseph Wheeler.

[2] Artemas Ward, the future general.

[3] Probably a work by the English minister, Ezekiel Hopkins (1633-1690).

[4] A work by the English Dissenter of London who died about 1717.

[5] William Fenner, *The Soul's Looking-Glasse . . . with a Treatise of Conscience* (Cambridge, 1640).

[6] John Brown (Harvard 1741), later the minister of Cohasset, 1747-1791. *Sibley*, XI, 12-17.

[7] The Reverend John Mellen of Sterling.

[8] The Reverend Ebenezer Morse of Boylston.

[9] John Britain of Marlborough.

[11] Thomas Fuller, *The Church-History of Britain* (London, 1655).

[10] Joseph Joslin.

18. I thought to have writ Something respecting our Controversie with the Church of Rome, and reasons against the Pretender—but my incumbrances etc.

19. Lieutenant Tainter came and inform'd Me that Sister Esther, my Brother Alexanders Wife dy'd on the 12th at Night, and was bury'd on Wednesday following. The Lord sanctifye his holy Hand to us all, but especially to my poor Brother and his only Child as they need Special Grace at Such a Time! A.M. on Eph. 2, 8. P.M. on Ps. 90, 1, because of the Troubles in England. My wife somewhat Better. Mrs. Kimbal of Hopkinton din'd with us.

20. Thomme to Mr. Barretts for Dr. Edwards Exposition on the Commandments.[12] Old Mr. Maynard here and wants I Should write his will over again a Third Time, which displeas'd me. Neighbour David Maynard junior, John Rogers, and Richard Barns kill'd Two Hoggs for me—one weigh'd 242. The other 225 when they were warm.

21. Very moderate weather. My wife not well yet, by reason of a Blister on her ankle, which does not heal up, but makes her very Lame. Captain Maynard at Evening.

22. Pleasant. Wrote to my Brother Alexander by Captain Maynard. Mr. Stratton[13] of Waltham here: He and his son Harrington din'd with me.

23. Sebastian Smith (the Spaniard) din'd here. Mr. John Garfield[14] came to acquaint me with the Death of one of the Twin Children of Mr. Daniel Warrin of Shrewsbury. At Eve Mr. Bowker here, likewise Mr. Aaron Hardy of Grafton. N.B. Reckon'd with Thomas Winchester and paid him all—and £4 old Tenor of Interest for his forbearance.

24. At the Funeral of Mr. Daniel Warrins Child.

25. Smart Storm—Snow, Wind, Rain, Hail, Thunder and Lightning. Captain Maynard here.

26. On Ps. 68, 1. On Occasion of the Rebellion in Scotland. Mr. Stratton of Waltham and Granny Forbush[15] din'd here. May we all be Convinc'd what Enemies of God We naturally are and may we obtain the renewing Grace of God that we may throw down our arms and submitt ourselves to Him!

27. At Neighbour Hardys and Rogers's in the Morning—rode to Eleazer Pratts p.m. and round by Bezaleel Smiths through a swamp over to Mr. Samuel Fay junior. N.B. his wife after above Two Years Confinement got about again. But their Youngest Child sick. When I came home Mr. Stephen Fay here. He is Still disturb'd about my having Minutes of what pass'd between his wife and me May 3, 1744, and divers other Things came in. 'Tis Matter of Grief that we are so frequently in Jarrs. The Lord pardon us for his Names sake!

28. A.M. at Ensign Bruce's and Mr. Beeman's. P.M. sent for to go to Mr. William Nurse's to see several Children Sick of the Throat Distemper. In returning call'd at Mr. Stephen Fays—and (he being present) I put sundry close Inquirys to his wife offering to the both that if She consent'd to the Substance of what had been written and did abide by that Reconcilement which was September 26 last I would blot out her name, but she would not make answer though repeatedly desir'd. Her Husband and I were much more happy in our Agreement by far than I expected.

29. Ante Meridiem: Recollections and Humilliations and [illegible] But was grievously interrupted by Dr. Gotts Mother (Mrs. Fairfield) Sally Gott and her Brother Benjamin as likewise Dr. Breck, all coming in a stormy Time (Raining hard) to see us, and I could not keep my Retirement. But I remember the wormwood and the Gall this Day Ten Years agoe.[16] But how amazing the Divine Longsuffering towards Me who am most unworthy!

30. They all lodg'd here. Dr. Breck to Boston. Mrs. Fairfield and the rest din'd with us, and towards Eve they return'd to Marlborough. At Eve Mr. Williams and Winchester here. Wrote Two Letters for Mr. Winchester. Late in the Evening came

12 A work of the great English Calvinist divine, John Edwards (1637–1716).
13 Several Strattons lived in Waltham at this time. Edmund L. Sanderson, *Waltham as a Precinct of Watertown and as a Town* (Waltham, 1936), pp. 138–140.
14 Of Shrewsbury.
15 Widow of Thomas Forbush.
16 The anniversary of the first Mrs. Parkman's death.

Captain Ephraim Williams junior—supp'd with me and hasten'd to Captain Maynards and he lodg'd there.

31. Mr. Samuel Hardy and William Rogers junior Swingling Flax. At Evening Mr. Phinehas Hardy of Grafton, who tells me that he and Mr. James Fay have exchang'd places. N.B. Mr. Fay has left us for many sabbaths.

## FEBRUARY, 1746.

1. Mr. Benjamin Fay here for me to go to Mr. William Nurse's Dauter Priscilla's Funeral, which I comply'd with.

2. On Ps. 68, 1. Mat. 11, 12. Widow Woods, Widow Thurston and Mr. Ithamar Bellows's wife din'd here. N.B. I hear there is one Mr. Manson a Barber from Sudbury, is hir'd by the School Committee to keep school in the South East part of the Town.

3. Town Meeting for Town Debts. N.B. I sent in a Paper to the Town to Consider the Dammages I sustain by the long delay of my Dues—especially £82 Old Tenor, from June 5 in the Year 1744 to October 20 of the same Year. Eli Forbush here. Letter from Mr. Jenison.[1] Deacon Forbush, Beriah Rice—all upon the Same Thing, viz. to have me teach Eli and Asaph Rice. Brother Hicks here. Sarah Henry at work here on Ebenezers Jackett etc.

4. Thunder and Lightning in the Night past. Brother Hicks to Cambridge.

5. Mr. Benjamin Burnap here and din'd. I visited Sundry of our Near Neighbours—old Mr. Maynard etc. Old Mrs. Rogers Sick of a Fever and I went to see her; Spent some Time with her: she has Strong Confidence that she is prepar'd to dye, and appears much resign'd to the Divine Will.

6. I preach'd at the Private Meeting at Lieutenant Tainters on Mat. 18, 18, 19. My wife rode with me. We din'd there. O that the Lord Jesus Christ might meet with us in all our Meetings! We were inform'd that Yesterday the Quarter sessions at Worcester abated the Rates of the Second Precinct to the Rate of £82 10 shillings to me from June 5 to October 20, 1744, and they gave Judgment also that the precincts proceedings had been invalid from the Beginning.

7. Noah How framing my Shed over my East Door. His Brother Benjamin a.m. assisted him. Mr. Goodwin[2] of Worcester here to request me to preach at Worcester. Dr. Gott with him.

8. I visited Mrs. Rogers again who is very low. Noah framing a.m.

9. On Ps. 68, 1. Eph. 2, 6. N.B. Mrs. Fay (Samuel juniors wife) wondrously recover'd after Confinement above Two Years, out at Meeting to Day. Both Mr. Fay and his wife din'd with us. N.B. Receiv'd from Mr. Pierpoint by Mr. Loring.[3]

10. A Precinct Meeting at which I was prepar'd to give an Answer to their Messages to Me last Year: But by what was determin'd last Week at Worcester Court in the Affair of the North precinct, this precinct were So alarm'd and Suspicious of the invalidity of their own Acts, as a precinct, from the Beginning, that they ventur'd not to do anything Further—save that they chose a Moderator and then pass'd every Vote after (upon the several Bills or Petitions which were carry'd in) in the Negative. No Opportunity was given (nor by my Friends desir'd) for my Answer. N.B. Reckon'd with Deacon Newton. William Bois of Blanford was married to Mary Hamilton (daughter in Law to Mr. Gamel).

11. I rode out to see old Mr. Rogers and his wife who were Sick. Then to see old Mr. Whipple, where was his son Francis. Talk'd of the present Confusion of the Town in both precincts. I went also to see Captain Baker, and Spent Some with him upon the Public Affairs in Town and Precinct. Debated amicably and parted Peaceably. Reckon'd with his Son Samuel. Neighbour Samuel Hardy Swingling Flax. Bright day but windy and Cold. N.B. I sent for Mr. Whipple and talk with him again upon the Confus'd state of the Town and precinct. P.M. was at Captain Maynards. N.B. About the Time a New Trouble Still blew up: which Neighbour Beriah Rice acquaint'd me with, viz. Robert

1 William Jenison, the former schoolmaster of Westborough.
2 James Goodwin.
3 The Reverend Israel Loring of Sudbury.

Bradish went from one house to another Exclaiming against Last Sabbath afternoon sermon, as being Corrupt and Damnable Doctrine—So much in Defence of Grace and to the Disparagement of Works in point of Justification before God. But 'tis a Favor that when this kind of Trial arises, I am complain'd of upon Such Occasion as This. The Lord grant me suffering Grace in Suffering Time!

13. Mr. Daniel Forbush[4] kindly to acquaint me with the disgusts of Some others with last Sabbaths Exercise in the afternoon—looking upon himself (as Mr. Rice likewise did) in Duty and Faithfulness bound, to do it.

14. Very much engag'd in my Preparations—and Collecting the Sense and Judgment of the most Celebrated men on the Great Doctrine of Justification by Faith alone.

15. [No entry].

16. On Eph. 2, 8. Added a Defence of this Doctrine from innumerable Authoritys not only to shew the Truth but the Importance and Weight of it. Read a Manuscript Extract of Mr. Lorings from Mr. Abraham Tailer[5] on Justification. P.M. Repeat'd the remainder of Exposition of Mat. 11, 12.

17. Paul Newtown and Mary Farrar[6] Marry'd. Jonas Child here to be Examin'd and taught in order to his joining with the Church.

18. I rode over to Mr. Biglo's to see his Daughter that was Sick; and I proceeded to Mr. Barretts—who (as I before conceiv'd would be) was going down to a Council at Framingham previous to the Ordination of Mr. Matthew Bridge.[7] I made a Visit to Captain Morris, who return'd with me to his sisters (Mrs. Barretts) with which we din'd. N.B. Their Sister Barrett's (Widow) House in an high wind took fire on the Roof—but by the help of the School Boys was Discover'd and Extinguish'd. I return'd home at Eve, and marry'd Thomas Patrick and Sarah Johnson. N.B. Neighbour Daniel Hardy riding with me inform'd that Mr. James Fay was this Day moving out of Westborough and Mr. Phinehas Hardy was moving in.

19. I rode to the Ordination of Mr. Matthew Bridge at Framingham. My son Ebenezer rode down also. Entertain'd at Ensign Stones. Great opposition by Captain Goddard[8] and others Yesterday and today. The Council consisted of 11 Churches. Mr. Loring Moderator and Mr. Stone Clerk. The Council repair'd to the Meeting House before noon. Mr. Cook of Sudbury pray'd. Mr Appleton[9] preach'd from 1 Cor. 13, 1, 2. Then the Clerk read the Councils Result. Mr. Loring gave the Charge, Mr. Williams[10] of Weston pray'd after the Charge, and gave the Right Hand. An Exceeding great Throng attended. May I have a suitable Impression upon my Spirits at the Remembrance of my own solemn Ordination! Visited old Madam Swift.[11] Mr. Cushing and Stone, and Mr. Briton the Clothier my Company in returning. We call'd at both Mr. Britons and Mr. Stones. Reach'd home in Comfort. D.G. Moderate comfortable Weather.

20. Great Change of Weather last night. Today very Cold and windy. Esquire Williams[12] of Stockbridge came at Eve, having left Mr. Lydius[13] at Boston, endeavouring to get french Prisoners, with which to redeem his Children from Canada.

21. Esquire Williams not well—too cold to undertake his Journey home.

22. The Day somewhat moderate. Esquire Williams accompany'd to Worcester—and then I left him to prosecute his Journey to Brookfield. I unhappily miss'd of Mr. Emmerson[14] who came from Worcester to preach at Westborough whilst I

went there to gratifie the Request of the Committe at Worcester in administering the Ordinance of Baptism among them. Lodg'd at Mr. Eatons.[15]

23. Cloudy—at length Snow. Preach'd at Worcester on John 1, 11 and Rom. 6, 13. P.M. baptiz'd the Children. See the Records.[16] At Eve at Dr. Brecks[17] and lodg'd there. In the Night the Wind rose exceeding high.

24. Wind very high and Cold. Broke fast at Colonel Chandlers. Visited Mr. Crossby at the Jayl. Return'd to the Colonel's and din'd there. P.M. return'd home calling in especially at Mr. Cushings, Major Keys and Colonel Nahum Ward.[18] At this last was Mr. Martyn.[19] N.B. Some free Conversation with them with reference to Westborough Town and Precinct Affairs: but fear what use they may make. It shall be a warning.

25. At Colonel Wards Sollicitation I din'd at Captain Maynards with the Field Officers, who met upon some Affairs of the Regiment. Cold Day.

26. Preach'd at Southborough Preparatory Lecture on Rom. 6, 13. Return'd at Eve. N.B. was in at Mr. Jacob Amsdens going and returning. Had a Mess of his boisterous windy Talk against—and manifesting dissatisfaction with me for my preaching and praying so much about the Spirit. N.B. Mr. Joseph Wood brought my Gold Buttons which I lost October 13, 1744, he having found them in the Road at Waltham last week. Captain Maynard at Eve.

27. Mr. Stone preach'd my Lecture on Mat. 27, 46. Mr. Jenison here at my House, but not a Lecture.

28. Mr. Aaron Hardy of Grafton here at Eve, as were also Messers James Maynard and Francis Whipple. Mr. Maynard as Collector Ventures Still to go on in Paying me notwithstanding the threatnings to break up the Precinct Transactions.

### MARCH [1746]

2. Sacrament and were favour'd by Providence with Moderate Weather, Yet Very few of our North side Brethren or Sisters at Communion. I confess I did not Send them over Express, written Word last Sabbath, For as I went from Home last Saturday it was not in my Mind. But I rested in this, that they could not but all of them know that it was our stated Cause. I preach'd a.m. and p.m. on Eph. 2, 8, first part. Deacon Fay and his wife and Deacon Newton din'd here.

3. Two Precinct Meetings on this one Day, one for Precinct Debts and to hear my answer—the other for Election of Officers. Mrs. Mary Brigham (Gershoms Wife) din'd here.

4. I went early to Mr. Beemans and paid him £30 old Tenor and took up my Bond. N.B. By his wife's assistance he was induc'd to forego the Whole of the Interest. I in the Mean Time promising to do him the like Kindness if he should stand in Need, and I be able. Catechiz'd both a.m. and p.m. at the Meeting House.

5. Young Mr. Emerson from Worcester here, and presently Captain Flagg[1] both from Worcester. P.M. I was designing to go to Marlborough but Mrs. Child (Jonas's wife) here to be examin'd. Brother Hicks from Cambridge. N.B. Though he has been down so long yet little Effected towards settling Accounts, but he tells me they were oblig'd to put in a Petition to the Judge to bring forward the Settlement of them.[2] At Eve he went to Sutton.

6. I preach'd at Deacon Jonathan Forbush's on Judg. 11, 35. My Daughter Molly went with me. Deacon Forbush acknowledg'd the Goodness of God to him in the Benefit he receiv'd by the Exercises Last Lords Day, and the Special Communion (he judges) he had with God that Day in his Ordinances. Blessed be God for such a Favour! O that when I have preach'd and Minister'd to others, I may not my Self be a Cast away! We were accompany'd back by Mr. Williams as far his House.

4 Son of Deacon Jonathan Forbush.

5 The Reverend Abraham Taylor was a dissenting minister of England.

6 Given as Paul Newton and Mary Farrour in *Westborough Vital Records*.

7 (Harvard 1741), minister of the church at Framingham, 1746-1775. Sibley, XI, 8-11.

8 Edward Goddard. These opposition charges were printed as *A Brief Account* (Boston, 1750).

9 The Reverend Nathaniel Appleton of Cambridge.

10 The Reverend William Williams.

11 Widow of the Reverend John Swift.

12 Ephraim Williams, a founder of Stockbridge. See Sarah C. Sedgwick and Christina S. Marquand, *Stockbridge 1739-1939 A Chronicle* ([Great Barrington]), 1939), pp. 22-24.

13 Johannes Lydius of Albany. See *Collections of the History of Albany* (Albany, 1871), IV, 144.

14 Joseph Emerson (Harvard 1743), later the minister at Pepperell, 1746-1775. Sibley, XI, 217-220.

15 Joshua Eaton, a lawyer of Worcester.

16 Parkman recorded no baptisms or other church activities on or near this date in the Westborough Church Records.

17 Parkman's brother-in-law, the physician of Worcester.

18 Prominent citizen of Shrewsbury.

19 The Reverend John Martyn of the north precinct of Westborough.

1 Captain Benjamin Flagg, Jr.

2 This concerned the settlement of the estate of Parkman's first father-in-law, Samuel Champney of Cambridge.

7. One Alpheus Spencer (alias Prinmus) of Concord here, as he is going to Cape Breton. My sons Thrashing Barley. Thomas Winchester here at Evening.

8. They sow'd some Peas in the Garden, and thrash'd Barley again.

9. A.M. on Tit. 2, 11. P.M. on Rom. 13, 1, with some Additions. Proclamation for Fast.

10. Robert Bradish here—proud and obstinate, and would have me produce my Witnesses—Pertly Controverts and debates the Point. Maintains that Good Works do go into the Conditions of Justification. A Storm of Snow, and Cold Rain. At Eve divers persons here who acquaint'd me with the remarkable peace and Dispatch with which the affairs of Meeting to Day were carry'd on. I am not without hope that my sermon yesterday p.m. might be of Some service (by the Blessing of God) to them.

11. A Meeting of the Commission officers at Captain Maynards for dignifying the Regiment. Mr. Cushing came with Colonel Ward, and Mr. Smith[3] with Colonel Wiliams;[4] The Colonels gave me also their Invitation to dine with them which I was oblig'd to Comply with, tho it was a very uncomfortable Interruption to me, and much prevented my Preparations for the Evening Fast.

12. Robert Bradish here but I did not Speak with him.

13. Public Fast[5] on Occasion of the horrid Rebellion in Scotland and of the Seasons of the Year before us. I preach'd on Jer. 6, latter part of 1 and 8. My wife ill again tho she tarried at Meeting, yet was ill there; and increas'd at Evening.

14. My wife (thro Divine Favor) grows Better. Ebenezer Sleds the Stones of the old Garden to the Well.

15. Stormy Day. A Season of Close application to study.

16. On Tit. 2, 11, 12. My Kinswoman Mrs. Winchester Sick of a Fever.

17. The Town was in Some perplexity by Means that the Summons to the Officers who were lately chosen for the Year, to be Sworn before Justice Baker, was not Dated, and the Days being run out which are sett by the Law, and they not Sworn, they chose them over again and So it happen'd that the Same Persons were Chose. I visited My Kinswoman Winchester, (dining at Mr. Grouts). Was at Mr. Benjamin Fays and Phinehas Hardy's. At Evening Edwards Whipple here learning to sing.

18. Catechetical Exercise to Young Women, on Eph. 2, 3, latter part. At Eve Mr. Frink,[6] but proceeded on his Journey to Mr. Cushings.

19. Early sent Ebenezer with a Letter to Mr. Frink. Thomas Winchester here to Work.

20. Wrote to Mr. Breck[7] of Springfield, in Reply to his of February 28, which was in return to Mine of August 23 last. Inclos'd it to Dr. Breck of Worcester for Conveyance. Thomas Winchester at work. My son Thomas carry'd our Barley to Mr. Mathis.

21. Mr. Joseph Batchellor[8] brought a piece of Strip'd Camblot[9] Stuff which he had wove for my Dauter Molly. Having taken notice that Robert Bradish insists upon my Making out the Grounds of Letter of Admonition to him, I sent for Mr. Beriah Rice to come to me, who came accordingly at Evening. And this Very Evening I receiv'd a Tart Note from Robert who thinks of Putting me to greater Trouble if I don't produce my Informers. Such his Insolence towards me, in addition to his Reproaches.

22. [No entry].

23. On Tit. 2, 11, 12, and Gal. 6, 14. Appoint'd a Lecture to Young Men next Thursday.

24. When Thomas Winchester was lately with me we agreed upon Thursday next to break up the Ground, round about the Settle, and have bespoke plough and Cattle, 4 Yoke accordingly but forgetting this appointment yesterday, I appointed the Same Day to be Lecture to Young Men. So perplexing is it to have

the Affairs of the Ministry and of a Farm to manage together. I was oblig'd to be up early this morning and go to Mr. Winchesters to Speak with Thomas who was going over to Upton for Several Days and thought my Appointment might be altered. And I had propos'd to visit his Mother this Morning, She still lying Sick. Thence I went to Mr. Harringtons about Rails: and I receiv'd their Testimony about what Robert Bradish said at their House February 11. Visited Mr. Miller who is sick. Dr. Gott return'd part of the way with me.

25. Molly and I rode to Marlborough—Lecture to young Men. I preach'd on Rom. 6, 13. Mr. Smith and I to Madam Woods's[10] after Exercise. Left Molly at Marlborough and Bekky Gott came home with me.

26. Robert Bradish by appointment here and his uncle Beriah and his wife, and Mr. Samuel Harrington and his Wife here and gave their Testimony against him. The Evidences were plain and direct; yet he did not yield. A number of people in the kitchen. After they went off I went to Captain Maynards. Reverend Bacon[11] of Ashuelot came from Wrentham, here and lodg'd.

27. Preach'd a Lecture to Young Men on Ps. 119, 59.

28. We broke up the Ground about the settle. Thomas Winchester and Nathan Maynard help'd us. We had 5 Yoke of oxen besides my own. A precinct Meeting to See whether the Precinct would pay the Charges layd on them by the last Quarter Sessions, arising from the Petition of the North side to be freed from paying that part of my sallery from June 5, 1744 to October 20, of the Same Year. The Precinct chose a Committee to seek Council.

29. Broke up Ground again at the Same Place with the Same Number of Cattle, by the Same Hands as yesterday—till noon. West yard broke up. N.B. Poor Jos. Clagg here, yesterday and to Day.

30. On Tit. 2, 11, 12. P.M. Gal. 6, 14. At Evening Mr. Martyn who lodg'd here.

31. Mr. Martyn gives his Answer to the North Precinct—in the Affirmative.[12] I rode to Cambridge. Found Mother Champney weak and feeble, yet able to walk about. I lodg'd there.

## APRIL [1746]

1. Visited Brother Barrett who has been infirm ever since he came from Cape Briton, but now is very low and wasting. The Lord grant both him and Me a lively Sense of our frail and perishing Nature, and prepare us for our Dissolution! Heard that Mrs. Miriam Cheever is Dead. O that Every Death of those I knew and Convers'd freely with might be a new quickening to Me! I was with Edmund Trowbridge Esquire[1] to consult him upon my Case with reference to the arrears of the Town of Westborough, and with respect to our Precincts Votes for my Sallery etc.—and some other Affairs of Difficulty with me at this Time. Proceeded to Boston; din'd at my Honoured Mothers, who thro the Tender Mercy of God is yet Living, tho Very feeble and not able to get up to Day till 3 p.m. Sister Betty much better than when I left her last. Lodg'd at Brother Alexanders. N.B. He is hot in Courtship already to Mrs. Rebecca Jarvis—but the Circumstances of his Family are very Urgent. The God of infinite Wisdom direct him and prevent his too soon forgetting the Great Design of the Sore Chastisement he is under! N.B. Sent my Horse to Cambridge by Mr. Larkins son.

2. Din'd at Cousen John Parkmans. N.B. Her Fervency for Children. But Lodg'd with my Kinsman Elias, who is yet with Dr. Delhonde. N.B. I was at Mrs. Martyns. Here was her son John—with whom I also took a long walk and talk [sic] with him about his telling of great and Strange Storys, etc.

3. Visited Mrs. Carns of whom I had (gratis) an old Greek Lexicon, which with my Table Bible I consigned to Mr. Nathaniel Procter to be new bound. Visited Mr. Gee[2] who is much impair'd in his Health. The Lord be gracious to him and restore

[3] The Reverend Aaron Smith of Marlborough.

[4] Abraham Williams of Marlborough.

[5] March 13, 1745, was proclaimed a day of fasting and prayer throughout the province.

[6] The Reverend Thomas Frink of Rutland.

[7] The Reverend Robert Breck, Jr.

[8] The weaver of Grafton.

[9] Camlet or camblet, a fine, closely woven fabric of camel's hair or perhaps mixed wool and silk. This was once commonly used for cloaks.

[10] Widow of Benjamin Woods of Marlborough.

[11] Jacob Bacon of Keene, N.H.

[12] See Kent, Northborough History, pp. 24-26.

[1] Lawyer of Cambridge.

[2] The Reverend Joshua Gee.

him! Such worthy men being (alas!) too scarce. Was at the Public Lecture. Mr. Webb preach'd on Eph. 4, 18. Din'd at Mr. Quincys[3]—where was also the Honourable Mr. Danforth[4] and Mr. Josiah Quincy.[5] Was also at Mr. Hubbards.[6] At Mr. Daniel Henshaw's, with Captain Samuel Waterhouse. At Evening Brother Alexander and his Mistress (Mrs. Rebecca Jarvis) at mothers, till late. Lodg'd at Mothers. I had Sent for my Horse, but kept him this Night at Brother Alexander's Stable.

4. My Honour'd Mother Decays and I fear whether She will Continue any Long Time. Her Discourse last Evening whilst Brother Alexander was there, very Noticeable. Behold I die (Sayd She)—but God Shall visit you (directing herself to us her Children and having respect to our Children also in Case, that is, that we and ours Should keep the way of the Lord, as She had taught and Commanded us) and Shall be with you etc. etc. with many Such like words, as the old Patriarch when solemnly taking leave of his Posterity. The Lord Let these weighty Sayings home upon my, and upon all our Hearts, that they may be ever duly observ'd and kept by us and ours! I took leave with Great Affection, and with Hearty Gratitude to God and Her. And O that God most Gracious and all-sufficient would be with her to Support and Comfort her, and safely conduct her to his heavenly and Eternal Kingdom!

I broke fast at my Kinsman Hearseys.[7] Din'd at Brother Alexander's. Improv'd Mrs. Stoddard to buy me a Calamanco Jacket and Breeches. N.B. Mr. Abbot of Andover at Mrs. Stoddards. N.B. Kinsman John Parkman presented me a Wigg of Considerable Price. Sett out upon my Journey from Cousen Procters—it began to Rain, after a drie Time. Storm increas'd So that I turn'd in at Captain Winchesters—and again at Mr. Richard Gardners[8] during the Time of Terrible Thunder and Lightening. Lodg'd at Mother Champneys.

5. Return'd home. N.B. din'd at Mr. Patersons at Subdury. Mr. Cook's[9] wife very low—thot to be in a Consumption. The Lord prepare her for his holy Will! Found my Family well. Blessed be God our preserver! N.B. Thomas Winchester came to work for me last Wednesday noon to make up the month which he fell behind in our Agreement last Year. N.B. Mr. Stephen Maynard return'd home from the scout to Lake.

6. On Hosea 13, 9. Old Sermons which I had too Little Time to Correct, as it happens likewise in many of my Repititions—for tho I am not well pleas'd with the Composition of many of my sermons after I have deliver'd them yet am oblig'd to repeat them with too little Alteration. O that God would pardon my many and great Defects and Miscarriages; and bless my imperfect, mean Endeavours!

7. Thomas at work—ploughing stubble. P.M. Mr. Davis[10] of Holden lodg'd here.

8. Mr. Davis and I rode over to Association at Hopkinton. Mr. Loring,[11] Mr. Cushing and Mr. Stone[12] were all (except Two Young Gentlemen) that came besides. Mr. Seccomb, who was to have deliver'd the Concio, did not come. Mr. Barrett repeat'd his sermon at Mr. Millens Ordination. Mr. Bridge of Framingham told us a Council call'd by the Dissenting party, was to sit at that place tomorrow, and he desir'd advice. The advice given him was not to concern himself with them. The Council which had ordain'd him having sufficiently Examin'd him already.

9. Mr. Davis preach'd the Public Lecture on Acts 5, 31. Mr. Loring and Mr. Davis came home with me and lodg'd here.

10. Mr. Davis went home A.M. Mr. Loring preach'd my Lecture on Jer. 23, 6. An Excellent Savoury Sermon. The Lord be pleas'd to make it Savingly usefull and Beneficial to us! At

Evening Mr. Loring went to Marlborough, not without my hearty gratitude for his kind assistance. Lieutenant Tainter came and offer'd to Cutt my Colt which by the Help of Some Persons here he Effected.

11. Captain Maynard returns from Boston and brings word that my Honoured Mother grows worse.

12. Fine weather. Thomas Sow'd Barley. Might Grace Spring in our Hearts!

13. Sacrament. Preach'd a.m. on Luke 24, 46. P.M. Hosea 13, 9. N.B. At Communion we sung Rev. 5, 10, at which Mrs. Whitney cry'd out—but we went on without stopping to the End of what was propos'd—and she was still at the Blessing. O might it please God to give us all a lively sense of his infinite Love and our great Obligations to him therefor! O that we might walk worthy of him to all well pleasing! N.B. Deacon Fay, Widow Woods, Mrs. Collister[13] and Mrs. Bowman[14] din'd here. N.B. Many of the North side were absent from Communion. We were in much Expectation that Mr. Martyn would have brought his wife over to us this Evening—but he came not.

14. Thomas sowing Rye. Isaac Amsden sues William Rogers junior before Nahum Ward Esquire. Ebenezer Graffing.[15] Mr. James How of Worcester here to buy Cyder. N.B. his smart Arguing in behalf of the Arminians.[16] N.B. My Wife rode over to Mr. Caruth's.

15. Rain A.M. Catechetical Exercises to Young Women— The fore part of what I deliver'd was (without writing) on the Moderator and his Offices in general. The Latter part on the Office of a Prophet in particular and under that Head improv'd a Considerable part of my sermon on Isa. 61, 2, viz. the Beginning to Page 7 and the Heads of Application in page 25 and 26, omitting many of the particulars under those Heads. P.M. My Dauter Sarah taken ill.

16. A Dark Morning by means of the Storm of Rain—but far darker by means of the Most Sorrowfull Message Receiv'd by Letter from my Brother Samuel Parkman by the Hands of Mr. William Ward of Southborough (My Brother having given Ten Shillings to Convey me the Letter)That last Lords Day Evening about 6 o'Clock our Honoured and dear Mother departed this Life: and that tomorrow was appointed to be the Funeral. Tho we have long had warnings yet O how shocking when at last it comes! An Excelling Woman, as acknowledg'd by all that I have heard speak of her: Friends or Foes; especially in wisdom and steadiness and Piety. God was pleas'd to Bless her with a Tenacious Memory, which she had to the last, and remembring recent Facts as well as antient. God made her a great and rich Blessing to us all, and we had much Happiness in her. She was one of those Vertuous Women whom her Children think themselves in Duty Bound to rise up and call Blessed. The Lord be with us in the Great Duty of holy Mourning now incumbent! We waited while the Rain Slacken'd; and p.m. My Wife and I set out and rode to Marlborough. At Esquire Brighams[17] we borrow'd a Chair, and Lodg'd at Dr. Gotts.[18]

17. Just after sun rise we rode from Marlborough to Boston and din'd at Mrs. Keggells. Hasten'd to Brother Alexanders where we put up our Chair and Horse. The Funeral was put by because of the Fowl weather Yesterday which was thought would prevent my Coming. I went to my Brother Samuels to Consult him about Necessary Preparations but hasten'd to take a View of the Dear and much Esteem'd Remains—which tho So long breathless were not greatly alter'd from Life. The Lord Convince Me of my own Frailty, Since most certainly I am the Same as she from whom I came! The Lord prepare me for the awfull Time! In the Evening my Brethren were together at Mothers and we pray'd together. My wife and I lodg'd there.

18. Was much engag'd the fore part of the Day in buying black Cloth for a Coat—at length Suited myself at Mr. Lawtons £8 and 5 shillings per yard: improv'd Mr. Owen to make it—but because it was not possible to get it ready for the Funeral, my

---

[3] John Quincy (Harvard 1708) of Boston.

[4] Councillor Samuel Danforth.

[5] (Harvard 1728). *Sibley*, VIII, 463-475.

[6] Nathaniel Hubbard (Harvard 1698), Justice of the Superior Court. *Sibley*, IV, 406-408.

[7] Tabitha Parkman, the Reverend Mr. Parkman's niece, married Israel Hearsey, Nov. 13, 1740.

[8] Of Cambridge.

[9] The Reverend William Cooke of Wayland.

[10] The Reverend Joseph Davis.

[11] The Reverend Israel Loring of Sudbury.

[12] The Reverend Nathan Stone of Southborough.

[13] Mrs. John McCollister of Westborough.

[14] Mrs. James Bowman.

[15] Graff is an old variant of graft.

[16] Believers in the doctrines of Arminius.

[17] Joseph Brigham.

[18] Benjamin Gott, the physician.

Brother Samuel was So friendly as to lend me a Black Coat till my own could be made. This Eve The Remains of my Honoured Parent were decently interr'd. Mr. Gee not able by reason of illness to be there; but Mr. Webb and Mr. Eliot were. The Bearers were Deacon Procter and Elder Baker, Deacon Hunt and Deacon Townsend, Deacon Larraby and Dr. Archibald. After we return'd and the Company, except near Relations, gone, we again pray'd together. And O that now both Father and Mother Forsake us the Lord would take us up! N.B. Mr. Gee (by means of Deacon Larraby) Sent to me to preach for him next Sabbath—which I was not against if I did preach any where in Town. Lodg'd at sister Bettys.

19. Din'd at Brother Parkmans. Mr. Eliot Sent me a Messenger to Desire me to preach for him one part of the Day tomorrow, upon which I made him a Visit—and declin'd preaching for him at this Time because I felt but feeble and doubted whether I should be able to preach all Day for my Brethren expected me to give them some Exercise at Evening. I also Visited Mr. Gee who was in a low state of Health. Lodg'd at the Same.

20. I preach'd at the Old North a.m. on Rom. 6, 13, middle Clause. But yield themselves unto God, etc. Mr. Maccarty p.m. there on [blank]. N.B. din'd at Mr. Gees—and my wife there with me after meeting at Eve, From whence we went to sister Willards, where my late honoured Mother dwelt, and I had an Exercise to my Brethren and other Relatives on John 3, 23 latter part. May God make these Exercises usefull to us in our Sorrow and Mourning under our sore Bereavement! We lodg'd there. N.B. Brother Alexander brings Cousen Rebecca Jarvis freely among us, and she was with us this Evening.

21. Mr. Owen finish'd my Coat at Evening. After Sundry Visits in the Day I met my Brethren at sister Willards to read our Honoured Mothers Last Will and Testament, and attend upon the Duty Consequent, Particularly we valued the negro Pito: and as my Mother had given him leave to choose which of us should be his Master, he chose Brother Samuel—who took possession of him. N.B. P.M. we were at Mr. Eliots and Mr. Robert Brecks, etc. etc.

22. We din'd at Brother Samuels and Mr. Jabez Fox[19] of Casco with us, who informs us of the Mischief done by the Indians at Gorham Town. 4 killed and 3 carry'd Captive. At Eve we Supp'd at Brother Samuels with Brother Alexander and Mrs. Rebeca Jarvis—and lodg'd there.

23. My Horse for several Nights kept at my Kinsman Procters. We mounted from Brother Alexanders—din'd at Mrs. Keggells—made a visit at Judge Dudleys,[20] and proceeded to Cambridge before Night.

24. Brother Hicks Set out from Cambridge with us. We rode to Dr. Gotts, and to Esquire Brighams, where we left our Chair. Captain Maynard there. Sorrowfull News of Mr. Antipas Brighams Death at Grafton. Some bad News also from our own Family at Westborough That a few Days agoe my Young Cow (whose Calf was newly kill'd for the sake of the Milk) was a few Nights agoe drown'd in Mr. Barns's Swamp. We ourselves got home well, and found our Children and Whole Family Well; Sarah whom we left not well, comfortable, and Susè well wean'd. Blessed be God!

24. Mr. John Brown[21] from Cambridge here and lodg'd here. Tells us the sorrowfull News of upper Ashuelot besett by the Indians, and several Houses there in Flames. May God be mercifully present with them and save them and especially with Mr. Bacon[22] in this distressing Time.

26. Mr. Brown to Worcester where he preaches.

27. On the Occasion of the Death of my Honoured Mother, and Several other Bereavments (Ex. gr. Captain Forbush and Mrs. Byles mourn for the Loss of their sister Bruce and Ensign Bruce and Mrs. Miller the Loss of their Mother; Captain Baker and Captain Maynard and their wives the Death of their Brother Antipas Brigham, and Bezaliel Smith and wife the Loss of one of their Children) I preach'd a.m. on Rev. 14, 13, and p.m. on Ps.

19 (Harvard 1727).
20 Paul Dudley, Justice of the Superior Court of Judicature.
21 John Brown, Jr. (Harvard 1741), was later the minister at Cohasset, 1747-1791. Sibley, XI, 12-17.
22 The Reverend Jacob Bacon.

27, 10. May it please God to Concerr with both the Word and the Providence.

28. Mr. Martyn[23] here. He tells me the Day for his Ordination is appoint'd, and Churches to assist are chose. N.B. he asks me to preach on that Solemn occasion. He din'd here. P.M. he was to meet a number of Brethren who are preparing Letters to be Sent to the Churches, and he is about his Trading for a place to live on.

29. I Catechiz'd at the School House—about 45 Children. Visited at Mr. Childs, at Mr. Whitneys, Mr. Millers (whose wife is Sick yet) and at Mr. Daniel Forbush's.

30. A Number of Brethren from the North side here, viz. Messers Townsend, Allen and his Son, Matthias Rice and Silas Fay: and with them Mr. John McCollister desiring to be dismiss'd and recommended to the building a Church of Christ in the North part of the Town. I mention'd to them their Delinquency on Communion Days, their Injustice towards me respecting the arrears which were due to me from the Town, and the securing to me the Material Rights. At Length came Mr Wheeler, James Ball and Jacob Rice, who were opposite to the former and to their proceedings. Mr. Ball mention'd his Desire of a Church Meeting in order to have Some Conference and to sett all Things to Rights before we Divide and his proposal of a Meeting was agreed to.

### MAY, 1746

1. I preach'd at the Private Meeting at Deacon Newton's[1] on 1 John 1, 7. The rather because of the Languishing State of the Meeting much complain'd of Still, but yet not pitty'd and reform'd—tho I have been divers Times present with them upon this Very Ground. I Stop'd the Brethren after Meeting and talk'd to them upon that Head and earnestly Exhorted as well as admonish'd—hoping they would show some regard. We afterwards fell into some Discourse with relation to our North side and their Affairs. N.B. Molly rode with me. At Eve Thomas Winchester finish'd with me for last Years agreement—he having been paid therefor some time agoe.

2. Agreed with Thomas to help me from June 15 to August 15 and to have 22£ Old Tenor.

3. Mr. Stone here, going to Worcester to change with Mr. Brown.[2] P.M. Captain Forbush's wife.

4. I preach'd on Ps. 27, 10, all Day. Rainy. N.B. No Letter yet from Northside. Propounded Jonas Childs and Wife and Sarah Forbush, wife of Captain Forbush. Stop'd the Church and acquainted them with the Desires of 5 Brethren on the North side to be dismiss'd; and read the request of another five to have a Church Meeting. Church meeting appointed to be 2 p.m. Next Wednesday.

5. I visited Mr. Adams's little son who had been much burnt at a Cole-Pitt. Mr. Stone[3] in his journey from Worcester here, and it being rainy he lodg'd here.

6. Mr. Stone return'd home.

7. The Church met at the Request of Mr. Joseph Wheeler and Four others, Brethren of the Church to have Some Conference with those 6 Brethren who desire Dismission. See Records of the Church.[4] Not being able to come to a Vote to dismiss the Brethren desiring it, the Meeting was adjourn'd to Next Monday Morning 8 o'Clock.

8. I found there was a Considerable Frost last Night. Rode to Shrewsbury and Consulted Mr. Cushing[5] upon our Difficultys in the Church. Din'd there. Settl'd my account with Mr. Parker Shoemaker—was at Mr. Thomas Smiths whose wife is making me a Calamanco Jacket and Breaches. When I got home Neighbour Eliezer Rice concerning the Ministerial Meadow. Mr. Daniel Warrins (alias Spriggins). They were in Sorrows for 2 of his wife's Brethren who dy'd at Cape Breton.

23 The Reverend John Martyn of the north precinct.
1 Josiah Newton.
2 John Brown (Harvard 1741), later minister of Cohasset, 1747-1791. Sibley, XI, 12-17.
3 Reverend Nathan Stone of Southborough.
4 The Westborough church did not at this time vote the dismission of the north side people.
5 Reverend Job Cushing.

9. In the Morning rode to Eliezer Rice's and sent my son Ebenezer to work with him and a son of Lieutenant Forbush's, in Mending up the Fence of the Ministerial Meadow.

10. Greatly hinder'd by Mr. Josiah Bowkers being here to be Examin'd in order to his joining with others in laying the foundations of a Church in the North Precinct, but I advis'd him to wave it; besides that the Time was So short that there could be no opportunity for him to come again—and there would be enough for a Church without him. A Warm Day. At Eve came Mr. Carns[6] of Boston, who had been [on] a Journey to New Haven.

11. Mr. Carns a.m. on Mat. 16, 24. Let him Deny himself. P.M. on Col. 1, 27. Christ in you the Hope of Glory. Mr. Jenison at Meeting and here at Evening.

12. Mr. Carns's Horse not fit to go his Journey by reason of the Swelling of his Back. Church Met according to Adjournment. See Church Records.[7] I was full of deep Concern to See the Church so perplex'd—and I became faint and weary before we had done. But (by the Help of God) I endeavour'd to Manage every affair with the utmost Impartiality and refus'd to Vote, My Self, in any Article, but yielded all to them. Mr. Carns din'd with me. Mr. Martyn visited me. I urg'd him to provide Some Body else to preach the Ordination Sermon, and especially because of the uncertainty of the Councils allowing our Church votes. I enquir'd what he might intend by preventing Jealousies and Suspicions in his Letter to me, Since I had given No Cause for any? He invited my Wife and Dauter to Ordination. Mr. Martyn left me to go to a Number of his Brethren who were to meet in the Northside to Day. Mr. Carns lodg'd here. N.B. Mr. Jenison with Mr. Martyn to Day.

13. Cloudy and drizly in the Morn. P.M. did not rain, but it being Easterly weather Mr. Carns did not Care to go his Journey home. Mr. Jonas Child here, upon the Affair of his Relation but I could not write for him. School begins by Mr. Jenison at old Mr. Maynards.

14. Mr. Carns ventur'd to undertake his Journey home. Brother Hicks and his wife, his Company. P.M. Mrs. Forbush (Captain's wife) here to get her Relation writ. While I was engag'd in her Business came Mrs. Edwards of North Grafton and Major Pomeroys grandson. With them came also Reverend Mr. Bridge of Framingham—and Lieutenant Tainter. The Last inform'd me of the Sorrowfull Fall of Mrs. Betty Loring,[8] being six months gone with Child by Manson[9] the Barber at Sudbury. More sad news from the Frontiers—the Indians have wounded Several persons at Colerain and Husack, and led away Captive Deacon Brown and another man from lower Ashuelot.

15. Mrs. Edwards and the Lad with her went to Boston. Lieutenant Aaron Forbush to get a Letter writ by me to his son Noah. Mr. Daniel Warrin at stone Wall. Came at 10 a.m., yet he built me (as he said) 7 Rod—for which he ask'd me 7 Shillings tho by the Rod it would have amounted to half as much more.

16. Mr. James How of Worcester here for Cyder. I sold him 2 Barrells filled up for 20 pence per Barrell.

17. Ebenezer and Thomme Shear'd Sheep.

18. On Tit. 2, 12. Rev. 22, 20. Ebenezer goes to the Private Meeting of Young Men.

19. Mr. McAllister here for his Certificat; and Mr. Matthias Rice here with a Letter from Mr. Martyn concerning my preaching his Ordination sermon which I had already consented to in Case the Council Should advise that we Should join in the work of that Day. I rode over to Mr. Allens, and there (at the Mill) wrote a Letter to Mr. Barrett,[10] Seconding a Letter from Mr. Martyn desiring him to come prepar'd to preach in Case etc. I din'd at Mr. Palatiah Rice's. Bought peas at 16 shillings and wheat at 18 pence per Bushel. Was at Mr. Thomas Warrins, at the widow Coolidge's, at Mr. McAllisters, Gershom Fay's,

Lawrence's and Mr. Nathan Balls. N.B. his Son Ebenezer lyes by with a broken Thigh. I proceed'd (according to my main Design in going out to Day) to visit Mrs. Livermore who is in a Wasting Condition. In Return was at Mr. James Balls. There were Mr. Wheeler, Mr. Jacob Rice, Lawrence, etc. contriving and preparing to oppose the Ordinance call'd at Mr. George Smiths and Timothy Fays. N.B. in their Talk of Mr. Martyn I was every way endeavouring to mollifie etc., and should they make the worst of it they might Remember the Story of St. Augustine who did not preach till he was 35. When I came home I found Mr. Bridgham[11] of Brimfield and his Mother, who lodg'd here.

20. Mr. Bridgham with his Mother from Boston. At Eve Mr. Gay[12] of Suffield and his sister Ballantine in their Journey to Dedham, here and lodg'd here. Town Meeting. Mr. Francis Whipple chose Representative. I sent for Lieutenant Holloway[13] and talk'd with him for his Reproachfully declaring in Town Meeting that I would take more than Lawfull Interest. He made a mean and unsatisfying Defence.

21. Rainy Morning. Mr. Gay and his sister set out when it was moderated. Mr. Barrett here going to the Ordination. My Wife went over with me. Met at Lieutenant Holloways. Messers. Prentice, Cushing, Gardner,[14] there already. Mr. Loring and Mr. Hall[15] did not come, So that there were but 5 Churches. Mr. Prentice Moderator. Mr. Barrett Clerk. The Church of Westborough refus'd to join in the Council till the Votes of Said Church were Scann'd and judg'd of. The Council judg'd them Valid; yet they requested the advice of the Council whether all Things consider'd it could be, nevertheless, advisable for them to Act? Who Still advis'd to it. Upon which they join'd in Council. Objections were brought in (about 12 o'Clock) by Messers Wheeler, Jacob Rice, and Timothy Fay, but when debated on by the Council they were Voted in sufficient to be any Barr to proceeding. We went to meeting ½ after 4 P.M. Mr. Barrett began with prayer. I preach'd on Heb. 13, 17. Mr. Gardner gather'd the Church which consisted of Ten, viz. Ephraim Allen, John McAllister, Joshua Dowsing, Jonathan Livermore, John Caruth, Matthias Rice, Gershom Fay, Silas Fay, [blank] Shepherd and Samuel Allen. Mr. Prentice gave the Charge, Mr. Cushing the Fellowship of the Churches. Sung Ps. 66 from number 17 one staff and ½. It was almost night when we broke off. An unhappy accident befell a young man by the Fall of one of the Supporters of the Gallery. He was knock'd down to the Ground and seem'd Stunn'd for a while, but he was taken up and grew better. It was that son of Mr. Nathaniel Oake who has already met with Many Sad Disasters—but God be prais'd he yet survives! After Supper we were accompany'd home by Sir Williams and three young scholars more. Baldwin,[16] Cook,[17] and Richardson,[18] who all lodg'd here. And thus we have seen another Church founded in this Town and another Pastor ordain'd: And may the God of infinite Mercy forgive all my unfaithfulness to those who have been under my Care! may all that has been unrighteous, and blameworthy in them be pardon'd of God! May that Church be a Pure Golden Candlestick and the person Set up therein be a Starr, a burning and Shining Light! May we all be united in Faith and Love! that we may have Sweet Communion, mutual assistance and Consolation here, and meet together in the heavenly Glory at last—through Christ Jesus. Amen! Besides my having So much Company of late to Shorten my Pasture, a Number of Horses, chiefly from Captain Maynards, have broke in for Several Nights.

22. Sir Williams etc. had not left us before we were favour'd with Mr. Barretts Company, who tarried and din'd with me. N.B. a Council Sat at Framingham on Tuesday last, and sits at Hopkinton to Day, at the Call of the Separating Partys.

[6] John Carnes (Harvard 1742), later the minister of Stoneham, 1746-1757. *Sibley*, XI, 137-142.

[7] Through some oversight Parkman made no entry in the Church Records between May 7 and May 18.

[8] Elizabeth, the daughter of the Reverend Israel Loring.

[9] Richard Manson and Elizabeth Loring were married June 6, 1746.

[10] The Reverend Samuel Barrett of Hopkinton.

[11] Reverend James Bridgham.

[12] Reverend Ebenezer Gay.

[13] William Holloway.

[14] Reverend John Gardner of Stow.

[15] Reverend David Hall of Sutton.

[16] William Baldwin (Harvard 1748).

[17] William Cooke (Harvard 1748).

[18] Gideon Richardson (Harvard 1749).

P.M. Brother Hicks and his wife from Cambridge and lodg'd here.

23. Sent the Young Creatures to Sutton, under the Care of Brother Hicks.

24. Ebenezer and Thomme draw Stones for Well. Mr. Jenison goes to Worcester.

25. Sacrament. Luke 24, 46. 2 Cor. 5, 20. The Opposing Brethren of the North Side here at Communion, and Mrs. Laurence, Mrs. Fay (Samuel Junior's wife) Mrs. Chamberlin (John's wife) besides Captain Fay din'd here. O that we might not enjoy our happy privileges in Vain! nor liberation in Religion without some good Effect! I call'd heaven and Earth to witness, in Communion Exercise, that we did now Solemly Covenant and bind ourselves to be the Lords! May we have grace to abide by it!

26. Somewhat Cold. No School. Mr. Jenison not come from Worcester.

27. Early in the Morning I rode over to Mr. Williams to see his sons Wife and Child who had the Throat Distemper. Mr. Francis Whipple the Representative was with me, and we thence prosecuted our Journey for Cambridge and Boston. We rode to Mr. Liscombs[19] (at Southborough) to Mr. Stones—to Colonel Buckministers—rain'd at Weston—din'd at Woolsons Tavern. There came Mr. Cushing, and Mr. Whitney of Nitchewaug. My Company rode along, but much more on the Road, Colonel Stoddard,[20] Chandler[21] etc. We stopp'd at Saltmarsh's—and then many more; Brigadier Dwight,[22] Colonel Porter, Mr. Breck, Mr. Chester Williams. Afterwards Dr. William Clark of Boston etc. I proceeded as far as Cambridge and lodg'd at Mother Champneys.

28. Rode to Boston, put up my Horse at Mr. Samuel Procters. Visited my sister Willard, who has been in a poorer state of Health than usual, ever since Mother's Death. The sermon to Day was by my Excellent Master Barnard of Andover. Din'd with Brother Alexander. P.M. at the Convention. Dr. Sewal Moderator and Mr. Checkley Clerk. Voted an address to the King on Occasion of the Rebellion. Supp'd at Sister Bettys with Brother Alexander and his mistress. Lodg'd at Sister Willards.

29. Mr. Gay of Hingham preach'd to the Convention on John 3. The Collection (I think) amounted to 232£. A peaceable Meeting. Blessed be God! Din'd at Mr. Checkleys with Mr. President, Mr. Barnard of Marblehead, Mr. Appleton, Mr. Bridgham and Mr. Maccarty. At Convention P.M. we met to finish the Address and distribute the Collection. At Eve rode to Cambridge and lodg'd at Mother Champneys. N.B. Sister Lydia at Boston.

30. Went over to College for the Sake of Mr. Cushings Company, and to Mr. William Morse's to have a shooe put on to my Mare. Spent some little Time in the publick Library. We din'd at Mr. Stearns's in Watertown: and call'd at Matthias Rice's. Found my Tabernacle in Peace. Blessed be God!

31. Mr. Rand (now of Kingstown) came and din'd with me. Afterwards came Mr. Buckminster. The design'd Expedition to Canada now no longer a secret. The Lord be pleas'd to give all needed Direction, and prepare all the Hearts of his people for his great Mercy!

### JUNE [1746]

On Mat. 10, 39. He that Saveth is Life etc. and Ch. 12, 41. The Man of Nin—O might there be a suitable Effect, by the Gracious Concurrence of God.

2. Rainy. Frequently bad news from the Frontiers. Many people from Wrentham etc. riding to upper Ashuelot to the aid of the women. At the Evening came Mr. Devotion[1] of Windham and lodg'd here.

3. Mr. Devotion for Suffield. The Catechetical Exercise: but I could not begin my preparations till noon, when I sat down and wrote the minutes of what I deliver'd.

4. Rode to Mr. Ebenezer Rice's Shop. His Father Charles changes my Firelock. N.B. This Day about 7 or 8 o'Clock in the morning Mr. Samuel Harrington (and divers others) Saw in the South West a blazing Meteor, which Soon was Extinct.

5. Mr. Breck[2] of Springfield here and din'd with me. Cold Season.

6. Mr. Appleton[3] and with him Mr. John Wendall[4] of College here. The north Company train'd. I pray'd with them. At Eve Mr. Appleton, etc. went down with me to Captain Maynards. The Expedition to Canada Engrosses all Conversation.

7. Mr. Appleton and Mr. Wendall to Worcester. P.M. refreshing Rain and Moderate Thunder.

8. On Tit. 2, 12, and p.m. repeated on Acts 13, 36. Mr. Miller din'd with us.

9. Noah Forbush[5] here who gives me a distinct account of the Skirmish with the Indians at No. 4 last Saturday was fortnight when 5 Englishmen were kill'd, one wounded, and one carry'd away Captive. N.B. Noah was in the hottest Engagement, and broke thro the Indians tho in a Lane, and 70 Rod from the Fort. So memorable the Goodness of God towards him that he got in Safe.[6] N.B. Tho the Thunder last Saturday was So Moderate here, yet at Mr. Joseph Wheelers an Horse was kill'd. Training of the South Company and I din'd with the Officers at Captain Fays.[7]

10. Rainy. My Cattle grow very troublesome by breaking in upon my Corn, whilst Ebenezer and Thomme were gone a fishing. Mr. Eliezer Rice hobbled my Ox which was the Ringleader in the Mischief. At Eve Mr. Ebenezer Rice here and whilst he wants Privileges in the Church discovers to me the great Disadvantage his Character had been brought under by Lydia Pratt of Grafton.

11. Brother Hicks from Cambridge tells me they are in a way of settling the Affairs at Mother Champney's.

12. Preach'd to Young Men from Jer. 46, 10 former part, but herein us'd Sermon 3 and 4 on Isa. 61, 2. Tho the Subject was very moving yet there were but few to hear. O that God would quicken and awaken up all of us!

13. James White and Robert Cook[8] here; they with Some others going out to the Frontiers. May the Lord Sanctifie them and protect them. Thomas Winchester here at Evening to desire he may not begin with me at the Time agreed for, but may take Care of Mr. Abraham Temple's[9] Work and Affairs for a while, he being come out in the Troop, to the Frontiers. Out of Compassion therefore I yielded to a Weeks Delay.

14. The Sow missing yesterday and this morning—at length found by the Side of a great Pine Logg in the Hill, with Ten Piggs. P.M. a Storm of Thunder and rain: but bore away to the South, and south East. Reverend Mr. Smith here requesting me to go to Worcester in his Stead, but I could not well go. He proceeded to Shrewsbury.

15. Rest of Sermon on Acts 13, 36, and p.m. on 2 Tim. 2, 3.

16. Mr. Smith of Marlborough was here, and din'd with me. P.M. I went to the Funeral of Mr. Eliezer Rice's Child.[10]

17. My Wife and I were purposing to Visit Mr. Martyn and his, but Mr. Buckminster[11] with his spouse came a.m. and din'd with us, but we prosecuted our Design. At Mr. Martyns were Mr. Goss[12] and his Wife, and Mr. Martyns Landlord and Landlady Sawyer. I beg of God that the Correspondence which I now settle may be for his Glory and our mutual good, and that of the Societys respectively under our Care! At Eve when we return'd home my wife was ill, and full of Pain.

18. Hard Thunder in the Morning but it did not seem very nigh, and accompanying it was a great Storm of Rain. Mr.

---

[19] Samuel Lyscom.
[20] John Stoddard (Harvard 1701) of Northampton, a Councillor, and Chief Justice of the Circuit Court of Common Pleas. Sibley, V, 96–119.
[21] John Chandler of Worcester.
[22] Timothy Dwight of Hatfield.
[1] The Reverend Ebenezer Devotion.
[2] The Reverend Robert Breck, Jr.
[3] The Reverend Nathaniel Appleton of Cambridge.
[4] (Harvard 1747).
[5] Son of Aaron Forbush of Westborough.
[6] "We hear from No. 4. of the Narragansett-Townships, that on the 24th of May past, four Men were killed by the Indians; another was dangerously wounded, and two more are missing. . . ." The Boston Weekly News-Letter, June 5, 1746.
[7] John Fay, a deacon of the Westborough church.
[8] Son of Cornelius Cook of Westborough.
[9] Of Marlborough.
[10] No record of death in Westborough Vital Records.
[11] Reverend Joseph Buckminster, minister of the First Congregational Church in Rutland.
[12] The Reverend Thomas Goss of Bolton.

Cushing here and is desirous that instead of preaching a Lecture to his young people I would preach the Lecture Preparatory to the Sacrament among them.

19. Preach'd at Shrewsbury Lecture on Rom. 6, 13. Yield yourself to God. N.B. Not many at meeting. There was a Training yesterday and another to be tomorrow—besides that it was good weather for Business after much hindrance by the late Rains. N.B. Captain Caleb Johnsons[13] House was greatly wreck'd by the Thunder Yesterday Morning and the Lives of the Family marvellously Spar'd. N.B. Lieutenant Stone[14] came to Speak with me about my Letter, lately Sent to Mr. Cushing in which it was Suppos'd I severely check'd the Young Society there for their undutifulness to their pastor. I had prepar'd an Answer and deliver'd it by Lieutenant's Hands. At Eve when I return'd to my own House I found there Mr. Elisha Whittlesey of Wallingford and Mrs. Sarah Noyes[15] of New Haven who lodg'd here.

20. Rain a.m. held up p.m. After Dinner our Company went off. Sorrowfull News that Benjamin Tainter is either kill'd or Carry'd away Captive, by the Indians who have besett Massachusetts Fort at Hoosuck.

21. About 10 o'Clock at night comes Mr. Thomas Marsh[16] from College to request me to go to Worcester to preach in Mr. Stevens's[17] Stead. The Circumstances of the Case being Singular (as he related the matter with regard to both Mr. Stevens and himself)—tho he had undertaken to come, yet it was only to Exchange with Some Neighbouring Ministers, and if I could not he must go to Mr. Cushing or somebody for he could not preach there himself. I told him Mr. Cushing preach'd there but last Sabbath and Especially I know Mr. Cushing could not go because it was his (appointed) Sacrament. As to his being so late in his Journey, the President and Fellows sat upon an affair of some Difficulty till one o'Clock, and after that he had to dine. I at length consented to go, and In the morning I rose so Early as to ride a mile from home before sunrise. Got to Worcester about 7 o'Clock. Preach'd all Day on Gal. 2, 20. N.B. Colonel Chandler, who came up last night, confirms the News which Mr. Marsh brought that the Duke of Cumberland is Slain in Battle against the Rebells at Inverness. Din'd at the Colonel's. Supp'd at Dr. Brecks. Rode back to Mr. Cushings at Eve and lodg'd there.

23. Home Early. Mr. Marsh not gone. Thomas Winchester was to have come but did not till nigh noon, and I had sent the Oxen home which I had order'd to be got together to cross our Ground by the Settle. It prov'd Rainy also, So that Thomas could do but little today. Pamela which Colonel Chandler lent to Molly.

24. We cross'd the foresaid Ground with Neighbour Tomlins, Neighbour Hows and my own Oxen and Mare. Yet 'twas somewhat Rainy. Mr. Samuel Forbush of Upton here to be Examin'd. Mrs. McAllister and Mrs. Dowsing here, would have Dismissions from our Church.

25. Thomas and Ebenezer Hoaing and Mowing. They finish'd the Second Hoing. The first good Day for Hay that has come. I visited Lieutenant Tainter[18] and his Family in their Distress for Benjamin, who, as they conclude, is carry'd away Captive by the Indians. Captain Maynard brought old Christian (Squa Widow of George Misco) from Grafton to dwell at his House. Frequently bad news respecting our poor Englishmens Sufferings in the Indian Wars. We hear of another Skirmish at No. 4, and that a Trooper Shot himself with his own Pistol. Lieutenant Hezekiah Ward here at Evening.

26. Thomas and Ebenezer Mowing: a good Hay Day. P.M. Mr. Martyn here. After School Mr. Jenison. At Eve I walk'd to Captain Maynards to See Old Christian.

27. Rain a.m. Considerable Hay lyes expos'd. P.M. held up.

28. No School yesterday or to Day.

29. On 2 Tim. 2, 3, a. and p.m. N.B. Lieutenant Tainter receiv'd a Letter from Aaron Warrin at Fort Pelham informing and Certifying of the onset of the Indians on Hoosuck or Massachusetts Fort, and killing or carrying away Benjamin Tainter. N.B. Captain Thomas Steel, one that has Beating Orders for Canada, at meeting here.

30. Journeyed to Boston. Din'd at Mr. Patersons in Sudbury with Sir Williams. Sir Bass my Company from thence to Roxbury. Lodg'd at Brother Alexanders who marry'd Mrs. Rebecca Jarvis on the 5th Day of this Month.

### JULY [1746]

1. Visited my (only) Sister Willard, who through divine Goodness is better, and talks of going to Westborough with me. Din'd at my Kinsman John Parkman's. At Eve to Cambridge. Mother Champney but weak and feeble. Brother Hicks at work there.

2. At Commencement. Along with the Governor were Admiral Warrin[1] and Sir William Peperell. Every Body rejoic'd at the refreshing News of the Defeat of the Rebels in Scotland, and the Taking the young Pretender Prisoner. P.M. the Joyfull News Confirm'd by another vessell with Duplicates of the Letters lately receiv'd by the Governor respecting a Squadron of English Men of Warr and Troops about to sail from England for Canada Expedition. Thus God mixes Mercy with Judgment, and makes us, tho unworthy, to rejoice one Commencement after another. At Evening again heard something sorrowfull so Checker'd our State. A Lad was drown'd as he went into Water to Day. Brother Samuel Parkman lodg'd with me at Mother Champneys.

3. My Brother rode with me to Boston. Some of us who are Heirs to our deceas'd Mothers Estate were inclin'd to be together to Day to prepare (as we Should be able) for a Settlement. But Brother Alexander was not ready with his account So that it was prevented. Receiv'd one of Mr. Edwards's Books at Mr. Green's[2] for which I pay'd 28 Shillings Old Tenor. Din'd at Brother Parkmans. At Eve my sister Willard and I rode to Cambridge where we lodg'd.

4. My Sister rode Home with me. We Stopp'd at Mrs. Bekky Walkers, at Dr. Robys[3] and at Wards Tavern. Got up somewhat after 2 p.m., they having din'd but little before. N.B. John Hicks junior and Mrs. Molly Whittemore here before us. They went to Sutton. After them came Dr. Breck and Mr. Colton[4] Schoolmaster at Springfield, who at Eve proceeded to Worcester. N.B. Both Companys of Foot together this Afternoon. Lieutenant Hezekiah Ward beats up for Volunteers. Thomas Winchester trains p.m. N.B. Mr. Hastings[5] of Shrewsbury and Mr. Sparhawk[6] of Sutton in Company.

5. [No entry.]

6. On 1 Thess. 5, 19 (repeated) a. and p.m. O that God would add his Special Blessings Especially to my own Soul, that I may never, especially not finally quench the holy Spirit! Mr. Jenison came in at Evening. I was exceedingly tir'd and had a poor night.

7. Lieutenant Hezekiah Ward, surveyor, came at my request to look up the Bounds of the Ministerial Meadow. Warn'd Mr. David Maynard junior, Eliezer Rice and James Maynard of it, and they each of them attended upon it. Heavy rains beat us off when we had Spent but about one Hour. We retir'd to Dinner: and met again p.m. At about ¼ after 3 we finish'd the Lines of the 10 Acres, and with some Conversation upon the 3 Corner'd piece laid on upon the South Line towards the Spring of Water; and the northeast Line taking in Some of what Mr. Maynard has been wont to mow, we parted. A Storm of Thunder, Lightning and Rain arose before Night. N.B. Lieutenant ask'd me 20 shillings for his work. Without Saying much to him he

---

[13] Of Shrewsbury. Ward, *Shrewsbury*, p. 336.
[14] Isaac Stone was at one time selectman of Shrewsbury.
[15] Wife of the Reverend Joseph Noyes of New Haven.
[16] (Harvard 1731). Tutor of Harvard College. Sibley, IX, 67–70.
[17] Benjamin Stevens (Harvard 1740) was later minister of Kittery, Me., 1751–1791. *Sibley*, X, 535–539.
[18] Deacon Simon Tainter.

[1] Pepperrell and Warren had just returned from Louisburg.
[2] Timothy Green, the printer, of Boston published a number of the works of Jonathan Edwards.
[3] Ebenezer Roby, the physician of Sudbury.
[4] Jonathan Colton (Yale 1745) was later the missionary for the Society for the Propagation of the Gospel for Hebron and vicinity. Dexter, *Biographical Sketches*, II, 35–36.
[5] Daniel Hastings.
[6] Joseph Sparhawk.

took up with 14. N.B. Mr. Whittlesey[7] of Wallingford and Mr. Williams (junior)[8] of Longmeadow here whilst I was at the Meadow. Mr. Jenison keeps school again. Molly return'd Pamela volume 1 to Colonel Chandler by Mrs. Lucy Stearns.

8. Thomas etc. Hilling my Corn. A Boy from Mr. Wadsworth of Grafton to buy Cyder of me.

9. Captain Maynard comes for Thomas to go into the Service. Offers to send his own Young man a fortnight in his stead if he will be willing to go then. To which he Consents if he can't get anybody else. Old Mr. Axtel of Grafton dines here. Very Hot.

10. Fast on account of the Expedition to Canada. I consider'd the Business of the Day in these Two Lights—First to humble ourselves under Gods Sore Judgment (viz. the Sword of War) and then his Message to us to Repent etc. Accordingly preach'd on Jonah 3, 5 to 9. Secondly to beseech a great Mercy of God—such wisdom and Direction as was now needed, and success in so great an Enterprise as was now propos'd—but yet it was what we did not deserve, but might rather expect that God would be against us and therefore it concern'd us to look into our Case and endeavour to remove what might be a just Ground of Fear that God would not be with us nor prosper us—and therefore p.m. I preach'd on Ezek. 5, 5 to 9.

11. Rain. Yet Mr. Prentice and Mr. Ebenezer Wadsworth of Grafton came with a Boy to drive their Team and had 6 Barrells of Cyder of me; and Considering how late in the Year, yet it was boil'd and the Barrells were fill'd up (which took another Barrell) they agreed to give me 25 Shillings per Barrell even tho it was not of the Best.

12. [No entry.]

13. Sacrament. Preach'd on Luke 24, 46. P.M. Repeated Sermon on Eph. 5, 32. N.B. Mr. Jenison, Deacon Fay, Mrs. Whipple and her sister Lambson, and Mrs. Holloway din'd here.

14. Considering the Extremity among people on account of the Scarceness of men to Labour I did what I could abroad which yet was but very little for I was soon worry'd. My work was chiefly turning some Hay, and raking up and poling in Barley which lay greatly expos'd to a great storm of Rain which came up suddenly and pour'd down most heavily.

15. Had a poor night after my Labour. Lent my Mare to Mrs. Barns to send to her Father in Law for Help to Hill their Corn. I went to her House and to Neighbour Rogers's. William, John and Jonathan (as well as Neighbour Barns) being out in the Service. Lieutenant Ward din'd here. He brought Molly the second volume of Pamela from Colonel Chandler. Towards Evening my wife and sister to Captain Maynards. My wife bought and paid for 20 lbs. of wool of Mr. Thomas Ward, at 8/6 per pound. I walk'd down there to see Old Christian as well as to wait on them back. N.B. Captain Maynard not in the best Humour.

16. Captain Maynard Came and said why he was ruffl'd yesterday—viz. He had another Warrant (or Order) to press 4 more men—and he believ'd Thomas Winchester must now go. I work'd several Hours a.m. in turning, opening and raking Hay. P.M. Catechetical Exercise. I repeated from Isa. 1, 9.

17. Thomas and Ebenezer went to the Meadow. I walk'd down to Captain Maynards to see what he had done in pressing Men. He told me he had press'd several men but that one of them had paid his money; and therefore he Sees no way but that Thomas must go. So difficult as it was with reference to Cutting my Meadow, I resign'd the Affair—return'd soon, din'd, and Sent Thomas Word to come Home. I hasten'd to Mrs. Joslins[9] where I had appointed to Catechize. She was troubled and disappointed that I did not dine there. Thirteen Children was my whole Company—but I hope they will increase both in Numbers and Qualifications. Visited old Mr. Garfield[10] who had been Sick—and return'd home a little after Sundown. Thomas came home at noon Time, and is gone to Grafton to prepare to go away to the Colonel's tomorrow.

18. Ebenezer and Thomme are gone to the Meadow. A little before noon Thomas Winchester came preparing to sett out upon his Journey. It was very difficult as to my Business to part with him, but so it must be and I desire to committ myself to a Mercifull and faithfull God. It was also Somewhat difficult to part with one that had been of my Family so long and had endear'd himself to us by his good Conduct. The Lord go with him and give him to return to us again in Safety! I went after him to Captain Maynards and Saw him Still again at Mr. Chamberlins.

19. Late in the forenoon came Elijah Warrin and afterwards Mr. Dunlop came and reap'd my Winter Rye, and bound it and got it in to the Barn. Exceeding good Rye for the bigness of the Piece. Blessed be God! The Girls also pull'd the Flax—which was more than ordinary thin. Yet its more that I deserve. Ebenezer brought home one Load of Hay from the Meadow.

20. The Troubles and Interruptions of this week past have been Very many, and prevented my preparing for the Sabbath. I repeated both parts of the Day what I had deliver'd heretofore. A.M. on Zech. 12, 8, 9. P.M. on Gen. 17, 25.

21. Mr. Ebenezer Chamblins Wife here with a present of String Beans. My Sons at the Meadow to Day. I went over to Mr. Whipples who informs me that the Petition of the Select Men pass'd in the Lower House but was not granted in the Upper, which is directly Contrary to the State of Things heretofore: the Board being ready to grant and the House not. As he was going down this Eve I deliver'd him a Paper which I directed to him for his own Reading.

22. My Interruption great by Cattle breaking into my Corn. Ebenezer and Thomme at Meadow. Read four Necessary Cases of Conscience of daily use by Mr. Thomas Shepherd,[11] in a Letter to a Friend of his—with a Discourse of that Friends added—viz. R. H. [blank], which the Lord make Spiritually useful to me! Finish'd the second Volume of Pamela. See some Remarks I would draw up, on this Latter Piece.

23. Look'd very likely for Rain, but there was no more than a Sprinkling. Ebenezer and Thomme to the Meadow. Ebenezer brought home one Load of Hay a.m. Very Hot Season. Deacon Keyes p.m. One of my Oxen very troublesome in breaking in upon the Corn.

24. Ebenezer cutt off his Hair. He and his Brother to the Meadow. P.M. Rain, Thunder and rain till night. At Eve Captain Maynard here.

25. Rain. At length it clear'd off and instead of Ebenezers going to work for Elijah Warrin at his Fathers, I was oblig'd (tho Friday) to go over myself to Mr. Warrins to begg his Patience with regard to our helping him this week for his sons reaping, who was ready to oblige me. Was also at Deacon Newtons as I return'd home.

26. Various Incumbrances and Avocations so that I could Study but little.

27. On Micah 6, 2. P.M. on Luke 19, 9. This latter Sermon, tho I have deliver'd it at several private Houses (Mr. James Fays and Mr. Matthias Rice's) Yet I think I never have in Public till now.

28. [No entry.]

29. I Visited Mr. Tenney who is Settled with us in the room of Mr. Jedidiah How. Proceeded up to Mr. Daniel Warrins to get him to reap—but in Vain. Rode up to Mr. Cushings where was Mr. Stevens (who preaches at Worcester) but Mr. Cushing not at Home. I went to Serjeant Taylors to Speak with Mr. Parker the Shooemaker. At Mr. Robert Keys's to have my Mare Shod. Din'd at Home. At Eve was at Mr. Amsdens to get Reapers.

30. Morn Clouds gather, yet afterwards clear'd off—no reaping—but my Sons at the Meadow. Ebenezer Early to Meadow with the Team—2 Loads of Hay.

31. Morn much as yesterday, no reaper, yet the Day prov'd fit. My Sons to the Meadow. This Day I thought I would even go to the Meadow to see what they did there, and towards night I did so.

[7] Reverend Samuel Whittlesey (Yale 1705), the minister of Wallingford, 1708–1752. Dexter, *Biographical Sketches*, pp. 40–44.

[8] Stephen Williams, Jr. (Yale 1741), later the minister of West Woodstock, 1747–1795. Dexter, *Biographical Sketches*, pp. 695–696.

[9] Mrs. Joseph Joslin.

[10] Benjamin Garfield.

[11] This obscure work of the famous Puritan divine Thomas Shepard (1605–1649), was published under the title *Four Necessary Cases of Conscience of Daily Use* (London, 1661?).

## AUGUST, 1746

1. Isaac Amsden and Jonathan Devereux (the latter Sent by Captain Maynard) reap'd a.m. but the Rain came upon them and beat them off for this Day.

2. Bright good Day. The Rye Cutt yesterday to be turn'd and taken up. Considerable Hay lies in swarth at the Meadow—and wheat to be reap'd So that I have no little Care upon me to interrupt me tho I can do none of the Labour. Cattle and Hoggs often breaking in. How many Times my Soul is oppress'd in this manner!

3. A.M. on Micah 6, 2. P.M. on Ps. 145, 17, and under this Text us'd Collections from Mr. Charnock,[1] made Some years agoe; and in the remainder of the Exercise repeated Several passages from sermon on Gen. 18, 25, page 7 to 12.

4. Sister and I rode to old Mr. Whipples. My wife p.m. to Deacon Newtons to get her Side saddle mended against her journey to New Haven. My Boys mowed in my low Ground at Home. Several Women here while my wife was gone, viz. Mrs. Dowsing, Mrs. How, Mrs. Mercy Chamberlin.

5. P.M. rode over to Mr. Martyn's—the morning being Cloudy—but neither Mr. Martyn nor his wife at Home. Their Daughter said they were gone to Mr. Matthias Rice's—upon which I went there to meet with them but in vain, they were not there. Therefore I return'd home without seeing either of them.

6. Rainy Morning. Thunder at a Distance. P.M. Clear'd up and I went to Deacon Newtons, Serjeant Warrins and Merchant Rice's.

7. Foul weather Still in the Forenoon as it has been every Day for some Time and when breaking away a little, yet showers following the Shines to Spoil our haying. Somewhat Engag'd in my preparations for the Sabbath.

8. The fairest Day that has been a great while. Ebenezer and Thomme rak'd in the low Grounds at Home. I gave them a Short Spell in the Afternoon myself. The sun very hot so that I could not stand it long.

9. Mr. Chamberlin help'd Ebenezer get home a Load of Hay from the Meadow, and Ebenezer him a Load from his. P.M. Abraham Batchellor and Noah How mow'd for me in my Meadow. Ebenezer and Thomme a Load in from the Low Ground at Home. Thunder Storm arose partly over us and the Lightning very terrible, but bore away to North East and East.

10. On Habak. 3, 17, 18, and p.m. Repeated from Ps. 145, 17, latter part of Sermon on Gen. 18, 25, from page 12 to 18. Mr. Jenison din'd here. N.B. Mr. Thaddeus Gale came to me and acquainted me with the wonderfull Mercy and Goodness of God in preserving him when Struck down by the Lightning yesterday. It pass'd under him and plough'd the Ground for more than a Rod, yet was he unhurt.

11. Ebenezer to the Meadow—Thomme at Home. Rode to Mr. Cooks, Captain Warrins, and then visited Mr. Amsdens[2] Family, So marvellously preserv'd last Saturday in Time of most awful Thunder and Lightning. The Effect very noticeable—a Furrow in the Ground of 30 feet—the Boards of their Bee House Shiver'd and plough'd—one Hive Split—Two of the Posts of the Bee House Splitt also—one of them from Top to Bottom etc. May God sanctifie his providence to them! May we all Truly Fear this Great Omnipotent Being and be ever ready for His Will. Mr. Martyn and his Dauter here p.m. N.B. our Conversation about the Ministerial Rights, he told me that he was not willing to make a formal Quit Claim, because he fear'd it would displease his mother and bring upon him the Odium of his Friends in his precinct; but that I might rest Easy for that he Should never Disturb me in the Improvement of them but we spoke especially with regard to the Meadow.

12. A great Frost last Night. My Sons to the Meadow. They Spent part of the Day in Clearing a Cart way for the Hay in the upper end of the Meadow.

13. Ebenezer to the Meadow a.m.—mow'd p.m. Some Swamp Grass, had of Mr. Eliezer Rice, and Edwards Whipple was so good as to mow with him gratis. And at Eve he brought home the Eighth Load out of the Meadow, but came home, to my grief much too late. Thomme helped Thomas Rogers p.m.

14. Thanksgiving on account of the Suppression of the Rebellion in Scotland. May God prepare our Hearts! Honourable Colonel Chandler coming from Boston and bound for Worcester came in the morning—was at meeting with us and din'd with me. I preach'd on Ps. 132, 16. May God accept our Offering! and bless His Holy Word to His People! N.B. Having Sung 100th Psalm Tune and Com't Tune, and not willing to Sing either of them again, I propos'd and Set 100 New, or Anthem. Colonel towards Eve went to Worcester. News of the King of Spains Death.

15. Cloudy a.m.—but not raining to hinder, Ebenezer to the Meadow. More sorrowfull News from No. 4 that besides 2 men Shot by the Indians, one at No. 4 another at Northfield our Troopers Horses most of them kill'd. Mrs. Caruth and her son here and din'd with us: Mrs. Hayward[3] and Mrs. Billings,[4] all of them want their Dismissions from our Church. Towards Evening with Joy (viz. Mr. Ebenezer Phillips of Southborough) I saw a Number of our Westborough Troopers return from No. 4—but on foot, their Horses being of them that were lost in the late Encounter. They handed me a paper containing an Account of Several Particulars—which I Soon copy'd—and afterwards Sent Mr. Kneeland.[5]

16. Ebenezer and Thomme again to the Meadow, and brought home a Load of Swamp Hay which I have of Mr. Eliezer Rice.

17. On Consideration of the Singular Mercy and Goodness of God to Such a Number of my nearest Neibours, in Sparing them in the late Engagement against the Indians at No. 4, and not having been able seasonably to finish my propos'd preparations I repeat'd a. and p.m. Sermon on Ps. 68, 20. The widow Woods din'd with us. N.B. Neighbour How and his son Daniel Sick of Fever and Flux.

18. Mr. Dowsing here in the Morning. The Boys to the Meadow. I rode there myself but they rak'd up but little of the Hay before the Rain prevail'd, and they return'd. Was at Mr. James Maynards and at old Mr. Whipples in the Rain.

19. A very rainy Time. Yet Mr. Cushing and Morse being come I rode to the Meeting of the Ministers at Southborough. But there were no more than Two come Besides—Messers Barrett and Smith. N.B. I intimated that we had been too Partial in the late Times; particularly against Mr. Whitefield—this Somewhat rais'd Mr. Barrett and Mr. Smith. This produc'd a Challenge to me to show if I were able any one Instance—with Impatience they heard me read an Extract from Bishop Halls Meditations and Vows,[6] wherein he calls an Evil Man half a Beast and half a Devil, page 35 Folio Edition. N.B. Mr. Morse ask'd advice touching their Ministerial Lands—viz. what was his Duty now that his precinct had seiz'd upon them and sold them. I ask'd their Advice also, respecting the Dismission of our North-precinct sisters who had been delinquent, and some of them frequently absent from the Communion but not Sent their requests to have their Relation transferr'd to the Second Church. N.B. Mr. Smith Concio from John 8, 12.

20. Mr. Loring came. Mr. Morse preach'd on Ps. 144, 15. N.B. Mr. Loring has lately been at Worcester and convers'd freely with New-Light People and he is wondrous Charitable respecting them, and in his Trial fears that under the Notion of New-Light all true Religion is in Danger of being exploded—An Enigma of the Devil! says he.

21. Mr. Martyn din'd with me and preach'd my Lecture on Ps. 63, 8—an Excellent Discourse! I pray God to bless it to me and all that heard it. I stopp'd the Church after Lecture and obtain'd a Vote for the Dismission of 12 North-side sisters.

---

[1] Stephen Charnock (1628-1680) was a famous English non-conformist minister, whose writings were published posthumously. [Edward Veal and Richard Adams, editors], *The Works of the Late Learned Divine Stephen Charnock* (London, 1683-1684).

[2] Isaac Amsden of Westborough.

[3] Mrs. Simon Hayward.

[4] Mrs. Thomas Billings.

[5] Samuel Kneeland, the printer at Boston, and publisher with Timothy Green, Jr., of *The Boston Gazette or Weekly Journal.*

[6] Joseph Hall, successively Bishop of Exeter and Norwich wrote *Mediation and Vowes, Divine and Morall* (London, 1609). It appeared also as *Newly Enlarged with 10 Vows and Meditations* (London, 1609). Still another enlarged edition was published in 1621.

N.B. Mr. Wheeler, Daniel Hardy and David Maynard junior were against it and some others did not Vote for it.

22. Visited Mr. Cooks and Barns's Familys, and William Rogers who are ill of Fever and Flux.

23. Ebenezer brot home about 7 Cocks of Hay from the Meadow, which was all that was worth bringing since the Storm —the Rest lying out in swarth—and 'tis grown too late to cut any of the North-side of the Brook, the Grass is so dead. So that we now finish at the Meadow for this Year.

24. Sacrament. I preach'd a.m. on Luke 24, 46. P.M. on Habac. 3, 17, 18. Mr. Benjamin Rugg of Northfield din'd with us. Captain Fay absent from Dinner. P.M. Mrs. Whitney cry'd out in the middst of the sermon. I pray'd her to be as compos'd as possible; and she was not long a Disturbance. At the Evening I was at the Funeral of a Child of Mr. Cook (his Lydia) which dy'd of the Fever and Flux. This Distemper begins to Spread among us; one of Mr. Barns's Children also is Dead. The Lord prepare His People for His holy Will!

25. My wife and son Ebenezer undertake their Journey to New-Haven. Ebenezer setts out presently after Dinner to get some Things in order at Mr. Parkers in Shrewsbury, but my wife tarrys a while, till I go to the Burial of Mr. Barns's Child which is one of his Twins:—and behold the other Twin is also deceas'd, and they bury both in one Coffin! Mrs. Barns is also ill and another Child. Mr. Cook and Several of his Children are sick. Some other Familys are visited. May God be mercifull to us in a Day of Such Distress! As to my wife, she set out after 3 o'Clock and propos'd to lodge at Worcester tonight; Dr. Breck and his Wife to be Company as far as Mr. Devotions in Windham. May they have a prosperous Journey by the will of God! N.B. Abraham Batchellor help [sic] Thomme get up a Load of Hay from the Swamp, which was the Finishing Load.

26. Catechetical Exercise. I deliver'd the latter part of the sermon on Isa. 1, 9. Am greatly concern'd for my poor Neibours who are sorely afflicted. Another of Mr. Cooks Children dyes— his little Sarah of about [blank] years.

27. Went to the Funeral of Mr. Cooks little Daughter; and such was the will of God his little son Solomon is dead also! Deacon Newton and some others seem desirous to have 'em both bury'd to Day, tho the latter dy'd but this morning. It was, however, deferr'd till tomorrow when they Saw that I was not free to Countenance it. It might soon have caus'd evil Report of Mr. Cook that he Should so soon hurry his Children into the Grave, as if having many of them and being an odd man he was afraid they should come to life again. I visited Mr. Barns's, as I have been also at Neighbour Rogers's, where there are Two Children sick; and Neighbour Hows, where most of them are out of Case: but especially their grandson Jonathan. N.B. Last night there was a Third Frost, and in Some places more destructive than the preceding. N.B. Deacon Moore[7] of Worcester din'd with me. He had been to Mr. Stone to see whether he could not administer the Lords Supper to them but he is design'd for Harwich.

28. A Rainy Day, yet in the Rain I went on Foot to Mr. Cooks little Solomon's Funeral: having Catechiz'd the Boys at Meeting House a.m. No Girls p.m. it was So Wet and stormy. Captain Warrins Young Child (I hear) very bad.

29. A very Wet stormy Day again. This Day was appoint'd for a Fast at the Widow Rice's at Hopkinton on account of her youngest son, Samuel Whood, who has a grievous sore in the lower part of his Back, has lain long and is thought to be consuming away. Mr. Barrett has sent also to Mr. Stone to assist him with me. I walk'd to Mr. Williams's afternoon. He had offer'd me his Horse to go to the Fast. I rode over. Mr. Stone in his last prayer of the former Exercise. Mr. Barrett was not return'd from Boston. I carry'd on the Latter Exercise: preach'd on Isa. 38, 2, 3. The poor young man very grievously afflicted, and in a Dangerous Condition. The Lord accept our Offering! I return'd at Eve to my Family.

30. At the Funeral of Captain Warrins youngest Child. My Dauter Molly ill and full of pain. Ever since Wednesday Night.

[7] Nathaniel Moore, an early settler, was often elected selectman.

She seems to have the Same Distemper with my Neighbours. N.B. I was at Neighbour Ebenezer Maynards in the morning and pray'd with his wife who is Sick also. Neighbour Rogers's Betty dy'd last night.

31. Could not prepare my Discourse design'd for to day, by means of my many Hindrances all the Week long. Preach'd on Rev. 6, 8 a.m. without any material Alteration except a few Passages omitted, respecting the Distemper. P.M. On Eph. 5, 6. A great deal of the Beginning without more writing than a few broken Hints; the body of the sermon was from Page 19 to 28 of sermon on Eph. 2, 3, latter part. O that God might sett home on the Hearts of all, especially on Children those fervence Exercises! Mr. Jenison din'd with me. At noon the Church was Stopp'd to lay before them the Consideration of a Day of Fasting and Prayer in this gloomy Time. They freely and readily came into it and seem'd glad of it. A Vote pass'd and Thursday next (by Divine Leave) appointed herefor. After sermon p.m. I recommended the Same to the Congregation and published the Church's Vote and Purpose. And O that God would please to prepare all our Hearts thereunto! At Eve I attended upon the Funeral of Neighbour John Rogers's Daughter Betty. Rainy Evening. N.B. Ebenezer Maynard went to Dr. Gott for his wife and brought physick for Molly which she took.

### SEPTEMBER, 1746

1. Wrote a Letter at the fervent Desire of his Wife to Mr. John Rogers (now a soldier at or near Winchester) to inform of the Distress of his Family and the Death of his Child Betty, and the sickness of little Persis. I wrote also a Number of Letters to Neighbouring Ministers to desire their Assistance at the propos'd Fast. Lieutenant Tainter here. Kill'd my old Ram. Molly took another part of her purge, and I hope she is better. *Deo Soli Laus!* A long Time of Foul Weather. Tis not a little dull without my Dear Consort—but how is it with them who part for 5 nay 10 Times so long? How lonely soever I am, yet how happy is She in the Embraces of her dear Pierpoint? She has so many articles to reveal and to hear that She can have little Leisure to think of what She has left behind. But how Ardent and United were we this Day Nine Year ago! when our Nuptials were Celebrated at Mr. Pierpoints at Boston. The Lord has pleas'd to overlook the many miscarriages and Defects which we have been chargeable with since, especially my own! and make us Mutually Blessings, and Helps to the Kin of God! O how soon the Time will come when there will be neither marrying nor giving in Marriage, but the Saints shall be as the Angels of God!

2. Very Rainy the greatest part of the Day. Clear'd off late p.m. Mr. Daniel Maynard of Marlborough informs me that Captain Moses Rice is gone down the Road from Boston, a post from Deerfield to inform that Hoosuck (or Massachusetts Fort) was lately Burnt and Destroyed by the Indians.

3. Visited Mr. Hows[1] Family again, they being all ill. Their son Benjamin also is taken. Was at the Funeral of anther of Mr. Barns's Children and visited Mr. Cooks Family. There heard of Madam Shirley's[2] Death, a great Loss to our Province because of her influence with the Duke of New Castle.

4. This Day was observ'd by us in this Parish as a Time of Solemn Humilliation Fasting and Prayer on account of the great Mortality among us. I Sent to all the Neighbouring Ministers, but Mr. Barrett and Mr. Stone only came. Mr. Martyn had appointed a Lecture on this Very Day, and had engag'd Mr. Cushing to preach it. A.M. I pray'd and Mr. Stone preach'd on Heb. 3, 7, 8. P.M. Mr. Barrett both pray'd and preach'd: his Text, Ps. 37, 2. A Considerable assembly. Some Number of Strangers. O that God would accept our Offering and answer our fervent Supplications—that He would pardon our Defects and grant an abiding Effect of his Word upon us! May our Souls be heal'd, the Hand of God sanctify'd and when it Shall be best, the Affliction remov'd! May this Day be Some Suitable Preparatory for the Special Work before me tomorrow also—the Lord give Me wisdom and Instruction!

[1] Parkman's neighbor and old friend, Hezekiah How.
[2] Frances Barker Shirley, wife of Governor William Shirley of Mass.

5. Vide Natalitia. P.M. I visited both Familys of Hows, widow Tomlins[3] Grand Daughter (Mercy Wait) who is sick, and Mr. John Chamberlins son John in a Dangerous Condition.

6. Captain Winchesters Troop return from No. 4. Nathan Maynard help'd with the Women and Children. Thomme mended up the Partition Fence against the North lower orchard.

7. On Ps. 90, 5, 7. May God give an Effectual Blessing to these Exercises that both old and young may receive Saving Good and Benefit thereby.

8. Visited divers Sick. Neighbour Tomlin[4] came and desir'd me to go to Mr. Chamberlins to See his little son who was near his End, they fear'd. I went, but he had gasp'd. I minister'd to them as I was able, in Exhorting etc. Pray'd with them and proceeded in my Visit to Meeting with Messers Howe. At Eve Eli Forbush borrow'd Tully's Orations—and having heard that Mr. Barns has lost their Fourth and last Child, I improv'd Eli to go to Mr. Barns and acquaint them that Mr. Chamberlin had fix'd the Time for his Son's Funeral to be (God Willing) tomorrow at 2 o'Clock; and that therefore they must avoid appointing their Child's to be at the Same Time.

9. I expected word from Mr. Barns's but none came. I attended the Funeral at Mr. Chamberlins. N.B. Dr. Smith there, their Dauter Betty being ill. He brought Ebenezers Hatt from Mr. Cushings.[5] N.B. Mr. Winchester a Letter from Joshua Winchester a Soldier at Deerfield, who informs that Thomas is not well—is posted at Pelham Fort. The Lord graciously preserve him and defend him!

10. At Eve I visited Mr. Barns and his wife, whose House lately a place of great Joy and Life, is now become a solitude and a Desert. Mr. Jenison pray'd at their Child's Funeral yesterday.

11. Captain Maynard here to inform me from Dr. Breck that his Sister and my son were well last Friday was Sennight at Hartford: and he tells me he Saw a Copy of a Letter Sign'd by Mr. John Norton[6] late preacher at Hoosuck Fort which informs that the French and Indians besieg'd their fort, slew Thomas Knowlton and captivated all the rest. Read the account of Canada in six Chapters with an appendix lately published. Thomme by the help of Nathan Maynard made Cyder. One of my Oxen still very mischievous.

12. Neighbour Edwards Whipple helped Thomme bring Home Two Barrells of Cyder. Mornings have been foggy and some Days of late misty—but yesterday and to Day pleasant sunshine. Hear of Several Deaths in our North Precinct, viz. Mr. Jacob Rice[7] has bury'd one—and now Mr. Matthias Rice's little Foster son which they Set their Hearts much upon. Receiv'd (per Hand of Mr. Ebenezer Johnson of Southborough) a Letter from my Wife, when She was at [illegible], brought by Dr. Brown.

13. Wrote a Letter to my Wife but had no Opportunity to Send it. My sister is so indispos'd that She is afraid She is going to have a Distemper.

14. On Habac. 3, 17, 18 and p.m. repeated sermon on Mat. 10, 29, 30. Mr. Jenison and Mr. Dunlop din'd here. N.B. A Letter from my Wife (per Hand of Mr. Daniel Forbush[8]) Dated at New Haven. Most truely welcome. I grow not a little uneasy at their Absence. God be pleas'd to protect both her and my son and return them in Safety! Dull weather now and then Showers.

15. Mr. Tainter here to see my Sister and invited my Sister to Spend a few Days at their House. Mrs. Fay (Captain's Wife) here, with a large Present viz. a Cheese, 3 pounds Butter and Two Considerable pieces of Salt Pork. Visited Neighbour Chamberlin's Daughter Betty. Had Mr. Tomlins Mare to go

to Mr. Eleazer Bellows to see his Dauter Forbush[9] in her great Trouble by her Husbands Captivity and sickness of her Child.

16. Disappointed of Lieutenant Forbush's Horse by his being chose Jury man yesterday, I was at some Trouble to get another, to go up the Road and meet my wife. Mr. Barns lent me his. But Lieutenant Tainter came over with his Chaise to convey my sister to his House and I was oblig'd to accompany them and dine there. After dinner I rode up to Shrewsbury designing to go to Dr. Brecks, with expectation of meeting my wife there; but she had come to Worcester last night (from Springfield) and was now so forward as almost to Captain Hows[10] in Shrewsbury. I met them with much pleasure and satisfaction, for they had had the Favour of Health and success through their whole Journey. Blessed be God! At Mr. Bezaleel Eagers earnest Entreaty we turn'd in there to see his sick Children. One of them was near her End. I pray'd with them and commended them to the Divine Mercy.

17. A very Rainy Day all Day. Reckon'd with Nathan Maynard for his Mare which my wife had in her Journey and paid him 40 shillings old Tenor.

18. Fast at Mr. Jacob Gibbs's in Hopkinton: after visiting Several sick Familys (Mr. Chamberlins, Captain Maynards, Mr. Pratts and Mr. Jonah Warrins) I rode over to those Exercises. Mrs. Gibbs lyes in a miserable Condition by a Cancer in her Breast. Mr. Barrett began with Prayer. Mr. Prentice[11] of Holliston preach'd on Mark 7, 37. He hath done all Things Well. P.M. I pray'd and preach'd on Phil. 1, 21. And O that God would pardon our Defects and accept our Offerrings through Jesus Christ and have Mercy upon his Handmaid for his Name's Sake. As I return'd I found that one of Mr. Warrins Children[12] was dead; and the other which was sick, growing worse. The Lord Sanctifie his holy Hand to my afflicted Neighbours and to all of us, for our great awakening; and prepare us for his holy Will!

19. Took up our old Hive of Bees which was pritty well Honey'd.

20. [No entry.]

21. I preach'd on Heb. 12, 24, and on Acts 9, 6. Mr. Jenison din'd with us. O that God would make his holy word Effectual for our Saving Good. Mr. Chamberlin has lost his other son.

22. I understand that the Sickness is so sore and grievous on t'other side of the Town that three lie dead in one House (Timothy Fay's) and his Brother Silas has lost another. Mr. Martyn here to desire me to attend a Fast in their Precinct next Thursday. At Mr. Chamberlin's sons funeral. N.B. There are 5 Funerals this Day in Town. God be Mercifull to us miserable Sinners and prepare us for what is yet to be laid upon us! Mr. Whipple here at Evening. We talk'd of the Brest Squadron —and I Said to him, No Doubt but One Month will bring about great overturnings. N.B. Lieutenant Thomas Forbush here, and angry that his son Samuel of Upton and his wife could not be admitted to the privilege of Baptism for their Child. Rakes up old Things in his Fathers Days, to my Sorrow, and will have it that I have pick'd his son out etc., whereas I have endeavour'd to do nothing by Partiality. But the Lord Sanctifie this Trouble to me!

23. Mr. Benjamin Eager, Colonel Nahum Wards Messenger, comes Express amongst us and tells me that a French Fleet were yesterday within half a Days Sail of the Light House, and a Post came to the Colonel for 500 Men out of this Regiment— and I hear that 36 are requir'd out of this Company. We were going to plough with Lieutenant Forbush's Cattle but I sent them back again: and Ebenezer to Sutton. Bekky[13] borrow'd an Horse and went to Sutton also. It is a Day of great Trouble and Distress in all likelihood at Boston; and God only knows how Soon it may be among our Selves. May we all be suitably Prepar'd for the Divine Will in all Things! P.M. Catechetical

[3] The widow of Deacon Isaac Tomlin.

[4] Isaac Tomlin, Jr.

[5] Reverend Job Cushing of Shrewsbury.

[6] Reverend John Norton (Yale 1737) was serving as chaplain to the soldiers in various forts in western Massachusetts. At Fort Massachusetts, within the present township of Adams, Norton was taken captive, Aug. 20, 1746. He later published the narrative of his captivity and release. John Norton, *The Redeemed Captive* (Boston, 1748). See Dexter, *Biographical Sketches*, pp. 587-588.

[7] Eunice Rice died Sept. 5, 1746.

[8] Son of Deacon Jonathan Forbush.

[9] Sarah Bellows had married Phinehas Forbush.

[10] Daniel Howe. See Ward, *Shrewsbury*, p. 312.

[11] Reverend Joshua Prentice.

[12] Elisha, the son of Jonah Warrin died Sept. 18, 1746.

[13] Rebecca Hicks, Mr. Parkman's niece.

Exercise, but 13 present. I read to 'em sermon on Hos. 4, 12. At Eve I was very faint, and my feverishness greatly increas'd —but I bestir'd myself what I could. Took up an Hive of Bees. Was as chearfull as I could in Conversation. Lieutenant Aaron Forbush from Brookfield, Neighbor Ebenezer Maynard, here. But my illness increas'd. I had no stomach, nor much rest all night—but beg Grace to enable me to repose my Self in God.

24. Not So ill to Day as I fear'd from So bad a Night. Blessed be God! Our Forces mov'd down to Wards at Marlborough. Wrote to my Brethren by Mr. James Maynard. I walk'd over to the South Road—visited Ensign Newton and others in the Neighbourhood. N.B. Mr. Prentice rides with Captain Willard before Grafton Company, going to Boston. Towards Evening Reverend Gay of Suffield and his Wife, and Mr. Caleb Hitchcock at the Gate, but would not tarry with me. Ebenezer return'd from Sutton.

25. Sent Ebenezer to Boston. Fast in the North Precinct. But before I went over I visited little Joel Maynard (son of Ebenezer) and pray'd with him being dangerously sick. At the Fast Mr. Martyn pray'd and Mr. Cushing preach'd on Isa. 26, 9. P.M. Mr. Morse[14] pray'd and I preach'd on Rev. 6, 8. O that God would hear in Heaven his dwelling place, and when he hears forgive, Pity, and appear for his people not only on account of the Sickness but the fear'd Invasion! N.B. Sister Willard rode with me, and my Daughter rode with Mrs. Tomlin (widow) over to the Fast. At Eve Mr. Daniel Forbush here. Wrote by him to Brother Samuel Parkman to Secure Sister Willards Interest among them. Some Soldiers return from Boston.

26. Daily in Concern for our Friends at Boston. Half the Companys of Some Regiments dismiss'd return home.

27. Little Joel Maynard ill and I visited him. At Eve Mr. Whipple came for me to go and see Mrs. Persis Rice (wife of Eliezer) who is ill of the Same Distemper (Fever and Flux) which is so Common among Children. At Eve also our Son Ebenezer return'd from Boston. Our Friends all well except sister Betty who is remov'd to Reading. The Town is very kind to the Soldiers. Several Small Vessells are sent out to see what Fleet it is that lies off, but they are not yet come back, So that they are wholly uncertain Still.

28. In the Morning I rode over to Mr. Martyns, and he rode hither. I preach'd to the Second Precinct a.m. on Ezek. 5, 5 to 9. P.M. on Rom. 6, 13. N.B. Several Soldiers travelling back from Boston, being dismiss'd for the present and sundry of Westborough men viz. Billings, Jacob Rice, Paul Newton, Mr. Ephraim Allen likewise. The 3 former at Meeting. Mr. Martyn on Mat. 10, 28 and on Eccl. 7, 1 latter Clause. Each return'd at Eve to our respective Familys.

29. Visited Mrs. Rice and Joel Maynard who 'tis thought is dying. N.B. I had sent a Letter to Mr. Samuel Forbush of Upton that he might go otherwhere for Special Privileges since his Father was not well Satisfy'd with my Methods here; This brought him here to Day; but I Still Decline encouraging his coming here till there is some better Satisfaction. Mr. Whitney here and informs that Some Vessel is come in to Boston which certify that it is a French Fleet that was discover'd and that they are turn'd in to an Indian place not far from Annapolis. Mr. Martyn here P.M. Towards Eve I was at Neighbour Eliezer Rice's who brot up the News—he Confirms it, and that the people of Boston are very courteous to soldiers.

30. At Joel Maynards funeral. N.B. Sister Breck[15] from Worcester, here with Mr. Golding. My wife rode with sister Breck to Marlborough.

## OCTOBER, 1746

1. Sent for to Mrs. Rice who grows very bad. N.B. her, and her Husbands Mutual Forgiveness. N.B. her declaring how Easy and comfortable is her View of Departing till I put Some Close Questions about her Faith, Love to God etc. Upon which she seem'd to be much damp'd and Confus'd: Yet maintain'd a strong

Hope. Rain; yet Mr. Cushing came and preach'd my Lecture on John 3, 16. Wife and Sister Breck return'd from Marlborough in the Rain and did not go to Meeting. Sister Breck tarry'd all night.

2. Rainy. After Dinner (it holding up) Sister Breck setts out for Worcester, and Ebenezer waits on her as far as Mr. Cushings. Young Solomon Prentice here with a Team to bring the Barrells which they borrow'd of me. Stormy Night.

3. Bright Morning: but the Day prov'd very Windy. Solomon Prentice went home with his Team. P.M. Mr. Abner Newton here and acquaints me that his Sister Rice is yet alive, tho as they apprehend, is dying, and desires Me to visit her once More. I went—on my way saw several of our Soldiers return'd, who Say that all Colonel Chandlers and Colonel Wards Regiments are dismiss'd. As to Mrs. Rice I found her in the Valley of the Shadow of Death, and as she said freely, ready and willing to Depart. She gave her Testimony to the usefulness and Expediency of our attending upon Divine Ordinances. Said that God had graciously manifested his Mercy to her since she came to that Bed. I mix'd some Caution with my Consolation notwithstanding. But she fully expected Soon to be remov'd to Glory. After Prayer I gave Exhortation to all present—and particularly to the Children. Return'd sometime before sundown.

4. Sent Lieutenant Thomas Forbush a Letter respecting his unseasonable Disquietments with me with Reference to his son Samuel of Upton.

5. Sacrament. Preach'd on Rom. 8, 31, a. and p.m. Deacon Fay and Mrs. Joslyn din'd here. I hope this Day was not in vain. Mrs. Rice is yet alive. N.B. Mr. James Fay and his wife from Grafton here at Communion.

6. Mr. Nathaniel Trask[1] who has preach'd at North Sutton din'd here. P.M. Asa Brigham and his wife here. Mrs. Rice was thought to be dying about Noon, but Reviv'd.

7. Warm Day. I visited a.m. Mrs. Rice who is Somewhat better. Two of their Children taken sick. Their little Thimmè very ill: but is at his Uncle Seth's. I rode to Mr. Whipples, Mr. James Maynards, Mr. Seth Rice's, but he was not at home, his wife in great Trouble because of her Husbands Distractions: was at Ensign Rice's—neither was he at home. I proceeded to Mr. Bellows whose wife was ill, and their Daughter Sarah Forbush's Child. Visited also Mrs. Fay, Messers Green, Edwards Whipple whose Child is ill—and then hasten'd over to the southside. Din'd at Mr. Jonas Childs (from its Convenience to the School House) attended the Catechizing of above 50 (if I mistake not 55) Children of that part of the Town. Was at Mr. Daniel Forbush's at Catechizing. N.B. Mr. Millers Company part of the way Home, for I turn'd away to Deacon Newtons.

8. The Weather much alter'd—a Cold Air like Winter. Was at Mr. Hows, Tomlins, Chamberlins and Captain Maynards a.m. At old Mr. Maynards p.m. Neighbour David and his Sister Hannah went to Boston at Eve by whom I sent to Mr. Greens for Mr. Edwards's Books on Religious Affections which I so long ago subscrib'd for. Mr. Samuel Williams here at Evening. My Sons have pick'd up our Apples, gather'd the Beans, and this afternoon some of the Corn.

9. Rain. Hear that Mrs. Persis Rice[2] is Dead.

10. I was not well in the Early Morning So great Pains in my Bowels and working that I fear'd whether I should go out to Day; but I grew better, and tho it was a Cold, Raw, Rainy Day, yet (it holding up at the Time of my going and being abroad) I went to Mrs. Rice's Funeral, and visited Mrs. Edwards Whipples Child. N.B. Christian, the Widow of Old George Misco, Indian, expir'd. Deacon Whittemore of Cambridge at Eve, and lodg'd here.

11. Very Cold. It snow'd a Little yesterday, but last Night so as to cover the Roofs.

12. I with my wife went to the Funeral of old Christian. She was bury'd in a very decent manner by Captain Maynard, from his house. Samuel Brigham Esquire, Edward Baker Esquire, Captain Timothy Brigham, Messers Jotham and Charles Brigham and many others (besides a Number of Indians) attended. She

[14] Reverend Ebenezer Morse of Boylston.
[15] Mrs. Samuel Breck, Parkman's sister-in-law.

[1] (Harvard, 1742). The first minister of Brentwood, N. H., 1748-1789. Sibley, XI, 172-173.
[2] Wife of Elizer or Eleazer Rice.

was carry'd to our South Burying Place. At Eve Mr. Edward Bass, Schoolmaster at Lancaster came to see us, my wife being a Relation. Bekky Hicks watch'd with Neighbour Edwards Whipples little Dauter which dy'd in the Night. Not being able by means of many Interruptions to finish my Preparations without much Difficulty, and hurrying what I wanted to take Some Time about, I threw them aside for the present and preach'd again my sermon on Job 22, 21, a. and p.m. N.B. No Proclamation till I was going into the Pulpit P.M.

13. Mr. Bass, who had kept Sabbath with us, return'd to Lancaster, a Sober modest young gentleman, and I perceive is something observably Skill'd in the Hebrew. May God be pleas'd to make him a great Blessing in his Generation! P.M. was at the Funeral of Mr. Edwards Whipples Dauter. Visited his Brother Francis' Dauter Abigail who is taken sick. We have observ'd that the Child bury'd to Day is the 24th that has died in Town since August 23, when Mr. Cook's first (which dy'd) expir'd. Our Children Billy and Suse are somewhat indispos'd with Flux, but (thro Divine Goodness) run about yet. Ebenezer made Cyder at Mr. Hows.[3] At Eve had a Quarter of Beef from Mr. Jonah Warrin. Stormy and some snow.

14. Snow'd and Rain'd last Night, but this morning rains hard.

15. Mr. David Batherick's Child bury'd. I attended upon it with my sister Willard. [This is the 25th since August 23.] In our way we call'd at Mr. Jonas Childs, and at Deacon Newtons. At Eve came Mr. Bacon[4] of Ashuelot.

16. Publick Fast on Occasion of the Distresses the Province is under by the War, and especially the Great French Squadron appearing in North America; the Hopes also we are in of an English Fleet for Help. Mr. Bacon preach'd all Day. A.M. on Ps. 50, 15. P.M. on Zech, 7, 5. O that God would hear in Heaven and answer and defer not for His own names sake!

17. Mr. Bacon left us for Wrentham. P.M. Visited Abigail Whipple and Hepzibah Rice. Ebenezer got home our Cyder, 7 Barells, from Mr. Hows Mill. N.B. We have made in all this Year something more than Nine Barrells. More than ordinary Cold and Raw Weather—very uncomfortable for people that labour abroad. My son gather'd some of the Corn.

18. The Earth covered with Snow—a Stormy Day. Thomme Carry'd Barrells and Chairs to Mr. Whitneys—and brought Turnips from Mr. Pratts. N.B. Billey has a Bloody Flux, but helps about House.

19. On Rom. 8, 31 a. and p.m. the Entertainments I design'd for the late Fast Day. May God accompany them with his Blessing! The Snow goes off. Billy about yet.

20. The Snow has wholly disappear'd. A Very pleasant warm Day. My sons Carted Stones in the fore part of the Day, and then gathered Corn. Mr. Goss of Bolton, and with him one Mr. Carter and a Lad here, journeying to Narragansett. Mr. Jonathan Burnap din'd here. Mr. Stone p.m. going to ministers meeting at Rutland.

21. Held a Catechetical Exercise on the Benefits of those that are Effectually Call'd, repeating in sermon on Eph. 3, 8 from Page 17 to 24.

22. Ebenezer and Thomme cart Stones from the Settle Field; p.m. Ebenezer Carted home 6 Barrells of Cyder from Mr. Whitneys, 5 of which I have of him and one (Gratis) from Mr. Jonas Child. I visited Abigail Whipple who is very ill of the Common Distemper. My little Billy is ill also of the Same, yet runs about.

23. Ebenezer fetch'd 4½ Bushel Turnips from Mr. Hezekiah Pratts which with 1½ receiv'd already was my 6 propos'd Stock of him (at 3/6 per Bushel) but he afterwards sent Me a Bag more which were his present to Me. P.M. my Sons gather'd the rest of the Corn. I rode to Shrewsbury upon Several Small Affairs, but perceiv'd that people were gone to Lecture (which I had heard nothing of) whereupon I Snatch'd the Opportunity and went also. Mr. Martyn preach'd on John 8, 23. Those words—Ye are of this World. N.B. His Wife with him. We return'd to the parting of our Roads together. N.B. I was with Colonel Ward and Requested his Chair to wait on my sister Willard to Boston; who Consented to it without Difficulty.

[3] Neighbor Hezekiah How.
[4] Reverend Jacob Bacon of Keene, N. H.

24. Wondrous pleasant weather from Day to Day. As I last night had Some Discourse with Deacon Newton and Mr. Elisha Ward about my Circumstances with relation to the Town and this Precinct, so I had to Day with Captain Warrin. But I find no likelihood of a precinct meeting presently—unless I am my Self more Strenuous. N.B. Mr. Tinney was a work here in the Morning, mending the roof of my House.

25. Still admirable Weather. My Sons harrow'd my Settle Field. Also We Cover'd up about 3 Bushel of Turnips and about a Dozen and half of Cabbages in a Vault prepar'd for that Purpose.

26. On Tit. 2, 12, those words, "So live soberly", and repeat'd on p.m. the last part of sermon on Job 22, 21. At Eve came Mr. Grindal Rawson[5] a School Master and preacher at Worcester, who had preach'd at Southborough the preceding Day, and he lodg'd here.

27. Mr. Rawson went to Worcester. P.M. I visited old Ensign Newton and Mr. Abner Newtons Family, who are Sick of the Bloody Flux. The Ensign and a little Boy of 4 or 5 years very bad. I rode to Mr. Samuel Fays and to Mr. Grouts and Whitneys.

28. What Patience and Longsuffering of God are we call'd to Celebrate and magnifie Since we have been indulg'd now Two and Twenty Years in Church State and Relation. The Lords Name be prais'd with my whole Soul, and by all his people of this place! But may we be truely humbl'd for our Shamefull unprofitableness! And O that we might obtain the Quickening Grace of God that we may become More fruitfull and faithfull under our Sacred Bonds and Obligations and unspeakable Advantages! I endeavour'd to take some Notice of the Day—but alas with much Brokenness and Interruptions. Towards Eve Mr. Millen[6] of Chauxit here. My Wife rode to Mr. Grouts. Ebenezer to Colonel Wards of Shrewsbury for his Chair. I walk'd at Eve to see Ensign Newton again, who seem'd a little reviv'd and Easy—was in at Deacon Newtons. May God fitt us all for sickness and Death!

29. Rode to Cambridge with sister Willard[7] in Colonel Nahum Wards Chair. My Dauter Molly also on Mr. Tinneys Horse.

30. Rode to Boston in the Morning. Sister Betty very ill. She was brought home from Lieutenant Williams's (of Lynn End) last Saturday. Was much griev'd as were all her Friends to see her so much concern'd about her Daughter Eliza's having her design'd Share of the Estate; and was in agony to have Elias to take his Pen and Ink and Sett down what Eliza should have. I din'd at Mrs. Keggells, and rode with her over to her Brother Bass's at Dorchester. Return'd at Eve. Horse kept at Procters. Visited sister Betty, who had been yet more uneasy in the afternoon before a multitude of people in her Chamber, about her son Elias—but was now calmer. I made opportunity to talk freely with her alone. She took it thankfully. Mr. Joseph White (her uncle) came to see her also and he talk'd in a savoury Manner. I Lodg'd with my Kinsman. Sent Mr. Tinneys Horse home with Mr. Phinehas Hardy.

31. Took my Final Leave of Sister Betty—being convinc'd that I should never see her again, for the Season of the Year obliges me to return home, and we know not but she may lye so several Days. Din'd at Brother Alexanders—and having dispatch'd my Business rode with Molly in the Same Chair I came down in, to Cambridge.

### NOVEMBER, 1746

1. As we were going to mount in order to return Home, my Kinsman Nathaniel Parkman[1] came with Speed to acquaint me that Sister Betty dy'd this Morning. My Dauter and I Set out upon our Journey, fearing the weather might change and my Limbs be more affected. But upon second Thought we turn'd down the Road from Captain Wells's. I return'd to Boston to my mourning distress'd Friends. May God Sanctify the Breach to us all, as to my dear Young Kinsfolk—Special may the Lord take them up! may they have wisdom to Conduct! may they live

[5] (Harvard 1741). Later the minister at Ware, 1751-1754, and of Yarmouth, 1755-1760. *Sibley*, XI, 58-64.
[6] The Reverend John Mellen of Sterling.
[7] Parkman's sister, Mrs. Josiah Willard.
[1] Parkman's nephew, the son of William Parkman.

in Love and Peace! Captain White kindly ask'd me to put up my Chair into his House and my Mare into his Stable. Lodg'd with my Kinsman.

2. Preach'd a.m. at New North on Luke 19, 10. Mr. Webb[2] p.m. on [blank]. Din'd at Mr. Eliots.[3] At Eve I preach'd at my Brother Parkmans on Song 1, 4.

3. At Eve at Mr. John Brecks where came Mr. William Owen and my Brother William. Brother and I went to Elder Cheevers's—where was Mr. Wigglesworth[4] of Ipswich Hamlet.

4. P.M. rode over the Neck with Captain Whites Lady in my Chair: and at Eve at Dr. Colman's Lecture. Mr. Wigglesworh preach'd on Eccl. ult. ult. Din'd at Brother Williams. Lodg'd at Brother Samuels.

5. Din'd at Brother Alexanders. Weather exceeding various. After Dinner especially the Sun shone, but yet clouded up and rain'd toward Eve. Sister Betty Bury'd.

6. My Horse has been kept till now at Captain Whites. An Exceeding Cold wind in the Morning, yet Molly and I set out in the Chair and rode home, having stop'd and been kindly refresh'd at Mr. Thomas Dana's,[5] Mr. Patersons[6] and at Mr. Darlings.[7] Got home well and found my Family well. Blessed be God! But in my Absence It has pleas'd God to take away Ensign Thomas Newton and his wife, and one of their Son Abners little sons of the Fever and Flux.

7. Snow, Cold, Blustering—and yet Sun shine. Sent Colonel Wards Chair Home by my son Ebenezer—who brought Monsieur Calmetts Dictionary[8] volume I from Mr. Cushings. 'Rody and Jonathan Devereux help'd my sons husk at Eve, but twas very Cold.

8. Very Cold. Mr. Samuel Williams here—brought me the Return of the Deacons and Committee of the precinct concerning the Request of Captain Moses Rice of Deerfield.

9. On Occasion of Ensign Newtons and my sisters Death I preach'd on Ps. 39, 4 and P.M. on 10, 3, but us'd the sermon on Ps. 119, 59 from page 12.

10. Mr. Francis Whipples Dauter Lucy and son Nehemiah sick. I visited them. Lieutenant Tainter kill'd a Cow which Mr. Grout bought for me of Mr. Jonas Brigham for ƒ16.10.0.

11. I rode to Grafton—din'd at Mr. Prentice's—where was Mr. Thomas Harringtons wife of Waltham. Mr. Prentice and I walk'd to Mr. Joseph Batchellors—at Mr. Brooks[9]—at Mr. Winchesters.[10] Visited old Mrs. Tabitha Fay[11] who is taken very bad. At my own house and Barn Elizer Rice and 4 or 5 more are Husking, it being very moderate Weather.

12. Wrote by Lieutenant Tainter to Mr. Edwards of Northampton. Nurse Sherman din'd here. Captain Maynard here at Eve. We reckon'd and settl'd. Gave him a note to his brother James the Collector.

13. A.M. I rode to Deacon Newtons. Visited old Mrs. Tabitha Fay. P.M. proceeded to Mr. Francis Whipples whose Family (a Number of them) is sick. Thence I went to Mr. James Maynards and to Ensign Rice's. N.B. Mrs. Rice's inveighing against Mr. Martyn; against his prayers at Ensign Newtons Funeral. She is greatly displeas'd with me for assisting in his Ordination. I rode up to Colonel Ward,[12] who was too generous to ask anything for his Chair to Boston. Was also at Dr. Smiths[13] as I return'd.

14. At Eve Mr. Noah Brooks[14] of Grafton here—being in much perplexity and Difficulty not knowing what was his Duty respecting their approaching Sacrament. Since he and others had com-

plain'd of Ezekiel Cole[15] for his preaching and the Church had condemm'd him as disorderly, yet had lately voted him forgiveness if he would reform, notwithstanding they have had no Signs of his Repentence—nay have reason to fear he has had not Conviction of his offence.

15. Great Storm of Rain. Strong Winds, and great Flood.

16. On Ps. 39, 4, and 84, 1. Captain Warrins wife din'd here.

17. Monsieur Calmet engages me not a little.

18. At Mr. Whipples[16]—his son Nehemiah of about a Twelve month old dy'd. Pleasant moderate weather. Some of our Cattle have been hous'd but we are not yet ready for the Rest.

19. A great storm of Snow. Mr. Whipple's Son was to be bury'd to Day but I could not attend upon it in Such Weather.

20. Ebenezer and Thomme build a new Hoval at the East End of the Barn. The Cattle were all hous'd. Thomas Winchester is come from his station at Fort Pelham to visit his Friends.

21. Mr. Samuel Harrington here. I traded with him for one of his Hoggs, and am to give him 15 d. per pound (old Tenor).

22. Captain Maynard here after a Tedious Journey with his Team to Boston. Deacon Forbush here about his son Eli. Abraham Batchellor my Team p.m.

23. On Tit. 2, 12, all Day. Mrs. Mary Steward and Mrs. Sarah Forbush (Phinehas's wife) din'd here. Might it please God of his infinite Mercy to bring me off from a Life after the Flesh! that I might live according to the Rules of Christian Temperance in all Things!

24. The Boys thrash Wheat, which they find much Eaten by Vermin, besides that it was much Blasted. Sarah Henry here turning an old Black Coat of mine to make a Coat for Ebenezer. Mr. Jones of Western lodg'd here.

25. Mr. Jones to Western. My wife gone to Mr. Edwards Whipples wifes Labour. At Eve they had a son born. Eli Forbush wants to lodge here when the School comes into the Middle of the Town. Sarah Henry here.

26. Captain Daniel Ward of Worcester for Mr. Maccarty[17] but he did not come. Rainy. Sarah Henry.

27. Public Thanksgiving. I preach'd on Ps. 48, 1, 3, 7, 9, 11. Disappointed of those whom we had design'd to dine with us—and had no Body but our own Folks. I would fain remember those who are in Affliction or are slenderly provided. For what we have receiv'd the Lord make us truely Thankfull, and of the Number of those Children of Judah who Spiritually rejoice in Gods Judgments! At Eve came Sir Williams from Marlborough and lodg'd here. N.B. He brought up Dr. Watts Sermon for me.

28. Sir Williams bought my Volume of the works of the author of the whole Duty of Man for 8£, and he had my Dr. Clark's Letters to Mr. Dodwell[18] for Dr. Watts Sermon. He return'd to Sudbury. Mr. Jenison came over from the Northside to keep School in the middle of the Town.

29. Sarah Henry here again.

30. Sacrament. Preach'd on 1 Pet. 1, 18, 19. N.B. Mr. Jenison at Sermon but not at Communion. Deacon Fay and Mr. Kendall[19] of Suffield din'd here. P.M. repeat'd Sermon on Ps. 119, 106. O may the Blood of the Son of God be precious to me and Since we have again Sworn it, may God afford us Grace to Perform etc!

### DECEMBER, 1746

1. I Catechiz'd both A. and P.M. at the Meeting House. P.M. Mr. Daniel Forbush came with some Hearthstones and new laid my Kitchen Hearth. Mrs. Sarah Henry here. Mr. Jenison keeps at Mr. Barns's and Eli lodges with him at Captain Forbush's.

2. Mr. David Maynard and his Brother Ebenezer came and kill'd Two Hoggs for me. One weigh'd 232. The other 202. Mr. Harrington also brought a Hogg which I bought of him lately—

---

[2] Reverend John Webb.

[3] The Reverend Andrew Eliot.

[4] The Reverend Samuel Wigglesworth of Hamilton.

[5] Of Cambridge.

[6] Joseph Patterson of Watertown.

[7] Thomas Darling of Framingham.

[8] Augustin Calmet, *An Historical, Critical, Geographical, Chronological, and Etymological Dictionary of the Holy Bible* (London, 1732), 3 vols.

[9] Ebenezer Brooks of Grafton.

[10] Benjamin Winchester.

[11] Mrs. Samuel Fay.

[12] Nahum Ward of Shrewsbury.

[13] Joshua Smith, the physician of Shrewsbury.

[14] Son of Ebenezer Brooks.

[15] An uneducated preacher who was later ordained. He became the minister of the Separatist Church in Sutton, 1751-1799.

[16] Francis Whipple.

[17] The Reverend Thaddeus Maccarty of Worcester.

[18] Samuel Clarke, D.D., *A Defense of an Argument made use of in a Letter [by Dr. Clarke] to Mr. Dodwel, to Prove the Immateriality and Natural Immortality of the Soul* (London, 1707). There followed an exchange of views in a series of pamphlets by Clarke and Henry Dodwell (1641-1711).

[19] Joshua Kendall, an early settler.

which weigh'd 335. In all 769 pounds of Pork cutt and Salted up this Evening. N.B. Mr. Whitney here with Mr. Harrington. N.B. Mr. Cushing absent last Sabbath from his people by reason of the sickness of his son Jacob at College.

3. Very Cold. I rode by Mr. Thomas Goodenows (where I call'd) to Mr. Jesse Rice's of Marlborough. Return'd to his mother[1] Mr. Fenner on Conscience.[2] Din'd at Mr. Smiths—he not at home. At Dr. Gotts reckon'd with him and paid all. N.B. Captain Brintnall[3] and Lieutenant Cleveland[4] at the Doctors. As I return'd home visited Mr. Jacob Amsden who has been very ill, and still confin'd. When I came home found Mr. Maccarty here from Worcester. N.B. A post went to the Governour to Day with Letters from Albany of Several of the Mohawks going to Quebec with Pretences of Friendship to the French but return'd with Scalps to Albany etc.

4. Mr. Maccarty tarried and din'd with me and then return'd to Worcester. At Evening Elijah Warrin here, and (it raining and freezing) he lodg'd here.

5. Mr. Upham[5] (of Sturbridge) and his Dauter here in their Journey downwards.

6. [No entry.]

7. On Tit. 2, 12—to live Righteously. P.M. repeated on Rom. 8, 6. Mr. Jenison and Mrs. Grow din'd here. At Night after Family Devotions read Mr. Edwards on Religious Affections.

8. Deacon Forbush here to ask me to go over to his son Solomon Woods there having been an odd Occurrence there, for when Mrs. Woods had lain in and got Joanna Fay from Southborough to Nurse her, on the Fourth Day the Nurse (an unmarried, Young Woman) falls into Travail and was deliver'd of a Child. Yesterday morning it dy'd—and they who were nearly Concern'd would now have me Visit her and be at the Funeral. I went accordingly—talk'd with the Girl who seem'd penitent but would not tell who was the Father of her Child. After Prayer I return'd to Lieutenant Tainters and thence to Captain Bakers. N.B. My wife rode with me as far as Captain Bakers and waited there till I came. We Supped there. N.B. Young Men's Society met this Evening at old Mr. Maynards to settle their accounts etc.

9. Mr. Pratt and Neighbour Ebenezer Maynard kill'd an old large sow which weigh'd 267. Read Mr. Edwards on Religious Affections, and find him much Study'd in his subject.

10. Lieutenant Tainter had encourag'd me that he would take the Care of marketting the Pork (kill'd yesterday) if I send it to Boston by my son Thomme; we accordingly got ready. Ebenezer got the Mare shod at Mr. Cooks and went over to Lieutenants—acquainted him we had kill'd, and to know his Purpose; but it prov'd dull misty and Rainy Day, and it being a very heavy and difficult Load and Lieutenant not to go till late, together with diverse other Things which perplexed us, therefore we deferr'd it till another Day. N.B. Mr. Ebenezer Baker of Marlborough here and din'd with us. At Eve my Son was at old Mr. Maynards and Ebenezer Maynard offer'd to go to Boston with our Pork, tho his Design was to trade with Nathan if he had been at home.

11. Rainy yet. Neighbour Ebenezer came; we tackl'd and loaded, and he went off—but before noon he return'd—the Rain and bad road discourag'd him. He din'd with us but would take nothing for his Pains about the Pork. At Eve we Salted it up. N.B. Our Two first Hoggs weighed 232 and 202. Mr. Harringtons 335. This Sow weigh'd 261. In all that we Salted up 1030.

12. Exceeding Cold Morning. At Eve Thomas Winchester here, lately return'd from his Station at Fort Pelham.

13. Very Cold Day.

14. Preach'd all Day upon Micah 6, 8, those words—but to do justly—carrying on from thence the Same Subject which I have

been lately on from Titus 2, 12. Mr. Stratton[6] of Waltham din'd here.

15. Precinct Meeting—partly to receive a Memorial from me which I sent—but they did not see Cause to do anything at all upon it.

16. Very Cold from Day to Day. Dr. Gott here. My sons thrashing. P.M. tho Cold yet my wife and I rode over to see old Mrs. Whipple and tarried till Eve among the Whipples.

17. Ten Young Men Cutt wood. James Bradish (by his Proxy Mr. Daniel Hardy) Jonas Bradish, Noah and Daniel How, Benjamin Whipple Meradach Devereux, Elijah Warrin (by his proxy his Brother Aaron) Nathan Maynard, Jonathan Bruce, and Silas Newton. P.M. I went over to Mr. Whipples to meet with the precinct Committee who were there except Mr. Abner Newton. There was also present Neighbour Benjamin How. I discours'd with them of my late Memorial which was Sent to the precinct last Monday. I ask'd Deacon Newton, and Mr. Whipple whether the Representation which I therein made of what they said to me when they came to my House the Evening after that Precinct Meeting (there referr'd to) was a just and true Representation? And they reply'd in Terms of Consent, that it was. I ask'd Captain Warrin and Mr. Williams also, who Said that they remember'd that being at the Said precinct Meeting they did perceive that That was the precinct Meeting, viz. that my Sallery Should be that Money which pass'd before the Soldier Money (in 1744) was made, which was according to Gold at 4. 18 shillings per ounce—but I could not prevail with any of them to Sign any Line of Memorandum of it. When I got home young men all gone home.

18. The last Night and this Day were More than ordinary Cold. Should have expected Mr. Maccarty from Worcester to preach my Lecture to Young Men, had it not been so extreme Cold. I preach'd myself on Rom. 8, 6 former part to a few that Ventur'd out. Mr. Jenison spent the Evening with me and Supp'd here. N.B. I ask'd him why he was not at Communion last Opportunity? He said he did not know that it was to be Communion Day, till the Day before.

19. Continues very Cold. Ebenezer much taken off by Tooth ach. Thomme cyphers again.

20. [No entry.]

21. All Day upon Micah 6, 8 going on Still with the Subject from Tit. 2, 12. Mr. Jenison, Mrs. Mary Steward,[7] Widow Thurston, and Mr. Zebulon Rice's Wife[8] din'd here. My God grant us these dire principles to Love one another, and to delight in shewing Mercy!

22. A.M. I rode over to the Southside of the Town. Was at Mr. Beriah Rice's, Deacon Forbush's[9] where was Mr. Child of Roxbury, Glazier. Visited Mr. Dunlop who is Sick; This and to Speak with the Glazier were my Chief Errands: was also at Mr. Martin Pratts—din'd (as I return'd home) at Lieutenant Tainters. Very Raw Cold towards Night—but Lieutenant Hezekiah Ward came with a Plott of Land he had laid out for me of 7½ Acres by the Burying place, and would have me go and See it. I went just before sunsett. At Mr. Nurses at Eve and as I return'd home I visited Jonathan Maynard who is ill of a Dropsie.

23. Very Cold. Storm of Snow. P.M. Mr. John Child the Glazier came to work.

24. Bright Day, but Cold and Windy. Mr. Child at Work—last night he work'd very late, finish'd my new Study window, and this morning put it up; Mended my Windows thro out the House, which was no Small piece of work.

25. Mr. Child finish'd his work So late and it being very Cold he went not away till this Morning, which proves also a very Cold

---

[1] The widow of Joseph Rice of Marlborough.
[2] William Fenner, *The Soul's Looking-Glasse . . . With a Treatise of Conscience* (Cambridge, 1640). Another edition appeared in 1643.
[3] William Brintnall of Sudbury.
[4] Josiah Cleveland of Watertown.
[5] Ezekiel Upham.

[5] David Stratton.
[7] Daughter of Daniel Steward of Marlborough.
[8] Zebulon Rice married Abigail, daughter of Daniel Forbush of Westborough.
[9] Jonathan Forbush.

Day. My own common Exercises in my study without going out save to the Yard to chop a little etc.

26. Captain Maynard who grows cool and almost a Stranger here. Some Evenings the Boys Cypher.

27. My Sons frequently Sledding wood and little enough to maintain 3 Fires this Cold Season.

28. Go on with my Subject from Tit. 2, 12. Am now upon Living Godly—but the Text improv'd to Day was 2 Tim. 3, 12 one Clause. Mrs. Rice (Beriahs Wife) din'd here. Earnest Beg that to Days Exercises may have some Suitable Influence upon us!

29. Was at Mr. Jenisons School a.m. Visited Mr. Adams's[10] Family. Din'd with Mrs. Beamans after which Abimaleck (Indian) his Daughter Deborah having a Child Dead in their Wigwam and having desir'd Mr. Jonah Warrin to Send for me, I went to them pray'd in the Wigwam and went to the Grave. I gave them Severe Admonitions and Earnest Exhortations. Was at Mr. Williams's.

30. Dr. Breck here and din'd as he did Yesterday also whilst I was gone from home. Deacon Forbush Mr. Moses Pratt of Shrewsbury and Mr. Samuel Warrin of Grafton here, and wants a petition to be drawn to be presented to the General Court for their Compassion towards their Captive children and Friends. At Eve (tho it snow'd) I was at Captain Maynards. N.B. His Wife puts me in mind of my not having visited Mr. Abner Newton since the death of his Father, Mother and little Child: which I was a little surpriz'd at, but told Mrs. Maynard 'twas Neglected with no Particular Design, but I would endeavour soon to make them a Visit.

31. Captain Maynard as he was going to Boston gave me his hints and Resentments of my neglecting to visit Abner Newton—but he soon went off. I consider'd with myself that I visited them Some Number of Times in their Affliction, one Day after another — and when I came from Boston preach'd a Funeral Sermon on Purpose. But have been of late more than ordinarily fill'd with perplexing Cares and important Business—as particularly my Bond with Mr. Jesse Rice of Marlborough; the weighty Affairs of my settlement with this Precinct; the Sickness at Mr. Whipples; the troublesome Affair, and great Disappointment about my Pork; but especially a Daily anxiety about my Cattle my Hay being very Short and my Stock much increas'd. My Corn also Much Shorter than Ordinary; which has caus'd me to ride much more than I should have done, and yet without success. It was Somewhat Rainy this Morning, but was moderate air, so I delay'd no longer, but made a Visit to Mr. Abner Newtons. He was not at Home; his wife much confin'd by Lameness. She manifested no uneasiness that I had not been to see 'em, but said that they had hop'd I would, and I cant but remark that tho I have occasionally seen Mr. Newton, and did of very late yet he has shown no Disgust nor was I aware that they had any Special Expectation of me—tho I acknowledge I should have done well to have gone— and am Sorry I neglected it. I told Mrs. Newton I hop'd they would not be offended—and She manifested her Satisfaction and ask'd me to come again to see her. Call'd at Deacon Newtons. Return'd and din'd at home. It has been more than Ordinary Cold, difficult Weather, So that I could go out but little unless upon pressing Occasions. Was disappoint'd and hinder'd by the Cold when I was out.

The Year Ends with this Uneasiness of my Nearest and most bountiful Neighbours—which I am sorry for—but I can't but fear there is, and has been of late, a great Dissatisfaction on another Score; and I fear Some Disposition to Watch for my halting. There has been no sweetness I believe Since the Ordination of Mr. Martyn, or as my Neighbour calls him Esquire Martyn. But God forgive what has been amiss in me! quicken me to my Duty and enable me to walk inoffensively—that the Ministry be not blamed!

[10] Benjamin Adams of Marlborough.

## JANUARY, 1747

O that I might be made Suitably Sensible of the Flight of my Life. How soon alas! my Days on Earth will finish! and I shall be here no more! I could not retire (as I much desir'd) to Spend this Day by my Self for I was called in Providence to preach from home. But the Lord enable me to Consider his infinite Mercy to me, and my unspeakable Obligations to Him therefore! In Special through the Changing Scenes of Last Year. I rode to Shrewsbury and preach'd the Lecture there, on Ps. 39, 4. A Cold, especially very windy Day, and not many at Meeting. Return'd at Eve, and being Cold I call'd at Eagers[1] to warm me. N.B. Many Load of Stores gone and going up for the Forces in the Westward. Blanketts, Kettles, Arms etc. and yet its Doubtfull whether the Expedition will go on. At my House Thomas Winchester brings a message from Timothy Warrin (who was with me lately to buy my oxen) that he did not depend on them. Lieutenant Tainter brought up Six of Mr. Edwards on Religious Affections.

2. Nothing So observable as my close Engagement in my Studys and Preparations for the Sabbath. Mr. Jenison gone to preach at North Rutland.

3. Mr. John Chamberlin[2] here. Makes offers for my young fatting Sow.

4. I went on still with my Subject of the Gospel teaching us to live Godly from Tit. 2, 12, but I us'd for my Text to Day (as last Lords Day) 2 Tim. 3, 12, former Clause. Snowy Day, few attended. Mrs. Whitney and Mr. Jonathan Forbush's wife din'd with us. So few Young Men at Meeting that their Society did not Meet at Evening. Stormy Night.

5. No body comes to cutt wood as was expected. My Hay so very short that my mind is full of Concern. A.M. my sons thrash'd Rye. I rode into the Neighbourhood to enquire after Hay. To Neighbour Eliezer Rice, Williams's, Pratts. At Old Mr. Maynards at Eve—Old Mr. Whipple and Captain Maynard there. No Success as to Hay.

6. A.M. Mr. Chamberlin buys my fatting Sow alive. He offers 18 d per pound when kill'd, or 12 d alive. She weighed 108 a live and comes to 5£ 8 shillings of which he pays me 4£ old Tenor. My sons thrash Rye. P.M. I rode out again after Hay. To Eliezer Rice's, Ensign Rice, Eliezer Bellows, Joseph Knowltons (N.B. his wife ill). In returning I was in at old Mr. Green's for Corn. Agree with Joseph that what I have of him I must give 12 shillings per Bushel for. At my House found Timothy Warrin and Eliezer Rice about my Cattle, and I sold em to Neighbour Warrin for 44£ and a Days Work ploughing Stubble in the Spring. He gave me Bond to be paid September 29 with Interest—but I engag'd that if he would pay me by March 10 there should be no Interest at all. He promis'd also to bring me a Load of Rails from Mr. Harringtons.

7. Cold for some Days past—today Clear, Windy, Cold. Mr. Warrin took away the oxen he bought last night. My sons thrashing Rye. The Day appointed for the Ordination of Mr. Reed[3] over the second Church in Framingham. But I kept at home for I fear what Grounds they go upon. I grew very Cold especially towards Night.

8. Robert Bradish here in the forenoon, and is uneasy still. He wanted Opportunity for further Discourse. I told him those men which he improv'd before, viz. Deacon Newton and Neighbour Stephen Fay, would do very well for him to take Advice of again: and I purpos'd to be at Mr. Fays in the afternoon where he might be also if he pleas'd with any Body else that he should choose. Mr. Ebenezer Baker of Marlborough here and din'd again with us. P.M. I rode to Mr. Abner Newtons. Robert Bradish came in there, but I was going. Mr. Newton said nothing in the world of any Disquietments even tho we had talk of their Family Afflictions—of his Fathers affairs etc. I went to Deacon Newtons, having sent his Barnabas for Mr. Beriah Rice. I rode up to Mr. Stephen Fay's, who being gone to Boston we were much disappointed. I proceeded to visit old Captain Fay who is under

[1] James Eager of the north side of Westborough.
[2] Of Westborough.
[3] Solomon Reed (Harvard 1739) was the minister of the Second Church (Separatist) of Framingham, and later Titicut Separatist Church of Middleborough, 1756-1785. *Sibley*, X, 398-400.

a great Infirmity and kept from the House of God. Return'd to Captain Bakers who is under Confinement by great Pains in his Limbs. But hither resorted Robert Bradish, Deacon Newton and Beriah Rice—but Captain Baker was not willing to have the affair open'd to him, because of his great Indisposition—so it was adjourn'd. I went to Merchant Rice's and thence came Home. In the Evening came Lieutenant Thomas Forbush and in better Frame than last Time and was (to sum up in short) desirous that none of his Children might suffer for his Sake, and we parted in Peace. Mr. Reed ordain'd at Framingham.

9. [No entry.]

10. [No entry.]

11. I go on with the Subject of living Godly from 2 Tim. 3, 12. Nobody but my own Family din'd with me. P.M. Repeated from Rom. 8, 6, latter part. N.B. Mr. Prentice of Grafton absent from his people, and many of them here at meeting. I was exceedingly tired at Eve, and perceive that I have a bad Cold—Rheumatic Pains in my Limbs.

12. Clear but Cold. Am under indisposition of Body—but can read and write, all Day, through the great Goodness of God. The Rye Ebenezer has got out is 10 Bushels which (with 2 Bushel got out before and sown before winter) makes our Winter Rye 12 Bushels. At Eve came James White (late of Upton) and Joanna Fay (late of Southborough) her Brother Moses accompanying and were marry'd. Robert Bradish also came, and with him Deacon Newton, Captain Warrin and Mr. Wheeler; and tho they were not of my choosing yet I consented that the Cause should be heard by them—which was therefore accordingly rehears'd on both sides; and Mr. Beriah Rice was here to give his Testimony, which he gave plumply and Earnestly, By Word of Mouth, and deliver'd the Substance of it in Writing also, Sign'd by both himself and his wife. By this joint Testimony thus given in I look'd upon myself and conceive that all others did, as fully justify'd as to the Ground and Cause of my writing my Letter to Robert Bradish, and proceeded to argue that in Case Said Bradish was laid under any Burden which he ought not to bear, it was laid on him by some Body else and not by me; but that if what was testify'd was true, (and the Testimony of the Two is True) then I was to be look'd upon as under a great Grievous Burden of Reproch from Said Bradish. I shall not think it worth while to take much notice of what Strange Pleas and Exceptions he made against the Evidences—their being in my Hand writing etc. whereas the Harringtons and his wife's were (of which I had little need) yet Mr. Rice's and his wife's were recharg'd here by their own mouths to Bradish (where we were together heretofore) before any word of theirs was writ—and when it was written, it was while all partys were present and at the general Desire of all concern'd. In Brief, the Judges took the Case—and after Some Time spent alone by themselves we had their Request (instead of any Sentence) praying that for peace sake we would throw all up and go no further. Bradish was willing to—and when it came to my turn to answer, I spoke to this purpose, that under my Case I had discharg'd My Duty (as I apprehended) in a proper manner to him who had done me Injury—that I abide by it—and pray'd God to give His Blessing—wish'd heartily he might see his Error: but inasmuch as they who had heard the Case did Desire this Earnestly that it might be carry'd no further, I would accordingly Cease from anything further. If he had not Design'd to reproch me on what was deliver'd in my preaching and would labour after a sound understanding of those great and weighty Truths which had been mention'd—there being signification of Consent hereto, I gave him my Hand. We burnt the Papers and we parted without further Jarr.

'Tis true I had more reluctance than can easily be express'd, because he very much deserv'd severe Reprehension and needs humblings; for which I can't but think I had great advantage in my Hands and had no need to fear anything that he could in any wise be able to do. Nor can I conceive why those gentlemen which heard of the Case, unless their minds wrought towards him as he was a most turbulent fractious piece, and was now forthwith, tomorrow morning, to go off into the service, a soldier in Colonel Dwights[4] Regiment. But I could not withstand their pressing

Instance for peace; and I did not want to have anything more, in way of Contest, to do with him. Yet I may repent (for ought I know) of my too great Gentleness towards him. But may God be pleas'd to help me in subduing and denying myself, and my inward Corruptions; and grant forgiveness of what has been amiss; Sanctifie this Trial to me; and give the poor man to see his Pride and Wickedness, that he may repent of it. N.B. Mr. Chamberlin took away the young Sow which he bought of me a few days ago and sent her to Boston alive in a small Drove.

13. Very Cold Season. Ebenezer thrashes Barley. Thomme to Mr. Johnsons Mill. I read Fullers pisgah sight;[5] and at Eve transcrib'd the Applicatory Part of the last sermon on Tit. 2, 12. My Wife in great pain and Swell'd in on Legg and Foot. Nor am I free from Pains of Rheumatism. Diverse also of the Family complain of Agues in their Faces—Molly and Bekky particularly.

14. Exceeding Cold season. The Snow deep, but the last snow light. The air very sharp, and somewhat windy. Yet Billy goes to School. My wife confin'd with pain and Lameness, which with her pregnancy makes her Case very grievous to her.

15. Thomme to Mr. Johnsons Mill. Ebenezer Thrashing Barley. Not So Cold as Yesterday.

16. Mr. Raymond[6] of Hadley here. Very moderate pleasant Day.

17. Mr. Chamberlin came home from Boston. He informs me that my Kinsman Elias[7] was marry'd on New Years Night. May they be espous'd to Jesus Christ and live together as Heirs of the grace of Life. He brought me also a pair of stout Deer Skin Gloves from Mr. Stansbury in Boston.

18. A Thaw. Rainy. I preach'd a. and p.m. on Tit. 2, 13, a solemn word! Mrs. Patience Woods[8] din'd here. Lieutenant Tainter kind in helping my Children to meeting through the wet.

19. Mr. John Mead in the morning. Ebenezer gone, and Noah How with him to help him, to get slabbs for sides of an Horse sled at the ministerial Lot. My wife in much pain. Mr. Jenison return'd from Brookfield at Evening. Eli having kept school to Day also. Mr. Jenison was in here and acquaint'd me that the people of Worcester were this Day to meet and were likely to Endeavour after Mr. Maccarty, either settle [him] or at least to preach [him] another month.

20. I visited Mr. Ebenezer Baker at Captain Maynards—ill there of Gout or Rheumatism. Examin'd Taylor of Original Sin. A smooth and subtle Man!

21. Rode abroad this fine Day, which is very rare. Went as far as to Jonathan Fays, was at Mr. Grouts, old Mr. Samuel Fays, and was at Stephen Fays, where was his Brother James. Grafton, by his Representation, in a poor Miserable Condition. May God be gracious to them under their sad Divided Circumstances!

22. Very Considerable Storm of Snow. At noon as I sat at Table I had a sudden Indisposition which depriv'd me of my Dinner—but I did not faint; through Divine Mercy I reviv'd and went to my Chamber. My Sitting most of the Day might be very much the cause of Stagnation.

23. After a Great Storm, a fine, bright pleasant Day. P.M. Mr. Jenison going his Journey up to Brookfield; the Snow so deep he takes time. Mr. Stone[9] of Southborough here also, returning from North Shrewsbury where there has been a Council of Three Ministers. (Mr. Campbell,[10] Mr. Cushing and Mr. Stone) to hear and advise upon some Difficultys and Differences which have arisen there between Mr. Morse[11] and divers of his Neighbours, Especially Mr. Isaac Temple, which tis hop'd may be hereby in some Measure compos'd. Captain Maynard was also here. Tells me Mr. Ebenezer Baker still continued ill at his House. Ebenezer brings home an Horse sled made by him and Noah How.

24. Somewhat pleasant.

[4] Joseph Dwight. *Sibley*, VII, 56–66.
[5] Thomas Fuller, *A Pisgah-Sight of Palestine and the Confines thereof, with the History of the Old and New Testament Acted thereon* (London, 1650). Another edition was published in London in 1662.
[6] Josiah Raymond. See Sylvester Judd, *History of Hadley* (Northampton, 1863), p. 558.
[7] Parkman's nephew, Elias Parkman of Boston, married Abigail White.
[8] Mrs. Solomon Woods of Westborough.
[9] The Reverend Nathan Stone.
[10] The Reverend John Campbell of Oxford.
[11] The Reverend Ebenezer Morse of Boylston.

25. On Tit. 2, 13, have now finish'd what I have been so long upon. May God most gracious add his Blessing. P.M. repeated sermon on Rom. 8, 6. N.B. I have twice repeated an old sermon in the afternoon that I might deliver more unbrokenly my whole preparations in one Exercise, tho it has been very long and cost me much the more pains. O that we might be Spiritually minded— that we might have true and Eternal Life and Peace! Captain Flagg[12] and Mr. Joshua Child of Worcester here at Meeting and at my House afterwards. Captain Flagg pursued his Journey Home.

26. This is the third Monday that we have been Expecting woodcutters, and have not come. Snow deep. Mr. Stephen Fay here and had one of Mr. Edwards' Books on Religious Affections. Mr. Joshua Child here. Thomme to Grafton to Mr. Batchellors.

27. I rode over to Mr. Martyns and din'd there. P.M. he rode with me to Mr. Smiths at Marlborough. I went also to Mr. Joseph Williams sadler to talk with him about my son Thomme's living with him to learn his trade, and he readily consented. At Dr. Gotts at Eve. Return'd home. A Letter came from Mr. Pierpoint with his account of Esquire Lee's Debt Sworn—and a Power of attorney to me to recover.

28. It had been pleasant weather for 2 Days but now it is very likely to be stormy. 3 Teams came and number of Hands to Cutt wood. The Teams Mr. Bowman, Mr. Harrington and Mr. Phinehas Hardy, David Batheric—Jonathan Forbush, Solomon Woods, Tim Warrin, Zebulon Rice, Judah Rice, Nathaniel Whitney and Josiah Grout. They had not gone I think above 2 Turns after Dinner before the Storm prevail'd so that they broke off and went home. A Great Storm of Wind and Snow at Evening.

29. Latter part of the Night the Snow turn'd to Rain. This Day remember the wormwood and Gall and my soul is humbled in me.[13] *Jejun and previ.* Mr. Stephen Fay here at noon to my Discomposing.

30. Stormy Snow. Stephen Fay (at my sending for) came here, and again talk'd with me about taking up the Strip of Common Land, about 4 acres, on the South side of the Road by the South Burying place. N.B. Lieutenant Wood had told me that he, Mr. Abner Newton and Mr. Stephen Fay had all pitch'd on it, but the Two former would give up their pitch to me if Stephen would—but this the last was not willing to because he had the land which join'd to it, out to both the other Roads. But he made me this proposal, that if I would engage before hand to sell it to him, he would give me 25 shillings per acre for it and bear the charge of laying it out—or he would give me Rights to take up as much Land other where and Ten shillings, or instead of the 10 shillings he would give me one acre of that very Land clear and free. I told him I would do nothing underhand, but would acquaint Mr. Newton so far as should be needful that I might have his free Consent.

31. Captain Maynard is return'd from Boston thro the tedious Storms and Roads and his Team under his sons Care is coming. The Snow very deep. Captain Maynard brings me a Letter of the 23rd from my Brother Parkman informing me of their sorrows by the extreme illness of his Daughter Emms,[14] but Captain Maynard adds that Brother Samuel inform'd him that she dy'd on Thursday morning last. The Lord Pity the Bereav'd Husband and parents, and Sanctifie the frequent Breaches in our Family to us all who are related!

### FEBRUARY, 1747

I had so mislaid the first Leaf of the sermon which I design'd for the forenoon that I was not able to find it when people were coming to meeting, So that I was oblig'd to take up an old sermon and go to meeting. It was that on Eph. 1, 4. On Election. P.M. I found the Leaf I had mislaid and preach'd on Dan. 2, 35 last Clause. Captain Tainter[1] of Watertown and his Brother the Lieutenant[2] din'd here together with Mr. Jenison. N.B. people came, many of them upon Ratchetts[3] to Meeting.

2. Snowy, but it was not Cold. I went over to Mr. Abner Newtons[4] and made my way clear about taking up the Land, which we were talking of last Friday. Who was free that I should do what I would with it. Neighbour Stephen Fay had been there and was gone to Southboro to Lieutenant Wards. I immediately follow'd him tho the Snow was deep. I committed my Plott of 7 acres to Neighbour Stephen to be carry'd into the proprietors meeting to Day; and Lieutenant consenting, the other affair of the 4 acres was left with them to Lieutenant to prepare the Plott and to carry it to the meeting—upon which I return'd home. And 'twas well I did for the Storm prevailing very much. I went as soon as I had din'd (Mr. Whitney dining with us) to Neighbour Hows and paid him for Rights in Commons which I had before agreed with him for—viz. 3£ old tenor. The Storm was very great. Wind blew the Snow very much and when it clear'd away towards Eve it was very Cold and high gusts of Wind through the Night. My wife so near her Time that I was full of Concern but we rest'd (through Divine Goodness and protection) in Safety.

3. Very Cold and Blustering. Roads fill'd and little stirring. Mr. Jenison on Racketts.

4. More Moderate. School at Captain Maynards but children couldn't go by reason of the deep Snow. Eli din'd here. Mr. How came and sign'd the Conveyance of Rights. At Eve Stephen Fay here—informs me that both the plotts I committed to his Care were accepted at the Proprietors Meeting on Monday last. Eli Forbush and Asaph Rice came at Eve to Lodge and board here.

5. Bright and comfortable. I finish'd reading Mr. Lowth[5] on the prophecys. At Eve I visited Mr. Baker again, at Captain Maynards, Mr. Jenison also being there. I pass'd along on Banks most commonly as high, and many Times above the Fences. Mr. Baker much recover'd.

6. Mr. Richard Barns of Marlborough lyes Dead. The Lord convince me of my own Frail and dying Nature! and O that I might be ready. At Eve Mr. Jension, and supp'd here.

7. Thomme carry'd a Letter to Mr. Bezaleel Eager for Conveyance, which I have directed to Mr. Stephen Fessendin[6] at Worcester and containing Mr. Pierpoints Account of Esquire Lee's Debt. N.B. Mr. Jenison went this morning over to a Corner of Bolton and Marlborough to preach there. Eli and Asaph recited to me therefore.

8. A moderate, pleasant Day—not a few came to meeting on Racketts. I preach'd again on Dan. 2, 35.

9. Ebenezer work'd for Mr. Chamberlin. A.M. somewhat cloudy. P.M. pleasant.

10. I visited Mr. Richard Barns on consideration of the Loss of his Father. I rode also to Mr. Cushing at Shrewsbury and din'd there. N.B. The road from my House to the Country Road but Steppings through deep Snow, but the Great Road very Smooth. N.B. Mr. Prentice[7] of Lancaster ill, and has not preach'd for Some Sabbaths. P.M. I Rode to Worcester. Deliver'd Colonel Chandler his third and fourth volumes of Pamela with my Dauter Mollys gratitude. We went to his son Johns and Drank Tea. In the morn I set Johnson to do me a small jobb, the mending a small ironing box. Went to Dr. Becks.[8] We spent the Evening chiefly at Mr. Fessendens. Lodg'd at the Doctors. N.B. Mr. Fessendens Poem on the taking Louisbourg.[9] N.B. Worcester without preaching 3 Sabbaths. N.B. The Time for the Claims to Esquire Lee's Estate, out 3 Days before my Letter to Mr. Fessenden last Saturday.

11. After Breakfast the Doctor and I rode to Mr. Hedge's. I went to borrow a volume of Mr. Henry[10]—but it was at Sutton: but he set a Time for me to Send for it. I din'd at Colonel Chandlers with Major Keys[11] etc. I read the Colonel Mr. Fessen-

---

[12] Benjamin Flagg.
[13] The anniversary of the death of his first wife.
[14] Martha, daughter of Parkman's eldest brother, William, married Joshua Emmes.

[1] John Tainter.
[2] Deacon Simon Tainter of Westborough.
[3] Racket, a word used for snow shoe.

[4] Son of Thomas Newton.
[5] William Lowth, D.D. (1661-1732), the distinguished English theologian, wrote a number of works on prophets and prophecies. These works appeared separately at first and then in several collected editions.
[6] (Harvard 1737). A lawyer in Worcester.
[7] The Reverend John Prentice.
[8] Samuel Breck, the physician.
[9] This was not published.
[10] Matthew Henry (1662-1714), a learned, dissenting minister of Cheshire, England, was the author of many theological works.
[11] John Keyes of Shrewsbury.

dens Poem on Louisbourg inscrib'd to Governor Shirley—which the Colonel promis'd to present to the Governor. Major Keyes my Company to Shrewsbury. Receiv'd a Pair of black Shoes for my Dauter Molly and paid Mr. Parker[12] all to this Day, viz. 4£ 1. 6. Home at Eve. My wife still in her usual State which she has been of late.

12. A Rainy and thawing Day, but Thomme went to Mr. Johnsons Mill at Southborough.

13. Bright, but Windy, as it was very much last Night. Mr. Simon Tainter[13] of Grafton here with a Letter from that Church to me requesting me to join with four other ministers viz. Reverend Messers Martyn, Hall,[14] Webb[15] and Stone,[16] to advise them in their Difficultys. The Day appoint'd is the 24th Instant, the place of Meeting the house of Mr. Joseph Rice[17] in Grafton. I return'd that I would endeavour to if my Family Circumstances did not prevent which they might be like to know more of by next Thursday.

14. Mr. Jenison leaves the School again this Morning to go over to Mr. Jones's to preach there tomorrow. So that Eli and Asaph are oblig'd to recite to me.

15. All Day again on Dan. 2, 35 last Clause. Mr. Joseph Knowlton, Mrs. Tainter and Mrs. Miller din'd here as well as Eli and Asaph. Comfortable Day my wife at Meeting—but has been for this long Time in great Pains. N.B. Mr. Joseph Miles' son Joseph of about 8 was taken sick last Thursday his Father being gone to Boston, and dy'd the next Day before his Father return'd home.

16. Rainy, as it was all night. My wife very full of pain. This Morning I sent Ebenezer for Mrs. Forbush.[18] Eli was not here last night but came in the forenoon. Asaph recited to me there being no Schoolmaster. P.M. they were both dismiss'd and they went to Captain Forbush's. A Number of Women here. Mrs. Hephzibah Maynard and her sons wife, Mrs. How, Mr. David Maynards wife and his Brother Ebenezers, Captain Forbush's and Mr. Richard Barns's. My son Ebenezer went for the most of them. At night I resign my Dear Spouse to the infinite Compassions, allsufficiency and soverign pleasure of God and under God to the good Women that are with her, waiting Humbly the Event.

17. A mustering there was in the Night, but my Wife grew Easy again and I saw her in the Morning. But her pains returning I retir'd. God almighty most gracious and mercifull be pleas'd to extend His Pity and Help! About 7 o'Clock a.m. a Fourth living Son was born, and my wife liv'd through it and becomes Comfortable through the tender Mercy and Goodness of God—to whom be all Honour, praise and Glory! The women broke fast with me—and the morning being pleasant—divers of them walk'd home others rode. Mrs. Forbush Stay'd and din'd. Eli and Asaph went to Captain Forbushs yesterday but today return'd and din'd with us. Mr. Jenison did not return'd [sic] from where he preach'd last Sabbath till late this forenoon. P.M. Brother Hicks happen'd to come from Sutton on purpose to see and lodg'd here. N.B. Mrs. Forbush went home p.m. and would take no pay. N.B. Child the Glazier here and I paid him all. N.B. Mr. Jenison supp'd with me. N.B. Sad Thieving of Cattle and sheep of late by Jonathan Willard[19] and [blank] Cutting[20] of Shrewsbury.

18. Very pleasant Day—the Snow has Shrunk by the late Rains and the present Warmth, at no Small rate. Brother Hicks went Home. P.M. Mrs. Chamberlin (wife of John) here. Had talk with her about her being disgusted at my desiring my Wife might be excus'd from being at her last groaning—it being sabbath Day and when I was not very well.

19. Very pleasant Day. Ebenezer breaks flax. I was somewhat devoted to my Preparations but was interrupted almost all the afternoon by a Visit from Mr. Ebenezer Baker. Yet he

behav'd with great Civility. At Eve Mr. Francis Whipple and his Wife here. He acquaints me that Lieutenant Tainter was a far more hurtfull opposer of the Petition which was lately put into the General Court by a Great Number of Inhabitants of this Town respecting my Salary, than even any person of the north side whosoever; especially in his Discourse at Boston with the Honourable Joseph Wilder Esquire the chairman of the Committee to whom the said Petition is referr'd.

20. Bright—but raw cold East Wind.

21. [No entry.]

22. On the occasion of the Baptism of my Infant I preach'd on 1 Chron. 29, 19. I would earnestly Sett myself to the Great Work of renewing the Covenent with the Glorious God: and infinite Thanks are due to Him that I may have this Honour and Privilege. O that God would grant Me a Perfect Heart in all I undertake! in Special in the Work now incumbent—and I beseech God to grant to each of my Children graciously given to Me, a perfect Heart also: in a particular Manner to the Child we this Day dedicate to Him by the Name of Alexander, In Commemoration of my Mothers Father, and my youngest Brother. N.B. After Sermon p.m. I read the Act of the General Court against profane Cursing and Swearing.

23. A very fine Day. I sent Thomme to Marlborough to visit Mr. Williams the Sadler, and to Deacon Andrew Rice's. I visited Neighbour Rogers—and their Son Johns Wife, and Mrs. Garfield wife of Ebenezer, her Husband not being at Home. Dr. Gott here and din'd with me. Ebenezer cutting Post Stuff in the Ministerial Lott. N.B. A second young Lamb dead.

24. Mr. Martyn came, and in Conformity to the Request of the Church in Grafton we rode up there, first to Reverend Mr. Prentice's where was Mr. Stone and thence to Mr. Joseph Rice's, where we were entertain'd. Mr. Webb of Uxbridge came also, but Mr. Hall of Sutton came not. After Dinner we had something of Formality, and they chose me Moderator and Mr. Martyn Scribe. I pray'd—their Grievances were then laid before us.

25. Tho we were adjourn'd to 8 A.M. yet no Business was done till noon. Mr. Hall came. We sent messages to the five Separating Brethren praying 'em to let us Speak with them: viz. to Messers Jacob and Joseph Whipple, Joseph Goodell, Nehemiah Batchellor and Thomas Axtell. N.B. The Church Sent to them—and our messages accompany'd Theirs. Only the first and the last came, viz. Jacob Whipple and Thomas Axtell, and with them we had Some considerable Discourse, but I Suppose to be little Effect. Josiah Lyon also appear'd and our Conference with him was drawn out to Considerable Length. They judg'd the very Ground work and gathering of the Church in Grafton was not according to the Gospel. They Vindicated the Doctrine of Knowledge of one another by the union of Love etc. etc. Not to bed till very late.

26. Tho we were adjourn'd to eight o'Clock this Morning yet the Church did not come together till noon, nor any of the offended in any season for us to begin our Business. The Remainder of the Hearing was up in Neighbour Rice's Chamber. Towards Evening Mr. Hall return'd Home—tho our Business was extreme arduous. We apply'd ourselves with some Resolution to prepare our Judgment and gather up a Result. In this we spent the Whole Night—I never put off my Cloths, yet Mr. Martyn and Mr. Stone Slept not at all.

27. In the Morning When Mr. Prentice came, we were much retarded about our Result, by the happy Effect which our Endeavours had met with in him: for he was Convinc'd of his Errors and Misconduct and was ready to come into some Retractions. We (the Ministers) all went out among the people (who waited all Day for our Result) to see how they were temper'd towards Mr. Prentice—but there was some Number that would not consent to receive him again as a Minister, tho they would as a Brother. P.M. we drew up our Result and at Eve the Scribe read it. Mr. Stone concluded with prayer and after a little stop at Mr. Prentice's with his wife, we rode home. N.B. we were so belated by the bad riding that we call'd at Captain Fays. There was Mr. Solomon Pain[21]—but we didn't know him till after he

---

[12] Stephen Parker of Shrewsbury.
[12] Son of Deacon Simon Tainter of Westborough.
[14] David Hall of Sutton.
[15] Nathan Webb of Uxbridge.
[16] Nathan Stone of Southborough.
[17] He lived in the part of Grafton that later became the town of Millbury.
[18] Granny Forbush often served as midwife.
[19] This man, presumed to be a descendant of the distinguished Major Simon Willard of Lancaster, later moved to Greenfield. See Ward, *Shrewsbury*, pp. 477-478.
[20] Several persons of this name were then living in Shrewsbury.
[21] A preacher without a college education who became the minister of the North Society in Canterbury, Conn.

was gone out of the Room and (I suppose) to Bed. Through Divine Goodness I got home safe—but my wife has had a bad Turn—and has been ill ever since I went away. Mr. McCarty has been here in his Journey from Worcester to Boston.

28. Closely Engag'd in my Preparations for tomorrow.

### MARCH [1747]

1. I preach'd on Ps. 51, 18, and on Exod. 18, 21. Mrs. Sybil Child,[1] Mr. Jonathan Forbushes wife and Eli and Asaph din'd with us. I am exceedingly afraid of the Mischief Mr. Solomon Pain will be able to do in Grafton just now.

2. Town Meeting. Mr. Wheeler and Nathan Ball came to request me to go to prayer with them. Lieutenant Holloway here, and pleasant. Sad News from Annapolis, but Time will certifie us. Reckon'd with Deacon Newton and with his son Silas.

3. In the forenoon came Mr. Aaron Hardy from Grafton and din'd here. He gives but a dark account of Things among them— tells me Mr. Solomon Pain is (as I greatly fear'd) among them and preaching. The Separation likely (by these means) to increase there. At Evening came Mr. Harwood,[2] of Grafton Church who had been over to Mr. Martyn for the Result, and had with him a Copy for the Church and for Mr. Prentice.

4. It was Somewhat drisly—but I rode over to Mr. Martyns and preach'd his Lecture, from 1 Pet. 1, 18, 19, and return'd at Eve.

5. Mr. Martyn preach'd my Lecture on [blank]. Take heed how ye hear, a very usefull, savoury Sermon and which I hope God is pleas'd to make use of for our awakening and quickening. May it especially be profitable to my own Soul!

6. Thomme accompany'd by Ebenezer rode down to Marlborough to live at Mr. Williams's, the Sadler. May God be pleas'd to Smile on this attempt for his Benefit! and make him serviceable in his Generation! Ebenezer brought me 50£ Old Tenor from Deacon Andrew Rice, borrow'd of upon Bond, to pay my Brother Samuel Parkman.

7. [No entry.]

8. Sacrament. On 1 Pet. 1, 18, 19. Deacon Fay, Eli and Asaph din'd here. P.M. got Deacon Newton to read (in part) the Act of the General Court against profane Cursing and Swearing again. He read Slow and the people began to drop away so that I finish'd it myself. Receiv'd a Letter from Mr. Stone dated February 28 about our Result.

9. A.M. at Mr. Whipples and got him to come and kill a Calf of 7 weeks old for me, and he din'd with me, as did Mr. Prentice of Grafton who came down to see me under his heavy Burdens. He freely tells me that now he can have no Thoughts of tarrying in Grafton. Their Church is to meet tomorrow and he thinks he must ask a Dismission: his wife having been to hear Mr. Solomon Pain; and last Saturday Morning declar'd for the Separation. N.B. Mr. Samuel Forbush of Upton here and Examin'd in order to his owning the Covenant. Mr. Daniel Fisk also of Upton here and carry'd off the Pork which he bought of me.

10. Neighbour Edwards Whipple carry'd his Loading to Boston on my Mare he taking with him my Calf to market it for me, and 70£ Old Tenor to Brother Samuel Parkman. N.B. I was at Neighbour Eliezer Rice's this morning and improv'd him to take a Time to go and buy me a pair of Steers of Mr. Timothy Warrin. Mr. James Maynard here, but he can't finish his account with me. Mr. Wheeler here and acquaints me with the Death of Mr. Benjamin Rugg last Night at his House, and with his wife's Request to me to attend his Funeral tomorrow, but I gave Mr. Wheeler divers Reason why I could not, being pre-engag'd.

11. Mr. Wheeler yesterday instead of going to Reverend Mr. Cushing or Morse to attend the Funeral of Mr. Rugg, Sought only to Mr. Jenison, who left his School and went. Mr. Benjamin Harwood (of Grafton Church) here, in the Morning and he informs me that their Church met yesterday and voted our Result, tho I perceiv'd that it was but a Slender Majority of 20 against 18. Mr. Harwood in his own and others behalf, desires the Ministers

would discover their Judgment touching some Doctrine pass'd over in the Result, by means of Mr. Prentice's Retractions. I rode to Southborough to Meet Mr. Martyn and Mr. Stone together upon the Grafton affair. Din'd at Mr. Stones with Mr. Martyn. The Latter preach'd on Mat. 11, 23. N.B. Mr. Morse of Shrewsbury came to Lecture. After Lecture Mr. Morse laid before us his Difficultys—he having thrown up his Contract with his People and they have not, and tis thought will not make any new provision for him. I was design'd to Marlborough but Mr. Stone sollicited much that I would stay tonight and that we all would, that we might have Time to Confer upon both the Grafton Affair and Mr. Morse's Case also. We accordingly all of us lodged there.

12. We drew up and sign'd a Letter to the Reverend Mr. Prentice of Grafton advising him to ask a Dismission. When we parted Mr. Morse for Medfield, Mr. Martyn to go and preach at Shrewsbury first Parish, and I went to Marlborough to Mr. Williams's to see my son Thomas, who seems well contented as yet; to Dr. Gotts where I din'd—to Deacon Andrew Rice's to change several Bills, and call'd only at the Door of Dr. Smiths, he not being at Home. N.B. Saw Deacon Rice at Mr. Jonathan Brighams. In returning I call'd at Mr. Thomas Goodenow's. At Home I found that Mr. Edwards Whipple had Come back from Boston last night. He sold my Calf for £3. 2. 6 without the Skin. N.B. Old Mrs. Whipple and Mrs. Amy Maynard[3] here.

13. Strange Alteration of Weather. Night and Morning Stormy. Cold and Snow. When the Day got up it clear'd off and was bright tho Cold. Mr. Hardy from Grafton here for a Return from the Ministers lately met at Mr. Stone's. I committed the Letter to him. At Evening Brother Hicks and Mr. Daniel Champney[4]—came and lodg'd here. They inform me that Mr. John Sparhawk[5] lately dy'd on board of a Vessel at Boston, newly come from Annapolis, and was bury'd in Boston.

14. Brother Hicks and Mr. Champney at Sutton.

15. On 1. Cor. 1, 24 and p.m. on Mat. 5, 33 to 37. Mr. Jonah Warrins wife and Mrs. Beeman[6] din'd here. May God give his Blessing to my Weak Endeavours! I desir'd prayers in the Congregation for my Brother Alexander who I hear is sick.

16. Visited Jonathan Maynard. Dr. Gott din'd with us. Meeting to choose precinct officers. Major Williams[7] of Stockbridge lodg'd here. He was marching his Company down in order to his going to Annapolis but receiv'd Counter Orders on the Road—his men return'd back, but himself proceeding to Boston.

17. Major Williams on his Journey. At Mr. Tinnys and Jesse Brighams to buy oxen but do not succeed. Visited at divers places—Levi Brighams Charles Woods—William Rogers's. Ebenezer morticing posts. 40 at this beginning to do a days Work at it.

18. Rainy Day.

19. Bright and pleasant. Ebenezer holding Posts. Mrs. Garfield (Ebenezer Garfields wife) had my mare and so prevented my riding up to Mr. Wheelers to visit the widow Rugg, and p.m. came Mr. Samuel Forbush's wife from Upton to be examin'd. Mrs. Maynard (James's wife) brought a great Rarity to us, 8 fine fish out of their Brook, chiefly (if not all) Pickerell and Somewhat large.

20. Rode to Mr. Jesse Brighams—to Mr. Martyns: to Mr. Simon Haywards—to Mr. Wheelers to See Mrs. Rugg: to Mr. Crawfords—and was at Bezaleel Eagers.[8]

21. [No entry.]

22. Rode over to Mr. Martyns according to agreement last Friday, and preach'd for him from 2 Cor. 3, 15 and p.m. 10, 14. He preach'd for me on [blank]. P.M. It rain'd So that (tho he return'd home), yet I did not, but lodg'd there.

23. Din'd at Mr. Martyns; it being misty and rainy, but p.m. he and I rode to Mr. William Goddards[9] and I bought a pair of Steers of him nigh 4 years old for 34£ old Tenor. I return'd to my own House at Eve.

---

[1] Mrs. Jonas Child.
[2] Benjamin Harwood.
[3] Mrs. Ebenezer Maynard.
[4] Of Cambridge. The cousin of Parkman's first wife.
[5] The former schoolmaster of Plymouth and Shrewsbury.
[6] Mrs. Eleazer Beemon or Beamon.
[7] Ephraim Williams, the leading citizen of Stockbridge.
[8] All of the people in this entry resided in the North Precinct.
[9] He lived in that part of Marlborough that later became the town of Berlin.

24. Rainy Still. Attended the Catechetical Exercise to young Women but there were So few that came (only 6 besides my own Girls) that we went not to the meeting House. I discours'd to them next to Extemporarily on the Moral Law, the 10 Commandments, in general the manner of God's delivering them etc., for I hardly expected anybody to come such wet Weather. N.B. I hear that Eliezer Rice went out of meeting last Lords Day as soon as first prayer was over—because it was Mr. Martyn, and I hear that Mr. Jenison instead of preaching last Sabbath at Mr. Jones's[10] (of Marlborough) as he has been wont of late, chang'd with Mr. Goss.[11]

25. Sent Ebenezer to Mr. Goddards for the Steers I lately bought of him and paid him 15£ old Tenor. Mr. Martyn and his Wife made us a Visit and din'd here; as did Mr. Williams[12] of Weston likewise, he being on his Journey from Worcester (where he had preach'd for Mr. Maccarty) to Framingham, to See old Colonel Buckminster who draws near his End. Eli Forbush brought from Worcester Mr. Hedge's[13] Henry volume 5.

26. Catechized a. and p.m. at the Meeting House. 14 Boys (with my own) in the whole. 5 Girls including my Dauter Lucy, and no more. N.B. Mr. Willson[14] of Upton (an Irishman) here, in affliction, by the Sickness of his Son (who was in the late fight at Manis) and he din'd here. Mr. Levi Brigham here p.m. on the Affair of his and his Wife's joining to the Church.

27. Ebenezer trys, with Billey riding the Mare, and himself putting up the New Steers to Split Indian Hills.

28. [No entry.]

29. On Mat. 13, 9, 10, 11. P.M. My wife having through Gods great Mercy and Goodness got out to Day, after her lying in, I repeated those Sermons on Ps. 116, 9, and do desire to renew my Engagements as David did to walk before the Lord in the Land of the Living. May God be pleas'd graciously to enable me hereto, and keep it in the Imagination of my Heart continually! Levi Brigham and wife and Samuel Forbush and wife propounded.

30. A Cold I have had increased upon me insomuch that my Voice is exceeding Hoarse. Did something in the Garden. The season forward.

31. A.M. Visited Jonathan Maynard again, and Joshua Townsend came from Mr. Wheelers to desire me to visit Asa Rice[15] and Aaron Wheeler[16] who are sick of a Fever, and having Captain Maynard's Mare I went. Found them bad; yet sensible and penitent. Visited also Mr. Silas Rice's wife who lies sick of a Fever likewise.

### APRIL, 1747

1. Continue to read Taylor on Original sin. P.M. Mr. William Goddard of Marlborough here. Foul Day.

2. Exceeding pleasant. Warm, excellent Weather. Mr. Dunlop came from Lieutenant Tainters with an Horse for my wife and me to ride over there to Day. He Stay'd the forenoon and wrought in my Garden. According to Lieutenant Tainters Request my wife and I din'd there, and p.m. I preach'd to the private Meeting there, on Mat. 16, 26 to page 12, and the application, page 21. Ebenezer Carted Stones a.m. Harrow'd p.m.

3. Rain'd hard last night and this Morning, but about 10 clear'd off and Mr. Dunlop came to work in my Garden. Ebenezer Sow'd Some Barley and ploughs it in with the Mare. N.B. Billey begins more manfully to ride to plough. N.B. Some talk with Mr. Phinehas Hardy about his Son Constantine.

4. Ebenezer Sow'd the rest of the Barley and Some Early Peas.

5. On Mat. 13, 12 and p.m. on Rom. 12, 11. Appointed the Communion to be next Lords Day—tho it would be but the fifth Sabbath since the last Communion, yet the sixth Since the First Sabbath of March. Mrs. Mary Steward and Mr. Jonas Warrin's wife of Upton din'd with us. Frosts hard from one night to another.

6. Cool Day, but the Season wondrous forward. Apple trees

begin to put forth their Leaves. Mr. Dunlop came Early to work at my Garden, but went away about 3 in the afternoon, being oblig'd upon some unavoidable Business at Hopkinton. And was So generous as to give all his work these Several Days—making more than a Day and a half. Moses Pratt came with those oxen from Eliezer Rice's which Timothy Warrin bought of me, and with my Team join'd thereto plough'd my Stubble. Dr. Daniel Warrin also came p.m. and built Stone Wall, before the Ground where my old House stood. N.B. Captain William Brintnall[1] here; and informs me that old Colonel Buckminster[2] now lyes Dead. Deacon Forbush's wife here and brought me excellent Flax seed, a peck and half, and Eli half peck from his uncle Tainters, all of it gratis. I engag'd Moses Pratt[3] to work for me next Hay Time.

7. Mr. Warrin lodg'd here last night and works for me again to Day at building Stone Wall: part of the forenoon where he wrought yesterday: the rest of the Day at the northeast part of my Improvements. Neighbour Hezekiah Tomlin ploughs here with his oxen join'd to my Team. Mr. Jenison comes over from the northside and goes to keep School in the South part of Town. Asa Rice continues very low (I hear) but not worse. Aaron Wheeler much worse and very dangerously ill. My son Thomme came up from Marlborough to See us. Mr. Bacon[4] from Ashuelot (upper) came and lodg'd here. He brings the sorrowful News that a Number of Indians the night after last Sabbath was Sennight came to Mr. Shattucks Fort,[5] and fir'd it. They burnt down the Fort at Number 2 or great meadows[6]—and burnt an House of Colonel Josiah Willard. That their Town as well as the other Ashuelot[7] were broke up and come off—as was Winchester also. That Captain Melvin[8] and 26 men went out after the Indians, and discover'd 14 and packs of about 20. That Captain Stephens[9] with 50 men had been gone about 3 Weeks and no news of him but twas hop'd he was at No. 4.

8. Thomas returns to Mr. Williams's at Marlborough. Mr. Bacon left us to go to his Fathers[10] at Wrentham. Planted Some Bush Peas which he brought.

9. Publick Fast. A.M. on Joel 2, 12. P.M. on Jer. 12, 4, former part chiefly, and us'd some of the Improvement of Sermon on Ezra 10, 10, 11, 12.

10. Ebenezer a.m. graffing Pear Cyons[11] in Apple Stocks, but the Trees rather too forward, as is all Nature. Every Thing wondrously putting out. God's name be prais'd who pitys His People, and in the Middst of wrath remembers Mercy!

11. Rainy Morning. When it held up, tho the Sun broke out but now and then yet was it a growing Season.

12. Sacrament Day, yet this Morning just as I was going out to Meeting (with my Hat in my Hand), comes Levi Brigham with his and his wife's Relations which must be look'd over etc. A number of other Persons came, divers of them to my House, with various Cases—all by word of mouth which caused me to Speak to the Congregation to bring their Desires written—and when they have Business that takes any Time, they must not defer it till the Lord's Day. A.M. preach'd on Isa. 1, 18. P.M. from Rom. 12, 11, first Clause, but us'd the Heads in sermon on Mat. 20, 6, from page 24 to 31, resolving the Doubts which old men might frame against converting and becoming Religious. N.B. Mr. Jenison was at the sermons, and Sat in my Pew, but withdrew from the Communion. No fresh Occasion of Disgust that I know of. Deacon Fay, Mr. Nathan Balls wife, and Mr. Zeublon Rice's wife din'd here.

13. Very rainy. A.M. Mr. James Eager here to inform me of the Death of his Brother, Aaron Wheeler, who expir'd last night

---

[10] Samuel Jones.
[11] The Reverend Thomas Goss of Bolton.
[12] The Reverend William Williams.
[13] Elisha Hedges.
[14] John Willson.
[15] Son of Thomas Rice, Jr.
[16] Son of Joseph Wheeler.

[1] Of Sudbury.
[2] Joseph Buckminster of Framingham.
[3] Son of Isaac Pratt.
[4] The Reverend Jacob Bacon of Keene, N.H.
[5] Daniel Shattuck's garrison house was within the limits of the present town of Hinsdale, N.H.
[6] No. 2 township, sometimes known as Great Meadows, was incorporated as Westmoreland, N. H., in 1752.
[7] Lower Ashuelot was incorporated as Swanzey, N. H., in 1753.
[8] Eleazer Melvin.
[9] Phinehas Stevens.
[10] Thomas Bacon.
[11] An obsolete form of scion, a term sometimes used for a graft.

about Sunsetting. A Sore Bereavement to his Father and Mother, who, he being their only Son set their Hearts much upon him. May God Sanctifie this heavy Affliction to their highest Good. I had rather they would have sent to Mr. Martyn, but Mr. Eager said that they had determin'd to send to Mr. Jenison if I could not go. He informs me likewise that Asa Rice lyes at the point of Death if he be living. O that all young persons, and mine in Particular might take warning! renounce their Vanitys and prepare for Death and Judgment! P.M. I was at Neighbour Garfields, whose wife was just before brought to Bed of a Dauter. Finish'd Mr. Stoddards and Mathers Controversy about Right to the Lords Supper.[12]

14. Rode (with Deacon Forbush and his Wife) to Mr. Martyns and ask'd him to go with me to the Burial of Aaron Wheeler to which he immediately consented and went. I din'd at Mr. Wheelers. Asa Rice yet alive, there, tho very low. I pray'd and took leave. N.B. Mr. White[13] of Lancaster and his wife (who was a Ball) accompany'd me to Lancaster. Mr. Prentice much out of Health. Ministers Meeting had been put by, but I had not receiv'd the Letter, Said to be sent to me. Several ministers there notwithstanding—Mr. Cushing, Buckminster,[14] and Davis.[15] The 2 last went to Harvard. Mr. Cushing and I stay'd. Mr. Prentice pleasant at Evening—as he was also

15. In the Morning but tis fear'd his Disorders prevail. Visited Judge Wilder—talk'd of Westborough arrearages—to little purpose—he did not design to go to the General Court again. Din'd at Mr. Goss's—and it rain'd So that I was oblig'd to lodge there also.

16. Early in the Morning Mr. Goss and I rode to Mr. Seccombs,[16] and breakfasted there. N.B. brought from thence several books—Seldons Table Talk:[17] Warders Monarchy of Bees[18] etc. And from his Garden Box trees and a Variety of Curious Graffs etc. Din'd at Mr. Goss's (his wife gone from home)—call'd to Mr. Martyns (who was gone afishing). Return'd home in Safety my Self thro Gods tender mercy. But whilst I was abroad heard Sorrowful Tidings of the Indians assaulting the Garrison at Saratoga, and they kill'd and carry'd off Captive 40 Soldiers—and at Kenderhook kill'd and Captivated 11. N.B. Jonathan Maynard worse—visited him this Evening. At home whilst I was at Lancaster, a large promising Steer coming 2 years old, for which I had lately got a mate of Mr. David Maynard, was drown'd at a meadow where my young Cattle went to feed.

17. [No entry.]

18. [No entry.]

19. On Isa. 1, 18. P.M. on Thess. 5, 4. Mrs. Byles of Grafton din'd here.

20. Rain. Read Seldens Miscellaneous Discourses, or Table-Talk.

21. Dr. Gott here. Preach'd at old Mr. Maynards on occasion of his son Jonathans Sickness and confinement—and to Young Mens Society there. Text Luke 19, 10. A crowded House. May God give a Blessing, that the Word may do us good as it does the upright! Frost last night.

22. Ebenezer ploughing the rest of the Stubble. N.B. Neighbour Benjamin Hows Oxen with mine—and his brother Daniel drove. A greater Frost last night than the night before.

23. Rainy Day.

24. [No entry.]

25. Mr. Chamberlin at work here carting out muck. N.B. I visited Jonathan Maynard in the Morning.

26. On Mat. 13, 13, 14, 15. P.M. on John 21, 15. N.B. Mr. Nathan Maynard came in the morning to call me hastily to see his brother Jonathan and I went immediately. At Evening Jonathan Maynard dy'd. My [?] went to see 'em presently after his Expiring.

27. Ebenezer work'd at Mr. Tomlins. I rode to Marlborough and pay'd the remainder of the Bond at Mr. Jesse Rice's, and the Interest and took up the Bond. N.B. Mr. Joshua Wheeler of Boston and his wife there. Thence I rode to Bolton (Calling at Captain Barnards[19]—din'd at Mr. Benjamin Lawrence's (who lately dwelt at Westborough.) N.B. visited her sister Esther Russell who has lain Sick for Some Years and has not spoke a word ever since last March was Two Years. I proceeded to Mr. Joseph Tainters at Marlborough and at Colonel Williams[20]—call'd also at Mr. Amsdens[21] at Westborough. Got home before the Storm set in, which prov'd very great in The night. Fear'd my Barn would be blown down by the Strong Winds.

28. A great storm of Rain, and high winds. Jonathan Maynard bury'd. Nobody came to a Catechetical Exercise which was appoint'd to be today.

29. Ebenezer went with my Team to Ensign Rice's, and got some more Hay about 8 or 10 Hundred. Mr. Townsend[22] brot a Letter from Mr. Martyn requesting me to preach his Lecture tomorrow—but I have appointed a Catechizing of children, which prevents. Mr. Ebenezer Garfield[23] had my mare to go to Shrewsbury. Neighbour Jonas Brigham and his wife here to be Examin'd etc. Could do but a little for 'em because they came so near night. N.B. Mrs. Hannah Warrin (wife of Daniel) of Shrewsbury here.

30. In the morning visited Mr. Joslin who has been Sometime not well. Catechiz'd both forenoon and afternoon. A.M. 30 Boys; p.m. 24 Girls. Nathan Maynard work'd here for Noah How. N.B. Ebenezer p.m. Searching about for 2 Yearlings which were missing. At Eve he rode up to Mr. Adams's[24] at Shrewsbury.

## MAY, 1747

1. A.M. I rode to Shrewsbury after my Two Yearlings which yesterday follow'd Moses Brigham's Drove—but stopp'd at Shrewsbury by Major Keys's. I obtain'd of the Major to take em in his pasture till I could send for 'em. Din't at home. Noah How at work for me.

2. Rainy a.m. Ebenezer to Shrewsbury for the 2 Yearlings. Stopp'd at Major Keyes. Mr. Reed[1] of Framingham and Company here waiting on his new spouse home. P.M. Mr. Cushing came here and I rode to Shrewsbury.

3. I preach'd at Shrewsbury a.m. on 2 Cor. 3, 15 and p.m. 10, 14 and 17. It rain'd at Eve yet both Mr. Cushing and I return'd home. Mr. Cushing preach'd at Westborough and propounded my Dauter Mary to be join'd in full Communion with the Church. Blessed be God for such Tokens of his Grace as are appearing in her! O that they might be increas'd more and more!

4. So rainy our Cattle did not go to Sutton.

5. Mr. Jonah Warrin had my mare for his son and they drove up my young Cattle (seven of them) to Sutton. Mr. Smith[2] came this way in going to Shrewsbury, where the Association met this Day. I rode Noah Hows mare, Ebenezer using mine daily in ploughing. N.B. a long and warm disputation with Mr. Buckminster of Rutland, he affirming (if I could understand him) that men who are of Shining powers and Advantages, and that are in a Natural State, do not contract Guilt according to the Talents they are entrusted with and their abuse of them. N.B. This Debate arose from some passages which Mr. Seccomb had inserted from

[12] The controversy between Solomon Stoddard and Increase Mather began in 1700. Mather's Order of the Gospel (Boston, 1700) was followed by Stoddard's Doctrine of Instituted Churches (London, 1700). Mather published an "Advertisement, Directed to the Communicants in the Churches of New England" in Thomas Doolittle, A Treatise Concerning the Lords Supper, The Twentieth Edition (Boston, 1708). This was an answer to Stoddard's The Inexcusableness of Neglecting the Worship of God (Boston, 1708). Mather responded with A Dissertation wherein the Strange Doctrine Lately Published in a Sermon . . . is Examined and Confuted (Boston, 1708). Then came Stoddard's An Appeal to the Learned. Being a Vindication of the Right of the Visible Saints to the Lord's Supper (Boston, 1709). Later Mather wrote an epistle which was prefixed to Stoddard's A Guide to Christ (Boston, 1714).

[13] Deacon and Captain Joseph White had married Patience, the daughter of James Ball of Westborough.

[14] Joseph Buckminster of Rutland.

[15] Joseph Davis of Holden.

[16] The Reverend John Seccomb of Harvard.

[17] John Selden, Table-Talk (London, 1689). Numerous editions followed, one as late as 1892.

[18] Joseph Warder, The True Amazons, or the Monarchy of Bees (London, 1713). This went through 8 editions by 1749.

[19] Robert Barnard, who lived in Marlborough near the Bolton line, was a miller and kept a public house.

[20] Abraham Williams, Parkman's brother-in-law.

[21] Jacob Amsden.

[22] Joshua Townsend of the north side of town.

[23] Of Shrewsbury.

[24] Jonathan Adams lived near the Westborough line.

[1] The Reverend Solomon Reed.

[2] The Reverend Aaron Smith of Marlborough.

Cruttenden[3] concerning John Taylor's Book of Original Sin.[4] N.B. Most sorrowful News from Brookfield, Captain Buckminsters[5] Negro Girl having murder'd her Bastard Child last Lords Day. N.B. Lodg'd at Mr. Cushings.

6. Mr. Martyn and Mr. Maccarty came. The former tells us that Mr. Goss under his Lameness by a late Fall from his Horse, was now gone home to Bolton. At a Motion of mine to have the Association bring their Answers to any particular Questions which any member Should desire to have consider'd, the ministers voted to prepare their answers to this following, viz. What Shall best be done by us to prevent the Degeneracy and Back sliding in Religion which now awfully Threatens? N.B. This is not at all to hinder the Collections as usual. N.B. Several Gentlemen seem'd to think hard of my having the Collections repos'd with me; and therefore rested not till they obtain'd a Vote to have 'em from henceforth distributed: and those which were brought at this Meeting were accordingly distributed. When we were going out to meeting (and Mr. Barrett[6] to preach) came Joshua Townsend and presently after him Jason Badcock from Mr. Wheelers (of Westborough) who request'd me to make all haste to visit him before he dy'd, so that instead of going to meeting I went there. Mr. Wheeler was very low, but he wanted me more to assist him in drawing his Will over again than to help him in his Spiritual Work; which greatly engag'd my Thoughts—to See a man So apprehensive that he was going into Eternity So easy and quiet about it—saying that if he was not ready before now, it was now too late to do anything. N.B. I drew over his will, and made the Alterations which he desir'd. And as my office was, I conceiv'd it suitable to recommend some Charitable or Pious Deeds, to a Man that was able to leave such an Estate: I mention'd his leaving something to the Church—a good Bible—a Flaggon—or if he would he might leave something to the poor of the town. He pitch'd upon the first Thing, a Bible, which was accordingly inserted, his wife being by and several Times declaring she was heartily free for it. N.B. Jason accompany'd me through the Barrs and humbly ask'd pardon for all his old ill Behaviour and seem'd very penitent. Upon which I gave him my Hand, and we were reconciled. He ask'd my prayers and was full of good Resolutions. I call'd at Mr. Martyns, where Messers Loring,[7] Stone and Smith had stop'd. My Family in peace. Blessed be God!

7. Preach'd at Captain Fays the remainder of sermon on Mat. 16, 26. May God write these moving Things upon our Hearts. N.B. Mrs. Whitney crying out in the Orchard after Meeting. My Dauter Molly rode with Nabby How. I was at Captain Bakers at Eve. He not at home.

8. Rode over to see Mr. Wheeler, having many things lying very heavy upon my mind respecting his Case. I went first to see Betty Ball (dauter of Mr. James Ball) who lyes very Sick of a Fever. Sh was very thankfull to me and behav'd with a great Deal of Decency. She confess'd her Youthful Vanitys on the Lords Day especially, and pray'd me to Exhort and Charge her Brothers and sisters—which I did—pray'd with her and them. Din'd there and went from thence to Mr. Wheelers. Found him very weak and low. Dealt as freely as I could with him—ask'd him plainly what his sentiments were about the Doctrine of Election, and Original Sin, whether he believ'd them and he said he did etc. etc. Pray'd with him and the rest of his Family. O that God would graciously afford me Courage, widsom, and assistance to discharge my Ministerial Duty to particular persons with faithfullness! N.B. Stephen Maynard was so kind as to come with a Team and a Boy, and plough'd in my Field, a.m. Ebenezer furrow'd out p.m.

9. Warm Day. Ebenezer began to plant Indian Corn. But I don't suffer myself to be disturb'd with it having had so many avocations and Impediments.

10. On Mat. 13, 16, 17. P.M. repeat'd Mat. 16, 15.

11. Ebenezer ploughing. Captain Maynard kindly sent Rodney Smith and his brother Jonathan to help him and they finish'd before they din'd. P.M. Training. Captain Maynard himself came and view'd my Arms etc. which I expos'd to him, to his Satisfaction. Mr. Jenison was with him, and I walk'd out with them (at the Captain's earnest request) and pray'd with the Company. After which we went down to Captain Maynards—where was (among others) Captain Buckminster of Brookfield. News of the Mohawks taking 6 Scalps near Crown Point.

12. Rain a.m. Ebenezer plant'd potatoes. P.M. my wife and I rode over to Mr. Martyns. Dr. Smith there.

13. Ebenezer sow'd Peas. P.M. he wash'd Sheep. N.B. School at Eliezer Rice's.

14. Molly rode to Mr. Batchellors[8] at Grafton and was at Mr. Prentice's.[9] N.B. One John Remington a Lincolnshire man, of 92 years (as he says) here and din'd with us. He was here some years agoe—says he is a Burst man and goes about upon Charity.

15. Rain. Major Jones, Esquire Brigham and Mr. Simon Goddard[10] here. Brother Hicks towards Eve from Cambridge. Confirmation by the News papers of the dreadful Earthquake at Lima.

16. Brother Hicks to Sutton. Captain Maynard breakfasts here on Bacon etc.

17. On Mat. 13, 24, and p.m. before the admission of my Dauter Mary into full Communion with the Church. I repeated (with many alterations) my sermon on Mat. 19, 10, 22, the drift of which is to remove objections which are wont to discourage young people from being early religious. And Blessed be God, who I humbly hope has taken hold of the Heart of my dear Child, and engag'd her to Himself! O that the work of Divine Grace may be carry'd on in her Soul, and that she may have Divine Strength, Comfort and Establishment. And O that He would please to impart His Heavenly Grace to my other Children! This being infinitely the most Valuable and precious Gift for me to desire for them. Nor can anything give me such joy as to see my children walking in the Truth. O how Cutting was it to Samuel when it was Said to him, Thy Children walk not in thy Ways! and how wounding is the Thought to me if any of mine Should forsake the way of the Lord and finally miscarry!

18. I rode to Grafton to Speak with Mr. Joseph Batchellor—met with him at Mr. Winchesters. Rode with him up to Mr. Prentice's. Spent a great part of the afternoon with Mr. Prentice and his wife. She declar'd herself a Separate. I endeavour'd to discharge my Duty to her, to convince her of her Error; (especially Knowledge of the Spiritual Status of Persons looking on the Church in Grafton no Church of Christ. Her irregular Separation, She having never laid anything before that Church or Christian society esteeming themselves a Church of Christ, for their Conviction). I endeavour'd also to warn her against Defect in Relative Dutys in the House; and giving occasion to others to suspect criminal Freedoms with the other sex, under the splendid Guise of Spiritual Love and Friendship. I bore my Testimony against Visions and Revelations—and with Mr. Prentice, as to his appointing the Communion to be next Lords Day, whilst there is so great Confusion among them by the Vote only of 8 or 9 members, the Body of the Church were against it, I told him it would not do; there could be no Validity nor propriety in it. Parted very brotherly. A great storm seem'd to be rising. I got to Mr. Winchesters before it pour'd down. N.B. Mr. Brooks,[11] Mrs. Willard and a number of them there, going to Market to Boston. After the shower I went to Phinehas Hardy and thence home. N.B. Town Meeting at Westborough, chose Mr. Francis Whipple again their Representative.

19. Ebenezer plough'd the lower south side and planted little Beans. P.M. Mr. Charles Brigham[12] was here to talk with me about their sorrowful State in Grafton.

20. A.M. sent Ebenezer over to Mr. Goddards to desire further

---

[3] Robert Cruttenden may have commented on Taylor's work in one of its several editions, or Parkman may have had reference to *The Experience of Mr. R. Cruttenden* (London, 1744). This was reprinted in Boston in 1744.
[4] John Taylor, *The Scripture Doctrine of Original Sin Proposed to Free and Candid Examination* (London, 1740).
[5] Thomas Buckminster.
[6] Samuel Barrett of Hopkinton.
[7] The Reverend Israel Loring of Sudbury.

[8] Joseph Batcheller.
[9] The Reverend Solomon Prentice.
[10] Of Shrewsbury.
[11] Ebenezer Brooks of Grafton.
[12] An original proprietor of Grafton, a frequent office holder, and sometime Representative in the General Court. Pierce, *Grafton*, pp. 463-464.

Time—and to Mr. Martyn to request him to preach my Lecture tomorrow. Mr. Joseph Wheeler dy'd.

21. Rain yet Mr. Martyn came and preach'd my Lecture from John 7, 17. N.B. tho Mr. Martyn preaches very well yet some of my people are so disgusted with him that they will not hear him. James Maynard and Eliezer Rice when they came so near the Meeting House as to know who preach'd they turn'd back and went their way. This I am heartily griev'd for. May God give them a better Mind!

22. Rode over and attend'd (with Mr. Martyn whom I went to, and took with me) the Funeral of Mr. Joseph Wheeler, who is the seventh of the 12 original members who have deceas'd. I pray'd abroad with the people—the Corps being Set before us. The Lord Sanctifie this Death to us all! After Prayer, Mr. Martyn accompanying the Corps to the Grave, I rode over to see Betty Ball who is very low and dangerous and pray'd with her. Thence to Captain Eagers where the mourners in their Return halted and retir'd to have me read the will of the deceas'd Mr. Wheeler. O that God would truely awaken us, and fit us for our own Turn!

23. Mr. Crosby[13] has made a pair of shoes for me, as he work'd at Captain Maynards. My mind greatly disquieted by my own negligence in sermonizing: but my Cares and encumbrances are unavoidably very great.

24. The Lords Supper was administer'd—Preach'd on 2 Cor. 13, 5, repeating with omissions and alterations sermon on 1 Cor. 11, 28 to page 10. P.M. on Mat. 13, 25 to 30. Captain Fay, the widow Thurston[14] and old Mrs. Tabitha Fay[15] din'd with us. O that God would graciously quicken us!

25. Mr. Daniel Warrin work'd here. A.M. he built wall at the rear pasture. N.B. A.M. Mrs. Porter of Salem Village and her sister Suse Batchellor here—broke fast with me. P.M. I was at Mr. Cooks[16] (Smiths) Shop.

26. Visited Mrs. Joslin[17] in her sickness—proceeded to Mr. Stones of Southborough. He was not at home—pursued my Journey to Framingham. Visited Mrs. Farrar[18] (formerly Swift). From Weston had Mr. Rice[19] (of Sturbridge) his Company to Watertown. Lodg'd at Mother Champneys. She herself Still very weak and wasting.

27. Rain in Early Morning. When it slack'd I rode to Boston. N.B. My Brother Alexander never mention'd my little Boy, which with so much affection I nam'd after him. Dr. Chauncy[20] preach'd on 2 Sam. 23, 3. Din'd at Brother Samuels with Captain Maynard. My Brethren Seem desirous to take this Opportunity to consult together respecting the settlement of Mothers Estate—but Brother Alexander seems very unquiet and unmanageable and will consent to nothing, but what is in his particular Scheme. To this Disturbance and Ruffle about the Estate, I attribute his Disregard to my little son. But I am not willing to take any Notice of it. Was at the Convention—Dr. Sewal[21] Moderator and pray'd, Mr. Checkley[22] Clerk. Mr. Josiah Cotton[23] desires to be remov'd from Providence. Letter of Dr. Avery[24] on the Subjects of his presenting the Address of the Convention of Ministers last year to the king and the Affair of Mr. Torrey, read—voted Thanks to Dr. Avery for his Pains and Care. At Eve at the North End. Lodg'd at Dr. Parkmans[25] (who was marry'd some months ago) and his sister Eliza just by it, to one Mr. Cowel, a Cooper. N.B. Mr. Winget,[26] Mr. Chase[27] and Mr. Wellman[28] lodg'd there also.

---

13 David Crosby of Shrewsbury.
14 Mrs. Joseph Thurston.
15 Mrs. Samuel Fay.
16 Cornelius Cook, the Westborough blacksmith.
17 Mrs. Joseph Joslin.
18 Major John Farrar married Martha, the daughter of the Reverend John Swift. See Temple, *Framingham*, pp. 544-545.
19 The Reverend Caleb Rice.
20 Charles Chauncy.
21 Joseph Sewell of the Old South Church.
22 Samuel Checkly of the Second Church of Boston.
23 The minister of the First Congregational Church in Providence who later served the third church in Woburn, 1747-1756.
24 John Avery (Harvard 1706) was the minister of Truro, 1711-1754. He was also a physician. *Sibley*, V, 302-305.
25 Elias Parkman, a physician of Boston, was Ebenezer Parkman's uncle.
26 The Reverend Paine Wingate (Harvard 1723), the minister of the West Church in Amesbury, 1726-1786. *Sibley*, VII, 287-289.
27 The Reverend Stephen Chase of Lynnfield.
28 James Wellman (Harvard 1744) was the first minister of Millbury, Mass., 1747-1760.

28. Mr. Prescott[29] preach'd to the ministers on Rom. 3, 28, an Extremely long sermon. The Contribution 304. 19. 0. I din'd at Mr. Foxcrofts.[30] N.B. the late renowned Mr. Pembertons Relect, now Loyd,[31] and her Dauter Mrs. Vanns[32] din'd here. At Eve to Cambridge.

29. Rode over to College and smok'd a Pipe with Mr. Mayhew.[33] Talk'd with him about Eli Forbush. In returning call'd at Mrs. Bekky Walkers shop. Rain and Thunder whilst I stop'd at Baldwins. N.B. Mr. Cheney[34] and his Brother Samuel Cotton,[35] and Mr. Seccomb of Harvard came there. The two first came home with me and lodg'd here.

30. Mr. Cheney went home. Ebenezer has done next to none of the weeding. Does something of it to Day.

31. On 2 Chron. 15, 2 with alterations, etc. Rom. 6, 13.

### JUNE, 1747

1. Noah How work'd with Ebenezer at Weeding.

2. Noah How again. Mrs. Porter widow, and her sister Suse Batchellor here.

3. Rain a.m. Noah p.m. helping Ebenezer weed. N.B. Mr. David Batherick here again bargain'd to get my Meadow (viz. to mow and rake) for 8£. Mr. Breck came towards Eve. And at Eve Mr. Stephen Williams and his son—and Mr. Wadsworth[1] of Hartford—and they all lodg'd here. N.B. pastur'd 3 Horses in Captain Maynards.

4. Mr. Breck, Williams, Wadsworth and Williams [sic] went off. Noah How still at Weeding. Lieutenant Tainter and his Joseph Bowker, and Mr. Samuel Harrington with good Team came and got Wood, a good pile. Lieutenant at 4 p.m. went to Mr. Whipples to private meeting. The rest stay'd. N.B. Mr. Whipple here, and talk'd (to my grief) respecting the Common Medium of Trade, etc. Towards night came Mr. Wellman, preacher at Sutton, and lodg'd here.

5. Noah How. Mr. Wellman went to Sutton.

6. N.B. Noah How and my son Ebenezer had acquainted me that Mr. Jenison had offer'd to read one of his sermons to the young men at their meeting next Sabbath Evening if I was willing. I consented but not to his preaching. But to Day I saw him and spoke with him about it. P.M. he was here and very chearly but no word of this matter.

7. A.M. on Mat. 13, 29, 30 and 39 to 43. P.M. on 2 Cor. 13, 5 using Sermon on 1 Cor. 11, 28 from page 10 to page 21. After Evening Service I Stop'd the Church and having read the Letter from the Church of Worcester requesting our assistance in the Ordination of Mr. Maccarty, I ask'd for a Vote whether they comply'd with it, and for better Discovery desir'd those who voted it to move into the womens Seats—upward of Twenty appear'd for it and but 13 against it. Captain Baker[2] was also chose the Church's Delegate. Mr. Jenison at my House after Meeting but Said nothing of his meeting with the young men. But I understood afterwards that he went in among them and talk'd with them concerning my unwillingness etc. But that he would Speak with me himself about it.

8. Early in the Morning came Mr. Jenison and we had some Discourse together about my unwillingness that he Should preach. Mr. Whitney here afterwards—gave him some admonitory Caution about keeping to such word as he gives about Work, if not promising yet encouraging his Customers to have it done—and if it be in little Things yet to have proper Regard to it. Mr. Josiah Bowker call'd to see me just before I mounted to go to Marlborough. I call'd at Mr. David Brighams and at Levi's. Din'd at Mr. Smiths. Went to Mr. Williams and talk'd with him on the

---

29 Benjamin Prescott of Peabody.
30 The Reverend Thomas Foxcroft of the First Church of Boston.
31 The widow of tutor Ebenezer Pemberton (d. 1718) married John Campbell and then Henry Lloyd of Long Island.
32 Mary, the daughter of Ebenezer and Mary Pemberton, married Hugh Vans.
33 Joseph Mayhew (Harvard 1730), a tutor and later minister at Nantucket, 1761-1766. *Sibley*, VIII, 730-734.
34 The Reverend Thomas Cheney of Brookfield.
35 Brother of Cheney's second wife, Mary Cotton.
1 Daniel Wadsworth (Yale 1726), the minister of the First Church in Hartford, 1732-1747. Dexter, *Biographical Sketches*, pp. 340-341.
2 Edward Baker.

Affair of binding Thomme—but he would insist for my finding his Cloths. We did not proceed—but suspended it for the present. Was at Dr. Gotts and call'd at Mr. Matthias Rices. Barrs for my Book of the Platform etc.

9. I visited Millicent Rice[3] again in her Sickness at Captain Fays. I also visited Mrs. Miller (Mr. James Millers wife) who is in a Languishing Condition. At Eve I rode down to Mr. Cooks Shop.

10. Captain Baker accompany'd me to Worcester. Ebenezer was disappointed of his Cloths which could not be made, and he resign'd his Horse to his sister Molly who therefore went. Thomme also (who came up from Marlborough last night) went to Worcester. Mr. Williams[4] of Weston was chose Moderator and Mr. Gray[5] of Boston Clerk. N.B. Colonel Chandlers interpretation of that part of a Paper which Mr. Maccarty had Sign'd relating to Itinerants, viz. not to intend orderly ministers and of good standing in the Church of God who may Journey etc., but rambling Fellows that go about preaching. We went to Meeting in procession. Mr. Campbell[6] began with prayer. Mr. Maccarty preach'd on 1 Thess. 2, 13. Mr. Moderator pray'd and gave the Charge, and Mr. Cotton[7] of Newton the Right Hand. Handsome Entertainment at Colonel Chandlers. N.B. Mr. Flynt[8] and his Nephews son Henry Quincy[9] in Company with us from Mr. Cushings. A great many Clergy men at the Installment. I design'd to have return'd home this Eve, but my Dauter Molly was not well. She lodg'd at Colonel Chandlers but I lodg'd at Dr. Brecks. N.B. Mrs. Breck lately lain in of a Dauter.

11. Was at Mr. Fessendens who tells me that our Claim upon Esquire Lee's Estate is allow'd by the Judge, but the Administrator has not made up his Accounts yet. Broke fast at Mr. Maccartys with Mr. Gray and his Delegates, Mr. Bridge, Messers Newman and Thomas Greenough. I return'd home before we din'd. N.B. Mr. David Braynard, Missionary to the Indians on the Forks of Delaware under an ill habit of Body journeying for his Health was here and din'd with me, together with Miss Jerusha Edwards[10] of Northampton. Mr. Braynard gave me an account of the original of his mission and the success of it. To the glory and Honour of the Great Author of all Goodness and Mercy! N.B. Noah How[11] with Ebenezer Digging a Drain from my home Meadow into the Barns Swamp. Ebenezer Mow'd the Garden and fore yard.

12. Incomparable Weather. O that my soul bore any proportion to the State of Nature without!

13. News of more Spoil on our Enemys by the Mohawks.

14. On Mat. 13, 31, 32, 33 and 44. P.M. on 2 Cor. 13, 5, using further the latter part of sermon on 1 Cor. 11, 28 from page 21 to 28. Rainy Day, yet a Considerable Assembly.

15. Deacon Newton[12] and Mr. Francis Whipple here to induce me to Sue the Town for their arrearages to me. P.M. Mrs. Persis Brigham[13] here and was examin'd. At Eve Josiah Bowker here in Soul Concern. N.B. A Lye voluntarily confess'd. God grant remission! The conviction was ripen'd by Yesterday afternoon sermon.

16. I rode to Sudbury to Ministerial Meeting there. As I went I call'd at Mr. Cornelius Cooks Shop and got a Shooe put on to my Horse. At the meeting there were Mr. Cushing, Gardner, Barrett, Stone, Smith, Morse, Millen, Goss, Davis, Seccomb. See Association Records for what we did except my asking their Advice upon the article of my Suing the town of Westboro for my Sallery, in which they were to a Man Warm and Zealous against it. This I did not See meet to enter any Thing of in our Records.

17. Mr. Swift, Mr. Bliss[14] and Mr. Minot[15] came to Ministerial Meeting. Mr. Seccomb preach'd a Savoury and moving Sermon upon John 4, 41, 42. It seems indeed to have been Compos'd in A Strain which many would Term New-Light, but there was not much ground, if any at all for any one to make Exception. But I saw plainly that it did not go down well with Some Gentlemen. I am heartily sorry that there are any Remains of the Bitter root among us. I returned by Marlboro home.

18. Expected Mr. Barrett to preach a Lecture for me to my young people but he did not come. I preach'd my Self on Ps. 109, 4, latter part; and do beg it may have Effect, both on my Heart and the Audience! N.B. Neighbour Jonathan Rogers kill'd a Calf for me this morning. Captain Warrin and Neighbour How a Quarter apiece, Neighbour Chamberlin and Neighbour Cook a Quarter between them. N.B. after Lecture Captain Warrin, Messers Whitney, Abner Newton, Batherick and a number more stopp'd at my Barn and drawd up the Joints which were out to place, and pinn'd them and sett up shores to keep it from wrecking any more. N.B. To my great sorrow heard the Storys confirm'd of Mr. Prentice beating his Wife again; Ensign Pratt[16] of Grafton being here: who likewise desir'd me to desist with Mr. Ebenezer Rice's request for special Privileges, till he could talk with him a little. Mr. Jenison supp'd with me, and he attended Two Marriages here this Evening, viz. Mr. Tomlins[17] and James Miller[18] junior's. N.B. Mr. Jenison pray'd after the Covenant was administer'd to the last Couple.

19. Mr. Jenison active amongst young men in the Neighbourhood to persuade 'em to come and help me in my Farm Business. Ebenezer has done a part of the second hoeing and to Day ploughs the chief of the rest.

20. Goodhew, Daniel How, Nathan Maynard, Benjamin Whipple and Rody Smith came in the morning and hoed my Corn and my Beans and had done by 11 a.m. a great Kindness, and Relief tho it took but so little Time. P.M. Mr. Smith of Marlborough came to 'change. Mr. Whipple our Representative who came up to Day tells us that a Post is gone down to Boston with News from the Mohawks that 3000 French and Indians have come over the Lake. This will put us into new Distresses by pressing out our men again at this busy Season. I rode to Marlborough and lodg'd at Mr. Smiths.

21. I preach'd at Marlborough on Rom. 8, 7, a. and p.m. Mr. Smith at Westborough on Phil. 3, 8. We each return'd home this Evening.

22. Ebenezer begins the other mowing and strikes into the South side. Eli Forbush came here to board and to be instructed. P.M. Mr. Wellman from Sutton here and lodges. N.B. Shews me his Answer and Proposals to the people in Sutton that had call'd him to settle with them in the Ministry.

23. Mr. Wellman and Mr. Jenison journey, to Waterton and Cambridge. I visited Mrs. Miller again. She thinks She is grown better, but I fear it is self-Flattery. Was at Mr. Charles Rice's. Got him to choose a Scythe for my son at Ebenezer Rice's. Was also at Lieutenant Tainters. He requests me to write a Letter to Benjamin in Canada, if yet alive. Ebenezer mowing the Southside.

24. The Press very hot in Town, for 7 out of the first Company and 6 out of the second to go to Hatfield besides a Commission Officer to conduct them. A Sore Frown of Providence this Busy Season. Ebenezer mowing and getting in Hay. Eli help'd him pole in what was fit to go in.

25. Preach'd Mr. Martyns Lecture from Rom. 8, 31. Return'd at Eve.

26. Eli Forbush is with me this week to be instruct'd—and tho I rejoice in his Learning Yet it is a great avocation and Impediment to me in my studys.

27. [No entry.]

28. On Matt. 13, 45, 46, and on Eph. 6, 18, forepart.

[3] Daughter of Thomas Rice, Jr.
[4] The Reverend William Williams.
[5] Ellis Gray (Harvard 1734), the minister of the New Brick Church in Boston, 1738–1752.
[6] John Campbell of Oxford.
[7] John Cotton.
[8] Henry Flynt, the famous tutor of Harvard College.
[9] The grandson of Judge Edmund Quincy, Flynt's brother-in-law.
[10] The daughter of the Reverend Jonathan Edwards. She was betrothed to David Brainerd, the Indian missionary.
[11] Son of neighbour Hezekiah Howe.
[12] Josiah Newton.
[13] Mrs. Jonah Brigham.
[14] Daniel Bliss of Concord.
[15] Timothy Minot (Harvard 1718) was a Concord schoolmaster who preached occasionally in a number of towns. Sibley, VI, 257-258.
[16] Phinehas Pratt.
[17] Hezekiah Tomlin married Martha Maynard.
[18] Miller married Elizabeth, the daughter of Samuel Hardy.

29. Eli Forbush here. P.M. came Dodge[19] (of College) here. He tells us very terrible storys concerning Mr. Prentice of Grafton and his beating his wife.

30. Din'd at Mr. Jonathan Lorings[20] at Marlborough. Mr. Smith came to me, and we rode down to Reverend Storer[21] at Watertown and lodg'd there.

### JULY, 1747

1. Mr. Smith and I rode to Cambridge. I went over to Mother Champneys. N.B. They tell me Brother Champney has Sold the Place to one Mr. Fletcher, Merchant in Boston. Remarkable and Joyfull News again this Third Commencement. What we have now is that the Admirals Anson and Warrin had destroy'd 11 Sail of French Men of Warr, and it comes with such Tokens of probability that most Gentlemen believe it. N.B. What We had last Year was the Defeat of the Rebels by the Duke of Cumberland: and what we had the Year before was the Taking of Cape Breton. I din'd at Dr. Wigglesworths.[1] N.B. Mr. Searing[2] Minister of Rhode Island there, as also Mr. Bours, a very well bred, pleasant, free Gentleman of the Same place. P.M. at Meeting. N.B. Mr. Abraham Williams[3] disputing against the Respondent Mayhew,[4] and advancing that the Christian Religion was opposite to Reason because of its maintaining the Doctrine of original Sin, Mayhew tho newly ordain'd at Boston answer'd *Utraque pare, Domine, Vera est.* Lodg'd at Mother Champneys and was very much indispos'd. Perhaps Evening air in my walk over the Causey after the Days Melting Heat might be the Cause of my Disorders.

2. Rode to Boston. Visited my new marry'd kinswoman, Mrs. Cowell, after I had din'd with Brother Samuel. Note well, Settled accounts with Brother Samuel and paid all his Demands to this Day. I was exceeding griev'd to find that Mr. Joseph White, my sister Hannahs Brother in Law is dead. The Lord quicken all of us to be ready for that awful Time! I visited Mr. Brainerd missionary to the Indians who lies very low and like to die at Mr. Bromfields. I rode to Watertown and lodg'd at Captain John Tainters, but was not very well.

3. I rose early and was refresh'd with my Rest, Blessed be God! I got upon my Horse I suppose by Sun rise for tho I had requested Mr. Stone to preach my Lecture to Day yet I know not what might fall out; and therefore hasten'd home. Broke Fast with Mr. Seccomb at his Father Williams at Weston. He (and Mr. Cheney afterwards came up) was my Company as it was at Election Time. I call'd at Captain D. Baldwins and both he and his wife were full of Courtisie. I din'd at home. Reverend Mr. Stone came to my House just as I came myself, he going in at one Door whilst I did at t'other. He preach'd my Lecture on Jer. [blank]. I have sent unto you all my Prophets rising Early etc., but ye have not hearken'd. Understood that Thomme came up on Commencement Day to work at Home.

4. Felt very feeble and much dishearten'd. Full of deep concern about both my work tomorrow and my inward state. But my eyes are (in some measure) towards the Lord.

5. Sacrament. On Mat. 13, 45, 46 and on Rom. 12, 12, last words. Repeat'd sermon on Ps. 109, 4, last part.

6. Ebenezer and Thomme Hilling. Mr. Joseph Williams of Marlborough here to finish our agreement about Thomme. The Indentures were Sign'd at this Time But Thomme is to Stay with me 3 weeks to help me get my Hay. Letter from Mr. Taylor[5] of Milton to request me to send him all I could collect about Benjamin Tainter, he being about to write to a Gentlemen in Canada. Mr. Loring came from Sudbury and lodg'd here.

7. We went to the Council at Grafton. Only 3 Churchs came, viz. the Reverend Mr. Lorings, Mr. Goddards[6] and ours. We were entertain'd at Mr. Joseph Rice's. N.B. Grim and formidable Evils related concerning the Reverend Mr. Prentice's[7] Conduct towards his Wife and the rest of the Separatists, so lately as last Lords Day Eve—Tore her Gown, Struck them that resisted him etc. But among us to Day he is amicable and Sweet.

8. 9. Constantly devoted to the public hearing of the grievances and Difficultys among them leading the Church into the properest steps we could. One of those Evenings Mr. Ebenezer Wadsworth came and acquaint'd me with Mr. Prentice's Conduct and that he was about to prosecute him. The other of these Evenings Madam Prentice came and was at Supper with us, together with her Husband. We hear that Two Canterbury Exhorters were come into Town, viz. Samuel Wadsworth[8] and one McDonald. I lodg'd from night to night at Mr. Joseph Rice's.

10. There was a meeting (we heard) at Mr. David Wadsworths[9] this forenoon, but it was impossible for us to regard it being most closely engag'd in our private review of what we had been several Days hearing in Publick. N.B. Mr. Loring thinks that Mr. Prentice is not to blame for baptizing after Objections were made by 3 (Two Deacons and one particular member with them) and after the Church had shown Man by Man their Desire that Mr. Prentice would ask a Dismission. He and I had a few words upon this. P.M. we drew up our Result. Mr. Goddard Said he could not recommend him to the work of the Ministry again. Neither was there anyone found that could. Upon the public reading the Result Mrs. Prentice's Voice was Suddenly lifted up and she scream'd in the assembly—the Chief was in defence of their (the Separatists) Convenanting together and to exhort and pay the Members of the Council not to fight against God. Mr. Prentice reflected very hard upon the Council as doing what was very unjust; and especially towards Mr. Fletcher[10] and he further added that he took notice how some of the Council Whisper'd with the disaffected, a foolish aspersion! After the Assembly we went into his House: Where upon my Saying I hop'd I had done in Integrity what I had done. He reply'd that he Saw very little signs of it. I took leave of the Town this Evening and repair'd Home, accompany'd to Westborough by Deacon Newton and Mr. Whitney the Delegates.

11. Neighbour Batherick began to cut my Ministerial Meadow. The Boys made an End of Hilling the Corn.

12. Mr. Loring is left at Grafton to preach there to Day, though his own people were without; there being great Danger in Grafton that those two Canterbury Teachers would do much mischief. I had made part of a sermon but could not finish it and therefore preach'd on Eph. 2, 21, 22. Mrs. Wheeler, of the north side din'd with us, she is in new sorrows by the Death of her son in law, Mr. Asaph Wilder, a likely man—his Death seems to be much lamented.

13. In the Morning I rode over to Mr. Dunlop to get him to come and reap. Found him at Lieutenant Tainters. Our Girls Bekky Hicks[11] and my Lucy pull'd Flax. Mary Bradish came and pull'd another Piece of Flax. Old Mr. Axtell[12] from Grafton here. He tells me Mr. Loring is gone along, fearing the Storm which threatens. He says Mr. Prentice sat in the Pulpit—divers at meeting in the forenoon that were not in the afternoon. N.B. Jonas Brigham[13] here on the Affair of his joining to the Church.

14. Captain Willard[14] and Mr. Brooks[15] here going to Mr. Martyn to wait upon him with the Church's vote of him for their Standing Moderator. Ephraim Sherman here to acquaint me with their Desire that I would preach in Grafton next Lords Day and

---

[19] Ezekiel Dodge (Harvard 1749). He later became the minister of Abington, 1750–1770.

[20] The son of the Reverend Israel Loring of Sudbury.

[21] Seth Storer (Harvard 1720), the minister of Watertown, 1724–1774. *Sibley,* VI, 412–414.

[1] Edward Wigglesworth, Professor of Divinity at Harvard College.

[2] James Searing (Yale 1725), the minister of the Second Congregational Church at Newport, 1728–1755. Dexter, *Biographical Sketches,* p. 318.

[3] (Harvard 1744). The son of Colonel Abraham Williams of Marlborough.

[4] Jonathan Mayhew (Harvard 1744), the minister of the West Church in Boston, 1747–1766.

[5] The Reverend John Taylor (Harvard 1721), the minister of Milton, 1728–1750. *Sibley,* VI, 569–571.

[6] David Goddard of Leicester.

[7] Solomon Prentice of Grafton.

[8] An uneducated preacher who was ordained and served the third church at South Killingly, Conn., 1746–1762.

[9] David and Ebenezer Wadsworth were members of the separatist group in Grafton.

[10] Eleazer Fletcher of Grafton.

[11] Rebecca was the daughter of Parkman's brother-in-law, John Hicks of Sutton.

[12] Thomas Axtell.

[13] The son of David Brigham of Westborough.

[14] Joseph Willard of Grafton.

[15] Ebenezer Brooks of Grafton.

that they had got Mr. Wilson of Hopkinton to preach in my room. N.B. Noah How and Nathan Maynard p.m. mow'd for me. I suppose Nathan works for Mr. Abraham Batchellour who design'd to give me a Lift. Ebenezer and Thomme went to Cart Hay from the Meadow. They brought one Turn. N.B. Catechetical Exercise.

15. Ebenezer and Thomme Carting Hay from the Meadow to Day also. Batherick with 2 more Hands mowing the meadow. My wife and her Babe gone with Mrs. Whipple to see Old Mrs. Knowlton[16] at Shrewsbury. Ebenezer and Thomme Two more Load from the Meadow. I rak'd and tended Hay some part of the Day as I could bear it. Mrs. Persis Brigham (wife of Jonas) here on the Affair of her joining to the Church also. At Eve my wife return'd in safety. Mr. Francis Whipple came to see her well home.

16. My Boys work'd at Home. They Cutt the Barley. A great deal of Hay in Making. P.M. a thunder Storm arose which drew out all Hands of us to work. Bekky and I pol'd in what was round the Barn and near at Hand. The Barley in part rak'd and Cock'd, the rest left in Wind-rows. A part of our Hay we were forc'd to leave spread around. And Neighbour Batherick did not pretend to go to the meadow till the Afternoon, if he went then; So that doubtless the great Quantity of Hay there is wash'd. But the Storm went chiefly to the South. We had not a great deal of Rain. Another Thunder storm in the Evening went mostly South also. This working in the Hay worry'd me not a Little— But I hope I got over it.

17. Mr. Dunlop and Mr. Martin Pratt came to reap Rye for me. P.M. Joseph Grout came to reap also. They got the South-side down and Load in, the other part was Shock'd in the Field. Ebenezer and Thomme are getting the Barley into a Stack, with Joseph Grouts Help. Great likelihood of Thunder storm, but it went over. Mr. Batherick rakes and Cocks the South part of the Meadow. Molly rode over to Mr. Martyns with Hannah Forbush,[17] and return'd at Evening and Hannah lodg'd here. These Two Days have been extreme Hot, and it seems as if men could not undergo their Labour.

18. Assisted what I could in raking Hay. My whole House has lent an Hand before a storm. At Eve I stood dress'd in order to go up to Grafton but the Showers and Thunder prevented. Neither did Mr. Wilson whom I expect'd from Hopkinton come till about nine o'Clock. So that I was forc'd to lay aside going till the Morning.

19. Early in the Morning I rode away to go to Grafton—but nigh Mr. Grouts I perceiv'd I had left my Baggs—was oblig'd to go back for them and then proceed'd to Captain Willards. De-sign'd to have preach'd on Song. 1, 7, 8, but perceiving that Some of the people were so very wavering and not able to bear at present the least Severity I drew up a Conclusion to treat them with great Gentleness and therefore preach'd a.m. on 1 John 17 and p.m. on Rom. 6, 13. Mr. Prentice at meeting—and all the Deacons, even Deacon Cooper,[18] who it was fear'd would go to Day to the Sep-arates. I din'd at Mr. Isaac Harringtons—about which Time there was a very great Storm of wind, Rain and Thunder. N.B. I baptiz'd Manoah son of Thomas Drury and Elizabeth, Daughter of Abraham Temple. After Exercises I went up to Mr. Prentice's. Dodge of College with me. After a while came in Mrs. Prentice from her Separate Meeting, and a Number along with her—Mr. Hedge of Worcester etc. above half a Dozen Men and Women. Presently Mrs. Prentice stretch'd out her hand and declar'd how she, and their Society had enjoy'd the glorious presence of God among them this Day etc. I told her I hop'd there were Some good Tokens among us, and reasons to conceive that the Lord had been in our Assembly to Day. She soon went on in her Strain. Dodge and I went to Captain Willards and after refreshment, Prayer and Singing I return'd to my own House. N.B. I earnestly cau-tion'd Mrs. Winchester against Separating. Mr. Wilson[19] preach'd a. and p.m. at Westborough.

20. Mr. Smith of Marlborough and his wife rode here in their Chaise and din'd here. P.M. they went to Shrewsbury. Neigh-

[16] Mrs. Joseph Knowlton.
[17] The daughter of Deacon Jonathan Forbush.
[18] Samuel Cooper.
[19] Presumably John Wilson, an Edinburgh graduate, minister of Auburn, N. H.

bour Eliezer Rice with Neighbour John Rogers helped me in Carting home Hay. My sons with my Team—in all 5 Turns.

21. As I was reading Mr. Brainerds Journal, he appear'd at my gate, his brother Israel and Mrs. Jerusha Edwards of Northamp-ton with him—'twas just at Eve. I rejoic'd much to see him yet alive. They all lodg'd here. Mr. Beriah Rice brought us Some Metheglin.[20]

22. When the Morning Clouds were clear'd off, Mr. Brainerd and his fellow Travellers got upon their Journey. I rode with them as far as to Mr. Cushings where after a little Halt we parted. In my returning lit of Mr. Sergeant of Husatunnock, who with his Wife's sister Elizabeth Williams was going to Boston.

23. Ebenezer work'd for Mr. Eliezer Rice. Visited Mrs. Miller (who is almost gone) after I had been at Mr. Benjamin Fays and settled with him and din'd at Mr. Harringtons.

24. [No entry.]

25. [No entry.]

26. Preach'd a. and p.m. on 2 Cor. 11, 3. On occasion of the Errors and Disorders at Grafton. May it be follow'd with a divine Energy for our general Benefit!

27. A.M. came my Friend Mrs. Keggell of Boston with her son, and accompany'd by Mr. Edward Bass. They din'd with us. I Catechiz'd at Mr. Joslins. 5 Boys and 7 Girls in all. N.B. Brother Hicks and his wife here in the morning going to Cam-bridge.

28. Mrs. Miller extremely low. I went to see her again. Mr. Bass with me, in the Chaise which they came up in. My wife and Mrs. Keggell visited Mrs. Maynard. They lodg'd with us.

29. Our Friends rode to Worcester and my wife and I accom-pany'd them. Mrs. Sarah Whipple[21] taking Care of Alexander. N.B. my mare went in the chair and drew the Two Women. Mr. Barns lent me his mare and Captain Maynard lent Mr. Bass his horse. We din'd at Brother Brecks[22]—drank Tea at Mr. Mac-cartys, Mr. Maccarty being gone to Boston. We met him on the Road. I only call'd at Colonel Chandlers office. My wife did not so much as that. Mr. Campbell of Oxford Stop'd with me and I suppose stay'd over night—but we all return'd to Westborough. Through divine Goodness we found our Habitation in Peace.

30. Mrs. Biglo here to be examin'd. Am inform'd that Mrs. Miller dy'd last Evening. The Lord awaken us all to a serious and reallizing Meditation of Death and Judgment. Mr. Bass and I rode over to Mr. Martyns. Din'd (tho late) there. Thence we rode to Mr. Wheelers (who wanted to see me upon the Affair of the Great Bible etc.) we went to both the Ball's. We went and came by Mr. How's.

31. Our Friends undertook their Journey to Boston—having had fine Weather all the Time of their being here. Ebenezer sow'd the West Yard with Turnips.

### AUGUST [1747]

1. Neighbour Batherick cut the Northside of the meadow.

2. On 2 Cor. 11, 3. Mrs. Thurston din'd here. P.M. repeated with many Alterations sermon on 1 Cor. 15, 58.

3. Hear that Mr. Wilson preach'd at Grafton yesterday. A Very refreshing Shower in a very dry Time, but Mr. Batherick had got my Hay in Cock, except 4 Cocks before the Rain came. At Eve came Mr. Hancock[1] and Mr. Thomas Marsh[2] from Cam-bridge and lodg'd here.

4. The Two Fellows left us to go to Sutton and Worcester. Deacon Kimball[3] of Hopkinton here. P.M. Mr. Bowker and his wife from the Northside. Mr. Jenison—several Neighbours more. Forbush with his Theme. My son Thomas went to Marlborough, Apprentice to Mr. Joseph Williams. At Eve Mr. Beriah Rice came (when we were short enough as to grain) with a Bushell of Indian Corn and a Bushell of Rice. N.B. Captain Maynard sent Rody and Jonathan Devereux to Mow for me the forenoon.

5. Very dry Time. Ebenezer to the Meadow for the Last of the Hay. One very large Load. Mr. Edwards Whipple help'd

[20] A beverage made of fermented honey and water that was sometimes called mead.
[21] Mrs. Edwards Whipple.
[22] Parkman's brother-in-law, Dr. Samuel Breck.
[1] Belcher Hancock, the tutor of Harvard.
[2] (Harvard 1731). Another Harvard tutor. *Sibley*, IX, 67–70.
[3] Ebenezer Kimball.

him and work'd till night upon the Hay and Home, which a.m. I tend'd myself. P.M. Mr. Martyn here, and tarry'd till Eve. Brother Hicks does not return from Cambridge yet, I fear what may be the Cause of his Stay.

6. We are so belated in our Haying that after Morning Studys I went to raking Hay with Ebenezer and my little Billy. P.M. Came Brother Hicks and his wife. They inform me that Mother Champneys Thirds are settled and Mr. Fletcher (the Purchaser) comes to the place. N.B. as I was raking (p.m.) came Mr. Jonas Brigham and his wife to have their Relations writ. Mr. Brigham took my Rake whilst I wrote for his wife. Load got in. At Eve came Mr. Prentice of Grafton. He shews me a Letter of Invitation to Easton and wants something should be done about the Article in our Result where in we cannot recommend him. Brother Hicks and his wife lodg'd here, but Mr. Prentice went home.

7. Neighbour John Rogers help in with one Load of Hay. Jonathan Devereux help'd Ebenezer get in 2 Load of Hay. Mrs. Rogers (John's wife) had my mare to go to her Fathers. Mr. Bridge of Framingham here, going to Rutland. Mr. James Keys's wife (heretofore Rugg) from Shrewsbury here, about her souls Distresses.

8. Eli Forbush here, and being able to go to live at Cambridge took leave. At Eve Mr. Wilson of Hopkinton going to Change with Mr. Martyn is stop'd by a Letter from him and therefore goes, tho with great Reluctance to Grafton himself.

9. On 1 Cor. 15, ult. with divers alterations and additions. Widow Woods din'd here. P.M. on Gen. 2, 17. Repeated sermon on Heb. 9, 27, on occasion of my hearing that Mr. Thomas Ward late of Westborough is deceas'd. He dy'd last Thursday morning at Plainfield; the messenger that brought the News to Captain Maynard was at meeting with us. Refreshing Showers p.m. Some Thunder and Lightning also in a Time of Dryness, especially in Some Places.

10. Ebenezer still about the Hay. P.M. Mr. Jonas Brigham here about his Relation.

11. Association at Mr. Morse's, north Shrewsbury. Met Mr. Martyn at Mr. Josiah Bowkers. A Considerable Number at Meeting. But Father Prentice yet languishes and cannot get there. Mr. Goss read his Concio on John 21, 15. N.B. Mr. Marsh of Narraganset, with his Brethren that were against him, the principal of them came with their Grievances and Difficultys. This took up most of our Time to Day. They were advis'd to choose a Council. With this they comply'd, and chose the churchs under the pastoral Care of the Reverend Messers Loring, Cushing, Williams of Waltham, Stone and Smith.

12. Mr. Campbell of Oxford came, and made proposals about erecting a New Association. Mr. Loring preach'd the Public Lecture on Acts 3, 22. After Dinner, when I had invited the Association to my House next meeting I perceiv'd that it was mov'd by one and another that it was Mr. Marsh's turn to preach—but I privately Signify'd to Mr. Loring that I should be dissatisfy'd if they Should impose Mr. Marsh upon me. Mr. Loring consented that the Turn might proceed in the order in which it would if Mr. Marsh was absent—viz. Mr. Loring and Mr. Millen to perform the Exercises, and thus it was left without any formal Act or Vote. Mr. Loring, Stone, Seccomb, Goss, Smith, Martyn and I rode together after meeting to Mr. Martyns. After I came home there arose a great storm of Thunder and Lightning with some Rain. One Flash of Lightning exceeding Sharp, as we sat in the Kitchen after Evening Prayer—it came in among us as if very near indeed—but thro divine mercy did no Hurt. N.B. Ebenezer finish'd Mowing to Day.

13. Mr. Martyn and his wife came over with Mr. Seccomb and din'd with me. Mr. Seccomb preach'd on John 7, 37. N.B. Rainy yet Mr. Martyn etc. return'd home and Mr. Seccomb with them. N.B. Mrs. Wheeler here about the Bible and offers me 18£. Mrs. Biglo brought her Relation. Ebenezer has yet one Load of Hay that lyes abroad.

14. Deacon Meriam and Mr. James Whipple of Grafton here in their Way over to Mr. Martyn and want a Copy of the late Councils Result, and of divers important Votes which I got ready for them when they return'd. N.B. Mr. Martyn accepts the Modera-

torship. Continues to rain and mist till towards night. A Token of great Goodness from God! May we have Grace to make a proper Return! Sent Ebenezer with a Team to Deacon Newtons for six Bushels of Lime, which has stood there this Year or Two. Mr. Williams brought us the first pidgeons which he has caught or which we have seen this Year. Ebenezer went to Deacon Newtons for 6 Bushels of Lime, repos'd there, but brings only one Bushel and half.

15. Ebenezer gets in the Last of the Hay at Home.

16. Sacrament. I preach'd on [blank]. P.M. from Gen. 2, 17. Repeated sermon on Heb. 9, 27. N.B. Brother James Fay, now of Hardwick, attempting to tarry at Communion. Deacon Newton withdrew. Divers other Brethren Shew'd their dissatisfaction likewise—viz. Brother Tainter, Brother Miller, Brother Daniel Warrin—upon which I desir'd Mr. James Fay to withdraw, which upon his doing I sent for Deacon Newton, and he return'd to his Duty and Office accordingly. N.B. Brother James Fay din'd with me. P.M. I appointed a Church Meeting upon his affair to be tomorrow 4 o'Clock p.m. and Catechizing at the Meeting House next Friday.

17. In the morning went to Deacon Newtons about the Lime—bought and paid for 2 Bushels. Deacon Kimball of Hopkinton came to whitewash and spot my Kitchen, and Lath and plaister my new Study. Mr. Martyn and his Brother Marritt[4] of Cambridge here. P.M. My wife and I went to Esquire Bakers to raising of west end of his House, and before 5 was at the Meeting House, few members being come—but presently more—between Twenty and Thirty at Length. Brother James Fay present. His Affair was laid before the Church, and his Desire of his own and his wife's Dismission to the Church at Hardwick. After some Debate he acknowledg'd himself to blame for his going to the separate meeting at Grafton. His acknowledgment was writ by me, and Sign'd by him—upon which he was restor'd and his request granted. At Eve Brother Daniel Forbush and Brother James Bradish junior here, complaining that Deacon Newton (from what he said in Church Meeting) had not done his Duty to Brother James Fay, in private dealings with him, when Fay first told him of his going to the separate meeting. They hinted also that John Rogers Should be dealt with for neglecting to make his peace with the Church.

18. I Catechiz'd the Children at the Meeting House a. and p.m. About 70 Children of both sexes, viz. about 44 Boys and 26 Girls. N.B. Mr. Benjamin How at work for me a.m. Casing my study window, putting up a Shelf. N.B. I sent a Letter to Deacon Newton upon his not dealing previously and privately with Brother James Fay. Deacon Kimball at work here and lodges again.

19. Deacon Kimball finish'd today and went home at night. Mrs. Winchester here p.m. tells us that about 170 Captives are Come from Canada to Boston, and that Benjamin Tainter is come, but that Phinehas Forbush is Dead. Betty Ball[5] here to be examin'd.

20. In the morning I rode over to see Deacon Forbush and his Dauter in Law the widow of his son Phinehas to mourn with them under their Bereavement and pray'd with them. Went to Lieutenant Tainters to rejoice with them but was somewhat troubled to see Lieutenant's Indifference about going down to Boston for his son. I did not 'light—but, hasten'd home and rode over to Mr. Martyn's. Mr. Morse preach'd his Lecture from 1 Cor. 6, 11—alas I was much too dull and heavy in my attendance! The Lord pardon it for Jesus' sake! N.B. The Church then chose their Deacons. Mr. Livermore[6] and Mr. Matthias Rice. N.B. Mr. Morse's wife with him. I return'd at Eve. N.B. Neighbour Benjamin How picks Apples in my Orchard to make my Cyder (this early) to the Halves.

21. Benjamin Tainter, I hear, got home. Ebenezer mow'd Rowing. I was somewhat feeble.

22. Benjamin Tainter came to see me and gave me a narrative of his Captivity and Return. P.M. I rode to Worcester. Met Mr. Maccarty going to Westborough. Lodg'd at Mr. Maccarty's.

[4] The Reverend Mr. Martyn had married Mary Marrett of Cambridge.

[5] The daughter of James Ball.

[6] Jonathan Livermore.

23. I preach'd at Worcester on Luke 19, 10, a. and p.m. Baptiz'd a child of Mr. Ebenezer Flagg. Mr. Maccarty preach'd at Westborough but he return'd home at Eve. After Exercises I went over to Dr. Brecks but Supp'd and Lodg'd at Mr. Maccartys.

24. After Breakfast Mr. Maccarty and I went over to Dr. Brecks. N.B. Changed my Two octavo Volumes of Baileys Dictionary[7] with the Doctor for his Folio of the Same Work and gave him 45/ old Tenor Difference. Din'd at Colonel Chandlers. In returning home call'd at Mr. Cushings,[8] but he was not at home. Found my Family in Peace. Blessed be God!

25. One Mr. Abner Ely of Springfield here. P.M. Joseph Bowker examin'd. At Eve Dodge (of College) here. He gives me a notable account of Mr. Williams of Eston preaching last Sabbath at Grafton and disputing with the Separatists.

26. Ebenezer about the Rowing and cutting Stalks.

27. Mrs. Hardy (Phinehas's wife)[9] here with her Sister Hannah Rice[10] of Sutton, with her son Thomas Rice, and they all din'd here. P.M. I preach'd at old Mr. Graves's[11]—his wife having been long confin'd from public ordinances. Acts 20, 21, was the Text. N.B. I deliver'd a particular Address to the old Woman, She having been ordinarily but too insensible. N.B. Reverend Mr. Barrett there and pray'd after Sermon.

28. [No entry.]

29. Thomme came up from Marlborough to see us.

30. On Mat. 13, 47 to 50. Dr. Gott here and din'd with us, as did Captain Willards here from Grafton. P.M. Repeated with some Alterations and additions sermon on Ps. 126, on occasion not only of Benjamin Tainters but a great Number of Captives returning from Canada. Mr. Norton their Chaplain being among them.

31. I carry'd Molly as far as Esquire Brighams[12] at Marlborough (she having the Toothach) in order to her going to Dr. Gotts. Thomme went with us part of the way to Carry my Portmantle. I went on my way to Cambridge. Mr. Maccarty overtook me at Marlborough, and rode with me to Cambridge Bounds and then proceeded to Boston. I went to Mr. Danforths and to Mr. Boardmans, gave Bond and receiv'd a Letter of Guardianship for my Children. Lodg'd at Mother Champney's.

### SEPTEMBER, 1747

1. Rode to Boston with Brother Champney in order to go to Mr. Fletcher who had bought his place; and we were accordingly with him. We din'd at Brother Samuel Parkmans. A Sickly Time in Boston. The Venerable Dr. Colman[1] dy'd Suddenly last Saturday. Cousen Lydia Draper also is Dead—her Funeral I attended this Evening. Was with my Brother Alexander at Mr. Fletchers also, and I receiv'd of him 108£ 4 shillings old Tenor, being the remainder of what was due to my Children out of the two thirds of Father Champneys Estate. N.B. We went also to Judge Sewalls.[2] I lodg'd at Brother Alexanders. N.B. Brother Champney led my Horse to Cambridge.

2. Mr. Samuel Checkley[3] junior was ordain'd at old North. Din'd with the multitude at Mr. John Brecks. P.M. Dr. Colman was bury'd. When such pillars fall, how the Whole Fabric Trembles! Help Lord! What threatening aspects! A vast procession at the Funeral! Twas observ'd that 66 Couple being the Males of the Church and the Colleague pastor in deep mourning before the Corps: Six senior pastors Pall Bearers with Hat bands down: 100 Couple of mourners and men—among the Latter, the Council, a great number of ministers—4 Episcopal, among which Mr. Hooper[4] newly from England—46 Couple of women. 4 Coaches in the first of which the Governor. 8 four wheel Chaises and 7 Common. May the God of the Spirits of all Flesh grant

double portions of His Spirit and quicken all surviving ministers to the work the Works etc! [?] I supp'd at widow Jarvis's with my Brother Alexander and his wife. Lodg'd at sister Willards. N.B. Cousen Nathaniel Parkman not well. Gone to Nantucket.

3. Mr. Webb[5] preach'd the Public Lecture bewailing Dr. Colmans Death, from Rev. 1, 18. I din'd at Brother Alexander's. My Horse was Sent down to Mr. Procters by Brother Champney. Sarah Tyley lodg'd at Mrs. Keggells in order to be ready in the Morning to ride with me. I lodg'd at Brother Alexanders who kept my Horse also.

4. Sarah Tyley rode with me to Westborough. We stop'd at Cambridge—at old Mr. Livermors in Weston, and at Mr. Darlings[6] nigh Marlborough. Found my Family well, through God's great Mercy and Goodness. To His name be Glory! N.B. my Young Cattle are brought Home from Sutton, except a Young Steer.

5. I devoted the forenoon as much as I could to Such recollections etc. as I have endeavour'd to employ this Day in—but was oblig'd to do what I could in preparing a Sermon for tomorrow. See Natal. [The following appears in the Natalitia for the date of September 5, 1747.]

I could not Spend the Day (being Saturday and when I had been at Boston in the week and so was not prepar'd for the Sabbath) as I Should have been glad to do; but mindful in some measure of my Custom on this Day, but more I hope of the infinite Obligations I am under to the great God, who upholds my Soul, I gave myself as I could the fore part of it to recollections and Prayer. And O that God most gracious and merciful would thro the merits of Jesus Christ accept my (tho scanty) Penitence, and my imperfect Devotions! O that God would kindle up in me holy affections, and enliven me in this way! Might I be in some fit manner sensible how certainly I must die, and how uncertain the Time when. May the Death of that eminent Man Dr. Colman, whose Funeral I have been this week attending on, rouse me to work the works of him that has Sent me while the Day of Life lasts, and to be ready when the Night shall overspread me! O that I might enter into new Resolutions and may the almighty Grace of God be sufficient for me to enable me to keep them!

6. I preach'd a.m. on Heb. 9, 27, a repitition. P.M. on Mat. 24, 45, 46. On Occasion of Dr. Colmans Death. N.B. Mrs. Harwood din'd with us.

7. Old Mr. Baker[7] of Marlborough here.

8. Mr. Baker again. P.M. Catechetical Exercise on the first Commandment. At Eve came Mr. James Wellman and lodg'd here.

9. After Dinner Mr. Wellman went to Sutton. He tells me that tomorrow is to be a fast with his people in order to gather a Church. Mr. Campbell, Mr. Hall,[8] Mr. Webb,[9] and Mr. Maccarty are to assist in it. At Eve Joseph Bowker brot me a Letter from Barrett which manifests some uneasiness on account of his coming to Mr. Graves t'other Day when I preach'd there. I immediately wrote him an answer, and sent it by the same Hand.

10. Would have gone to Worcester to preach Mr. Maccartys Lecture but it rain'd all Day, and prevented me. I gave myself to reading, Meditation etc.

11. Bekky Hicks rode my Mare to Cambridge. Deacon Forbush and his wife and Mrs. Tainter here, as they return'd from Suffield. N.B. Mr. Nortons Letter to Deacon Forbush concerning his son Phinehas that dy'd at Quebeck.

12. Mr. Buckminster here and tells me his mother dy'd last night.

13. Mat. 24, 25 and p.m. repeated on Ezra 10, 10. Mrs. Phillips of Southborough and Mrs. Thurston din'd here.

14. Fowl morning. Mr. Buckminster din'd here.

15. Benjamin Tainter and Molly rode in Chaise to Cambridge. At Eve Mr. Bacon and Brother Hicks here.

16. Mr. Bacon and Brother Hicks go off. Sarah Henry makes Billey Leather Breeches. 26 pound of Beef of Mr. Rogers at 12 pence pound. Night Thunder Lightning.

---

[7] Nathan Bailey, the eminent English philologist, published *An Universal Etymological English Dictionary* (London, 1721). At least 10 editions appeared by 1742.
[8] The Reverend Job Cushing of Shrewsbury.
[9] Prudence Warren.
[10] Mrs. Noah (Warren) Rice.
[11] John Graves.
[12] Samuel Brigham.
[1] The Reverend Benjamin Colman of the Brattle Street Church.
[2] Stephen Sewall, justice of the Superior Court of Judicature.
[3] (Harvard 1743).
[4] William Hooper was the minister of Trinity Church in Boston, 1747-1767.

[5] John Webb.
[6] Thomas Darling.
[7] Joseph Baker.
[8] The Reverend David Hall of Sutton.
[9] The Reverend Nathan Webb of Uxbridge.

17. Mr. Cushing preach'd my Lecture to young people on 1 King 18, 12.

19. Ebenezer with the assistance of Nathan Maynard part of yesterday and part of to Day made six Barrells and Half of Cyder; of which Neighbour John Rogers had Two and Ebenezer boyld Two. At Eve came Captain Ephraim Williams to see me—but would not lodge here but would go to his Cousen Mr. Samuel Williams and he accordingly lodg'd there. He tells me that Dr. Chauncy. and Mr. Jackson of Boston parted at Eagers and would go to Marlborough and keep Sabbath there, against his Sollicitations to let him pilot them here.

20. On Mat. 24, 25 and P.M. on Ezra 10, 11. At Evening I read to the Church a Letter from the Second Church in Sutton desiring our Assistance in their approaching Ordination. Upon which our Church voted Compliance with their Request, and confirm'd it by asking whether any body objected? But all being Silent, we then proceeded to appointment of the Delegates, and Two were offer'd to be the Number, and try'd by Vote; but there were So few voted, that I enquir'd what might be the Matter? Captain Warrin answer'd that seeing the Church had no Returns made 'em of what was done when they sent out to Councils and such like, he did not know whether it was worthwhile to send any more. I soon found by Ensign Bruce's warm Speech (that follow'd as well as went before Captain Warrins) it was my not reading the Grafton Result that had given such Disgust. I told 'em That we had not the Custom with us, nor in the Churches where I had been concern'd that I know of, that when we had ever done it it was a special occasion for doing it; That indeed I had Some Reasons against Reading Results abroad round the Country, to Spread at great Distance (it would be some times) the miscarriages of Christians and Ministers etc. But yet I was free and ready to gratifie 'em in the present Case; either at my own House or otherwise when desir'd and was sorry they would make Such a Difficulty as that to clogg the present Duty (or to that purpose). Lieutenant Forbush said a man had told me that he ask'd me to read it—but that I did not. I reply'd that I had not a Copy at first, when I came Back from that Council—and that afterwards it seem'd late to read a Result; and I did not know there was any uneasiness about it, and could not take it well that the first Discovery of uneasiness Should be in such a public manner as this. Captain Baker mov'd that being it was the sabbath it might be better to defer it to some other Time. Lieutenant Tainter said he saw not why the Business might not go on, for this was a different work from that of going to Councils upon Differences etc. But twas urg'd that we should be together again at the Thursday ensuing, and we had best wave anything further about it till then. So it was deferr'd accordingly to that Day. (the Day of the Lecture). But note well, that when Brother Stephen Fay and Brother Daniel Hardy said they believ'd there was not a Vote, it made me recurr from that to the first vote, (of granting the request of the Letter) and observ'd to them that I esteem'd that vote to have been pass'd, for I had put it both ways, and desir'd if there was objection it might be shown. But at this Time there was no Objection made against that Vote. I look upon that therefore as doubly confirm'd. When I came home Captain Ephraim Williams was at my House and tarry'd with us over night. About nine o'Clock there was a storm of Thunder and Lightning But the Lord preserv'd us in safety.

21. Captain Williams went over to his Cousens and I accompany'd him. I went to Mr. Ebenezer Nurse's and he went with me to the Cedar Swamp which Brother Hicks has offer'd to Sell, and we went to the further end of it: but was greatly dissatisfy'd with it, and determin'd not to have it on any such Terms as Brother expect'd.

22. [No entry.]

23. [No entry.]

24. Mr. Wellman of Sutton did not come to preach my Lecture as I had Sent to him to do, but Mr. Martyn came, and he preach'd for me on John 4, 10.

25. Ebenezer went to Sutton and brought home the Young Cow which Brother Hicks wanted to have for his Cedar Swamp,

and he brought also a young Steer which had been left out of the Drove.

26. Ebenezer picking Apples—tho a scarce year with others, yet plentifull with me. D.G. But many are sadly wasted and rot away.

27. Sacrament. Preach'd on Mat. 13, 51, a.m. On Jer. 8, 4, 5. Deacon Fay, old Mr. Bellows,[10] and Mr. Cutter of Brookfield and Mrs. Deliverance Fay[11] din'd here. At Evening had Some more peculiar Meditations and Resolutions respecting a Closer Walk with God and self Reflection—but alas! how weak and slender is all that I can do! Read at night Sir Matthew Hales Discourse on Religion[12] and Letters to his Children.[13]

28. Visited old Mr. Fay. Was at Mr. Whipples, Lieutenant Tainter, at Mr. Jonah Warrin's and at Mr. Williams's. N.B. at this last House (Mr. Ebenezer Nurse being by) we had some Discourse concerning the vast alteration of the Price of all sorts of Things, and the great Distress it reduces Ministers in a peculiar manner to: But twas plain that Mr. Williams was disquieted with it and did not love to hear of it; whereas considering the Evidence and palpable Injustice done me in particular by the Precincts Delay to consider my Case, it is an aggravation of the Evil, that it can't be mention'd without giving Disgust. May God give me Wisdom and Patience, and Fidelity!

29. I walk'd down to Mr. Cooks and there wrote a Letter to my Dauter Molly at Cambridge and sent it with 12£ of money by Eli Forbush. A number of Hands came and gather'd my Corn. Mr. Samuel Fay junior, Joseph Green junior, Edwards Whipple (who was a first mover) and p.m. John Chamberlin, John Rogers, Benjamin Tainter, Joseph Bowker. Had Mr. Tinneys Cart as well as my own. P.M. visited Stephen Maynard. N.B. Dr. Greenleaf there to see him. At Evening husk'd. I know not of more than a small Number, and we provided accordingly, but there came (as I think they were counted) 34. Yet God was pleas'd to bless our Provision and he had Considerable left. N.B. they finish'd at 10 o'Clock. Sang latter part of Ps. 4 in Tate and Brady. Thro the Bounty of Providence a good Crop.

30. Ebenezer carts up the Corn from the Barn to the House. Hir'd Mr. Chamberlin, who came about noon and help'd us till night.

### OCTOBER, 1747

1. Very rainy Morning. Troubled about our Hoggs, which have one Time after another got in upon the Heaps of Apples. Read Dr. Watts's Ruin and Recovery[1]—borrow'd of the Reverend Mr. Davis.[2]

2. Ebenezer carted 2 Load of Apples over to Mr. Hows Mill.

3. Was greatly interrupted by my meddling with the Little House yesterday and to Day.

4. A.M. on Matt. 13, 52. P.M. repeated sermon on Isa. 26, 9. Many Grafton people at meeting; no preacher there. N.B. My great Distresses last night and this morning on account of my Negligence and unpreparedness. But the Lord be merciful to my unrighteousness and remember not against me my Transgressions. O may the Blood of the Great Sacrifice be accepted to make atonement. N.B. Captain Maynard here in the morning and informs me that his son is sick—and that my Dauter Molly is ill at Boston.

5. Visited Stephen Maynard and was at Mr. Hows. Ebenezer making Cyder there. Timothy Warrin here and by paying the money for my Oxen took up his Bond. Lieutenant Tainter return'd a Blanket which Captain Maynard borrow'd for Stephen when a Soldier. The Morning very Cold.

6. Conceiving it somewhat probable that I may be call'd to give the Right Hand to Mr. Wellman tomorrow I took a little Time to prepare a few Hints. Lieutenant Tainter here and cut a young Calf, and din'd here. Tells us that he heard at Watertown that Mr. Stearns[3] of Lunenbourgh is Dead. Mr. Stone and his

---

[10] Eleazer Bellows.
[11] Daughter of Samuel Fay, Jr.
[12] Matthew Hale, *The Judgment of the late Lord Chief Justice Sir M. H. of the Nature of True Religion* (London, 1684).
[13] Matthew Hale, *A Letter from Sir Matthew Hale . . . to his Children* (London, 1684).

[1] Isaac Watts seems not to have published a separate work under this title. It appeared, however, in his *Discourses, Essays, and Tracts on Various Subjects*, VI (London, 1753), 177–320.
[2] Joseph Davis of Holden.
[3] The Reverend David Stearns.

Delegates here in their way to Sutton, but I was not ready to go with them nor had I design'd to go so soon in the Day, my Circumstances being very pressing and difficult at this Time. Hir'd Thomas Rogers to help in picking Apples. Ebenezer got out 5 Barrells and a part of a Barrell at Mr. Hows Mill. One Barrell sold to Mr. Chamberlin and 1/2 Barrell I sent to old Mrs. Crouch, widow and Blind. 4 Barrells and Some Water Cyder, were put into the Cellar. Dr. Gott here P.M. Just at Evening (I suppose Sundown) I set out on my Journey alone. Reach'd to Captain Lelands, and lodg'd there. N.B. Mr. Isaac Glezon[4] of Framingham there.

7. We were Somewhat disturb'd by a Crew of Indians with a Violin last night while we were o'Bed. But thro Divine Mercy I rose well and rode (alone) to Mr. Samuel Brecks in North Sutton. Mr. Turners[5] Church in Rehoboth did not come. But the following Churches came, viz. of Oxford, first in Sutton, first in Westborough, of Uxbridge, second in Lynn, Southboro, Worcester, Wilmington. Reverend Campbell was chose Moderator and I was Chosen Scribe. N.B. My Brethren Williams and Miller satisfy'd themselves about joining with the first Church in Sutton, by discoursing with Mr. Campbell. Mr. Wellman was somewhat carefully examin'd yet gave the Council good Satisfaction, both praying and delivering part of a sermon before the Council also. In the public Assembly Mr. Chase[6] deliver'd a very good sermon on Rev. 1, 20, those words, the angels of the Churches. N.B. Mr. Stone was appoint'd to pray after the Charge, but he not sitting in the pulpit, the Moderator did himself, but (an unusual thing) he did not lay on Hands in said last prayer, and therefore none of us did. Soon after supper (at which Mr. Webb pray'd, and Mr. Stone in returning Thanks omitted to mention what he had receiv'd) we mounted to come home. Called at my Cousen Fullers, and at Captain Lelands.[7] My Family in Peace. Blessed be God. N.B. Ebenezer at Ordination and supp'd at Mr. Hollands. N.B. We hear again from Lunenbourg that Mr. Stearns is not Dead.

8. Rainy. Ebenezer made some Cyder at old Mr. Maynards but was beat off by the weather from proceeding. Miserable Mrs. Wakefield[8] I suppose hang'd, this afternoon at Cambridge.

9. [No entry.]

10. [No entry.]

11. (Being the Lords Day) in the morning came a Chair and who should be in it but Mr. Cowell and his wife (my Niece) who having tir'd their Horse yesterday were forc'd to Lodge at Wards in Marlborough. I preach'd on Jer. 8, 4, 5. P.M. on Ch. 3, 22. Return O backsliding Children etc. Repeating Sermon on the Ps. 28, 5 from page 25 nigh the bottom to page 33.

12. In the morning I rode to Lieutenant Tainters, who had kill'd a mutton and they put up a side of it in my portmantle. I brot it home. Had a Quarter of Beef of Mr. Jonah Warrin. Price of both the Mutton and Beef 12 d. Mr. Joseph Batchellor brought home a piece of 21 yards of part Callimanco and part pladd for me a Gown, and for Lucy another. P.M. I visited and pray'd with Jesse Maynards youngest Daughter, Sick at his Fathers. My Kinsman Cowell and his wife and Cousen Sarah Tyley rode over to Mr. Ebenezer Rice's, and my Wife was also of the Company, and she went as far as to Captain Fays, with design to provide some Salt Pork against Ministers Meeting. Our own Pork (notwithstanding we laid up So much) being almost out.

13. Mr. Cowell and his Wife went away, for Boston. The Association met at my House, viz. Mr. Loring, Cushing, Barrett, Martyn, Stone, Seccomb, Smith, Morse, Davis, and Wellman. See the Records of the Association. N.B. Jesse Maynards Child dy'd last night. Mrs. Jerusha Wood very low. While we were at Supper a messenger came for me to go and see her. I found her drawing near to Death, yet she was very desirous of Life, but with resignation to the will of God. She had not assurance, but seem'd to have a well-grounded Hope. She dy'd before morning.

14. Some Difficulty about my having desir'd Mr. Loring to preach my Lecture today, it being Mr. Marsh's Turn (as they would have it)—especially Mr. Smith was warm, Mr. Morse and

Mr. Davis also in behalf of Mr. Marsh. In opposition to them I declared my resolution against him. A vote was passed (which was to my great Satisfaction) that Mr. Loring should preach today. Accordingly he preached. His Text Ezek. 36, 26. An excellent Discourse—many much affected—God grant the Impressions may continue and be ripened! After Lecture and Dinner and some Time in Conversation the ministers went home. N.B. Jesse Maynards Child bury'd from his Fathers; Mr. Martyn officiated, (for I could not leave the ministers nor my work as Clerk, but was obliged to Stay at Home.) At evening I went down there—another of the Same Children taken sick.

15. Ebenezer undertakes to make some more Cyder but was so beat off again by the Rain that he could only Squeeze out a part of a Cheese, three Barrells though Neighbour John Rogers helped him part of the afternoon. Mrs. Jerusha Ward was bury'd—I attended tho twas raining, and the storm prevailed very much at Evening; and in the Night. Fast at Grafton. They send to Messrs. Martyn and Hall, Eaton[9] and Frost.[10]

16. Was at Neighbour Pratts, and Maynards about the making Cyder—send Ebenezer again to go on with it and went to Mr. Batchellor and got him to rig up my Casks—visited Neighbour Stephen Maynard who is ill yet. Proves a bright tho windy Day. Am griev'd at my interruptions, but cannot, I think, avoid them.

17. Ebenezer proceeds in gathering and laying up winter Apples. I went to the Funeral of Mr. Timothy Warrens youngest Child. The Third Funeral this week, but yet tis not a Sickly Time among us. P.M. came Mr. Stephen Frost[11] of Cambridge going to Grafton if he could not obtain of any Body to Change with him. I was oblig'd to deny him, my particular Circumstances being such that I could not go. Yet there are so many Exceptions made there against the ministers and preachers that go there that tis pity ordained ministers can't go in their stead, to instruct and direct them in this difficult Time! And by means of the Continual Interruptions and hindrances this week, every Day of it, I needed to change. My Soul is often bowed down with my Burthens—not being able to take Care of my Family without more impediment to my Studys and even to my whole Ministerial work then ought to be suffered.

18. A.M. I went on with the Subject from Mat. 24, 25. P.M. repeated a Number of Articles in the 4 Applicatory Head in sermon on Ps. 28, 5, viz. from page 33 and onward to the End of the particulars respecting Reformation of Life and Conversation, but with various alterations which I had not Time to write down there in. O that God would please to overlook my many Defects and give His blessing to my weak Endeavours! At Eve read the two first Judge Hale's Letters to his Children I would learn of him to concern my self for the highest Good of mine.

19. Lowery and Sometimes Showered and looked like a rainy Day and therefore Ebenezer deferred making Cyder to Day. Yet afterwards it held up, and I was Sorry we did not go on because the mill at old Mr. Maynards is left for me when others are depending. Neighbour Pratt in particular, and because I want to go to Boston this week with Cousen Sarah Tyley. P.M. I went over to Mr. Martyn—but both he and his wife were gone over to Bolton.

20. Mr. Ebenezer Chamberlain Collector came and brought me £17. 1/ of Old Tenor. A Cold Time for Ebenezer who makes Cyder to Day. At eve Mr. Goddard of Leicester here, with his Brother Benjamin. N.B. Our Neighbour Nathaniel Whitney here also.

21. Bright Day. Ebenezer making Cyder at Old Mr. Maynards Mill. This Day I Suppose the Council meets at Narraganset number 2, by reason of the Difficultys there with Reverend Elisha Marsh. The Lord be with them and grant all needed Wisdom and Understanding, Counsel and Fear of God. And may there by an happy Event!

22. Cousen Sarah Tyley and I set out for Boston. The occasion of going to Day rather than next Monday, as I designed, was this, Mr. Jesse Maynard brought a message last night from

---

[4] Gleason.

[5] David Turner (Harvard 1718), minister of Rehoboth, 1721–1757. *Sibley*, VI, 287.

[6] The Reverend Stephen Chase of Lynnfield.

[7] James Leland of Sutton.

[8] Elizabeth Wakefield was hanged "for the Murder of her spurious Offspring." *Boston Weekly News-Letter*, Oct. 15, 1747.

[9] The Reverend Joshua Eaton of Spencer.

[10] The Reverend Amariah Frost of Milford.

[11] (Harvard 1739). A schoolmaster of Lancaster and an occasional preacher. *Sibley*, X, 369.

Mr. Martyn, that I Should have his Chair if I could not do without, but that he had rather not lend it. I concluded (charitably) that it must be because of feebleness of the Wheels; but if otherwise, and it was but half granted it was better not to accept of it: and another reason is I foresee I shall want to be at home next Wednesday. We called at Mr. Ebenezer Chamberlins, who being Collector, had money to pay me. We called also at Captain Goddards. N.B. his Chaise was gone down and not returned, but he readily lent it to me if I lit of it. Molly was at Mother Champneys and pritty well. Cousen Sarah and I proceeded to Boston, to her mothers—But I lodg'd and my horse kept at Brother Alexander's.[12]

23. I made a few Visits, dispatched a little Business, dined at cousen Elias's with Madam Delhonde,[13] bargained with my Kinsman for Pools Synopsis 3 last volumes for his Debt to me. Bought my Wife a plad Gown at brother Sam Parkmans (9 yards for 9£) and paid him for it and for everything else I had there. Was with Mr. Whipple at Mrs. Keggels at Eve, and hastened to Cambridge (tho it rained somewhat) and lodged there. N.B. Ward of College with Molly.

24. It rained, yet I set out determining to ride as I could bear and as the storm Should permitt, tho it were no further than the Next Town. Stop'd at Justice Harris's in Watertown. Din'd at Mr. Cooks[14] in Sudbury—called at Mr. Darlings and reached home in some Comfort, tho sometimes it rained hard, and was wet all the day. Found my Dwelling in Peace—tho bad News round—for Mrs. Chamberlin (Johns wife) lost her Pocket Book in Boston with all her money of her Marketing (10 or 12£). But this was a Small thing compared with the accident at Grafton last Thursday, when Mr. Boynes was about to blow up a Rock in a Well of Mr. Charles Brighams the Train took fire by his picking of the Rock—Mr. Prentice's son Solomon was greatly wounded and his Leg despaired of. Several others were much hurt yet one man who was in the well, along with Mr. Boynes escaped.

25. Mr. Martyn here in the morning going up to Grafton to preach there. Mr. Stephen Frost for him. N.B. News that Solomon Prentice is Dead. I preached a. and p.m. on Rev. 20, 12, those words the Books were opened, and another Book was opened which was the Book of Life. At Eve Mr. Martyn returned and supped and lodged here. N.B. Mr. Prentice Sent me a message per Mr. Martyn to transcribe the Papers of the Council for him, but no word of his son's Funeral nor Desire that I or any of mine would attend it.

26. Mr. Martyn left us before Noon. No rupture about his Chair. N.B. Mary Bradish here, about having a Sermon at her House when she first goes into it. But we agree that the Private Meeting which is appointed to be at her Fathers next week be at her House, which is close by, to avoid Superstition and Ostentation.

27. Ebenezer fetched Clay from Mr. Abner Newtons to mend my Chimney Back. Read various things—in particular read part of Mr. Jerimiah Borroughs of Gospel Remission.[15]

28. Took some Notice of the Lord's long Patience towards me, and his Church here, these 23 Years. O that God would forgive my great unprofitableness and quicken and assist me in all his Works! And O That I might observe how my precious Time wastes, and Eternity long Eternity hastens upon me! I felt but poorly in the Day, but had especially much indisposition of Body thru the Night. Ebenezer dugg Potatoes. We are laying up for winter of every Store we can. O may we lay up in Time for Eternity!

29. Much indisposed in Body, but I thank God my mind not greatly sunk.

30. Rain. As we have been blessed with a good Crop of Corn, so likewise of Turnips, which are now Cutting. Mr. Cushing on his Journey home in the Rain, here at Evening.

31. Thomme came at Evening.

[12] Parkman's brother, Alexander.
[13] Wife of Louis Delhonde, the physician.
[14] The Reverend William Cooke of East Sudbury, which later became the town of Wayland.
[15] Jeremiah Burroughs, *Gospel Remission, or a Treatise Shewing that True Blessedness Consists in Pardon of Sin* (London, 1668).

NOVEMBER, 1747

1. I deliver'd the whole of my Preparation in the forenoon that the Congregation might have at one View what I could think further proper from Mat. 24, 46 and on occasion of beginning a New Year of Sabbaths and Gospel Privileges. May the Lord impress especially my own Heart herewith and not only make me a faithful and wise servant but enable me to continue and persevere to the Coming of the Lord that I may be among those Servants who shall be truely Blessed! P.M. I repeated Some parts of sermons on Jam. 1, 21. N.B. Mr. Jenison[1] come into Town again and at Meeting here.

2. P.M. at Merchant Rice's, dining there with the Officers, Captain Baker etc. At Eve pray'd with the Company before they were dismiss'd. N.B. Brother Hicks among us. Mr. Hall[2] of Sutton on his journey to Concord, spake with him on the Road. He informs me that the people of his Parish lately voted him 400£ (Old Tenor) for this Year. N.B. Mr. Loring preach'd at Grafton yesterday but he was not here either going or returning. N.B. Reverend Mr. Reed call'd here with his wife's Mother from New Haven (whilst I was from home) and brought me a Letter from Mrs. Pierpoint.

3. Brother Hicks and I reckon'd, about my Cattle which he had kept in the Summer and I pay'd him 33 shillings old Tenor for keeping Six: and we reckon'd also on account of the Cow that calv'd at his House, whose Calf he kill'd and whose milk he had till Ebenezer fetch'd the Cow home and he allow'd me but 3£ for both the Calf and the milk, but I yielded to anything he would propose least we should by Some Means or other get angry, which would be worse than all the Controversy was worth. I dreaded the dangerous Minute! Thomme return'd to Marlborough. N.B. by him I sent to Deacon Rice[3] 10£ Old Tenor being the full of 50£ borrow'd of him last March.

4. Ebenezer plough'd a little part of the Day. My Wife and I rode over to make Mr. Martyn a visit and din'd there. We after Dinner walk'd to their Meeting House, the workmen being then about the Pulpit and Mr. Martyns Pew. At Eve we return'd in Safety and Peace. Blessed be God! O the Sweets and Charms of Mutual Love and Friendship! May nothing ever invade or disturb this Sacred Calm! I afterwards went to Mr. Hezekiah Hows and bought a Couple of Geese for Store. Gave 18 shillings for the Couple.

5. Rainy yet I rode to the Private Meeting which was appointed to be at old Mr. Bradish's but we met at his Dauter Mary's. N.B. She had newly got into her House. I preach'd on Mat. 6, 33. Not many attended, but of elderly persons there were besides Mr. Bradish and his wife Justice Baker, Deacon Forbush and Deacon Newton, Captain Warrin, Lieutenant Tainter—Several women, and young people of both sexes.

6. I preach'd my Lecture from Neh. 10, 29.

7. Mr. John Chamberlin here.

8. Sacrament. Before I went to Meeting came the Reverend Mr. Caleb Rice of Sturbridge. I preach'd a.m. on Song 2, 4. Mr. Rice p.m. on Col. 3, 3. Mr. Rice lodg'd here.

9. Mr. Rice left us to go to Marlborough. My wife and I accompany'd with old Mr. Whipple and his wife rode up to see old Mr. Thomas Knowlton and his wife. In my way I went to Mr. Eleazer Bellows to admonish his Dauter Charity for her Repeated Fornication, which Duty I (as I was able) discharg'd and she thank'd me for it. We call'd also at Mr. Joseph Knowltons. We din'd at Mr. Abraham Knowltons, they having provided purposely very plentifully. As we return'd we call'd at Mr. Joseph Miles's and at Mr. Gershom Brighams and at Mr. Francis Whipples. At Eve we return'd in Peace. D.G.

10. This Day met here the Committee of Ministers appointed by the late Association to look over the Answers which had been given to the Question: What had best be done to prevent the Threatening Defection in Religion and gather out what may be reduc'd to practice. They were Mr. Loring, Mr. Cushing and Mr. Stone. They din'd here. Mr. Loring pray'd before we began the work. But we could go no further than to mark and minute the

[1] William Jenison.
[2] The Reverend David Hall.
[3] Caleb Rice.

principal Heads without drawing up any Report. Mr. Loring stay'd all night. At Evening came one Mr. Rosebrook[4] from Grafton with a Letter from Mr. Prentice desiring Copys of all the Papers of his Case. But I wrote to him to come here.

11. A Remarkable Morning, for the Conversation with Mr. Loring upon Christian Experiences—in which he was pleas'd to Relate much of his own. Mr. Loring din'd with me; as did also Mr. Prentice. N.B. They Two were together whilst I went to the Meeting House and Catechiz'd the Boys. P.M. Catechiz'd the Girls—the few that came. Ebenezer sows Rye about this Time.

12. I visited Martha Ward[5] who is in a weak state. I was also at Mr. Abner Newtons, and at Evening at Deacon Newtons. Whilst I was gone from home Samuel Hicks[6] was here as he return'd from Cambridge. N.B. On Monday morning last I Sold a Young Cow to Mr. John Chamberlin for 15£ old Tenor and last night a Spring Calf for 4£ of like money.

13. I rode up to Mr. Bezaleel Eagers to send a Letter to Deacon Whittemore[7] about his looking out for a Chair for me: and sent it to Captain Saltmarsh's[8] by one Randal. At Eve Mr. Benjamin Goddard here. N.B. His Discourse that Man by Adam Lost all—Natural Powers and all.

14. As it rain'd hard last night, so to Day. Yet at Evening I rode to Southborough and Mr. Stone hither.

15. I preach'd at Southborough on 2 Cor. 3, 15, p.m. on 10, 14, 17. Return'd home at Eve. Mr. Stone preach'd on Mat. 16, 24 and he also return'd home at Eve.

16. Neighbour Ebenezer Maynard kill'd a Pigg for me which at home Weigh'd 64. His Brother Nathan at Eve went with it to Boston. My wife and I at Mr. Whipples, his Dauter Lucy[9] being married this Evening there. We had an agreeable Supper and Company. O may we remember the Midnight Cry!

17. I read Mr. Hurrion's sermons on particular Redemption.[10] After Dinner I sat down and wrote some Sketches on the second Commandment which I deliver'd at a Catechetical Exercise to young women this afternoon. After the Said Exercise I visited Martha Ward who is in a languishing Condition.

18. Nathan Maynard who carry'd a Pig to Boston for me, return'd last night and tells me that there was a great uproar and Mobb in Boston by Reason of a certain Man of War coming in there and pressing a great Number of Men the night before. A very rainy Time till p.m. towards Night. N.B. Mr. James Bowman was going down with an Horse for Forbush at Cambridge and a Letter to Molly—but he was prevented by the Rain. I went down myself as far as to Mr. Bavericks. N.B. My Cambridge Cow which we are fatting, Sick and lame. Captain Maynard here and at Eve Mr. Daniel Forbush informs that his Brother Jonathan as well as Bowman is going to Boston so that he can lead Molly an Horse down if I desire it.

19. I rode down to Neighbour Bavericks and Captain Warrins. Sent my mare and Sidesaddle by Mr. Bowman to Molly at Cambridge. Lieutenant Tainter here to see what is the matter with my Fat Cow.

20. Grows Cold, yet it is a pleasant bright Day. Mr. Jonathan Rogers thrash'd out some of my Rye for himself to Sow. He din'd with us.

21. Bright and pleasant but Cold and blustering. Expect Molly from Cambridge and she came at Evening with Forbush from Mr. Strattons at Waltham where they lodg'd having come from Cambridge the Evening before. They brot me Turretine's Theol. Elenct.[11] 3 volumes quarto which Mr. Eliot bought for me of Captain Wadsworth for 5£ old Tenor.

22. A. and P.M. on Jer. 8, 4, 5. O that God would give us a true sense of our Backslidings and recover us that there mayn't be a perpetual Backsliding!

23. [No entry.]

24. My wife and I visited Martha Ward—and from thence (Lieutenant Tainter there for us) we went over to the marriage of Samuel Baker and Susanna Tainter, at her Fathers.

25. At Evening came Two Gentlemen with a Letter from Mr. Edwards of Northampton. By the Letter I found em to be Messers Spencer and Strong, who were on their Journey to Boston, being Sent for by the Commissioners of the Corporation for Propagating Christian Knowledge in order to their going upon the mission to the Mohawks. They lodg'd here but I sent their Horses to Captain Maynards. By my Interruptions

26. was not able to finish my intended Discourse for the General Thanksgiving, which was on this Day, but was oblig'd to take a sermon I preach'd heretofore. It was on Lev. 3, 1 but made several alterations and large Additions. O that God would be pleas'd to accept the Sacrifice of Praise presented throughout this province to Day! and grant us Grace to improve Divine Benefits and Mercys to the Glory of the Great Bestower. In the Evening I had Opportunity to converse with our Two Strangers. Shew'd 'em Dr. Cotton Mather's Joyful Sound reaching to both the Indies; containing also an account of the Mission to Malabar, and Dr. Mathers Literary Correspondence with the Missionarys.[12] This Book I presented to the Mission to the Mohawks.

27. Messers Spencer and Strong pursued their Journey to Boston. I visited Martha Ward again, who continues very weak and low in mind and Body. She can't bear anything about her being in Danger of Death, but fills herself with Hopes that She Shall recover to Health. Forbush was here at Evening and brot a Letter from Mr. Martyn desiring we might Change next Lords Day.

28. Went down to Captain Maynards to Satisfie him for keeping the Horses I lately Sent there (viz. Messers. Spencers and Strongs) but I could not see him, being gone out from home, but I offer'd his son and his wife pay, tho they would not take it. I Sent Martha Ward a Fowl by Daniel Cook, Mr. Nurse's Boy.

29. I rode over to Mr. Martyns and preach'd to his people. A. and P.M. on 2 Cor. 3, 17, 18 and finish'd that Subject, which I began among them on March last. He preach'd to my people on Ezek. 18, 32 carrying on the Same Subject as he also began when we chang'd before. N.B. In the Northside meeting house a pulpit to preach in. Comfortable Day tho somewhat Cold. We both of us return'd home at Evening. May God to pleased to own and Bless our Endeavours! N.B. at Eve I understood that Eliezer Rice went away from Mr. Martyns Exercises again. Neither was his wife at meeting in the afternoon.

30. A Cold, windy, but bright Day. I am not a little concern'd about my keeping such a large Stock of Cattle for tho I have sold a Cow and one of the last Spring Calves yet have we 18 Horn Cattle besides our Horses and Sheep, and I fear my Hay will be short for them all, I therefore walk'd out toward Evening to see if I could either buy Hay or promote the Sale of Some of them or get some kept through the Winter. I went to Mr. Elijah Rice's and to Mr. Tennys. Call'd at the Shoomaker Garfields and at Neighbor John Chamberlins. We finish this month with a great deal of Comfort and Health both in person and in Family. Blessed be God!

### DECEMBER, 1747

1. We din'd early and my Wife visited old Mrs. Crouch (Mrs. Rogers's mother) in her Blindness and lameness. I also call'd there and took her with me (Mrs. Crouch not able to go) to old Mrs. Dorcas Forbushs,[1] where, according to appointment made in my Name by the Reverend Mr. Martyn last Lords Day I preach'd to the Said Widow Forbush. Text John 9, 4. A Considerable Assembly. O that the word of God might have free Course and be glorified! After the Exercise we visited Martha Ward again and pray'd with her.

2. Lieutenant Tainter and his son Benjamin came over and kill'd my Cambridge Cow. Weigh'd 413, the Quarters—Hide 65, Tallow 35. Lieutenant was very kind and obliging—not only gave me freely his pains, but knowing my straights for winter

[4] James Rosborough of Grafton.

[5] Daughter of Increase Ward.

[6] The son of John Hicks of Sutton.

[7] Samuel Whittemore of Cambridge.

[8] Thomas Saltmarsh, an innkeeper of Watertown.

[9] Lucy Whipple married Moses Pratt of Hardwick.

[10] John Hurrion (1675?–1731), an English Congregational minister, wrote *The Scripture Doctrine of Particular Redemption Stated and Vindicated in Four Sermons.* When this first appeared is uncertain but it may have been in his *Discourses*, 3 vols. (London, 1727).

[11] Franciscus Turretinus, *Compendium Theologiae Didactico-Elencticae* (Amsterdam, 1695).

[12] *India Christiana. A Discourse, Delivered unto the Commissioners, for the Propagation of the Gospel among the American Indians* (Boston, 1721).

[1] Widow of Thomas Forbush.

keeping for my stock, he took home a Cow to winter for me. N.B. A Sorrowful accident befell us in the Night. My son Ebenezer being greatly fatigu'd with his worrying in the Day, sat sleeping by the fire after we were come up to Bed, with his Head upon his Arms on his Knees: his Elbows slip'd from his Knees and his Chair slip'd away from under him, and he fell into the Fire—his Hands were both burnt, his right Hand especially which threw him into great pain and smart. For his Relief I immediately kill'd a Cat and he wash'd his Hands in the Blood. God be prais'd he was awak'd and enabled to get out of the Fire! May the Providence of God be Sanctify'd to both him and us!

3. A.M. Messers Spencer and Strong here in their Return from Boston and are now engag'd in the mission to the Mohawks, upon the Donation of Dr. Daniel Williams. As a Token of my Hearty good wishes I presented the Missions Calvins Institutions, an handsome large Octavo Edition. May the Hand of the Lord be with them and give them good success! P.M. My Wife rode with me to the private meeting at Captain Baker's. I preach'd on Mat. 7, 13, 14. A greater Number of hearers than I expected. I am very glad they can find in their Hearts to come together so roundly, tho it is a Second Time this week. May God give an efficacious Blessing! We supp'd their—Lieutenant Tainter with us. A snow storm to go home in. The storm increas'd very much, both the Snow and Wind. The Night was very Tempestuous. The House Shook exceedingly. But God safely preserv'd us. To his Name be Praise and Glory! N.B. After Exercise I desir'd their Help in getting Wood next Monday, because of my sons Lameness.

4. A very difficult Morning. The Snow deep—my son lame and unable to go to the Barn. I was oblig'd to go myself. We were also very much out of wood, but Neighbour Ebenezer Maynard and his brother Nathan came and both cut and sledded for me. And at Eve came Mr. Benjamin Tainter and offer'd to tarry over night to help me tomorrow notwithstanding his purpose to come with his Father and others to get wood next Monday. I bless God for those kind Tokens from my Neibours! May I have grace suitably to improve them!

5. Benjamin Tainter came, and brought with him Noah How, who (together) having a Large Saw, saw'd off a Stout Pine Logg for the sawmill. They din'd with us and p.m. Benjamin Cutt and sledded down some wood. The Cold increases.

6. A pritty Cold Day, but few at Meeting. I preach'd all Day upon 1 Cor. 10, 31. Mr. Winchester and widow Sarah Forbush, (Phinehas's widow) din'd with us. It was so cold that I finish'd the Exercises early about 3.

7. Old Mr. Maynard informs me that Martha Ward dy'd last Evening. A Very Cold Day. There came only the few following Hands to cutt Wood (N.B. Not one Team came to sled) Messers Jonah Warrin, and Daniel Hardy, Solomon Baker and Benjamin Tainter, Charles Rice junior, and Timothy Newton. Benjamin Tainter took my Oxen, mare and sled and sledded down 8 Load. N.B. The first of the Hands came about 11 a.m. the rest at near Noon. Captain Maynard here at Eve whilst I sold Mr. Jonah Warrin (of whom, and his son Elijah, I had this last Fall 178£ of Beef at 12 d. per pound) Two Steers, one coming 3, the other coming 2 for 21£ old Tenor. Twas Captain Maynards Judgment that they were worth so much, and offer'd to give it for 'em if he hadn't 'em. N.B. I offer'd the Captain pay for keeping the Horses I sent to him at Thanksgiving Time, but he would not take it.

8. Cold Day. My Dauter Molly rode with me to the Burial of Martha Ward. May every Instance of Death awaken and quicken us! and in Special our Youth! After Burying we went to Deacon Newtons, and I sat there whilst Silas Sow'd a Soal, upon one of my Boots.

9. Last Night snow'd; this morning very Cold, but bright more moderate and pleasant afterwards. Read Dr. Owen of Apostacy.[2]

10. The Cold continues.

11. Snow'd again.

12. Very Cold. Old Mr. Maynard came repeatedly and chop'd wood for us at the Door, Ebenezer not being able to handle an Ax

to any purpose—but he tends the Cattle. A dozen Fowls kill'd to send to Boston by Neighbour Richard Barns next Monday morning. P.M. Jonathan Grout came and chop'd wood for us at the Door. A great Kindness that my Neighbours thus help me in this the small article, it would otherwise take up so much of my Time since my son is so lame. N.B. We have the sorrowful News that the Town House in Boston was burnt last Wednesday.

13. A very Cold Day. On John 17, 4, and p.m. on Eccl. 8, 8. Our Exercise short for I am not able to undergo the Cold without much Care. The Lord accept up (wherein through Grace we are sincere) through his Dear son! Lieutenant Tainter and one Mr. Bond din'd with us.

14. A Very Cold Storm of Snow. Mr. Barns does not go to Boston. Precinct Meeting to call in Debts and to Consider my sallery—but was adjourn'd. (See Lee's Solomon Temple on Ministers Maintenance[3] which I read at Even.)

15. Bright and pleasant but Cold. A very tight severe Season. But God is the preserver of Man and Beast.

16. A Cold Storm of Snow again. Ebenezer went at Evening to old Mr. Maynards, the young men meet to Settle their accounts for the year.

17. Exceeding Cold and stormy Some Hail and Rain and forms a Crust. Ceas'd storming p.m. but very Cold; as almost any weather that Comes. In the Evening Captain Maynard here. Winds exceeding high. N.B. I am inform'd that the Reverend Mr. Cheney of Brookfield is to be bury'd today (the 17th).

18. A very Severe night we have pass'd through, but God's Mercys are new this morning which is bright without Clouds, and silver'd by the Icicles everywhere shining and the Trees glistening. But it is still Cold. As the Day gets up the Wind rises. 'Tis as much as we can do to take Care of ourselves and the Children, provide for and Tend the Fires, and the Cattle. But our Eyes should be to the Lord our never failing Support. Benjamin Whipple came, and got wood out of the Snow and cut it for Me. The Evening somewhat moderate.

19. Several Neibours were so good as to come and assist in cutting wood for the Sabbath and getting in Loggs. Old Mr. Maynard—Neighbour Barns and Neighbour John Rogers.

20. It Snow'd again last night—but to Day bright very pleasant and Comfortable. On Mat. 13, 53 to the End of the Chapter. P.M. on Eccl. 8, 13. Mr. Stratton of Waltham and Mr. Samuel Fay juniors wife din'd here. O that God would help us suitably to Entertain the Lord Jesus Christ and not by our Unbelief Prevent Him in the mighty works of his Grace and Spirit upon our Souls! and O that we might not be of the wicked, that vainly imagine they shall prolong their Day. May we remember that our Days are as a shadow and may we fear before God that it may go well with us!

21. A Moderate Day. Benjamin Tainter came before we were out of wood, and with my son got a little more to the Door. Mr. Cushing here and Captain Maynard towards Evening. The Chief I did today was reading Limestreet Sermons, some of which I can't but very highly esteem.

22. Heard there was a Man found dead on Boston Neck about last Wednesday, Suppos'd to have perish'd in the Cold. I rode to Merchant Rice's—and had further Conversation with him about his Case respecting Lydia Pratt of Grafton. I visited Mr. Jonathan Fay's wife who lyes sick. Call'd at Mr. Grouts where was Mr. Phinehas Hardy. But I made it my Business, according to my Intention when I went out from Home, to visit Neighbour Eliezer Rice, and talked with him about his going away from Mr. Martyn's Ministrations here, both when he preaches my Lecture and when we change. I desir'd his Reasons. He gave me these following, and Said that these were they, viz. That he had always understood that a minister should be blameless and of good character, but he heard Mr. Martyn had not, in the former part of his Life been so, and was not of good Report, and Secondly, he reckon'd that Mr. Martyn did not act like a man of good Conscience in taking that Money which was gather'd from those

[2] John Owen, *The Nature of Apostasie from the Profession of the Gospel* (London, 1676).

[3] Samuel Lee, *Orbis Miraculum; or, The Temple of Solomon* (London, 1659).

familys who had mov'd out of that Precinct. I endeavour'd to answer both these Reasons. N.B. In our Conversation Mr. Rice would by no means allow that any Man who had been vicious when young tho thro the Grace of God ever so penitent, and furnish'd with Gifts Should be admitted into the Ministry; or that any minister who Should fall into Scandal might on any Terms be restor'd to his ministry, but to the Privileges of a Brother only. I dealt plainly with him—and may God Succeed what I Said.

23. Neighbour Eliezer Rice came with Neibour Edwards Whipple and they kill'd a Sow which weigh'd 167 and a Barrow which weigh'd 175. They did it gratis. N.B. Captain Maynard and I had some Talk of visiting Father Prentice at Lancaster, but the Weather was such as I could not venture out in.

24. Cloudy and rainy.

25. God grant that I and mine may be happy partakers this Day with all those who Sincerely celebrate the Nativity of Jesus Christ! We had Captain Maynards Team, to join with mine and draw down Wood from my Hill. Mr. Biglo, Noah and Daniel How, Rody Smith, Benjamin Whipple, Nathan Maynard, Silas Newton, Jonathan and Robert Cook, Jonas Bradish, Jonathan Bruce, Samuel Warrin, Josiah Walker, Samuel Bumpso (Indian) and Elijah Bellows came and Cutt Wood. Receiv'd a Letter by Mr. Barns from Brother Samuel Parkman informing that Dr. Parkman had a Son born on the 9th instant, and which they have call'd Elias. May God make him a great Blessing!

26. [No entry.]

27. On Mat. 14, 1 to 4. P.M. repeated the first sermon on Eph. 5, 16 from Col. 4, 5. Mrs. Tainter and the widow of Nehemiah How din'd with us. Snowy Day.

28. Snow Storm. At Eve Mr. Benjamin Fay here to inform his aged Father was very low.

29. A Bright pleasant Day. Was at Merchant Rice's. Visited Captain Fay and din'd there. Pray'd and took solemn leave of him. N.B. his son James there. Call'd at Mr. Williams's he being confin'd by Rheumatism.

30. [No entry.]

31. I preach'd to the Young people, especially to the Society of Young Men, from Eph. 5, 16. This I thought seasonable at the Conclusion of the Year—for alas! how far have we been from rightly improving this precious Talent. If God Shall grant the Continuance of it to me, will He please to afford with all, the Grace rightly to husband it!

# ❧ III ❧

## WESTBOROUGH AT MID-CENTURY

### 1748-1755

## JANUARY 1748

I would heartily bless God for His Sparing Mercy and Goodness! Having spent part of the Day in Rest and Exercises of Religion and Abstinence, (See Memoirs etc.) Lieutenant Perez Rice of Sutton came to acquaint me with the Desire of Captain Fay to see me. I comply'd and went. Found him very low and scarce capable to Converse, could get only a word or two and then he would drop into sleep presently—I prayed and soon I took leave and bid him farewell, he reply'd Farewell—and we could hear a few words more such as, "God bless you, Support you, Succeed you"—(and may God be pleased to hear this dying prayer! Oh might we all be ready for such an Hour!) I went from there to old Mr. Samuel Fays (after I had eat something with 'em at Dinner)—Had some talk with Mr. Fay about the old Disgusts, and prayed we might come to a thorow Reconcilement. Talked with Jeduthun and his wife about their Delays. N.B. Jeduthan put into my Hand, at coming away, a Token of his Regard in Two Bills amounting to 20/6 Old Tenor, saying withall, that he could not come to help me get wood nor assist me as others, and would therefore pray me to accept that. So slow riding it was near night when I got home, the weather being thick fogg, southerly wind and warm.

2. [No entry.]

3. On Mathew 14, 4 to 12. although I had prepared as much as might have served for Two Exercises yet I chose to deliver the whole in one, though I was the longer and spoke the faster. P.M. Repeat'd on Psalm 90, 9 last Clause.

4. This day the precinct met together by adjournment upon the affair of the depreciating of the Bills of Credit in which my Sallery was paid. I went to the Meeting House myself, being desired by the Meeting. Mr. Miller was the person the Moderator sent. I read Two papers which I had drawn up to lay before them, and after a few words I returned. Lieutenant Forbush together with Captain Forbush and Ensign Bruce informed at eve, that they had considered the depreciating of money according to the Act of the General Court, and had allowed me 12£ 10 shillings per cent, that is 27£ and conceiving that this would not suffice they had chosen a Committee to Consider of my papers and make report to the precinct Committee for raising Meeting that they might raise another Meeting to see what the precinct will do further, they not being able to do any more now by vertue of the present Warrant. Said Committee for Considering my papers are Captain Warrin, Mr. Miller, Deacon Newton, Mr. Whipple, and Mr. Abner Newton. And thus this Day went over, on which so much seemed to be depending. However, there seemed to be good humour and respect. N.B. The Day was a very Cold Day, yet many attended the Meeting. N.B. Mr. Ebenezer Chamberlin Collector here and paid me 34. 4. 9 old Tenor.

5. Snow Storm. Went to Captain Maynard's to see Jeremy Goodhue the cooper who is sick there. Heard that Captain Fay is Dead. About 8 or 9 in the evening came Rody Devereux to call me to go and see Goodhue who is grown far worse. He soon after I spoke to him, got into a very peculiar Frame, expressing in a wondrous Tone, his Experiences at Ipswich, his Behavior since, and his present hopes and assurances. I felt he was somewhat delirious. I rather thought so by his praying Lord whilst I was at Prayer, (at his Desire) and continuing to pray when we had done.

6. Rained last night, and a Thaw ensues. Thunder and Lightning. Dr. Gott here after his visiting Goodhue.

7. In the Morning Mr. William Goodhue of Holliston was here to desire me to go down to Captain Maynard's, his Brother would be glad to see me. I complyed and the Special Reason of his sending for me was to assist him in Making his will. His Senses were sound—he confirmed what he said to me t'other night of his Experiences of the Divine grace at Ipswich, and was earnest in his Defence of the late work of God in the Land. My taking Minutes of his Will detained me till past Noon and was obliged to dine there. After prayer I returned home and drew the will. At eve I went to him again and compleated it. Having prayed with him again at Captain Maynard's earnest Desire, I

came home. Forbush from College here, he tells me he keeps School in Town to make up some of Mr. Jenison's Time.

8. Snowy again. N.B. sent Mr. Stow the original of Result of Council at Narragansett by Mr. John Bent of Framingham. Mr. Jeduthan Fay here to Desire me to attend the Funeral of Captain Fay today. He dined with us, and then both my wife and I went. It was a large Funeral, and Twas very sorrowfull to bury such an old Friend, such a pious, useful, good tempered man, and the principal Deacon in the Church. The Lord awaken us to be in readiness ourself. I am told by the Deacon's Son James that they could not discern that he was any clearer about his Spiritual state till he dyed, than he was when I was with him. Such was the Sovereign will of God!

9. [No entry.]

10. A.M. and P.M. On Occasion of the Death of Deacon Fay I preached on Gen. 25, 8. Mr. James Fay and his mother, the Widow dined here. N.B. At noon received a letter from the Honorable Judge Wilder[1] informing me of the Death of their Reverend and dear Pastor Mr. John Prentice and desiring my assistance at the Interment of his Remains next Thursday. An heavy stroke this, upon not only that Town but this part of the Country! The Lord Sanctifies it to all of us, and to me in Special! Snowed and Stormed especially at Night and I was concerned about my journey to Lancaster.

11. Sent for Captain Maynard—who consented to go with me if I would venture, at least he would go with me as far as Shrewsbury. It was a rugged Day—The Snow deep, the air somewhat sharp, the wind blew about the Snow—but we ventured to Shrewsbury. Mr. Cushing and Dr. Smith[2] with their Wives were going. I was exceedingly well wrapped up, and we ventured with them. Stopped at Deacon Jonathan Keyes',[3] Mr. Morse's,[4] and at Moore's[5] (in Chauxitt) arrived at the House of sorrow in the evening where I lodged. Mr. Gardner of Stow there, having preached there the day before. Captain Maynard lodged at Colonel Oliver Wilder's. N.B. Disquietment among Mr. Prentice's children by reason of their Father's will.

12. The Funeral Obsequies of Reverend Mr. Prentice Solemnized. Mr. Loring prayed. Mr. Loring, Mr. Gardner, Mr. Stow, Mr. Seccomb Mr. Mellen[6] and I were Bearers. (Were favored with moderate weather. A considerable number of Ministers.) The Church and Congregation (males) walked before the corps. Mr. Thomas Prentice made a short Speech after covering up in the grave. The Parish bore the Expenses of the Funeral so far as 200£ old Tenor. Judge Wilder by Request was with the Bearers at the Drawing up of Character and took the Care of transmitting it to the Printer. A most Sorrowfull and Mournful Time! The Lord repair the wide Breach! and comfort all the Bereaved and grant them to study peace and Love! Lodged there again.

13. In Returning today, dined at Mr. Morse's and (though it snowed) we tarried and attended his Lecture. I preached on John 17. 4. N.B. Colonel Nahum Ward,[7] Mr. Cushing, and Mr. Maccarty[8] with us. Captain Maynard and I called at Mr. Cushing's and at evening returned home, through God's mercy in Comfort and safety and found our Familys in peace. D.G.

14. Read Mr. Joseph Stevens's[9] Sermons preached at Charlestown and Cambridge and reviewed my College Almanacks and Journals—with great Sorrow and Shame.

15. Captain Forbush here and objects against his Cousin Cooks enjoying Baptism for his Child.

16. Moderate and pleasant. Mrs. Rice (Eliezear's wife) had my mare to Mr. Beeman's. N.B. Captain Forbush's wife here and objected against Mrs. Cooks enjoying special privileges.

17. It Snowed this Sabbath also. I preached A.M. on John 12, 35, on the Death of Reverend Mr. John Prentice of Lancaster.

[1] Joseph Wilder, a deacon of the Lancaster church.
[2] Joshua Smith, the physician of Shrewsbury.
[3] Of the north precinct (Boylston) of Shrewsbury.
[4] The Reverend Mr. Ebenezer Morse of Boylston.
[5] Deacon Joseph Moore.
[6] The Reverend Mr. John Mellen of Sterling.
[7] The magistrate of Shrewsbury.
[8] The Reverend Mr. Thaddeus Maccarty of Worcester.
[9] Joseph Stevens, *Another and Better Country even an Heaven: in Reserve for all True Believers* (Boston, 1723).

N.B. for a character of him I took the original of what was delivered to Judge Wilder to be printed. But O might we all who survive Consider our remaining Advantages, and have Grace to improve 'em whilst the Lord is pleased to continue them. May we also have proper apprehensions of those Dark Days that threaten us! I delivered the whole of my preparation in one Exercise, for though 'twas very long I could not divide it. And preached P.M. on Mathew 26, 20. and intimated to the people that it was a Repetition. And may God be pleased to remember this His gracious promise for our Support in these Cloudy Times: and when such a number of Ministers have been within this six months taken away from us! When we came home at Evening it snowed very hard and was very Windy and Cold—the Night a Windy, Cold Night.

18. And such a Day followed as the Night was which rendered it a tedious Time. I kept close to my Study all Day, read Dr. Increase Mather's Order Of The Churches In New England vindicated[10] Mr. Jeremiah Burroughs of Gospel remission.

19. Brother Hicks came from Cambridge.

20. Brother Hicks went home. Mr. Martyn came and dined with us. Tarried till evening when Captain Eager came to wait on him home. N.B. Mr. James Fay has been here and brought me a piece of black shalloon from Mr. Harwood[11] of Hardwick and Mr. Edwards's sermon on the Death of Mr. Brainerd.[12] At eve Mr. Daniel Forbush[13] was married to Mrs. Mary Parker of Shrewsbury.

21. A fine Day. My wife set out for Boston on Captain Forbush's horse. Little Alexander was carried at Night to Mrs. Amy Maynard.[14]

22. Although I was much concerned last Night about my wife's Journey, I was much less anxious to Day it being a very fine, warm Day. Mr. [blank] Woods[15] of Summers was here with Deer Leather and dined, I bought a Large skin for which I gave him 13£ old Tenor.

23. A somewhat Cold Day, but conceiving it to be my Duty to use my best endeavor to get to Lancaster, I first rode to Mr. Cushing's dined there and obtained of Mr. Cushing to send his son Jacob along with me who accordingly was my Fellow-traveler. The Snow was so deep before we got to Deacon Jonathan Keyes that I was obliged to dismount several Times, my Mare worrying sometimes pritty much to surmount or get thro the Banks. Mr. Morse came to Westboro, and Mr. Stevens[16] went to Mr. Morse's. We arrived at Lancaster by Daylight.

24. It Snowed all Day. I preached A. & P.M. on John 12. 35. On the Death of their late worthy pastor. May the Great Shepherd of the Sheep, the Chief Shepherd, Compassionate their State, hear and accept their humble Supplication in their late Test. (Last Thursday) provide for their guidance to a Resettlement and may they walk while they have the Light—Darkness may not come upon you. N.B. A sorrowful Accident this morning. My Mare Slunk [?] 2 Colts.

25. Dr. Stanton Prentice[17] has been very kind in looking after my Mare. Breakfasted there—before I left Lancaster, Dr. Stanton came over to his Mother's to take Leave and I perceiving that there was disquietment among them on account of Mr. Prentice's Will, gave 'em an Earnest Friendly Exhortation. Cushing and I rode to Mr. Silas Brigham's at the Mills and dined there. Mr. Brigham rode with me home, we called at Mr. Morse's and at Mr. Cushing's. My wife had returned safely from Boston last Saturday Night, brings me News that my Brother Alexander is in a poor State of Health and my sister

Willard but feeble and lives alone much broken and decayed. Nabby also (Elias's wife) in but a weak and low condition.

26. [No entry.]

27. Sarah Henry at Work here making Billy a Bannian.[18]

28. Snowed. A Public Fast on account of the Judgment of God upon us in the Continuance of the War. The perplexity of the province Affairs and the burning of the Courthouse. I preached on Heb. 12, 29 A.M.; P.M. on Romans 11, 26 repeating the latter part of sermon on 1 Thess. 1, 10. Sarah Henry lodges here.

29. A Day to be remembered. Twelve Years ago my dear wife Mary died, may I never lose the sense of God's holy Dispensation toward me and mine, but I was not able to devote this Day as I would have inclined to by reason on my unavoidable Engagement in preparing for the next Sabbath. Sarah Henry takes my plush coat to pieces in order to New line it. P.M., Ebenezer to Marlboro to get him a great coat cut out and pay Deacon Andrew Price the full of the Interest of my Bond to him and brought it home. I am now again out of Debt, (a few Dribbles, etc. excepted) and my obligation to my own Children.

30. Sarah Henry.

31. Preached on John 12, 35 A. and P.M. It was a bright Day which we have not had for public Assembling this very great While. But may we see the Glorious Sun of [illegible] and delight in the Lord. Tis of no small consequence to us that we improve the Light while we are indulged with it, for our contempt of it will provoke God to send a dreadful Darkness upon us and this Land has Reason to fear it. Mrs. Dunlop dined here.

### FEBRUARY, [1748]

1. Went to the Funeral of Mr. Jonathan Fay's young Child. Dined at merchant Rice's. Sent by Mr. Abner Temple for 3 volumes of Pools Synopsis from Boston. My wife went to Marlboro on Mr. Nathan Maynard's Mare, and returned at Eve. Sarah Henry at work here. Town Meeting falls through for want of a third selectman. At Eve I rode over to Neighbour How's. Mr. Wellman[1] came and lodg'd here. He is going down to get Mr. Chase's[2] sermon at his Ordination printed. Wants my Right Hand.

2. Mr. Wellman left us. Mr. Bezaleel Eager brought Mrs. Bekky Gott. Mrs. Dunlop in spiritual Troubles here and dined with us. Ebenezer preparing Timber for a Slay. This Day Twelve Years my dear wife was buried. I remember the wormwood and the gall and my Soul is humbled within me—but the Continual interruptions of Company prevented my Retirements.

3. Mr. Dunlop and Ebenezer thrash Barley. At Night came Joseph Biglo for Sarah Henry (who was making a Great Coat for Ebenezer) and carried her away. Mr. Jenison here from Worcester Supped with us but did not lodge.

4. Mr. Dunlop and Ebenezer thrashed Barley. My wife and I went to the private meeting at Mr. Grouts. I finished the discourse I began at Captain Baker's, on Mat. 7, 13, 14. Snowed hard when we returned home.

5. Forbush here at Eve, and lodged here.

6. The Extremest Cold Day, I think that we have had this winter. Mr. Henchman came for Mrs. Bekky Gott[3] and carryed her home.

7. Cold Day. On Matt. 14, 13, 14. John 5, 28, 29. Mrs. Tainter and Forbush dined here.

8. Bright and Comfortable. Nineteen persons came to get wood for me, viz. Mr. Grow, Harrington with his team, Daniel Forbush, Ebenezer Miller, Samuel, Daniel and Phinehas Hardy, Zebulon Rice, Tim Warrin, Joseph Grout, junior, Samuel Baker and Benjamin Willson, Benjamin Tainter for James Bradish, Martyn Pratt, Robert Dunlop, Jonathan Forbush, Solomon Woods, John Kelly for Beriah Rice, William Pierce. N.B. We had Mr. Richard Barr's oxen to go with mine to make up a second

[10] *The Order of the Gospel, Professed and Practiced by the Churches of Christ in New-England, Justified* (Boston, 1700).

[11] John Harwood.

[12] Jonathan Edwards, *True Saints, when Absent from the Body, are Present with the Lord* (Boston, 1747).

[13] Son of Deacon Jonathan Forbush of Westborough.

[14] Mrs. Ebenezer Maynard.

[15] Probably Deacon James Woods of Somers, Conn.

[16] Benjamin Stevens (Harvard 1740). Later the minister of Kittery, Maine, 1751–1791. *Sibley*, X, 535–539.

[17] Physician of Lancaster. Son of the Reverend Mr. John Prentice.

[18] A loose flannel gown, jacket, or shirt.

[1] The Reverend Mr. James Wellman of Millbury.

[2] The Reverend Mr. Stephen Chase of Lynnfield.

[3] The daughter of Dr. Gott of Marlborough.

Team and they brought up to the Door about 30 loads. N.B. They cut it in Mr. Barr's swamp. Mr. Phinehas Hardy went to him to know his mind, besides my message to him to come up to me, by my Billy. By both which we had free leave.

9. Snowed again. A parcel of wood being left in the swamp cutt yesterday We went and sledded up with 3 Cattle 7 Turns. Thomas Rogers assisted. Mr. Davis[4] of Holden here on his Journey to Boston. Ebenezer p.m. making a Slay. At Mr. Hows.

10. I rode to Mr. Garfield's[5] and settled with him. To Mr. Benjamin How's.

11. Snowy Day. Ebenezer at Mr. How's still upon the slay. Captain Daniel Ward of Worster here.

12. Ebenezer at Mr. How's. Mr. Peam Cowel[6] of Boston came. N.B. Lieutenant Ward of Southboro here, I paid him in full of 24£ old Tenor, for 6 yeards of Blue Broad cloth which my wife bought of him at Boston. Mr. Ebenezer Maynard brot up a variety of Things for us—Sugar, Molasses, Chocolate and a Box from Brother Samuel Parkman's containing 3 volumes of Synopsis Criticicorum and a Black Coat which Brother offers to sale for 10£. Mr. Cowell lodged here.

13. Mr. Wellman here, on his Journey to Sutton. Ebenezer at Mr. How's again. Interruption by Company prevented my preparing a second sermon.

14. I preached a.m. on John 5, 28, 29. P.M. Considering the Affair of Tomorrow I repeated sermon on Phil. 4, 7. Mr. Cowell and old Mrs. Whipple at dinner. O might the Peace of God ever reign in our Hearts!

15. Mr. Ebenezer Rice here in the morning with Mr. Cowell. Mr. Cowell left us to go to Boston. N.B. The Precinct met to make answer to my Two last Papers sent in to them and to see whether they would build a New meeting House within 30 Rods of the Burying place. Affairs of such weight and Consequence (as I humbly apprehend) read the direction and influence of Heaven which may God's people obtain! Molly and Lucy to Mr. Martyns.

16. Deacon Whittemore[7] and John Hicks junior here in the morning, they having lodged at Captain Maynard's last night. Mr. Stone[8] going to Oxford and Cushing (Jacob)[9] here. These last dined here. Sent home Mr. Cushing's Calmet, Volume I.[10] Snowed p.m. Ebenezer at Howe's.

17. The snow storm continues.

18. I would have gone over to Mr. Martyn's to preach his last sermon but could not get there. Sometimes shines and sometimes snowy, cold, and snow deep. Ebenezer finished the Slay.

19. Ebenezer went to Mr. Johnson's mill.

20. A Very great storm of snow. The greatest that has come, perhaps these seven years. Now 31 years since the Great snow.

21. Few at Meeting. On John 5, 28, 29. P.M. repeated latter part of Sermon on Phil. 4, 7. Lieutenant Tainter and his daughters Sarah and Elizabeth dined here. Some that were at meeting in the forenoon came not in the afternoon. Mr. Francis Whipple who read the psalm came not: or Captain Maynard where as it was better coming when the way was broke. But 'tis a very tedious Time.

22. A fine Day though the snow is deep. Lieutenant Tainter came and killed me an Hog. Weighed 245. P.M. had a great deal of Discourse with Lieutenant about the sorrowful Divisions in our precinct. I observed it the rather because: Captain Maynard came, but understanding that Lieutenant Tainter was here would not come in. N.B. Dominique Dyer, a young Frenchman of Chandelieu, here.

23. Snowstorm again, and snowed fast for great part of the Day. A great Body of Snow on the Earth: the Ways are very much blocked up: little Stirring but Neighbour Ebenezer Maynard

here most of the afternoon. Discourse was chiefly concerning the precinct's late proceedings particularly with reference to my Affair. He tells me that Yesterday was the Day appointed for the Committee and Surveyor for finding the center of the precinct to attend that Business.

24. It being a pleasant Day tho the snow was deep, I attempted to ride over to the South Road. Called at Neighbour Pratt's and Mr. Williams proceeded to Captain Baker's, dined there. We had no small conversation, (But in Harmony) about the Precinct's Affairs. He showed me the papers of their later proceedings. One paper was the Report of the later Committee (viz. Deacon Newton, Captain Warrin, Mr. Whipple, Mr. Miller, and Mr. Abner Newton) which the precinct would receive but in part, but were ashamed to let me know some articles of. They exhibited therein that they were uneasy that I did not give them a Discharge for or else. N.B. Squire Baker's earnest Advice to discharge the Town, tho they do not pay me, and by no means to sue, endeavor to recover from the Town in a Lawful way the Debt for my service four months and 15 Days before the Town was divided: again they were uneasy at the vote of the precincts in which they promised me 500£ in Case etc. and that I preach old Sermons. This last I have not met with any man til now that would discover to me, nor own. When I left the Squire I went to Deacon Newton's. Talked over the same things. N.B. The Deacon not pleased with any proposals of Discharging the Town, so well as with my suing the Town. He says a just War must be upheld. I remarked to him my unhappy Praemunire: it being impossible to please them either way. And viewing the Case and its grim aspect upon our dearest Interests I very solemnly said, The Lord look down upon us in Mercy etc! It was evening, and, calling at Mr. Ebenezer Rice's (where came Dominick Dyer) and at Neighbour Pratt's (of whom I got a Leather Apron for Billy) I returned home.

25. The deep Snows prevent my going to Worcester to preach Mr. Maccartys Lecture tho tis fine Weather overhead. At Evening Ward was here and lodged.

26. Ward went home after morning prayer but before Breakfast.

27. Thomas came up from Marlboro to stay over the Sabbath.

28. A.M. on Matt. 14, 15–18. P.M. on Acts 26, 8. Dominick dined here.

29. Bright a.m. Thawy toward Eve. Rain at Night. Mr. Jonathan Forbes, Junior, came and brought 2 pound of Flax from his Mother and gave me his part towards 400£ salary, viz. 35 shillings over and above what he had paid the collection (Old Tenor).

MARCH, 1748

1. It being a fine pleasant Day, my Wife rode with me in the New Slay, to visit old Mrs. Crouch, at Mr. Rogers's. I find the snow very deep.

2. Thomas returned to Marlboro fitted out with a new pair of Shooes, a New Silk Handkerchief—35/ and a Linen Ditto 9/.

3. Mr. Wellman of Sutton came and preached my Lecture. His Text, Mat. 5, 6. My son Ebenezer has been indisposed and done Little for several Days—having a sore throat, etc., but is a little better.

4. Mr. Wellman bought 3 Volumes of Pools Synopsis Criticorum of me viz: on the Haggiographa and on the New Testament[1] (I having duplicates of them) for £3. 15, New Tenor, and he carried away one of them with him.

5. [No entry.]

6. On Song. 2, 4, latter part. Sacrament. The two Deacons and widow Thompson dined here. P.M. on Acts 26, 8, on the Resurrection. May God grant that we may all be really under and experience the happy Benefits and Comforts of Christs Banner and may We be Confirmed in the Great Doctrine of the Resurrection and our Hearts and Lives be influenced always thereby!

7. I prayed at the Town Meeting. Mr. Bowman and Billings being the persons sent by the Town to me to request it. N.B.

---

[4] The Reverend Mr. Joseph Davis.

[5] In Shrewsbury.

[6] Parkman's niece, Elizabeth, married Peam Cowell.

[7] Samuel Whittemore of Cambridge.

[8] The Reverend Mr. Nathan Stone of Southborough.

[9] (Harvard 1748). The son of the Reverend Mr. Job Cushing of Shrewsbury who later became the minister of Waltham, 1752–1809.

[10] One of the works of the French theologian, Augustin Calmet (1672–1757).

[1] Matthew Poole, *Synopsis Criticorum aliorumque S. Scripturae interpretum*, 4 vols. (London, 1669–76). Additional editions followed.

After Prayer I stood on the Stairs and addressed the Town with an Exhortation to Peace and Righteousness, and concerning my own affair, I intimated how long and how patiently I had waited for my Dues from them and prayed that they would take such motions as might prevent my being obliged to use Disagreeable measures to recover those arrears. I afterwards sent a paper, by old Mr. Whipple, to the Moderator to be lodged with the Town Clerk containing the Drift and Design of what I had said. Heard that Mr. Asa Bowker's wife (a worthy woman!) dyed yesterday at Shrewsbury of a cancer. And that Mr. John Brainard, brother of the late Mr. David, preached for Mr. Martyn, designing to have come to me if he could have got here, but the snow is so deep, no Horse (I suppose) can pass between here and Mr. Eagers Tavern.

8. I walked out in the Morning on the Snow to visit divers of my Neighbours—was in at Mr. David Maynard, Junior's, at Mr. Eliezer Rice's, where I tarried some time. At Mr. Jonathan Whipple's, but most of them were from Home. At Mr. Stephen Fay's (which was a main End of my going Out). N.B. His Dissatisfaction with Sallerys and Rates: At Mr. Samuel Bakers: Called at Merchant Rice's (he having newly been to Mr. Fleet[2] for me about my news)—At Deacon Newton's who told me that they did not read to the Town the paper which old Mr. Whipple carried from me to them on the 7th, but they acknowledged it to be the Drift of what I had said—and it was in the Clerks hands. I went to see Moses Nurse who was in a weak and feeble condition and 'tis feared consumptive. N.B. The Day was so bright and pleasant and the sun so warm that I had bad slumping in the snow some times.

9. Ebenezer took the sleigh and carried 8 bushels of barley for malt to Mr. James Woods of Marlborough. I went to see old Mr. Crouch; and neighbor John Rogers giving both to him and his wife solemn warning of their delaying Repentance and Humiliation. Snow melts a great pace. Captain Maynard brought me a sorrowful letter from Brother Parkman with the heavy tidings of the death of my dear Brother Alexander on the 6th at evening of a bilious cholic. Oh that God would by this Providence which is so near me prepare me for my own turn.

10. [No entry.]

11. [No entry.]

12. [No entry.]

13. On John 11, 23, 24, 25. On occasion of the Death of my Dear Brother Alexander. God grant I may have true and living faith in the Resurrection and in Him Who is the Resurrection and The Light that I may have in part in the Resurrection of the Just!

14. It was somewhat late in the morning before I set out upon my journey. Called at Captain Warrins to meet Mr. Ebenezer Chamberlin, the collector. Was also hindered a little at Mr. Jacob Amsden's. Had one Lockhart's company from Marlboro to Waltham. Went to see Mr. Warham Williams[3] and lodged there. It was raw cold 'til evening and then snowed. N.B. Fire burnt in the floor of Mr. Williams's study, but was discovered as we sat in the lower room under it, and was soon put out.

15. I rode to Justice Harris's on account of a piece of all wool cloth I had sent him to be dress'd: and called at Mr. John Hunt's where was Mr. Thomas Marsh[4] of College. Dined at Mother Champney's, P.M. at College. Stormed Hard—I attended Prayer at the Chappell. Put up my Horse at Deacon Whittemore's, lodged with Mr. Hancock[5] at College.

16. It had hailed and snowed in the night. I attended morning Prayers in the Chappell. Broke fast with Mr. Hancock. Dr. Breck[6] came there and was going to Boston. I had his company. N.B. His account of a late difference between him and Mr. Maccarty: which led me to resent his whispering to Mr. Abraham Williams what had passed between Mr. Campbell[7] and me about

him—the grand Haretick Williams whereas I had reference to what he personated at commencement. I visited Dr. Parkman in his affliction—his wife remaining in a very languishing condition. Dined at my eldest Brothers. Visited Sister Willard,[8] and my newly widowed Sister Beckky and my bereaved niece Esther. Lodged there. N.B. Mr. Edward Brattle Oliver[9] there. N.B. Kept my Horse there.

17. Mr. Welsteed preached the public Lecture on the Royalty of God our Salvation from (I think) Ps. 10, 16. Dined at Brother Samuels at evening at Dr. Parkmans, it proving raining I could not go to the South End—spent the Evening at Captain White's and at Mr. Eliot's.[10] Lodged with my Kinsman. His wife very weak and languishing in danger of death and very full of distress, being afraid to die.

18. Visited Mrs. Betty White (Mr. Joseph's dauter) who is wasting away in a consumption. I went up to the burying place and what a multitude even of our own family are there in the Congregation of the Dead. The Lord make me ready for my turn which hastens! Visited my sister Willard. N.B. Sisters discourse with me about her dauter Sarah and my Ebenezer. Was at Cousin John's. N.B. He offered me silver enough for a spoon for my dauter Sarah at £3 Old Tenor an ounce and to give me the making which I accepted of and paid him £4. 13. 0 for one and on consideration that Dr. Gott had given her about 56/ several years ago, I ordered it to be marked as his gift to my child. I dined at Mr. Stoddard's P.M. As I hastened out of Town I called at Mr. Bagnal's about my watch and at Mr. Fleet's and began anew for his Paper. At Sister Beckky's, where was Mr. E.B.O. who presented me a considerable quantity of brown biskitt—and at Mr. Snow's (who married Mrs. Susanna Sharp)[11] where I bought me a large blue handkerchief. for 58/ and hastened to Mother Champney's where I lodged.

19. As I returned home I called at Mr. Dix's[12] (who married Sarah Bond) and was well entertained with smelts and he bountifully sent up several dozen to my wife. Was at Mrs. Beckky Walkers and I dined at Mr. Paterson's[13] at Sudbury. Called also at Mr. Darling's.[14] Very heavy riding and breaking through the deep snow from Marlboro home but arrived well and found my house in health and peace. Blest be God!

21. A Precinct Meeting by adjournment both about answering my two last papers, and concerning building a Meeting House but it dropped through and they did nothing. But before they dispersed, and were gone home I understood that another meeting was agreed to and that they designed nothing about any grant of money for me wherefore I stopped Captain Warrin and Lieutenant Forbush at the road and insisted that something relating to a grant of money to me be inserted in the Warrant. They consented and sent their minds to the rest of the committee by Mr. Nathaniel Whitney and Mr. Stephen Fay.

22. This morning Ebenezer set out upon a designed journey to Connecticutt after flax and was to have gone with Mr. Samuel Baker but when he was at Esquire Baker's he understood there were several men, come down with flax, who gave a most discouraging account of the river and that there was no room to expect any flax on this side under 4 shillings the pound. He therefore returned home, and my wife and I rode over to the said Esquire's and we (the Esquire and I) bought a Bagg of 200 weight—their price was 5/ per pound but they threw in 40 S in the whole Bagg and 3 pound and 1/2 of over plus weight. So that we did not give quite 4/9 the pound. After this Esquire Baker and I went to Deacon Newton's to obtain his consent to put into the Warrant for the designed Meeting the abovementioned article about a grant. Deacon Newton would consent to it if I desired it, but not of his own motion—his reason was that the block must be removed out of the way (meaning that the

[2] Thomas Fleet, the printer of the *Boston Evening-Post*.

[3] The minister of Waltham.

[4] The tutor at Harvard College.

[5] Belcher Hancock, the Harvard tutor.

[6] Samuel Breck, the physician of Worcester.

[7] The Reverend Mr. John Campbell of Oxford.

[8] Parkman's sister, Susanna, the widow of Captain Josiah Willard.

[9] Parkman's niece, Esther, married Oliver later in the year.

[10] The Reverend Mr. Andrew Eliot of New North Church.

[11] The daughter of Captain Robert Sharp of Brookline.

[12] James Dix of Watertown.

[13] James Patterson.

[14] Thomas Darling of Framingham.

82. 10–0 of arrears must be first sued for) or he could not go forward. There ensued warmer talk than ever I had had with Deacon Newton. I urged him to consider how unreasonable it was that he would not do his present duty for the support of the ministry in this Precinct, because somebody else did not do their duty some years ago: and that they should quarrell with me not for suing and straining upon them in the Law, but because I was charitable and compassionate and would not. My Wife went to Mr. Abner Newton's while the Esquire and I were at the Deacon's. I went to her and dined there but Mr. Newton was gone to Boston and we dined with his wife. Spent some hours there and heard her tell of her husband's dissatisfaction about my preaching old sermons. I perceived that Mr. Francis Whipple had been among them. I gave her many Reasons for my Doing it. She mentioned nothing else, we parted in peace. Called at Mr. Samuel Williams where was Neighbour Eliezer Rice. Mr. Williams brought on discourse about the precinct's present circumstances and especially with regard to my Sallery and the building a Meeting House. N.B. Neighbour Rice offered to pay me before that very night the sum which the Town was indebted to me if I would give him the power which I have to recover it in a Court of Law. But I refused to accept of it. We returned home at eve in safety.

23. Early came Mr. Jonas Brigham to call me to Mr. Charles Woods' child (Phoebe) of about 3 years old in dying Circumstances. I went tho very difficult passing through the snow banks. Called to see Neighbour Rogers and Neighbour Barns. Snow Storm came up before I got home. P.M. Mr. Ebenezer Maynard here. I gave him as treasurer receipt for 220£ for last year's Sallery, instead of the receipt given last July 21 to Mr. Benjamin Fay.

24. Lieutenant Tainter here—he acquainted me with the foolish and mischievious conduct of a number of young men on March Meeting night at his house (about 10 or 11 of them) he being gone on a journey at that time: and he wanted my advice. I advised him to keep it as private as he could but to go and discourse with the youngsters themselves and with their parents. I refused to know who they were till he should take these steps and if these steps were not successful it would then be time enough to expose them.

25. Ebenezer now built the boxes at the front of the house and sowed them with parsley, radishes, and cabbage. But though the ground is bare a little before house and particular spots yet it is very deep in general. At eve came Brother Hicks and lodged here.

26. Brother Hicks went home. Ebenezer cutting down timber for Posts at ministerial lot.

27. I was much indisposed yet went through the exercises after my Fashion. A.M. on Matt. 14, 19 to 21. P.M. Heb. 9. 27, Latter clause,—improved then in some passages out of sermon on Eccl. 11, 9, latter part, viz. pages 3, 4, 5, and 12, 13, with alterations and inverting the order of the articles as was most agreeable. After the last exercise read the Act of the General Court against profane Cursing and Swearing, and gave reasons why it was not read last Lord's Day nor the Lord's Day before. At eve I was much out of Ease. Only prayed in the family and Ebenezer read the 25th of Saint Matthew. I was often aguish or as if I had taken Cold.

28. Lent my Mare to Neighbour Barns to go to Marlboro and his young man brought her back by noon, at which time I rode to Mr. Charles Wood's on occasion of the funeral of one of his children (Phebe). A warm day, snow wastes apace.

29. A very fair warm pleasant Day. In the morning I assisted Ebenezer in sledding down several Load of wood and conceive that such a strring myself might be useful to me under my present Indispositions. N.B. Mr. Ephraim Sherman here and told me he was going over to Mr. Martyn where a subscription which I reckoned up to be £45 15/ Old Tenor for the printing his sermon on October 25 last. Jacob Garfield here to be examined in order to his receiving Holy Baptism. N.B. I received an admonitory letter from the Reverend Mr. Stone of my mistaking the time of the Committee of ministers meeting at his house which I conceive was to be on the 16th but was on the 9th and a new appointment made to meet at Mr. Smiths on Association morning at 8 o'clock.

30. I rode over to Mr. Martyns. Tho the snow was much gone in open ground here and there, yet in the woods it was very deep. I found it very difficult passing on the east side of Liquor Hill, and from the new Meeting House in the lane to Mr. Martyn's brook. I dined there but his wife gone to Groaning. He went with me over to Mr. Lulls and was one of the witness of his wife's signing of the several deeds which her husband had given me of land in Townsend. Returned at evening, air smoaky and warm. The snow flows off apace.

31. Warm and pleasant. Went down a little way into the ministerial lot with Mr. Batchellor who wants stave timber of me. P.M. Mr. John Rogers at length comes to confess his fornication. The Lord grant him Repentence unto Life!

Month after month my life consumes away!
Lord! Make me timely learn by what I may
Be always ready for the extremest day!

### APRIL, 1748.

1. A Warm Day—but little snow to be seen in open Land, and what remains mercifully wastes apace. May this month be spent to God's Glory! Mr. Jonathan Bellows, pressed to go out a soldier and upon his march, here to desire prayer. Ebenezer putting up Fences and getting Riders.

2. Last Evening the Weather changed very much and became Cold; and the morning Cold. It may sett the springing grass back—but all Eyes wait on God who is the mercifull preserver of both man and beast. Ebenezer sowed some peas.

3. On Mat. 14, 22, 23. P.M. Heb. 9, 27. Captain Willard[1] of Grafton and his sister the widow How, dined here. N.B. I publickly appointed a Catecheticall Exercise to Young Women to be next Tuesday at 2 p.m. Not knowing that that is the time, by warrant, for the precinct meeting.

4. Dr. Gott here. Wrote by him to Mr. Martyn not to come over (as proposed) on Tuesday to visit us, but to come on Thursday, and prepared to preach at the private meeting at Lieutenant Tainter's. P.M. I walked to Captain Maynard's and thence over to Mr. Seth Rice's on purpose to visit his mother and wife. N.B. I sent word about that the appointed Catechetical Exercise is put by. My wife rode to Deacon Forbush's.

5. An Important Time! When this precinct met upon the affair of my sallery and a new Meeting House—Mr. Grout and Lieutenant Tainter being sent to me to desire me to Pray with them. I went after prayer. They passed no vote about the former article respecting me, but they desired the Committee of the Precinct would at evening come and Confer with me, and enquire of me what I thought my Circumstances would require, and I could chearfully go on in the work of the Ministry with—and so adjourned that affair to the 18th Instant. And accordinly at evening the said Committee (4 of whom, viz. Edward Baker, Esquire, Captain Warrin, Lieutenant Forbush and Mr. Benjamin Fay) came to me and insisted upon my saying what would suffice maintenance. Note well, they said the precinct would Expect that if the Precinct should comply and make a grant of what I should say would suffice for the Year Currant, then I should give 'em a Receipt in full. I answered that I was averse to saying anything of a particular Sum—but they insisted that I would. I replyed that I insisted on it that the Precinct would Explain their Expression (in their Votes at the Contract) wherein they say that the "Yearly sallery 55£ New Tenor money so called, not Soldier money, so called" and as to the Present State of Things—what I would have. I said there was a very different manner of Maintaining the Gospel—There was what would barely do it; there was also what would do it with some handsomeness and Decency; and there was a manner of doing it with a Generousness, when persons were in their Hearts enlarged unto Bountifullness. I did not therefore care to proscribe, nor go about to set a summ. However, upon their further insisting, for they said they must make some Report to them that had sent them, I told them I could offer thus much for their Consideration, that as all the Necessarys of Life had so exceedingly risen as they had for several years past especially. I humbly conceived that

[1] Benjamin Willard.

it would take double or nigh it (in Denomination of Bills) to do the same as used to be done. Esquire Baker answered that then they understood me that it would now take 440£ old Tenor to have the same done which 220£ used to do. I answered that it could not take less than 400£. Mr. Fay understood me that if the precinct should vote that summ, yet I could not do the whole work nor should go on Chearfully. I replyed to this that if they should vote that I would endeavor (as God should please to enable me) to go on with all parts of the work and would go on chearfully—at least would try this year—and if it would well do I should, I hoped given God the Glory and them all suitable Thanks, and if it did not do, I would let them know. But it growing late, I told 'em that I would take the matter into Consideration, and they should have Some Return from me when they should sit again. This Concluded the present Conference. As to the other important matter upon which the precinct met today, viz. The Meeting House, they voted that a New Meeting House should be built upon the South Great Road, a little below the Burying place.

6. Lowery. Ebenezer has been ploughing a little in the Days past, and now a little 3 yearling calves sick, probably with what they eat abroad yesterday. Very growing season and the grass appears very pleasant. Mr. John Rogers's wife here, and examined.

7. Mr. Martyn (whom I expected to visit me today and go with me to the Family Meeting) sent me a line that he could not come. I preached at Lieutenant Tainter's on Gen. 17, 7, to the end of page 12. My wife was with me. After Exercises Captain Baker discoursed with me about our precinct Transactions with me and respecting the 500£ vote in special. My wife and I visited Neighbour Eliezer Rice's wife (who is sick) at Evening.

8. Mr. Dunlop works in my Garden, sows parsnips etc. Ebenezer splitting Hills.

9. Ebenezer sledding off Stones from the Field by the House, A.M. P.M. ploughed there and took up Flax. Neighbour John Rogers here. I gave him what fervent Cautions and Exhortations I could. O that God would give his Blessing!

10. On Mat. 14, 24 and Heb. 9, 27. Mr. Berriah Rice's wife dined with us. N.B. Mr. John Rogers and wife propounded in order to their Humilliation, etc.

11. Mr. Dunlop again works for me in the Garden. Ebenezer ploughing stubble. Mr. Wellman came P.M. N.B. our reading Dr. Gauden's Hieraspistes.[2]

12. Mr. Wellman (having lodged here) rode with me to the Ministers Meeting at Marlborough early in the Morning. I went so early because of an appointment made at Southboro by the other members of the Committee to meet at 6 o'clock this morning to finish our Report. But they did not come in season nor did Mr. Loring come till nigh 11 o'clock today. So that we could accomplish but very little before Dinner and the association Exercises came on. See the minutes of the Association.[3] At Eve a most unhappy occurence! It was this, Mr. Jenison had sent a letter to Mr. Smith[4] to be communicated to the association, and he came himself. As the Moderator (Mr. Loring)[5] began to read the letter, came in his son Jonathan.[6] Mr. Buckminster,[7] perceiving that there was in the room one who did not belong to the association (viz. said Mr. Jonathan Loring) and knowing our practice not to read letters or transact association business while any stranger was present, stepped up to the Moderator and put the question to him, whether it was fit to go on till his son was retired. Mr. Jonathan Loring, mistaking him and not knowing our custom, flew into a sudden and violent passion with him—reproached him bitterly. Mr. Davis[8] offered to speak—Mr.

Loring fell upon him also. Insulted the whole association at a very intolerable Rate, nor did his own worthy and venerable father escape, who could do nothing to Effect in stilling him. But we saw how grievous and wounding it was to the good man, and for his sake we could not but forebear the Resentment which Jonathan deserved. We hardly ever saw such an Evening, any of us in all our lives. Mr. Jenison's letter was voted to be read tomorrow morning. Yet was it afterwards read to a number that remained to lodge at Mr. Smith's—because of Mr. Jenison's frequent and strong insisting—his plea that he was to go to Watertown early in the Morning. I lodged at Mr. Smith's but my horse was kept at Mr. Samuel Wards.

13. Mr. Jenison sent another letter to the association and demanded a Categorical answer. There was much debate about whether he should be answered and how.[9] Mr. Cushing preached the public Lecture on 2 Pet. 1, 10. N.B. Mr. Mills[10] late of Bellingham there. N.B. Heard the sorrowful News yesterday of Mr. Bridghams[11] house at Brimfield, burnt to the ground and little saved. P.M. Letter to Mr. Jenison drawn up by Mr. Morse and after many readings, voted. Mr. Loring goes from us to Grafton to preach there tomorrow. Mr. Cushing chose moderator in his room. Mr. Wellman rode home with me.

14. Mr. Wellman went home. Mr. Barrett was to have preached my Lecture but he disappoints me, as he has done several Times, and I was obliged to preach myself. Text, Gen. 17, 7, latter part. After Meeting the Committee of the Precinct at my Desire came So that I might have a Word of Conference with them. James Bradish and Mary Whitney were married. Ebenezer ploughed in the forenoon.

15. Mr. Campbell of Oxford came and lodged with us.

16. Mr. Campbell left us.

17. Sacrament, on Song 2, 4. P.M. Hos. 6, 6, made the Chief of the Exercise from Sermon on John, 17, 3, from page 12 to page 22.

18. This was the Day of the Adjournment of the precinct meeting on the affair of my sallery at which I had great hopes the people would have considered my Circumstances Comitting the matter however to the Glorious God to do his pleasure. I drew up a paper of answer to the Committee's request to me in behalf of the precinct that I would say what I would have to support my Family? This paper I gave 'em, and it was read to the precinct. Yet they did nothing—adjourned again to the last Monday in Next Month. It was very provoking to me that they should trifle with me and abuse me at this rate, and this under colour of the most slender pretence, which was this—that "They had not a Discharge for their part (which they had paid) of the 82. 10 whereas it was expressly inserted in my paper of Reply to the Committee this Day—as a Postscript to it—(but I understood afterward that it was excepted against because it was said "this precinct". This precinct not having a Being at That Time.) Whereas no Quibble could be more trifling than this, What I had written in said P.S. being only to intimate my sense of what I was ready to do, respecting those who now make up this precinct, not as if they were to be considered as a Precinct in the Instrument of Discharge, but Inhabitants of the Town. But I saw that Anything would serve 'em to shift this unacceptable Business off.) Divers of the Committee came in here after the adjournment. Deacon Newton, Esquire Baker and Mr. Benjamin Fay who acquainted me with the adjournment. I was in some Chagrin and hastily stepped aside and wrote and signed a paper by itself assuring them of my readiness to give full Discharge. God grant me patience, Humility, Resignation to his holy Will and grace to improve the Frown of his providence upon me!

19. I visited at Captain Forbushs and Neighbour Cooks on account of the difference subsisting between the women. Was at Lieutenant Forbush. N.B. Am told a Committee is seen in the Morning. Very warm Weather.

[2] John Gauden, Hieraspistes: a Defence, by Way of Apology, for the Ministry and Ministers of the Church of England (London, 1653).

[3] Among other things Mr. Morse of Boylston told the ministers he had not had any salary for more than a year. Allen, Worcester Association, p. 28.

[4] Aaron Smith of Southborough.

[5] Israel Loring of Sudbury.

[6] Jonathan Loring (Harvard 1738) was a lawyer of Marlborough. Sibley, X, 288-289.

[7] Joseph Buckminster of Rutland.

[8] Joseph Davis of Holden.

[9] The Association records note "A Contemptuous letter of Mr. William Jennison was treated with the neglect it deserved." Allen, Worcester Association, p. 28.

[10] Jonathan Mills (Harvard 1723), the minister of Bellingham, 1727-1737. Sibley, VII, 239-241.

[11] The Reverend Mr. James Bridgham.

20. Catachized at the Meeting House A. & P.M. N.B. There were about 8 girls besides my own. They were Lavinia Baker, Susanna Newton, Hephzibah Rice, Persis Crosby, Jemima Maynard, Ruhamah Pratt, Rachel Pratt, Jemima Brigham. I hope the warm admonitions etc., especially in the forenoon were not without some Effect. The Lord bless these means for their highest good! A very warm day—and it proves a very dry Time. Noah How works here.

21. Mr. Eliezer Rice's Wife continues so very ill. I visited her again. Dr. Smith there. N.B. Read Plutarch's Life of Marc. Marcellus. Noah How and Ebenezer mend Fence.

22. Killed a Pigg that weighed 7 score and 19 pound. I stuck it myself. Noah How and Ebenezer dressed it. Noah and Ebenezer upon the Fences. At Eve Dr. Stanton Prentice and Dr. Smith called here. Understand that Mrs. Wheeler who lies ill over at Lancaster is in way of Recovery.

23. Mr. Eleazer Pratt here to desire me to attend the funeral of Mr. Francis Whitney who was taken suddenly ill the Day before yesterday—was soon after insensible—and yesterday P.M. deceased. The Lord sanctify such sudden strokes! I went accordingly tho, it being Saturday, I went not quite to the Grave.

24. A.M. on Mat. 14, 25, 26, 27. P.M. On Hos. 6, 6, but repeated Sermon John 17, 3, from page 23 to 28. Deacon Woodberry[12] of Sutton on his journey from the General Court dined here. O, that God would grant to us the true, influential, affective Knowledge of Him! That we may both know God and be and do accordingly. N.B. Very refreshing, merciful Rain last night after a very dry Time.

25. Frost this Morning. Ebenezer mending Fence on the lower South Side. Major Keyes[13] here P.M. to visit me.

26. [No entry.]

27. My Colt came home of himself from Mr. Grouts.[14] Noah How brought a plough which he had made for me at Ebenezer's Desire, tho we had one of Captain Warrin's make. P.M. Mr. Barns[15] here. I told him his new Fence had come in upon me about the North East corner of my new piece of woodland. We agreed to review our marks and plotts. Very sweet refreshing Rain. N.B. Ebenezer planted Beans and Cucumbers in the back yard. —But may my mind and Heart be turned from Earthly things and be suitably prepared for the Solemnity approaching!

29. Public Fast. I preached all Day upon Hos. 6, 6, composed on the occasion tho for the Exercises on the last Sabbaths from this Text I repeated as before is said. N.B. A number of Gentlemen at Meeting who sat in Captain Maynard's and other seats. May God accept our offerings and teach us the true, influential Knowledge of Him!

29. I went to Captain Maynard's and understood that Dr. Joseph Pyncheon[16] was one of the Gentlemen that kept Fast with us, but he was gone upon his journey homeward. Mr. Martyn came to see me. I went down to the woodland, joining on to Mr. Barns, and Mr. Martyn and Ebenezer with me. I called also my Neighbour Stephen Maynard and we all saw that my marked Tree was cutt down and laid into Mr. Barns's New Fence. Mr. Martyn dined with us.

30. I have sent a letter to Mr. Smith about our changing (He had mentioned it at the Time of the Minister's Meeting without Determining what Day). I rode to Marlboro, calling at Judge Ward's[17] to consult him about my Plott which he had drawn of my land joining to Mr. Barns, and he discovered to me that Mr. Barns had not trespassed etc. Was at Mr. Smith's, but as to our changing, tomorrow is appointed to be a Sacrament Day with them. At Dr. Gott's. There I obtained Mr. Wilson[18] to preach for me tomorrow. Mr. David Warrin shod my Colt. Dr. Gott gave the shoes; Mr. Loring paid for the work and engaged to

treat the workman. Went to see my son Thomas. Mr. Williams not at home. Returned at Eve to Westboro.

## MAY, 1748.

1. Mr. Wilson preached for me. A.M. on Mat. 16, 26. P.M. 1 Thess. 4, 14. He returned to Hopkinton at eve.

2. Joseph Bowker came to work for me for 4 months, Wages 50£, Old Tenor. Ebenezer and he brought my Cow (with her Calf) that had been kept at Lieutenant Tainter's. I walked over to Mr. Whipples. N.B. Mr. Silas Walker of Nichewog there. Mr. Whipple was so kind as to lend me his Horse to ride to Mr. Joseph Knowltons. I visited his Wife and pray'd with her. Visited Elijah Bellows[1] Sick of a Fever and pray'd with him. A Thunder Storm arose and kept me there and at Mr. Whipples till it was late in the Evening.

3. Sent 8 Cattle by the Whipples etc to Nitchewag, under the Care of Mr. Silas Wheeler. Captain Warrin sent his sons Nahum and Jonathan with Two Yoke of Oxen and Hay to keep 'em, to plough for me. Sent by Captain Maynard to Boston. P.M. my Team also ploughing. N.B. Mr. Jonathan Green[2] here, and desires me from his Mother Wheeler to take the Care of getting the Bible given by Mr. Wheeler to our Church, let it Cost more or less; he tells me he has money lying by him for that use.

4. Lieutenant Ward here. Mr. Whitney also. N.B. had very free Talk and with some Earnestness about the Backwardness of people throughout the Land to Support their Ministers. Mr. Martyn came with his wife to see us—and din'd with us—Spent the p.m. here and went home at Eve. I griev'd that so little was Said of the State of Religion in our own Flocks. He brought me Mrs. Wheelers earnest Request to visit her.

5. Joseph and Ebenezer are ploughing and mending Fence. The Weather from Day to Day so Cloudy and cold and sometimes Rains that we declin'd planting Indian Corn. A.M. Visited Mr. Eliezer Rice's Wife, who now grows better.

6. The Weather forbids planting Still. My Hay I think is now wholly done but had some Kindly from old Mr. Maynards. Lieutenant Holloway here—we talk'd of his sister Wheeler who is at Lancaster still.

7. We planted some of the Ground. Isaac Amsdens Child dy'd in bed with them Suddenly last night.

8. On Mat. 14, 28 to 31. P.M. on Heb. 9, 27. John Rogers and his wife restor'd to Charity,[3] and his wife Baptized. O that God would keep alive the Impressions made this Day; and might they be Saving! Heard Mrs. Wheeler is better. Gave public Notice of the Funeral of Isaac Amsdens Child to be tomorrow morning 8 o'clock. N.B. I wrote to Mr. Martyn at noon, and sent it this Eve after meeting by Mr. James Ball to let him know of this Funeral—we having agreed to go tomorrow morning over to Lancaster to see Mrs. Wheeler before she dyes; but now I may not hinder his going, tho I be prevented myself by the Funeral aforesaid (Tho I fear whether some Evil mayn't come of it, that I have written upon the Lords Day.)

9. Funeral of Isaac Amsdens Child at 8 a.m. After Prayer there rode over to Mr. Martyns who was not gone to Lancaster. I din'd there, and p.m. I return'd home, he concluding to go over to see Mrs. Wheeler tomorrow morning.

10. Read the Chief part of the Independent Advertisers[4] that have come out. Borrow'd of Mr. Martyn.[5]

11. Preach'd Mr. Stone's Lecture at Southboro on Song 2, 4. Visited old Mr. Johnson, and was exceeding plain with him. Return'd home at Evening.

12. My wife and I rode to Sutton and din'd at my Cousen Fullers,[6] and Trasks.[7] Preach'd the Lecture on Rom. 6, 13. After

---

12 Benjamin Woodberry.

13 John Keyes of Shrewsbury.

14 Joseph Grout.

15 Richard Barnes.

16 The physician of Springfield.

17 William Ward of Southborough, a justice of the peace.

18 John Wilson (Harvard 1743), a physician of Natick, who settled in Hopkinton in 1750. The doctor occasionally preached in nearby pulpits. *Sibley*, XI, 96–97.

1 A son of Eleazer Bellows.

2 Green's wife, Sibyl or Sibil, was the daughter of the late Joseph Wheeler.

3 In the church records Parkman noted "John Rogers and Elizabeth his Wife offered their humble Confessions of the Sin of Fornication, and were restor'd—the Latter own'd the Covenant and, was baptiz'd herself and then their Children Persis and John were also baptiz'd."

4 A weekly paper established Jan. 4, 1748, in Boston by Gamaliel Rogers and Daniel Fowle. It continued to be issued through Dec. 5, 1749.

5 The Reverend Mr. John Martyn of the north precinct of Westborough.

6 Jonathan Fuller.

7 Samuel Trask had come with Jonathan Fuller to Sutton from Salem.

Lecture Mr. Wellman rode with us first to Mr. Singleterrys,[8] where we were kindly entertain'd and refresh'd, and then to Mr. Halls[9]—where was Mr. Aaron Hutchinson (of Connecticut) Preacher at Grafton, who had preach'd the Lecture this Day for Mr. Hall. We all lodg'd at Mr. Halls. N.B. Mr. Hall had had a Church Meeting on account of the Separatists among them.

13. Mr. Hall and his Wife, Mr. Wellman and Mr. Hutchinson went with us down to Brother Hicks, who also came to show us the way to his House. We all din'd there. In the Afternoon Brother Hicks and his wife mounted and rode with us as far as to Deacon Hall's,[10] whither we all went. My Spouse and I parted from the rest of the Company at Deacon Halls and we rode, with Mr. Hutchinson accompanying to Deacon Whipples[11] in Grafton, where this Gentleman lodges. Our Conversation was chiefly on the Melancholly Subject of the Separations—both at Sutton and at Grafton. Mr. Hutchinson show'd the Ministers who were together today his Credentials—sign'd by the Clerk of the South Association in Hartford. We Stopp'd at Winchesters so long as to Eat. We found our Habitation in Peace. D.G. In special our little Alexander who has been weaning ever since Monday Night.

14. Joseph and Ebenezer building Stone Wall on the South side of the Road before and below the Barns. The Face of the Creation is Wonderfully beautify'd and forward. Might the work of Grace flourish in my Soul no less!

15. On Mat. 11 the 31 verse ad finem. P.M. Hos. 6, 3.

16. I rode to Lancaster to see Mrs. Wheeler. Mr. James Ball went with me. I visited Judge Wilder likewise. Was at Madam Prentice's[12] but she was gone to Boston. Expected to see Mr. Abraham Williams who preaches there, but he was gone to Lemister. Was at Dr. Stanton Prentice's. He gave me an imperfect Scudders daily walk.[13] Return'd home at Night. Found the Missionary Strong at my House, both he and Mr. Spencer had been at Boston. They had been to the Commissioners to acquaint 'em that there was no Encouragement to go up with Mr. John Brainerd to the Indians on Susquehannah River. He lodg'd here.

17. Mr. Strong left us to go to Northampton. Town Meeting to choose a Representative, but they conclude not to send. N.B. Mr. James Ball and Mr. Jacob Rice pay their part to the old Arrears, and paid nigh double in denomination. At Eve came Mr. Cotton[14] of New Town.

18. Mr. Cotton left us.

19. Rainy. Mr. Cushing preach'd my Lecture on John 6, 51. N.B. I was Sleepy at Meeting, the Lord forgive this sin!

20. At Mr. Whipples with my wife at the Raising of his Barn.

21. [No entry.]

22. Sacrament. A.M. on Song 1, 12. P.M. Repeated on John 5, 6. Took in all the paragraph.

23. Was at Deacon Newtons—din'd there. Mr. Buckminster here P.M.

24. In the Morning I asked in Honourable Joseph Pyncheon and the Reverend Mr. Jones,[15] who broke fast with me and I set out with them on my Journey to Cambridge, but I turn'd away to Mr. Ebenezer Chamberlins the Collector. N.B. Thunder stop'd me at Mr. Mixtows[16] in Southborough. Call'd at Captain Buckminsters[17] in Framingham. N.B. Din'd at Wolsoms with Colonel Ward, Dr. Pyncheon and Mr. Jones. Rode to College with Colonel Ward. Lodg'd at Mother Champneys who lives at Brother Barretts House in Cambridge Town old—left my Horse with Brother Champney.

25. Rode to Boston. Mr. Lewis[18] of Pembrook preach'd to the

General Assembly on Isa. 22, 21. Din'd at Brother Samuels. At Convention P.M. N.B. Mr. Williams[19] of Weston Moderator. No Boston ministers at Dr. Sewals but Mr. Byles[20] only: who was therefore chosen Clerk. A Letter from Major Abbot[21] of Providence born by Deacon Belknap, to desire further assistance from the Convention, in supporting preaching among them. I heard the very heavy Tidings of the Death of the Reverend and worthy Mr. Joshua Gee, Senior Pastor of the Old North, a minister of primitive Stamp. *Alme Deus! Tales prefice ubique Gregi.* I went to see Dr. Parkmans Wife who remains in Very low and weak Condition, but is not worse. I lodg'd there with them.

26. At Convention. Dr. Wigglesworth[22] preach'd on Eph. 4, 11, 12. The Collection amounted to nigh 300£ Old Tenor. I din'd at Mr. Wellsteads.[23] Mr. Solomon Williams[24] and President Clap[25] give me account of Mr. Aaron Hutchinson now at Grafton. Mr. Chase's Sermon at Mr. Wellmans Ordination is now come out of the Press.[26] Bought Brother Alexanders Hatt for 8£ Old Tenor. Reverend Mr. Gee bury'd. Dr. Sewall pray'd before the Corps were mov'd. I walk'd with Mr. Lowel[27] of Newbury. Ministers, except the associated ministers of the Town had not Gloves: Yet the Church and Congregation gather'd plentifully to bear the Charge but it was very much expended on the numerous Family. After I had some free and warm Discourse with Mr. Loring, and hope I have Some Special Interest in his prayers. N.B. Something was Said by Dr. Parkman about my preaching to his wife this Eve—but he went to Dorchester to see his Child (had my Horse in Captain Whites Chair). Nobody spoke to me at Evening about it and I was very deeply engag'd in my mind about some other Things, So that twas too late to begin an Exercise. Captain White and his Lady were there, and I lodg'd there.

27. Mr. Kneeland[28] told me I Should not need to say anything to his Brother Green[29] about paying for the Journal, for I was not (he said) in the pay List. Was at Rogers and Fowls and receiv'd several Favours from Mr. Rogers. Din'd with sister Rebecca[30] and my Neece Mrs. Oliver. Bought my Brothers Hatt for 8£ Old Tenor and they presented me with my Fathers Cane, of Whales Tooth. Had Mr. Peam Cowells Chair for my Neece (Betty Parkman) who was ready to ride with me. We rode as far as to Mr. Cottons at Newtown. There we were kindly entertain'd and lodg'd. Mr. Jones of Western there.

28. We pursued our Journey. I was sometimes very sick at my Stomach by means, as I suppose, of drinking Tea (I believe Green) for Breakfast. We call'd at Dr. Robys[31] and were refresh'd. I grew better. It being a very hot Season (as it has been also all this Week) we stopp'd at Mr. Darlings, and din'd, and rested Two Hours I believe. Got home in season and Safety, Blessed be God! My Family also in peace.

29. I repeated a. and p.m. on Acts 1, 7. In prosecution of my Scheme on the last Judgement and now consider'd the Time when etc.

30. This Day the Parish met upon adjournment Concerning my Support among them. They pass'd a vote in the following words viz. Voted and granted to the Reverend Mr. Parkman our minister the Sum of one Hundred and fifty Two pounds ten shillings old Tenor—This with what they had heretofore granted was to make up 400£ Old Tenor—for his Support this Currant Year, provided Mr. Parkman will give the said precinct a full

---

[8] Amos Singletary was a justice of the peace and a representative of Sutton.

[9] The Reverend Mr. David Hall of Sutton.

[10] Percival Hall was a founder of the Sutton Church. He was a representative of Sutton.

[11] James Whipple.

[12] The widow of the Reverend Mr. John Prentice.

[13] Henry Scudder, *The Christian's Daily Walk in Holy Security and Peace* (London, 1637). There were many English editions.

[14] The Reverend Mr. John Cotton of Newton.

[15] Isaac Jones (Yale 1742), the minister of Warren, Mass., 1747–1784. Dexter, *Biographical Sketches*, p. 715.

[16] Benjamin Mixter or Mixer.

[17] Thomas, son of the late Colonel Joseph Buckminster.

[18] Daniel Lewes (Harvard 1707), the minister of Pembroke, 1712–1751. *Sibley*, V, 334–337.

[19] The Reverend Mr. William Williams.

[20] Mather Byles of the Hollis Street Church.

[21] Daniel Abbott, Jr., of Providence.

[22] Edward Wigglesworth, D.D., the Harvard professor.

[23] The Reverend Mr. William Welsteed of the New Brick Church.

[24] (Harvard 1719). The minister of Lebanon, Conn., 1749–1769. *Sibley*, VI, 352–361.

[25] Thomas Clap (Harvard 1722), the President of Yale College, 1740–1764. *Sibley*, VII, 27–50.

[26] Stephen Chase, *The Angel of the Churches* (Boston, 1748).

[27] The Reverend Mr. John Lowell.

[28] Samuel Kneeland, the printer of Boston.

[29] Bartholomew Green and Kneeland were the publishers of *The Boston Gazette and Weekly Journal*.

[30] Parkman's sister-in-law, Mrs. Alexander Parkman

[31] Ebenezer Roby, the physician of Sudbury.

Discharge from the Time said Precinct began their Contract with him for his Service in the Work of the ministry among them untill the fifth Day of June 1748. Josiah Newton Moderator. And then sent Two persons, viz. Mr. Samuel Williams and [blank] to desire me to go up to the meeting House that they might Speak with me personally. Upon which I went up. When the opportunity was prepared for me to speak, I desir'd the precinct, in order to my fulfilling the Condition abovesaid to give me (according to what was inserted in the Warrant for this meeting) some direct and plain answer to my reasonable Request last December (for so long this affair had been depending, which request was) that they would explain their Expression in their Votes of February [blank] 1744/5, wherein they Say that they will give me 55£ New Tenor Money so called etc. Upon my making this motion Several seem'd to be disgust'd; and even some that I suppose were friendly and were the means of obtaining to Day's vote, and some were ready to throw it up, or would have it re-consider'd. We had Some warm debate about that Explanation which the then Moderator (Deacon Newton) and the Clerk (Mr. Francis Whipple) had given me (by desire) that Evening after the Vote was made. N.B. When the Paper I had lately given the present Committee of the precinct (who were appointed to treat with me) was referr'd to and the words were recited from it which (as I conceive) the said Moderator and Clerk in February 1744/5 deliver'd me as the meaning of the vote which had been pass'd that Day, immediately Captain Warrin was in a great Heat, and express'd himself indecently—saying that That was a Corrupt Thing, pointing said to Paper. I therefore referr'd to myself to the very words of the Moderator and Mr. Whipple—but tho they said much the same things as heretofore in showing the Interpretation of the foremention'd vote, yet they now add that they did not hereby intend that the Precinct would keep up the Value of money according to Gold or silver; but that it Should be according to the Determination of the Court. And when they had said this divers others struck in, and Insisted that That was the true intent and meaning. Whereupon I reply'd that being Sensible I could recover nothing but what was written in the Votes how ambiguous Soever, I desir'd it might be wav'd for the present (for it was almost dark and the people seem'd uneasy that they might go home) and I would have the precinct to take a Time to settle our agreement; and concerning their Vote of today for supply this year Currant, I openly declar'd that I accepted of it upon the Condition therein inserted, and that I could do no otherwise, through the Necessity of my Case. No sooner was this Spoke, than new Displeasures arose—but I went to a window and wrote what I had said (viz. My Consent to the vote upon the Conditions therein express'd) on the paper of the Vote itself. Then the Moderator dissolv'd the Meeting. N.B. When I propos'd Corn and other Necessarys of Life to be a standard, if they did not like to have Gold and Silver, Brother Williams answer'd that then if there Should come ever so dreadful a Scarcity and if Corn Should be many pounds a Bushel I would have it of them to the full notwithstanding. I was griev'd at this answer and I hope my Reply was satisfying. N.B. Lieutenant Tainter and Mr. Eliezer Rice in a Contest, about something which the former affirms I said. Scil. that (on Consideration of the Difference among the people) I was ready to throw up the Precincts Votes without any Ifs and and's. Where as I told him it was upon Supposition that they would do Something else as good in the Stead thereof. It was a grief to me to find there were so many Disquietments and I was especially Sorry that when the people had granted as much as I expected (if it went not so much as was properly due) that I must accept it in such a manner as looks to them unkind and as if I was Still bearing upon them. Weeding Corn over.

31. Cousen Betty and I rode to Captain Bakers, to Deacon Newtons and to Lieutenant Tainters. We din'd (upon Lieutenants Invitations yesterday) at the House of this Latter, for I catechiz'd at the South School House. At Eve in returning Home I overturn'd the Chair between old Mr. Maynards and my own House. Dr. Breck and his Brother Cooley here while I was gone to Catechizing.

## JUNE, 1748

1. It has been the dryest Time we have known for a great While, but at night and

2. In the morning were refreshing Showers of Rain. A great Mercy and Blessing! a.m. I walk'd over to Eliezer Rice's—his Father in Law Bootman there. Mr. Breck[1] here, in his Journey to Springfield, and lodg'd here. Lent Neighbour Rice my mare for him to ride to Sutton tomorrow morning, with his Father in law and others. Joseph and Ebenezer Cabbage Plants etc.

3. Bright Day, Mr. Breck left us. Mr. Leavitt[2] of Sommers here and din'd. Neighbour Jonathan Rogers here again and I took pains with him in examining him for some Hours. Ebenezer and Joseph carting fencing-Stuff. Receiv'd a Proclamation for a Fast on account of the Drought, dated June 1 the very Day the Rain came.

4. Mrs. Joanna, wife of Jonathan Rogers here to be Examin'd. P.M. Divers Gentlemen from Grafton going over to Mr. Martyn in order to obtain a Church Meeting. They were, Captain Willard, Mr. Brooks[3] and Mr. Simon Tainter.[4] I sent my Desire to Mr. Martyn to Change Tomorrow (as I had done to Mr. Smith without success) but the Return was that Mr. Morse was already there to Change with him.

5. A.M. on Mat. 15, 1, 2. P.M. on John 6, 45. And they shall all be taught of God. Repeating some parts (the Heads much chang'd) of Sermon on John 17, 3. I began with page 33 Article 6 and then deliver'd the propertys beginning with the second. N.B. Omitted the Object in page 35. Us'd Some of the Hints of Application and added some other. Propounded Jonathan Rogers and his wife.

6. At Evening took a Ride in the Chair with Cousen Betty, and my Dauter Lucy beyond the Pond. Ebenezer and Joseph have been very much upon the Fences, ridering etc. Mr. Bootman[5] of Beverly here.

7. Ebenezer and Joseph undertook to kill a Fatt Calf for me.

8. Mr. Cook[6] here, Settled our accounts and paid him for his work.

9. In the Morning (being Publick Fast because of the Drought) came 2 Chairs. Mr. Gay[7] of Suffield and his Wife, his Brother also and Mrs. Ballentine with her little Daughter from Horns[8] at Southborough. Mr. Gay preach'd for me both parts of the Day on 2 Chron. 7, 14. After Early Supper and Prayers they left us to prosecute their Journey as far as Shrewsbury. I was very much griev'd that we were So turn'd aside from serious Meditation and that so much was done in Entertainments beyond the Nature of a Fast. The Lord forgive us that in our Fast we find pleasure!

10. Mr. Martyn here in his Way to Grafton, to hold a Church Meeting there. Mr. Lull and Townsend here going to see Jonathan Rogers who is Sick. A very hot Day. Ebenezer and Joseph who began their half—hilling on the eighth follow it again to Day.

11. [No entry.]

12. Deliver'd the sermons which I had design'd for the Fast, Scil. on Jer. 14, 22.

13. Visited Neighbour Jonathan Rogers who is sick of a Fever. Training of North Company. Rain at Night. I pray'd with them and din'd at Captain Maynards. Ebenezer and Molly and Betty rode to Colonel Wards.

14. Mr. Cushing, Mr. Morse, Mr. Davis and I rode to Hopkinton to the Association. No Concio. The Report of the Committee was read, but Mr. Smith and Mr. Mellen did So except against our Declaring ourselves respecting Doctrines that there was a great deal of Debate. At Supper a little Clash between Mr. Smith and Me how our People in Westborough were disturb'd at my not

---

[1] The Reverend Mr. Robert Breck, Jr., of Springfield.

[2] The Reverend Mr. Freegrace Leavitt (Yale 1745), the minister of Somers, Conn., 1748-1761. Dexter, *Biographical Sketches*, II, 43-44.

[3] Ebenezer Brooks.

[4] Simon Tainter, Jr., the son of the Westborough deacon.

[5] Numerous Bootmans, Butmans, and Buttmans lived in Beverly.

[6] Cornelius Cook, the blacksmith.

[7] The Reverend Mr. Ebenezer Gay.

[8] Robert Horne.

accepting (as 'twas reported) the 400£ which they voted me, and that 'twas understood I design'd to leave 'em.

15. Mr. Loring ask'd advice concerning his dismissing members to Mr. Solomon Reeds Church in Framingham. I preach'd the Public Lecture on 2 Cor. 3, 18. After Dinner we return'd to Consider the Report of the Committee and passing over what related to declaring our principles, we concurr'd pritty well in all the rest. In particular came into Resolves and votes about guarding our Pulpitts; and to send some of our Members to Cambridge and to the South East Associations, that we might have their Concurrence if it might be, or know their Minds and Methods touching Examining Candidates. As to Mr. Abraham Williams who had begun to preach, it was thought best to let him alone for the present. In returning home (Mr. Cushing my Company) I call'd to see old Mrs. Graves. Mr. Cornelius Biglo sick, and hear of divers others taken ill. But thro God's Goodness found my own Family in peace. N.B. Ebenezer and Cousen Betty Parkman set out this Morning for Boston. Molly went with them in the Chair to Marlborough. Bad News from many Towns that it is very Sickly, in Boston especially—one if not more meeting Houses shutt up Some sabbath past. Some Number of Ministers ill.

16. Visited Neighbour Jonathan Rogers who is very bad. P.M. preach'd to young people on 1 John 2, 15. Few at Meeting. After Exercise much Communication with serious Mr. Bradish. Sent by him to have Mr. Cook come to me tomorrow. Helped Joseph pole in the Yard and Garden Hay.

17. Mr. Cook came—after much Discourse I Said to him "If you do agree that Since the Conversation and Assistance of the Brethren that were together upon our Affair, (Mr. Bradish, Mr. Belknap and Mr. Chamberlin, at Mr. Cooks House Some Time ago) we wholly lay aside the Difference which Subsisted at that Time; and if you will Endeavour by the Grace of God to watch over yourself, and to walk as becomes the Gospel of Christ, then I consent to administer the Ordinance of Baptism to their Child." To this he answer'd that he did not consent thereto—and we parted this Time in peace.[9] P.M. I rak'd Hay for a good while with Joseph (N.B. a.m. he work'd for Neighbour John Rogers) between the House and Barn. Mr. Mellen of Chauxit here. Cherrys and Currans [sic] begin to be prey'd upon.

18. Thunder and Lightning. At Eve I rode to Marlborough. Met Mr. Smith on the Road.

19. Bad News from the Frontiers. Last Thursday 10 men assaulted by a great Body of Indians between Hinsdells Fort and Fort Dummer. Three kill'd and Seven Captivated. We hear also that Colonel Stoddard[10] of Northampton is dead at Boston. Mrs. Colson likewise (hitherto Abigail Boardman) dead at Boston. I preach'd at Marlborough on 2 Cor. 3, 15. P.M. 10, 14, 18. N.B. Mr. Jenison and Dr. Gott at meeting a.m. and not p.m. I return'd to Westborough at Eve. N.B. Dr. Gotts exceptions (made at his House before Colonel Williams[11] and Mr. Jenison) against the passage in sermon on 10, 15 page 7. "Faith Springs from the Love, Unbelief from the Hatred of God."

20 Visited Neighbour Jonathan Rogers again, who we think is growing better.

21. My Wife and I rode over to Mr. Martyns, to the raising of their New House. Ruth and Hannah Hicks[12] came to see us. Thomas Rogers borrowed money, 40 shillings. More Mischief by the Indians. The last News is from Kenderhook, 5 out of 7 English kill'd.

22. Catechetical Exercise on the Third Commandment. After the Exercise I went to Mr. Amsdens to the raising of his New House. My Wife not well and therefore could not go with me. N.B. Mr. Gale, Father of Thaddeus there.

23. Mr. Martyn in his way to Grafton Church meeting brought his Dauter to see us. She din'd here and tarry'd till Evening, till her Father return'd from Grafton. Neighbour Barns bought a

Barrell of boil'd Cyder. £3.10.0. P.M. marry'd Abijah Gale to Abigail Amsden. N.B. Mr. Amsden and Mr. Gale present, with many young people. Mr. Amsden excepted against that passage in the marriage Covenant, Obey him. This was clear'd up from Eph. 5, 24. My wife very ill all Day. Mr. Martyn at Evening. Sorrowful account of the broken state of Grafton—very nigh to breaking up the Church.

24. Exeeding Hott dry Season. Joseph and Ebenezer mowing and raking. P.M. came Mr. Stephen Fay with a Warrant from Captain Edward Baker Esquire with which he press'd Joseph Bowker, my Young Man, into the service! I went over to the Captain to see if nothing could be done to release him. The Captain said he would do his utmost: and accordinly Sent his son to try to hire Robert Cook,[13] and he should offer him 50£. Nay not come without him if 60£ would procure him. I am afraid of the Temptation of too great Anxiety—but I beseech God to enable me to put my Trust in Him! and Committing all to Him, to be at Rest! Joseph went to Lieutenant Tainters who I am perswaded would do what in him lies. Two or Three Things made this impressing feel the worse. Its falling out at this Season, when I cannot get any Body in his stead; and it being on Friday when I was more disturb'd: (It was So exactly when Captain Baker press'd Thomas Winchester) And when they want but one Man out of the whole Town. My Dauter Mary not return'd from Marlborough till this p.m. Dr. Gotts young man, Breed, and Mrs. Sally Gott rode up with her in Mr. Lorings Chair, but Breed and Sally return'd. N.B. They inform me that Mrs. Smith was lately seiz'd with a Lethargy—and her Friends from Cape Ann are Sent for.

25. Still exceeding Hot, but was oblig'd to turn out and Pole Hay both Yesterday and to Day also. Joseph Bowker is oblig'd to go to the Frontiers and accordingly left us. May God be his Guardian and his Helper, and return him in Safety! The Interruptions I have had prevent my preparing more than part of an Exercise for tomorrow.

26. Another very hot Day and the Earth exceeding Dry. Unless the Lord have Mercy on us the Event must needs be very terrible. A.M. on Mat. 15, 3–6. P.M. repeated sermon on 1 John 2, 15 latter part. N.B. Mr. Daniel Forbush[14] brought me the very Sorrowful Tidings of the Death of sister Hannah[15] on the twenty third at 5 in the Morning. An unspeakable Loss to my Brother and his Family; and to us all! She was a very worthy person and a great Blessing among us. My Brother was marry'd to her when I was so young, that she has always seem'd as a Blood Relation. The Lord Sanctify the wide Breach to my dear Brother and his Children. And since we are all so frequently Smitten, O that we might be more and more in Readiness! Lord make me know my End! O might I be as one that waits for his Lord!

27. The Heat Continues. Ebenezer began hilling. Wrote to Brother William on occasion of his Wife's Death. Mr. Maynard made us a Visit and brought Mr. John Nichols of Boston and his Spouse. Mr. Barns and his man fetch'd away the Cyder which he bought on the twenty third.

28. Visited Neighbour Jonathan Rogers. Mr. Jason Whitney here and desires me to write to Colonel Ward about recalling Joseph Bowker; and I comply'd with it, and Sent it by him. A very great Dew and some distant Thunder last night, and Somewhat Cloudy this morning also, yet it clears off and is hot and Dry. P.M. after Some Time of distant Thunder, there came up a great Storm here, and we had several very hard Claps of thunder accompany'd with sharp Lightning and Some very refreshing Showers of Rain. Blessed be God! Towards Eve Captain Warrin was here to discourse with me. Our subject was those disagreeable Contradictions we had at the precinct meeting May 30th last.

29. The Great Mercy of God is magnify'd in the Refreshing Showers again. Cloudy all Day. Rain'd most of the afternoon.

---

[9] Abigail, the daughter of Cornelius and Eunice Cook, was not baptized until Aug. 17, 1748.

[10] Colonel John Stoddard.

[11] Abraham Williams of Marlborough.

[12] Daughters of Parkman's brother-in-law, John Hicks of Sutton.

[13] The son of Cornelius Cook of Westborough.

[14] The son of Deacon Jonathan Forbush.

[15] Parkman's sister-in-law, Mrs. William Parkman of Boston.

30. I greatly expected Mr. Martyn to preach my Lecture but to my considerable Disappointment he did not come. I preach'd from 1 Cor. 11, 24, last Clause—but was oblig'd to repeat my old sermon 2 on Luke 22, 19. I was requested to stop the Church that the Deacons might acquaint them with the Deficiency of the Contributions to Supply the Communion Table. N.B. I Spake to the Congregation just before the Blessing, to the following purposes. "In my present peculiar Circumstances I am obliged to acquaint the Inhabitants of this Precinct that my Help being taken away I must depend upon you to help me. I must depend upon you respecting my Temporals, if you would have me attend to your Spirituals." After meeting Lieutenant Tainter here, and spake Comfortably of Sending Help, but tho others were here no one else Spoke a word of it. I desire to rest in Gods Providence. N.B. Mr. Jason Whitney brought a Letter from Colonel Ward[16] to Captain Baker about recalling Joseph Bowker as I suppose. A bright good Day. Ebenezer mowed a.m. round the Great Field, and partly round the old Well etc.

## JULY, 1748

1. Bright Day. Air cooler much than of late. Thomas Rogers came to hilling along with Ebenezer the forenoon for Josephs work for his Brother John. I was oblig'd to turn out and tend Hay, and pole from some distance for notwithstanding what I said yesterday nobody came to work for me. Some rain towards Eve. Deacon Sparhawk[1] of Cambridge came to see us and lodg'd here.

2. Deacon Sparhawk return'd to Cambridge. Mr. Townsend[2] here, acquaints me that Mr. Martyn was ill on Thursday and had 8 Hands Come to work for him.

3. Sacrament. By reason of my great Difficulties and incumbrances, I was oblig'd to go on in repeating sermon on Luke 22, 19 but did it from 1 Cor. 11, 24. P.M. deliver'd an Exposition of Mat. 25, 7, 8. One Mrs. Margaret Chadduck din'd here. Thomme came up last night and kept Sabbath with us.

4. Mr. Samuel Harrington kindly came and hoed for me, and Samuel Forbush came for Lieutenant Tainter. It rain'd a while—but they were not much beat off. Thomme tho he was not well, yet plough'd for them great part of the Day. N.B. Thomme tells me that this master thinks he might be excus'd more from out door work if his Indentures were thrown up. N.B. Ebenezer by going down into the Well to hook up the Buckett, took Cold and was Sick at Eve. The Discharge by Vomit a great Favour. A Storm of Thunder, Lightning and Rain at Night.

5. Rose very early by Candle Light, and soon Set out upon my Journey to Cambridge. Stopp'd at Mr. Cooks and got a Shooe put on my Colt (which I now first rode to Boston); at Mr. Chamberlins and receiv'd 25£ New Tenor, hastened to Mr. Bridge's[3] who was gone before me but his wife there. I din'd at Watertown, at Captain Tainters.[4] Stop'd at Saltmarshs, by reason of Mr. Nichols and his Spouse, Mr. John Gerrish and his Spouse, Messers Marsh[5] and Nathaniel Gardner[6] of College there. I rode to Cambridge to see my honour'd mother in Law at Brother Barretts. Visited Brother Champney—but lodg'd, and my Horse was kept at Deacon Sparhawks. N.B. On the fifth Deacon Newton Sent Timothy and Mr. Charles Rice sent Charles to help us in hilling our Corn. On the seventh he sow'd the South field with Rie.

6. Attended Commencement. Was chiefly at Sir Wards[7] and Sir Cushings.[8] Din'd in the Hall. The afternoon prov'd very rainy and into Night. The Presidents Oration was a Lamenting of the disadvantages and Disrepute which Learning was fallen under in these Times, and Satyrical Invective against those who

were the Sad Causes of our gloomy state. N.B. Neither the Governor nor the Lieutenant Governor present. The former gone his journey to Albany. I lodg'd at Mother Champneys.

7. Samuel Sparhawk junior brought my Horse in the Morning and I rode to Boston. I stop'd at Proctors and would have been glad to have had my Horse kept there this Visit. And I made it my Business to go and see bereaved Brother William to mix my Tears with his and his Childrens. But I din'd at Mr. Olivers, and my Horse was taken care of there. P.M. at the Auction of Dr. Colmans[9] Books—bought 7 folios: 4 quartos and 4 octavos. Supp'd at Mr. Olivers—was to have lodg'd with my Brother but was (to my grief) too late; turn'd in the Doctors and lodg'd with him, his wife continuing in a low Condition.

8. Very early went over to my Brother. Had a good Morning with him. And visited also his son John. Hasten'd to Dr. Colmans to pay for my Books. My Kinsman Hearsey help'd me move them to his House. Din'd at Mr. Cowells. Mounted from Mr. Olivers, who and his Spouse were very generous and bountiful in Special by a very handsome Hatt for my Alexander as well as Pickled Oysters, Mackrell, fine Biskitt for my wife. I sett out between 3 and 4 o'Clock. Mr. Thomas[10] of Marlborough my Company. Stop'd at Mr. Edward Harringtons in Watertown to see Mr. Ebenezer Bullard[11] who lyes languishing and pray'd with him, and it Seem'd as if the Conversation was (by Divine Blessing) made profitable. We stop'd again at Mr. Darlings tho it was late. Heard of Mischief done by the Indians at Lunenbourg—burning the Garrison and several persons. Got home somewhat after Midnight; and was in a Measure of Comfort—my family also well. Thanks to God.

9. Not only tired with my Journey but interrupted with Company both a. and p.m. Mr. Hall and Mr. Wellman here a.m. and broke their fast here. Mr. Rawson[12] din'd here in his way to Chauxitt. N.B. heard there was an Alarm last night at Chauxitt, which was answer'd as low as Marlboro.

10. Preach'd a. and p.m. on Mat. 20, 6 to page 6 and from page 32 to the End. N.B. old Mr. Eleazer Bellows had dy'd Somewhat Suddenly and was bury'd in the Course of the last week. N.B. Mr. Cushing from home, many Shrewsbury people were at meeting here. Dr. Smith and his wife and Sir Cushing din'd here.

11. My Dauter Mary rode with me to the South East Corner of Town. I visited all the Familys there. Din'd at Mr. Chamberlins—and Catechiz'd at Mr. Joslins. N.B. some difference among them about the place where I should Catechize. N.B. Thomme went to Worcester for his master with Two Horses to get Rie. Billy rode with him to Dr. Brecks. Letter from Mr. Edwards[13] about his publishing Life of Mr. David Brainerd.

12. Rainy Day. Just before night I rode to the Southside of the Town as far as Mr. Dunlops. Call'd at Several Familys—but made no great Stay at either, tho it has been long since I was in that Neighbourhood. Thomme and Billy return'd from Worcester.

13. Tended Hay part of the forenoon and rode as far as Ephraim Bruce's p.m. Visited at Mr. Millers, Mr. Daniel Forbush, Solomon Woods (by whom I sent for my still at Deacon Drowns at Boston) and Mr. Bowmans. N.B. Thomme left us.

14. Sarah Henry at work here.

15. Mr. Dunlop came and reap'd in my Rye Field. Ebenezer assisted him. At Eve he went to Marlborough to carry Thomme a Jacket of Home made Cloth, and a Pair of Breeches of Camlett—and to buy him a sickle.

16. Ebenezer return'd. He reap'd, and various Jobbs took up the Day. I am greatly hindred [sic] and my Cares and Perplexitys many. Dauter Mary drooping from Day to Day—and my wife much indispos'd.

16 Nahum Ward of Shrewsbury.

1 Samuel Sparhawk.

2 Joshua Townsend of the north side.

3 The Reverend Mr. Matthew Bridge of Framingham.

4 John Tainter.

5 Perez Marsh (Harvard 1748).

6 (Harvard 1739). A Boston schoolmaster and teacher of French at Harvard College. Sibley, X, 366–368.

7 Artemas Ward of Shrewsbury.

8 Jacob Cushing, the son of the Reverend Job Cushing of Shrewsbury.

9 The Reverend Mr. Benjamin Colman.

10 William Thomas.

11 The step-son of Mr. Edward Harrington.

12 Grindall Rawson (Harvard 1741), later the minister at Ware, 1751–1754, and at Yarmouth, 1755–1760. Sibley, XI, 58–64.

13 Jonathan Edwards published An Account of the Life of the late Reverend Mr. David Brainerd (Boston, 1749).

17. On Mat. 15, 9, 10, 11. P.M. on Col. 3, 20 but was oblig'd to make very free use of sermon on Eph. 6, 1, 2, 3. Mrs. Chaddock and Mr. Martin Pratts wife din'd here. I was much tir'd at Night.

18. Mr. Dunlop came and reap'd a.m. and Samuel Burnap so came gratis and mow'd. Rain part of the Day. They got in one Load of Rye before the Rains. Mr. Dunlop went away p.m. after reaping a while. They all (of 'em) got down the Rie. I visited Mrs. Tomlin and Neighbour How, and at the same time endeavour'd to inform my neighbours of the Design a Number on the Southside have to mow my meadow tomorrow (if it be fair) and therefore I shall need Rakers. Forbush (who keeps School at Mr. Joslins) here, and the Rain prevailing, he lodg'd here.

19. Rainy Night and Morning. No expectation of mowing. Visited Mr. Jonathan Rogers's wife who is very ill of a Fever. Dr. Smith there. Very sorrowfull News from the westward—of nineteen of our men passing between Hensdalls and Fort Dummer[14] but 2 are come in. Mr. Hall of Sutton, his wife and son David din'd here.

20. Six Hands mow'd in my ministerial meadow—viz. Mr. Bowman, Mr. Pratt, Phinnehas Hardy, Solomon Woods, Jonathan Forbush and Zebulon Rice. I waited on them both a. and p.m. at the Meadow and endeavour'd they Should have every Thing for their Comfort that I could. Deacon Whipple[15] of Grafton brought Mr. Wainwright and they din'd with us.

21. I rode about for Rakers—but only Benjamin Whipple (for Mr. Tomlin) went. I went from Mr. Barns (after visiting Mr. Rogers) to Mr. Cooks, Mr. Nurse's, Mr. Pratts, to Mr. James Maynards.

22. I rode out in the morning as I think it is my Duty, considering my Circumstances, first to Mr. Nurse's for Some shooing of my Colt then to divers Neighbours to look up Rakers. N.B. Merchant Rice can't go himself, but Sends a Bottle of Rum (nigh a Quart) to encourage them that did. Amos Whitney, Jonathan Devereux (from Captain Maynard) and Mr. Beriah Rice's Son Timothy, together with my Ebenezer rak'd in the Meadow. P.M. there went divers others viz. Mr. Jonas Child and Jonathan Grout and near night Mr. Eliezer Rice lent a Hand. N.B. Some uncomfortable Discourse with Neighbour Eliezer Rice in the forenoon about the precincts agreement with me about my annual Stipend. I had an afternoon of great Labour and worry among my Hay at Home.

23. I rose early and went to Captain Bakers to desire him to Cart for me—Since my Hay was now ready: but (tho he went to Stephen Fay's to get his Cattle for it) he could not. I proceeded to Lieutenant Tainters. He agreed to go to Day if Captain Baker went to Day—but he chose to deferr it till Monday. I had considerable of work in my Hay to do at Home, tho it be Such a Day in the Week—but in providence Mr. Dunlop was passing from Marlborough, and I laid hold on him. Ebenezer and he got in 2 Load of Hay that was at Home—and then went to the Meadow to rake what was left and to bring home 1 Load of Hay. He did the Latter but omitted the former. I was ill at Eve.

24. I had a bad Night and rose so indisposed this morning that could hardly imagine I should go to meeting—but tho I was very lax in my Body much pain'd and faint, yet considering how the people would be Scatter'd and the Lords Day thrown away if there was not a minister, I ventur'd to the Public Prayer, was short—the Exposition on Mat. 20, 12, 13 was about 34 minutes long. P.M. I attempted again repeated (from Col. 3, 20) Sermon of the Duty of Children from page 9 to the End. Flying News that Joseph Bowker was kill'd by the late Body of Indians between Hensdells and Fort Dummer.

25. Am still but weak and pain'd. Flux attending me from Day to Day. Mr. Samuel Harrington with Cart and one Yoke of Oxen, and Benjamin Tainter with the Like Carted Hay for me from the Meadow. Harrington 2 Turns 13 Cocks each, and once with 14. Tainter with 13 Cocks all 3 Turns: Ebenezer 13 Cocks 2 Turns and his last turn being in the Dark was but 11 Cocks.

N.B. The Cocks in general large. A great Kindness this of my Neibours. The Lord reward 'em for it. I visited Thomas Rogers who is sick. A letter subscribed Eli Forbush,[16] desiring free Liberty to discourse with Molly without giving Offence.

30. Ebenezer grows so bad with the poison that he can do nothing.

31. On Mat. 15, 14 and Mat. 25, 46 former part. Thomas Rogers thot to be near his End. At Eve both my wife and I visited Thomas Rogers and pray'd there. He was not able to give any answer or I suppose understanding any thing—convulsive motions increas'd greatly—and after we came away, perhaps an hour or Two, he dy'd. A great loss to his parents who have set much by him, and depended much upon him. He was 19 and half—a very lively, active and mannerly Youth: but I can say little else. The Lord sanctifie this providence both to the parents and the Neighbourhood, especially our young people.

## AUGUST, 1748

1. I got Neighbour Hezekiah How and Abraham Batchellor to help in with Hay at home a.m., Ebenezer being unable to do anything.

2. Thomas Rogers bury'd. Hot Day, the Corps very offensive—many attended, of old and young—after prayer as the Corps stood abroad I had a brief address to the Youth. Lucy rode with me to the Funeral—visited Mrs. Williams[1] who is ailing, in our return. After 3 p.m. Noah How and Merodach Devereux mow'd the remainder of my meadow, viz. the North Side of the Brook. At 4 the Same afternoon Captain Maynard who sent Jonathan, a little Hay, about 10 Cocks which I had rak'd into winrow.

3. Neighbour Baverick mow'd the last of my Grass at home, and gave me half the Day. I pay'd him 10 shillings old Tenor for the other half. A.M. I rode to most of the houses as far as Mr. Joseph Knowltons in order to get somebody to rake what was mow'd yesterday at the meadow and, to cart it home. Mr. Knowlton sent two sons to rake this afternoon.

4. Mr. Gershom Brigham carted home one Load of the Meadow Hay with my Team. Phinehas Maynard helping him pole and Load—and Phinehas Maynard with Ebenezers Help got home the last. The Drought very great—notwithstanding some Sprinkling at Eve. N.B. The Neighbours very kind to Mr. Rogers Since the Loss of his son in mowing, Raking and Carting his Hay both at home and his meadow—hay in which I much rejoice.

5. Hezekiah Bellows, about 14 years old, came and gave me a Days work, raking and Carting at home. Ebenezer mowing the Flax ground over, the Flax coming to nothing nor any of it pulled. At Eve Lieutenant Ward[2] and Mr. Chapin[3] of Grafton here.

6. Ebenezer to Marlborough for our Malt, at Mr. James Woods's. The pastures exceedingly burnt up. Captain Maynard assisted Ebenezer in getting in the last Load of Hay.

7. A.M. on Mat. 15, 15 to 20th. I Spake to the Congregation to take some more special Care to prevent Disorders at Noon Time and in returning home at Evening that the Sabbath might not be profaned especially by young people; and that in particular Injury might not be done in thy Neighbourhood. If there was any Tithing Men present I recommended it to Such in a peculiar Manner, Their having been complaint one Time after another. Mrs. Child (Jonas's wife) din'd here. P.M. on Prov. 22, 6. The former part of the Sermon without writing, the rest partly from sermon on Eph. 6, 4, page 5 to 11, adding the Applicatory Heads in page 32.

8. One Mr. Skinner of Needham here. Tells me of the Alarm from Nichewoag on Saturday; and the mustering yesterday at Worcester to go out. P.M. I rode as far as Mr. Bezaleel Eagers,

---

[14] Within the present town of Brattleboro, Vt.

[15] James Whipple.

[16] The son of Deacon Jonathan Forbush. Eli (Harvard 1751) changed his name to Forbes and was ordained at North Brookfield June 3, 1752. He married Mary Parkman, Aug. 5, 1752. Pierce, Forbes and Forbush Genealogy, pp. 33–36.

[1] Mrs. Eleazer Williams.

[2] Hezekiah Ward.

[3] Benjamin Chapin.

and understood the matter more Clearly. Signs of Rain go over—the Drought very Great.

9. Refreshing Showers of Rain in the Morning. Thanks be to God. Clear afternoon. Asaph Rice[4] here—afterwards Dodge[5] of College. Wrote to New Haven—to be sent to Boston for Conveyance.

10. [No entry.]

11. Mr. Wainwright[6] sent me word he could not preach my Lecture being pre-engaged to preach for Mr. Hall of Sutton. I preach'd myself Repeating sermon on 1 Cor. 11, 16 to page 8. N.B. it was Mr. Cushings and Mr. Martyns Lecture and otherwhere also. N.B. Letters from Joseph Bowker from Fort Pelham.

12. [No entry.]

13. [No entry.]

14. Sacrament. I Spent the whole of my Preparations on Mat. 15, 21 to 28, tho I stood some time above an Hour. P.M. on Parents Duty repeating Sermon on Eph. 6, 4, from Prov. 22, 6. At night much tir'd.

15. I rode to the South Road; to Deacon Newtons in particular and borrow'd 20£ old Tenor of him, to accomodate my wife in her going down to Boston. Din'd at Captain Warrin's, where Jonathan Rogers's Child lay sick. Call'd at Mr. Amsdens. Proceeded to Marlborough to Mr. Williams[7] and got my Saddle pad new stuff'd in and in other respects Mended—which he did gratis. He told me of Thomme's being out too late some nights, complain'd of his being too much acquainted at Uriah Amsdens.[8] He said something of throwing up the Indentures—but that went over. Call'd at Dr. Gotts.[9] Mr. Smith[10] gone to Cape Ann. Call'd at Lieutenant Beemans[11] who is sick. My Neighbour Jacob Amsden with me there—but he left me and went back to the Doctors having forgot something. This disappointed me of an opportunity I intended to make of free Discourse with him.

16. Early I visited old Mr. Rogers. Then proceeded to Ministers meeting at Holden. N.B. overtook Mr. Reed[12] of Framingham and Mr. Ebenezer Goddard[13] with him. At Mr. Davis's there was Mr. Frink,[14] who wanted we should read his papers—but our Affair of the Report of the Committee to the Quarter: about Degeneracy took up our Time after we had heard Mr. Mellen's[15] Concio from Rom. 9, 15 (which Exercise of his disgusted the most if not every one that heard it) and the Collections. The Several Articles of said Report were come into beyond Expectation—and all but Mr. Mellen consented to 'em as they now stand.

17. Mr. Harrington[16] (who has received a Call from Lancaster) preach'd the public Lecture on Mat. 12, 36. Every idle word etc. Mr. Maccarty came when meeting was ended. Mr. Frinks papers were read according to his request last night before he went away. At Mr. Davis's before Dinner came upon the Table, Opportunity was taken to talk with Mr. Mellen; during which Time Mr. Maccarty and Mr. Harrington were desired to be in the other Room—but Mr. Maccarty was highly affronted. Pursuant to our above Report the Association agreed to set about the Reading the Scriptures in Public—and to begin a Course of Fasts next April. I return'd home. Abraham Batchellor sick. Mrs. Patty Ward and Mrs. Molly Martyn[17] here.

18. I went to see Mrs. Wheeler. In my way I visited Mr. Martyn (whose Dauter with Mrs. Patty Ward lodg'd here last night). N.B. The Talk of Joshua Townsend who was desirous to be baptiz'd, but full of Murmurs against Mr. Martyn—that they are oppress'd etc.

19. [No entry.]

20. Mr. Wellman[18] came from Sutton and din'd here. I rode up to his Parish and Stopp'd at Mr. Isaac Barnards—they were very Courteous and I lodg'd there.

21. I preach'd at Sutton on 2 Cor. 11, 3, a. and p.m. Din'd at Captain Carters, but after Meetings I repaired to my Kinsmans Mr. Jonathan Fuller, and Supp'd at my Cousen Samuel Trasks. N.B. Mr. Fullers Dauter Moreton and her Dauter Moreton, also there—and was exceeding glad to see a woman of whom I had heard so much: Mrs. Moreton being the person Mr. Clark[19] of Salem Village wrote his printed Letters about Infant Baptism to. I lodg'd at Captain Carters.

22. In returning from Sutton I first visited Captain Robert Goddard[20]—had Mr. John Hollands Company to Worcester. I carry'd home Mr. Hedge's Henry, the Volume on Evangelists and Acts[21]—but Mr. Hedge not at home. Visited Mr. Maccarty—din'd at Dr. Brecks.[22] My Studdy Lock to Johnsons to mend the Key. At Colonel Chandlers.[23] And at Shrewsbury was at Mr. Edward Goddards for Cheese, at Dr. Smith's[24]—where was Mr. Cushing Cornet Hayward and Mr. Jonathan Green. Heard that My Dauter Molly accompany'd by Mr. Wellman had been at Colonel Wards and with Mrs. Patty,[25] was gone to Mr. Morse's. But they return'd at Night.

23. Mr. Wellman went home to Sutton.

24. Engag'd early in my preparations on Public Reading the Scriptures.

25. Catechiz'd the Children at the Meeting House. Colonel Ward and Mr. Cushing call'd at Noon as they were going to Mr. Benjamin Fays to a meeting of Officers and desir'd me to give 'em my Company. Mr. Martyn and his wife made us a visit today also. N.B. Mr. James Whipple and Mr. Noah Brooks here for advice about their Grafton difficultys. I waited upon the officers after my catechizing. Ensign Bruce made Lieutenant and Mr. Miller Ensign. Also Mr. Bezaleel Eager made Lieutenant of the North Company.

26. Visit old Mrs. Crouch, Adams and Beeman. Captain Baker lent me 30£ old Tenor.

27. Tho I was far advanc'd as well as deeply engag'd in my preparations, I was glad to have the help in providence Sent me, for Mr. Frink came.

28. Mr. Frink preach'd for me all Day. A.M. on Mat. 5, 29, 30 and p.m., Mat. 5, 14. Two serious warm discourses. May God give his Blessing!

29. Mrs. Parkman and Lucy early to Boston. Mr. Frink to Marlborough where his family is at present. P.M. Mr. Buckminster, his wife and child—and lodged here—Abigail How[26] lives here this week.

30. Mr. Buckminster to Framingham. Visited Mrs. Thankfull Maynard[27] who is sick. Dr. Gott here. Held a Catechetical Exercise—preach'd on Joel 3, 13, a Repitition.

31. Visited Mrs. Maynard and Mrs. Rogers. The Drought continues and is now become very distressing.

### SEPTEMBER, 1748.

1. Went out with Lieutenant Hezekiah Ward to look up some Common Land, towards the Cedar Swamps. Visited widow Thurston, Grow and Harrington. Din'd at Home. Sir Isaac

[4] Son of Beriah Rice.

[5] Ezekiel Dodge (Harvard 1749).

[6] John Wainwright (Harvard 1742).

[7] Abraham Williams, Parkman's brother-in-law.

[8] The son of Abraham Amsden of Marlborough.

[9] Benjamin Gott, the physician of Marlborough.

[10] The Reverend Mr. Aaron Smith of Marlborough.

[11] Abraham Beaman of Marlborough.

[12] The Reverend Mr. Solomon Reed of Framingham.

[13] The son of Edward Goddard, a prominent citizen of Framingham.

[14] The Reverend Mr. Thomas Frink had been the minister of Rutland and Plymouth (Third Church). At this time he was living in Marlborough. In 1753 he was made the minister of Rutland District which later became the town of Barre.

[15] The Reverend Mr. John Mellen of Sterling.

[16] The Reverend Mr. Timothy Harrington (Harvard 1737) had been the minister of Lower Ashuelot (Swansey, N. H.), 1741-1748. He served Lancaster, 1748-1795. *Sibley*, X, 188-195.

[17] The daughter of the Reverend John Martyn of the north precinct.

[18] The Reverend Mr. James Wellman of Millbury.

[19] The Reverend Mr. Peter Clark of Danvers had published *The Scripture-Grounds of the Baptism of Christian Infants* (Boston, 1735).

[20] He lived in that part of Sutton that became Millbury.

[21] One of the works of Matthew Henry (1662-1714), the English noncomformist minister.

[22] Samuel Breck, the physician of Worcester.

[23] John Chandler, Jr., the prominent office-holder of Worcester.

[24] Joshua Smith, the physician of Shrewsbury.

[25] The daughter of Colonel Nahum Ward of Shrewsbury.

[26] The daughter of Hezekiah How of Westborough.

[27] Mrs. Stephen Maynard.

Newton on Daniel.[1] Everywhere Complaints of want of Water.

2. Mr. Biglo here clearing out my well, and paid him 10 shillings old Tenor for his work only part of the forenoon. Mr. Israel Stevens of Grafton here and din'd with us. A very reviving Rain—thro the Mercy of God! after long and distressing Drought. At Eve Mr. Abner Newton here about some Boards he wants of me. Mr. Elihu Spencer designed Missionary to the Mohawks here, and brought a Letter from Mr. Edwards of Northampton. He lodg'd here.

3. Three Letters from my wife informing that on Tuesday last Mother Champney was seiz'd with the Numb Palsey, could not speak nor did know any Body, was alive and that was all: and that on Thursday morning She dy'd—but was uncertain when she would be bury'd. She has been a most loving, kind Mother to me. I hope she receives a glorious Reward. She was very Timorous but desir'd to trust in Christ. May God please to Sanctifie her Death to me and mine, and to all more nearly connected! I wrote by Mr. Spencer to Mrs. Parkman—the happy Showers this Morning detain'd him a little, but he set out for Boston. Ebenezer went over to Mr. Martyns for the portmantle which my wife has Sent up in his chair.

4. I preach'd on 1 Thess. 5, 17 a. and p.m. Earnestly recommending the Duty of Public Reading the holy Scriptures. Mrs. Fay (Samuel junior's wife) din'd here.

5. Fine Showers again last Night, and rain'd Plentifully this morning. Blessed be God who has permitted me to finish my 45th Year and to see the Light of this Morning. *Vide Natalitia.* [The following is recorded in the Natalitia for September 5, 1748.]

I observ'd this Day (in some Measure) religiously—by retiring and going through (in a broken imperfect manner) various acts of Devotion, viz. Praise and Thanksgiving, Confession, Petition, Resignation etc.

Besides what respected my Self, my Family and my people, there was a great and important Affair which I had to Spread before the Lord this Day; Scil. The Sitting of the Council at Grafton tomorrow; their Affairs being very peculiarly Difficult, and lying much upon my Heart, as I have been unavoidably oblig'd to have their Matters with me from Time to Time. The Lord therefore be pleased to prepare my Heart, and all of the Council, and grant to us all, Such Wisdom and Direction as We need! point out what their Case and the present State thereof is; and Shew us what is the best Method for the Church thence to take both with respect to the Separation, and with regard to their Re-settlement of the Gospel Ministry among them. May God be pleas'd to impart to us what to Say to them And incline and dispose their Hearts to receive it and conform to it! That so there may be some happy Event of the Councils Meeting at this Time!

6. Waited some Time for Mr. Martyn, but at Length I went without him. Deacon Newton[2] and Brother Nathaniel Whitney, from Mr. Grouts accompany'd me to Grafton, we being warned to Meet there to sit in Council upon their affairs, by adjournment. Mr. Loring (who is Moderator) came, but brought no messenger. Mr. Goddard[3] of Leicester came not, nor any Delegate, so that we did not sit as a Council. We neither acted, nor dissolv'd. But the Church of Grafton had, by vote, desir'd several Neighbouring Ministers to come and join with the Elders of the Council to hear their Affairs. We therefore had the Church together and Reverend Messers Martyn, Hall of Sutton, and Eaton[4] of Leicester being with us we formed, and Chose Mr. Loring Moderator, and the same meet to choose their Clerk—and the Church was adjourn'd to tomorrow 9 a.m. to the Meeting House.

7. We met at the Meeting House. Mr. Hall (according to Turn) pray'd. Such of the Separatists as had any Things to offer, who had not opportunity heretofore, were call'd; and while the Moderator was attending upon one or Two who presented themselves, a Certain Woman (Mr. David Wadsworths Wife) from

behind cry'd out and came up the Great Alley crying out "O Dear souls in the Name of my great Lord and Master, have a Single Eye etc." With much ado the Moderator Still'd her. Dr. David Batchellor openly declar'd himself a Separatist; and the rather because we had resisted (as he judg'd) the Ordinance and will of the Lord in not suffering that sister to go on with her message. We din'd at Deacon Whipples. P.M. the ministers call'd in several of those who had been wont to clogg the church in dealing with the Separatists, and conferr'd with them—viz. Mr. Abner Stow, Joseph Batchelour, Gideon Baker and several others. At length the whole Church and all the people were call'd in: and Deacon Merriam[5] was interrogated. Mr. Eaton pray'd, before the Church was dismiss'd at Night.

8. Mr. Davis of Holden being by providence among us, pray'd in the morning. The Weight of forming the Result was thrown upon Me. I retir'd and (with some assistance in one sentence from Mr. Hall, and in the Exhortation from Mr. Martyn) I drew it up. It was voted unanimously. Mr. Loring preach'd a Lecture on Mat. 5, 4, and after Lecture I publish'd the Result to the Congregation. The Church stop'd and voted their acceptance of the Result about 4 or 6 Dissenting. But Deacon Merriam voted. After dining we Dissolv'd and Return'd home. At home found my wife and dauter Lucy from Cambridge together with Brother and Sister Hicks[6] who came from thence with them and they lodg'd here.

9. Brother and sister Hicks to Sutton. I went to see Captain Warrin and his wife who are very bad—and their son Jonathan likewise ill. Visited also Captain Maynards Family, Six of which are ill, viz. Stephens wife and son John—Rody Smith, and Josiah Lock, Hepzibah Crosby and Hepzibah Rice. Mr. Edward Whipple brought home my brindled Cow, from Nichewoag Cutt. A Great Frost last night. Prisoners broke Jayl last night at Worcester. A vile Woman and a man—both committed for Theft.

10. A great Frost again last Night. Asa Rice came p.m. from Mrs. Wheeler requesting me to visit her. I went. She was very low. Took very Solemn Leave of her—return'd to Mr. Martyns and lodg'd there.

11. I preach'd for Mr. Martyn and he for me. My Text Heb. 9, 27 former part. His Text John [blank]. I return'd at Eve.

12. Captain Warrin[7] dy'd last Night. An heavy Loss! He was a worthy Man. The Lord sanctify it to us all! Lieutenant Ward survey'd a piece of Land nigh the Cedar Swamps for me. Neighbour David and Nathan Maynard Chain Men. Mr. Bliss[8] of Concord here. He and Lieutenant Ward din'd here. I rode down to see Mrs. Amsden who is Sick. Went to the House of Death, Captain Warrins, pray'd with the sick there, and the sorrowing Neighbours that were there together. At Eve sent to Boston by Asa Brigham.[9]

13. In the morning at Captain Maynards. Mr. James Eager came to inform me that Mrs. Wheeler[10] dy'd last Night and I was desir'd to attend the Funeral tomorrow. My Wife and I to Captain Warrins burying. While we were at the House of Mourning Message from Mrs. Amsden that she was near her End. After prayer and the Corps moving out to go to the Grave I went down to Mr. Amsdens[11]—and pray'd there she being exceeding low. Return'd and met the Mourners as they were on the Road home. Left 'em the solemn Charge of David to Solomon 1 Chron. 28, 9. Visited Mrs. Rogers and pray'd with them. Sarah Henry at work on a Coat for Ebenezer.

14. My Wife and I rode over to Mrs. Wheelers burying. We first went to Mr. Martyns, and din'd there. Mr. Martyn rode with us to the House of Mourning. Though I was ask'd to pray on that occasion yet I repeatedly desir'd Mr. Martyn to perform it in my Stead but he as often refus'd. Tis a very desolate House

---

[1] *Observations upon the Prophecies of Daniel and the Apocalypse of St. John* (London, 1733).
[2] Josiah Newton of Westborough.
[3] The Reverend Mr. David Goddard.
[4] The Reverend Mr. Joshua Eaton of Spencer.

[5] Joseph Merriam.
[6] Mr. and Mrs. John Hicks of Sutton.
[7] Daniel Warren.
[8] The Reverend Mr. Daniel Bliss.
[9] Son of neighbor David Brigham.
[10] The widow of Joseph Wheeler.
[11] Mrs. Jacob Amsden.

and the Hand of God is observable! In how short a Time, from remarkable prosperity, to this sorrowful Desolation! God grant the surviving Children and all of us to see what the Great God has done. Rain at mounting to return. Mr. Batheric came to work but was soon call'd off to make a Coffin for Mrs. Amsden.

15. I went to Marlborough tho it was something showery. In returning I attended upon Mrs. Amsden Funeral. N.B. at Dr. Gotts to Day there was brot one John Brigham of 22 Years, whose arm he himself had shot with a Pistol, and tis thought it must be cut off. Mr. Batheric[12] at work here upon the shed at my North Door, and Sarah Henry at work here.

16. Mr. Batheric here again—Sarah Henry still. I visited Daniel Warrins Son Daniel and was at Mr. Knowltons. Visited Lydia Bellows Sick at Ensign Rice's.

17. Sarah Henry. Visited Mrs. Warrin and the Lads there who are sick yet. Dr. Greenleaf[13] there. I have been, I think Every Day this week abroad. I have however some Preparations for the Sabbath. But

18. I Chose to go on with the Parental Duty from Prov. 22, 6, as I deliver'd it before from Eph. 6, 4, a. and p.m. reserving what I had writ upon Mat. 25, 46 to another Time. N.B. We this Day began the public Reading of Scriptures. A.M. after Prayer, before singing I read the first Chapter of Genesis and p.m. the first Chapter of Matthew.

19. I was up extreme early—prepar'd a Deed which Neighbour Hezekiah How sign'd delivered Me of the Right to his fifth Division of Common Lands without the Cow Common. I rode to Marlborough, to Mr. Eleazer How and traded with Benomi Bailey for a second Hand Saddle—for which I am to give him 4£. I din'd at Mr. Smiths[14]—attended the Proprietors Meeting, but neither Lieutenant Ward, nor those I am to border upon being there I did not present my Plott. Went to Mr. Joseph Williams about Benomi's Saddle but Mr. Williams had lent it. I return'd home having the Second Volume of Dr. Doddridge's Family Expositor[15] of Mr. Smith and I immediately began it in my Family.

20. Lecture to Young Men on Ps. 90, 5, After burying Mr. Thaddeus Gales youngest Child and dining at Mr. Warrins. Sarah Henry finish'd a blue Jacket for me. Mr. Buckminster and wife here in Lecture Time.

21. Ebenezer to Worcester and return'd at Night.

22. Ebenezer to Worcester again return'd at Night. Great Showers at Night. Visited at Ebenezer Rice's and Mr. Charles Rice's. Examin'd Benjamin Tainter[16] at Mr. Ebenezer Rice's.

23. [No entry.]

24. Thomme brought the Saddle I bought of Benomi Bailey.

25. Read a.m. the second Chapter of Genesis and preach'd on Prov. 22, 6. P.M. Read second Chapter of Matthew and preach'd on Mat. 25, 46. Southboro people at meeting. Mrs. Liscomb[17] and Mr. Moses Johnsons[18] wife din'd with us. Great Frost Night after Night.

26. Mr. Townsends wife being Sick, her Father Rogers (as her mother had done some time ago) requested me to go and see her; it was also her express Desire and sent over to Day She being in a low Condition So that p.m. I rode over there, calling at Mr. Martyns both going and coming.

27. Mr. Barns[19] here, and I took the Opportunity to go down with him to that part of the Meadow east of my Improvements—and it being the most unprofitable, (not worth mowing) but within my Fence, and what old Mr. Barns in his Life Time had consented in presence of Witnesses Should be my property, and settled it so by the Bound-Mark on the Nole Close by it, Yet inasmuch as the Said old Mr. Barns mention'd Bounds up as

far as the Corner of my Field, I told his son that for the Ease of my own Mind I would give him Ten Shillings as a Consideration for that Land which would be included within even that Line which a Bound from thence (From a Tree near the Corner of my Field) would include—Notwithstanding that the Affair was all wholly settled as aforesaid by old Mr. Barns in the presence of witnesses, and he could have no Demand at all upon me. But then he should not oblige me to run the Fence from the marked Tree upon the Nole to the North East Corner, on the Side of the Ridge and in the hollow, as a Straight Line would carry it, but Should allow me to make my Fence on the Top of the Rigdge [sic], tho it be Somewhat rounding, but it would be so much better for both him and me. To all which Things he freely consented, and I accordingly gave him the Ten Shillings. N.B. Mr. Martyn here in his way to Grafton Church Meeting, in which tis propos'd to suspend some of the Separatists. My Daughters Molly and Lucy went over to Mr. Martyns. Ebenezer gathering Winter apples. Mr. Mede here. Mr. Martyn here at night. He informs me the Church in Grafton have passed a Vote to suspend 24 members (Men and Women) and appointed a Fast. N.B. Troopers entertain'd this Evening at Mr. Benjamin Hows in this Town. Mr. Martyn told me the Church of Grafton had appointed a Fast, and desir'd my Assistance with others.

28. Visited Mrs. Warrin, who tis hopeful is on the Recovery; as is Jonathan likewise: but Nahum was in great Extremeity and Nigh his End when I went there. I pray'd with them—and after some solemn and Serious Discourse took leave: but before I mounted, word came out that Nahum was just gone. I went in again, and saw him give up the Ghost. N.B. Mr. Jonas Warrins Exhortation and Admonition to me, as God was now taking away both Sheep and Lambs out of my Flock. I took it kindly—thank'd him, and do pray God to bless it to me. N.B. The Same Mr. Warrin deliver'd to me the request of the people in Upton to go over and preach to them, at such Time as I could best attend it. Soon after I came home Mr. Abraham Williams[20] came with a Packet from New Haven—containing besides the Commencement Papers, a Letter from Mrs. Pierpoint[21] and therewith a silver Snuff Box, the Gift of Mrs. Pierpoint to my Daughter Sarah. On the Said Box were engraven the Arms of the Pierpoints with that instructive and quickening motto PIE REPONE TE, which is the Same as are worn by the Duke of Kinstone. May God reward her abundantly in Spiritual Blessings for all her Love to me and mine! He left us, tho it rain'd, to go to Marlboro.

29. A.M. at the Burial of Nahum Warrin[22] (so far as to be at the House an Pray and Exhort). May this Death be a further warning to us! Especially to our Young People! Mr. Martyn and his Wife din'd with us. He preach'd my Lecture on Ps. 89, 7 with special reference to the Lords Supper. Towards Night came Mr. Fuller of Sutton who marry'd my Kinswoman, and his son in law Mr. Isaac Putnam, and they lodg'd here.

30. My Kinsmen proceeded in their Journey towards Salem. Moses Warrin came for me to visit his Mother[23] who grows worse again: at Evening I was there. When I return'd found Mr. Breck[24] of Springfield and Mr. Ballantine[25] of Westfield, on their Journey to the Ordination (next week) of Mr. Gad Hitchcock.[26] They lodg'd here.

## OCTOBER, [1748]

1. Cold Day. Mr. Breck and Ballantine proceeded for Boston. Dr. Gott din'd here. P.M. Mr. Edwards Whipple brought home my young Cattle which came from Nichewoag: and receiv'd a Letter from the Church of Rutland to go to Council there. My many avocations greatly perplex me. May the Lord graciously Commiserate all my state!

2. I was in a very dull and Lifeless Frame especially a.m. Read the third Chapter of Genesis in the Assembly. Repeated

[12] Daniel Batherick of Westborough.
[13] Daniel Greenleaf, a physician of Boston. James E. Greenleaf, Genealogy of the Greenleaf Family (Boston, 1896), pp. 206–207.
[14] The Reverend Mr. Aaron Smith.
[15] Philip Doddridge, The Family Expositor; or a Paraphrase and Version of the New Testament, with Notes (London, 1739).
[16] The son of Deacon Simon Tainter.
[17] Mrs. Samuel Lyscom of Southborough.
[18] Of Southborough.
[19] Richard Barnes.
[20] Abraham Williams, Jr., of Marlborough.
[21] Mrs. James Pierpont of New Haven.
[22] Son of Daniel Warren.
[23] Mrs. Daniel Warren.
[24] The Reverend Mr. Robert Breck, Jr.
[25] The Reverend Mr. John Ballantine.
[26] (Harvard 1743). The minister of Hanson, 1748–1803. Sibley, XI, 231–236.

sermon on 1 Cor. 10, 16 from page 9 to page 15. Administer'd the ordinance of the Lords Supper. Divers Southborough people here. Deacon Forbush sick. Mr. Jonathan Whipple Waited in his stead; and he and the widow Woods din'd with me. P.M. read the third of Matthew. Preach'd on Mark 9, 44, carrying on the subject of the Grand Result of the Last Day.

3. Ebenezer carting apples to Mr. Hows[1] mill. Aaron Warrin hir'd into the House to make Shooes. Mrs. Josselyn here with a quarter of young Mutton. She din'd with us. At Evening in a Private Manner Rebecca Hicks[2] was marry'd to Mr. Elijah Warrin. We had a small supper. They lodg'd here. God grant they may be both espoused to one Husband, the Lord Jesus Christ! And may we all be ready for the midnight Cry, and the Coming of the Bridegroom!

4. Aaron Warrin works here. My wife began to still Cyder, having borrow'd a large Iron Pott of Mr. Eliezer Rice for that Purpose. P.M. I rode to Mr. Daniel Warrins to see his brother in law Abraham Bond who is sick at a Fever. Was at Mr. Knowltons who was very kind favouring me with Rie meal and a Quarter of Mutton which I brot home with me for we had great need of them being in hopes of divers Hands tomorrow to gather and husk my Corn—and had no Body that I could send so far to mill as Mr. Drury's.

5. My Wife stilling. Aaron Warrin at work. Benjamin Tainter only came to gathering Corn a.m. Some others p.m. viz. Neighbours Edwards Whipple, Joseph Green junior, Thomas Whipple, Mr. Elijah Warrin. I visited Deacon Forbush who is ill but not bad, has Erisypilas Fever. Several Hands came in the Evening to Husk, but it had rain'd so in the afternoon that they had gather'd but part of the Corn, and the Company chose to come again. There were about eleven.

6. I visited the widow Warrin who is very low, as is likewise Jonathan Warrin. My wife and I rode over to Mr. Martyns. I preach'd his Lecture on Song 2, 4. At Eve Rain. Some Number of Hands dropp'd in till into the Evening and some of them had gather'd more Corn, but the south Field yet to gather. But neither did they incline to husk this night. I taught 'em something about singing. Aaron Warrin here.

7. Rainy. Aaron Warrin makes a pair of shooes for Bekky. Rainy. Disappoint'd of gathering the rest of my Corn. A Letter from the Church of Grafton, signed by Deacon Merriam, desiring me to assist in a Fast there, in concurrence with Reverend Messers Hall and Maccarty on the 13th instant. Towards Evening Storm clear'd off.

8. Ebenezer gathering more of winter apples. The Bridegroom (Mr. Elijah Warrin) came at Eve.

9. Preach'd all Day on Mat. 25, 46 former part. May God most merciful and gracious add his almighty Blessing to render the word Effectual to the awakening of every one! Read a.m. fourth of Genesis. P.M. the fourth of Matthew. Mr. Daniel Forbush's wife din'd with us. The Widow Warrin dy'd last night. This is the Third out of the Four who were Sick in that (now) very desolate House.

10. Aaron Warrin at Work in making Shooes. The Bridegroom and Bride having kept Sabbath here together were preparing to go to Sutton when Brother Hicks came, Supposing me to be going to Cambridge. But because of Mrs. Warrins Funeral, and because of the other sick persons among us I deferr'd it. Brother Hicks and his Children went from us. P.M. at the Funeral. N.B. several young men turned away from the procession and came up to help Ebenezer in gathering my Corn, viz. Abraham Batchellor, Phinehas Maynard and several more. 32 persons assisted in Husking. Finish'd the work by about 10 o'Clock. After Supper we Sung latter part of Ps. 4 and pray'd before the Company went off.

11. Preparing a sermon a.m. on Jer. 3, 15 for Grafton Fast. P.M. I din'd with the South Company Officers—Lieutenant Bruce[3] had the Command by Means of Captain Bakers[4] being

engag'd as one of the Referrees upon the Case of Messers Nurse[5] and Cook.[6] The other Referrees Captain Eager[7] and Lieutenant Hezikiah Ward the other Two. In my returning home at Eve went in to old Mr. Maynards to See Neverson Warrin (son of Daniel from Watertown) who is very ill and much Swell'd and convuls'd. He was about House in the forenoon, but has not been well this fortnight.

12. Was call'd up as soon as 'twas Light to go down to Neverson Warrin, who dy'd while I was present. He was in his Eleventh Year. Mr. Hezikiah Pratt afforded me the help of his Boy Cornelius Cook and his Team to get up the Corn from the barn. Ebenezer and Cornelius hard at it all Day. Aaron Warrin making Ebenezer a pair of German Pumps Monday and to Day. Mr. Daniel Bond here from Watertown and bought me a Specimen of 3 Sorts of Cornet Bright Apples. My wife p.m. rode over to Mr. Seth Rice's.

13. Rainy morning. Mr. Ballantine came. It held up and I left him to go to Grafton Fast. I sat in the Pulpit sometime waiting for Mr. Hall and Maccarty. At length I began with Prayer. Mr. Maccarty came and preach'd from Hebrew. Follow Peace etc. We were entertain'd at Serjeant James Whipples. P.M. Mr. Hall pray'd and I preach'd from Song 1, 7, 8. At Evening return'd. Mr. Edwards Whipple accompany'd me. We call'd at Mr. Winchesters[8]—Mr. Goddard[9] of Grafton there, who with Mrs. Winchester was in Defence of Separatists.

14. Neverson Warrins Buryal. My Interruption very great.

15. Jonathan Warrins Buryal. Deaths so oft—we had need take warning. At Evening came Cousen Samuel Procter from Boston, his Brother Joseph his Company but went to Captain Maynards.

16. A.M. repeated on Eccl. 9, 12. P.M. preach'd on Act 16, 29, 30. Read a.m. the fifth of Genesis and p.m. the fifth of Matthew. Both Procters din'd and supp'd here, but Mr. Joseph would lodge at Captain Maynards. He left a Bill which we found to be 40 shillings old Tenor.

17. The Procters sett out for Sutton. Ebenezer began to make our late Cyder. I rode to Mr. Josselyns who kindly lent me 20£ old Tenor. I proceeded on my Journey to Watertown. Rain'd at Eve. Was at Cornet Brights to see his Pippins and other rich Fruit. I design'd for Cambridge but it rain'd so hard I turn'd back to Mr. Daniel Bonds and lodg'd there.

18. In the Morning I visited Mr. Storer. Went to Cambridge to Brother Champneys—din'd there. We went over to sisters Lydia and Barrett. Read Mothers Will in which gives her Cloths to sister Hannah and makes sister Lydia Executrix, but She Refuses to Stand or have the will till she knows what the Debts amount to. I rode to Boston. Put up at Procters.[10] Was at Mr. Fletchers who paid me 140£ old Tenor for Brother Champney. Lodg'd at Brother Samuels.

19. Broke fast at Hearsys.[11] Din'd at Cowels.[12] Visited my Neece Lydia Tyley now Davis.[13] Was at Mr. Olivers—his Father and Mother etc. there. At Eve at Mr. Owens and at Mr. Quincys.[14] Lodg'd at Brother Williams.

20. Mr. Barnard[15] of Marblehead the public Lecture on Rom. 5, 12. Din'd at Dr. Sewals: who shew'd me Mr. Moorheads[16] Letter in Defence of himself against Mr. Buckminster.[17] P.M. at

---

[1] Neighbour Hezekiah How.
[2] The daughter of John Hicks of Sutton.
[3] Abijah Bruce.
[4] Edward Baker.
[5] William Nurse.
[6] Cornelius Cook.
[7] James Eager.
[8] Benjamin Winchester.
[9] Benjamin Goddard.
[10] Parkman's niece, Mrs. Samuel Proctor.
[11] Another niece, Mrs. Israel Hearsey.
[12] Another niece, Mrs. Peam Cowell.
[13] Robert Davis.
[14] Edmund Quincy.
[15] The Reverend Mr. John Barnard.
[16] John Moorehead, minister of the Arlington Street Church (Presbyterian), Boston, 1730-1773.
[17] The Reverend Mr. Joseph Buckminster of Rutland. Someone of the Rutland church complained that the Reverend Mr. Moorehead "has lately done great Mischief in this Place, by making Separations and Contentions among us." He "continues his wicked dividing work; and as we hear, intends to administer the Lord's Supper to his separate Company next Sabbath." *Boston Evening-Post*, Supplement, Sept. 19, 1748.

Deacon Bouteneau's Garden. At Eve rode over the Neck with Mr. Dunbar. I proceeded to Cambridge. Visited Deacon Sparhawk whose Wife is much disordered. Lodg'd at Brother Champneys.

21. The Heirs of Mother Champney together and we made Computations among ourselves and agreed. Sister Lydia took administrations (not in form of Law) and gave us Security. I din'd at Brother Barretts.[18] After I had drawn the writings I smok'd a pipe with Judge Danforth[19] for his approbation. Past 3 p.m. I undertook my Journey. Got to Mr. Bridge's[20] at Framingham and lodg'd there.

22. Mr. Bridge rode with me as far as Mr. David Bruce's—talk'd with his wife (heretofore Hannah Pierce) being under the Frowns of the Southborough Church. I din'd at Colonel Williams[21] at Marlborough. P.M. found my family in Peace. *D.G.* Rebecca Gott[22] came to live here on the 20th instant. Ebenezer finish'd making Cyder, in all 18 Barrells.

23. Preach'd a.m. on Acts 16, 29, 30. P.M. on 10, 31 but repeated part sermon on John 3, 36. Mr. Samuel Crosby and Mrs. Tainter din'd here.

24. Mr. Graves[23] Messenger from the Church of Southborough here without Mr. Stone,[24] his eldest son being ill of the Throat Distemper. Captain Baker and Ensign Miller came (as Delegates of our Church) and we went to Rutland. On the way din'd at Mr. Cushings,[25] and stopp'd again at Captain Biglo's.[26] Got up in Comfort and lodg'd at Mr. Buckminsters. The Council was call'd on account of uneasiness and irregularitys among some of the Brethren, particularly Messers Samuel Stone, and Simon Davis. John Stone also and Jones were join'd therein: and on account of the Conduct of a Number of Ireland[27] people who were members of the Church in Rutland; but without Dismission or acquainting the Church with it, drew off and join'd with others who Sett up another Assembly in the Town by the assistance of Mr. Moorhead.

25. The Council was form'd. I was their unwritten Moderator. Mr. Hall of Sutton was Clerk. We went to the Meeting House a.m. I opened the Meeting with prayer. We read the Paper of Grounds of uneasiness which Samuel Stone had exhibited to the Church some time ago. Great Debate whether that Paper should be the beginning of our Business in Hearing. Adjourn'd—din'd and repair'd to the public Hearing. Mr. Buckminster chiefly took up the Time. Mr. Williams[28] of Weston pray'd when we broke up this session at Night.

26. Mr. Campbell[29] pray'd at the opening the forenoon session. Mr. Samuel Stone chiefly this forenoon, with his Friends. We were again in hearing p.m. giving fair opportunity to the Irish etc to answer if they pleas'd. Evening Mr. Hall pray'd, when we had adjourn'd to Mr. Buckminsters where we sat again the Same Night till very late—Reading over, debating and Voting—and appointing a Committee to draw up a Result. The Committee were the Reverend Messers Williams, Hall and Eaton.

27. We were not ready with the Result till late p.m., for another Affair arose before us—viz. a Quarrell between Captain Edward Rice and Deacon Eleazer Ball. A Number of the Council went to the Meeting House to assist the Church in reconciling those Brethren—but in Vain. At Evening about Sunsett we went to the Meeting House and publish'd our Result partly by Daylight and partly by Candle. N.B. Captain Baker and Ensign Miller were dismiss'd to go home. The Church voted Acceptance of the Result. The Stones thank'd us for our Pains and promis'd to Consider of what was done, and in the Mean Time to return to

Mr. Buckminster's administrations.[30] But this was not the Conduct of the Irish. We were late up with the Affair of the Captain and the Deacon.

28. And Next Morning but without Effect tho we sat upon it p.m. also; and till toward Night. The Council appointed a Committee to hear it, viz. Mr. Campbell and myself, with Colonel Larnard, Mr. Brown of Leicester, and Esquire Baker, and then we adjourn'd without Day. It was so late and Misty that Mr. Buckminster and others from Time to Time earnestly requesting it, I stay'd; and Mr. Williams and I visited Mr. Frink in the Evening. I would not utterly forget the important Transactions of this Day 24 Years ago when I was solemnly Ordain'd. The Lord Grant me forgiveness of my many Defects; and make me Wise and Thankful!

29. A very rainy Night and Morning. But Mr. Buckminster went to Westborough and both Mr. Williams and I stay'd at Rutland.

30. I preach'd at Rutland a.m. on 2 Cor. 3, 14, 15. Mr. Williams p.m. on Phil. 1, 9, 10, 11. Mr. Buckminster at Westborough on [blank]. Sundry people came to Mr. Buckminster at Eve. Mr. Frink, Captain Howard etc.

31. Mr. Williams and I (who had all this Time lodg'd together) rode together to Holden. Old Mr. Clark my old irish Neighbour Scourg'd us. Call'd at Mr. Davis's.[31] Mr. Williams to Lancaster. Mr. Phelps my Company to Shrewsbury. I visited Mr. D. Warrin of Shrewsbury and his wife who were very sick and low, the latter especially. Got to my Family in safety—blessed be God for his great Goodness! But we are under Affliction by my wife's Lameness, which came only by a little Scratch in her Ankle. Found Mr. Pierpoint from New Haven at my House.

### NOVEMBER, [1748]

1. Mr. Pierpoint to Boston. Visited Mr. John Rogers's dauter Suse who is sick. Dr. Gott etc. here.

2. Visited Captain Maynard[1] who is still confin'd by sickness. At Mr. Hows. Ebenezer a Load of Pine.

3. Visited Mr. D. Warrin and his wife again—and Mr. Samuel Crosbys son, and din'd there. P.M. to the private meeting at Lieutenant Tainters—on Mat. 26, 14. N.B. My Dauter Mary with me. Supp'd there with divers Men and Women from Waterton and Waltham.

4. Very Cold Morning. Rain p.m. Ebenezer making a Bee-House.

5. [No entry.]

6. On Jer. 3, 15 all Day. N.B. I have been wont to take some Notice of the first Sabbath after October 28 (the Day of my Ordination A.D. 1724) to treat of some Ministerial or other proper subject; but was detain'd from home last Sabbath. No preaching at Grafton. Mr. Isaac Richardson[2] who was to have preach'd there to Day having been taken sick and dy'd. Captain Willard[3] din'd here.

7. Neighbour Rogers here and tells me his little Dauter is something better. At Captain Maynards at Evening.

8. Neighbour Rogers assist'd my son in killing a Cow (brindled which I some Years ago bought of Mr. Aaron Forbush). P.M. I rode to Mr. Bathericks and Mr. Cooks.

9. At Eve Mr. Abner Newton and his wife made us a Visit; and this Eve also came Mr. Cotton[4] of Newtown who informs me that his Dauter Cheney was married last Thursday to the Honourable Joseph Pyncheon Esquire.

10. Mr. Cotton for Newton. N.B. his son and Mr. Cook, his Neighbour at Newtown, with him. Mr. Grow and Batherick at

[18] Parkman's brother-in-law, John Barrett.

[19] Samuel Danforth of Cambridge.

[20] The Reverend Mr. Matthew Bridge.

[21] Abraham Williams, Parkman's brother-in-law.

[22] Daughter of Dr. Benjamin Gott of Marlborough.

[23] Joseph Graves.

[24] The Reverend Mr. Nathan Stone of Southborough.

[25] The Reverend Mr. Job Cushing.

[26] Joseph Bigelow, a selectman of Shrewsbury.

[27] Ulster Presbyterians.

[28] William Williams.

[29] John Campbell of Oxford.

[30] The Presbyterian minister of Boston, John Moorehead, had charged that Buckminster was not orthodox in his Calvinism. This council found him orthodox and called the Presbyterians "unchristian and disorderly." *Sibley*, X, 349.

[31] The Reverend Mr. Joseph Davis of Holden.

[1] John Maynard.

[2] (Harvard 1726). An itinerant schoolmaster, who preached occasionally at various places. *Sibley*, VIII, 92–95.

[3] Benjamin Willard of Grafton.

[4] The Reverend Mr. John Cotton of Newton.

work a.m. on my back porch. They din'd here, as did Reverend Mr. Stone,[5] Two Tainters and their Kinswoman Joanna Tainter[6] of Watertown. Mr. Stone preach'd the Lecture on Phil. 2, 8. I Stopp'd the Church to read the Rutland Result and a Letter from Lancaster. N.B. Mr. Ebenezer Chamberlain brought me two living Ducks to keep. At Eve Mr. Nathaniel Whitney here to ask me whether if they should gather but a small part of the Money due to me from the North Side, among them in their South Neighbourhood, I would give a Receipt in full? (They having heard from Lieutenant Tainter that I would.) I told him I was not ready to make any direct answer to it.

11. [No entry.]

12. [No entry.]

13. Read the ninth of Genesis and preach'd on Mat. 22, 37, 38. Administer'd the Lords Supper. Deacon Newton, old Mrs. Tomlin and Mrs. Patience Woods din'd here. P.M. read ninth of Matthew. Preach'd on Mat. 25, 46, last part. Deacon Newton requested the Church before the Congregation to excuse him from the service of Delegate, and nominated Brother Baker, but no sooner was the Matter propos'd than Ensign Bruce objected and said it was not according to Custom to propose such Things before the Congregation. I gave him the Reason—viz. it was So late and Cold—but immediately I stopp'd the Church, and then dispatch'd it. I perceiv'd afterwards that Lieutenant had some Disgust with the Captain about their Military proceedings.

14. Mr. Batherick here to work upon my shed, or back porch. At Eve I visited Captain Maynard who has of late grown Worse.

15. Bright fine Day. Captain Baker and Ensign Miller accompany'd me to Lancaster to the Installment of Mr. Timothy Harrington.[7] We din'd at Mr. Nathan Balls. I lodg'd at Colonel Willards.[8] Mr. Maccarty[9] my Bedfellow.

16. The Council form'd at Captain Willards. Mr. Hancock[10] Moderator and pray'd. Mr. Harrington was examin'd by Mr. Loring respecting his principles. Mr. Storer[11] pray'd publickly. Mr. Hancock preach'd on 1 Cor. 9, 19. Mr. Loring[12] gave the Charge, Mr. Gardner[13] pray'd after it; and Mr. Appleton[14] the right Hand of Fellowship. Were entertain'd at the Colonels and at his son's. At Eve visited Madam Prentice[15] and the Doctor,[16] but lodg'd as Last. Mr. Trowbridge[17] of Groton lodg'd with me.

17. Went to Mr. Martyn and his wife, at Mr. Townsends; and we all and a Number more din'd at Mr. Goss's.[18] Mr. Martyn and his wife in their Chair my Company homeward as far as their House. Found my family safe at Evening. N.B. I understand that Esquire Baker is about buying at Bolton.

18. Mr. Charles Rice here. Tells me Lieutenant Ward has laid out his Land for me, that he has 16 acres upon that plain. Ebenezer digging a Vault.

19. A very bright moderate Day. The Earth open yet, and a fine Opportunity to provide for Winter. N.B. Mr. Stephen Maynard brought me from Major Henchman, a New Folio Bible which the late Mr. Joseph Wheeler presented to the first Church in Westborough to be at the Dispose of the Pastor thereof for the time being. The price I understand is 20£ old Tenor. At Eve came Mr. Bridge of Framingham. Mr. Buckminster[19] is to preach for him. Mr. Maccarty to go to Rutland, Mr. Martyn to Worcester and tis propos'd I Should preach for Mr. Martyn.

20. Mr. Bridge on Eccl. [blank] and on [blank]. I rode over to the North Side and preach'd a. and p.m. on John 5, 28, 29.

[5] Nathan Stone of Southborough.

[6] The daughter of Captain John Tainter.

[7] The minister of Lancaster, 1748-1795.

[8] Aaron Willard of Lancaster.

[9] The Reverend Mr. Thaddeus Maccarty of Worcester.

[10] John Hancock of Lexington.

[11] Seth Storer of Watertown.

[12] Israel Loring of Sudbury.

[13] John Gardner of Stow.

[14] Nathaniel Appleton of Cambridge.

[15] The widow of the Reverend Mr. John Prentice.

[16] Stanton Prentice, the physician of Lancaster.

[17] The Reverend Mr. Caleb Trowbridge.

[18] The Reverend Mr. Thomas Goss of Bolton.

[19] Joseph Buckminster of Rutland.

Baptiz'd Elizabeth of Jonathan and Sibyl Green. Return'd at Eve. Mr. Bridge supp'd with us and then left us to go home.

21. I rode down to Mr. Cooks Shop. Was inform'd there that it was proprietors meeting at Marlborough, but I could not go, it being precinct meeting here, about my Support (So they are pleas'd to call it again) and they voted 180£ old Tenor, to be added to the 220£ which they call my Sallery. Justice Baker brought the Return to me of it and said it was chearfully voted. And they have voted also to build another Meeting House. N.B. Mr. Buckminster here.

22. Ebenezer to Sutton to assist in bringing Rebecca Warrin to her own Home at Upton. My wife and I went to see old Mrs. Brigham who is sick; and call'd to see Several others. Moderate Season. At Eve Sir Henchman[20] and Mr. John Brigham of Sudbury (whose Arm Dr. Gott cutt off) Supp'd with us. Rebecca Gott to Marlborough.

23. Rain. Thomas came home. A variety of presents from my Neighbours. But by means of the pressure of Family Cares, and many hindrances by my Circumstances, my mind was greatly confus'd—could make but little way in my preparations for the approaching solemnity.

24. I was in a great Deal of Confusion, and my Soul greatly bowed down, so that I was very unprepar'd for the solemnity of the Thanksgiving, and yet thro the kind assistance of a gracious God I was mercifully carried thro. But I desire to humble myself before the Lord for my backwardness and unpreparedness; and may the Blood of the Great Saviour make Atonement! I preach'd on Ps. 17, 43. O might I have the Grace wisely to observe the divine Dispensations towards the Children of Men, and might I come to understand and not only Speculatively, but Experimentally and sensibly the Loving Kindness of the Lord! We invited Mr. Daniel Warrin (of the other precinct) and his wife and desir'd him to bring not only his wife but his Children to our House but none of them came. Rebecca Warrin was at our Table. At Eve Thomas Winchester was marry'd to Mary Pratt.[21]

25. Mrs. Brigham grows worse—her son Levi came in the Morning to call Me. I went—convers'd with her, and pray'd (as I did also when I visited her on the 22). N.B. Mr. Benjamin Carryll here with the Petitions of his Brother in Law David Woodwell for a Contribution that he may be able to redeem his Daughter from the Hands of the Indians. At Eve came Mr. Jonathan Green and Mr. James Eager, sons in law to the late Mr. Joseph Wheeler, and approving of the Bible which Major Henchman had provided and sent, they presented it to the First Church in this Town according to the Tenor of the Testament of the Deceased; which I thankfully receiv'd of them in behalf of the Church.

26. A very fine pleasant Day. The Earth yet open. Sir Henchman brought up Bekky Gott. He and I walk'd to Captain Maynards; the Captain lying Still in a weak and low Condition. Molly rode yesterday to Mr. Warrins—returns to Day.

27. Read Gen. 11 and preach'd on Mat. 25, 46, latter part. P.M. read (the first Time in the Great Bible) Mat. 11, and repeated Some of my brief Sketches on the Mediator from Heb. 12, 24. N.B. A Nuisance from the Gallery over my Pew—Tobacco Spittle druling down upon my Dauter Mollys Hand. Read to the Congregation the petition of David Woodwell of Hopkinton. Molly and I visited old Mrs. Brigham at the Eve.

28. Mr. Chapin[22] from Grafton din'd here. Shews me a Letter which they had prepar'd to send to Mr. Hutchinson:[23] he wants to have the Neighbouring Ministers also to write to him; whereas I conceiv'd 'em to be fervent enough themselves he insisted upon it—but I finally refus'd. P.M. Mr. Martyn here.

29. Held a Catechetical Exercise: only instead of explaining the Catechism I deliver'd 'em another Sermon on Joel 3, 13, (put ye in the Sickle) without reading that or any other Text previous to it. A.M. at Lieutenant Tainters to see him in his Lameness.

[20] (Harvard 1747).

[21] Of Grafton.

[22] Benjamin Chapin.

[23] Aaron Hutchinson, who was to become the minister of Grafton.

30. My wife attempted to ride with me—but she alighted at Neighbour John Rogers's. I went to see Mrs. Brigham[24] before She dy's, and pray'd with her. Rode over to Mr. Martyns and din'd there. Return'd at Evening.

### DECEMBER, 1748

1. I rode over to Upton. Forbush[1] went with me. We din'd at Jonas Warrins. Preach'd a Lecture on John 3, 36, and baptiz'd Two Children, one of them the Child of Moses Wood, the other of Samuel Wood, their wives being Members of the Church. Was at Captain Sadlers[2] his wife (who is my kinswoman) was very urgent to have me tarry all night, for it began to rain. But I chose to get as near home as possible. It was very dark and rainy before we got to Mr. James Bradish's. Then we lodg'd.

2. Return'd home. I have heard of some Frolicks of late at Merchant Rice's. On the Trooping night, and last Friday night. I (before I went home) rode up to Mr. Rice's and (taking him aside) talk'd with him and warn'd him. He assur'd me there Should be no more Frolicks of Young People at His House. I understand that Mrs. Brigham dy'd yesterday.

3. Tis now a very alter'd Air. Cold and Windy. Molly and Lucy rode together and Bekky Gott rode with me to the Funeral of Mrs. Brigham. This is now the Ninth Death that has been in this Parish of Late. May God make me sensible of my own Frailty and Mortality! My Thoughts have been of late greatly discompos'd, and I don't know that I have ever felt so inwardly sunk and disheartened and unable to sustain my Infirmity. What has brought me into this has been my inability to do for my Children, when they come to be of age. My son Ebenezer in particular. All my schemes and Designs respecting him fall to the Ground. He has chose to be a Farmer, but I have not a Farm to give him that is handy or desirable (No other than that at Townshend). Nor has he strength of Body to drudge and bring to a place. My Family is so large as to need what I have at home and more too. But I beg grace to enable me to cast my Care upon God who Careth for us.

4. Read Gen. 12. Preach'd on Mat. 25, 46 last Clause. Old Mrs. Whipple, Bekky Warrin din'd with us. P.M. Read Mat. 12. Sermon on Ps. 2, 6 and made use of some Preparations which I had deliver'd to young women. A Colder season than of late, by much.

5. Rose very Early and tho it was very Cold went over to Mr. Martyn, who is going to Cambridge, with Letters to Deacon Whittemore (who Sends me word he has got me a Chair) and to Sister Lydia Champney. I both breakfasted and din'd at Mr. Martyns—for after I had taken leave I was met and detain'd on the Road by Captain Amsden; I had also forgot something or at least omitted to speak of something which I was desirous Mr. Martyn should do (respecting bringing up the Chair, if the Affair was fully Clear and I must have it) So I return'd and din'd there. P.M. returning home I visited Captain Maynard who is recovering. Old Mr. Joseph Green with me, in difficulty about his Spiritual state. I visited Mr. Samuel Bakers wife who is very weak and low. Visited at Mr. Williams's in the Evening. When I came home found Mr. Wellman[3] here, on his Journey to Concord to the Ordination of Mr. Lawrence.[4]

6. Mr. Williams prosecuted his design for Concord. Cold Day. Old Mr. Green here again in Spiritual Troubles. After telling me his Condition he earnestly ask'd me whether I thought there was any Hope for him? The Lord pity his miserable State, but I conceive him to be over timorous, and born down with his scruples. Went with Mr. How a while to look up the Bounds of the Ministerial Lot next to him and Me, especially the West End.

7. Another bright Cold Day. I expected that the Young Men of the private society would have come to cutt wood, for so they had appointed to do—but there came only the Eight following. Daniel How, Benjamin Tainter, Timothy Newton, Rody Smith

(or Devereux) Jonathan Bruce, Moses Warrin, Phinehas Maynard, and Aaron Warrin. At Eve my wife and I were at Captain Maynards.

8. My Wife and I went over to Neighbour Hows to the Marriage of their son Noah to Mary Walker, and we Supp'd there.

9. [No entry.]

10. Mr. Martyn sent Thaddeus Fay[5] to desire me to change tomorrow. The same Lad brought me several Letters—one from my Brother Parkman bewailing the Death of his son John Parkman,[6] goldsmith who was well last Sabbath, but being seiz'd with a Fever, deceas'd yesterday. My God Sanctify the frequent, sorrowful Breaches upon that Family! and may we all who are related, be shown wherefor the Lord contends with us! and be exited to an actual Readiness for our own Turn! Another Letter from Deacon Whittemore of Cambridge in Answer to mine of the fifth informing me what he had done about a Chair.

11. I preach'd at the North side on Heb. 9, 27, a. and p.m. to page 20th. Return'd home at Eve. Mr. Martyn preach'd to my people on Acts 9, 11, and Rom. 12, 18. He tarried and lodg'd here.

12. Mr. Martyn return'd home. Joseph Bowker din'd here. I reckon'd with him and paid him all. Rainy.

13. Rain a.m. Clear'd off p.m. So that I Set out on a Journey to Boston. Call'd at Mr. Stone's—his wife ill. Proceeded to Framingham. Mr. Bridge[7] and wife from Home. By means of one Isaac Clark I was conducted to Mr. Thomas Stone's who marry'd Mrs. Betty Andrew of Cambridge—and by this Time it was So far in the Evening that I lodg'd there. N.B. Said Isaac Clarks wife dauter of Mr. Stone separated from her husband, and residing there.

14. Drizly—but I pursued my Journey. Din'd at Captain Tainters at Watertown. Went to Deacon Whittemores to see what he had done about a Chair: it Rain'd harder, yet I went to Charleston and over the Ferry in the Dark and Rain with my young Horse that had never been in a Boat before. Hasten'd up to my Kinsman Olivers—Supp'd at Captain Davenport Walkers, but lodg'd at Olivers and had my Horse kept there. Was not well, being kept up late after so much fatigue.

15. After a Night of Disorder, and tempestuous Storm of Wind and Rain, wak'd early. Shav'd at Mr. Mallow's. Had Some Contest with Major Henchman for his not sending any Return to my repeated Letters. He resented my last. I took it again. Public Lecture by Mr. Wellsteed[8] on Ps. 51, 11 or 12 of our Need of the Gift of the Holy Spirit. Din'd at Brother Samuels. Visited Mrs. Mary Bennett (who was so good as to make me a present of Tea)—visited my poor Mourning Niece—but the prizers were there. After visits to my other Relations—Supp'd at Olivers, my Two Brethren also there. N.B. Talk in private with my Brother Parkman; concerning the Grounds of the Reproachful Storm in most people's mouths of his Conduct towards his sons widow, and especially the very night of the Funeral. I rejoice to hear him declare his Innocence. Lodg'd at Olivers; my Horse kept here Still. N.B. Old Mr. S. Clark the Builder bury'd and Mr. Joseph White's widow (sister Hannahs sister) dy'd.

16. Din'd at Brother Samuels—did not see Dr. Parkman tho I was at his House yesterday—not having Time to Day to go to the North End. Saw sister Lydia Champney in the street in Boston, I being on my Horse and coming out of Town. At Cambridge call'd at Brother Champneys. Lodg'd at Deacon Whittemore's.

17. In the Morning my Horses Lampsas[9] burnt by Mr. William Morse. The Deacon and I at Mr. Ebenezer Bradish's about the Chair. Have deliver'd the Deacon 60£ old Tenor for it. Left Cambridge about 11 a.m. Din'd at Mr. Nathaniel Harrington's. Mr. Bridge and his wife gone to a Funeral and could not see him going or returning to know whether he designs to preach my Lecture to Young Men. Was at old Clark Johnsons at Evening.

---

[24] Mrs. David Brigham.
[1] Eli Forbush, or Forbes.
[2] John Sadler.
[3] The Reverend Mr. James Wellman of Millbury.
[4] William Lawrence (Harvard 1743), the minister of Lincoln, Mass., 1748–1780.
[5] The son of Gershom Fay.
[6] The son of Parkman's eldest brother, William.
[7] The Reverend Mr. Matthew Bridge of Framingham.
[8] William Wellsteed of the New Brick Church.
[9] Lampas, or lampers, is an inflammation and swelling of the roof of the mouth of a horse.

Mr. Eleazer Bellows my Company Home. My Family Well. To God be Glory!

18. Preach'd a. and p.m. on Rom. 1, 18, repeating some part of Sermon on Tit. 2, 11, Scil: from page 19 to 33, tho with divers omissions, Additions, Transpositions and alterations.

19. Rain. Kitty Grout here making a New, cloth-colour'd Riding Hood for my Wife, and altering my Wife's Scarlet Riding Hood for Molly.

20. Kitty Grout.

21. I had reason to look for Mr. Bridge to preach my Lecture to the young people, but he came not. Mr. Martyn and his wife came. I got him to preach. His Text Mat. 22, 5. They Stay'd into Evening.

22. Kitty Grout went home a.m. Molly rode with me over to Mr. Martyns and Mr. Martyn rode with me to Harvard. N.B. we din'd at Mr. Townsends—went up to Lancaster—and I proceeded with Mr. Martyn to Mr. Ebenezer Beeman's, and buying Bricks of him, I bought a few with him. We lodg'd at Mr. Seccombs.[10] N.B. Mrs. Seccomb a Fitt at Eve.

23. We left Mr. Seccombs and came to Mr. [blank] Keys's, and I made some proposals to him about his taking my son Ebenezer to learn the Business of a Gunsmith, which he accepted of. We din'd late at Mr. Goss's. It was Evening when Molly and I return'd home. Here was Mr. Caleb Upham who is our Schoolmaster; he supp'd and lodg'd here.

24. Mr. Upham to his School at Mr. Hezekiah Pratts. Finish'd reading in the Family Dr. Doddridge Family Expositor[11] Volume 2 and next morning began it again.

25. Read Geneisis 15. Gave some brief Expository Hints. Preach'd on Mat. 25 last Clause of 10, 46. Mr. Upham, Mrs. Rogers and Mrs. Steward din'd. P.M. read Mat. 15 and my Exercise was an Exposition of the latter part of it. Mr. Upham here after meeting—tarry'd to Supper and lodg'd here.

26. A very pleasant Day. I rode out p.m. as far as Mr. Ebenezer Rice's and Deacon Newtons—finished reading Εικων Βασιλικη Δευτερη or the Portraiture of King Charles the second.[12] Ebenezer thrashing Rye.

27. The weather greatly alter'd to Cold and Windy, tho bright. Ebenezer thrashing.

28. I visited Lucy Pratt (heretofore Whipple) in her Mourning for the Loss of her husband Moses Pratt at Hardwick. I was also at Mr. Eleazer Bellows's, at Mr. Daniel Warrins in Shrewsbury; at Mr. Crosbys; Deacon Miles's,[13] and din'd there. At Mr. Joseph Miles's[14] to bespeak the making a Cart; went over to Mr. Benjamin Willards at Grafton and bespoke Joshua Winchester[15] to come and live with me next season—was at his Fathers—from thence went to Mr. Nathaniel Whitneys to see his son Oliver, who was lately hurt by a Tree. At my Returning home in the Eve, receiv'd a Letter from Mr. Upham inclosing a piece of Poetry which he stiles the Choice. N.B. our people begin to stir in getting Timber for a Meeting House.

29. Wrote a brief answer to Mr. Upham. P.M. Deacon Newton came and we reckon'd and I paid all and his son Silas's account likewise by a Note to the Collector Mr. Daniel Hardy. N.B. Mr. Caryl from Hopkinton here to see whether we had done anything in Contributing for the Redemption of his Brother Woodwell's Dauter out of Captivity—whereas this was one part

---

of Deacon Newtons Business with me, to acquaint me that the Deacons and Committee of the Precinct did advise to my publickly proposing it, to our Congregation next Sabbath. I was sorry we were so late; for other Congregations round about had collected already, and they now (who were concern'd) were receiving it, that our Bills may be Exchang'd into Silver. This afternoon it began to snow there having been no Snow, if to cover the Ground, yet not to lye this Year till now. At Night the storm increas'd.

30. Considerable Cold Storm of Snow. My Care at present is to provide for my sons going off to Harvard to live with Mr. William Keyes to be a Gun Smith. Ah wretched Harvard to which I had design'd him! But this will be I hope, *non invita Minerva*.

31. Extremely high Gusts of Wind last Night. But thro God's Mercy we are all well this Morning. Proves a very Cold blustering Day.

Thus through the tender Mercy of God I have finish'd another Year. Blessed be his glorious Name! But when I look back and see what I have done in this further Measure of divine Forbearance, alas! What reason for Grief and shame that I have been so unprofitable; having brought so little Glory to the name of God—done so little for my own Soul, and been so Slenderly Beneficial unto others! May God be pleas'd to grant me true holy Mourning and Sorrow; and may I by Faith be enabled to repair to and depend on the atoning Blood of the son of God which Cleanseth from all sin! May I have part in the Merits of his Righteousness and Obedience when my own is so defective; nay, have none at all! And O that the glorious High Priest who ever lives to make Intercession might allow and enable me to come to God by him—and notwithstanding all my infinite unworthiness Save me to the Uttermost. Amen.

### JANUARY, 1749

Blessed be the Lord who continually upholds my Soul in Life and especially has conducted me through the changing Scenes of the Last Year—has granted me also to see Chearful Light of another New Years Day! that we have also the Day of Grace and the means thereof, at the Same Time; and that we have another of the Days of the son of Man! How undeserv'd! how discriminating His Mercy and Bounty! This forenoon I read publickly the 16th chapter of Genesis: and preach'd on Neh. 9, 6, using the Body of the Sermon I formerly deliver'd on that Text, but had both a new introduction and an application for Improvement of the Day. Mr. Joseph Stratton of Waltham din'd with us. P.M. I read Mat. 16, preach'd on Ps. 17, ult carrying on the Subject of the Happiness of the Saints in Heaven. May God grant to us the principle of Holiness and divine Love here, which shall be in Such Glory in the future World! The Weather is grown very Cold. The Snow hard enough for people to run upon. God only can Sustain us, for who can Stand before his Cold.

2. Another very Cold Day. Mr. Hall[1] of Sutton here with a Letter from the first Church there requesting me to assist in a Fast next Week on Account of Various Difficultys among them by reason of the Separations increasing and on Consideration of a Late Council at Oxford, met at the Request of one of the members of the 1st Church in Sutton (one Davidson) under the Censure of Said Church. But I was oblig'd to refuse, both because of my own uncertain Health, and my wife's present Circumstances. The widow Sarah Forbush[2] here to work for us—Spinning. Ebenezer is Sledding Wood.

3. Not altogether So Cold as yesterday. Ebenezer Sledded Two Oak Loggs to Maynards Saw Mill. I rode up to Mr. Knowltons to obtain one of his sons to come and live with me, Ebenezer being about to go to Harvard. Din'd at Mr. Knowltons. Was also at Mr. Bellows's, Mr. Greens and old Mr. Whipples. Very Raw Cold, and begins to snow before I got home. Billy began to

---

[10] The Reverend Mr. John Seccomb of Harvard.

[11] Philip Doddridge, *The Family Expositor* (London, 1739).

[12] Εικων Βασιλικη Δευτερη *The Portraiture of his sacred Majesty, King Charles, II* (London, 1694).

[13] Samuel Miles of Shrewsbury.

[14] A brother of Deacon Miles.

[15] The son of Benjamin Winchester of Grafton.

[1] The Reverend David Hall.

[2] Mrs. Samuel Forbush.

learn Latin. May God be pleas'd to grant it may succeed. Mr. Amos Pratt[3] of Shrewsbury dy'd yesterday.

4. The Morning was Somewhat snowy, but Elijah Bellows according to appointment came to go with Ebenezer to Harvard to bring back the Horse. And therefore my son went Scil. to Mr. William Keyes's to learn what he can of the Gunsmiths Business. And God most merciful be gracious to him and be the Guide of his Youth! Mr. Joseph Roberts[4] from Boston, a young preacher at Grafton (accompany'd by Mr. Simon Tainter of Grafton) came to see me—din'd with us, and tarry'd over Night (Mr. Tainter going to his Father Bruce's).[5] Elijah Warrin return'd safe with the Horses from Harvard.

5. Mr. Roberts, Mr. Upham and Mr. Tainter din'd here. P.M. though a very Cold, blustering Day, Mr. Roberts return'd to Grafton.

6. Cold Season. Very difficult to be without help. P.M. at my Request Mr. Pratt sent his Cornelius to assist in Cutting Wood, etc.

7. Very Cold. Mr. Solomon Woods came—brought a pair of Bellows from Cambridge and mended 'em. Din'd here. P.M. Mrs. Forbush (Phinehas' Widow) here till now. She had my mare to ride home, and went for me to Mr. Daniel Hardys to get me some money, he being Collector of the money granted for the last Year, and tho he has had the Rates from Month to Month, yet he brings me none. Nathan Knowlton does not come as I expected.

8. Very Cold Day. No Nathan. Tending the Cattle at this extreme season very troublesome to me, having been so very unus'd to it—but my little Billy has been some help. At noon came Cornelius Cook (by desire) to take Care of the Cattle. At noon likewise one of the Chimneys took fire. I read in the publick service part of the 17th chapter of Genesis and preach'd on Ps. 17, 15 of the Happiness of Heaven. P.M. read part of the 17th of Matthew. Preach'd on 2 Cor. 8, 7 (repeated), on occasion of the design'd Contributions for the Redemption of the Dauter of Mr. David Woodwell. But by reason of the Extremity of the Season I (not without advising upon it) thot it prudentest to adjourn it to another Sabbath. N.B. Deacon Forbush was the person I talked with—he din'd with me, as did his daughter in law (widow Forbush) as well as master Upham.

9. A very cold Night indeed. Nathan Knowlton came in the forenoon. His Father afterwards, and din'd here. The Day Somewhat moderater. At Eve Thomas came home.

10. Difficulty to get grinding. Thomas to old Mr. Johnson's mill, but brot nothing home. P.M. came Mr. Joseph Williams from Marlborough in a Disquietment about Thomas—in Special his being at Uriah Amsdens (where he had contracted acquaintance by means of the womans being a Westboro woman) after he had forbid him. And nothing would Satisfie with him or Thomas but throwing up the Indentures, which after much Debate therefore We did. Thomas acknowledging his Fault in using Amsdens House against his (his masters) will: and his not coming home from Horns of Southborough (at the Time of the late trooping there) along with Silas (his fellow 'prentice) but riding home with Said Amsden—and some other Indiscretions—and Williams acknowledged he had not done well in speaking to Thomme's Disparagement undervaluing his Time, and was sorry that in his passion he should Express himself So. This is a New Affliction, but tis unavoidable. I desire to acknowledge the hand of God in it, and Submitt to His holy will. O that God would grant Repentence and forgiveness for what has been amiss!

11. Nathan Knowlton to Drurys Mill with Success. A.M. pleasant, P.M. clouded. Sheriff Taylor[6] of Southboro and Several others for his aid, is conducting Jacob Newton (of the Same Town) up to Worcester Goal to committ him for Theft.

12. Neighbour Ebenezer Maynard kill'd an Hogg for me, my son Thomas and Nathan Knowlton assisting. A pleasant Day though Somewhat Cold. P.M. I rode as far as Mr. Daniel Hardys (who is Collector) and to Lieutenant Tainters.

13. Thomas (and his Sister Molly with Bekky Gott) rode in the Slay to Marlborough. Instead of his bringing up his Chest and all his Things from his late Master Williams's he gives in to his [kind] Entertainment, leaves his Chest and hearkens to Mr. Williams's Discourse of employing him again. N.B. Sally Gott instead of Bekky[7]—in a snow Storm. At Eve Mr. Samuel Harrington to see how I was on't, for wood etc., and he helped me in getting in Loggs etc. before the Storm was too hard.

14. Stormy a.m. Clear'd off p.m. Neighbour Eliezer Rice came kindly to see whether I did not want help about my Wood, Loggs especially and about my Creatures. I took it very kindly tho I did not Stand in need at this Time.

15. A.M. read the latter part of Genesis 17 and gave some Exposition (as I have done several Times) and I preach'd on Mat. 25, 46 latter Clause. Mr. Upham[8] brought his Father to dine with me. P.M. read the latter part of Mat. 17 and deliver'd part of Several Expositions of Mat. 6 but from 2 Cor. 8, 7, and after Sermon we Contributed for the Redemption of the Dauter of Mr. David Woodwell of Hopkinton. The Lord bless his word, and accept of our Offering!

16. Master Uphams Father here. Sudden News from Dr. Gott, by Sir Henchman that Sally must go home. Mr. Cushing[9] and his wife to See us, and din'd here. P.M. Sally return'd with Henchman, to our great Disappointment. At Eve came Mr. Stone who had visited Mr. Martyn. N.B. Deacon Newton was with me to count the money gather'd yesterday and it amounted to a few Shillings above 20£ old Tenor. The Precinct had a Meeting to appoint a Committee to treat with Lieutenant Brigham, the proprietor of the Land which they have voted the Convenientest Spot for a Meeting House.[10]

17. Mr. David Woodwell here on his Return from Deerfield to Hopkinton. He tells us that last week dy'd Mr. Benjamin Doolittle[11] the pastor of Northfield. Many Southern Neighbours came to Cutt and Sled wood for me. My Son Thomas went also with my own Team. The Company were Mr. Samuel Harrington with a Team, Mr. Timothy Warrin and Team, Benjamin Tainter (for his Brother Jonathan Forbush—but) with his Fathers Team, Mr. Growe, Mr. Bowman, Mr. Daniel Hardy, Mr. Phinehas Hardy, Mr. Zebulon Rice, Messers Solomon Woods, Jonas Child, Samuel Baker, Eleazer Williams, besides which were Robert Cook, Nathaniel Whitney junior, Joseph Grout, Judah Rice, Thomas Hardy, and Samuel Bumpso. And they got down 34 Load to the Door. Sorrowful News of the Death of Mr. Daniel Cooks son, at Newton, his only Child, who was here not long since with his designed Father in Law, Reverend Mr. Cotton. My wife continually in much pain particularly in her Side: but especially o'Nights—I fear the Event. The Lord be pleas'd to prepare us for his holy Will!

18. A.M. being a bright pleasant Day I assisted Thomas in Sledding home 2 load of the Wood which the people yesterday left cutt in the woods; for there is danger of its being cover'd up if there should come another Snow. P.M. I rode in my Slay to Mr. Cooks with Irons (given last year by Mr. Cowell) to shoee it. At Eve Cold. Thomas informs me that there is no water to be found at the Springs; tho he cutt quite through the Ice he meets with nothing but Mudd. My wife continues very full of pain in her side.

19. Cold Morning. Sent my son Thomas to Mr. Cooks to finish Shooing the Slay.

20. Mr. Dyer of Worcester brought me Mr. Thomas Emlyn's—Tracts Volume I.[12]

21. Lieutenant Ward here to see me about the Plot of 19½ Acres.

[3] Formerly of Westborough.

[4] Joseph Roberts (Harvard 1741), a schoolmaster of Weston and the minister of Leicester, 1754–1762. Sibley, XI, 65–68.

[5] Tainter had married Mary, the daughter of Lieutenant Abijah Bruce of Westborough.

[6] Several Taylors lived in Southborough. Whitmore, Massachusetts Civil List, does not indicate any sheriff of this name.

[7] Daughters of Dr. Benjamin Gott of Marlborough.

[8] Caleb Upham, Westborough's schoolmaster.

[9] The Reverend Job Cushing of Shrewsbury.

[10] In Dec., 1748, the first precinct appropriated £600, old tenor for the construction of the new meeting house. In Jan., 1749, a piece of land five rods long and eight wide, near the present center of Westborough, was purchased from Nathan Brigham of Southborough. DeForest and Bates, Westborough, p. 133.

[11] (Yale 1716). The minister of Northfield, 1717–1748. Dexter, Biographical Sketches, pp. 151–154.

[12] This learned English divine and supporter of Arianism published many works. Parkman probably made reference to A Collection of Tracts relating to the Deity, Worship, and Satisfaction of the Lord Jesus Christ (London, 1719).

22. Read Genesis 18 and gave some Extracts from Mr. Ainsworth[13] and some Observations of my own for an Exposition. Preached on John 12, 26. Mr. Upham[14] and Dodge[15] from College din'd here. P.M. read Mat. 18 with some brief observations, and preached from 2 Pet. 1, 5, 6. The former part too unprepar'd, the body of the Discourse was from sermon on Titus 2, 12,—add to their Knowledge of Temperance, from page 55 to 68. Because of what I had lately heard of some persons being overtaken with Drink, and some of them members of the Church.

23. A.M. Dodge here. In my Defence of my Sermon on Eph. 5, 14, awake that Sleepest etc. against what Dodge had heard diverse people say of it, I read him the chief of the Notes. P.M. Deacon Newton came to review the counting of the late Contribution for Mr. Woodwell, and he brought somewhat more which a person put into his Hands, who was not at Meeting on the Day of the Contributions—the whole sum now amounts to £29.11.2. The precinct also met today to hear the Report of their Committee about the Land which they have pitch upon for the new Meeting House to Stand on: but they are at present at a stand by reason of the Objections of those Rice's who are fellow-heirs with the late wife of Lieutenant Nathan Brigham of Southborough, who is the present possessor or Claimer of the spot. N.B. At Eve Several men were in here, after the meeting. Mr. Daniel Hardy paid me the full of 152£ 10 s. to make up for last Year. And I gave the precinct a Receipt in full from the Beginning of the precinct to June 5 last. Lieutenant Forbush was here and he was the first who mention'd to me any Dissatisfaction of his own, with my public Reading of the holy Scriptures in public. Captain Forbush and Daniel Hardy also offer'd something in my hearing of the like nature. I endeavour'd further to Vindicate it—and we had fervent argument upon another Point likewise. Scil. the Beginning of the Sabbath. I was griev'd to find such a Disposition to Objecting and finding fault—for Lieutenant Said he believ'd we Should not only come to reading the Scripture, but to reading Prayers, for we were got to reading our Notes, whereas our Charge was to preach—not read. No word in the Bible that we should read, as for singing, he said I had preach'd about it some Time ago and recommended the Duty very much, and that they should all have their Psalm-Books—but now we were going (he thought) to turn it out of the worship, by degrees, for we had got to singing but one Stave. I answer'd that this was only in extreme Cold Day, or while they were so short that we needed to redeem time, and to Satisfie such people as had most frequently been very uneasy that they could not get home to their Cattle sooner. And therefore it was exceeding unreasonable to complain of that. May the Lord pitty and pardon us, for his names sake! My Wife in the Meantime was extreme full of pain, and when the Company retir'd home I rode to Mr. Maynards and would have got Nathan to go for Mrs. Forbush (the Midwife) but he was not at home. His Brother Ebenezer offer'd to go; whilst I went myself for Captain Maynards wife: and those Two women were here all night.

24. Mrs. Maynard return'd home. Mrs. Forbush tarrys. The weather changes to a Snow Storm. Yet I rode to Mr. Joseph Knowltons after his son Jacob to hire him for the year. Heard there that Mr. Samuel Crosby dy'd last night, a considerable Loss! I was at Mr. Bellows's, Mr. Samuel Fays, Mr. Greens, and Mr. Francis Whipple's. My wife, at my return, much the Same as when I left her.

25. Cold, clear Day. Mrs. Forbush here still—my wife in great pain—but very chiefly in her side. A time of much Distress with her. May the Lord prepare our Hearts with Suitable Frames to wait his holy will! Very Cold at Night.

26. My Wife has somewhat more distinct Travail pains, but desires to consult Dr. Gott. Thomas rode to Marlborough with a Letter to him. He went also to his Master Williams's, to bring up some More of his Things, and to know more of his Mind, since he had put a Stop to bringing away his Chest. Thomas carried likewise a Letter directed to the Reverend Mr. Loring, to be lodg'd at Mr. Jonathan Lorings for Conveyance. P.M. My Wife desires the Assistance of Neighbouring Women. I tackled up the Slay and went for old Mrs. Whipple and Mrs. Kitty Rice, then for Mrs. How and her Dauter Molly. Old Mrs. Maynard being notify'd came again; and I had the help of Nathan Maynard to bring Captain Forbush's Wife. Thus we were waiting upon the Divine Pleasure this Evening. Thomas in Return from Marlborough has brought a Letter and Druggs from the Doctors, and word from Mr. Williams (of Marlborough) that he will Shortly come and see me.

27. About 4 this Morning came Captain Forbush's Wife to my Bed Side, and waking me wish'd me Joy with my new Son which was newly born, a lusty Child and the Mother in great Comfort. The Name of God be glorify'd! for tho weeping may endure for a Night, yet Joy comes in the Morning. May this Child (with all my others) graciously given me of God, be the Lords! Devoted to his Service and an Instrument of his Glory! A very fine pleasant Day. Thomas waited on Mrs. Whipple, and Mrs. Eleazer Rice's wife home in the Slay. The Rest went home o'foot. Thus I had very little Trouble in gathering the Women, or waiting on 'em home. Thomas brought the widow Mary Fay[16] to nurse, and she watch'd.

28. Thomas rode to Mr. Edward Goddards[17] and brought me 3 large Cheeses all of them being 37½ weight at 3 Shillings per pound. Mercy Maynard[18] watch'd.

29. Tis now 13 Year since my dear wife (Mary) dy'd—but God has turn'd our Sorrows into Joys. A.M. I read Genesis 19, and gave some brief glances upon it. Preach'd on Neh. 9, 6, repeating my old sermon on that Text. It was Seasonable after what we have lately experienc'd. Mr. Upham and Granny Forbush[19] din'd here. P.M. I read and briefly remark'd upon Matthew 19. Preach'd on 1 Tim. 2, 15. N.B. I began it with a very Cautionary Introduction extempore, but I think there was no great need of it. My Twelfth, Eleventh living, Child was publickly dedicated to God and baptiz'd. In Honour of my worthy and Reverend Father in Law[20] and excellent Friend I call'd him Breck. May the Lord graciously accept of him and bless him! and make him a Blessing in his Generation! The Granny and not the Nurse held him up. The Young Widow, Sarah Forbush Stay'd and watch'd. N.B. My Wife has been somewhat faint and weak, but was got up to Day. At Eve, She having endured a great deal of pain in her Hipp (She supposes tis the same flatulent pain which had before been so troublesome in her Side) and nothing past thro her since last Thursday, I sent my son Thomas to Dr. Gott, and had Return from him the Same Night.

30. Endeavour'd some Retirement and Abstinence on Consideration of the Troubles I was in when my former wife lay dead. I would not forget the Wormwood and the Gall: and may my Soul be humbled in me! Brother Hicks here. It happened to be a Sad Interruption to me—by Enquirys about the Settlement of Mother Champneys Estate; but Especially by uneasiness about a particular trifling article of the Goods which put me out of Frame to see him so Stiff and Disobliging to me—only about Father Champneys old Sword. I desire to bewail my ill frames on Such Days! Mrs. Fay, our Nurse, watched herself, again.

31. P.M. visited Mr. Abner Newton who has been sometime confin'd by Indispositions. And was also at Mr. Ebenezer Rice's. Mrs. Hannah Maynard rode home with me and Watch'd. N.B. The Neighbourhood full of Talk of Robert Cook and Sarah Crosby, Two Young Things who propose Marriage.

### FEBRUARY, 1749

1. I went over to Neighbour Hows. Sarah Crosby[1] having liv'd here awhile I warmly inveigh'd against the Libertys allow'd to Young people. No watcher with my Wife.

2. My Wife grows better, one Day after another. Reflected on the Sorrows of my Family when my former wife was bury'd, this

---

[13] Henry Ainsworth (d. 1622) was a prominent non-conformist minister who belonged to the Brownists. He wrote many works which were published in England.
[14] Caleb Upham (Harvard 1744).
[15] Ezekiel Dodge (Harvard 1749).

[16] The widow of Captain John Fay.
[17] An early settler of Shrewsbury.
[18] The daughter of David Maynard.
[19] The widow of Thomas Forbush.
[20] The late Reverend Robert Breck, Sr., of Marlborough.
[1] The daughter of David Crosby of Shrewsbury.

Day 13 Years agoe. Old Mr. Maynard here just after we had weigh'd the Infant, weight 10½. At Eve Mr. John Chamberlin here. Also Mr. Eliezer Rice and wife—these last supp'd with me.

3. Mr. David Woodwell here and receiv'd the Contribution of our Congregation for the Redemption of his Dauter out of Captivity, viz. £29.11.11 old Tenor.

4. The Child Sore Mouth.

5. Read the 20th of Genesis. I preach'd on John 12, 26. P.M. read 20th of Matthew and preach'd on Heb. 12, part of 10, 22 and 23. N.B. Mrs. Susanna Tainter of Watertown din'd here. Hephzibah Crosby watch'd.

6. Town Meeting to call in Debts. I sent the Town a Paper respecting my arrears in the year (44) per hand of Captain Maynard.[2] Marry'd Robert Cook[3] and Sarah Crosby at his Fathers.

7. I rode to Southborough and din'd at Mrs. Stone's.[4] His Wife had the Mid-wife with her, but the Women had dispers'd to their Several Homes. I proceeded in my Journey to Sudbury—to Deacon Mores to get him to die a large Deer skin for me. I went at Eve to Mr. Lorings,[5] his son Nathan's Wife ill. The old Gentleman in Trouble about some New Dissentions in his Parish (Several members of Mr. Bliss's Church at Concord desir'd to partake at their Communion but were deny'd). I lodg'd there.

8. I found the way to Mr. Jotham Browns—but he was not at home—din'd with his Wife and talk'd about my son Thomas's living there. P.M. I went to Mr. Abijah Haynes's—and the Storm increasing very tediously I consented to their repeated Invitation to tarry there—lodg'd with one Puffer in that House on a Visit but belonging to Castle William. N.B. read the new Act about Silver Money—account of Lord Lovat.[6]

9. A rugged morning—went to Mr. Browns again. He agreed to take Thomas. I had Mr. William Rice's Company from Mr. Lorings. Din'd at Deacon More's. When I got up to Dr. Gotts heard that Mr. Stones[7] Spouse is given over. Call'd at Mr. Smiths.[8] When I got home found there had been Three sorrowful messages. A man from Mr. Stones to desire me to visit him in his Affliction. One or Two from Mr. Tomlin, his Child being Dead, and a Letter from Holden concerning an appointed Fast there on occasion of the Throat Distemper at which they desire my assistance.

10. In the morning visit Brother Stone—his wife departed yesterday p.m. A very sore Breach upon him—May God Support him and afford all needed Mercy to him and his dear Children! Mr. Noah Brooks[9] here going to Mr. Martyn to desire him to administer the Lord's Supper to the Church of Grafton. Our Infant Child has a somewhat bad Sore Mouth. Attended the Funeral of Mr. Tomlins Child. Mrs. Thankful Maynard watch'd.

11. Disappointed of Changing tomorrow with Mr. Martyn. I did what I could to prepare my Self. But at about 11 at night came Mr. Ebenezer Johnson from Southboro requesting me to change tomorrow with Mr. Minot[10] of Concord, who would preach at Acton and Mr. Swift[11] for Mr. Smith, Mr. Smith would come to supply my place whilst I should go to Southboro. Accordingly

12. I rode to Southborough and met Mr. Smith coming here. I preach'd for Mr. Stone (who was present) on occasion of his dear Spouse's Decease. Text a.m. Ez. 24, 16. P.M. on Mat. 24, 44. Mr. Nicols of Boston among us. I return'd at Eve.

13. This was the Sorrowful Day of the Funeral of Mrs. Judith Stone, the amiable and lovely Spouse of my Brother Stone of Southborough. Mr. Cushing and Mr. Martyn came and though a Snowy Time I went with them to the House of Mourning. The

Reverend Mr. Loring pray'd. The Pall Bearers were plac'd thus Mr. Loring and Mr. Cushing, Mr. Barrett[12] and I, Mr. Martyn and Mr. Smith. The carrying Bearers were Justice Liscomb[13] and Deacon Amsden,[14] Deacon Woods[15] and Captain Brigham.[16] There were several other ministers besides the foremention'd. Mr. Perkins[17] of Bridgewater, Mr. Cotton[18] of Woburn, Mr. Swift of Acton, Mr. Reed of Framingham, besides Mr. Weld[19] of Attlebury who was the deceaseds Brother in Law. May God take up his Dwelling with and Comfort the Mournfull Husband, take up the Motherless Children and remember them in his gracious Covenant and awaken all survivers to a diligent preparation for our own Decease! Mr. Cushing return'd home with me. Found my son Ebenezer from Harvard, there.

14. I rode up to Mr. Cushings, who was sent to also by the Reverend Mr. Davis and the Church and people under his Care, to assist in the Services of the intended Fast at Holden, on account of the Throat Distemper lately among them. We had a Cold Ride—called at Mr. Phinehas Haywoods—found 'em all well at Mr. Davis's, tho their Neighbours were very distress'd. An exceeding Cold Night.

15. In the Morning came Mr. Buckminster[20] and Mr. Maccarty. The Public Exercises of the Fast were carry'd on thus, Mr. Davis began with prayer. I preach'd on Rev. 6, 8. Mr. Buckminster pray'd after sermon. P.M. Mr. Maccarty pray'd, Mr. Cushing preach'd on [blank] and I concluded. Mr. Cushing and I lodg'd at Mr. Davis's.

16. The Weather somewhat Moderator. Mr. Cushing was my Company to Shrewsbury. We went in to see Mrs. Crosby (Mr. David Crosbys Wife) and in talking of the Marriage of her Dauter Sarah to Robert Cook, I told her that his Brother Jonathan Certify'd me in the presence of the Company at the wedding that she (Mrs. Crosby) did give her Consent to it: but Mrs. Crosby said she did not, but that Robert had obtained her Leave to court her Dauter, and nothing else but that he had come and ask'd her Pardon, as to anything he had offended her in. Din'd at Mr. Cushings—preach'd the Lecture for him on Rom. 8, 7. Cold and Stormy P.M. and at Eve. I rode home in a snow storm. Mrs. Molly Martyn here. She came yesterday—she was brought by Ebenezer and Forbush—and there had been considerable Company besides here.

17. Cold and blustering. P.M. Mr. Martyn sent his Lad for Mrs. Molly, who therefore accordingly left us. N.B. I brought home from Holden the bloody Assizes in the West,[21] and an Epitome of Ecclesiastical History.[22]

18. Mr. Martyn here in his way to Grafton. N.B. he is going up in order to administer the Lord's Supper there.

19. Read Gen. 22. Mat. 22. Preach'd on Mat. 25, 46. Mr. Upham.

20. Mr. John Mead here. Mr. Wellman.[23] Mr. Martyn in his return from Grafton. Ebenezer rode up to Worcester o'mind to see Mr. Johnson the Smith.

21. Visit Mr. Benjamin Hows Family, 2 or 3 of his Children being under the Throat Distemper, especially Betty. At Eve Mr. [blank] Stone of Lexington (about to marry Hannah Holloway) here, with Gideon Hayward, to invite Ebenezer and Molly to Wedding tomorrow, but Ebenezer was gone (this Day) to Harvard again. My Mare Lame which proves no small Trouble.

22. At the Funeral of one of Mr. Thaddeus Gale's Twins, and

[2] John Maynard.

[3] The son of Cornelius Cook of Westborough.

[4] The Reverend Nathan Stone.

[5] The Reverend Israel Loring of Sudbury.

[6] Simon Fraser, twelfth Lord Lovat (1667?-1747), was a notorious Jacobite schemer and the author of numerous works published in England.

[7] The Reverend Nathan Stone of Southborough.

[8] The Reverend Aaron Smith of Marlborough.

[9] The son of Ebenezer Brooks of Grafton.

[10] Timothy Minot (Harvard 1718), a Concord schoolmaster who preached occasionally. Sibley, VI, 257-258. See Shattuck, Concord, p. 164.

[11] The Reverend John Swift, Jr., of Acton.

[12] The Reverend Samuel Barrett of Hopkinton.

[13] Samuel Lyscom or Lyscomb, a justice of the peace.

[14] John Amsden.

[15] David Woods.

[16] Timothy Brigham.

[17] The Reverend Daniel Perkins (Harvard 1717), the minister of Bridgewater, 1721-1782. Sibley, VI, 208-211.

[18] The Reverend Josiah Cotton (Harvard 1722), the minister of Woburn, 1747-1756. Sibley, VII, 50-56.

[19] The Reverend Habijah Savage Weld (Harvard 1723), the minister of Attleborough, 1727-1782. Sibley, VII, 268-272.

[20] The Reverend Joseph Buckminster of Rutland.

[21] James Bent, The Bloody Assizes: or, a Compleat History of the Life of George Lord Jeffries (London, 1689). There were several later editions.

[22] [John Shirley], An Epitome of Ecclesiastical History (London, 1692). Shirley had previously published Ecclesiastical History Epitomized . . . Part the First (London, 1682).

[23] The Reverend James Wellman of Millbury.

after the Funeral I visited Mr. Abner Newton who is still confin'd. Mr. Upham moves from Captain Bakers to Captain Maynards and keeps School there. Mr. Nurse blooded my mare. Snow'd exceeding Fast.

23. Mr. Martyn and his Spouse made us a Visit, and din'd here. Mr. Upham also—and Spent the Evening with me. At Neighbour Hows—Betty grows worse.

24. I rode over to Deacon Forbush's—din'd at his son Jonathan's—proceeded as far as to Mr. Thomas Chaddocks (at Hopkinton)—agreed with him about his Son Thomas's living with me. This was an Affair of great Necessity because my son Thomas has tarried so long at home that there are several Dangers by means of it; and I foresee that I can't go in the beginning of the week—but then indeed my son must (if possible) go away. Yet it was not without some regret that I left my study having been almost throughout the week hitherto, so hinder'd. At Lieutenant Tainters at Evening.

25. A message from Mr. Hows that Betty is dead, and to be bury'd today. I attended the Funeral. Hephizibah Crosby has been here for some Days spinning. Mrs. Fay here nursing still, for my wife gets well slowly.

26. Oblig'd to take some old preparations for both a. and p.m. What I had endeavour'd to prepare not being ripened. I therefore repeated sermon from Ps. 78, 11 on Occasion of the Throat Distemper being among us again at Mr. Hows—Betty How dead and 2 more Children sick there. Mr. Upham, Mr. Lawrence and Mr. Chaddock din'd here. Mr. Chaddock brought his son Thomas to live here with me.

27. It being proprietors meeting at Marlborough to Day, I thought it best (as Solomon directs Prov. 25, 9) to go over to Mr. Charles Rice's to talk with him about the Land which Lieutenant Hezekiah Ward had taken up for me on the plain. He shewed me his Deeds, but had not the Plott which was needed. Sent by Mr. Ebenezer Rice for some Number of Things to Boston. Call'd to visit Mr. Williams.[24] My Mare Lame yet. Stopp'd the Church to offer Mr. Lawrence[25] and Mrs. Oak's[26] Desire to be dismiss'd to Bolton, and to quicken the Church again in contributing at Communion.

28. Sent my son Thomas to Mr. Jotham Brown of Sudbury, Sadler, to work with him, and Lieutenant Tainter, kindly, rode with him and brought back my Horse. Mrs. Rice very bountifully gives me the greatest part of her Nursing here now more than a Month instead of 5£ She takes only 42 shillings old Tenor.

MARCH, [1749]

1. Din'd with the Officers at Captain Maynards, at the Invitation of Colonel Ward some Days ago. Messers Chushing, Martyn, Smith, Roberts and Upham there. Captain Willard receiv'd a Major Commission. Hepzibah Crosby here this week also. N.B. Dr. Gott here likewise but return'd not well.

2. Should have Expected Mr. Maccarty to preach my Lecture, but it was a very rainy Day and he did not come. I preach'd (to a thin assembly) on John 7, 4.

3. Mr. Roberts, who preach'd for Mr. Martyn yesterday, din'd here. Mrs. Fay now left us, and Still would take nothing more than I had given her for her Nursing. Hepzibah Crosby talks with me about her making a profession. My wife has gone a little into the Kitchen for several Days.

4. Mrs. Fay (our Nurse) came at Evening to Stay with us over the Sabbath.

5. A.M. I read Genesis 24 in part. Preach'd on Mat. 22, 37, 38, and administered the Lords Supper. Mr. Upham did not dine with us being gone to Grafton. P.M. I Read Matthew 24 in part. Preach'd on Mat. 25, 46.

6. Town Meeting. At their request I pray'd with them. At Evening Mr. Daniel Hardy was in a Sudden Flame at my House, because I offer'd to return him a bad 5/ Bill which I had took of him.

7. Mrs. Fay tarried with us till today. I carried her to her son Benjamin Fays. I visited old Mr. Samuel Fay. Din'd at

Mr. Phinehas Hardys. Visited at Mr. Samuel Hardy and James Millers. Proceeded to Upton to the Funeral of Mr. Samuel Forbush's Child—a Second Child of theirs which has dy'd of the Throat Distemper. Tarried a little at Ensign Millers. After Burying visited Mr. Abner Newton who is still confin'd.

8. Preach'd at Southboro Lecture on Song 2, 16.

9. Read Life and Character of the late Reverend Dr. Colman.[1] Admirable weather.

10. Hepzibah Crosby discourses with me about her joining with the Church.

11. As we were at Morning Exercise came the Reverend Elihu Spencer,[2] Missionary to the Mohawks on Onohaughguage. I persuaded him to stay and keep Sabbath here—for I was in very Special need of him to preach for me. He breakfasted with me and consented. Mr. Upham here p.m. At Eve I ask'd him to come tomorrow Evening.

12. Mr. Spencer preach'd a.m. on Eph. 2, 8 after I had read the 24th Chapter of Genesis and offer'd my Observations on the whole. Mr. Upham din'd here. P.M. Mr. Spencer preach'd on John 1, 11, after I had read Matthew 24 and made my Observations on the whole of it. A Rainy Time. Mr. Upham here at Eve as I had invit'd him, and he stay'd over night. Mr. Spencer in his Conversation goes on in the Accounts of what he did and went through at Onohoughguage. N.B. In public I read the Act against Cursing etc.

13. Mr. Spencer to Boston. I attended the Funeral of Mr. Thaddeus Gales other Infant Twin. Mr. Maccarty made us a Visit and tarried over Night.

14. Mr. Maccarty to Boston. Lieutenant Tainter[3] came and winnow'd out my Barley.

15. Rode to Marlborough to Deacon Tainters[4] and din'd there. Went to Mr. Joseph Williams to get some Things for Thomas but could not get at 'em by reason that the Lock seem'd to have been Strain'd, whether by anybodys trying to open it or by what other means can't be found. From thence I proceeded on my Design'd Journey to Mr. Jotham Browns, who with his Lads were gone to a Raising at Mr. Dakins—going there I was compell'd to tarry and sup with 'em; and then (though it was by this Time Candle-Light) I was oblig'd to visit and pray with his aged Mother. One Mr. Buss of Concord was going home, with his Wife and they were my Company, in the Evening Ride further. Mr. Buss accompany'd me to Mr. Bliss's[5] where I lodg'd.

16. In the Morning Mr. Bliss was going to a Fast at Mr. Farrars[6] and my own Business requir'd me to make Dispatch. Was a little while at Mr. Minots. But my Design was to find out one Mr. Isaac Taylor, a Gunsmith, with whom I desir'd my son Ebenezer Should live a while to learn that [crossed out] and what else falls into that Trade. I accordingly went to him and talk'd with him, who deferr'd determining, and promis'd to send me a Letter. Visited Mr. Whiting,[7] and Captain Peter Prescott[8]—din'd with the Latter—brought from him the works of Machiavell—also a Number of Roots, Cyons and Branches to propagate Mullbery Trees, and Pear Trees etc. Call'd at Deacon Rice's in my way up. Mr. Stone of Southborough came there. We rode together to Marlborough. I lodg'd at Mr. Smiths.

17. Home. Captain Maynard had come, and with Lieutenant Tainter kill'd a Young Swine of between 7 and 8 score. Neighbour Rogers salted down our pork, and Mr. Daniel Warrin of Shrewsbury brought me an Hive of Bees.

18. I rode up to Worcester against a very Cold wind. Got up in season.

---

[1] Ebenezer Turell, *The Life and Character of the Reverend Benjamin Colman, D.D.* (Boston, 1749).

[2] (Yale 1746). Spencer had been ordained in Boston, Sept. 14, 1748. He later served numerous Presbyterian parishes in New Jersey, New York, and Delaware. Dexter, *Biographical Sketches*, II, 89–92.

[3] Simon Tainter, Jr.

[4] Simon Tainter, Sr.

[5] The Reverend Daniel Bliss of Concord.

[6] Deacon Samuel Farrar.

[7] The Reverend John Whiting (Harvard 1700) was the minister of Concord, 1711–1737. He opposed the Great Awakening, and New-Lights, pressing a charge of intemperance, secured his removal through an ecclesiastical council in October, 1737. *Sibley*, IV, 532–535.

[8] (Harvard 1730). He practiced law in Boston and Concord, served in the Louisbourg campaign of 1745, and in several others of the French and Indian War. Prescott was also the clerk of the proprietors of what became Peterborough, N.H. *Sibley*, VIII, 772–774.

---

[24] Eleazer Williams.

[25] Both Mr. and Mrs. Benjamin Lawrence were dismissed to the Bolton church.

[26] Mrs. Nathaniel Oake.

19. After a very cold Night a very bright morning. I preach'd a. and p.m. on Eph. 3, 8. N.B. Mr. Putnam,[9] a Lawyer, diets at Mr. Maccartys. N.B. The Church Stop'd at Noon an send me a prayer desiring me to give public Notice of their agreement to have a Contribution on the approaching Fast, for a person that had in years past dwelt in Worcester, but whose dwelling was lately consum'd. This I comply'd with—as well as their Custom of Reading publickly the holy Scriptures. I had purpos'd to tarry over the Sabbath and till Monday at Worcester, but because of the Fast approaching and the great likelihood of another storm, I set out at Eve and rode to Shrewsbury. Met Mr. Maccarty (who preach'd for me on 2 Cor. 6, 2, and 2, Epistle of John 10, 4. I lodg'd at Mr. Cushings, because of the Snow Storm which now came on. N.B. Master Job[10] went off Friday night was sennight. Mr. Maccarty read Chapter 26 of Genesis and Matthew at Westborough. N.B. My wife went to meeting today; first after her Lying in. God's Name be prais'd!

20. When I return'd home Several Letters were deliver'd me which my Brethren had sent me. My Eldest Brother[11] in great concern for his only son[12] who droops again and in much affliction by Mr. Nathaniel about his deceased son John's Estate. Mr. Martyns boy here with a Letter to change next Sabbath.

21. Snow Storm again. Neighbour Pratt took my oxen to keep, for a short Space. Daniel Hastings came with his Cousen Benjamin Tainter, and agrees to work for me, without determining how long, or for how much but leaves it with his uncle Tainter. Little Breck not well.

22. Mr. Upham here. Several Neighbours came to get wood for me. Neighbour Eliezer Rice came with his Team, and my young man Daniel Hastings went with mine. Those that cutt were Messers Tinny, Noah How, Elijah and Adonijah and Edmund Rice and Benjamin Whipple. They got me a good pile of Excellent Solid Wood. N.B. Mr. Simon Tainter of Grafton here and brought me a Letter from Mr. Hall of Sutton, inclosing a Remarkable one from Mr. Edwards of Northampton to him to be communicated to me containing Extracts from Letters from Scotland of the Good Tokens repecting Religion in some very eminent Persons in Great Britain—some of the Royal Family, the Archbishop of Canterbury—Esquire West etc.—and in Holland, the prince of Orange. A great Interruption by the Company today in my preparations for the solemnity approaching. N.B. The school ceases.

23. Public Fast. I preach'd on Isa. 58, 1 to 7. N.B. Abraham Bond fainted in the Assembly.

24. In the Morning Mr. Upham here before he went home to his Fathers at Leicester.

25. Daniel is preparing and bespeaking Cattle, that we may have a Team to break up. As for myself, am oblig'd to be closely Employ'd in my Preparations for the Sabbath.

26. My Thoughts had wrought very much about my Preparations, having had but little Time, and many avocations and Encumbrances, in so large a Family. Yet God was pleas'd to assist beyond all my Deserts [sic]. I desire to bemoan my slothfulness and Negligence but would humbly rely upon the infinite Grace and Mercy of God in Christ to pardon my many Defects. I preach'd upon 1 John 3, 3 a. and p.m. Mrs. (Beriah's) Rice and Mrs. (John) Chamberlin din'd here.

27. I went abroad very Early because of what we had before us. Was at Mr. Nurse's[13] where I had a plough, and at Ebenezer Rice's. With the following Team and assistance we broke up the ground next to the Swamp. Besides Daniel with my own Oxen, Neighbour John Rogers with his, Neighbour Tomlin with his, and Nathan Maynard with theirs; to which add Neighbour Benjamin Hows. P.M. Nathan Maynard drew off, and Stephen Maynard came to work in his room with another Yoke of Oxen, so that we had p.m. 12 Oxen and turn'd it over pritty well. Mr.

Tomlin and Stephen Maynard gave in their work and their Cattle—Neighbour Rogers was very moderate in his Demands. Mr. Dunlop in the Garden the same Day.

28. Ebenezer came home from Harvard. I went over to visit Mr. Martyn p.m. but he was gone to Boston. Dr. Gott sick at Boston.

29. A.M. Visit Mrs. Deborah Brigham. P.M. to widow Crosby's to buy a Cow, but did not succeed. At Mr. Joseph Knowltons. At Eve Mrs. Deborah Brigham worse, sent for me. I went at 9 Evening, Ebenezer with me. I conceive her to be under hysterical Disorders: But She Said it was thro the Distress of her soul concerning her Eternal Condition.

30. Lecture to Young People on Ps. 119, 136. The widow Lucy Pratt,[14] (heretofore Whipple) here about her Souls State. Deacon Miles from Boston, here at Even.

31. Rain, Snow, Hail.

## APRIL, 1749

1. Snow. Receiv'd a Bundle of Young Vines, Trees and Branches from Monsieur [Stephen] Boutineau of Boston. Mr. Eliezer Rice here, who ask'd me whether I was to preach at the north side. I told him, yes.

2. Preach'd at the North side on Mat. 25, 46, former part. Mr. Martyn, for me on 1 Pet. 3, 18. I lodg'd at Mr. Martyns.

3. Return'd home. Ebenezer and Daniel making Wall on the Southside of my Land joining to my Neighbour Ebenezer Maynard. Old Mr. Willson of Bolton here. Talk'd with him about his joining to the Church of England. Mr. Putnam of Worcester, Lawyer, here with a Letter from Mr. Maccarty desiring me to preach his Lecture on the 13, which I am oblig'd to deny because of the Fast at Sudbury and our own Lecture the same week.

4. Should have gone to the Funeral of Abijah Gale's Child, but the Rain and some Rheumatick indispositions prevented. Edward Baker Esquire made me a visit, to ask me to preach at his House next Thursday.

5. Was somewhat troubled with Rhuematic pains. Hephzibah Crosby here. Neighbour David Batheric here. Mr. Jesse Maynard came here in behalf of Brother Jotham to carry away the Cart wheel which I had borrow'd of Captain Maynard.

6. Preach'd at Edward Baker's Esquire, on Mat. 26, 41, and after Exercise I read some part of Mr. Edwards's long Letter of Extracts etc. respecting Religion in Europe. At Merchant Rice's at Evening—Daughter Molly with me.

7. Daniel Splitting thills[?], up by the House.

8. Ebenezer ploughing Stubble Ground. P.M. Rheumatic Pains increas'd much in my right arm. A great hindrance to me—at Night especially.

9. At first waking I did not expect to go to meeting. Yet growing better when I got up, I did; and preach'd all Day—Text 1 Tim. 6, 12. Lay hold on Eternal Life. N.B. Mary Garfield[1] of Shrewsbury (of about 22) fell into fitts in the Meeting House, was carry'd out and remov'd to my House. Her fitts were repeated in the Evening. She had some Number of them. Her mother and Two Brothers here; Mrs. Garfield and son Moses here with Mary over night. My son Ebenezer went about 9 at Night to Dr. Smith[2]—but he would not come.

10. Mary Garfields fitts are not only Histeric but convulsive—increas'd to strong Convulsions. At length her Father came. They undertook to get her home. Mrs. Miller (James junior's wife) here to be examin'd. P.M. Mr. Batherick on the like account. Very Warm and Spring like. Ebenezer graffing Cyons from Cornet Bright of Watertown. Daniel ploughing Stubble ground.

11. Ebenezer a.m. works for Samuel Bumpso. Daniel ploughing stubble ground. A very fine pleasant, warm Day. P.M. Ebenezer graffing. Forbush who has been sick at College, here.

12. Undertook a Journey to Sudbury, it being the Day appointed by the Association for the First Fast on Consideration of the sad Signs of threatning Degeneracy and Defection in Reli-

[9] James Putnam (Harvard 1746), a native of Danvers, was just beginning his practice in Worcester. He became attorney general of Massachusetts, but fled from the province in 1776 because of his Loyalist sympathies. Lincoln, *Worcester*, pp. 192–193.

[10] The son of the Reverend Job Cushing of Shrewsbury. See Ward, *Shrewsbury*, p. 253.

[11] William Parkman of Boston.

[12] Nathaniel Parkman. Three other sons in this family had died.

[13] William Nurse.

[14] Lucy, the daughter of Francis Whipple of Westborough, had married Moses Pratt of Hardwick.

[1] The daughter of Daniel Garfield.

[2] Joshua Smith, the physician of Shrewsbury.

gion. Rode first to Mrs. Deborah Brigham and pray'd with her. Thence (concluding Mr. Smith was gone) I went hastily to Deacon Tainters[3] in Marlborough and so to Mr. Lorings. But he was surpriz'd to see me, he having put by the Fast by reason of his wife's illness, and of this he had writ me a Line as he had done to other Members of the association but which I had never receiv'd nor knew one Lisp of till I got to Sudbury. After dining there, conversing with Madam Loring (who is Yet very low and weak) and Spending a little Time with Mr. Williams[4] of Weston who (in his way to Harvard) call'd there, I return'd to Marlborough. A storm arising made me call at Mr. Jabez Wards—where was Mr. John Weeks, and others. Mr. Ward is selling his Place and going to New-Marlboro. Mr. Weeks intimates to me that they grow sick of Mr. Jenison[5] who has hitherto kept School and preach'd among them. Stop'd a little with Mrs. Sally Gott[6] to enquire about her Father. At Mr. Smiths[7] into Evening yet got home and lodg'd at my own House. To God be praise and Thanks!

13. Mr. Abraham Williams[8] here. Tells me he has a Call at Sandwich—argues against the Duty of Fasting—calls it dressing up Religion in frightful Figures to terrifie Men—Says getting a Neighbour to kick ones shins or thrash one with an Horsewhip will do as well etc. He is going to Worcester to demand of Dr. Breck[9] the Legacy his grandmother Breck left him.

14. Mr. Cushing preach'd my Lecture. His Text Ps. 130, 3, 4. Ebenezer and Daniel cart muck a.m. and after Lecture.

15. Mr. Hancock of College call'd to know the Way to Mr. Martyns that he may Change with him tomorrow, by going to Grafton; and ask'd me to go next Sabbath.

16. Sacrament. Read Genesis 29. Preach'd on 1 Cor. 11, 31. Mr. Twitchell[10] and wife (who are lately come to dwell in this precinct) widow Woods and Bekky Warrin din'd here. P.M. I read Mark 1. Preach'd on 1 Sam. 16, 5, those words "Come with me to the Sacrifice." The Body of the Exercise was sermon on 1 Cor. 10, 16, from page 16 to the End of page 22. Mr. Martyn here both going to and returning from Grafton to Day—tells me Deacon Cooper has been dead this fortnight.

17. A Precinct Meeting—partly to provide for raising the New Meeting House, and among divers other Things to See whether they would pull off the Covering and Closing of the old Meeting House and Use them upon the New—but could not obtain a vote to meddle with it.[11] N.B. I sent in a Letter, which the Moderator (Esquire Baker) receiv'd; but without reading to the precinct, order'd to be return'd to me, which Lieutenant Forbush accordingly did. N.B. Captain Maynard here a.m. Also Mrs. Batherick. N.B. Mr. D. Heminway the Carpenter began to work in Framing of the New Meeting House. In the Morning I visited Mary Garfield who is now very weak and low, but expresses herself very sensibly and graciously.

18. Catechiz'd at the Meeting House both a. and p.m. Very Cool Weather. Ebenezer and Daniel ridering the upper Fence.

19. Last night rose out of my Bed and marry'd Joseph Rice[12] and Eunice Harrington. This morning a great Frost. Brother Hicks here. My wife and I rode over to Mr. Martyns—carry'd little Breck—we din'd there. Mr. Cushing came there. Return'd well at Evening.

20. Ebenezer and Daniel digging Stones for the South Wall between Mr. Ebenezer Maynard and me. Dr. Breck and his Wife came to see me. Doctor had unhappily turn'd over his Chair in coming and hurt one of his Hands: he was sick at Dinner and rose from the Table. Old Mrs. Whipple and her Granddauter Pratt here. Mrs. Pratt in Distress about her Spiritual State. N.B. Forbush[13] here—wants opportunity to talk with me, and with my wife that all Grounds of Offence in his acquaintance with Molly and his Conduct about her may be removed. Being in a low State of Health, he is going over to live at Dr. Scammells.[14]

21. Ebenezer and Daniel making Stone Wall, on the South side. A very warm Day. There seems to be great Need of Rain: but God who is the Father of Rain takes Care.

22. Though I sent by Brother Hicks on the 19th to Mr. Belcher Hancock of College that I could not well change with him yet he came at Evening. My English Hay is gone (having kept my Young Horse over Winter) which was beyond my Design, and hereby I became too much straitened. N.B. Ebenezer and Daniel making Stone Wall on the Southside, and not finish'd yet.

23. In the Morning I rode to Grafton for Mr. Hancock. Was entertain'd at Mr. Isaac Harringtons. I preach'd a.m. on Jer. 3, 15. At the Earnest Request of Mr. Joseph Axtell[15] and his Wife I preach'd to her at Evening at their House, She having lain Sometime under great Affliction and long confin'd from the Public Worship. My Text 1 Thess. 1, 10 last Clause. Rode home the Same Night following. Mr. Hancocks Text 1 John 3, 19.

24. Mr. Hancock and I rode over to Mr. Martyns where were Mrs. Monis and the late Colonel Vassals[16] widow (who came up with him last Saturday) and I waited on them a few Miles—Mr. Martyn and his wife further, in their Journey to Cambridge. I returned home by the way of Ensign Rice's and prevail'd with him to Spare me some Hay. N.B. Captain Maynard came to See me at my House and we have much Discourse about our Trouble by the Meeting-House being carry'd away from us. Samuel Bumpso worked with my Young Men in finishing the Wall on the southside and building a wall at the Back of my House. N.B. It grows a very dry Time. Very high winds. The Fires raged last Night and this at Hopkinton.

25. Read the Life of Colonel Gardner.[17] Daniel finishes the Wall in the back Yard from the East to the orchard Barrs. Ebenezer begins to plough for planting.

26. Mrs. Hephzibah Maynard[18] here a.m. Much Troubled about the New Meeting House place. Ebenezer work'd with Noah How, getting out Rails for him in Lieu of an 100 which he says my Hands carted away from him—but inadvertently. Daniel ploughing. P.M. Mrs. Lucy Pratt here, on her Spiritual Concerns. N.B. Brother Hicks here from Cambridge. He confirms the sad news of Mr. J. Davenports House as being burnt in Watertown on the 24th and of other Burnings in divers Towns. N.B. He and I finish'd a Troublesome affair that had lain some time between him and me.

27. Daniel ploughing. Ebenezer variously employ'd about the fences round the Yards etc. In the forenoon I was oblig'd to go down to Mr. Cook's to fasten my Horse's Shooes. Mr. Daniel Forbush[19] was there. He took Notice I had not yet been to the Timber (where they were framing the Meeting House). I told him I was going to preach to Mr. Martyns people. He said he believ'd the Committee would be glad (he doubted not) of Such an opportunity to Send a message by me to Mr. Martyn. He spoke in much Earnestness and intimating that they were at the Frame, who would thus be glad, and that they would send to my House. I went from thence to see old Mrs. Forbush[20] (nigh 85 years of age). But when I came out from her, I thought it would be best to ride round by the Meeting House place to give 'em opportunity and prevent their Sending on purpose to my House and as Mr. Forbush aforesaid intimated they would. I therefore came home that way. Captain Baker and Lieutenant Bruce[21] were very complaisant. I enquir'd whether the work went on well and how forward they were etc.? They told me the Time that

---

3 Joseph Tainter.

4 The Reverend William Williams.

5 William Jennison, sometime preacher, had kept school at one time in Westborough.

6 Sarah was the eldest daughter of Dr. Benjamin Gott of Marlborough.

7 The Reverend Aaron Smith of Marlborough.

8 The son of Colonel Abraham Williams of Marlborough. He accepted the Sandwich call.

9 Samuel Breck, the physician.

10 Jonas Twitchell, Twitchel, or Twichel.

11 The precinct voted "to provide Half a barrel of Roum, by the cost and charge of the precinct, for the Raising the frame of the meeting-house . . . Voted Capt. John Maynard, Lieut. Simon Tainter, Lieut. Abijah Bruce to be a committee to take care to provide the Roum." DeForest and Bates, Westborough, pp. 133-134.

12 The son of Josiah Rice.

13 Eli Forbush or Forbes as he spelled it.

14 Samuel Scammell, a native of Portsmouth, England, came to America about 1737. He served as a schoolmaster and then became well-known as a physician of Milford, Mass. Adin Ballou, History of the Town of Milford (Boston, 1882), II, 1004-1005.

15 The Axtells took up residence in the north part of Grafton about 1730. Pierce, Grafton, pp. 451-2.

16 John Vassal (Harvard 1732) of Cambridge had died Nov. 27, 1747. Sibley, IX, 229-235.

17 Philip Doddridge, Some Remarkable Passages in the Life of the Honourable Col. James Gardiner, who was Slain at the Battle of Preston-Pans September 21, 1745 (Boston, 1748).

18 The wife of Parkman's neighbour, Captain John Maynard.

19 The son of Deacon Jonathan Forbush.

20 The widow of Thomas Forbush.

21 Abijah Bruce.

they had last night agreed upon for the Raising Day—viz. Next Wednesday—But that they intended to send to me and to the Neighbouring Ministers, But as there was but one of the Committee there, Captain Baker, there could be no public message as yet to Mr. Martyn. I put em in mind to Send without Fail to his Spouse also. One Mr. Hastings, a Carpenter, brought me their bottle and offer'd to give me a Dram—which gave me occasion to talk with them about their offering (as I had heard) their Bottle to Travellers to beg of them as they pass'd in the high way: I talk'd with the Chief Workman Mr. Hemingway, but he vindicated himself. I told him I had rather give em, myself, Every Penny of what they Should so Collect—and I took out my Book to pay him what they Said had been given tho they Said it was only by Such as had turn'd aside to see them and that only by Two persons—one of which gave 3/, the other 1/. I parted as decently as I could professing my Concern to have Every Thing carry'd on in Righteousness, Peace and Honour. Esquire Baker, in his Conversation, inform'd me that at the Meeting last Night (which was of Such of the Inhabitants of the precinct as pleas'd to Show their Minds about the Provision they would make for the Raising) Some that were disaffected brought in a Petition to the Committee to raise a Meeting, if possible to remove the Spot for the Meeting House. But it was too late, and he said it could be thought no other than Vexatious, design'd so—by its being brought at this Time. Molly rode with me over to Mr. Martyns—Mr. Cushing and his wife came. We din'd there. The Drought So great that I turn'd my Thoughts from other Subjects, and preach'd (the Lecture) from Jer. 14, 22. The Lord grant us to acknowledge Him in all His Dispensations and wait on Him alone for Supply and Relief! In returning at Evening was in Danger at the Bridge by means of my Horse's Fright and Springing, at the loose Planks, especially one that was broken, but was safely upheld and got over without hurt.

28. Daniel finish'd ploughing the Field a.m. and plough'd the Yards by the House. The Beds of the Garden, by the Drought and by the Fowl, chiefly destroy'd. Mr. Walker of Nichewoag, who took Care of my Cattle last Year, was here. Agreed to give him 45 shillings for the Care of the Cattle, and 20/ for his pains after one of them could not get up (by 8 miles) At the Time of Driving up.

29. After great and distressing Drought, there came this Day a refreshing Rain. Colonel Hendsell[22] and his Spouse came in, but tarried not long. Ebenezer and Daniel planting the Yards. Had the Comfort of being seasonably prepar'd for the Sabbath. Deacon Newton came and in the Name of the Committee of the Precinct invited me and my wife to the Raising of the Meeting House next Wednesday.

30. Preach'd all Day upon Ps. 119, 60. Read a.m. Gen. 31, p.m. Mark 3, N.B. I gave the People a fervent Caution and Exhortation respecting their Conduct on the design'd Raising of a new Meeting House.

## MAY, 1749

1. Ebenezer and Daniel began to plant the Fields of Indian Corn. Mr. Phinehas Hardy kindly Sent his Son Noah to assist in it. Visited Mrs. Tainter who is ill, and din'd there. N.B. Benjamin Kicked and hurt by one of their Horses but revived.

2. Visited Mrs. Deborah Brigham who is yet ill. P.M. Was Sent for by the Society at the Framing the design'd Meeting House, to go and pray with them as they were now going to lay the Groundsills of the House. The persons who came with the message were Messers Biglo and Daniel Hardy. I went and pray'd with them and after prayer I put them in mind of what I had Said to them on the Lords Day past. N.B. a very Cold Wind—fear I took Cold. Indeed my Heart was too Cold, at least was very difficultly brought to this Work. I find Indeed a great deal of Wisdom and Grace to go through what is now called for. O that God would grant that as the Day is So my Strength may be! Finish'd planting.

22 Ebenezer Hinsdale (Harvard 1727) of Deerfield, had been the chaplain of Fort Dummer and missionary to the Indians. In 1742 he built the fort in what became Hinsdale, N.H. At this time Colonel Hinsdale was the representative of Deerfield. *Sibley*, VIII, 141-148. See Herbert C. Hinsdale, *Hinsdale Genealogy* (Lombard, Ill., 1906) pp. 84-87.

3. A.M. came Mr. Martyn and his Wife; Mr. Cushing also, and Mr. Stone and din'd with us. After Dinner we all rode over to the Raising of the New Meeting House. Mr. Barrett likewise came: and a great Concourse of people. The Frame went up well; and through God's great Goodness, Neither Life nor Limb lost. The only Hurt I have heard of was by the Fall of a Board which graz'd a man's forehead but Slightly. But the Impudence of Young Men with the Young Women was with them very Shameless. I was oblig'd to go and reprove several. Reverend Mr. Cushing, Barrett, Martyn and Stone refresh'd themselves with me at Deacon Newtons.[1] Mr. Cushing (when all the Timber was in place and the Frame compleated) Pray'd and gave Thanks. After which we sang Ps. 132, 10, 13-16 and there was a plentiful Entertainment. Mr. Barrett carved; Mr. Martyn Return'd Thanks after Supper. When the Company drew off we repair'd again to Deacon Newtons. N.B. Forbush brought a message from Mr. Frost[2] of Mill-River to desire me to change with him next Lords Day. I Spake of it to the Ministers, and Mr. Barrett oppos'd it, without Mr. Frost would retract his having an Hand in ordaining Mr. Reed[3] of Framingham. Mr. Martyn Seconded him so that I sent this return that I could not, but would be glad to see him and converse with him.

4. Daniel did not come to work today, many Watertown Friends of his being at his uncles. Mr. Joseph Phillips of Oxford here and din'd with us. P.M. Ebenezer went to help Neighbour Ebenezer Maynard. David Forbush and Anna Whitney[4] married. At Eve Daniel came and Sarah Harrington. Nathan Maynard and Benjamin Whipple in the Name of their Society (together with Ebenezer) presented me Daniel as desirous to be admitted among them, but I was not ready for an Answer, he having been but a little while among us.

5. Rainy a.m. Daniel makes a pair of Shooes for Alexander. P.M. Showery yet Ebenezer and Daniel went to the Ministerial Meadow to mend up the Fence.

6. Considerable Storm of Rain. My Mare foal'd.

7. A.M. read Genesis 32. Preach'd a. and p.m. on Ps. 119, 60. P.M. was very much mov'd. *Verba fuerunt Ardentia.* May God set them home on the Hearts of the Heavens! P.M. read Mark 4. N.B. Old Mrs. Whipple din'd with us.

8. Daniel Hastings sett out o'foot for Watertown. A.M. Mr. Mede[5] here. Lent Mr. Mead my Dult. Histor. both volumes. P.M. I went over to Neighbour Elijah Rice's, Tinneys,[6] and John Chamberlins—gather'd some Hair.

9. Five of my Cattle were driven by Mr. Francis Whipple etc. to Nichewoag. Ebenezer assisted as far as Shrewsbury. Ebenezer upon the Fences—middle Pasture. P.M. I rode round by Mr. Cooks to Mr. Nurses's, to Mr. Eliezer Rice's (his wifes sister being lately dead) and to both the Whipples. N.B. Old Mrs. Whipples Hair.

10. Molly went to Cambridge with Mr. Beriah Rice and his son Asaph. I accompany'd her as far as Mr. Daniel Warrins. Ebenezer a.m. looking up the sheep. P.M. he Carted Stones for Wall. Dr. Crawford and his Brother with their wives here. Sam Bumpso buying Land of Mr. Axtell, desires me to lend him money, which I did. Mrs. Miller here again. Reading Sir Isaac Newton on Daniel and the Revelations.

11. I rode over to the Northside. Din'd at Mr. Jacob Rice's—he not at home. He was gone to Lancaster to fetch Brick for Mr. Martyn. I went to Mr. James Balls to look of an Heiffer (which I bought) his price and which I agreed to was 20£ old Tenor. N.B. David Bates, an Young Man, there, who was bit by a Rattle snake last Tuesday. I was at Mr. Billings's[7] and at Mr. Asa Bowkers where was Mr. Cushing. Return'd at Evening.

1 Josiah Newton.

2 The Reverend Amariah Frost (Harvard 1740), the minister of Milford, Mass., 1742–1792. *Sibley*, X. 494-496.

3 The Reverend Solomon Reed of Framingham was a New-Light preacher. *Sibley*, X, 398-400.

4 The daughter of Nathaniel Whitney.

5 James Mead, an uneducated teacher and preacher, founded a New-Light church in Middleborough in 1756. Thomas Weston, *History of the Town of Middleborough* (Boston, 1906), p. 467, 475.

6 Stephen Tenney.

7 Thomas Billings.

12. Town Meeting to Choose a Representative. Mr. Francis Whipple Chose. At Eve Cousen Nathaniel Parkman (Ame and Daniel Hastings)—my Kinsman much out of Health: is come to tarry a while with us for Change of Air.

13. Very Hot. P.M. Mr. Cushing here. I rode to Shrewsbury.

14. Preach'd at Shrewsbury a. and p.m. on Jer. 8, 4, 5. I read there a.m. Genesis 36, p.m. Mark 8. Baptiz'd Two Children. Job son of Deacon Miles,[8] and Submitt of Benjamin Maynard. At Mr. Cushings Desire I acquainted the Church etc. with the design'd association Fast, and invited them to attend. At Eve I went in to Colonel Wards[9] to Weep with him and his Family, he being bereaved of his son Ithamar, of about 28 or 9 years by the Small Pox. He dy'd at the Pest House below Boston. I return'd home. Mr. Cushing was on *if once the Master of the House be risen up and put to the Door*, etc.

15. Daniel and Ebenezer look'd up and walk'd sheep a. and p.m. Wall behind the House p.m.

16. Held a Catechetical Exercise. Exposition of the Sixth Commandment. Daniel and Ebenezer on the wall northwest of the House.

17. My Kinsman and I rode to Shrewsbury Mr. Stone with us—to the Association Fast on the Account of the Declension in Religion. There were present Messers Loring, Cushing, Martyn, Stone, Seccomb, Smith, Davis, Mellen. Mr. Cushing pray'd (in publick) and Mr. Mellen preach'd on John 13, 17. P.M. Mr. Davis pray'd and Mr. Loring preach'd on Heb. 3, 2. N.B. There came a Letter to the Association sign'd Edward Goddard, Bragg, Simon Goddard and Benjamin Goddard manifesting their Dissent to the Fast—but no Notice was taken of it by the Association. N.B. Colonel Nahum Ward went to Boston the same Day— and said something to me of the ministers giving their people so little warning of the Fast—intimated also that he thought we had better lay the matter before our Churchs. N.B. Mr. Maccarty admitted. Mr. Swain[10] among us. N.B. The Association voted to have the Report of the Committee which contains the sum and substance of the answer etc. to be inserted in the Book of their Minutes. We return'd at Evening.

18. My Son Ebenezer and Daughter Lucy, together with my Kinsman rode over to Upton.

19. Daniel carry'd out the whole of our Ashes upon the New Ground, planted with Indian Corn.

20. Ebenezer and Lucy with our Kinsman return'd from Upton. Ebenezer work'd with Daniel p.m.

21. A.M. Read Genesis 34. Preach'd on Prov. 14, 19. P.M. read Mark 6, and repeated (for a sermon) with alterations (omissions and additions) my Exposition on Mat. 14, 1–12 which is the parallel to Mark 6, 14–29.

22. Was at Mr. Cooks, and likewise visted Neighbour Abner Newton under his Confinement and illness, and I din'd there— p.m. My Kinsman and Ebenezer rode over to Mr. Martyns. Daniel is clearing the lower end of the South Orchard. Mr. Samuel Williams and Mr. Charles Rice here. Abigail Baker making Stays here.

23. Ebenezer and Daniel began to weed. My Kinsman rides Every Day; and has somewhat better Stomach but is often in Sinking Dejection. A.M. frequently in some Trouble about young people's disorderly night walking: have now Such a Number (My son Ebenezer, Daniel Hastings, Abigail Baker[11] and Sarah Harrington) of young persons in my own Family that it causes me some Perplexity when my own do walk contrary to the advice and Counsel which I am frequently giving them.

24. Jonathan Bruce[12] was marry'd to Hannah Beeman.[13]

25. Preach'd the Lecture myself on 1 Cor. 11, 29. N.B. I us'd the answer to Scruple 4th in Sermon on 1 Cor. 10, 16 page 27 to 31.

26. Kinsman went home with Abigail Baker.

27. Thomas came from Sudbury, to See us. Tells me how extreme the Drought is at Sudbury.

28. Sacrament. Read Genesis 35. Preach'd on 1 Cor. 11, 31. P.M. read Mark 7. Preach'd on 1 Sam. 16, 5, using sermon on 1 Cor. 10, 16, from page 23 to 27 and from 31 to the End, with Additions on Rom. 14, 23.

29. My Kinsman Nathaniel (on Mr. James Bowman's Horse) Set out with me for Boston. We din'd at Mr. Farrars[14] in Framingham after a turn of Fishing in his River—lodg'd at Captain Tainters at Watertown—my Kinsman being much worn with the Journey thus far.

30. Went into Boston. Put up my Horse at Mrs. Keggells.[15] N.B. We had Stopp'd a While at Cambridge, and gave Deacon Whittemore order to deliver my Chair to Benjamin Hastings of Watertown; which I understand since, he accordingly did. Din'd at Mr. Procters.[16] Mr. Sweetzer has made me a new dark brown Wigg. Besides the Hair I provided, it cost me £4.14.0, and Mr. Eaton a Bever Hatt, 12£.

31. Mr. William Balch of Bradford preach'd the Election Sermon. The Day exceeding Hot. Din'd at Mr. Olivers—his Father and mother, and Brother and sister Lowden din'd there also. P.M. at Convention. Mr. Barnard[17] of Marblehead moderator. The Report of a Committee appointed last year, to consider of a Fund for society for Propagating the Gospel among the Indians took up much of the Time and was adjourn'd. Lodg'd at Brother Parkmans.

## JUNE, 1749

I attended the Convention. Was at the sermon. Mr. Barnard[1] of Andover preach'd on 2 Cor. 4, 1. The Contribution amounted to £ [blank]. I din'd at Mr. Cooper's.[2] P.M. I was so unavoidably taken up with my affairs that I could not go again to the Convention. My Horse was kept in the New North Meeting House Yard. Supp'd at Mr. Olivers. Lodg'd at Dr. Parkman's. The Distresses by the Drought very great. I meet with no man, not the oldest, that has ever known Such a Drought so Early in the Year.

2. I Set out from Boston (Mrs. Keggell having been so handsome as to charge nothing for my Horse keeping). The Heat was very great—call'd at Captain Sharps.[3] Mr. Cotton Brown[4] lodges there. I din'd at Mr. Benjamin Hastings in Watertown. Ephraim Holland p.m. my Company great part of the way up. Got home in the Night.

3. Our Hearts are pained for the parch'd Earth and wither'd Grass. I understand that some people are oblig'd to turn their Cattle into their mowing ground.

4. Read (by Mistake) Genesis 37—preach'd on Micah 6, 2. P.M. read Mark 8. At Eve visited Bethia Tylor who lys sick at Mr. Tennys.

5. Visited Neighbour Tomlin and Bethia Tyler. Catechiz'd both a. and p.m. at the Meeting House. The Earth is grown extremely dry. May God have Mercy on His people!

6. I feel very poorly—Weak and faint. Hot, burning Season.

7. Mr. Swain (preacher at Grafton) came to see me, and din'd here. P.M. Mr. Breck[5] came and Mr. Swain to Grafton. In the Night refreshing Showers. To God by the Glory! Thunder and Lightning. May God grant us the Grace we need, that we may improve his Favours to his Glory! and may He be pleas'd to grant further needed supplys!

8. Mr. Breck set out for Springfield. Cool bright Day. But I feel heavy whilst universal Nature is reviv'd and rejoic'd.

9. Sarah Henry came up from Boston, her aunt Hastings her

8 Samuel Miles.

9 Nahum Ward. Ithamar, returning from sea, died unmarried on Governor's Island in Boston harbor. Ward, *Shrewsbury*, p. 459.

10 Joseph Swain (Harvard 1744) later the minister of Wenham, 1750–1792. Myron O. Allen, *History of Wenham* (Boston, 1860), pp. 181–184.

11 The daughter of Edward Baker, Esq.

12 The son of Lieutenant Abijah Bruce.

13 The daughter of Eleazer Beeman.

14 Major John Farrar, the proprietor of a grist mill, held several town offices and in 1774 was named to Framingham's committee of correspondence. Temple, *Framingham*, pp. 544–545.

15 Mrs. Abel Keggell, the cousin of Mrs. Parkman.

16 Samuel Procter.

17 The Reverend John Barnard. _____

1 The Reverend John Barnard.

2 The Reverend Samuel Cooper (Harvard 1743), the minister of the Brattle Street Church in Boston.

3 Robert Sharp of Brookline.

4 The Reverend Cotton Brown (Harvard 1743), the minister of Brookline, 1748–1751.

5 The Reverend Robert Breck, Jr., of Springfield.

Company, who with her Son Benjamin came up in my Chair. The Honourable Captain Goddard[6] and his son Benjamin here, in their way to Framingham. Benjamin Hastings, Sarah and Elizabeth Tainter lodg'd here. Showers in the Night. Ebenezer and Daniel getting Rails and Posts.

10. Mrs. Hastings and her son Benjamin, Sarah and Elizabeth Tainter din'd with us. Several Excellent Showers very reviving and refreshing. Glory to God! Neighbour Eliezer Rice here. He pretends to ask my Leave for Dr. Green[7] to preach at his House—but I warn'd him against it. Ebenezer and Daniel setting out Cabbage and Tobacco Plants—and began to half-Hill the Indian Corn. Receiv'd Sundrys from Molly by Mr. Ebenezer Rice.

11. I read Genesis 36 and Mark 9 to 10, 30. Preach'd a. and p.m. on Prov. 14, 9 former part. Some Number Din'd with us. Mrs. Tainter and her sister Hastings, Benjamin Hastings, Eli Forbush, Mrs. Chaddock, Mrs. Deborah Brigham and Rebecca Warrin. Read the Proclamation for the public Fast.

12. Daniel and Ebenezer hoeing. A.M. I visited Bethiah Tyler and Mr. Tomlin. P.M. Cornelius Biglo junior came for me to visit his aged Grandmother Graves.[8] I went but She dy'd before I got there. Visit Neighbour Jonah Warrins Daughter Betty—and Neighbour Hezekiah Pratts infant who are sick.

13. The Drought very great. An hot Morning. Lieutenant Hezekiah Ward, was by appointment at Mr. Charles Rice's to measure the controverted Land, but he was content to wave the work and return home, and he did so. I visited Mr. Abner Newton. I talk'd earnestly against Dr. Greens preaching among us: I hope to Effect. My Young Men are at their half-hilling to Day, and Neighbour John Rogers helps them. They finish'd some time before Sun setting. There goes a great Storm of Thunder and Rain to the Northward. Scarce any Drops here.

14. At Mrs. Graves's Funeral a.m. Very Hot. Ebenezer and Daniel mowing. I have but little Time to prepare for the Fast approaching.

15. Public Fast on Account of the Great Drought. I preach'd on 2 Chron. 6, 26, 27, 31. I thought it best to deliver my whole Preparation in one Exercise, tho it takes me an Hour and quarter to deliver it,—then to break the Discourse, and loose the warmth and Force by dividing it. P.M. from Amos 4, 6 and 7, I also have given you etc.—Yet have ye not return'd unto me saith the Lord. I undertook to Shew that tho God had inflicted on us many Judgments yet we did not turn to Him as he justly might expect we Should, and tho it might seem to us that we did much in returning to Him, yet he Saw and knew us better—and I Enquired into this Matter more distinctly, to see what men might do, and yet there might be no true returning, and for Reply to this Enquiry, I used again those Articles in sermon on Acts [blank] from page 3 to page [blank]. And I hope it was, by Gods Blessing somewhat Beneficial. But O that God would give us the Grace to see what we are, turn us, and have mercy on us!

16. My Wife and I (now first) rode out in our Chair to visit Mr. Tomlin and Bethiah Tyler—but we proceeded as far as to Mr. Martyns and din'd there. We made our propos'd visits as we came back. I was indispos'd when I went out, and by means of the Great Heat, I grew much worse. When I return'd home, Mr. Charles Brigham was here; but I was So ill, I could not converse with him. I appointed him a Time to come again.

17. After a very ill night I rose somewhat comfortable. Blessed be God! The prospects abroad extremely Melancholly and sorrowful. My people mowing—but yet next to nothing for their pains. I gave them order to fence off Some of the ground for pasture. Mr. Samuel Harrington sent me with veal, a present to me—which was very acceptable—my Stomach being very poor. Very Hot Time—as if we should be burnt up with the Drought. I was little more than hanging about all Day.

18. In the Morning I rode over (according to agreement) to Mr. Martyns, and he came hither. I preach'd to his people on

Heb. 3, 17, 18 and p.m. what I deliver'd to my own the afternoon of the Fast from Amos 4, 6, 7. Mr. Martyn on 2 Pet. 3, 18. Extreme Hot Day. (So that Cakes of Chocolat melted on the Shelves tho they lay Single. It was So both at my House and at Mr. Martyns.) In returning at Eve we met at Mr. Tomlins, and pray'd with him.

19. Another Hot Day Still, but not so hot as Yesterday. Mr. Charles Brigham of Grafton examin'd. Aaron Warrin came to desire me to go over immediately to see his sister Betty—went on Captain Maynards Horse. A multitude gathered there to See her. Dr. Miles there. Mr. Daniel Hardy paid me above sixty five pounds old Tenor. Forbush came home with me. Brother Hicks here going to Boston in the Night.

20. Clear but cooler. Reckon'd with Captain Maynard and settl'd with him not only for the Year last past, but likewise in the Affair of his Rate in the 82£ which Mr. Billings was to have gather'd for the Year 44 from June 5 to October 20. Mr. Beton putts on Clouts upon the Axeltree of my Chair.

21. I rode to Sudbury to Association Fast. But few there. Only Mr. Stone, Mr. Smith and Mr. Davis. Afterwards came Mr. Gardner.[9] Not even Mr. Cook[10] there. P.M. Mr. Bridge[11] of Framingham came. Mr. Loring pray'd a.m. and Mr. Davis preach'd Text Rom. 2, 25. P.M. Mr. Smith pray'd and Mr. Gardner preach'd Text Rom. 2, 25. P.M. Mr. Smith pray'd and Mr. Gardner preach'd. Text Habac. 3, 2. N.B. Ebenezer and Forbush went in my Chair, in order to go to Cambridge, but they turn'd in to Sudbury meeting in the Afternoon. It prov'd an Hot Day. I return'd as far as Marlborough; lodg'd at Mr. Smiths with Mr. Davis.

22. Was at Mr. Ephraim Brighams, at Mr. Edward Barns's (where I bought Cheese) din'd at Deacon Matthias Rice's[12] (whose wife presented me with a Cheese) and then I return'd home. Here had been Mr. Solomon Reed and his Wife from New Haven and brought a kind Letter from Mrs. Pierpoint. Brother Hicks from Boston. Sorrowful Accounts of the Prevalence of the Drought. From Different Parts of the Province we hear that the Fish die in the Rivers through the Scantiness and heat of Waters. Hear that people in Marlborough have met (divers of them) to Fast and pray, and propose to again tomorrow.

23. Daniel mows over much Ground for only a Cock or Two of Hay.

24. Was at the Funeral of Elizabeth Warrin. Daniel did not work p.m.

25. Preach'd a.m. on 2 Sam. 21, 14 last Clause. P.M. on 1 Thess. 4, 7, repeating part of Sermon on Titus 2, 12, from page 47 to 54 inclusive. We read Genesis 40 and Mark 11. Propounded Mr. Charles Brigham of Grafton in order to his joining in full Communion with this Church. Mrs. Margaret How din'd with us.

26. Daniel mow'd and rak'd behind the Barn. Before night he broke off to go to Mr. Ebenezer Rice's. It look'd like Rain but signs go over.

27. Daniel began his hilling. Sometimes lowering, and dropp'd but not enough to lay the Dust. Heard that at Lieutenant Tainters divers people met to pray together. I had recommended it to him on sabbath Eve last. I visited Mr. Stephen Fay—his uncle—and was at Mr. Benjamin Fay's: also at Mr. Pratts to see his sick Child.

28. I rode to Mr. Bavericks and Spent some Time with his wife about her Spiritual State. Rode to Marlborough and preach'd the Lecture for Mr. Smith on Hab. 3, 17, 18. It was a Cloudy Day and Sometimes Misty, but did not rain much. At Evening in the Mist I rode over to Mr. Stones and lodg'd there. Alas how different his House is become!

29. In the Morning Mr. Stone and I rode over to the Fast at Mr. Smiths[13] at Hopkinton. He desir'd it on account of his two sons Nathaniel and Richard, and Two Dauters likewise, who had fallen into very gross, familistical Errors. We went first to Mr. Barretts[14]—and thence to Mr. Smiths. Some of the Children

---

[6] Edward Goddard, a prominent citizen of Framingham.

[7] The Reverend Thomas Green was the minister of the Greenville Baptist Church in Leicester. He was also a physician. Emory Washburn, *Historical Sketches of . . . Leicester* (Boston, 1860), pp. 111-113.

[8] Mrs. John Graves.

[9] The Reverend John Gardner of Stowe.

[10] The Reverend William Cooke of Wayland.

[11] The Reverend Matthew Bridge.

[12] One of the founders of the church in the north precinct of Westborough.

[13] Richard Smith.

[14] The Reverend Samuel Barrett of Hopkinton.

were there in the forenoon—all of them in the Afternoon. Mr. Barrett pray'd in the first Exercise, Mr. Stone preach'd from Isa. 63, 17. And Mr. Porter[15] of Sherbourn concluded with prayer. P.M. Mr. Bridge pray'd. I preach'd from 2 Cor. 11, 3, and Mr. Prentice[16] of Holliston concluded. After the Exercises we had some Discourse with Nat Smith[17] but to very little purpose. I lodg'd at Mr. Barretts.[18] N.B. Mr. Webb[19] of Chatham there, a Candidate for the Church of England.

30. Rode home Early. Brought over Mr. Henry[20] Volume 1. Daniel has been hoeing and he has finish'd the Long piece, and the New Ground. Ebenezer does not come from Cambridge. Have heard it is Commencement there to Day. Hot and Dry Weather still. May the God of infinite Mercy and pity look upon his Weary Heritage!

### JULY, 1749

Yesterday and the Day before when I was at Hopkinton there was considerable said in Conversation, of poor Mr. Woodwell that went to Canada for his Daughter: fearing he was lost—but last Night he came to Captain Maynards and this morning was at my House. But his Dauter was not with him: he had not obtain'd as yet, her Redemption. At Eve came Ebenezer and Forbush in my Chair, drawn by Lieutenant Tainters Horse, from Cambridge, Having been gone 10 working Days: but no Evil had befallen him as I began to fear there had. An Hot and very drying Day. Corn curls pritty much. Every Thing looks very languishing but English Grain.

2. A Very burning Day. A.M. read Genesis 41 and preach'd on 2 Sam. 21, 14. P.M. read Mark 12, and in preaching carry'd on the Same Design of the forenoon, but made great use of sermon on Tit. 2, 12, tho with many alterations, frequently mixing Reflections and Exhortations to Repentance. Our Prayers were fervent for the Divine Compassion under the sore and grievous Drought. A Storm, with Thunder and Lightning arose at Eve, but there was but a gentle Shower of Rain. N.B. One of my Young Geese in the Road was found gasping and dy'd—either by the Heat or for Thirst: the Throat, the Grass in it being dry and hard.

3. In the Morning Daniel mow'd the Barley, of which there seems to be, through Gods Goodness, a midling Crop. Ebenezer and Daniel mow'd in the Lower Orchard, Northside the Road. There was a sprinkling of Rain in the Morning, but the Clouds soon grew thin. I have been inform'd that Dr. Green is like to preach at Mr. Eliezer Rice's, and that tomorrow is to be the Day. I wrote a Letter and got it ready to lodge at one or other of the Houses where he practices Physick—and again I heard it was put off. But I took my Horse and rode to the several Houses viz. to Mr. Abner Newtons and Mr. Hezekiah Pratts—but found he was not to come again till they sent for him: but that the Mutual Desires aforesaid about his preaching were the Same.

4. I visited Mr. Tomlin and Bethial Tyler. Ebenezer and Daniel Hilling and mowing. About Noon came Mr. Jotham Brown with my son Thomas from Sudbury—the Times being so distressing, he had neither work nor plentifull provisions—and since he had Nothing to do in the shop, he thought if my son work'd abroad, it ought to be for Me, and not for him—but when

it Should please God to raise us out of this Calamity then he would Send for him again.

5. Ebenezer and Thomas reaping Rye, of which I have a very likely piece. D.G. Daniel Hill'd. Mr. Martyn and his Spouse, together with Mr. Barrett din'd here. Mr. Barrett preach'd my Lecture on Ps. 42, 4. The Lord quicken us hereby.

6. The most reviving Morning that we have seen this long Time, for through the undeserv'd Mercy and Goodness of God, we had a fine Rain. It prov'd a rainy Day. Blessed be God! Went P.M. to Lieutenant Tainters and preach'd at the Private Meeting. Text Mat. 26, 41. After Exercise there was an handsome Entertainment at which were Esquire Baker and his wife, and some Number besides. Call'd at Mr. Williams's to see his wife.

7. Daniel Hastings here. I reckon'd with him and paid him all (for 3 Months and 4 Days—Scil. 10£ old Tenor per Month, and for the odd Days 10 shillings per Day) 32£ old Tenor. Cloudy Day, but little Rain. Ebenezer and Thomas plough'd the Barley Stubble, there being much Barley left among the stones which they could not rake.

8. Rain in the Morning. Clear'd off afterwards So that Ebenezer and Thomas hoed Rye into the Indian Hills—but could not meddle with the Hay that lies out both in Cock and Swarth. N.B. A Letter from Mr. Buckminster[1] of Rutland giving my Information of Dinah Downing.

9. A.M. read Genesis 42. Preach'd on 1 Cor. 11, 31. P.M. read Mark 13. Preach'd from Hos. 3, 5—fear the Lord and his Goodness—but partly carry'd on my Scheme from 2 Sam. 21, 14. Administer'd the Lords Supper also this Day. Mr. Ezekiel Upham and Daniel Hastings brought Elisha Coolidge[2] of Watertown to dine here. Bad News of Mr. Abraham Williams[3] of Sandwich being lost.

10. An heavy Rain. Showery great part of the Day. Daniel after Dinner rode off for Watertown. Neighbours Eliezer Rice and Edwards Whipple here. Ebenezer and Thomas mow'd and then Hoed a little.

11. I went out a.m. to visit Several Familys. Was at Mr. Moses Brighams and Mr. Eleazer Pratt's—Mrs. Pratt follow'd with her Fits yet—last night she was much Exercis'd with them. Din'd at Mr. Grouts. My Horse was put out at Mr. Jonas Childs (who expected me to have din'd there) while I went to my Exercise. Catechiz'd at the South School-House—about 56 or 58, Children attended. After Exercise I was refresh'd at Mr. Jonas Childs and Forbush was with me. We went also to Ensign Millers, where Forbush read his account of the Ordination or anointing of one Hovey[4] at Mill-river. In my returning home I understood that Dr. Green was So conversant with Stephen Fay that it was very likely, he would Shortly preach among us. News of Mr. Abraham Williams that he preach'd at Concord last Lords Day. The Face of the Earth is much renew'd since the late Rains. Showery all Day. Some Hay has laid out till tis almost rotten—it being a very muggy growing season.

12. Sir Dodge here. Confirms the account which Forbush gave of Mill river, he also having been present at Said Ordination. Mr. Jonas Warren of Upton here in order to get Dodge, a new Batchelour, to preach which I disswaded. At Night Daniel Hastings return'd and brought me very Sorrowful News of Mollys being very Sick and nigh to Death (if yet alive) and desiring earnestly to see me.

13. Hinder'd in the Morning so long as to have my Horse's Shooes rectify'd and fasten'd, and one Shooe put on. Got down to Mr. Hastings's at Watertown so as to dine there—to Cambridge about 2 p.m. My visit was to my Daughter though the Crowd was going by to the Gallows with Mary Rogers,[5] alias Elizabeth

---

[15] The Reverend Samuel Porter (Harvard 1730), the minister of Sherborn, 1734-1758. *Sibley*, VIII, 769-772.

[16] The Reverend Joshua Prentiss.

[17] The following indicates who Smith was and how mad he was. Franklin B. Dexter, ed., *Extracts from the Itineraries . . . of Ezra Stiles* (New Haven, 1916), p. 418. "Sept. 18, 1793, Old Nat Smith died 2 or 3 y. ago, Æt. 80 & supra. He lived an old Bach. in Hopkinton near Edge Medfield. He was one of Old [Shadrach] Ireland's Men & of the Company of a doz. or 15 wild Enthusiasts who about 50 y. ago lived in and about Medfd., Sutton, Uxbridge & declared themselves IMMORTALS: of which Rev. Mr. Prentice's Wife of Grafton was one. She used to lie with Ireland as his spiritual Husbd.

"Formerly they walk round Hopkinton Meetinghouse sounding with Ramshorns and denouncing its Downfall, in vain.

"Nat Smith proceeded to assume & declare himself to be the Most High God & wore a Cap with the Word God inscribed on its front. His Great Chair was a Holy Chair & none but himself must sit in it. He had a number of Adorers and Worshippers, who continue to this day to believe he was the Great God."

[18] The Reverend Samuel Barrett of Hopkinton.

[19] Benjamin Webb (Harvard 1743) of Eastham, was baptized in Christ Church (Episcopal), Boston in 1750. He did not become a minister, but rather spent fifty years as an itinerant schoolmaster. *Sibley*, XI, 326-327.

[20] A work of the English divine, Matthew Henry (1662-1714).

[1] The Reverend Joseph Buckminster.

[2] The son of Deacon John Coolidge.

[3] Parkman had been concerned about his nephew's being lost spiritually (see diary for April 13, 1749), but here made reference to the fact that Williams had been reported lost at sea in 1749. The newly ordained minister survived, however, and served Sandwich until his death in 1784.

[4] The Reverend Samuel Hovey of the Milford Baptist Church.

[5] "The Woman under Sentence of Death for Theft, who has been in Prison at Cambridge, for some Months past, having had several Reprieves, was on Thursday last carried to the Place of Execution, where a Pardon was read to her, and she accordingly discharged." *The Boston Weekly News-Letter*, July 20, 1749.

Richardson, alias etc. My Molly was very low, having Fever and sore Throat. N.B. Forbush got down by 10 a.m. As to the vile Woman who was carry'd up to the place of Execution She Seem'd somewhat affected but Said very little—tho the Terrible Instruments of Death were before her, the Rope about her Neck, her Coffin before her etc.—and the Sheriff bid her prepare for Death, for he had no further Reprieve for her—But Colonel Brattle[6] read her Pardon and Mr. Appleton[7] pray'd. I went home with Mr. Appleton and Mr. Sheriff; there was also Colonel Wendell[8] at Mr. Appletons. I visited the President[9] likewise. After visiting divers Friends and Spending Some Time with my Dauter, I repair'd to Mr. Appleton's where, at his repeated Sollicitations I lodged; my Horse also was kept in his Pasture.

14. All the Morning perplex'd and fatigu'd about my Horse, which had got out of the Pasture and could not be found; till Sir Appleton[10] took his Fathers Horse and rode to Watertown; the Horse was found in old Lieutenant Coolidges Yard. I did not get away from Cambridge till noon. Call'd at Captain Sharps—where was Mr. Cotton Brown. I proceeded to Boston. My Brethren well etc. Lodg'd at Brother Samuels. My Horse at Mrs. Keggells. Molly a poor Night, but better Morning.

15. Cousen Nathaniel Setting Sail for Chebucto in partnership with William Willson. I broke fast at Mrs. Keggells, where was Mr. Edward Bass. I consulted Dr. Davis who has the Care of Molly. I thereupon ventur'd to return when I had Seen, examin'd and encourag'd her what I could: refresh'd at Mr. Hastings's and Captain Tainters—also at Colonel Buckminsters[11]—was stopp'd by rain and Thunder at Mr. Morse's[12] in Framingham and was Shav'd there. The Storm came on so impetuously that I lodg'd at Mr. Nichols's.[13]

16. Rose very Early and Set out before sunrise. When I got to Mr. Stones[14] at Southboro, he offer'd to go to Westborough in my Stead. I consent'd. I preach'd at Southborough a.m. on 2 Sam. 21, 14. N.B. Heavy Rains both last night and to Day. P.M. on Gal. 2, 20. I live by the Faith etc. Mr. Stone read Genesis 43, Mark 14 and preach'd on 1 Pet. 4, 18. I baptiz'd Bartholomew Son of William Newton.

17. Daniel Hastings resides here yet. Mr. Dunlop was So kind as to Reap gratis for me (which Joseph Bowker had done also whilst I was from home last Week). A pritty good Crop of Rye, thro the Divine Bounty. Daniel trys to break my young Horse to the Chair.

18. Visited Mr. Tomlin and Mrs. Bethiah Tyler.

19. I rode very early to Mr. Smiths at Marlborough for his Company to the Association Fast at Stow. His Wife and her sister went in their Chaise; and he himself rode with me. There were at Mr. Gardners this Meeting Messers Loring, Cushing, Martyn, Stone, Seccomb,[15] Smith, Swift,[16] Goss:[17] and Mr. Hutchinson of Connecticut, preaching at Grafton. Mr. Gardner began the public exercise with an Excellent prayer. Mr. Stone preach'd a good, useful Sermon on Mal. 3, 16. P.M. Mr. Goss pray'd and Mr. Cushing preach'd on Mat. 6, 10. Thy Kingdom come. At Eve Mr. Martyn and I rode to Justice Whitman's[18] and Mr. Pierce's[19] where we lodg'd.

20. Rain'd hard. Din'd at Mr. Pierce's, tho I had very much design'd to have gone to Southborough Lecture to have heard Mr. Hutchinson. In returning home, call'd at Captain Graves's—at Peter Hows[20] (because of the Showers), and at Mr. Smiths. Found my Family in a measure of Comfort. Blessed be God!

21. Lowery yet—a wonderful growing season tho very bad for Hay. Mr. Hutchinson[21] (preacher at Grafton) din'd here.

22. I was much in Suspense about my going to preach at Upton. It having been propos'd that Mr. Jonas Warrin should go to provide Mr. Minot of Concord to come to Marlborough and Mr. Smith[22] hither: but neither Mr. Smith came to preach here, nor Mr. Warrin to acquaint me with it. Hear that Molly is better.

23. I preach'd a.m. on Hosea 3, 4. But my Aim was against Envy. Read Genesis 44. P.M. read Mark 14, from the 32. Preach'd by Desire on Infant Baptism, repeating my sermon on Luke 18, 15, 16.

24. Mrs. Parkman exceedingly worried from Day to Day, being without a Maid so long. To Day engag'd in much Slavish work. Ebenezer begins to mow the Meadow. Daniel Hastings so kind as to give a Days Work there. P.M. Mr. Martyn here. At Eve Mr. Tinney came for me to visit his Sister again, Bethiah Tyler. I went—and found her both low in Body and distress'd in Mind.

25. Went Early to Mr. Cooks to get my Horse Shod; was at Neighbour Barns's and Captain Forbush's.[23] My sons went away to rake at the Meadow, but were soon prevented by Rain.

26. Great Rains a.m. When the Rain was over Ebenezer and Thomas went to the Meadow to look after the Hay there. Samuel Bumpso gave half a Days work. P.M. my Wife rode with me to the South part of the Town: to Mr. Harringtons, the Widow Woods's, to Mr. Daniel Forbush's, and (which was my Chief Design) to Mr. Millers[24] who was married to the widow Margaret How.[25] At Lieutenant Tainters in returning at Eve, who presented me with a side of Lamb against tomorrow. Got home safely though somewhat Dark. Three of Mr. Barns's Cattle very troublesome one Night after another and now get into the Corn.

27. A.M. Ebenezer and Thomas to the Meadow to rake. I am inform'd that Several Inhabitants of this precinct Went up to Grafton yesterday to hear Dr. Green preach.

28. Ebenezer and Thomas at the Meadow. At Eve they got home one Load. There is Scarce a Day but that it rains more or less,—but today the Showers not Such as much to hurt the haying. Colonel Nahum Ward here p.m.

29. Sent Billey to Mr. Allens (the miller) with Letter to Mr. Jonathan Goodale about Cart Wheels. Mr. Charles Brigham of Grafton here with his Relation. Ebenezer and Thomas to the Meadow. 2 Load more of Hay home. Billey return'd frustrated as to Mr. Goodale: but from Mr. Martyns with Dissenting Gentlemans Answer to Mr. Whites Letters[26]—and Esq. Prior on Tar-water.[27]

30. Mr. Brigham was not here as expected to be taken into the Church. I read Genesis 45, gave long Exposition. Preach'd on Jam. 3, 16. P.M. read Mark 15 and gave Exposition (as I have done for a great while) and preach'd on Ps. 34, 13, but therein improv'd Sermon on Tit. 2, 11, 12 from page 81 to 85, and Sermon on Isa. 33, 14, page 15, 16, but both these assistances were with great Alterations and additions. I find a great Deal of Difficulty in providing for so many different kinds of Exercises, with the vast Encumbrance and avocations by my Large Family while my wife has no Maid.

31. Din'd at Deacon Newtons. P.M. I visited Mr. Bradish, and thence rode to Mr. Garfields. His son Jacob and Wife had been desirous of Special Privileges, and had been at My House, when I was from Home. I now enter'd into Examination of her first, because of her Circumstances (being near her Time) and then afterwards of him but briefly concerning Some Objections which would be like to be rais'd against him. But he was Soon So plain as to tell me that if What I had had from him at My House and

[6] William Brattle (Harvard 1722), lawyer, representative, Councillor, later a general, and finally a Loyalist, who left Boston in 1776. *Sibley*, VII, 10-23.
[7] The Reverend Nathaniel Appleton of Cambridge.
[8] Jacob Wendell, a Boston merchant of Dutch background, was a colonel of the militia and a councillor.
[9] Edward Holyoke, the President of Harvard College. *Sibley*, V, 265-278.
[10] Nathaniel Appleton, Jr. (Harvard 1749).
[11] Joseph Buckminster, the prominent citizen of Framingham.
[12] Jonathan Morse.
[13] Joseph Nichols kept a tavern in Framingham.
[14] The Reverend Nathan Stone.
[15] The Reverend John Seccomb of Harvard.
[16] The Reverend John Swift, Jr., of Acton.
[17] The Reverend Thomas Goss of Bolton.
[18] John Whitman, a Justice of the Peace.
[19] William Pierce of Stow.
[20] Of Marlborough.
[21] Aaron Hutchinson.
[22] The Reverend Aaron Smith of Marlborough.
[23] Samuel Forbush.
[24] James Miller.
[25] Mrs. Nehemiah Howe.
[26] [Michaijah Towgood], *The Dissenting Gentleman's Answer to the Reverend Mr. White's Three Letters*, fifth ed. (Boston, 1748).
[27] Thomas Prior, *The Authentic Narrative of the Success of Tar Water, in Curing a Great Number and Variety of Distempers* (Boston, 1749). The first edition was published in London in 1746.

now (when indeed we had but a few words) did not Satisfy me, he should not trouble me any more, he should go other where, Intimating (as I apprehended) that he design'd to go over to Mr. Price[28] at Hopkinton, and hereby manifesting as he has done by several Things besides that his Mind was upon External Privilege and administration rather than upon inward Benefit or Qualification. Ebenezer and Thomas to the Meadow to Day.

### AUGUST, 1749

Ebenezer and Thomas to the Meadow again. Deacon Forbush here. Desires me to preach at his House next Thursday. I made a Business (of set purpose) of visiting Brother Stephen Fay and his wife to talk with them about going to the Separate Meetings, and having Lay-Preachers and mention'd particularly Dr. Green. Mr. Cushing and his wife at my House—and din'd with us. N.B. Billey met me when I was on the Road from Mr. Fays and inform'd me of Mr. Cushing etc. otherwise I Should have visited Mr. James Maynard again. Mr. Batherick here just at Eve—and Mr. Simon Goddard[1] and wife. N.B. A Letter from his honour'd Father.

2. Visited at Mr. Twitchells and Mr. William Rogers's. P.M. at Captain Maynards, Tomlins, and Tennys to see Bethial Tyler. When I return'd in the Eve found that Billy had been brought home Lame from the Meadow, for he had been with his Brothers there—and Silas Rice[2] had accidentally cutt his Legg with a Scythe. A fifth Load Hay home.

3. Early to Dr. Smith to come and Dress Billys Legg which he comply'd with. N.B. The Doctor's Discourse against Original Sin. P.M. I preach'd at Deacon Forbushs on Eph. 1, 4. After Exercise I went to Mr. Kellys to see his Dauter Jane, and then to Mr. William Pierce's to see 2 of his Children, they being Sick. N.B. Forbush with me. Ebenezer sixth Load Hay.

4. Rainy. Out of Rye. Ebenezer and Thomas P.M. thrash'd.

5. Ebenezer and Thomas to the Meadow. P.M. to raking. Daniel went away Yesterday but return'd here this Evening.

6. I preach'd a. and p.m. on Mal. 3, 7. Read Gen. 46 and Mark 16. By means of Mr. Charles Brigham very long relation we were very late at Evening.

7. Rode to Mr. Jonah Warrins, to Mr. Harringtons and got him to take my Horse down to Boston with him in order to bring up a Maid from Mr. Thomas Clarks. Din'd at Deacon Forbush's. Mrs. Batherick here.

8. I expected Mr. Martyns Company but he came not; I proceeded alone to Grafton Fast preparatory to Calling a Minister. I began the Exercises with Prayer, Mr. Hall[3] preach'd on Jer. 8, 22. Went to Ensign Whipples[4] at Noon. Mr. Maccarty[5] pray'd p.m. I preach'd on 2 Cor. 11, 3. As we supp'd at Ensign Whipples, thither the Church came to take Advice of the Minister what Steps they Should now take. N.B. Mr. Wellman, Mr. Hutchinson and Sir Dodge[6] there. Old Mr. Whipple accompany'd me back in the Evening when I return'd.

9. Rode up to Shrewsbury in my Chair, with Billy to have his Leg dress'd. When I return'd Mr. Daniel Forbush was here with my Horse which Mr. Harrington led to Boston for a Maid from Mrs. Clark—but the Endeavour was frustrated. The woman could not be found. P.M. I went to the Meadow to see the last of the Haying there.

10. Neighbour Batherick here to be further Examin'd, p.m. The Precinct Met and Voted to pull the old Meeting House down. The Time to go about it next month. N.B. Mr. Eliezer Rice came to me and told me Mr. Lyon of Grafton was gone over to see Bethiah Tyler. Wouldn't I go to him? for he said he thought it might be to no good for such Men to be here, nor did he like he should come. After looking up to God and Considering the Matter, I got my Horse and rode after him, designing and expecting to Meet him at Mr. Tennys, but I met with him on the

Road in his Return from thence. When I ask'd what Business he could have there, he told me they had sent for him; the Young Women in particular several Times. After Talk a long Time in the Mist on the Road I return'd home and he with me—he came in, and he tarried till it began to be Darkish. He deny'd that he pretended to have authority to preach—he deny'd his being in any Antinomian Errors, but declar'd he denounc'd them—affirm'd himself to be desirous to be in the way of Shepherd Hooker etc—before he went off, there thronged in Many into my House as they went from precinct Meeting. Ebenezer and Thomas picked apples part of the Day.

11. Mr. Andrew Farrand[7] of Kingstown in Hampshire County, here to buy my Young Horse—but does not come to my price which because of the Extremity of the Time as to Hay I ask'd him but an hundred for—nay offer'd him for ninety pounds old Tenor. Ebenezer the ninth and last Load from the Meadow.

12. Mr. Mead here. N.B. I hear of base misrepresentations of my Conference with Lyon. P.M. Daniel return'd here.

13. On. Mal. 3, 7, a. and p.m. Read Gen. 47 and Luke 1. Showery again.

14. Daniel went to Watertown for either Molly or the Maid from Mr. Clarks—in my Chair and his uncle Tainters Horse. I rode to Mr. Ebenezer Rice's where Mr. Farrand had left word about my Horse and there also Mr. Phinehas Hardy who had sold his Horse to said Farrand and if he did not consent to dispose of mine, would himself have him. Din'd at Home. Mrs. Tenny and her son Josiah din'd here. Showery to Day also. My sons mowing Bushes and Weeds.

15. Mrs. Miller (James juniors wife) here again to be examined. Much Difficulty in her Case, because whilst she desires to come to the Lords Supper yet she tells me She does not pretend to a Saving Change. N.B. Ebenezer Maynard here and kill'd a Ewe for me.

16. Association Fast here. I pray'd in the forenoon and Mr. Maccarty preach'd on Ps. 119, 126. P.M. Mr. Buckminster pray'd and Mr. Barrett preach'd on Mal. 4, 2. Those who came were Messers Loring, Cushing, Barrett, Martyn, Stone, Smith, Buckminster, Maccarty, Mellen,[8] Hutchinson. There came also of Scholars, Sir Cushing[9] and Forbush.[10] Mr. Loring and Mr. Mellen tarry'd over Night. O might God accept our Offerings and Humilliations! Especially may He grant that we mayn't by all provoke him the more and derive upon us a Curse instead of a Blessing! N.B. Messers Ebenezer Rice, Phinehas Hardy, Benjamin Fay, and Burnap here when very late at Night in their way from Worcester. And Mr. Hardy having put away his Horse to Mr. Farrand, but under some Discouragement about his Character, says Something about my Horse, yet refuses to buy him unless I will take Farrands Note. I offer to do this if he will give me 100£—he consents not to this—offers 25. This I refuse and still insist for 100 if I must be under such a Disadvantage as he himself was So uneasy with. The Affair was deferr'd till the morning, that he might See the Horse, and if he did not like him to be wholly quitt. Daniel Hastings brought up Molly from Cambridge. Sarah and Elizabeth Tainter assisted my Wife, but at night went home.

17. Mr. Farrand had sent me word that if I could not dispose of my Horse better I might Send him up to Worcester and he would give me 90£ to be paid at December 25 and he would wait for me til 12 o'clock: And Mr. Woolly of Holden with whom I had agreed to make me a Cyder Mill may very likely be at Mr. Cushings putting up his Mill. These Things induced me to think that way, being especially very loath to loose an opportunity to Putt away my Horse—but many incumbrances, perplexing Thoughts about getting up the Maid from Boston, writing to Mr. Minot about changing at Upton, and to Mr. Jotham Brown of Sudbury about Thomas—Company here (Mr. Loring and Mr. Millen) with many other Things made me late; and Mr. Martyn had also engag'd me, if

---

[28] Commissary Roger Price.

[1] Of Shrewsbury.

[2] The son of Eliezer Rice.

[3] The Reverend David Hall of Sutton.

[4] James Whipple of Grafton.

[5] The Reverend Thaddeus Maccarty of Worcester.

[6] Ezekiel Dodge (Harvard 1749), later the minister of Abington.

[7] Andrew Farran and his brother Thomas operated a grist mill in the region called Kingstown, which was incorporated as the town of Palmer in 1752. It is in Hampden rather than Hampshire County. J[osiah] H. Temple, History of the Town of Palmer ([Springfield], 1889), pp. 140, 445-446.

[8] The Reverend John Mellen of Sterling.

[9] Jacob Cushing (Harvard 1748), later the minister of Waltham.

[10] Eli Forbes.

I could, to preach his Lecture? I e'en gave up the Affairs of Worcester and Shrewsbury. Visited Mr. Tomlin in his Languishment and preach'd at the Northside on 1 Cor. 11, 31. N.B. Mr. Martyn and his Spouse So much Expected me (Yet I told him he might not depend upon me) and also to See my Wife with me, that they were greatly disappointed, and I seem'd to be hardly welcome without her. After Meeting I rode to Deacon Matthias Rice's, he being this Evening going to Boston. I left him my Horse to lead down for the Maid, again: I came home o'foot. Daniel Hastings here yet—but is unsettled as to any Business whatever.

18. Ebenezer Carts Apples to Mr. Charles Rice's Mill. Daniel setts his Pidgeon Net, but without any Success.

19. Thomas went to Deacon Rice's to accompany the Young Woman hither if she be come, but she is not come. She could not ride. Ebenezer press'd out Six Barrells Cyder and got 5 here. N.B. Sent one Barrell to old Mr. Maynard.

20. A.M. read Genesis 46 with Exposition. Preach'd on Isa. 63, 10. P.M. read Luke 1, 10, 39 to the End with Exposition in the sermon on Isa. 28, 16. Those words—a Sure Foundation. N.B. us'd Sermon on Eph. 3, 10, from page 12 to 18. This Day Ebenezer is 22. O that he might be born again! Molly got to meeting among us a.m. Billy also got out to meeting to Day. Blessed be God for all his Goodness towards us! Mr. Bradish din'd with us. Daniel Hastings with us Still.

21. I rode to Shrewsbury a.m. Colonel Ward[11] ask'd me into his House, and I smoak'd a Pipe. N.B. He is full of their Affair with Dr. Smith which is to come before their Church to Day. I went to Mr. Cushings about the Cyder Mill, which Mr. Woolley is to make for me. I find it needfull to go to him to Holden. Mr. Cushing lent me his Horse (mine being pritty Dull with his late Journeys)—din'd at Mr. Woolleys. As I return'd at Evening I visited Mrs. Martha Warrin[12] who is sick. Ebenezer went to Boston in my Chair, drawn by my Mare—set out at 9 or 10 at Night.

22. Captain Sadler[13] here to see my Horse—din'd here—agrees to give me 90£ old Tenor if he is not better Supply'd by this Day sennight. P.M. Daniel Hastings reckon'd, and took Leave. May God be gracious to him and keep him from snares.

23. Some heavy Showers. Ebenezer return'd in the Chair and brought to us Elizabeth Grice, widow, to Serve us as a Maid. Mr. Francis Whipple's wife here and brought us about 2 pound Butter, and Rebecca Warrin brought a small Cheese and some Cucumbers, but nothing else was brought by anybody for the Thanksgiving.

24. Public Thanksgiving for the Rain. I preach'd on Ps. 68, 9. I am full of fear lest, if we provoke the Lord by these Services, He will bring upon us yet Sorer judgments. He has begun upon us now gradually, and waits to See when we will return to Him. Last Year there was Drought; This Year a much greater—such an one as the oldest doth not remember; perhaps the Next may be a Proper Famine. Prepare to Meet thy God O Israel! Began Mr. Brainerds Life[14] at Even.

25. Ebenezer and Thomas a.m. mow Weeds for Fodder. P.M. Cutt Stalks. Neighbour Batherick here with his Relation. We Need Indian Corn—borrow'd a Bushel of Lieutenant Thomas Forbush, and Neighbour Batherick went to Mr. Allens Mill with it. My Neighbours full of Animosity about the removing of the Meeting-House, and it gives me no small Anxiety. But I hope to leave it with the holy, sovereign Providence of God.

26. A.M. came Edward Baker Esq., Deacon Newton and Lieutenant Tainter to acquaint me in private Capacity, that the Precinct had determin'd by their vote at their late Meeting, to take down the old Meeting House next Monday; So that I might be at no loss, or put to Difficulty the Lords Day following if I preach at the New Meeting House, they would invite me and Such of my Family as should go to Meeting, to their Houses, till there Should be some proper provision made for us by the precinct. I acknowledged their Goodness, and thank'd 'em kindly for their Offer. And we took opportunity to enter upon some

11 Nahum Ward.
12 Mrs. Daniel Warrin.
13 John Sadler of Upton.
14 Jonathan Edwards, *An Account of the Life of the Late Davis Brainerd* (Boston, 1749).

discourse about the Difficultys I must unavoidably undergoe the Ensuing Winter if the Meeting House we now use be taken down. And after their relating to me the Debates of the last Meeting—Two of them (viz. Esq. Baker and Deacon Newton) undertook to go among the Opponents (Captain Maynard etc.) to see whether they did so desire the suspending the design'd work till next Spring, as that if they should be gratify'd therein, they would then acquiesce, at least not molest them in their Proceeding. N.B. My Saying the Dividing the Town was the Thing that gave the Fatal Stabb to my Interest (explaining it of my Temporal Interest) among them. Mrs. Batherick here with her Relation. Mr. Stephen Sadler din'd here, came to look on the Horse, which his Father talks of buying of me. Ebenezer went over to Mr. Martyns for Bricks for an Oven and brought them. Two Barrells of my new boild Cyder sprang Leaks—much was wasted—oblig'd to get another Barrell, rinse and Shift what we could of the Cyder. Betty Grice, who seems to be but an infirm Body, is indispos'd and lyes by.

27. I arrive at this Day with a great deal of heavy Pressure upon my Spirits. I find it necessary to compose myself in the middst of many Temptations and Trials. There is Some reason to fear it will be the last Sabbath we shall ever have in this Meeting-House. The Morning was Cloudy and rainy. I was deceiv'd by my watch and went to Meeting late But I was also behind hand in my preparations as any one would justly conceive, having so very little Time to Study in the week. For the forenoon Exercise I deliver'd (with alterations) Sermon on Ps. 144, 15th. Read Genesis 49. P.M. Luke 2. Admitted Mr. David Batherick and Wife into the Church and administer'd the Lord's Supper. Very late, full Two o'Clock when we came out of the Meeting House (nor was it much more) I requested the Communicants to return Somewhat Sooner to Meeting again than usual after Sacrament because I perceiv'd it was very late. P.M. Deacon Newton inform'd me that their Endeavour yesterday among those who were against the taking down the Meeting House, in order to peace, was not successful. I preach'd on Rev. 3, 3, former part, but I did not finish the Subject. But O that God would enable us to comply with such needful Counsel as this word exhibits. N.B. Mrs. Grice lyes by.

28. Early in the Morning as soon as there came any to the Meeting House I stept up and pray'd that they would give me Opportunity to Speak with the Precinct before they proceeded to their work. Mr. Jonas Brigham, one of the Committee for the work, was there and said they would Stay, that I might. Others Said the Like. I hasten'd back and while I was writing was call'd—the Committee (Said Mr. Brigham, Mr. Benjamin Fay, and Mr. Timothy Warrin) being below. I went down—they Said they were come to See whether I had any thing to offer. I told 'em (having my paper in my Hand) that I wanted to Speak with the precinct before they proceeded to take down the Meeting House. They answered that they were the Servants of the Precinct—and Seem'd desirous to hear it and were in haste to go to work. I read it and still said I wanted to Speak to the Precinct. They undertook to answer with respect to the last article, which respected my Near Neighbours—but said nothing to the rest of the paper, but in an hurry added that they did not see any Thing but that they might go up to the work and So left Me. N.B. Lieutenant Tainter was also present and heard what I read. Captain Maynard and Ensign Josiah Rice came in a little Time from the Meeting House and wanted to know Something of a propos'd, peacefull meeting—and intimated that they thought themselves impos'd upon—and hop'd I would now see that there was a flame—acquainting me that word was brought to the Meeting House (as Deacon Newton, they Said, inform'd them) that they had Sent a Message to me and the return was that I had Nothing to Say. (N.B. Captain Baker had been here and told me that his Saturday Endeavour was not to Effect, so that laying with this what Deacon Newton told me yesterday as I went up the Pulpit stairs p.m., I concluded there was nothing of meeting or Conference to be Expected.) Upon Captain Maynards saying this, I wanted to see the Deacon that I might know how it could be so understood. Captain went up and brought the Deacon to

me. Others of the Neighbours Came and I endeavour'd to make them Sensible that I had prepar'd something and would fain have gone up to the people if I could have had opportunity but was disappointed thro these means. The House was uncover'd, unclos'd after the Pulpit, Pews and seats were taken down— Several Carts kept going all Day. A Melancholly Sight! But Many that came in would express their Compassionate Hopes and Wishes. Most of all my Dependence be on the God that has in Providence brought me here and protected and provided for me hitherto! N.B. Mr. Martyn[15] here as he went to Grafton Church Meeting to choose a minister. At Eve Mr. Josslyn[16] here complaining of my Lateness at Meeting on the Sabbaths. Mr. Ebenezer Chamberlin with him, whose wife Said that Sabbath was Sennight it was 4 o'Clock p.m. when we went to Meeting (for Second service of the Day), whereas, as I remember, the sun was about an Hour and half high when we left off—that is, about 5 o'Clock. What Service was performed took up not much less time than Two Hours and half So that we went not at much after 1/2 past Two. Yet were they Confident that we began past 4. Mr. Martyn came in and acquainted me that at Grafton they had chose Mr. Hutchinson.

29. Rain a.m. They go on to take down the Frame of the old Meeting House. I gave the Committee leave to lay the Timber on my Land. Neighbour John Rogers was to have gone for my Cyder Mill, but is prevented by Weather. Captain Sadler neither came nor sent about the Horse. Mr. Ephraim Woods here to look upon my Horse. Mrs. Grice is ill yet and confin'd.

30. Visited Mr. Beriah Rice's Children sick of the Throat Distemper, visited Mr. Jonas Child who is sick. There I saw Dr. Scammell.[17] Got him to Look on Mrs. Grice and give Directions. She had a Fit while the Doctor was here—and much Trouble afterwards. N.B. Neighbour Rogers went, with his Oxen and mine and Neighbour Hows Cart, to fetch my Cyder-Mill from Mr. Woolley's of Holden; and brought it. The Affliction about Mrs. Grice is, however, the great test of all, for going up to see her in the Night, my wife being then with her, I gave her a few affectionate Words exhorting her to Repentance and Consider her Danger. She made me very unbecoming Answers, So that tho I wanted it much I could have no agreeable Opportunity to talk with her.

31. Forbush came in the Morning (according to Agreement last night to carry Mrs. Grice back to Boston) he being about to return to College, and Lieutenant Tainter offer'd his Horse (if we could not do better with her) to draw her to Boston. The Doctor had said to Me, that she could by on Means be fitt to keep here, but get her to the place from whence she came. I found She grew ill-humour'd, and us'd indecent Language—abusing my Kindness to her—So that I was oblig'd to put on a stern Air; and with a Resolute Mind got her from her Bed. My Horse follow'd after to assist if there be need. Thus I bid adieu to her who had been so great a Vexation to me. But what was very Cutting was, that She seem'd averse to hearing anything about her Soul, her sins, or another World. The Lord who alone is able, be pleas'd to awaken her to Repentance. Ebenezer return'd home before Night, having Seen her along as far as into Sudbury—but he brought me a very grieving Letter from Mr. Jotham Brown of Sudbury that he had not work enough; and that his Circumstances were such that he could not take Thomme again. But Let the Lord do what seemeth [to] Him good!

### SEPTEMBER, [1749]

1. Old Mr. Rogers[1] came with an Earnest request to go and see his son William who Seems to be in a very bad Frame—yesterday would have made himself away by running into the Pond and drowning himself but his Brother John went at that juncture to the Pond to water his Horse, and prevented him. He got loose also a second Time and ran into the Pond Waste deep but his Brother got him out, and with help led him up to his Fathers where he was watch'd all night by two Men. I visited him ac-

[15] The Reverend John Martyn of the north precinct.

[16] Joseph Joslin.

[17] Samuel Scammell, the physician of Milford, Mass.

[1] John Rogers.

cordingly and pray'd with him. N.B. Mr. Ebenezer Chamberlins Wife met me in returning home, to give me some clearer account about what her Husband and Mr. Joslin had Said from her about its being so late when I went to Meeting the Sabbath before last: and Says it was what Captain Forbush's wife told her. Ebenezer and Thomas cutting Stalks—Thrashing Rye etc. At Eve Lieutenant Tainter came, in the Name of the Committee to inform me that the new Meeting House would be So put in order by the Sabbath that they expect'd the Services to be perform'd there: and he, for himself desir'd that I would dine at His House on that Day—but I thank'd him and declin'd it.

2. Ebenezer and Thomas went to Mr. Abner Newtons to fetch a Load of Clay for an Oven. Benjamin Tainter came up from Cambridge with my Chair and brought a Letter from Forbush that he got down well with Mrs. Grice but without sister Lydia Champney[2] whom I now hop'd for; and it was a great Disappointment that she did not come. He brought me from I know not who a Considerable Box of Pipes. N.B. Neighbour Hezekiah How here in much Frett about the Meeting House.

3. This Day we first met in the New Meeting House. Molly and I with Suse and Alex rode in the Chair, Thomas and Lucy rode upon the Horse, Ebenezer and Billy went o'foot—Thus eight of us got to Meeting. In the Exercise us'd the Lords Prayer. I read 1 King 8th Chapter, but (according to desire) expounded Genesis 49 which was read last Lords Day. Sang Psalm 92, 12 ad. fin. Preach'd on Rev. 3, 3. Din'd at Edward Baker Esquire's— but my Children all went home. P.M. read and gave Expository remarks on Luke 3. Sang Psalm 132, 4 to the End of the 10th omitting the 16th. Preach'd once More on Rev. 3, 3. Baptiz'd 3 Children of Mr. David Bathrick, and one of Mr. Eleazer Whitney. O that we might have the Grace to review, hold fast, and repent! We got home in good Season. I grieves me that Such a Number of my near Neighbours were absent from Meeting.

4. Master Minot[3] of Concord who preach'd yesterday at Upton here, with one Mr. Wheeler of Concord and with them Mr. Jonas Warrin of Upton. Near Night came Mr. Wooly to put up my Cyder Mill. Wrote to New Haven.

5. Blessed be the Lord who from Year to Year, both preserves me and loads me with his Benefits! vide Natal. Mr. Woolley at work, with Ebenezer, putting up the Cyder Mill. Mr. Cushing and Mr. Davis[4] came and we rode together to Southborough, Association Fast. Mr. Loring, Mr. Smith and Mr. Millen were all that came besides the foremention'd. I was oblig'd to preach a.m. Text was Jer. 8, 5. P.M. Mr. Millen preach'd on Rom. 2, 28, 29. A variety of Cases at Evening—Mr. Cushings relating to Dr. Smith, Mr. Loring about general Petitions for and against Church Meetings, etc.

[The following is from Parkman's Natalitia, Sept. 5, 1749.]

I seem now to be growing old apace. I am fill'd with grief and astonishment at the Swift, unavoidable Flight of my Time! Alas! Whether I look backward or forward I am thrown into no small Anguish of Heart. As to my past Life, how empty and sinful has it been! As to what is to come, I am amaz'd at the Apprehension of the Brevity and Uncertainty of it, as likewise what is like to be the Eternal Event! O that I might be suitably affected! and might indeed be ready for the work and will of God! Our Association Fast on account of the Signs of Degeneracy among us, was this Day at Southborough; and I attended on it. It was my place to preach on that Solemnity. My Text was Jer. 8, 4, 5. May the Lord Himself please to awaken us, and prevent our falling into a Perpetual Backsliding!

6. A.M. I return'd home, with the same Company that I had in going. Mr. Woolley.

7. Mr. Woolley. Old Mr. Garfield here to desire me to go to the Funeral of his son Jacobs Child.

8. Mr. Woolley went home. Mr. Millen here. Ebenezer makes Cyder at the New Mill.

9. Visited Neighbour William Rogers—heard Mrs. Garfield was very bad, therefor went forward and visited her nigh her End. Return'd back to Mr. Cooks to have my Horse prepar'd for my

[2] Parkman's sister-in-law.

[3] Timothy Minot, a schoolmaster of Concord, and an occasional preacher.

[4] The Reverend Joseph Davis of Holden.

Design'd Journey. Whilst there, Mr. Minot came to me. He din'd with us. P.M. I rode to Upton. Entertain'd at Captain Hazzletines.[5]

10. I preach'd at Upton a. and p.m. on Ps. 110, 3. Din'd at Captain Sadlers. May God please to make it the Day of his power with my Soul! and with all that hear me! Call'd at Mr. Elijah Warrins—and at Mr. Jonas Childs at Evening. Supp'd at Home. 1 Cor. 14, 1. Mr. Minot din'd at Esquire Bakers.

11. Mr. Minot left us. Mr. Bucknam[6] going to Brookfield calls here and dines. At the Funeral of Mr. Jacob Garfields wife. Visited Neighbour Abner Newton.

12. Molly and I rode in the Chair to Concord—din'd at Mr. John Weeks[7] at Marlborough and got to Mr. Minot's seasonably—made a visit to Colonel Minot—but both my Dauter and I lodg'd at Mr. Timothys. But my Principal Errand was with Mr. Gold the Sadler, to see whether he would take Thomas to perfect him in the Trade of Sadler. He took it to Consideration of.

13. Mr. Minot very Courteous, accompanying me from place to place and particularly to Mr. Whitneys—where I bought Voetius's Select Disputations,[8] 2 volumes for 25/ old Tenor. Mr. Gold settles his Terms that Thomas must either live with him a Twelve month and pay 30£ old Tenor, or live with him 18 Months. Din'd at Mr. Minots, call'd at Mr. Bliss's.[9] Was at Mr. Jotham Browns, and at Mr. Ebenezer Newtons in returning—got home, thro God's Goodness in Safety.

14. Catechiz'd at Mr. Josselyn's.

15. Rain'd hard. Mrs. Bekky Gott[10] and Mrs. Bekky Williams[11] from Marlborough to visit us, and lodg'd here.

16. The Young Ladys return'd. Young Cattle out of the Woods. Rode up to Grafton in Complyance with Mr. Hutchinsons Request, but I not having Sent him any word, I was oblig'd to ride up as far as Captain Lelands[12] before I saw him, and then to Mr. Holbrooks[13] before he to Westborough. N.B. He lodg'd at Captain Baker's: I at Mr. Holbrooks.

17. Preach'd at Grafton on 2 Cor. 3, 15. P.M. 10, 14, 17, 18. Din'd at Mr. Isaac Harringtons. Baptiz'd 4 Children—viz. of Mr. Abner Stow, Mr. John Sherman, Mr. Moses Eager, and Mr. Abijah Allen. At Eve rode as far as to Mr. Winchesters, refresh'd there—afterwards Supp'd at Home. May God be pleas'd to cause his word to make a deep Impression on both my own heart and the hearts of his people. Mr. Hutchinson tarried—the Town of Grafton being to meet to Morrow to choose a Minister or rather to see whether it will concurr with the choice of the Church.

18. Mr. Hutchinson to Mr. Martyns. Mr. Bucknam here in his return from Mr. Hardings[14] Ordination. P.M. I went to Proprietors Meeting at Marlborough with a plot of 13¼ acres, which lyes South East of our new Meeting House—which they granted: and I left it with Colonel Williams to be recorded. At Mr. Smiths in my return home.

19. Took my Son Thomas with me in my Chair, to Concord. We din'd at Deacon Rice's and were entertain'd Courteously and handsomely. Call'd at Mr. Jotham Browns, Thomas having much longing after them. We went to Mr. Goolds and, by the Assistance of Mr. Minot with whom they were lodg'd, enter'd into Articles of Agreement with said Gould—and after Several visits in the Neighborhood, I return'd to Mr. Goolds, and tarried with them all Night.

20. Set out from Concord for Boston. Call'd at old Mr. Hancocks[15] at Lexington, but only the old Lady at Home. Thence to Cambridge and din'd at Deacon Whittemores[16]—thence to Boston. N.B. a Cold Night. Bells rung for Fire. The Chief noise in Boston is about the Money lately come in to re-emburse for Charge of Cape Briton.

21. Mr. Cowell[17] presented a black Hickery or Walnutt Stick. My late Kinsman John Parkmans Widow made me a Present of her late Husbands Rocculo,[18] which was a little the worse for Wear. Mr. John Breck presented me Εικων Βασιλικη Δευτεα and Mr. Edwards of Northampton Sent me by Mr. Bromfield, his Book against his Grandfather.[19] I beg grace to be truely Thankfull to God for so many favours. Sister Lydia Champney rode with me to Cambridge—my Mare and Chair taken Care of by Brother Champney—but I lodg'd in sister Lydia's Chamber.

22. We Set out early (Sister Lydia and I in my Chair) from Cambridge. Din'd at old Mr. Livermore's at Weston. My Mare very Dull—very hardly expected that She would hold home, but we arriv'd in Safety at Evening.

23. [No entry.]

24. Somewhat rainy and raw Cold Air. The Meeting House too open, difficult to undergoe it. Read Exod. 2. Preach'd on Eccl. 5, 1. Din'd at Esq. Bakers. P.M. read Luke 6, and preach'd on Luke 6, 31, repeating my Exposition on the parallell place in Matthew. Daniel Hastings here.

25. Rain. The precinct by their Committee Sold the old meeting House Frame.

26. Mr. Martyn I hear is gone to Boston with his wife to see his mother who is ill. I visited Mr. Tomlin[20] who seems to be near his End. Daniel Hastings kill'd a Steer for me. He left us and return'd to Watertown.

27. Ebenezer makes Cyder—getts in Rowing—I assisted him—Mrs. Mary Sherman.

28. Captain Maynard came to desire me to go to Mr. Tomlins who is still living. At Eve Mr. Thaddeus Gale here to discourse with me about his joining to the Church.

29. Mr. Tomlin dy'd last night. He was an innocent harmless man, and seriously inclin'd, but was Somewhat liable to be discomposed in his reason, and doubted much of his Sincerity and Faith. The Lord Sanctify his holy Dispensation for our awakening and quickening!

30. Mr. Tomlin bury'd. Receiv'd a Letter from the first Church in Sutton to assist in Council there on the 17th of next Month. It was deliver'd by Lieutenant Peres Rice.[21]

## OCTOBER, 1749

1. A rainy Day. Rain'd down upon me in the Pulpit. Din'd at Deacon Newtons. A.M. read Exod. 3. Preach'd on Eccl. 5, 1, but made up of Exod. 3, 5, as my Text at this Exercise. P.M. read Luke 7th. Preach'd from Eccl. 5, 1. A Somewhat tedious Day to undergoe. But God be pleas'd to grant me the Wisdom and Patience necessary for me under my Circumstances! When I read the Letter from Sutton, I told the Church that I could not well go, because of the Difficultys respecting my uncertain Health, and my great uncertainty what would be like to befall me as to my attending upon Meeting this Winter approaching—to look after the Preparations for which I had but little Time before me: for the ensuing Week would be chiefly taken up in Ministers Meeting, and the Committee's Business at Rutland. Yet I told the Church I would not hinder their going to Sutton if they saw best. But Deacon Newton objected that Sutton first Church had an hand in setting up the Church in Framingham which is under Mr. Solomon Reed, and so were divers of the other Churches which were sent to on this Occasion, and therefore he was not free to Send. Upon the whole, when it was put to Vote, no Hand at all was lifted up.

2. Lieutenant Peres Rice came from Southboro and receiv'd our Negative Answer to the Church in Sutton. Sister Lydia road out with me. We din'd at Lieutenant Tainters. P.M. I had his Horse to visit James Miller juniors wife: Mr. Samuel Hardy's and Mr. Zebulon Rice's Family—Two Children in the last Family

[5] John Hazeltine of Upton.
[6] The Reverend Nathan Bucknam of East Medway.
[7] A prominent citizen who later became a colonel.
[8] Daniel Voet, *Disputationem Selectarum Decima-Quartae* (1656). I have found no reference to an English translation.
[9] The Reverend Daniel Bliss of Concord.
[10] The daughter of Dr. Benjamin Gott.
[11] The daughter of Colonel Abraham Williams.
[12] James Leland.
[13] John Holbrook of Grafton.
[14] The Reverend Elisha Harding (Harvard 1745), the minister of Brookfield, 1749-1755.
[15] The Reverend John Hancock.
[16] Samuel Whittemore.
[17] Peam Cowell.
[18] The roquelaure was a cloak-like garment often of bright and gay colors. The name was spelled and misspelled in a bewildering number of ways. "Roculo" was one variant. See Alice M. Earle, *Two Centuries of Costume in America* (New York, 1910), pp. 264-265.
[19] Jonathan Edwards, *An Humble Inquiry into the Rules of the Word of God, Concerning the Qualifications Requisite to a Complete Standing and Full Communion with the Visible Christian Church* (Boston, 1749). This was an effort to counteract the Halfway Covenant and relative liberalism of his maternal grandfather, the Reverend Solomon Stoddard of Northampton.
[20] Hezekiah Tomlin.
[21] Formerly of Westborough, but now a resident of Sutton.

sick of Throat Distemper. Dark chairing home in the Evening yet call'd at Merchant Rice's to receive Money of Mr. Daniel Hardy Collector.

3. In going up to Holden I was desir'd to go in to Mr. Benjamin Eagers to see a poor Sick, despairing Man, one Clark from Westfield. Got to Holden (in Company with Mr. Cushing) seasonably, and we kept the Day as a Fast. Mr. Davis pray'd, Mr. Smith preach'd on Ga. 5, 7. P.M. Mr. Maccarty pray'd and Mr. Seccomb preach'd on Acts 9, 3, 4, 5. I lodg'd at Mr. Davis's with Mr. Smith.

4. N.B. Mr. Buckminster of Rutland had mistaken the Time of my going up there and therefore appointed a Church Meeting there at 9 a.m. whereas I had appointed to be there in the afternoon and had writ so to Mr. Campbell[1] and the rest of the Committee. Accordingly having din'd at Mr. Davis's, p.m. I rode up to Rutland. Lieutenant Brown[2] of Leicester was there, and Deacon Davis[3] of Oxford (instead of Colonel Larnard[4]) came before Night. We went to the meeting house this Evening. Mr. Buckminster pray'd and tho Captain Rice[5] was much against submitting his Case to our Cognizance, yet the Church and Deacon Ball[6] requesting it we adjourn'd to tomorrow morning and Mr. Cambell and I lodg'd at Mr. Buckminsters.

5. Met at the Meeting House, both the Church and Committee of the Council and found Captain Rice willing to submit their Controversie to us—adding Deacon Davis to us instead of Colonel Larnard—but N.B. Esq. Baker did not come at all. P.M. carry'd on the Hearing again. N.B. Captain Rice and the Church were reconcil'd to Day. At Night the Committee were at Mr. Buckminsters reviewing and debating, till late.

6. Deacon Ball came to us early to see whether his Wife, who had been distress'd all Night might not come to us and declare her Mind. We consented but Captain Rice must be present. He was therefore sent for, came and we labour'd with them all, after which drew up our Report and advice, and did our utmost to reconcile 'em. But now the Tables were turn'd; our Difficulty was with Captain Rice no longer, or with his son (John). Deacon Ball was the person that now appear'd inexorable, and not to be satisfy'd with our Judgement and award. The Church who had met in the forenoon, and again in the p.m. were call'd together after sun setting and we went into the Meeting House, read what we determin'd—and Captain Rice and his son accepted it; and the Church by their Vote also approv'd of it, but Deacon Ball stood out to the last. Mr. Campbell pray'd and we broke up; our Hearts griev'd that we are forc'd to leave any Remains of the Contention. But blessed be God for any Measure of success! Very Cold Nights one after another. We lodge still at Mr. Buckminsters.

7. Visited Mr. Frink[7] as we came off. I was at Mr. Feltons[8] to see whether some of my stray Cattle are not there: but am not enough acquainted with my marks to know them. N.B. Mr. Feltons wife was a Trask. Din'd at Mr. Davis's.[9] Return'd home at Eve, and found all in peace. Blessed be God!

8. Another very rainy, Stormy Sabbath. Administer'd the Lords Supper—the first in the new Meeting House. Read a.m. Exod. 4, preach'd on 1 Cor. 11, 26 a Repitition—having no Opportunity to Prepare. My wife, sister Lydia and Dauter Molly din'd at Deacon Newtons. P.M. read Luke 8 repeated an Exposition on Mat. 8, 23 to 27. Very tedious returning home at Night. N.B. Reasons for Consenting to Shrewsbury Letter (requesting our assistance in Council) were it is near—we can't keep denying—and no objection against that Church as there was against Sutton. A terrible stormy Night of Wind and Rain.

9. A.M. I rode over to Mr. Harringtons for the 2 Volumes of

Mr. Flavells[10] works which he had brought up for me from Mr. Daniel Gookins[11] of Boston. Also visited Mr. Jonah Warrins Family, one of his Children being ill. Mr. Death[12] of Framingham here to buy my Young Horse, but goes away without him. P.M. rain. Ebenezer to Rutland after the stray Cattle.

10. Clear, and Cool. Sent a Number of my Books last night and to Day in order to their being carry'd to Mr. Gookins's to be sold. Honourable Esq. Goddard here at Eve, going with his son Edward to Shrewsbury. At Eve likewise came Mr. Devotion[13] of Windham, and Coggswell[14] of Canterbury here, and lodg'd with us.

11. Mr. Devotion and Cogswell to Boston. Mr. Whipple, one of the Delegates of the Church, came and accompany'd me to Shrewsbury. Captain Baker the other Delegate came afterwards. There met at Colonel Nahum Wards the following Churches. Mr. Lorings,[15] Mr. Williams's[16] of Weston. Mr. Gays[17] of Hingham, Southborough, second of Bradford, and first of Westborough. We waited all the forenoon for the old South in Boston and the first Church in Cambridge, but they came not. After Dinner we form'd into Ecclesiastical Council. Mr. Loring was chose Moderator. Mr. Williams and I were chosen Clerks. Then proceeded to the Meeting House. Moderator pray'd and we had an Hearing of the Cause—the Complaint was by Mr. Isaac Stone[18] against Dr. Joshua Smith,[19] touching Original Sin. N.B. Mr. Balch[20] pastor of a church in Bradford, and of the Council, was observ'd to turn Advocate for Dr. Smith. At Eve I return'd home, there being a great Number of young Men husking my Corn this Evening.

12. In the Morning to Shrewsbury. Debating in Council, yet passing several Votes—went not from Colonel Wards all Day. Lodg'd there also. N.B. Messers Gay and Balch dissented from the rest.

13. Hard at it—all Day—the Result was read by Candle Light, at Colonel Wards. N.B. Mr. Balch and his Messenger went off for Bradford in the Morning. Mr. Gay and his Messenger drew off before voting the Result and were absent at the Reading of it. I pray'd after reading the Result. Return'd at Eve in Company of Mr. Stone and Esq. Liscomb of Shrewsbury, and Esq. Baker and Mr. Whipple of this Town. N.B. the Council was adjourn'd without Day.

14. Making Some preparations for the Sabbath. Ebenezer has carry'd up the Corn into the Garret, and we have great Reason to Bless God for his abundant Goodness and Bounty to us, especially considering the terrible Drought, for we have a competent Crop. May we have grace to improve it to the Glory of the Giver!

15. Read Exod. 4 from 10, 18. Text 2 Tim. 4, 3 former part. Molly and I din'd at Deacon Newtons. P.M. read Luke 8 from 10, 26. Text Eph. 2, 5, repeating sermon on Eph. 2, 8, to page 10, and including the Application entitled Reflections at Page 8. Refuse to read a paper of William Rogers. No Result to read.

16. Mr. Martyn and Deacon Livermore[21] here as they were going to Council at Sutton.

17. Ebenezer to the Trooping at Marlborough. Nathan Maynard help'd me in raking our Husks into Heaps and Cocking them before the Threatening Storm.

18. Between 3 and 4 in the Morning Mr. Samuel Hardy call'd me out of my Bed to visit Mr. Jonas Warrin of Upton who is

[1] The Reverend John Campbell of Oxford.
[2] John Brown.
[3] Samuel Davis held a number of town offices.
[4] Ebenezer Learned was a selectman and representative of Oxford. Daniels, *Oxford*, pp. 586–587.
[5] Edward Rice of Rutland.
[6] Eleazer Ball. See Reed, *Rutland*, p. 139.
[7] The Reverend Thomas Frink of Rutland District, later Barre.
[8] Joseph Felton of Rutland.
[9] The Reverend Joseph Davis of Holden.

[10] John Flavell (1627-1691), a popular English dissenting divine, was the author of numerous books. Parkman may have referred to *The Whole Works of . . . J. Flavel . . . Now First Collected Together*, 2 vols. (London, 1701). Several other editions followed. Numerous individual works by Flavell were published in Boston, but there was no American edition of his collected works.
[11] A bookseller located near the Old South Church in Boston.
[12] Oliver Death.
[13] The Reverend Ebenezer Devotion of Windham, Conn.
[14] The Reverend James Coggswell (Yale 1742), the minister of Canterbury, 1744-1771. Dexter, *Biographical Sketches*, pp. 701-704.
[15] The Reverend Israel Loring of Sudbury.
[16] The Reverend William Williams.
[17] The Reverend Ebenezer Gay.
[18] Lieutenant Stone was one of the first selectmen of Shrewsbury.
[19] The physician of Shrewsbury.
[20] The Reverend William Balch of Groveland (Second Church in Bradford) was an Arminian in theology.
[21] Jonathan Livermore was one of the first deacons chosen at the organization of a church in the north precinct. Kent, *Northborough*, pp. 278-280.

thought to be near his End. I went, got there about sun rise (a stormy Morning. Snow'd hard). He discours'd admirably well when I first went in, of his going to Rest—his praising forever and ever. But by the force of his Distemper he afterwards became delirious, and his Mind was clouded and sadly distracted—after Prayer I return'd home, calling at Mr. Grows, Lieutenant Tainters and Merchant Rice's. Ebenezer has made 3 Barrells more of Cyder, which is the last (of clear Cyder) and makes up the Number of 19½ Barrells for the Year.

19. Joseph Bowker returns from Townsend, whither he went last Monday with Lieutenant Tainter to look of my Land there, and he brings me word that Lieutenant Tainter acquaints him that my 10 Acre Lot is gone. The Hampshire Men had met at Groton and drawn their Lotts, and for this among the rest, as 'twas Suppos'd.

20. Sent Ebenezer with a Team to Lieutenant Eagers Tavern to carry a Barrell of Cyder Here for Mr. Davis of Holden. I rode up myself and proceeded to Colonel Wards, to Mr. Cushings and to Mr. Edward Goddards—bought 42½ pounds of Cheese. Return'd p.m. Mrs. Mehitable Brigham[22] here again to discourse with me about her joining to the Church—interrupted by Mr. Martyn who was come from Council at Sutton and Mr. Hutchinson who expects to give his answer to Grafton next Monday.

21. Some Competency of Turnips rais'd and cutt by ourselves. Mr. Francis Whipple here to bring Intelligence of my lost Cow, suppos'd to be found at Lambstown at one Weeks's.[23]

22. Rainy—yet rode over to Mr. Martyns, we having agreed on the 20th to change on this Day. I preach'd all Day on Mat. 25, 46 latter part. Mr. Martyn preach'd for me on 1 Thess. 5, 19. Quench not etc. Mr. Martyn has news of his mothers being ill. I return'd home by 9 o'clock before Every Body was o'Bed.

23. A rainy and stormy Day.

24. Another very rainy Day, which prevents my going to the Association Fast at Harvard, and am afraid it will many others. However, I desire to have my Heart with them. Did somewhat that way in the forepart of the Day, but was afterwards variously interrupted. John Rutherford here to make a Letter-Garter-Loom. P.M. divers others here. Yet may God of his infinite Mercy pardon my great Defects! and accept of those who this Day call upon his Name! for I would hold Communion with them.

25. Ebenezer rode early to Shrewsbury on his Journey to Lambstown to look up my Stray Cow. Dr. Smith here. Major Keyes also. A.M. Sorry the Doctor is Still in So Disturb'd a Temper. May God be pleas'd to open his Mind, and dispose him to receive the Counsel which has been given him!

26. Daniel How p.m. diggs Potatoes. Mr. Ezekiel Dodge here, with his sister Maynard. He tarry'd to Supper. He read some Letters from Cambridge which inform of divers late Severe Laws made by the Corporation especially against Absence from College beyond the Liberty granted. Very fine Day. Mrs. Elizabeth Miller[24] here.

27. Pleasant Weather. Sister Lydia Champney and Molly rode over to see Mrs. Warrin at Upton. At Eve Brother Hicks, and lodg'd here. N.B. Mr. Carryl from Hopkinton here in behalf of his Brother Woodwell and din'd with us. Ebenezer return'd and brought home the Cow. He paid 40/ old Tenor to Mr. Weeks of Lambstown for her keeping. He can hear nothing of other Young Creatures that are still missing. At Night came on a storm of Rain, but

28. In the Morning the Ground was cover'd with Snow. Cold and Raw, and looks dismally. Brother Hicks went over to Upton to invite sister Lydia to his House. I have great Reason to magnifie and praise the Name of God for his Great Mercy and Goodness which he has shewn in lengthening out the Day of His Patience towards Me and towards this Church and people, it being this Day 25 Years since the Church was gather'd and I was ordain'd the Pastor of it. And at the same Time I have great reason to be deeply humbled before God for my Unfaithfullness, Slothfullness, Barrenness, and Unprofitableness. May God be

[22] Mrs. Moses Brigham.

[23] Thomas Weeks of Lambstown Plantation, which had become the town of Hardwick in 1739.

[24] Mrs. James Miller, Jr.

graciously pleas'd to grant me his holy Spirit to quicken me to both true Gratitude for the Lenity, and deep Repentance for my great Defects and Miscarriages! And may God grant all needed Influences of His Spirit also to qualifie and furnish for his Service, and to excite to it hence forward in a much more fruitfull Manner than heretofore! and May the Long-suffering of God prove salvation. May God be very gracious to the dear Flock! and grant sucess of the Word and Ordinances among them. An inasmuch as it is a Day of peculiar Difficulty, Burden and Charge, by the Building of the New Meeting House and my Remove, May it please God to vouchsafe needed Wisdom and Grace to guide and direct in those Important Affairs: and Smile upon and prosper our Endeavours for Re-settlement that it may in his own good Time be in Righteousness and Peace!

29. Through Gods tender Mercy we began another Year of Sabbaths. May we have Grace to keep them aright! I read Exod. 6 and gave a large Exposition. Preach'd once more on Eccl. 5, 1, applying and improving the Subject according to the season But spent my Preparations in the forenoon service. P.M. read Luke 9 from 10, 28, and repeat'd instead of a sermon Expositions on Mat. 8, 19 to 22. (being Number 141, 142.) Was a pritty raw Air, and the Meeting House very uncomfortable, So many great Windows being open yet, and the Doors unhung.

30. A fine pleasant Day. Ebenezer first help'd Mr. Edwards Whipple kill a Beeve and then Mr. Whipple came and help'd him kill a Young Heiffer for me. Neighbour Stephen Fay here at Evening.

31. I rode over to Mr. Whipples, and made a Visit to Mr. James Maynards—who has for some Time been absent from our Meeting—but he was not at home. Din'd at Mr. Ebenezer Rice's. He and I went down to the plain and view'd the Land South and South East of the Meeting House. I visited Mr. Solomon Woods, Several of whose Children are ill of the Throat Distemper. Had opportunity to Day to talk with Mr. Asa Brigham about Some Meadow and with Mr. Beriah Rice about some of his.

## NOVEMBER, 1749.

1. Exceeding Cold last Night and this morning for the Season. Deacon Forbush here and had an Hebrew Bible for his Son at College. Mr. John Rutherford here again and teaches Lucy to weave Letter'd Garters. Ebenezer work'd for Neighbour Noah How. P.M. Visited Mr. Martyn. In returning call'd to see the Two Widows Tomlin.

2. Mrs. Hitty Brigham here again. Neighbour Rutherford after Dinner left us, generously refusing to take anything for his Pains in teaching Lucy to weave Garters. Molly return'd from Upton and Mrs. Warrin with her. P.M. my wife and I rode in the Chair to the Private Meeting at Mr. Francis Whipples. I preach'd from Isa. 55, 7. After Supper there, Lieutenant Tainter came home with us. The Air pritty Cold. The setting in of the Cold thus makes me very sollicitous and Concern'd about Keeping for my Stock. But I confide in Him who made the Meal in the Barrell and the Oyl in the Cruse last, and provid'd so much for us in the season past, beyond our Fears will Still extend his Care of us and bless our Store as he has done before.

3. Considering the Dangers my Neighbour James Maynard is in of throwing up his Profession of Religion with us, and turning to the Communion of the Church of England, I attempted again to make him a Visit, and found him at home. But the most of his Discourse was to this purpose that Things had gone wrong in this Town for many Years—above Twenty—yet he Said it was not because of any Disquietment he had with me that he broke off. This he said three Times in the Conversation. But he dwelt most largely upon the Conduct of Things in the Days of Mr. Elmer,[1] for he had little to say in his own Defence. I din'd there—neither was there any Angry Ruffle. Finally, I entreated him to Suspend absolutely determining to leave us till there might be some Opportunity improv'd to look into his Complaints and Difficultys; and if things did look to him, in the mean time too disagreeable for him to go to Meeting with us, he would rather go to meeting at Shrewsbury, which was near to him;

[1] The Reverend Daniel Elmer who had preceded Parkman as a preacher in Westborough.

than to Hopkinton, to Mr. Price[2]—and desir'd him to come and See me. To which he reply'd that he did not know but he Should. I left him with much Concern for him. May God most mercifull be pleas'd to pitty him and rescue him! P.M. rode to the Burying of Mr. Solomon Woods's little Dauter which dy'd of the Throat Distemper. At Eve Brother Hicks brought sister Lydia from Sutton.

4. Brother Hicks return'd home to Sutton. Mrs. Hitty Brigham here again. P.M. Mr. Hutchinson here, and I rode up to Mr. Ebenezer Brooks's in Grafton and lodg'd there.

5. Mr. Hutchinson preach'd at Westborough. N.B. He and sister Lydia din'd at Lieutenant Tainters. I preach'd at Grafton on Rom. 8, 7, all Day. And Baptiz'd Timothy the son of Abraham Temple, and Mary Dauter of John Adams. At Eve Mr. Hutchinson return'd to Mr. Brooks's where I lodg'd. Major Willard[3] Mr. Cutler[4] and Mr. Aaron Hardy came in, and had much Discourse with Mr. Hutchinson. N.B. Mr. Hutchinson seem'd not freely willing to let the Town know whether in Case he should come up to the proposals he had made to them he would even accept of them.

6. Mr. Hutchinson preparing to Set out this Morning for Hebron. I return'd to Westborough. N.B. call'd at Major Willards—Mr. Temples,[5] Mr. Winchesters and Jonathan Fays. Training of the first Company. After praying with them I din'd with the Company at Mr. Eliezer Rice's. P.M. at the Burial of Mr. William Pierce's little Dauter Sarah who dy'd by the Throat Distemper. Return'd to the Officers at Eve—but they were dismiss'd before I got to them. At Neighbour Williams in returning home.

7. A Comfortable Warm Season for several Days. My Wife and I in the Chair rode over to Mr. Martyns and din'd there. Return'd at Evening and visited Mrs. Martha Warrin. N.B. at Mr. Martyns were several visitors p.m. particularly Mr. Asa Bowker[6] of Shrewsbury and his Brother and sister Davis[7] of Marlborough.

8. Ebenezer is and has been variously employ'd in Carting out Muck and Spreading it etc. I read Plutarchs Life of Demosthenes —and part of Demetrius. At Eve Lieutenant Tainter and his son Benjamin brought in Mary Woodwell the Captive return'd from Canada. They left her and she lodg'd here, and Lieutenant brought home my steer which had been missing from Thurstons at Reads Farm, having found him at Brookfield.

9. Lieutenant came and kill'd a Cow for me—weigh'd 16 score. He and Mary Woodwell after Dinner left us, that She might go over to her Father at Hopkinton.

10. Closely engag'd in Preparations.

11. [No entry.]

12. Read Exod. 7 (tho the former part of it was read by Mr. Hutchinson last Lords Day) and I gave a large Exposition which was the whole forenoon Exercise. Molly and I din'd at Deacon Newtons. P.M. Molly Woodwell's thanks were offer'd in our Congregation—also prayers for no less than Six Children that are sick—3 of Neighbour Beriah Rice's—who have a malignant Fever. The rest have the Canker or Throat Distemper. Read Luke 10 from 21, and ended at 29, and gave the Exposition on Mat. 11, 25, 26. Somewhat drizly Weather then Shiny at Times.

13. Early visited Mr. Ebenezer Rice's Child, Sick, but is better. Was at Mr. Abner Newtons. Broke fast there—ask'd him to sell part of his place. Mr. Child the Glazier, glazing the Meeting House. Was call'd to visit Mr. Beriah Rice's Children. Judah was the Messenger and the same Eve was taken ill. I was at Mr. Jonah Warrins whose Dauter Anna is ill.

14. Captain Maynards Company train'd—pray'd with them and Eat with them. N.B. Lieutenant Eager first appointed.

15. The weather Still favourable. John Dunlop call'd me to visit Sarah Rice, and it was Evening—I went. 6 of them are ill.

16. Snowy and Cold. Public Thanksgiving. Preach'd on Deut. 32, 15. Sarah Rice, Dauter of Beriah dy'd this morning

and Timothy, another son is taken. N.B. Asaph Rice last night brought up a Letter from Cambridge to Sister Lydia in which inform'd that Brother Champney has lost a Dauter.

17. Neighbour Batherick is making a Sink in my back Porch. Tis now grown Cold and the Earth wears the Face of Winter. At the Burial of Sarah Rice.

18. N.B. Assist'd Mrs. Miller about her Relation. Did this at Lieutenant Tainters.

19. Was much disquieted with Mrs. Mehitabel Brigham who neglected to bring her Relation to me till this Morning, nay till I was going into the Meeting House. Read Exod. 8, preach'd from Ps. 26, 6, improving and repeating the Heads in Sermon on 1 Cor. 11, 26, from page [blank] to page [blank]. Administered the Lords Supper. Din'd at Deacon Newtons also my wife, and Sister Lydia. Molly and Lucy were at the Deacons but had dinners of their own. P.M. omitted the reading—and instead of a Sermon gave the Exposition of the forenoon Chapter; Somewhat enlarg'd. It was a Somewhat Cold Day—and I stood it with Difficulty: But would bless God for that measure of Strength and Comfort which I am favoured with. Was at home some while before sunsett. I reflect with a great deal of shame and sorrow on my scantiness and Barrenness; but the Week past has been a Time of much Engagement, and I could not well imagine I Should have full Preparation for the Sabbath. May God pitty my Weakness and forgive my great Defects!

20. Nineteen persons, older and younger, Three with Teams, to get me wood. They got down to the Door 29 Load. They were Lieutenant Tainter with his Team and his Son, Mr. James Bowman with his Team and his son, Mr. Harrington with his Team and his son; Messers Martin Pratt, Daniel Hardy, Cornelius Biglo, William Pierce, Jonathan Forbush junior, Solomon Baker, Joseph Grout junior, Elijah Hardy, Thomas Hardy, Seth Miller, Daniel Forbush junior, Joseph Bowker, and Samuel Bumpso. P.M. there came up such a snow storm as made 'em break off a little earlyer than they otherwise perhaps would have done. I took Cold by being out among the People in the Snow.

21. Sister Lydia purposing to go down, but being the Preparation etc. for going was not affected till after one o'Clock p.m. therefore tho it was an inviting pleasant Day, Yet I conceiv'd it too late to set out to Day and perswaded her to adjourn it till tomorrow morning. My wife and I rode in our Slay to Lieutenant Tainters to the marriage of Joseph Bowker.[8] Mr. Hutchinson from Grafton there. I was much afflicted with Toothach, Rheumatic Pains, and I was feverish—was not well, at Home or abroad. Went to bed much indispos'd. Ebenezer gather'd our Sheep home. In all 16.

22. Early in the Morning Stormy; but afterwards it clear'd off, and very Cold. Ebenezer in Lieutenant Tainters least Slay waited upon his Aunt Lydia[9] to Cambridge. I am much indisposed with Pains in my Teeth, and at Times Rheumatic Darts in my Limbs: yet able, through Mercy, both to write and read. It proves exceeding Cold at Night. My little Son William putt up the Cattle and meated them himself tho so very Cold.

23. Neighbour William Rogers here again importuning me to suffer him to join with the Church. Catechiz'd at my House. Only six Boys besides my own in the forenoon: and in the Afternoon the Weather being Cold and the Roads bad, there came no Girls at all. At Eve Lieutenant Hezekiah Ward here, and put up with us for the Night. Josiah Lock[10] (at my Request) is here to help my Billy in tending the Cattle and cutting Wood; and lodg'd here.

24. Lieutenant Ward left us towards noon, and Ensign Millar here and bought Two Spring Calves, for 6£ old Tenor. The Weather a little Moderater. I am still indispos'd, but Somewhat Easier: so that I go out, tho with Care.

25. A very Cold Night, and this morning very sharp. Captain Maynard sent Joshua Winchester (who lives with him) to Cut Wood at the Door and assist Billy about the Creatures. At Eve Ebenezer came home, having had a tedious Journey to Boston and Concord: he came from Concord to Day. N.B. a Letter

[2] Commissary Roger Price.
[3] Joseph Willard, a founder of Grafton.
[4] James Cutler of Grafton.
[5] Abraham Temple of Grafton.
[6] Asa Bouker or Bowker married Martha Eager of Marlborough.
[7] Eleazer Davis married Abigail Bowker.

[8] Bowker married Sarah Tainter, the daughter of Lieutenant Simon Tainter.
[9] Parkman's sister-in-law, Lydia Champney.
[10] The son of Joshua Lock of Westborough.

from Thomas of the abusive Detractions of Mr. Williams of Marlborough at Jones's Tavern at Concord. From Mr. Whiting Fullers Worthys.[11]

26. A raw Cold, cloudy Day—but I was so much more Comfortable than I have been (tho Still indispos'd) that I ventur'd to Meeting. Read Exod. 9, gave some brief Observations only. Preach'd on 2 Tim. 4, 3, former part a. and p.m. P.M. read latter part of Luke 10. My wife din'd with me at Deacon Newtons. Got home in Comfort at Night. Blessed be God! We are much burthen'd with Stray Sheep.

27. A.M. Robert Cook[12] here to be examin'd etc. Sent 1/2 Dozen Fowls to Boston by Neighbour Ebenezer Maynard: being oblig'd to Sell and kill off every Thing that I can Spare, in order to preserve what live Stock may remain.

28. This Day in the Year 1730 my Honoured Father Deceas'd. I would not only remember the Death, but the Sudden manner of his being Seiz'd, and would beg of God so to prepare me, that I may be always ready for his Summons. My Wife and Dauter Mary made a visit to Lieutenant Eagers wife, it being good slaying. The Precinct (as Captain Maynard who came in, in the Evening Inform'd me) met together this Day to Consider my Circumstances—Yearly Support, and Entertainment on Sabbath noons. What they have done I expect to hear more particularly in due Time. In the mean While I desire to committ myself to God and his good Providence. The Lord careth for me. May I have grace, also, to put my intire Confidence in Him!

29. Neighbour Robert Cooks wife here in the Day Time, and He again in the Evening—A very Troublesome Case.

30. I have receiv'd no message from the Precinct. P.M. I rode over to Deacon Newtons to discourse with him about hiring part of his House, but he was not at Home. While I sat there Esq. Baker came in. After some Discourse we walk'd over to Neighbour Abner Newtons. Our Discourse there was also about my moving if I could find any Convenient House. Call'd at Merchant Rice's at Eve to see his sick Child. Rode around to Mr. Eliezer Rice's and left my Young Horse with him to be kept. The Season looks at present very terrible. Tight Shut up with Snow and some Days very Cold. It fills many (I suppose) with Concern. But we must remember Jehovah.

### DECEMBER, 1749

1. Comes in with a strong Storm—rain'd all Day. Domestic Conversation about our Moving—appears no Small Matter.

2. Bright and pleasant. My wife finish'd a Cloth colour'd Russell Gown for me.

3. Read Exod. 10 with Exposition, and preach'd from 2 Tim. 4, 3. Din'd (by his renewed invitation to me, but no mention of any of the rest) at Deacon Newtons. Molly and Lucy and Billy tarry'd at the Meeting House. I enquir'd of Mrs. Newton what was become of them and she manifested concern and Disappointment for she had ask'd them (heretofore) and did Desire they might be with us at Dinner, and said she spoke to Billy (to Day) at the Meeting House Door, to come. (But I suppose they knew not upon what foot they were to come and therefore did not. It is a pity that this Affair has made any Difficulty.) P.M. I read part of Luke 11, viz. to 13, and after a few glances upon it, I wav'd the rest, to the sermon which was upon those words in 2. When you pray, say, Our Father etc. in which I improv'd what I had upon Mat. 6, 9. For tho I had writ more than might have serv'd for one Exercise, upon the Subject in the Morning yet I much rather chose to deliver as much of it as I well could at once. May God please to pardon my Defects, and own and bless my imperfect, if sincere Endeavours preventing misunderstandings of what has been offer'd, that men might be prejudic'd against seasonable Truth. May God enable us to see and embrace it as it is in Jesus, and be sanctify'd thereby! N.B. Besides Neighbour James Maynards going over to the Church of England, we hear sorrowfull News from Hardwick of some Number of those who

[11] Thomas Fuller, *History of the Worthies of England* (London, 1662).
[12] The son of Cornelius Cook.

went from this Town (Mr. James Fay[1] etc.) Separating from the Church there and setting up John Roberts[2] late of Grafton, for their Preacher if not Teacher: and some among ourselves hankering to go after them.

4. [No entry.]

5. Mr. John Child Glazier here, mending etc. Stormy Day. Neighbour Eliezer Rice here p.m.

6. Mr. Robert Cooks wife here again. I acquaint her with Difficultys in the way of proceeding to propound her. Ephraim Whitney and Thankful Harrington marry'd a.m. Neighbour Hezekiah How and Neighbour Daniel Warrin assist my son in killing 3 Swine, one weighing above nine, another above 7, another almost 4 Score. Foreseeing I must give some of my Corn to my Cattle and Horses by reason of shortness of Hay, I chose to kill my Pork early tho it be small—have laid up the more Beef. N.B. Mr. Phinehas Hardy has brought 1/2 an Hundred and 8 pound of Iron from Sutton for me, and Mr. Samuel Williams borrows part of it of me. At Eve Mr. Billings, Mr. Bezaleel Eager, Captain Forbush and Lieutenant Thomas Forbush here. The last of them came to know whether I desir'd the Committee of the Precinct would call a precinct meeting to Consider of my Remove nigher the Meeting House, and would send them any Writing on that Hand. I told him I chose they Should themselves consult and advise what would be best to be done.

7. Sent Billy to Mr. Billings, who last night took a wrong Hat. He went also to Mr. Martyns to inform him of Mr. Maccartys preaching to our young men next Wednesday—and ask him and his wife to let us wait on them this Time. For I would by all means promote and strengthen the Bonds of our Fraternity.

8. Tis a great Favour in Providence that we have open and moderate weather again. Deacon Forbush here, and din'd with us. I am sorry there has been Trouble with Deacon Newton about my Dining at his House.

9. Lieutenant Tainter came to acquaint me that the Committee of the Precinct would meet at Esq. Bakers next Monday etc. to desire me to give them my Company there at that Time to confer with me about our Affairs and Circumstances at this Day: and especially with reference to my removal—also in the Name of Esq. Baker he desir'd I would henceforward till next May, myself and as many of my Family as Should please, would dine at his (Esq. Bakers) House on Lords Days. This was the Result of a Meeting which a Number of Southern Neighbours had at Lieutenant Tainters last Night, when likewise they had Discourse with Deacon Newton for his Conduct about this Affair. Lieutenant remark'd to me and strongly affirm'd that Deacon Newton, when three of them came to my House the Saturday before taking down the old Meeting House to desire and invite me to dine at their Houses on Sabbath Noons, (that then the Deacon) did not invite—as I had suppos'd and had often said.

10. Mr. Eliezer Rice sent my Horse in the Morning for us to Meeting. A.M. read the 10th Chapter of Exod. with some Expository remarks, but read P.M. Luke 11, from 14 to 36 without [?]. Preach'd a. and p.m. on 2 Tim. 4, 3, 4, which I have this Day Seen much more the need of, than while I was composing the Sermons. My Wife and I din'd at Esq. Bakers. I am inform'd that Neighbour Stephen Fay,[3] since the forenoon sermon of last Lords Day has been so warm about leaving us and moving to Lambstown, that seat of Disorder and Separation, and principal subject of Discourse at this Time, that he last week went up and brought him a place there. God grant him Grace to make a good use of the seasonable word he has heard to Day! And may it be bless'd as a Solemn Warning to us all!

[1] Son of the late Captain John Fay of Westborough. Stephen Fay, who had settled in Hardwick in 1746, was a founder of the Separatist Church, Congregational, in Hardwick, in 1750. Deacon Fay was named as a Tory in 1775 by the Hardwick Committee of Correspondence. George H. Johnson, *One Branch of the Fay Family Tree* (Columbus, O., 1913), p. 25.
[2] Roberts was not a college graduate but a lay-preacher or exhorter. There is no record that the Separatist Church of Hardwick had a settled minister. In 1761 Roberts and some others of the Congregation voted to move to Bennington, Vermont, and there they formed the first church in the state of Vermont. Paige, *Hardwick*, pp. 225-230.
[3] The brother of James Fay, who had already moved to Hardwick. Stephen became an innkeeper and prominent citizen of Hardwick. He later moved to Bennington and kept the Green Mountain House there.

11. P.M. according to the Request brot me by Lieutenant Tainter last Saturday I rode over to Esq. Bakers and Met the Committee of the Precinct viz. Esq. Baker, Lieutenant Tainter, Lieutenant Thomas Forbush, Messers James Bowman and Phinehas Hardy. The Business was, They wanted to know whether I expected or desir'd the Precinct to do any Thing for me about my Remove from my present Dwelling to the New Meeting House, which I certify'd them I depended upon their assistance. Was at Merchant Rice's and had some Talk there with Lieutenant Nathan Brigham of Southboro about the Land round the Meeting House and he seems willing to grant it.

12. Was at Captain Maynards.

13. Cold. Mr. Martyn and his wife made us a Visit, and din'd here. Mr. Maccarty came from Worcester and preach'd a Lecture to Young Men from Luke 16. If they hear not Moses etc. My son Ebenezer Set the Psalm: and Nathan Maynard read it. Mr. Stone[4] and Mr. Smith[5] came from Shrewsbury and din'd here but neither they nor Mr. Martyn or his wife went to Lecture. Mr. Edward Goddard came for a Copy of Mr. Isaac Stones Complaint. Hear that Job Cushing is come home.

14. Mr. Maccarty left us, to return home to Worcester.

15. [No entry.]

16. Court held at Esq. Liscombs,[6] Mr. Abraham Temple and others having prosecuted a Grafton Bridegroom and some of his Attendants for abusing his son Joseph who with other youngsters from Mr. Jonathan Fays in this Town, broke forth Sounding an Horn etc. as the nuptial procession went up into Grafton from Esq. Bakers where their Marriage was Solemnized.

17. Cold and rugged Weather. Mrs. Chamberlin rode with my wife and Dauter Lucy and me in our slay. Read part of Exod. 12 and made the Exposition to be a.m. Sermon. My wife and Billy and I din'd at Esq. Bakers. I lengthen'd the Time to an Hour and half Intermission. P.M. read Luke 11, 14 to 37. Preach'd on Jer. 6, 16. Neighbour Eliezer Rice and his wife (tho so Cold a Day) went to Meeting at Grafton. My Lucy din'd at Mr. Abner Newtons. But O that we may be made willing to undergoe unavoidable Difficultys in getting to the Place of worship for the Sake of Communion with God. I have lov'd the Habitation of thine House, says David, and the place where thine Honour dwelleth.

18. Court held at Esq. Wards,[7] the Opposite Party to those which prosecuted on Saturday, viz. Captain Drury and now prosecuter Temple's son, Eleazer Whitney and Two of Mr. William Nurse's sons, for their Behaviour. Samuel Bumpso here to borrow money, but declar'd himself to have been clear, not so much as a witness, nor any way concern'd, only that he ow'd his Landlord Fay some Money, and he now wanted it. I lent him 82/. A very Cold Day. P.M. Mrs. Ann Maynard made us a Visit, and it was at the Time when Oliver Whitney[8] and Dorcas Forbush[9] were marry'd. Neighbour Noah How came and took away Eight stray Sheep to keep, and legally Stray 'em.

19. My wife and I rode over to visit Mr. Beriah Rice's Family. Asaph[10] is now confin'd to his Bed. We were also at Mr. Jonah Warrins and at Neighbor Pratts, whose youngest Child is Still in a weak state.

20. The season is somewhat Severe—Close Time for Spending Hay. But we are in the Hands of God whose tender Mercys are great. At Mr. Rice's Desire I wrote a Letter to President Holyoke concerning Asaphs confinement, and sent the pedigree of Mr. Secretary Wyllys[11] of Hartford. At Eve Captain Maynard here—made a Business of Consulting him about the Circumstances of my Remove, and desir'd him to Sell me some Land which lys near.

21. Very Cold. I kept myself very Close this Week to preparing my Sermons; and did accordingly get forward therein.

22. Somewhat moderater. Had prepar'd of Sermons as much as might well serve for Two Exercises—besides some Thoughts Expository of the Paragraph of the Chapter which we are next to read. At Eve was sent for to visit Mr. Hezekiah Pratts youngest Child, which Seems to be dying—went and pray'd. Some others of the Neighbours and their Wives being there also.

23. Added Somewhat more, by way of Reflection—to my Preparations. Very much wish and desire I could always Enjoy my Saturdays as now. But then it very much takes me off from other Studys. N.B. Mr. Warrin and his feeble wife here, and Mrs. Bowker; and din'd here.

24. The Weather somewhat troublesome. A.M. I read Exod. 12, 11 to 20, gave some brief unwritten Remarks or Glances—preach'd a. and p.m. on Jer. 6, 16. Din'd at Esq. Bakers, Molly at Mr. Ebenezer Rice's, and Lucy at Mr. Abner Newtons. P.M. read Luke 11, latter part. In returning home at Eve call'd in at Mr. Hezekiah Pratts, whose youngest Child lyes dead. N.B. It gave me great Relief to be so seasonably prepar'd for the Sabbath and Exercises were perform'd with much more pleasure. My Heart also was not altogether unaffected. Blessed be God for it.

25. At the Funerall of Mr. Pratts Child—carry'd Lucy, Billy and Sarah in the Slay. Lieutenant Bruce[12] was here about the Stables which Several of them had join'd to raise at the Meeting House and had done it last Friday, on the Land which I am buying of Lieutenant Brigham of Southboro.

26. Somewhat Cold but bright. My wife and I rode in the Slay to visit a Number of Neighbours viz. Captain Forbush,[13] Old Mrs. Forbush,[14] Lieutenant Bruce, Mr. Amsden, where we din'd—My little Alexander being with us. Then we proceeded to Elisha Wards and return'd by Isaac Amsdens. Were at Mr. Beemans and Eliphalet Adams's. Were oblig'd to leave the rest of the Familys to some other Time. But alas that no more good is done for the Souls of Men!

27. I think it was the Coldest Morning we have had this Year. But yet towards Noon came Neighbour John Rogers with his Team, and help'd Ebenezer draw two Pine Loggs to the Saw-mill, before Night.

28. It was very Cold—and somewhat Windy But I was oblig'd to provide another place (than Mr. Eliezer Rice's) for the Entertainment of my Horse. I undertook a walk—was at Mr. Pratts and Mr. Williams without success. N.B. Reckon'd with Mr. Ebenezer Rice, and din'd there—walk'd up to Mr. Grouts—in returning call'd at Moses Brighams—visited old Mrs. Fay—Exhorted Jeduthun and his wife to attend to their Duty in making a Profession of Religion and that their Children might be baptiz'd—of which they now have five. Call'd also at Neighbour Eliezer Rice's.

29. Ebenezer is fitting a pair of Runners for the Chair to be plac'd on. Colonel Nahum Ward here. Wants Copys of Papers in the late Council at Shrewsbury. At Eve had account of the Free masons late procession at Boston.

30. Spent myself so much in my Expository Preparations that I was belated in preparing for p.m. but my mind had been before engag'd upon it.

31. A moderate pleasant Day. A.M. I read Exod. 12, 29 to 36. The Exposition was the forenoon Exercise. I din'd at Esq. Bakers. My Wife and Children return'd home in the Slay. P.M. I read Luke 12 to 21. Sermon on Jer. 6, 16. In both the Exercises I had reference to the Concluding of the Year. May God accompany etc. Had some lively sense of our Mortal state. May God impress my Soul thorowly! That when not only Years, but Time itself Shall finish, I may be ready! may be Secure and Happy—But I see I had need to be awake, and diligent for the Grand Period hastens upon Me apace. May God almighty and most mercifull grant His needed Grace!

---

[4] The Reverend Nathan Stone of Marlborough.
[5] The Reverend Aaron Smith of Southborough.
[6] Samuel Lyscom of Southborough was a Justice of the Peace.
[7] Nahum Ward of Shrewsbury.
[8] The son of Nathaniel Whitney.
[9] The daughter of the late Thomas Forbush.
[10] Asaph Rice (Harvard 1752).
[11] George Wyllys, Secretary of Conn.
[12] Abijah Bruce.
[13] Samuel Forbush.
[14] The widow of Thomas Forbush.

## JANUARY 1750

With all hearty Gratitude and praise I would magnifie the Name of God who through his Wonderful Patience and Longsuffering has Still protracted my worthless, unprofitable Life to the Commencement of yet another Year. I would Spend a little Time in Meditation on human Frailty and Mortality, and Compare the Divine Unchangeableness and Everlastingness. I would Consider the unsuitableness of immoderate Sollicitude and Anxiety about future Events in this World, but beg Grace to committ to God all that concerns me. I beg pardon through the Blood of Jesus the great Atonement of all Numberless Offences past, especially through the Course of the last Year: Entreat I may be enabled, and more quickened than ever to serve and Glorifie God in holiness, fruitfullness and faithfullness. But inasmuch as I may be call'd to some special Trials this Year (if my Life be preserv'd) in the Affair of my Remove from my present Dwelling, to be nearer to the New Meeting House, I beseech God to save me from Temptation or make a way for my Escape that I may be able to bear it! I spent the Chief of the Day retir'd, yet too brokenly.

2. Mr. Edward Goddard here in the Morning. The Society of Young Men came and Cut Wood for me, viz. Nathan Maynard, Daniel How, Jonas Bradish, Aaron Warrin by proxy scil Josiah Walker, Merodach Smith, Daniel Cook, Phinehas Maynard, Moses Warrin, Joseph Grout junior—but there was no other Team than my own which was manag'd by my son part of the Day—but it being warm and pleasant weather the Snow became at length too soft and sticky so that he left off Sledding. P.M. Sam Bumpso came to Cutt. At Evening we Sang. May God increase all grace and Goodness in them and make them all to be rich Blessings in their Generation!

3. A.M. to Southboro to Lieutenant Brighams[1] to Speak with him again about the Land near the Meeting House, but he was not at home. I din'd there and then return'd home as soon as I could that I might get upon my Journey p.m. to Upton. Mr. James Bradish accompany'd me to Mr. Elijah Warrins, and Mr. Marshall Baker from thence to Captain Hazzletinc's[2] where I lodg'd. But neither Mr. Hall[3] nor Mr. Frost[4] nor Mr. Dodge[5] (who were expected) were there.

4. Fast at Upton in order to Calling a Minister; and that they might be better prepar'd for that, to renew Covenant as a Church. No Minister came till afternoon to assist. Mr. Frost came in service Time, and with him Mr. Hutchinson.[6] We had but one Exercise. I preach'd on Jer. 3, 15 and after Mr. Frosts praying, the Church very solemnly declar'd their Consent to the Covenant (which had been before hand prepar'd and agreed upon) the men by rising up and lifting up their Hands; the women by rising up. Of men there were present, and thus transacted, Eleven: of women but Three. It was a very solemn season. I hope we had the presence of God. May He be pleas'd to pardon what was amiss, and accept the offering of his People. We sung the Close of Ps. 118. We retir'd to Captain Sadlers[7] and supp'd. And at Eve the Brethren of the Church who had transacted as aforesaid, Sign'd the Covent. N.B. Mr. Benjamin Palmers Offence with me remov'd. N.B. a Number of Separatists at Captain Sadlers, who himself did not (I think) go to meeting. I rode to Mill-River with Mr. Frost, and one Mr. Bointon. We call'd at Captain Tylers[8] and Dr. Scammells.[9] I lodg'd at Mr. Frosts; and Mr. Bointon kept my Horse. A Cold Night.

5. A very Cold Morning, but journeyed Home, calling at many Houses—Mr. David Tylers, where I din'd—Mr. Matthew Tafts, Mr. Gasketts, Mr. Chaddocks, Deacon Forbushs, and Lieutenant Taynters. Found my Tabernacle in peace. D.G.

6. Snow. An Exposition on Exod. 12, from 37 is all I can prepare.

7. A.M. Exposition Exod. 12 from 37. My wife and I din'd at Esq. Bakers. P.M. read Luke 12 from 22. Distinguish'd 33 and repeated Exposition on Mat. 6, 19, 20, 21. A considerable Cold Day, but God sustains us.

8. A very Cold Day. Mr. Jeduthun Fay came and bought seven Sheep of me, (3 of them Lucy's) for 12£ old Tenor and took a poor Ewe with Lamb to winter for me. Mr. Thomas Whitney was to take my Horse to keep.

9. A very tedious Cold Snow Storm. The Mercifull God have Compassion on the miserable and Distress'd! Whilst Blessed be his Name for our Comforts!

10. A Lovely Day. I rode to Mr. Elisha Wards about the Land (which he holds in Common with Lieutenant Brigham) round our New Meeting House. Cold at Eve in riding home. N.B. The Conduct of William Rogers to Day at my House would not so much do the least Neighbourly Kindness, E. g. Stand at a place to stop the Geese when we wanted to catch one but went away in a Strange Frame. I went and talk'd with his Parents and Brethren. Sent to Brother Samuel Parkman 20£ old Tenor by Nathan Maynard.

11. At Mr. Ebenezer Rice's—obtain'd of Mr. Rice to go to Mr. Stephen Fay and endeavour to trade with him for his Land on the Plain before the Meeting House. Thence I went to Deacon Newtons and reckon'd with him. N.B. Mr. Benjamin Fay there. When I came home found Lieutenant Tainter here (who was here also to see me last night, endeavouring then in vain) to speak with me about keeping some of my Cattle, and to Comfort me under my Circumstances with hopes of what may be done by the precinct for my remove.

12. Mr. Simon Tainter of Grafton here, but he did not take any Cattle as I expected. Mr. Ebenezer Rice makes me some Return from Neighbour Stephen Fay—that he was willing to sell the Land for £160 old Tenor. At Eve came Rev. Mr. Campbell of Oxford and lodged here.

13. Rainy. Yet Mr. Campbell set out for Sutton.

14. Clear'd up pritty Cold. Read and Expounded Exod. 8. Lucy and I din'd at Esq. Bakers. Molly dines at Mr. Ebenezer Rice's. P.M. read Luke 13 and preach'd on Exod. 13 Two last verses. Manning,[10] a junior Sophister, who keeps School at Mr. Daniel Warrins, Supp'd and Lodg'd here, at Ebenezers Invitation.

15. A Remarkable Day! The Parish came together at the Meeting House to consider and provide for my Remove from my present Dwelling. N.B. Lieutenant Tainter here. Captain Maynard (came at my Desire). I ask'd him (as I have of late Several Times) to sell his Land nigh the Meeting House but he refuses—is very much out of Humour, to my Grief, as he has been a worthy neighbour; and I fear he will be very much incapacitated by this Ruffle, to receive any good. I sent a Paper to the Precinct by Lieutenant Tainter. Tho it was a Cold Day I rode over to Deacon Newtons. At Eve came in (to Deacon Newtons) Mr. Ebenezer Rice and inform'd me (agreeable to my Desire) that Neighbour Stephen Fay would be at my House tomorrow to finish the Bargain about the Land aforesaid, and afterwards came in the Deacon, Esq. Baker and Lieutenant Tainter. They inform'd me that the people at their meeting made no Vote upon my Affair. But all Things relating to my Remove are left in Confusions, their Minds being very much Divided. Many persons were for granting no more than 500£ naked and according to the present Value, nor would they vote that to be put into a Rate without I would manifest myself contented with it. We had a great Deal of Discourse at the Deacons upon what had pass'd in the Day—and the Tendency of those Things.[11] N.B. talk'd with the Deacon alone concerning the Paper which a Committee (of which he was one) prepar'd us a message from the precinct to me in answer etc. but tho it was not voted yet doth said paper lye among the papers of the precinct to my great Disadvantage and Reproach. I therefore desir'd the Deacon to take Care that it be destroy'd; or else let me have the Benefit of putting in a Reply to lye along with it. My Wife and several Children much indispos'd.

16. Mr. Stephen Fay came here and brought his Plotts that I might make the writings respecting the Land I have propos'd to buy of him, provided we can agree upon the Terms. He din'd

[1] Timothy Brigham.
[2] John Hazeltine.
[3] The Reverend David Hall of Sutton.
[4] The Reverend Amariah Frost of Milford.
[5] Ezekiel Dodge (Harvard 1749), a young preacher. *Sibley*, XII, 367-369.
[6] Aaron Hutchinson, the preacher of Grafton.
[7] John Sadler of Upton.
[8] Nathan Tyler of Milford.
[9] Samuel Scammell, the physician of Milford.
[10] Joseph Manning (Harvard 1751), later a chaplain of the Continental Army.
[11] See DeForest and Bates, *Westborough*, p. 135.

here. But Mr. Fay loaded our Bargain with Demands which Mr. Rice had never told me of, viz. that I must throw up my Expectation of the Condition of his possessing the Three Acres which were laid out to me, but which now he obliges me to buy at So dear a Rate of him, which Condition was, that he should make over Right to me to take up Three Acres of Common Land instead of it: Yet even this I conceded to hopes to make the Bargain easier in other respects, scil. respecting the Money and Time of payment. We made several proposals, but finally I agreed to go to drawing the Instruments against Tomorrow p.m. leaving a Space to insert that of the Terms he propos'd to my Choice, which I should like best. And thus he left me. One of the ways or kinds of Terms he had left me was, that I should give Such a Bond as those had give who had lately been buying of him, Such as Esq. Baker etc. Nigh Evening I rode to Esq. Baker to Consult him about those Bonds. In Conversation with him he gave such Account of the Temper of the Precinct Yesterday, and the little prospect of its being better—that, considering this and therewith the Difficulty about the Payment, I hearken'd to the Esquire's Council not to Engage, if I could fairly desist; and defer it a little while, till I should be able to see what would come out of my Circumstances among this People. I first appriz'd Mr. Rice of it, and then went to Mr. Fay. I acquainted him that since he left me I had met with what had much mov'd me to come, and desire him to wave the Bargain for a while, or, as the Case now Stood with me with Regard to the Parish and as there was so much difficulty in knowing what could be just and safe in the Payment in so very Critical a juncture, I must desire him to throw it up. He told me he had as lieve as not—Upon which it was all dissolv'd and the Whole Affair fell to the Ground. Hear that Dr. Breck[12] is very ill.

17. At Eve Master Manning brought me a Letter from Mrs. Pierpoint[13] of New-Haven. Several Children yet indispos'd, but my wife is about again.

18. A Cool Day, but I was oblig'd to go and look after my Horse at Thomas Whitneys. My wife and I took the Opportunity in my Chair upon Runners, to visit several Familys Mr. Grouts, Jonathan Fays, his uncle Benjamin Fays.

19. Rugged Weather. Mr. Josiah Jones[14] of Stockbridge here.
20. [No entry].
21. We rode in the Chair upon runners—a Cool Day yet the sun shin'd. Fewer at Meeting than usual a.m. More p.m. A.M. read Exod. 14, 1–20. Gave an Exposition. My wife din'd with me at the Justice's. Lucy at Mr. Ebenezer Rice's, Billy at Mr. Abner Newtons. At noon receiv'd a Letter from sister Breck of Worcester of the Doctors illness. P.M. read Luke 14, and for a Sermon repeated the Exposition on Mat. 6, 21, and Luke 12, 34.

22. My Wife and I rode to Worcester to See Brother Breck. Find him Somewhat better. Din'd there. P.M. at Mr. Maccartys.[15] He rode with me to See Mr. Joshua Biglo whose House and Two Children were burnt last Saturday morning: at which he and his wife were much Scorch'd and confin'd to their Beds. At their request I pray'd with them. At Eve Mr. Maccarty and I were at Colonel Chandlers but he was from home. My Wife Sat up watching with her Brother. I lodg'd at Mr. Maccartys.

23. Brother Breck is considerably reviv'd and in a much more hopefull way. I din'd at Colonel Chandlers, and Mr. Maccarty and his wife likewise. N.B. the Colonel much disappointed that my wife did not come: Whereas her Brother was so fond of his Company that he would by no means consent to it. P.M. we return'd home. N.B. Call'd at Mr. Cushings[16] and at Lieutenant Eagers[17] both going and coming.

24. Mr. Jacob Rice, Constable for the north part of the Town here, and Saluted me in a perfectly New Manner, viz. with my son Ebenezers Rates—to the Province Tax, viz. £3.4.4. I have

Daily new Hints of the Great Disquietments in this Parish by means of the Affair of my Remove. But God grant me the Patience and Wisdom necessary for me! My Wife much indispos'd and taken off.

25. Mrs. Tainter and Daniel Hastings din'd here. P.M. Captain Maynard brought me a sorrowfull Letter from my Eldest Brother of the Dangerous Condition of my sister Willard[18] is in, and that if I would see her alive I must hasten down. Deacon Forbush here to talk with me about the uneasiness in the Minds of people touching the Charge of my Remove. I walk'd with the Deacon, went as far as Mr. Pratts and got him to go for my Horse, who accordingly brought him from Mr. Jonathan Fay's. N.B. Word Sent by Mrs. Tainter to Mary Woodwell not to come to live here.

26. Set out Early for Boston. Call'd at Mr. Tim Warrins where was Lieutenant Tainter with money for me. I left a Line in his Hands directed to one of the Committee of the Precinct touching the Business of next Wednesday. Call'd at Mr. Stones[19] at Southboro—at Mr. Livermores[20] at Weston—at Captain Tainters[21] and Mr. Dix's[22] at Watertown. Put up my Horse at Mr. Blakes in Boston where Mr. Whipple lodg'd; and thence I hasten'd to my Sister who was as yet alive tho very ill of a pleuratic Disorder and peripneumony.[23] She was also much distress'd in her Mind, and under apprehension that Death can not be far off. Brother William has been ill, but is recovering. D.G. Lodg'd at Dr. Parkmans. N.B. Mr. Taylor[24] of Milton dy'd this Morning! Molly went over to Mr. Palatiah Rice's and brought Martha Pannell to live with us.

27. Visited my Sister, who remains in much the Same distress'd Condition as last Night. Din'd at Brother Samuels and Mr. Whipple with me, who took Care of my Horse till Monday when he is to ride him Home. With my dear Sister at Eve who is Still in great Distress and grows weaker. Yet She entertains an Hope in God thro Christ which is as an Anchor fasten'd etc. And were it not for her burthen'd Mind, could bear the anguishes of her Body, even tho She despairs of continuing in this World. Thinks She shall never See another Sabbath after this which (I intimated to her) is now begun—(But I keep my reckoning of Time here, after a Roman Manner). Lodg'd at the Doctors again.

28. Visited my Sister in the Morning. She told me She had had an horrible Night. Complain'd of the Vilest Things entering into her Mind which She Seem'd to be full of Indignation at. She desir'd Prayers at both Meeting Houses. I wrote Several Notes. Attended at the New North. Sat in Brother Samuels Pew, where was Mr. Whipple also. Mr. Eliot[25] preach'd on John 15. Of the Spiritual Union to Jesus Christ. In Sermon Time Mrs. Kelland came under the Window and gave us to understand we must return to my Sister. Brother Samuel and I went accordingly. Sister was Still breathing, but, not Sensible. We commended her to God by Prayer. She expir'd just as we finish'd, About 1/2 past 11 a.m. and hope She Sleeps in Jesus. One of the most affectionate of Women. May God of his infinite Mercy grant this Providence mayn't go over without Special Benefit to my own Soul! I had determin'd not to preach to Day: but Mr. Webb[26] sent his Son with So urgent a Letter that I went to him and din'd with him. He was So ill that I thought it my Duty to comply—for that weeping ought not to hinder Sowing. I preach'd therefore as I was able p.m. on Gal. 2, 20. At Eve at Brother Parkman's, our remaining kindred being together and Some few Friends, (Colonel Cotton,[27] Mr. Thomas Stoddard,[28] etc.) I delivered an Exercise on John 12, 35. Lodg'd at the Doctors.

---

[12] Samuel Breck, the physician of Worcester, was Parkman's brother-in-law.

[13] Mrs. James Pierpont, Jr.

[14] Deacon Jones, one of the first white inhabitants of Stockbridge, was also called Captain Jones. Electa F. Jones, *Stockbridge, Past and Present* (Springfield, 1854), pp. 148-150.

[15] The Reverend Thaddeus Maccarty of Worcester.

[16] The Reverend Job Cushing of Shrewsbury.

[17] Bezaleel Eager of Westborough.

[18] Parkman's sister, Mrs. Josiah Willard.

[19] The Reverend Nathan Stone of Southborough.

[20] Joseph Livermore was frequently a Representative of Weston.

[21] John Tainter, the brother of Deacon Simon Tainter of Westborough. Bond, *Watertown*, I, 597.

[22] James Dix, who kept a shop in Watertown. Bond, *Watertown*, I, 199.

[23] Peripneumony or peripneumonia, an old name for inflammation of the lungs, or pneumonia.

[24] The Reverend John Taylor (Harvard 1721), the minister of the First Church in Milton, 1728-1750. *Sibley*, VI, 569-571.

[25] The Reverend Andrew Eliot.

[26] The Reverend John Webb of the New North Church in Boston.

[27] Roland Cotton (Harvard 1719) was a Clerk of the House of Representatives, a Justice of the Peace, and a lieutenant colonel. *Sibley*, VI, 298-304.

[28] Sometimes called Captain Stoddard.

29. In the Morning early walk'd up to Mr. Blakes to Send another Letter per Mr. Whipple to my wife, but he was gone. I took Cold by walking in the wet Streets—din'd at Mr. Cowels[29]—felt but poorly, yet visited divers Friends—Elder Cheever[30] etc. Lodg'd at Brother Parkman's. N.B. I remember the wormwood and the gall of this Day, 14 Years since.

30. Walk'd out—but was much indispos'd—went as far as Mrs. Negus's and din'd with her. At Eve among divers Friends—Mr. Thomas Stoddard very kind—daily visited the Corps of my dear Sister. Lodg'd as last Night.

31. Din'd at Mr. Stoddards—A.M. much better than I was—may God Sanctify his holy Hand upon Me! 'tis heavy work now before me. Attended the Funeral of my dear and only Sister. My Brother Samuel led Sarah Tyley and I led sister Rebecca. Brother Parkman was confin'd. The Bearers were Deacon Larrabee, Messers Leazonby, Stoddard, Grant, Greenough and Bradford. Brother Samuel and I went to Brother Parkmans and Spent the Evening together—in Conversation according to the season. May God prepare me for my Turn! Lodg'd at the Doctors.

### FEBRUARY, 1750.

1. Foul Weather, but I went to the Public Lecture Mr. Checkley of the old North preach'd on Ps. 40, 1,2, 3. May God forgive my wanderings and bless it to my souls profit! Din'd at Brother Samuels. P.M. I visited the Honourable Thomas Hubbard.[1] Mr. Eliot there. Mr. Hubbard (I think) had been himself at the Funeral of our dear Friend and Class-mate Mr. Taylor of Milton, Yesterday, whose Death is much lamented. I heard of the Funeral seasonably but could not attend it, having the like work to do, where I was yet more nearly concern'd. May all have a proper Effect upon my poor insensible Heart! Visited Dr. Sewall[2] and Mr. Prince.[3] When I return'd at Evening to my Brother Samuels Mr. Cook of Westborough had been there with my Horse, and a Letter from my dear Spouse at Home, which inform'd of my son Thomas ill at Concord. My Horse was kept at Mr. Thomas Stoddards Stable; but Mr. Cook brought both Hay and Provinder for him. I lodg'd at Brother Samuels.

2. Undertook my Journey from Boston about 10 a.m. Din'd at Brother Champney's at Cambridge. Call'd at Mr. Stephen Prentice's[4] who was confin'd to his Chamber; and at Mr. Hancocks[5] at Lexington, but he was not at home. The old Lady receiv'd and entertain'd me kindly. At Concord at the first of Evening. My son had been much indispos'd, and weaken'd by Vomiting, bleeding at the Nose, and purging—but was Somewhat better, through Gods Goodness. Mr. Minot[6] at Mr. Goolds. Visited the Colonel. Lodg'd at Mr. Bliss's[7] who also kept my Horse.

3. After a Visit to my son, I Set out again on my Journey home. Din'd at Mr. Smiths[8] at Marlborough. Found my Family well—Blessed be God!

4. Read Exod. 14, 21 to the End. Preach'd a. and p.m. on Tit. 2, 13. N.B. was mov'd exceedingly p.m. May God grant it may be abiding on my own Spirits, and have a Suitable influence upon all the Audience! P.M. read Luke 15. My wife and I din'd at Justice Bakers—Molly at Lieutenant Tainters, William at Mr. Williams's. Ebenezer and Martha Pannell came home. At Eve, Master Manning at Supper, and into the Evening. Snow Storm in the Night or

5. Morning. Ebenezer return'd my Horse to Mr. Jonathan Fays to be kept there again. Mr. Whitney came to discourse with me about the precinct Affair. N.B. they adjourn'd their late meeting to February 13 as I am inform'd. Mr. Whitney seems much dispos'd for Peace, while others, it seems, are in Ruffle

especially Some in the South East Corner. The Weather clears up very Cold, and it grows a distressing Time among people, respecting their Cattle; Hay being So very Short, there is reason for much Concern,—but must Confide in God.

6. I visited Mr. Martyn—found him confin'd by his taking Physic. Din'd with Mrs. Martyn[9]—return'd before sunsett. Mr. Francis Whipple and his wife made us a Visit. Master Manning at Eve and lodg'd here. N.B. he finish'd school keeping.

7. Ebenezer in the slay to Concord for Thomas. Cold morning moderate p.m.

8. Thomas brought home by his Brother. Drisly Weather p.m. At Eve Mr. Daniel Hardy here and pays me more money. Old Mr. Whipple and his wife make us a long visit and Sup with us.

9. Lieutenant Tainter here to acquaint me that the Precinct had adjourn'd their late meeting to Tuesday the 13th of the Month. He beseeches me to remember the old Mens Council to Rehoboam, and Speak kindly to this people etc. At Eve Colonel Ward here, for whom I had transcrib'd the papers of the late Council at Shrewsbury, for which he oblig'd me to take a 20/ Bill, though I once and again refus'd to receive any Thing. N.B. I received a Letter from Mr. Stone of Southborough giving me his advice about the 500£ vote of this precinct, and what I had best intimate to them.

10. My Son Thomas is Somewhat better I hope—but seems dull and inactive yet.

11. Read Exod. 15, beginning, but not having as yet given the Exposition of the Close of Chapter 14, which exhibits the Ground and Occasion of that famous song, I made that the Exercise for the Forenoon instead of a Sermon. My wife and I din'd at Justice Bakers. P.M. read Luke 16. Preach'd on Numb. 23, 10. Occasion'd by the Death both of my dear Sister Willard and old Mr. Thomas Knowlton a very godly and worthy man, whose Decease, tho he was very aged and infirm is greatly to be lamented; and we have much reason to wish our Death and last End might be like his. My son Thomas at meeting p.m.

12. Visited Mr. Abner Newton, who has relaps'd. P.M. wrote a Line to Mr. Stone in reply to his of the 5th instant, by one Barton. At Eve Ebenezer taken very ill, Shaking and great pain in his Side follow'd with Fever and Thirst. N.B. he had winnow'd some Quantity of Indian Corn in the Day and very probably took Cold by it.

13. Ebenezer So ill that I sent for Mr. Stephen Maynard to go for Dr. Gott,[10] who accordingly went for him. While my Neighbour was gone the Pain in Ebenezers Side was very extreme. The Doctor himself came not, but his young man Frink,[11] who blooded my Son. He was Somewhat easier and I walk'd over to the Meeting about my Affairs. The Moderator Sent for me desiring that I would go in to the Meeting. I went in accordingly. Utter'd my Mind to the precinct by word of Mouth: the Substance of what was Said I have writ out. Retir'd to Mr. Abner Newtons. A Committee came to me there, viz. Messers Phinehas Hardy, Eliezer Rice, and Jonas Brigham; their Errand was to know whether I had ever accepted the Precincts Votes of February 5 and 8, 1744/5? I Sent word "that I always look'd upon myself as having accepted them." This I wrote and Sent by them, and added by word of mouth (which I desir'd 'em to take notice of) that the particular manner in which I accepted, has been exhibited partly in my paper of February 8, 1744/5 (which the precinct had and read that Day) and partly in a paper which was my design'd, and full answer, which always lay ready for them.

14. As to Ebenezer, the pains are moderated, but he has a Strong Fever. Dr. Gott came and blooded him. Storm of Snow. Captain Maynard came to See us in our Affliction. At Eve Ebenezer very restless; has been all along very Thirsty: and his Case throws us into much Concern.

15. We watch with Ebenezer ourselves; One setting up the fore-part, another the latter part of the Night. In the Morning he Seem'd to be Somewhat Comfortable, but it was not long before he grew worse. Neighbour Eliezer Rice came kindly to see

[29] Parkman's niece, Elizabeth, married Peam Cowell of Boston.

[30] Joshua Cheever, a deacon of the New North Church.

[1] (Harvard 1721). Hubbard, one of Parkman's classmates, was treasurer of Harvard College, Justice of the Peace, and Commissary General of Mass. Sibley, VI, 490-495.

[2] The Reverend Joseph Sewall of the Old South Church.

[3] The Reverend Thomas Prince of the Old South Church.

[4] A former selectman of Cambridge. Paige, Cambridge, p. 630.

[5] The Reverend John Hancock.

[6] Timothy Minot (Harvard 1747) was keeping school in Concord. He became a well known physician there. Sibley, XII, 194-195.

[7] The Reverend Daniel Bliss of Concord.

[8] The Reverend Aaron Smith.

[9] The Reverend John Martyn of Northborough.

[10] Benjamin Gott, the physician of Marlborough.

[11] John Frink, the son of the Reverend Thomas Frink of Rutland, Mass., did not have a college education, but he later practised "physic" in Rutland. Reed, Rutland, pp. 98-99.

us: went home and return'd again to cutt Loggs at the Door. But Ebenezer grew so bad, and at Times Somewhat Delirious that I Sent Mr. Rice to Dr. Gott; who came up with him p.m. My son is much distress'd about the State of his Soul. At his Special Request I pray'd with him. N.B. Mr. Pratt kindly Sent Cornelius Cook to cutt wood at the Door. At Eve Deacon Newton, Lieutenant Tainter, snd Mr. Francis Whipple came as a Committee (they were the Majority thereof, Captain Baker and Lieutenant Thomas Forbush being the other two that came not) to inform me of Two Things from the Precinct, one which had pass'd into a Certainty: if I would accept of it: namely that this Precinct had voted that the grant of 500£ old Tenor made in the Year 1744/5 Should be put into a Rate, to be gather'd and paid me. The other Thing was not Voted, but much talk'd of, and they (the Committee) were desir'd by a great many to propose it to me, namely, whether I would rather choose to tarry where I am, if the precinct will give me an hundred pounds old Tenor per Annum more of Sallery? N.B. They acquainted me that what was voted, as above, was with freeness and Love. I desir'd Time to consider of what they had said. They each of them for their own particular parts gave me their Advice that I would take up with it cheerfully for they had reason to hope that many people would fall in and generously assist. N.B. Martha Pannells Brother Moses Pannell and her Cousen Abraham Black here to see Martha, but by reason of the Trouble in my House they lodg'd at Captain Maynards. I Sat up till between 2 and 3 o'Clock with Ebenezer who is very ill.

16. Sent for the Two Young Men aforesaid who were at Breakfast with me. Very Cold Day, yet Neighbour Jonathan Rogers is moving his wife and Children to Day, up to Mr. Lulls at Ware River. Ebenezer very ill yet. Thomas, through divine Goodness, able to tend the Cattle, But is not free of pain and Indisposition. At Eve came Forbush and afterwards Benjamin Tainter,[12] and they by turns watch'd with Ebenezer. The weather very Extreme.

17. Ebenezer more Shatter'd and delirious when he wakes up; his Fever somewhat off in the morning but returns very Strong at about 10 a.m. as it did also yesterday. The morning exceeding Cold, So that the Doctor did not come: Sent Master Frink who tells me the Doctor judges it will go hard with my son. The Troubles of my Heart are greatly enlarg'd: O that God would bring me out of my Distresses! My Neighbours kind and ready to assist us. Neighbour Eliezer Williams came p.m. to help us about wood, as Benjamin Tainter assisted a.m. Joshua Winchester came at Night.

18. Joshua Winchester having watch'd acquaints us that Ebenezer tho very bad in the fore part of the Night, yet slept considerably well the latter, and Seems better this morning. The Glory be to God, who seems to appear for his Help. Dr. Gott came before Meeting. Says he sees no Dangerous Symptoms but hopes there is an imperfect Crisis: only he does not know what to say of his Spitting bloody matter. I went to Meeting—read Exod. 15 and gave some Exposition. Preach'd on Numb. 23, 10. Rode home at noon. Martha Pannell din'd at Captain Bakers but the rest of my Family at Home. Ebenezer's Fit does not come on as fear'd. P.M. Read Luke 17. Said a few Things Extemporaneously on it. Preach'd on Heb. 4, 7, improving Some part of Sermon on John 6, 12, Scil. from page 6 to 18. At Eve Forbush, but return'd (to his uncle Holloways).

19. Aaron Warrin watch'd last Night with Ebenezer who we hope is thro Gods great Mercy a little better. Neighbours Edwards Whipple and Eleazer Williams came and kindly sledded wood. It was the more kind and seasonable as it proved a considerable stormy Time p.m. yet they were not beat off, but got to the Door 10 Turns, the wood being already Cut to their Hands. They din'd with us, as did Mr. Stone of Southboro who kindly came to see us. The Snow prevail'd pritty much towards Eve. It put us in Mind of the Great Snow storm which came this Day 33 Years agoe. Ebenezer Spitts bloody matter to a greater Degree. My Son William taken ill, having took Cold Yesterday (most probably) in coming from Meeting. Mr. Daniel Hardy,

Collector for the last Year, paid me the last of what he was to gather for my Sallery and support for the Year past.

20. Was Somewhat concern'd about Ebenezers spitting Blood, but this Morning it disappears. Abraham Batchellor had watch'd. Billy seems better in the first of the Morning, but afterwards droops again. Dr. Gott here. He gives Billy a Purge. Lucy complains and is laid by. P.M. Mr. Martyn and his Wife came to see us in our Affliction. He pray'd with us. We have much Reason for Serious Reflection. In this Day of Adversity we Should Consider. May God grant us the Grace needed!

21. Ebenezer considerabley better—blessed be God! Lucy much indispos'd Still, but Billy is at his Lessons again. Captain Maynard and Deacon Forbush here. P.M. Lieutenant Tainter he informs me that he finds he shall be very short of Hay and must get some other place for my Two Heifers which he has in keeping. Thomas trims apple Trees etc.

22. Rode to Southboro—at Mr. Johnsons to Buy Corn for my Horse at Mr. Fays. Din'd at Mr. Stones. N.B. Mr. Thomas How and his despairing Wife there. Rode to Marlborough. Deacon Tainters,[13] Dr. Gotts (for Bitters for Ebenezer) at Mr. Smiths, Colonel Williams's.[14] Heard of the Death of Moses How of Rutland Esq., a Gentleman I was well acquainted with.

23. Justice Baker here to see us in our Affliction, but my Children are thro Mercy better. Thomas had a Ratteen Banyan made by Mrs. Lucy Bowker. Mr. Samuel Fay junior brought me an English Cheese from Boston.

24. Very fine Spring like weather for several Days.

25. Great Rains a.m. and the Roads being exceeding Hollow I did not go to Meeting—but perform'd divers Exercises in my own Family. Neighbour Noah How came and join'd with us. He din'd with us. Deacon Forbush came from the Meeting House at noon, the Rain slacking. I went to meeting p.m. Read Luke 18, preach'd on Numb. 23, 10 and may God grant us both to live the Lives and die the Deaths of the Righteous!

26. Letter from Rev. Mr. Maccarty containing a Request in behalf of Mr. Joshua Biglo for a Contribution here. Mr. Hutchinson who preach'd at Southboro Yesterday, din'd here. P.M. Mr. Stone to Esq. Baker, as Answer to the Committee who were lately with me to acquaint me with what the precinct had voted about the 500£ being put into a Rate. Lieutenant Holloway came to see Ebenezer. He informs me that David Willson has elop'd.

27. I was at Esq. Bakers and Ebenezer Rice's. I call'd there a.m. At Mr. Martyns P.M. to desire him to preach my Lecture. My wife at Mr. John Chamberlins. Brother Hicks here.

28. Thomas return'd to Mr. Goolds at Concord. P.M. my wife and I made a Visit to Mr. Abner Newton who is in a Languishing Condition. N.B. He put into my Hand a 20 shilling Bill New Tenor. I took the more Notice of this because of the State of my Mind to Day: Reflecting on the Trials I meet with in this Parish about my Remove, I nevertheless did in some Measure acquiesce in the will of God as being wisest and best.

### MARCH, [1750].

1. Fine Day. Mr. Cushing here and wants Advice in their Troubles which increase rather than diminish. Mr. Isaac Stones[1] uneasiness So great that he moves for a Dismission and Colonel Ward[2] is not far from asking the Same. Mr. Martyn here likewise. The both din'd here. The Latter preach'd my Lecture. Text Eccl. 1, 2. They went from Meeting, to Southborough.

2. Tho yesterday and for several Days, it had look'd like Spring, yet this Morning has a winter Face again. Brother Hicks[3] din'd here.

3. Ebenezer So far recover'd that today he came out of his Room and din'd with us. Blessed be God for this Token of His Goodness!

---

[12] The son of Deacon Simon Tainter.

[13] Joseph Tainter of Marlborough.

[14] Abraham Williams of Marlborough.

[1] Lieutenant Stone was one of the first selectmen of Shrewsbury. Ward, *Shrewsbury*, pp. 423-424.

[2] Nahum Ward, the magistrate.

[3] Parkman's brother-in-law, John Hicks of Sutton.

4. A.M. read Exod. 16. Exposition with Application to the Occasion of the Communion which was administer'd today. I din'd at Justice Bakers. My Wife and Dauter Molly tarry'd at the Meeting House. P.M. on Eph. 1, 3. Have but two low and dull sense of these great Things. O that God might raise and quicken me by his almighty Grace and Spirit!

5. Having appointed the Catechizing to Day at the School House on the South part of the Town I rode over to attend upon it. At Deacon Newtons Desire I din'd at his House. N.B. had no message from the Town meeting about my Prayer with them. Know not whether there was any at all. At Catechizing about 45 Children. Mr. Ezekiel Dodge here at Eve. He lodg'd here. N.B. his Call at Abington.

6. Rode with Mr. Dodge to his uncle Joseph Knowltons, and din'd there. Proceeded to see his aged grandmother, and uncles Abraham and Ezekiel. At Eve in returning I call'd at Mr. Francis Whipples. N.B. his Discovering to me the Temper and Proceedings of the late precinct Meeting about my Removal and their Endeavours to have the grant of 500£ loaded with new and hard Conditions before they would vote to enter it into a Rate. He also discover'd to me that he had in his Hands my Paper of March 3, 1745/6 which was my Answer to the Precincts renewed Call—which had it been seen or remember'd at the Time of the late meetings about my Affairs would have prevented much Trouble. Mr. Daniel Hardy riving out Posts for me.

7. Rode to Mr. Ebenezer Chamberlins etc. Visited a sick Child of Mr. Joslyns.

8. My Wife and I rode to Mr. Martyns Lecture. Mr. Eliezer Rice favour'd me with his Mare. Din'd there. Mr. Smith there also—but Mr. Cushing preach'd on John 6, 26. At our Return Esq. Baker took Mr. Rice's Horse to deliver him to his Master. N.B. Lucy at Mr. John Chamberlins while her Huband is gone to Boston.

9. Raw Cold. Several Cold Nights of late. Mr. Chamberlin return'd last night from Boston. N.B. he paid 6£ old Tenor to Mr. S. Procter for Cheese for me—also 14 shillings for Chocolat and 6 shillings for Rice.

10. [No entry.]

11. Read and briefly expounded Exod. 17. Preach'd on Eph. 1, 3, a. and p.m. My Wife and I din'd at Justice Bakers, where was also Mr. John Nichols of Boston. P.M. read Luke 19 from number 28.

12. Rode to Mr. Elisha Wards and to Lieutenant Brighams. Lieutenant Tainter with me, endeavouring to trade with owners of the Land round about the Meeting House. I din'd there. P.M. rode up to our Meeting House the Precinct being met there for the choice of Officers, and I desir'd to know their minds respecting Two Requests I had Receiv'd—one from Revd. Mr. Maccarty in behalf of Mr. Joshua Biglo in Worcester whose House was burnt, and another from Revd. Mr. Stone in behalf of the widow Richards of Southborough, who was lately burnt out also. The Moderater desir'd me to go in. I comply'd, but tarry'd not long. They voted there Should be a Contribution for the Widow. N.B. Captain Maynard and I renewed Bounds near the Burying place. N.B. Mr. Whipple had from me Three papers of mine which had been heretofore put in to the Precincts Book. Cold, Raw, Searching Air. Mr. Jeduthan Fay took my Oxen to keep.

13. By Agreement Lieutenant Brigham and I met on the Land by the Meeting House, and look'd up the Bounds of his Land there; and we pitch'd upon a Time to draw the Writings.

14. Sent to my son Thomas by Charles Miles of Concord. Deacon Miles[4] of Shrewsbury here at Eve, by whom had return from Boston of Messages to Brother Samuel Parkman and Mrs. Stoddard.

15. Public Fast. Preach'd on Jer. 5 from number 20 to 25 and read number 29 a. and p.m. P.M. I improv'd some Heads in sermon on Isa. 33, 14, viz. from page 5 to 14. Sometimes only here and there a Sentence, as particularly from page 9 to 12. My Wife and Lucy walk'd to meeting; Molly rode with me on the Mare. It prov'd very Cold: at length snow'd. I went to Deacon New-

tons at Noon. My wife, Molly and Lucy stay'd at the Meeting House, because of the storm. After Meeting the storm being exceeding Strong, the Snow beating very vehemently, my wife rode home with me, Esq. Baker kindly Sent a Son with an Horse to help Molly home, and Mr. Eliezer Rice kindly help'd Lucy home, So that we got home in Some Comfort to what it would have otherwise been, but I think it was more tedious than any Sabbath thro the Winter. May God be pleas'd to forgive our Defects bless his holy word; hear our Supplications and be reconcil'd to us! N.B. I was not only oblig'd to undergo such a storm after preaching, but to look after my Creatures at the Barn. My Health has been much expos'd to Day.

16. Indispos'd, dull and unactive—having been so expos'd to the storm yesterday—Ebenezer so feeble, tender and confin'd yet that he can't go to the Barn in any rugged Weather.

17. Bright pleasant Morning. Brother Hicks at Eve from Cambridge. Lodg'd here.

18. Rugged Morning. I rode over to the North Precinct. Sent my Mare back from the Country Road by Joel Rice.[5] I read (at Mr. Martyns meeting) Exod. 31, and preach'd on Ps. 17, 15 first part, carrying on my Discourse on the Happiness of Heaven begun heretofore on Mat. 25, 46 latter part. It prov'd a rainy Day. P.M. I read Luke 16. Preach'd on John 12, 26, managing another Head of the same subject. Contribution in that assembly for Mr. Joshua Biglow of Worcester, amounted to about 13£ old Tenor. Mr. Martyn preach'd for me on 2 Tim. 3, 5. He and his wife din'd at Justice Bakers. N.B. he did not read in public, a. or p.m. Contribution in the South parish was for the Widow Richards in Southboro, and amounted to [blank]. N.B. It was so rainy, and having no Horse, I lodg'd at Mr. Martyns, who return'd home at Eve. N.B. Brother Hicks at our House.

19. Stormy morning. Yet I return'd home; a little way on Mr. Martyns Horse, and meeting Billy on my own mare coming for me Chang'd Horses. Brother Hicks went away this morning. N.B. Lieutenant Bruce[6] here he being about buying Mr. Cornelius Cooks[7] place, and offers it to me for the Same.

20. Storm of Snow so great that considering the great Straits of many people for Hay, it is very sorrowfull and distressing. Deacon Newton here in the Morning and brought the Contribution of our Parish for the Widow Richards—it amounted to £13.16.10, but very few large Bills—only 1 20/Bill in the whole—one 14/—and but a few 10's. 2£16/ of Hampshire. £2.13.6 Rhode Island, of which a considerable number were of the condemned Bills. It grieves me much. Yet I am glad they did anything Since we are at this Day so many ways burden'd. The Lord accept our offering! but if any have knowingly offerred to the Lord a Corrupt Thing, the Lord be pleased to detect it to their Consciences, give 'em the Grace to repent of it, and in great Mercy forgive it!

21. Storm continues Still. Mr. Jeduthun Fay return'd my Oxen home. Was at Merchant Rice's and paid all, clearing myself and my Children wholly of all other-Government Money. P.M. Mr. Ithamar Bellows here to acquaint me with the Death of Mr. Josslins Daughter Patience. Before Night the weather clear. N.B. Neighbour Ebenezer Maynard digging a Cellar in order to build a new House on the Land which was heretofore Brother Hicks's.

22. Bekky Warrin[8] here to See us with her Babe, and lodg'd here last night.

23. My Wife rode with me to the Funeral of Mr. Joslins Daughter Patience. After the burying, and the people gone off, my wife and I Spent a little Time in viewing the Land round the Burying Place, and meeting House, that we look up a place to build on; but all seem'd to me so barren and undesirable, that I can have little Encouragement. But I desire to repose my Self in God. N.B. Ebenezer waited on Cousen Bekky with her Babe, to her Father Warrins.

[4] Samuel Miles. Ward, *Shrewsbury*, p. 368.

[5] Son of Josiah Rice of Westborough.
[6] Abijah Bruce of Westborough.
[7] Westborough's troublesome blacksmith.
[8] Parkman's niece, Mrs. Elijah Warrin of Sutton.

24. Rain. Thunder. The Earth very full of Rain.

25. So rainy Night, and in early Morn, I was so indispos'd I was not determin'd to go to meeting: but I was afterwards better, and the weather Clear'd; so that I went to Meeting; but having onely one Horse but few of us got to meeting. I carry'd Lucy and Ebenezer, and William went on Foot; all the Rest tarried at home a.m. N.B. Public Thanks for God's great Goodness in restoring my son: this being the first of his going to meeting since his sickness. I read Exod. 18, with some considerable of Exposition and Observations. Preach'd about an hour on Jer. 5, 20, 25, 29, and did not break off till about half after Twelve—but ask'd their pardon for detaining them so long. Din'd at Justice Bakers. Rode before his wife to Meeting. P.M. read Luke 20, and since I chose rather to deliver all my Preparations in one Exercise than to divide it; and Because of the Paragraph in the Reading of our Lords Answering the Pharisees concerning the Resurrection, I therefore took the latter part of my Exercise on the Resurrection, and repeated instead of a Sermon or Exposition. After the services I gave a Warning to such of the Congregation as in the late Contribution put in Bills of poor Credit. But as the forenoon Sermon was very moving, May God be pleas'd to impress all our souls deeply with what was then deliver'd!

26. Grass begins to Spring. Mr. Buckminster[9] of Rutland here. Their Divisions, especially Captain Rice[10] and Deacon Ball's[11] Still continue.

27. Great Rain. Lieutenant Tainter with us.

28. Was at Captain Maynards—his Discourse gave Some Trouble, as he endeavour'd to blacken the Characters of Several principal persons in the parish, and perswade me that there was some Number of persons who do not desire my Continuance here. Gave me very Strong Caution and warning not by any means to depend upon or Expect one farthing more of the Parish towards my Remove than the Naked 500£. Besides this there was much more of the same Nature. N.B. Captain had been out after his Brother James's Son John who was suppos'd to be run away.

29. Ebenezer got 600 of Hay at Ensign Rice's, a.m. N.B. Captain Maynard help'd him get it home. P.M. Lecture to young Society from Ps. 63, 8, repeated with many Alterations and Additions. May God humble and quicken us all! At Eve Lieutenant Bruce here again, to let me know he had now got a Deed of Mr. Cornelius Cooks place, and offers it or any part of it to Me, at the Same rate that he bought it of Mr. Cook.

30. Ebenezer So weak yet, and indispos'd that he can't bear Work. Being a Warmish Pleasant Day, we are invited to gardening. Patty Pannell does what she can in making Beds and Sewing some early Seeds. My Mind is greatly fill'd with a Variety of heavy, perplexing Cares and Troubles. I endeavour in Some Measure to committ myself to God and repose myself in His Graciousness and Faithfullness.

31. Mr. Thomas Stoddard of Boston came up to See us. Though I was glad to See him yet I was Sorry it happen'd to be at Such a Season of Engagement in My Preparations, it proving very much of an Interruption to me.

### APRIL, 1750.

1. A.M. on Exod. 19. I din'd at Justice Bakers. Mr. Stoddard din'd with my Wife at Home. P.M. I read Luke 21, and gave brief Exposition of my Hints. Preach'd on Ps. 26, 9, former part, and use of Sermon on Isa. 33, 14 from page 29 to 47 omitting from page 37 to page 40 near the bottom, and omitting from page 42 to middle of page 46.

2. I waited on Mr. Stoddard to Captain Maynards, and rode with him as far as Lieutenant Brighams—return'd home to Dinner. N.B. Two Foot Travellers from Medfield brought the sorrowfull Tidings of the Death of my dear Friend the Reverend Mr. Henry Messenger of Wrentham, who deceas'd last Saturday of a Fever. They inform likewise that old Deacon Bellows[1] of Southboro dy'd this Day. Mr. Seth Hudson whose Horse Mr.

Thomas Stoddard had bought, was here: Judge Ward made me a Visit. N.B. Mr. Jonathan Fay brought home my Young Horse, he having kept him hitherto and asks me 30/ old Tenor per Week.

3. Was at the Funeral of Mr. Jonathan Bruce's infant. Din'd at Lieutenant Tainters. P.M. at Mr. Nurse's. View'd divers Tracts of Land, in order to procure Something to settle on; but cannot be suited. All is as yet very Dark.

4. Took my Horse at Neighbour Hezekiah Pratts, who kindly kept him last night, and rode to Mr. Benjamin Fays for keeping, for him but in vain—din'd at Mr. Moses Brighams. At Eve heard that Mr. William Jenison[2] is dead.

5. Rose early and rode to Lieutenant Brigham's and obtain'd a Deed of the Land which I have been so long about, and made up 59£ of the Money (Old Tenor). N.B. Mr. Daniel Warrin to keep my Horse.

6. My Mind and Heart very much burthen'd and afflicted from Day to

7. Day by reason of my present Difficultys—but would humbly wait on God.

8. Read Exod. 19 from number 7, *ad fin.* and Exposition of which was the forenoon Exercise. I din'd at Justice Bakers; my Wife and divers others came home. Patty Pannell and little Susan stay'd at the Meeting House. P.M. read Luke 22 and to 38th number and since there have been Such a Number of Deaths of Late (which I have been inform'd of) of persons I have been acquainted with, but especially that I might drop a Tear over my Friend Mr. Messenger. I preach'd on Zech. 1, 5, and my own Soul be suitable affected and profited hereby!

9. Took a Walk first to visit Nathan Maynard who is Sick: to old Mr. Whipples where I din'd. P.M. was at Deacon Newtons and got him to go with me to view Mr. Cooks Island—we had Lieutenant Bruce and Mr. Cook there to shew the Bounds. At Eve at Mr. Nurse's. N.B. he has got a Barrell of Tar, to make Tar-Water.

10. I went to Captain Maynards—he grows Still crosser, and appears angry at Every Thing. Nay even at Goodhues rates being mix'd with his on the Same Paper, tho I was desir'd one Time after another to have Goodhue's reckon'd at the same Time, Mr. Stephen Maynard being to Act for him—But the Captain would have nothing to do with Goodhue's Affairs.

11. Mr. Richard Barns has my Young Horse to go to Boston. Agreed with Lieutenant Bruce for the Cook Island. 250£ old Tenor for what he has of Mr. Cook, being at least 7 Acres; and 300£ old Tenor, if I have the whole Island, and which he assures me I shall when he can be able to give a Title to it.

12. Visited Nathan Maynard who is very ill. Mr. Stone din'd with us and preach'd my Lecture. His Text, Rom. 5, 6. After Meeting we view'd Several Parts of my new bought Land to find a suitable Place to build an House on.

13. This Day 4 Years ago my ever honour'd and dear Mother dy'd. May I ever remember her Example and imitate her excellent Vertues! My Horse is return'd to his Boarding place.

14. Jonathan Fay here for Corn for keeping my Horse. Have let him have 3 Bushels.

15. Read Exod. 20, to number 18. Expository Exercise on the Commandments in general and on the first and second in particular—and the application adapted to the Occasion of the Lord's Supper. My Wife and I din'd at Justice Bakers. P.M. on Zech. 1, 5. Not a few Strangers among us.

16. My Wife and I rode up to Mr. Winchesters to see their Dauter Prudence who is consuming away. We din'd there. In returning call'd at Mr. Benjamin Fays. N.B. Mrs. Miles of Concord there in a very gloomy disconsolate Condition. Catechiz'd at the Meeting House, 43 Children, males and Females. My wife waited for me with the Chair, at Mr. Fays and at Deacon Newtons. The Earth wears a pleasant Green again. Blessed be God!

17. Mr. Ezekiel Dodge came here last Night from Abington with Letter to our Church to request Assistance in his Ordination, and with a Special Request to Me in particular which I am full of Fears I can't comply with by reason of my great Perplexity about

[9] The Reverend Joseph Buckminster.

[10] Edward Rice was an original settler of Rutland. Reed, *Rutland*, pp. 111–113.

[11] Eleazer Ball. For the disputes in Rutland and the stormy career of the New-Light, Reverend Thomas Frink, see *Sibley*, VII, 70–75.

[1] John Bellows.

[2] Jenison (Harvard 1724) had preached and taught at various places including Westborough. *Sibley*, VII, 371–374.

my Building. P.M. I made a visit to Mr. Stephen Fay and his Wife who are tomorrow to move to Lambs Town. N.B. Neighbour Benjamin Fay and Neighbour Eliezer Rice there when I talk'd to them. In returning I call'd at Esq. Bakers. N.B. Consult him about my Building. N.B. Strange accounts about Mr. Jonas Child, his Conduct about his bargaining away his place and beating his wife and Children.

18. Rainy—rode to Deacon Matthias Rice's, to Mr. George Oakes, where lodges Mr. Woods late of Sudbury, Clothier, that I might secure Some Brick among them for my intended Stack of Chimneys and thence I made a Visit at Mr. Martyns.

19. I rode down to Mr. Amsdens[3] to get his son in law Abijah Gale to go into the Ministerial Lott and cut Timber for my intended House. He consents and I procure Neighbour John Rogers to go with him.

20. Messers Gale and Rogers go into a Ministerial Lott as agreed Yesterday but they find only Two sticks and cutt but one of them. It rain'd also and beat 'em off in the forenoon. I rode to the South Side as far as Mr. Charles Bruce's—din'd at Mr. Bowmans. Proceeded to Mr. James Bradishes accompany'd by Mr. Bowman and engag'd him to work on my intended Frame. Was at divers Houses besides, promoting the Same Affair. For the Time of preparing to build is so far elaps'd that unless I am very industrious and Successfull there can be little Hopes of getting into an House before next Winter. But I meet with considerable Encouragement—and especially from Mr. Bowman, who likewise presented me a Bushel and half of Indian Corn, and carried it to Lieutenant Tainters, in order to its being Sent to Mill. Visited Mr. Bonds[4] Family who are newly come into Town.

21. Brother Hicks here from Cambridge and brings me the very Sorrowfull News of the Death of my Reverend and valuable Pastor, Mr. Webb of Boston. May God Sanctifie this Dispensation to me, to the Bereaved Flock at the New North in Boston, and to the bereaved Colleague, and Family in particular! We have great reason to mourn and grieve for the Interest of Religion in this Day when such Sound, pious, usefull Men are, one after another removed from us. O that God would have mercy on us when So many Sad Aspects appear! N.B. Remarkable Gusts of Wind.

22. A.M. read Exod. 20 from number 18—gave some Exposition of the Second Commandment—din'd at Justice Bakers. Walk'd up and back. P.M. read Luke 23 to number 27. Preach'd on Eph. 2, 8 latter part. Us'd my Sermon on the forepart of this number from page 10 to 16 with many alterations and added some Account of Reverend Mr. Webb. After the Exercises read the Letter from Abington, requesting the Church to assist in the Ordination of Mr. Dodge[5]—the Church votes Complyance.[6] But some did not vote among the Rest Deacon Newton,[7] who gave this Reason that the Church had no Return made 'em of Shrewsbury Council's Proceedings—No Result. This answer of the Deacons Troubled me because the Deacon had several Opportunitys to have Spoken to me in private but never gave me any hint of disquietment.

23. Mr. Martyn brought Mrs. Molly, his Dauter here, and rode himself to Grafton—Church Meeting which was concerning the Ordination of Mr. Hutchinson. N.B. Mrs. Sibyl Child in distress about her Husband, Mr. Jonas Child, who is Supposed to be delirious. She Sends for me and I went today. Din'd at Mr. Harringtons—went to Mr. Grows and Ensign Millers. I went also and talk'd with Deacon Newton. Mr. Martyn here at Night.

24. Rain is very seasonable.

25. Neighbour William Rogers junior work'd for me. I rode to Mr. Jonas Brighams to Send an Answer to a Letter from my Brother William concerning Captain Stansbury's Negro. But they Set out Early—however I put on hastily after them and proceeded down the Road till overtook Mr. Twitchell with the Team. From thence I rode to Mr. Stones but he was again gone to Boston. Was at old Mr. Johnsons and at Mr. Amsdens and took particular Demensions of the Timber for my House, of Abijah Gale whom I employ'd to undertake my Frame. When I return'd, Mr. Morse of Shrewsbury was here and din'd with us. N.B. Joseph Bruce came to work for me this afternoon. N.B. Mr. Jeremiah Fowler and Captain Maynard here. The former brought a Jackal, an Entertaining Sight. How wondrously are the Works of God diversify'd! How manifest are thy Works, O Lord! in wisdom hast thou made them all!

26. Joseph Bruce works for me. Mr. Martyn and his Spouse made us a Visit. My wife and I, in our Chair, wait on them in theirs, over to the Meeting House Ground, to see the places which are recommended for my building Spot. N.B. We went round by Mr. Ebenezer Rice's, where was Mr. Fowler with his Jackall, who invites us up Chamber to See him and his pranks. So many resort there to see this Strange Creature that I am doubtful what the Event will be. N.B. Mr. Martyn as Moderator of the Church in Grafton draws Letters Missive to the Churchs which they invite to the Ordination of Mr. Hutchinson.

27. Mrs. Sally Gott[8] and her Sister Betty came to See us. Din'd here. Joseph Bruce works here. They begin to plant Indian Corn.

28. Forbush (from College) lodg'd here last Night. Ebenezer and Joseph ploughing and planting. Extraordinary high Gusts of Wind.

29. Read Exod. 21. Gave an Exposition of the Third Commandment a. and p.m. Din'd at Justice Bakers; my Wife, Ebenezer and Molly, Lucy and Sarah and Alexander likewise. Joseph Bruce and Patty Pannell, who were all of my Family that were at meeting—came home to Dinner. I rode to meeting p.m. on Justice Bakers Horse. P.M. I read Luke 23 throughout. O that we might not take the Name of our God in Vain in our religious Services! and that we might not miss of the Blessing of the Sabbath! Very weary at Night So that I lay down.

30. Rode to Mr. Dunlops to see him in his Sickness. Lieutenant Tainter blooded him. I return'd with him to his House, as a terrible Storm of Thunder and Rain arose. Din'd at Lieutenant Tainters. P.M. visited old Mrs. Dorcas Forbush. N.B. Mr. David Batherick fell upon me as I was coming out of the Door with bitter Resentments of Abuse, because when I yesterday, for the last singing in Publick appointed Mean Tune to be sung, and he instead of Mean, Set Canterbury (as I thought through either Mistake, or because he could not strike upon Mean at that Time) I set the Tune mention'd myself. Nor did I know that this or the other Triple Time Tunes were displeasing to any, till he now makes it one aggravation of the Offence that I knew that people did not like it and yet I would Sett it. N.B. Mr. Batherick Said there was one who said he would go out if that Tune was Sung. I answer'd that (who ever he was) he was (or would be if he Should do so) a Blockhead for his Pains. N.B. Lieutenant Thomas Forbush sat by and heard his Bitterness. N.B. I was very much mov'd, and gave him Some deserv'd Correction. But the Lord forgive what was amiss in me at this Critical Juncture. When I came home, I found here Mr. Samuel Haven[9] of Framingham who desires he may come and board at my House and study Divinity.

## MAY, 1750

1. Very pleasant after the Rain. All Nature blooming and flourishing whilst (alas!) my Heart is as a barren Wilderness. Mr. Haven left us to go back to Framingham. My Wife and I rode to Mr. Twitchells.[1] Ebenezer and Joseph Mending Fence ploughing and preparing the Fields for Planting.

2. Wondrous pleasant and Delightfull. A beautiful Prospect all round; the Air every where perfum'd by the Blossoms; and a Tunefull Chorus of different kinds of Birds, which Sing their Makers Praise. Lord! all thy works praise thee; and may thy Saints bless thee! Bless the Lord O my Soul! Agreed with Joseph

---

[3] Jacob Amsden of Westborough.

[4] Jonathan Bond had lived earlier in Waltham and Mendon.

[5] Ezekiel Dodge (Harvard 1749) had been a supply preacher in several towns of central Massachusetts.

[6] The church voted to send Francis Whipple and Simon Tainter to Abington ordination. Westborough Church Records, April 22, 1750.

[7] Josiah Newton.

[8] Sarah, the daughter of Dr. Benjamin Gott of Marlborough.

[9] (Harvard 1749). The son of the prominent office holder of Framingham, Joseph Haven. Temple, *Framingham*, p. 579.

[1] Jonas Twitchel (Twitchell), of Westborough.

Bruce to live with me for three months; from yesterday, till the first of August, for 41£ old Tenor. But then by taking in the Days that he had work'd for me before this month came in on one hand, and allowing him two Days to Spend for himself of the Time to come, on the other; we agree that I shall pay him 42£ in the whole, when his Term shall be up. N.B. Sent home Mr. Dyers Emlyn[2] by one Ephraim Bacon of Dedham.

3. Consulting all the authors I can, on the Sabbath. Visit Mr. Cushing and din'd there.

4. Ebenezer finish'd planting Indian Corn. P.M. Ebenezer and Molly to Mr. Martyns.

5. A.M. Ebenezer went for a pair of Cart Wheels to Mr. Joseph Miles[3] and brought 'em Home. Price 10£ Old Tenor.

6. Read Exod. 22. Expounded the Fourth Commandment a. and p.m. My Wife and I din'd at Justice Bakers, he having provided and handed an Horse ready tackled for us both. P.M. read Luke 24. After Exercises Mr. Charles Bruce brought me the Earnest Desire of Mrs. Kelly (wife of [blank] Kelly a member of the Church of England in Hopkinton) to visit her, She being very sick—I comply'd. Rode to Deacon Forbushes in my Chair, left my Daughter Molly there, and borrow'd Mr. Jonathan Forbush's Horse, and with Mr. Bruce to pilot, I saw her and pray'd with her. Return'd home the same Evening.

7. My wife rode with me to see Adonijah Rice,[4] sick of a Fever; and thence to Marlborough. Deacon Tainter making me a black Cloth Jacket out of an old Broadcloth Coat. We din'd at Dr. Gotts. N.B. the Doctor gives me his Hand in token of reconcilement. Design'd a Visit to Mr. Smith but he was gone to Cape Ann. N.B. Mr. Hezekiah Bush[5] who suddenly drop'd down dead last—Saturday a.m. bury'd to Day. A very awful and awakening Dispensation when a man is taken away So very Suddenly! The Lord quickens us all hereby! that we may be in an immediate Readiness. Visited Colonel Williams and return'd at Eve in safety. Thanks be to God!

8. As the Earth has needed Rain notwithstanding the late Rains, this Day increases the Dryness.

9. But especially this, which is very warm—the sun burns as in Summer. Finish'd Secret History of Europe[6] Part 1, which is volume 1.

10. A good Air, but burning sun. Brother Hicks and his Daughter Betty going to Cambridge. At Eve Rain, Thunder and Lightning. Lieutenant Tainter here; wants to know where people shall lay the Timber which they provide for me. Jonas Child in sad Distraction Still.

11. [No entry.]

12. Captain Maynard and I renewed Bounds where the old Meeting House stood and agreed that the Stake and Stones, exactly East of the old Meeting House East Door, Should Stand where we have now placed it, till it Should appear by a Survey with Instruments that it is not according to the Plott. Reverend Mr. Joseph Bellamy[7] of Woodberry in Connecticut came to See me, and he brought a Letter to me, and another to the Church from Mr. Edwards[8] of Northampton requesting us to assist them in Council on June 19 next. Revd. Mr. Stone came P.M. N.B. Mr. Stone came in answer to my Desire to change tomorrow, but when he perceiv'd how, in divine Providence I was Supply'd, he went over to Mr. Martyn and Succeeded. Brother Hicks also here, from Boston and brought me a kind good Letter from Mrs. Pierpoint. I bless God for this Correspondence! I am fill'd with Shame and Grief that I can Sustain it no better. O that God would manifest His Grace towards me and qualifie me!

13. Read Exod. 23. Mr. Bellamy preach'd from Job 22, 21. He din'd with me at Justice Bakers. P.M. I read John 1. Mr.

Bellamy from Luke 16, 30. His Exercises were very moving as well as enlightening. Would fervently pray and hope there may be a Saving Influence of the Spirit of Grace accompanying. N.B. I am much concern'd for our Brother Jonas Child, who I hear is often making attempts upon his Life. If it did not rain So hard this Evening I Should not rest without going to See him: yet he was at meeting to Day, and Set the Tune, Sweetly and agreeably as ever. Savoury and entertaining Conversation with Mr. Bellamy, whom I find an ingenious as well as Pious Man.

14. Accompany'd Mr. Bellamy 2 Mile or more on his Journey. Was at Mr. Beemans at the moving of his Barn. Oblig'd to improve every Opportunity to forward my Building—I must undertake it under So many disadvantages. P.M. to Deacon Tainters and Dr. Gotts at Marlborough. At Eve at Mr. Bradishs who and his wife likewise are sick. I was not very well while I was there.

15. Lieutenant Forbush and I went to view the Ridge or Nole, which joins to the Land I lately bought of Lieutenant Nathan Brigham, and he Stak'd out how much I Should have if it Should Suit me to build upon it. P.M. Mr. Martyn here. My Concern very great about Mr. Hutchinson[9] settling at Grafton. Rain Eve. I have been hinder'd visiting Mr. Child.

16. Was at Mr. Jonas Childs, but neither he nor his Wife at home. Hear that Mr. Biglo has taken him with him to Marlborough to work at a Stone-Wall, which I hope will prove a good thing, and proper means of diverting his Mind and helping his Body. Ebenezer and Billy went up to Brother Hicks's with 5 Young Cattle. I visited old Mr. Fay. N.B. Colonel Buckminster and Lady here when I was from home, They being in their Journey to Brookfield and Rutland. N.B. Captain Maynard fences the old Meeting House Ground.

17. My Wife rode over to Mr. Woods (the Clothier) with a Message from Me, of my Dependence upon him for Bricks. She was also at Mr. Martyns. I rode to Mr. Twitchells and to Mr. Bradishs, for Girders for my design'd Building. N.B. Mr. Broad of Natick here. N.B. Mr. Cushing at my House (while I was absent and knew it not) waiting Some Hours to Speak with me concerning going to Mr. Dodge's Ordination and that he purpose to preach.

18. Ebenezer over at Mr. Benjamin Hows, making a Cart. Mr. Hutchinson din'd here—have more Satisfaction about him and their Affairs at Grafton than I had.

19. Mr. Martyn, in his way to Grafton Stops here; he approves of the proposal that Mr. Hutchinson preach for me tomorrow and I to the Northside. Mr. Hutchinson here at Eve and lodg'd here.

20. Mr. Hutchinson preach'd for me, and I for him at Mr. Martyns. N.B. I preach'd on Mat. 25, 46, latter part all Day. Honourable Samuel Watts[10] and Colonel Richards[11] at Meeting, and I ask'd 'em to dine with me; which they comply'd with. At Eve I return'd home—as did Mr. Martyn also. Mr. Hutchinson lodg'd at my House.

21. Mr. Hutchinson to Grafton. My Wife and I to Mr. Beemans raising his Barn. Ebenezer and Joseph there. After Dinner we went to Lieutenant Bruce's to move his Barn. Whilst I was there came Lieutenant Tainter, and told me we had Some other Duty to attend, for that poor Jonas Child had hang'd himself and was Dead: and it was desir'd that I would go to his House forthwith. I did So, Mrs. Parkman with me. I went up to the Scaffold and Saw him (miserable Creature!) a ghastly, lifeless Corps. How awful the Dispensation! One of the Members of the Church! God's Judgments are a great Deep! unsearchable! and his Ways past finding out! A multitude were gather'd, and the Coroner came, Lieutenant Hezekiah Ward, the distress'd widow and Relatives desiring it, I pray'd with them and took Leave. May the Lord (of his infinite Mercy) Sanctifie this terrible Stroke to us all! Tis very worthy of my Notice that I have never had opportunity to Speak with this poor Man in all this Time of his

[2] Possibly a work by the English Unitarian minister, Thomas Emlyn (1663-1741), which belonged to Jonathan Dyer of Dedham.

[3] Of Shrewsbury.

[4] Son of Charles Rice of Westborough.

[5] Of Marlborough.

[6] The editor has not located a record of a work with this title. There are, however, a number of "secret histories" of specific reigns, etc.

[7] Bellamy (Yale 1735) became the first minister of the church in the northern part of Woodbury (now Bethlem) April 2, 1740, and served this parish for 50 years. Dexter, *Biographical Sketches*, pp. 523-529.

[8] The Reverend Jonathan Edwards.

[9] The Reverend Aaron Hutchinson.

[10] Watts was a leading citizen of Chelsea, a justice of the peace, and councillor of the province.

[11] Joseph Richards (Harvard 1721), a class-mate of Parkman's, practiced medicine in Dedham, served as selectman and Representative, and was lieutenant colonel of the Suffolk regiment. *Sibley*, VI, 553-555.

perplexity and Temptation tho I have been to his House to see him one Time after another. It fills me with Grief and Trouble. O that we might all be quicken'd—to a consciencious Discharge of every Duty; careful improvement of the Day and Means of Grace; watchfulness against the Snares and Temptations of the Devil; against quenching the holy Spirit of Grace, or so much as grieving the Spirit or provoking Him to withdraw from us. Jury Satt up all night.

22. Verdict "in a Fitt of Distraction." Tho I was full of Sorrow yet having promis'd to go over to Mr. Martyn my wife and I went; and din'd there. P.M. Mr. Martyn and I rode to the Mason Hastings,[12] and thence to Mr. Morse's[13]—but neither of them at Home. Went to Mr. Bush's, Representative, but the Town do not send.

23. At Mr. Jonas Childs Funeral. A great and a sorrowful Burying.

24. Mrs. Bowker[14] (heretofore Sarah Tainter) taken leave and goes to live at Summers. Mr. Hutchinson came up from Boston and preach'd my Lecture. Text John 14, 16, 17. After Exercise Mr. Hutchinson my wife and I were refresh'd at justice Bakers. N.B. Brother Edwards Whipple Set the Psalm.

25. Mr. Bellamy din'd here upon his return from Boston to Northampton: tells me that neither Mr. Foxcroft,[15] nor Mr. Wigglesworth[16] will go to the Council at Northampton but hopes Mr. Hobby[17] will. Mr. Bellamy did not tarry. I was forced to Send a Denyal to Mr. Edwards. N.B. Ebenezer and Joseph Weeding.

26. Justice Charles Brigham[18] here. I enquir'd of him why his Children were not baptiz'd? He answer'd that many Things had occurr'd to his Disappointment. Towards Night came the Reverend Mr. Samuel Hopkins[19] of Springfield and his Dauter.

27. I administered the Lords Supper. A.M. read Exod. 25 to number 23. Mr. Hopkins preach'd on 2 Cor. 6, 1 a. and p.m. He was with us at Communion. Mr. Hopkins my wife and I din'd at justice Bakers. P.M. I read John second Chapter. N.B. Brother Edwards Whipple set the psalm. N.B. When the Church was transacting the Affair relating to the Ordination of Mr. Hutchinson at Grafton the Choice of one of the Delegates was much clogg'd. Deacon Forbush was nominated, but the vote not clear—he excus'd himself. Lieutenant Tainter was nominated, but no vote. At length Brother Whitney was chose; Scil: together with Esq. Baker.

28. I waited on Mr. Hopkins and his Dauter as far as Mr. Bathericks, on their way to Boston. Thence I visited the Sorrowful widow Child and din'd there P.M. Visited Adonijah Rice who is still weak and low; his Case dubious. Catechiz'd at the Meeting House, at 3 p.m. 40 Children if I mistake not. Ebenezer and Joseph finish weeding. From Mr. Nurse's, Sent by Mr. Samuel Fay to Mr. Kneeland,[20] an Account of Mr. Jonas Child.

29. My Kinsman Nathaniel Parkman[21] accompany'd by Daniel Hastings came to See me. My Son Thomas also came home to See us. They all lodg'd here; and their Horses are all kept here. N.B. A Most Shocking Account of Mr. William Williams[22] of Weston. And hear of Sudden Deaths from Day to Day.

30. Endeavour'd to keep Election at home. After Dinner we Sung part of the eightieth psalm. P.M. came old Mr. Maynard and old Mr. Whipple to see me. Read 'em those parts of Mr. Prince's Chronology[23] which contains the Beginnings of the

Plymouth and Massachusetts Colonys. Endeavour'd to be myself and to make my Family etc. sensible of God's Favours to New England. The Lord make us truely Thankfull for them preserve them and grant Grace to improve them!

31. Mrs. Nanny and Beckky Gott, Mr. Martyn and wife and Mr. Morse and wife here. My Son Thomas cutts off his Hair. He and his Brother to Upton. My Kinsman Nathaniel went over to Lieutenant Tainters to dine there and did not return. Every Day confirms and increases the sorrowful News from Weston. N.B. My Wife's Neices lodge here.

### JUNE, 1750.

1. Thomas return'd to Concord; and Mrs. Nanny and Beckky Gott with him as far as Marlborough. Ebenezer and Joseph put up a Partition Fence from South to North in the upper part of the Great Pasture. I finish'd the Life of Miley Ismael Emperor of Morocco.[1] P.M. Mr. Millen[2] and his Spouse, accompany'd by Mr. Palmer,[3] Schoolmaster, here. The Weather, especially in the Nights, very Cool for Some Time.

2. Wrote, and sent to Mr. Ebenezer Rice's for Conveyance a Line to Mr. Hutchinson concerning his preparing a Confession of his Faith against his Ordination.

3. Read Exod. 25, 23, preach'd on Rom. 11, 33, latter part, a. and p.m. Din'd at Justice Bakers. N.B. an Horse is provided for me and my wife stately to ride up to Dinner. P.M. read John third.

4. Cousen Nathaniel and I rode to Mr. Twitchells. P.M. came Mr. Samuel Haven to dwell here. He was accompany'd by his uncle Deacon Burnap of Hopkinton.

5. A Day to be remember'd—as for my Accepting the Call of the Town in the Year 1724. So now for my undertaking to begin the World again on the South Road—a Number of Neighbours came to Clear and plough down the Knoll which I purpose to build on. It was very much owing to Lieutenant Bruce, and accordingly a.m. there was a number to clear the ground, Scil. Neighbour John Rogers, Thomas Frost, and Abraham Beeman, besides my own Ebenezer and Joseph, and p.m. a considerable Number with their Cattle to plough and levill it. Lieutenant Bruce and Oxen Mr. Timothy Warrin with Oxen both his own and his Brother Daniels, Mr. John Rogers with Oxen, which with my own oxen made up Ten. Other Hands were Ephraim Bruce, Ebenezer Forbush, Neighbour Cook, Eleazer Williams, Timothy Warrin, Samuel Harrington, Simon Tainter, Abner Newton, Junior. N.B. Lieutenant Forbush and I transacted the Affair of our Conveyance of the Title to the Knoll and Land adjoining. He gave me a Deed of an Acre and Quarter—for 11£ old Tenor.

6. My Wife, Mr. Haven, Son Ebenezer and Two Dauters Molly and Lucy rode in the Rain, in Company with Mr. Martyn, his wife and Daughter, to Grafton to the Ordination of Mr. Aaron Hutchinson. Council met at Mr. Ebenezer Brooks'. Consisted of the following Churches. West Church in Sudbury, the 2 Churches of Westborough, First Church in Sutton, Church in Southborough, and the First in Hebron, and the Church in Worcester. Mr. Loring Moderator, Mr. Martyn Clerk. Moderator pray'd, Mr. Hutchinson was examin'd. Mr. Ebenezer Wadsworth came and objected against our proceeding. N.B. Captain Sadler and his wife, his witnesses on the one part, to prove falsehood upon him. Mr. Joseph Batchellour and his wife were to be the other, but they could not be had, nor were prepar'd—but if they were, the Subject Matter of the Difficulty was not thought to be sufficient to retard the Council. About 2 p.m. went to Meeting. Mr. Martyn pray'd, Mr. Pomroy[4] of Hebron preach'd on Acts 20, 28. Mr. Loring gave the Charge. Mr. Hall[5] pray'd after the Charge. The Right Hand I deliver'd was much the same with that which I prepar'd for and gave at Mr. Buck-

---

[12] Daniel Hastings of Shrewsbury.

[13] The Reverend Ebenezer Morse of Boylston.

[14] Mrs. Joseph Bowker.

[15] The Reverend Thomas Foxcroft of the First Church of Boston.

[16] The Reverend Samuel Wigglesworth of Hamilton.

[17] The Reverend William Hobby of Reading.

[18] A prominent citizen of Grafton. Pierce, *Grafton*, pp. 463–464.

[19] (Yale 1718). Hopkins was the minister of the First Congregational Church of West Springfield, 1720–1755. Dexter, *Biographical Sketches*, pp. 184–187.

[20] Samuel Kneeland, publisher with Timothy Green of *The Boston Gazette and Weekly Journal*.

[21] Parkman's nephew, the son of William Parkman of Boston.

[22] Williams was accused of "heinous miscarriages," and a church council of Oct. 24, 1750, which dismissed him, found him guilty of "gross Lasciviousness in Diverse instances." Sibley, V, 297–298.

[23] Thomas Prince, *A Chronological History of New England in the Form of Annals*, 2 vols. (Boston, 1736–[1755]). The second volume was published with the title *Annals of New-England*.

[1] John Harrison, *The Tragicall Life and Death of Muley Abdala Melek, the late King of Barbarie* (Delph, 1633).

[2] The Reverend John Mellen of Sterling.

[3] Joseph Palmer (Harvard 1747) kept school in Westborough and neighbouring towns for about 2 years. He was the second minister of the First Church in Norton, 1753–1791. Sibley, XII, 197–199.

[4] The Reverend Benjamin Pomeroy of Hebron, Conn.

[5] The Reverend David Hall of Sutton.

minsters Ordination at Rutland. N.B. Thunder Storm at night when we got home. Mr. Martyn etc. Stay'd till it was over. Mr. Smith of Marlborough tarry'd over Night. N.B. Mr. Haven and Mr. Dodge went up to Sutton, and carry'd my two Daughters to Esq. Goddard's;[6] and Deacon Burnap of Hopkinton came hither, and led home Mr. Havens Horse. Thus have we Seen the Vacancy at Grafton, which has given the Churches so great Trouble, from Year to Year, thus far happily made up; and God grant the Joy may not diminish! N.B. Wrote to Mr. Pierpoint by Mr. Bliss of Concord.

7. Mr. Smith tarried and din'd with us. Dr. Gott came and accompany'd him. At Night our Young People return'd from Sutton. N.B. Dodge lodg'd here. I was so very ill, with a bad Cold, feverish etc. thro the Night. My Kinsman Nathaniel Set out for Boston.

8. Mr. Dodge din'd with us. My son Ebenezer ill with a Cold. P.M. a Number of Neighbours went to my Knoll, with Two Yoke of Cattle besides my own, and with Shovels Hoes and Barrs to levell it further. They were chiefly Mr. Charles Rice, Lieutenant Thomas Forbush, Lieutenant Bruce, Lieutenant Tainter, Mr. Grow, Bowman, Harrington, Simon Tainter Junior, Jonathan Forbush, Charles Bruce, Ephraim Bruce, Adams, Rogers (with oxen), Timothy Warrin, Abraham Bond, Samuel Forbush junior [blank] Miller, Eleazer Williams, Abner Rice, and Daniel Forbush junior with a Cart and Oxen. N.B. Neighbour Ebenezer Maynard raised his House this Afternoon. I supp'd there. A Time of remarkable and great Colds.

9. A Cool Air—most people oppress'd with Colds. Ebenezer unable to do any great matter. Mr. Dodge came p.m.

10. Read Exod. 26, and gave some Exposition of it. Mr. Dodge preach'd on Prov. 3, 17. He, my wife and I din'd at Esq. Bakers, where was Mr. Thomas Cheevers[7] of Lyn. Mr. Haven din'd at my House. P.M. Read John 4. Mr. Dodge preach'd on Heb. 2, 3. I gave Notice to the Church and Congregation of the Association Fast next Tuesday at Mr. Martyns. N.B. Mr. James Maynard was at Meeting.

11. Very rainy. Mr. Dodge left us, a.m. Mr. Jonah Warrin here; tells me he has got me 6500 Shingle. I gave him a Note to Lieutenant Tainter for 26£ old Tenor.

12. Mr. Haven and I rode over to Mr. Martyns it being Association Fast there. But a few Members came, viz. Mr. Cushing, Mr. Goss,[8] Buckminster and Maccarty. Afterwards for the last service came Mr. Barrett—and when we came home at Eve Mr. Seccomb.[9] As to the Exercises, Mr. Martyn pray'd and Mr. Buckminster preach'd on Rev. 2, 3, 4. P.M. Mr. Goss pray'd and Mr. Maccarty preach'd on Mat. 16, 28. It was committed to me to draw up an Answer to the Letter which was sent us from the Association of which the Reverend Mr. Townsend[10] of Needham was Moderator in reply to a Message from us to them by a Committee which we sent them upon the Affair of guarding our Pulpits and Examining Candidates. I lodg'd with Mr. Maccarty at Mr. Martyns. Most of us indispos'd with a great Cold.

13. I walk'd over from Mr. Martyns in the Morning to Mr. Gideon Haywards and talk'd with Mr. Lull about my Land in Townsend. Says he'll go over with me to Townsend as soon as Hay Time is over. Mr. Haven who rode home to my House last Evening in my Chair, return'd to Day (at my request) to carry me back. N.B. Mr. Barrett with me most of the p.m.

14. Ebenezer and Joseph are mowing Bushes. I rode to Mr. Bonds and left a Letter for Mr. Beriah Rice about his meadow in Chauncy. Was at Lieutenant Tainters who was mowing. Money extreme difficult to be got; receiv'd 30£ old Tenor when the whole sallery should be finish'd.

15. Brother Hicks brought up sister Hannah Champney[11] from Cambridge. Ebenezer and Joseph Clear over by the new Meeting House.

16. Brother Hicks goes up to Sutton with Sister Hannah. Ebenezer and Joseph clear again over at the New meeting House. Samuel Bumpso lends 'em an Hand.

17. My illness was so much increas'd that I did not go to Meeting without a great deal of Difficulty. My wife and I rode in the Chair, and Mr. Haven and Molly on the Horse. I read Exod. 27, and preach'd on Exod. 20, 8. Din'd (together with my wife) at Esq. Bakers. P.M. read John 5, and carry'd on the Exercise on Exod. 20, 8. Very much indispos'd and worried at night.

18. Mr. Martyn here. He rode with me to my new Knoll. At Eve he carry'd Molly over to his House as to tarry a few Days with them. Joseph half-hilling p.m.

19. Mr. Haven rode with me to old Mr. Fays. We din'd there. Took up Mr. Fay into my Chair to see how he could bear to ride in one. Mr. Haven and I rode to Mr. Winchesters—would have had Prudy ride in the Chair, but she was too Weak. We return'd to Mr. Moses Brighams Raising of his Barn, and were well entertain'd there. Mr. Ebenezer Rice undertakes to get me the 4 Beams of my intended House, and Mr. William Pierce to hew the 4 Girts (which are wanting). Mr. Daniel Hardy finding the Timbers.

20. Mr. Noah How hoed here at half hilling.

21. Ebenezer did so much as to mow the Garden and foreyard a.m. I rode to Mr. Martyns—din'd there. Thunder storm arose and detain'd me an Hour or Two. Brought Molly home. Mr. Martyn came with me. Lecture to young men was appointed to be at 4 p.m. but we were 34 Minutes after, when we began being hinder'd by the Storm. Mr. Martyn preach'd on Josh. 24, 21. N.B. I rode out at Eve by Express Desire to a woman (one of the Members of the Church who has try'd to hang herself) this Day. A most astonishing power which the Devil has among us!

22. [No entry.]

23. I had agreed with Mr. Martyn to change with him tomorrow, but Mr. Stone coming here and desiring to Change I sent him to Mr. Martyn that he might Supply my place at the North Side, and I rode to Southborough.

24. I preach'd at Southborough on Prov. 14, 9, and p.m. on Mat. 16, 26 to page 15, and baptiz'd Miriam, of Manasseh and Dinah Stow. At Eve return'd home. Mr. Martyn preach'd for me on Regeneration from John 3, 5.

25. Funeral of Joseph Rice's Child. N.B. At the House of Mourning heard the astonishing account of the fearful Judgment of God on Robert Woodberry of Beverly, who having in his Lifetime been us'd to profane Cursing, and wishing persons might go to Hell and blare like a Calf especially would often curse his worthy Mother in this Manner—and carry'd it very basely and cruelly to his Wife, sicken'd and dy'd, and when the Corps had lain a Suitable Time to be laid out, a horrible Sound broke forth from the Corps, blaring like a Calf. This Story is Said to be sufficiently attested to be credited. After the Funeral I visited old Captain Forbush who has been ill of late; and he receiv'd my advice to him affectionately and gratefully. N.B. William rode to Marlborough with Lucy and brought up Mrs. Sally Gott.

26. Mr. Martyn and his Spouse here and din'd with us. Towards Eve my Wife undertakes the Weaning of little Breck; and to accomplish it the better, she and Sally rode to Worcester. When I was preparing to go to bed, came Mr. William Rogers and desir'd me to go to Mr. David Brigham, whom I found past Speaking. He Expir'd while I was there between 11 and 12 o'Clock. A serious man and I hope dy'd in Christ. He was taken ill on the Sabbath a.m. at meeting. Twas thought to be the Effect of the great Cold that goes about. He was So comfortable this Day that p.m. the Sun about Two Hours high, he walk'd into the other room; yet a little after sunsett was not able to Speak any more, nor understand any Thing. So Sudden was the Summons. I return'd home about midnight.

27. It rain'd all Day. Ebenezer and Joseph fixing up the New Cart with Ladders.

28. Rode with Mr. Eliezer Rice and his Wife to Mr. Brighams and had discourse with her referring to her Temptations. Attended the Funeral of Mr. David Brigham there being now but 3 of the first 12 members who were in the Foundation of this

6 Robert Goddard of Sutton.

7 Cheever was a prominent citizen who had represented Lynn in the General Court several times.

8 The Reverend Thomas Goss of Bolton.

9 The Reverend John Seccomb of Harvard.

10 The Reverend Jonathan Townsend.

11 The first Mrs. Parkman's oldest sister.

Church, Surviving. May be truely sensible of our hastening into the Eternal World, who commonly are So extremely fond of this! And O that our practices and Experiences might bear some proposition to our high and Sacred Professions! After Funeral I rode over to Mr. Martyns. Captain Eager and Lieutenant Holloway and Mr. Jacob Rice in Company. My Wife and Mrs. Sally Gott came from Worcester to Mr. Martyns after we had din'd, but Seasonably for Lecture. I preach'd on Hos. 6, 6. I desir'd the Knowledge of God more than Burnt Offerings.

29. Mr. Goodhue came from Hopkinton Requesting me to visit his Brother Jeremy who lies very bad at his House; (yet is, at Madam Dench's, where he has hired). I accordingly went. Din'd with Mrs. Barrett. Found Jeremy not altogether so bad as I fear'd. Talk'd with Mrs. Dench about her Mothers Apparition to Mr. Cutting a Gentleman from Barbadoes in Boston, at Eve returning home and calling at Mr. Barretts (who was not come home yet) had some Conversation with Mrs. Price (Commissarys Lady). Met Mr. Barrett on the Road—could not get from Hopkinton till some time after sunsett and therefore was late home; but safe. Blessed be God!

30. Ebenezer and Joseph mowing Day by Day Except that Ebenezer was at Times indispos'd. N.B. Colonel Chandler and his Lady here, in their Journey from Boston to Worcester. By the various accidents and avocations of this Week have been exceedingly interrupted and impeded in my Studys and Preparations for the Sabbath.

### JULY, 1750.

1. Read Exod. 2, 8 to verse 29, and Preach'd on Rom. 6, 13. Yield yourself to God—repeating what I had heretofore compos'd and deliver'd on that Subject. My Wife and I din'd at Esq. Bakers. P.M. read John 6 to number 34, and in preaching did the remainder of the forenoon Discourse.

2. Joseph plough'd for Hilling. Ebenezer much indispos'd and works but little. P.M. My Wife and I in the Chair and Mr. Haven on my Young Horse undertake a Journey, designing for Boston as Soon as with Convenience we can get there. A Thunder Storm came up, and we were Stopp'd at Mr. Elisha Wards till near Sunsett. Proceeded as far as Mr. Stones at Southborough and lodg'd there.

3. Rode to Framingham and broke fast at Mr. Joseph Havens.[1] We call'd at Colonel Bakers. Another storm came up by that Time we arriv'd at Mr. Benjamin Hastings at Watertown. We din'd there, and proceeded to Cambridge. I tarried and lodg'd at sister Lydia Champneys. Mr. Haven waited on my Wife to Boston and brought back the Chair to me. Kept my Mare at Brother Champney's.

4. This being Commencement I contracted Some acquaintance with Two of the Young Batchellours who were ingenious and Sober Men. Sir Fish[2] and Sir True,[3] but I was entertain'd chiefly at Sir Cotton's[4] (where I broke Fast) and at Sir Gardner's.[5] Was Sent for by the Corporation to give my Testimony concerning Mr. Hutchinson of Grafton. N.B. Sir Dudley's[6] Oration was pronounc'd, but very indifferently. Din'd at Mr. Monis,[7] for the Sake of Mr. Martyn as well as to honor my old Master. Conversation very much turns upon Mr. Edwards Dismission from Northampton. P.M. the President in his Oration exceedingly laments the miserable State to which Learning and the Ministry are reduc'd—by means of the Niggardliness of people. Complains of his own Miserable Circumstances. N.B. Lodg'd at the Same place and Mr. Haven with me.

5. I rode Early to Boston. Mr. Barnard[8] of Marblehead preach'd the Lecture on 1 Tim. 3, 16. I din'd at My Kinsman Oliver,[9] who has a son (Alexander) lately born. But Sorrowful accounts of the Conduct of Jonathan Coarser[10] in his Life Time, towards his Wife; and of his Miserable End. N.B. Her sister Lydia is embarking to go to her Husband (Mr. Davis) at Chebucta. At Eve Mrs. Harris, Widow of Captain William Harris was at Brother Samuels with Brother William who is publish'd to her. N.B. Revd. Mr. Gay[11] of Hingham was with us at supper. It was indeed expected that my Brother would have been marry'd this Evening to the Said Lady but by means of one of her sons going to sea She would not get ready. My Wife and I lodg'd at Brother Samuel's, My Horse at Mr. Stoddards, my Chair at Mr. Eatons.

6. Mr. Oliver went with Me to one Mr. Maxwells in Kings Street where I bought Two Cheeses, one Glocester (of old England) the other Rhode-Island, both weighing 32£ at 3/ old Tenor per pound. We din'd at Judge Dudleys,[12] baited at old Mr. Livermores in Weston, called at Colonel Buckminsters[13] at Framingham and lodg'd at Mr. Joseph Havens. N.B. an exceeding violent storm of Hail etc. on the fourth, p.m.

7. Mr. Samuel Haven returns with us to our House. In our way Call'd at Mr. Reeds; and Mrs. Wharton gives me an account of Mrs. Pierpoints Troubles about Mr. Curtis,[14] the preacher who is there with them. Stopp'd at Mr. Nichols's: din'd at Mr. Stones and return'd in Safety, finding my Family well. Blessed be God! Ebenezer and Joseph have finish'd the hilling of Indian Corn this Week—having had Mr. David Maynard junior's Horse to plough.

8. An hot Day. Mr. Martyn and I chang'd. He preach'd on John 3, 5. I preach'd to his people on 1 John 3, 3 and 1 Tim. 6, 12. He read Exod. 28 from number 29 and John 6 from number 34, as I also read in his Course for him. Each return'd at Eve.

9. Prudence Winchester being Very low and like to dye, Sends for Me and I went. Found a wonderful Change in her, and hope it is a Saving. All last night indeed She was in terrible Distress, but this Morning had gracious Discoverys of the mercy and Graciousness of God to her. Ebenezer and Joseph mowing. Manning lodg'd here.

10. Mr. Martyn and his wife, with me and mine, visited Mr. Barrett at Hopkinton.

11. Tended Hay as I was able. Near Night rode over to Mr. Woods about my Bricks fearing I shall be disappointed of them. And went to Mr. Martyns.

12. A.M. did something at the Hay. P.M. preach'd the Lecture before Sacrament on Luke 24, 46 to page 11. After Lecture I rode to Grafton and supp'd with Mr. Hutchinson who to Day brought home his Spouse. Of ministers there was only Mr. Cushing, of Ladys none besides Mrs. Betty Hall, and the Town people to wait on them. I lodg'd there. Ebenezer and Joseph reap Rye and did not go to Lecture.

13. Hot weather from Day to Day. In returning home, Mr. Hutchinson with me, as far as to Winchesters where we call'd to see Prudence, and he pray'd with her. N.B. Her Consolation not without some Darkness and Difficulty. N.B. Mr. Haven lodg'd at Deacon Forbush's last Night. Ebenezer and Joseph, besides what they do about the Hay, reap'd and got in part of the Rye. It has been, now for Some Time a wondrous growing Season. Might our Hearts be as fruitful and flourishing!

14. My Incumbrances and Cares, my Indispositions of Body and Distress of Mind So grievous and pressing when I discern my Preparations to be short of what they ought to be, that at Night I was much distress'd.

---

[1] Selectman and Representative of Framingham.

[2] Elisha Fish (Harvard 1750) became the second minister of the First Church in Upton, 1750–1795. *Sibley*, XII, 550–556.

[3] Henry True (Harvard 1750) became the first minister of Hampstead, N.H., 1752–1782. *Sibley*, XII, 588–592.

[4] Nathaniel Cotton (Harvard 1750) taught school at Weston, served as a military chaplain in Nova Scotia, turned Anglican, and was made "chaplain and minister" of Pensacola, West Florida. *Sibley*, XII, 540–543.

[5] Henry Gardner (Harvard 1750), the son of the Reverend Henry Gardner of Stow, became the first Treasurer of the State of Mass. *Sibley*, XII, 558–560.

[6] Thomas Dudley (Harvard 1750), son of the Honorable William Dudley of Roxbury. *Sibley*, XII, 543–544.

[7] Judah Monis, the Hebrew tutor at Harvard, was the brother-in-law of the Reverend John Martyn of Northborough.

[8] The Reverend John Barnard.

[9] The Reverend Parkman's niece, Esther Parkman, had married Edward Oliver.

[10] The Reverend Parkman's niece, Elizabeth Tyley, had married John Coarsa.

[11] The Reverend Ebenezer Gay.

[12] Paul Dudley, justice of the Superior Court of Judicature.

[13] Colonel Joseph Buckminster, Jr., a prominent office-holder. Temple, *Framingham*, p. 490.

[14] Jeremiah Curtis (Yale 1724) was the minster of Southington (Third church of Farmington). He was a zealous Old-Light and alienated his parish which dismissed him in 1755. Dexter, *Biographical Sketches*, pp. 300–301.

15. Administered the Sacred Ordinance of the Supper—And as to the Common Exercises of the Lords Day Read Exod. 29, and preach'd on Eph. 1, 3. P.M. read John 7 and for the Sermon, though I had by me a considerable Preparation upon the Subject I have begun Scil. of the Fourth Commandment yet the Argument not being finish'd, I chose not to deliver it till I could in one View, at least the Same Day; and considering likewise that the Subject I was upon last Lecture Day was so much more suitable for the Day, I therefore went on with that, and repeated from Luke 24, 46. N.B. Mr. Haven, invited by Esq. Baker, din'd there with us (viz. with my wife, Dauter Molly and I). O that we might have both a suitable apprehension of the Sufferings of Christ and have fellowship with him therein, that we may be also Blessed with all Spiritual Blessings in heavenly Things in Christ Jesus!

16. Forbush[15] begins to keep School at Mr. Eliezer Rice's, and lodges here. Catechiz'd at Mr. Joslins. Carry'd my Wife with me and visited all that neighbourhood except old Mr. Garfield; dining at Mr. Chamberlins. We were also well entertain'd at Mr. Joslins after the Exercise. May God add his Blessing to my weak endeavours to promote His Kingdom and enable me rightly to improve the Benefits which I receive from his people!

17. Mr. Haven and I rode to Association Fast at Worcester. N.B. the people of Worcester desir'd there might be but one Exercise and therefore we kept the Fast ourselves at Mr. Maccarty's House a.m. at which Mr. Maccarty himself pray'd, and Mr. Morse preach'd on Ezek. 3, 1 to 5. And p.m. we went to the meeting House where Mr. Morse pray'd, and Mr. Martyn preach'd on Luke 19, 44. A very moving and profitable Discourse! May we never loose the Benefit of it! Mr. Haven and I lodg'd at Dr. Brecks, who is gone a long Journey to look out another place to live in.

18. Mr. Haven was examin'd and approbated by the Association. P.M. We return'd home, but N.B. Mr. Morse's both yesterdays and to Days Conduct towards me with reference to Mr. Marsh[16] of Narraganset Number 2 who Mr. Morse Says will not come to this Association because I am of it: and acquaints us that Mr. Marsh Spoke further to my dishonour. To which I reply'd I fear too warmly that His reproches instead of being to my Dishonour I esteem'd Commendation, his Invectives Panegyrics. N.B. visited Captain Maynard who is confin'd by illness.

19. Visited Mr. Eliezer Rice's wife and carry'd Mr. Hows works, folio, Volume 2. Visited Mrs. Beeman who by a fall from an Horse, broke her Legg and is confin'd. Ebenezer and Joseph mow'd a.m. some Grass which Mr. Eliezer Rice lets us have.

20. They go and mow in the ministerial meadow.

21. Mr. Stone, at Ministers Meeting, had desir'd me to change with him the next ensuing Lords Day, inasmuch as he was going a Journey further; whereupon I depended on his coming here; but he went to Holden, and sent Mr. Davis[17] to preach for him. I rode therefore to Southborough.

22. Preach'd at Southborough a.m. on Mat. 16, 26 the remainder of the Discourse which I began there the last time I preach'd there, and p.m. on Hebr. 9, 27 former part. N.B. Judge Ward[18] din'd with me and with me after the Exercises. N.B. I baptiz'd Two Children; Ruth, of Jonathan Newton; and Stephen, of Isaac Johnson. Return'd home in the Evening. Mr. Davis preach'd for me on Mat. 13, 30 or number 40 and over.

23. Mr. Haven rode with Mr. Davis; the latter going to Boston, the former to his Fathers at Framingham. N.B. Anna Bradish here on Examination in order to her joining with the Church. Ebenezer and Joseph mowing and raking Hay at the Meadow. P.M. Mr. Edward Bass and his Cousen Henshaw from Leicester here.

24. Was call'd to Visit Mr. Abner Newton, who lies in a de-

lirious State. Joseph brought home one Load of Hay which they mowed at Mr. Rice's, and 2 Load of Meadow Hay. I read Prideaux's Life of Mahomet.[19]

25. Read Stackhouse's Abridgment of Burnets History of his own Times.[20] A.M. Joseph brought home 2 Load more of Meadow Hay. N.B. my wife, accompany'd by Mrs. Hephzibah Maynard and Mr. Eliezer Rice's Wife rode to Mr. Abraham Knowltons and Mr. Joseph Miles's; and sent her side Saddle with immediate success to be Mended by Peter Butler, in Shrewsbury. P.M. Molly and Lucy went to the Funeral of Prudence Winchester, who dy'd yesterday Morning. Mr. Winchester and his wife sent for me but I could not go. Colonel William Ward lodg'd here.

26. Visited Mr. Abner Newton who is exceeding bad Still and incapable to Converse with me. Neighbour Eliezer Rice and his son reap'd my Wheat A.M. and Ebenezer and Joseph mow'd etc. for him.

27. Ebenezer and Joseph work at the Meadow—but p.m., Ebenezer came and got in part of the Wheat.

28. Joseph brought home 2 Load of the Meadow Hay. He got in the Wheat likewise. P.M. Mr. Haven came from Framingham. Rain Setts in P.M. so that they were beat off from work at the Meadow.

29. Rain, Thunder and Lightning. Read Exod. 31 and tho I had prepar'd a sufficient Number of pages on the subject I have in Hand viz. the Beginning of the Sabbath, yet not having compleated the whole of what I design upon that Argument I thought it best to defer delivering any part of it; and the Instances of suicide in this Country, a. and p.m. increasing (to my Knowledge and Observation) Mrs. Rice also still under very great Temptations and strange assaults, I preach'd from Luke 11, 4, latter part, repeating mainly my Expositions of Mat. 6, 13 former part with alterations and additions. Read P.M. John 8 to number 25. N.B. it rain'd so exceeding hard that my Wife and a Number of my Family besides tarried at the Meeting House. But Esq. Baker invited Mr. Haven to dine with me at his House—which he did. By the Evening there fell so much Rain that there was a great Flood. But thro the Merciful preservation of God no hurt done among us by the Lightning.

30. Anna Bradish further Examin'd by me. Mr. Jonas Warrin of Upton came and invited Mr. Haven to preach at Upton which he consents to do after some Time. Tho it rain'd hard I rode over to See Mr. Abner Newton who was near his End. N.B. terrible Struggles. Convulsive Motions and Groans. May God grant me to be ready for my own Turn!

31. News came in the Morning that Mr. Newton dy'd about Midnight, last. Ebenezer and Joseph to the Meadow. Visited Neighbour Benjamin Hows sick Child.

### AUGUST, 1750

1. We have Still so much to do at the Meadow that Joseph Bruce, though his Time agreed to be out, yet at Ebenezers Desire, I detain to work for me. Mr. Abner Newton was buryed. A large Funeral. He dy'd in the middst of his Days, being in his 42nd Year. I hope he dy'd in Christ, and in him I have lost a very valuable and generous Friend. The Lord Sanctify it to Me and to the Neighbourhood, who Seem sensibly to feel the Loss. Mrs. Newton requested that my Wife and I would return to her House after burying which we did and Supped with the Mourners, Bearers and the other Friends.

2. Bruce helps us: also Mr. John Rogers with his Team helping us get home Hay from the Meadow. But by means of the late great Rains the Meadow was So soft that they were mir'd and much worried; they made but Two turns in the whole Day. That is, they brought home in all to Day by both Teams 4 Load. I rode over to See Mr. Woods and Oake, and talk with them about my Bricks for my intended House. They excuse themselves and plead themselves wholly off; So that I give the Affair up with them. I din'd at Mr. Martyns. He tells me Ensign Bartlet spake with a Post who last Night went down the Road for Boston, and

---

[15] Eli Forbes.

[16] Elisha Marsh (Harvard 1738), minister of the First Congregational Church of Westminster, then a frontier plantation known as Narragansett No. 2. Marsh was a liberal in theology and he opposed New-Light fanaticism. Parkman had moved to prevent Marsh from preaching at a Marlborough Association meeting in Aug., 1747, and thereafter Marsh refused to attend Association meetings. *Sibley*, X, 300–306.

[17] The Reverend Joseph Davis of Holden.

[18] Justice William Ward of the Court of Common Pleas, Worcester County.

[19] Humphrey Prideaux, *Life of Mahomet; with a Discourse for the Vindicating Christianity from the Charges of Imposture* (London, 1697). Several other editions were printed, but none in America.

[20] Thomas Stackhouse, *An Abridgement of Bishop Burnet's Own Times* (London 1724).

gives an Account that a Number of Indians are designing to fall upon our Frontiers. Rains, thunders and Lightens before I came yet home; but soon increases to a terrible storm. A very sad, catching Time for Haying. But the Earth brings forth in Great Plenty.

3. Bruce works this one Day more for us.

4. Bruce works for Neighbour Eliezer Rice. Much letting Weather. He return'd at Eve. He returns at Eve and keeps Sabbath here.

5. Read Exod. 32. Preached a. & p.m. on Exod. 20, 8. The Beginning of the Sabbath my wife and I rode up to Esq. Bakers and din'd there. It was Showery as it is almost every Day. I have heard that divers persons were So Tenacious heretofore of their opinion that the Sabbath begins in the Morning, that they were very impatient at but the Expectation, Shall I Should mention the Contrary. But I leave it unto God. P.M. read John 8 latter part.

6. Joseph Bruce left us. I am indebted to him 42£ 8/ old Tenor. P.M. Mr. Haven rode to Framingham. Neighbour Robert Cooks Wife here to be further Examin'd in order to owning the Covenant. Mr. Nathaniel Adams of Worcester here. Mr. Francis Whipple made me a Visit and tarried into Evening.

7. Forbush goes home, having lodg'd here.

8. Rode to Mr. Cornelius Biglo to induce him to undertake to provide stones for my Chimney but I try in Vain. Ebenezer worked for Neighbour John Rogers A.M. and Rogers for him with his Team p.m. They brought home the Two last Loads of Hay from the Ministerial Meadow. N.B. Molly to Mr. Martyns alone.

9. Ebenezer mows at home. Molly and Lucy rode in the Chair to Mr. Twitchells. Mrs. Cook here about her son Roberts Affair. I gave myself to my Study (as much as I well could) the whole Day.

10. Mr. Chapin of Grafton here with a Question: What is the meaning of St. Paul to the Corinthians, 1 Ep. 7, 14, last Clause. What kind of Holiness is that? Federal—or to more Legitimacy? P.M. Mr. Haven returns from Framingham

11. Hot: and has been so for several Days: but today it is remarkably so.

12. Another very hot Day: but some Showers, with Thunder at Evening. A.M. read Exod. 33 of which I gave Some brief Expository Hints and preach'd on Exod. 20, 8, 9. The Sanctification of the sabbath in which Exercise I was somewhat long, but it was not sufficient to divide—and yet it had taken up my Time very much, to prepare this one Exercise, as I had many authors to consult upon it. Mr. Haven (by express Invitation) din'd with me at the Esquire's. P.M. read John 9 and briefly expounded. And considering what a Day of Temptation it has been, and remains with a Member of our Church before mention'd, I repeated my Expositions on Mat. number 11, 31, 32, both the Exercises in one. For tho the Exercise was longer and more worrying to me, yet it gave the more complete View of the Subject. But what will avail without the divine Concurrence? May God therefore add His Blessing. N.B. I gave the Congregation Notice of the Association Fast to be (God willing) next Tuesday at Marlboro.

13. Very Hot a.m. P.M. Clouds gather'd. Mr. Haven and I help'd Ebenezer get in Hay. Mr. Haven help'd in a second Load. Old Mr. Dodge came to see me, and walk'd with me to see Captain Maynard.

14. Association Fast at Marlborough (and I suppose at Rutland at the same Time.) A pritty Hot Day, but Rain at Night. The Exercises were carry'd on thus, Mr. Smith pray'd (but I was so unhappy by several accidents on the Road as to miss of it, and arriv'd in singing Time, at meeting), Mr. Goss[1] preach'd from Mat. 11, 23. P.M. Mr. Gardner[2] pray'd—and Mr. Loring[3] preach'd on Hos. 9, 14, last Clause. May the Lord accept the Offerings and Bless His Holy Word to our, and his peoples highest Good. Advis'd with the Association about Robert Cooks Case. Mr. Martyn my Company part of the Way in returning Home; but after he left me, Rainy and Dark, but not too late for my Family.

15. Rode to Mr. Ebenezer Rice's and Lieutenant Tainters to forward the getting Timber for my House together—din'd at Lieutenants. Sent by him to Boston for divers Things—but next to No Money to be had any where. Mr. Bowman carrys the Two Plaits to the place. Was with Mr. Jonathan Forbush at his mill looking over the stuff—viz. Boards and slitwork. At Eve when I return'd I understood that Mr. Martyn and his Spouse had been here—whereas I did not expect 'em till Friday. Jeduthun Baldwin here to acquaint me with his Circumstances and when he can come to work for me. He lodg'd here.

16. I rode out again about stuff—went to Hopkinton to Mr. Joseph Woods mill, and to Deacon Burnaps—din'd at the Deacons. Was at Kellys and Pierce's. Ebenezer Carted Boards from Mr. Forbush's Mill. 600 of Oake Boards of what I have of Mr. Forbush and 220 which I have of Mr. Daniel Miller and [blank] which I have of Mr. Samuel Harrington. I was at Mr. Ebenezer Rice's as I return'd home, to get stuff for window Frames. N.B. Mr. Daniel Forbush brought a long, oake Cill.

17. Rode to Mr. Timothy Warrins to try for white Pine Boards—was at Mr. Beamans, whose wife is still confin'd by her broken Legg. Mr. Jonathan Forbush here and we reckon'd—what I had of him of Boards and slittwork comes to 9£ old Tenor. He desir'd and I gave him a note for 4£ and he gave me the other 5£ which was his Proportion according to the Rates (he says) towards what he thinks the precinct ought to do more than they have done towards my Building etc.

18. Ebenezer got in the last of the Hay at home; and this finishes this part of his toilfull work at home.

19. Mr. Samuel Haven began to preach. He preach'd for me all Day, on Colloss. 3, 4. May God Bless his labour and make him an able Minister of the New Testament! He and I din'd at Esq. Bakers; my wife and the rest of my Family went home.

20. Am now concern'd to set forward my Building; rode to Deacon Matthias Rice's to Speak with Jeduthun Baldwin. I din'd at the Deacons. P.M. Jeduthun came to my House to look of Stuff for window Frames, but which would not do. Great Rains.

21. Measur'd out the House plot, in order to having the Cellar dugg. N.B. this was done by the motion of Samuel Bumpso. P.M. at the Funeral of Neighbour Benjamin Hows Child.[4] At Eve came Mr. Edwards of Northampton, together with Revd. Mr. Tuthil of Bedford[5] in the upper County, and Mrs. Martha Edwards, sister of Mr. Edwards of Northampton and they lodg'd here. N.B. Mrs. Edwards Horse extremely lame.

22. It rain'd most of the Day. Yet the Company chose to proceed on their Journey. Mrs. Edwards left her Horse, and I supply'd her with my Mare. Ebenezer went with Mrs. Edwards lame Beast to Mr. Barns's for his Advice and Counsel, as last Night Mr. Tuthil went to Captain Maynards for his. P.M. I preach'd the Lecture on Isa. 1, 18. I was peculiarly fervent; and could not but be so—do earnestly beg it may be bless'd to my own Soul, and to all the Audience; especially to Mrs. Hitty Rice who was at meeting. At Night Mrs. Edwards Mare (as it ought to have been writ before) is so bad that we fear whether she will live till morning.

23. Lieutenant Tainter came over, at my Request, to see Mrs. Edwards's Mare. Mr. Pratt came likewise to see her: I sent also for Captain Maynard who came, and tis concluded that She is hipp'd. Mr. Martyn having gone to Boston and left the Care of his Lecture with me I rode over—din'd there, and preach'd his Lecture on Isa. 1, 18. Nigh Sunsett Mr. Martyn came home. As I return'd I visited the Two widows Tomlin.

24. Mrs. Edwards Mare notwithstanding our bathing, etc. I think Swells more and more. N.B. Neighbour John Rogers made Cyder at my Mill. At Eve came my Kinsman Mr. Daniel Needham from Norwich, having been Sick a long Time and Still remaining in a very feeble and weak State.

25. Ebenezer making Cyder for ourselves.

26. Read Exod. 35. Preach'd on Eph. 1, 3. Administer'd the Lords Supper. Mr. Haven and I din'd at the Justice's, my Kins-

[1] The Reverend Thomas Goss of Bolton.
[2] The Reverend John Gardner of Stow.
[3] The Reverend Israel Loring of Sudbury.

[4] Elizabeth How died Aug. 19, 1750.
[5] Moses Tuttle (Yale 1745) was the minister of Granville, Mass. (then called the plantation of Bedford), 1747-1754. Dexter, *Biographical Sketches*, II, 66-69.

man and wife went home. Molly din'd at Deacon Newtons. P.M. read John 11 to number 30 and I preach'd on 1 Pet. 4, 6, but us'd the Discourse on Eph. 5, 14 from page 11 to 27. N.B. at Eve my Kinsmans Spiritual Conversation which may God be pleas'd to Bless, as well as what has Perform'd in the Day! N.B. Mrs. Edwards mare put into Captain Mainards Pasture.

27. I early rode up to Mr. Obadiah Newton[6] and engag'd him to build my Chimney. Had Neighbour Eliezer Rice's Mare, my Horse needing to be shod. Was at Sherman's[7] Saw-Mill for Stuff: at Mr. Hardys in Grafton. I din'd at Mr. Hutchinsons.[8] He and his wife came with me as far as Major Willards[9] in my returning home. Ebenezer had got out 4 Barrells of Cyder—and boyl'd Three of them.

28. Rode to Mr. Gales[10] in order to his coming to view my Timber and he went accordingly towards Night, and Saw that it was so chiefly there that he agrees to begin the framing next Thursday. P.M. Mr. Martyn and his Dauter here. He goes over with me to See what I am about to do in preparing to build. My son Ebenezer very much laid by, with pain in his Back by Reason of a Strain in lifting the Beam at the Cyder Mill last week, and now getting Cold.

29. Samuel Bumpso with me at the place of the design'd Cellar, and after Squaring and Setting out, he began to digg. I rode to Mr. James Bradish's and din'd there, but he was not at home. Rode over to Elijah Warrins to Speak with Bradish, where I found him, and he engages to come to my work. N.B. One son of Mr. Samuel another of Mr. Phinehas Hardy came to the digging before noon. I provided a Dinner for Samuel Bumpso at Mr. Ebenezer Rice's, but not knowing of the Two Hardys coming, did not provide for them. P.M. came Charles and Abner Rice and Phinehas Maynard from Mr. Ebenezer Rice's. At Eve Solomon Baker and Samuel Bumpso with a Number more came and dugg—Mrs. Rice (Ebenezers wife) encouraging their coming and treating em for it.

30. Messers. Gale and Bradish began to Frame by House. Samuel Bumpso and Martyn Pratt dugg at the Cellar. N.B. Early in the Morning I went to Noah How and Elijah Rice and got them to go into the Ministerial Lot and hew'd one Post. Noah had my Team to carry it over, but could not perswade him to do any more work to Day, tho we wanted Hands very much. I catechiz'd at the Meeting House. At Eve Visit Mr. Lewis Brigham's sick Child. Mrs. Edwards return'd from Boston, accompany'd by Mr. Tuttle and Mrs. Martha Edwards.

31. Mrs. Edwards having rid an Horse from Baldwins at Sudbury which belongs to Mr. Joseph Child at Worcester. At my Frame were Messers. Gale and Bradish, Mr. Grow and Mr. Simon Tainter junior, and P.M. Mr. Harrington. N.B. No body at the Cellar today. Mr. Haven return'd.

SEPTEMBER, 1750.

1. Messers. Harrington and Twitchell dugg at the Cellar. Messers. Gale, Bradish, Grow, Tainter junior, Sam Hardy, old Mr. Charles Rice, and P.M. Lieutenant Tainter, at the Frame. Mr. Haven went to Upton. Prepar'd part of an Exercise, but found I must throw it by: Such were the Impediments of this Week—and I am oblig'd to improve some former Preparations.

2. Read Exod. 36. Preach'd from 1 Pet. 4, 6, former part and us'd Sermon 3 on Eph. 5, 14. My wife din'd with me at Esquire Bakers. P.M. read John 11 from number 30 and carry'd on the Same Subject in preaching as in the Morning from 1 Pet. 4, 6, answering the objections against the propriety of preaching the Gospel to them that are Dead—see Sermon on Eph. 5, 14, Page 34 to 44. Mr. Haven preach'd at Upton.

3. Messers. Gale, Bradish, Grow, Tainter junior, Harrington— work'd at the Frame. I attended the Burying of Mr. Bezaliel Smiths Child. P.M. came Mr. Haven. P.M. Thomas Whitney of Shrewsbury work'd at the Frame. Ebenezer under bodily indis-·

positions and very unfit for Business—but a considerable Number of Hands digging in the Cellar at Eve, he was with them.

4. Gale, Bradish, Grow, Tainter junior, old Mr. Charles Rice, Mr. Nathaniel Whitney, David Batherick, John Rogers and Jonas Warrin of Upton wrought at the Frame. P.M. Samuel Bumpso at the Cellar. Justice Baker carted stones, six Load. Mr. Benjamin Fay and Mr. Eleazer Williams dugg in the high way and in divers places in the Interest of the Esquire. I rode to Mr. Daniel Forbush's[1] and to his Father, and they gave me Encouragement to begin the Stoning of the Cellar tomorrow Morning.

5. See Natal. I went not over to the Workmen, but sent over as usual which was daily Beer and Cyder, and a bottle of Rum; some Days Bread and Cheese for Bait; and p.m. dinner for Two or Three, the rest bringing for themselves. Deacon Forbush came to the Cellar, but I think did not work. P.M. his son came—but neither did he much, the digging was not completed, where their work was to be: Yet there was Samuel Bumpso and Nathan Whitney at Digging. At the Frame, there were Whitney, Messers. Gale, Grow, Bradish, Tainter, Batherick, old Mr. Charles Rice, Mr. Nathaniel Whitney and Neighbour John Rogers. N.B. Sam Bumpso wrought to Day on Deacon Newton's account. N.B. Ebenezer and Mr. Eliezer Rice's son Silas carted Stones and Mr. Pratt Sent Cornelius Cook to digg them.

[The following appears in the Natalitia for September 5, 1750.]

I endeavour'd to Spend the Day in a Separate and religious Manner—Seriously reflecting on my past Temper and Conduct— especially since this Day Twelve Month, and whilst I gratefully recognized the Divine Benefits, do penitently confess and bewail my own bareness and vileness, my negligence and unfaithfulness, which I would earnestly beg of God, in His infinite and adorable Mercy to forgive, through a great Propitiation!

My manifest unfaithfulness, together with finding so very little of good Motions or Dispositions in me, fill me with deep and distressing Concern about my Spiritual Condition, But desire to referr all to the boundless Mercy and Goodness of God thro Christ, hoping that my principal Desire and aim and longing is to be Conform'd to the Blessed and Holy Nature and will of God.

Special Errands in Prayer were, my undertaking to Build another House and the Dividing the Association.

6. Deacon Forbush and his son Daniel at Stoning the Cellar, and Samuel Bumpso, employ'd by me, diggs in the Cellar and tends Mr. Forbush with Stones. At the Frame Messers. Gale, Grow, Bradish, Tainter, Charles Rice, Jonah Warrin, Bowman, Harrington, Bond, Ephraim Bruce. Since it is concluded upon to raise tomorrow, I very earnestly entreated every one who was at the Work to notifie all the Several Quarters of the Parish which they liv'd in. I made a Business especially of going to Captain Maynards to invite him and all his that could come. Captain was gone to Brookfield—but I invited Stephen and Joseph Winchester. I took all the pains I could to Send every where, that none might be excepted. I rode over to the other side of the River, Spake and Sent word to Every One, that way: particularly both Sent and went to Mr. James Maynard and to Mr. Seth Rice, and Spake with them both. N.B. Mr. Haven with me, and we rode over to Mr. Martyns. Ask'd him and his Spouse—and brought over Mrs. Molly to our House.

7. Deacon Forbush a.m. and his son Daniel at the Cellar. Deacon Newton tends 'em. At the Frame, Messers. Gale, Bradish, Grow, Tainter, Batheric, Charles Rice, Nathaniel Whitney, Bowman, Harrington, Jonah Warrin, John Rogers, and [blank] who all gave their Work of this forenoon. Mr. Martyn and Mrs. Molly din'd with us, Mr. Haven went briskly to Mrs. Martyn and brought her over (Mr. Martyn having come without her). P.M. My Neighbours rais'd my New Frame and we sung part of Psalm 127. Scil. one Stanza and Psalm 128 (second meetre) except the last half stanza. Sundry Neighbours Sent and brought Cheese, Cake, Wheat Bread, etc. which with Some Apples Pyes which my Wife provided, made up our Entertainment. Mr. Martyn crav'd and Mr. Haven return'd Thanks. N.B. Mr. Gaskitts Son, Seth, came and requested me to go this Evening to their

[6] Of Westborough.
[7] Ephraim Sherman of Grafton.
[8] The Reverend Aaron Hutchinson of Grafton.
[9] Joseph Willard, an early settler and official of Grafton, was a major of a Worcester regiment. Pierce, Grafton, p. 604.
[10] Abijah Gale of Westborough lived on the road to Southborough.
[1] The son of Deacon Jonathan Forbush.

House to See Two Children who were dangerously Sick of Throat Distemper and (tho I was oblig'd to leave all my Affairs to my wife and son and to take leave of my Company and Comforts in returning to my Seasonable Rest after Such a Day of Care and Fatiegue) yet I Cheerfully rode over to 'em. Return'd home tho late at Night. Mrs. Molly Martyn Still with us. Thanks to God for the Favours and Salvations of this Day!

8. Bright good Day. Ebenezer mows a little more Rowing. Mr. Haven to Upton. I rode to Grafton. Mr. Hutchinson not ready. He expected a Line from me. He borrow'd an Horse having Lent his own. It all made him late to Westborough.

9. Preach'd at Grafton on Ps. 110, 3 all Day. Mr. Hutchinson went from my House this morning over to Mr. Martyn and according to agreement preach'd for him: Mr. Martyn for me. N.B. at Grafton p.m. there was Some interruption in the Time of Worship; Thieves (it was Said) had begun to rifle Mr. Phinehas Rice's House. After Meeting many persons went in Search of them. Mr. Hutchinson return'd home, tho it was Somewhat late when he arriv'd.

10. Mr. Hutchinson rode with me to make Some Enquiry after five of my Cattle which lye about Still in that Neighbourhood. We went to Charles Brigham Esq., from thence I went to Captain Drurys[2] and Mr. Aaron Hardys, as I return'd home. Was at Mr. Amsdens at Eve to get Mr. Gale to come to Work for me in Covering my House, which he consented, at length, to, if he could hire any man to Work for him in his Husbandry.

11. I rode over to the New House hoping to meet Lieutenant Hezekiah Ward, but he came not. Went to Mr. Harringtons and din'd there. Thence to the Burial of a Child of Mr. Eleazer Whitney.[3] Thence with Lieutenant Ward (who came by that time) to view a piece of Swampy Land east of my New House which he says is common Land. We did no more than view it. Ebenezer taken very ill with Pain in his Bowels, vomiting, etc.

12. Ebenezer very ill yet. Messers. Grove and Simon Tainter work at the New House in putting up Short Studds. Samuel Bumpso proposes to digg me a Well, which is necessary to be done before my Chimney can be built.

13. Laid out the Well. Samuel begins to digg—upon the following Terms. He says he must have five pounds If he digg Eight foot wide, and digg till he come to a good Spring. If we Shall not agree about the Spring, that he Shall Choose a Third, a majority of which Shall decide the Matter—That Samuel Shall find himself Diet; but I promise to allow him a Dram for each Day. Samuel to find Windlass and Crotches; and I am to find Tub, Chains and Rope. To these I consent. My wife rode over to Mr. Martyns a.m. I rode to Mr. Levi Brighams Child p.m.—went to Deacon Rice's,[4] to Ensign Bartlets,[5] and to Mr. Martyns at Eve.

14. My Neighbour Thomas Frost at work for me P.M. Ebenezer being Still unable to work. Esquire Baker brought down my Cattle (which had run in Grafton) from Esq. Brighams[6] who had put 'em into his Pasture. N.B. Sam Bumpso.

15. Samuel Bumpso at the Well. Mr. Frost again p.m. Lieutenant Tainter brought home from the woods, a Steer which he had kept all winter, and driven up to Sommers for Summering; and this as well as the keeping of Several Cattle for me last Winter was I Suppose Gratis. Ebenezer Somewhat better.

16. Read Exod. 37, 38 and 39 Chapters, a Verse or Two of Each with some Remarks on Repititions—preach'd on Exod. 20, 10. Din'd with my Wife at the Esquire's. P.M. Read John 12 and from Ez. 18, 32, repeated sermon on Eph. 5, 14, and hope it may not prove unuseful. May God add His Blessing, on which all depends!

17. Messers. Samuel and Phinehas Hardy, and Benjamin How began to work on the Roof of my New House, to board and Shingle. Sam Bumpso at the Well, a great and Solid Rock appears in the Well. I visited Rufus Hardy who has had a Sore on his

Knee for about Seven Weeks. N.B. Mr. Haven came to us again.

18. Messers. Samuel Hardy and How on the roof and Mr. Phinehas Hardy a.m. I got Mr. Wyman[7] of Shrewsbury to come and blow the Rock in the Well and he Split it to pieces. He blow'd also a Rock in the Cellar, Sam Bumpso assisted all Day. Ebenezer Shingling p.m. N.B. They got the south side of the Roof done by night.

19. Messers. Samuel and Phinehas Hardy, How, Daniel How (who has often heretofore work'd at Day Labour for me) work'd upon the Roof; as did Ebenezer also. Samuel Bumpso with help from the Carpenters got out of the Well the Great Pieces of the Rock which was blow'd yesterday and, thanks to God, without Dammage. P.M. Sam came from Dinner to work but little before Night. I rode over to Deacon Forbush[8] just at Eve to See if he could come to underpinn the New House. At my return home found my Brother Samuel Parkman and with him Mr. Holland[9] of Boston on their Journey home from New-London. Frost this Night.

20. Waited on my Brother and Mr. Holland as far as Marlborough. Din'd at justice Brighams.[10] In returning call'd to see Eliphalet Adams and his wife, and at divers of their near Neighbours—having heard that Said Adams was to have a Separatepreacher to be at his House on Some Day appoint'd and preach there. I therefore warn'd and Caution'd them against so great Evil; and found them ready to Comply (verbally) with my Counsel: and Adams assur'd me there was not a direct appointment though something had been Said to one Joseph Ward, late of Marlborough about Mr. Hovey[11] of Mill River his coming, but now promis'd me he Should not come. At Night very Cold. My son Thomas came up from Concord.

21. Messers. Samuel and Phinehas Hardy closing my new House with Boards. Samuel Bumpso at the Well. Then came also Mr. Dunlop to digg in my Cellar, besides whom there were three Youths viz. Jonathan Grout and a Son of each of foresaid Hardys to digg in the Cellar. Messers. Bezaleel Smith and Eleazer Pratt, each with a Team Carting Stones for the Cellar, whilest Thomas Whitney and Isaac Tomlin (this last was sent by Mr. Reuben Maynard) dugg Stones for me. And all but the Two Carpenters and Mr. Dunlop brought themselves Dinner. But Some time before Night it rain'd; Yet I desire to submit to the will of God under the Disappointment.

22. Rain over, Sam was at the Well and had Nathan Whitney and Charles Rice junior to help him. Mr. Haven to Upton and Molly with him to See Bekky Warrin.

23. Read Exod. 40. Preach'd on Rev. 10 former part. My Wife and I din'd at Justice Bakers.[12] P.M. I read John 13, and preach'd on the Same subject that I was upon in the forenoon, but from another Text, Scil. Lev. 19, 30, and by means of my continual avocations at the New House Business I was oblig'd to repeat part of what I formerly deliver'd from that Text, viz. from page 14 to 20. N.B. a Very Cold Day for the Time of the Year. N.B. Gave Notice of the Association Fast to be next Tuesday at Hopkinton.

24. Samuel at the Well just before noon, and he had got Phinehas Maynard to help him. Visited Mr. Daniel Forbush's Dauter Sarah who lyes at her uncle Jonathans sick of the Throat Distemper. N.B. Mr. Harrington ask'd me to dine at his House, but I refus'd that I might hasten along with Mr. Daniel Forbush to see his Dauter—by which means I miss'd of dining to my Hurt—Yet they did ask me to Eat both at Mr. Jonathan Forbushs and at Mr. Bonds, but both under great Disadvantages So that I did not accept thereof. At Evening Mr. Haven return'd home with Molly from Upton by the Way of Grafton.

25. Mr. Davis[13] of Holden and Mr. Haven accompany'd me

---

[2] Thomas Drury was a Selectman of Grafton. Pierce, *Grafton*, p. 475.
[3] Deborah Whitney was only 1 year old.
[4] Matthias Rice of the north precinct.
[5] Jonathan Bartlett of the north precinct.
[6] Charles Brigham was an early settler, town officer, and Representative of Grafton. Pierce, *Grafton*, pp. 463–464.
[7] Ross Wyman. See Ward, *Shrewsbury*, pp. 482–483.
[8] Jonathan Forbush of Westborough.
[9] Samuel Holland was a prominent member and later deacon of the New North Church.
[10] Charles Brigham of Marlborough was a Justice of the Peace.
[11] Samuel Hovey, an uneducated preacher, was ordained minister of the Baptist Church in the Mill River precinct of Mendon in 1749.
[12] Edward Baker, a selectman of Westborough.
[13] The Reverend Joseph Davis.

to Hopkinton Association Fast. Found only Mr. Loring[14] there. Nor did there come any other Minister. Mr. Barrett[15] pray'd and Mr. Davis preach'd on Hab. 3, 2. P.M. Mr. Loring pray'd and I preach'd on Ps. 110, 3. Mr. Davis to Framingham. Mr. Davis and I came home. N.B. Some Water in the Well.

26. Mr. Davis having din'd with us return'd to Holden. I rode to South East Corner of the Parish and visited old Mr. Hudson and his Wife at Mr. Ithamar Bellows: and old Mr. Garfield[16] and his wife. Was at Mr. Joslins[17] about Stones. He is willing to give me Stones, but does not appear very forward to help me in digging and Carting them. Whereas divers men who are nearer have offer'd me Stones gratis, but the Difficulty is at this busy Time of Year, to get them to the place where they are to be us'd. Mr. Benjamin How and Ebenezer boarding the New House. Sam Bumpso and Mr. Pierce make a Frame to digg in, in the well.

27. My Son Thomas left us to go to Concord again. Billy rode with him as far as to Deacon Jonathan Rice's in Sudbury, to bring back the Mare, on which he rode. Visited Rufus Hardy[18] who is dangerously Sick. Din'd there. P.M. attended the Funeral of little Sarah Forbush dauter of Mr. Daniel Forbush. She was almost nine years of age: a very agreeable forward Child. Bury'd from Jonathans where she had liv'd for Two Years. Mr. Benjamin How and his Brother Noah, together with my Son Ebenezer boarding the New House. Mr. Pierce and Sam Bumpso digging at the Well. N.B. It had cav'd in, before they got a Frame, about 4 feet. They have got out a great part of it to Day.

28. Rain Storm. Under a great Disappointment having striven much Yesterday for men to digg in my Cellar, that Mr. Forbush might finish Stoning it, and might do the underpinning of the House and get ready for Mr. Newton to be about the Chimney—and I had provided Two, viz. Benjamin Whipple (of Hardwick) and Aaron Warrin. Messers. Benjamin and Noah How p.m. at boarding the New House, and Ebenezer with them. Sam Bumpso diggs an Hour or Two before night in the Cellar. At Eve Benjamin Whipple and his wife with their Children here. We took up 3 Hives of Bees. A great Frost this Evening.

29. Sam Bumpso having nobody to work with him at the Well, work'd at digging the Cellar. Messers. Benjamin and Noah How boarding the House. Ebenezer work'd there also part of the Day. Mr. Bond Cart'd 3 Load of Stones. Lieutenant Tainter, Mr. Nat Whitney, Mr. Harrington, Aaron Warrin and [blank] dug Stones in Mr. Jonah Warrins Lot, and at Grind-Stone Hill. I attended the Funeral of Rufus Hardy. Mr. Haven came to my House and I went to Upton for him. Lodg'd at Captain Hazzletons.[19]

30. A great Frost last night, and the Ground much frozen this morning. I preach'd at Upton on 1 Thess. 1, 10 a. and p.m. Din'd at Captain Sadlers[20] (the Captain gone to Church at Hopkinton). P.M. I baptiz'd Elizabeth Warrin, Dauter of Elijah and Rebecca Warrin; on her Mothers Right, being Member of the first Church in Cambridge. Was at their House in the Eve, and lodg'd there. N.B. Mr. Haven preach'd for me on John 3, 36.

OCTOBER, 1750

1. I went from Mr. Elijah Warrins to Mr. Beriah Rice's—Mr. Marshal Bakers—Mr. Jonas Warrins, Mr. James Bradishs, Mr. Dunlaps, Mr. Gashets[1] and Mr. Chaddocks[2]—to Lieutenant Tainters. N.B. Sam Bumpso a d Phinehas Maynard work'd at the well a while, but it growing too heavy for one person to draw at the Windlass, they broke off. Dr. Breck[3] at my House while I

was from Home. N.B. We have had [blank] Bushel of Winter apples of old Mr. Maynard.

2. Deacon Forbush and his Son at the Cellar. Mr. Frost, Levi Jummers and Charles Rice junior from about 10 o'Clock a.m. Two of them in the Cellar digging and tending the Masons; and the other of them with Samuel Bumpso and Phinehas Maynard who work'd all Day at the Well. A.M. oblig'd my self to run up and down to get the Hands together and tend upon them. Water increases in the Well.

3. Deacon and his Son at the Cellar, Neighbour Frost, Levi Jummers and Charles Rice, junior from about 10 o'clock a.m. Two of them in the Cellar digging and tending the Masons; and the other of them with Samuel Bumpso and Phinehas Maynard who work'd all Day at the Well. A.M. oblig'd my self to run up and down to get the Hands together and tend upon them. Water increases in the Well.

4. Mr. William Pierce came to stone the well and Sam Bumpso to tend him, but they judg'd that the Water was not deep enough, tho they Spent much Time in drawing; and I assisted what I could a.m. but Charles Rice junior came p.m. N.B. Mrs. William Pierce p.m. would fain have prevented her Husband, and not without much difficulty perswaded to give way to his coming tomorrow to stone the Well. Was in an uncommon Manner perplex'd for want of Money—after divers fruitless Endeavours borrow'd some of Mr. Ebenezer Rice's wife which I pay'd to Mrs. Pierce, wife of Mr. William Pierce. They began to Stone towards Night. Mr. Charles Rice got a Cart Load of Moss for the Well.

5. Mr. Pierce and Samuel Bumpso Stoning the Well. Joseph Grout junior help'd them. N.B. Two foot of Water in the Morning. N.B. The Well 22 feet Deep. Mr. Haven and I rode over to Mr. Martyns and din'd there. I went especially to take Measure of his Entry and stair Case and Fire places. Return'd about 4 p.m. Ebenezer has been Carting Apples etc. No corn gather'd yet. But we suffer'd great Dammage by the Cattle; all of them 12 in Number broke out of the Cow Yard last night—were in the Corn, among the Apples, Cabbages etc. N.B. the Weather has been very Cold for several Days.

6. I am much afflicted with Toothach. Bright but cool weather. Jonathan Smith helps Ebenezer Thrash Rye. Mr. Haven to Upton p.m. Nobody at work at New House or Well but Mr. Daniel Forbush at the Cellar.

7. Much afflicted with Toothach. Had a sorrowful Night of Pain. Drew a Blister but it did not give me Ease. I went to Meeting thro much Difficulty, and thro Divine Goodness went thro the Exercises. Read Levit. 2 and gave Some account of that Book and the Contents of the first Chapter but enlarged on the Meaning of the second, preach'd on Lev. 19, 30 repeating in part what I formerly deliver'd on that Text, from page 20 to 22, nigh the Bottom; but with great additions on the Hand of Reading the Sacred Scriptures. None of my Family besides me din'd at the Esquires to Day. P.M. read John 15, and preach'd on the fourth Commandment but us'd the Same Text as the Morning, and us'd likewise the passages in those Sermons which are in page 22 near the Bottom, to page 25. Many Strangers, especially from Southborough among us at the Worship.

8. Expected Masons but they came not. I provided Two Hands, Mr. Frost and Thomas Whipple to tend 'em but was oblig'd to employ em in throwing out the Cobbling Stones out of the Cellar, which may do for the Well; and p.m. to digg Stones for the well. I was much indispos'd, yet made a shift to ride over. Found no Mr. Pierce at the Well. Jonathan Smith thrashes with Ebenezer. A.M. they gather Corn. P.M. a Council of 3 ministers Sit at Shrewsbury to Day. Revd. Dorr,[4] Martyn[5] and Harrington.[6] P.M. receiv'd a Letter dated September 29 with Clerk of Study, from Mr. Edwards[7] of Northampton. N.B. the Town met at the North Side to see what to do with those who took down the

[14] The Reverend Israel Loring of Sudbury.
[15] The Reverend Samuel Barrett of Hopkinton.
[16] Benjamin Garfield.
[17] Joseph Joslin.
[18] The son of Phinehas Hardy.
[19] John Hazeltine, an early settler, selectman, and Representative of Upton.
[20] John Sadler, a frequent office-holder in Upton.

[1] Daniel Gaschet, Gassett or Gashitt.
[2] Parkman meant Isaac Shattuck.
[3] Samuel Breck, the physician of Worcester.

[4] The Reverend Joseph Dorr of Mendon.
[5] The Reverend John Martyn of Northborough.
[6] The Reverend Timothy Harrington (Harvard 1737), had served the First Congregational Church at Swanzey, N.H., and since August, 1748, had been the minister of the First Congregational Church of Lancaster. Sibley, X, 188-195.
[7] The great Jonathan Edwards.

Meeting House. Lieutenant Tainter here, with Resentments of high Seasoning concerning the meeting. At Eve Lieutenant and Mr. Daniel Forbush here when they were returning from Town Meeting. Town did nothing about the old Meeting House. I was in much pain, which Mr. Forbush Seeing, acquainted me with a Remedy used by him with observable Success, which he communicated the Knowledge of; and which tho very Disagreeable, yet the more clearly Methods (Blister etc.) us'd by me, failing, and my affliction great, I yielded freely to—viz. Cow dung fir'd in Hoggs Fatt—and lay all Night with my Face on't Despicable as it seems; it gave me Relief. D.G.

9. My Wife and Dauter Molly rose early and rode to Worcester to Dr. Brecks to visit them before they leave these parts of the World. I had a comfortable Day, thro Gods Goodness, tho I was pritty much confin'd to the House. Dispatched Clark on Study and made a few Remarks thereon; having begun it Yesterday. Towards night interrupted with Company—Samuel, Ruth and Hannah Hicks from Cambridge. Jonathan Smith at work with Ebenezer in cutting up Corn.

10. Jonathan Smith helps Ebenezer Still, in getting in the Harvest. It was So cloudy and dull weather that tho I was much eas'd of my Pains yet I was feeble and did not go out.

11. Expected Mr. Pierce to Stone the New Well. Sent Ebenezer over to tend him but he came not—so Ebenezer after throwing Some of the Cellar Stones to the Well return'd home. Heard afterward that Mr. Pierce came and found no Body to tend him and therefore went home.

12. Sent Billy on the Mare to Worcester with a Letter to Brother Samuel Breck about his Servant Girl but without Effect, he not accepting my offer for her. Ebenezer rode over to Mr. Pierce but to no purpose. Jonathan Smith work'd here getting in Corn. Towards Evening came home my Son Thomas from Mr. Goold of Concord, with a Letter from Mr. Minott.[8] I thank God my son has been carry'd out, thro the Agreement and that no Evil has fallen upon us to Grieve us. Three Sons and Two Dauters, with Patty Pannell husk Corn in the Barn this Eve, and Except Molly, they Stay till Eleven o'Clock.

13. [No entry.]

14. Read Lev. 3, and preach'd on 1 Cor. 11, 20, administering the Lords Supper. My Wife and I din'd at the Justice's. P.M. read John 16, and preach'd on 1 Pet. 46 latter Part. At Eve (blessed be God) I had some peculiar Sense of Divine and Eternal Things. O that they might abide and increase!

15. I rode over to my New House. Mr. Daniel Warrin to tend on Mr. Pierce. At length came Mr. Pierce to go on with stoning the Well. Got Mr. Charles Rice to send a son till I could get another Hand to tend Mr. Pierce. By 11 o'Clock sent Samuel Bumpso to the Work. Mr. Obadiah Newton came to build my Chimney. P.M. my Son Ebenezer tended Mr. Newton. Mr. Jeduthan Fay working at the high way Sent for his Man and Team about 3 or 4 p.m. to come and draw stones which they had dug in the high way, and it prov'd a great kindness to me: especially as he wrought with his Team Gratis. At Merchant Rices at Eve with Mr. Obadiah Newton, Fay, etc.

16. Mr. Newton and Forbush at the Cellar Wall which is the Foundation for the Chimney. Jonathan Smith works there, at the Cellar and Well, Mr. Pierce being at the stoning the Well. Sam Bumpso tends him. Yet want another Hand. Jonathan Smith So oblig'd to help at the Well that the Masons are forc'd to tend themselves a great Part of the Time. As for me I rode about and waited and waited on the Work at Cellar and Well from Early Morning till into Evening—was especially at Mr. Timothy Warrins and talk'd with the widow Sarah Forbush[9] who is going to marry Josiah Walker,[10] an unbaptiz'd person,—he desir'd to talk with me about Deacon Burnaps[11] being offended with him—and said he had acknowledg'd his Fault to the Deacon. N.B. Sent 12£ old Tenor to Mr. Daniel Gookin Bookseller at Boston, by

Mr. Batheric. I din'd at Ensign Millers.[12] We are so out of **Meat** in the Family that I bought a Quarter of Beef of him. N.B. **Mr.** Bogle[13] of Sudbury there. Call'd to see Mr. Daniel Forbush's Children Sick of Canker. Lieutenant Tainter sent his Team **with** Stones by William Dunlop.

17. Mr. Newton (who dines at his sisters, but lodges at various Places in the Neighbourhood) and Mr. Forbush at the Foundation of the Chimneys Still—are now got even with the Ground. Jonathan Smith tends 'em. Mr. Pierce stoning the well, Samuel Bumpso and Thomas Whipple tend him. Well caves in frequently upon the work. Deacon Newton and Cornelius Cook cart Stones for the Well all Day. Neighbours Harrington, Tainter and Charles Rice are carting Stones for the Chimney. I was among them all Day (except Dining Time)—provided dinner for **only** Mr. Pierce to Day. At Neighbour Eliezer Rice's at Eve, His **Wife** seems to be under strange Disgusts but I know not as yet **what.** Sent my Son Thomas p.m. to Worcester to get Bricks for **Oven** and Topping Chimney, but he could get none. Am full of various perplexitys. Ebenezer making Cyder.

18. Very Rainy. No body at Work. Held up p.m. Catechiz'd at Meeting House. N.B. at Mr. Eliezer Rice's at Eve: and **Mrs.** Rice taxes me with being worldly.

19. Messers Newton and Forbush. Jonathan Smith **tends.** Mr. Pierce stones the Well about 2 foot above Ground—Clears out the well—asks me 7£ Old Tenor. Afterwards he took **less.** Ebenezer works there, and Mr. Joseph Green junior and Abner Whipple digg and Cart stones—with Mr. Edward Whipples yoke of Oxen. Mr. Obadiah Newton came to our House at Night.

20. Mr. Newton at the Chimneys. Mr. Forbush also; and Jonathan Smith to tend 'em. I rode over to Mr. Martyns, and thence to Bolton. Din'd at Mr. Benjamin Baileys. Proceeded **to** Mr. Robert Fosgits[14] for Brick for my new Ovens and for topping out my Chimneys. Mr. Fosgit not at Home, but his wife went with me to the Kiln where I picked out 600 and some odd Bricks, and Two Dozen of Tile. The Bricks at 7£ old Tenor per Thousand, The Tile 1 Shilling a piece. Agreed with Mr. Bailey to cart 'em to his House and Mr. Goddard to cart them Home, to my own. Return'd at Eve to Mr. Martyns. Mr. Stone[15] there, to Change with Mr. Martyn. I lodg'd there.

21. Mr. Martyn in the Rain to Southborough. Mr. Stone came and preach'd here a.m. on 1 Pet. 4, 18. P.M. on Eph. 5, 16. He read Levit. 4, John 17. I preach'd for Mr. Martyn a. and p.m. on Jer. 6, 16. I return'd home at Eve.

22. A very Cold windy, freezing Day. Mr. Newton came to work, and Jonathan Smith to tend him; but the Mortar was So froze and the Cold so increasing that they were scarce able to stand it. They built up some Defences against the Cold wind yet it was too Cold. It was so broken a Day, they both threw it in, and went home before Night. Mr. William Goddards Sons brot me 600 of Brick and 2 Dozen of Tile.

23. Windy, but somewhat more moderate weather. Mr. Newton and Mr. Forbush at work, and Ebenezer tending. Association Fast at Bolton, but I could not go by reason of the work which is doing at my new House, and expect Huskers at Night, but it was put by. Lieutenant Tainter proceed according to Law with sundry persons for their Rates and had Deacon Newton with him. I charged Lieutenant to use Moderation with Mr. Hezekiah Pratt because of the Affliction he is under by his wifes sickness. They went to Mr. Barns and Mr. Pratt. N.B. A Sour Message to me from Mr. Barns to go to him and settle accounts with him before Night or he would send an Officer. I wrote him an answer which my wife carry'd with a 3£ Bill old Tenor to pay him for an Ox which he had bought for me at Boston last Spring when I let him have my Horse to go there; and for which he had never paid me, nor had ask'd me for his Money, but had concluded to Set it off in the Rates.

---

[8] Timothy Minot (Harvard 1747), a schoolmaster and later a physician of Concord. *Sibley,* XII, 194–195.

[9] The widow of Phinehas Forbush of Westborough, who had died at Fort Massachusetts, July 16, 1746. Pierce, *Forbes and Forbush Genealogy,* pp. 31–32.

[10] Listed as Joseph Walker of Hopkinton in *Westborough Vital Records.*

[11] Jonathan Burnap of Hopkinton.

[12] James Miller of Westborough.

[13] Thomas Bogle.

[14] Fosgit, or Fosgate, owned the first brick-yard in Bolton. Soon there were several others operating in this town.

[15] The Reverend Nathan Stone of Southborough.

24. Mr. Newton and Forbush at the Chimneys. Ebenezer tends. Hear that Lieutenant Tainter[16] with assistance of Deacon Newton[17] etc., Strain'd upon Mr. James Maynard, and actually laid him in Jayl. I rode down to Mr. Daniel Warrins, Mr. Joslins, etc. to get some stones dugg and Carted. Was at Mr. Bradish's, at his Morning Prayer. Din'd at Mr. Joslins. P.M. at the New House desir'd Rody Smith to ask Mr. Barns to come and husk to night. A Number were ask'd, but there were but six only who came, scil. Neighbour Benjamin How and his Brother Daniel, Neighbour John Frost and Samuel Forbush, Cornelius Cook and John Pratt. Lieutenant Eager here at Eve, with a message from Mr. Edwards of Northampton to send the Lame Mare to his House tomorrow.

25. Mr. Newton and Forbush at the Chimneys—Jonathan Smith tended. Joseph Rice came and offer'd to help me to Day. Thomas and he carted and sledded stones about the well. I rode to Lieutenant Tainters to acquaint him with Mr. Edwards of Northamptons Message; and he sent the Mare to Lieutenant Eagers. P.M. Expected Hands to level the Banks from the New House to the Well, but there came no one but Ebenezer Forbush. I fear'd Mr. Pierce (who was at the projecting this and appointing the Day) would not come; and therefore I Expressly Sent for Mr. Biglo to help in raising up the Wall of our Well, and he and Ebenezer Forbush work'd till Evening. Mr. Nathaniel Whitney informs me that Mr. William Williams of Weston was dismiss'd from his people by the Advice of a Council last night. A most shocking Event in the Course of Divine Providence! The Lord Sanctifie it to all! N.B. My Neighbour Pratt greatly disturbed with me for Lieutenant Tainters proceeding with him but most unjustly, because I besought him on Pratts behalf. At Evening Edwards Whipple here. A.M. Neighbour How assisted Ebenezer in getting 3 Mantle Trees, and p.m. Ebenezer help'd him dig potatoes. N.B. Mr. Daniel Warrin and Mr. Ithamar Bellows brought 6 Load of Stones.

26. Ebenezer Carted the 3 Mantle Trees which were hew'd yesterday—and tended Mr. Newton and Forbush at the Chimneys. I visited the Sick—viz. Two Children of Mr. Eleazer Whitneys, 3 of Mr. Daniel Forbush, and the Widow Woods. Din'd at Mr. Jonathan Forbush's. P.M. at Mr. Hezekiah Pratts that his wife might shew her mind to me for Lieutenant Tainters proceeding with her Husband. N.B. Mrs. Whipple and Mrs. Hannah Maynard came in and were witnesses of my Discourse with Mr. Pratt and his wife; who (all) manifested Satisfaction. Mr. Haven return'd to us. Joseph Winchester and Jonathan Smith husk'd with my sons at Evening till 10.

27. Mr. Haven left us again, and is to preach at Medway tomorrow. My Condition very afflictive, while I have so many Difficultys, to conflict with so many avocations and Disturbances from almost all Quarters. May God Sustain and help me! Whilst I was so grievously born down, especially with regard to my preparations for the Sabbath approaching (which is a Day to be observ'd by me throughout my Life) Mr. Barrett came at Evening Expecting to change with me tomorrow. I rode over to Hopkinton and lodg'd at Mr. Barretts.[18]

28. This Day Twenty Six years ago I receiv'd holy ordination. Blessed be God for His Longsuffering towards so unprofitable and unfaithfull a Creature! and O that the Lord would pardon, through the mediation of Jesus Christ, my great defects and miscarriages! May he be pleas'd to quicken me by His Spirit, assist me, Support and strengthen me for his Mercys Sake! I preach'd at Hopkinton a. and p.m. on Jer. 8, 4, 5. May God grant Success, that those serious, weighty Things may duely affect us all! and especially be profitable to my own Soul! Mr. Barrett din'd at Esquire Bakers. My wife not at meeting. Mr. Barrett read Levit. 5, omitted reading p.m. We return'd home at night. I lodg'd there.

29. I early return'd to Westboro. Call'd at Mr. Biglo's. N.B His Fray with Mrs. Pierce which I did something to compose. Mr. Newton and Forbush at the Chimney. Ebenezer and Sam

Bumpso tend them. Was oblig'd to visit Mr. Jonathan Forbush's Child Jonathan who is very sick. N.B. have heard that Mr. James Maynard, Eliezer Rice and Joseph Rice went to Church at Hopkinton yesterday—and that to Day Revd. Roger Price is come over to visit in Westborough. Mr. John Rogers makes Cyder at my Mill. Neighbour Rogers husks with my sons in the Barn this Evening. N.B. I went to Neighbour Barns's to talk with him, but his wife said he was gone to Marlborough. P.M. Molly and Lucy rode in the Chair to Colonel Wards[19] at Shrewsbury.

30. Mr. Newton, Mr. Forbush and Jonathan Smith, together with my son Ebenezer at the Chimneys. I rode over to the New House. I rode up to Captain Bakers, to get him to Cart Some more Stones who says he will go tomorrow. N.B. I call'd in at Mr. Pratts with Mr. Abraham Knowlton; and there was Mrs. Whipple to See further into the Discourse of Mr. Pratt of late, but he was not at Home. P.M. Mr. Barns call'd here. He denys he Sent me such a Message as on the 23 yet Deacon Newton and Lieutenant Thomas Forbush have testify'd that they heard him. Neighbour Rogers making Cyder here. Thomas thrashes Wheat. Molly and Lucy return'd from Colonel Wards, where they lodg'd last Night. Mr. Joslin and Mr. Jonathan Bellows dug the Stones at Mr. Joslins to Day, while the Teams were going—3 Turns apiece. At Eve came Lieutenant Tainter and brought me in Money Notes and including Several Small parcells of Money which he had before paid, in Old Tenor Value 62£. N.B. his son Benjamin came from Sommers with his new Marry'd Wife. Rain at Night.

31. Messers Newton and Forbush at the Chimney, my Son Thomas and Jonathan Smith tended 'em. Lieutenant Tainter sent us a Quarter of Mutton at Evening besides which there was not anything Sent us for the approaching Thanksgiving. But I thank God who inclin'd him to Send; and that we had in the House wherewith to make decent Provision, were but our Hearts in a Suitable Frame. Which may God with whom is the Preparation of the Heart, grant to us!

### NOVEMBER [1750]

1. Thanksgiving. How numberless, and how vast the divine Benefits! O for a Truely devout and grateful Sense of them and that we might be able to attend to the Obligations we are under to our glorious Benefactor! Rain'd hard especially in Meeting Time and when we came home from the worship. Text was 1 Thess. 5, 16. May God grant the Joy of this Day may not go over with the Day, but that we may long protract it—nay rejoice evermore, both in this world and the future!

2. I went early to the New House. Mr. Newton and Forbush came to the Chimneys. Mr. Newton brought Sam Bumpso to tend—and Ebenezer was there also. The Parish meet to consider my Support—grant the Same as last Year, but do it chearfully, which gives me the much greater pleasure. May God enable me to improve to His Glory as he is pleas'd to vouchsafe! At Eve rode down to See Mr. Daniel Warrins Son Daniel who is sick.

3. Messers. Newton and Forbush. Samuel Bumpso helps my Son in tending them but I was not over to See what they are doing to Day. My Son Thomas (Mr. John Rogers affording Some assistance, and dining here) finished the making up of Cyder, from our own Apples—but Neighbour David Maynard has brot a parcel of Apples from his Sister Tomlins, which are partly for our Supply with Cyder is not making enough ourselves to fill our Casks.

4. On Jer. 6, 8. (the Subject I design'd for October 28th). May God be pleas'd to add his Blessing! Din'd at Justice Bakers. Snow'd very fast, so that the whole Earth appears mantled for Winter. I think I remark'd on Lev. 5 and 6th and John 18, read. (This was writ sometime after.)

5. Was early at the New House. Messers. Newton, Forbush and tended as before, but by reason of the Cold make Slow Work. Rode over to Mr. Jonathan Forbush's to see his Sick Children. Widow Newton gave me Alpheus's digging and Carting Six Load of Clay: and this afternoon he goes with a Yoke of Oxen and

---

[16] Simon Tainter of Westborough.

[17] Josiah Newton.

[18] The Reverend Samuel Barrett.

[19] Nahum Ward.

assists Ebenezer in digging and Carting 3 Load more. Towards Eve I visited Mr. Beeman who is very bad. Was also at Mr. Warrins to See Daniel—in returning home I call'd at Mr. Bathericks.

6. Was early at the New House. Messers. Newton and Forbush—Ebenezer and Sam at the Chimneys. The Weather more Moderate. A.M. Cloudy and Cold p.m. P.M. I visited at Mr. Eliezer Rice's, who tho the last Time I was there parted with me in very good Friendship, yet has Seem'd to be in very great Disgust—by his absenting himself from our Meeting Two or Three Days—had warm Talk at first—but were calmer afterwards, and he walk'd with me to Mr. Whipples and back. Parted also in peace. His Disgust was rais'd from a misapprehension of my Discourse the last Visit.

7. Messers. Newton and Forbush at the Chimneys. Ebenezer lyes by great part of the Day. Thomas goes to the New House and by the help of Samuel Bumpso tends the Masons. Towards Evening Set out to visit Mr. Beeman: but when going heard he dy'd in the forenoon. Nevertheless I proceeded to visit the widow and the distress'd Children. Was likewise at Mr. Daniel Warrins, whose son Daniel dyed also this afternoon. When I came home in the Evening found Mr. Prentice[1] of Easton here and lodg'd with us. Martha Pannell return'd here from Mr. Rice's.

8. Messers. Newton and Forbush at the Chimneys. Ebenezer tho not Well, and Thomas tended. Mr. Prentice left us. N.B. Lieutenant Bruce[2] here before Mr. Prentice went away. N.B. Mr. Hutchinson[3] sent his Desire (By Letter last Night) to me to preach his Lecture to Day: but I could not go, being oblig'd to look after my workmen, and to wait for a message concerning the Funeral of Mr. Daniel Warrin; not knowing but it would be to Day; Mr. Beemans being also appointed to be tomorrow, So that I Should have little Time to prepare for the Sabbath. Nor could I well go because of a Lame Leg, which was bruised yesterday, and I suppose have got Cold in it. Besides that my Horses are smooth, whilst the Roads are Slippery. At Night Nigh 11 o'Clock came Mr. Harrington to call me, Mr. Bowman being apprehended near his End. I went with him. Got there about midnight—found him alive, and a little reviv'd, but very low—discours'd and pray'd with him and them present. Lodg'd at Ensign Millers. N.B. Revd. Mr. Curtis[4] (who marry'd a Bass) having attempted to go to Poquoag Ordination but without Success, call'd here in his way to his aunt Buckminsters at Framingham.

9. Early in the Morning went from Ensign Millers to Mr. Bowman, who was further reviv'd. Discours'd and pray'd with him—and went to my New House where Messers. Forbush and Newton were at work: and my two sons with Cornelius Cook tending them. P.M. at the Funerals of Mr. Beeman[5] and Daniel Warrin junior which were carry'd on thus, we went to the House of the late Mr. Beeman and pray'd there. (N.B. his only Son Abraham is taken Sick and so bad he keeps his Bed) then I hasted to Mr. Warrins, and both the Corps were Sett in the Yard on their Biers, and I pray'd again there. A Sorrowful Sight—both the hoary Head and the blooming Youth going to the House appoint'd for all the Living. After the Funerals, my Wife (who was with me) and I rode to Mr. Eliezer Rice's. Lieutenant Ward, who had survey'd 5 acres and 36 Rods of Swampy Land, being there, with the Plan of it. N.B. the Masons having rais'd my Chimneys as high as the Roof, break off for this Season: and after so much Toil we heartily rejoice.

10. Rain. About 10 at night my Wife went to Mrs. Ann Maynards[6] Groaning and return'd not till after we were gone to Meeting (this) Next Day.

11. I read and gave (as I usually do) some observations upon Levit. 7. Preach'd on Lev. 19, 30 repeating from my sermon on that Text page 25 to the End of 31 with alterations and omissions and additions. Din'd at Justice Bakers. P.M. Read John 19. Preach'd on Exod. 31, 13.

12. My sons make Cyder of Apples brought from the Widow Tomlins[7] by Mr. David Maynard. At Captain Bakers Request I pray'd with his Company and din'd at Mr. Ebenezer Rice's with the Officers. After which the Captain accompany'd me in a visit to Mr. Bowman who is still sick. N.B. Proprietors Meeting at Marlborough. Sent a Plan of 5 Acres and 36 Rods of Land lying South of Chauncy Meadows and west of the Cedar Swamp to be accepted; but it was objected against by Neighbour Richard Barns as what he Should claim a part of. N.B. I sent the plan by Neighbour Eliezer Rice. N.B. Mr. Martyn here and din'd with my Wife while I was with the Officers. He brought the Answer of the Association to my Question Sent to them respecting the Baptizing of the Children of Justice Charles Brigham.

13. Mr. Maynard had Two Barrells and we have Two, of the Cyder made from his Sister Tomlins Apples, but were it not so Cold weather there had Perhaps been another Barrell. At Eve Mr. Benjamin Tainter[8] brought his wife to visit us. Their Brother Bowker[9] and sister Elizabeth were then come from Sommers. They (except Bowker) supp'd here: as did Neighbour Obadiah Newton (who this Eve, plaster'd my Study Jaums anew; and pointed the Jaums in the Kitchen) and Samuel Bumpso. Reckon'd with Mr. Newton who tells me he must be paid for nineteen Days, 20/ old Tenor per Day.

14. Mr. William Rogers makes Cyder here, and dines with us. Mr. Larkin Williams[10] of Marlborough likewise. He tells me that Lieutenant Beeman lyes dead. A very observable providence! P.M. I visited Mrs. Beeman (widow of the late Eleazer) and her son Abraham who is Sick, but grows better. Visited also Two Children of Mr. Adams which are taken sick. At Lieutenant Bruce's in the Eve. Rode home accompany'd by the widow Smith, alias Devereux.

15. Went down to Mr. Stephen Maynards to view a large Quantity of White Pine Boards there. P.M. Church Meeting on the Affair of Robert Cook. There were but Eleven Members came, and those very late. We adjourn'd to Monday next. My Son Thomas went to Concord to fetch up the rest of his Cloths etc. My Legg is full of Smart and gives me great Trouble.

16. With much ado Study at all, my Legg So very bad. At Eve Brother Hicks[11] here.

17. Brother Hicks to Sutton. Thomas return'd from Concord. Dr. Gott call'd and dress'd my Legg. Dr. Smith[12] also came here, by Billys Means at Mr. Whipples. P.M. Captain Maynard here, having been to Boston, and bought sundrys for us.

18. So bad with my Legg in the Morning that it was with Difficulty I rode to Meeting. Omitted Reading publickly a. and p.m. Preached a.m. on Exod. 31, 13. My wife and I din'd at Esq. Bakers. P.M. I preach'd on Zech. 1, 4 repeating Sermon on Ps. 119, 60 to page 13. In returning home at Eve one Felly of a Chair Wheel broke out and oblig'd me to stop at old Mr. Maynards till an Horse was brought for me.

19. We kill'd a Steer of 5 past–21 score. Mr. Jonathan Rogers assisted. P.M. Church meeting according to adjournment, exactly at 2 p.m. on the Affair of Robert Cook. Both he and his wife declare their Innocence. After all that we heard from them and the witnesses, the Number of Members of the Church who

[1] The Reverend Solomon Prentice, the former minister of Grafton.

[2] Abijah Bruce of Westborough.

[3] The Reverend Aaron Hutchinson of Grafton.

[4] Philip Curtis (Harvard 1738), the first minister of the First Congregational Church of Sharon, 1741–1797. He married Elizabeth, the daughter of Joseph Bass of Dorchester, Sept. 6, 1744. *Sibley*, X, 282–284.

[5] Eleazer Beeman.

[6] Mrs. David Maynard, Jr.

[7] The widow of Deacon Isaac Tomlin of Westborough.

[8] The son of Deacon Simon Tainter.

[9] Sarah, the daughter of Deacon Tainter, married Joseph Bowker, Nov. 21, 1749. Her sister, Elizabeth, married Stephen Sadler of Upton, Nov. 19, 1750. Dean W. Tainter, *A History and Genealogy of the Descendants of Joseph Taynter* (Boston, 1859), pp. 23–24.

[10] The son of Colonel Abraham Williams of Marlborough, Parkman's brother-in-law. Hudson, *Marlborough*, p. 470.

[11] John Hicks of Sutton, Parkman's brother-in-law.

[12] Joshua Smith, the physician of Shrewsbury.

declar'd themselves unprepar'd yet to vote, the Church Meeting was again adjourn'd to Thursday next after Lecture. At Eve my Wife and I at Lieutenant Tainters at the Marriage of their Daughter Eliza to Mr. Stephen Sadler. N.B. Mr. Fish[13] (who preaches at Upton) and Captain Sadler there. Those last came home with us and lodg'd here.

20. Snowy morning but the Earth soon appear'd again. Captain Sadler and Mr. Fish to Upton. P.M. old Mr. Maynard here. Anna Bradish[14] with her Relation.

21. Ebenezer went to Bolton. Thomas a.m. carts wood; p.m. husks. William to Mr. Britons with a Piece of Cloth to be full'd for Riding Hoods. My wife visits Mrs. Ann Maynard. My Legg very full of Smart, especially after the dressing: and continues very painful till Night. Fear I have got Cold in it, or else it might be too plentifull use of the precipitate.

22. A Storm of Snow. Mr. Cushing came and preach'd my Lecture. I did not go out by reason of my Lameness which is very bad. Mr. Cushing[15] in my Name mention'd the deferring Anna Bradish's Admission into the Church till Lords Day notwithstanding the Vote at the Church Meeting—and the Adjournment of the Church Meeting till next Monday come Sennight. Ebenezer return'd home at late Evening.

23. Mr. Benjamin How and Ebenezer laying Floor in the Stable. Thomas sledded Wood part of the Day. William to Mr. William Goddards Mill. My Legg somewhat easier. Dr. Smith voluntarily called to see me at Eve. We had Some Discourse about his Affair which was laid before the Council at Shrewsbury last Year.

24. It grows very Cold. My sons variously employ'd—some bank the House.

25. My Leg is Still So Sore that I know not how to go out. But the Consideration of the State of the Congregation if I Should not, and especially of the Church if I Should not administer the Lords Supper on the Day appointed therefor pressing me I resolv'd to do what in me lies, and accordingly under took with dependence on the Goodness of God to carry me through. I omitted the public Reading to Day also, both a. and p.m. Preach'd on 1 Cor. 11, 20 latter part. N.B. Before the administration of the Sacred Supper was taken suddenly with Such a Laxness in my Body that I was oblig'd to go out of the Meeting House. When I return'd I proceeded to the administration without admitting Anna Bradish, but my wife came near and whisper'd it to me—upon which I stopp'd, and took her into the Church before I pray'd and then went on. My wife and I din'd at Captain Bakers. P.M. preach'd on Zech. 1, 4, delivering the Chief of the rest of the Discourse begun last Lords Day p.m. The Day was raw and uncomfortable, but guarded myself what I could against the Cold and hope I have receiv'd no Harm.

26. The Parish met on the Affair of Treasurer Ebenezer Maynards not paying Revd. Mr. Price[16] of Hopkinton Mr. James Maynards Rates. Mr. Job Cushing din'd here. Billy brought 46 pounds of Salt Fish from Mr. Jonah Warrins. Ebenezer work'd part of the Day for Mr. Benjamin How.

27. Storm of Rain. At Eve came Mr. Haven. Patty Pannels father also and lodg'd.

28. Storm of Snow. Mr. Pannell return'd—but Mr. Haven with us. To Day My Neighbour Ebenezer Maynard Treasurer for this Parish, was Sued by Revd. Roger Price of Hopkinton for the Rates of Mr. James Maynard, before Colonel Chandler at Worcester.

29. Mr. Haven, after dinner, went to Framingham. My son Thomas much taken off from Business by Ague in his Face and Teeth, both yesterday and to Day.

30. Billy as he was cutting Wood at the Door, cut his ankle. The wound was Somewhat Cross-wise, and bled very much. It was in the Forenoon and when his Brothers who were able to do any Thing were gone from home, Ebenezer to work for Mr. Rogers, and Thomas to Mr. Goddards Mill. We try'd Puff Ball to Stopp the Bleeding, but to no purpose. After some Time, the Blood running fresh Still, we took off the Bindings, and fill'd the Sore with Sugar—but neither did this Succeed. We Sent about Noon for Mrs. Hephzibah Maynard. Both the Captain and his Wife came. It Seem'd to be Stanched for a while, but flow'd again. He had now bled So much that we were much Concern'd at the Event. Thomas was groaning with the Tooth Ach and wanted to go to Dr. Smith to get his Tooth drawn out. I therefor hasten'd him, tho it was past Evening, to bring the Doctor to Billy. We having also try'd scrapings of Tann'd Leather and Scorch'd Cotton, and still fresh Puddles appear'd. N.B. Several Times when it was open'd, the Blood Spurted out as in Phlebotomy. While Thomas was gone and tarried long, our Fears arose higher, for Billy had lost so great a Quantity of Blood that he began to turn pale and we did not know but that it was still running. I ardently committed him and his Case to God who is a present Help in Time of Trouble. After a while the Blood ceas'd, as we conceiv'd, nor did any more appear throughout the Night. Blessed be God for his Sparing Mercy! Thomas did not come till past Nine o'Clock, and no Doctor with him; but got his own Tooth out, or rather part of it, for it broke in the Jaw. Molly is also in great Anguish with Tooch ach So that with my own Lameness, we have no Small Trouble in the House. But would humbly wait on God. My wife watch'd with Billy.

DECEMBER [1750]

1. Billy Somewhat chearful tho we dare not let him Stir for fear of his Bleeding again. We let him lie in the Blood, which we now hope is Stopp'd. Lieutenant Bruce here, and upon his asking a Note to the Collector I read him what I wrote of our Agreement last April 11, respecting the Cook Island; and he consenting to it, I gave him a Note for Twenty Seven Pounds and Ten Shillings old Tenor. P.M. Ebenezer rode to Dr. Gotts[1] on Billy's Case.

2. Dr. Gott being ill, his son Benjamin came and dress'd Billy's Leg, which (thro Gods Mercy) was effected without any more bleeding. In the Public Service (to which I went somewhat late, 7 minutes after Eleven when I got here) read Lev. 8th. Preach'd on Ps. 23, 4, a. and p.m. Din'd at Esq. Bakers. N.B. Walk'd up, rode back. N.B. Astonishing Accounts of Mr. Benjamin Lawrence's[2] cruelty to his Boy Seem confirm'd. P.M. read John 20. Of both the Chapters which we read, I gave some brief Exposition.

3. A pleasant Day—The little Snow which has lain a while on the Earth wastes away, and the Roads dirty and hollow. Billy bears the Dressing his Leg very well, is Sensible of but very little Pain. Ebenezer and Thomas husking P.M. Church Meeting. About 23 or 24 present. Robert Cook was not there; nor his Father etc. The whole Church seem ready to Vote. The Vote was written and read over and over. Whether Robert Cook and his Wife Should enjoy Special Privileges of the Gospel in this Church without an acknowledgement. No Hand was lifted up for it. I said upon it, that they all seem'd to be of one mind—viz. on the Negative. Had any one any Thing to offer? There was a profound Silence. The Meeting clos'd with Prayer and Blessing, Was after Meeting, at Deacon Newtons, Mr. Ebenezer Rice's. Mr. Pratts and old Mr. Maynard's.

4. My Wife and I rode p.m. to Mr. Martyn's. Mr. Martyn was gone to the Funeral of a Child of John Oakes, and return'd not till Eve: but we found there Revd. Mr. Trowbridge[3] of Groton, Revd. Mr. Goss and his wife, Mr. Caleb Richardson[4] and Mr. Marritt[5] of Cambridge. We tarried till the moon was up and Supp'd there. N.B. the Story of Mr. Benjamin Lawrence was

[13] Elisha Fish (Harvard 1750) was the second minister of the First Congregational Church of Upton, 1750–1795. Sibley, XII, 550–556.

[14] Daughter of James Bradish.

[15] The Reverend Job Cushing of Shrewsbury.

[16] Commissary Roger Price.

[1] Benjamin Gott.

[2] Of Bolton.

[3] The Reverend Caleb Trowbridge.

[4] The son of Joseph Richardson, Jr., of West Newbury.

[5] Amos Marrett was a man of considerable wealth. Paige, Cambridge, p. 604.

true but in part. This Eve the select men of this Town meet in order to Relieve the Boy, as they were the Guardians of the Child and had bound him out to Mr. Lawrence.

5. Benjamin Gott here and dresses Billy's Legg. P.M. I rode to Mr. Amsdens[6] to make him a Visit since the Death of his two Brethren, Beemans, and to see his son Abijah Gale who has been Sick. I was also at Mr. Adams's because of the late Sickness of their Children, and call'd at Mr. Twitchells in my returning. At home was Mr. Daniel Forbush by appointment to reckon. I am to pay him for 23 Days work at 18 shillings but he found himself his Dinners.

6. Somewhat Rainy and misty—but I rode over to the private Meeting at Deacon Forbush's and preach'd there; the rather because Mrs. Mary Steward is confin'd by Illness there. Text John 12, 26. May we all enjoy that Blessedness to enjoy the presence and Gracious Rewards of Christ!

7. Mr. Maccarty[7] and Mr. Wellman,[8] came from Mr. Beans[9] Ordination at Wrentham, were here and din'd—Sent home to Mr. Cushings Father Calmets Dictionary[10] Volume 3. My Sons finish'd husking.

8. Mr. Cushing came so near night that I could not Sett out till near sunsetting—passing by Mr. Daniel Warrins after sundown, and they Still at work in shingling the House, I besought 'em to break off, expressing my Regret for my own riding so late. They answer'd that they would soon break off. N.B. Mr. Cushing had stopp'd to visit Mr. Daniel Hemingway who was Sick at Doctor Smiths. I call'd there also at Mr. Cushings Desire—lodg'd at Mr. Cushing.

9. Rainy Day. Preach'd at Shrewsbury a.m. on Rom. 8, 7 from page 19 to the End, and p.m. on Ps. 110, 3. After the Eve came on and family Exercises over, Mrs. Cushing walk'd with me to Mr. Artemas Wards[11] who had invited me after meeting to come to see him. N.B. Dark and rainy.

10. At Dr. Smiths—Mr. Heminway better. I return'd home. My wife informs me that Mr. Cushing rode away from the Meeting House Yesterday in order to go to Marlborough, to her great Surprize, at the Funeral of a base-born Child, at Mr. Francis Whipples. The Mother is from Boston: I ask'd her what her name was, but she desir'd to conceal it. At Eve Lieutenant Tainter here.

11. A number of Young Men, chiefly the religious Society, came and chopp'd Wood. They were Daniel How, Merodach Smith, Phinehas Maynard, Moses Warrin, Joseph Grout junior—and Mr. Cornelius Biglo and his Son, very kindly came with them. My son Ebenezer Chopp'd with them and Thomas carted part of the Day. Sent a Letter to Mrs. Stoddard at Boston with 14£ of money by Mrs. Mary Maynard (James's Wife) to buy my Daughter Lucy a Riding Hood.

12. Ebenezer a.m. fits up an House for the Doves, which were lately presented me, and p.m. Swingled Flax. Thomas to mill a.m. Cut Wood at the Door p.m. Billys Sore begins to digest a little. P.M. I went to Mr. Hezekiah How's and got him to go with me to view my North East Bounds, which border on him and on the Ministerial Lot and on Mr. Richard Barns. N.B. To Day Mr. Solomon Wood was here and settled our Accounts. I ow'd him 12£ 13 Shillings Old Tenor and gave him a Note to Lieutenant Tainter. Mr. Wood informs me likewise of the Death of the Widow Thurstons[12] Daughter Experience.

13. Ebenezer and Thomas at the New House, clearing Ground. P.M. Molly rode with me to the Funeral of Experience Thurston. N.B. She was almost 19 years of age, and after a few Days illness fell into Fitts and dyed Suddenly.

14. A Storm of Rain which rais'd the Floods.

15. Ebenezer and Thomas variously employ'd about the Cattle, Firing etc. Mrs. Mary Maynard brought up a Camblet Riding Hood from Mrs. Stoddard at Boston. Wrote on Exod. 20, 12 chiefly this Evening and Night till 12 o'Clock.

16. Read Levit. 11 with Some Expository remarks. Preach'd on Ps. 23, 4. Din'd at Esquire Bakers. My wife at Mr. Williams. P.M. read Acts 1. Preach'd on Exod. 20, 12.

17. Rose a little after 4 o'Clock. Ebenezer and Thomas went over to clearing at the New Place. Mr. Ebenezer Rice cutting Ship Timber at Mr. How's—and desires to cutt in my Lot also.

18. Ebenezer and Thomas Clearing at the New Place.

19. Ebenezer assisted by Neighbour Ebenezer Maynard kill'd a Sow for me which had never had any Piggs and which weigh'd 224. Clearing P.M.

20. Mr. Martyn and his wife din'd with us—and p.m. he preach'd the Lecture to my Young People from Ps. 100, 3. My Wife made a Discovery to me this Evening which gave me some surprize.

21. Cold uncomfortable weather.

22. Very raw.

23. A cold raw Storm. I doubted much in the Morning whether it was my Duty to go to Meeting. I concluded to try; and found that tho it was tedious and difficult, yet I could undergo it. There was a considerable assembly, which gave me fresh Encouragement. Of Levit. 12 I read only the first 10 and proceeded to Some Remarks. Preach'd on Exod. 20, 12. My wife din'd with me at the Squire's and Martha Pannell at Deacon Newton's. P.M. I read Acts 2 and preach'd on Exod. 20, 12. But this Exercise was little other than a Recapitulation of what I had deliver'd and repeated Some Time ago, of the Dutys of Children and Parents, from Eph. 6, 1, 2, 3, 4. But I made many alterations, transpositions and necessary Corrections etc.

24. My Wife rode with me to visit the Two Widows Tomlin: and thence we went to Ensign Rice's. N.B. The little Boy was there which Mr. Lawrence of Bolton had So Severely whipp'd. His Back was Stripp'd for me to See it. There were bad Signs all over it and Two or Three large and plain Scarrs. We went to Mr. Martyn's, and tarry'd to Supper with them there being a pleasant Moon to come home by.

25. I hear that Several of my Neighbours, particularly Eliezer Rice and his Wife are trapesing over to Hopkinton to keep Christmas there.[13] Were any of them rationally and Sincerely Enquiring and Examining into the Grounds of the Controversie between the prelatists and the Dissenters it were a far different Case; but they manifest only a Spirit of unsteddiness. May God grant 'em a Sight and Sense of their Folly and Childishness! P.M. Mr. Martyn and Mr. Smith of Marlborough made us a Visit and tarried till Evening. My Son Thomas is gradually providing him Tools etc. for setting up his Trade. His prospering herein is a Matter that lyes much upon my Mind from Day to Day. May God afford us the wisdom which may be profitable to direct!

26. Storm of Rain. Forbush[14] begins to keep School at Captain Maynards and lodges there.

27. Molly and Lucy undertook to walk over to Mr. Martyn's. Mr. Joseph Haven (accompany'd by Deacon Burnap of Hopkinton) made us a Visit. Paid me 15£ and 2 shillings old Tenor on account of his Sons lodging here. He acquainted me with Some of his Difficultys with Mr. Reed, which rather increase and advance. Tarried to supper but return'd to his Brother Burnaps.

28. Ebenezer got out Flax. Mr. Frost broke it, and he Swingl'd. At Eve Ebenezer and Thomas rode over to Mr. Martyns to bring him their Sisters, which they did tho it was very Cold.

29. They Clear'd at the New Place. Brother Samuel Breck[15] here and din'd with us. He keeps School and practices at Sheffield.

---

[6] Jacob Amsden of Westborough.

[7] The Reverend Thaddeus Maccarty of Worcester.

[8] The Reverend James Wellman of Millbury.

[9] Joseph Bean (Harvard 1748), the minister of the First Congregational Church in Wrentham, 1750–1784. Sibley, XII, 240–242.

[10] Augustin Calmet, An Historical, Critical, Geographical, Chronological, and Etymological Dictionary of the Holy Bible, 3 vols. (London, 1732).

[11] The future Major General and first commander-in-chief of the Continental Army.

[12] The widow of Joseph Thurston.

[13] The celebration of Christmas by the Anglicans led by Commissary Roger Price was deplored by the Puritans.

[14] Eli Forbes (Harvard 1751), the son of Deacon Jonathan Forbush of Westborough.

[15] Parkman's brother-in-law, who had practiced medicine in Worcester, was now living in the north parish of Sheffield, which was set off as the town of Great Barrington in 1761.

30. Very Cold. Read a few verses in the Beginning of Lev. 13, and a few Remarks thereon: preach'd on Prov. 29, 15, repeating Sermon on Eph. 6, 4 from page 21 to page 27. My wife and I din'd at Esq. Bakers. P.M. Read Acts 3. Preach'd on Gen. 17, 18 and repeated Sermon on Eph. 6, 4, from page 27 to the End. N.B. I had formerly repeated the other parts of these Discourses on the Dutys of Children and of Parents, but had not these Sermons but now Mention'd, and therefore I chose to finish the Repitition of these rather than omit them altho I had prepar'd on the Duty of Magistrates for one part of the Day, and in other parts of my Time I gave myself as much as I could to Reading, viz. Mr. Reyners Rules of the New Creature,[16] Travels of Cyrus by Ramsay,[17] Popes Essay on Man[18] etc.

31. My Sons are clearing at the New Place. I rode over to them to Lieutenant Tainters—visited at Mr. Nurse's,[19] he having been several Times absent from Meeting. At Eve Mr. Williams and Mr. Whipple here. I perceive there is much Strife among the People on the Affair of the Law-Suit depending between Revd. Mr. Price and this Precincts Treasurer for Mr. James Maynards Rates—21 Persons having Sign'd against the Proceedings of the Precinct at their last Meeting, at which they voted that their Treasurer Should Stand Mr. Price. I am very much griev'd for this Contention, as it very much frustrates the End of the ministry among a people. O that the God of infinite Mercy would grant us wisdom, grace and Peace! We finish this Year with these Sorrowful Reflections and with many Fears of what we are about to meet with unless God Himself be pleas'd to interpose and prevent.

### JANUARY, 1751

Every Year brings fresh occasion of Praise to the great, unchangeable, and incomprehensible Being who upholds the Universe! Let me especially praise and adore Him who preserves my Soul and Sustains my Body; who confers richest Favours on the vilest Ingrate!

To Thee Supreme, Omnipotent!
May universal Nature rise!
"Homage To thee, with one Consent,
From whom we all have all Supplys!"
But thou, My Soul, as thou'rt most bound,
Thy Breath and Being chearfull Spend.
The Great Jehovah's Praise resound
To Ages that shall never End!

At Eve my wife and I rode over to Mr. Francis Whipples and assisted at the Solemnizing the Marriage of his Daughter Lucy to Nathan Maynard.[1] N.B. She was born this Day 22 Years Since. An handsome supper, and though a Cold Night, yet it was (thro the Smile of Providence) a pleasant, joyfull Time. As I would bemoan my Ingratitude, Barrenness, Senselessness, So I would beg of God to quicken, pardon and help me! To God I would committ all the Events of this Year! But! I know not what a Day may bring forth!

2. Cold, raw Day. The Earth open still and good Clearing. Ebenezer and Thomas improve it. I was much employ'd with Ramsays Cyrus and (except yesterday) for Several Days. It shews a Strong, bright Genius, and is writ with much Elegance. Old Mr. Maynard came to invite me, and my wife also to his House at Even, his Son Nathan having brought home his Bride. We went and Supp'd with them.

3. Ebenezer Thrashing Wheat—which has Suffer'd by the Rotts of the Barn. Thomas a.m. to Mr. Wymans for Several Sadlers-Tools which he has made for him. P.M. he thrash'd with his Brother. A Cold Season.

4. Bright and pleasant—and not altogether so Cold as the Days past. My sons thrashing Still. Lucy to Mrs. Mehitable Brighams[2] to obtain her to help in making her new Riding hood—and stays all Night.

5. Read a Letter from Mr. Elijah Collins concerning my Watch, and from my Brother Parkman[3] concerning his Marriage last July 19 to Captain Harris's Widow, his near Neighbour, and took her to his House the 31. That her Son, William Harris's Brigantine was lately ashore on Plumb-Island, where his Father was cast away, and lost a Brigantine which my Brother was part owner of.[4]

6. I rode over to Mr. Martyns and he came hither. He read not publicly either a. or p.m. His Texts Dan. 2, 21, and Mat. 6, 33. He return'd home at Eve. I at his meeting read a.m. Lev. 25, and preach'd on Jer. 6, 8. P.M. read Acts 2 and preach'd on Numb. 23, 10. At Eve I was very much tir'd, and it being very dark when I had refresh'd my Self at Supper with Mr. Martyn, I tarried and lodg'd there. I had design'd also to go to Bolton next Morning.

7. It prov'd a very Stormy Morning—it blew and Snow'd and became very tempestuous. I yielded to their Importunity to Stay till noon. After Dinner I ventur'd out, and got home safely—my Family also in Comfort. But Captain Maynard came towards Eve, and had a fresh Debate about the precincts pulling down the old Meeting House.

8. The Storm goes over—but very cold and snow blow'd about.

9. Mr. Whitney here—reckon'd with him for his work, about my New House—gave him a Note to Lieutenant Tainter for 5 Days—2 at framing and 3 at digging Stones—15/ per Day—in all £3.15.0 old Tenor. Thomas making another New Pillion. Ebenezer sledded Wood. I kept to my Preparations with some Diligence.

10. My Wife and I design'd to have rid to Marlborough, but a young Dog antickly Seiz'd upon the Lining of the Chair (which was to be set upon Runners) and tore it wholly out of the Back: which exceedingly defac'd it. However we rode over to the widow Newtons[5] and din'd there. Captain Eager[6] there also. At Eve my son Thomas rode over to Robert Cooks—I thought upon Business, but (as I came to understand afterwards) to an House-warming.

11. Ebenezer Sledded Ship-Timber for Mr. Ebenezer Rice. Thomas thrashing.

12. Rain. Ebenezer with Neighbour Benjamin How and his Brother Noah, go to the Meeting House to put up Some Sort of Steps or stairs into the Gallery. Thomas went to Lieutenant Tainter who promis'd to Send £7.3.10 old Tenor to Esquire Hazzletine of Upton.

13. Very Rainy. The Rain with the Snow upon the Earth make it very difficult going to Meeting. A few of us arrive there. A.M. read several parts of Lev. 13. Scil. the heads of the paragraphs and gave Some Expository Observations. Preach'd a. and p.m. on 2 Sam. 33, 3. So very rainy at Noon that I acquainted the Congregation that I Should not go out of the Meeting House, and desir'd them that went out to come in again, in ¼ of an Hour. I eat a bit of Bread and Cheese which my Maid handed to me in the Pulpit, and I was much refresh'd. P.M. according to my proposal to the Congregation I went not out of the House, but began the Second Service as soon as the people gather'd in. Read Acts 4, and gave Some glances upon it. Preach'd as aforesaid. Got home safely tho it was very tedious to me. However I bless God for my many Comforts which I am favour'd with! After Supper and the Evening Exercise in my Family I read to them Mr. Baxters Preface to his Call. May God grant His Awakening Spirit to accompany it and render it profitable!

14. Cloudy, Misty—exceeding bad Stirring. My Mare troubl'd with a large Swelling which is become an hard Bunch, upon her Breast.

[16] Edward Reyner (1600–1668), an English minister, published *Precepts for Christian Practice* (London, 1645). This was designated as the second edition, but is the earliest edition this editor has found. The eighth edition bore the title *Precepts for Christian Practice; or the Rule of the New Creature new Model'd* (London, 1655). There were at least eleven English editions of this work.

[17] Andrew Ramsay (1686–1743), a French author, wrote *Les Voyages de Cyrus, avec un Discours sur la Mythologie des Payens* (Paris, 1727). English translations were published in London in 1730 and 1733.

[18] Alexander Pope's famous work appeared first in London in 1734 and several other English editions were soon printed. By 1751 there had also been published Philadelphia editions in 1747 and 1748.

[19] William Nurse.

[1] The son of David Maynard.

[2] Mrs. Moses Brigham.

[3] William or "Elder" Parkman of Boston married Hannah Harris.

[4] *The Boston Gazette, or Weekly Journal*, Dec. 4, 1750, reported "One Day last Week, a Brigantine deep laden from the West Indies, in bad Weather, ran ashore on Plumb-Island, and tis feared will suffer much Damage."

[5] The widow of Ensign Thomas Newton.

[6] James Eager of the north precinct.

15. The Storm continues (ever since last Saturday) and rains all Day. My 2 Sons can employ themselves to but small purpose. I was both yesterday and this Day engag'd on my preparations. William gets to School through the Wet and Dirt. Master Forbush here at Eve and lodg'd here.

16. Mr. Stephen Fay here—din'd with us and tarried till almost Night. The Storm not over, but rains Still. A very unusual Time. The Earth Extremely hollow, and fill'd with Water.

17. According to appointment I met Mr. Stephen Fay at Justice Bakers Tho it was rainy Weather and bad Stirring abroad. I din'd at Deacon Newtons. I went down with Justice Baker and Mr. Stephen Fay to look of the Land within my Plot of 4 acres and 57 Rods. Mr. Fay and I agreed to go on and give each other a Deed; I him of 3 Acres and 37 Rods of this Land, and he me of Three Acres Right of the sixth Division, to take up Common Land other where. We finish'd the Affair at Mr. Ebenezer Rice's. N.B. Mr. Rice's Young Man (Dudley) and his wife's brethren, had been at the Great Pond, though foul Weather: and caught a great Number of fine Fish—the Pickerell, Some of them very large. They made me an handsome Present of 3 large ones. At Deacon Newtons as I return'd home, but tarried not long. N.B. Ebenezer at Mr. Cornelius Cooks[7] assisting him in making a stubb scythe, a Whipple-Tree Chain and several other Things.

18. The first fair Day ever Since this Day Sennight. This Day, Ebenezer and his Brother Thomas go a Fishing at the Great Pond (mov'd by yesterdays News about Fishing). They return to Dinner. Ebenezer goes this afternoon to looking up Trees for Loggs to be carry'd to the saw-mill; his Brother goes (on Foot) to Mr. David Felton at Marlborough and bought an Horse side of Leather price 30/ old Tenor; and return'd home at Eve. Deacon Newton here. We reckon'd my Debts to him was 8£ 4s, 6d. He threw in 10/6 and I gave him a note to Mr. Samuel Williams for the rest. N.B. I press him to Peace in the Affair relating to Mr. James Maynard and Rev. Mr. Price. P.M. reckon'd with Aaron Warrin—his account £4.10 old Tenor. Gave him a Note to Mr. Williams.

19. Ebenezer and Thomas go into the Woods to Cutt Loggs.

20. A pleasant Day. I read Lev. 14 to number 32 with long Expositions. Preach'd on Tit. 3, 1. Din'd at Justice Bakers—my wife and several of the Family tarried at the Meeting House—Billy din'd at Mr. Ebenezer Rice's. P.M. read Acts 5, with some brief Exposition. Not having altogether finish'd my Preparations for the Afternoon Exercise, tho I began early in the Week and continu'd more than usual at the work, yet by Reading Dr. Hoadly[8] etc., and my meditations enlarging, yet being desirous it might not be more than Two Exercises; I wanted also some more moving Subject for the afternoon—I therefore repeated to page 8 of sermon on 1 John 2, 14, latter part.

21. Daniel How assisted Ebenezer and Thomas in Killing Two large Hoggs. Each 12 Score, 11¾. P.M. my sons thrash'd Wheat and Swingled some small matter of Flax. Mr. Phinehas Hardy, afterwards Mr. Samuel Hardy, Mr. Grow and Mr. Harrington, were here, reckon'd with them for work and Stuff about the New House and gave each of them a Note to Lieutenant Tainter. Captain Maynards Wife made us a Visit. At Eve I rode over to Mr. Williams and receiv'd £9.10 old Tenor of money from him. The forepart of this Day was exceeding pleasant.

22. The Early Morn began with Storm. As the Day got up it grew exceeding Tempestuous. The Wind at South, very Stiff, and sometimes like meer Hurricanes, raining very hard also. It beats extremely against, and into the House. The Lord hath his way in the Whirlwind and in the Storm, and the Clouds are the Dust of his Feet. Nah. 1, 3. Stormy Wind, fulfilling his Word. Ps. 148, 8. Storm prevails till The Middle of the Day: then the Clouds Scatter and the Sun appears; yet it continues very windy. In the Storm, Two Apple Trees (which were defective) were blown down; the Roof of the Bee House was blown off. The Well-Crotch, Sweep and Pole were laid flatt, one Leaf of the front Gate was forc'd from the Post and thrown down;

and it was wonderful that the Roof of the Barn was not carry'd off and destroy'd. The Rain beat through the Windows of the House so much that there were great Puddles in the Rooms and Chambers, but especially in the Great Entry; and had the Wind and Rain continued with Such Violence for a little while longer, it look'd as if the sashes of the Windows would have been forc'd down and the House laid open that we could have had little or no Comfort. But Blessed be God who in the middst of Wrath remember'd Mercy! He that raised the Stormy Wind, made it obey and fulfill his Word. We have reason to fear there is much Dammage done by this terrible Storm. I hear already of the Desolation of Mr. Daniel Forbush's Barn which was blown down to Day when the Cattle were in it, and he himself gone to Boston.

23. A.M. Ebenezer and Thomas got Wood. P.M. they went into the Woods to prepare Loggs for the Saw-Mill. Mr. Charles Rice with me and reckon'd. N.B. a Letter from Mr. Henry Goold[9] of Concord for Money. At Eve Mr. Stephen Sadler[10] and his wife and they lodg'd here; as did Master Forbush also; there being an Entertainment or Frolick, of some young people at his Lodgings (Captain Maynards) to Night.

24. Moses Warrin[11] was married to Persis Rice, Daughter of Mr. Seth Rice. Some of the Company (without any Knowledge) took in the Key which offended a Number of persons who came to see 'em married, and particularly Jonathan Smith was so much displeas'd that he got an Horn, and when the Bridegroom with his Bride and attendants were returning home, he began to blow, even before they had got all of them away from the Road before my Gate. I therefore went out and Smartly reprov'd him for his Impudence and Folly. P.M. my wife and I, tho it was very cold, took a Ride to See old Mr. Fay in his illness and confinement. We also went to Benjamin Fay, and examin'd into their suffering Young people to have a Frolick a little while ago at their house. At Eve we were at Mr. Nathaniel Whitneys and we made a Visit also to Mr. Daniel Forbush, where I saw Some of the Sorrowful Effects of the late storm, which blew over his Barn.

25. 26. Sharp Weather.

27. Read Lev. 14 from number 33 with Remarks. Preach'd on Nahum 1; 3. Din'd at Justice Bakers. P.M. read Acts 6, and repeated the Rest of Sermon to young men on 1 John 2, 14, latter part.

28. Martha Pannell went from us to live at Mr. Benjamin Hows.

29. Was at Mr. Bathericks and Sent by Mr. Bezaleel Smith 20£ old Tenor to Mr. Henry Goold. Visited Mr. Bradish.

30. My wife and I rode to Marlboro—as we went we call'd at Deacon Rice's[12] and din'd there. Renew'd my Desire to Jeduthan Baldwin to work for me in finishing my New House. We visited Dr. Gott who is in a waste and much confin'd. We went also to See Cousen Sally Brigham at Justice Brighams.[13] I was likewise at Mr. Smiths[14] and Supp'd there with one Mr. Osgood of Andover. N.B. Judge Dudley[15] lies dead. Captain Boardman bury'd this Day. We lodg'd at Dr. Gotts.

31. A very Snowy forenoon. I went to Mr. Benjamin Woods[16] but returned and din'd at the Doctors. I wish I could deal more plainly with the Doctor about his intemperate use of Spirituous Liquors—yet had it over and over with him and gave him what Charge I could that he should abstain—but I fear it is all in Vain. Mrs. Rachel Bowker there. Everyones Heart bleeds—but we must leave it to God! P.M. we visited at Mr. Smiths (Mr. Osgood not gone) and went in to See Mrs. Williams to mourn with her under the loss of her Father. At home in the Evening.

[7] Westborough's blacksmith.
[8] Bishop Benjamin Hoadly (1676–1761) was a controversial figure who published numerous works.
[9] Parkman's son had been apprenticed to Gould.
[10] Of Upton.
[11] The son of Daniel Warrin of Westborough.
[12] Caleb Rice of Marlborough.
[13] Charles Brigham, a justice of the peace.
[14] The Reverend Aaron Smith of Marlborough.
[15] Justice Paul Dudley of the Superior Court of Judicature died Jan. 21, 1751.
[16] A leading citizen of Marlborough.

## FEBRUARY, 1751

1. [No entry.]

2. At Eve in much Trouble. A Cow ready to Calve missing: and my young Horse lam'd himself in the Stable. He was hung by one of his fore feet in the floor of the Manger, and after much Striving fell down on the outside of the Manger, in great pain—but was heard and Seasonably reliev'd—but the Cow (which I bought of Mr. James Ball) missing all night tho we search'd up and down the woods till about midnight, and considerable Snow upon the Ground.

3. The little black Cow, missing last night, found this morning with a Calf, in the woods—was late at meeting by Reason of trapsing (in the Snow) so late last night. Read but the Two first Verses of Lev. 15, and gave some Observations upon it. Preach'd on Tit. 3, 1, a. and p.m. Din'd at Esquire Bakers and p.m. read part of Acts 7.

4. This Day concludes the School kept by Forbush at Captain Maynards. Ebenezer with Neighbour John Rogers's Help and his Oxen join'd to my Team carry Large Loggs to Mill.

5. Worcester Court at which we expect the Case of our Treasurer Mr. Ebenezer Maynard by Appeal against the Reverend Roger Price, for Mr. James Maynards Rates, is expected to come on. Mr. Haven came to see us at Evening. N.B. Ebenezer and Thomas, Mary and Lucy gone to dine at Lieutenant Tainters and wait upon his Daughter Sadler[1] in her going home to Upton.

6. Mr. Haven and I rode over to see Mr. Martyn. Mr. Cushing came there also. Call'd at Captain Eagers about Clabboards for my New House. Ebenezer and his Brother and Sister return'd from Upton.

7. Mr. Haven bought of me Dr. Atterburys Two Volumes of Sermons.[2] He leaves us to go to Brookfield, North part of it, to preach on probation there. Mr. David Baldwin of Leicester sold me 1000 of White Pine Boards for £15.10/Old Tenor for which I paid him 10£ old Tenor. As I Sat at Captain Maynards came in the Reverend Mr. Price from Court—tells me they gave him the Case yesterday, as he was sure all men of any Reason and Justice would. Captain Maynard urg'd me much to dine there but I return'd home. P.M. nigh Evening I visited Mrs. Pratt. When I came home had Mr. Jonathan Bond with me. N.B. Ebenezer and Thomas carried Loggs to the Saw Mill, and Boards to the New House.

8. Ebenezer in the Woods about Loggs. Thomas to Marlborough and bought an Horse Hide of Mr. Felton—cost 58/. He paid Lieutenant Nathan Brigham 21£ old Tenor in full for the Land I bought of him by the Meeting House. Thomas brings word that Cousen Sally Brigham was brought to Bed this Morning and bore a Son, being (I think) thirty Weeks Since her Marriage.

9. Ebenezer works for Neighbour Rogers, with the Oxen. At Night I was with Joseph Grout junior who is Sick of a Fever, till nigh 12 o'clock.

10. Many of Hopkinton People at Meeting with us Mr. Barrett[3] being Sick. A.M. read Levit. 16. Preach'd on Rom. 12, 18. Din'd at Justice Bakers. Deacon Kimbal[4] and others of Hopkinton din'd there also. P.M. read Acts 7 from number 26, gave short Exposition each part of the Day. Preach'd on Rom. 3, 24—freely by his Grace—(and by Reason of my Interruption last Eve did not finish the Subject which I was then engaged upon) I us'd from page 16 to 24 of sermon on Eph. 2, 8. My Wife this Day 34 Years old. May God grant her the Grace so to number her Days as to apply her Heart to Wisdom.

11. Rainy. Ebenezer a.m. goes a Fishing at the Great Pond. At Eve the Storm increases the Wind Southerly and to the East of South, very Strong for several Hours.

12. Am running over Some of Esquire Wests Observations on the History and Evidences of the Resurrection of Jesus Christ.[5]

13. I rode to Hopkinton to See Mr. Barret in his Sickness—find he is much better. I din'd there. The Desolations in Hopkinton by the great Storm much greater than among us. Mr. Barretts, Mr. Price's, and 10 or 11 Barns more in that Town blown down. Mr. Barretts Cattle, and his Negro Man also in the Barn at that Instant. I was at Lieutenant Woods where lay ill Phebe Chamberlin and at their Request I pray'd with her. At Aaron Warrins Shop for a large Cargo of mended Shooes. Call'd at Mr. Hezekiah Pratts, whose wife wastes very much. My Son Ebenezer breaks Flax. Thomas at his Trade.

14. A fine Day after a Sharp Night, but the prospect of my Debts, Building and Family Expences very gloomy and distressing. P.M. rode out—designing to visit Lieutenant Tainter; and yet what can he be able to do for me in these uncommon Times of Difficulty and Straitness in the Province! and especially in Times of Such Trouble and Division in the Parish! As I pass'd by Mr. Nurse's Lieutenant passed along in the Common Road and went to my House—but carry'd no money for my Relief. As Soon as I was inform'd that Lieutenant had passed along the Road I turn'd my Course (from going to his House) and it being probable that the Lieutenant Saw, and was inform'd that it was I, that was at Mr. Nurse's, yet that he had no Special Business with me, I went to Mr. Ebenezer Rice's and reckon'd with him. I Should have proceeded up the Road to visit Joseph Grout, but heard he was better—had no fit Since Lords Day Evening. Lieutenant Tainter here while I was abroad.

15. Snow. Old Mr. Maynard and old Mr. Whipple here. By Mr. Whipples Discourse I perceive there are new Disgusts with Lieutenant Tainter—that he doth not take Steps towards Mr. James Maynards Rates being Sunk by the Precinct: there being a Warrant up for a Meeting and nothing of Mr. Maynards Affair in it; nor to Consult the Precinct about it.

16. Exceeding high westerly Winds—Sometimes Rain, Sometimes white flying Clouds.

17. I read (and gave Some Expository Hints on) Levit. 17. Preach'd on Rom. 12, 18. Din'd at Justice Bakers. My wife has for a long Time refus'd to dine with me there fearing to be burdensome, tho the Justice has repeatedly manifested his uneasiness at her not coming, and Said that she gave him more trouble as she did not dine there. P.M. read Acts 8, and tho I had provided sufficient for another Exercise on the same subject which I preach'd on in the forenoon, yet being unwilling to harp too much on that string at this Time, I conceiv'd it best to wave what remain'd for the present, and chose to finish the Subject I was upon last Lords Day a.m. and therefore deliver'd the Rest of that Discourse (without the Reconcilement of St. James and Saint Paul) on Eph. 2, 8 from page 24 to page 36, from Rom. 3, 24. Which may God be pleas'd to add his Blessing to! N.B. I publicly notified a meeting at Mr. Hezekiah Pratts next Wednesday.

18. Was in a great deal of Anxiety on Account of my Family Circumstances, being in divers Straits and Difficultys—much in Debt already (by means of my New Building chiefly) and unwilling to keep my Creditors out of their dues, yet oblig'd to keep plunging much deeper if I would go on with my New House and place—and no reason to say any word to the Parish, they being so involv'd, and in Such Contention. But I took a Walk to Mr. Whipples, Mr. Williams's (to each of their Houses) to Deacon Newtons, Widow Newtons etc. In the middst of my disconsolateness on outward Accounts, desire I may not leave trusting and reposing myself in a Mercifull and faithful God: who I pray may be my Supporter under all!

19. Wrote to my Kinsman Davis[6] and to Captain Charles Morris at Halifax. P.M. I rode to Mr. Grouts to See his son Joseph who is still sick, and pray'd with him. In every Conversation yesterday and to Day, with the Parishioners, endeavour to my utmost to promote peace and agreement, and to engage others to do what in them lies with those immediately concern'd, that the Contention may go no further. Was at Esquire Bakers at Eve. He is going into Connecticut with Mr. Shattuck Flaxtrader—who is there, to sett out in the morning—wrote to Mr.

---

[1] Elizabeth Tainter married Stephen Sadler of Upton.

[2] Francis Atterbury, *Sermons and Discourses on Several Subjects and Occasions*, 2 vols. (London, 1730).

[3] The Reverend Samuel Barrett.

[4] Ebenezer Kemble.

[5] Gilbert West, *A Defence of the Christian Revelation . . . as Contained in . . . Observations on the History and Evidences of the Resurrection of Jesus Christ* (Boston, 1749). This work first appeared in a Dublin edition of 1747.

[6] Parkman's niece, Lydia Tyley of Boston, married Robert Davis, June 9, 1748.

Pierpoint.[7] Solomon Baker[8] designing to go to Boston in the morning, Sent my Watch by him to Mr. Moses Peck by him to have a Glass fitted to it. N.B. My son William this Day ten years old—he goes over to Mr. Benjamin Hows, and at Eve Ebenezer and Thomas go over there, and to my Grief tarry (all of them) too late. P.M. Ebenezer thrashes Barley.

20. Manifested to my sons Somewhat of my affectionate Concern for them. Ebenezer acknowledges. Thomas more insensible. P.M. at Mr. Pratt and his Wife's Desire, and agreeable to public Notice, given last Lords Day, preached to a Considerable Assembly at Mr. Pratts, his wife lying in a languishing Condition, and long confin'd from public Worship. I us'd Luke 12, 40 for the Text. Pick'd the Exercise out of Sermon on Mat. 24, 44, and added Two Extracts from Mr. Flavels Touch-stone.[9] Viz. Mr. Sedgwick's and Mr. Sydenham's Marks in brief. N.B. old Mr. Whipple and Lieutenant Tainter tarried at Mr. Pratts after the Exercise, and I endeavour'd to have some misunderstandings removed and peace promoted. I advis'd Lieutenant to make Mr. James Maynard a Visit. O that the God of peace would give peace! At Eve Mr. Jedediah Hows of Brookfield here, and Neighbour Stephen Maynard.

21. After several Days of Springlike weather, we have now gentle warmish Rain.

22. Neighbour Batherick here and with Ebenezer hewing Timber for a Privy. Mrs. Warrin of Upton and her child here.

23. [No entry.].

24. Read Levit. 18. Preach'd all Day on Rom. 12, 16. Din'd at the usual place, tho the Justice was gone a Journey to Connecticut. N.B. Deacon Newton invited me to dine at their House, but I conceiv'd it not so well to leave Mrs. Baker now when she needed me most. P.M. read Acts 9.

25. Mr. Batherick and Ebenezer frame a Privy. At Captain Maynards about some Affairs of Plotts of Land, it being Proprietors Meeting at Marlborough to Day. Visited the widow Sibyl Childs. Din'd at Lieutenant Tainters. Settled with Joseph Bruce and paid all.

26. Rode to Mr. Fosgitts[10] and picked out 325 more Brick, and paid him £8.12 old Tenor, being in full. Paid Mr. Goddard 20/ old Tenor for Carting the former parcell of Bricks. N.B. both din'd and supp'd at Mr. Martyns.

27. Ebenezer went with Neighbour Benjamin How to clear a new Road for foot people to Meeting. Lieutenant Tainter carry'd to Boston a Calf for me, which he came and kill'd last Night.

28. Mr. Fish[11] of Upton preach'd my Lecture on Ps. 107, 9. My wife not well at meeting.

### MARCH, 1751

Cold Day. Mr. Fish left us to go to Upton. Samuel Bumpso came hither in order to his and Ebenezer's going to Sam's Swamp to get a Stick of White Pine to make Two Troughs for my new House. They both went but did not Succeed in Sam's Swamp; but obtain'd Two in Mr. Bradish's,[1] which they cutt down and partly hew'd one of them. [Two words crossed out] by the help of Mr. Daniel Warrin to hew for them. At Eve Lieutenant Bruce came here and I gave him a note to Lieutenant Tainter for 72£ 10/ old Tenor, which with 27£10/ of the like Tenor paid some Time agoe makes 100£ old Tenor in part for Cook Island, which he promises to give me a Deed of upon Demand.

2. Lieutenant Tainter here, who carry'd a Veal for us to Boston. Ebenezer to Mr. Bradish's Swamp with Mr. Daniel Warrin to hew Troughs.

3. Read Levit. 19. Preach'd on Rev. 1, 8. Administer'd the Lords Supper. My wife (being ask'd by Esquire Baker) din'd with us—Mr. Williams also invited both of us to dine at their House. Molly din'd at Deacon Newtons. Some of the Hopkinton

people here at meeting, Mr. Barrett not being well yet. P.M. read Acts 10. Repeated sermon on 1 John 3, 3.

4. Town Meeting was at the North Meeting House—Tedious Storm of Snow. Mr. Edwards Whipple has bought us 25 pounds of Flax at Northampton at 5/ and asks 1/6 for bringing—comes to 8£2.6.

5. The Storm yet more tedious, Snowing, blowing and Cold, all Day and Night. I was chiefly engag'd in reading Expositors and other writers on my design'd Text and Subject—a faithfull minister. Read especially Davenant on the Colossians.[2] I bless God my own Soul not altogether unaffected! Find I have great Reason for Deep Humilliation for my unqualifydness and great unfaithfullness—the Lord pardon me, thro the Great Saviour! N.B. I had appointed a Catechizing at the Meeting House to Day, but the Storm prevented going out.

6. Stormy morning—but the wish'd for Sun appear'd before Noon. The Snow is deep, and the air very Cold. Read Gilbert West Esquire on the Resurrection of Christ. (It is Mr. Martyns[3] and I would fain return it tomorrow.) Ebenezer takes Care of the Cattle, gets wood, and is busy'd about various Choars. Thomas makes Whipps but can't get Deer's Hair for Saddles.

7. I rode over to Mr. Martyns and din'd there. Preach'd his Lecture—Text 1 Cor. 11, 20, latter part. May God be pleas'd to add his Blessing! Call'd at Ensign Rice's at Evening. N.B. Mr. John Caruth there.

8. John Caruth junior here, from Mr. Martyn. Sent Tar, to make Tar-Water. My sons sledding wood most of the Day. N.B. one of our Geese, instead of Setting, was found Dead near the Currant Bushes—when open'd we found her Eggs were broke within her.

9. Misty.

10. Read, with some brief Observations Lev. 20. Preach'd all Day on Col. 1, 7. Din'd at Justice Bakers—P.M. Acts 11. A very Rainy Day, and very difficult getting to and from Meeting.

11. I was at Mr. Ebenezer Rice's to pay them Rum which I had borrow'd of them chiefly for raising my New House, my Well, Cellar and Chimney work. N.B. the Precinct Meeting for their Annual Election of officers, thrown up. At Eve came Mr. Haven from Brookfield and lodg'd here.

12. After Dinner I undertook a Journey to Leicester—call'd at Mr. Maccartys,[4] met Mr. Lull in Shrewsbury with a Drove of Hoggs, reach'd Mr. Goddards[5] and lodg'd there. The Roads very bad, I was so late as to ride great part of the Roade from Worcester to Leicester in the Dark and Mudd.

13. From Mr. Goddards to Mr. David Baldwins. Bargain'd with him to make my Window Frames and Sashes, 13 of the former and 15 of the Latter, 24 Squares in Each Window 7 by 9 Dimensions of Glass and to lodge 'em Safe at Captain Maynards at Westborough, not exceeding the first week of June, for 48£ old Tenor Money, and 4 inner Doors, double rais'd pannells at the price which Mr. Goodwin Housewright in Worcester shall sett. Return'd to Worcester—din'd near 5 o'clock at Mr. Maccartys. Horse kept at Captain Daniel Wards. Mr. Maccarty and I walk'd to Colonel Chandlers but he was not at Home. Spent the Eve with his Lady. Lodg'd at Mr. Maccartys. N.B. was in great Grief and Trouble by means of the bitter Lamentations and Complaints about Dr. Breck. N.B. News that Colonel Samuel Willard[6] of Lancaster was struck last night with the Numb Palsey.

14. Was with Mr. Putnam[7] (as I was yesterday with Mr. Doolittle,[8] and Mr. Waters[9]) on the Affair of Dr. Breck. N.B. in my returning home, had Discourse with Mr. David Crosby[10] about his son and Dauter Cook,[11] who are under the Frowns of

---

[7] James Pierpont, Jr., of New Haven.
[8] The son of Squire Edward Baker of Westborough.
[9] John Flavell, *The Touchstone of Sincerity: or the Signs of Grace and Symptoms of Hypocrisy* (Boston, 1731). This appeared originally in a London edition of 1678.
[10] In Bolton.
[11] The Reverend Elisha Fish.

[1] James Bradish.

[2] John Davenant, *Expositio Epistolae D. Pauli ad Colossenses* (Cantab., 1627). Two other Latin editions were published in 1630 and 1639.
[3] The Reverend John Martyn of the north parish.
[4] The Reverend Thaddeus Maccarty of Worcester.
[5] The Reverend David Goddard of Leicester.
[6] Willard was a leading citizen, a justice of the peace, and judge of the Worcester County Court of Common Pleas, and Lancaster's representative for many years.
[7] James Putnam, the lawyer of Worcester.
[8] Ephraim Doolittle of Worcester.
[9] John Waters of Worcester.
[10] Samuel Crosby of Shrewsbury. Ward, *Shrewsbury*, p. 255.
[11] Sarah Crosby married Robert Cook of Westborough. Their conduct was a concern of the Westborough church for many months.

our Church. Have heard to Day and yesterday of Several sudden Deaths—but when I got home (instead of finding Mr. Martyn and his wife, to dine with me, as I expected) found Forbush[12] from College there, who came up with Tidings of Asaph Rice's[13] illness at College. But especially—O Especially! with the heavy and grievous Accounts of the Death of my Dear Kinsman, and rather Brother or Son than Nephew Elias Parkman who was taken ill Friday night was sennight of a Pleurisie, Soon grew delirious—continued all Wednesday after and expir'd—was interr'd the next Saturday. May I be suitably affected with this Holy Dispensation—remember and prepare for my own Decease! May God remember dear Nabby, and her Maker be her Husband! and with him may the dear Orphans find Mercy!

15. Rainy—Thomas carry'd 19£ Old Tenor to Mr. Obadiah Newton. Captain Maynard here from Boston, but no Letter from any one.

16. P.M. I rode over to Mr. Martyns and desir'd him to change tomorrow, which he consenting to I tarried there.

17. Mr. Martyn preach'd for me, and I for him. My Text a. and p.m. Dan. 2, 35. His was Isa. 5, beginning. I return'd home at Eve and he lodg'd with us. N.B. a Letter from Brother Parkman of the Death of the Doctor the Day, he dy'd, by the Date of it.

18. Mr. Martyn and I chang'd Watches, mine being so much worn and having prov'd very expensive to me to keep it in repair; and he also having lately bought Lieutenant Ephraim Brighams—but I Suppose he can sell mine, but his watch being by him valued at 10£ more than mine, and the Chain 40/ I gave him Bishop Hopkins'[14] works, Kennets Roman Antiquities;[15] and lively Oracles by the Author of the Whole Duty of Man.[16] P.M. Mrs. Newton, widow here. Mr. Abijah Gale and wife here. She was Examin'd.

19. I was with Neighbour Stephen Maynard as he and Neighbour Benjamin How measur'd Mr. Baldwins Boards.

20. Ebenezer and Thomas digging stones East of the Barn.

21. Publick Fast. Preach'd all Day upon Hos. 2, 8, 9. At noon refresh'd at Deacon Newtons. At Eve my wife and I returning home call'd to See Mrs. Pratt who grows weaker and weaker.

22. Was at old Mr. Maynard's a.m. At Noon Mr. Ebenezer Harrington[17] and Ensign Stone of Framingham were here, but did not stay to dine. P.M. Mr. Benjamin Lull. Ebenezer drawing stones with the Young Horse put in with the Rest of the Team; and tho it be the first Tryal does very well.

23. One Mrs. Davidson here from Needham, who informs that Mr. Peabody[18] very bad, and it is doubtful whether he will ever recover.

24. Read Levit. 21, omitting number 18, 19, 20, but gave a general account of what they contain'd—preach'd a. and p.m. on 1 Chron. 29, 15 on occasion of the Death of my dear Kinsman Dr. Elias Parkman[19] of Boston. May God bless these meditations to me for my highest Profit! Din'd at Esquires. P.M. read Acts 12.

25. Undertook a Journey to Boston. Din'd at Mr. Stone's[20] at Southborough. Call'd at Colonel Buckministers at Framingham, but Mrs. Buckminister not at home. Rode to Natick—found Mr. Peabody poor and weak. Lodg'd there—with his son of Roxbury.

26. Prosecuted my Journey—aiming to go to Mr. John Child's, Glazier at Roxbury. N.B. one Cook of Needham or Dedham piloted me, to his Grandfathers Captain Robert Cook in Needham

—to Mr. Stephen Winchester in Newton bad with a Cancer—and to Mrs. Hastings's who formerly carry'd me up to Newtown in her Lap—N.B. her mother Davis alive—accounted 116 last October. There was a Mr. Childs at Madam Dudley's—put up my Horse at Cousen Cowels—visited my Kinsmans Widow—Roxbury, her Negro man dy'd to Day—little Elias very ill of a Fever. Lodg'd at Brother Samuels.

27. My Brother Parkman, Cozen Cowel and I attended the Funeral of poor Roxbury. I lodg'd at Brother Parkmans, and rejoice in his New Spouse.

28. The Town very much alive with people who throng into it to put off or Change their Province Bills. I attended the Public Lecture. Mr. Cooper[21] preach'd on Luke 18 chapter, 9 to 14. The Pharisee and Publican. Din'd at Dr. Chauncy's,[22] where also din'd Judge Sewall,[23] Mr. Cook[24] of Sudbury and Mr. Peabody[25] of Roxbury. Visited Mrs. Oliver and Captain Devenport Walker. Was at Mr. Foxcrofts etc. Lodg'd at Cousen Cowells.

29. A.M. at Mr. Eliots[26]—Mr. Welsteeds[27]—Mr. Clark[28] of Salem Village came there. Settled my Account with Brother Samuel and paid what appear'd to be the Ballance. Lodg'd at Brother Samuels. My Horse kept at My Kinsman Cowels till this Night; when he was kept at Mr. Stoddards. Visited Mr. Jeremiah Condy.

30. Sett out from Boston after Noon about 10 minutes,—rain'd somewhat while I pass'd thro Watertown—got to Mr. Nathaniel Williams at Weston by half after Two. Got to Mr. Bridge's[29] in Season to have come home, but he was desirous we should change: at least he would go to Southborough, and Mr. Stone (having been Spoke to already to do it in Case I should need) to come to Westborough. So that I tarried at Framingham.

31. Preach'd at Framingham a.m. on Prov. 14, 9. P.M. on John 12, 26. Exceeding Cold Wind. Mr. Samuel Haven din'd and lodg'd with me. Ensign Stone and Mr. Farrar[30] came to see me at Eve. Mr. Bridge, who came to Westborough did not return home till after I was in Bed. N.B. Mrs. Bridge's fall from the Horse Block, by reason of the Wind.

## APRIL, 1751

1. Breakfast at Colonel Buckminsters. N.B. Mr. Bridge, Mr. Haven[1], together with his Father, and one Mr. Hale of Brookfield, consulting with me about Mr. Samuel Havens preaching with them (as he had done) in order to his settling there—whereas he had a Call at part of Medway, and therefore, he (justly) refuses to encourage those of Brookfield till he has done with Medway. Mr. Hale rode home with me. We din'd at Mr. Nichols in Framingham.

2. I was at Mr. Jeduthun Fays. Mr. Cushing here while I was from home.

3. I was employ'd partly upon some Books I brought from Boston. Night Thots etc.

4. Preach'd Mr. Cushings Lecture at Shrewsbury on Song. 1, 12. Return'd at Eve. Ebenezer sowing Rye. It has been very searching Cold Weather for some Time. I have taken Cold and went to bed ill. N.B. Lieutenant Bruce went up to Grafton to meet the Reverend Mr. Prentice,[2] and expected me to have gone.

5. Somewhat better a.m. but was indispos'd p.m. Remains Cold. Ebenezer and Billy plough at Cook Island.

6. A.M. A great Snow Storm. The Snow nigh a foot deep. Ebenezer fetch'd nine Bushels Lime borrow'd of Messers. Woods and Oake, northside.

[12] Eli Forbush, who was keeping school in Westborough.
[13] (Harvard 1752). Rice practiced medicine for a time in Brookfield and later served as the minister of the First Congregational Church of Westminster, Mass., 1765-1815.
[14] Ezekiel Hopkins, D.D. (1634-1690), Bishop of Raphoe and Derry, was the author of numerous books. Posthumously, there was published *The Works of . . . Ezekiel Hopkins . . . Collected into One Volume* (London, 1701). Two other English editions appeared by 1710.
[15] Basil Kennet, *Romanae Antiquae Notitia; or the Antiquities of Rome* (London, 1696). At least 11 English editions had been published by 1746.
[16] [Richard Allestree], *Whole Duty of Man* (London, [1658]). Many other editions followed. *The Lively Oracles Given to Us* (Oxford, 1658) was also published anonymously and in several editions.
[17] Selectman of Framingham.
[18] The Reverend Oliver Peabody of the First Congregational Church of Natick.
[19] Parkman's nephew.
[20] The Reverend Nathan Stone.

[21] Samuel Cooper of the Brattle Street Church.
[22] The Reverend Charles Chauncy of the First Church of Boston.
[23] Justice Stephen Sewall of the Superior Court of Judicature.
[24] The Reverend William Cooke of Wayland.
[25] The Reverend Oliver Peabody (Harvard 1745), minister of the First Congregational Church in Roxbury, 1750-1752. *Sibley*, XI, 563-564.
[26] The Reverend Andrew Eliot of the New North Church.
[27] The Reverend William Welsteed of the New Brick Church in Boston.
[28] The Reverend Peter Clark, the minister of Danvers.
[29] The Reverend Matthew Bridges of Framingham.
[30] John Farrar, a prominent citizen of Framingham.

[1] Samuel Haven (Harvard 1749), the son of Joseph Haven of Framingham, taught school, read divinity with the Reverend Mr. Parkman, and became the minister of the Second Congregational Church of Portsmouth, N. H., 1752-1806. *Sibley*, XII, 382-392.
[2] Solomon Prentice who had been dismissed by the Grafton church in 1747.

7. Read Lev. 22. Preach'd on 1 Cor. 4, 1. Din'd at Esquire Bakers. P.M. read Acts 13. Preach'd on 1 Pet. 3, 5. Those words—Love as Brethren, be pitiful, be Courteous. Us'd (with alterations) Sermons on Tit. 2, 12, from page 85 to 95. Stop'd the Church, and they voted the Dismission of Samuel and Susanna Baker to the Church of Bolton. N.B. Mrs. Rachel Pratt[3] grows much weaker.

8. The weather being unfit for our masonry little expect Mr. Newton today, Yet I went over to the New House. Ebenezer and the Team also. Ebenezer fetch'd a Load of Clay from Mr. James Maynards, Mrs. Newtons Clay Pitts being filled and Surrounded with water. I was at Lieutenant Tainters—visited Mrs. Pratt.

9. The Snow being chiefly gone, my masons came, Mr. Obadiah Newton and Mr. Edward Willson to top out my Chimney, but they were beat off by the Rain. Din'd them at home. P.M. about 4 they go to work again. They lodg'd here, and I kept their Horses. N.B. Ebenezer and Thomas tended the Masons.

10. Masons go to work, but were beat off again Several Times before noon. I carry'd them their Dinner. Ebenezer and Thomas tended them again to Day. P.M. they broke off about 4 or between 4 and 5 o'Clock (I suppose) it raining very hard—and they went away both of 'em to Shrewsbury. I rode with Mr. Holbrook of Grafton to Mr. Amsdens—and discours'd with each of the Gales and their wifes concerning their making a profession of Religion. N.B. Sent a Letter by Mr. Holbrook to Mr. John Avery at Boston, Merchant respecting my Young Horse.

11. Lieutenant Wood of Upton and [blank] Chase (a young practitioner in Physic and who has taken up Lodging at Captain Bakers) din'd here. We are terrify'd with more than ordinary Gusts of Wind—and the weather is very Cold.

12. Lieutenant Tainter cutt my Two Year old Colt, and Gratis, as he has been always wont generously to do all such work for me. Ebenezer and Billy go to ploughing a.m. at the Cook Island. Bright, but windy and cold. Preach'd the Lecture on Hos. 10, 12, former part, omitted page 1. Proceeded to the End of page 12. After Lecture my wife and I call'd to See Mrs. Pratt, and before we came home we went to See Mr. Eliezer Rice and his wife (who had not been to Lecture either of them) to discourse with them especially with her concerning some Conversations She had had about me at old Mr. Whipple's Some Time since. He not being in the House, I desir'd her to Send for him to come in, which She did, and he came. I told him I wanted to Speak with him, and we walk'd out, to his Gate. Upon my acquainting him with my End in coming, he was Soon in a Ruffle. He tax'd me with impudence in coming now, for that I ought to have come before. I answer'd that it was but newly that I was inform'd of the persons She Spake in the hearing of, So that I was not able to Say any Thing of it besides, I was not willing to mind it or make any Thing of it, Considering the Frame she was in when I suppose she Said what she did, but that it best to let it dye—but Seeing She came again to the Communion and She was now more in her right mind; but especially Seeing it was got about and it was Concluded by people that I had talked with her, I was desirous to know what she now had to say of it; or who the Men were that She had Said told her what She reported. He ask'd me whether I thougt it convenient to talk with her now, about what she had said when (as I conceiv'd) she was not altogether herself? He also Said that he acknowledg'd he had been brought under great Trouble and Affliction in the providence of God, and he was Sorry to find that his Neighbours especially that his Minister should add Affliction to the Afflicted, and he added (most unjustly) that he thought I took a delight in it. He utter'd divers other grievous Sentences. It was so Cold we could stand no longer abroad. We went into the House—but having intimated my purpose was to talk with his Wife, I let him understand that I was not willing to be with her alone. He Said he design'd to be with her when I did talk with her. Mr. Edwards Whipple was in the House, and I talk'd with Mr. Rice then only about our Reckoning together—which we finish'd—except that when he ask'd me whether It was much better if I did not get

3 Mrs. Hezekiah Pratt.

home till Evening I told him it was Friday and I wanted to go home—but was very willing if they had any Thing to Say, or I could serve them in any Thing, to stay as long as it should need, and I waited a while, but he was silent—So that I took leave.

13. Drizzly Morning. Broke away afterwards. Ebenezer goes a Fishing till noon.

14. Read Lev. 23. Preach'd on Rev. 22, 16. My wife and I din'd at the Justice's. Sacrament. P.M. Read Acts 14. Preach'd on John 15, 14, repeating in part but with many alterations and additions what was deliver'd before my ordination on the Text.

15. Rain. No Masons. At Eve came Mr. Maccarty—after him Mr. Campbell,[4] Maccarty, Wellman[5] and I rode to Sudbury, the Association Meeting to Day at Mr. Lorings.[6] There were besides, Messers. Cushing, Gardner,[7] Martyn, Smith, Morse,[8] Goss,[9] Davis. Mr. Loring for a Concio read Sermon on Ps. 90, 12. N.B. Mr. Campbell and Wellman's Difficulty with Mr. Martyn and Stone, complaining of their Result at the late Council at Sutton. Mr. Stone not present the Affair not heard by the Association as such; but afforded Mr. Campbell and Wellman assistance to effect a Reconcilement between them and Mr. Martyn, which was with success, and they made up all the Matter. I lodg'd at Mr. Lorings. I rode to Concord—broke fast at Mr. Minots. Paid Mr. Goold the full of the written agreement, viz. [blotted]—which added to the former 20£ old Tenor which I sent him was the whole—and gave him a promisory Note for 18/ Lawfull Money to satisfie him for Thomas's Rates at Concord. I return'd to Sudbury by 11 o'Clock the Time of Lecture which I attended and Mr. Cushing preach'd on John 13, 34. After Dinner came Mr. Bridge of Framingham, and Mr. Samuel Haven. Mr. Haven asks advice touching the admission of Mr. Joseph Haven into the Church. In returning home, called at Dr. Gotts and Mr. Smiths—very Cold Night.

18. Ebenezer ploughing Stubble. P.M. I catechiz'd at the Meeting House, about 36 Children, Males and Females.

19. 20. We are much troubled about the Chimney of the New House, there being so high winds and frequent Rains,—So that we can't keep it Safely cover'd.

21. Cold. Read Levit. 24. N.B. had prepar'd more than Sufficient (for quantity) for one Sermon on the Duty of people to their ministers; but thought it not prudent to deliver it till I had finish'd the whole on that Head—and therefore after much deliberating and weighing things I concluded it to be best to lay it aside for the present and took some Sermons on living Godly in the Discourse on Tit. 2, 12, and deliver'd them, from page 96 to 110 with alterations from Acts 5, 20 latter part (both a. and p.m.) Din'd at Justice Bakers. P.M. read Acts 15. N.B. Mr. William Pierce's young Child (of about 2 months old) well last night after sunsetting, dy'd before Day this morning.

22. Rain—yet attended the Funeral of Mr. Pierce's Child. Mr. Ebenezer Chamberlin here in the Eve.

23. I went over to the New House with Ebenezer to direct and assist in planting Elms and Plumb Trees. No ground fenc'd thereof. Sett no Apple Trees. P.M. Mr. Martyn and his Wife here. Afterwards Mr. Abijah Weld[10] of Attlebury, with his son. Mr. Martyn and his wife tarry'd to Supper but the other to Shrewsbury. N.B. The Youth is infirm—going to Dr. Greens.

24. Went to Lieutenant Bruce's about Mrs. Cooks Signing his Deed. At Mr. Warrins. Timothy gave me 20 young Apple Trees which I set out in vacant places of my orchard at Home. Mr. Haven din'd and lodg'd here.

25. Mr. Haven with us. N.B. The Watch I lately had of Mr. Martyn Stop'd in the last Night and I can have no further good of it. Mr. Weld returning home from Leicester to Attlebury, here, and after Dinner he and Mr. Haven took leave together. N.B. The Season unusually Cold and Somewhat windy but Ebenezer (having deferr'd it long already) Sowed Wheat.

4 The Reverend John Campbell of Oxford.
5 The Reverend James Wellman of Millbury.
6 The Reverend Israel Loring of Sudbury.
7 The Reverend John Gardner of Stow.
8 The Reverend Ebenezer Morse of Boylston.
9 The Reverend Thomas Goss of Bolton.
10 The Reverend Habijah Weld (Harvard 1723), the minister of Attleborough, 1727-1782. Sibley, VII, 268-272.

26. Ebenezer Sows Flax—and p.m. Carts muck. Thomas helps him p.m. Mr. Ebenezer Rice here. Mr. Cook. N.B. Captain Maynard brought a Letter which came from my Kinsman Davis at Nova Scotia.

27. Cool windy weather yet. Ebenezer and Thomas Sowing Barley and Carting Muck.

28. I have prepared about 16 pages (6 or 7 is an ordinary Exercise) on the third Article of the people's Duty to their Ministers, viz. and Honorable Maintenance. My heart has labour'd very much about the delivering it—I much reluct at it—am asham'd I have So much fear of displeasing the people. But being Sensible it is my Duty to preach on this Subject, have begg'd of God to direct me how I shall conduct my self in this matter—and that I might deliver no Line but what is His. I endeavor to divest myself of my own Concern in it as much as I can, that I may deal impartially—Have conceiv'd it would be best to deliver but one Exercise upon this Head, though I have much more prepar'd. Accordingly committing myself and my work to God, I went to meeting. Read and gave some Expository Observations on Lev. 25, and then preach'd on 1 Cor. 4, 1. Deliver'd some passages concerning the Duty of Obedience to Ministers from Sermon on Heb. 13, 17, but only glancingly—and proceeded to treat of maintenance—but could not deliver all that I had prepar'd, by 4 pages—or more. Din'd as usual. P.M. read Acts 16. Repeated Sermon on Tit. 2, 12., page 111 to 121, from Acts 5, 20. Baptiz'd Mrs. Abigail Gale.[11]

29. Visited Mr. Moses Brighams wife who is very weak and low. Mr. Martyn while I was gone.

30. My Wife went to Marlborough and was blooded. She return'd at Eve.

### MAY, 1751

1. Having receiv'd a Letter from Mr. Stone[1] to preach his Lecture I went and preach'd on 1 Cor. 11, 26 to page 11. In returning at Evening call'd at Mr. Amsdens,[2] his Dauter Abigail brought to bed before her Expected Time. N.B. Mr. Amsdens indecent Discourse and Conduct. Was at Lieutenant Bruce's and gave him a Bond for 150£ old Tenor and received a Deed of Cook Island.

2. My Wife and I rode over to Mr. Martyns. Mr. Morse[3] and his Spouse there. We all din'd together. P.M. at the Public Lecture. Mr. Morse pray'd and preach'd on Eph. 1, 3. We return'd at Evening. Found our Tabernacle in peace.

3. Mr. Holbrook of Grafton here and din'd with us.

4. We have now had five Calves, and four of them has [sic] come on Saturday. There has been So much of windy, Rainy, Cold weather that people don't Care to plant yet.

5. Read Lev. 26 with some Exposition chiefly extracted from Mr. Henry,[4] as has been my method for some time. Preach'd a. and p.m. on 1 Tim. 6, 17, 18, 19. I din'd as usual. P.M. read Acts 17.

6. A.M. at the New House. Mr. Jonathan Forbush and Mr. Ebenezer Rice there with me. Mr. Forbush prizes Mr. Rice's Boards which he has spar'd to me. The price falls so much below Mr. Rice's Expectation that I agree not to use 'em till he is better Satisfy'd. Mr. Biglo Spends Some Hours in building a Wall against the Bank of Gravel which came out of my Cellar. N.B. frequent high Winds. Towards evening I visited Eliezer Rice who is Sick of a Fever. He and his wife also were so very fervent for forgiveness and Reconcilement that I gave him my Hand—but as to the Doctrine of Original Sin, I told him, I would wave every Thot at present, as he was not now able to undergo Discourse and Dispute. We part'd friendly. Brother Hicks[5] had been at my House and was gone to Cambridge. When I came home, found Mr. Edwards[6] of Northampton, who was in his

Return home from Boston. He and Colonel Timothy Dwight[7] have been endeavouring to have a Council to sit at Northampton next week to advise the small part of people there whether it is best to have Mr. Edwards install'd over them, or not.

7. Mr. Edwards left us. Dr. Breck[8] here and din'd with us. P.M. went to Worcester. N.B. Expected Martyn[9] and wife to go to Grafton—but they did not come.

8. Fine Weather; blessed be God! Ebenezer and Thomas are gone to Bolton for Lime. They have Mr. Richard Barns's Oxen added to our own Team. They have a tedious Journey (undertaking it in one Day) and return not till late in the Night. Mr. Fish here and din'd with us. Brings Letter respecting his Ordination.

9. My sons begin to plant the Field. A very fine Day. Patty Pannell, brought a present, of a Quarter of Veal from the Widow Tomlins with whom she lives.

10. Warm, bright and exceeding pleasant, after a night of plentifull Rain. My sons go on with the planting. N.B. Brother Hicks and his Dauter Elizabeth here. Visited Neighbour Eliezer Rice.

11. Another very fine Day. My Sons finish'd planting at home, this morning. N.B. Thomas has work'd with his Brother for Several Days—to Day for himself in his Shop. Brother Hicks and his Dauter return home. Mr. Levi Brigham sent us a wild Goose which he kill'd in the pond. Ebenezer p.m. sow'd the rest of the Flax.

12. Ebenezer watch'd last night with Neighbour Eliezer Rice. In the public Assembly read Lev. 27. Preach'd on Jam. 2, 5, a. and p.m. Din'd as usual, myself; but my wife, Thomas, William, Sarah and Susanna tarried at the Meeting House. P.M. read Acts 18. Some Number of Strangers at Meeting. Captain Cummins, who is Delegate from Mr. Wigglesworth's[10] Church to the design'd Council at Northampton. Lieutenant Steward,[11] from Marlborough, Mr. Smith[12] being absent, and some Number of others.

13. Went to Mr. Eliezer Rice's—Mr. James Maynards, Mr. Seth Rice's, etc. Ebenezer harrows the Ground at the Island. An unusual hot Day. Mr. Bowman and his Brother Thaddeus din'd here. N.B. Gave to Treasurer Ebenezer Maynard per Hand of Lieutenant Tainter a Receipt of the whole of my last Years Sallery, £53.6.8 or 400£ old Tenor, but this Receipt the Committee return'd and I destroy'd.

14. We finish'd planting at the Island. Was there myself p.m. Captain Forbush there and dropp'd Corn. Mr. Silas Brigham with me, about his Affair with Mr. Morse.

15. My wife and I, together with my two sons Ebenezer and Thomas attended the Marriage of Mr. Abraham Batchellor to Mrs. Sally Newton, only Dauter of the late Mr. Abner Newton; which was Solemniz'd at the Widow Newtons p.m. N.B. My Dauter Lucy was invited also, (and not Molly)—Molly rode over to Mr. Martyns, agreeable to Appointment Some Time ago, and Lucy tarried at home with the children. I can't but remark what a changing world we live in. What an House of Sorrows that was for a great while, which is now of so high Joy.

16. Ebenezer shearing a few Sheep.

17. Mr. Abraham Knowlton come from Boston call'd here. 'Tis Said that the Prince of Wales is Dead. Lucy went over to Mr. Martyns for Molly and they came home at Eve.

18. Ebenezer and Thomas a.m. to the New House to take Care of the Boards and Lime there.

19. In the Morning Alexander struck a Ram that return'd the Blow and knock'd him down, and repeated it as often as he endeavour'd to rise—till my Dauter Molly running to his relief, was struck down likewise; So that they were both in Some Danger; till I went to their Succour. In Public read Numbers Chapter 1 with some Exposition. In the forenoon I thought to have preach'd for the Comfort and Support and Direction of the poor,

---

[11] The wife of Abijah Gale of Westborough.

[1] The Reverend Nathan Stone of Southborough.

[2] Jacob Amsden.

[3] The Reverend Ebenezer Morse of Boylston.

[4] Matthew Henry (1662–1714), the learned dissenting divine, was the author of numerous works published in England. Several of his writings had been published in America.

[5] Parkman's brother-in-law, John Hicks of Sutton.

[6] The great Jonathan Edwards.

[7] Dwight and other friends and supporters of Edwards were working to establish a new church in Northampton for the dismissed preacher. James R. Trumbull, *History of Northampton* (Northampton, 1898, 1902), II, 228, 233–234.

[8] Samuel Breck, the physician of Great Barrington.

[9] The Reverend John Martyn of Northborough.

[10] The Reverend Samuel Wigglesworth of Hamilton.

[11] Daniel Stewart.

[12] The Reverend Aaron Smith of Marlborough.

on the Duty of Contentment—and accordingly read Several Essays on that Subject. But after all, chose to wave writing upon it, till I come to the Tenth Commandment and would also be glad to See Mr. Burroughs's[13] Treatise hereof. Therefore I repeated with some alterations my Exposition on Mat. 6, 25 to 30 omitting number 27. Din'd at Justice Bakers, where also din'd Justice Liscomb.[14] N.B. Lucy, Sarah and Susanna carry'd their Dinners. P.M. read Acts 19. Preach'd on Prov. 16, 31. After Divine Service, read Letter from Upton for Ordination of Mr. Fish.[15] N.B. I nominated Justice Baker.

20. Mr. Martyn came a.m. to talk about his people's Conduct in the Affair of his Sallery. He din'd and tarried till Eve. N.B. He is greatly mov'd and very resolute in the affair aforesaid. Mr. Harding of Brookfield likewise here, but did not tarry long.

21. I visited old Mr. Bradish and din'd there. Visited Mrs. Dunlop who is Sick. Was at Deacon Forbush's. N.B. Mr. Solomon Woods (Tything man) complains of my son Williams's Rudeness at Meeting on Lords Day. Was at Mr. Williams's. Call'd to see Mrs. Pratt. My son Ebenezer about a well Crotch, Sweep etc. Thomas not very well. William setts out Cabbage Plants and goes to Mill at Mr. Allens.

22. Preach'd my Lecture myself—on Hosea 10, 12. Though with many omissions, alterations and additions—especially on account of the Death of the Prince of Wales. After Lecture my wife and I visited Neighbour Eliezer Rice who is still sick, and was in one of his Fitts. Several Neighbours here to raise the Well Crotch and Sweep.

23. This Morning, according to appointment, my Masons were to come, but to my great Disappointment they did not come. Ebenezer mending Fences, after he had done the well-pole.

24. Ebenezer at the Fences, a.m. At Neighbour Bathericks Barn-raising p.m. I was in a great Deal of Trouble about Sending to Mr. Willson, the Mason, again. Neither of my Two Eldest sons return'd from Raising till late at Night.

25. Instead of their rising Earlier than usual that I might Send one of them this Morning to Mr. Willsons, my Sons, both of them were so sound, that when awak'd they are disturb'd—and not without Great Difficulty Ebenezer goes up to him to know the Reason of his not coming to my Work. The many Troubles, Difficultys and Disappointments I meet with together with the Confinement I am under by the Work and Business of my Sacred Office, whilst so many and Important Affairs are depending. But especially the impudent Conduct of my Sons, render me very Impatient So that I am scarcely able to contain myself which is to my greater Grief because of the present Season, just before the holy Supper. Thomas rode to Marlborough to get Pannell Crooks and to bring home the rest of my Malt from Deacon Woods.

26. Read Numb. 2. Preach'd on Rev. 22, 16 a. and p.m. Administer'd the Lords Supper. Din'd at Justice Bakers—and my wife with me. P.M. read Acts 20. N.B. Gave Warning to old and young respecting the Election and requested Young Women to dismiss Seasonably the Young Men that wait upon them.

27. Mr. Willson came to work—work'd up my Bricks—got but one Brick above the ridge of the House. Ebenezer tended him. At Eve paid off both Mr. Willson and Mr. Obadiah Newton who came this Eve in order to go to work tomorrow—but they both went home. Mr. Breck[16] of Springfield came and lodg'd.

28. Mr. Breck to Marlborough. I undertook my Journey afterwards. Called at Mr. Timothy Warrins to receive money of Lieutenant Tainter. At Mr. Gale's to get Horse Shooes mov'd etc. N.B. One Pierce of Sutton who had been a Delegate at Northampton Council, travelled some Miles with me. Mr. Breck and I call'd to see Mr. Warham Williams but his Spouse acquainted us how hurtful it was to him to see Company, So that we did not desire to disturb him. At Saltmarsh's we saw Mr.

Roberts Breck of Boston and his Wife with other Company who had rid out so far for their Diversion. Heard that Captain Joseph White, Elias's Father-in-Law, was dead: and my Cousen Cowells Son Peam dy'd suddenly last week; being taken sick on Thursday and dy'd on Friday. About three years old. I put up my Horse at my Kinsman Procters in Boston and lodg'd at my Brother Samuels.

29. Another Token for Good from God to New England, in that we enjoy the present Anniversary. Mr. Welsteeds[17] Sermon on Ps. 47, 9, very disgusting to many people in Boston, as therein he much commended what the late general assemblys had done in Sinking the Paper Currency and bringing us into a Silver Medium. I din'd at Brother Samuels. Attended the Convention p.m. N.B. Mr. Prince read divers Letters from England—especially touching a Correspondence propos'd to be kept up between our Convention and the united Dissenting Brethren in England, particularly the Committee of Deputation there. I lodg'd at Nabby's.

30. At the Convention Sermon; preach'd by Mr. Wigglesworth of Ipswich on 2 Cor. 11, 2, and the Collection for the Support of the Gospel Ministry which I fear was Small. Din'd at Mr. Eliots.[18] N.B. Mr. Kneeland[19] acquaints me with a present from Scotland to Mr. Edwards of Northampton which will turn to be nigh 1000£ value old Tenor. He likewise tells me he will undertake to print the Collection of Poems which I have propos'd to him—and this (if I understood him) whether there be any more subscribers or not. Supp'd at Cousen Olivers with some Number besides—Mrs. Davenport. He lodg'd at Brother Samuels.

31. Bought a Box of London Crown Glass 7 by 9 of Mr. James Pitts for 45£ old Tenor. Bought a piece of Garlix etc. of Mrs. Stoddard. N.B. Mr. Moses Peck has mended my Watch. Endeavour'd to get upon my Journey but was Stopp'd at Eve, when I design'd to have gone out of Town, by Storm of Thunder and Lightning and Rain. Lodg'd at Cousen Procters. N.B. Mr. Gooldsbury[20] of Wrentham there.

### JUNE, 1751.

At five in the morning set out from Boston. Broke fast at Mr. Dix's[1] in Watertown. Visited Mr. Williams[2] of Waltham who is very low. Pray'd with him. N.B. Mr. Cotton[3] of Newton and Dr. Convers[4] there. Visited Mr. Williams of Watertown. He seems very much humbl'd—yet defends himself in many respects. Din'd with Mrs. Baldwin in Sudbury; her Husband Captain Baldwin from Home, but her sons there. Was again refresh'd at Mr. Jonathan Strattons in Marlborough. Before I got up to Amsdens it rain'd hard—stop'd a great while in the Storm at Mr. Amsdens—before dark set out again, but the rain pour'd down so violently I was oblig'd to turn in to Lieutenant Bruce's—Pray'd with them, lay'd down and Slep'd. At 11 o'Clock attempted to ride Home—and arriv'd in Safety. Blessed be God!

2. Read Numb. 3. Preach'd on Job 36, 24, a. and p.m. Din'd as usual. P.M. read Acts 21.

3. Lieutenant Tainter was here—wants a Receit of the whole Rates, altho above one hundred pounds behind; he offering me his Note of Hand—I comply'd and gratify'd him. Mr. Grout here—Mr. Grout desires a note to the Collector for 40/ which is the price of the Timber which he got me for the Frame of my New House. It was so contrary to my Expectation from one who pretended to be so generous, that I was surpriz'd at it. I was also in a great deal of Consternation at the view and prospect of our Family Circumstances—my sons Ebenezer and Billy not able to accomplish our Weeding at Home—yet have the Cook Island to tend besides—my Mind could be in no Composedness

13 The Reverend Jeremiah Burroughs (1599–1646), an English Congregationalist, was the author of numerous works published in England. The following was published in Boston. *The Rare Jewel of Christian Contentment, Containing Eighteen Rules for the Obtaining this Excellent Grace* (Boston, 1732). Another Boston edition appeared in 1742.

14 Samuel Lyscomb, a justice of the peace.

15 The Reverend Elisha Fish.

16 The Reverend Robert Breck, Jr.

17 William Welsteed, *The Dignity and Duty of the Civil Magistrate . . . Preached May 29th, 1751. Being the Anniversary for the Election* (Boston, 1751). The minister of the New Brick Church in Boston deplored the effects of inflation and expressed approval of the resumption of specie payment in this sermon.

18 The Reverend Andrew Eliot of the New North Church.

19 Samuel Kneeland, the printer and bookseller of Boston.

20 Samuel Goldsbury.

1 John Dix, the selectman. Bond, *Watertown*, p. 199.

2 The Reverend Warham Williams, who died later this month, June 22, 1751.

3 The Reverend John Cotton.

4 Josiah Convers (Harvard 1723), a physician of Watertown. *Sibley*, VII, 159–160.

for the Exercises of the Solemnity of Ordination at Upton which approaches—told Mr. Grout I did not see but that I must Stay at Home and hoe. I took my Horse and rode out—din'd at Lieutenant Thomas Forbushs. Was at Mr. Ebenezer Rice's etc.

4. I rode over to Mr. Cooks and to Mr. Martyns in the Morning—Then to the Island with Victuals and Drink, supposing I should find Some Hands at Work there—but tho it was not (I suppose) past 10 a.m. A number had been there and had finish'd the work. Lieutenant Tainter and Mr. Charles Rice ploughed and young Mr. Tainter, Mr. Joseph Woods, Two Hands from Mr. Ebenezer Rice's, Two from his fathers, and one from the widow Newton, in all Seven that Hoed. Young Mr. Jeduthun Baldwin, my Carpenter, and his Prentice John Woods came about Noon—they Eat with us and went to work to finish the New House. Whilst I was gone from home came the Reverend Maccarty and Major Keyes. Also my kinsman Mr. Needham and his wife. Mr. Breck of Springfield and Mr. Martyn and his Dauter. Mr. Haven also—but went with Forbush. Baldwin and his Man lodg'd at old Mr. Maynards. Mr. Maccarty and Major Keyes went home: the rest lodg'd here.

5. Mr. Martyn and his Dauter rode with me and my Dauter Lucy and son Thomas to Upton Ordination. The rest went their respective ways. But by means of So much Company I was later in setting out than I had appointed. The Churches met and Mr. Dor[5] was chose Moderator. N.B. My Enquiry, in the Council, whether Mr. Fish had been at the Shepards Tent? which was Satisfy'd by Mr. Owen,[6] his Pastor who gave a good Testimony of the Candidate. N.B. Mr. Fishs having sign'd an agreement with the people about Church Government which I could not approve of; yet did not think it sufficient to break Communion and therefore proceeding. Mr. Hall[7] open'd the public Exercise with Prayer. Mr. Owen preach'd on Eph. 4, 12. Mr. Dor the Charge. I pray'd after the Charge. Mr. Barret[8] gave the right Hand. N.B. our Entertainment was at Lieutenant Woods. We return'd to Westborough at night and Mr. Martyn and his Dauter lodg'd here.

6. Mr. Martyn etc. din'd here. Lucy Bowker at work here for Ebenezer turning his Camblet Coat.

7. Visited Mrs. Pratt. Read to her my sermon on Ps. 23, 4. But having been much worried of late and broke of my Rest, I was very dull and drowsy. Ebenezer finish'd weeding at home. P.M. hir'd William Wood to work at the New House to clear out the stones from the Chambers etc. Lucy Bowker still.

8. Ebenezer Carts Boards from hence etc. to the New House. N.B. My Carpenters diet at Deacon Newtons till this Eve.

9. I preach'd for Mr. Martyn on Prov. 14, 9, a. and p.m. Mr. Martyn for me on Isa. 5, fore part. Rain at Eve and I lodg'd there.

10. Return'd home. My Carpenters diet at Widow Newtons; the Deacon and his wife going from Home this Week. Lucy Bowker, who went home Saturday Night, here again to Day. N.B. Saw Lieutenant Tainter who seems offended that I said, last Monday, that I saw not but that I must go to hoeing instead of going to Ordination on Wednesday, but I endeavour'd to render him some answer to his Opposition as well as Some Thanks for his Assistance in the work done for me.

11. I rode to Shrewsbury to ministers meeting. N.B. Mr. Morse and Mr. Davis[9] indecently laugh'd out at reading my Collection—which was Judge Dudleys Elegant Translation of Dr. Thomas Burnets Dedication of his Archaeologia to King William[10]. I return'd home at Night. N.B. Mr. Morse asks advice in his Case with Mr. Silas Brigham, one of our church.

12. Went to my New House to know how my Carpenters proceeded. Visited Mr. Pratt. Visited Neighbour, Eliezer Rice whose Infant is ill. They desire it may be baptiz'd in private— but I was going to the association. Rode to Shrewsbury to

Association Lecture—call'd at Mr. Charles Woods's. Mr. Loring[11] preach'd on Tit. 3, 5. The sermon an hour and 36 minutes long. Captain Flagg[12] of Worcester we hear is dying. Mr. Edwards of Northampton call'd to see us. He is appointed Missionary to the Indians of Houssatunnock to whom he is going. I ask'd advice of the Association respecting my Baptizing of Eliezer Rice's Child, especially if he should declare himself against the Commonly recognized Doctrine of Original Sin. Some advis'd one way and Some another. In returning home I went to Mr. Martyns, in Company with Mr. Loring, Mr. Stone and Mr. Seccomb.[13]

13. I went to Mr. Eliezer Rice's whose Child is Sick. He still ask'd me what I thought of his proposal about baptizing it? I told him that if he was in Charity, and profess'd what he us'd to do; (and the like was offer'd to his wife) I was willing—There ensued a discourse concerning original Sin and how for the Belief of it was a Term of Communion. He plainly deny'd both the Imputation and Corruption: his wife did neither but profess'd as she us'd to do. I told Mr. Rice that if I was even of his opinion and ever so willing to administer, yet as it was the first Instance, it would not do to do it without laying it before the Church, to prevent Disquietment. But especially to do it in private would be altogether impudent but if he would consent to it I would do it on his wife's Right, but he refus'd. I offer'd to do any Thing within my power to oblige him. He desir'd it might be laid before the Church, and I consented on Condition he would send his Request in Writing; which he promis'd. N.B. Mrs. Hannah Maynard the Nurse was present. P.M. at New House and visited Mrs. Pratt. N.B. Jonas Bradish undertakes to Split a Stick of Timber of nigh 40 feet long for a Trough with his Saw; but gives out.

14. With Mrs. Pratt who grows still weaker. Ebenezer and Thomas yesterday and to Day at Half-hilling. P.M. at the New House to see what becomes of the Timber-sawing; and there was Mr. Biglo and Alpheus Newton at it. N.B. Great frustration about Clabboards—from 1400 which are needed, am reduc'd to 7 or 8 hundred. N.B. Boards for my Floor prove too hard, knotty, unequal in Thickness—and Difficult to find fit Boards for another Floor—viz. the West Chamber, but they have laid the west lower room floor. Tho there are so many Boards provided, Those which Lieutenant Tainter brought, which were design'd for the floor having been thrown by as much too knotty: O how perplexing and incumbering these avocations and Disquietments to a Minister! It is very grievous to be thus kept from my Studys. Yet I meet with Some other Things which are of a different Kind: Scil. Mrs. Pratt in her Languishment of Body, Shows a flourishing Soul; and seems to be full of affectionate Regard to me—Says She has been hopefully thinking she shall be part of my Crown in the Great Day—which Expression of hers fill'd me with deep Humiliation at the Sense of my own infinite unworthiness of any such Honour and Happiness—but fervent Desire and Longing that it might be so!

15. Sent Billy with a Letter to Mr. Ebenezer Chamberlin about Clabboards—and another to Jonas Bradish. Mr. Cook here and reckon'd with him. P.M. attended the Funeral of Mr. Abijah Gale's Infant Child. N.B. Mr. Biglo in the morning finish'd Sawing the Trough. Baldwin with his son John came home to me: but Parkhurst went to Deacon Newtons.

16. Read Numb. 4. Preach'd on Prov. 16, 31. Din'd at the usual place, my wife and Sundry Small Children Stay'd at and nigh the meeting House. P.M. read Acts 22. In preaching, repeated sermon on Tit. 3, 12, from page 121 to 127 from Gen. 17, 1. An Hour after the public services I went to Mr. Hezekiah Pratts and read to his wife some of my Notes on Mat. 11, 28. She having express'd to me divers Times that she receiv'd much of the Benefits of God's Ordinances thereby. A Number of Neighbours also were present.

17. David How junior of Sudbury here to acquaint me that the Designed Council is put off to Some future Time. Ebenezer So out of Health that he goes to Day to Dr. Smith,[14] is blooded

---

[5] The Reverend Joseph Dorr of Mendon.
[6] The Reverend John Owen (Harvard 1723), the minister of the First Congregational Church of Groton, Conn., 1727–1753. *Sibley*, VII, 244–247.
[7] The Reverend David Hall of Sutton.
[8] The Reverend Samuel Barrett of Hopkinton.
[9] The Reverend Joseph Davis of Holden.
[10] Burnet's work first appeared as *Archaeologiae Philosophicae: sive Doctrina Antiqua de Rerum Originibus* (London, 1692). Other editions, some in English translations, followed. The editor has found no record of publication of the translation of the dedication by the late Justice Paul Dudley.
[11] The Reverend Israel Loring of Sudbury.
[12] Benjamin Flagg, Jr.
[13] The Reverend John Seccomb of Harvard.
[14] Dr. Joshua Smith of Shrewsbury. Ward, *Shrewsbury*, p. 436.

and took Physick. A Showery Day. At Eve came Mr. Zebulon Baldwin in behalf of his Father David Baldwin with a Load of Work and stuff for my New House, viz. 13 Frames and 15 setts of Sashes (Jeduthun Baldwin makes the 2 Frames for the Garrett But Mr. Baldwin of Leicester all the Sashes) he brought also 3 inner Doors—and 425 feet of white pine Boards which I bought of him at 30/ old Tenor per Hundred. He and his Team were entertain'd here over night—and

18. In the Morning put in my Three Creatures and carry'd over the Load to my New House. N.B. Lieutenant Tainter there and paid me 15£ old Tenor which I paid Mr. Baldwin for his Father. N.B. Lieutenant Tainter was very Sharp upon me about the pride of Ministers, when he saw the Window Frames—and tho I reprov'd him, for the unseasonableness of it, being before such a Number of Strangers, yet I endeavour'd to let him know that I was myself griev'd that the windows were so large and I have often said it that I wish'd they were less—but I was much more surpriz'd and troubl'd when I found that the posts of the House were a full foot shorter than I gave orders for and depended upon. This was a Disappointment which Somewhat mov'd me—being laid with a number of other Afflictions—but may God grant patience! Mr. Cushing[15] and Mr. Martyn with their wives, here; I and mine waited upon them to Southboro to See Mr. Stone and his New Spouse.[16] We all din'd there; Mr. Loring also with us; and return'd at Eve. N.B. Mr. Elisha Jones[17] of Weston here, but did not lodge. Sister Hannah Champney[18] here from Sutton, brought by Brother Hicks who return'd home.

19. Ebenezer not well—but mow'd a little—the Yard and Garden. I Sent my son William to the Island with my Mare to plough to Day under the Guidance of Mr. Williams who with Esquire Baker and a son of his with an Horse and Plough, Mr. David Maynard junior and a Son, Mr. Eleazer Williams, Mr. Benjamin Fay, Adonijah Rice, Abner Whipple, Daniel Grout. These plough'd and hoed till between 10 and 11—when they finish'd it. I waited on them with some refreshment and acknowledg'd my great indebtedness to them for it. P.M. Mr. Benjamin Fay here. He desires, in behalf of the Committee that I would step to them which I did—they Sat at Mr. Ebenezer Maynards. What they requested of me was to give them a Receipt in full of the Grant in February 8, 1744/5 and which I offer'd to do for them if they could assure me it was the Desire of the Precinct that I Should do it; which they did—or at least, they desir'd it in their Name. Whereupon, I comply'd therewith though I did not deliver it now; but told 'em I would write over again, what I had written and it was requested that I would give it to the Precinct Clerk, Mr. Benjamin Fay. I made them also several offers of my part with a Number (if Such would join) and poor as [illegible] I am and Family as I have yet would stand Equal with the richest in the precinct to put an End to the Quarrell with Mr. James Maynard. Some of the Committee gratefully acknowledg'd themselves oblig'd to me—but Deacon Newton Said he did not think the precinct expected or desir'd Mr. Parkman to be burden'd with that Affair, but would do their Duty about it themselves. N.B. sent to Boston for Colouring by Thomas Whipple. Lucy Bowker at Night.

20. Lucy Bowker works here again for Ebenezer. Thomas to Sutton, to the Raising of their New Meeting House. I Catechiz'd a.m. at the School-House, but no one ask'd me to dinner anywhere; so that I return'd home, din'd with my own Family. P.M. I rode over to the North End to get short Clabboards of Captain Eager, but he, as was also Mr. Martyn and his wife at private meeting at Lieutenant Holloway's. So that I went there also—did not succeed about more Clabboards—went home with Mr. Martyn. Send by him (if he goes to Boston next Monday) to Mr. Kneeland concerning the Collection of Poems which is propos'd to be printed. Supp'd with them by Day Light and return'd home. Ebenezer still not well.

21. Part of the forenoon assisted Ebenezer in mending Fence in the furthermost Pasture—a large Steer being very unruly. My wife is grown much lamer ever since we rode to Southborough. Sarah Sick—no doubt by eating Currans and Cherrys. P.M. Necessity obliging I rode to Mr. Whipples[19] for Nails, Bradds and Colours, brought up from Boston by his son Thomas. Carry'd 'em to the New House—rode to Mr. Twitchells at Eve. My son Thomas return'd from Sutton Meeting-House-Raising.

22. Ebenezer is better: he mows between the House and Barn. Thomas mows over the Clear'd ground at the New House. Lucy Bowker here still. P.M. Mr. Hutchinson,[20] in complyance with a Letter which I sent him Yesterday, came—but it was So late I did not get up to Grafton before Sun Setting. By Mr. Hutchinson's Desire I call'd to see the Child of Mr. Samuel Cooper and at Mr. Cooper's request I pray'd with them. N.B. Dr. Morse[21] there. I lodg'd at Mr. Hutchinsons.

23. I preach'd at Grafton a. and p.m. on Mat. 16, 26, and Baptiz'd Nehemiah, of John and [blank] Adams. Return'd to Westborough in the Night. Mr. Hutchinson preach'd at Westborough on Rev. 1, latter part of number 5 and on [blank]. He din'd at Lieutenant Tainters.

24. Ebenezer mows at home. Thomas carrys a Barrell of Cyder to the New House and mows over the Clear'd Ground to it. Neighbour Eliezer Rice, in his Feebleness here, more Discourse about his Childs Baptism. P.M. I visited Mary Lattiner who lies sick at Deacon Forbush's. N.B. Jonas Bradish leaves Word that he cannot get me the Clabboards which my work-men are now ready to call for, which Disappointment putts me into no Small Difficulty. N.B. Lieutenant Tainter and his son, Messers. Harrington, Solomon Woods and Zebulon Rice came a little before night and pulled away Some of the Gravel at the fore side of my New House. Dr. Smith at Eve.

25. My Wife growing very Lame, I waited on her to Lieutenant Bezaleal Eagers,[22] where She was blooded by Dr. Smith. I left her and proceeded up the Road to enquire after Clabboards—hearing of Some at Worcester I road up there—call'd at Mr. Cushings and at Captain Jennisons[23]—din'd at Mr. Maccartys. Bought a thousand of White Pine Clabboards of Captain Chandler, for 20£ old Tenor. Return'd to my Wife at Eagers, were both of us decently entertain'd: and, with my mind much reliev'd by my Success, came home in peace. Another Swarm of Bees, or Two which Captain Maynard hives—and is much Stung.

26. Sent Mr. John Rogers with my Team for Clabboards at Worcester, who brought 'em, though in the Night first. N.B. Mr. Robert Jennison (William Parkhursts Master) here, with his Wife and Brother. Mr. Stephen Maynard here, and we reckon'd. His Mother also was here. N.B. Their Extraordinary bountifulness in the Reckoning particularly in sinking the account of 43 pounds of Butter to 23, and this at 4/ per pound when I suppose the price is not much less than 5/—and in throwing in the bringing up of the Box of Glass for my New House; and in some other Respects, which Things are besides many presents of Meat, Cheese etc.

27. Brother Hicks here and Carrys Sister Hannah Champney to Cambridge. Ebenezer and Thomas mowing. Ebenezer hangs a New, Small, Grindstone of 40/ old Tenor. I visited Mrs. Pratt and Eliezer Rice's Child.

28. The Young Men who finish my New House are daily at Work, but can't go to See 'em every Day.

29. Brother Hicks from Cambridge din'd here. Sent by him to Mr. Benjamin Fay, the Precincts Clerk, a Receipt in Full for the 500£ grant. This I have done at the Committees Desire for peace sake. Baldwin and John Woods at Eve.

30. Read Numb. 5. Preach'd on Prov. 16, 31. Din'd as usual. P.M. read Acts 23. Preach'd on Lev. 19, 32. Appointed the Communion but put by the Lecture.

---

[15] The Reverend Job Cushing of Shrewsbury.

[16] The Reverend Nathan Stone of Southborough married his second wife, Mary, the daughter of the Reverend Peter Thacher of Middleborough, May 16, 1751.

[17] Jones held various town offices and later represented Weston in the General Court.

[18] Parkman's first wife's sister, who had been visiting her sister, Mrs. John Hicks of Sutton.

[19] Francis Whipple of Westborough.

[20] The Reverend Aaron Hutchinson of Grafton.

[21] Dr. Benjamin Morse, the physician of Sutton. Benedict & Tracy, *Sutton*, p. 698.

[22] Of the north precinct, and later a representative of Westborough, Kent, *Northborough*, pp. 280–281.

[23] Israel Jennison of Worcester.

## JULY, 1751

1. Mr. Twitchell and Mr. Daniel Warrin of the west-side, got stones and built upon the Wall at the West End of my Dwelling House. P.M. Mr. Davis[1] of Holden and his Wife. Afterwards Mr. Maccarty[2] and Mr. Wellman,[3] here in their Journey to Commencement. A Clap of hard Thunder. At Eve I rode to Mr. Martyns for my Watch (which he has made to go again)—and return'd immediately.

2. Mr. Cushing and his Wife here on their Journey to Cambridge. Ebenezer and Thomas also rode down. I visited Mrs. Pratt. Din'd at Deacon Newton's where my young Carpenters board. I visited at Mr. Ebenezer Rice's where two Children have the Throat Distemper. Was at Mr. Charles Rice's and at Captain Bakers. An hot Day. At Eve I was much tir'd with my Walks. Wrote to Mr. Edmund Quincy[4] about my Collection of Poems.

3. Keep Solitary Commencement at Home. It was Mr. Martyns Lecture and he has ask'd me to assist him in it: but I was not without apprehension I should be oblig'd to attend upon the private meeting (if I tarry in Town); and therefore refus'd him: but if I could have forseen my not going to Cambridge I should have both appoint'd our own Lecture, which I Should have endeavour'd to have him preach, and likewise have assisted him to Day in his. P.M. marry'd Adonijah Rice[5] to Hannah Crosby.[6]

4. Last night were heavy rains and high winds. This morning very rainy, even to floods. P.M. came two of Brother Hicks's Dauters, viz. Hannah and Betty. Would have gladly attended the private Meeting, which I hear is at Mr. Whitnys, but I expected an Invitation and an Horse, if they desir'd me; but neither Word or Horse had I. Yet I do not resent it; for possibly they know not I am in Town—tho I may think that enough has been Said to Spread the Knowledge of it. It was also somewhat Showery. P.M. Several Neighbours join'd together to levell the Bank of Gravell at the West End of my New House. They were Neighbour Ebenezer and Nathan and Phinehas Maynard. John Rogers and John Frost and Cornelius Cook. Mrs. Pratt sinks yet lower.

5. Rainy Day again. Mr. Ebenezer Rice and his wife Sent for me; their youngest son being dead by the Throat Distemper, and their little Dauter ill also of the Same. At the New House in my Return. Very letting season.

6. Our Kinswoman (Hicks's) return home to Sutton. Weather dull yet. Ebenezer and Thomas return'd from Commencement. They came from Marlborough this Morning, having lodg'd at Dr. Gotts. P.M. Funeral of Mr. Ebenezer Rice's youngest Child. Dy'd by the Throat Distemper.

7. Had not compleated what I design'd for the Sacramental Exercise, and by Reason of my Circumstances, together with my indisposedness (not without too Criminal Indisposedness of Mind and Negligence) could prepare no other; and therefore repeat'd both a. and p.m. Read Numb. 6. Preach'd on 1 Cor. 5, 7. Administer'd the Lord's Supper. My Wife and Dauter tarried at the Meeting House. I din'd at the Justice's. P.M. read Acts 21. Preach'd on 1 Cor. 5, 6, 7, 8. N.B. I expressly told the Audience it was not what I had design'd, but what they had had before. Appointed Church Meeting and Catechizing at Mr. Joslins.

8. Church Meeting at one p.m. at the Desire of Eliezer Rice, who wants to have his infant Child baptiz'd but acknowledges himself tho not utterly to deny Original Sin, yet to be most apt to deny the Imputation of Adams Guilt to his Posterity. Mr. Rice did not appear to be very expert in the Controversy: and was therefore perswaded to take things into better Consideration. After Meeting call'd in to see Mrs. Pratt (as I frequently do passing backwards or forwards) but she is now as a breathing Corps. Sir Forbush was with me—and Mr. Martyn and his wife were

at our House. N.B. Mr. Martyn Show'd me the Advertisement which is publish'd by my Direction of Proposals to print a Collection of Poems, etc. He informed me also of a Fast which Dr. Gott proposes to have kept at his House next week, by the assistance of Mr. Smith, Mr. Martyn and Mr. Stone.

9. Visited Mrs. Pratt who revives a little. Visited Mr. Jonah Warrin who is ill. P.M. attended the Funeral of another of Mr. Ebenezer Rice's Children, which has dy'd by the Throat Distemper, and Mrs. Rice is in some measure troubl'd with it. P.M. my workman Baldwin went to Shrewsbury. He return'd and lodg'd at my House.

10. Very hot Day. My Sons Ebenezer and Thomas are daily Hilling and Mowing, except when the Rainy weather which is indeed frequent prevents.

11. Rainy at different parts of the Day. But the forenoon Ebenezer and Thomas attend the Hilling. I rode over to the New House, and down to the South East Corner. Eat at old Mr. Garfields, for Dinner. Catechiz'd at Mr. Joslins. 20 Children. Was generously entertain'd. May God reward 'em! My Sons Ebenezer and Thomas go over this afternoon to Hopkinton to the Marriage of Edmund Rice to Hannah Gashit.

12. It being rainy, or Cloudy, and letting Weather, Ebenezer a.m. Carted over some slit work for stairs—and Boards to the New House. When he returns he tells me that a very considerable number of persons—Lieutenant Tainter etc. have been to Day and Hill'd my Corn at the Cook Field. N.B. Mr. David Maynard junior brot me 12£ of Putty from my Brother Samuel Parkman.

13. Somewhat bright Day but we do nothing at all about Hay. Ebenezer and Thomas after killing a Lamb, went to Hilling. Sent Billy to Mr. Martyns and to Mill.

14. Read Numb. 7. Preach'd a. and p.m. on Isa. 7, 14. P.M. read Acts 25. Din'd as usual, at Justice Bakers. N.B. Mr. Eliezer Rice proposes to offer his infant Child to Day on his Wife's Right, but understanding that I Should Say so in the Congregation he resisted—and being willing and desirous to gratifie him I stop'd the Church to ask them whether it would not Satisfie them (Since they had known how the Case was, and they so would know that it was only on the Mothers Right) if I should proceed to baptize that Child when it shall be offer'd without saying anything Publickly at the time of the Administration. Their Silence was propos'd should give Consent; and it did so. I publickly desir'd the Members of other Churches would get their Dismissions.

15. Undertook Something of glazing—one Small Garrett Sash completed. P.M. Mr. Abijah Gale and his wife here with their Relations. Thomas lies by, not well.

16. Exceeding hot. Thomas much out of order. P.M. I set the Glass of another Sash. Visit Mrs. Pratt, and Mr. Ebenezer Rice's Son who has the Throat Distemper.

17. Lieutenant Tainter here in the Morning and deliver'd me 22£10/ old Tenor. My Wife and I rode to Captain Bakers, where lodges Mr. Thomas Chase, a young Practitioner in Physick and Surgery. My wife blooded by him. Neighbours John Rogers and John Frost reap Rye, p.m. but do not get it down, tho it be but an Acre. Mr. Fish of Upton here to ask me to preach his Lecture next Friday; but I am oblig'd to deny him.

18. I rode over to Mr. Martyns, but he with Mr. Smith of Marlborough were gone to visit Mr. Morse. Thomas takes a Vomit. Neighbours John Rogers and Frost reap'd again, a.m., and din'd with us. P.M. Mr. David Baldwin here. N.B. he counts the Doors which he made for me (which are four pannell, and raised and quarter rounded on both sides) at 2 Days work apiece—and at 3£ 5/ whereas Mr. Goodwin (who was the prizer of them from the account I gave him) had set them at far less.

19. Ebenezer to the Meadow to Cart Hay; Mr. Samuel Hardy who has taken it to Cut and rake it having been with 4 Hands, the Day before yesterday to mow, and Two Hands Yesterday to rake. Mr. David Baldwin and I reckon'd—and he consented to take an hundred pounds old Tenor for work and stuff which I have had of him paid him 20£ old Tenor (which makes up 45£ of what I have paid him in Cash) receiv'd his Order to pay Mr. Stephen Manyard 40£ and gave him a Note for 15 more (old

---

[1] The Reverend Joseph Davis.
[2] The Reverend Thaddeus Maccarty of Worcester.
[3] The Reverend James Wellman of Millbury.
[4] Squire Quincy (Harvard 1722) of Braintree.
[5] The son of Charles Rice of Westborough.
[6] The daughter of David Crosby of Shrewsbury.

Tenor). Mr. Morris made us a visit—Mr. Stone and his Spouse with him. But my wife exceeding ill: vomiting etc. The Company din'd with us. Mr. Morris lodg'd here. My wife grew better. Blessed be God!

20. Mr. Morris din'd with us, and Sir Forbush waiting upon him to show him the way to Mr. Martyns, he p.m. went there. N.B. Sent Mr. Eliezer Rice word by Forbush (as he return'd to his Father) that I Should not be at home tomorrow. (Otherwise, I should have expected him to bring out his Child to be baptiz'd on his Wife's account). Ebenezer brought home Two Load of Hay to Day.

21. I preach'd at the North End on Hosea 2, 8, 9 and on John 6, 12. Read Numb. [blank] and Acts [blank]. Mr. Morris with us. At Noon and at Eve heavy showers of Rain. I rode to Marlborough to see Dr. Gott who is in a very low State. I lodg'd there. Talk'd plainly to the Doctor—left him. N.B. Overtook Barnes; gave him 8/ old Tenor and we were reconcil'd.

22. Call'd at Mr. Smiths: broke fast at Deacon Matthias Rice's and came home in Safety. Thanks to God! Ebenezer and Thomas Mowing—part of the Barley. Benjamin Gott came up with a Chair and carry'd down his aunt to See his Father. Mrs. Mary Bradish pulls Flax. Neighbour John Rogers, with his Oxen added to my Team, went with Ebenezer to Meadow and brought home Two Load of Hay. Molly to Deacon Forbush. Sent my Horse to Boston per Ebenezer Forbush for my Brother William. N.B. On the 22nd at Eve, while I was in great Concern of Mind about Mrs. Rachel Pratts State (apprehended to be dying and yet uncertain whether she was ready) She receiv'd gracious manifestations and discoverys of the preciousness of the Lord Jesus Christ and her Interest in Him. Glory be to the Name of God!

23. The rest of the Barley cut down. P.M. Solemnized the Nuptials of the Reverend Mr. Fish[7] and Mrs. Hannah Forbush.[8] My son Ebenezer and Dauter Molly there.

24. Ebenezer got home another Load of Hay from the Meadow, got in Barley etc. Cousen Proctor[9] to Oxford in the Morning. As we rose from Dinner came my Brother Parkman and having refresh'd himself began to assist me in putting my Glass into the Sashes. N.B. He informs me that my Cousen Oliver[10] has lost her Alexander and that Samuel Bradshaw junior[11] lies very Sick.

25. Ebenezer and Thomas Spend the forepart of the Day in mending the Fence at the Island. Molly with Sir Forbush, to wait on the Reverend Mr. Fish and his Bride to Upton. I rode over to Mr. Martyns, and borrow'd his Chair, in which I went to Marlborough to Dr. Gotts for my Wife. The Doctor was insensible as in a Dying State. We attempted to come away, but when we were dining at Mr. Smiths, came a Messenger that the Doctor was dying. We return'd and tarry'd till after 4 p.m. and left him Still breathing. Came home in Comfort. To God the Glory! My Brother sett Glass to Day.

26. My Brother to the New House. Ebenezer mows. Thomas and William reap Rye. Mr. Samuel Brigham came in the Morning and told us that the Doctor dy'd yesterday about ¾ after 5 p.m. Mr. Samuel Procter return'd to us from Oxford—in his Way to Boston. Din'd and lodg'd here.

27. My Dauter Lucy and I rode down to Marlborough (using by his leave, Mr. Martyns Chair) to the Funeral of Dr. Gott.[12] Mr. Smith[13] Said he was not well, and desir'd me to pray—but I refus'd. Mr. Martyn and Mr. Stone being there the former of those pray'd. Mr. Smith, when the Corps was carry'd forth, took the other Ministers home to his House. I walk'd with Colonel Williams to the Grave. When we return'd from the Grave I refus'd to tarry to Supper, because the Sabbath was so nigh. We made haste home.

28. This week past also I was So prevented Studying that I was oblig'd today to preach old Sermons. N.B. my Brother

William sabbatizing with us. A.M. I read Numb. 6, 8 and preach'd on Heb. 1, 3—upholding all Things etc. P.M. read Acts 26, and preach'd the Sermon on Col. 1, 21 to page 14 but from 2 Cor. 5, 18. My Wife, my Brother, Son William, Jeduthan Baldwin and John Woods din'd with me at my New House.

29. Deacon Newtons son Peter very bad of the Throat Distemper and three more are ill. In the morning visited there. My Brother who is setting Glass at my New House, and my Two workmen there, dine at Deacon Newtons. Ebenezer and I dine at the New House. When they return from Dinner they bring sorrowful News that little Peter is dead. At Eve the Rain prevail'd so that my Brother and I lodg'd at the New House all Night; Ebenezer having carted over Bed—Bedstead and Bedding. Baldwin and his man ran up to the Widdow Newtons and lodg'd there: for Deacon Newtons House was now in no fit state to entertain them any more.

30. My Brother and I work at the New House, about the Glass. Mr. Eliezer Rice call'd me hastily to Mrs. Pratt who is thought to be dying—yet she reviv'd by that I got to her. Deacon Newton invit'd both me and my Brother to dine with him. My Brother accept'd and din'd there accordingly but I din'd at home yet hasten'd to the Deacons, his son John being very ill. P.M. Peter Newton burying. After Burying we return'd to our work at the Puttying Windows. Baldwin and his man lodg'd at the New House. Brother and I came home. The Waters are exceedingly rais'd by the heavy Rains of last night.

31. Rain again. Brother and my son Thomas to the New House. Ebenezer getting a Well-Crotch for the Well at the New House. P.M. I was there myself rubbing and cleaning Glass, as my Brother was engag'd in pinning it in. Thomas with his Brother mow'd, Some part of the upper South Side.

## AUGUST [1751].

1. At Deacon Newtons[1] whose son John is thought to be very dangerously ill. At Mr. Pratts. Neighbour Stephen Maynard going to Boston with his Team, my Brother after Spending the forenoon about my new Windows, and dining with us rides my Mare to Boston. Ebenezer Carts a Well-Crotch, Bed, Powdering Tubb with Pork etc. to the New House. Boards also from the Mill. Thomas and William reap Wheat. P.M. they rake Hay in the Southside and Ebenezer mows.

2. John Newton sends for me being near his End. Went: he wants I Should repeat to him the Discourse I had with him yesterday. Pray'd with him. Stephen Newton[2] is taken ill with the Same Distemper. Call'd at Mrs. Pratts—she is just gone—has inward Comfort, but great outward Trouble. Molly and Sarah go over to tarry at the New House to dress the Carpenters Diet. They lodge there; a Second Bed being Set up there. P.M. heavy Showers of Rain.

3. John Newton dy'd last Night: and Stephen's illness increases. May God in his great Mercy look upon that afflicted Family and Spare them! Neighbour Stephen Maynard brings my Mare back from Boston, which has been very troublesome to him, and was the occasion of his Cart's being over-turn'd. He brot me 11½ Gallons of Rhum.

4. Read Numb. ninth Chaper A.M. and preach'd the last Sermon on Col. 1, 21 from page 31 with additions. Din'd with my Family at the New House. P.M. read Acts 27 and preach'd on Job 15, 11, with a View to the Afflicted Cases of Several Familys in the Parish.

5. Deacon Kimball[3] of Hopkinton came to Plaister the West End of my New House. Mrs. Rachel Pratt, the Wife of Neighbour Hezekiah Pratt, dy'd about 1 P.M. I was with her a.m. and we talk'd of her Decease—she having comfortable Evidence of Grace. Mr. Pratt has carry'd himself in a very exemplary Manner towards his Wife; and his House is now turn'd into a Bochim.[4] The Lord Sanctifie this Death not only to them but to all of us! Stephen Newton Sick of the Throat Distemper but is thot to be better.

---

[7] Elisha Fish of Upton.
[8] The daughter of Deacon Jonathan Forbush.
[9] Parkman's niece, Mrs. Samuel Proctor.
[10] Parkman's niece, Mrs. Edward Oliver.
[11] The son of Parkman's niece, Mrs. Samuel Bradshaw.
[12] Benjamin Gott, the physician of Marlborough, was Parkman's brother-in-law.
[12] The Reverend Aaron Smith of Marlborough.

[1] Josiah Newton.
[2] Another son of Deacon Newton.
[3] Ebenezer Kemble.
[4] Judges, II, 1–5.

6. Deacon Kimbal at the New House. Baldwin and his Man John all this Time there and my Dauter Molly lodges and works also, tending upon the Workmen in their Meals etc. Mrs. Pratt was bury'd and with much Lamentation. May it please God to enable us to improve this Breach. Mr. Martyn[5] came here while I was gone to Mrs. Pratts Funeral.

7. Deacon Kimball, as well as the Carpenters. I am over there Daily. Go to Mr. Bradishs and fetch upward of 200 Lath upon my Horse before me. Ebenezer Carted Stuff for Cellar Stairs, and for a Stack Yard. Thomas assisted him part of the Day.

8. Deacon Kimball etc. Ebenezer and Thomas Carted Two Load of Hay from the Meadow to the New Stack Yard which was mow'd last Saturday was sennight, and was made up the Friday following—being drench'd by the Storms of Rain. Enough for Some Number of Cocks was left finally, and lost. Yet I suppose Mr. Samuel Hardy (who had the work in his Hands) took what Care he could but it prov'd a very wet Season.

9. At the New House. Deacon Kimball, and his Son Ebenezer lay on the Plaistering. Cornelius Cook[6] tends them. The Carpenters Still there and Molly and Susé to provide for us. Ebenezer and Thomas Cart one Load more from the Meadow to the New Stack-Yard—having stack'd up the remainder of the Hay at the Meadow, there till some better Season for Carting it. Towards Night they came home to mowing. Have much of our haying to do, when many others are done. Deacon Newton came for me to visit his son Stephen who grows worse. Went according and discours'd and pray'd with him. Visited also the Widow Newton.[7] At Night the Walls of my New House being so green and damp, with the New Mortar, no body cares to lodge within them. Deacon and Baldwin make up a Couch in the unfinish'd part of the House. Molly and Suse go to the Widow Newtons. Others disperse otherwise.

10. Ebenezer mows, and tends Hay all Day. I am in the morning in no small Trouble for an Hand to tend Plaisterers. Am forc'd to Send Thomas. They finish to Day.

11. Read Numb. 10 and preach'd on 1 Cor. 6, 9, the first 4 pages, which I deliver'd in the Year 1727/8. My Family din'd at the New House. Mr. Stephen Maynard at noon came for me to go up to Stephen Newton who is nigh expiring and I comply'd. P.M. read the last Chapter of Acts. Went on with 1 Cor. 6, 9, 10, 11. Deliver'd page 5 and from page 13 to 19. (For altho I had prepar'd in part on Job 15, 11, Yet I could not finish it, having So many Different Cares and Encumbrances at the Time of So many workmen, and at such a Distance from home.) Stephen Newton Expir'd p.m.

12. At the New House with the Carpenters. P.M. at the Funeral of Stephen Newton. N.B. had Din'd at Mr. Martyn's— and Committed to his Care a paper for Subscriptions to My Collection of Poems, he being about to go to ministers Meeting at Stow tomorrow, or likely to see several ministers in their Journey there. Hot Day.

13. Hot Weather; and yet I go to the New House my Workmen finishing for the present, what they can do for me.

14. Jeduthun Baldwin and John Woods go over to work at the Meeting House at the North End of the Town. Their Tools carry'd over in Mr. Martyns Chair, drawn by my mare. I agree to give Baldwin 18/ old Tenor per Day for 60 Days, to his Journeyman, William Parkhurst, 15/ per Day, 26 Days and to his Apprentice, John Woods 10£, lumping the Latter part of his Time. (The former part he was so new and raw, nothing more than his Diet could be expected.) In all, my Debt to Baldwin is 83£10s., old Tenor—his Credit 3£10. This Day due to him 80£. N.B. he offers to take 75£ if I pay him 40£ within a Month, and 35 within 2 months More, or give him Bond for it. The Same Day My Son Thomas carted over my Desk, Study Table, and a Number of Books, etc. Ebenezer went over and with Edwards Whipple and a few more, rais'd the Well-Crotch and sweep. P.M. They went to their Haying at home.

[5] The Reverend John Martyn of the north precinct.
[6] The son of Parkman's neighbor.
[7] Mrs. Thomas Newton.

15. Molly has liv'd at the New House ever since we dieted the Workmen, to Day she went home, and after much hard work in the Day return'd at Eve. I visited Mrs. Martha Warrin[8] in the Morning. Over to the other House to point sashes tho I do but little of it. I tarried all Day at the New-House. Din'd there alone, but went back to Mrs. Parkman at Night: She being full of pain; has strange Cramps. Has also Indications that her Travail is not far off. The Lord prepare her and all of us for the Changes before us. Rainy and stormy Night. N.B. my mind in much Exercise by Reason of the great Urgency that we remove and yet our House and place there exceedingly unfit to receive us. The Hearth's unlaid, the Banks of Gravel at Each Door unlevelled. No pasture for a Cow, or feed or Hay for an Horse etc. etc.

16. Exceeding rainy and stormy Morning. Thomas lodg'd at the New House last Night and remains there this morning to clear out the Cellar, Shavings etc. Ebenezer goes to him to join with him therein. I rode over. Six of us dine here, and here I must begin to Study. Clearer weather p.m.

17. I lodg'd at the New House. My Family here and Molly, Susé and Alexander. A very fine clear Day. Ebenezer in the Morning brought over another Barell of Cyder, and Severall Boxes of Books and Pamphletts. Mr. Samuel Harrington and Mr. Phinehas Hardy brought each of them an heavy Load of Large Flatt Stones from Mr. Harringtons Quarry, for my Hearths and passage to the Well, etc., both which were gratis. Daniel How din'd with us.

18. Read Numb. 11, preach'd on 1 Cor. 6, 11. Din'd at the New House. P.M. read Rom. 1. I gave an account of the Epistle and the Contents of the first Chapter. Preach'd on Job 15, 11. Return'd to the old House at Eve, with Mr. John Green[9] who (as also old Mr. Joseph Green) din'd with me to Day.

19. At the New House in the morning—when I came back rode up to Mr. Asa Brighams to desire Mrs. Brigham to release Hannah Pratt to nurse my wife. N.B. was at Mr. Gershom Brighams who made me a present of Cheese—and visited Mr. Samuel Fays Wife: but din'd at Mr. Joseph Knowltons who gave me ¾ Bushel Rye. When I came home, found Mr. Cushing, and Several Women, our near Neighbours to see Mrs. Parkman, who is every Day and Night in great Pain, and has been for some Time. Here was also Mrs. Patty Haven, and with her Deacon Burnaps[10] Dauter. Those last lodg'd with us.

20. The Young Women rode with me to the New House, and we din'd there p.m. I rode back and brought my Wife here to the New House, where now we take up our Dwelling, for the present, at least. O may God be pleas'd to take up His Dwelling with us. Rainy morn. They work part of the Day in Clearing out Shavings and Dirt out of the New House. At Eve, while we were in our New Circumstances, came Mrs. Peggy and Mrs. Isabella Breck, wifes of Messers. John[11] and Robert Breck[12] of Boston; (accompany'd by Captain Maynard) and they lodg'd here.

21. I waited upon the Ladys as far as the Edge of Southborough in their Journey. My sons Ebenezer and Thomas go to mowing at the Island—but by Various Hindrances, did not begin to mow there till late in the forenoon. My Wife grew so ill that we were glad to See Mrs. Forbush[13] (the Midwife) coming to See us. And we detain'd her all night. Mrs. Bekky Warrin with her Child here, and tarrys to her Aunts Labour.

22. Mrs. Forbush tripp'd away home just after break of Day. But my wife grew so bad that I hastily rode away for her again and brought her. It proves a very hot Day; but we must gather the Neighbouring Women. I rode up the Street and alarm'd the four nearest, and proceeded for Mrs. Baker—likewise for Mrs.

[8] Mrs. Daniel Warrin.
[9] This was perhaps a man by that name, referred to as "a sore trial to the thrifty farmers who had to 'entertain' him by turns, and who appointed successive committees in town meeting to ascertain whether he belonged of right in town, and whether he had no relatives anywhere who could support or relieve him." DeForest and Bates, *Westborough*, p. 105.
[10] Benjamin Burnap of Hopkinton.
[11] Mrs. Parkman's cousin, a merchant of extensive business, often engaged in the Newfoundland fishery. Samuel Breck, *Genealogy of the Breck Family* (Omaha, 1889), pp. 18-19.
[12] This cousin of Mrs. Parkman was a cooper of Boston.
[13] Old "Granny" was the widow of Thomas Forbush.

Nurse and Mrs. Williams who came—and Suddenly about 11 o'Clock a.m. a Son was born. My Twelfth living Child, and my Sixth living Son. The Name of the Lord be magnifyed! May I obtain the Grace to walk in Wisdom and faithfullness towards all the Children which he has graciously given to me! P.M. I preach'd the Sacramental Lecture from 1 Tim. 6, 2. "Partakers of the Benefit." It prov'd a very trying Time to me: But may God Support me through! After Lecture I got Mr. William Nurse to lead up my Mare to Mr. Eleazer Pratts for his Dauter Hannah, who came at Evening to Nurse my wife.

23. Our Hay both at the Island and at home, wet. At Eve very heavy Rains. N.B. Mr. Charles Rice (who came and hoop'd our Bear–Barrell, and does various Chores at different Times) with divers others who came likewise, fitted a Draught-Pole for the Well.

24. Mr. Daniel Forbush came and laid the west Chamber Hearth. My mind greatly Exercis'd on Account of the Great Solemnitys before me; especially considering how very slender my preparation is, in all respects.

25. My Great Care was that both my Wife and I might trans-act aright with the glorious God in the Important Work of this Day. Read (publickly) Numb. 12. Preach'd on 1 Pet. 1, 19. The precious Blood of Christ. Deacon Forbush,[14] his sister Byles,[15] and Mrs. Eleazer Harrington, (Mrs. Bonds Sister) din'd with us. P.M. read Rom. 2. Preach'd on Job 15, 11, and bap-tiz'd my Son Samuel. And may God accept him and make him a Great and rich Blessing to us! I have call'd him by this Name, out of respect and Affection to my Brother Samuel at Boston. May he be so endow'd as to be worthy of it!

26. Ebenezer Carted over my principall Book Presses, and several Boxes more. And it seems now like something of Remove. I was at Morning Prayer with my Children at my former Dwell-ing. After Exercises I gave them Exhortation and Solemn Charge to keep the Way of the Lord. May they have Grace to attend to it and observe it! Before we parted from home, came Mr. Martyn and his Wife, accompany'd by Mr. Michael Dennis, Bookseller in Boston. Who all went with me to the New House. Where came also to visit us Mr. Miller and Mrs. Harrington each with a Cheese. Thomas to the Island a. and p.m. Ebenezer only latter part of P.M. Lieutenant Wood of Hopkinton here.

27. Ebenezer and Thomas Cart 3 Load of Hay from the Island and stack it at the New House.

28. Rode over to Mr. Martyns and din'd there. I preach'd a Lecture at the North End, on Ps. 116, 9, and at Eve return'd home.

29. Mr. Frost and Rogers mow'd with Ebenezer in the Swamp at home, endeavouring to cutt down all to Day that we can come at to mow. Nathaniel Whitney and his Brother in their going with a Team to the Meadow, brought me two Load of stones for the underpinning the East End of my New House. Mr. Daniel Forbush work'd here in laying the west room Hearth but did not finish it. Brother Hicks here.

30. At Night reckon'd with Lieutenant Tainter and with Merchant Rice, and Settled our accounts.

31. I walk'd over to my Farm House, having no Horse here at the New, from thence I might Set out for Southborough whither I went towards Evening—got there when the Sun was about an Hour high, and Mr. Stone[16] came to Westborough. N.B. Madam Thatcher[17] of Middleborough there. N.B. She Show'd me the Notes of her Husband, of his Father, and his Grandfather.

### SEPTEMBER, [1751]

1. Preach'd at Southborough—a.m. on 2 Cor. 3, 15. P.M. on number 14, 17, and baptiz'd David, Son of David Newton. Mr. Stone at Westborough on 1 Tim. 4, 8. He also read. At Eve we each of us return'd to his respective home. May the Lord pardon what has been amiss; and accept and bless what was agreeable to His Will!

14 Jonathan Forbush.
15 Mrs. Joseph Byles of Westborough.
16 The Reverend Nathan Stone of Southborough.
17 The widow of the Reverend Peter Thacher of Middleborough.

2. I sent Billy with a Team to the North-End-Meeting House for a Cyder screw made by Deacon Livermore[1] for me—one of those made by Woolly having Scal'd and Split so much that it is useless; and it is lodg'd at the North Meeting House, under the Care of Mr. Jeduthan Baldwin, who is at work there. I rode after him least some Disaster Should befall him. I din'd at Cap-tain Eagers. A.M. reading Ansons Voiage round the world by Walter.[2] Ebenezer and Thomas mend the Fence of the Pasture at the Island and bring a milk Cow, and Two fatting Creatures to pasture there.

3. Mr. Daniel Forbush came and wrought at the underpinning of the East End of the House, and in the Evening finish'd the Hearth in the West Room. N.B. Reckon'd with Mr. Bowman and with Mr. Biglo. Ebenezer gets up the Swamp Hay at home: and Some Rowing. Billy cutts Stalks.

4. Mr. Biglo Sent his Son Cornelius to cutt Stalks at the Island. P.M. a number more of Lads came, viz. Joseph and James Bowman: Samuel and Joseph Harrington, Thomas Hardy, and Daniel Grout, who cutt the rest of the Stalks at the Island and Pik'd up those which were cutt in the forenoon by about 5 o'clock P.M. At Evening reckon'd with Mr. Samuel Hardy, for his cutting and raking and cocking Hay at the ministerial Meadow, and instead of 8£ old Tenor which he took it for, I allow'd him nine; and this even altho, by Divine Providence there was a Considerable Quantity was never rak'd at all, and Some Loads which were Carted home, or stack'd at the Meadow, were so wash'd with heavy Rains that it was of but little Value. Mr. Samuel Haven here and went over to t'other House to lodge. Ebenezer has kill'd some Veal and brought us a part.

5. I observ'd the Day in some Religious Manner. (Vide Natal.). Mr. Haven din'd here. I was in some Difficulty to break off from my retir'd Employment to wait upon him, and not discover my Engagedness another way. I remember'd the words of the Lord in Mat. 6, 18. That thou appear not to mean to fast: and agreeably I went down, convers'd, and eat somewhat at Table—but fearing this interruption I improv'd all the fore-part of the Day as Separately as I could. But alas! all is too broken, uninfluencing, ineffectual! God of his infinite Mercy and Graciousness, pitty and pardon, and grant His Grace and Mercy to Me for the great Redeemers Sake! At Eve Mr. Whipple and Mr. Biglo here.

[The following appears in the Natalitia for September 5, 1751:]

I Endeavour'd to employ myself Separately and religiously—chiefly in the following Acts of Thanksgiving and Praise; Humilia-tion and Penitence; Supplication and Intercession; Self-Dedica-tion and renewing Covenant with God; Resolutions; Considera-tions of Frailty and Morality. In Petitioning and Supplicating the Throne of Grace, Special Subjects were, Pardon and Sancti-fication, Ministerial Qualifications and Success, That God would Sanctifie my present new Circumstances in my beginning the World again in this New Habitation, and particularly Direction and Wisdom to Conduct as all my present state and Case is, Grace to Discharge Relative Dutys, The Spirit of God to Prepare for Death and Eternity, Intercession for especially My Wife—Children—each of them—the Infant—Flock—for Ministers—State of Religion—Friends and Relations.

6. I wrote a Letter to Mr. Pierpoint of New Haven, wraping up in it a Catalogue etc. I rode to Lieutenant Eagers for Con-veyance. Din'd with my Children at my former Dwelling. I hop'd for some Body to come and take up my stalks at the Island, but saw no one. Neighbour How has been burning his Bricks this week.

7. Alexander so ill with Cough and Sore Throat that I had my Cloths on the Chief of the Night.

8. Read Numb. 14. Preach'd a.m. on Job 15, 11. P.M. read Rom. 4 and deliver'd an Expository Exercise on the sixth Com-mandment. Alexander was so comfortable as to go to Meeting.

9. Mr. Samuel Hardy here digging Stones, and I got Charles Rice junior to join with him in digging and drawing Stones till night, for a wall by my House.

1 Jonathan Livermore.
2 George Anson, *A Voyage round the World in Years MDCCXL, I, II, III, IV,* Com-piled by Richard Walter (London, 1748).

10. Charles Rice and his Brother Abner drawing Stones part of the forenoon. Captain and Lieutenant Forbush gather'd up and pik'd the rest of my Stalks at the Island.

11. Ebenezer went with my Oxen in the Rain to Mr. Adams's to help him move his Barn. I rode to Lieutenant Woods at Hopkinton to attend a Fast there at his House and was agreed when he was at our House a fortnight ago, but I found they had had an Exercise there at the Time first appointed. I din'd at Mr. Barrett's[3] and return'd.

12. Was at Mr. Hows Brick Kiln. Went to Mr. Martyns and return'd him his Book of Lord Ansons Voiages. Was at Mr. Wymans to Speak with Mr. Edward Willson. Visit Edmund Rice, and again visited Granny Maynard in her Sickness: her Husband not at Home.

13. Had word that Mr. William Goss at Shrewsbury had Floor Boards which hew'd lay at my Door for a small Matter of ready Money. I borrow'd 3 Dollars at Squire Bakers, and sent Mr. Aaron Nurse to Mr. Goss; but without success—for when he come to see his Boards, he found they had taken Dammage through ill-sticking. But this Affair was a great Interruption to my Studys and Perplexity to my mind. P.M. Eliezer Rice, Mr. Fortner etc.

14. Understand that Ebenezer is now got to making Cyder.

15. Read Numb. 15, and made the Exposition of it for the present. N.B. Neighbour Eliezer Rice was not at Meeting with us. Preach'd from Col. 3, 12, on Mercifulness and Meekness; both in pursuance of my Exposition of the sixth Commandment and because it was just before the Superior Court in this County at which our people are like to have Several Cases. At Night Rain.

16. Very Early in the Morning came Mr. Richard Barns—he tells me that whereas Deacon Newton had sued him for money, and he had resolv'd to withstand him on account of Exorbitant Interest, yet the Deacon after the sermon, yesterday p.m. Spoke to him as soon as they came out of meeting, and desir'd he might See him early next Morning that they might agree, he was now going up to him—But he had an Affair of yet greater Difficulty, for Mr. Gamel (he said) was going to throw him into Jayl and the Execution has been already serv'd upon him, and he must go unless he could this Day obtain 60£ old Tenor value in silver; therefore pray'd me to help him, and offer'd me part of his Land on Sale: would let me have 3 or 4 acres of the Land next to mine. I told him I did not care to Trade with him at Such a Time as this was, with both him and me. With him, as he was in Such a Straight that he would be oblig'd to Sell cheaper than it was worth; and with me, as I was already plung'd deeply into Debt both for Land and for my New House. But he still insisted—and told me that he knew where I could get the money, but he could not upon which he induc'd me to go to Marlborough. As I went I eat at Deacon Matthias Rice's—made the Rest of my Dining among Dr. Gotts Children. It was Proprietors Meeting at Marlborough. I attended it and presented the plot of 5 Acres etc. joining to Chauncy Cedar Swamp and Meadows. Captain Maynard oppos'd it again, as did Ensign Josiah Rice, and tho it was put to vote, it did not pass. I was oblig'd to defer it, and I soon retir'd; try'd to hire money for Neighbour Barns. Succeeded at Mr. Jacob Felton's[4]—receiv'd 28 Dollars. N.B. Could get but 250 whole Bricks at Neighbour Benjamin Hows.

17. Neighbour Barns Sign'd a Deed for 4 Acres of Swamp and Upland joining to my old place: and paid him 27 Dollars for it. Hannah Pratt, our Nurse went away. I went over to Neighbour Hows again about Bricks. Job Cushing junior there from Day to Day with 3 Teams—so that I cannot be Supply'd—for the Kiln turns out poorly, many being broke. Both Cushing and I pick'd out many halves. The whole ones 15/ per Hundred. At Night Rain—in the Rain and Dark came Mr. William Winter of Boston, and Dr. Parkmans Widow, and Mr. Henry Newhall's Wife—Two Chairs. Not having got our Beds from t'other House I was oblig'd to go with Mr. Winter to Mr. Ebenezer Rice's and we lodg'd there.

18. Heavy Rains. The Company din'd with us. P.M. Mr. Winter to Worcester Court. My Kinswoman and Mrs. Newhall to the other House.

19. Mr. Edward Willson works in topping my Chimney—and Mr. Daniel Forbush in building the Wall at the West End of the House. Abner Rice tends Mr. Willson. P.M. came a small Number of Young Men and Lads who help'd me a few Hours in levelling the Banks of Gravell. They were Nathaniel Whitney, Joseph Dudley, Samuel Harrington, Joseph Harrington, Daniel Forbush, Adam Rice. My Kinswoman and Mrs. Newhall here. N.B. A Blunder about Dinner. A Lamb kill'd but was brought afternoon. They return'd to the other House, and I supp'd with them there. N.B. The Case of Mr. James Maynard and Lieutenant Tainter etc., try'd at the Superior Court and Maynard obtain'd Judgment.

20. Mr. Willson and Abner Rice on the Top of the Chimney A.M. but having work'd up my few Bricks, it is left still unfinish'd. The Company return'd to Boston: Molly accompany'd them to Marlborough. N.B. Neighbour Eliezer Rice here at Evening and asks for another Church-Meeting. I give him Several Reasons why it is at this Time utterly unsuitable—especially considering the present frame of many persons by Reason of the Contentions at Court—besides that it is but a little while since we had one at his Desire. Nor was there any Time for me to think of it, my Preparations for the Sabbath being now in Hand, and have but little Opportunity for them. But he went away dissatisfy'd. See a loose paper.

21. A great Frost last Night. My Mind much taken off with Neighbour Rice's Conduct last Night, which was the more to my perplexing as I am thereby So much hinder'd in my Preparations for the Sabbath. Out of wood—and no where to go to get any—forc'd to pick up, round about the House. Have taken Cold and have a grievous Pain in my back.

22. Very Cold Morning. Very great Frost. Sometimes doubted whether I could venture to Meeting, having Such a Pain in my Back. With much Difficulty I went. Read Numb. 16. Forenoon Exercise was an Exposition of the former part of the chapter to number 15. P.M. Read Rom. 6. Made some brief Observations upon it. Preach'd on Col. 3, 7, 8. Made use of the greatest part of what is under Doct. 4 from 1 Cor. 6, 11, but with Alterations and Additions. Heard that Mrs. Mary Bennett, Shopkeeper in Boston dy'd lately. May God Sanctifie this to me, as I was considerably acquainted with her! She was a person of uncommon Abilitys and Attainments.

23. Mr. Hezekiah Pratt kindly brought me a Load of Wood—he had my Oxen with his. Sir Forbush[5] goes to Boston by whom I wrote to my Brother William. Was at Mr. Clafflands. P.M. I visited Neighbour Bathericks Family—Mr. Daniel and Timothy Warrin—Mr. Twitchell—and Patty Pannell being Sick I visited her also at Mr. Jonas Brighams. When I return'd at Eve, heard that my little Breck is ill.

24. Went to See little Breck at t'other House—found him better. Mr. Jotham Maynard came from Mr. Joshua Townsend to desire me to attend the Funeral of a Child of his (about 5 Years old) who has dy'd of the Throat Distemper—He having bury'd his son Joshua, near 10 years old, of the Same Distemper—Mr. Martyn gone to Stow. I rode over, and din'd with Mrs. Martyn. N.B. Messers. Whitney (of Nitchewog)[6] Maccarty, Davis, and Humphreys[7]—going to the Ordination at Weston. Mrs. Martyn rode with me to the Burying at Mr. Townsends. N.B. very few males only 2 from the Neighbourhood there, till they were oblig'd to send out for Neighbours to come and assist by which means they made it late.

25. This Day Mr. Woodward[8] (as I understand) is to be ordain'd at Weston in the Room of Mr. William Williams but I could not go.

[3] The Reverend Samuel Barrett.

[4] At one time a lieutenant and a selectman of Marlborough.

[5] Eli Forbes or Forbush, the son of Deacon Jonathan Forbush of Westborough.

[6] The Reverend Aaron Whitney of the plantation called Nichewoag, which became the town of Petersham in 1754.

[7] The Reverend James Humphrey (Harvard 1744), the minister of Payquage or Pequoig plantation (later the town of Athol), 1750-1782. *Sibley*, XI, 416-418.

[8] The Reverend Samuel Woodward (Harvard 1748), the minister of Weston, 1751-1782. *Sibley*, XII, 349-352.

26. The Reverend Mr. Maccarty din'd here. Tells me that the Ordination went on yesterday without any Lett. The Reverend Mr. Townsend[9] of Needham preach'd on Mat. 11, 16, 17. Sam Bumpso undertakes to mow Bushes on the North East part of my Brigham Lott. Mows a little, and moves off about his Scyth—See no more of him to Day.

27. After a turn of Frosts and rugged Weather, a very fine Warm Day. My Wife went over to the other House, to See Breck who has been ill—and about some necessary Affairs. Mr. Joseph Knowlton and his Wife with a Present (a Legg of Pork, large piece of Pork, a Cheese, and a parcell of dry'd Huckleberrys.) N.B. Mr. Knowlton rode over to my other House and brought back my wife.

28. Fine Warm Weather. Sam Bumpso part of the Day mowed shrubb Bushes.

29. My Wife thro Gods Goodness, So happy as to go to Meeting again—we offer public thanks. Read Numb. 16 from 15 to 35, and for the forenoon Exercise, gave Exposition. P.M. Read Rom. 7, and preach'd on 1 Sam. 2, 1, 6, repeating Somewhat Considerable of Sermon on that Text, but now adding in many places; especially in the Close. But it was a Subject so Suitable (Hannah with her Samuel now come to the House of God) that (as I conceiv'd) I could not resist it. May God pardon what is amiss and graciously accept of me and mine.

30. Samuel Bumpso mows Shrubb Bushes all Day. P.M. This Parish met. I sent a Memorial to the Meeting at the very juncture that a Committee (Mr. Williams and Ensign Miller) were coming to me to see if I had any Thing that I would communicate to them. By and by Lieutenant Tainter came to me from the people to acquaint me that they had granted no otherwise than they us'd to do (400£ old Tenor). I Sent a Reply and Request in Writing. At Eve Captain Baker and Mr. Whipple came and acquainted me that they had consider'd what I Sent to them and had granted 50£ old Tenor more. But had done Nothing about the Wood, That being an Article which they could not manage by virtue of this present Warrant: But people would have it in their Thoughts—and doubtless prepare themselves to Say Something about it when there could be Preparation Time for it.

### OCTOBER, 1751

1. Fine Weather Still. Let Mr. Jonathan Forbush junior have 212 feet of White Oake Boards, to go to Boston, to Mr. James Allen Merchant, Taylor.

2. I rode to Grafton and preach'd the Lecture on Eph. 1, 3 and return'd home at Eve.

3. Preach'd my own Lecture on 1 Cor. 11, 26, from page 12 to 19, from Jam. 4, 8. Sir Forbush brought me from the Reverend Mr. Commissary Price[1] Deism Reveal'd volume 1.[2]

4. 5. [No entries.]

6. Read Numb. 16 from number 35 to the End. Preach'd on Jam. 4, 8. Us'd Sermon on 2 Cor. 11, 26, page 19 to 23. Administer'd the Lord's Supper. P.M. read Rom. 8 and preach'd on Isa. 7, 14.

7. Rode over to Mr. Gashitts for Lath—was at Mr. Chaddocks also. Rain at Deacon Forbush and at Neighbour Bonds.

8. Mr. Hutchinson came and rode with me to Ministers Meeting at Mr. Martyns. N.B. Sir Forbush examin'd (as well as Mr. Jacob Cushing[3]) and approbated. Several Brothers of Mr. Lorings[4] Church. Mr. Loring inexorable.

9. Mr. Stone[5] preach'd the Public Lecture on Eph. 2, 11.

10. Mrs. Esther Edwards[6] at the other House and lodg'd there, but I saw her not. Heavy Rains. The Day appointed to gather my Island Corn but disappointed by the Weather.

11. Mr. Martyn and his Wife (tho a wet Day) with their Sister Monis[7] din'd here. Mr. Gay[8] and his wife lodg'd last night at t'other House, the last night and to Day they Set out in the Rain.

12. Exceeding Cold, yet no Wood. Sent to Mr. Jonah Warrin, but none came. Pick'd up pine and what I could find, for the Sabbath. N.B. Packet from New Haven by President Burr,[9] but he was not here.

13. Mr. Martyn here and preach'd on Mat. 11, 16 and onward and read Numb. 17. P.M. Luke 12, 1, and read Rom. 9. I rode over to the Northside and read both a. and p.m. Preach'd a and p.m. on Eph. 1, 3, concluding the subject. Return'd at Eve —but miss'd of Mr. Martyn. At Mr. Joslins etc. at Eve.

14. I rode to Lieutenant Tainters to see what was like to come of my Island-Corn. N.B. Mr. Charles Rice makes a Corn-Binn with poles brought by my son Ebenezer.

15. Lieutenant Tainter with his Team (a Load of Wood, Quarter of Lamb and a present of Salt Pork) to cut up and Cart home my Island Corn. Joseph Grout junior with his Team, my William also came with our own—8 Load of Cutt up Corn were brought home. Old Mr. Rice and his sons (3 of them) and his son-in-law with a small number more, came in the afternoon and Evening and husk'd—till about Nine o'Clock at Night—a very Cold Evening. Mr. Breck[10] of Springfield here and lodg'd here.

16. My Corn was laid expos'd where there was no fence, so that I rose Early to look after it. Mr. Breck went to Marlborough to carry up Cousen Betty Gott[11] to live with him. Mr. Jonathan Bellows came and work'd for me to Day, in taking Care of the Husks, building up the Corn Bin etc. N.B. Ephraim Bruce, Barnabas Newton and Jonathan Bellows. P.M. Sent Billy into the Whipple Corner for help in Husking. Nobody came till about 4 p.m. when Mr. Samuel Fay junior, Mr. Joseph Green junior, and four Ladds—viz. Abner and Francis Whipple and two sons of Mr. Fay aforesaid came and husk'd. N.B. Mr. Amsden came to see us.

17. My little Dauter Susan very much Indispos'd—but we ventur'd to go to Mr. Martyn with the Child, having appointed and engag'd it. The last night so cold that the Horse was not able well to break the Ice through the Brook at Widow Tomlins. Din'd at Mr. Martyns. Mrs. Eager and her sister, Mrs. Patty Ward there. We return'd at Eve. Susen so ill we sent for Dr. Chase—who came. May God prepare us for his holy will!

18. Warmer Weather. Mr. Ithamar Bellows at work here in making my garden-yard—Carting and stacking stalks etc. P.M. Lieutenant Tainter brought another Load of Wood and helps clear the Island Field, of Pumpkins, Beans, Turnips. Mr. Charles Rice cover'd and Secur'd my Corn Binn. Suse took a Vomit.

19. Susen very bad (of a Fever) Dr. Chase[12] tends upon her diligently. God prepare us for His holy will! hear that several Children and Youth are ill of Fever also. The air much Warmer. Susen (D.G.) better.

20. Read Numb. 18. Preach'd on Exod. 20, 14. Many Grafton people with us. P.M. Sir Forbush, Mr. Joseph Miles, and his son Abner, and Mrs. Twitchell din'd here.

21. Ebenezer with the Team brought Boards from Maynards Mill—and Two Turns from Forbush's Mill—viz. 700 of Mr. Joseph Woods's Boards. P.M. Mr. Jeduthan Baldwin and his apprentice John Woods came to work, to finish my East Room. Sir Forbush to Boston on the Affair of Stockbridge. Grows colder.

22. At the Widow Beeman's[13] (who was very bountiful, Sending Pork, Beef, and Cheese to my Wife). N.B. The remarkable Number of Teams and market Horses going to Boston, yesterday

---

[9] Jonathan Townsend.

[1] Roger Price of Hopkinton.

[2] [Philip Skelton], *Deism Revealed* (London, 1751).

[3] Jacob (Harvard 1748), the son of the Reverend Job Cushing of Shrewsbury, became the minister of the First Congregational Church of Waltham, 1752–1809. *Sibley*, XII, 252–257.

[4] The Reverend Israel Loring of Sudbury.

[5] The Reverend Nathan Stone of Southborough.

[6] Esther, the daughter of the Reverend Jonathan Edwards, later married the Reverend Aaron Burr, the president of the young College of New Jersey.

[7] Abigail Marrett of Cambridge, who married Judah Monis, was the sister of Mrs. John Martyn of Northborough. Kent, *Northborough*, p. 287.

[8] The Reverend Ebenezer Gay of Hingham.

[9] Aaron Burr of the College of New Jersey.

[10] The Reverend Robert Breck, Jr.

[11] Elizabeth was the daughter of the late Dr. Benjamin Gott of Marlborough.

[12] Thomas Chase, born in Sutton, April 3, 1732, studied medicine with Dr. Benjamin Morse of Sutton. He lived and practiced in Westborough in the 1750's. Some time after 1760 he moved to New York.

[13] Mrs. Eleazer Beeman.

and to Day—no less than 19 Teams only from Sutton yesterday. P.M. visited Samuel Hardy junior who is very ill of a Fever. Was at Mr. Moses Warrins, Mr. Grouts, Phinehas Hardys, etc.

23. Susen So well that the Doctor ceases his visits, and generously gives his Medicines and visits also. Sorrowful News of Two Young Women, Dauters of Mr. William Brewer[14] of Shrewsbury, who were drown'd yesterday at Lancaster as they were going to visit a Relation. Ebenezer design'd to have an Husking this afternoon but being belated in his Invitations was oblig'd to defer it.

24. The Wind high and Southerly, the House, especially my Chamber, So fill'd with smoke that I was oblig'd to put out my Fire; this is to my great Disappointment after so much trouble and Charge to obtain Good Chimneys. Sam Bumpso Clearing by the Stack Yard. N.B. Mr. Phinehas Hardy goes to Bolton for Lime, for Deacon Newton and me, and return'd at Night empty, bringing only a Bag of Hair from Mr. Samuel Bakers. P.M. 25 Hands help'd Ebenezer husk. N.B. Baldwin, John Woods and Sam Bumpso went.

25. [No entry.]

26. Sir Forbush return'd from Boston ill. N.B. Letters to him from Colonel Dwight[15] and Pyncheon.

27. Rainy. Read Numb. 19 and Rom. 10. Preach'd all Day on Exod. 20, 14. Mr. Mead and Daniel How din'd here.

28. Visited Sir Forbush. Training. I din'd with the officers after Prayer with the Company. P.M. visited Mr. Jacob Amsden sick of a Fever.

29. Rode Mr. Williams's Horse to visit Mr. Amsden again; Mr. Rogers etc. Din'd at my other House with Mr. Martyn whom I accompany'd hither also. Lieutenant Hezekiah Ward here. N.B. Jonathan Bond junior (a Lad) who with my Billy and my Team plough'd in Rye at my Island. N.B. Mr. Grout, Lieutenant Tainter, Mr. Phinehas Hardy, Samuel Harrington, and Mr. Beriah Rice here. Consult about a Shed over my Kitchen Chimney and North Door.

30. Jonathan Bond and Billy plough'd in Rye again. Mr. John Beaton din'd here. Mr. Bliss[16] and Deacon Miles[17] of Concord here, going to a Council at Sutton. N.B. Mr. Hezekiah How help'd Ebenezer kill the Cow which I bought some Years ago of Ebenezer Maynard. Baldwin yesterday and to Day about the Garrett Stairs. It grows very Cold and we are Scanted for Wood; nor can I as yet tell what way I am like to have supply.

31. Mr. Harrington brought a Load of Wood. So faithful and bountiful is Divine Providence and so kind and unwearied this good Neighbour (under God) to assist me! Billy brought over a side of Beef. Samuel and Hannah Hicks in their Return here. P.M. walk'd to Deacon Newton; and thence to Justice Bakers. Had his mare to visit Samuel Hardy junior, and old Mr. Fay. Mr. Bliss return'd from Council at Sutton and call'd but I was not at home. Mr. Baldwin for 2 or Three Days about the Garrett stairs.

### NOVEMBER, 1751

1. Wind at South West and my House fill'd with Smoke. See October 24. N.B. Mr. Joseph Woods here and reckon'd with him for 750 feet of Boards at 16/ per hundred. N.B. His Objections against the people's adding the 50£ lately granted to be added to my Sallery and Support. Nay and against the people's paying 500£ towards my Remove to this Place. Exclaims against my New House and thinks that it is too big, and that it is too high. He thinks there needed to be no Chamber over the room we were sitting in etc., etc. P.M. Baldwin to Shrewsbury and return'd to t'other House.

2. Baldwin built the Cellar stairs. John Woods about the Garrett Floor. Mr. Robert Cooks wife here and din'd with us.

3. Read Numb. 20, and Rom 11. The Exposition of the forenoon Chapter took up both parts of the Day in the room of sermons.

4. Mr. Eleazer Kimball came and lath'd my Chamber in Ceil-

[14] Abigail and Elizabeth Brewer were drowned "in a saw mill pond" in Lancaster. Ward, *Shrewsbury*, p. 245.
[15] Joseph Dwight of Hatfield.
[16] The Reverend Daniel Bliss.
[17] Samuel Miles.

ing. Baldwin and his man John preparing the East Room for the Masons. Ebenezer help'd in making Mortar.

5. Sent Mr. Jonas Twitchell to Worcester for Bricks. A very fine Day. Ebenezer makes Cyder. Sam Bumpso has been thrashing wheat and Rye for Ebenezer for some Time. N.B. Deacon Kimball came, and with his son lath'd and plaister'd my East lower Room: Part of the afternoon Robert Claffland waited on the Masons, and did divers Chores. At Eve Alpheus Newton tended the Masons with Mortar, to plaister the East Room, and North Closet in the Chamber.

6. Alpheus tended the Masons. Baldwin trys for an Horse to go to Sudbury but in vain. Works part of the day. John p.m. to Marlborough. About 3 p.m. the Masons break off and before Night go home. Twitchell does not return from Worcester till Eve. The Weather moderate for my plaistering. N.B. Lieutenant Tainter and Solomon Baker Cart Wood from Moses Brighams. Lieutenant 3 Times: the other 2 Turns. So many Various affairs depending, and so much Noise and Confusion in every part of the House, that I Snatch Opportunity to study with great Difficulty.

7. Thanksgiving. After a very rainy Night, a Very Rainy Morning. Lieutenant Tainter brought a Loin of Mutton. We somewhat expected Mrs. Nanny Gott but she did not come. The sermon to Day on Ps. 4, 7. May God accept our Sacred Offerings and grant us true Gladness in our Hearts from the sense of his Special Favour and the Light of His Countenance upon us! My Children all here together with us. Blessed be God for Family Mercys and for the Measure of Health particularly we enjoy! (altho Alexander is somewhat Rheumatic.)

8. Settled with the Collector, Mr. Williams. Visited Adonijah Rice. Ebenezer brought over the Bricks which Mr. Twitchell brot from Worcester the Night before last. He also brought 10 Barrells of Cyder. Mr. Robert Cook here in further Preparation for his Confession and owning the Covenant. N.B. Lieutenant Ward waits upon Captain Maynard and Lieutenant Bruce to the Cook Island to settle the Measure and Bounds of it. Captain Maynard also goes with Lieutenant Ward to view the Bounds of the last Plott of Land by Chauncy Cedar Swamp. Mr. Ezekiel How there with a Letter from the aggrieved in the Church of West-Sudbury desiring a Council etc. N.B. Baldwin did not work at Evening.

9. Rainy Day. I broke fast and din'd with my children at t'other House. Sir Forbush there and pray'd in the Morning. A. and P.M. read Numb. 28, and Rom. 8. Mr. Martyn rode hither, and read Numb. 21, and Rom. 11, but Sir Forbush preach'd (his first sermons) a. and p.m. on 1 Cor. 15, 55. I tarry'd and lodg'd at Mr. Martyns that I might confer with him about the Council to be at Sudbury on Mr. Lorings Case, Mr. Martyn being Sent to likewise.

11. In the Morning it rain'd. But so heavy did the Affair of Sudbury lie upon us that Mr. Martyn and I determin'd to ride to Southborough and Conferr with Mr. Stone who was another sent to: we stop'd at my other House where were Messers. Noah How and Daniel Garfield junior who at this Time bought my Fat Steer—agreed to give 13 pence old Tenor for him Hide Beef and Tallow. We call'd also to see old Mr. Rogers, with whom I pray'd. When we came to Southborough Mr. Stone was gone abroad. We sent after him—din'd and tarry'd there until sunsetting but saw him not. We drew up a Letter to the Sudbury Committee and to Mr. Loring. In my return home, call'd to see Mr. Amsden. John Woods return'd to work here p.m.

12. Mr. Martyn and his wife came here, in hopes to see Mr. Stone here, but he did not come.

13. I think Ebenezer has finish'd his making Cyder.

14. Lieutenant Ward here laying out Land for me: he setts off an acre for me south of the Meeting House: and the Four Acres which I lately bought of Mr. Richard Barns. He also laid out a little Bit of Land which was Common between the ministerial Lot and my Land, being 27 Rods. At Eve I was at Mr. David Maynard juniors.

15. Lieutenant Ward laid out another Scrap of Land joining to the Road south west of the Meeting House, and bounding on

the Burying Place. 43 Rods. P.M. Mr. Claffland work'd for me; is making an Hovell for my Cattle. Captain Tainter[1] of Watertown and his Wife here. Sir Forbush is gone to Brookfield to preach.

16. Mr. Claffland all Day—upon the Hovell etc. Wondrous fine agreeable weather and thus it has been for Some Time. Captain Richardson and Mr. Cornelius Woods of Sudbury here to confer with me on the Affair of their design'd Council they having receiv'd my Letter of Denyal last Night. They din'd here, but I still persisted in Denying them and finally refus'd to go. Baldwin begins the Outside of the Door—pediment, Pillars etc.

17. Moderate Weather Still. Read Numb. 22. Preach'd on 1 Thess. 4, 4 carrying on my Exposition of the seventh Commandment P.M. read Rom. 12. Preach'd on James 2, 24, using in part, Notes which were deliver'd under Eph. 2, 5 last Clause.[2]

18. Exceeding fine Weather. I committed my Plotts of Land lately taken up to Captain Maynard to be presented to the proprietors. Visited old Mr. Rogers—both broke fast and din'd at t'other House. N.B. Mrs. Molly Martyn and Mrs. Betty Williams there, and din'd with us. P.M. at Captain Maynards. At Eve Lieutenant Tainter and Mr. Harrington with their Teams, and a Number of Neighbours (Pratt, Ebenezer Maynard etc.) to the Number of 14 or 16 more, besides my Two oldest sons, Spent the Evening in Levelling the Banks on the fore side of my House.

19. Very fine Day—got Lime from Mr. Jonathan Forbush's and from Lieutenant Bruce's to Top my Chimneys and Sent Ebenezer at Eve for Mr. Willson, at Evening (after he had accompany'd Mrs. Molly Martyn home) and he lodg'd at Mr. Willsons. Mr. Daniel Forbush work'd at the Stone-wall south west of the House and at the North underpinning. Near Night came Mrs. Nanny Gott[3] to See us, and lodg'd here.

20. Ebenezer return'd from Mr. Willsons (of Shrewsbury) and it being a Cloudy Morning Mr. Willson did not come. It proves a dull Day misting and likely to bring on a Storm. Mrs. Nanny p.m. to t'other House and lodges there.

21. Baldwin on the Head of the Door yet. John covering and closing a little House. Mrs. Rachel Bowker[4] who came into Town with Mrs. Nanny Gott, came to see us a.m. Mrs. Nanny also return'd here. Sir Forbush came and din'd with us. P.M. he preach'd my Lecture on Isa. 50, 10. May God accept of him, and both bless him and make him a great Blessing! Mrs. Bowker and Mrs. Nanny to Marlborough. Baldwin did not work at Evening. But went to t'other House and lodg'd there.

22. Mr. Ebenezer Kimbal here a.m. lathing the Stair way. By him I sent the Reverend Mr. Price of Hopkinton Deism Reveal'd volume 1. Baldwin rode my Horse to his Fathers. John Woods about the little House.

23. Mr. Ebenezer Rice brought part of my Books from Mr. Daniel Gookins Bookseller in Boston, which have lain there some time to be sold. Samuel Bumpso work'd gratis at the Vault of the little House. But it grows very Cold.

24. Read Numb. 23. Preach'd on Ps. 4, 7. Lords Supper. P.M. read Rom. 13 and finish'd the Discourse on Ps. 4, 7. Cold Day. Read Sudbury Letter to the Church.

25. Proprietors Meeting at Marlborough. Sent 3 Plotts by Captain Maynard, viz. one of 5 acres and [blank] Rods, which has been depending these Twelve Months: the second was of 27 Rods joining to the Ministerial Lot; the third of 43 Rods by the road South West of the Meeting House. They were granted, with this Exception in the Last, of Liberty for Stables on the Front of it. Lucy Bowker at work for my sons at the other House. Mr. Daniel Forbush lays the East room Hearth. Baldwin finish'd and paint'd the Front Door. Cold Day. At Night Snow.

26. The Snow went off; chiefly by noon. P.M. Mr. Claffland finish'd the Hovell. At Eve at Lieutenant Forbush's.

27. Mr. Edward Willson came to top out my Chimney, the morning being pleasant: and my son Ebenezer here to help him. But by that Time the Staging was compleated, the weather was So Cold, he quitted it. Samuel Bumpso here and din'd with us. P.M. they all clapp'd to and finish'd the Vault of the Little House, and bank'd it up. Mrs. Nabby Baker at work here, making my wife a plad gown. P.M. I Catechiz'd at the Meeting House. P.M. Baldwin and John Woods left us. For this turn of their Work am indebted to Jeduthan Baldwin £4.13.4, or 35£ old Tenor—in all £9.6.8, or 70£ old Tenor this Day. N.B. His whole work comes to £113.10 shillings old Tenor.

28. Mr. Claffland works here; putting up a Sort of Shed on the Northside of the House. The Cold beats him off p.m. He makes a Cask for the Well and goes home. N.B. Old Mr. Maynard and Mr. Whipple din'd here.

29. Comfortable Day. Messers. Brown and Ballard from Boston call'd at the Door. Billy has been not well for some time. Pain in his Neck and Face.

30. Grows Very Cold. At Eve it Snow'd fast.

### DECEMBER, 1751

1. The most Snowy, winterlike Morning that we have had all this Season. Altho I had not any extraordinary hindrances in the Course of the week yet by one affair, or Concern or Care or Other I was so far interrupted that I finish'd but one sermon. Read Numb. 24. Preach'd on Mat. 19, 4, 5, 6. P.M. Read Rom. 14. Repeated Sermon on Mal. 3, 17, to page 8.

2. Various weather. Early Morn fair. Cloudy generally through the Day, and not very Cold—but the Earth with a very Winter Face. Mr. Hall[1] of Sutton din'd here, in his Way to Concord. Sent Mr. Henry Goold 7£ old Tenor by him. Read Sir Hovenden Walkers journal of his Expedition to Canada.[2] Mr. Samuel Harrington here in the Evening. Ebenezer and Thomas brought a Side of an Hog, kill'd at t'other House—weigh'd (the whole Hog) 11 Score and 17 pound.

3. Ebenezer went to Grafton after our two stray piggs, but in vain, he returns at Evening without 'em.

4. Was at Deacon Newtons at Eve and reckon'd with him. N.B. his boarding my Workmen Baldwin, Parkhurst and Woods one hundred Days (or 14 weeks and Two Days, taking them all, together) at 25/ per Week, was, in old Tenor £17.18.0.

5. Last Night and to Day Very Cold. Rode Lieutenant Tainters Horse to Mr. Bradish's to the Private Meeting there. Preach'd on Jer. 6, 16, to page 13. N.B. The Company Besides Mr. Bradish, his Wife, son and Dauter were Deacon Forbush, Deacon Newton, Lieutenant Tainter and his son—and Four Women. At Night snow'd hard. N.B. Mr. Abraham Temple who brought from Boston Lining and Trimming for a Blue Cloth Jacket for me, din'd with us. At Eve Mr. Biglo, Mr. Daniel Hardy and Mr. Benjamin Winchester here. Billy not well, but is better.

6. Thick Cloudy; sometimes Mist, Sleet, Rain—but not so Cold as Yesterday. Billy writes a Days, and helps a little about the Cattle etc.

7. Reverend Mr. Hall of Sutton din'd here. N.B. He paid Mr. Henry Goold 18/ lawful Money, and brought me my Note—and 5/ Change (old Tenor). And thus I have wholly finish'd with Mr. Goold. N.B. I had sufficient Preparations made Seasonably before the Sabbath—which was a great Comfort to me. However I Still added as New Thoughts were Supply'd, especially in the Heads of Application.

8. Bright and Cold. Read Numb. 25. Preach'd a.m. on Mat. 19, 6. Patty Pannell din'd here. P.M. read Rom. 15. Preach'd a Sermon I now added to that made on Occasion of my Dauter Elizabeths Baptism upon Mal. 3, 17. At the Close of it read from passages in the Boston Gazett or Weekly Journal No. 1655.[3]

---

[1] John Tainter was the brother of Deacon Simon Tainter of Westborough.

[2] In the Westborough Church Records for Nov. 17, 1751, Parkman noted that "Robert Cook and Sarah his wife offer'd Confession of their being Guilty of the Sin of Fornication, and likewise their Aggravating it by Denying it; upon which they were restor'd to Charity and Own'd the Covenant."

[3] Anna, the daughter of the late Dr. Benjamin Gott of Marlborough.

[4] The daughter of John Bowker of Marlborough.

[1] The Reverend David Hall.

[2] A Journal . . . of the late Expedition to Canada (London, 1720). Admiral Walker commanded the ill-fated expedition against Quebec in 1711, which ran into stormy weather, lost 8 transports and 900 Men in the Gulf of St. Lawrence, and then returned to England.

[3] Evidently Parkman read all or part of a moralizing piece that appeared under the title "From a late Magazine."

9. Cold. I rode up to Mr. Samuel Hardys to See his Daughter Sarah, who has been Sick of a Fever some Time. N.B. I call'd at Mr. Benjamin Fays. N.B. I Saw two persons of the Neighbourhood there drinking Drams (Adonijah Rice[4] and John Dunlop), and I gave them a Brief Word upon it. I call'd also at Mr. Phinehas Hardy's to see him after his Recovery from his Wounds by the Fall of a great Log upon him. N.B. We began to keep Geese here at the New House. For Ebenezer brought a Gander from the other House, and I bought a Goose of Mr. Ebenezer Rice. Mr. Daniel Hardy brought a Load of Wood.

10. Somewhat Pleasant Day. Sir Forbush (being come from Brookfield) din'd here. Mr. Simon Tainter brot a Load of Wood from Elijah Rice's Swamp. Mr. Phinehas Hardy a Load from his own place. Lieutenant Forbush and Neighbour Batheric here and want to talk about the affair of Sudbury Council, and have been displeas'd; what they have been disquieted with was (as they apprehended) my not giving the Church Liberty to Send if they had been o'Mind to. Whereas they acknowledg'd that I gave Space for them to speak if they had had Disposition to Say any Thing: but what they complain of is that I did not ask the Church to Speak, as I have indeed sometimes done, when I have Seen them as I thought too Backward. But however, as to Sending, it was not expected of us, after what I had Said to Captain Richardson and therefore the Reading of the Letters was merely to oblige them. N.B. Ebenezer and Thomas are gone to wait on Dr. Chase, who, to Day brings his Wife[5] from Sutton. Mrs. Lucy Bowker P.M. at Work making me a Cloth Jacket.

11. Rain. I was inform'd that a Number of Young persons lodg'd last night at my other House. Mr. Halls son and Dauter, Mr. Minot's son—and one Mr. Hale[6] of Sutton. Lucy Bowker here at work.

12. A fine pleasant Day. Sir Forbush dines with me, and p.m. preaches to the Young people on [blank]. Take heed that the Light which is in you be [blank]. In which he takes his Leave of the Society. Lieutenant Holloway here after Meeting. May God give His Blessing to the Word deliver'd! N.B. one of the Heifers which we have been wont to keep here, calv'd—Samuel Bumpso kind and helpfull about the Calf—that it may be Comfortable in the Hovel: Billy being gone to Mill at Southborough with the first Grist of Corn that we ever sent from this House.

13. Mr. Harrington and Eleazer Whitney going to Chauncy-Meadows for Hay, brought each of them a Load of Wood. P.M. Mrs. Forbush, the Deacons Wife, fell from Mr. Wymans (of Shrewsbury) Horse, a little South of the Stables. She was much stunn'd. Mr. Wyman and I took her up in an arm Chair and brought her into my House. Sent for Dr. Chase, who came: he let her Blood. She by Degrees came to. I sent by her son Bowman to her Husband. He and his son Jonathan and Mr. Tainter brought a Whirrey, and they carry'd her Home. N.B. Mrs. Rachel Rice[7] came to our help. N.B. I talk'd with her upon the sorrowful Subject of her Childrens Drinking.

14. Mr. Jonathan Forbush came and gave me account of his mother, that she is much as she was last Night—does not recover, tho she has her sense.

15. Rugged Season. Read Numb. 26, omitting Some number in the middle of the Chapter by reason of the Cold. Preach'd on Jer. 31, 18, 19, 20, a. and p.m. Read P.M. Rom. 16. Dauter Molly tarried with us over Night—the Night exceeding Cold.

16. Exceeding Cold. Reckon'd with Aaron Warrin. His account was £11. 10.4 old Tenor. But the Glass which he had of me came to 42/—gave him a Note for 9.8.4. Lieutenant Holloway here. Spoke to him of the Towns Debt to me. He own'd it to be just—said he would talk with the Select Men about it—and forward it with those of the precinct that he could.

17. Weather Somewhat moderated, but it is a Cold Day. Finish'd Life of Oliver Cromwell.[8] Sent by Mr. Nathaniel

Whitney a Messenger to Mr. Jacob Felton in Marlborough. Cold Night.

18. Very Cold—Am Somewhat Rheumatic. Daughter Mary and Breck who have been here ever since the Sabbath, return'd home.

19. Sent by Mr. Jacob Whipple[9] of Grafton to Mr. Thomas Fleet,[10] printer, concerning my Young Horse. See his Paper of Last Monday. At Eve Ebenezer and Lucy came over and Supp'd here. N.B. My Discourse with Ebenezer about his Settling in the World. I made him various offers for his Encouragement and he acquainted me with his Desires to Marry.

20. Snowy Morning—a Dark, misty, Cold Day.

21. Very rainy Morning. Mr. Jacob Whipple with a Letter from Brother Samuel Parkman concerning my Horse.

22. A Cold Season—very Slippery. Read Numb. 27. Preach'd a. and p.m. on Jer. 31, 18, 19, 20. P.M. read 1 Cor. 1.

23. Visited Mrs. Vashi Newton[11] and reckon'd with her. Visited Mrs. Forbush (Deacon's Wife) and Supped there. N.B. Sir Forbush there. Pray'd with them. N.B. Exceeding Slippery riding—rode in much Danger, but the Lord sustain'd and preserv'd me. I return'd home in safety—D.G.

24. Last Night and this Morning considerable Snow storm. Cold and blowing. P.M. Messers Benjamin Fay and Simon Tainter here to see us and how we far'd in the storm. At Eve Sir Forbush Supp'd with me.

25. Stormy and Cold. Mr. Beeton here. He brought home various pieces of Work—a shovel, in particular the wood of which Ebenezer had made. I went over to the other House (not having been there for a great While). Ebenezer (I conceive) going to Boston with my Young Horse, to Mr. Thomas Goldthwait—but to my disappointment he is not going. Sir Forbush from the North Side, where he went not without Expectation that there was a Lecture appointed. The proposal was Lieutenant Holloways—but Mr. Martyn forgot it.

26. I went over to t'other House again and Sent off Ebenezer with my Horse to Boston—he himself riding the Mare. A.M. It was a Snow Storm, but it was clear by that he was out of Town. My urgency arose from our being in Danger of loosing this Opportunity—and we are short of Hay. When I return'd Mr. Joslin was here—brought money.

27. Fair, which is rare, but cold—a tight Season. May God uphold us!

28. Mr. Simon Tainter brought (as he call'd it) a Small Jagg of Wood from Elijah Rice's—he and his son din'd here. Stormy. Snow—rain—p.m. came Deacon Mellen[12] of Hopkinton with a Letter from the Church in Holliston to our's to sit in Council there on January 8, next; there having arisen Difficultys among some of their members—viz. Captain Ephraim Littlefield and Mr. Daniel Mellen.

29. Ebenezer return'd from Boston last night—and brings News that Brother Samuel Parkman is ill of a Fever. Read Numb. 28 and gave some observations preach'd a.m. on Job. 33, 27. P.M. read 1 Cor. 11, and preach'd on number 2. Us'd sermon on this Text, which were compos'd when I was young (viz. June 1724). I therefore made great alterations and additions (in delivering altho not in Writing) proceeding to page 8. After the usual Exercise I stopp'd the Church and read the Letter from the Church in Holliston, and ask'd for a Vote, but there were but very few Hands—after repeatedly requesting that they would offer Some Reason which I might Send with our Answer, for our not complying, Justice Baker Said he believ'd there was Some Difficulty among ourselves which was the Reason—and after further Enquiry, I found it was, and with respect to Me, he himself and others being dissatisfy'd with my so suddenly dismissing the Church when I had read the Sudbury Brethren's Letter on November 24. Mr. Francis Whipple Stops to the Same Purpose. I answer'd (in Substance) that if I had given the Church Ground of Offence it was altogether undesign'd, and I was utterly insensible of it, at the Time of it: that I conceiv'd I gave Time eno'

[4] The son of Charles Rice of Westborough.

[5] Thomas Chase married Mary White, Sept. 26, 1751. John C. Chase and George W. Chamberlain, *Seven Generations of the Descendants of Aquila and Thomas Chase* (Derry, N.H., 1928), p. 102.

[6] Jonathan Hale.

[7] Mrs. Charles Rice.

[8] No biography of Cromwell had been published in America. It is impossible to determine which of many works Parkman may have read.

[9] The son of Deacon James Whipple.

[10] Publisher of *The Boston Evening-Post.* The issue of Dec. 9, 1751, contained the following advertisement: "To be sold, a good Draught Horse. Enquire of the Printer."

[11] Vashti was the wife of Abner Newton.

[12] Henry Mellen.

for any Body to Speak if they had desir'd it. But that indeed Such were the Nature and Circumstances of the Affair, that I did not expect any Thing would be Said—For what I design'd in Reading those Letters and in acquainting them with what I had done about them was, to oblige the Sudbury Brethren and to gratifie the Church also hoping for their Satisfaction and Concurrence in what I had done if they approv'd of it, or otherwise, to have the Church's Sentiments and apprehensions about what was my and their Duty. So that I was So far from designing to give any Offence, that it was all done out of Respect and to avoid all manner of Ground and of Offence: That I could freely appeal to the Consciences of all that I was always Stanch for order; and tho I would vindicate the Authority of the Ministry, yet made Conscience of not invading the Privileges of the Church—and as to this present Article, it was (as I apprehended) wholly owning to a Misunderstanding of the Design I had in Staying the Church. And if the Time which I gave for any Brother to Speak (if any one inclin'd to) was Short, yet I thought it as long as was at all needfull or could be desir'd in such short Days and Cold Weather (N.B. it was Sacrament Day also), when people are uneasy to get home—So that I had no imagination that any one was disquieted. But if they any of them were then uneasy, it would have been much more proper to have manifested it before now; either at the Time of it, or at least to have come to See me and Speak to me of it (as Several had done, and I had satisfy'd them) than to let it alone all this Time; and now make it Such an Obstruction to our Duty. I Said I hop'd they were not fond of Divisions, and of having Councils to come here too for we ought to learn by the Evils which others suffer'd ourselves to beware. These Things were Said at divers Times, in replying to Brother Baker and others—but to him chiefly—little else being offer'd but what was by him—And I added, that if the Space which was given (however I apprehended it) between reading the Letters etc. and my dismissing the Church, was verily too short, I was Sorry for it, and I ask'd their Pardon. But Justice Baker said that did not satisfie him; but he would take a Time to come and see me; which (that we might make Short) was propos'd to others also to do, and to do it in this ensuing Week—that So this Hindrance being remov'd we might next Lords Day Act upon the Holliston Letter.

This Obstruction was a Trouble to me; but that the Brethren should be so much disquieted as this came to, and yet keep it from me so long, till I am far less Capable of making Defence, did not a little Disturb me.

30. Very Cold Season. I went over to t'other House, and receiv'd Ebenezers Account of his late Journey, in which he sold my Horse for 90£ old Tenor. It Storm'd and Snow'd hard. Zachary Hicks[13] was here from Sutton and lodg'd here. Ebenezer assisted by Mr. Barns[14] kill'd our Chamberlin Cow.

31. The cold grows very intense. Zachary Hicks to Cambridge. The Frost is exceeding perceptible. The Year finishes with Weather Some of the most tedious and extreme. We hereby perceive how great and powerful God is! Surely with Him is terrible Majesty!

## JANUARY, 1752

Through the amazing Patience and Longsuffering of God, I am permitted to begin another New Year. Blessed be His glorious Name! May God be pleased to continue his great Mercy and Goodness, choose out our Changes for us, and prepare both me and mine for all His holy Will! This last Night and this Morning were intense Cold. I think I scarce ever was more sensible of the frostiness of the Air at any Time whatsoever. The Lord extend his pity to the poor, and whoever are in Distress at this so uncommon season! Ebenezer came over with a side of Beef, being part of our Chamberlin Cow. Mr. Whitney[1] was here and said something of the Difficulty last Lords Day, showing himself to be one of those who was in some measure dissatisfyed about the Sudbury affair; but after hearing what I had to say, he was so easy as to say no more about it.

2. At Deacon Newton's[2] a.m. The Deacon did not begin with me, but I with him about the uneasiness in the Church about the Sudbury affair; and being the private Meeting was to be at his House this Afternoon I would have him tell the Brethren when they are there—that I was perswaded they mistook my Design that Sabbath, but however, since I now know their minds, and that their inclination was to have had opportunity to pass a vote—if it were to do again, I would not do as I did. Least the Deacon should mistake my meaning I sent Billy with a note—at Eve came the Deacon, as if I had unraveled by my paper what I had spoke by word of mouth. With him came Captain Baker, Lieutenant Tainter, Lieutenant Bruce, Mr. Francis Whipple, Mr. Daniel Hardy, and after them Lieutenant Bruce[3] and Mr. Batheric.[4] By what they said I was so convinced of my omitting to deliver some things concerning my Conference with Captain Richardson etc. that I believed my Conduct at that Time when I dismissed the Church appeared exceptional and as if I bore upon their privilege. I told 'em it must needs be thro such omissions that I was sorry—they all listened satisfyed but I had a night of oppressing Thought, and sinking Faintness at my Heart, which was very distressing. Mr. Isaac Harrington here to tell me my piggs were at Mr. Thomas Axtell's.

3. It was still exceeding Cold. Messers. Harrington, Jonathan Forbush and Eleazer Whitney brought each of them a Load of wood, as they went to the meadows for Hay. Judge Ward[5] dined here and Zachary Hicks who lodged at t'other House was here also.

4. Cold. Ebenezer to Mr. Thomas Axtell's with a Whirry and brought home my piggs which had been so long lost; he having shut them up and fed them as his own.

5. Read Numb. 29. Preached on Job 33, 27. P.M. Read 1 Cor. 3 and preached on 1 Cor. 2, 2. Church stayed on the Holliston letter. I spoke somewhat for their Satisfaction and they voted smoothly. Had a night of Deep Concern about my Spirit and Eternal Condition.

6. A variety of Interruptions. Sent Billy to Ebenezer that he may improve the sledding. Mr. Beeton here and very helpfull. At Eve Batherick and Bumpso.

7. A.M. at the other House—Mr. Daniel Bond of Watertown with Ebenezer. Ebenezer has Mr. Barns's Cattle and Sled and sledds Loggs to the saw-mill. P.M. Parish met and one article, but at no motion of mine, is my wood for the year Currant passes in the Negative. Messers. Samuel and Daniel Hardy a Load of wood [illegible]. Lieutenant Tainter dined here; and was very helpful to get me an Horse for my Journey to Holliston. Had his Mare which he had delivered to Justice Baker for him; and he provided him another. I rode to Hopkinton and lodged at Mr. Barrett's.[6]

8. Captain Baker and Lieutenant Tainter called me at Mr. Barrett's and we rode to Captain Littlefield's in Holliston. All the Churches met there; and p.m. we formed into a Council and went into the Hearing of the Partys. Mr. Buckman[7] was chosen Clerk—We were up till past midnight. The first Church in Medway and Framingham.

9. In the Council, we still go on in hearing the partys till Evening, but adjourned at noon to Mr. Mellen's where we dined and spent the afternoon, and began our Debates and Votes of Council there in the Evening. I was very faint and worn.

10. We proceeded in our Debating, but we understood that by means of some unseasonable Discovery of the votes of the Council last night, Deacon Mellen was much dissatisfyed, and at Eve he came into the Council and indecently vented his Disgust and was sharply rebuked for it. My spirits were roused with this, but in general I was much worried and waited. Mr. Bucknam and I lodged together at Captain Littlefield's throughout the time of the Council.

11. The Council has been very unanimous. Finish our Result and publish it before Dinner. The Church and the other partys

---

[13] Zachariah was the son of John Hicks of Sutton. Benedict and Tracy, *Sutton*, p. 660.
[14] Richard Barns of Westborough.

[1] Nathaniel Whitney, a selectman of Westborough.

[2] Josiah Newton.
[3] Abijah Bruce.
[4] David Batherick.
[5] Justice Nahum Ward of the Worcester County Court of Common Pleas.
[6] Samuel Barrett.
[7] Nathan Buckman of East Medway (Millis).

retire while we dined. Return and manifest their Gratitude and acceptance. Except Mr. Mellen who desires a little Time to think of the first articles. We return home—calling at Mr. Barrett's a short space where I was informed that as to the Fast at Lieutenant John Woods (to which I was desired to come and assist) Yesterday, Mr. Stone[8] of Southborough preached, and they had but one Exercise.

12. Read Numb. 30, and 1 Cor. 4. Preached on John 12, 35. Acquainted the Church in the face of the Congregation that I was not prepared to lay before 'em what the Council at Holliston had done, but I hoped I should be enabled by another Lords Day—for I had not an whole copy of the Result, but expect one from Mr. Bridge[9] of Framingham.

13. A very Cold, Windy Day—feel very poorly—faint and weak. An ill Night.

14. My daughters Molly and Lucy were last Wednesday at Mr. Martyns, and heard their Disgust at my not having been to see 'em for so long time. They pitched upon to Day for us to go, and they would stay at home for us—but tho it was a most agreeable Day and fine slaying, yet I was so very ill that I could by no means go. Mrs. Parkman and Molly went. I grew so ill, so faint, feverish etc. that I sent for Dr. Chase[10], who came. N.B. The Vagrant Baker dined here: and I gave him some friendly admonition, he seemed to thank me and to take it kindly. Mr. Thomas Axtell of Grafton here about his keeping of my piggs. He leaves it to Mr. Phineas Hardy to judge between us.

15. I had a Night of Sleep, and yet had a Morning and Forenoon of Sinking Faintness and Illness. Sir Forbush from Waltham dined with me, and I dined somewhat agreeably. P.M. a little better, yet am exceeding low. At Eve marry'd Ebenezer Miller,[11] but thro much Difficulty.

16. Another Comfortable Night (thro Divine Mercy) yet very faint Morning. I perceive I go down Hill apace. Tho Dr. Chase is very faithful and very generous, yet he is young and I am not content without further advice. Sent for Neighbour Pratt, that he might go to Dr. Scammell;[12] he came but could not go for the Doctor. He went to Deacon Newton and he consented and went. He returned at Evening without him, but brot a portion of Rhubarb corrected with oyl of Cinnamon. Memorandum. I consumed Number 1.2.3.4.5.6. of Journals from February 19, 1719 thro to April 1723 containing numberless puerilities and better destroyed than preserved.[13] As Mr. Jonah Warrin brot a Load of Wood on the seventh at Evening and on the eleventh Day Mr. Sam Harrington another, this Day Mr. Samuel Hardy and James Miller junior brot each of them a load as they went to the meadows for hay. At Eve Dr. Chase here and advises to take the Rhubarb ut Supr. N.B. Sir Forbush receiv'd a call from Brookfield and is here at Eve.

17. Was not quite so faint. Took the Rhubarb, it worked once. Dr. Chase here, Mr. Isaac Harrington. Billy to Horns mill. At eve Captain Eager. A more comfortable Day in general (thro Divine Goodness.)

18. Exceeding low and faint at first waking which was long before Day and continued so till I got up, and some time in the morning about 11 a.m. came Dr. Scammell. He says I have no Hectick, advises to Bitters and nutritious Diet, but forbids all Volatiles. I sent for Dr. Chase but he was gone out of town. Dr. Scammel to Colonel Nahum Wards and returned p.m. Captain Maynard[14] visited me. Mr. Jacob Cushing[15] came to assist me tomorrow and lodged here. In general I was better thro the Day than I expected. D.G.

19. A bright Day, but too Cold and searching for me to go abroad. Mr. Jacob Cushing preached for me, a. and p.m. on Job 22, 24. He read Numb. 31 and 1 Cor. 5. I was in some Comfort—yet weak and feeble. Mr. Cushing went to the other House with my Children to lodge there.

20. Somewhat stormy in some parts of the Day; yet such the goodness of Brother Stone that he came to see me in my lowly, feeble state. Dined here, he also prayed with me. At Eve Captain Eager[16] and afterwards Justice Baker[17], Mr. Hastings[18] of Watertown and his wife and others to see me. Was very feverish, weak and faint. N.B. Justice Baker prayed with me—the Lord accept the offering!

21. Thro God's great Mercy I had a considerable comfortable Day. Mr. Bridges of Framingham here. P.M. my wife and I rode out to Deacon Newtons and to the Widow Newtons. Felt so comfortable that I greatly rejoiced. The Glory to God. May I obtain the Grace suitably to improve it!

22. Mr. Francis Whipple a large load of wood. N.B. Mr. Williams here. P.M. Mr. John Martyn junior and his sister, my son Ebenezer and Daughters Molly and Lucy here. I rode out again as far as Mr. Clafflands. N.B. Lieutenant Tainter carry'd to Boston a Calf for me which he killed the Eve before last. Was not in general so well as yesterday. May I wait the Will of God! N.B. Dr. Smith[19] and Granny Forbush[20] here.

23. Cold Snowy Day. Mr. Martyn, Mr. Cushing and his wife visited me and dined with us. Mr. Ebenezer Chamberlin brot a Load of Wood. Mr. Pratt very kind. Mr. Cushing prayed with me. I had had but a poor night and forenoon, but was better p.m. and Eve. D.G.

24. A stormy Day—snowing all Day. Thro the divine Goodness I enjoyed much comfort. O for grace to improve my Strength to divine Glory! for I find myself extremely prone to wax cool again tho I have been deeply Concerned and very fervent. At Eve Lieutenant Tainter from Boston where he had marketed a poor calf for me—brot me Madera for Bitters.

25. Had another good Day (thro the great Mercy of God!) P.M. Mr. David Maynard[21] brought Dr. Samuel Gardner[22] (the School-Master) to board here.

26. Mr. Jacob Cushing going yesterday to Southborough that to Day he might preach for Mr. Stone. Mr. Stone was so kind as to come up this morning and preached all Day for me, two seasonable sermons on Isa. 27, 9, and I had the Liberty to the House of the Lord again for which I would praise his Name with rejoicing. Mr. Stone read a.m. Numb. 3. I read p.m. 1 Cor. 6. N.B. Judge Ward was at Meeting here. He and widow Child[23] (besides the above mentioned) dined with us, who (with my own Family, all of them together) make a considerable Company. Mr. Stone returned to Southborough this Evening—the Lord graciously reward him for his Labor of Love and bless his endeavors among us! especially to me who am now immediately concerned in it.

27. The School begins at Mr. Hezekiah Pratt's, and Billy and Sarah attend it. Mr. James Miller junior brings a Load of Wood.

28. Brother Hicks and his son John here. They are going down to Cambridge to old Mr. Hicks's[24] Funeral. Mr. Whitney here with 10 chairs which he has bottomed for me, Two arm chairs and 8 others. Mr. Eliezer Rice here, he desires to discourse with me and asks Mr. Whitney to go along with us. He asks a Church Meeting again and I immediately grant it. I say all I can safely to him for reconcilement. He says there is nobody that takes any care of his Soul, (referring, I suppose, to his absenting himself from meeting without anybody minding it, for which reasons might be given). N. B. He asked whether we should not strive to forget as well as forgive—when there had been nothing ripened so far as forgiveness. I asked him whether he was sorry for his passed Conduct and would endeavour after true affectionate regard to me hence forward? but he made me

---

[8] Nathan Stone.

[9] Matthew Bridge.

[10] Thomas Chase, Westborough's young physician.

[11] Ebenezer Miller of Upton married Hannah How.

[12] Samuel Scannell, the physician of Milford.

[13] It is regrettable that Parkman destroyed these early years of the diary, kept while he was at Harvard College and before he accepted the call to Westborough.

[14] Parkman's old friend, Captain John Maynard.

[15] Jacob (Harvard 1748), the son of the Reverend Job Cushing of Shrewsbury, became the minister of Waltham in 1752. Ward, Shrewsbury, p. 254.

[16] James Eager of the north precinct.

[17] Edward Baker of Westborough was a justice of the peace.

[18] Joseph Hastings, a selectman.

[19] Joshua Smith, the physician of Shrewsbury.

[20] The widow of Deacon Thomas Newton.

[21] Parkman's old friend, one of the original settlers of Westborough.

[22] (Harvard 1746). Gardner, the son of the Reverend John Gardner of Stow, kept school at various places before settling as a physician in Milton. Sibley, XII, 27.

[23] Mrs. Jonas Child of Westborough.

[24] Zechariah Hicks, a carpenter of Cambridge, died Jan. 27, 1752, aged 94. He was the father of John Hicks of Sutton. Paige, Cambridge, p. 580.

no answer to it. He goes away temperately. My Daughter Molly came and lodged here in order to my riding abroad with her Mother to Marlborough if I be able—but the weather proves too rough and Cold.

29. This Day 16 year Was a most gloomy time when I lost my former wife. I would remember the wormwood and the gall, and my soul has reasons to be humbled within me. But how gracious God has been in preserving and sparing me so long! May God grant me His Grace to enable me to improve his long suffering! Mr. Smith[25] came from Marlborough to see me, and brings a young lady with him, one Mrs. Lydia Coit of Boston. Their coming prevented our going abroad to Day also. They dined here and tarryed till nigh night when it snowed and the storm increased. At Eve Mr. Williams and Mr. Batherick here. N.B. the errand which the latter acquaints me with from Daniel Bond of Watertown concerning Mrs. Elizabeth Harrington. Ebenezer here likewise. N.B. Messers. Daniel and Jonathan Forbush, Martin Pratt, and Elijah Rice, brought each of them a load of wood, and Mr. Edward Whipple ditto.

30. Messers. Charles Bruce and Eleazer Whitney, each a Load of Wood. Mr. Edward Whipple came with his mare, and putting her into my slay drove my wife and me to his House, and we dined there. I read Dr. Souths sermon on January 30, there. Mr. Walker has made me a pair of Boots. We went to Mr. Eliezer Rice's, he was not at home, but I discoursed with his wife, she having lately lost her mother by sudden Death. Ebenezer drove our slay home.

31. Cold Weather, yet thro God's Goodness I am very comfortable and able to read and write again. Dr. Gardner goes to Marlboro after school and I sent a mesage by him to Mr. Jacob Felton; and a letter from Mr. Josiah Swan[26] at Lancaster about Eusebius which I bought of his mother in his name some years ago. Thus I finish the first month of this year, in which I have gone through both deep affliction and memorable mercy. May God afford his Grace that I may walk in newness of life.

### FEBRUARY, 1752

1. Mr. Eliezer Rice was here and brought me a written request for a Church Meeting. Brother Hicks lodged at t'other house last night, here today.

2. Read Numb. 38 and preached on Job 33. 27, last clause. P.M. read 1 Cor. 7. to number 24 omitting the rest. Stopped the Church and read the Holliston result and Neighbour Eliezer Rice's request for Church Meeting. At Eve was very much worryed and tired, but I bless God He has enabled me thus far, May His Grace be perfected!

3. Rain. I attended the Church Meeting at which Mr. Eliezer Rice gave a paper containing his opinion about Original Sin. I made some reply to it which the Church was desired to show their minds whether he should enjoy the priviledge of baptism for his child. No hand was lifted up.[1] N.B. Dr. Gardner returned from Marlboro last Eve to t'other house.

4. Cold and blustering weather. The season is still severe. Read second volume of Secret History of Europe. Mr. Grow here and brought me £12, 12 shillings, Old Tenor. Never were the times more difficult with me than now respecting money when I owe so many and have so little to pay 'em with. This troubles me chiefly that I should be so unrighteous especially when not only a professor but a preacher of Righteousness. Lord deliver me out of this snare!

5. Dr. Gardner would find Horse while I find slay to ride to Mr. Martyn's. His horse proves too untractable. We put in my Mare. It is cloudy and cool and nigh Eve but we got over comfortably and lodged there. N.B. Mr. Martyn has bought Ridgely etc.[2]

6. We feared a Storm but have a very fine Morn. Return home. N.B. Sir Forbes[3] has received a call from the town of Waltham and he is come up. Captain Baker was here in the morning to acquaint me that the private meeting is appointed to be at his house today and yet that he must unavoidable be at Worcester—therefore requests me to be in his stead. I accepted and preached there—Jer. 6. 16 from page 13 on. Lieutenant Tainter came home with me. The sorrowful news of Mr. Peabody's[4] Death which was confirmed,

7. next morning; and t'is said that he is to be buried this Day. Help Lord! May this Death be sanctified to Thee in particular that since I live I may live unto the Lord. Mr. John Witt of Brookfield lodged at my other house last night and is here and meets Sir Forbes today here.

8. Mr. Ebenezer Harrington[5] of Framingham and his wife here.

9. Read Numb. 34. Preached on Rom. 14.8. P.M. read 1 Cor. 8. Preached on 1 Cor. 1. 30, using mostly the first sermon on 2 Cor. 12. 2. N.B. Daniel Hastings dined here and went at Eve to the other house.

10. My Wife this Day 35 years old. I went over to the other house. Daniel Hastings there. He assisted Ebenezer in killing two swine, one nigh fourteen the other near thirteen score. P.M. Carryed Molly over to take her mother's place whilst my Wife and I rode in the slay to Grafton. Mr. Hutchinson[6] just gone to Sutton. Tarried with Mrs. Hutchinson til nigh night. In returning at Eve it was cold. Called at Mr. Winchesters[7] and at Mr. Benjamin Fay's[8] and the presents made us did well reward us for our trouble.

11. My Wife and I rode to Marlboro and carryed the child, Mr. William Winter and his Wife and his Wife's Sister at Colonel Williams[9]—the ladys are fleeing to Worcester from the smallpox which is now in Three familys in Boston. I went to Mr. Jacob Felton's. My wife and I dined at Colonel Williams. Visited Mr. Smith and Dr. Samuel Brigham[10] who has marryed our Neece Mrs. Nanny Gott.[11] Mr. Smith and Mr. Stone came to us at the Doctor's in the Eve. We lodged there.

12. Cold Day. We dined at Esquire Brigham's, the Doctor and his wife and his Brother Uriah and his wife being there also. P.M. In returning home called at Mr. Jacob Amsdens—found our habitation in peace. To God the Glory!

13. Read Sydenham on smallpox.[12]

14. [No entry.]

15. The School finishes at Mr. Pratts. Masters David Maynard junior and Jacob Rice here P.M. to pay Dr. Gardner.

16. Mr. Martyn[13] and I had agreed to change if it was not foul weather or very cold, but it proved so very sharp a morning and was so very slippery that I despaired of his coming out; and therefore although I depended much upon changing I did not venture to go, but turned my mare home that my children might come in the slay to Meeting. However in case Mr. Martyn should be o'mind to come I remember 1.) We had agreed that if it looked doubtful whether the other would set out, yet he that was so disposed should stir early and give the other sufficient time. 2.) I know I could take his horse and ride as far as my other house and there take one of my own. (And thirdly) I put myself into all the preparation I well could by reading over my Notes which I designed to deliver to his people, skirting, etc. but we were all of us sure, by what he has said in times past, that it was too slippery for him to ride. Yet at more than half after

---

[25] The Reverend Aaron Smith. The matter concerned the future marriage of Elizabeth and Ebenezer, Jr.

[26] Swan (Harvard 1733) had been the minister of Dunstable, 1738–1746. He was now keeping school in Lancaster. Sibley, IX, 331–332.

[1] There was some debate over Rice's petition and Parkman opposed it. Westborough Church Records, Feb. 3, 1752.

[2] Thomas Ridgley, D.D. (c. 1667–1734), a nonconformist English divine, was the author of several works, none of which was published in America. The work mentioned here may have been A Body of Divinity: wherein the Doctrines of the Christian Religion are Explained and Defended, 2 vols. (London, 1731, 1733).

[3] Forbes did not accept this call but later in the year was ordained at North Brookfield.

[4] The Reverend Oliver Peabody of Natick.

[5] A Framingham selectman.

[6] Aaron Hutchinson of Grafton.

[7] Benjamin Winchester of Westborough.

[8] The son of the late Captain John Fay of Westborough.

[9] Abraham Williams, the prominent office-holder of Marlborough, was Parkman's brother-in-law. Hudson, Marlborough, p. 470.

[10] The son of the prominent Marlborough citizen, Samuel Brigham, Sr.

[11] Anna, the daughter of Dr. Benjamin Gott of Marlborough, married Brigham, Jan. 9, 1752. Hudson, Marlborough, p. 373.

[12] Thomas Sydenham, the English physician, was the author of numerous medical works in Latin and in English. The reference here may have been to Walter Lynn, An Essay towards a . . . Cure in the Small Pox . . . and a Review of Dr. Sydenham's Works (London, 1714).

[13] John Martyn of Northborough.

nine o'clock, Mr. Martyn came—and understanding that I was not dressed, nor did expect to go, he was so moved that if I had not used, not only entreatys but force, he would have gone back. I took his horse as I had purposed and rode to my other house, where I left him and took Ebenezer's mare and proceeded to the north side. Got to Meeting in good Season and broke off in season likewise. A.M. read the chapter of my text, viz. Jer. 31.18.19. 20 which I preached on both parts of the Day. P.M. read 1 Cor. 4. Baptized Eli son of Thomas and Persis Goodenow. I tarried not a great while after Meeting before I returned to my other house, for I was much afraid of the evening cold. Mr. Martyn and Dr. Gardner came to me there; and after some refreshment we parted—but it proved a very sorrowful day to me to see Mr. Martyn so extremely raised for I did not in the least refuse to go; nor was it so late but that I got there in proper season and although he found me at home, yet there was much reason for it, it was also the first time that he had ever come to me thus; whereas I have time after time been at his house before he was in any readiness at all, yet I showed no resentment. No, not when he was lingered and delayed so long that he has made it altogether too late, quite!!, when he began the Divine Service for me. But I fear what this will prove the beginning of! *Deus avertat omen!*

17. Stormy morning. Dr. Gardner lodged over at t'other house—gone p.m. with Molly and Lucy to Mr. Stone's[14] of Southboro. I rode to Mr. Pierce's to see two children sick of the throat distemper.

18. Sent letters to my Brethren at Boston and an advertisement to put my other house and place upon sale. Mr. Pierce's youngest child which I saw last evening is dead; another very bad and two more are taken sick. Dr. Gardner left us and went to Marlboro. Mr. Grow brought £8.10.0 Old Tenor. The weather foul; Snow, Rain, Snow, etc.

19. The weather is become very Fine, but it setts the snow aflowing. Mr. Martyn and his wife came to see us—dined here; Mrs. Nabby Baker made Mrs. Martyn a gown here. P.M. I went to the funeral of Mr. William Pierce's child. Sir Forbush here, being come from Waltham and goes today upon his journey to Brookfield. N.B. I sent £10 Old Tenor to Jeduthun Baldwin per Mr. Samuel Harrington. Mr. Martyn and his Wife returned home at Evening.

20. Mr. Haven and his sister Patty lodged at t'other house, and came here a.m. as did Captain Waters[15] of Sutton and his wife, Dr. Chase and his wife and Mrs. Newton. These last all went away before dinner. Mr. Haven and his sister dined here. N.B. His answer to the South Church in Portsmouth, New Hampshire.[16] The Waters flow exceedingly. N.B. Molly brought Breck here, who has canker in his mouth, yet plays about in the house and abroad. N.B. An odd kind of note—Mr. Grows from Mr. Thaddeus Gale for money which I do not owe.

21. Bright and moderately Warm but very windy. Low grounds, especially hollows exceedingly filled with waters, the snow disappears apace.

22. Mr. William Pierce's little son Aaron buried but by reason of the storminess of the weather I could not go to it. This child also died of the throat distemper.

23. Read Numb. 35. Preached A.M. on Thom. 14. 8. P.M. read 1 Cor. 9, and took some notice of the providence of God which has ordered these two Chapters to be read the same day. Preached on Rom 6.21. We took into the Church Messers. Jonathan Bond and Eleazer Whitney, Mary Bond, Margaret Chaddock, and Lydia Twitchell.[17]

24. Billy to Mr. Allen's Mill and to Mr. Woods' fulling Mill with a pair of blanketts to be fulled. Came home so late P.M. that I could not go to Mr. Pierce's to see his son William who is sick. In the morning I went to Mr. Ebenezer Rice's and talked

with his wife about her drinking which she denies herself guilty of.[18]

25. The weather grows very springlike. I went to Mr. Pierce's. William is so bad t'is doubtful whether he will live or no. Mr. Edward Willson here. Wrote to Mr. Prince[19] of Boston per Mr. Hall[20] of Sutton.

26. Although I sent to Mr. Hutchinson to come and help me in my lecture today, yet I was obliged to preach it myself. Text— 1 Cor. 1—Used the notes on 2 Cor. 12.2 with a new plan and many alterations and additions. And oh that the Blessings of God may accompany the serious things that were spoken for the highest good of all! That we may both be in Christ and have the great Happiness and Comfort of well grounded Evidence that we are so! N.B. Samuel Bumpso and an hand with him, viz. Elijah Hardy clearing behind the Meeting House. A.M. they dined here. And Sam took a small turn at the same work after lecture.

27. Samuel Bumpso and with him Charles and Abner Rice and Constantine Hardy came and cleared the bushy land behind the Meeting House. My sons Ebenezer and Thomas also came and helped. N.B. Sam and Constantine dined here. P.M. Mrs. Nabby Baker[21] here and my wife took opportunity to take discourse with her about some reports with regard to my son Ebenezer courting her.

28. Sam, Charles and Abner cleared again. Sam dines here. The others go home. Mr. Hall of Sutton here, bought Two Cloth for Thomas of him. Ebenezer was here at eve.

29. Sam Bumpso brought a parcel of Apples here from Mr. Jonathan Fay's and from Mr. Grout and dined with us but did not work. Mr. Winchester comes from Boston here. Smallpox doth not spread as t'was reported. May the Lord Pitty his People! Thus has the Lord carried us through the tedious Winter and the changes of it. Blessed be His Name for all his Goodness to Us!

MARCH, 1752

We begin not only with a Sabbath but a Sacrament day. I read the last chaper of Numbers. Preached on John 1, 41, A. and P.M. It was a rainy day and but few women at communion. P.M. read 1 Cor. 10. Oh that God would please to bless these happy seasons to all our Souls—to my own in particular! Deacon Forbush[1] and Mr. Thomas Kendal[2] dined with us. Deacon Burnap[3] of Hopkinton with us, Mr. Barrett[4] not well.

2. Town Meeting. I was at Captain Maynard's A.M. but returned seasonably to pray with the freeholders at their assembly. Captain Forbush and Mr. Grout were their messengers. A great deal of company at my house all P.M. and Eve—among the rest Mr. Joshua Townsend[5]—who was extremely full of Talk, and unmannerly with his Hatt, which since he us'd to be our Schoolmaster I took the more Notice of and as decently as I could, hinted to him. N.B. Reckon'd with Messers. How and Daniel Garfield, who bought a steer of me last fall. Mr. Grow here and paid me so much in Money and Notes as amounted to above 68£ Old Tenor. Sam Bumpso with Jonathan Grout and Abner Rice clear'd part of a.m.

3. Rainy. Mr. Forbush here from Brookfield.

4. I rode to Mr. Stones; I went by the way of Deacon Matthias Rice's,[6] who is confin'd by Illness; is doubtless delirious but Shews great Distress of Mind. I pray'd with him. It rain'd yet I proceeded to Southborough, din'd at Mr. Stones. Preach'd his Lecture on Rom. 14, 8. I return'd (in the Rain) at Eve. Call'd at Mr. Amsdens. N.B. Exceeding hollow and miry Roads.

[14] The Reverend Nathan Stone.

[15] Jonathan Waters.

[16] Samuel Haven (Harvard 1749) became the minister of the South Church of Portsmouth, N. H., 1752-1806. *Sibley*, XII, 382-392.

[17] These new members had been dismissed from other towns as follows: Jonathan Bond and Lydia Twitchell from Watertown; Eleazer Whitney from Waltham; Margaret Chaddock from Hopkinton; Mary Bond (wife of Jonathan) from Mendon. Westborough Church Records, Feb. 23, 1752.

[18] Anna, the daughter of Charles Rice of Westborough married Ebenezer Rice of Southborough, March 23, 1743. This couple made their home in Westborough but were evidently not admitted to the church.

[19] Thomas Prince of the Old South Church.

[20] Parson David Hall.

[21] Abigail, the daughter of Squire Edward Baker, later married John Martyn, Jr., of Northborough.

[1] Jonathan Forbush.

[2] Thomas Kendall of Suffield, Conn., had married Susanna Tainter of Westborough.

[3] Jonathan Burnap.

[4] Samuel Barrett of Hopkinton.

[5] See Parkman Diary, Dec. 12, 1726.

[6] Of Marlborough.

5. Am Reading old Mr. Niles of Braintree against Mr. Briant.[7]

6. The Adjournment of Town-meeting brought much Company and Interruptions Particularly Mr. Kelly[8] of Hopkinton (of the Church of England) here. Mr. Bezaleel Eager brought Me (from Mr. Davis[9] of Holden) Mr. John Taylor of Original Sin[10] At Eve came Mr. Grout, Lieutenant Tainter and Mr. Samuel Harrington, who propose to assist me in getting Timber for a Barn, also to help me in breaking up Land for an Orchard.

7. [No entry.]

8. Read Deut. 1, and 1 Cor. 11. Text a.m. Rom. 6, 21. P.M. Rev. 2, 2—hope there were Some good Impressions: but all is with God.

9. Went in the Morning to t'other House. Thence to Mr. Francis Whipples to See him under his broken Bones—but they were newly sett, and he was asleep, I refus'd to have him 'waked. I was at Mr. James Maynards but he was not at home. P.M. Pray'd at the Precinct Meeting. Private Baptism was desir'd for an infant Child of Mr. Solomon Woods—I took the opportunity of the people's being together to go into their Meeting and consulted (such of the Church as were there) upon it. There appeared an hearty Concurrence. I propose tomorrow, 11 a.m. to do it. N.B. Captain Maynard here and talks with me about buying my old place.

10. A.M. very cold. Catechiz'd at the Meeting House. 27 Males: 15 Girls. Rode to Mr. Woods after Catechizing and din'd there, the Child very dangerously ill. P.M. in Presence of a number of the Church and others I Baptiz'd it—the Name was Patience. I introduc'd the administration with Some short Exercise on the Work and Duty of a Parent on such Occasion—and after the Exercise we sung part of the 143 Ps. Concluded with the Blessing. Artemas Ward Esquire[11] there and came home with me. It Snow'd very Hard and the Ground soon cover'd. Wrote by Esquire Wards Brother Thomas Trowbridge[12] of Groton, to John Stevens Esquire of Townsend about the Plott of Lott Land.

11. Mr. Forbush from Waltham, here; and wants immediate advice about Brookfield.

12. In the Morning having thought of Mr. Forbush's Case with regard to Brookfield Proposals, I rode over to Mr. Martyns whither he was gone to meet a Brookfield Messenger, Mr. Cutter; and I din'd there. Mr. Forbush prepar'd his answer, which had some Conditions inserted respecting Wood and Sallery—and he sent it by Mr. Cutter. P.M. I rode to Marlborough accompany'd by Forbush who is returning to Waltham. I pay'd Mr. Felton 22£ 5, shillings old Tenor and obtain'd of Mr. Ephraim How to pay him the rest, as he Should want it. I return'd home by Deacon Matthias Rice's who is grown much better.

13. Mr. Thomas Axtell here, and with him Mr. Aaron Hardy. Mr. Axtell here many Hours—he din'd here—with much Ado we came to an agreement. I engag'd him 4 Bushels of Indian Corn for what he had given my Piggs. At Eve I rode to See Mr. Moses Warrins Wife in her low Condition and apprehended to be dying—but she reviv'd. N.B. had Widow Newtons Mare. Lieutenant Tainter from Boston, when I got home.

14. Impossible for me to prepare Two Sermons this Week, have so many Impediments and Interruptions. My mind much exercis'd with it.

15. Deut. 2. Read a.m. and preach'd on Rom. 6, 21. P.M. read 1 Cor. 12. Preach'd on the Death of Louisa Queen of Denmark, King George's Youngest Daughter and improv'd Sermon on Ps. 39, 8. N.B. Widow Child din'd here.

16. The Reverend Mr. Wellman[13] and Mr. Amos Case din'd here. Sent by Mr. Wellman to Mr. Prince at Boston, and by Mr. Case to Mr. wilkins[14] of Souhegan.

17. Sorm of Rain and Wind.

18. Storm continues—increases—a considerable Snow—and very Cold.

19. Forbush from Waltham again, and wants further Advice. P.M. I preach'd to Young People from Mat. 18, number 19, 20. At Eve Mr. Abijah Gale here.

20. Sent to Boston by Mr. Jonas Bond of Sutton; and bought 7 Yards Tow Cloth of him. P.M. Mr. Noah How and his wife here to be examin'd—but I am oblig'd in Conscience to put them by and request them Still to take further Pains. We hear that the Small Pox greatly Spreads in Boston.

21. Snow'd a.m. Rain'd p.m. but at 3 p.m. rode to North Sutton. N.B. Ebenezer and William went to Mr. Daniel Matthews with our Barley to be Malted. N.B. Mr. Greenwood of Sutton rode with me at Evening to Mr. Wellman's.

22. I preach'd there on Rom. 8, 7. Mr. Minott[15] Schoolmaster din'd with me. At Eve I rode up to See my Kinswoman Mrs. Fuller[16] who through God's Goodness is yet alive and was able to be at Meeting p.m. There came Mr. Holman and Mr. Fish—they follow'd me with Questions for the Explanation of the Sacred Scriptures till 10 o'clock. I lodg'd at Cousen Trasks,[17] and Master Minott with me. N.B. No Proclamations till to Day. I baptiz'd a Child of William Wait. N.B. Mr. Wellman preach'd at Westborough on Gen. 19, 14, and Ps. 19, 11.

23. My Kindred full of kind Endearments. But we must part. My Kinsman Trask rode with me to Grafton. I proceeded to Mr. Hutchinsons where was Mr. Wellman and we din'd together. In returning home I made a Visit at Mr. Moses Warrins, whose wife is low and weak yet, but is somewhat better. When I came home understood that Captain Witt and Mr. Barns of Brookfield had been here to see Mr. Forbush but he was not here. They seem determin'd to have him at Brookfield. N.B. Mr. Wellman tells me that Cousen Nat Parkmans Wife at Boston has the small pox.

24. My Wife went to t'other House and return'd at Eve. Captain Witt etc. here again but it still happens to be when I am absent. Mr. Forbush comes to me still to advise with me in the weighty Case before him: For Brookfield do not accept his Conditions, but do make further proposals to him, which are such as make the Matter no better than it was before.

25. Dr. Samuel Gardner to see us (having lodg'd at t'other House) and din'd here. We hear the Small Pox So spreads that they begin to inoculate in Boston. May God in infinite Mercy Shew his Compassion to the Distress'd Town.

26. Publick Fast on occasion both of the Small Pox and the Season. I preach'd a.m. on 2 Sam. 24, 14. In my preparations I Spent my Time upon the forenoon sermon. P.M. preach'd on Zech. 12, 10, to page 7, and made Some Additions according to the Business of the Day. A rainy Day, yet considerable many People out: I wish it might be to Some good Purpose. N.B. Not only Mr. Seth Rice went out of Meeting from the forenoon sermon, but Mr. Robert Bradish also. N.B. My Dauter Lucy has stay'd at home from Public Worship several Days—she has now an ague in her Face, and has been pritty much troubl'd with it.

27. Exceeding rainy Day.

28. Mrs. Lucy Bowker here A.M. Mr. Winchester from Boston and brings us account that now the Small Pox prevails there very much. I am dissatisfy'd with Mr. Prince's misimprovement of the Materials etc. which I Sent him about Mechoachan.[18]

29. Read Deut. 3 and 1 Cor. 13. Preach'd on Rom. 6, 21, last Clause, a. and p.m.

30. Prepar'd Something in reply to Benevolentius in the last Boston Gazette.[19]

---

[7] Samuel Niles, *A Vindication of Divers Important Gospel-Doctrines . . . against the Injurious Reflections and Misrepresentations . . . of the Rev. Lemuel Briant's* (Boston, 1752).

[8] Richard Kelley.

[9] Joseph Davis.

[10] *The Scripture Doctrine of Original Sin Proposed to Free and Candid Examination* (London, 1740). There were subsequent English editions.

[11] The future major general and commander-in-chief.

[12] Artemas Ward married Sarah, the daughter of the Reverend Caleb Trowbridge of Groton, July 31, 1750.

[13] James Wellman of Millbury.

[14] Daniel Greenwood, of the north parish of Sutton.

[15] Timothy Minot, a Concord schoolmaster and occasional preacher.

[16] Mrs. Jonathan Fuller.

[17] Samuel Trask was an adopted son of Jonathan Fuller of Sutton. Benedict and Tracy, *Sutton,* p. 735.

[18] Sometimes spelled mechoacanna. Any of several plants of the morning-glory family with roots used as cathartics.

[19] The *Boston Gazette or Weekly Journal,* Dec. 17 and Dec. 24, 1751, contained an article entitled "The Cure of Cancers," taken from the *Gentleman's Magazine* for July, 1751. Parkman became involved in a dispute over the nature of phytolacca, poke-weed, and mechoacan. A note from Parkman appeared in the issue of Feb. 18, 1752, in which the Westborough minister asserted "That at New Haven *he made a Business of discoursing with Capt. Dickerman; who told him, it was Mechoacan that he used for his Cancer in his Cheek.*" Another correspondent, "Benevolentius," argued that Parkman was mistaken. *Boston Gazette,* March 24, 1752. The March 31 issue of the paper did not contain Parkman's response and there are no known copies of the next 2 issues.

31. Kill'd a young Sow to Send to Boston, but sold it to Mr. John Beeton, Smith; weigh'd 152. Mr. Beeton to Boston. Sent by him to invite Mr. Stoddard to come up to us this Small Pox Time. Sent by Mr. Richard Kelly the like to Brother Samuels Children and to Dr. Parkmans Widow—to this last because: She had writ to my Dauter Molly that she had rather come here than go to Weymouth. And Sent a Letter to Mr. Kneeland, for the Press,—in Vindication of Captain Dickerman.

### APRIL, 1752

1. Rode to Mr. Gashetts about a breaking up Plough, but he was not at home. In my way I call'd at Mr. Bonds—Mr. Martyn Pratts, Chaddocks, Dunlops, Charles Bruce, Bowmans, Harringtons etc. N.B. Ebenezer here when I return'd and took home his Mare. Ebenezer brot about ½ a Load of Swamp Hay from Eliezer Rice, who he had gratify'd with part of a Barrell of Cyder.

2. Ebenezer here again to bring his Mare, and take Care of the Hay brot last Evening—Rain. I rode to Mr. Grouts—See Mr. Phinehas Hardy, Endeavour'd to obtain his son Constantine. Was at old Mr. Whipples. Mrs. Hitty Burnap was here and is gone to t'other House.

3. Mr. Claffland came to digg Stones, but being alone I ran to 3 or 4 near Neighbours for an Hand but in Vain. He was forc'd to return home again. N.B. he was to have brought Mr. William Pierce, but Mr. Pierce was gone to hewing Timber in Mr. Sherbourns Lott for my Barn. For (by Lieutenant Tainters and Mr. Harringtons Means chiefly) a Number of Hands have freely gone and got a considerable Part of the Great Timber—and this Day Lieutenant Harrington brought Two Load of it to place, and Joseph Grout brought another Load—in all 22 Sticks—which is all the Large Timber for the Barn except Two posts, which another person is to provide. A Singular Smile of divine Providence. May God reward them for their Bounty and grant me grace to make a good use of it to divine Glory! The three Carters din'd here with us. P.M. my wife to See Mr. Edwards Whipples.

4. The Weather has been very Cold; and the Nights frosty for Some time. This Morning very Cold. Mr. Winchester returns from Boston—as does Mr. Kelly who was at my Brother Samuels and deliver'd my Letter—but he brought me no Return. Mrs. Hitty Burnap is Still over at t'other House. P.M. Mr. Whitney here.

5. Read Deut. 4. Preach'd a.m. on Mal. 4, 1. P.M. read 1 Cor. 14. Preach'd on Mark 9, 44 repeating sermon on Heb. 9, 27 from page 28 to 36.

6. Mr. Claffland and Mr. Pierce came and dugg Stones out of the Ground I design to break up for an Orchard. Mr. William Rogers junior work'd with Ebenezer at holing posts. Constantine Hardy came to live a little while with us. Mr. Batherick, being disquieted that we sung Mear Tune Yesterday.

7. Mr. Pierce and Elijah Rice work for me partly in digging and drawing Stones, and partly in building Stone Wall at the Front Corner next to the Road. Mr. Harrington came with 4 Oxen, Mr. Simon Tainter came with his Fathers Team with 4 Oxen and brought Mr. Gashetts Plough, Mr. Grouts Son came with 4 Oxen, Mr. Pratt came with a Yoke of Oxen, and all these with my own join'd to them made up a Team to break up, and follow'd it all Day—they broke up a Piece of Ground for a Garden Spott—and a Field in which I purpose to plant an Orchard, but it not being wholly compleated, they agree to come again all of them (but Mr. Grouts Son) tomorrow morning and finish the Work. Mr. Pierce stays and lodges here. N.B. Mr. Joseph Hagar from Waltham here with a Letter from Captain Livermore[1] concerning Mr. Forbush. Mr. Eliezer Rice here and asks for a Copy of the Votes of the Church respecting him. Merodach Baladan Smith[2] was married to Abigail Bruce.[3]

8. The Breaking up Team came again this Morning and finish'd their Work. Mr. Ebenezer Nurse's came with his son Moses, viz. 4 Oxen, instead of Mr. Grouts. N.B. Mr. Pratt gives his man

Cornelius's Work tother Day in my Cellar and his oxens work yesterday and this morning, but asks pay for one Day for himself. Mr. Nurses Team with Moses tarrys all the forenoon. Mr. Pierce and Elijah Rice at the Stone Wall to Day. My Son Ebenezer first begins to plough for sowing at the old place. I rode to Grafton Lecture and preach'd on Rev. 22, 16. Return'd at Eve. Ebenezer here at Eve and rode home his Mare. N.B. Talk'd of his taking the place to the Halves etc.

9. Billy is forc'd to go to plough at t'other House. Neither Ebenezer nor Constantine Hardy came to Lecture. Mr. Hutchinson preach'd it, from Luke 22, 15, 16. I wrote to Sir Forbush at Brookfield concerning the Contents of Captain Livermore's Letter from Waltham.

10. Receiv'd Two Letters per Mr. Winchester from Brother Samuel Parkman, dated the third Instant—one of them writ by Billy Bows, who with his sister Nabby and Cousen Sarah Tyley were inoculated on the second. As soon as I had read I burnt both the Letters. N.B. Mr. William Rogers and his wife apprehended and carry'd before Justice Liscomb[4] for Stealing (as it is suspect'd) Flax out of Mr. Jonas Brighams Barn, and at Night the Man was committed to Jayl.

11. Mr. Richard Kelly brings Word from my Brothers that yesterday the Pox was come out favourably upon Billy etc.

12. Read Deut. 5. Preach'd on John 1, 41. P.M. administer'd the Lords Supper. Read 1 Cor. 15 and with alterations etc. deliver'd the first of the sermon on number 22. My Mind wrought tumultuously through the last Night from a deep Sense of my Negligence, Slothfulness and unfaithfulness—But I humbly make my Flight to the Glorious Redeemer, relying and depending on his Merits and Righteousness for Pardon and Acceptance with God. N.B. Deacon Newton sick of the Throat Distemper. I call'd Brother Tainter to officiate in his Room, which he did. At Eve I visited the Deacon and found him very ill.

13. Old Mr. Dunlop came to work in my New Garden, to dig out the Roots which the plough has left, and prepare it for the Rake. His son John also wrought for me. They both came late. John Singled Flax. At Eve at Deacon Newtons—Justice Baker there also—now a bad Fever and is an ill man. N.B. Mr. Maccarty[5] came to my House and lodg'd here.

14. Thomas and Molly ride to Cambridge to see their Aunt Lydia.[6] Thomas rode on Mr. Samuel Fay's Beast: Molly on her Brother Ebenezers. I had word from Deacon Newtons that he was worse. Mr. Maccarty, and afterwards Messers. Cushing,[7] Martyn and Buckminster[8] rode to Ministers Meeting at Hopkinton but I was oblig'd to stay and visit Deacon Newton, but he not being (as I conceive) altogether so bad as others apprehended, I rode to Hopkinton where I was through the Day and over Night. N.B. The Affair of Father Loring[9] took us up the Chief of our Time; except what Deacon Mellen[10] and his son Daniel had. N.B. The Night exceeding Cold.

15. The Morning unseasonably Cold. The Ground Froze at an unusual rate. N.B. Mr. Maccarty lodg'd at Commissary Price's.[11] He preach'd the public Lecture from Josh. 24, 24. After Exercise Mr. Bridge of Framingham discover'd to me what he heard of Some of the Conduct of Deacon Millen at a certain neighbouring Ministers House, with regard to the late Council at Holliston, calling 'em Numbskulls and Villains etc. whereupon I took opportunity and talk'd with him, and acquainted him with the Vote of the Council there "that he Should not speak again in that Council except he first make an acknowledgement of his bad Conduct etc." As to Mr. Loring it was resolv'd that 2 or 3 of the Association make him a Visit and discourse with him upon his great Disgust with us, and that Messers. Cushing, Barrett and Parkman go to him, and a Day was agreed upon—but I objected against my going, and propos'd Mr. Martyn; but it was not freely accepted. My own private Affairs are at this Time,

[1] Nathaniel Livermore.
[2] Merodackbaladin was the son of Jonathan Smith of Marlborough. Hudson, *Marlborough*, p. 446.
[3] The daughter of Lieutenant Abijah Bruce.
[4] Samuel Lyscomb of Hopkinton, a justice of the peace.
[5] The Reverend Thaddeus Maccarty of Worcester.
[6] Lydia Champney was the sister of Parkman's first wife.
[7] Job Cushing of Shrewsbury.
[8] Joseph Buckminster of Rutland.
[9] Israel Loring of Sudbury.
[10] Henry Mellen of Hopkinton.
[11] Roger Price of Hopkinton.

in my new Circumstances, too much incumber'd to pretend to go abroad. Messers. Cushing, Martyn and Maccarty came home with me. Mr. Dunlop has work'd in my New Garden, in digging up Roots, and subduing it; this is now the third Day. Deacon Newton, I hear, is somewhat better.

16. Was oblig'd to do something in the Garden myself. Sow'd a few seeds etc. Am Preparing on the Eighth Commandment. At the Funeral of Mr. Bezaleel Smiths Child.

17. Thomas and Molly return'd from Cambridge. Thomas had drop'd his great Coat from his Horse in Roxbury—and did not find it. Mr. Winchester from Boston informs that many die of the Small Pox there, and Some Number of those who were inoculated: particularly we hear that Mr. Robert Breck being inoculated, is dead.

18. Mr. Bezaleel Smith and Mr. Eleazer Pratt brought Girts for my Barn from Mr. Reuben Maynards that Neighbourhood having join'd together and got 'em.

19. A.M. read Deut. 6. Preach'd on Exod. 20, 15. P.M. read 1 Cor. 16. Deliver'd again the second Sermon on 1 Cor. 15, 22. Stop'd the Brethren and read another Letter from Sudbury agriev'd Sign'd by Josiah Haynes and Samuel Dakin. Dated March 26, 1752, and it was left to Consideration.

20. In the Garden again. Am reading Dr. Youngs Sermons volume 2[12] borrow'd of Mrs. Barrett at Hopkinton.

21. Early in the Morning to Mr. Clafflands, Warrins, and to Mr. Bonds, to get Teams to fetch Rails from Rody Smiths and Elijah Rice's. Visit old Mrs. Dorcas Forbush.[13] P.M. Catechiz'd at the School House. 37 Boys and Girls. After the Exercise was at Mr. Grows and Harringtons.

22. It has been very Cold, especially the Mornings very frosty—but today the Sun is very Warm, and is the most Spring-like Day we have had this Spring. Mr. Bond brought 35 Rails from Rody Smiths, and Mr. Simon Tainter 50 from Elijah Rice's. Daniel Hastings of Watertown dines with us. Mrs. Parkman is gone to reckon with Patty Pannell and paid her all that was due.

23. Mr. Edward Wilson came, and at last finishes the Topping out of my Chimney—had Cornelius Cook for a Tender. Another very warm Day. I was oblig'd to go to Mr. Jonathan Forbush's for another Bushel of Lime. Was put to Difficulty for Clay to plaister the inside. Try'd at Widow Newtons Clay-Pitts without Success.

24. Ebenezer brought over a Load of Clay from Mr. Hows hither; Mr. Willson came again, to plaister the Chimney; and Cornelius Cook tended. They work'd from a little before noon till Evening—paid Mr. Willson 40/ old Tenor in part. Hot Still, even like in Summer. Ebenezer return'd home after Dinner. P.M. I rode to see old Mr. Rogers who is thought to be near his End. A Letter etc. from Mr. Forbush at Brookfield.

25. Mr. Phinehas Rice of Grafton returns from Boston. Informs that it is a most sorrowful Time. Mr. John Gardner, Brazier, Son of the Reverend Mr. Gardner[14] of Stowe is dead, but tis doubtful whether Mrs. Breck is deliver'd. N.B. remarkable Hot Weather for Some Days but towards Eve of this, chang'd.

26. Read Deut. 7. Preach'd on Exod. 20, 15. P.M. read 2 Cor. 1. Deliver'd the third Sermon on 1 Cor. 15, 22, but from Rom. 5, 12 with some alterations. After Exercises we attended the Funeral of old William Rogers, who was thought to be in his 82nd Year. May God Sanctify it to our aged people of whom we have some Number yet living.

27. Mr. Joseph Gambel work'd for me, and p.m. he employ'd John Frost to help him—but would have it all to be set down, but a days Work. Near Night I marry'd Joseph Far and Eunice Bradish. Ebenezer brought in the Morning a Load of Posts and plough'd at the Island the Ground that was plough'd this Time Twelve Month, and lay Fallow.

28. Ebenezer plough'd there again, and harrow'd it p.m. with Mrs. Newtons Harrow. He had done before Night. Exceeding difficulty to get any Body to Cart Rails which I have bought of

Rody Smith and Elijah Rice. The Ground by my New House design'd for a pasture lys open to the Flocks of Sheep. A Letter from Mr. Josiah Swan about Eusebius.

29. My Business abroad all lys Still, except what I can do in Gardening. Chief of my Reading is the Free-Thinker.[15]

30. Made Return of Marriages to Mr. Francis Whipple, whom I Saw at Mr. Williams. I din't at old Mr. Rice's. A Dry Time—Signs of Rain, but they Seem to fail and go over. It may put us in mind of our Conduct towards God with many Signs of Graciousness in our Profession, but very barren and unprofitable in our Hearts, and in our Conversation. Mr. Winchester from Boston and his Wife from Cambridge bring News of Colonel Brattle's Lady's[16] Decease by the Small Pox.

### MAY, 1752

1. Thro the great Goodness of God we have had a rainy Night, and it showers this Morning to the great reviving of the Earth. Granny Forbush is gone by, to Mr. Stone's, his wife being in Travail. In the Mount, may the Lord be seen! The Day proves chiefly a rainy Day; tho it rains not hard, yet, it wetts steddily. Mr. Joseph Gambet diggs in my Garden P.M.

2. It was too cloudy to view the Eclipse which occurs to Day. At about Sunsetting Mr. John Rogers brought 6,000 of Shingles.

3. Read Deut. 8. Preach'd on Deut. 5, 19. P.M. read 2 Cor. 9. Preach'd on Phil. 1, 27, A Sermon which was first deliver'd in the Year 1725, now with many alterations and additions. At Night, 9 o'clock came Mr. Ezra Taylor of Southborough to desire me to go to the Funeral of Mr. Jonathan Brewer[1] of Framingham who Yesterday Morning cutt his own Throat with a Sickle.

4. I din'd at Mr. Stone's at Southborough. His Wife (who had newly lain in) was exceeding Weak and low. P.M. I attended the Funeral of Mr. Brewer at Framingham. A most Solemn Time! Mr. Barrett there also, and pray'd. N.B. Mr. Bridge[2] gone to the Ordination of Mr. Haven[3] at Portsmouth: and Mr. Stone to the Funeral of the Widow of old Mr. Daniel Newton. N.B. Whilst I was gone to Framingham Mr. Martyn came to our House and had 28 lbs of Sugar which I got for him at Mr. Ebenezer Rice's at 22£ old Tenor per Hundred.

5. Mr. Solomon Baker with my Cart, but his own Oxen brought me 40 Rails from Rody Smiths: and Mr. Simon Tainter 45 from the same. The former of those was gratis: for the Latter Mr. Tainter ask'd 15/ old Tenor. My Wife went to Mr. Jonas Brighams, and met Patty Pannell there. Mr. Zebulon Rice here, and we agree upon the Time of beginning to Frame my Barn. Mr. George Bruce of Mendon and Mr. Hall of North Sutton here.

6. Richard Kelly work'd here instead of John Dunlop. He setts up the Fence from the Meeting House, Northwest. I visited the Widow Rogers who is going to leave us: and the Widow Hannah Rice, Sister of that Mr. Brewer, bury'd on the fourth.

7. Richard Kelly work'd again (for John Dunlop) in Setting up Fence for me etc. Cornelius Cook (on Mr. Hezekiah Pratt's Account) work'd for me in carting out some Muck and ploughing at my Island.

8. Mrs. Mary Johnson, Stay-maker, came to work here. Old Mr. Joseph Sever[4] of Framingham came to me about the Cancer in his Leg, that he might know how to use Mechoachan or Poke Weed. He din'd here. Mr. Phinehas Hardy setts up Fence for me: and he and his son Elijah (together with my son William) Planted the Grounds at the Island.

9. Mr. Robert Claffland, with my Oxen and a Yoke of Mr. Jonah Warrins, brought 50 Rails from Mr. Elijah Rice's. P.M.

---

[12] Edward Young (1643-1705) was a Fellow of Winchester College, Rector of Upham and Dean of Salisbury. The work mentioned here was probably *Sermons on Several Occasions*, 2 vols. (London, 1702, 1703). Another English edition appeared in 1706.

[13] The widow of Thomas Forbush.

[14] John Gardner.

[15] *The Free-thinker, or Essays on Ignorance* was first published serially in London, March 24, 1718, to July 28, 1721. Collected editions in 3 volumes appeared in London in 1733 and 1739.

[16] William Brattle (Harvard 1722) married Katherine, the daughter of Governor Gurdon Saltonstall on Nov. 13, 1727. The Brattles lost five daughters and a son to the throat distemper (probably diphtheria), and Mrs. Brattle was ill with the same disease. She recovered only to succumb to smallpox April 28, 1752. *Sibley*, VII, 10-23.

[1] Brewer, who was in his 64th year, had lived in Framingham since 1717. Temple, *Framingham*, p. 481.

[2] Matthew Bridge of Framingham.

[3] Samuel Haven (Harvard 1749) had been reading theology with Ebenezer Parkman, keeping school and preaching in numerous pulpits in Massachusetts and New Hampshire. He was ordained in the South Church of Portsmouth, May 6, 1752. *Sibley*, XII, 382-392.

[4] Joseph Sever or Seaver, a long time resident, had been a town officer.

Mr. Warrin himself with the Same Team, brought 50 more. Mr. Forbush here—goes to preach at Southborough.

10. Read Deut. 9. Preach'd on Deut. 5, 19. P.M. read 2 Cor. 3. Repeated with many Alterations another sermon on Original Sin (from Rom. 5, 12) in the Discourses on 1 Cor. 15, 22. O that God would please to add his special Blessing!

11. Was early at Mr. Whipples. Lieutenant Tainter and Mr. Samuel Harrington drive Cattle into the Woods at Leicester. They take 3 of mine, 4 other Young Creatures of Mine cannot be found this morning that they might go. Perswaded Mr. Edwards Whipple to Send his Boy with 22 of my Braces for My New Barn, Saw'd at Mr. Maynards Saw Mill. Mr. Zebulun Rice and Samuel Bumpso came; and they began to Frame my Barn. I went over to Mr. Hows and din'd there. Mr. David Maynard assisted with my son Ebenezer in cutting Principals.

12. Mr. Zebulon Rice and Samuel at the Frame. There came also Mr. Phinehas Hardy and Mr. Simon Tainter, and gave me a Day's Work at it. There has been some prospects of Rain; but the most was a Fog or Mist and went off with Cold Raw Weather. Mr. Stephen Maynard here, but without his Account that we might reckon, though I have taken unwearied pains to obtain it. Mr. Batheric and Benjamin How with Ebenezer hew the Principals and Thomas brings 10 of them over.

13. Mr. Zebulon Rice, and Messers Phinehas Hardy, Simon Tainter and Samuel Bumpso work at the Frame, and to Day came likewise Mr. Jonah Warrin. Receiv'd a Letter from Brother Parkman, dated April 28 or 29. I visited Deacon Newton[5] who is much recover'd. My son Ebenezer brought 10 more Principals. My Wife went to Marlborough. At Night came a Young Man Odoavdo Thomas for Mrs. Molly Johnson, but she went not with him.

14. This Morning came Mr. Zebulon Rice, and Mr. Simon Tainter. Afterwards came old Mr. Charles Rice, and Mr. Jonathan Forbush to the Frame. Mrs. Molly Johnson left us at Evening.

15. Mr. Zebulon Rice at the Frame. Added to him afterwards were, Mr. Batherick, Mr. Grow—old Mr. Graves, and Mr. Simon Tainter—who work'd and din'd with us. In the afternoon by the help of a Sufficient Number of Hands (about 70 Great and Small) we rais'd the Barn. 30 feet long and 28 wide—and thro the Goodness of God there was no Evil Accident. I had provided only for about a Score, yet I hope no one went away without some refreshment. It was only Cake and Cheese and Butter etc.

16. Billy works at t'other House so that I am alone to take Care of things and put all to rights after the Raising. Wet myself and then took Cold.

17. Sir Forbush preach'd for me a. and p.m. on Jam. 1, 5. May God be pleas'd to Add to his Graces and accomplishments and make him an happy Instrument of Saving Good to Many Souls! May he be abundantly fitted and prepar'd for the very awful and Solemn Charge he will (God willing) in a short Time receive! At Night I was very much indispos'd.

18. In the Morning much better. Blessed be God! The Day was lowery and Misty. A great Favour after much drie Weather. Town Meeting. Chose Esquire Baker[6] representative.

19. Wettish Weather, but no great Matter of Showers. Visit old Mrs. Dorcas Forbush. Messers. Bliss[7] and Hobby[8] at the Door, in their Journey to another Sutton Council.

20. The Reverend Mr. Fish[9] and his wife here p.m.

21. Samuel Forbush carted Two Load of Boards, Oake and Pine from Mr. Maynards Mill. Disappointed of the help I expected I undertook to preach my Self the Lecture preparatory to the Lords Supper—from 1 Cor. 11, 26. Having no Watch I preach'd too long. Solemnized the Marriage of Mr. Daniel Adams[10] to Mr. Daniel Hardys only Child, at Mr. Hardys. The Weather Exceeding Cold. N.B. Our Kinswoman Mrs. Sally Brigham[11] here and din'd with us.

22. Sir Forbush Sends his Chest (containing a number of Valuable Books which I have sold him, viz. Hammond,[12] Saurin,[13] Edwards[14]) by one Ball to Brookfield.

23. I find it impossible under my incumbrances to prepare two Sermons in a Week, in the Manner I conceive they ought to be compos'd and written. But I have, I hope, Some sincerity towards God in what I have done.

24. Read Deut. 11. Preach'd on Mat. 1, 21. Somewhat long but I chose to deliver it all (that I had prepar'd) at once. Administer'd the Lords Supper. Mrs. Molly Johnson here with us. P.M. read 2 Cor. 5, and on Consideration of a number of persons being rais'd from Sickness, and brought to the divine Worship again, Not less than 6 within these 8 Days. I preach'd Eph. 5, 20. After Sermon read Letter Missive from Brookfield, second parish respecting Mr. Eli Forbush's Ordination.

25. Messers. Batheric, Phinehas Hardy and Daniel Adams work'd on the Covering my Barn. Mr. Gashitt Sollicits me to go with him to Mr. Ross Wymans[15] to bind Henry Gashitt, which we did—din'd at Wyman's. P.M. visited Mr. Cushing who was not able to preach yesterday. When I return'd, found Mr. Martyn and his wife here; and that Mr. Stone and Madame Thatcher[16] (his Mother in Law) had been here likewise, having come before Dinner. Mr. Forbush to Brookfield.

26. Mr. Adams all Day. Mr. Batheric p.m. I went to Mr. Rogers and talk'd with him about the Narrowness of the Shingle which I have had of him. N.B. Mr. Edmund Greenleaf of Newbury call'd at the Door, in his Journey to Sutton.

27. The General Election is at Concord, because of the Small Pox at Boston. At Mr. Martyns Importunity I din'd at his House. I rode home in Mr. Martyns Chair which I borrow'd for Ebenezer to go to Watertown. Ebenezer and Thomas plant our South Field over again, it having been rooted up by young Piggs. At Eve it rain'd: Billy did not return from his play at Mr. Martyns. I rode to Mr. Jonah Warrins and brought home my Molly and Mrs. Molly Johnson (who is still at Work here) but Lucy lodg'd there. At Night came old Mr. Fuller of Sutton, in his return home from Middleton and lodged here. N.B. Mr. Winchester from Boston; he has left my Watch still with Mr. Atkinson.

28. Mr. Fuller goes home. The We [?]

29. Ebenezer brought Mrs. Eliza Harrington to dinner here. She was not well. They rode to Watertown in Mr. Martyns Chair. Tis thought he courts her. I earnestly pray that God may be Guardian and Director of my Dear Son in this important Matter before him!

30. I was not So well as usual: and have Such a Weight of Care and Trouble but chiefly on account of my Ministry and Great Account that I am much Sunk.

31. Was much indispos'd last night and to Day. The Weather Cold and Rainy. I notwithstanding went to Meeting both Parts of the Day. A.M. read Deut. 12. Gave some Observations. Preach'd on the eighth Commandment from Eph. 4, 28, first part. P.M. read 2 Cor. 6, and altho I had preparations for the p.m. sermon yet such person or persons as the Discourse would more immediately concern, being absent by the Rain I deferred it—and preach'd on 1 Cor. 15, 22, latter part! being sermon 6 from page 28 to 33. N.B. Mr. Eli Forbush and Mr. Hannah Fish dismiss'd.[17]

### JUNE, 1752

1. Am weak and feeble, yet keep about. The Parish met to Day in order to Petition the General Court to Establish all their Legal Acts, notwithstanding their Misstep at first setting out

---

[5] Josiah Newton.

[6] Edward Baker was a frequent office-holder of Westborough.

[7] Daniel Bliss of Concord.

[8] William Hobby of Reading.

[9] Elisha Fish of Upton.

[10] Daniel Adams of Shrewsbury married Abigail Hardy of Westborough.

[11] Mrs. Parkman's sister, Sarah Gott, married Uriah Brigham of Marlborough, July 12, 1750. Hudson, *Marlborough*, p. 373.

[12] A work by the English divine and Canon of Christ's Church Oxford, Henry Hammond, D.D. (1605-1660). None of his numerous writings had been published in America.

[13] Jacques Saurin (1677-1730), a celebrated French Protestant preacher, had been the minister of a Walloon church in London, and after 1705 a minister in The Hague. His work had not appeared in an American edition.

[14] Some writing or writings of the great Jonathan Edwards of Northampton.

[15] A blacksmith of Shrewsbury.

[16] The Reverend Nathan Stone of Southborough had married Mary Thacher, daughter of the late Reverend Peter Thacher of Middleborough. May 16, 1751.

[17] Parkman entered in the Westborough Church Records, May 31, 1752: "The Church was Stop'd and Voted Dismission of Mr. Eli Forbush to the work of founding and Settling a Church in the North East Part of Brookfield, or to the Church there, if there be one gather'd; in order to his being ordain'd the Pastor thereof. And the dismission of Mrs. Hannah Fish (heretofore Hannah Forbush) to the Church in Upton."

(which I'm told was by reason of Justice Wards giving them a defective Warrant for their first parish Meeting). N.B. Mr. Grows account of a slanderous Report of the Frolicking of my sons but I perceive it arose from a Family that were affronted because their Son was not invited to the Wedding of Abigail Hardy. Being so weak and feeble I sent Thomas to Mr. Martyns that he must prepare to preach at Brookfield on next Wednesday. Sister Lydia Champney came up with Ebenezer from Cambridge.

2. Deacon Forbush and Lieutenant Tainter accompany'd me to Bezalleel Eagers, where we were join'd by Mr. Whipple, to go to Brookfield. I was very weak and faint, but hop'd I Should be better by riding. Mr. Martyn and his Delegates join'd us likewise. We din'd at Sergennts at Leicester and got up to Captain Witts in Brookfield before Night.

3. Mr. Eli Forbush's Ordination. A most important Day with one whom I am nearly concern'd for! May God be almightily present with him, and his grace sufficient for him! But it is a Comfort that there is no Objection likely to arise. Captain Ayres[1] does not join, but he does not oppose. We did not form into a Council till it was late in the Day, because the pastors and Deligates of Several Churches did not come Seasonably: and when they came, Several Pastors were unwilling to perform any of the public Service. Mr. Forbush gave the Council to their universal Satisfaction an Account of his Principles; and his Views in undertaking the Ministry. N.B. The Confession of his Faith, contain'd an humble Declaration of his own Hope: and it was to acceptance. N.B. When Mr. Forbush's Call was read, the Church declar'd that the meaning of those Words "While he shall continue in the Work of the Ministry" did mean, as long as he had the pastoral Care of them, and not merely as long as he was able to preach. In public Mr. Jones[2] of Western began with Prayer. Mr. Martyn preach'd in my stead; his Text [blank]. I gave the Assembly an Account of our Proceedings in Enquiring into the Qualifications of the Candidate, and the regular steps which the people had taken in ripening Matters thus far. To satisfie them all likewise we went over them again, from each party transacting. I gave the Charge. This was the first Time I ever perform'd this Service: and did it Memoriter. Mr. White[3] of Hardwick pray'd after the Charge. Sung last part of Ps. 118. I hear there was much order and Decency among the people afterwards. May God accept our Offerrings, and may the Ordain'd especially have Grace to keep the Solemn Charge! Nor may any of us ever forget these solemn actions! Through Gods great Goodness, my feeble Body was sustain'd and carry'd thro in a measure of Comfort. So that my Evening was pleasant. N.B. Mr. Breck[4] of Springfield—Mr. Pynchon[5] of Brookfield there.

4. I rode over to Brookfield Town when the Company was gone with Deacon Forbush to visit Lieutenant Aaron Forbush under his terrible Cancer. [N.B. We call'd in to see Captain Ayres.] The sore which Lieutenant is distress'd by has altered him extremely—but he is much Supported. I lodg'd at Dr. Pynchons,[6] but the Doctor not yet return'd from Court.

5. I preach'd to Lieutenant Forbush on Mat. 24, 44, which may God please to Bless to us all! N.B. I din'd with Mr. Harding[7] at Captain Buckminsters[8]—return'd at Evening with Captain Witt and his wife to their House and lodged there.

6. Captain Witt rode with me to See Mr. Jedidiah Hows Family. We din'd there.

7. I preach'd at Brookfield for Mr. Forbush and he at Westboro for me. My Text a.m. Heb. 13, 17. P.M. Rom. 6, 13. An Hot Day. At Eve I was very faint—was forc'd to lie down—could not attend family prayer—but Committ myself to God.

8. Was more comfortable thro the Goodness of God. Undertook my Journey Home. Witt accompany'd me till one Mr. Walker of Brookfield first Parish met us, and then he was my Company to Mr. Eatons[9] of Leicester. This Man was in much Spiritual Trouble, and wanted to open his Mind to me, and therefore devoted himself to wait upon me. Wish I may have given him any Suitable Direction and Instruction and may God grant his Blessing! N.B. Admonish'd George Harrington for his being in Drink, as we went up to Brookfield last Tuesday, and may God succeed it! Very hot Day. I could reach no further at noon than Mr. David Goddards, where I din'd. At Worcester talk'd with Mr. Sergeant of Leicester joiner about making an handsome sett of Chest Drawers, for Molly. At Mr. Maccartys and altho the Ministers Meeting draws nigh yet I thought it not wise to stay, having been gone so long from home. I rode as far as Mr. Cushings, and a Thunder storm with heavy rains coming up, I lodg'd there.

9. Return'd home in the Morning. Found (through God's Goodness) my Tabernacle in peace. Mr. Forbush preach'd for me last Lords Day, and baptiz'd Two Children. The first was Eli, the other Mindwell.[10] I am inform'd that last Friday, 17 Hands came a.m. and wed my Corn. They were those following—Mr. David Maynard and 2 sons, Mr. Eliezer Rice and his son—Messers. Nathan Maynard and Hezekiah Pratt. Mr. Ebenezer Chamberlin and son—Mr. Joseph Woods and Son. Mr. Joslins Boy—Lieutenant Tainter and Grandson—Mr. Harringtons 2 sons—and a Son of Ensign Miller.

10. Great Rains. Mr. Forbush din'd here. My Heart with the Association though bodily absent.

11. I din'd at t'other House with my Children, sister Lydia and Mrs. Molly Johnson.

12. Dr. Samuel Brigham and his Wife here, and din'd with us, as did Mr. John Green of Boston, printer. Hear that Cousen Peam Cowell is dead by small pox.

13. Billys Hair cutt off. Mr. Winchester returns from Boston and brings confirmation of Cousen Cowell's Death. He brings my Watch from Mr. James Atkinson, but with the Chrystal broke.

14. A.M. but feeble and weak. Yet went to meeting and perform'd the Services both a. and p.m. Nay, in the forenoon went through a double Service, for I not only deliver'd the sermon which I prepar'd for last Lords Day p.m., but added as much more; and it being upon Usury (Text Eph. 4, 28) I exerted myself to the utmost, and deliver'd both at once. Read Deut. 13, P.M. I deliver'd a sermon on James 1 (which I made and deliver'd before I was ordain'd, viz. September 1724) but with many alterations as indeed were very necessary. N.B. read 2 Cor. 7. Was exceedingly worry'd and fatigu'd; with my forenoon sermon especially. Poor Night.

15. Mr. Stone[11] and his Delegates going to a Council at Woodstock. Mr. Phinehas Hardy 300 Boards. This Morning early Mrs. Newton takes Mrs. Molly Johnson to her House. I Din'd at t'other House. Sister Lydia lives almost wholly over there. Ebenezer has met with several Checks upon the Field of Indian Corn on the south side of the Road. The piggs rooted it up a while ago so that he was forc'd to plant the chief of it over again: and now as soon as it is come up again a Flock of Sheep has broke in upon it and crop'd it down. P.M. Billy in the Rain went as far as to Mr. Seth Hudson[12] for Tobacco Plants.

16. After a rainy Night, a rainy Morning, and continues wet all Day.

17. Doubtful what the weather might prove, yet (late in the morning) came Mr. Jonah Warrin, Daniel Adams, Batherick and Claffland to covering my Barn. I rode over to Mr. Martyns and din'd there. Preach'd his Lecture on Rev. 22, 16. Return'd home at Eve. May God follow the weak endeavours of the Day with his Special Blessing. May my own Soul have the Light and Comfort of that glorious Morning Star.

[1] William Ayers or Ayres of Brookfield.

[2] Isaac Jones (Yale 1742), the minister of Western (now Warren) Mass., 1744-1784. Dexter, *Biographical Sketches*, p. 715.

[3] David White (Yale 1730), the minister of Hardwick, Mass., 1736-1784. Dexter, *Biographical Sketches*, pp. 419-420.

[4] The Reverend Robert Breck, Jr., of Springfield.

[5] Joseph Pynchon of Brookfield.

[6] Dr. Joseph Pynchon (Harvard 1726), the physician of Springfield and justice of the Hampshire County Court of Common Pleas. *Sibley*, VIII, 90-92.

[7] Elisha Harding (Harvard 1745), the minister of the First Congregational Church of Brookfield, 1749-1755. *Sibley*, XI, 561-562.

[8] Thomas Buckminster of Brookfield.

[9] The Reverend James Eaton of Spencer.

[10] Eli was the son of Jonas Brigham; Mindwell was the daughter of Samuel Forbush of Upton. Westborough Church Records, June 6, 1752.

[11] Nathan Stone of Southborough.

[12] Of Marlborough. Hudson served as a lieutenant in the militia and at one time commanded Fort Massachusetts. Hudson, *Marlborough*, p. 399.

18. Messers. Adams, Claffland and Pierce at Work on the Barn.

19. Adams and Claffland closing the Barn. At Eve I fell on one corner of the Corn Barn and greatly wounded myself.

20. [No entry.]

21. Lame and poorly: I went to meeting—read Deut. 14. Preach'd on Eph. 4, 28. P.M. read 2 Cor. 8, and preach'd on James 1, 22, a Sermon which I have chose to make from this Text rather than preach the second of those I began with last Lords Day.

22. Mrs. Parkman to t'other House. Ebenezer to Watertown and Cambridge.

23. I rode to Lieutenant Tainters. Din'd at Mr. Whitney's—was at Mr. Grouts, and most of the Houses on this Side.

24. Lieutenant Tainter came and brought an Horse, plough and Lad to plough my Island. Mr. Williams also plough'd, Ebenezer Rice junior led, and Eleven Hands hold—viz. Messers. Grow, Harrington, Jonathan Forbush and Daniel Grout, Joseph Baker, William Stone, James Bowman, Jonathan and Thomas Bond, Abner Warrin came and half hill'd my Corn at the Island; and they finish'd by half after 9 a.m. P.M. came Jeduthun Baldwin. Took up both my notes with him, by giving him one that is of 60£ old Tenor. P.M. Rain.

25. Rainy Day.

26. Lieutenant Bruce here, about the Land at the Island. The Reverend Mr. Hall of Sutton and young Master Minot here. Mr. Phinehas Rice (of Grafton) from Boston brings me Dr. Nathaniel Williams late of Boston, his Method of Practice in the Small Pox.[13]

27. I understand that Ebenezer return'd last night from Cambridge and Watertown and has brot up a Lad from Cambridge to dwell with him, viz. John Barrett, junior. It was bright a While in the Morning and Ebenezer begins to mow a little, but it proves very rainy p.m.

28. Thro my Indispositions and Infirmitys of Body, and the many Cares and Troubles which perplex my mind, I prepar'd for only a.m. This was, once more on Eph. 4, 28. N.B. read Deut. 15. P.M. read 2 Cor. 9. Repeated much of Sermon 1 Cor. 15, 22, from page 33 to the bottom of page 38, from John 10, 10, latter part. It was a Time of very great Rain, Thunder and Lightning. N.B. Sister did not come from t'other House.

29. A very Clear Day. Mr. Martyn came here—and (slenderly) din'd with us. At Eve Sent a Number of Letters to Boston, committing them to the Care of Mr. Winchester unseal'd—viz. to Mr. John Breck, Mr. William Winter, Mr. John Phillips, junior, and to Brother Samuel Parkman.

30. Fair, hot:—N.B. Billy assisted a Drover (one Boardman of Exeter) with a Flock of Sheep and went so far with him as put us in great Consternation. I visited old Mrs. Dorcas Forbush and borrow'd Lieutenant's Horse to ride after Billy. Went as far as Mr. Elisha Wards and found him there. He had been as far as Mr. Jonathan Strattons. In returning we din'd at Lieutenant Bruce's. I sent Billy to the other House to help his Brother this Afternoon.

### JULY, [1752]

1. Billy at t'other House helping his Brother Ebenezer at night returns. Sister Lydia rode here with my Daughter Molly, and din'd here. At Eve return'd to t'other House. The Weather very hot.

2. Publick Fast on the Account of the Small pox and other Malignant Distempers at Boston and divers other Towns.[1] N.B. We had no proclamation, but read what is inserted in the Boston Gazette. However there was So much Said of there being no Proclamation in the County of Worcester, and that in several parishes there would be no Meeting, as at our North End; at Shrewsbury etc. that I doubted of an Assembly (some number did go to work and came not at all: some came from their work in their Sweat and Dirt). I therefore threw aside my design'd sermon for the forenoon, and took that on 1 Pet. 5, 6 which I deliver'd. But there was So considerable a Congregation that

I took Heart, and p.m. preach'd on 1 Kings 8, 37, 38, and may God please to all his Blessing! N.B. Dr. Willson[2] of Hopkinton here at Eve.

3. Mr. Batherick mow'd a.m. part of the Island. Deacon Forbush assisted in the Underpinning the Barn posts.

4. Alpheus Newton[3] gave an half Day, mowing at my Island—and the great likelihood of foul Weather made me conceive it to be my Duty, part of the p.m. to assist my son William in raking. If the rain should come upon that sort of thing, it would be of very little value: but this was the Chief of the English Hay I should have to trust to. And I was fully apprehensive that I should not be able to prepare more than one sermon for the sabbath.

5. Read 2 Cor. 10 a.m. Omitted reading, p.m. Preach'd a.m. on Mat. 1, 21. Administer'd the Lords Supper. P.M. preach'd on the Same Text, but us'd much of the sermon on 1 Cor. 15, 22, viz. part of page 39 and from page 41 to 45. N.B. Sister Lydia Champney[4] not at meeting tho Communion Day.

6. Mr. Martyn Pratt work'd for me a.m. and Cornelius Cook for Mr. Hezekiah Pratt till past 10 o'Clock a.m. We got our Hay from the Island—it amounted to one good Load—and we secur'd it in the Barn.

7. [No entry.]

8. I thought it most adviseable personally to see and talk with Mr. Beriah Rice about the Meadow, and therefore rode over to Upton. Din'd at Mr. Rice's. Did not buy the Meadow, but hir'd the Grass for this Year for 20/ old Tenor per Load. Visited Mr. Fish and call'd at Captain Sadler[5]—was mistaken in my Road home—came by Boons and Kellys.

9. Mr. Claffland and Daniel Adams mow'd in the Ministerial Meadow, the Weather hot, and very tedious to hard labourers—but now is the principal Season of Vigourous Engagement. P.M. came up a violent Storm. Thunder and Lightning. N.B. Mrs. Mary Steward visited us and left a present in silver (50/ old Tenor) in new linnen Cloth for Shirts for several of my little Children, and in some Rie meal, to the Value of near 5£ old Tenor.

10. Mr. Samuel Williams with my Mare, and with Billy to lead, plough'd among my Indian Corn: and Mr. Eliezer Rice came with plough, Horse and Boy and plough'd likewise, but there were but few Hoers—only Mr. Edwards Whipple and his Boy which made me go to Mr. Clafflands and get Robert to help. The Men broke off about ½ after 10 a.m. The Boys viz. Robert Claffland, Moses Sever and my Billy hoed all Day, but did not finish the work. N.B. Sow'd Rie, which I had of Mr. Hezekiah Pratt, at the Hilling. This work was gratis, as was Alpheus Newton's also, who mow'd at the Island a.m. Mr. Jonathan Bellows (upon hire) mow'd and rak'd at the Meadow, and Mr. Eliezer Rice help'd him rake p.m. changing work with us. N.B. Mr. Eli Forbush here, and paid me 10 Dollars for Books which he has had.

11. Rak'd Hay at the Island. Billy finish'd the Hilling there. P.M. Mr. Aaron Nurse help'd us get in a Load of Hay from the Island. It was very hot and tedious to me to bear—but I think it my Duty to do what in me lies having so large a Family and so little help. At Eve rode to Grafton and Mr. Hutchinson[6] came here.

12. Preach'd at Grafton on Ps. 4, 7, a. and p.m. Return'd home at Night. [N.B. Mr. Forbush and my Dauter Molly were publish'd at Westborough.] Mr. Hutchinson return'd home likewise. We met at Mr. Abraham Temple's whose young Child is in a Miserable Condition, and has been so from its Birth, by a Tumor on the Back.

13. John Kelly of Hopkinton work'd for me instead of Mr. Martyn Pratt. The forenoon I sent him to work for Mr. Eliezer Rice. P.M. he work'd (with my sons Thomas and William) in raking and Carting home Hay from the Meadow—they got home Two Load this p.m.

14. Rode about for Labourers to work in the Ministerial

[13] *The Method of Practice in the Small-Pox, with Observations on the Way of Inoculation* (Boston, 1752).

[1] A study of the extent of smallpox at this time may be found in John Duffy, *Epidemics in Colonial America* (Baton Rouge, [1953]). pp. 57-61.

[2] John Wilson or Willson, the physician.
[3] The son of Abner Newton.
[4] Parkman's first wife's sister.
[5] John Sadler of Upton.
[6] The Reverend Aaron Hutchinson.

Meadow, and to take to the Halves the Grass of Mr. Beriah Rice's Meadow which I have hir'd. Succeeded with Joseph Bruce to take half of this latter. Was at Messers. Daniel Forbush's and Harrington's: at Ensign Millers, Messers. Phinehas Hardys and Grouts—the last two consent to help me next Week, to mow in the Ministerial Meadow.

15. Rode out again a.m. to get Labourers but have little success.

16. I rak'd Hay and Barley p.m. at the other place, and re-turn'd home at Eve.

17. Sermonizing—Except the Time when I was interrupted by Mr. Obadiah Newton who came p.m. to make me a Visit. My Wife gone to Captain Maynards. Benjamin Hastings of Waterton brought her home at Eve.

18. At my Preparations. Joseph Bruce and I step'd down to view Mr. Beriah Rice's meadow.

19. Read Deut. 16. Preach'd a.m. on Mat. 1, 21. P.M. read 2 Cor. 11. Preach'd home at Eve on Job 7, 9, made up of several parts of sermon on John 5, 28, 29 (as See upon the first page). Benjamin Hastings[7] and Anna Tainter[8] of Watertown din'd with us.

20. Rode early to Mr. Dunlops to offer them some of Mr. Beriah Rice's Meadow, Seeing Mr. Dunlop had urg'd he might have part. Return'd and visited Mrs. Twitchell. Went over to Mr. Martyns and din'd there. Return'd at Eve. Mr. Batheric joins with John Bruce and they mow in the Rice Meadow.

21. In the Morning walk'd to the Ministerial Meadow, hoping to find a Number of Hands there, but there was only Mr. Phinehas Hardy mowing there. I went to Mr. James Maynards to get a Hand to be with him, but succeeded not—to Mr. Joseph Green junior and prevail'd. He mow'd p.m. I din'd at Mr. Edwards Whipples p.m. I went down into Chauncy Meadows and passed through the Rice Meadow. My undertakers there who rake to Day what they mow'd Yesterday, complaining much of it. Consulted Lieutenant Forbush about it. N.B. Lieutenant Forbush complains to me of my strictness in Examining Candidates for Admission into the Church. N.B. My Wife to Mr. Martyns—but return'd home at Night.

22. Aaron Warrin mows, makes, and Carts from Ministerial Meadow. I walk'd there, and to Mr. Greens. Rode his Horse to Mr. Knowltons. His son Henry works in the Meadow p.m. Aaron Warrin got home one Jagg of 11 Cocks—ventures into the Meadow with the Team for Second and getts mir'd, boggled and belated—came home with 8 Cocks in the Rain and Dark—and is sick in the night o'bed. Ebenezer Forbush brings me 12 Cocks from the Rie Meadow and Joseph Bruce helps unload it.

23. Morning Cloudy, doubtfull Weather—but Aaron goes to the Meadow again. P.M. I rode down to Messers. Daniel and Timothy Warrin, to get them to Cart for me Some of the Hay from the Rie Meadow.

24. Aaron and Billy at the Meadow—Two Jaggs of Hay. The Warrins Daniel and Timothy brought, each of them, a Small Load of Hay from Mr. Beriah Rice's Meadow. Aaron at Eve goes to his Fathers.

25. Aaron and Billy to the meadow. Thomas goes there with the Team and carrys home to the other House, a stout Load of Hay from the Meadow. Lieutenant Bruce kindly brought me the last Load from Mr. Rice's Meadow, and this was a large Load of 18 Cocks. So that I have now got all my part of that Hay and my mind greatly reliev'd.

26. I was much impeded by a Cold yet it did not hinder my public speaking, but my Limbs are much pain'd and my Stomach deprav'd—but I desire humbly to place my Confidence in God. Read Deut. 17 and preach'd on Mat. 1, 21. P.M. read 2 Cor. 12. Preach'd on Prov. 3, 9. May God please to add his Blessing!

27. Somewhat poor Night—am stiff and in pain this Morning. So that I don't stirr about without Difficulty. Thomas and Billy rak'd a Load of Hay which Aaron mow'd and carted it to t'other Barn. My wife to Ensign Millers to Mr. Harringtons and Lieutenant Tainters—borrows his Chaise for some of us to go to

Watertown on Mollys Account. Sister Hicks and her Dauter Hannah at t'other House.

28. A poor Night again with pain. A.M. to Mr. Ebenezer Rice's to get Mr. Dunlop to reap, he having long disappointed me, yet it is Winter Rie and suffers. Mr. Jonathan Bellows reaps from about 11 a.m. till night—and p.m. Mr. Dunlop and Short Richard Kelly come from Mr. Ebenezer Rice's and reap. My son Billy also reaps. Sister Hicks etc. are still at t'other House. Mrs. Hannah here at Evening and lodges here.

29. Exceeding poorly—Know not how to go to my intended Journey. Sister Hicks and her Dauter dine here. N.B. Mr. Parsons[9] of Newbury calls at the Door when we are at Dinner but he will not come in. About 4 P.M. my Dauter and I undertook a Journey in Lieutenant Tainters Chaise.

## AUGUST, 1752

[There are no entries in the diary for the period August 1–15, 1752.]

16. A very melancholly Sabbath! I had an exceeding poor Night. Feverish, profusely Sweating, and extreme faint. Yet the Lord upheld me till the Morning, and my pains are much abated. N.B. Ebenezer is published to Mrs. Elizabeth Harrington. Lieutenant Tainter watch'd at home. I was somewhat reviv'd in the Day, But this Day was peculiarly Dark as there was no Preacher. Dr. Willson was to have come, but he was prevented by several Patients. There was a Meeting at our Meeting House a.m. They read Dr. Watts[1] on Job 23, 3, 4. But all the Meeting p.m. was at my House, 5 persons besides my own Family—who pray'd and Read and sung.

17. But a poorish Night, yet my wife tended me. Wrote by Deacon Newton[2] to Dr. Scammell[3] [my wife wrote just before Day]. Ebenezer gets in the last of my Island Hay, and the Flax. The Deacon carrys his Dauter Sarah to the Doctors. Less pain a.m. Eat something of Dinner. N.B. Mr. Pierce of Stow his wife and Mrs. Martyn din'd here. P.M. I was very full of pain in my right Knee. N.B. In Deacon Newtons return from Dr. Scammell, I find the Doctor will have it that I have the Gout as well as Rheumatism. Captain Maynard here at Evening. Mrs. Lucy Bowker makes a Coat for Alexander gratis—and watches with me.

18. Another very feverish, Sweating, faint Night the last. Several Neighbours to See me. Somewhat freer of pain. William Woods watches.

19. The best night that I have had since I was Sick. Blessed be God! Sister Lydia and my Daughter Forbush here, din'd and Spent p.m. with us. N.B. Mr. Abiel Richardson here. Mr. Nurse a generous present of Salt Pork. A great Frost abroad. My pains shift from Limb to Limb. John Frost watches.

20. A.M. pretty good night, but the Pain rises in my left Knee. Several of our Neighbours go into Boston. Divers Visitants, of persons in Town and otherwise. P.M. Mr. Martyn he pray'd with me. Mrs. Baker here—my wife discourses with her about Patty Pannells Tattle. Ebenezer came and watches.

21. Not so comfortable Night as lately. My left Knee and Foot full of Pain. I wrote to Dr. Scammell by Captain Tyler.[4] Alas! how dull and discouraging! I am so wasted, that there appears to me Danger of consuming away. But I would humbly confide in the infinite Goodness of God. Thomas watches.

22. A pretty good Night for Sleep, and yet this morning full of pain chiefly in my left Hip, Shoulder and Foot. Great Frost last Night. Dr. Scammell came while I was at Dinner. P.M. pains increase exceedingly especially in my left Shoulder. May God almighty sustain me and prepare me for his sovereign Will. My little Samuel a Twelve Month old. May he be born again in the Blessed Spirit of God! The Evening and night were most distressing with pain that ceased not, no not in any Situation whatever, a Circumstance which I have not, I think, at any Time

---

[7] Hastings married Mary, the daughter of Deacon Simon Tainter of Westborough, April 14, 1726.

[8] The daughter of Captain John Tainter of Watertown.

[9] The Reverend Moses Parsons of Newbury (Byfield Parish), 1744–1783.

[1] One of the numerous writings of Isaac Watts.

[2] Josiah Newton.

[3] Samuel Scammell. the physician of Milford.

[4] Nathan Tyler of Mendon.

had till now. I put on a Blister upon the upper part of my arm—which by Divine favour gave me

23. By the Morning some Relief. A portion of Rhubarb also which I took last Night works to Day, and I am easier of pain, but reduc'd to be very weak and faint.

A Melancholly Sabbath! a Second Disappointment by Dr. Willson, whom I earnestly sent Mr. Ebenezer Chamberlin to, last Thursday, and had return by the Same on Friday Eve that he would certainly come unless some Case of Life or Death occurred. But the people watch'd till it was late, and then some went to the North End etc. and some attended at the Meeting House the Deacons carrying on both a. and p.m. N.B. they read Dr. Watts on Col. 3, 3. N.B. Mr. Bradish pray'd with me in the Evening, and my Dauter Forbush watches. It proves a Night of Fever, faintness and frequent waking.

24. Freer of Pain, but very weak and feeble. N.B. ventur'd to Shave not having been shav'd since my Confinement till now. Rain. Mr. Daniel Bond here, complaining of my son Ebenezer. N.B. he went to Ebenezer last Saturday to warn him before Two Witnesses not to marry the person he was publish'd to. Child carry'd away to be wean'd at t'other House. Deacon Newton pray'd at Night.

25. Last Night was exceeding tedious not for pains so much as Faintness, especially towards Morning I was exceeding low. My Wife watch'd. The forenoon was of apiece with the Morning. My wife stills a miscellany of Meat, Herbs, Roots, seeds etc. by the Doctor's Direction. But my Eye and Heart are to God to Show Mercy. Dr. Chase waits upon his Father here. P.M. I was more lively and comfortable. D.G. Very free of pain—a better Evening and Night.

26. My wife tends me o'nights and supply's me with Breast-Milk. Rain'd hard last night. The Thumb of my left Hand seiz'd this morning. We presently put on a Blister to my Wrist. Days of deep Affliction and Distress, tho now and then intervals of Comfort. May the Lord look upon me and be gracious to me! P.M. Captain Forbush and divers others here. I sent for Justice Baker who came to confer with him about Sending to Mr. Minot[5] of Concord to come and preach next Lords Day. My Hand grows much worse.

27. So that I had a Night of grievous Trouble and Exercise till the Morning. My Hand somewhat easier in the Day, and I was more comfortable and lively. But these are Days of Darkness and sorrow. Mrs. Molly Brigham (Gershom's wife) brot some bak'd Bear with Sauce which I could Eat of tho I have a most deprav'd appetite and have eaten next to no Meat these Two Days. Mr. Baxter visits me and pray'd with me. He tells me Noah Hows has been with him about his Baptism. Mrs. Hepzibah Maynard visits me. A.M. Mrs. Rachel Rice and her son Abners Wife here, but no particular Notice was taken of the latter one way nor another. At Night my Hand still very sore and much swell'd, yet not so as to prevent my sleeping. But a Blister a little below my Knee has more prevented my walking in the Room, thereat almost any Time of late.

28. Somewhat broke off my Rest by Company too late here last Evening. Yet the Day was not very bad. Walk but little because of my Blister aforesaid in my left Hand remains much swell'd, but not very painful. Mrs. Dolly Rice here, and nigh Eve came my Dauter Forbush and sister Lydia and lodge here.

29. A very good Night last, for sleep. D.G. Yet its followed with a Day of faintness. Mr. Beeton carrys a Letter for me directed to Lieutenant Taylor[6] of Townshend. Mr. Joseph Woods din'd here. Towards Night sister Lydia and my Dauter went back.

30. Another tolerable Night for sleep, yet remain faint and weak only my appetite is Somewhat better. I am humbly waiting the will of God. But it is Another Melancholly, sorrowful Sabbath. A meeting is held at the Meeting House, but few attend it. The School-Master, Mr. Jonathan Ward reads a. and p.m. Dr. Watts on Ps. 42, 2. At Dinner we had Deacon Forbush and old Mr. Bradish. At Eve Mr. Eliezer Rice desirous of Dr. Scammell

(if he Should come here) for his Young Child. The Nights are Cold and frosty.

31. I had a very Good Night—but am weak and faint in the Day. Kind Letter from the Reverend Brother Morse[7] recommending a Remedy which he had taken with Success. Mr. Francis Whipple tells me he publish'd my son yesterday at the North Meeting House. Thus have I been carry'd thro this Month of deep and distressing Sickness and Pain. May it please God to engage my whole Soul in holy Gratitude and Praise to Him who has been my only Saviour, my Refuge and Support! And might it please him to perfect the begun Mercy in my thorow Restoration and Recovery!

### SEPTEMBER, 1752

1. I have Somewhat comfortable Nights, and my Appetite is somewhat reviv'd, yet I am faint and weak, and have an inward Fever attending me, I suppose continually. I humbly wait the Divine Will. I am inform'd that divers Bears are about, and that one lay in my Field at the other Place lately, and has done Damage in the Corn.

2. Somewhat dull and heavy. Yet Mr. Stone and his Wife and Mr. Forbush from Brookfield and my Dauter, were here to see me and din'd with me. Near Night came Dr. Willson and Deacon Burnap from Hopkinton to see me also. Little Samuel brought home from Weaning.

[There are no entries dated September 3 to September 13, 1752 because of the change in the calendar.]

14. I remain feeble, yet I hope recruiting by slow Degrees. Mr. Forbush Studys here to Day, being about his preparations for the Sabbath—Billy has been about the Stalks, which he having cutt, he is gathering and Piking as he is able. By Reason of the late Frosts the Bushes are so Brown'd that the Year is advanc'd into the Fall even more than in proportion to the Alteration of the Date. Rain at Evening.

15. Mr. Forbush takes Leave and goes to Brookfield, appointing to return 4 Weeks from next Monday. P.M. Mr. Martyn here and Mrs. Winchester. At Eve I wrote a Letter to Dr. Scammell, Deacon Newton the Bearer.

16. This being the 51st Day in Old Style I would consider as being my Birth Day; and Bless God who has so wonderfully preserv'd me, and graciously born with me thro such a long Space as 49 Years. Vide Natalitia.

[Under the date of September 5, 1752 the following appears in the Natalitia.]

I attended in Some poor, broken manner upon like Exercises with those which have been wont to employ me on these Days. But am now under the holy Frowns of a righteous God afflicting and chastizing me by the Remains of illness, pains and weakness, which may it please God to Sanctifie and remove! And Blessed be His glorious Name, that in the Midst of Wrath he has remembered Mercy; and that I am in Some Measure reliev'd and hope I am in a Way of Recovery. If it shall please Him to restore me to His service, May my Life be devoted to Him and to His Glory at another Rate than ever heretofore! But desire humbly to yield myself to the Sovereign Will and Pleasure of the most high! I will, by his Grace enabling Me thereto bear the Indignation of the Lord for I have sinn'd against Him.

[The entry for September 16, 1752, continues in the diary.]

My Thumb on my left Hand begins to be in Pain; and it increas'd more and more. P.M. Mr. Joseph Manning comes from Concord and informs me that Mr. Minot, to whom I sent to preach for me tomorrow cannot come, it being Sacrament Day there. Deacon Newton brings me Directions and a little vial from Dr. Scammell.

17. Nobody to preach Still. How Melancholly, how Solitary! They read at the Meeting House Dr. Watts on Rom. 1, 16. Mrs. Tainter and Mary Biglo dine here. My hand exceeding full of Pain. At Night I put on a (Ninth) Blister.

18. My Hand much easier. D.G. Young Mr. Minot and Mrs. Bekky Hall[1] dine here, in their Return to Sutton. As did Mr. Daniel Forbush who is laying the Front Door Stone. P.M. I

---

[5] Timothy Minot, schoolmaster and supply preacher.

[6] Daniel Taylor. See Ithamar B. Sawtelle, *History of the Town of Townsend* (Fitchburg, 1878), pp. 154-155.

[7] Ebenezer Morse of Boylston.

[1] Rebecca was the daughter of the Reverend David Hall of Sutton.

wrote to the Reverend Mr. Haven of Portsmouth concerning my Townshend Interest—sent it per Mr. Joseph Manning. Ensign Millers Wife here.

19. Ebenezer waits upon his Aunt Lydia to Cambridge in Sergeant Maynard[2] of Shrewsbury's Chair. Mr. Manning with them. Mr. Wellman[3] din'd here. Billy goes to t'other House to take Care of Things and Creatures etc. there. Mr. Samuel Morris of Dudley here.

20. The Weather being clear and Warm I ventur'd to walk out abroad; and the Air was balmy and refreshing. Blessed be God for His great Goodness to me in raising me from so low and afflicted a State to so much Ease and Comfort.

21. My Wife went over to t'other House. The Reverend Mr. Price of Hopkinton now from Worcester, here, to make me an offer about Books of his I had Spoke to him of; but he spent the Chief of his Time with me in vindicating the Church of England. At Eve Mr. Newton—and divers others here to see me. Mr. Winchester brot a kind Letter from my Brother Samuel Parkman and several Presents, therewith. I walk'd abroad again.

22. My son Ebenezer came up from Watertown last Night and brot his Bride, Mrs. Elizabeth Harrington, the Dauter of Mr. Joseph Harrington of Watertown, with him, for they were marry'd yesterday p.m., and Mr. John Rogers came with the Team loaded with her Goods. May God please to make 'em an happy pair! A.M. Mr. Samuel Harrington being here I took the Opportunity to ride a few Rods on his Horse. P.M. Thomas came with a Chair and drove me over to See the New-Married and I din'd with them. He also brought me back before Night; so that I receiv'd no harm as I hope.

23. One Smith of Medfield here, enquiring about the Remedy for Cancers, his Father in Law, one Mr. Hammond having one, which has already destroyed one of his Eyes and now eats his Cheek. Wrote to Mr. Martyn to preach here tomorrow if Mr. Frink[4] preaches for him. The return was that he must preach at Marlboro. I wrote also to Mr. Cushing having been inform'd that Mr. Swan[5] is to preach for him: the return was that to-morrow will be their Sacrament, but that he will not prevent Mr. Swans coming to us. Billy brot over divers of our Goods from t'other House.

24. Through the great Goodness of God to me I went to His House, and was enabled to perform divine service both a. and p.m. but omitted Reading: I preach'd a.m. on Mic. 7, 9. P.M. (my son Ebenezer appearing Bridegroom) I preach'd a.m. on 1 Chron. 29, 19. Nor was I at Eve Extremely overcome. Blessed be God for His great Goodness and Mercy to me! O that I might never forget His Benefits! and might it please Him to perfect the recovery—that the Soul may be restor'd and have Eternal Life. N.B. Mr. John Martyn junior din'd with us.

25. I am not any thing (apparently) worse for the Exercise Yesterday: but my Knees are still weak, and my Left Hand is not without some Pain and stiffness. Noah Hardy came to plough my Stubble at the Island: but Billy was so late in bringing the Team from t'other House that they did little in the forenoon. P.M. they kept to the Work. The School has been kept several Days at Mr. Eliezer Rice's.

26. It is in General a very dry Time: very little Water in our Well—but there were considerable Showers of Rain last Night. P.M. Deacon Newton here and gives me a distinct account of their late proceedings at the Superior Court.

27. Bears are rife about: another is kill'd in Town. As to my-self, I hope I gather Strength in the Main, but it is Slowly. I can read and write longer than I could a while agoe. I desire to be heartily thankful to God for it. May I have the Grace to make a due Improvement of it! I almost daily endeavour something in my Preparations for the Sabbath. Billy goes to Mill to Cap-tain Drurys.[6] Write to my Brothers. P.M. Mr. Winchester.

28. Constantine Hardy ploughs with my Team the rest of my Field at Cook Island. At Eve Mr. Samuel Harrington here, and

acquaints me that he has brot home one of the three young Cattle that were turn'd into the Woods last Spring. The other two are missing, viz. a Three Year old Heifer and a Two Year old. They were under the Care of one Mr. John Curtis of Leicester, upper part.

29. A Number of men were here who had been hunting Bears which they See the Tracks of in many places about us. Mrs. Hephzibah Maynard to see me.

30. I feel Some pains in my left Shoulder, and Hand, and my Knees are weak. After a considerable Drought there comes a great and plentifull Rain.

### OCTOBER, NEW STYLE, 1752

1. It prov'd very rainy and confin'd me at both a. and p.m., a sore Frown of God's holy Sovereign Providence that I am thus chastiz'd. I design'd to have preach'd again upon Mic. 7, 9, but am forbid. May I have Grace to utter my Text my Self! Dr. Watt's sermon 18 of volume 1 read (on Rom. 1, 16). The Weather clears up about 4 or 5 p.m.

2. I rode to Mrs. Newtons (who had handsomely invited me to her House as soon as I Should get abroad again) and I din'd with her. P.M. I went to Deacon Newtons and borrow'd of him 18 Dollars with a View to my Paying Mr. Felton of Marlborough. When I return'd home Mr. Martyn came to see me.

3. I prepar'd my Self to go over to Mr. Martyns, but not hav-ing an Horse, I went not. In order to get an Horse I walked to Mr. Nurse's and thence to old Mr. Maynards. I proceeded fur-ther to my t'other House. N.B. I was without an Horse because Billy was gone to Mill, and I suppos'd Ebenezer to be gone to Leicester to look up the young Cattle which are missing: but the Cattle at Home were so unruly that he went not—but by that Time I got there it was too late. I rode to Mr. Richard Barns, and made him an offer of Two Thirds of the Lands which I bought of him, if he would procure and pay the Money which remains due by me to Mr. Felton but he would not accept my offer; not tho I repeated it over and over. I din'd with my Children at tother House and Mr. Grow with us. I return'd home before Night, I hope in safety, tho it was windy and somewhat searching to my poor crazy Limbs.

4. A fine Day. Mr. Daniel Forbush brot me Mr. Samuel Harringtons Horse for me to go and See his Wife who lyes in a low Condition. I went and found her in a gracious Frame, and tho very weak in Body yet I am full of Hopes for her Recovery. N.B. Captain John Tainter[1] There. Mr. Harrington sent his son with a Load of Wood to my House. At noon I rode to my other House and by Lieutenant Maynards urgent Invitation I went to their House, Colonel Ward being there to give out Commissions to several Officers in the New Troop lately rais'd out of Shrews-bury and this Town. Mr. Cushing[2] there and we had an hand-some Entertainment. My Son Ebenezer went this Morning up to Leicester Woods to look up our stray Cattle. His wife rode home with me and thence she rode to her Brother Bonds to tarry a Day or Two there. N.B. Mr. John Oake,[3] who has so long been under a terrible Evil of Cancer, was bury'd this afternoon.

5. A fine Day—p.m. I rode to Lieutenant Bruce's and reckon'd with him and his son Ephraim. I am still weak in my Knees and my left arm is somewhat Lame.

6. Another fine Day. I rode to Mr. Jonas Brighams[4] to see his sister Mrs. Deborah who has been ill for some Time. Thence I went to Marlborough. Settled with Mr. Jacob Felton, paying him the Money which I took up of him last Year to pay Mr. Richard Barns for 4 acres of Land which I bought of him, adjoin-ing to my old Place. Din'd at Colonel Williams's was at Mr. Smiths[5] and Dr. Brighams.[6] Return'd at Eve. N.B. Ebenezer return'd last night from Leicester and the lost Cattle are brought home. Lieutenant Tainter brought a Load of Wood and a Barrell of Cyder.

[2] Simon Maynard was one of the founders of the Shrewsbury Church.
[3] The Reverend James Wellman of Millbury.
[4] Thomas Frink of Rutland.
[5] Josiah Swan, formerly the minister of Dunstable, and now a schoolmaster of Lancaster.
[6] Thomas Drury of Grafton.

[1] Of Watertown. The brother of Deacon Simon Tainter of Westborough.
[2] The Reverend Job Cushing of Shrewsbury.
[3] Of Westborough.
[4] The son of David Brigham of Westborough.
[5] The Reverend Aaron Smith of Marlborough.
[6] Samuel Brigham, a physician of Marlborough.

7. A Storm of Rain arose towards Night, which grew impetuous.

8. It continued Stormy and rain'd all Day. But I could not bear that the people Should be again Destitute. I wrap'd my Self up exceedingly, had an Horse brot to my Door, and rode to the Meeting-House Door; by which means I attended and perform'd the Public Worship both a. and p.m. My Text Mal. 7, 9. N.B. I still omitt the Reading; and as to naming what Tune to sing, I acquainted the Congregation that the more special End which I had in going into that Custom having been, Some time Since, answer'd I should leave it to him that should sett the Tune to sing what he should think proper. I desire to bless God that at Evening I find no inconvenience by going out to Day. May God accompany the Word with the special Energy of His Holy Spirit—and especially make it profitable to my own Soul; that I may bear the Indignation of the Lord! I have the utmost Reason to because I have sinn'd against Him.

9. This Day was appointed and agreed upon by Lieutenant Tainter and others to gather my Corn at the Island, but the storm continues; and nothing can be done altho there is reason to fear it will rot.

10. The storm ceases a.m. but I am not able to attend the Association at Rutland to Day. Mrs. Martyn din'd with us. P.M. came her brother Marritt[7] of Cambridge. My Dauter Forbush[8] here and prepares to go to Cambridge.

11. The Weather Doubtfull and no Money for my Dauter's Journey—but at length the Air was clearer; and Esquire Baker came and lent me some Gold. Molly came but depended on her Brother Mr. Daniel Forbush to go with her, who did not come as expected. She went to his House. After the middle of the Day they Set out from hence to Cambridge and Boston. P.M. Mrs. Witt, my wife's Niece, and her sister Betty, came to us; but return'd to Marlboro.

12. Billy goes with my Team to Mr. Tainters for a Load of Cyder, and brings home a pair of Guinea Fowls from Mr. Daniel Forbush's and 30 Rails from Mr. James Millers junior. Mr. William Rogers works for me, clearing about the East Part of the Barn Land for tho it is fair yet my Corn is not fit to gather. Mrs. Lucy Bowker here p.m. cutting out several Garments for the little Boys. Mr. Elijah Rice of Shrewsbury here, with a Note from Mr. Nathaniel Livermore of Weston.

13. A Fair and pleasant Day for our Harvest. D.G. Lieutenant Tainter, Mr. Jonathan Forbush, Joseph Bowman and Isaac Miller cut up my Corn; and my Son William with my Team to Cart it; and afterwards Mr. Harrington with his Team; So that they got it all home before noon. Lieutenant Tainter, Joseph Bowman and Isaac Miller din'd here. Mrs. Lucy Bowker lodg'd here last night and is at work here to Day, making several of the Garments which She Cutt out Yesterday. Instead of Brother Samuel who was expected to come up on my Mare, my Brother William came. Brother Samuels Dauter Nabby being dangerously ill. P.M. a number of Hands husk'd out my Corn. Old Mr. Maynard and his sons, Ebenezer and Nathan, old Mr. Rice, Joseph Bowman, Isaac Miller, Mr. Bonds 2 Sons, 2 from Mr. Jonah Warrins, Daniel Grout, Constantine Hardy and some others, made up the Company. The Husking was over by that the Evening came: but they tarried so long as to thrust the Husks into the Barn. N.B. the Widow Newton and Mrs. Molly Johnson here. My Brother went over to the other House and lodged there.

14. Billy with assistance putts the remainder of the Husk'd Corn into the Barns. It was so Spoil'd with the Drought and with the Frost that there is but here and there a good Ear among it. But God is holy and Sovereign. My Brother with me again. Rain p.m.

15. I had not prepar'd, by Means of my Indispositions and Avocations (partly; and partly I fear through my too great Negligence—which may God in infinite Mercy forgive through Jesus Christ)! I took a Text conformable to the general Subject which I had been of late upon, viz. the eighth Commandment—honouring the Lord with our substance: the Text was Ps. 11, 7 and I us'd my Expositions of Mat. 6. P.M. I repeated Sermon

on John 17, 3 to page 12. N.B. My Brothers Expressions (denoting Assurance) in the Morning before we went to Meeting. N.B. he din'd at Deacon Newtons.

16. Tho under Pains and Infirmitys and the Day Cloudy, p.m. and Mr. Fish of Upton here, yet I visited the Widow Pierce: She is very bad, yet no great Signs of Repentence. Her Case very Deplorable! God be Mercifull to her! My Brother returns to Boston.

17. I am troubl'd with Rheumatic Pains Day by Day; especially in my left Arm.

18. Mr. Hezekiah Pratt has brought up my Mare from Boston and left my Dauter there.

19. I preach'd the Lecture. I make a Practice of delivering Sermons on these Occasions, which I have heretofore deliver'd for I cannot, under my Encumbrances and Difficultys, prepare fully, even so much as for the Sabbaths. What I deliver'd to Day was on Hos. 6, 6. Neither my Son Ebenezer nor Thomas were at Meeting; and but few others.

20. P.M. Mr. William Pierce acquaints me that his Mother is dead. At Eve Rain. Mr. Daniel Forbush brings up in his Cart, Brass, Pewter etc. from Boston for my Dauter.

21. A Bright Morning after a Stormy Night. O might I enjoy the like Favour in Spiritual Respects! I was not very well, but it being a bright good Day I ventur'd out to the Funeral of the Widow Pierce of Hopkinton. This prov'd a very great Interruption to my Studys—so that (to my great Grief) under my Infirmitys and Difficultys I can get but one Sermon ready for the Sabbath.

22. Preach'd on Heb. 9, 15, and administer'd the Sacrament of the Lords Supper. P.M. I repeated Sermon on 1 John 3, 23. Mrs. Emma Maynard din'd with us. May God be magnify'd that we have again this Solemnity!

23. I din'd early at home, and Catechiz'd at Mr. Joslins. 13 Children, Boys and Girls together. May God seal the Instruction!

24. I visited old Mr. Samuel Fay[9]—and Mrs. Harrington, they having desir'd Prayers last Lords Day. The first of them recovers to his usual State; the other languishes. My left Arm grows more Rheumatic Day by Day.

25. I din'd at home, but p.m. rode over to see Mr. Martyn, not having been there of a very great while: yet my pains were Successless: They both, Mr. Martyn and his Wife were gone to Southboro. I soon return'd—it was well I did: my little son Breck was carry'd home lame from School by Mr. Eliezer Rice—tis fear'd his Leg is broke. May God Sanctify!

26. Breck is no easier. Storm of Rain. Mr. Aaron Nurse with my Billy puts up my Husks from the Barn Floor. N.B. Uncommon Storm of Wind and Rain in the Night.

27. Breck's Leg no better: from the Discoverys I could make no Bone is broke, or put out of Joint, but I conceive the Tendons are strain'd, and perhaps the Ligaments at the Ankle. Mr. Grout, and old Mrs. Maynard at my Desire, came to See Breck, being feverish and not able to stir his Leg. I Sent by Mr. William Nurse for Dr. Brigham, who came, and I hope his anointing and bathing him was beneficial. Sent Billy to Mr. Joseph Goodale at Grafton for a pair of Chair Wheels, the time Sett being more than up. At Eve he returns, but without 'em. N.B. Ebenezer brought over part of the Young Cow which he kill'd yesterday—the whole Creature weigh'd 16 Score wanting one Pound. N.B. Mr. John Beton brought a Pair of Andirons for my Daughter Forbush, weigh'd 36 at 4/ per pound. N.B. one of our Guinea Fowls carry'd off in the Night by Some Animal of Prey.

28. My sons wife din'd here and tarried the Afternoon. Mr. Grout came kindly to See Breck, who is much as he was yesterday. I have been so interrupt'd in my studys by Brecks Lameness that I have not been able to touch any sermon for p.m. tomorrow—to my great sorrow and Grief.

29. A very Cold Day, and I have So much Pain in my left Arm, especially have in the Nights distressing Trouble with it, that I am much concern'd about the Event; yet I ventur'd to Meeting both Parts of the Day. Preach'd a.m. on Heb. 9, 15. P.M. I went on with a further Exercise about Alms etc. from

---

[7] Amos Marrett was the older brother of Mrs. John Martyn of Northborough.
[8] Mary Parkman had married the Reverend Eli Forbush or Forbes of Brookfield.

[9] Samuel Fay, Jr., nephew of the late Captain John Fay of Westborough.

Mat. 6, 4 repeating my Expository Attempts on that Passage from page 6 to 10.

30. The Reverend and Learned Mr. Clark[10] of Salem Village here, in returning home from Sutton, where he, with two more ministers, Mr. Dor[11] and Mr. Hobby,[12] had been assisting Mr. Wellmans Church and some agriev'd Brethren to a reconcilement and tis to be hop'd with some success. One Mr. Bartlett was with him and they din'd here. P.M. Mr. Moses Warrin[13] and his wife here and were examin'd.

31. Mr. Forbush came last Night to the Other House, and hither this Morning—but hastens away to Boston (his wife being still there) and carrys with him John Barrett; he has Mr. Martyns Chair and my Mare. Ebenezer makes an Husking this Evening. I am but lame yet in my left Arm. And we are much put to 't for Wood, but we have some Loggs and we pick about and get one Thing and another. Yet it is difficult because the season is unusually Cold, and I am so infirm. But I desire to trust in the careful faithfull Providence of God!

### NOVEMBER, 1752

1. A fine Day. I rode abroad tho my Arm is upon many Occasions thrown into great Pain. Was at Esquire Bakers; visit Mrs. Harrington and din'd there—at Deacon Forbush's, Elijah Rice's—visit Mr. Pierce's Family—his Wife and son Seth sick—the latter very bad. Mr. Pierce was my Company home, and I had some free Conversation with him. N.B. Lieutenant Tainter brought me a Load of Wood. Mr. Moses Warrin another.

2. Messers. Elijah Rice and Martyn Pratt break out and swingle Flax. And Charles Rice and John Frost digg stones. P.M. at Mr. Bradish's, Private Meeting. N.B. There were few there, even tho I waited long for their Coming. It arose from a Mistake about New and Old Style. We pray'd and Sung, but the design'd Sermon was omitted. When I return'd home Mr. Martyn was here. He had been to see his son, Mr. John who is now sett up a Corier[1] among us, and begins to work. N.B. Dr. Brigham came to see Brecks Leg, which he can't yet go upon.

3. Billy went with the Team and brought home from Mr. Jonathan Fay's, his present a Barrell of Cyder which Ebenezer Nurse presents me, and further Lieutenant Tainter brought a Barrell of Cyder which Mr. Bowman has given. I desire thankfully to acknowledge the Goodness of God in stirring up the Minds of His People to bestow thus bountifully upon me who am so unworthy. My wife went to Mr. Joseph Batchellors in Grafton. Mr. Ephraim Sherman (come from Boston with his Team) din'd with me.

4. My son Ebenezer draws Stones with my Team, for underpinning the Barn and Billy assists him. Mr. Forbush and his wife tarry at Boston or Cambridge yet.

5. A very pleasant Day. I preach'd a. and p.m. on Heb. 9, 15. N.B. Ebenezer and his Wife went home to the Other House to Dinner. Old Mrs. Whipple din'd here. After the Exercises p.m. I Stop'd the Church and read a Draught of a Letter which I had prepar'd to Send in my own Name to the Committee of the aggrieved Brethren in the West Church in Sudbury. But it was desir'd they might have some Time to take it into Consideration before they discover'd their Thots upon it.

6. Messers Biglo and Claffland came a.m. to underpinning my Barn. P.M. we all go to the Burying of Mr. William Pierce's son Seth, his wife and Two more sons sick of the Same Fever.

7. Messers Biglo and Claffland at work here again, underpinning the Barn and making a Stage or Causey to go into the stable Door. They also face the Well. I visit Mrs. Pierce and her sons. N.B. I was at Justice Bakers to get him to pay Captain Chandler of Worcester for me 20£ Old Tenor and he tells me he will do it.

8. Mr. Forbush and his Wife came from Boston, where my Dauter has been, now a long Time providing for her keeping

House. They lodg'd at t'other House, as did Mr. [blank] Taylor of Brookfield from Captain Witts with a Team for Mrs. Forbush's Goods.

9. Mrs. Nabby Baker making and altering Gowns for Lucy. She, with Mr. Taylor[2], Mr. Bartlett[3] of Sutton din'd here. My Dauters Goods which are here, loaded up in Mr. Taylors Cart: and he goes to t'other House to lodge. Mr. Forbush etc. here with us, and both dine and lodge here—which is a Rarity!

10. After Mr. Forbush etc. had din'd here they went to Upton to visit Mr. Fish[4] and his Wife, tho there was great likelihood of Rain.

11. Rain a.m. Mr. Forbush and his wife return'd from Upton P.M.

12. Mr. Forbush preach'd a. and p.m. A.M. on Isa. 64, 6, that Clause "And we all do fade as a Leaf." P.M. on Rom. 16, 7—"Who were in Christ before me," insisting chiefly on those words, "who were in Christ." N.B. My Dauter was not well and did not go to Meeting.

13. So great Rain p.m. especially that we little expected Company. Yet at Eve came a number of persons from Brookfield, viz. Captain Witt, Messers. Bartlett and Abraham How. The two former lodged here. Mr. How lodg'd at Captain Bakers. Several Persons came also to t'other House—viz. Jeduthan Baldwin, who rode in a Chair for Mr. Forbush and my Dauter, and one Mr. Smith. Two others also who lodg'd at [blank]. Mrs. Nabby Baker here making and altering Gowns for my Dauter Lucy.

14. Early in the Morning Mr. Forbush and his Wife, with the Company who came to wait on them together with a Number from us, My Son Ebenezer and his Wife, Thomas and Lucy—Messers. Daniel and Jonathan Forbush and their Wives, took leave of us for Brookfield, designing to dine at Sergeants[5] at Leicester; the weather Fair, and Everyone, through Mercy, in Health. Lucy is gone with her sister to tarry with her this Winter. May God be gracious to them, and give them a prosperous Journey by the Will of God! and may their Joys be never diminish'd! I visited Mrs. Pierce and her Children that are sick. P.M. Antoine Cussuc, a Deserter from the French Forces at Chignecto, or from Crown Point, here. At Eve I marry'd Mr. Francis Harrington[6] and Mrs. Deborah Brigham,[7] at her Brother Jonas's, and I supp'd there.

15. Ensign Josiah Rice made me a present of a pair of Turkeys and a Bag of Turnips. N.B. Billy, and Mrs. Molly Bond[8] are all that keep House at my other House.

16. Publick Thanksgiving. I preach'd on Ps. 50, 22. O that we might truely offer praise, so as that we may indeed Glorifie God! and so order our Conversation that we may all See and enjoy the Salvation of God! N.B. Mr. Edwards Whipple who has been wont to set the Tune, having set 100 new at the first singing, Mr. David Batherick was so displeas'd that at the Next Singing he rose up and Set a Tune that would please himself better, and thus likewise at the last Singing, to the great Disturbance of many. At Evening cames Messers. Williams, Francis and Edwards Whipple, Nathan Maynard and Mr. Jonathan Ward,[9] the Schoolmaster to visit me.

17. Mr. Nathan Sergeant of Leicester who has been at Work for me in making some Joiners Ware for my Daughter Forbush in his way to Boston din'd here.

18. The Turkey Cock was Stole away by a Fox as we suppose.

19. On Ps. 11, 7, a.m., and when I nam'd that Psalm to be Sung expressly desir'd Mr. Edwards Whipple would Set the Tune, and added that considering how awful those Words are, may no one presume, on what Pretence So ever to interrupt the Sacred Worship. P.M. repeated Sermon 308 to 310, on 2 Cor. 3, 15, in

---

[10] Peter Clark of Danvers.
[11] Joseph Dorr of Mendon.
[12] William Hobby of Reading.
[13] Moses, the son of Daniel Warrin of Westborough, had married, Jan. 24, 1751, Persis, the daughter of Seth Rice.

[1] Corier (or coriar) was an obsolete form of currier, meaning one engaged in the trade of dressing and coloring leather.

[2] James Taylor of Sutton.
[3] Richard Bartlett.
[4] The Reverend Elisha Fish.
[5] Jonathan Sargent kept a tavern in Leicester. Emory Washburn, *Historical Sketches of Leicester* (Boston, 1860), p. 391.
[6] Of Worcester.
[7] The daughter of David Brigham of Westborough.
[8] The daughter of Jonathan Bond.
[9] The son of Hezekiah Ward of Westborough.

one Exercise. And may God please to fasten and ripen the Impressions which arise hereby!

20. Rainy. No one but Billy and Molly Bond to keep House and take all the Care of the Stock etc. at t'other Place. At Eve came Several Brethren of the Church to See me (and it was agreeable to my Desire Signify'd to Deacon Forbush) and converse about the Sudbury Affair. They were Lieutenant Tainter, Ensign Miller, and Mr. Whitney: afterwards came Deacon Forbush. They were of opinion that there was no need of the Churchs acting any Thing formally about it. The Authors of the Sudbury Letter had requested Nothing but that we would consider of our own Conduct, which it no doubt behoves us to do: Let the Pastor of this Church if he pleases do So much as inform one of them that their Letter has been laid before us. Those Brethren aforesaid made some Business of discoursing about Brother Bathericks Conduct on the late Day of Publick Thanksgiving. They agreed that Deacon Forbush Should go and talk with him—and if he should appear unconvinc'd of his Error, they conceiv'd it must be laid before the Church. But if he was Sensible, and would do so no more, this being discover'd to the Pastor, they were willing it should be passed over. Left Arm so Painful I put on a Blister.

21. Esquire Baker here. Informs me that he has paid Captain Chandler of Worcester 20£, 13, 4, Lawful money, for me. It being for 1000 Clabboards which I bought of him last year. He Signifys to me at the Same Time that Captain Chandler express'd uneasiness at my long Delay. I gave Esquire Baker a note till the first of next April. Sometimes rainy. The Weather exceeding windy—Sour—and therefore So uncomfortable that I am much confin'd whereas I had otherwise gone to t'other House to See how Billy Conducts there, or to Mr. Pierce's seeing another, Francis, lies now Sick among them—Five, in all, now Sick. May God be mercifull to them. At Eve came Mr. Marrit of Cambridge, and smok'd a pipe with me, but he lodg'd I suppose at Justice Bakers.

22. North West Wind very Cold this morning—Tis the Day appointed for the Ordination of Mr. Jacob Cushing[10] at Waltham. May he be strong in the Grace which is in Christ Jesus! Am debarr'd the pleasure of Waiting upon it, but may God be with me in my Solitude! Mr. Joseph Goodale and his Wife, from Grafton, for Boston din'd here. Billy from t'other House informs me that his Brothers return'd from Brookfield last Night. Billy rides p.m. to Mr. Joseph Batchellors at Grafton.

23. The Coldest Morning hitherto. The Earth is now froze hard. P.M. Snows hard. Mrs. Persis Warrin, wife of Moses Warrin, here. At Eve, he himself—both of them that I might gather Minutes from them for their Relation to the Church. My Lameness in my left Arm very troublesome. Can't pull off or put on my Cloths. My Affairs Somewhat perplex'd. My son has not come to me since his Journey to Brookfield and winter is come upon us before I am ready—No place to put up my Cattle o'nights, how cold or Stormy Soever. No small Wood at the Door, but some Pine which being lately cut down is unfit to burn. But my wife went to See old Mrs. Dorcas Forbush[11] and get Lieutenant (her son) to let his Team go, and Samuel Forbush now prevail'd with to bring up a Load before Night. May the Lord look on my very Afflicted State and appear for my Help and Relief as he has numberless Times done!

24. The morning bright, and the whole Earth round us in its Winter White. As to me altho I am not able to dress my Self in my upper Cloths, yet I thank God I feel so well in my Stomach and am able to read, write, Study, go to the Door; and So far look after my Affairs. My Confinement however, gives me many Disappointments. May I have the Grace to exercise the Patience call'd for!

25. But may God be pleas'd to grant me a Suitable Frame of Temper under all his Dealings with Me and Mine! At Eve came Three of our Young Kinswomen, viz. Ruth, Hannah and Elizabeth Hicks[12] from Salem and Cambridge in their return Home to Sutton; and lodge here. N.B. This is the first Night of our tying up Cattle in my New Barn. We now put up three Cows.

26. Our Kinswomen keep Sabbath with us. I preach'd on Ps. 11, 7, a. and p.m. At Eve our Kinswomen went home with Ebenezer. O that we might be truely righteous that we might have the reward and be blessed with the Righteous!

27. A bright pleasant Day. I walk'd up to Mr. Ebenezer Rice's to reckon with him; but he was not at home. I visited Sarah Newton[13] lately cur'd of a Polypus[14] in her Nose: Din'd there (at Deacon Newton's) but the Deacon not at Home. At Mr. Nurse's also. In the Eve Ebenezer was here, and we had some talk of our Settling our Affairs—his Labour on the place as taking it to the halves etc. I gave him Two Ridgling Piggs of last Spring, over and above, but we defer the Exact Settling.

28. Our Kinswomen, who have been a Night or Two past at t'other House, return hither and go over to Upton, designing from thence Home to Sutton. The Weather frequently wet: the Day in general Dark, windy and uncomfortable. My Arm I think is somewhat better through the Favour of God, but my Wife dull, disconsolate. May God Himself, Support, Strengthen and Comfort her!

29. I was at Mr. Biglo's and convers'd with Captain Ephraim Littlefield of Holliston there, concerning the present state of the Church there. I din'd at Mr. Elijah Rice's. Went from thence (in the Rain) to Mr. Pierce's. Mr. Barrett[15] there, praying with the sick. I also pray'd with them before I came away.

30. Rainy, but Mr. Hutchinson[16] came and din'd with me, and preach'd the Lecture on Heb. 13, 20. After Sermon Moses Warrin and Persis his wife were admitted into the Church, also Amy Mainard Wife of Ebenezer Mainard. N.B. This was done agreeable to a proposal of it made to the Church and consented to last Lords Day. They were admitted before the Congregation because the Day was So short, and Dark Night soon coming on. Furthermore, the Brethren were stop'd to see what they would incline to do about the Sudbury Affair. Their Minds were, to let it drop, so no Vote was pass'd about it. N.B. I ask'd the Churchs Minds respecting my appointing or desiring a Person to sett the Psalm, and they voted that they were Satisfy'd with what I had done in it, particularly with my having desir'd Brother Edwards Whipple to Sett the Psalm. I moreover requested that they would Shew their Minds respecting the Tunes which we had usually Sung—Triple-time Tunes were especially intended, viz. Mear Ps. 100 new etc. They voted Satisfaction thereupon. At least I conceiv'd there was a Vote, because nobody objected against it: but otherwise, I am not altogether clear in it, that there was a Majority of Hands.[17] N.B. Mr. Silas Brigham here; and I gave him an Extract from the Reverend Mr. Morse's[18] Letter about him.

At the Close of this Month I would take Notice of the great Goodness of God in that I enjoy Such a Measure of Ease and Comfort as I am favour'd with; having good Appetite to my Food and in my Breast, Strength and Vigor, Notwithstanding that in my Limbs I have Sometime; the Blister I lately us'd upon it having reliev'd me but a little. But my Family Cares are heavy and Perplexing, and especially the deep and distressing Concern for my Everlasting well-being, and that of my dear Wife, Children; and to these I would not fail to add my dear Flock. O what shall I do that this greatest of all Interests may be Secur'd! and that true, Spiritual Religion may indeed flourish among us! Blessed be God that we are still permitted the invaluable Privileges of the Means and Season of Grace, notwithstanding my great unprofitableness; and our indifference in Matters of Religion in general. O that God would please to pour out His Spirit upon us; and that I might especially myself experience the happy Effects of it!

---

[13] The daughter of Abner Newton.

[14] A polyp, a mass of swollen mucous membrane.

[15] Samuel Barrett of Hopkinton.

[16] Aaron Hutchinson of Grafton.

[17] In the Westborough Church Records, Nov. 30, 1752, Parkman entered: "The Brethren also voted that they were Satisfy'd in the Pastors having desir'd Brother Edwards Whipple to Set the Tune; and in the Tunes which we have been wont to Sing in this Congregation. N.B. These last Votes were occasion'd by Some late Disturbances in our Singing."

[18] Ebenezer Morse of Boylston.

---

[10] Jacob (Harvard 1748), the son of the Reverend Job Cushing of Shrewsbury, served the First Congregational Church of Waltham, 1752–1809. *Sibley*, XII, 252–257.

[11] Widow of the late Thomas Forbush.

[12] Daughter of John Hicks of Sutton, Parkman's brother-in-law.

## DECEMBER, 1752

1. The Rain continues Still. Billy goes to School to Day to Mr. Jonathan Ward at Mr. Eliezer Rice's. Samuel Bumpso Bushel Turnips. P.M. Sun breaks out I improv'd the Day in Study, prayer and Self Reflection. At Eve Mr. Batherick here. Tells me he is sorry for what he did on the late Day of Thanksgiving, and that he will do so no more.

2. Ebenezer and his wife watch'd at Mr. Pierce's last night It remains an House of great Distress. Ebenezer Pierce is now taken ill. Mr. Hezekiah Pratt a Load of Wood, when we were much Straitned. Mr. Grout another.

3. Having finish'd both my Sermons last Night, my Mind is happily freer to Day. Thanks be to God who has enabled me thus far. I preach'd a.m. on Isa. 9, 6, first Clauses. Administer'd the Lord's Supper. Deacon Forbush din'd with us. P.M. on I Cor. 6, 9, 10, the unrighteous etc. Shall not inherit the Kingdom of God. This finishes the eighth Commandment. N.B. Deacon Forbush dines with us. The Weather Comfortable a great Favour considering how late in the Year. O might I suitably profit by the services of this Day! Be humbl'd for all my unrighteousness, and repair to and copy after Jesus the righteous, and escape the punishment of the unjust!

4. Mr. John Martyn[1] bore me a Message from his Father desiring me to preach his Lecture next Wednesday. The Town Met to Day at the North Meeting House, to consider and provide Money to pay Town-Debts. N.B. We this Day gave out the Last of the Corn in the Corn-Barn (which was the Island Corn) Nor is there any left of all the Indian Corn that I rais'd here, excepted a few Ears in the Garrett which were trac'd up. Billy gets out Corn for our Eating, at t'other House. At Evening Snows—in the Night the storm prevails, and by Morning the Snow is pritty deep. But God protects and guards Supplys and comforts us.

5. A very Winterlike Morning. The Day bright by 10 a.m. but Cold. I examin'd Some Number of Authorities yesterday and to Day on the ninth Commandment and am writing Something of an Exposition of it. Read also Stackhouse's Body of Divinity.[2] It grows exceeding Cold.

6. Messers. Martyn Pratt and Elijah Rice, get out Flax. Neighbour Eliphalet Adams also. N.B. Mr. Jonathan Forbush brot me about 254 feet of Plank which he had sav'd for my stable and Cow House. N.B. It was So Cold I did not venture to go over to preach Mr. Martyns Lecture to Day. I desire to be humbled under the Frowns of God's Providence whereby I am detain'd and prevented.

7. Rainy, and raw Cold. Lieutenant Tainter and his son Simon, and Neighbour Eleazer Williams kill'd an Hog for me of 253. I catechiz'd at the Meeting-House, but had only Two Children besides 4 of my own. Lieutenant at Evening. Salted up my Pork.

8. Lieutenant Tainter assisted my son Ebenezer in killing and dressing a Cow, at t'other House. I visited Mr. Pierce's Family. Ebenezer Pierce extreme bad. N.B. Mr. Whipple's Mill-stone from Hopkinton.

9. Cold Searching Winds, and very uncomfortable Weather to poor Rheumaticks. Lieutenant Hunt[3] of Concord, Brother in Law to Deacon Merriam[4] of Grafton, here; chiefly on the Affairs of Acton, from whence he wants to be dismiss'd. The uneasiness which he and others have with Mr. Swift,[5] much the Same with the Sudbury Brethren with Mr. Loring.[6]

10. Extreme high Winds last night. A Cold, uncomfortable Air, tho bright. I preach'd a.m. on Exod. 20, 16. I had prepar'd what I conceiv'd to be Sufficient for both Exercises, but that I might not be So long in the Exposition of this Commandment as I was of the last, I strove hard, and deliver'd the whole in one. P.M. I form'd an Exercise from 2 Cor. 5, 11, first part. N.B. I

deliver'd all that related to the Chapter and what was peculiar to the tenth of the Text, without writing. And for the Body of the Subject us'd Sermon on Heb. 9, 27, from page 21 to 28, and 37, 38. And O that the Exercise might prove awakening and instructing unto all of us!

11. The Parish met and made the like Grant of 60£ Lawfull Money, as last Year; and voted to finish the pulpit, ministerial Pew, Stairs, Gallery Floors, and Breast work.[7] Ebenezer brot over 3 Quarters of the Cow, he with Lieutenant Tainter help kill'd last Week—the 4 Quarters weigh'd 18 score wanting one part.

12. My sons wife goes over to her Brother Bonds to stay a few Days. I walk'd up to Mr. Charles Rice's. Reckon'd with Merchant Rice and I am this Day indebted to him about 12£ old Tenor. Cousen Samuel Trask here.

13. Visited at Mr. Pierce's. Ebenezer somewhat reviv'd had desir'd me to come. I was at Dinner with them. Was p.m. at Mr. Bonds and at Mr. Warrins.

14. Heard of the Sudden Death of Venerable and aged Mr. Hancock[8] of Lexington. May God be pleas'd to show me convincingly and Effectually that I must also put off this my Tabernacle! At Evening marry'd Joseph Bruce to the Widow Child.[9]

15. A very Cold Morning after a Cold Night. Mrs. Molly Martyn din'd with us. She came over on foot, and p.m. goes up to Justice Bakers. Ebenezer Pierce dy'd about noon in his twenty second Year, accounted the most hopeful in the Family.

16. The Season becomes very Cold, and we are so unhappy as to have but a Small Woodpile: but I desire the Grace suitably to depend upon the kind Providence of God, who has always taken Care of me.

17. I provided very sufficiently for each part of the Day, especially for such a Short, Cold Day—but I was afraid my Expositions of this Commandment would take up too many Exercises, and therefore Strove hard to do as last Lords Day, even though I had now more pages than then, and deliver'd it all in the a.m. on Exod. 20, 16. P.M. repeated Sermon on Mat. 25, 46, on the Extremity of Hells Torments. O that God might please to accompany it with his Special Blessing!

18. At the Funeral of Ebenezer Pierce. A Sorrowful Time! This Death Seems to be much lamented. Many more attended it than I expected because of the fears of the people are under of being Seiz'd with the Same Fever. Mrs. Pierce and their Dauter Hannah lies sick yet. O might these Providences issue in the divine Glory, and their, and all our highest Good! And especially may our young people be Suitably awaken'd, and abiding Impressions be made upon them hereby! Alexander to School to Captain Maynards.

19. My Wife and I rode over to Mr. Martyns—din'd there, and tarry'd till almost Evening. Mr. Martyn has lately bought a Variety of New Books. I borrow'd of him Martins Phylosophical Grammar.[10] At Evening we stop'd at t'other House, and talk'd with Ebenezer[11] about his Circumstances and Manner of living there, and gave him what Encouragement I could. I feel a great deal of deep Concern for both his Temporal and Spiritual Good. May God direct me what to do for him, for the Securing both, but especially the latter! N.B. Lieutenant Tainter brought a Load of choice Walnut Wood. My Sons Father in Law, Mr. Joseph Harrington, on his Journey to Connecticut call'd here, while we were absent.

20. Mr. Hezekiah Pratt and Mr. Aaron Nurse assisted in Killing my other Hog. Weigh'd 9 Score and Six Pounds. At Eve Mr. David Maynard assisted in Cutting it out. Mr. Samuel Harrington a Load of Wood.

[1] The son of John Martyn, the minister of the north precinct.

[2] Thomas Stackhouse, *A Complete Body of Divinity . . . Extracted the best Ancient and Modern Writers* (London, 1729). A second edition was published in London in 1734.

[3] Simon Hunt.

[4] Joseph Merriam, one of the pioneers of Grafton, married Ruth Hunt of Concord. Pierce, *Grafton*, p. 532.

[5] John Swift, Jr.

[6] Israel Loring.

[7] At this precinct meeting they also voted "to sell the pews; the highest payer in the two years they were building to have the first choice. Chose a committee to mark out the pews and to dignify and set a price upon each pew. Voted that the pew room on the floor next to the walls, and the room where the four hind seats should be, shall be called Pew-Room." DeForest and Bates, *Westborough*, p. 137.

[8] John Hancock died Dec. 5, 1752.

[9] Sibyl (Cibel, Sibel) was the widow of Jonas Child of Westborough.

[10] Benjamin Martin, *The Philosophical Grammar; being a View of the Present State of Experimented Physiology, or Natural Philosophy* (London, 1735). Another edition was published in London in 1738.

[11] Ebenezer, Jr., who had married Elizabeth Harrington of Watertown, Sept. 21, 1752, was living in the old parsonage located on the hill where the Lyman School now stands.

21. I went over to t'other House. My 3 sons are trimming over the New swamp the Ground being open and froze. I din'd there. I gave Ebenezer my Yoke of Oxen, and Two Young Heifers coming Two: also a last Year Calf. Alpheus Newton brought Two Load of Wood. Mr. William Rogers cutt up a Parcell of Wood at the Door, which was a Considerable Kindness. Cousen Winchester here.

22. A Cold Day. Old Mr. Dunlop din'd here. Billy at t'other House. They kill'd one of the Ridgling Shoats which have been some Trouble to us. Ensign Rice sent another Turkey Cock to t'other House—price 20/ old Tenor.

23. Raw Cold. Ebenezer brought over in the Team 4 Sticks for Sleepers to lay my Barn Floor, and he hung my Small Door on the South Side of the Barn. Mr. David Goodenow here. He brings a Petition (drawn up by Mr. Martyn) Sign'd by himself requesting a Charitable Contribution for him.

24. Preach'd on Exod. 20, 16 a. and p.m. Mrs. Grow din'd here. N.B. I had Some Discourse with Mr. Richard before I consented to baptize his infant Child. He assures me his wife and he are well reconcil'd, and he promises to walk orderly and soberly as becomes a Christian. P.M. after the Exercises, immediately before giving the Blessing, I read Mr. Goodenows Petition for a Contribution. I desir'd the Deacons of the Church and the Committee of the Parish to meet at my House tomorrow Eve, that I may have their Thoughts about it.

25. I rode to Mr. Amsdens to Mr. Thaddeus Gale's son Jacob who lies Sick. N.B. Dr. Robinson[12] of Marlboro there. Din'd with him at Mr. Amsdens Table. N.B. Instead of Resentments with Mr. Gale, who has been of a long Time represented by Mr. Grow as offended Mr. Gale came to me and thank'd me for my Visit etc. and then presented me with a double Toasting Iron requesting I would come again and See them. At Eve Deacons Forbush and Newton, Lieutenant Bruce and Mr. Phinehas Hardy (who with Deacon Newton made up a Majority of the Precinct Committee) met here at my Request publickly yesterday, to confer and give me their Thot, what would be best to be done with regard to the Contribution which Mr. David Goodenow had petitioned for. Mr. Grow was also here. They, upon the whole, could not advise to it by Virtue of that Petition, the reason they gave was, he did not appear humble, and blaming himself for his poverty, but the Contrary, and rather casting Blame where he ought not. And they Thought it left that I Should write to him.

26. Deacon Newton returns to me this Morning further to strengthen what was Said last Night. P.M. Deacon Newton carry'd a Letter from me to Mr. Goodenow—he went also to Mr. Martyns. My wife to old Mr. Rice's at Widow Newtons—I went to her at Eve. At Eve Ebenezer here and brings me an Hat which he brought from Mr. Doolittle's. Had still some further Discourse with Ebenezer about his Circumstances—occasion'd by his own Desire to know how he must be settled. Mr. Israel Walker here in the Evening desirous that I would take Boards of him to pay Thomas for a Saddle, or at least in part.

27. Deacon Newton here to give me account of his Journey to the North Side; and Says he saw but little alteration, by his Discourse, with Mr. Goodenow. I read Martyns Phylosophical Grammar. Ebenezer brought 4 more Sleepers for my Cow-House floor. My Wife to Captain Maynards.

28. Mr. Joseph Harrington (my Brother in law) here—Supps with me but goes to Mr. Bonds to lodge.

29. A Severe Storm of Snow. At Eve Sundry Men here; particularly Three of the Committee laying out the Pew Ground in the Meeting House who have been upon that Business to Day. They were Mr. Grow, Lieutenant Bruce, Mr. Jonathan Bond. The other Two of the Committee are Messers. Francis Whipple and David Maynard junior.

30. Billys face remains So broke out that it is very Sore, but goes up to Mr. Winchesters in Grafton. John Maynard tertius brings a piece of Beef. It may be noted and remember'd that I have receiv'd from the people above an hundred Valuable Presents and kind Assistances, which I have writ down, Since August 3, when I began to be confin'd by Rheumatism. I desire to take a grateful Notice herefor. Would bless God who has inclin'd and open'd their Hearts hereunto. May God be pleas'd to reward them abundantly for all their Bountys, and give me and mine the Grace to make a right use and Improvement of them!

31. I preach'd on Deut. 32, 29, a. and p.m., but could not finish my design as to a full and large Application and especially dilating in the Meditations on our Last Day of Life, and on the Last Day of the World: but must leave it to another Time. However, I went into Some brief Hints hereof to the people, and endeavoured more peculiarly to exercise myself therein in the Evening when the Year was closing up.

### JANUARY, 1753

I desire humbly to wait upon God for the Great Grace necessary to make a right use and improvement of the Swift Flight of Time—Time which is So exceeding precious! How prone am I to depend on what I am my Self doing when nothing is or can be vainer! How prone I am also to depend upon having another Year to Spend as I have had the former, whereas infinite Wisdom has advis'd that I boast not of So much as tomorrow, because I know not what a Day will bring forth. As I would heartily praise God for this Day, So would devoutly resign to Him, whether I shall enjoy any more, or how many; and what shall befall both me and mine. Mr. Daniel Hardy brot me a Load of Wood.

2. Mr. Daniel Adams and my son Thomas are at Work upon a Floor in my Barn for my Cattle. Mr. Jonathan Forbush brought a Load of Wood.

3. Mr. Adams and my son Thomas again. N.B. 4 more Cattle brought from my other place to keep at this new Barn. Weather very Cold. Simon Tainter tertius and his Brother (2 Boys) brought a Load of Walnut Wood with their Steers and little Sled.

4. A Storm of Snow. Mr. Adams and Thomas Still. All the Plank laid but the floor not finish'd. We put up 7 Cattle. My wife and I to the private Meeting at Lieutenant Tainters. Preach'd on Ps. 23, 4. Storm increas'd at Eve.

5. One Mrs. Goold, a Widow, at Mr. Clafflands, Sent for me, She being in a very low Condition in great Distress. Mr. Joseph Manning din'd with us. Mr. Jeduthan Baldwin from Brookfield at Eve, and brought us comfortable News of the Welfare of my Children there. D.G. He Lodg'd with us.

6. Baldwin left us—wrote by him to Mr. Martyn about the Contributions for Mr. Goodenow.

7. Cold Day. I read publickly Deut. 18. Preach'd on Deut. 32, 29. Deacon Forbush and Mrs. Mary Green (wife of Joseph junior) din'd here. P.M. read 2 Cor. 13, and preach'd on number 5 of the Same, making use of Sermon on 1 Cor. 11, 28. O that God would please to grant an abiding Impression!

8. The Weather Cold and Raw. Visited Mrs. Grant, who is ill, and din'd there. P.M. was at Mr. Ebenezer Millers on occasion of the Funeral of his Infant.

9. My son Thomas went to Sutton for shirting. Mrs. Parkman to Esquire Bakers preparing for a Journey. I din'd at Lieutenant Forbush's being on a visit to his aged Mother. Rode his Horse to Lieutenant Bruce's. Deliver'd him an order to Mr. Grow for 60£ old Tenor. At Eve Mr. Jedediah Fay from Ashford with the Flax. I bought 11£ weight of him. Mr. Ephraim Bruce, Collector, here, and pays me (for the first time) 19. 15. 10 old Tenor. N.B. heard that the Reverend Mr. Goddard's Wife[1] is bury'd this Day. May God be with him in drinking the Wormwood and Gall!

---

[12] Jeremiah Robinson, who did not have a college education, married Eunice, the daughter of Thomas Amsden of Marlborough. Robinson practiced medicine in Marlborough for many years.

[1] Mercy, the wife of David Goddard of Leicester, died Jan. 4, 1752/3. Town records incorrectly give 1751 as the year of her death.

10. Mr. Eleazer Whitney a Load of Wood. My Wife to Boston with Lieutenant Tainter in his Whirry. Mr. Grow brought a Guinea Cock to supply the Place of That which (as we suppose) a Fox killed, a while agoe.

11. Sarah has worried through the Night with the Child (tho he has not been well for Some Time). Alexander is at t'other House, and the rest I took into my own Chamber last night in their Mothers Absence.

12. Exceeding pleasant Day. Fear t'is a weather breeder. William and many more go afishing at the great Pond—they catch a great Number of Pickerell. Sarah is my House keeper and manages very agreeably—But am oblig'd myself to attend more peculiarly to the Family Circumstances. Mr. Grow and his son Whitney here, and bring me another Load of Wood.

13. A Thaw: Southerly Wind and Rain. The Snow goes off apace—fear my Wife with her Fellow-Traveller, has an heavy Journey. About Sun setting Lieutenant Tainter and my Wife arriv'd in Safety. D.G. They lodg'd at Captain Tainters at Watertown the first Night—she lodg'd at Brother Samuels at Boston the Second, and at Brother Harringtons at Watertown the last—they din'd at Colonel Buckminsters to Day, and in general have had prosperous Journey. The Child, Samuel, has also done pretty well with us. N.B. Sorrowful News of the Sudden Death of the Reverend Mr. Ellis Gray[2] of Boston, being Suddenly Seiz'd with a Numb Palsie last Lords Day morning and dy'd the Same Day, to he inexpressible Surprize and Grief of the whole Town.

14. Exceeding Cold. The Wind very cutting. Read Deut. 19, preach'd on Ps. 78, 36. P.M. read Gal. 1, and preach'd again on 2 Cor. 13, 5, making use of the latter part of Sermon on 1 Cor. 11, 28, with omissions, alterations and additions.

15. Jacob Garfield here; and tho he pretends he has come with great earnestness about the Affair that has lain so long between Mr. Parkman and him and he wants to have it issued and done with, yet can't stay to be examin'd, but must attend upon other Business;—but he thought he would call and see whether it would be now, or no.

16. Billy goes to School to learn to write, the School being kept at Captain Maynards. The Precinct meet to Day to enquire into their Debts and grant money instead of Mr. James Maynards Rates to make up my Sallery for last Year. Mr. Martyn and his Wife came p.m. and tarry over night. At Eve Mr. Stephen White of Waltham and Mr. Walker of Brookfield.

17. Mr. Martyn and his wife din'd here. P.M. I visited at Mr. Daniel Garfields, Noah Hows and Captain Maynards. Was at t'other House—am deeply concern'd about my son and what will become of him—but desire to committ him and his, to the God who careth for us!

18. I visited Mr. Martyn Pratt, who is Sick. In returning I din'd at Mr. Bond's.

19. Difficult Stirring with a Team yet our Wood draws near to an End.

20. Mr. Claffland brot us a Load of Wood, when I began to determine to Speak to the Congregation about it.

21. Read Deut. 20. Preach'd on Tit. 3, 2. P.M. read Gal. 2.

22. Mr. Bond brought Plank for my Thrashing Floor and to fill out what is wanting in the Stable. N.B. Mr. Elijah Rice gave the Timber. Messers. Moses Brigham and Daniel Forbush draw'd the Loggs to Mill; and Mr. Jonathan Forbush saw'd them. N.B. I sell my Turkeys to Mr. Bond for Rye. The Turkeys at 20/ apiece and Rye at 25 per Bushel. I have a more Strong and lively Sense of the Mortality of my Body etc. than usual (for me). O that it might be continued and improv'd! I visited at Neighbour Frosts[3]—there are 3 of them there—and their sister Ruth. I paid her what I have for some time ow'd her—was at Neighbour

Barns's etc. at Lieutenant Bruce's and gave him a Note to Mr. Grow for 54£ old Tenor and to his son Ephraim for 26£ of like money. N.B. Mr. John Rogers at Thomas's procuring, to assist him in providing for a Frame for a Shop. Part of P.M. Cutts Timbers.

23. Lieutenant Bruce[4] Shewed me the Bounds of the last Survey of the Island. Mr. Stone[5] came to See us and din'd here. At Eve Mr. Jonathan Ward our School-Master. N.B. I have kept my Mare at the New Barn for Some Time. The Earth Open and Roads heavy.

24. Am reading Martins Grammar Still. A usefull piece.

25. Very rainy. Lieutenant Bruce here—calls in Quarter the Terms of our Bargain, but finds himself under a Mistake, yields, and goes away Easy.

26. Rainy Still. Mr. Hall[6] of Sutton here, and informs that Brother Samuel Breck[7] was lately at his House, came from Rhode Island through Upton—was going to Worcester—and from thence home.

27. Our Wood very Short; but a Stick or two left at the Door, and yet a Stormy, raw Cold Day—p.m. Snowy. Lieutenant Tainter came to See how 'twas with us as to wood, and went to Deacon Newtons and Esquire Bakers to See whether they would not bring some—but there came none. But I was oblig'd to make what we had in the House and the few Sticks at the Door, do over the Sabbath.

28. Read Deut. 21. Preach'd on Tit. 3, 2. P.M. read Gal. 3. Mrs. Hannah Pratt din'd here. The Weather is become comfortable. May God enable us to improve our advantages and Comforts to His Glory! Shunning carefully the Sins which his holy word has prohibited and humbling ourselves for what has been Chargeable upon us—as the Sin of Slandering and defaming has been very much So. I had (to God be Glory!) some peculiar Sense of the Vanity of Life, and the Greatness of Things Eternal. O that it might be preserv'd and increas'd!

29. A more than ordinary fine Day. Messers. Jonah Warrin and Jonathan Bond and Joseph Grout, brought, each of them, a Load of Wood. The wood of the two first and partly the Cutting, am beholden to Lieutenant Tainter for. Mrs. Newton Sends Milk again; and from Esquire Bakers a Gallon ditto. I rode out to visit Mrs. Adams (Eliphalet's Wife) and Mrs. Beeman (Abraham's Wife) was also at Lieutenant Bruce's who gave me up my Bond of 145.10/old Tenor and I gave him a new one of 100£ old Tenor. He gave me also a new Deed including 9 Acres and 1 Rod of the Island. N.B. I owe him 1£ 11 s., 8 d, old Tenor, besides the Interest and besides the Remainder of our old Reckoning.

30. Another very fine Day. My Wife goes to t'other House, my sons Wife being much indispos'd. I reckon'd with Deacon Newton, and gave him a Note for the whole of my Book Debt.

31. After We din'd at home, my Wife and I rode to Mr. Clafflins and celebrated the Nuptials of Alpheus Newton[8] and Elizabeth Clafflin, after which we had a plentifull Entertainment. The Weather fine and the Company pretty large—but we came away in the first of the Evening and Captain Benjamin Wood of Hopkinton waiting on the Bridegrooms Mother. Thus we finish this Month with much chearfullness and Joy but it becomes us to rejoice as tho we rejoic'd not.[9]

---

[2] The minister of the New Brick Church died at the untimely age of 37.
[3] Thomas Frost.
[4] Elijah Bruce.
[5] The Reverend Nathan Stone of Southborough.
[6] The Reverend David Hall.
[7] Parkman's brother-in-law, the physician of Great Barrington.
[8] The son of Abner Newton and his wife made their home in Westborough.
[9] The remainder of the diary for the Year 1753 cannot be located.

## JANUARY, 1754.

Through the Tender Mercy and Longsuffering of God I see the Morning of another New Year, and am at Brookfield. Esquire Howard had Sent a Message to me Yesterday, and this Morning came himself to invite me and my son Ebenezer who is with me, as well as Mr. Forbush[1] and his Wife, to a New Years Dinner. It prov'd a fine Day, which with good Company, and fine Eating, made it a chearful Time. Thanks be to God for his great Goodness in which He is rich unto all! May it be a truely happy New Year! Captain Wit[2] and I rode from Esquire Howards up to Mr. Abraham Smiths to talk with him about his place, with a view to my son Ebenezer's living there. At Eve return'd to Mr. Forbush's.

2. Am upon the Business of Mr. Smiths place. Mr. Forbush and Lieutenant Gilbert[3] accompany us, as Mr. Smith shews us his Bounds. But the Snow being on the Ground we can't See the Soil. At Eve Mr. Benjamin Ruggles,[4] preaching now a Days at New Braintree came to Mr. Forbushs. I preach'd an Eve Lecture at the Meeting House there on Luke 29, 10. Mr. Ruggles pray'd. N.B. This was the first Time Mr. Forbush got out since his Fall. May God make his word effectual for our saving Profit! Mr. Ruggles lodg'd with me at Mr. Forbushs.

3. It was an exceeding fine Day Yesterday, but to Day a Storm. Ebenezer and I rode to Lieutenant Abraham Hows; din'd at Mr. Smiths; at Eve was at Captain Witts.

4. Rain. Agree with Mr. Smith. Take a Deed of him and give him a Bond, to give him a Deed of my House, and nine acres and 1/2 of Land in Westborough. Late in the Day leave Brookfield and rode to Mr. Eatons[5] in Leicester—were well refresh'd there, and though it was wet at Evening proceeded to the Reverend Mr. Goddards[6] and lodg'd there. Through the divine Favour am also in good Comforts of Body, altho my mind has been exceedingly agitated in my trading with Mr. Smith fearing whether it will be suitably improv'd by him and turn to his good. But whilst I am thus concern'd for him pay him a great Price for his and sell my own but at very low rate. His Wife also very backward to sign.

5. Wet, uncomfortable riding from Leicester, home. Call'd at Mr. Maccartys.[7] Din'd at Mr. Cushings.[8] Arriv'd in Safety, and found our Dwellings in Peace. D.G.

6. Rain. People came late to Meeting. Omitted reading a.m. Preach'd a. and p.m. on Rom. 6, 21. P.M. read Heb. 6. Deferr'd the Contribution because of the Rain.

7. I made a Visit to my old Neighbour and Friend Captain Maynard to acquaint him with what I had done with Mr. Abraham Smith and take his Advice. Seeing likewise when I parted with Mr. Smith and saw how lost his Wife was, I told him that if I could do better, and his Wife should grow no easier, I Should still desire to throw up; I therefore relating the matter to Captain Maynard, ask'd both him and his Son whether they would by my whole (old) place, in Case Smith would release the Bargain; but they declin'd it, but especially refused the House. Captain Wood[9] of Hopkinton brought a Letter from Mr. Barret[10] requesting me to assist there at a Fast by reason of the malignant Fever, which exceedingly rages and proves very mortal in Holliston, and begins to rage in Hopkinton. N.B. Ten lay dead in Holliston last Friday. Mrs. Prentice[11] was bury'd on Saturday last, but Mr. Prentice is recovering. For want of Help, So many being

Sick and Dead, they draw some Corps to their Graves on Sleds.[12] N.B. Mr. Griffin here.

8. A.M. visit Mrs. Fay once more, but now take Solemn Leave of her. P.M. marry'd Phinehas Maynard to Dorothy Rice.[13] Exceeding fine Weather.

9. It rain'd hard; but I rode to Hopkinton found Messers. Stone and Smith with Mr. Barret. Mr. Fish came also. Mr. Barret pray'd a.m. and Mr. Stone preach'd on Rev. 6, 8. N.B. about 20 pray'd for. The rain prevail'd so that we all lodg'd there. At Eve Dr. Wilson among us; who tells us that in this Fever there is much of pleurisy and peripneumony.

10. Bright morning—visit Captain Wood and his Brother Lieutenant John Wood who has the fever. I pray'd with him. Mr. Fish[14] went to a Fast to Day at Mill-river in Mendon. In my return home call'd at John Kelley's to get Loggs for some choice Floor Boards—din'd at Mr. Daniel Hardys. At Eve Mr. Ebenezer Chamberlin here, and Mr. Daniel Forbush. They offer a Motion for a Fast here.

11. At Eve Deacon Forbush here. He observably breaks and wears away. Lieutenant Holloway here also.

12. Mr. Samuel Fays (junior) wife dy'd, and I hope in Christ. Mr. Griffin of Oxford here.

13. I read part of Judg. 6. I spent so much time in my Preparations for the Afternoon that I could not prepare for the forenoon only a brief Introduction of the Repitition of Sermon on Rom. 6, 21 from page 37 to 46, but from Jam. 1, 15 last Clause. To this I was induc'd the rather because of my last repetition Concerning the unprofitableness and Shamlessness of Sin, have appear'd to be acceptable and useful, and I heard it wish'd that there might be more: and again I was induced hereto also because of the Mortality in Neighbouring Towns. P.M. read Heb. 7, and preach'd on Rev. 10, 6 latter part on occasion of our Contributing for the Relief of Alpheus Newton and his Wife, lately burnt out;[15] which Contribution was this afternoon, and may God accept the offering of his people and sanctifie His holy Dispensations.

14. Rain a.m. Clear'd up p.m. went to the Funeral of Mrs. Deliverance Fay, wife of Mr. Samuel Fay junior. Rode Alpheus Newtons Horse. After burying at Deacon Newtons and Mr. Francis Whipple with us, counting the Money gather'd yesterday, and it amounted to 44£ 15 shillings and 6d old Tenor.

15. Exceeding pleasant, warm and bright till Eve; but then Rain. I was at Eve reckoning with Mr. Ebenezer Rice at his House while Daniel Williams and his Squaw, who are come from Dudley to wigwam among us, came, at my sending for, to See me, but I saw them not.

16. Rain. Ebenezer comes over, in trouble for his little son, who is sick: and they fear'd of the Throat Distemper; but tis hop'd otherwise. Two of Mr. Baldwin's prentices (Jones and Wyman) here. They go to lodge at t'other House.

17. I receiv'd a Letter from Mr. John Parkman of Cowes in the Isle of Wight.

18. Much Company interrupting especially at Eve. Mr. Timothy Warrin in Defence of Samuel Bumpso, so far as to prevent his going to Jayl, if getting posts and Rails next March might Satisfie on an Execution and Note of last October the third follow'd by continual Ingratitude, negligence and unfaithfulness. One Mr. Moon of Lebanon here, tells me Dr. Eliot[16] of Killingworth is dead.

19. [No entry.]

20. Read Judg. 6, from number 25. Preach'd all Day on 1 Cor. 15, 25. Read p.m. Heb. 8. N.B. had the Sorrowfull news of the Death of Reverend Mr. David Goddard of Leicester. He ex-

---

[1] Parkman's son-in-law, the Reverend Eli Forbes.

[2] Ebenezer Witt.

[3] Benjamin Gilbert of Brookfield.

[4] Benjamin Ruggles (Yale 1721) had been the minister of Lakeville, 1725-1753. Because of an insufficient salary, Ruggles asked for and received his dismission. He was called to the town of New Braintree where he served, 1754-1782. Dexter, *Biographical Sketches*, pp. 255-256, and *Sibley*, VII, 646-650.

[5] The Reverend Joshua Eaton of Spencer.

[6] David Goddard of Leicester.

[7] The Reverend Thaddeus Maccarty of Worcester.

[8] Job Cushing of Shrewsbury.

[9] John Wood.

[10] The Reverend Samuel Barrett of Hopkinton.

[11] Mary, the wife of the Reverend Joshua Prentiss of Holliston. This town was very hard hit in this epidemic, and Prentiss wrote an account of the sickness there. See Mass. Hist. Soc., *Collections*, 1st Ser., III, 18-20.

[12] Modern authorities regard this as another outbreak of diphtheria, which was a problem in various parts of New Hampshire and Massachusetts. See John Duffy, *Epidemics in Colonial America* (Baton Rouge, [1953]), pp. 125-126.

[13] These were both Westborough people: Phinehas was the son of James Maynard, and Dorothy (or Dority) the daughter of Seth Rice.

[14] The Reverend Elisha Fish of Upton.

[15] The Westborough Church Records, Jan. 13, 1754, reveal that Newton's house was burned down "in the Night between the 24th and 25th of December last."

[16] This reference is puzzling, for the Reverend Jared Eliot of Killingworth, who also served as a physician, lived until 1763. Two of his sons who also practiced medicine there died in 1741 and 1747.

pir'd yesterday at his wife's House in Framingham, after a very short illness of a violent Fever which prevails in Framingham. He preach'd last Sabbath at Southboro, and was taken ill the next Day. N.B. I was desir'd by Deacon Forbush to think of a Fast here. After the Exercises I stop'd the Church and propos'd it. The Deacon aforesaid manifested his Desire again—but I could not without Difficulty obtain of the Brethren to Speak their Minds about it, and yet when I put it to Vote, it was voted unanimously as far as I could discern.

21. Mr. Ephraim Woods of Southborough here. Mr. James Ball—I paid him what I ow'd him. 12£ old Tenor. Mr. John Fay brot a Letter from Mr. Stone[17] to desire my assistance at the Fast among them Thursday. At Eve Lieutenant Tainter brought wool and Cards which he had bought for us at Boston.

22. After a considerable Space of fine Moderate weather comes an Exceeding Cold Day—bright but high Winds and Sharp Air that can Scarcely be sustain'd. Mr. Benjamin Goddard came to desire me to go to the Funeral of his Brother (Reverend David) tomorrow, at Framingham.

23. Mr. Joseph Bruce here on occasion of his son in Law Child his Thigh broke. I sent a Line by him to Mr. Francis Whipple containing my Desire to have a Clause inserted in the Warrant for the next Town Meeting relating to their Arrears. I went to the Funeral of the Reverend Dr. David Goddard of Leicester; who was bury'd from his Wife's House in Framingham. The Reverend Mr. Read[18] pray'd. He and the Reverend Messers. Stone, Bliss[19] and Bridge,[20] with Dr. Ebenezer Hemingway[21] were the other Bearers. Mr. Ebenezer Goddard lies very bad of the same Fever. News also came that Mr. Benjamin Goddard, who was with me yesterday, was taken sick as soon as he got home; and for the Time is very ill. May a gracious God fit us for His holy will! In the Eve the Mare I rode, Stray'd away from Colonel Buckminsters[22] where we turn'd in to warm us, and drew up some account of Mr. Goddards Death; which was committed to Mr. Bliss to carry Mr. Kneeland at Boston to publish.[23] I lodg'd at the Colonel's.

24. It snow'd in the Night and Morning, but I walk'd up to Dr. Hemingways who lent me his Horse to Southboro—found mine at Mr. Andrew Newtons, and proceeded to the Fast in Southborough, on occasion of the sickness. Mr. Stone pray'd first. I preach'd from Mat. 24, 44. Mr. Smith pray'd after sermon, then we sang part of Ps. 37. Mr. Bridge pray'd after singing—for we had but one Exercise. In returning home (Lieutenant Tainter my Company) comply'd with Lieutenant Nathan Brighams earnest Desire to turn in and see his son Nathan, who lay very sick of the Fever, and pray'd with him.

25. At Evening which I much depended upon for Studying, came Mr. Benjamin Tainter and his Wife to make us a Visit, therein waiting upon her Father, Mr. Josiah Woods from Summers; and soon after came his Brother and they tarryed and Supp'd here. Mr. Samuel Fay junior here this Eve also. Billy thrash'd with Ebenezer.

26. Lieutenant Ward din'd here. A fine Day. Hands at work helping Alpheus Newton frame. Billy thrashing with Ebenezer.

27. Read Judg. 7. A.M. on 1 Cor. 15, 25. P.M. read Heb. 9, and preach'd on 1 Cor. 15, 26. Appointed Wednesday next to be a Day of Solemn Fasting and Prayer on Consideration of the Malignant Sickness in Neighbouring Towns; we having also many Evils among ourselves—and that God would please to revive his Work here.

28. Dr. Perkins[24] of Framingham informs me that Mr. Benjamin Goddard,[25] who was with me last Tuesday, dy'd last Night. Alpheus Newton's House rais'd. Captain Eager ask'd

me to go up, and I did so. Some refreshment at Deacon Newtons[26] by Captain Eager. Mr. Hezekiah Rice came to request me to go to Mr. Goddards Funeral. N.B. some Discourse with Deacon Newton and Mr. Francis Whipple about my addressing the Town for the remains of my Sallery in the Year 1744. N.B. James Eager brings a Message from Mr. Jonathan Greene.

29. I visited Mrs. Dodge wife of Mr. Jabez Dodge. Also a Lad ([blank] Childs) at Mr. Hezekiah Pratts, he having broke his Thigh Bone. I went to the Funeral of Mr. Benjamin Goddard. Mr. Cushing not sent for. I reprov'd them for their Neglect. N.B. Colonel Nahum Wards private Talk with me about Mr. Cushing. N.B. Mr. Jeduthun Baldwin and [blank] Cutler from Brookfield.

30. This Day was observ'd as a Day of Humiliation and Prayer by this Parish.[27] I began with Prayer. No minister comes tho I had sent to most of those round about, it being a dark, stormy Day. Mr. Stone[28] came in Prayer Time. He preach'd on Ps. 39, 4. Mr. Cushing came also in prayer Time. In time of the last Prayer a. m. came Mr. Barret.[29] Neither did any other come. P.M. Mr. Barret pray'd. Mr. Cushing preach'd on Hos. 4, 7. Captain Brigham, Deacon Burnap[30] and Mr. Ephraim Wood Supp'd here. O that God would graciously accept our Offerings; pardon our sins, revive His Work and remove from His People His sore Judgments. Preserve us still in this Day of Evil, and prevent Spiritual Judgments falling upon us! May the Goodness of God to us lead us to repentence and prevent our abusing His Mercy.

31. I rode over to Mr. Jonathan Greens. In going by Captain James Eagers swamp I perceiv'd there was a great Number of men getting shingle for Abner Newton. I din't at Lieutenant Holloways. Mr. Green and his wife both gone from home. Visited Mr. Martin. His wife and Daughter confin'd by illness. Call'd at Ensign Rice's who was gone to Boston. N.B. She desires me to talk with her Husband for Azuba.

### FEBRUARY, 1754

1. Mr. Timothy Warrin here, on Sam Bumpso's Account. He brings Sam's Gun here; which I take and give up Sams Note to Mr. Warrin. Wrote to Mr. Cushing to Change next Lords Day and sent it to t'other House—but it did not go.

2. Mr. Clafflin here, and tho I ow'd him but Twenty odd Shillings yet at his Request I gave him a Note of above four pounds (old Tenor).

3. Fowl Day. Read Judg. 8, and for sermon had prepar'd on Psalm 51, 11 in chief part for one Sermon, but considering our present threatned Circumstances with relation to the Fever, which now spreads much in Southborough and very mortally, I took and altered some old sermons on Ps. 119, 120, and deliver'd the substance of them a. and p.m. Read p.m. Heb. 10 to number 18. At Eve I was not well.

4. Had a poor night; and was ill all Day. Have symptons of Distemper.

5. Feel but poorly, yet hope I am better. Ebenezer kill'd 5 Swine. One of 13 Score, a sow of nigh 11 Score, and three pigs of 5 or 6 score. Three of those swine he sent to Mr. James Allen of Boston, Tayler, per Lieutenant Maynard. At Eve came here Foster from Holliston and lodg'd here. Mr. Clafflin went off last Night.

6. Mr. Foster puts his Horse into my Chair and rode with Lucy to t'other House. They return at Eve, and Mr. Foster leaves us. I sent Billey over to Mr. Jonathan Green with Sufficient silver to pay his Demands of Samuel Bumpso, viz. £6.11.0, old Tenor. I recover slowly. P.M. Mr. Ebenezer Maynard Treasurer here; and gave him Receipts agreeable to his Mind, respecting instead of what was given to Collector Grow.

7. I went down below to Day and din'd with the Family. Blessed be God! Lieutenant Tainter here. Settled my accounts

[17] Nathan Stone of Southborough.
[18] Solomon Reed of Framingham.
[19] Daniel Bliss of Concord.
[20] Matthew Bridge of Framingham.
[21] Ebenezer Hemenway was a physician of Framingham. Clair A. H. Newton, *Ralph Hemmenway . . . and his Descendants* (Naperville, Ill., 1932), I, 16.
[22] Colonel Joseph Buckminster, a leading citizen of Framingham.
[23] This news item appears not to have been published.
[24] Richard Perkins (Harvard 1748), a physician, was the son of the Reverend Daniel Perkins of Bridgewater and the brother-in-law of the Reverend Matthew Bridge of Framingham.
[25] Of Shrewsbury.
[26] Josiah Newton of Westborough.
[27] This fast was held "on Account of a Malignant Mortal fever raging in many Neighbouring Towns." Westborough Church Records, Jan. 30, 1754.
[28] Nathan Stone of Southborough.
[29] The Reverend Samuel Barrett of Hopkinton.
[30] Benjamin Burnap of Hopkinton.

with him. Had I been well I should have endeavour'd to preach to Day at Mr. Grows. But in divine Providence am prevented but desire to have my Heart with my Brethren that Seek the Lord there. May God graciously assist them and accept their Offering!

8. Through divine Goodness grow better but am interrupted with divers Visitants. Colonel William Ward din'd here. P.M. Mr. Ammiel Weeks of Brookfield. Mr. Cornelius Biglow much engag'd in gathering and bringing Money and Notes. Snow. Mr. Hezekiah Maynard from Marlborough from Mr. Smiths[1] to desire my Help at a Fast there next Wednesday.

9. Mr. Biglow here again. I let him have Sam Bumpso's Gun for 7£ old Tenor, he promising that if either I, or Sam or Mr. Timothy Warrin repay him this Money, we may have it again.

10. Winds very high in the Night. I ventur'd to the Meeting tho Cold. A.M. read Judg. P.M. read Heb. 10, 19 to the End. Preach'd on Ps. 51, 11. Mrs. Beeman din'd here. Mr. Joslin and Mr. Ithamar Bellows Wife and Several Children in that Corner of the Town, Sick; and tis fear'd of the Distemper. My son Ebenezer not at Meeting, he having cutt himself lately.

11. Ebenezer here at Eve. He seems Somewhat Sick of the Bargain with Mr. Smith of Brookfield and yet does not appear Willing to throw it up. He hopes I will Send for no more Indian Corn from the Other House.

12. Another Very Cold Tuesday. Sent by Mr. Ephraim Sherman to Boston—for Mr. Fleets Paper as well as Mr. Kneelands.[2]

13. Went to the Fast at Marlborough tho it was very Cold. Overtook Lieutenant Tainter who was going likewise, and he return'd with me at Eve. Mr. Stone preach'd a.m. on 1 K. 8, 37 to 40. Mr. Gardner[3] pray'd p.m. and I preach'd from Ps. 119, 59. May God hear in Heaven forgive and Bless his people for His Name's Sake! As we return'd at Eve in the Cold, we visited Mr. Jacob Amsden,[4] who Seems to have met with a great deal of Trouble and Affliction which may God Sanctifie to him for his Spiritual and Eternal Good!

14. Lucy rode with Ebenezers Wife to See Mrs. Martyn[5] and Mrs. Molly her Daughter who, we hear, are not well yet. Lucy brings me at Evening a most bitter Letter from my Brother Martyn, full of Misrepresentations and hard Reflections. God grant him to See his Errors and retract them! But Darts foreseen may be better warded off. I confess I have been full of fears Time would come when our Peace would be broke up. I was early premonish'd what I might Expect from him; and have all along been watchfull and upon my Guard—and have been very far from Willingly giving the least Ground of Offence. Have always defended him when I have heard any Word to his Disparagement, and been ready always to give him a good Character; or oblige him in any Thing in the World that lay in my Power, or any of his: and would Still Serve him with my whole Heart. I therefore look upon this as a sore Frown of Heaven: and do beg of God to Sanctifie it to me; and Since it bodes exceeding ill with regard to the Interest of Religion among us, I would heartily mourn and grieve for it. May God avert the Omen! These Things came upon me a little the more heavily because I had in the Day preceeding receiv'd an undesirable Letter from Mr. Abraham Smith of Brookfield, in which he tells me he shall come down with his Family the beginning of next Week if he does not hear from me and it contains also some Threatenings. I went over presently to Ebenezer P.M. but he was gone to help Mr. Daniel Maynard drive to Marlborough the Cattle he had bought of my Son (the Oxen I gave him) for 75£ old Tenor—but Ebenezer Came over in the Evening. I visited old Mrs. Rogers who is sick.

15. Thomas and Lucy ride Ebenezer's Mare to Brookfield and they carry a Letter from me to Mr. Abraham Smith to prevent his coming and if he pleases throw up the Bargain: Ebenezer being much against going there, tho he was So much for it before:

Says he would give Smith 50£ rather than not throw up. P.M. I borrow'd Lieutenant Forbush's Horse and visited Mr. Chamberlins, Ithamar Bellow's, and Mr. Joslins Family, because of their Sickness—and old Mr. Garfield who is very bad tis fear'd of a Malignant Fever. N.B. Mr. Chamberlin with me from House to House.

16. Having Sent a Letter by my Son Thomas yesterday to Mr. Cushing to desire him to Change, he came here and I rode there. N.B. was Shav'd by Dr. Smith[6] at his House. A Somewhat Cold Time but I got up safely, and rested Comfortably, D.G.

17. I thought it very Seasonable to preach on Mat. 24, 44, a. and p.m. considering the Sickness had entered into the Town of Shrewsbury and Mr. Benjamin Goddard had dy'd there and others had been taken ill of it. But it happened likewise to be the Next Lords Day after the Funeral of the Honourable Edward Goddard[7] Esquire (and but a little while since the Death of his aged Wife) at Framingham: but his son Edward and Family now desir'd Public Prayers. O that I myself might be ready for my own Decease! At Eve I return'd home.

18. Wrote some proposals and offers to my son Ebenezer which I sent by Lieutenant Tainter, having understood that both son and his wife were under Discouragement. Lieutenant Tainter has taken fruitless pains with Mr. Grout for an Horse for my Wife to ride to Boston upon. And altho I depended upon my son Ebenezer to go down with his Mother instead of Thomas who is gone to Brookfield; and that he might wait upon his Father Harrington respecting our Trading with Mr. Smith. Yet he also throws it by. Lieutenant Tainter therefore strikes in and proposes to go with my Wife in my Chair, with my own Mare. This therefore

19. They undertake, a.m. But p.m. was the most violent Storm of Wind and Rain, So that I was exceedingly concern'd about 'em. But they (as I heard afterwards) got safely to Colonel Buckminsters and lodg'd there.

20. Lieutenant Forbush brought me his Horse on which I rode to old Mr. Nathaniel Hudsons[8] Funeral. He was in his 85th Year according to his Children's Reckoning. I went from the House of Mourning to visit old Mrs. Garfield who lies very bad of the Pleuretick Fever which has been of late very Mortal in Neighbouring Towns. Mr. Grove and Mr. Joseph Woods din'd with me, and Mr. John Brighams wife here all the afternoon.

21. My Son Thomas return'd from Brookfield last night to t'other House without Lucy, but with Mr. Abraham Smith. P.M. I went over to Mr. Smith and spent the afternoon there. I return'd home at Evening not a little troubled that after all my Endeavours to gratifie my son, both he and his wife are not willing to Venture to go to Brookfield, but however my son does gratefully acknowledge what I wrote to him by Lieutenant Tainter. My Thoughts are deeply engaged on these Matters. We talk'd of Recanting the Bargain with Mr. Smith, who seems willing if we might both of us be just as we were before we began—and I thought to take him but left it untill the next Morning. Finish'd a Letter to Mr. Martyn in Answer to his of the 12th.

22. A very fine Day. My Wife return'd from Boston while I was gone to the Funeral of old Mrs. Garfield, widow of the late Mr. Benjamin Garfield. N.B. Mr. Smith din'd with me. Tells me the meaning of his Talk yesterday (of our recanting upon Such Terms as to have both of us in the same State as we were when we began), was that I pay him what Damages he sustains if he does not go forward—which I refus'd to comply with but would willingly recant for both his and my sons sake, if he saw Cause. This he rejected, and went to Sudbury to see his Parents. My son Thomas rode to Marlboro with him.

23. Mr. Smith was to have return'd that he might go home to Brookfield but did not.

24. Read Judg. 12. Text Ps. 51, 11. P.M. read Heb. 11 from number 17, and Repeated Exposition (with Alterations) on Mat.

[1] The Reverend Aaron Smith of Marlborough.
[2] Thomas Fleet published *The Boston Evening-Post*; Kneeland, *The Boston Gazette*.
[3] The Reverend John Gardner of Stow.
[4] Of Westborough.
[5] Wife of the Reverend John Martyn of Northborough.
[6] Joshua Smith of Shrewsbury.
[7] Goddard, a prominent citizen, held numerous town offices, was a justice of the peace, and a member of the Council of the province. Temple, *Framingham*, p. 566.
[8] Of Marlborough.

9, 12, accommodating it to the Present Time of Sickness—for tho we are very much spar'd in this place thro Gods great Mercy, with regard to our Bodys, yet are we under sore spiritual sickness. May God grant us to be sensible of it and perswade us to repair to the Lord Jesus Christ for Healing!

25. Roger Bruce work'd here p.m. in Clearing. Mr. Abraham Smith came p.m. and his Father with him. They Spent the Eve here, and then return'd to lodge at t'other House. Dr. David Barns,[9] Schoolmaster came and lodg'd here.

26. Went over to my sons, the Smiths being there; and find 'em much against having their Line to run to the North so far as the Settle. They want a Notch behind the Barn to take in the low Ground Behind the Barn. We all din'd at my sons. P.M. we find we cannot agree about the Line there having been nothing Said in the written Bargain about this nor by Word of Mouth only that it Should go as far East as the West End of the Barn and I conceiv'd nothing but that he would Choose to go North; except that likewise I insisted that my Land should not be cut into bad forms and notches. We therefore broke wholly off—writ it and sign'd it. So old Mr. Smith took his Leave and went home, parting in peace. But his son stayed and when I was going away he ask'd me to walk down to the Barn which I comply'd with. And no sooner were we come to the East End of the Barn than Mr. Smith started a new Proposal for the Line of his 7 Acres—and to include the Barn for his Over plus—this I hearkened to; but not being well, and much worry'd would Say nothing to, to Night. Mr. Smith tarry'd and lodg'd there. In my way home visited Mr. Dodge and his wife and Neighbour Hezekiah Pratt and his new Wife. N.B. Roger Bruce Clear'd to Day, and lodges here.

27. A Stormy Night and Morning. Roger went off. My son and Mr. Smith came here. My son appear'd Willing to go to Brookfield and offers to go if I can trade with Mr. Smith still. Provided I will give him a Deed of Such as comes to the proportion of a Thousand Pounds in our Bargain, and will let him have the use of my remaining part for Two Years free of Interest. Hereupon Mr. Smith and I reviv'd our Bargain and settled it, and wrote and sign'd it and he is to come down next Week with his goods. John Dunlop here and wants to let himself to me.

28. Ebenezer goes to Brookfield with Mr. Abraham Smith. Mrs. Parkman to t'other House, She not having been there ever since Peach Time till now. Such is her Encumbrance by the Children and Business of the Family. Mr. Bartlett[10] of Sutton here and tells me that Mr. Edmund Greenleaf of Newbury dy'd about a fortnight agoe. May God please to teach me to number my Days so as that I may apply my Heart to Wisdom!

### MARCH, 1754.

1. Roger Bruce, John Dunlop with two more Hands with him viz. Richard Kelly and Joseph Chaddock, come and Clean next to Captain Maynards Swamp. Thomas brot about 30 Rails with Ebenezers Team from the Ministerial Lot.

2. Thomas brings a Load of Goods from t'other House—storm of Snow.

3. Read Judg. 13. Preach'd on Jer. 31, 23, a. and p.m. Widow Woods din'd here.

4. I went over to t'other House, a.m. Ebenezer and I measur'd the Lines of the Piece of Land mark'd out for Mr. Smith. P.M. I pray'd with the Town at their Meeting and receiv'd at Eve another uncomfortable Letter from my Brother Martyn.[1] This Paper War with this Gentleman is the Grief of my Heart: it being the most peculiarly happy thing for ministers in the Same Town to be well united, and the most grievous when tis otherwise. Witness Woburn and Sutton nearer home.

5. I visited Mr. Jonathan Bellows who is sick and din'd there. Went to Southborough to carry Mr. Stone a little money for the Newton Meadow, but Mr. Stone was gone to Boston—left 8£ old Tenor with his wife and return'd. Billy begins the Accidence[2] again. Mr. Abraham Smith and his Wife are come from Brookfield to t'other House.

6. Thomas waited on his Sister, Ebenezer's Wife, with my Chair and Mare, tho in heavy Roads, to her Father Harringtons at Watertown. Mr. Hutchinson[3] preach'd my Lecture from John 12, 23, and may God Himself add a Blessing.

8. Snowy. Captain Timothy Brigham here. Brought the Journal of the House of Representatives.

9. Thomas return'd to t'other House last night and came here with Mr. Smith and Mr. Jeduthun Baldwin who is come from Brookfield with a Chair from Mr. Forbush to carry us his Mother. P.M. Captain Timothy Brigham returns here, and I pay him £5.5/ for Reverend Mr. Stone.

10. It was appointed last Sabbath to have the Communion to Day—But because of the Extremity of the Season, Snow, Rain etc. the Sacrament was put by. I read Judg. 14 and for a. and p.m. Exercises expounded and improv'd the Chapter and especially number 14. Deacon Forbush and Lieutenant Thomas Weeks of Weston din'd with us. Ebenezer is observ'd to be very down.

11. Precinct Met for Choice of Officers—No Prayer ask'd. Ebenezer comes at Eve—tells me that Mr. Abraham Smith notwithstanding all his Bargain with me and giving me a Deed of his Place, has actually mortgag'd it to Mr. Aaron Boardman of Boston. He is this Day gone on my sons Mare to See his Father at Sudbury and to return tonight.

12. I made a Visit to Mr. Smith to enquire into his Conduct Colonel William Ward[4] here with whom I advis'd respecting; Mr. Smiths Treatment of me. I rode to Mr. Bradishs to See his Wife, and to Mr. Ithamar Bellows. A fine Day overhead, but exceeding bad Road—snow, Mud etc. Billy brought over four Sheep and [blank] Lambs from t'other House. Mr. Jeduthun Baldwin here from Sudbury, returning to Brookfield. Told him I was very sorry that when Mr. Forbush[5] and he knew of Mr. Smiths Mortgaging his Place to Mr. Boardman yet that they did not prevent his moving his Family hither, or Send one word of it.

13. Ebenezer rode (on Mr. Smiths Stallion) to his Father Harringtons at Watertown where his Wife has hitherto continued. And Billy is over at tother place taking Care of his Brothers Cattle. Mr. Edwards Whipple here at Eve. Acquaints me with Base Coin stirring; Some of it passed by Mr. John Dunlop, but chiefly by Abraham Rice of Brookfield, and Moses Pannell of Colrain, who are principally Suspected.

14. I visited in the South part of the Town. Din'd at Mr. Harringtons. Was at Mr. Bowmans, both Twitchells, but especially went to see Mr. Dunlop who is sick. Lieutenant Maynard and others are gone to Brookfield to Abner Rice's to detect the base Coiners. Receiv'd an affectionate Letter from Brother Samuel Parkman on the Death of Captain T. Davis.

15. Ebenezer return'd home at Eve with his Wife and Child in my Chair. My Wife visited Mrs. Smith at t'other House.

16. John Dunlop here (after his Journey to Brookfield) tells me the New Coiners are Two sons of the late Mr. Thomas Newton[6] formerly of this Town; and they made the Money at Hunting Hills[7] beyond Deerfield. Company are here every Day, and not a few—which is a great Interruption to me. Mr. Daniel Forbush here about making Satisfaction to Reverend Mr. Barret.

17. A bright Day, tho raw Cold North wind. Read Judg. 15. Preach'd a.m. on Judg. 14, 14. Administered the Lords Supper. Deacon Forbush and Mrs. Brigham (Gershoms Wife) din'd with us. P.M. repeated with Alteration Exposition on Mat. 8, 21, 22.

---

[9] (Harvard 1752). Barnes was ordained later this year at Norwell (Second Church in Scituate). Hudson, *Marlborough*, p. 317. In Nov. 1753, Westborough was presented at the Court of General Sessions in Worcester for not having maintained a school for over a year. Feb. 5, 1754, the Westborough selectmen testified before the court that a school master had been hired. The town was dismissed after "paying costs."

[10] Richard Bartlett.

[1] John Martyn of Northborough. The editor has not discovered in this diary, in local histories or in church records any clue relating to the cause of this dispute between Martyn and Parkman.

[2] A book containing the rudiments of grammar. Probably one of the famous Latin grammars of Ezekiel Cheever.

[3] Aaron Hutchinson of Grafton.

[4] Ward of Southborough was a justice of the peace. Hudson, *Marlborough*, p. 460.

[5] Parkman's son-in-law, the Reverend Eli Forbes of Brookfield.

[6] Thomas Newton, Jr., had moved to Sunderland in 1742; he was in Deerfield in 1756. The editor has not determined the identity of the other Newton counterfeiter. Ermina N. Leonard, *Newton Genealogy* (DePere, Wisconsin, 1915), pp. 74-75.

[7] The plantation called Huntstown became the town of Ashfield in 1765.

God grant we may be quickened to cast off all procrastinations and Delays and apply ourselves to the Work of God, as we are respectively called thereto!

18. I went over to Mr. Smith and talk with him—and inasmuch as he pretends that Mr. Boardman of Boston is ready to take off the Mortgage, he must go to him forthwith and do it, otherwise it will be too late for this Year. I think it also a great Wrong and hardship that Mr. Smiths Horse is kept in my Barn since our Hay is So Short and it is difficult for me to go for Supply otherwise. Visited at Mr. Whipples, both Houses. Mr. Edwards Whipple talks of helping me get Timber for a Kitchin. Ebenezer and his wife and Child here at Eve. Thunder and Lightning. They lodge here.

19. Mr. Smith to Boston to see what Mr. Boardman will do. Wrote to my Brother Samuel to assist me; that I may not be deceiv'd. Desir'd Lieutenant Maynard to receive from my Brother an Account of their Proceedings. Din'd at Mr. Amsdens. Mr. Abijah Gale gives me Dimensions for a Leanto. Visited Mrs. Twitchell after the Death of her Mother. Return'd by t'other House. Mrs. Smith very dull—though neighbours come to see her yet she removes into another room and shuts the Door that she may be alone. I went in to take leave of her, and found her under Discouragement. Lieutenant Tainter brought saw'd stuff for Barn Doors. N.B. much Noise about Abner Rice and his Brother in Law Moses Pannell being apprehended, and one Newton likewise. All brot before Colonel Chandler,[8] for making money—and are committed to Jayl.

20. Greatly engag'd and troubled in my Mind about Mr. Smiths Conduct, and much perplex'd what Course to take: to throw up will tend much to the ruin of Mr. Smith however he has brot it upon himself in giving me so great Reason for it: on the other Hand to go on is exceeding Dangerous: and it will soon be too late for my son to go to Brookfield. May the Lord influence my Mind and Heart and direct me what Course to take. Visit Captain Forbush's Wife, mourning for the Loss of her sister Sawin.

21. Esquire Baker came here kindly to tell me that he heard Smiths Land in Brookfield was under an attachment and that there were several Executions out against him. Catechiz'd at the Meeting House, A. and P.M. N.B. I gave the Congregation a quickening Word last Lords Day to send their Children. And a.m. I had 51 Boys. P.M. it snow'd yet 23 Girls. Mr. [blank] Park of Sutton din'd here. Lieutenant Tainter and a Number besides with their Teams brot a great Stone for the principal step at the Front of the Meeting House. My wife but poorly— may God fit us for His Will! At Eve Mr. Ebenezer Rice here. I wrote a Line to Mr. Abraham Smith to apprize him that I must be oblig'd to tell the Select Men of his Coming.

22. Sent by Ebenezer to Mr. Whipple[9] Town Clerk Information of Mr. Smith and his Family being in my House—to be Communicated to the Select Men. N.B. my Paper return'd because the Wife's and Dauters Names were not inserted. Mr. Hill of Sherbourn brot me a Letter from Mr. Morse[10] of Shrewsbury requesting a Contribution for the Relief of Mr. Asa Hill of Shrewsbury who was lately burnt out. Mr. Stone's son Nathaniel here and din'd with us. At Eve I was with Deacon Newton, another of the selectman, and gave him a Paper which had the Names of Mr. Smiths Wife and Dauter but did not leave it.

23. In the Morning I went to Esquire Baker and consulted him on the Smith Affair and wrote and left with him (another of the select Men) an information in Writing certifying when Mr. Smith his Wife and Dauter came into Town. N.B. last Night Mr. Daniel Forbush came here from Brookfield and tells me that Mr. Smith was come up from Boston, and brought up a Letter (which he also delivered me and which was from Mr. Andrew Boardman of Boston informing me that he Should Send up Mr. Barker on Monday to transact the Affair of taking off the Mortgage from Smiths Brookfield Land. Mr. Smith came here and I imediately Sent for Esquire Baker who came. They din'd here. A warm Debate ensued. I insist for security besides a Deed if

[8] John Chandler of Worcester.

[9] Francis Whipple.

[10] The Reverend Ebenezer Morse of Boylston.

we go on; Seeing Mr. Smith has So deceiv'd me, in the Matter of the Former Deed. Captain Baker thinks it very Reasonable and Necessary. Smith resists it. When the Esquire was gone I offer to leave it to 3 indifferent Men. N.B. I receiv'd another Letter from Mr. Boardman attested by him to be the Copy of what he had sent by Mr. Smith. This came by the help of my Brother Samuel.

24. A.M. read Judg. 16 and the Expository remarks upon it were our forenoon Exercise. P.M. read James 2 and by reason of my perplexing Difficulties with Mr. Smith repeated Exposition on Mat. 5, 38, and part of 39. At Eve receiv'd a Letter from Mr. Smith, dated yesterday, in which he intimates his rejecting Still my proposal of a Bondsman. Read to the Congregation a Letter from the Reverend Mr. Morse of Shrewsbury requesting a Contribution for one Mr. Asa Hill who was lately burnt out. Left it with Deacons and Committee to advise upon. I thought it agreeable to Christian Principles, and that Meekness and Mercifulness which I had been recommending in the Day preceding, to Consider Mr. Smith's Case as well as my own; and being perswaded that Mr. Barkers Coming up here (as may be expected on the Ensuing Day) will be in Vain, I desir'd my son Thomas to prepare and go with a Line to Mr. Smith and take an Horse (if Mr. Smith desir'd also) and go away now in the Night to Boston and stop Mr. Barkers Coming to prevent needless Charge. And he went away accordingly about a quarter after 12 in the Night.

25. Thomas return'd: Mr. Smith not accepting my Offer. I went to Esquire Bakers to Consult him again upon my present Affairs; and to desire that the Select Men would defer their Warning Mr. Smith out of Town and especially if Some of his Friends would give Security respecting the Infant now expected; which he comply'd with, and at my Request he sent one of his Sons to Mr. Bezaleel Smith with a Note from me to have him come to Me or to his Kinsmans; and he came. N.B. Captain Maynard and Mr. Benjamin How look out a place in my Land by the Meeting House to set stables. I went over to see Mrs. Smith. She says now that she is willing to sign a Deed. But her Husband I find in the Same Disposition as he was, and increasing in self Vindications and Resentments. Asks me to let his Goods remain in my House, while he carrys his Family to his or her Fathers, to which I consent, but will not be answerable for them. N.B. His dread of Lying as he and I stood in the Road talking in the hearing of his Cousen Bezaleel. I return'd home. N.B. Mr. Ebenezer Maynard brought me a Load of Posts from the Ministerial Lot, and carry'd 'em to the Island. Mr. Batheric, Noah Forbush and my son Ebenezer Splicing Rails at the Ministerial Lott. At Eve Mr. Smith comes here and brings Mr. Barker. We effect no thing—but increase sin and Trouble. The Lord shew Mercy! and extend forgiveness! Tis a Day of sore Temptation. May God most gracious Help! Mrs. Smith sent me a Letter in which She complains of great unkindness—which verily I never shewed her but the Contrary.

26. Mr. Barker came with Mr. Smith. N.B. Mr. Barker tells me Mr. Smith at the Time when he (Barker) went up to take a Mortgage of him did not acquaint him that he had given me a Deed, but said he was under Obligation to me—whereas Mr. Smith has told me he did inform Mr. Barker that he had given me a Deed. Mr. Barker returns to Boston without effecting any Thing; for neither are the Conditions of my Bond fulfilled nor is there any security. N.B. Mr. Bezaleel Smith here and Confronts Abraham with respect to the different Account he has given of the Sum which the place in Brookfield is mortgaged for. Noah Forbush not well: does no great matter of Business to Day.

27. Mr. Ebenezer Rice levys an Execution on Mr. Abraham Smith to the value of an hundred Twenty odd Pounds old Tenor in behalf of one of the Hitchcocks in Springfield. My wife was over there to see Mrs. Smith who takes but little Notice of her. P.M. I rode down to Colonel William Ward and got him to take Mr. Andrew Newtons Deed that it may be acknowledged. Went to Mr. Ephraim How of Marlborough and paid him Six Pounds Old Tenor Interest.

28. Went over to t'other House and talk'd with Mrs. Smith. Her Husband is gone to Boston again, that he may obtain a

Power of Attorney for Colonel Chandler or somebody else that may take up the Mortgage for Mr. Boardman, and by what he has Said I apprehend he designs also to go to his Mother that she may sign his Deed; he had also sent to Brookfield to have the Land there measur'd. His wife manifests Satisfaction and Reconcilement with me and her Consent at least, if not Desire also to have me go to their Fathers. I rode to Mr. Smiths Father in Sudbury and lodg'd there, but the man himself was not at home: was gone to Boston. The Woman was almost overwhelm'd with Trouble about her son before I began. N.B. Mr. Bezaleel Smith there and had sufficient Ground to confirm what I said.

29. Left a Letter for Mr. Amos Smith at his House, rode to Mr. Francis Wheeler's and din'd there. He gave me from under his Hand and witness'd that the Child which might be born of his Dauter in Westborough Should not be a Town Charge. I call'd at Lieutenant Dakins, who favoured me with a pint of Hotspur Peas; but especially was desirous to acquaint me with their present Difficultys with Mr. Loring and their purpose to have a Council. I call'd at Mr. Lorings[11] in Marlborough—receiv'd of him his Chandlers History of Persecution.[12] Was at Mr. Benjamin Woods's.[13] Paid him 30/ old Tenor in full of all Demands. At Eve return'd home in Safety. D.G.

30. Have had so many avocations that I could not prepare more than one sermon.

31. Mr. Smith came up from Boston last night, but has not been to either of his Fathers, nor Seen his Mother. Read Judg. 17. Preach'd on Ps. 51, 11. P.M. read James, and repeated on Mat. 8, 34. N.B. The Deacons and Committee who met last Thursday to Confer about Mr. Asa Hills Case, as mention'd last Lords Day, made me no Return.

APRIL, 1754

Richard Kelly works here. Noah Forbush here still at Shooe-work. Ebenezer plough'd [in my Garden and split] the Indian Hills at my New Barn—and carry'd out some Muck from the stables. P.M. Mr. Abraham Smith and his Brother Francis Wheeler here. Mr. Nathaniel Green Coroner, with an Assistant here after Mr. Smith. Mr. Smith and I return our writings which had past and reciprocally burn our Agreement and give mutually Full Discharge. Mr. Green I suppose arrested or seiz'd him and they went all off together. I fear the Event with poor Smith. The Lord pitty, convince and forgive him! and may I be in a proper Frame towards him. May God forgive me wherein I have offended in my trading with him!

2. My wife went over to t'other House. Mr. Smith having given I know not what Satisfaction to the Officer, Green, is there till this Morning probably by reason of Mrs. Smiths being so near her Time, growing ill last night they had the midwife: But when they had din'd they all rode away—viz. Mr. Smith and wife, and Child, and her Brother Francis Wheeler, for Sudbury. Richard Kelly setts up, and mends, Fence at the Island, and prepar'd Beds in the Garden two long Beds for Hotspur Peas. Mr. Simon Tainter junior, who fell into a Fit yesterday, is greatly recover'd to Day.

3. Wrote to Mr. Hutchinson[1] to change next Sabbath.

4. Public Fast. A.M. on Jer. 12, 2. P.M. on Ez. 18, 30, latter part. Improv'd Some parts of Sermon on Jer. 31, 18, namely from page 6 to 15.

5. I visited Mrs. Williams (Mr. Samuels wife) who has of late lost a number of Relations, and some of them very near and dear to her, at Sherbourn, by the mortal fever that has rag'd among them. N.B. Mr. Abraham Smith at the other House to answer to Mr. Ebenezer Rice, sheriff. He lodg'd (as I heard) at Lieutenant Bruce's. N.B. Mr. Ephraim Bruce here, and tells me that Mr. Smith had told Such Things at their House, as if true, he Should be greatly Disaffected to me for: but when I came to understand

what they were, it was even astonishing that ever a professing Christian Should pervert and misrepresent the Truth so. Particularly that when our Agreement to throw up all our Bargain, was So clear, and in presence of his Brother Wheeler as well as others he Should so exceedingly misrepresent the plain and express'd Terms thereof. Thus when it was propos'd that we Should throw up all, it was expressly mention'd that a Bag of Feathers which he sent to my Dauter Forbush (of 50£ weight at 7/6 old Tenor per pound, but was thrown in for 10£ in our Bargain) should be given in—and this was the least he could do Since he lay expos'd to an action in Law for Breach of Covenant and for Dammages by his presumptiousness coming into my House; Yet Mr. Smith tells 'em at Bruce's that this was not mention'd till after Signing the mutual Discharges; and that tho he told me he had forgot that Article, yet I was so unfair and hard as to refuse to Consider it.

6. Receiv'd an insulting Letter from Mr. Smith, but God grant me Wisdom, Meekness and Patience. I rode to Grafton. Mr. Hutchinson in his New House, tho very unfinish'd.

7. Preach'd at Grafton a. and p.m. on Ps. 51, 11. Mr. Hutchinson here on Job and on [blank]. In returning at Eve call'd at Mr. Winchesters.

8. Captain Maynard and Lieutenant Bruce run the North Line of the Island, and set up Stakes.

9. Receiv'd a joyful Letter from my son Forbush that on the Night before last (the night after the 7th) my Dauter Mary was delivered of a Dauter, and both Mother and Child well. All glory be to God our Saviour and Deliverer. May He perfect begun Mercy! Richard Kelly at work again on John Dunlops Account. He setts up the Fence on the Line before mention'd. My Wife to Mr. Harringtons and brought seven Dollars which I borrow of him to pay the Reverend Mr. Stone for Newton Meadow.

10. Kelly at work here: and finishes for John Dunlop. Lieutenant Forbush Setts out 90 Apple Trees South west of the Barn—70 out of my own Nursery and 20 from Mr. Whitney. Showery p.m. P.M. a Cow which Ebenezer had of Mr. Abraham Knowlton and which I have had to keep a while, was Mir'd in the Swamp which I took up a few Years ago, near the Cedar Swamps; but we got her out again alive. Before Welch[2] in Boston Jayl is hang'd (the Day for his Execution being tomorrow) another barbarous Murder is Committed, and by another Irishman.[3]

11. Rode to Mr. Daniel Mathis's to a Fast kept there on Account of his Sciatica and Discouragements. Mr. Stone[4] was there, but no Minister besides. I preach'd a.m. on Ps. 51, 11, and pray'd both before and after Sermons. Left Mr. Stone to carry on the remaining Exercises: being oblig'd myself to hasten to my own Catechetical Exercises to Young Men. About 24 persons attended: I deliver'd Number 5 which is from page 17 to 22.

12. To my great Sorrow Mr. Abraham Smiths Goods which Mr. Ebenezer Rice seiz'd on an Execution, were sold at Vendue at Captain Maynards. Billy work'd part of the Day at Mr. Nurse's.

13. Mr. Moses Morse plough'd my Stubble at the Island, with 4 Oxen and his large Plough. At Eve my Kinsman Mr. Daniel Needham[5] came from Norwich and is travelling to Salem. He is much out of Health.

14. Read Judg. 18. Preach'd on Ez. 18, 30, repeating with alterations and additions Sermon on Jer. 31, from page 15 to the End. P.M. Read Jam. 5, preach'd on 1 Thess. 4, 17, last Clause, and chiefly made use of Sermon on Ps. 17, ult. The Happiness of Heaven from the Company: Especially of the glorious God

---

[11] Jonathan Loring was the son of the Reverend Israel Loring of Sudbury.

[12] Samuel Chandler translated the following work by Philippus van Limborch, *The History of the Inquisition*, 2 vols. (London, 1731). Chandler also published *The History of Persecution, in four Parts* (London, 1736).

[13] A leading citizen of Marlborough. _____

[1] Aaron Hutchinson of Grafton.

[2] William Welch, also known as George Kelly, was tried and convicted of the murder of Darby O'Brien "in November last by stabbing him in the Belly" *The Boston Weekly News-Letter*, March 14, 1754. Welch was executed in Boston April 11, 1754.

[3] "Last Saturday in the Afternoon Two Men at the South End having some Dispute about cording Wood on a Wharf, one of them struck the other on the Head with one of the Sticks, so that he fell down Speechless and expired soon after. The Man that gave the Blow surrender'd himself up to Justice, and, after Examination, was committed to Prison: The Jury of Inquest have found it wilful Murder." *The Boston Weekly News-Letter*, April 11, 1754.

[4] Nathan Stone of Southborough.

[5] Parkman's oldest sister, Mary, had married Daniel Needham.

Himself—from page 73 to 82. The Reason of my using old sermons to Day (tho I made great Alterations) was I was preparing on a difficult Text, viz. Rom. 5, 12, and by means of many Interruptions as well as the Subject I could not accomplish my Preparations. N.B. My Kinsman was so ill that he went not to Meeting at all.

15. Mr. Nathan Maynard plough'd my Island stubble with Mr. Nurse's and his own Oxen. My Kinsman still but poorly, but behaves as a Christian. Sent his Horse to Mr. Bathericks to be kept.

16. My Kinsman goes on his Journey. Rode to Shrewsbury Ministers Meeting at Mr. Cushings. Mr. Stone, Morse, Maccarty,[6] Buckminster,[7] and Davis[8] there. Mr. Buckminster the Concio on 2 Cor. 2, 15, 16. Mr. Martyn not there to Day. Mr. John Brighams wife came to us.

17. Mr. Martyn and Mr. Smith came to Association. Mr. Davis preach'd on 1 Cor. 16, 13. We went in a Body to see Colonel Ward,[9] at his request, he being in a low State of Health. I pray'd with him. His Dauter also ill. Mr. Millen[10] my Company home, but he goes to Hopkinton. Mr. John Child and his Lad and Dr. Jenison[11] lodge. I Sent my Mare to Captain Bakers and Dr. Jenisons to Deacon Newtons.

18. Mr. Child glazes my sons shop. Dr. Jenison to Leicester. Lieutenant Hezekiah Ward din'd. P.M. Mrs. Molly Martyn. Unusual Cold Weather.

19. Exceeding Cold. Ebenezer's weak Cow brings a Calf. The Cold is more Severe, and the Ice thicker than I think I have ever known it.

20. The Weather moderated considerably, yet 'tis Cold. An unusual Time! Mr. Greenwood[12] of Sutton, from the General Court calls and takes the Journals of the House of Representatives which he had lent me; and acquaints me with the proceedings of the Court.

21. Read Judg. 19. Preach'd a. and p.m. on Rom. 5, 12. Read P.M. 1 Pet. 1. Acquainted the Congregation that I perceiv'd it was the mind of those I had Convers'd with that it is not adviseable to have among us, a public Contribution for Mr. Hill of Shrewsbury (who was burnt out and whose Request was read some Sabbaths ago) not only because of our Circumstances here, but Mr. Hill has receiv'd pritty full Supplys; and it is not expected from us, all Things considered. But yet if any persons are still So inclined as to Contribute Money or Necessarys of Life, they may use their Discretion.

22. Thomas rides to Hopkinton upon my Mare. He desires to use some severity with Mr. Israel Walker who keeps him out of his Money from one Year to another. He was to have return'd the same Day but did not.

23. Thomas return'd—does nothing with Mr. Walker.

24. My wife makes a Visit to Mr. Martyns P.M. and return'd at Eve.

25. Mr. Barrett[13] preach'd my Lecture on Ps. 34, 8. N.B. Captain Wood[14] came with him, who also, and Dr. Brigham of Marlborough din'd with us.

26. Mr. Jacob Foster here in his Way to Brookfiled. Alpheus Newton disquieted with my Sheep.

27. Trouble with my Creatures breaking in to Neighbour's Meadows.

28. Read Judg. 20 to number 25. Preach'd on 1 Cor. 15, 24, 27, 28, a. and p.m. P.M. read 1 Pet. 2. May God pardon our sins and graciously accept us! My Neighbour Williams's Wife

ill of the Fever (as it is Suppos'd) which so many of her Relations have dy'd of at Sherbourn.

29. Thomas help'd me at the Garden a.m. Catechiz'd Children at the Meeting House both a. and p.m. Visited Mrs. Williams in the Morning and prayed with her. Was at t'other House at Eve. Gave Lieutenant Maynard a Note to Mr. Biglow of 8£ Lawfull Money. Mr. Foster came back from Brookfield but goes to his Brother Twitchells to lodge. N.B. We were almost wholly out of Hay.

30. Mr. Foster came here and rode with me to Mr. Jonas Brighams who moves a Barn from the East side of the Road to the back of his House.

### MAY, 1754.

1. I visited Mrs. Williams and pray'd with her. She is very bad and grows much weaker. Visited Mrs. Barrett of Hopkinton who is Sick. Return'd at Evening.

2. I preach'd at Lieutenant Tainters, by his Desire, the sermon and on the Text I preach'd from when Neighbour Newtons House was burnt, viz. Lam. 3, 22, 23. My wife went with me. Before I got home Mr. Eleazer Williams meets with an Horse to Visit his Mother. I went and pray'd with her; she is hastening away apace, and was Sensible. Discours'd like a good Christian. Gave her Testimony to the Truth of the Christian Religion and to the Expediency and usefulness of waiting upon divine Ordinances. Mr. Williams desir'd me to return again in the Morning—

3. Which I did—but his Wife was a Corps laid out. She departed after Day break this Morning. Mr. Eleazer Whitney brought me forty Rails, ten of them being beyond the Number I expected, and not Splic'd. Still exceeding dry Weather. Mr. John Freeland Taylor makes a Coat of Blue Broad Cloth for Thomas. This Day is a week since Mrs. Williams was confin'd—She was at Lecture yesterday was Sennight.

4. Mrs. Williams bury'd. May God Sanctify this breach! Mr. Freeland here till he went to Mrs. Williams Funeral.

5. I have been preparing upon the Doctrine of Original Sin, comparing Mr. John Taylor,[1] Dr. Watts (Ruin and Recovery),[2] Turrettine,[3] Van Mast., Mr. Willard[4] etc. and cannot finish in season what I propos'd. Therefore on this Consideration and on Consideration of the Extraordinary Drought preach'd a.m. on Jer. 14, 22 and p.m. on Occasion of the Death of Mrs. Williams and another of Mr. Nathaniel Whitneys Brothers and I preach'd on Job 14, 14. The public Reading was Judg. 20, from number 26, a.m. and p.m. was 1 Pet. 3.

6. Here the Woods at Wachusett are much on Fire in this terrible Drought, and 'tis thought they approach nearer. The burnt leaves by means of the strong Winds reach even hither. Mr. Jonas Twitchell works for me, carrying out Dung—my sons Ebenezer and Thomas also hard at it. Have Ebenezers Cart and Oxen and my Mare for the Team: and borrow Deacon Newtons Cart. Mr. Bigelow and Timothy Warrin here at Evening. Mr. John Freeland finishes Thomas's Coat and goes home.

7. Our sheep continue troublesome to Alphy Newton and Mr. Francis Whipple comes to me on his Account. The Shower of Rain tho but Small exceeding comfortable and reviving.

8. Warmer Weather. Many People are planting to Day. I walk'd up to Lieutenant Fays and to Engisn Fay's. Hear that Colonel Nahum Ward dy'd Yesterday. A great Loss to his County!

9. Held a Catechetical Exercise to Young Women, of which forty one attended. At Eve was at old Mr. Maynards.

10. Ebenezer's Mare which I have now the Care of, is kept at Mr. Bonds whilst Ebenezer has mine to work—that I may help

---

[6] Thaddeus Maccarty of Worcester.

[7] Joseph Buckminster of Rutland.

[8] Joseph Davis of Holden.

[9] Justice Nahum Ward of Shrewsbury died a few weeks later, May 7, 1754.

[10] The Reverend John Mellen of Sterling.

[11] William Jennison, who did not have a college education, studied medicine with Dr. Stanton Prentice of Lancaster. He began to practice medicine in Mendon in May, 1753, but "afterwards engaged in trade." Bond, *Watertown*, II, 802.

[12] Daniel Greenwood. Benedict and Tracy, *Sutton*, p. 653.

[13] The Reverend Samuel Barrett of Hopkinton.

[14] John Wood.

[1] John Taylor, *The Scripture Doctrine of Original Sin Proposed to Free and Candid Examination* (London, 1740). Other editions followed.

[2] Isaac Watts, "The Ruin and Recovery of Mankind," *Discourses, Essays, and Tracts on Various Subjects*, VI (London, 1753), 177–320. The Ruin and Recovery evidently did not appear as a separate imprint.

[3] This was probably Franciscus Turretinus, *Compendium Theologiae Didactico-Elencticae* (Amsterdam, 1695). Parkman owned this volume. See Diary, Nov. 21, 1747.

[4] Samuel Willard, D.D., minister of the Old South Church and Vice-President of Harvard College, was the author of numerous works. The editor has not discovered a work with reference to original sin in the title. Many of Willard's writings were collected by Joseph Sewall and Thomas Prince and published as *A Compleat Body of Divinity in Two Hundred and Fifty Expository Lectures* (Boston, 1726).

him what I can. His Father Harrington here. Lucy came from Brookfield with Mr. Baldwin last night. I rode up to Shrewsbury to the Funeral of Colonel Nahum Ward. A very great number of people attended—many Gentlemen from Neighbouring Towns—except Ministers, there being no Minister from the Neighbouring Towns or Parishes but my Self. Mrs. Patty in a low Condition. I supp'd with the Bearers and other Gentlemen at the Widows. Justice Baker and Lieutenant Fay my Company home. N.B. We had a very refreshing Rain gently distill'd most of the Afternoon. A Seasonable Blessing this exceeding dry time.

11. My Cattle break in to the Meadows So often it gives great Disquietment. Mr. Nathaniel Whitney in particular greatly offended, and in intemperate Anger, which gave me much trouble. Last Night Watertown New Meeting House burnt.

12. Read Judg. 21. Preach'd a. and p.m. on Rom. 5, 12. P.M. read 1 Pet. 4. Showery. We praise God for this Great Blessing. May it please God to pour out abundantly His Holy Spirit! and may Doctrine distill as the Rain, and Knowledge flow down among us!

13. A most mercifull growing Season! P.M. Mr. Baldwin came from Sudbury.

14. [No entry.]

15. Mr. Hezekiah Pratt plough'd at the Island. I was at t'other House. Ebenezer has begun to plant one piece. I was at Mr. David Maynards with old Mr. Green. N.B. I wrote to Colonel Chandler concerning my Collection of Poems[5] and sent him the Paper of Subscriptions. Wrote also to Mr. Forbush of Brookfield. These were sent by Elisha Jones. Mr. Baldwin and John Woods begin to work at the Meeting House. They undertake the Pulpit in the first place. Frequent Showers of Rain, rendering it a wonderful season, thanks be to God! O that Grace might Spring in our Hearts! Mr. Nathaniel Whitney here and seems very Calm. I read him a paper containing Several Offers which I make him. To which he makes me no Reply.

16. Showery this Morning also. Lucy lodg'd at t'other House. I went into the Neighbourhood to get somebody to plough or harrow my Ground, but without Success. I was at Mr. Daniel Warrins—but he offer'd a Bushel of Indian Corn. N.B. I had din'd at Lieutenant Tainters with Master Hezekiah Coolidge[6] who came the Day before Yesterday to keep School, and keeps at the School House. Mr. Baldwin here at Eve, and aks Leave to Spend a little Time with my Dauter Lucy.

17. Still Showery. Mr. David Maynard junior with his son David and a Team, ploughs by the Barn.

18. Very rainy.

19. Read Ruth 7. Preach'd on Rom. 5, 15, 18 a. and p.m. Read Pet. 5.

20. Town Meeting to See whether the Town will Send a Representative. They vote not to. Billy must furrow out for ploughing; he has Benjamin Rice to help him; but they prove insufficient—forc'd to get Mr. Jonathan Forbush to hold plough and we plant part of the piece by the Barn. Mr. Hezekiah Coolidge visits me and lodges here.

21. Greatly fatigued and disappointed about Oxen to plough my further Field at the Island. I Seek to above half a score Neighbours in Vain. We are also out of Rye, and when I was about to go out P.M. Mr. Isaac Johnson of Southboro came to desire me to go and see his Father in his last Minutes (as they apprehend), Mr. Stone being gone with his Wife to Mr. Martyns. It was exceeding difficult for me to go, yet I went. Return'd at Eve.

22. Lieutenant Gilbert of Brookfield here. N.B. my Horse was kept last Night by Mr. Batherick. Lieutenant Thomas Forbush plough'd for me. Abner Warrin wash'd 5 of my sheep, which were all that were wash'd. P.M. my son Forbush here. He

goes at Eve to t'other House. Deacon Haynes[7] of Sudbury brings a Letter to our Church for a Council.

23. Billy has Eben Rice to help him furrow and plant: and they almost finish.

24. [No entry.]

25. Mr. Israel Hearsy[8] from Boston here going to Oxford to See his Wife. I rode to Southborough (at Mr. Stone's[9] Desire by Mr. Ebenezer Rice).

26. I preach'd at Southborough on Eph. 5, 14, a. and p.m. Mr. Stone here, on Nahum 1, 2. Return'd home at Eve. I lodg'd at his House.

27. Andrew Newton Sign'd and seal'd and deliver'd another more fairly drawn Deed, and his Wife also in presence of Messers. Biton and Lock, their near Neighbours. Din'd at Mr. Bridge's[10] in Framingham on part of a large Turtle or Tortoise. Showery—yet rode to Captain Livermore's[11] at Waltham and lodg'd there.

28. Visited Mrs. Williams (widow of the late Reverend Mr. Williams)[12] and Mr. Cushing[13] and his Wife. Proceeded on my Journey to Cambridge (having been refresh'd at Watertown at Mr. Benjamin Hastings) din'd at Brother Champneys[14] late in the Day—Rain prevented my going to Boston. At Eve at President Holyokes[15]—and at Mr. Spragues. Lodg'd at sister Barretts: Sister Lydia[16] being there also, but my Mare (Ebenezers) was kept at Brother Champneys.

29. Early to Boston. Put up my Mare at Mr. Procters. Dr. Mayhew[17] the Election sermon on Mat. 25, 21. Din'd at Brother Samuels and went to the Convention P.M. Dr. Sewal Moderator and Pray'd. At Eve at Brother Samuels my Brother William also. Sweet Conference together about our Affairs, which are in Common. I lodg'd there.

30. Conference with my Brethren and Messers Oliver and Briant[18] at Mr. William Winters office upon settling what our honoured Mother had given us, and we agree with the Executor, or Eldest Brother. Broke fast at Olivers.[19] Return'd to Convention and attended the public meeting. Mr. Williams[20] of Long Meadow preach'd on Exod. 25, 8. The Collection follow'd. I din'd at Dr. Sewalls.[21] Present Messrs. Flynt,[22] Niles,[23] Williams (that preach'd), Townsend[24] of Needham, Byles,[25] Quincy (Edmund)[26]—P.M. at Mr. Prince's,[27] and at Mr. Foxcrofts.[28] Supp'd at Cousen Edward Langdons—and lodg'd at Brother Parkmans. Return'd Mr. Pierpoints Letters to Mrs. Derricut.

31. Variously employ'd still in Town. Din'd at Mr. Stoddards. At Eve rode to Brother Harringtons in Watertown and lodged there.

### JUNE, [1754]

Set out Early in the Morning from Brother Harringtons. Stop'd at Mr. Woodburns[1] Tavern in Waltham, and wrote a Letter by him to Brother Samuel Parkmans. Cross'd Charles River and went to Captain Josh Fullers. Proceeded up to Natick. Refresh'd at the Reverend Mr. Badgers;[2] visited Mrs. Peabody:[3] and Mr. Hezekiah Coolidge having invited me to his Fathers in Sherbourn, promising to come up with me—I therefore rode

7 Josiah Haynes.
8 The husband of Parkman's niece, Tabitha.
9 The Reverend Nathan Stone.
10 The Reverend Matthew Bridge.
11 Samuel Livermore.
12 Warham Williams of Waltham had died, June 22, 1751.
13 The Reverend Job Cushing of Shrewsbury.
14 Parkman's brother-in-law, Samuel Champney of Cambridge.
15 Edward Holyoke of Harvard College.
16 Parkman's sister-in-law, Lydia Champney.
17 The great Jonathan Mayhew.
18 Joseph Bryant had married Parkman's niece, Elizabeth Parkman.
19 Edward Brattle Oliver, who had married Parkman's niece, Esther Parkman.
20 Stephen Williams.
21 The Reverend Joseph Sewall of the Old South Church.
22 Tutor Henry Flynt of Harvard College.
23 The Reverend Samuel Niles of Braintree.
24 The Reverend Jonathan Townsend.
25 Mather Byles of Boston.
26 (Harvard 1722). "Squire" Quincy, the great landowner and office-holder of Braintree and Boston.
27 Thomas Prince of the Old South Church.
28 Thomas Foxcroft of the First Church in Boston.

5 Parkman's hopes of publication of his poems, which have been lost, never did materialize.

6 (Harvard 1750). He was the son of a tavernkeeper and selectman of Sherborn. At Harvard, Coolidge had been punished for fighting, card-playing, and gambling. After making his humble confession and graduating, he kept the Roxbury Grammar School for a time. At Westborough he frequented taverns and gambled, and was soon dismissed from the school. *Sibley*, XII, 539-540.

1 Samuel Woodburn.
2 Stephen Badger.
3 The widow of the Reverend Oliver Peabody of Natick.

there; but he was not at Home. It was said he was gone to his Uncle's, Major Coolidge. It was about noon when I left Mr. James Coolidges and proceeded to the Majors—but neither was he there. I din'd there, and hastened to Colonel Buckminster's. From whence Dr. Wilson⁴ of Sherbourn rode with me some miles—and gave me an account of Some of Coolidge's late Conduct at Coltons Tavern in Cambridge—his gaming etc. In Southboro a storm rising (after I left Mr. Stones) I was oblig'd to stop at Lieutenant Brighams. Arriv'd in Safety and found my Family well. D.O.M. Gratis.

2. Read Ruth 2 and 2 Pet. 1. Repeated sermon on Jer. 8, 4, 5, a. and p.m. Captain Storer of Boston in his Journey from Connecticut attended with us, and din'd here. He lodg'd at Mr. Ebenezer Rice's.

3. Mr. Nurse's Piggs (being unyoked), root up great part of my Field by the Barn to our great Grief.

4. [No entry.]

5. Preach'd my own Lecture on 1 Cor. 11, 31 to page 10. Read the Letter from the aggrieved Brethren at Sudbury—and left the Affair to further Consideration. After Lecture Came Justice Liscom⁵ to acquaint me that old Mr. Johnson⁶ is dead and Mr. Stone being gone to Harwich, the survivors desire me to attend the Funeral next Saturday. N.B. Inform'd concerning Brother Abijah Gales Conduct towards Mr. Isaac Amsdens wife; and desire he would stay from the Communion till the Cause can be heard. At Eve came Messers. Williams and Breck of Springfield and lodge here. Lieutenant Tainter took my Billy with him to lead the Horses to his Barn.

6. The Horses fetch'd by Billy, and the said Springfield Gentlemen leave us. N.B. Mr. Ebenezer Rice repeatedly request he may cutt two or three large Trees for Timber in the Ministerial Lott—I advis'd yesterday with several of the selectmen, and to Day with Esquire Baker. I am not so free to sell any stick off from that Lot; but Mr. Rice tells me they are such Trees as are not likely to be of so great profit and Service any other way. It was also desir'd that Mr. Marly were appriz'd of it, that there might be no Disquietment, even altho he has verbally declar'd he Should not trouble himself about the Ministerial Rights. But Mr. Rice said he could not have Time to go over to Mr. Martyns⁷ or Captain Eagers about it. Whereupon I told him he had heard what anyhow the Case was; he must use his Discretion. He said if he did cut 'em he would pay all Damages that Should ensue, every manner of the Way.

7. [No entry.]

8. Ensign Whipple of Grafton brot a Letter from Mr. Hutchinson about their Difficultys and desiring Help.

9. Sacrament. Read Ruth 3, 2 Pet. 2. Preach'd on Isa. 9, 6, his Name Wonderful. P.M. on Rom. 6, 1, 2. After the Exercises the Church stop'd upon the Sudbury Affair. Voted not to Send. But those who were for sending and were the minor part, were in some Chafe, especially M. Grow and Lieutenant Bruce. Esquire Baker and Mr. Whipple earnestly for it. However there was no withstanding so evident a Vote.

10. My son Thomas help'd me. Had Mr. Williams's Cart and Oxen to carry out the ashes to the Island Field. My sons plough'd with my Mare and Lieutenant Forbush's plough. P.M. Messers. Chamberlin and Joseph Wood, with Two or Three sons apiece, hoed what was to be hoed at the Island.

11. Rain. Yet I rode to the School House and Catechiz'd the Children there, at 4 P.M.

12. Mr. Martyn came here in order to go with me to Grafton. No word nor Lisp of either Side respecting the Epistolary Acrimony. At Grafton we join'd with Messers. Cushing and Hall⁸ in hearing the Matters of Difficultie between a Number of the Church and Mr. Hutchinson,⁹ who they conceive, was chargeable with Falsehood in saying that the Selectmen had agreed and determin'd to move Mr. Arnolds Shop and at Such a Time—

when they had not. See the Minutes of the Council. Mr. Carter,¹⁰ Father in Law to Mr. Hutchinson there. Mr. Hall at Eve went home. The rest of us lodg'd there.

13. Mr. Hutchinsons Confession new drawn—we were at the Meeting House Twice. The Church accepted by a Majority of those present. I pray'd at the Conclusion. After Dinner we parted. Mr. Martyn and I rode to Westborough together but no word of our own Troubles. Call'd at Winchesters—and at Captain Bakers. When I came home marry'd Cornelius Biglow junior to Sarah Miller.¹¹ Billy to School at the School House. Mr. Hezekiah Coolidge Master.

14. Captain Bakers¹² Company together in pursuance of Beating Orders to go to the Eastward; I pray'd with the Company. Captain Timothy Brigham of Southborough and others here after the Company was dismiss'd.

15. The Busness of the Week and the Circumstances of my Family prevent my making the fully of mý Ordinary Preparations for the Sabbath. Mr. Jonah Warrin here Early and desires me to write a Letter to his son Samuel which I gratify'd him in. Receiv'd a Letter from Daniel Millen to be Communicated.

16. Read Ruth ult. Preach'd a.m. on Isa. 9, 6—shall be call'd Wonderfull. P.M. read 2 Pet. 3. Repeated on Mat. 22, 37, 38. Stay'd the Church and read the Letter from Daniel Miller and the request was answer'd.¹³

17. Sundry Neighbours, viz. Mr. Jonathan Warrin, Daniel Hardy, Phinehas Hardy, Solomon Woods, and Ebenezer Rice junior. Samuel Harrington, Jonathan Bond, Moses Nurse's Boy little Ebenezer came and gave a lift in Weeding my little Field by the Barn. The Precinct Met (among other Things) to See whether Mr. Jonathan Forbush Should retain his Right in the Meeting House Seating, if he Conveys his Right in the Pew which he drew for me, equal to what he would have had if he had done nothing about said Pew. They sent for me—upon Esquire Bakers informing me in the middst of them that the Money for the Pew must be immediately paid, I insisted to have a just Title convey'd to me I would See to the answering it—Upon its being intimated that they wanted the money forthwith and maybe I could not pay, I answer'd that altho this precinct, as a precinct had paid me their Dues (that is, with regard to Sallery) yet this Body, namely as Members of the Town were yet indebted to me; and that as much or more than the Pew came to. Lieutenant Bruce answer'd Sharply, and coarsely, asking me with great Anger Why I Upraided them with this? Whereas I spake of my just dues only when forc'd to it, and with all Meekness in my just Defence. But I soon retir'd from them and would not stay to contend with them.

18. The Association met here, viz. Messers. Cushing, Martyn, Stone, Smith, Maccarty. Lieutenant Tainter kill'd one of my Lambs. Captain Baker sent a side of Lamb. Mr. Ebenezer Rice's Wife sent a dozen and half of Biskett—French Turnips, Potatoes and Salletting. As for the Exercises and the Conversation see the Association Minutes. Mr. Maccarty lodg'd at Esquire Bakers; the rest lodg'd here. The Horses were sent 1 to Esquire's, 1 to Lieutenant Tainters, 1 to Mr. Nurse's and Two to Mr. Pratts.

19. Mr. Maccarty pray'd at the public Lecture and Mr. Cushing preach'd on 3 John 4. Mr. Hutchinson, here and Mr. Hezekiah Coolidge din'd here. Mt. Hutchinson and I confirm'd an Agreement to Change next Lords Day.

20. Catechetical Exercise to Young Men, Number 6 from page 22 to page [blank]. N.B. That I might not hinder the Carpenters at the Meeting House, I took the Young Men to my own.

21. Having heard that Messers. Harrington and Daniel Forbush and some others were disquieted with what I mention'd of late at the Precinct Meeting concerning the Towns arrears with me, I went to see 'em and talk with them and did so, and made a Visit likewise at Mr. Nathaniel Whitneys. Am growing Feeble and out of Health.

22. Another Letter from the agriev'd Brethren in Sudbury,

⁴ John Wilson (Harvard 1741) practiced for a time among the Indians at Natick and then settled in Hopkinton. Sibley, XI, 96–97.
⁵ Samuel Lyscomb of Southborough.
⁶ William Johnson of Southborough.
⁷ The Reverend John Martyn of Northborough.
⁸ David Hall of Sutton.
⁹ Aaron Hutchinson.
¹⁰ Margery Carter of Hebron, Conn., married the Grafton minister.
¹¹ The daughter of James Miller of Westborough.
¹² Edward Baker of Westborough.
¹³ Daniel Millen of Holliston had requested assistance in a council to be held July 2.

which I am the more sorry for as they Seem to have some bad Design in it; or at least it will be like to have a bad tendency among us, some of the Brethren of our Church being in some Ruffle already about their Affair. But its coming now when I am going out of Town, and there will be no other Lords Day in which it can be done, I thought it best to acquaint Deacon Newton with it, that he might tell the Church—but I wrote what I said to him and left it with him, telling him with all that the Letter was at the Churchs Service, being left with my wife for them if they Should desire to have it. Then I rode to Grafton.

23. Preach'd at Grafton on Rom. 12, 28. If it be possible etc. Mr. Hutchinson at Westborough. I baptiz'd a Dauter of Mr. Andrew Adams, and a son, Abner, for Mr. Charles Bruce. Rainy Day, but at Eve it increas'd, but especially was violent in the Night. Yet Mr. Hutchinson return'd home which I could not. Mr. Hutchinson preach'd on Gen. 3, 22, 23, 24. Heb. 11, 4.

24. Great part of the forenoon rainy, but I set out for Westboro. At Captain Bakers found that he and Francis Whipple were disquieted with me about the Sudbury Letters not being read, whereas Deacon Newton was told that it was at the Churchs service. N.B. Deacon was at the Squires, and I think own'd that I told him where they might have the Letter—but he said he had promis'd me he would Say nothing but what I had writ. I offer'd to warn a Church Meeting this Day to be towards Night, and to hire a man to do it if that would satisfie; but it was not accepted. I left 'em ruffl'd. P.M. saw Mr. Abraham Smith with his Father ride upwards.

25. This Day the Churchs are to meet at Sudbury for Council. Mr. Campbell[14] of Oxford, and Deacon Davis here on their way thither. N.B. Mr. Nathaniel Whitney's Discourse of Sudbury Affair. Jonah and the Storm. Send Mr. Nurse my Chair to carry his Wife to Salem.

26. A very menacing Letter from Mr. Abraham Smith, threatning to prosecute me for telling him he was a Lyar and had told a Lie.

27. Mr. Adams at work making a pair of Great Doors for the Barn. Sent an answer to Mr. Smiths Letter, by Mr. Phinehas Rice of Grafton. Was over at t'other House.

28. Mr. Adams finishes that work. Mr. Samuel Livermore junior here, going to Cold Spring. I wrote by Mr. Livermore to Mr. Forbush on the Smith Affair. Mr. Phinehas Rice brings me another blustering Letter from Mr. Smith.

29. I was in a poor feeble, relax'd State, but got through my Preparations somewhat Seasonably and largely. D.G.

30. Read and expounded for the a.m. Exercise 1 Sam., chapter 1. P.M. read 1 John 1, and preach'd on Rom. 6, 3, 4. Forenoon Exercise finish'd Somewhat before 12. Altho I was Still but in a weak State yet had today Some Appetite to my Dinner which I have not had for some time. Stay'd the Church at Eve and related to them what I had done about the Sudbury Letter, and so endeavour'd to remove all misunderstandings among them about that Affair, and I said that if any one of them had any Thing to offer there was Opportunity but no Body Spake. So the Church was dismiss'd with Blessing, and I desir'd that those who were appointed Delegates to the Holliston Council would Seasonably attend that service.

## JULY, 1754.

1. Messers. Martyn and Maccarty and their Wives here p.m. Neighbour Eleazer Williams plough'd at the Island, and Mr. Benjamin Tainter hoed. Send Two Calves to be kept at t'other Place: Mr. Tainter assisted in getting them over and took my Mare to keep at his own Pasture.

2. My Mare was brot from Mr. Tainters: and Lieutenant and I rode to Holliston. Neither heard nor saw any Thing of Esquire Baker, the other Delegate. At Mr. Daniel Mellens who had call'd us, we found the Reverend Messers. Bucknam[1] and Bridge,[2] and their Delegates, viz. Esquire Adams[3] for Medway first

Church, and Esquire Haven,[4] Deacon Pike[5] and Ensign Stone[6] for Framingham. We got together by about 10 a.m. so that we settled all our Preparatory Business respecting the Churchs Committee who were ready with us to attend upon the Council when we should be form'd—we form'd—(tho I earnestly besought I might be excus'd leading in the Work, and try'd a Vote for Mr. Bucknam), yet I could not escape. Mr. Bucknam chose Scribe and sent a written Message to Captain Littlefield to attend if he pleas'd. These Things before Dinner. P.M. Mr. Mellen gave us a long and too confus'd Account of his Case. At Eve were in our Debates—Could find no Method to proceed in: both Esquire Adams and Esquire Haven went home. We remain'd wholly incapable of drawing up anything, till we dispers'd. I only, lodg'd at Mr. Mellens. Lieutenant Tainter at Captain Littlefields. I was in a most feeble, weak, trembling State thro the Night and had but little sleep. But (Mr. Mellen lodging with me)

3. In the Morning I had some Discourse with him which open'd a Way for us to proceed in—I wrote—it took; with Mr. Bridge's Help it was ripen'd—and we had a result which succeeded (D.G.). Mr. Mellen Consented. The Ministers din'd at Mr. Prentice's. P.M. went to Lecture. I pray'd before sermon. Mr. Bucknam preach'd on 1 Sam. 4, 13, for his Heart trembled for the Ark of God. After Sermon the Church was Stop'd and our Result was publicly read by the Scribe. Mr. Mellen renewed his Acceptance, Submission etc. The Church also voted their Concurrence. And Mrs. Mellen publicly consenting was also restor'd by the Church to Charity and privileges—all which gave us great Joy and cause of Praise to God. We left 'em cheerfully and Lieutenant Tainter and I rode to Southborough. I wanted to Consult Mr. Ezra Tailor on the Smith Affair. Found him at Captain Timothy Brighams, and read him the Letters which had pass'd between us. He said he would go and See Smith next Monday or Tuesday, with Mr. Ebenezer Rice. Lieutenant Tainter rode Home. I lodg'd at Mr. Stones being afraid to ride in the Evening Air. Had but a poor Night.

4. Lowery till 8 or 9. I return'd home when it clear'd up in Safety, except my feeble state. My wife tells me that 16 Hands came Yesterday forenoon and hoed the rest of my Corn over.

5. Am not altogether So faint and feeble. Can Study part of my Time.

6. Mr. Jason Haven,[7] a Senior sophister here; din'd with us. Sent an Answer to Mr. Smiths second Letter by Primus—Mr. Phinehas Rice's Negro. P.M. I attended the burying of Mr. Thomas Twitchells Infant.

7. Read and gave large Exposition of 1 Sam. 2. P.M. read 1 John 2. By the Extra Business of last Week was able to prepare but one Exercise—therefore p.m. repeated Exposition on Mat. 11, 29, 30, delivering two Exercises in one. Mr. Gershom Brighams wife din'd with us. At Eve read to the Church the late Result of the Council at Holliston.

8. Went to t'other House; my son Ebenezer began to mow between the House and Barn. Brought over Ebenezer's Mare for Mr. Ebenezer Rice to go down with Mr. Ezra Taylor to Abraham Smith of Sudbury. At Eve Mr. Jason Haven came and lodg'd here. Thomas mow'd Bushes p.m.

9. Mr. Haven to Framingham. Thomas mow'd at the Island. Billy mow'd p.m. Mr. Forbush and his Wife and Child with their Friend Deacon Cutler and his Wife came from Brookfield to t'other House last Night, and this Day here, with Mrs. Brown (Mr. Zechariah Browns Wife) broke fast and din'd here. P.M. Mr. Forbush to Cambridge and the rest of the Company left us except My Dauter and her Child. Master Coolidge and I rode over to Mr. Eliezer Rice's to See the Ministerial Meadow, and find that some of the Grass is now fit to be mow'd.

10. Expected Mr. Stone to preach my Lecture but he did not come. I preach'd myself on 1 Cor. 11, 31. Thomas and Billy at the Island part of the Day.

14 The Reverend John Campbell.

1 Nathan Bucknam of Millis.
2 Matthew Bridge of Framingham
3 Elisha Adams.

4 Joseph Haven, selectman and representative.
5 Moses Pike was a prominent office-holder. Temple, *Framingham*, p. 670.
6 Hezekiah Stone.
7 (Harvard 1754). Haven became the minister of Dedham, 1756–1803.

11. Mr. Phinehas Hardy here about the Affair of the Pew; and he seems inclin'd to have me resign the matter to Mr. Jonathan Forbush that he may take the Pew and Pay the Money. I visited Captain Forbush and other Neighbours as far as Jonas Twitchells. N.B. came home on Foot. Thomas and Billy mowing and raking at the Island.

12. Mr. Arnold of Grafton here, and obtains of me a Copy of Mr. Hutchinsons Second Paper (or Confession). Thomas and William mowe and make Hay at the Island, and Lieutenant Tainter Carts up a few Cocks of it. It is So Cloudy Weather and now and then Sprinkles of Rain, that the Hay does not make as we could wish. Mr. Baldwin Strikes me up an Extempore Gate before my House. Plants in fore yard.

13. Thomas finish'd mowing at the Island. Dull weather a.m. brighter p.m. I hiv'd a Swarm of Bees my Self, my sons both of them gone to the Island.

14. Read 1 Sam. 3. Mr. Forbush preach'd for me on 1 Cor. 11, 29. I administer'd the Lords Supper. P.M. read 1 John 3. Mr. Forbush preach'd on Eph. 5, 8. They went to their Father Forbush at Evening.

15. Went to the Ministerial Meadow and found there Messers. Jonas Twitchell and John Rogers mowing. Rody Smith was gone to Captain Maynards for Rum but mow'd the rest of the Day. My son Thomas got in a Jagg from the Island and then mow'd at the Meadow p.m. P.M. I rode with Mr. Forbush to Waltham and lodg'd at Mr. Isaac Brown's.

16. Set out from Mr. Browns early; broke fast at the Reverend Mr. Adams's[8] at Roxbury. We proceeded to Mr. John Barkers at Boston, whom Mr. Abraham Smith I Suppose has dependence upon to testify against me; but who in Discourse, tells me he was astonish'd at Smiths Impudence that Night he was at my House, and the next morning likewise, than ever he was in his Life; and says he doth not remember that he so much as once heard me express my Self towards Smith in any unbecoming manner. To this Mr. Forbush was Witness. Thence we went to Dr. Pyncheons[9] and din'd there. Spent the Chief of the p.m. at Brother Samuels, Captain Storers, and Mr. Kneelands.[10] We return'd as far as to Mr. Adams's and lodg'd there. At home Thomas and Billy rak'd at the Meadow a.m. P.M. prov'd rainy, and at night a great Storm of Thunder and Lightning and Rain.

17. Commencement. Mr. Forbush and I set out early from Mr. Adams's and went to Cambridge. Mr. Forbush took his second Degree. I din'd in the Hall. We lodg'd together at Sister Barretts having left our Horse and Chair under the Care of Brother Champney. Thomas and Billy, and Rody Smith rak'd at the Meadow, and on 18 Neighbour Eliezer Rice, Hezekiah Pratt and Edwards Whipple brought three Load of Hay from the Meadow.

18. Subscriptions for my Collection of Poems promoted by Mr. Forbush who got a Number of them among his Acquaintance and others, and at Mr. Hancocks[11] Chamber, Mr. Tucker[12] and Mr. Webster[13] subscrib'd. Din'd at Mr. Appletons[14] where I also mention'd the Collection. N.B. Mr. Walker Merchant of Boston there, with whom I have much Conversation. Mr. Forbush and I rode up to Mr. Woodwards of Weston, and lodg'd there.

19. We Set out early from Mr. Woodwards, and broke fast at Mr. Isaac Baldwins. N.B. Jeduthun there. We fish'd in the pleasant Pond beyond the Garden. Mr. Forbush took Ebenezers Mare which Baldwin rode down, and rode to Abraham Smiths to talk with him, as well on his own as on my Account. Baldwin rode home with me in the Chair. Found all well and Comfortable. D.G. Neighbour Eliezer Rice brought home another Load of Hay from the Meadow. Thomas and Billy work'd part of the Day for Neighbour Eliezer Rice, and part of the Day at the Meadow. N.B. Mr. Jonas Twitchell work'd 2 half Days for me.

20. Thomas and Billy at the Meadow. Mr. Forbush went to Upton. I rode to Shrewsbury and prevail'd with Mr. Cushing to go in my stead to Worcester: Mr. Maccarty having obtain'd of Mr. Forbush to supply his Pulpit; but if I would undertake it, he would Supply mine.

21. I preach'd at Shrewsbury for Mr. Cushing on Acts 3, 19, a. and p.m. N.B. read a.m. the Chapter of the Text. P.M. read Mat. 18. Mr. Fish[15] preach'd for me in the room of Mr. Forbush. I return'd home at Eve. Molly and her Child gone to Deacons.

22. Thomas and Billy at Work at the Meadow. Ebenezer carted one Load of Hay from thence. I went to Neighbour How's. Billy breaks out with Poison. Mr. Forbush and Wife to t'other House and lodg'd there.

23. I rose Early and went to Esquire Bakers and to the Fays for Teams to fetch home Hay. They agree to go p.m. But by noon it began to rain, and rain'd exceeding hard the rest of the Day. Mr. Forbush and his Wife and Ebenezer's Wife rode to Mr. Martyns, but the former return'd here at Eve and lodg'd here. Thomas went over a.m. to work for Ebenezer.

24. Thomas work'd part of a.m. for me. P.M. late he went to Ebenezer to hoe for him. Jonathan and Joseph How came to hill for me, the former but a little before noon. N.B. greatly put to 't for plough and for Horse—sent Billy to t'other Place for my own Mare. Thomas Stay'd to Plough which was one of the Reasons of his being late to Ebenezer. Billy works with Difficulty because he is so much poison'd. Mr. Forbush and his Wife and little Daughter leave us to go to Brookfield. Fair Weather, but can do Nothing about my Hay at the Ministerial Meadow—Some of which is in Cock, and some of has lain over the storm in swarth.

25. Thomas and William bring home two small Jaggs of Hay from Ministerial Meadow, which make Six small turns from thence and is all of the South side of the Brook. N.B. Neighbour Eliezer Rice assisted—for which my sons work'd for him. Our Kinswomen Mrs. Sally Brigham and her sister Mrs. Betty Gott[16] came to See us—but return'd to Marlboro at Eve.

26. Thomas and Billy hoed at the Island Field.

27. Thomas and Billy hoed a.m. P.M. Thomas mow'd in Newton Meadow.

28. Read 1 Sam. 4, and made the Exercises of both a. and p.m. from thence. Rain'd hard. Read P.M. 1 John 4. Daniel How din'd here.

29. Fair. Thomas mow'd Bushes a.m., and in Newton Meadow p.m. N.B. Mr. David Batchellor and Brother Hicks din'd here. P.M. Visit little Elijah Rice who is Sick. Captain Maynard at Eve invited me to dine at his House tomorrow, a number of military Gentlemen having bespoke a Dinner there—and he Suppos'd his Honour (as he call'd Captain Baker but I thought he meant Colonel Williams) had Spoke to me of it, but no one had. Captain said if I would come he would find me a room etc.

30. At about 11 a.m. came Colonel Williams and with him Mr. Smith, Captain Uriah Eager, and two other officers with them, and the Colonel invited me to dine with him to Day. He said he had depended upon Captain Baker to invite me, having given him Order, to do it, or else the Captain had said he would, but he was gone over to Bolton. I walk'd over as far as Mr. Nathan Maynards in the middle and heat of the Day, but from thence had his Mare, which I also rode home upon. I din'd with Colonel Williams, Major Willard, and the other Officers of this Regiment, at Captain Maynards. The Design of their Meeting was to Consult about a general Meeting of the Regiment—agreeable to the Governor's Proclamation. Messers. Cushing (who came from the Funeral of Mr. Morse's Child) Stone and Smith, there. After 4 o'Clock (the Hour I appointed) I attended the Catechetical Exercise to Young Women at the Meeting House. N.B. Mr. Baldwin went yesterday to Brookfield, and Elisha Jones, one of his Prentice's, work'd for my son Ebenezer during the Absence of his Master. At Eve deliver'd Mary Latiner a Receipt from Mr. Abraham Smith of her Debt to Said Smith, but it was writ

[8] Amos Adams (Harvard 1754) served Roxbury, 1753–1775.

[9] Joseph Pyncheon, the physician of Boston and Springfield. *Sibley*, VIII, 90–95.

[10] Samuel Kneeland, the printer of Boston.

[11] Belcher Hancock, the tutor at Harvard.

[12] The Reverend John Tucker (Harvard 1741), the minister of Newbury. *Sibley*, XI, 78–91.

[13] The Reverend Samuel Webster of Salisbury.

[14] The Reverend Nathaniel Appleton of Cambridge.

[15] Elisha Fish of Upton.

[16] Sarah and Rebecca, daughters of the late Dr. Benjamin Gott, were Parkman's nieces.

as from Mr. Richard Barns. Thomas mows and rakes at Newton Meadow; but those who clear'd there left many Bushes unpick'd up, by which means it is very slow and bad mowing.

31. Before the Rain came heavy, I ran up to Mr. Elijah Rice who came with his Team and got in nine Cocks of Hay from my Newton Meadow but presently the storm came on and it was a very rainy Day. I had agreed yesterday with Mr. Stone to preach his Lecture to Day but the Rain prevented. But Mr. Baldwin came from Brookfield P.M.

## AUGUST, 1754

1. Joseph Bowman and Richard Kelly reap'd, bound up and with Mr. Timothy Warrins Team Carted in my Rye—Thomas and Billy helping them. My Wife rode to Deacon Forbush etc.

2. Thomas can make but very Slow Work at the Meadow it being bad to Mow—Billy helps him. At Night Mr. Solomon Stow brought me from Mr. Kneeland 6 of Clark on Infant Baptism.[1]

3. Thomas and Billy work at the Meadow.

4. Read 1 Sam. 5. Preach'd on 1 Sam. 4, 22. P.M. read 1 John 5. Preach'd on Isa. 9, 6. Mr. Foster din'd here.

5. Thomas and William at the Meadow Still. At Eve came one Mr. Jonathan Fuller of Oxford, and brought in a Chair my Neece Mrs. Tabitha Hearsey, who is in great Affliction by reason of her Husband—she is returning to him at Boston at least to See what his Pleasure is about her Goods which were allow'd her at their Parting. She has also her Dauter Hannah.

6. My Kinswoman etc. pursue their Journey. The Lord conduct and defend her! Being nigh out of Cyder I rode to Mr. Harringtons for supply. Thomas and Billy mow and rake a little at the Newton Meadow: and Neighbour Moses Nurse brings up a Load of Hay from thence. Mrs. Prentice,[2] I hear, at Grafton, and that her Exhortings have Success.

7. Thomas and Billy still at the Meadow.

8. Thomas and Billy at the Meadow this Day also. Neighbour Moses Nurse Carts a large Load of Hay from thence. Mr. Thomas Twitchell Examin'd.

9. Thomas and Billy went to the Ministerial Meadow and Mow'd the North Side of the Brook, and rak'd up about 9 Cocks, and left about as much more.

10. Thomas and Billy were going to the Meadow to rake the rest which they left Yesterday, and to bring it home but it prov'd a rainy Day. Mr. Bond brought a Load of Boards from Mr. Jonathan Forbush's Mill; the Boards of those Loggs which I had last Winter of Mr. John Kelley of Hopkinton.

11. Read 1 Sam. 6. Preach'd on Chapter 4, 22. Mr. Foster din'd here. P.M. read 2 John. Preach'd on Rev. 1, 18. May God add his Special Blessing!

12. Thomas and Billy went in the morning to the Ministerial Meadow to look after the Hay which they lately Cut there—but they were drench'd by that time they rak'd up the Rest of the Hay—a very Heavy Rain.

13. I rode to Mr. Thomas Chaddocks, who being ill had desir'd Prayers. N.B. Mr. Samuel Wood late Miller of Upton there. Visit at Gashitts also. When I return'd at Eve Mrs. Hephzibah Maynard here. Desires me to try what I can do to reconcile Abijah Gale and Isaac Amsden.

14. N.B. Thomas with Ebenezer's Team and Help brings home the last Load of Hay from the Ministerial Meadow. Thomas goes p.m. to help Ebenezer but is not well. I visited Ensign Mathis of Southborough and came home by Isaac Amsdens, Esquire Liscombs, and Mr. Abijah Gales, calling at those places; and endeavouring what I could a Reconcilement.

15. Lieutenant Tainter plaistering at the Sides of the Pulpit, din'd here. Mr. Thaddeus Gale here about his Brothers Affair.

Mr. Jonathan Bond comes from Boston with a Letter from Mr. Joshua Winter informing me that My Neece Mrs. Lydia Davis at Halifax dyed of a Dropsie July 3 last. Mr. Jonas Twitchell here to be Examin'd.

16. Sent Billy over to help his Brother Ebenezer in his Harvest and haying.

17. Very Rainy Day. Concern'd about Billy who went from his Brother's to Mr. Hows—and thence he went out upon the Great Pond a fishing, and did not return to them till Even, till Dark—and not to us till

18. Next Morning—when he came Safely. Read 1 Sam. 7. Preach'd on Rev. 1, 18 a. and p.m. Read third John. Mr. Foster etc. din'd here.

19. Sent to Mr. Barret by Mr. Daniel Hardy to desire his Company to Ministers Meeting to morrow morning at Mr. Martyns. At Eve Suse to t'other House. Read Universal Magazine.[3] Let Mr. Thaddeus Gale my Chair to go to Worcester.

20. Association at Mr. Martyns. No Mr. Barrett: but he sent me a Letter that he would endeavour to come at Eve or tomorrow Morning. Those who attended were Messers. Cushing,[4] Stone, Smith[5] and Davis.[6] The Conversation was chiefly with Mr. Davis about his Contract with his People and his Satisfaction with it. We all lodg'd at Mr. Martyns. N.B. Mr. Martyn much out of Health.

21. Mr. Barrett came not—I was oblig'd to preach the Public Lecture. Text was Heb. 11, 6. Major Keys and Sir Foster[7] with us. May God grant to all of us a Right and part in that better Country! and may we seek it in a proper Manner! N.B. Conversation after Dinner about Mr. Morse's Letter to me about Mr. Silas Brigham—it was advis'd that I let the Matter run and not meddle with it, till more be done by Mr. Morse[8] at Shrewsbury Church. When I return'd with Mr. Foster Stop'd at t'other House where was my Wife and we drank Tea there.

22. I sent Billy to work with his Brother, but being not well he return'd home. Early in the Morning I rode to Lieutenant Fays on my son Thomas's Affair. The Painter at the Meeting House having Colour'd the Pulpit 3 Times over return'd to Billerica from whence he came to us last Monday Eve. Dull Cloudy Weather. Prevents Ebenezers Busness in his Hay. P.M. made a Visit to Mr. Williams on the account of the great Changes and Sudden, in his Circumstances for tho he lost his Wife so lately, he is out-publish'd to another. At Eve Mr. Phinehas Hardy Treasurer for the Precinct, came to reckon, and he receiv'd a Receipt from me in full of what the Precinct had voted the Deficiency in Mr. Bigelows Rates but including the Deficiency in Bruces. Mr. Baldwin finishes his work at the Meeting House. The Pulpit and the fronts of the Gallerys, Ministerial Pew and Deacon's seat. Likewise Three Pews for particular persons, viz. Deacon Newtons, Mr. Bonds, and Esquire Bakers. Mr. Adams is building Three more.

23. Mr. Baldwin and his 'prentice comes to work for me—to plain and Joint Boards for Chamber floor—and a number of Small Jobbs. Sent Billy to Ebenezer.

24. Mr. Baldwin and his 'prentice are here at work. Mr. Thaddeus Gale return'd my Chair. (See on the 19th). His Father and Captain Elisha Jones din'd here. P.M. Great storm of Rain. I rode to Southboro at Eve and Mr. Stone came here.

25. Mr. Stone and I 'chang'd. I preach'd at Southboro on Heb. 11, 16, baptiz'd Edmund the Son of [blank] Moors—and Mr. Stone preach'd on Rev. 3, 18, and baptiz'd Mr. William Pierce's Dauter Mary. We each of us return'd home at Eve.

26. Mr. Baldwin and Elisha Jones went off. Trooping at the North End.

---

[1] Peter Clark, *A Defence of the Divine Right of Infant Baptism* (Boston, 1752). Earlier, Clark had published *The Scripture-Grounds of the Baptism of Christian Infants* (Boston, 1735).

[2] Mrs. Solomon Prentice was one of that fanatic band of "immortals" in the vicinity.

[3] *The Universal Magazine*, begun in London in 1747, continued to be published for the rest of the century.

[4] Job Cushing of Shrewsbury.

[5] Aaron Smith of Marlborough.

[6] Joseph Davis of Holden.

[7] Abiel Foster (Harvard 1756), later became the minister of Canterbury, N.H.

[8] The Reverend Ebenezer Morse of Boylston.

27. My Wife and I rode to the South part of the Town to visit Mr. Grow and his Wife who were Sick and Mrs. Mary Stewart—likewise Mr. Bowman and Mr. Thomas Twitchell. Return'd home at Eve. While we were gone Mr. Martyn here. N.B. Mr. Baldwin went to Brookfield. Billy helps Ebenezer.

28. Mr. Martyn and his Wife came and din'd with us, and he came to preach my Lecture which he did tho my asking him was but implicit and not direct—but he seems to be reconcil'd—but we act an odd part towards one another—afraid of lisping the least word of our uneasiness. He preach'd on Gal. 2, 20, a very good sermon—May God give his Blessing! I am much oblig'd to his Wife for her pains to have us reconcil'd. But my thoughts were much engag'd upon the Situation of the Affair. Our Conduct is as if nothing had happen'd. I am concern'd at the Frame we must needs be both of us in, especially as the Communion in their Church as well as ours hastens. But I have very much discharg'd my Duty, I think, in my last Letter to him: and I am taught by the Word and by the Example of Christ to be free to forgive even innumerable Trespasses: I learn that 'tis the Glory of a Man to overlook a transgression, and that Charity Covers a Multitude of sins. As to his making me Satisfaction for such undeserv'd Insults, tho I ought to claim it, yet I conceive I had better forego my own personal Right than endanger the Public Peace and the Success of our Ministry—on these Considerations and dreading the grim Mischiefs of our being at Variance, I deny myself and yield the matter of making Demands of him, or shewing any Resentments, Earnestly begging of God Grace, Directon and forgiveness to Each of us. And O that we might have Fellowship one with another and that the Blood of Christ would Cleanse us from all sin!

29. Billy is Still helping his Brother Ebenezer who is about his Hay yet.

30. Mr. Baldwin return'd from Brookfield and lodges here. Retir'd and Somewhat devoted—but alas! how Imperfectly!

31. Billy help'd his Brother Yesterday and to Day, and he is now almost done Haying.

SEPTEMBER, 1754.

Read 1 Sam. 8. Preach'd on Rev. 1, 18, and found it best to deliver my whole preparation tho I was oblig'd to Speak the faster and to continue somewhat longer than usual. Administer'd the Lords Supper, took in 3 persons into the Church. P.M. read Rev. 1. Repeated on Mat. 12, 33, 34, 35. Administered Baptism to Several Children and appointed Catechizing at the East part of the Town. Deacon Forbush and Sir Foster din'd here. Mr. Baldwin here at Eve and lodg'd here. O that God would grant us all to understand, and be confirm'd in, be influenced by, and have a Right to the Benefit of the Resurrection of Christ from the Dead!

2. Visited the Widow Thurston whose Son Samuel lies Sick. Was at Mr. Grow's again, that Family being Still under Affliction by Sickness. Visited also Mrs. Harrington lame by a Fall from her Horse; and Ensign Miller, whose paralytic Disorders increase upon him much.

3. Catechiz'd at Mr. Joslins—about 19 Children. Had visited the good old Mr. Bradish. After Catechizing Mr. Joslin went with me cross the Woods to Mr. Jabez Snow's—Mr. Snow with me to Mr. Abraham Beeman's. Was also at Mr. Adams's where they fill'd my Ears with Complaints (I mean the Mother and Dauter) against the Gales, against whom they had been, and were like to be again Summon'd to Court as Witnesses: but I was not willing to meddle with their Affair.

4. Sir Haven was here yesterday, and lodg'd at my sons last night. Was here again today and din'd with us. I have been in a great deal of deep Concern about how to dispose of Billy. He Seems not willing to resume his Books except I can keep him wholly to 'em—which our present Circumstances forbid. His Mothers Consent to Learning for him, is hard to obtain. It grieves me much to give him up—But as he was yesterday Clearing at the Island Pasture, So there he goes to Day. P.M. Mr. Jonathan Forbush here again about the Pew which he drew for me—is not willing to give me a Title to it except the Precinct

will let him have the Same privilege in the Meeting House as if he had not drawn it, since he drew it, as they all knew, for me, but appears desirous of it himself. Lieutenant Bruce comes here to conferr about building the Pews, and I agree with him to provide a Stick of Timber for My Part of the Foundation. I discern So much of the minds of persons about this Matter of the Pew that I am very much dispos'd to give it up, tho there are So many Reasons impelling to keep it. Such Tokens of Ingratitude are very grievous—But how much it is the Lot of Ministers in these days! May God himself be pleas'd to look with Pity on his own Cause!

5. Billy clearing at the Island part of the forenoon. P.M. Showery. My Wife and I walk'd together to Mr. Williams',[1] to Celebrate his Marriage to Mrs. Eleanor Gould.

6. Sir Foster brings Sir Dana[2] here—who is come up from Marlborough, where he keeps School. Billy cutts Stalks.

8. Read 1 Sam. 9. Preach'd on Phil. 3, 10. P.M. read Rev. 2. Judge Ward here, but goes to Mr. Nurse's.

9. Lieutenant Forbush being about to Sell Some Land to Mr. John Beeton, Blacksmith, he comes to acquaint me with it and asks me what I would my Self have for the Straitning or accommodating of my Lines. I go with him and agree where.

10. Lieutenant Ward here with his Instruments, and he with Mr. Nathaniel Whitney Measure this Piece of Land where my House Stands and the Lines agreed upon Yesterday. Robert Morton of Mendon here, with his Box, Glass and Prospects; and he Shews us his Sights, gratis. Master Richard Martyn[3] brought his Sister Molly here, and left her to Stay with us a little while.

11. Receiv'd the last Volume of the History of the Foundling[4] from Mr. Samuel Livermore by Mr. Samuel Harrington. At Eve came Dr. Perkins, and Mr. Hezekiah Coolidge and lodg'd here. Mr. Jeduthan Baldwin brought back Ebenezer's Mare which he himself had rid to Weston when he finish'd his Work and left us.

12. General Muster of Colonel Williams Regiment. 5 Southern Companys at Mendon with Grafton Troop: 8 Companys of Foot and one Troop at Westboro. I pray'd with Captain Bakers Company at the Meeting House. Had Captain Baker's Horse to ride over to the Field which was in Captain Maynards Pasture. Dr. Perkins and Mr. Coollidge rode with me. We proceeded to Captain Maynards—my Sons House was taken up by Dr. Brigham[5] for twenty Marlborough men. The Battalion was not form'd till some time in the afternoon. There were many Spectators. The Reverend Messers. Cushing, Martyn, Stone, Smith, Morse, Hutchinson there. The first of whom pray'd with the Regiment at about 4 P.M. and when the Colonel had read his Proclamation he soon dissolv'd the Battalion and the Companys march'd out of the Field. I din'd with the Colonel and the Ministers (except Mr. Hutchinson) who went to Lieutenant Fays, where, Captain Baker ask'd me to dine with him—but I requested he would contrive to dine with the Colonel and other Officers, for I should not be able to refuse them. Lieutenant Maynard had also bespoke me before Captain Baker; and I found it would greatly incommode me to go so far. N.B. Rumours about the Indians. Dr. Perkins, Mr. Asaph Rice and Mr. Baldwin, together with Mrs. Molly Martyn lodge here.

13. Dr. Perkins and Mr. Rice and Mr. Baldwin, as also Mr. Hezekiah Coollidge return home. N.B. Sent Mr. Badgers Family Companion[6] home by Mr. Coollidge. P.M. my wife carry'd Mrs. Molly Martyn as far as my other House where her Brother is to come for her. I went to Lieutenant Forbush's, and he and his wife sign'd me a new Deed of this Land where my House stands with the additions, and Judge Ward took their acknowledgements. Mr. John Beeton receiv'd a Deed likewise of an Acre joining to mine.

14. Frost last night. Beeton begins to Clear his Land. P.M. I rode to Shrewsbury and Mr. Cushing here. Very Cold Eve. I

---

[1] Samuel Williams of Westborough.
[2] Samuel Dana (Harvard 1755) was later the minister of Groton, 1760–1775.
[3] The son of the Reverend John Martyn of Northborough.
[4] Probably Samuel Silence, pseud., *The Foundling Hospital for Wit* No. 1–6, (London 1743–1749).
[5] Samuel Brigham, the physician of Marlborough.
[6] *The Family Companion for Health: or . . . Rules which . . . will . . . keep Families free from Diseases, and Procure them a Long Life* (London, 1729).

was Shav'd at Mr. Job Cushings. Bears are about very thick—many are kill'd.

15. I preach'd at Shrewsbury a.m. on Acts 3, 19. P.M. on 2 Tim. 2, 3. Mr. Cushing preach'd at Westborough on [blank] and on [blank]. We both return'd at Eve.

16. This being the fifth Day Old Stile I separated myself in some peculiar manner for Recollection and Devotions. O that God would pardon my brokenness and many Miscarriages! *Vid. Natal.*

[In the Natalitia the following under the date Sept. 5, "old Stile."]

I would bless God with my whole Soul for his adorable Patience and Longsuffering and in Special that I have been preserv'd through another Year, tho I have been So utterly undeserving, nay provoking to Him! I endeavour'd (in Some very broken manner) to acknowledge the Divine lenity and Goodness, and to humble my Self for my great Defects and unfaithfulness. I would also devoutly committ my Self the uncertain residue of my frail Life, humbly begging of God to make me faithfull in my Great Work, and enable me to Save my own Soul as well as those that hear me!

And whereas the Care of my Family lies with a peculiar Weight upon my Spirits, I would most earnestly beseech of God to enable me to Cast this Care upon Him, who cares for His own!

17. Mr. Abijah Gale came while we were in family Exercise—read a Summons to me to go up to Court to Day—and threw down his money. Being thus oblig'd to go, p.m. I went to Worcester—to Mr. Maccartys[7]—to Colonel Chandlers—lodg'd at Mr. Maccartys. N.B. Colonel Cushing and his Wife also there. N.B. Several Gentlemen are taken ill—Mr. Trowbridge,[8] who is the King's Attorney—Colonel Chandler is also ill, but crawls about a little.

18. I attended Court. Din'd at Captain Stearns's[9] with the Judges: Judge Sewal[10] not well. N.B. Messers. Joseph Green,[11] Nathaniel Bethune,[12] Isaac Winslow,[13] and [blank] Wheelwright din'd with us. N.B. They Subscribed for my Collection of Poems. P.M. came on the Cause, upon which I was Summon'd viz. of Isaac Amsden[14] plaintiff against Abijah Gale[15] Defendant; for that the Said Abijah assaulted the Plaintiffs Wife, attempted to discover her Nakedness and to have Carnal Knowledge of her Body—I was put under solemn Adjuration and was ask'd what I knew of the Cause Depending and especially Whether I had met with anything from Mrs. Amsden that was contrary to the Oath which She had taken? My answer was to this Effect—

That it was Surprizing to me to be summon'd, having had no Knowledge of the Case, till of late, Sometime Since the Prosecution or Complaint before Mr. Justice Liscomb that I know now no otherwise than by Report and Conversation as any other Neighbours might do. That from what was Said to me at my summoning I had no reason to Suppose any thing would be desir'd of me at this Court more than to be present to hear the Cause (being Mr. Gale's Pastor) and to give my Testimony of him which I could freely do, and did so, viz. that for any Thing I had ever known of him he was of unblemish'd Reputation till this Affair: and I might Say much the Same of Mrs. Amsden who was brought up in my near Neighborhood, and was of good Character among us. This Answer of mine was upon Colonel Brattle's interrogating me as upon Oath whether I knew anything of this Cause, or had heard this Woman Say any Thing different from what She had now Sworn? And this was also urg'd by the Chief Justice Sewal; to which therefore I further reply'd that I had indeed made Mrs. Amsden a visit and did put Some Questions to her, but I was not prepar'd to Say what her answers to me at that Time were:

and that I could not think it fit or just for me to utter what was so brokenly and imperfectly remember'd—So that I was not ripe to Say any thing of the Particular Expressions She us'd. When the Judge ask'd me whether I remembered that it was Opposite, or Contrary to her Oath? I answer'd that as I remember'd it was what did not carry the Matter so far as the Complaint She has made upon Oath—but I was not Ripe for offering any More of it. The Colonel chew'd upon that that I said I was not ripe—that I ought to say what 'twas—but I told him I would not be impos'd upon. For I conceiv'd it wrong to utter what was So unshapen in my Mind—and I said I perceiv'd that Mrs. Amsden at the Time of my Discourse with her was in such a Surprize and flutter that I did not know whether what She had answer'd was her real Mind—and She was So uneasy at my putting these sorts of Questions to her that I thought it best not to proceed, and therefore desisted—so that I conceiv'd it unjust for me to declare what I apprehended She did, under these Circumstances, Say. The Jurys Verdict came in against Gale; for it appear'd there was an Assault. It was late in the Eve—lodg'd at Mr. Maccartys again. N.B. Colonel William Ward in Jayl.

19. My Mare got out of Mr. Maccartys Pasture, but was found by Mr. Othniel Taylor, about two Mile and half off. Weather very hot. Was at Colonel Chandlers Office. Colonel deliver'd Me two Deeds, viz. Hezekiah Hows and Andrew Newtons, to me. Paid him 15/ old Tenor for both and lodg'd two more, viz. from Lieutenant Forbush and Richard Barns. I call'd at Mr. Dyars—din'd at Dr. Crawfords.[16] N.B. his son William at Learning. I stop'd at Captain Jenisons and wrote a Letter to Mr. Edwards at Stockbridge. Return'd home safe at Eve. Mr. Stone of Southborough had been to See Me. A Bear Was Seen by my son Thomas passing through my Land just below the Burying place, and went Cross the Road. N.B. Talk'd with Mr. Isaac Amsdens Wife about what she said to me at their House etc. See loose papers.

20. Mr. Nathaniel Whitney was here and I gave him Some Account of what I utter'd upon oath at the late Superior Court. Lieutenant Forbush here at Eve tells me of his Cattle being once and again in my Island—and to Day in the Corn.

21. Lieutenant Forbush now Setts the Fence between Beriah Rice and me in the Meadow.

22. Read 1 Sam. 11. Preach'd on Acts 1, 9. P.M. read Rev. 4. Repeated Exposition on Mat. 12, 36. Read publickly the Petition of Mr. Thomas Gleson[17] of Oxford and desir'd the Congregation that if any one had any thing to offer he would come and See me this week.

23. Mr. Stratton[18] of Waltham came to See me.

24. My wife dipps little John into Cold Water to cure him of his Ricketts.

25. Lieutenant Forbush kindly came and kill'd a fatt Calf for me. My Wife and I rode in the Chair to visit aged Widow Hannah Rice[19] and took little John with us. Call'd at Captain Maynards in returning home. Lieutenant Tainter carry'd down the Calf to Boston. Lieutenant Brigham of Southborough and his Wife here. N.B. He shew'd me an Instrument sign'd by his Children by which he was empower'd to take up and dispose of the Land which they had, otherwise, Right to from the Rights of Edmund Rice. John was dipped again.

26. John was dipp'd again, and we cease for a while. I had a Message last Eve from Mr. Cushing to preach his Lecture today, but it happen'd to be a Day appointed for the Catechetical Exercise to young men—which I attended—had 23. Mr. Foster came here after School, but return'd again.

27. Billy cutt up part of the Corn by the Barn.

28. Mr. Isaac Amsden of Southborough here to ask me whether I had not talk'd with Ezra Taylor about what his Wife Said to me at Major Howards on the 19th. I told him what it was and that I wrote it down that same Eve, and with all that I was ready to shew it [to] him, but he answer'd that twas no

[7] The Reverend Thaddeus Maccarty.

[8] Attorney General Edmund Trowbridge.

[9] Thomas Sterne of Worcester.

[10] Justice Stephen Sewall of the Superior Court of Judicature.

[11] The Reverend Joseph Green (Harvard 1746) of Marshfield. *Sibley,* XII, 28–30.

[12] (Harvard 1734). A Boston merchant. *Sibley,* IX, 386–389.

[13] (Harvard 1727). A prominent businessman of Boston, who was later a Mandamus Councillor. *Sibley,* VIII, 333–339.

[14] Of Southborough.

[15] The innkeeper of Westborough.

[16] Robert Crawford, the physician.

[17] Gleason had been "burnt out" lately.

[18] Joseph Stratton.

[19] Mrs. Jacob Rice.

matter, or to that purpose. P.M. Joshua Lock and his wife here, and offer'd a Confession of their Fornication. But it was very imperfect—he also was not willing to own the Covenant. Said he was by principle of the Church of England—did not care to be examin'd Strictly—his wife might own the Covenant and have the Child baptiz'd here. It was also late in the Day—therefore I did not proceed to gratifie them at this time.

29. Read 1 Sam. 12. Preach'd a. and p.m. on Acts 1, 9. P.M. read Rev. 5. Mr. Stratton of Waltham din'd here. Appointed a Contribution for Mr. Thomas Gleson of Oxford (by Mistake I said Dudley) to be next Lords Day P.M.

30. An unusual dry Time. Our well So low that we can't without much difficulty dip the Buckett. Messers. Batherick, Abijah Gale, Adams and Kimbal, Carpenters are at Work at the Meeting House building the seats in the Womens Gallery.

### OCTOBER, 1754

Was up at 4, morning, and Saw the Eclipse: and before Light took up a large, well-fill'd Hive of Bees. Mr. Jonas Twitchell work'd for me in clearing the Newton Meadow. Sent home to Mr. Samuel Livermore junior the fourth Volume of the Foundling; by the Hand of Mr. Joseph Stretton of Waltham. A.M. exceedingly perplex'd for want of money to pay my just Debts and especially for Spinning. I went to Ensign Fay to borrow, but very much in Vain. We are also out of Cyder, and I sought to him for present Supply; which I answer'd my End in—but remain in great difficulty on the other Account.

2. Mr. Jonas Twitchel at Work to Day also, clearing at my Meadow. William waits upon his Mother to Mr. Martyns, and Lucy undertakes to wean little John. Ebenezer here at Eve and has my Chair and Mare to go with his Wife and son to their Father Harringtons. Mrs. Miller (Ensigns Wife) here to bring me word that if I would have Cyder of him I must fetch it to-morrow or not at all, whereas not being warn'd of it my Barrells are not soak'd, nor do I know whether I can have either Man or Team, so that altho I want it much, and dont know but that I must go without if I have it not of him, yet I must Send him denyal. And this is also the Third Message which I have had of this kind, which because so Sudden I have been forc'd to deny. N.B. Received a Letter from Brother William Parkman dated July 10 last: brought by Dr. Crosby. N.B. Mr. Simon Tainter now of Sutton coming in to my Door fell down upon the Floor in a Fit—I Suppose Epileptic—but after a while came to, and he proceeded with his Wife and Child to their Father Bruce's.

3. Sent Billy to Mr. Garfields for pursely Water[1] for little John, and bagg of Apples from Mr. Joseph Knowlton—which he brought. I preach'd at Lieutenant Tainters on Hos. 2, 8, 9. May it please God to add his effectual Blessing! When I came home found Mr. Ball[2] of Grafton here, who had carry'd Mr. Bliss's[3] Stackhouse[4] for me. Mr. Fay brought a Barrell of Cyder.

4. In the latter part of the Night and Morning Some refreshing Showers, but clear'd off afterwards So that I rode over to Mr. Martyns and brought home my Wife. No word pass'd about our Epistolary Contests. At Evening came Mr. Benjamin Tainter with his Wife, his own Mother, and his Wife's Father, Mother and Brother. N.B. Thomas lodges at t'other House to my great Grief and Trouble, as there are Several young Women like to lodge there, and Mr. Foster is gone to Holiston to See his Father who we hear is Sick.

5. Putt to much Difficulty to draw Water out of our Well. Mr. Hall[5] of Sutton and his Dauter Hale here. Mr. Abijah Gale here to know what I thought was expected of him by the Church.

6. Read 1 Sam. 13. Preach'd a. and p.m. on Mark 16, 19, and Sat on the Right Hand of God. P.M. read Rev. 6. Mrs. Woods, Mother in Law to Mr. Benjamin Tainter, din'd here. Mr. Ephraim Bruce's Wife had a fit and was brought in here at noon. P.M. we had a Publick Contribution for the Relief of Mr. Thomas Gleason of Oxford.

7. Lieutenant Tainter, Messers. Jonathan Forbush, Eleazer Whitney, Thomas Twitchell, Amariah Thurston, with several Lads, Daniel Grout and Joseph Harrington came and cutt up my Corn at the Island, and Mr. Ebenezer Forbush with his Team brought it in. They made 4 Load of it and had done by noon. Four of them stay'd to dine. It was our purpose to have husk'd in the afternoon (for some persons said they Should choose it rather than in the Eve) and a few Neighbours were Sent to, but none came but old Mr. Maynard. So then we sent again, desiring they would come in the Evening, but neither did there come any but a few Boys who ran away home again. N.B. Mr. John Hicks of Cambridge and his Wife and little son Jonathan here, going to Sutton. Mr. Abijah Gale here at Eve with a Paper of Acknowledgement.

8. To Day some of my own Family who did not use to husk, put their Hands to it. Deacon Newton came in the Morning to assist in Counting the Contribution—Money. We found it to be £9.6.10 old Tenor. Noah Forbush part of p.m. husking—a number more came in the Evening, viz. Thomas Hardy, Alpheus and Abner Newton, Charles Rice and Ebenezer Rice junior—very frosty Night, they did not stay to husk the whole.

9. Mr. White, Painter from Billerica to Paint the Pulpit. Thomas and Billy husk. Joshua Lock here again about his and his wifes Confession etc. I endeavour to show him briefly the absurdity of his turning to the Church of England, unless he had better acquainted himself with the Controversie. Daniel Goddard[6] of Shrewsbury here to ask my Advice about his Learning Latin. He goes away disgusted because of my defending Mr. Cushing.[7] Mr. Fish of Upton and his Wife dine here. He preaches my Lecture on John 3, 14, a moving and profitable Discourse! May God add his Blessing. Mr. Hicks of Cambridge and his Wife and son from Sutton came and lodge here. Mr. White the Painter with Mr. Francis Whipple, Spend some Time in the Evening here. Thomas and Billy, and 3 Rices (Merchants Sons) husk in the Evening.

10. Mr. Hicks etc. return to Cambridge.

11. Hear that Mr. Whitefield[8] is at Boston. My Wife visits Mrs. Amy Maynard.[9]

12. Mr. White finishes his painting the Pulpit etc. Brushes over my Chair, gratis—dines with me—returns home to Billerica.

13. The Pulpit etc. are not dry. We make a convenient Station for preaching and Communion Table before the Deacons Seat. Many Shrewsbury people here—Mr. Cushing being gone a Journey. Mrs. Amy Maynard grows worse. Read 1. Sam. 14 to number 23. Preach'd on Mark 16, 19. Administered the Lords Supper. P.M. read Rev. 7, and having Spent my Preparations in the forenoon I repeated Sermons on John 11, 24. Deacon Miles[10] and his Wife, Mrs. Foster[11] of Holliston and her Daughter Twitchel[12] din'd here. At Eve I visited and pray'd with Mrs. Maynard, and My Wife watch'd with her.

14. Visited Deacon Newton to Settle with him for the Year past respecting my Note given him. P.M. Mrs. Judith Bellows here in a peculiar Domestic Difficulty, but deferrs opening the particulars to a Visit which She prays me to make with them. Mrs. Foster (the Schoolmasters Mother) with divers others here.

15. Sent the second Volume of the New Universal Magazine to Captain Storer at Boston per Mr. Ebenezer Rice. Mr. Davis came this way for my Company to Southboro. Rode down there to Ministers Meeting. Messers. Barrett, Martyn, Seccomb,[13] Smith—were the rest that attended. See the Minutes of the Association. At Eve our Conversation was upon the Qualifications for Communion at the Lords Table. N.B. Mr. Stone is Strongly in the Sentiments of Mr. Stoddard.[14]

---

[1] Purslane, a low, succulent herb.
[2] Nathaniel Ball.
[3] The Reverend Daniel Bliss of Concord.
[4] A work of the English divine, Thomas Stackhouse.
[5] The Reverend David Hall.
[6] The son of Edward Goddard. He evidently did not pursue his interest in higher learning.
[7] Job Cushing of Shrewsbury.
[8] The great George Whitefield.
[9] Mrs. Ebenezer Maynard.
[10] Samuel Miles of Concord.
[11] Mrs. Jacob Foster.
[12] Mary Foster married Moses Twitchell of Westborough.
[13] John Seccomb of Harvard.
[14] Solomon Stoddard, *An Appeal to the Learned. Being a Vindication of the Right of Visible Saints to the Lords Supper, though they be Destitute of a Saving Work of God's Spirit in their Hearts: against the Exceptions of Mr. Increase Mather* (Boston, 1709).

16. Mr. Martyn preach'd on Luke 9, ult. Many useful and awakening Thoughts on the great Evil and Danger of Apostacy—May God sett them home upon my own Heart! N.B. when we return'd to Mr. Stones, Mr. Davis a terrible Fit—shaking etc. N.B. Mr. Martyn desires me to Change next Sabbath to which I Consent. I return'd home by t'other House and Call'd to see Mrs. Amy Maynard, who grows worse.

17. Rainy Day. A.M. my Wife and I went to See Mrs. Mainard and found her much worse. She thinks she shall dye—she prays audibly, tho with low voice; very importunately, and pertinently. I can't tell whether She was aware that she Spoke So loud as to be heard by others. I receiv'd also her Testimony to the Gospel and the Ordinances thereof. Pray'd with her and left her in a very solemn manner. P.M. Catechiz'd at the School House.

18. Lieutenant Tainter and Solomon Miller brought home 6 Barrells of Cyder from Ensign Miller, at 20/ per Barrell. Went (by special Desire) over to Mrs. Maynards again, She being, as they think, dying. We endeavour'd to Commend her departing Soul to God by Prayer—but I left her breathing.

19. Mrs. Maynard dy'd about 10 o'clock last night. She is much Commended.

20. I walk'd over to t'other House and thence rode over to Mr. Martyns and preach'd there a. and p.m. on Ps. 119, 60. I read some Passages of the Psalm a.m. but p.m. did not read. Mr. Martyn preach'd a.m. on Eph. 5, 8, 9. P.M. on Ps. 57. He did not read either a. or p.m. We each return'd at Eve.

21. A.M. Mrs Amy (or Emma) Maynard was buried. Some Number of persons din'd here, among which Captain Maynard; it being inconvenient for them to go home after the Funeral because; there was to be a Precinct Meeting at 1 o'Clock. It was to Vote me Support and Wood. And when they came together they Voted to do as they did last Year—and Lieutenant Tainter came to acquaint me with it. I sent them a Line by him: which altho it did not induce them to alter their Vote, yet a Number of them were induc'd to subscribe Wood by the Cord—and it amounted to 20 Load. This was brought me by Mr. Ephraim Bruce, and he said it was freely and heartily done. So that I made no further Difficulty. My Brother Samuel Parkman from Boston waits on Reverend Mr. Gay[15] of Hingham here, and lodge. They are going to Leicester, to the Ordination of Mr. Joseph Roberts.[16]

22. Came the Reverend Messers. Barrett and Eliot[17] and with them Deacon Barret of Boston and his son, and Mr. Thayer of Boston also—and they din'd here. N.B. Deacon Barret ill and with his Brother returns to Hopkinton. The rest go to Leicester. P.M. came Mr. Joseph Briant from Stoneham and lodges here.

23. Mr. Briant to Leicester. Sent by him Lieutenant Nathan Brighams Deed to be recorded at Colonel Chandlers Office. At Night Mr. Solomon Baker brought up from Mr. Kneeland one of Mr. Edwards Enquiry[18] etc. Price 4/6, Lawful Money. The Reverend Joseph Roberts's Ordination at Leicester.

24. Messers. Eliot, Thayer and Young Barrett from Leicester—only call'd at the Door in their Way to Hopkinton. P.M. Went down to see Mr. Jonathan Bellows and wife; but he was not himself at home. I discours'd with his Wife according to her particular Case, and pray'd with her and Such as were in the House. N.B. Dr. Chase[19] was with me and he visited at Mr. Ithamar Bellows's their Daughter Elizabeth having the Rheumatism. I talked freely with the Doctor concerning his own Conduct; and wish a Blessing!

25. A very Rainy Day. N.B. Some Number more of Bears kill'd among us and on the Confines. The Whitneys have kill'd and assisted in killing 4 or 5 within a very few Days. Tis Said about 20 have been kill'd in this Town.

26. A Cool Morning after the Storm. My Wife goes on in

plunging little John in Cold Water. The Reverend Mr. Bliss of Concord here in his way to Upton.

27. John dip'd again. Read 1 Sam. 14 from number 24. Preach'd on John 1, number 16 a. and p.m. N.B. Jane Smith (Sister of Rody) fell into a fit in the Time of afternoon sermon was carry'd out, and carry'd to my House; there She remain'd in her Fitt for four Hours. A sorrowful Spectacle!

28. Mr. Henry Barns, Merchant in Marlborough, here. Is about to set up the Pot Ash Business in Hopkinton. Messers. Bliss and Fish here and din'd with us. P.M. Was at Lieutenant Forbush's.

29. Brother Samuel Parkman here in his Return to Boston, but I was not at home. At Eve Mr. Foster who lodg'd here. Mr. Samuel Fay junior acquaints me with Mr. Billings Case and Request.

30. Mr. Fay last night was so importunate to have me visit Mrs. Billing that to Day I went. Din'd at Captain Bezaleel Eagers. I found Mrs. Billings Case to [be] very deplorable both in Body and Mind. Pray'd with her. At Eve came Messers. Hezekiah Pratt with a Yoke of Oxen, Solomon Baker with a Plough and with 2 Yoke. Mr. Eleazer Williams, Joseph Baker—and my sons Ebenezer and Thomas.

31. I made a Visit to Mr. Eliezer Rice and to Mr. James Maynard. The former was not at home.

### NOVEMBER, [1754]

1. Brother Hicks[1] came p.m. and lodg'd. At Eve Mr. David Taylor of Concord with Letter requesting a Council on his Difficultys.

2. Brother Hicks after Dinner returns home. Mr. Whitney came with his Cart to bring me Turnips for Winter according as I had bespoke. I expected Mr. Henry Barns's Wife and her Mother in their way to Hopkinton, but they did not come. However my other avocations enough.

3. Read 1 Sam. 15. Preach'd a.m. (repeating) Mat. 12, 36, 37. P.M. read Rev. 9. Preach'd on John 1, 16. Many Southboro People at meeting here Mr. Stone being gone to the Cape.

4. I wrote to Mr. Bows of Bedford about Mr. David Taylor's Request. Mr. Abraham Beeman and his Wife here to be examin'd.

5. A very rainy Day. We have reason to fear little John is much troubled with Worms as well as Rickets: and is much oppress'd having very labouring Breath. May God teach us to profit by his holy Hand upon us.

6. Ebenezer has an Husking p.m. My Wife and I took John into the Chair and rode to Lieutenant Tainters—were well entertain'd and return'd.

7. I rode to Upton and preach'd Mr. Fish's Lecture on Ps. 51, 11. Return'd at Eve. N.B. a smart Assault by Long Kelly at Mr. Dunlops, respecting the Church of England; which made me late home.

8. A Second Appointment to Shovel the Gravel at the back of my House, but it was Cold and Dark, and but Two Came, Mr. Beeton and Jonathan Grout. They stood it till 9 o'Clock. Mr. Foster[2] came over; and lodg'd here. Sent by Lieutenant Tainter to Boston. N.B. He kill'd one of my steers, or rather one of his which he changes for one of mine that was a Rogue. He kill'd it at his House and brot me a Side of the Meat, the Hide, Tallow and Offal, and borrows half of the Meat to spend in his own Family. N.B. The Quarters he brought here were 90 & 86.

9. A very Cold Night the last—and this morning. Mr. Jonathan Fuller junior of Suton call'd to see me. Mr. Jonathan Forbush brought some Wood we being in a Straight, he brought also several Presents besides. Mr. Dodge Came with Money for a Token of Love to me. A cool Night again.

10. Read 1 Sam. 16 and gave Observations upon it for the Exercise a.m. Read p.m. Rev. 10. Preach'd once more on John 1, 16. Stop'd the Church at Eve, on the Account of Mr. Abijah

---

[15] Ebenezer Gay.

[16] Joseph Roberts (Harvard 1741) had preached at various places. He served Leicester, 1754-1762. *Sibley*, XI, 65-68.

[17] Andrew Eliot of the New North Church in Boston.

[18] Jonathan Edwards, *A Careful and Strict Enquiry into the Modern Prevailing Notions of that Freedom of Will* (Boston, 1754).

[19] Thomas Chase, the young physician of Westborough.

[1] Parkman's brother-in-law, John Hicks of Sutton.

[2] Jacob Foster, the schoolmaster.

Gale's Acknowledgement which was read and accepted, and he restor'd[3]—and on Account of Mr. David Taylor of Concord, late of Bedford, who wrote to this Church for Assistance under his present Distress: Voted.

11. Was at t'other House. Bid Farewell to Mr. Dodge and his wife who are moving to Framingham. Mr. Foster goes to keep School North Side. Mr. Daniel Adams examin'd at Eve. Mrs. Winchester here.

12. I rode to Concord alone. N.B. Mr. Stephen Prentice[4] of Grafton on the Road with me as far as Bruce's Tavern, very Troublesome. Captain Baker who was the appointed Delegate having Sent me word he could not go. At Mr. Taylor were the Reverend Messers Dunbar,[5] Martyn and Smith, each having a Delegate, viz. Deacon Putnam, and Messers. Josiah Fosset and [blank] Kidder, who were present at the Hearing of Mr. Taylors Cause. There came also from Bedford, Deacon Lane and Mr. Abbot, who were of Singular Service in informing and letting us into the Controversie. We found Mr. Taylor very desirous to have us hear not only the Difficultys which repeatedly withstood it, that being of Civil Nature and had been fully heard, and Settled in a Course of Law, which had run through the Courts. We conceiv'd it would be best to have something drawn up for Mr. Taylor to offer the Church of Bedford, which if it express'd a sutable [sic] Christian Frame in him, would be most of all likely to induce them to grant him a Dismission to Concord first Church, and put an End to the Contention; at least what subsisted between Mr. Taylor and the Church of Bedford. This was therefore what we bent our Minds to. One and another try'd to draught Something—and we discours'd with Mr. Taylor to perswade him to it, but it seem'd in Vain—it grew late and we retir'd to rest—the Bedford Committee returning home. Mr. Whitefield preaches at Upton. I sent him a Letter on three Heads—the last of them requesting he would go to poor Smithfield.

13. After frequent importunate Sollicitations I undertook to draw up Something for Mr. Taylor to make application with to the Church in Bedford: little imagining that it would succeed; yet it did, through the divine Favour, and as we had earnestly requested the Committee from Bedford to return again, So they came and Mr. Taylor having Sign'd the Address to their Church, They freely came in to it, and each of them engag'd to use their best Influence to have it succeed with the Church. Whereupon we gave Thanks to God, din'd, adjourn'd without Day, and parted with Joy. I rode to Marlborough and lodg'd there.

14. When I return'd home, understood that tho there was an appointment of Hands to come yesterday P.M. to level my Bank on the Back of the House, yet none came to the work but Mr. Kenny, and towards night Noah Forbush.

15. Very rainy last Night and this Morning but p.m. Clear. Visited Mr. Jonah Warrins Daughter Sarah who is much disorder'd in the Mind. Mr. Warrin told me he deliver'd my Letter into Mr. Whitefield's Hands, and that he saw him read in it.

16. Old Mr. Maynard cleaning the Meeting House, din'd here.

17. Read 1 Sam. 17 to about 31, 10. Preach'd on Col. 1, 16, 17. P.M. read Rev. 11 and by means of the Business of last Week was oblig'd to repeat Sermon on Acts 16, 29, 30. At Eve Mr. Jeduthun Baldwin here.

18. Rain—especially the latter part of the Day—at Night the Storm increas'd greatly. Mr. Baldwin lodg'd here to night also, being prevented by the storm returning.

19. Mr. Baldwin left us, it being a bright Day. Neighbour Moses Nurse plough'd Indian Hills for me in order to Sow Rye. At Eve Ebenezer here. N.B. Mr. Jonah Warrin being in great Distress for his Dauter Sarah, came for me. And I went. She had attempted Several Times to destroy her Self; but now was Somewhat calm and conversible. Dr. Brigham[6] here. I pray'd with them. The Doctor in returning din'd with us.

20. Mr. James Fay and his wife came to see me. I visited Mr. Daniel Forbush's Child under a grievous Scald, and pray'd with him. N.B. his Discourse about Mr. Whitefield, and of my Conduct with regard to him. At Lieutenant Tainters at Eve.

21. Ebenezer went to Brookfield after our young Cattle. He rode my Mare. Moses Nurse with 2 Yoke of Oxen, and my Billy helping, plough'd, sow'd Rye and harrow'd it in. Held a Catechetical Exercise to Young Women. At Eve Ebenezer and Samuel Forbush each with a Yoke of Cattle, Noah Forbush with my sons Oxen and a Drag, Elijah Rice, Moses Nurse and his Cousen Daniel and Abner Newton, came and plough'd and drew down Gravel from the back of my House. N.B. Much to 't for want of Wood.

22. The Friend at a Pinch, Lieutenant Tainter brought a Load of Wood. Mr. Jacob Foster here—gives up his School, and bids farewell to Westborough—tells me Mr. Benjamin Webb[7] is to keep in his Stead at North End.

23. Last Night is froze hard. Billy having harrow'd yesterday with Ebenezer's Oxen at the Island at Night went home with them. He this Morning return'd here with them, and Carted out Muck into the Garden and Grass Ground. Thomas help'd him a.m. but was ill p.m. Lieutenant Tainter another Load of Wood. P.M. Mr. Gleason of Oxford here. At Eve Mr. George Bruce of Mendon here. Had been serving a Writ on Richard Barns, who it is fear'd is hastening into Ruin. Ebenezer return'd.

24. Very Cold Night, the last. Read 1 Sam. 17, from number 32. Preach'd on Rev. 5, 9. At Dinner were besides Ebenezer and his Wife, Mr. Hezekiah How, and Mrs. Lydia Cutting. P.M. read Rev. 12, and by reason of my difficult Circumstances (especially being oblig'd to help yesterday in Carting out Muck) was oblig'd to repeat an old Discourse. It was an Expository Exercise on Mat. 12, 42. Omitted to appoint the Communion to my great Sorrow.

25. Storm of Snow. My Stray'd Steer brought home by Ebenezer.

26. Wrote to Mr. John Parkman in the Isle of Wight. Sent it by Mr. Jonathan Bond to the Care of my Brother Samuel Parkman in Boston. Mr. John Chamberlins Wife here from Stockbridge. She relates the sorrowful Story of the Indians besetting their House and killing two of her Children. At Eve Mr. Daniel Warrin, Collector, here. Tells me the Treasurer, Phinehas Hardy is advis'd not to give him Orders to pay me any Money till two Notes, viz. for 2£ each, on account of the Pew are Satisfy'd for—and yet the Precinct know that I am ready to pay them if they will but give me a Title to the Pew. They are especially Esquire Baker and Deacon Newton, who Mr. Warrin mentions are advising in the Manner aforesaid, and therefore altho my Dependence upon receiving Money of the Collector now, is greater than usual, and my Necessitys more pressing, yet he gives me little ground of Hope that I can be supply'd either as presently or plentifully, as my Straits require.

27. Cold Day. Winds high; Snow blowing about. Billy must needs go a Hunting, having long begg'd this Favour.

28. Thanksgiving. I preach'd on Ps. 150, numbers 1 and 2. N.B. appointed the Communion to be on the Next Lords Day—having omitted to do it last Lords Day—but gave Opportunity for any one to object if there were any that desir'd to. Ebenezer and his Wife with us. May we have a truly grateful sense of the divine Benefits and of our infinite Obligations therefor!

29. My Wife Saw Deacon Newton and call'd him in to talk with him concerning his Advice to the Treasurer as mention'd on the 26th. I also went down to him, and in my Discourse with him highly resented it. At Eve Mr. Solomon Woods here.

30. Have had a great deal of Trouble in my Mind and much Discourse with my Wife about Deacon Newtons Conduct; ever since my Conference with him Yesterday forenoon.

## DECEMBER, 1754

With much adoe my Mind was brot into some Composedness. Omitted reading both a. and p.m. Preach'd on Rev. 5, 9, a.m. On Acts 16, 29, 30 p.m. N.B. was oblig'd to deliver a great part of

---

[3] "A Paper was read to the Church (being Stop'd at Evening) Sign'd by Abijah Gale containing his acknowledgment of acting foolishly and imprudently with the wife of Isaac Amsden of Southborough; and the Church voted Satisfaction with what he offer'd." Westborough Church Records, Nov. 10, 1754. See Diary for Sept. 17-19, 1754.

[4] The brother of the Reverend Solomon Prentice, who had been dismissed by the Grafton church. Pierce, *Grafton*, p. 551.

[5] Samuel Dunbar of Canton.

[6] Samuel Brigham, the physician of Marlborough.

[7] (Harvard 1743). *Sibley*, XI, 326-327.

the latter Exercise without any Writing—the former part was a repetition of Sermon on the Text. N.B. Mrs. Chamberlin of Stockbridge, and Deacon Forbush din'd here. Mrs. Chamberlin lodg'd here.

2. Sent for Mr. Jonathan Forbush and acquainted him with what I had met with respecting the Pew. Agreed with him that he should pay for and build and improve the Pew as long as I liv'd—but at my Decease he shall return it to my Family and give them Legal Conveyance of it, they repaying him the price he pays and for the building it; and indemnifying him with respect to his Seat in the Meeting House otherwise. This is consents to—upon Supposition he outlives me, but does not bind his Heirs thereto if he decease first. This he also declar'd in the hearing of my Wife. N.B. Mrs. Chamberlin here. N.B. Town Meeting to Call in Town Debts; at which my son Ebenezer very hardly gets his Bill for boarding the Schoolmaster, Mr. Foster, granted. Is forc'd to abate from 35/ Old Tenor to 30/ per week.

3. My son Forbush here. My wife goes with him to Boston on Mr. Jonathan Forbush's Mare, and he takes Mrs. Chamberlin's which She was otherwise to have rid on. Mrs. Chamberlin remaining Still with us. N.B. Mr. Jonathan Forbush brought me my promissory Notes from the Treasurer Hardy given for the Pew, and so ends that Affair. Only now my son Forbush heard his Brother Jonathan declare (as yesterday in the hearing of my Wife) concerning giving up the Pew to my Heirs if he outlives me. N.B. Mr. Phinehas Rice of Grafton here and wants copys of the Papers against Mr. Hutchinson.

4. In the Morning had some Discourse with Treasurer Hardy concerning the Taking away the Pew from me in that violent manner. Mrs. Chamberlin left us to go to Captain Forbush's. Tho it rain'd I rode over to the North End and preach'd Mr. Martyns Lecture. Text Rom. 7, 9. I return'd at Eve. My son Thomas has been lathing his Shop. Mr. Gale having finish'd the work he had to do there in preparing for the Mason.

5. Bright and pleasant. I preach'd at Mr. Grow's, on the Same that I did Yesterday: Lieutenant Maynard, 3 Howes, Mr. Daniel Warrin (over the River) and Mr. Phinehas Maynard Set up Stables on my Land back of the Meeting House.

6. I wrote to Mr. Hutchinson concerning Mr. Rice's Desiring Copys etc. See on the third, and I sent it per Mr. Ezekiel Brigham of Grafton. My wife with my son Forbush returned in Safety. Blessed be God!

7. Mr. Forbush to Brookfield.

8. Read 1 Sam. 18. Preach'd on Rev. 5, 9, a. and p.m. Read p.m. Rev. 13.

9. Brother Hicks and his Daughter Hannah here. Lieutenant Maynard etc. finishing their Stables.

10. Visit Mr. Eleazer Pratts, Mr. William Nurse's, Mr. Smiths, Mr. Reuben Maynard's Family.

11. Mr. Adams and his wife here at Even. Sold 11 Sheep to Mr. Simon Tainter. Persis Fay Spins here.

12. Precinct Meeting to call in Debts and especially to See what they are indebted for the Meeting House. They grant 281£ old Tenor.

13. The Earth has been open for some time, but now Snow— p.m. Rain. At Eve came Brother Hicks and Dauter Hannah and lodged here.

14. Bright Morn, Brother Hicks and Dauter proceed on their Journey home. I rode up to Grafton. Directed Mr. Hutchinson to call at Captain Bakers and desire him to keep his Horse— which he did.

15. Preach'd there a. and p.m. on Rom. 7, 9. N.B. Consulted with the Deacons Whipple and How, Major Willard and 2 sons and Mr. Brooks and his son, about baptizing Mr. Hezekiah Taylors, and Mr. Jonathan Rolf's Child—and requested their Minds concerning my giving Copys of their Papers which were given in to the Ministers concerning Mr. Hutchinson: and they were generally of the Mind that it was best to wave it for the present—nay and not to gratifie anyone that would be likely to disturb their peace till the Church's Consent to it shall be obtain'd. P.M. I baptiz'd the following Children—Hannah, of Hezekiah and Abigail Taylor; Lucy, of Aaron and Elizabeth

Brigham; Elizabeth, of Jonathan and Abigail Rolf. At Eve came to see me Messers. Arnold, Isaac Harrington, and Stephen Prentice. Mr. Hutchinson return'd, having preach'd on Rom. 10, 10, and John 12, 46.

16. The Wind very high—call'd at Mr. Arnolds and at Mr. Brooks's in my Return home. When I came home found here my Cousen Sadler who came here yesterday noon to See me. At Eve Lieutenant Tainter and his Wife here at Supper.

17. P.M. Lieutenant Tainter came and waited on my Kinswoman Sadler to Ensign Mathis's in Southborough. N.B. Vendue at the Meeting House, at which are sold the Remnants of the Boards, Plank etc. now the Carpenters and joiners have finish'd their Work. Visited Deacon Newton who is ill, but mending.

18. The Reverend Mr. Wellman din'd here. I have receiv'd the whole six of Mr. Edwards's Enquiry. Rainy.

19. Visited Sarah Warrin who is yet out of order. Hannah Gold who lately lay in at Mr. Williams of a base born Child. My Wife walked to the other House to see my Dauter in Law, who is under some peculiar bad Circumstances and over runs her Time.

20. Vendue of Remnants of Boards etc. at the Meeting House. I went a little while. Very Cold Night.

21. [No entry.]

22. Read a.m. 1 Sam. 20. P.M. preach'd on Eph. 1, 7, each part of the Day. P.M. read Rev. 14. Widow Beeman, Persis Fay Still live here.

23. Lieutenant Griffin here going to Boston.

24. Visited Mr. Jonathan Bellows and his wife in order to compose their Strife. N.B. Mr. Ebenezer Chamberlin there and much disquieted with Mrs. Bellows. When I return'd home Mr. Martyn and wife here and din'd here.

25. Joseph Bowman came from Boston having done Several Errands for us, and call'd me up between 2 and 3 in the Morning. After Day exceeding Rainy.

26. At Eve Ebenezer came over for his Mother, his wife growing ill. About 10 o'clock at Night a Daughter was born to them. D.G.

27. My Wife has not return'd from the Groaning. P.M. I took my Daughter Sarah into the Chair and rode over to See My Dauter Eliza and her new born Babe. Left my Wife Still to tarry another Night, their Maid being not Sufficient and their Nurse not yet with them. N.B. 5 Bushels of Oats of Solomon Miller at 8/ old Tenor.

28. Sent Billy over to help his Brother in the forenoon. P.M. Mr. John Chamberlin of Stockbridge here. Brings my Volume of Chubbs Tracts[1] from Mr. Edwards. He informs me that Mr. Edwards is very weak and brought down by the Fever and Ague, which has follow'd for some months past, and that the Captain Cuncauput is return'd, a great many of the Stockbridge Indians, perhaps two Thirds of them are gone from the Town. Towards Eve my wife return'd from t'other House. N.B. Mr. Eleazer Williams brought a Load of Wood.

29. Read 1 Sam. 21. Preach'd a. and p.m. on Acts 9, 6 carrying on the Subject begun from Acts 16, 29, 30, but p.m. in Application endeavouring to stir up Conviction and Humiliation Shewing the Evil Nature of Sin. I us'd from page 2 to page 12 of Sermon on Job 33, 27. Mr. John Chamberlin of Stockbridge din'd here. N.B. my Son and Dauter gave Thanks for the little Token of the Divine Goodness to them. But what a Damp it is to my Joy that they have not lain hold on God's Covenant for themselves or their Offspring! The Lord give me an Heart Seriously to reflect upon it!

30. My Wife and I rode over in the Slay to visit our Children and dine there. Return'd at Eve home. N.B. My Daughter in Some Comfort, Blessed be the Lord who heals her! and the Child in a hopefull State. It was represented very Small, but by its Weight appears near middling (as they Speak) and tho they had many Thoughts to call it Mary, yet agree to call it Elizabeth.

31. A considerable storm of Rain and Snow. We are in Some Difficulty for want of Wood. Mr. Jeduthun Baldwin came here last Evening. He goes to Worcester this Morning in his Journey

[1] Thomas Chubb, *Three Tracts* (London, 1727) or *A Collection of Tracts on Various Subjects* (London, 1730).

to Brookfield. Three of my Sons having lain with Noah Forbush at t'other House, we fear have taken a Troublesome Distemper, and are using Some Means to drive it out if they have, and another which they have probably infected with them.

Thus Ends this Year, in which we have in General had thro Divine Mercy much Health of Body, but not a few Straits, Cares, and Difficultys. God be pleas'd to sanctifie them and prepare us for what we have yet to conflict with especially our final Departure out of this State which has many Scenes of Sin and Trouble.

### JANUARY, 1755

A true Sense of the Divine Dispensations would (methinks) fill my Soul with an holy astonishment at the Liberty and Goodness of God which is still protracted: and His Longsuffering is amazing towards So worthless and unfruitful a Creature. O that I might be rous'd and quicken'd! and O that God would vouchsafe after all, to pardon and Sanctifie me; and that He would please to direct and assist me in the great incumbent Dutys—that I may improve my Time, Serve the Souls of men, and Save my own soul as well as those that hear me! It was very Cold, yet Billy went to Ensign Woods the Clothier and to Allens Mill.

2. Very Cold—but Billy to Johnsons Mill. I have almost Every Day Deep Concern for both the Spiritual and Temporal Welfare of my Children especially my dear son Ebenezer. Would humbly lift my Soul to God on this Account and beg Grace to Committ my whole Cause to Him, who I know will do what is wisest and best. In That I would repose myself.

3. The Aged Judge Ward here and din'd with us.

5. Read 1 Samuel 22. Preach'd a. and p.m. on Ps. 39, 6. Read P.M. Rev. 16. On this Day my little son Samuel was observ'd to look Yellow.

6. More Notice taken of Samme's Yellowness, yet plays about and is brisk. At Eve Mr. David Maynard junior here, and gives me account of the unhappy Condition of his Brother Mason, who has lain for some time in Worcester Jayl.

7. Traded away sled sides to Lieutenant Stephen Maynard and brought 1000 shingles of him.

8. Samme, tho he sits at Table with us and plays about, grows very Yellow from Day to Day—to our Surprize he does indeed in some Measure fail in his Appetite.

9. At Captain Forbush's, heard that Mr. Daniel Hastings dy'd on the 7th having had the Mumps and took Cold. It was very Surprizing—may God sanctify it to us, as well as to his own Relations! He dys in the midst of his Glory and gaiety—was just going to be married—but that very Day his Thoughts perish.

10. Mr. Solomon Stow brought me 5 sheets of Tin (price 5/ a piece Old Tenor) for my Chamber Floor, next my Hearth.

11. Exceeding High Gusts in the Night—my old Barn is in great Danger, but God is our preserver; to Him I committ myself and my substance.

12. [No entry.]

[The remainder of the diary for January, 1755, and for the entire month of February, 1755 has been lost.]

### MARCH, 1755

1. Lieutenant Maynard with two Stout Teams, brought 6 Load of Wood. P.M. I attended the Funeral of Mr. Joseph Farr of Southborough, Mr. Stone being gone to Boston. I proceeded to Mr. Stones having agreed to change with him. He came home before Night—but so tir'd he tarried at Home.

2. In the Morning he rode up to Westborough and preach'd here. I preach'd at Southboro on Zech. 1, 5 and John 12, 35, occasion'd by the late Death of the Venerable Mr. Stone[1] of Harwich Aet. 88. At Eve I return'd home—call'd to see Mr. Ephraim Bruce's Child which he told me Yesterday had a Pin Stuck across the Throat—but now they can't tell what is come of it—they suppose it Swallow'd.

3. Altho it was Town Meeting Day, yet I went away Somewhat Early to Visit Mr. Zebulon Rice—call'd at Mr. Grouts and

Mr. Phinehas Hardy's. Mr. Zeublon Rice gone to Town Meeting at Upton—his Wife also from Home. Visit Mr. Ebenezer Miller and Mr. Moses Warrin din'd at the House of the Latter. N.B. My Wife indispos'd.

4. A great Storm of Snow. I would have gone over to the Funeral of Captain James Eagers Wife, if it had not been so exceeding stormy: and it is doubtful whether they will be able themselves to attend it. N.B. This Day 38 Year ago, old Stile, The Great Snow Storm.

5. I preach'd the Lecture from 1 Cor. 11, 20. At Eve my Wife and I went up to Captain Bakers[2] to the Marriage of Mrs. Betty to Mr. Jonas Wilder of Bolton. Stay'd to supper and made it late Home. Very Cold.

6. N.B. My Wife much indispos'd from Day to Day.

7. Captain Benjamin Wood of Hopkinton dines here. He gives me further Account of the perplext state of their Church. Snows again.

8. Lieutenant Tainter comes up from Boston but leaves his Whirrey at Waltham by reason of the deep Snows. My Watch useless.

9. Read 1 Sam. 28. Preach'd A.M. Isa. 9, 6. The mighty God. Administer'd the Lords Supper. P.M. Read Rev. 22, and preach'd on number 22. Had an Exceeding great Weight upon my Spirits last night especially concerning my own state and Frame. Had a great Relief in my Mind as to my sermons (their being prepar'd Seasonably) having Spent the week very much in Work—and got them done before the Sabbath. D.G.

10. Colonel Williams, Colonel Brigham and Major Ward met here—they are going to Mendon to give out Commissions there.

11. My Wife and I rode p.m. to See Lieutenant Bruce, who was lately very ill. Sent my Watch by Mr. Moses Brigham to Mr. Moses Peck at Boston.

12. I rode to Mr. William Nurse's expecting to hear Mr. Cushing there but the Meeting which was appointed to be there to Day was put by; the Snow being So deep and very uncomfortable Travelling. Mr. Ebenezer Nurse went with me. Visited the Widow Whitney, and at Mr. Eleazer Pratts. The Field Officers return from Mendon at Eve.

13. Heavy Rains the last Night: Smoaky Air to Day and rain frequently yet hearing Mr. Ebenezer Rice was confin'd by illness I went up to See him, and endeavour'd to discharge my Duty with tender Affection to him.

14. Mr. George Bruce Sheriff call'd here. He had been with an Execution against Jonas Bradish, who is Bondsman for Mr. Ebenezer Rice. It gives me much Grief, as Mr. Rice has behav'd himself So ingenuously among us. Mr. Bruce acquaints me that Mr. Dorrs[3] Family at Mendon is in great Affliction by the illness of Mrs. Katy, at her sister Tafts[4] in Braintree. It is far from a New Observation that this World is full of Changes, nor is it Strange that we are So unaffected with them.

16. Exceeding Cold Morning. Read a.m. 1 Sam. 28. Preach'd on Rev. 22, 17, a. and p.m. Several persons more than our own Family at Dinner. P.M. appointed a Church-Meeting for the Choice of a Deacon or Deacons to be next Thursday come sennight at 1 o'Clock p.m. In the Evening began my Preparations for the Fast.

17. Settl'd my Accounts with Mr. Ebenezer Rice.

18. [No entry.]

19. Mr. James Bowman again asks my advice about a School Master.

20. Public Fast. Preach'd on Mat. 24, 12. After the Exercises Captain Fay warn'd his Company to meet tomorrow to beat for Volunties.

21. Messers. Samuel Hardy and Simon Tainter here on the Affair of Mr. Tainters Debt to me for the sheep he bought of me. P.M. the Company Met.

22. Mr. Martyn Sent his Son Richard with a Letter (in Soft Stile) complaining of my not visiting them—to which I return'd a like answer: but as he also acquainted me therein that he could

[1] The Reverend Nathaniel Stone (Harvard 1690) had served Brewster (Harwich), 1700-1755.

[2] Edward Baker of Westborough.
[3] The Reverend Mr. Joseph Dorr.
[4] Katherine was the daughter of the Reverend Mr. Dorr. Her sister, Mary, married Moses Taft (Harvard 1751), the minister of Randolph, 1752-1791.

not change with me next Sabbath (being previously engag'd to Mr. Cushing) I was oblig'd to prepare as well as I could to preach at home.

23. Read (and Expounded as usual) 1 Sam. 30. Preach'd on Mat. 24, 12, but P.M. was oblig'd to repeat an old Sermon. It was on Heb. 3, 13.

24. Lucy ill with Swelling in her Mouth, Face.

25. My Wife and I rode over in my Chair to Mr. Martyns. Carry'd the Preceptor⁵ Volume 1, and din'd there, it raining hard p.m. and at Eve we tarry'd and lodg'd there. N.B. No word with him of the angry Letters of Last Year to this Day.

26. Bright Morn. We return'd, call'd at Ensign Rice's, and (both going and returning) at Mr. Masons. Call'd also at Captain Maynards, din'd at Ebenezers. P.M. I rode to Mr. William Nurse's and heard Mr. Cushing, on Contentment.

27. This Day the Church Met to choose Deacons. I prepar'd somewhat to deliver on that Occasion, but it was brief and broken. N.B. Mr. Whitney and Deacon Forbush are concern'd, and talk with me before the Meeting about Lieutenant Tainter, who they Say, would be like to be voted for, for one were it not for Something which divers Brethren have heard from him about his paying me (one way or another) a matter of 16 or 17£ upon the Score of the North sides Rates which Should have been paid me in the Year 1744: but which is not so accepted by me. I open'd the Meeting with Prayer. Read Acts 6 to 7, and 1 Tim. 3, 8 to 14 and deliver'd what I had prepared. Brother Whitney chose by 19 out of 25—then try'd for another, but the Votes were scattering, viz. 6 for Lieutenant Tainter, 6 for Mr. Francis Whipple, 6 for Mr. Jonathan Bond, the rest were for Esquire Baker, Jonathan Forbush junior, Daniel Forbush and David Maynard junior. We try'd again—but still no Choice: they were 12 for Lieutenant Tainter, 10 for Mr. Bond, 4 for Mr. Whipple. Try'd again also in Vain; there being now 12 for Mr. Bond, 11 for Lieutenant Tainter—2 for Mr. Whipple and one for Jonathan Forbush junior. We try'd once more and Mr. Bond was chose by 16 votes only 6 for Lieutenant, the rest for Whipple and Jonathan Forbush junior. Both Mr. Whitney and Mr. Bond modestly refus'd, but their answer was desir'd to be deferr'd to this Day fortnight to which Time the Meeting was adjourn'd. The Disposal of the Lot is of the Lord. At Eve Mr. Jacob Sweetzer of Rutland here, and lodg'd—his Horse at Mr. Nurse's. Billy brings home sad News of Betty Bimelock (Indian) Murdering her Child about six weeks old.

28. Mr. Sweetzer left us before Breakfast and before the Storm which came on when the Day got up.

29. [No entry.]

30. Read 1 Sam. 31. Text Isa. 9, 6. The Everlasting Father. P.M. no reading. The Exercise was from Rev. 1, 3 in which I deliver'd an Extract from Mr. Lowman on the whole Book of Revelation.⁶ N.B. Mr. Jonah Warrin in Distress about his Dauter Sarah again, came to me at noon and desir'd public prayers. N.B. One Mr. Sheldon of Litchfield in Connecticut at Meeting P.M. At Eve I visited Sarah Warrin and pray'd with her.

31. I visited Sarah Warrin again. The Difficultys in my own Family very great on account of our being kept out of Money and Wanting many necessarys—but Desire to keep up my Spirits, hoping in an infinitely Mercifull and gracious God. My Wife lame by the Humors falling into a Blister on one of her Legs, on which she was endeavouring to make an issue. N.B. at Eve a great Light as of Some Burning. It appear'd in the North East.

### APRIL 1755

1. Wrote out 12 Principal Articles of Religion for the Benefit of Candidates for Communion. News that the Burning last night was Captain Thomas Amsden's House in Marlborough. Suspected to be by his son in Law Dr. Robinson.¹ P.M. Captain Fays Company call'd together to beat for Volunteers at the Desire

of Captain Speakman of Boston. N.B. Mr. Henry Burns of Marlborough here.

2. It rain'd, had no Horse to go to the Fast Exercises at Mr. Jonah Warrin's till accidentally my Dauter in Law came with her Child. The Roads bad and it rain'd so that she did not go (as she design'd)—therefore I took her Horse and went. I pray'd first; Mr. Fish² preach'd on Luke 19, 10. He pray'd P.M. and I preach'd on Phil. 4, 11. Sarah Warrin in So ill a frame that before we began the Exercise I could not get it out of her that she desir'd that what we were undertaking, or concurr'd in it—however she did tarry with us. And at Eve desir'd to talk with Mr. Fish—and when I took leave she ask'd me to remember her as being, if not under Conviction yet under Temptations. My Dauter Eliza return'd home at Eve with her Child.

3. A brighter Day. I preach'd at the widow Newtons on Numb. 23.

4. [No entry.]

5. [No entry.]

6. Read 2 Sam. 1. Preach'd on Isa. 4, 6. P.M. no reading. O that I might have the Grace to submit myself to the Glorious Prince of Peace! and that a perfect Reconcilement on each part might be accomplish'd! not only submit myself but induce Others!

7. Lucy much out of order—breaks out in her Face.

8. Lucy and I ride to Marlborough to consult Dr. Brigham about her. She is blooded—we din'd there. I went to Captain Daniel Barns's³ and paid Mr. Barns the full of my Account there; which was about 6£ old Tenor. Visit Mr. Smith⁴—and also Mr. Ephraim How and pay my Interest there. We return home at Eve; find our Tabernacle in Peace. D.G.

9. I rode down to Mrs. Belknaps who lies Sick—found her in an Excellent Frame as to her Spiritual Frame, pray'd with her—Said what I possibly could to her Husband to induce him to Reflect on himself. Din'd at Chamberlins. N.B. their bitter Complaints of Mr. Jonathan Bellows's. At Eve Mr. Baldwin here—and lodg'd here. My Mare was kept at the Squire's.

10. In the Morning Mr. Whitney gave his Letter to the Church, containing his Denyal. Catechizing a.m. about 28 young Men attend the Catechetical Exercise. P.M. Church meeting by Adjournment to receive the Answers of the Elected Deacons. Mr. Bond after a modest refusal, and the Church insisting on their Choice, submitted. Mr. Whitneys refusal (in writing as aforesaid) was read but the Reason which is couch'd in it, not satisfying the Church we adjourn'd to this Day sennight after Lecture.

11. [No entry.]

12. [No entry.]

13. Read 2 Sam. 2. Preach'd on Mat. 5, 4, and therein deliver'd one of my former Expository Exercises with Alterations Accommodating it to a Scheme I have now in Hand, viz. the manner of the Souls Preparation and coming into Christ. P.M. read Gal. 1, and preach'd from number 15, 16. O what a great important and glorious Work this of bringing the Soul to be acquainted with and united to Christ is! May I myself be one of those who happily experience this—but alas! My Great Darkness and Perplexity!

14. Mr. Samuel Hardy and Mr. John Rogers work here setting up Fence at the Island a.m. and Digging stones behind the Meeting House p.m.

15. Mr. Cushing and I rode over to Hopkinton to Ministers Meeting at Mr. Barrets. It was very thin: none but Mr. Stone more. N.B. Mr. Barretts Troubles a.m. with his Peoples very great. Deacon Millen with Some Questions.

16. Mr. Stone preach'd an Excellent Sermon from Rom. 6, 17. After Lecture Deacon Millen came and left a Paper of Questions for the Association to Solve. N.B. Mr. Prentice⁵ of Holliston and his new Spouse, came and din'd with us. N.B. before we broke up, we that were of the Association had Some serious Dis-

⁵ Dodsley, Robert, *The Preceptor: Containing A general Course of Education*, 2 vols., (London 1748). A preface to this work was written by Dr. Samuel Johnson.

⁶ Moses Lowman (1680-1752) was an English non-conformist divine who published *A Paraphrase and Notes on the Revelation of St. John* (London, 1737).

¹ Jeremiah Robinson had married Eunice Amsden.

² The Reverend Elisha Fish of Upton.
³ Also a deacon in Marlborough.
⁴ The Reverend Aaron Smith of Marlborough.
⁵ The Reverend Joshua Prentiss married Margaret, the daughter of Nathaniel Appleton of Cambridge, Jan. 9, 1755.

course with Brother Barrett upon the late Complaints against him—which may God bless and render Effectual! Mr. Cushing my Company home. I ask'd both Mr. Cushing and Mr. Stone to preach my Lecture tomorrow, but in Vain.

17. My Lecture on Ezek. 5, 5 to 9. N.B. Mr. Eliezer Rice asks that his Children might be baptiz'd on his Wife's Account which is readily consented to. N.B. The Church stop'd according to Adjournment. Mr. Whitney persisting in his Refusal the Church proceeded to choose another Deacon. First tryal was scattering. 13 for Brother Tainter: 11 for Brother Jonathan Forbush junior, 1 for Brother Francis Whipple and 1 for Brother David Maynard junior—try'd a second Time—still too Scattering. 14 for brother Forbush, 13 for his Father Tainter again: 2 for Brother Whipple—try'd a Third Time: and then Brother Forbush was chose, viz. 15 out of 29, 11 of which were for Lieutenant Tainter, 2 for Mr. David Maynard and one (if I mistake not) for Mr. Whipple. Adjourn'd to next Monday come sennight 2 p.m. Deacon Bond and his Wife here after meeting.

18. My Wife to Marlborough on Ebenezers Mare, and tarrys over Night.

19. My Wife does not return a.m. by reason of the Rain: but it Clearing away p.m. She came in Safety. N.B. her Kinswoman, Dr. Brighams Wife, a third Child, the oldest not 3 years old till next August. N.B. Brother Hicks here in his Journey from Cambridge home. N.B. a Child of Mr. Robert Keys nigh Wachusett missing Some Days.

20. A.M. read 2 Sam. 3. Preach'd on Gal. 1, 15, 16. Administered the Lords Supper. P.M. omitted Reading. The Sermon was formed out of Number 130, 131 of Expositions on Mat. 7, 15–21. Ministers Meeting, the Lecture and Family Cares preventing my preparing anew for this Exercise. But my Soul in deep Engagement on my State and Frame. May God most gracious pity, pardon and accept me thro the Merits of the great Redeemer. Deacon Bond waited at Communion.

21. Mr. Samuel Hardy came to Clearing. He takes the work between the Pasture Fences to clear for a Dollar. P.M. Reverend Mr. Hall of Sutton here, going to Boston on account of Troubles he meets with by means of Mr. Elisha Putnam and Duncan Campbell Esquire. N.B. Mr. Keys's Child not found, tho some Hundreds of men were Yesterday and to Day in Search after her. A dozen went who belong to our Congregation.

22. I visited at Mr. Zebulon Rice's, Captain Fays, Mr. Whipples, Mr. Eliezer Rice's and Mr. Pratts.

23. This Morning my Wife, accompany'd by Deacon Forbush Set out on her Journey to Brookfield. She had Ebenezers Mare to ride on. I borrow'd old Mr. Charles Rice's to ride to Shrewsbury, to preach Mr. Cushings Lecture—din'd there—but Mr. Cushing[6] of Waltham being on a Visit to their Parents I conceiv'd it would be more agreeable for him to preach and therefore I requested him to—he comply'd and preach'd on Luke 12, 43. N.B. Discourse with Mr. Thomas Smith who went to a Wise-Man (Mr. Williams Wood a blacksmith in Scituate nigh Providence) to know where Mr. Keys's lost Child might be found. Call'd for my Account with Dr. Smith as I return'd at Eve.

24. Catechiz'd both parts of the Day at the Meeting House—35 Boys—28 Girls.

25. Mr. Moses Nurse with his Plough and 4 Oxen, assisted by Deacon Bonds Son Thomas and a Yoke of Oxen and from 4 o'Clock P.M. Barnibus Newtons Oxen broke up Some Grass Ground for me on the Island.

26. Alpheus Newton was to have come and Sowed Wheat for me, but disappointed me. Poor Mr. Samuel Coollidge,[7] brought up by Lieutenant Tainter, 2 or 3 Days ago, is in Town, that if he may be able he may keep School.

27. Read 2 Sam. 4. Preach'd on Josh. 7, 13. P.M. read Isa. 8, and preach'd on number 20 against the foolish and wicked practice of going to Cunning Men to enquire for lost Things. And may God succeed what has been Said! Poor Mr. Coollidge was very distracted last night. Lieutenant Tainter tarries at home with him to Day.

28. The Church met by Adjournment to receive Brother Jonathan Forbush juniors Answer—he desir'd to be excus'd, but his Reasons not Satisfying the Church, he submitted. Wrote a Letter to my Wife at Brookfield in Answer to hers by Deacon Forbush. Deliver'd mine to Mr. Francis Whipple who designs to Lambstown[8] tomorrow. N.B. I very affectionately let the Church know (at their meeting to Day that my Difficultys and Burdens are inexpressibly great, So that I was unavoidably forc'd to omitt many Things in my ministerial Work which I would most gladly perform—many Schemes and Designs for their Souls Good, I was forc'd to drop—and I could not but greatly lament it for their sakes as well as my own. I let 'em know that it was very much against my Inclination to be uttering Complaints—I was averse to putting Memorials to the Precinct. I therefore apply'd to Them as the Lord's People praying they would advise some way or other for my Relief. However at least to let me have their fervent Prayers to God for me. And thus left it.

29. Visit Lieutenant Forbush—and Captain Forbush. N.B. took him aside and talk'd with him closely, and may God render it Effectual! N.B. Mrs. Lucy Forbush (Ebenezers Wife) fell backward from her Horse before my House. I in part saw her—ran to her help—directed her into my House till she might revive and recover—she complains very much of her Hand aking extremely—Captain Tyler of Mendon with me. She recover'd so as to go home.

30. Mr. John Rogers comes with his Oxen and Plough—splits hills by the Barn and sows Wheat. Billy with my Mare helps him.

MAY, 1755

In the Morning I went to Mr. Jonah Warrins[1]—Sarah, his Dauter, exceedingly Set to destroy herself, being requested by him tho against her Inclination, I pray'd. N.B. She ran away into the Woods, and all hands after her. Neighbour Alpheus Newton a.m. sowd and plough'd in some more Wheat and some Peas at the Barn Orchard.

2. In the morning Captain Baker brot me a Letter from Mr. Forbush and my Wife (at Brookfield) urging me to go up there, and informing me that Mr. Benjamin Lull of the Manor of Peace would meet me Monday or Tuesday next at Brookfield. P.M. rode up to Mr. William Nurse's, on my own Mare, there got Daniel Nurse's, and left mine. Rode to Mr. Noah Brooks's and lodg'd—at their earnest Request.

3. Rode to Brookfield. Din'd at Mr. Roberts at Leicester.[2] N.B. Dr. Upham[3] Company from Mr. Eatons.[4] Found my wife and Mr. Forbush[5] and his in Health.

4. My People destitute (for I could not get up to Brookfield soon enough for Mr. Forbush to go to Westborough). I preach'd at Brookfield a.m. on Rev. 22, 16 and p.m. on Ps. 110, 3. Many of the other part of Town at Mr. Forbush's meeting, Mr. Harding[6] being absent, and his people in great Disquietment.

5. My Wife and I, with Mr. Forbush and his, at Dinner at Mr. Benjamin Adams's. P.M. Mr. Forbush and I rode to Esquire Fosters and to Mr. Henry Dwights—and Captain Buckminsters.

6. Preach'd a Lecture for Mr. Forbush from Judg. 14, 14. After Lecture came Mr. Lull to Mr. Forbush. Supp'd late at Lieutenant Abraham Hows, my wife, and Mr. Forbush, and his wife there also. Mr. Lull lodg'd at Mr. Jabez Ayre's.

7. Mr. Lull came and we made an agreement about his Pearl-Hill Lot in Townshend, and reciprocally gave Notes of Sixty five pounds Lawfull Money to stand to our agreement—then we rode up to the Town, an Ecclesiastical Council sitting to Day on the Affair of Mr. Hardings Dismission. I return'd with Mr. Forbush at Evening.

[8] Lambstown plantation had become the town of Hardwick.

[1] Of Westborough.
[2] The Reverend Joseph Roberts.
[3] Jabez Upham, a physician of Brookfield.
[4] The Reverend Joshua Eaton of Spencer.
[5] The Reverend Eli Forbes (or Forbush), Parkman's son-in-law.
[6] The Reverend Elisha Harding of Brookfield, who was dismissed by his congregation a few days later, May 8, 1755. Salary difficulties were behind this controversy. *Sibley*, XI, 561–562.

[6] The Reverend Jacob Cushing was the son of Job Cushing of Shrewsbury.
[7] Coolidge (Harvard 1724) had a checkered career as librarian at Harvard, sometime preacher and schoolmaster. See Diary, Sept. 8, 1744, and July 3, 1745.

8. My Wife and I Set out for home. Din'd at Captain John Browns in Leicester, and lodg'd at Mr. Cushings.

9. We came home Safely, and our Tabernacle and all in it in peace. D.G.

10. [No entry.]

11. Read 2 Sam. 5. Preach'd on Gal. 1, 15, 16. P.M. read Tit. 2, and preach'd on number 12, delivering an old Sermon out of a set of sermons from page 34.

12. We heard at Eve that this Morning the Spouse[7] of Brother Smith of Marlboro died—and somewhat suddenly. An heavy stroke!

13. [No entry.]

14. Colonel Williams[8] came from the Reverend Mr. Smith to desire me to attend the Funeral of his Wife tomorrow.

15. This Day 2 o'Clock p.m. was last Lords Day appointed to be the Time for the Catechetical Exercise to Young Women: but the Funeral aforesaid prevented it. I took very effectual Pains to Notifie the Young Women in the several parts of the Parish of it. And my wife and I rode down in the Chair to Marlborough. We stop'd and din'd at Colonel Williams as did Messers Cushing and Martyn[9] and their wives. The Bearers at the Funeral were the Reverend Messers. Loring[10] and Cushing, Gardner,[11] Martyn, Goss[12] and I. Mr. Cushing pray'd, Mr. Loring having a Cold. We return'd safe home at Evening.

16. Catechetical Exercise to Young Women—29 present. At Eve Mr. Ebenezer Cutler of Grafton requested me to go in the Morning to See his Son Ebenezer who is ill in Body and disturb'd in Mind.

17. Mr. Williams Wife has Fitts—he lends me his Mare and I rode to See the foresaid young man. Call'd at Mr. William Nurse's, and agreed with him to preach (by divine leave) at his House next Thursday. Din'd at Mr. Cutlers. At Mr. Bezaleel Smiths and at Mr. Eleazer Pratts in my return home.

18. Mr. Martyn preach'd for me a.m. on Job 31, 14. P.M. on [blank]. I preach'd for him a. and p.m. on Rev. 22, 17. After the Exercises I visited Captain James Eager, who languishes in Jaundice, etc.

19. Town meet to choose a Representative—they Chose Mr. Francis Whipple.

20. Was at the Funeral of Samuel Lyscomb, of Southboro, Esquire. N.B. a.m. was at Marlborough—at Mr. Woods, and at Mr. Smiths. Din'd at the House of Mourning.

21. Was at Captain Bakers, at Eve and married Mr. Jonathan Adams [13] and Mrs. Hephzibah.[14] N.B. Mr. Forbush from Brookfield here.

22. Preach'd at Mr. William Nurse's on Isa. 66, 2. Mr. Cushing and Mr. Hutchinson[15] there.

23. [No entry.]

24. Was at the Funeral of Mr. David Mathis of Southborough. Ebenezer rode to Brookfield to look of Mr. Harding's Place, or desire the refusal of it. N.B. old Mr. Graves, Deacon Amsden and Deacon Woods desir'd me to preach at Southboro tomorrow, Seeing Mr. Forbush would preach for me, and Mr. Stone[16] was gone to Hardwick.

25. Preach'd at Southborough. A.M. on Rev. 22, 14, and p.m. on Gal. 3, 10. Cursed is Everyone etc. Mr. Forbush for me on [blank]. I went in the Morn and return'd at Eve. N.B. In Southborough they had a Contribution for me.

26. At Eve came Mr. Breck[17] of Springfield and lodg'd here.

27. Mr. Breck, Mr. Whipple (the Representative of this Town) and I set out for Boston. Din'd at Mr. Woodwards[18] at Weston.

Lodg'd at Brother Samuels at Boston. N.B. Mr. Charles Frost[19] of Falmouth lodges there also.

28. Mr. Checkley[20] preach'd the Election Sermon on Zeph. 1, 15. A Day of Darkness. I din'd at Mr. Secretary Willards[21] where also din'd old Mr. White[22] of Gloucester, old Mr. Niles[23] of Braintree, Mr. Wigglesworth[24] of Ipswich, Messers. Nathaniel[25] and Daniel Rogers,[26] and Mr. Hemingway[27] of Townshend. P.M. Made a Visit to Colonel Mascarene[28] where my kinswoman Hersey[29] lives—and attended the Convention of Ministers. Mr. Prince[30] Moderator and Dr. Mayhew[31] Scribe. Visited my Kinswoman Olivers Family, but he was not at home. Poor old Scipio (one of my Brother Alexanders Negro Men) very low. Instructed and prayed with him. Visited my sister Rebecca,[32] at the North End; and lodg'd at Brother Williams.

29. Convention Lecture by Mr. Joseph Parsons of Bradford, on Mat. 5, 14, 15, 16. Din'd at Mr. Mathers, where also din'd a great number more, viz. Messers. Job Cushing, John Gardner, Parsons, Abbot,[33] William Balch,[34] Bradstreet,[35] etc. P.M. Visit my Kinswoman Langdon[36] lately widow'd, and the Deacon her Father in Law attended the Conversation a little while [but Mr. Lowel desiring me to go to smoak a Pipe with Dr. Chauncy,[37] I comply'd. N.B. The Conversation chiefly of Mr. Biles[38] and his wife in their violent squabbles. No word of our own Disgusts. I think this visit was on the 28th.] At Eve Brother Samuel and I visited Deacon Grant. Both return'd to his House, and there arose an unexpected Contest between him and me about Clark the Separate who had exhorted in Boston a few Years Since and was lately in Falmouth. Mr. Charles Frost present and join'd with him, very sanguinely. I Soon held my Tongue: and let it go off.

30. Set myself to hire Money in order to Purchase of the Reverend Mr. Harding of Brookfield for Ebenezer: but in vain. Visited Colonel Saltonstall at his Brother Cooks—he is exceeding low, and much distress'd. Pray'd with him and commended him to God. Visited Mr. Foxcroft—din'd with my Kinsman Winter. Mr. William Winter and I go to old Mr. Owen Harris to hire money, but the attempt there also was without any success. Visited Mr. Sutton who Shew'd me a mathematical Bellows. N.B. at the 3 Horse Shooes enquired after Francis Fogery—or Allagajo—could not find nor hear of Him—but there was Bartholomew—and Captain Lane an Interpreter. Lodg'd at Miss Dudley's.

31. A great Frost last night. Undertook my Journey home and I arriv'd well; found my Family in Peace. D.G. N.B. I din'd at Mr. Isaac Brooks in Waltham and rode most of the Journey home alone. Call'd at Dr. Robys,[39] and at the Widow Darlings.

### JUNE, 1755

1. Read 2 Sam. 7. Preach'd on Ps. 68, 1, a. and p.m. and p.m. read Ps. 66. N.B. Mention'd to the Congregation Judge Saltonstalls[1] Sickness, before Prayer.

2. Lucy and I rode to t'other House and din'd there. Mr. Eliezer Rice goes to Boston to See his Son Silas at the Camp, and

---

[7] Martha Smith, wife of the Reverend Aaron Smith.

[8] Abraham Williams of Marlborough held many town offices and was a justice of the peace.

[9] The Reverend John Martyn of Northborough.

[10] Israel Loring of Sudbury.

[11] John Gardner of Stow.

[12] Thomas Goss of Bolton.

[13] Of Shrewsbury.

[14] The daughter of Squire Edward Baker.

[15] Aaron Hutchinson of Grafton.

[16] The Reverend Nathan Stone of Southborough.

[17] The Reverend Robert Breck, Jr.

[18] The Reverend Samuel Woodward.

[19] (Harvard, 1730). Frost was a wealthy merchant and landowner, justice of the peace and representative of Falmouth, Maine. *Sibley*, VIII, 715–717.

[20] Samuel Checkley of the New North Church.

[21] Josiah Willard, Secretary of Massachusetts.

[22] The Reverend John White.

[23] The Reverend Samuel Niles.

[24] Samuel Wigglesworth, the minister of Hamilton.

[25] The Reverend Nathaniel Rogers of Ipswich.

[26] Daniel Rogers, the minister of Ipswich.

[27] The Reverend Phinehas Hemenway.

[28] Jean Paul Mascarene of Boston. See *New Eng. Hist. and Gen. Register*, X (January, 1856), 143–147.

[29] Mrs. Israel Hearsey.

[30] Thomas Prince of the Old South Church.

[31] Jonathan Mayhew of the West Church in Boston.

[32] Parkman's sister-in-law, Mrs. Alexander Parkman.

[33] The Reverend Hull Abbot of Charlestown.

[34] The minister of Groveland.

[35] Simon Bradstreet, the minister of Marblehead.

[36] Parkman's niece Mary was the widow of Edward Langdon.

[37] Charles Chauncy of the First Church in Boston.

[38] The Reverend Mather Byles of the Hollis Street Church. A modern authority says "that Byles's humor was enough to make a wreck of any woman." *Sibley*, VII, 479.

[39] Ebenezer Roby, the physician of Sudbury.

[1] Colonel Richard Saltonstall.

at his Request I wrote a few Lines of Instruction and Caution to the Youth. I visited at Mr. David Maynard juniors and talk with him about his getting Timber for a Kitchin, which he says he will forward. N.B. Whilst I was gone last week Mr. Phinehas Hardy brought 3 Posts for my Kitchin. Mr. Freeland at work here, turning a Coat for Billy.

3. Rode over to Deacon Bonds; at Eve Mr. Baldwin here.

4. I preach'd my Lecture on Ps. 68, 1. Very hot weather—and follow'd with Thunder.

5. Mr. John Rogers and Rody Smith digging Stones. Billy brought over Rails from t'other Place, and carry'd out Ashes to the Cook Field, and laid 'em on the New-broke ground. Thomas has been drooping for Several Days—today Seems worse. P.M. went to Mr. Daniel Forbush to the raising of a New House. Went in to Ensign Millers—who grows weaker with his Paralytic Shaking.

6. My Son Thomas has Fever and Ague.

7. Judas Rice here and paid Thomas and me in behalf of his Brother Asaph.

8. Read 2 Sam. 8. Preach'd on Gen. 49, 10 latter part. Administer'd the Lords Supper. P.M. read Isa. 44 and preach'd on number 5. N.B. my old Neighbour Mrs. Elizabeth How din'd with us.

9. Went over to the Funeral of Captain James Eager,[2] who dy'd last Saturday Morning in the 69th year of his age. My Company chiefly in going and returning was Captain Baker and his wife. N.B. My Kinsman Bryant of Stoneham, going to Grafton, call'd here. I would Seriously reflect upon my own Speedy Departure. O that God would fasten and ripen the Impressions upon Me!

10. Rody Smith work'd with Billy in hoeing Corn. Mrs. Prentice[3] and with her one Mrs. Logan, going to Charlestown, call'd here. I perceive they are plung'd very deep into Errors; and Yet Seem exceeding Spiritual, heavenly and Purify'd—at least Mrs. Prentice. 'Tis Said they are Nicolaitans, and yet Perfectionists. O the infinite Mischief done by such to the Church of God which they profess to have the most fervent Affection to! May God grant 'em a Discovery of the Evil; and may I and all others be preserv'd from their Mischievous Reveries! My Kinsman Briant call'd here in his Return.

11. Thomas Still lies by, with the Fever and Ague.

12. Was at Captain Fays Training—I din'd at his House; and he din'd all the Company and all that Came, on free Cost. N.B. I Spoke to the Company to avoid Intemperance and Disorders.

13. Mr. Kenny and his son Nathan I hir'd to hoe my Corn with Billy. P.M. Mrs. Winchester here, and requests me to write a Letter to her son John Chamberlin at Stockbridge, which I gratify'd her in. She also gave us a melancholly Account of the Conduct of Mrs. Prentice and her Party.

14. Mr. Batheric Shews himself one of a mutinous Spirit against Military Officers—this was in some Conversation I had occasionally with him near the Meeting House.

15. Read 2 Sam. 9. Preach'd on Isa. 44, 5, a and p.m. Lieutenant Bruce's wife ill: was pray'd for.

16. Variously hinder'd from visiting Mrs. Bruce. Chiefly was disappointed of what I expected from Mr. Bruce, an Horse to ride on to them.

17. My Son Ebenezer's Wife, with her young Child, and my Dauter Lucy rode in my Chair to Brookfield. Rode to Mr. Martyns and with him to Bolton, to Ministers Meeting—Messers. Cushing, Seccomb and Morse all that were at Mr. Goss's besides us. N.B. Mr. Morse perswaded in his Mind that God will remarkably bring down his Enemies and gave us a Concio to that Purpose. My Daughter Elizabeth snd Lucy rode to Brookfield in my Chair. Lodg'd at Mr. Goss's.

18. Mr. Stone and Mr. Mellen[4] came. I having never preach'd at Bolton, was urg'd to preach the Lecture, Seeing Mr. Barrett[5] who was appointed to do it was absent, and it being a remarkable

Juncture of the Forces marching to Providence to take Ship there, and many moving westward, and the Preparations ripening apace for the Expedition against Crown Point, I preach'd on Josh. 7, 4, 13. P.M. Mr. Martyn and his Wife were my Company back as far as their House, where, because of the Storm (of Rain) prevailing I Stop'd and lodg'd.

19. I return'd home. Attended a Catechetical Exercise to Young Men (about 24 of them) and afterwards visited Mrs. Bruce in her illness.

20. Ebenezer finishes Weeding. Billy comes home Sick from thence.

21. Dr. Willson[6] of Hopkinton having visited Mr. Daniel Warrin, return'd and din'd here.

22. Read Sam. 10. Preach'd a.m. on Eccl. 12, 13. P.M. read Isa. 46, and preach'd from number 8. N.B. made Some use of 2 pages of Sermon on Tit. 2, 6, viz. part of page 15, all 16, and part of 17. Deliver'd also 12 Articles of Religion which I recommended to Young People especially. N.B. a great number of Bills for Prayer and Thanks—but p.m. I happen'd to forget to take Notice of two of them that were put up then. They were Lieutenant Bruce's for his Wife; and Mr. Eliphalet Adams on occasion of the Death of his Mother: Lieutenant Bruce came into my House, and the Storm abroad was great, Thunder, Lightening, and Rain. Yet the Storm of Brother Bruce's Passions was more grievous; uttering many bitter and grievous Things; neither could I at all lay his Passionate Heat by anything I could Say. He went away talking and in a Rage, notwithstanding it was the Sabbath, and the Storm which Should have Struck Terror, into each of our Hearts. I could not Suffer him to go away in Such a Frame. I put on my Great Coat, and went to the Meeting House, ready to declare it was not with Design that I omitted the Note, but through forgetfullness—as I went I Spake to him at the Stables to Mollifie him—and entreated him and all others that were there to go into the Meeting House; but neither of them did. When I got into the Meeting House I was Somewhat out of Breath by my running through the Rain. There were many more in the Meeting House (probably) than I expected: Yet I then conceiv'd it best for the prevention of further Mischief to declare that it was thro my Infirmity and no otherwise that his Case was Neglected: I also mention'd to them the Reason of my coming to Speak of it to them, viz. the violent Anger which he was in, and continued in, though I did all in my Power to Compose and Satisfie him: and that he assur'd me he would never bring me any Papers (to desire Prayers) any more. When I return'd from the Meeting House, he being Still at the Stables, I Stop'd there again and there labour'd to pacifie him: but all was in Vain. So that I left him with telling him that I had done and Said enough (and indeed it was too much) I would not trouble my Self any more. This was a just Chastizement from God upon me, for my own Sloth and Negligence! the Lord be mercifull to me a Sinner! Mr. Elizer Rice's Wife Stop'd here because of the Storm and Supp'd with us.

23. I made it my Business to Visit Mrs. Bruce. But went to Mr. Adams's first, because he was poor. N.B. I Sent by the widow Beeman to Mr. Eliphalet Adams, that it was only thro forgetfullness that his Case was omitted in the Prayer. I visited the Widow Beaman also. As to Lieutenant Bruce, he now receiv'd me civily—no word of yesterday; only when I parted while I had him by the Hand I told him I would not have any Difficulty between him and me, and he answer'd Smiling, "with all my Heart." At Eve was at Captain Maynards. Lieutenant Maynard pitches upon Friday for Breaking up for Me. N.B. My Dauters Elizabeth and Lucy not return'd yet. Alpheus and Abner Newton a.m. draw off Stones from the Ground behind the Meeting House, with Six oxen. 2 Yoke Abners, and one Yoke Neighbour Zebulon Rice's.

24. Rode out to the Southward on the Affair of my Breaking up—and went to Mr. Jonah Warrins to See his Dauter Sarah, who yet remains under Disorders: To Deacon Bonds (whose wife lies in) and I din'd there: to Ensign Millers and had Some free discourse with him upon Original Sin, divine Decrees etc.: to

---

[2] An early settler of Westborough who had served as selectman.

[3] Mrs. Solomon Prentice of Grafton, at other times known as an "immortal."

[4] The Reverend John Mellen of Sterling.

[5] The Reverend Samuel Barrett of Hopkinton.

[6] John Wilson, the physician.

Captain Fays who is to lead in my Team next Friday, but he was not at Home. I find tis wish'd I had not troubled myself So much about Lieutenant Bruce's Anger last Lords Day.

25. My Wife and I, after Lucy came home with the Chair (N.B. she and Elizabeth came from Brookfield Yesterday) rode to See Lieutenant Bruce's Wife; and went to Mr. Timothy Warrins Raising of one Barn and removing another. Did not get home till late. N.B. Billy, tho drooping began to Mow a little. Thomas has his Fits of Fever and Ague yet. Dr. Joshua Smith extremely ill.

26. Mr. Benjamin Tainters Wife being in Travail, and like to expire sends in all haste to me to visit here. I rode there, and pray'd with her. After a few Pains more She was deliver'd of a Son. We gave Thanks to God, and at her Desire we Sang Gods Praise; Singing Ps. 116, 1–7.

27. We broke up about an Acre and half, behind the Meeting House. Our Team was of 20 Oxen. Captain Fay with 4. Lieutenant Brigham with 4. Deacon Bond 2. Lieutenant Tainter 2. Mr. Zebulon Rice 2. Ensign Miller 2. Mr. Samuel Hardy 2. My son Ebenezer 2. The Men who came were Captain Fay, Lieutenant Brigham, Lieutenant Maynard, Isaac Miller, the Lads were Thomas Bond, Joseph Rice son of Mr. Ebenezer Rice and had Lieutenant Maynards Plough. Lieutenant Maynard also at his Cost hir'd Mr. John Rogers p.m. to work for me among them. At Eve Captain Maynard Sent Quarter Veal and Several Pounds of Butter—all this was given freely.

28. Both Thomas and Billy not well.

29. I read 2 Sam. 11, and preach'd on Eccl. 12, 13. P.M. read Ps. 51, 17 before the Fast, fearing least I Shall be absent from here on that Solemnity. N.B. I read the Same Ps. publickly. And gave Notice at Eve to the Congregation that it was uncertain whether I Should be at home the ensuing Fast by reason of what I had engag'd before I knew anything of the Fast. Mrs. Mercy Chamberlin from Stockbridge here and lodges here.

30. Set out a little before Sun rise on my Journey to Groton; leaving Billy ill of (I Suppose) the Fever and Ague. Broke fast at Mr. Martyns, and call'd and baited at Mr. Goss's—din'd at Mr. Seccombs—supp'd and lodg'd at Mr. Trowbridge's.[7] It rain'd hard great part of the p.m. and was long detain'd by it—partly at Mr. John Stone's in Groton.—and I stop'd at Captain John Stevens's (late of Townshend, now in Groton). N.B. Mr. Lull there before me. N.B. The New Meeting House in Groton, a Superb Edifice and cost the Town above 13000£ old Tenor.

### JULY, 1755

1. Set out from Groton with Captain John Stevens Esquire, and rode to Townshend. Mr. Lull goes to Lieutenant Taylor in Townshend for the Plott of the Land which Mr. Lull would give me in Equivalence for the 70 acres which I lost; and he tells me that it lies on Pearl Hill about 2½ Miles from Lunenbourg Meeting House. Captain Stevens and I din'd at Mr. Hemenways. P.M. when Mr. Lull and Lieutenant Taylor (whom Lull had chose for his Arbitrator) came, and we set to the Business. But instead of the Lotts being on Pearl Hill as abovesaid, and as Lull had always told me, it was found in the Plott to be probably five Miles farther off, being 7 or 8 Miles from Lunenbourg Meeting House, and therefore I was dissatisfy'd with it. It was therefore agreed that Lull Should not only give me a Deed of his third Division, but of his Sixth also, and if they Should appear to be both of them more than an Equivalence for the 70 Acre Lot and my Dammages and Disappointment—also my Expences, which Mr. Lull Should have born in finding the Bounds of the 100 Acre Lott, then I engag'd by writing to pay as the Arbitrators Should judge. I also gave him from under my Hand to Quitt my Claim to the 70 Acres as Soon as I Should have my Equivalence for it in the Judgment of the Arbitrators. Said Lull accordingly gave me a Deed of the Said 2 Divisions, one containing 62 Acres and the other 35 Acres, which Captain Stevens took the Acknowledgement of. And we agreed that Since we could not view them to Day—and So not this Journey—The two Gentlemen above Said Should take a Time and View them and Judge of them when

they could with best Convenience. I pay'd Captain Stevens 24/7 for this Day. I lodg'd at Mr. Hemingways—but it was my great Grief that Mr. Lull went away uneasy because I would not be[ar] my Part of the Charge (not only of Viewing the Lotts when they Should be found but likewise) of looking them up. Thus this troublesome Day finish'd. May God please to discover what was amiss, and forgive it!

2. Set out (from Mr. Hemenways[1]) and went to Lieutenant Taylors; who rode with me to Lunenbourg. Visit Mr. Stearns.[2] Meet with Mr. William Jones (Brother of Captain Elisha of Weston) who tells me he can assist us in finding the Lotts, and their Bounds which I have of Lull. Din'd at Reverend Mr. Harringtons at Lancaster. Arriv'd at Mr. Martyns before Night but tir'd and unprepar'd to preach to my own people. Lodge there.

3. Publick Fast on Occasion of the Expeditions to Crown Point etc. Mr. Martyn preach'd for me; and I for him. My Text Ps. 51, 11. May it be accompany'd with a divine Energy to the Eternal Salvation of all of us! Mr. Martyn preach'd a.m. on [blank]. P.M. on [blank]. I came home at Evening. Billy, as well as Thomas, laid up with the Fever and Ague. My Wife tells me that Mr. Hezekiah Pratt and 14 others came last Tuesday P.M. and hoed my Corn.

4. Mr. Twitchell mows for me near my House, part of the Day and gives it. Captain Codman of Charleston was poison'd lately by a Negro. My Son Thomas has his Fitts yet, and Billy grows worse. May God prepare us for his Sovereign Will! At Evening Mr. Baldwin here. N.B. Mr. Beeton broke up his acre joining to me. He had 16 or 18 Cattle.

5. Mr. Baldwins Horse had got away in the Night; an Horse of Value; So that he is in Perplexity for Some Time this morning, but after a while finds him in the Burying Place.

6. Read 2 Sam. 12. Preach'd on Isa. 65, 24, a. and p.m. on Occasion of the Reduction of Chignecto, and Several other Places by Land by General Monkton, Winslow etc. and the Taking Several French Men of War by Admiral Boscawen on our Seas.

7. Mr. Jonathan Bellows's wife here complaining of Messers. Belknap and Chamberlin; at Eve They here inveighing against her.

8. Mr. Samuel Hardy mow'd here at home for me. My wife and I rode to t'other House and din'd there. Both Thomas and Billy their Fitt of Fever and Ague.

9. Little John taken ill—vomits, is feverish etc. I rak'd Hay which Mr. Hardy mow'd. N.B. Mr. John Brighams wife here and complains to me of the Church of Shrewsbury. I reprov'd her for her Disquietment with Mr. Cushing; and shew'd her her Duty towards the Church.

10. Samuel Harrington junior comes and mows instead of Mr. Moses Twitchell. Mr. Jonas Twitchell also Comes and mows.

11. Great Rains—all Hay making Suspended—Indian Corn generally very low. Many persons here and interrupting me. Mrs. Winchester here about her Dauter Chamberlins going to live at her Uncle Jonathan Brown's in Watertown in her Circumstances—both Pregnant and languishing; they being much displeas'd with it. At her Request I write a Letter to her son at Stockbridge.

12. Mr. Jonas Twitchell comes and rakes and Carts about 10 Cocks of Hay from the Island. N.B. Mr. Nurse's Team.

13. By Means of both my Sons Illnesses I have been so taken off from my studies that I was oblig'd to use some old Preparations part of the Day. A.M. read 2 Sam. 13, and gave in place of a Sermon, a long Exercise in Exposition. P.M. read Heb. 10 and preach'd on number 22. Mrs. Martyn Sick.

14. My Wife visits Mrs. Martyn p.m. Thomas his Fitts, Billy a little better.

15. My Wife and I rode to Boston. Call'd at Mr. Stone's, who was gone. We din'd at Colonel Buckminsters. N.B. Mr. Barrett of Hopkinton with us. We put up the Mare and Chair at Procters,

---

7 The Reverend Caleb Trowbridge of Groton, Mass.

1 The Reverend Phinehas Hemenway of Townsend.
2 The Reverend David Stearns.

and walk'd to Brother Samuels where we lodg'd. All our Friends are as well as usual. D.G.

16. My Brother Samuel rode with me to Cambridge, it being Commencement. N.B. Brother Champney is involv'd in Mr. William Fletchers Ruin. N.B. No Boston Scholar in the Class who take their first Degree to Day. I was almost melted with the Heat. Return'd to Boston at Night, my Brother Samuel with me; and my wife being at his House, I lodg'd there again.

17. Made several Visits among my Relations and Friends, particularly to Mr. John Osborn, a relation of my former Wife's. I attended the public Lecture. Young Mr. Checkley[3] preach'd—his Text Ps. 20, 7. He had importun'd me to preach, but I refus'd—din'd at Mr. Foxcrofts.[4] Mr. Conant[5] and Dr. Rogers of Ipswich din'd there also. I went to See Mr. Oxenbridge Thatcher, who had my Kinswoman Hearsys Case in his Hands: and he shewed me her Petition to the Governor and Council: assuring me he should do his utmost that she might be divorc'd. Nigh sunsetting we set out on our Journey—Reach'd Captain Thomas Prentice's (in time past of Lunenbourg and Lancaster) and we lodged there.

18. We din'd at Mr. Bridge's[6] in Framingham, call'd at Mr. Stone's, and at Lieutenant Bruce's: Mrs. Bruce being yet alive, and at 9 or 10 at night arriv'd at home—our House in safety (except Thomas and Billy's illness) D.G.

19. About break of Day came Mr. Forbush and Mr. Joseph Manning from Cambridge, and went to bed here. Mr. Joseph Woods brought a Complaint sign'd by Ebenezer Chamberlin and Mary (wife of Ithamar) Bellows; against Judith, wife of Jonathan Bellows. N.B. Lieutenant Bruce here and acknowledg'd he did amiss on June 22 and what he said was writ and sign'd.

20. Read part of 1 Cor. 11 from number 17. Preach'd again sermon on Heb. 10, 22, a. and p.m. Administer'd the Lords Supper. Deacons Bond and Jonathan Forbush junior and Mrs. Mary Stewart din'd here. P.M. read Ps. 139.

21. Visited Mrs. Bruce and Mrs. Martyn. They are both of them better. N.B. din'd at Mr. Bruce's. N.B. Mr. Jonas Twitchell denys me, tho he had led me along in Dependence upon him for mowing.

22. Read Mr. Hopkins's History of Housatunnock.[7] Mr. Ebenezer Chamberlins Wife here, and appears dissatisfy'd at my Lenity to Mrs. Judith Bellows: but hope she went away easy with my just Vindication.

23. Mr. Moses Twitchell came and mow'd for me. Part of the Day the remainder of the upland at the Island, and part in the Meadow near to it. Mr. Joseph Rice's wife and Joshua Lock's, came to See me but my Business in my Hay was so urgent I desir'd to be excus'd—and went to my raking. N.B. There was no Hand could be hir'd, and both my sons, Thomas and Billy incapable of any Labour at all.

24. In the Morning came Mr. Moses Twitchell to mow again—he undertakes to mow what remains to be mow'd (and which is the Chief of it) of my Newton Meadow, for two Days Work, to which I readily Consent. A.M. I visited Mrs. Judith Bellows. A most amazing scene open'd, when I enter'd into Examination of her and her Dauter Comfort. Mrs. Bellows constantly and very Solemnly Denys that she herself knows what became of the Things which Comfort stole from Belknaps: or that Comfort came by them in a dishonest way. Affirms that what she says is as true as that the Heavens are over her Head and the Earth under her Feet. Comfort with great sorrow and shame confesses She did take the Things in the Way complain'd of: and hopes and prays She shall never be left to such sin and folly again. She says that her Mother did know of it—know as much as She did of it: and knows what became of them. She can't Say her Mother did burn them but very seriously and solemnly declares that her

Mother told her She had burnt them, and can tell what her Mother said at the same time; and that was this, "But I will never be such a fool as to acknowledge it as You have done." Upon which the Mother added many bitter Reproaches;—persisting in denying what Comfort had affirm'd. I interrogated Mr. Bellows Strictly, whether from all that he had seen and heard about it, he did believe his wife had burnt the Things? He answered that he did. There arose very terrible Contradictions, and exceeding bitter Charges against him—so that I was oblig'd to turn to the Children and enquire of them—as, whether (since Mrs. Bellows complain'd bitterly of her Husbands beating her etc., whether) they had either of them seen their Father Strike their Mother? unless as He had Said he had been forc'd to do. This was prefac'd with Something very Solemn to them and expressing the great unhappiness of Such a Case etc.—They answer'd that they never had. The Woman oft times rose to Such transports of Rage, and behav'd so furiously that I was necessitated to rebuke her Sharply—(having us'd all manner of gentle Methods with her before), and was not able to do anything to any good purpose with her. To my great sorrow and grief left her: with serious Advice and Charge to the poor Man and his unhappy Children. May God of his infinite mercy and Goodness restrain, convince and recover her! P.M. held a Catechetical Exercise to Young Women. 30 Present. Joseph Chaddock kindly help'd me p.m. in Hilling and securing the upland Hay. Mr. Moses Twitchell lodges here.

25. Had Mr. Zebulon Rice's Teams, manag'd by his son Adam; and Mr. Twitchell loaded up all the upland Hay; which was safely brought home. About 10 Cocks. Mr. Thomas Twitchell came and work'd a while, but having rak'd about ½ dozen Cocks, and the Weather growing thick, they both broke off about 10 o'Clock and went home. It prov'd a very rainy Day. N.B. The Reverend Mr. Fish here, he having put a Bone out of Joint and been to a Bone-setters. We agree to Change next Sabbath, God Willing.

26. Mr. Solomon Prentice here. He din'd with us. I talk'd closely with him of his Wife's pretence to Immortality: he gives in to it, and thinks She is, as She declares, in the Millennium State. I also enquir'd strictly into their Sentiments and Practices respecting their Conjugal Covenant. He utterly denys Every Thing of uncleanness, Fornication or Adultery among them. P.M. I rode to Upton, Deacon Forbush in Company. Mr. Fish[8] came here.

27. I preach'd on Joel 3, 13. A.M. on Mat. 13, 39, p.m. I tarried there all night. Mr. Fish return'd home. O that the God of infinite Grace and Goodness would grant Success! but more especially that I might, myself, feel the Power and Efficacy of the Word of God and do Every Thing as reallizing Eternity.

28. I rose very Early and Brother Forbush and I return'd to Westborough. Lieutenant Tainter and a Young Man of his hiring—and two Boys also under him, in all four Hands, came and hill'd for me. There were also Ensign Harrington, Mr. Eleazer Whitney, Ezra Baker, Ebenezer Rice junior for Barnebas Newton, and William Bowman—nine in all—and they ended by baiting Time. Mr. Thomas Twitchel raking for me in the Newton Meadow, and Lieutenant Tainters two Boys help him. Both Thomas and Billy drooping yet; and their Fitts follow them. Thomas's Yesterday and Billy's to Day.

29. Mr. Nurse going to Dr. Willson, I sent Billy with him. And he endur'd the Journey without Injury. Brought a Letter from Doctor to Me—with Medicines particularly a Vomit. Cortex-Elixir Vitr. and a Saline Infusion. Mr. Thomas Twitchell and Jedidiah Woods rak'd, cock'd, pol'd and Carted the rest of the Hay that was now ready at the Newton Meadow being 3 Load. Had Ebenezers Team for one and Mr. Nurse's gratis for the other. Towards Night went to see the Ministerial Meadow which is now brown but I have No body to cut it.

30. Great Rains, a.m.

31. Neighbour Nurse very ready to help and oblige me in my little Husbandry. One Mr. Marshal of Somers, a Separate Teacher here. P.M. I rode in the Chair to Mr. Thomas Twitch-

[3] The Reverend Samuel Checkley, Jr., minister of the Second Church of Boston.
[4] The Reverend Thomas Foxcroft.
[5] Sylvanus Conant, the minister of Middleborough.
[6] The Reverend Matthew Bridge.
[7] Samuel Hopkins, *Historical Memoirs, Relating to the Housatunnuk Indians* (Boston, 1753). This appeared later in different form as *An Abridgement of Mr. Hopkins's Historical Memoirs* (Phila., 1757), and *An Address to the People of New-England* (Phila., 1757). The Philadelphia imprints were by Benjamin Franklin.

[8] The Reverend Elisha Fish of Upton.

ells. Carry'd Sarah and Susan to get Gowns made. Went to Mr. Richard Kelly to get him to reap my Rye. We had a dark ride home, in the Chair, not without Considerable Danger.

### AUGUST, 1755

1. Only Breck and I to rake Barley. Thomas and Billy yet ill.

2. Solomon Baker came in the Morning and with Mr. Nurse's Team got in my Barley: being but half a Load of it.

3. Read 2 Sam. 13, from number 19, and preach'd on the Same. P.M. read Ps. 20 and preach'd from number 7. May this be a most Seasonable Word! Both Thomas and Billy at Meeting a.m. but Billy had a fit p.m.

4. Mr. Richard Kelly and Mr. John Freeland came to reap for me: but it rain'd so hard they were prevented. They din'd with us. P.M. 3 hours they went to it and reap'd till night. I gave 'em 14/ old Tenor. Mr. Zebulon Rice work'd p.m. in taking out a Summer at my Stable which was broke, and put in One or Two others instead of it to bear up the Scaffold. N.B. Deacon Bond and Alpheus Newton help'd in Pitching off the Barley and Hay— and Mr. Ebenezer Chamberlin in Pitching it on again, to its place.

5. Mr. Moses Twitchell Mows for me at the Ministerial Meadow, and Mr. Daniel Warrin a.m. I visit old Captain Forbush: and Mrs. Bruce who is still sick. Was at Mr. Jonas Twitchells. He had given me Encouragement that he would work for me and he had told me he Should very gladly pay his Rates this Way—but when it came to, disappointed me. He allow'd he had said to me that he thought I might depend upon him. This was the Reason of my saying any thing to him. The Collector also having told me that this man would help me, I ask'd him now to help me but so much only of tomorrow as to bind and shock up my Rye (being but an acre and quarter of it) but he answered me indecently—So that I left him; and was much offended with him. Went to Mr. Rody Smiths, who was also to have work'd for me; but neither could I get him. N.B. I din'd at Mr. John Rogers. Mr. Batheric and Ebenezer Forbush reap'd the piece which the Reapers Yesterday had left. I call'd to see my Children at t'other House. Neither Ebenezer nor his Wife, nor youngest Child, have been well of late. At Evening Messers. John Rogers and Rody Smith assisted by John and Silas Frost, gather'd up and bound my Rye, and Neighbour Rogers came with his Team and brought it home. This was done gratis. Mr. Moses Twitchell lodg'd here.

6. Rode to Deacon Bonds, Mr. Jonah Warrins and to Mr. Barachias Morse's. P.M. Mr. Moses Twitchell, Jonathan Bond junior and Levi Warrin rake in the Ministerial Meadow. Billy and Lucy rode over to Mr. Martyns[1] and return'd at Eve. Billy no fit to Day.

7. Can't get any Body to Cart my Hay from the Ministerial Meadow, though I have taken a great deal of Pains. P.M. preach'd at Lieutenant Tainters on Mat. 13, 39. My wife, Thomas and Billy there. N.B. Mr. Francis Gardner[2] keeps school at the School House.

8. My Son Ebenezer went with his Team, and Moses Nurse with his, to the Ministerial Meadow, and brought thence a Load apiece of my Hay. But did not get home with it till nigh 10 o'Clock. At Eve Rain. Mr. Ebenezer Millers Wife was here and Examin'd.

9. Thomas and William are Somewhat better and Stronger. Blessed be God for it!

10. Read 2 Sam. 14. Preach'd on Ps. 20, 7. P.M. read Ps. 119, parts 7, 8, 9. Repeated Sermon on Ps. 119, number 54.

11. Deacon Bond tells me the News is confirm'd of General Bradock's Defeat and Death. A most Sorrowfull Stroke! may God of his infinite Mercy Sanctifie it to this Sinfull Provoking People! and be mercifull to His Servant Shirley[3] and the Forces with him; that they may not be dismay'd when they Shall hear of

it! Barachias and Seth Morse came and mow'd in the ministerial Meadow.

12. Seth Morse (having lodg'd here) works again for me, and Neighbour Moses Nurse fetch'd home one Load from the Ministerial Meadow. P.M. Mr. Francis Gardner made us a Visit.

13. Barachias and Seth Morse work for me—they get home 3 Load, 2 Load by half after 12. P.M. they rake and bring home another Load at Eve. Those were brot by our own Team: Ebenezers Oxen and my Mare. Having heard that my Young Cattle in the woods, had stray'd from their Keeper, I wrote several Letters and Advertisements about them.

14. Old Mr. Maynard makes another Will. Lieutenant Maynard brought me present of Fish from Mr. John Breck of Boston—and himself presents me a Load of Hay out of the Meadow on Rutters Brook. 'Kias and Seth mow at the ministerial Meadow again and this is the last, which they accomplish a.m. but because it was cloudy and they could not rake up what they had mow'd; they return'd home and P.M. reap'd my Wheat by the Barn, and got it in. N.B. Mr. John Chamberlin of Stockbridge here, and wants to hire part of my t'other House for his Wife, that She may ly in there: but I am not free for lest it Should hinder the Sale of the House. Am oblig'd to ride about to get a Team to Cart home my Hay. Receive a kind Letter from Mr. William Winter of Boston giving me a Clear Account of the Death of General Bradock, and the Defeat of the Forces with him on the fatal July 9th past, in their Expedition to Ohio.

15. 'Kias reaps for Ebenezer a.m. and for me in carting home Hay p.m. Seth work'd for me all Day. Had Mr. Pratts Team to bring home one Load, and with Mr. Samuel Fay juniors Oxen they brought home another. And this finish'd my Haying for this Year. Those Young Men agree to have 17/ per Day—I am indebted to them for 9 Days £7.13.0 Old Tenor. N.B. Mr. Ebenezer Chamberlin here again about Mrs. Bellows, urging for Church-Meeting.

16. Billy reaps a few Oates. Rain p.m.

17. Read 2 Sam. 15. Preach'd on Isa. 42, 23, 24, 25 on account of the Defeat etc. Sir Gardner din'd here. P.M. read latter part of Deut. 27, 26. I acquainted the Church (in hearing of the Congregation) that I had receiv'd a Complaint against Judith, wife of Jonathan Bellows—and appointed a Church Meeting to hear it, tomorrow come Sennight, at 2 p.m., and all concern'd must look upon themselves bound to attend.

18. Mr. Dunlop came to thrash my Wheat—finds it too damp. Thrashes only the out Sides of the Sheaves and leaves them to be dry'd. He with Billy reaps Oates. Ensign Harrington here a.m. Mr. James Flagg of Upton p.m. At Eve sent a Letter to Mrs. Bellows.

19. I rode to Marlborough. Din'd at Mr. Smiths.[4] Hear that Dr. Breck[5] was in Marlborough over the Sabbath, and went out of Town but this Morning to return home, and has not come to See his Sister. At Deacon Tainters and at Mr. Henry Barns's— Improve him to help me to a Chap for my old Place. Return home in the Eve.

20. Mr. John Freeland Taylor comes to work here to make me a Jacket and pair of Breeches. Mr. Dunlop also comes to take Care of my Wheat, drie and thrash some of it. Hear that Some of my young Cattle that had Stray'd away, are come to my Sons.

21. Mr. Freeland at work here. My oldest Steers come home. Very Cloudy Weather, unfit for the In-gatherings. Mrs. Judith Bellows here—also Mr. Joseph Rice's Wife. Thomas and William Somewhat worse again.

22. Mr. Freeland still here. My son grow somewhat better.

23. Mr. Freeland finish'd his work for me; and Something for Thomas. He ask'd me but 26/ old Tenor for all he had done, this Turn, for me—and having din'd he left us.

24. Read 2 Sam. 16. Preach'd on Isa. 42, 23, 24, 25, both a. and p.m. May God grant us Grace to attend to both his Word and Providence!

25. The Church met today on account of Mrs. Judith Bellows (wife of Jonathan Bellows) being Complain'd of by Mr. Ebenezer

---

[1] The Reverend John Martyn of Northborough.

[2] (Harvard 1755). He became the minister of Leominster, 1762–1814.

[3] Governor William Shirley of Massachusetts, was a lieutenant-general and commander-in-chief of British forces in America at this time.

[4] The Reverend Aaron Smith.

[5] Samuel Breck, the physician of Springfield, was the son of the late Reverend Robert Breck of Marlborough.

Chamberlin and Mrs. Mary Bellows (wife of Ithamar Bellows).[6] Before Meeting, Mr. Batheric gave me fresh Trouble about Singing (in the assembly) triple Time tunes; and would have Me lay this before the Church, but I told him we had so much Business today, it was not likely there would be Time for it. Lieutenant Tainter Carry'd to Boston 2 hind Quarters of Veal for me to some Friends there—Mr. Solomon Woods kill'd it—and took a Quarter for him and Lieutenant Tainter in token of Gratitude to them both.

26. [No entry.]

27. Remarkable Plenty Pidgeons—the Neighbours take them in their Netts in great Numbers.

28. Public Fast on Account of Gods Frown upon us in the Expedition to Ohio, and Still to Supplicate divine Favour in the Other Expeditions—viz. to Niagara and Crown Point. And O that we had a Spirit of Prayer that we might Cry aloud to God for His infinite Mercy—as our Necessity is! For in Him may we Confide, and in His Name go forth against our Enemies.

29. Mr. Martyn and his Wife to my great Pleasure at all other Times, but now to my great Interruption, made us a visit. Deacon Bond 'Listing orders.

30. I had not time to prepare any more than one Sermon for besides the Interruptions of Company I was much disquieted with toothach.

31. Read 2 Sam. 17. Preach'd on Luke 2, 25. The Consolation of Israel. Administered the Lord's Supper. Deacon Burnap and his Brother Daniel at Communion with us, Mr. Barrett being at Boston. Deacon and his Wife and Dauter Hitty were at Dinner here, also Mrs. Chamberlin of Stockbridge, who is Come to board at my sons. P.M. I repeated Sermon on Eph. 1, 3, to page 12. Took in also the 7th and 8th articles—and the Reflections in the Close of all.

## SEPTEMBER, 1755

1. Mrs. Chamberlin Sends for Mrs. Forbush, and women are gather'd for her Help. N.B. My Son has the Trouble and fatigue, tho unable to undergo it.

2. Rode (with Mr. Martyn and Stone) to Chauxit: the Association meeting at Mr. Mellen's.[1] I deliver'd a Concio on Gal. 1, 15, 16. Lodg'd at Mr. Mellen's.

3. The ministers (most of us) went to Mount Wachusett. Mrs. Mellen and her Sister Robbins with us and Mrs. Mellen had a Fall from her Horse but recover'd. We refresh'd ourselves on the Top of the Mount, Having carry'd up Bacon, Bread and Cheese, Rum. In Descending from the Summitt we stop'd a little and Sang a Stanza to the Praise of the Great Creator. N.B. A great multitude of persons happen'd to go up to the Mount to Day. We saw many Horses at the Bottom, and at Mr. Keys's. N.B. I went to Mr. Jonathan Wilders enquiring after my Young Cattle which have stray'd but Mr. Wilder was not at home. When I return'd to Mr. Mellens he came to me, and told me my Cattle he believ'd were at his Neighbours and promis'd he would take Care of them. N.B. my Mare was very lame by reason of her loosing one of her fore shooes, which exceedingly incommoded me, and retarded the whole Company. This Man had such Benevolence, Compassion and Generosity that he took off one of his own Horse's shooes, and sav'd and Straiten'd the Nails to put them into mine, which he so fasten'd on that it held me till I got to Westborough: a nobleness that was notic'd

by all, and may he be suitably rewarded for it! A Number of us in returning homeward visited the Mine[2]—digging by Mr. Christian Angel—a German from Ypres a Town on the River Rhine. Messers. Cushing, Martyn, Stone and I lodg'd at Mr. Morse's:[3] but I was greatly fatigu'd and had but little Sleep.

4. Mr. Stone and I din'd with Mr. Martyn at his House. When I return'd found that Mrs. Chamberlin (at my Sons) was deliver'd of a son on the 2nd, and yesterday, Mr. Willard Wheeler carry'd a Letter from me, to Captain Stevens of Groton, Signifying my acquiescence in his dropping the Arbitration between Lull and me: and Lieutenant Taylors Plan of 3rd Division in Townshend.

5. [No entry.]

6. At Eve Mr. Stone came here, Mr. Buckminster[4] being to preach for him.

7. I rode to Mr. Martyns, leaving Mr. Stone to preach for me. Mr. Martyn was gone to Mr. Morse's, Mr. Morse to Mr. Davis, and Mr. Davis to Rutland for Mr. Buckminster. I preach'd on Isa. 42, 23, 24, 25, and on Gal. 1, 19, 16 former part. Return'd soon after Exercise because Mrs. Chamberlin was in a very low and dangerous Condition.

8. Visit Mrs. Chamberlin who is reviv'd a little. I am again endeavouring to carry on the tilling my now broke Land, by providing for the harrowing of it.

9. Visit Mrs. Bruce who is yet very low—visit Mrs. Gale; din'd at Mr. Jabez Snows. Visit Mrs. Judith Bellows—but find her much the same. Went to the other Familys in that Corner to get em to help me to Timber for my Kitchin.

10. Harrow my new Ground; with 8 Oxen, viz. my sons, and Lieutenant Forbush, Samuel Forbush, and Mr. Rogers's. Mr. Rogers and John Frost were the Men that manag'd it. Mr. Benjamin Nichols work'd for me in Clearing at the Newton Meadow. Mrs. Lock here with her Confession. Mrs. Whipple and her sister and Mrs. Pratt made a Visit; Each with a Cheese. Nichols lodges here. Lieutenant Tainter kill'd a large Calf for me and carry'd part to Boston.

11. Many of the Soldiers of Captain Woods Company march being on their Journey to Crown Point. I held a Catechetical Exercise design'd to Young Men—but there were only 3 Youths came besides my sons Thomas and William. Nichols at work for me in Clearing etc. Captain Wood and Lieutenant Bond here as they went off. I deliver'd Lieutenant Bond Mr. Meads Almost Christian[5] for the use of those who go with him and into the Expedition from this Place. Esquire Charles Brigham here at Eve—I assist him in Making Return to Colonel Pollard of the Committment of poor Silas Rice.

12. It is a very dry Time; Water very low, and many low Grounds that at ordinary Times are wet, are now hard: and it is very hot like July. Mr. Nichols clearing still.

13. Mr. Gardner[6] of Stow having been at Windham brought from thence a copy of an Express from Albany that our Camp at Lake Sacrament was beset by French and Indians last Monday—and Men are very earnestly pushing along—many come to hear the Express.

14. I read 2 Sam. 18. Preach'd on Luke 2, 25—and p.m. because of the Recruits for Crown Point I preach'd on Ps. 18, 34, first part and us'd with variations, omissions and additions Sermon on 2 Tim. 2, 3 from Page 11.

15. Training Day—to See who would List, or if not Sufficient offers, then to press for Crown Point. I din'd with the Officers at Mr. Ebenezer Rice's. N.B. Another Post from Albany who informs there was a Smart Engagement last Monday but that our people drove off the Enemy, took their General, and slew (as I

[6] The following appears in the Westborough Church Records, Aug. 25, 1755. "The Church met (having been timely warn'd) to hear a Complaint Sign'd by Ebenezer Chamberlin and Mary (Wife of Ithamar) Bellows, and bearing Date July 18 last, against Judith (Wife of Jonathan) Bellows, all of them Members of this Church, setting forth in substance, that the Said Judith hath walk'd very Disorderly and Contrary to the Rules of the Gospel—In particular respecting her Daughter Comfort, who has confess'd her taking away certain Things from a Neighbour feloniously and that her Mother would not let her return said Things when She would have done it: and that said Comfort also declar'd her Mother had burnt them. The Complaint exhibited further that said Judith was guilty of False speaking about those Things etc. After prayer the Complaint was read, and the Partys respectively, and the Witnesses, were fully heard—the Church voted, 1. Respecting the first part of the Complaint that altho we cannot say She is guilty of Burning the Things referred to in the Complaint, yet we find upon all that has been Said, that She has Conducted in a very Evil Manner respecting her Daughter under her Guilt; and in that whole Affair respecting Said Things, and 2. Voted, as to the Second part of the Complaint, namely, her False speaking, that is Supported. This was voted universally. The Pastor read those votes to said sister Judith, and solemnly laid the Evil before her, and Call'd her to Repentence . . ."

[1] The Reverend John Mellen of Sterling.

[2] It was at about this time that various shafts were sunk into a hill in Sterling in anticipation of finding some mineral of value. A Brief History of Sterling (n.p., 1931), pp. 60–61, comments: ". . . Christian Angel a miner from Sweden was the principal workman." Specimens of ore were found to be without value and the mine abandoned. Fragments found in the twentieth century include plumbago, nickel, sulphates of copper and iron, garnets and carbonite of iron.

[3] The Reverend Ebenezer Morse of Boyslton.

[4] Joseph Buckminster of Rutland.

[5] Matthew Mead, The Almost Christian Discovered: or, the False Professor Tryed and Cast (Boston, 1730). Another edition was published in Boston in 1742.

[6] The Reverend John Gardner.

think) 1000 of them besides, to the Loss of 130 (as judg'd) of our own; and Colonel Ephraim Williams,[7] Colonel Titcomb[8] of Newbury, among the last. About 60 of ours wounded—and General Johnson[9] himself has a Ball lodg'd in his Thigh. May God be glorify'd for what has been thus far done, and prepare us for further Favours!

[The following is from the Natalitia, dated Sept. 5, 1755.]

Scarce any one has ever had greater Cause to bless and praise God and yet what Heart so Stupidly Sensless and ungratefull! and who that have Such Reason to grieve and mourn for Sin and wickedness, among all that profess to have any apprehensions of their Conditions, is So remote from this Duty! (My Flight is only to Jesus who gives both Repentance to Israel and Remission of Sins! O for the Spirit of Christ to qualifie me; and the Merits of Christ, His Righteousness, and his Sacrifice; for acceptance with God! My infinite unworthiness does not drive me to Despair, while the Sacred Scriptures assure me that the Blood of Christ cleanseth from all sin; and He ever lives to make Intercession for His People—and among them are Some of the Chief of Sinners.)

17. Mr. Nichols came to Work—he thrash'd Rye—Billy with him. N.B. Many Men who have enlisted for the 2nd Regiment of Recruits for Crown Point meet at Captain Fays to be viewed by the Muster Master Captain Josiah Richardson, but he came not—so that their assembling was in vain.

18. Mr. Nichols cleans up Rye and remainder of Wheat which Dunlop thrash'd, and mow'd Bushels in the New broke up Land. I catechiz'd at Mr. Joslins. After Catechizing came Mrs. Judith Bellows and was far from penitent. I told her I was offended with her myself—and this for two Things—namely, her ill Carriage to her Husband, and her not adhering to the Truth. As to the first, She had the assurance to Challenge me upon it. I therefore apply'd to Mr. Joslin who Soon confronted her, particularly with her Conduct that very Day that I had been at their House the time before Last. Mrs. Joslin also join'd with her Husband in it. Yet She remain'd incorrigible. I visited Mrs. Bruce and pray'd with her. Her Case is now fear'd to be desperate. When I return'd home met Brother Hicks[10] and his Dauter Hannah here. N.B. He has been perplex'd at Boston, by Mr. Elijah Collins, by means of a Bond of Mr. Oliver Wards in which Brother Hicks was also jointly bound. They lodg'd here. N.B. one of their Horses Sadly lame.

19. Brother Hicks and his Dauter endeavour to go home; but the lame Horse is very lame this morning. N.B. We have been much troubl'd by ten Hogs of Captain Samuel Forbush, which get into my Corn Field. Nicols still at work for me—mows bushes in the design'd Rye Field.

20. Nicols a.m. builds Some stone Wall in the Lane behind the Meeting House.

21. Read 2 Sam. 19. Preach'd on Luke 2, 25. Sir Gardner din'd here. Read p.m. 2 Cor. 3, and prach'd on number 6, designing to begin again to Read the New Testament. I insisted on that Expression in the number, repeating my first Exposition with additions.

22. In the Morning Mr. Jeduthun Baldwin here—he came last Night—is going to Crown Point—and takes leave accordingly. N.B. He tells me the Negro Man and Negro Woman who murder'd Captain Codman[11] of Charlestown, were Executed last Thursday, at Cambridge.[12] The Man was hang'd, and was afterwards to be hang'd in Irons on Charlestown Neck: the Woman was burnt to Death, a frightfull Spectacle! May all hear and fear! especially to be punish'd Eternally in the Flames of Hell May my own Soul be suitably affected with the Thought! Our

Parish met to Day to grant my Support, as they call it. I sent in a Memorial, that considering the Troubles [of] the present Time (by the War) I was willing to take up with what they did for me, as to sallery and Wood, last Year, if they would do it chearfully—but that I could not, with less. In Return they Sent me a Committee (Mr. Grow and Ephraim Bruce) with their vote in the following words viz. "(thirdly) Voted and granted to the Reverend Mr. Parkman our Minister for his Support for the Current Year the Sum of thirty two Pounds Lawfull Money including his Firewood." Sign'd by Thomas Forbush Moderator. This I did not well understand. The Committee Said the Precinct meant to make my whole sallery and Support to be in old Tenor £460. I told em I did not know what my Sallery was, if there [was] needed so much support to make it up that Sum. They said I had better go to the Precinct or write to them. I chose this latter—and accordingly wrote to them desiring them to let me know what they Suppos'd I meant by Support for I conceiv'd my Sallery was 55£ Lawfull Money. The Committee carry'd my writing to the people. I remark'd also to the Committee that this was not So much as they did last Year for there was here no Subscription for the wood. They went, but the meeting broke up without doing any thing further—either in answer to me—or about the Wood.

23. Brother Hicks here, going to Boston again on the Affair of Elijah Collins: it being left to Arbitration. N.B. We are exceedingly troubl'd by Captain Forbushes Hogs at my Cook Field—10 of them and have been in nigh 10 Times. I got Mr. Ebenezer Forbush to mend my Fence—and yet they got in. I went to the Captain's and they promis'd to Shutt them up.

24. I went to Mr. Whipples to See how my Slit work Boards etc. lay—Solomon Baker brought a Load—all the Braces were missing and some other sticks. Was at Mrs. Hitty Rice's, and din'd with her. To Day there is a Muster of Soldiers for Crown Point, at Captain Maynards—the Muster Master being Captain Josiah Richardson of Sudbury.

25. I made a Visit to Mr. Seth Rice's. He was not at Home. He is gone to Dr. Smiths. His Family greatly distress'd for him, being grown worse of late—pain'd in Body as well as discompos'd in Mind. Dr. Smith[13] came there. We rode together to see Lieutenant Stephen Maynard who is Sick of a Fever. His Son Antipas also Sick and the Family in much Trouble. Pray'd with them. N.B. Josiah Lock, of the Same Family, Set out to go to Crown Point.

26. A Great Frost last Night. Mr. Thomas Stoddard promoted to be a Captain of a Company going to Crown Point, was here and his son Boardman with him. N.B. I sent home the Three Universal Magazines[14] by him, which I borrow'd of Esquire Steel[15] of Leicester. Exceedingly encumber'd and Disappointed with respect to my design'd Kitchin—no Timber comes from Joslins as I expected—and my Field which I broke up in June—can't get the Fencing Stuff. My Son Ebenezer, instead of bringing Stuff here as I expected, goes to work for Mr. How without saying a word to me of it, which greatly disappoints and troubles me. Brother Hicks returns from Boston and lodges here. Another Frosty night.

27. Call'd away at Night to visit Elijah Rice's Wife, (who now live within Upton Bounds) She had been deliver'd of one Child, which was living; but there was another of which She could not be deliver'd. They had Mrs. Forbush and Mrs. Clark—and had Sent to Dr. Greenleaf.[16]

28. I tarried till after midnight—got home between one and two o'Clock—was but poorly Capable of preaching. Yet I went through the Service of the forenoon reading 2 Sam. 20. Preach'd on Luke 2, 25. P.M. read part of the Chapter of the Gospel of St. Matthew. Read with some alterations and additions Number 2 of my Expositions. More than 16 Requests for Prayers—about half of them respecting those who went to Crown Point. Contribution for Mr. Jesse Maynard of the northside.

---

[7] Of Stockbridge.

[8] Moses Titcomb had played an important role in the capture of Louisburg in 1745. John J. Currier, "Ould Newbury" (Boston, 1896), pp. 464–473.

[9] Sir William Johnson, the superintendent of Indian affairs. Johnson's account of the campaign in New York appeared in The Boston Weekly News-Letter, Sept. 18, 1755.

[10] John Hicks of Sutton.

[11] John Codman.

[12] Aug. 19, 1755, "Phillis, a Negro woman, and Mark, a Negro Man, Servants to the late Capt. Codman . . . were found Guilty of poisoning their Master." The woman was sentenced to be "burnt to Death," the man to be hanged. The Boston Weekly News-Letter, Aug. 21, Sept. 18, 1755. A Boston broadside of 1755 called attention to the "untimely end" of these miscreants.

[13] Joshua Smith, the physician of Shrewsbury.

[14] Published in London beginning in June, 1747. Booksellers in Boston often advertised it for sale.

[15] Thomas Steel (Harvard 1730) was a businessman who served as town clerk and representative. In 1756 he was appointed judge of the Court of Common Pleas for Worcester County. See Washburn, Leicester, pp. 179–180, and Sibley, VIII, 783–785.

[16] Daniel Greenleaf, a physician of Boston.

29. Deacon Jonathan Forbush junior here. We Counted the money gather'd Yesterday—found it £21.3 7½ old Tenor.[17]

30. I visited the Widow of the late Thaddeus Gale, and Mr. Abijah Gale mourning for his Brother. Also visited Mr. Abraham Bond and Mrs. Hannah Warrin mourning the Loss of their Father. Visited Mrs. Bruce again, who now revives a little.

### OCTOBER, 1755

1. My Daughter Forbush came down last night to t'other House, and with her Mr. Joseph Manning; they came here today. Mr. Manning and I visited Lieutenant Stephen Maynard who is Grown better, but he has two Children Sick. N.B. Mr. Hezekiah Pratt and Mr. Kenny (for Mr. Nurse), dug stones for the Wall behind the Meeting House, and this was gratis.

2. Mr. Abijah Gale and Mr. Batheric came and began to Frame a Kitchin for me, on the Back of my New House.

3. Mr. Alpheus Newton begins to dig a Cellar way for my Kitchin. Mr. Dunlop and Mr. Beeton and his Boy work at levelling the Ground where the Kitchin is to stand. Messers. Gale, Batherick, Grow and Zebulon Rice at the Frame. An Hot Day. Mr. Edwards Whipple (with the Assistance of my Son William and Steers) brought a Load of Boards and Eight Braces.

4. Messers. Gale, Grow, Rice and Batheric work at the Frame.

5. Read 2 Sam. 21. Preach'd on Jer. 7, 23, a. and p.m.[1]

6. Mr. Ebenezer Forbush dug in my Cellar way for the new Kitchin. Messers. Gale, Zebulon Rice, and Batheric at Work on the Frame. Towards Night we Rais'd—No Hurt—Thanks to God. N.B. No Mr. Grow to Day.

7. Our Well affords very little Water. My sons Wife and Dauter Susanna ride to Watertown with my Mare in the Chair. Messers. Gale and Batheric at Work in rectifying the Frame and preparing the Principals—which are not yet put on. The Reverend Mr. Cushing here and din'd with me. Desires me to preach at a Private Fast at Shrewsbury next Tuesday on account of Mr. Samuel Wheelock[2] who is in a gloomy, delirious State, and lately cut this Throat, but not mortally.

8. No Body at Work. Disappointed about sowing my Field, north west of the Meeting House: Can't get up the Wall nor Rail-Fence.

9. Lecture on Eph. 1, 3. N.B. Mr. Grow work'd a.m. Mr. Manning with my Dauter Forbush at Eve from Cambridge and Boston. My Kinsman William Bowes Parkman generous in sending Me another Pamphlet concerning Affairs in America. This is the Present State of North America—of the Discoverys of the English and French Claims Rights and Possessions etc.,[3] and therewith he sent me a Letter handsomely written. A great Trouble to be straitened as to Water. My Wife daily in Pain and her Life much afflicted, as her Time approaches.

10. Messers. Gale, Grow, Rice. Still finishing the Frame of my Kitchin and various things about it. Ensign Harrington a Load of stones, from his own Home, to Stone my Cellar Way.

11. Gale and Rice a.m. My Dauter returns here at Eve from her Father Forbushes. Very Cold night and A.M. likewise.

12. There was a great Frost last Night: A Cold Day for this time of the Year. Read a.m. 2 Sam. 22. Preach'd on Hag. 2, 7, those words—The Desire of all Nations. Mr. Manning, Deacon Forbush, Sir Gardner and Mrs. Chamberlin (who has now got abroad again). P.M. omitted Reading—preach'd on Exod. 17, 12, latter part and 13 with reference to the Expeditions against the French and Indians. N.B. My Dauter Forbush was dismiss'd from our Church to Brookfield 2nd Church. Mr. Manning Still with us. My Wife so indispos'd she Stays at home p.m.

13. Rain. The Rain increases till it is a very Wet time. Mr. Manning and my Dauter Forbush here. Draw near as to Wood.

14. Rain Still a.m. About noon It began to Clear So that I undertook my Journey to Mr. Samuel Wheelocks in Shrewsbury to assist in the Exercises of a Fast there on the Account of his Melancholly. The assembly (which there was) met at Lieutenant Stones. Prayer was over before I got there, and the last Syllables of the Psalm were singing when I went in. Yet Mr. Cushing would not excuse me from Preaching. Text was Rom. 11, 33. N.B. Altho Mr. Wheelock would not Suffer the Exercises to be at his House, neither could I obtain to see him before I went to meeting. Yet after we had done, he sent his son to desire me to go to him and Pray with him: only with this Caution that nobody must go with me. I went and pray'd with him, but could hardly keep him with me. He thinks there is no Such Sinner as he is—that he has Committed the Sin unto Death; and this was the Reason why he was against the Exercises—because it is added "I do not say You Shall Pray for it." My Visit to him was Short. Mr. Cushing, his Wife and I stop'd at Mr. Braggs[4] (They went first and waited for me). There we had Some refreshment—which I needed, for I had had a very wet and worrying Journey. I return'd home before I slept; my Wife's Circumstances forbad my Staying. My Dauters, Forbush and Lucy and Mr. Manning went over to Mr. Martyns, and lodged there; tho they were also Sopp'd with the Rain. N.B. It was Training to Day, at Lieutenant Brighams, but his Invitation was too late for me to attend it. I was pre-engag'd to go to Shrewsbury.

15. Mr. Manning P.M. brought Lucy from Mr. Martyns; Molly remains there, but he lodges at t'other House. I wrote by him to Mr. Lull in which I desire him to Send his Deed of Townshend Rights, to be acknowledged and Recorded; and to accept of Mr. William Jones of Lunenbourg to be one of our Arbitrators instead of Captain John Stevens of Groton. Dauters Eliza and Susanna from Watertown.

16. My Son Thomas finishes the digging of a Cellar Way from the Kitchin. Mr. Benjamin Tainter brings me 4 Barrells of Cyder, gratis—one Barrell from his Father, another from Mr. Daniel Forbush, a Third from Ensign Harrington and one from Mr. Solomon Woods. All Gratis. Little John Sav'd from Drowning. Bill had dug an Hole in Neighbour Barnabas Newtons meadow in the Time of Drought, which was now fill'd with Water; into this John fell and Samuel pull'd him out. *D. Grates plurimas!*

17. Before it was quite light in the Morning Lieutenant Tainter came and brot a Load of Wood fearing we Should Suffer—whereas Timothy Warrin had brought a Load last Eve. My Sons Thomas, and William undertake to gather our Corn, but it rains hard before they got home one Load. My Wife in Pains, expecting her Hour for which the Lord mercifully prepare us! Her Pains continue at Times, yet we go to Bed—we lie till after midnight—when She grew so ill that I fetch'd Mrs. Forbush—and then Mrs. Baker, in the meantime Sending along 3 Mrs. Rices.

18. Ebenezer brought his Wife in the Morning—and Messers. Phinehas Hardy and Batherick came to work on my Kitchin Roof (boarding and Shingling). About 9, or between 9 and 10 o'Clock a.m. my wife was deliver'd of her ninth, and my fourteenth living Child: her fourth, and my Seventh Daughter—a perfect Child and Well; and especially my Wife in great Comfort. Blessed be the Name of God! May we have a due Sense of the divine Mercy (So utterly undeserv'd) and may we have Grace to Walk accordingly! I threw by the Preparations which I was making, as Soon as the Child was born, and set myself to prepare on Gen. 22, 14, tho under many Disadvantages. The Women din'd here with us, and then went home o'foot Except Mrs. Forbush who was waited on by William with an Horse. Rachel Pratt watches.

19. Read 2 Sam. 22 from number 26. In preaching I went on with the Repition (with Some Alterations) of Sermon on Eph. 1, 3. Mrs. Chamberlin din'd with us. P.M. Read Mat. 2. Preach'd on Gen. 22, 14, and baptiz'd my New-born Daughter, Anna

[17] This contribution was "for the Relief of Mr. Jesse Maynard who was lately burnt out." Westborough Church Records, Sept. 27, 1755.

[1] In the Westborough Church Records, Oct. 5, 1755, Parkman wrote, "Abigail, heretofore Maynard, now Lock (the wife of Joshua Lock) made a Confession of the Sin of Fornication, and was restored to Charity. She also own'd the Covenant and Grace, her Dauter, was baptiz'd."

[2] The son of a deacon of the same name. It was he who died in Shrewsbury, April 8, 1756, although it is not ascertainable that this was a case of suicide. Ward, Shrewsbury, pp. 465-466.

[3] [Huske, Ellis], The Present State of North America (London, 1755). A Boston reprint followed in 1755.

[4] Ebenezer Bragg, an early resident of Shrewsbury, was a carpenter.

Sophia. May a gracious God pardon us and accept our Offerings! Mrs. Pratt (wife of Neighbour Hezekiah) watches.

20. Very Rainy. Messers. Edwards and Benjamin Whipple din'd here. N.B. The last is become a Separate at Lambs Town. I had Some free Talk with him upon it. At Eve my wife has Pains in her Breasts and Smart in her Nipples to a great Degree. These forebode ill. Mr. Zebulon Rices Dauter Abigail draws her Breast. My Dauter Lucy watching.

21. Deacon Forbush is Stoning my Kitchin Cellar Way. Sarah Watch'd. My Wife got up on the 21.

22. Thomas and William cutt up and bring in 3 Turns of Corn from the Cook Field. A great Frost last Night. My Wife distress'd with her Nipples. She got up, but she grows weaker by Reason of the Childs sucking her when her Nipples are So Sore.

23. Cold, Bleak Season. Messers. Phinehas Hardy, Zebulon Rice and Edwards Whipple here Shingling my Kitchin Roof. Am straitned for Wood, being near out this Cold Weather.

24. A Number of Soldiers from Lake George—whom I interrogate of their state and understand there is a great Force of Canadians at the Narrows.

25. Storm of Rain and Snow—and We without Wood except Some Timber of Ebenezer Rice which he had condemn'd and given me.

26. Read 2 Sam. 23. Preach'd on Hagg. 2, 7, a. and p.m. Sister Forbush din'd here. O that God would bless the Exercises to my own Saving Advantage! and to the Eternal Good of all the hearers!

27. Deacon Forbush again at the stoning my Cellar way. Mr. Thomas Twitchell tends him. Receiv'd Letters of the 13 and 16 from Mr. Jeduthun Baldwin at Lake George. Other Letters are come also; all Signifying that the Army is not like to proceed against Crown Point this Winter.

28. Mr. Grow finishes the Covering of my Roof. Mr. Nurse puts on the Iron of the Wheel-barrow made by Mr. Edwards Whipple for me. Mr. Martyn and his Wife here and dine with us. They carry home my little John. Cornelius Biglow junior (who was here upon some Cooper Business) din'd here.

29. The Cold Air we have had produces Snow. A Considerable storm. My Dauter Susanna goes over to Mr. Martyns. In the Night I had a Turn of distressing Pain. God be thank'd I am out of Hell! May these Trials be Sanctify'd to me for my thorough awakening that I may flee from the dreadfull Wrath which is to come!

30. The storm of Snow continues and increases. It prevents Deacon Forbush coming to finish my Cellar Way: It prevents also the Young Women coming to the Catechetical Exercise appointed to be to Day. Receiv'd a Letter from Mr. John Parker of Southborough, now at Lake George.

31. Mr. Hall[5] and his Delegate here, in their return from a Council on Mr. Reeds[6] affair at Framingham. Mr. Putnam,[7] Candidate, here, on his Journey to Pomfret. The Weather Fair, but every Thing wears a Winter Hue. I hear Mr. Eliezer Rice is return'd home from Lake George.

## NOVEMBER, 1755

1. Storms again. A Sorrowfull Time. Many have not gather'd Corn, nor made their Cyder.

2. Read 2 Sam. 24. Preach'd on Isa. 9, 12 latter part and number 13, a. and p.m. Mr. Eliezer Rice, Mr. Ithamar Bellows and William Dunlop, return'd Thanks for their safe Return home from the Service.

3. Mr. Stone and Colonel Timothy Brigham here in their Journey to Woodstock Council. Mrs. Judith Bellows din'd here. She Spends a great Part of the p.m. here—but is not convinc'd she has been in an Error. Mr. Daniel Warrin Collector here and reckons—pays £14.10.1 old Tenor, but has after this about 120£ to pay. Thawy Weather.

4. Dull Heavy Air. Visit Jonathan Bond who is Sick of Pleuretick Fever. Receiv'd Lieutenant Maynards account which I have sought for these Ten Months.

5. A Fine Morning—warm and bright—p.m. Cloudy. Jonathan Bond worse.

6. Am Sent for to Visit him—accordingly I went—he is Still delirious and his Fever changes to be Nervous. N.B. Mr. Eliezer Rice came to see me and gave Some Account of Affairs at the Camp at Lake George.

7. Deacon Forbush and Mr. Thomas Twitchell are Stoning my Cellar Wall, but do not finish it. Mr. Zebulon Rice P.M. hews Sleepers—and Mr. Eleazer Pratt Sets em into the Gains.

8. I wake with Some Serious Impressions of the Sparing Mercy and Long suffering of God towards Me and the Church I am related to: and desire to be deeply humbled on consideration of my Ingratitude, unprofitableness, and unfaithfulness. Would Spend what time can be spar'd from my preparations and unavoidable Cares of my Family etc., in Serious Reflections and Humilliations. And O that I had a Spirit of Grace and Supplications—and that God would have Mercy on me and grant Forgiveness through the Blood of Jesus Christ of my numberless and great Offences—and quicken and assist me in my whole future conduct! N.B. This is 31 Years since my Ordination. Mr. Thomas Twitchel here again and finishes the Stoning of my Cellar Way.

9. Read 1 K, 1. Preach'd on Rev. 3, 2, and in the Close p.m. I warmly represented to the people the Pressures I was under and Obstructions in the Work of the Ministry. See the Notes. May God grant Me relief and may we all do our utmost to strengthen the Things etc.

10. A very Rainy time. My Son Ebenezer has neither gather'd his Corn nor made his Cyder: and its So with divers others.

11. Rain a.m. P.M. Billy works at Mr. Nurse's in cutting Turnips. At Eve Nathan Kenny, and Solomon and David Maynard husk'd out the rest of our Corn. At Eve also Mr. Whitney and his Wife with their Brother Child return from the Funeral of his Sister Liscomb, who has dy'd Somewhat Suddenly. A valuable and gracious woman, one that when she was among us, conducted with much decency and Discretion and a good Friend to the ministerial Interest here. May God teach us all rightly to improve this and every Such sorrowfull Providence!

12. I went over to t'other House in my way to the North End. Ebenezer was cutting up his Corn: his Brother Thomas and Mr. John Frost help him. He informs me that my Mare was in an ill Situation on Lords Day Morning, being Cast in her Fetters and a great Rail in between them, and She had lain till She was almost Spent, when he discover'd her. I rode upon her to visit Mrs. Beeman who is Sick at her son Bruce's. I went also to Mr. Martyns, where is my little son John Still. Call'd to See Ensign Josiah Rice who is still lame in his Foot. Billy work'd a.m. for Mr. Nurse. Bright and Pleasant Weather.

13. Fair again. Billy with Mare and Steers work'd for Mr. Nurse all Day. Thomas for Ebenezer, who finishes getting in his Corn. Catechetical Exercise to Young Women, about 26 Present. N.B. What they Said the Proofs of were the Answers to the 22, 23, and 24 Questions. And they must begin next time both Young Women and Young Men at the 25th Question.

14. Rose Early and visited Jonathan Bond. Brought home Mrs. Bonds Oxen and Billy and Nathan (Kenny) plough with them and my Steers at the Cook Field. Mr. Nathaniel Whitney brought a Barrell of Cyder, and he brought one from Mr. Grout. These were gratis. At Eve came Isaac Miller with Two Barrells of Cyder more which were also gratis. One from Deacon Jonathan Forbush and the other from Ensign Miller, who also Sent me a large Piece of Beef and a parcel of Apples. May God reward His Servants and grant me Grace to make a proper Improvement of the Benefits I receive!

15. With many avocations am able to prepare but one sermon, Since this one obliges me to much Reading.

16. Read 1 Kings 2. Preach'd a.m. on Mat. 16, 24. Mrs. Joanna Forbush[1] (wife of young Deacon) din'd here. P.M. read

---

[5] The Reverend David Hall of Sutton.
[6] The Reverend Solomon Reed of the Second Church of Framingham, a fervent New-Light preacher, had salary problems, and the next year departed for other pulpits. *Sibley*, X, 398-400.
[7] Aaron Putnam (Harvard 1752) served the First Church of Pomfret, Conn., 1755-1802.

[1] Mrs. Jonathan Forbush, Jr.

Mat. 6. Repeated the Exposition on number 23. N.B. an unusual multitude of Notes put up, desiring Prayers and Offering Thanks etc.

17. Mrs. Hannah Ward (Dauter of Lieutenant Hezekiah) din'd here.

18. This Morning about a Quarter past 4 We were all wak'd up by a very Terrible Earthquake.[2] The shock Seems to me to be as great and to last about as long as the great Earthquake, October 29, 1727, but the manner of Shaking I think is different—That more horizontal, this partly Vertical. My Children rose and gather'd into my Chamber, where we gave Thanks to God for our Preservation, and begg'd His Mercy towards us. We heard another shock at 28 Minutes after 5. The Air was Clear, the moon bright, and a great Frost. God grant us grace rightly to improve His holy Dispensation! and prepare us for what is yet before us!

19. I rose early—rode to Southborough and preach'd Mr. Stone's Lecture at 10 a.m. on Isa. 9, 12, 13. Din'd there (N.B. his Mother Thatcher[3] there) and he rode with me and preach'd my Lecture at 2 p.m. on Eccl. 8, 11. May God bless these Exercises to our, and to his people's Saving Good!

20. Mr. Wellman[4] and his Wife came—they din'd here. Ebenezer has Billy part of to Day to help him.

21. Billy to Ebenezer.

22. At Eve about half after Eight was another Earthquake and which very much Surpriz'd me. Yet it was not above a third so long or strong as that last Tuesday morning. May God grant the impressions may be increas'd and abiding!

23. Read publickly Hab. 3. Preach'd a. and p.m. on Ps. 18, 7. Administered the Lords Supper. Both the Deacons din'd here—also Mrs. Chaddock and Mrs. Mercy Chamberlin. P.M. My Wife went to Meeting. D.G. Rain a.m.

24. Catechiz'd at the Meeting House a. and p.m. At Eve Mr. Joseph Stratton of Waltham and his Dauter Harrington, and give me Account of the Surprizing Effects of the Earthquake. Lieutenant Forbush desires me to go to Upton Fast on the 27th.

25. At Captain Forbushes—ride his Horse to Lieutenant Brighams, whom I visit, he being still confin'd by illness—din'd there. P.M. visit Eliz Biglow—who is sick of a Fever. N.B. Thomas and Billy at their Brother Ebenezers who has a Husking to Day.

26. Samuel Forbush carts out muck for me. Mrs. Molly Martyn dines here: She returns home at Evening.

27. I rode over to Upton Fast. On Occasion of the Earthquake. Mr. Zebulon Rice accompany'd me (on the 24 at Evening Lieutenant Burnap of Hopkinton here in Mr. Barretts[5] Name to desire me to assist at a Fast there, next Thursday, but Lieutenant Forbush was first). I began with Prayer. Mr. Hutchinson preach'd (an Hour and Half) on Deut. 5, 29. P.M. Reverend Mr. Dor[6] pray'd and I preach'd—taking for my Text Isa. 5, 25, and read also Chapter 9, 12, 13, and I pick'd my Discourse partly out of that of mine on Isa. 9, 12, 13, and partly from that on Ps. 18, 7, with Some additions and alterations. May God freely pardon what has been amiss, hear our Prayers and accept our Humilliations and Thanksgiving: and may the Word prove Savingly beneficial! I return'd at night.

28. A fine Morning. My Wife and Lucy are gone over to Mr. Martyns. At Eve they return and bring home my little John.

29. Billy so out of Order that he is incapable of any Business.

30. Read 1 Kings 3. Preach'd a. and p.m. on Isa. 5, 24, 25. But am heartily griev'd it was So defectively—especially as it was the finishing the Subject, and there can be no Opportunity for ever Supplying what has been omitted. May God forgive me my many Miscarriages and Omissions! Miss Mary Steward, Miss Patience Woods and Miss Grace Ball din'd here.

[2] This earthquake was felt on both sides of the Atlantic. The effects in Boston were described at length in *The Boston Weekly News-Letter*, Nov. 20, 1755, and *The Boston Gazette, or Country Journal*, Nov. 24, 1755. For the controversy over the causes see Eleanor M. Tilton, "Lightning-Rods and the Earthquake of 1755," *New England Quarterly*, XIII (March, 1940), 85–97.
[3] The Reverend Mr. Stone's mother-in-law, the widow of the Reverend Peter Thatcher of Middleborough.
[4] The Reverend James Wellman of Millbury.
[5] The Reverend Samuel Barrett of Hopkinton.
[6] Joseph Dorr of Mendon.

DECEMBER, 1755

1. One Mr. Stimpson of Hopkinton here and din'd with us.

2. Lieutenant Tainter here and din'd with us. He is so good as to come and see whether we had any service to be done at Boston, as his Custom has been, but I would not at this time trouble him with anything. I am heartily thankfull to God for the affectionate Kindness of this Good Man, who whether he is at home or goes abroad he is ever caring for us. This is to be noted before Thanksgiving.

3. Ebenezer came with two Barrells of Cyder which is all that I design to have of him more this Year—in all 3 Barrells. He says he has one more Cheese to make Still.

4. Public Thanksgiving. Preach'd on Ps. 150, number 2. May God give Success! Master Gardner din'd with us and Mr. Elijah Warrin and his Wife and their little son, here at Eve and supp'd with us. She and her son lodg'd here.

5. Mr. John Martyn junior here at Breakfast time. P.M. Mary Latiner here and Examin'd. Also Joseph Bowman.

6. It was very Cold, but having appointed to Change with Mr. Wellman I Set out upon my Journey a.m. Call'd at Captain Bakers and deliver'd him a Paper containing a brief Memorial to be laid before the Town next Monday, when they are to meet to bring in Town Debts; desiring them to pay Me what they owe Me. N.B. Captain Baker Said he would use his Best Endeavour to have it Succeed. I therefore repose my Affair under God in his Care. Din'd at Mr. Hutchinsons. Lieutenant Tainter came to me there and din'd with us. Met Mr. Wellman on the Road from Sutton to Grafton. I lodg'd at Mr. Wellmans, Lieutenant Tainter at his Sons.

7. I preach'd at Sutton for Mr. Wellman, and he for me at Westboro. My Text a.m. was Gal. 1, part of 15 and part of 16. P.M. it was Heb. 11, 16. A fine Day, as to Weather; might God grant us divine Refreshment and Joy from His Word and Ordinances! I baptiz'd Moses Son of Deacon Chase,[1] and having Consulted Mr. Wellman about it, who requested it, I appointed an Exercise in the Evening at Mr. Jonathan Fullers, where accordingly [I] preach'd to a crowded Assembly from Luke 12, 36, 37. N.B. After Exercise came in two Soldiers—one of them had Plans of the Forts lately built by our Forces. Fort William and Henry and Fort Edwards. I lodg'd at Mr. Samuel Trasks.

8. Rode to Mr. Charles Richardsons who copy'd the Plans which I borrow'd last night, for me. Mr. Wellman and Lieutenant Tainter came, and we all din'd there. P.M. Lieutenant and I return'd home, calling at Mr. Wellmans where I borrow'd Henry on the Historical Books of Old Testament[2] and at Mr. Hutchinsons with whom both I and Mr. Wellman are somewhat disquieted that he would not change with Mr. Wellman and go to Westborough in his Stead. I arriv'd safely thro God's Mercy, in the Evening. Thus I have perform'd this long design'd Journey for the Sake of my dear Kinswoman, Mrs. Fuller (who is about 82). And may God himself visit, Support and bless them and at last receive them to Himself!

9. Soldiers are continually returning from Albany.

10. Mr. Nathaniel Whitney here at Eve and tells me the Town Meeting on the 8th did nothing upon my Paper which I sent and was (he said) presented, by Captain Baker. But he tells me that Lieutenant Tainter takes off the Force of any Such Petition, for he says that he has paid 20£ old Tenor towards that Debt—and Harrington has some pounds more: so that there is very little remaining now. In answer to which I assur'd him (Mr. Whitney) that no Body had to my Knowledge paid a Farthing of that Debt but Messers. James Ball, and Jacob Rice, and Captain Maynard. Unless Lieutenant Tainter charg'd for keeping a Creature or two the Winter following the Drought. But yet he never said so to me; nor is there any Thing behind in my account with him except for some few Things which Lieutenant has bought at Boston for us, this Year: for as for last Year I discharg'd all Debt to him Unto the Day when I gave him a Note to

[1] Abel Chase.
[2] Matthew Henry (1662–1714), a noted English dissenting minister wrote *Exposition of the Historical Books of the Old Testament* (London, 1708).

the Collector of 15£ old Tenor. Mr. Whitney added that Lieutenant Tainter told him as above, yesterday.

11. Levelling the Bank of Sand which was dug out of my New Cellar Way.

12. Last Night it snow'd, which has been Somewhat rare—it being an extraordinary open Season. Am preparing again upon Mat. 16, 24. May God assist me in it.

13. Much interrupted by the Coming of Captain Thomas Stoddard from Fort Edward. He tells me he supposes Mr. Bowes, late of Bedford, one of the Chaplains in the army, to be by this time dead, he having been struck suddenly with numb palsey, and speechless when he was with him, as he came down upon his Journey. May God grant that I may myself be always ready! Since we know not the Day nor the Hour. O that I might wait for my Lord!

14. Captain Stoddard having lodg'd here, his son in Law, Mr. William Boardman came from Marlborough this Morning (from Boston Yesterday) to wait upon him. They tarried with us over the Sabbath. Reverend Mr. Bowes[3] Death is Several Ways confirm'd. I read 1 K. 4. Preach'd on Mat. 16, 24. P.M. read Mat. 7, and on Occasion of Mr. Bowes Death, repeated the remainder of what I began on Occasion of Deacon Newtons sudden Death last February, viz. from Deut. 32, 29. N.B. Deacon Bond, Mr. Cornelius Biglow and others return'd. N.B. After Meeting Captain Maynard came in to see Captain Stoddard—and took home his Horse. Which I took in very kind, good Part of him and wish it might please God So to Change his Heart as that he might be reduc'd to some Freeness and sweetness again.

15. Captain Stoddard and his son Bowman left us for Boston. At Eve Lieutenant Tainter return'd from below—I had writ by him to Brother Sam Parkman but he brought me no answer—and thus it has been divers times, that tho I write it is to no purpose.

16. Rain, and high Winds: as the Day advanc'd the Gusts were very Strong. The stormy winds fulfill the Almighty Authors Words. May God deliver Me from the Whirlwinds and Tempests of Gods Eternal Wrath!

17. Bright and Clear. In the great Storm yesterday Captain Maynards etc. Stables were wholly turn'd over so as to stand upon the Roof. At Eve Lieutenant Tainter here and I had some Talk with him about his having said that he had paid me some considerable Part of the North side Debt. And we had some considerable altercation but parted in Love and Peace. A Frosty Night which we have not had of a great while, nor anything severe.

18. Dr. Brigham[4] (who has been Doctor of Colonel Browns Regiment of Recruits to Lake George) din'd here. Sent 4£ 5/ old Tenor to Mr. Benjamin Nicols. At Eve Mr. Zebulon Rice at work putting up Partition in my Cellar. Mrs. Judith Bellows here, but as unrelenting, Self-vindicating as ever.

19. Billy not well, but thrashes Rye.

20. Many deep and Serious Thots of my Personal and family Circumstances both relating to present and future Life.

21. Read 1 K. 5, and gave an Exercise upon it. P.M. read Mat. 8 to number 13. Deacon Forbush, Mrs. Foster and Mrs. Chaddock din'd here.

22. Rode Mr. Nurse's Mare to Mr. Ebenezer Chamberlins to see his son who is dangerously Ill. I din'd there. Dr. Brigham also. At Mr. Jonathan Bellows—Mrs. Bellows extremely Clamorous. At Mr. Snows where I talk'd with Comfort Bellows in the hearing of Mrs. Snow and her son and Dauter. At Mr. Amsdens, Bruce's—Bathericks. N.B. Breck (the first time) went to Mill.

23. Pleasant Day, but grows Somewhat Cold. Mr. Edward Marrit[5] of Cambridge here. At Eve Lieutenant Forbush who having writ something for Mrs. Judith Bellows, wanted to apprize me of it (for she had clean worried him out to do it) but said he did not think it would do much good. Mr. Daniel Warrin

here and paid me 10£ old Tenor. Lieutenant Tainter, here and we retir'd and talk'd over our whole Affair, concerning the Northside Debt to me and what he had done towards it. He brought me from Esquire Baker, my Paper which I put in to the Town, with the Record on the back of it, of the Towns refusal to do anything about it. Lieutenant Tainter (now first of all) acquainted me with the Articles which he had given me with Design in his own Heart, towards defraying the Northside Debt; Except that he had hinted to me somewhat of his keeping a Cow for me the winter after the Drought, and which at the Time, as I remember I manifested my Dissent to. Thro divine Restraints we kept from being angry—supp'd together and parted in peace.

24. A Great Frost: and the Day proves an exceeding Cold Day. Am disappointed of all Carpenters coming, and by these Means my design'd Kitchin remains unclos'd, and my Cellar consequently greatly expos'd to the Frost notwithstanding all I have done in making a Partition between the New Part and the old. We now batten and Partition and carry down Coals, and all little enough; for the Frost is very great. Master Gardner, having been to Boston, brot me Several Letters, among which one from my worthy Friend Simon Frost[6] Esquire of Kittery, who inclosed Mr. Benjamin Lulls Deed of the 70 Acres; which Judge Frost had got recorded for me at Portsmouth. My Son William much indispos'd.

25. The Frost has got very much into the House: But the wind not so high abroad. Blessed be God for my preservation and many Comforts—and I would praise Him My Heart is in some Measure tender—I hope choosing and yielding to Him. Had some serious Thoughts on the Day, as kept by many in Commemoration of our Lords Nativity. And I desire to be one with all of them that are one with Christ, and who avoid the Superstitions and Excesses of this Day, and Serve the Lord in sincerity. May I and mine have part in the glorious Logos[7] who was made Flesh and dwelt among us! At Eve Dr. Joshua Smith here—receiv'd the News Paper in which have a frightfull Account of the terrible Earthquake at Cadiz and Seville; but especially Lisbon, St. Woes and Agazira. O may we learn Righteousness! fear God and give Glory to Him: and in peculiar since we are so mercifully Spar'd!

26. Somewhat moderater. My Son Ebenezer came and with Thomas's Help kill'd two Swine; which were but Small, one 126, the other 119, our Corn having been so cut off by the Frosts, both late in the Spring and early in the Fall. The Negro Gosport, Mr. Gardners Servant here, and din'd here. At Eve I walk'd to the widow Newtons and reckon'd with her—gave her a Note to Constable Forbush and reckon'd with Mr. John Beeton—Paid him 20 shillings old Tenor for Captain Drury[8] of Grafton, and gave a Note for the Shop work to the Collector Forbush. N.B. Several Returning from the adjournment of the Town Meeting came in to my House—viz. Deacon Jonathan Forbush junior, Messers. Solomon Woods and Benjamin Tainter—afterwards Ensign Harrington. Tis observable that Ensign Harrington never said one word of his having paid me any of that Debt: tho so much has been Said by others of his having declar'd he had. Some of them cut out my pork. All of them supp'd with me. Our Discourse was partly of the awful providences of Late in the Earthquakes—and likewise of unhappy Controversie of the Town with me, who refuse to pay their just Debt to me, or to settle with me. N.B. receiv'd a Letter from Mr. Charles Richardson of Sutton inclosing the Plans of the Forts lately built by the Army.

27. After a considerable time in which the Ground has been open, it Snows.

28. Read 1 King. 6, preach'd a.m. on Mat. 16, 24. P.M. on Occasion of the Earthquake and Inundation at Cadiz, Seville and especially at Lisbon preach'd on 1 Pet. 4, 7, repeating the first Sermon on that Text, with divers alterations and additions, and may God forgive my great Deficiency, and add His efficacious Blessing! N.B. after Meeting at Eve two Soldiers returning from Oswego, viz. James Johnston of Shirley, the other Timothy

---

[3] Nicholas Bowes (Harvard 1725) had been the minister of Bedford, 1730–1754. After being dismissed he taught school and served as chaplain at Fort Edward. He died at Western (now Warren) on his way home in December, 1755.

[4] Samuel Brigham of Marlborough.

[5] Marrett was a tailor, who later served as selectman of Cambridge, and as a captain of militia. Paige, Cambridge, p. 605.

[6] Justice of the Court of Common Pleas.

[7] See John 1, 1–18.

[8] Thomas Drury.

Canniston of Pepperrells Regiment here and desir'd Refreshments, which we chearfully gave 'em.

29. A.M. a great Heap of stones sledded from the West End of my Kitchin to make part of the Wall from the Well to the Barn. At Eve reckon'd with Barnabas Newton.

30. Very Cold Morning. Billy is ill with a Flux and confin'd most of the Day, to the House. P.M. Mr. Martyn made me a Visit. At Eve I walk'd up to Mr. Zebulon Rice's.

31. Captain Wood, return'd from Albany, was here with his Brother Jonathan in their Journey home; feeble and weak yet; and complains of Dizziness—but we are much rejoic'd to See him again, and so well as he is, we having heard he was Dead.

Thus this Year ends with nothing peculiar accomplish'd against Niagara or Crown-Point—the building of Some Forts—but the Troops are exceedingly wasted by Sickness and by their great Fatigues and hard Fare. We must now wait the Will of God in what is to follow. And may God fit me and mine for His holy Pleasure!

# INDEX